A History of The United States

E PLURIBUS UNUM

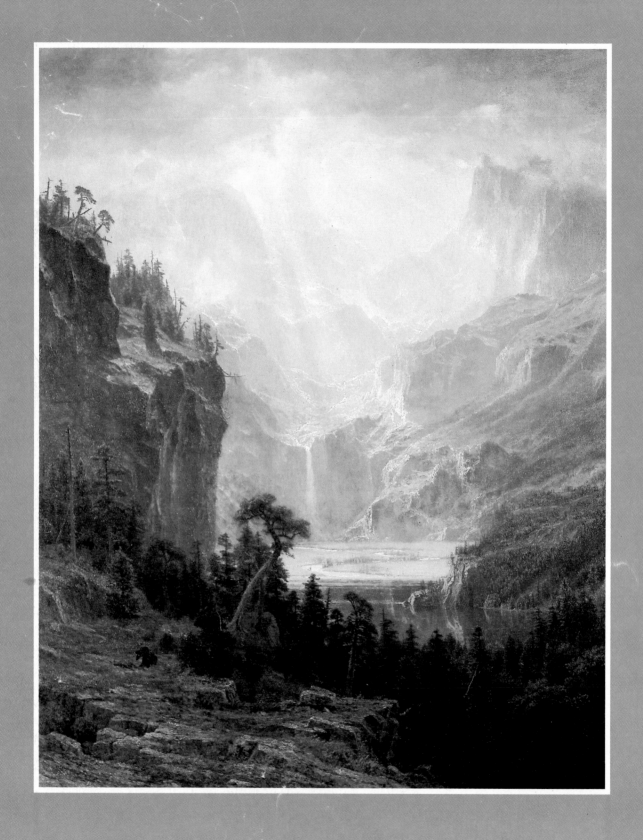

A History of The United States

Daniel J. Boorstin

Brooks Mather Kelley

WITH

Ruth Frankel Boorstin

PRENTICE HALL

Needham, Massachusetts • Englewood Cliffs, New Jersey

Credits

Executive Editor: Jeffrey M. Ikler
Project Editor: Mary Katherine O'Hare
Editor: David R. Zarowin
Editorial Services: Susan Feibelman, Joanna Gatanti, Mary Oates Johnson, Jane E. Shattuck
Production/Manufacturing Coordinator: Bill Wood
Copy/Production Editor: Pauline P. Wright
Product Marketing Director: Martha G. Smith
Product Marketing Manager: Darrell J. Kozlowski
Design Director: L. Christopher Valente
Design Coordinator: Stuart Wallace
Cover Design: John Martucci, L. Christopher Valente, Peter Brooks
Cover Photo: Peter B. Kaplan
Design: Carol H. Rose
Production, Design Services: Prentice Crosier, Carolynn Decillo, Nicole Schildcrout, Linda Dana Willis
Photo Researcher: Pembroke Herbert

Title page:

Albert Bierstadt, "Lander's Peak," Courtesy of Fogg Art Museum, Bequest of Mrs. William Hayes Fogg

Table of Contents Credit:

A Simon & Schuster Company

Time Line Text Credit:

"First Fig" (p. 514) from *Collected Poems*, by Edna St. Vincent Millay. Copyright © 1950 by Harper & Row Publ. Reprinted by permission of Harper & Row Publishers, Inc.

Time Line Credit:

65TL "Map of London, 1616" by C. J. Visscher (detail), By Permission of The British Library (B. L. Maps 162.0.1); 65TR "Paul Revere" by John Singleton Copley, Museum of Fine Arts, Boston, Gift of Joseph W., William B., and Edward H. R. Revere, 1930; 65B Machu Picchu, Tom Nebbia/Click/Chicago. 136 "A View of the South Part of Lexington, 1775" (detail) by Amos Doolittle, The Connecticut Historical Society, 137TL Second Continental Congress (detail), Historical Society of Pennsylvania; 137TR Great Seal of the United States 1798, National Archives. 204–205 "A View of New Orleans Taken from the Plantation of Marigny, November, 1803" (detail) by Boqueto de Woiserie, Chicago Historical Society, 205TL "King Andrew the First," Library of Congress; 205TR "Webster's Reply to Hayne" (detail) by G.P.A. Healy, City of Boston Art Commission, painting in Faneuil Hall, Boston. 276 "Lazell, Perkins & Co. Bridgewater, Mass." (detail) lithograph by J. P. Newell, The Corcoran Gallery of Art, Museum Purchase, Mary E. Maxwell; 277T Uncle Tom's Cabin, The Bettmann Archive; 277M "Geese in Flight" (detail) by Leila T. Bauman, National Gallery of Art, Gift of Edgar William and Bernice Chrysler Garbisch. 349TL "Mountain Jack and a Wandering Miner" (detail) by E. Hall, The Oakland Museum, Gift of Concours D'Antiques, Art Guild of the Oakland Museum Association; 349TR "The Emancipation Proclamation" (detail) by A. A. Lamb, National Gallery of Art, Washington, D.C., Gift of Edgar William and Bernice Chrysler Garbisch, 349B "A Rainy Day in Camp" (detail) by Winslow Homer, Metropolitan Museum of Art, Gift of Mrs. William F. Milton, 1923 (#23.77.1). 411TL "The Grand Display of Fireworks and Illuminations" (detail) lithograph by Currier and Ives, Art Resource; 411TR "The Yankee Horse Rake" (detail), The Oakland Museum; 411B "Cross Streets of New York" (detail) by Evertt Shinn, The Corcoran Gallery of Art, Gift of Margaret M. Hitchcock. 477TL McClure's 1903, Culver Pictures; 477TR "Dewey? We do!" (detail) Art Resource; 477M "On the Job for Victory" (detail), Library of Congress. 515TL McClure's, Culver Pictures; 515TR "Employment Agency" (detail) by Isaac Soyer, The Whitney Museum of American Art; 515B Lindbergh, Culver Pictures. 595 "Dust, Drought, and Destruction" (detail) by William C. Palmer, The Whitney Museum of American Art; 595TR Yalta, Franklin D. Roosevelt Library, Hyde Park, N.Y.; 595B "March in Remembrance of the Putsch" by Hugo Jaeger, LIFE Magazine © Time, Inc. 657TR IKE, Wide World Photos; 657TL MLK, Bob Fitch/Black Star; 657B Berlin, Fenno Jacobs/Black Star. 715TL Inagurall Ball, Black Star; 715TR LBJ, Fred Ward/Black Star; 715B Nixon, Wally McNamee/Woodfin Camp & Associates. 796 No Gas, Dennis Brack/Black Star; 797TL Woman Pilot, Rob Nelson/Picture Group; 797TR Reagan, Michael Evans/Sygma.

To All Americans
present and future
Who explore the past
To rediscover the New World

"It may be said, That in a Sort,
they began the World a New."
Jared Eliot, 1748

"The Eagle has landed!"
Neil A. Armstrong and Edwin E. Aldrin, Jr.
July 20, 1969, from the Moon

About the Authors

Daniel J. Boorstin, Pulitzer Prize-winning historian, educator, and author, and now the Librarian of Congress emeritus, directed the nation's library from 1975 to 1987. He had previously been Director of the National Museum of American History and Technology, and then Senior Historian of the Smithsonian Institution. Before that, he was the Preston and Sterling Morton Distinguished Service Professor of History at the University of Chicago, where he taught for twenty-five years.

Born in Atlanta, Georgia, and raised in Tulsa, Oklahoma, Dr. Boorstin received his undergraduate degree with highest honors from Harvard College and his doctorate from Yale. As a Rhodes Scholar at Balliol College, Oxford, he won a coveted "double first" in two degrees in law and was admitted as a barrister-at-law of the Inner Temple, London. He has served as a visiting professor at many leading universities throughout the world, and has lectured widely here and in many other countries.

Dr. Boorstin is an active author and editor whose books include the trilogy *The Americans*. The first volume of this work, *The Colonial Experience* (1959), won the Bancroft Prize. The second volume, *The National Experience* (1965), received the Parkman Prize, and the third, *The Democratic Experience* (1973), was honored with the Pulitzer Prize for History, and the Dexter Prize. *The Discoverers* (1983) is a history of man's search to know his world and himself. Dr. Boorstin is editor of the 27-volume *Chicago History of American Civilization*.

Brooks Mather Kelley is currently Research Affiliate in History at Yale University, where he has held a variety of teaching and research posts since 1961. He was University Archivist and Curator of Historical Manuscripts at Yale from 1964 to 1967; he has also taught American History at the Illinois Institute of Technology and has been a visiting professor at Brown University.

Dr. Kelley was born in Lake Forest, Illinois, and attended school there and at Deerfield Academy. He received his B.A. from Yale University and his M.A. and Ph.D. from the University of Chicago. His publications include *Yale: A History* and *New Haven Heritage: An Area of Historic Houses on Hillhouse Avenue* in addition to numerous articles and book reviews. In 1983 he was historical consultant for the WQED/Pittsburgh PBS television series "Freedom to Speak." Dr. Kelley also serves as President of the Connecticut Fund for the Environment.

EDITORIAL ASSOCIATE

Ruth Frankel Boorstin, a Phi Beta Kappa graduate of Wellesley College, went on to receive an M.A. in Social Science from the University of Chicago, where she ranked first in her class. She has worked at promoting the readability of technical literature in history and economics on the staff of the Cowles Commission, the Committee for Economic Development, and the National Opinion Research Center. Her publications include *The Peacetime Uses of Atomic Energy*, which she edited, and a weekly syndicated newspaper column for young people. Mrs. Boorstin has been an active collaborator on all her historian husband's books.

For her assistance as researcher, typist, and editor, we wish to express our deep appreciation to Suzanne Gray Kelley.

Contents

Ætatis suæ 21. A.1616.

12 The United States looks ahead 717

List of Maps

List of Charts and Graphs

A Note on American Pictorial Art

The illustrations in this book not only show the American past. They are selected especially to introduce you to American art. In every chapter, the paintings, drawings, engravings, lithographs, photographs, and objects shown come from the very period described in that chapter. They are authentic witnesses of our art—and of our history. To help you understand and enjoy the pictures in this book and to encourage you to visit your neighboring art galleries, here is a thumbnail history of American art.

Most early settlers of our country had little time for the fine arts. Building villages and clearing the wilderness kept them busy enough. But as the 17th century advanced, some of these new Americans had the leisure to enjoy the arts, and the money to commission a portrait. Of course they could not be photographed, for that invention was still two centuries in the future!

Portraits were the main form of painting in the colonial era. Over the years, portrait painters became ever more skillful. Among the best in the 18th century were John Smibert, an English immigrant, Robert Feke, Joseph Badger, John Singleton Copley, Charles Willson Peale, Ralph Earl, Gilbert Stuart, and Benjamin West. Copley and West left America and went to England, where they painted statesmen and wealthy aristocrats and won international reputations.

Benjamin West was one of the earliest American painters to focus on historical events, like the "Death of General Wolfe" (1771). Following his example, John Trumbull painted a whole series on the American Revolution. Citizens sometimes commissioned a view of their harbor or their city for proud display in the town hall.

In the 19th century, American artists became increasingly aware of the peculiar charms of America. Between 1829 and 1838, George Catlin, fascinated by the handsome Indians, recorded their colorful costumes and dances, and painted 600 Indian portraits. The skilled brushes of Karl Bodmer, Alfred Jacob Miller, and others depicted the Native Americans at home, on the hunt, and at war. John James Audubon's stunning 4-volume *Birds of America* (1827–1838, called "the elephant folio" because of its enormous size) still helps us identify our splendid American birds.

Meanwhile some artists were captivated by the romantic beauty of the American wilderness. Thomas Cole, Asher B. Durand, and other brilliant landscape painters came to be called "The Hudson River School." They were followed by Thomas Moran and Thomas Hill, both born in England, and Albert Bierstadt, a German—who traveled all over the West. Their gigantic canvases capture the wild continent which was everywhere then, but which now we must seek out in specially preserved wilderness areas.

After the Civil War, more American painters began to look to Europe, especially to the French Impressionists, for new ways of using color. Childe Hassam, Mary Cassatt, and others imported their techniques. Still Winslow Homer, Thomas Eakins, and Albert Pinkham Ryder resisted European influences and went their own American ways.

In the 20th century American painting has run the gamut from the photograph-like work of Andrew Wyeth and the pop art of Andy Warhol to the abstract expressionism of Willem de Kooning and Jackson Pollock, with just about every variation in between. These range from the seamy realism of Edward Hopper and the regionalism of Thomas Hart Benton or Grant Wood to the elegant abstractions of Georgia O'Keeffe.

We should not forget, in even the briefest survey, the so-called "primitives." These were the amateur artists who lacked formal training. For this very reason they gave their work a naive charm and offered a fresh insight into the American past. Most of their names remain unknown. Two whose names do survive are Horace Pickens and Grandma Moses.

Painting, of course, is only one kind of pictorial art. In the days before photography, the engraving and (beginning about 1800) the lithograph provided inexpensive copies of political cartoons, propaganda and advertising messages, romantic landscapes, battle scenes, and likenesses of George Washington for the home, the office, or the classroom. Nathaniel Currier and James M. Ives, for much of the 19th century, sold thousands of copies of colorful lithographs which recapture for us the pleasures of ice-skating, steamboat-riding, and horse-racing. Their works became less popular with the rise of photography.

The political cartoon has flourished ever since colonial days. German-born Thomas Nast and Austrian-born Joseph Keppler brought here their sharp eye for caricature. Their hard-hitting attacks made corrupt politicians miserable. Other cartoonists, over the years, have used a variety of styles to deliver a political or moral message—or just to poke fun at us. Among the more influential have been Daniel Fitzpatrick, especially in the 1930s and 1940s, Bill Mauldin (famous for his "G.I. Joe") beginning in World War II, and Herblock (Herbert Block), whose caricatures of Joseph McCarthy and Richard Nixon became classics.

Photography was introduced into the United States with an assist from the versatile painter-inventor Samuel F. B. Morse. In 1840 he reported from France on the daguerreotype process by which (in half an hour!) a photographic image could be captured on silver-plated copper. Mathew Brady, the great Civil War photographer, first worked with daguerreotypes, but then learned the more flexible (but terribly complicated) wet-plate process. Brady and the many photographers who worked for him, his team, wandering about with their "what-is-it" buggies filled with chemicals for developing their pictures made the first photographic record of warfare. And they risked their lives, too, because mystified soldiers in the field thought the camera was a new kind of artillery.

Not until the 1880s with easy-to-use dry and flexible film invented by George Eastman, and his simple box camera, could photography go everywhere. The Danish-born journalist-reformer Jacob Riis took his camera into alleys and tenements and then shocked Americans by his pictures of big-city slums. In the 1930s the power of the camera worked again—now through the photographs of the impoverished and the unemployed taken by Ben Shahn, Walker Evans, Dorothea Lange, and others under the auspices of the Farm Security Administration. World War II was brought home to the people of the United States by daring photographers like Robert Capa and Margaret Bourke-White. Capa lost his life to a land mine in 1954 while photographing the war in Vietnam.

Looking at pictures—paintings, drawings, photographs, even posters, advertisements and other commercial art—like reading or visiting museums and historic places, is a happy way of studying our past. We hope that the illustrations in this book and this brief note on American art will entice you to seek out and enjoy American artists, cartoonists, and photographers to open up vistas that you cannot find in words.

Thomas Moran, "The Grand Canyon of the Yellowstone," 1871.

National Museum of American Art, Smithsonian Institution, Washington, D.C. U.S. Department of the Interior, National Park Service

Prologue

American history is the story of a magic transformation.   How did people from everywhere join the American family?   How did men and women from a tired Old World, where people thought they knew what to expect, become wide-eyed explorers of a New World?

Our history is the story of these millions in search of what it means to be an American.   In the Old World people knew quite definitely whether they were English, French, or Spanish.   But here it took time for them to discover that they really were Americans.

What does it mean to be an American?   To answer that question we must shake hands with our earlier selves and try to become acquainted.   We must discover what puzzled and interested and troubled earlier Americans.

What has been especially American about our ways of living and earning a living?   Our ways of making war and making peace?   Our ways of thinking and hoping and fearing, of worshiping God and fighting the Devil?   Our ways of traveling and politicking, of importing people, of building houses and cities?   These are some of the questions we try to answer in this book.

Discovering America is a way of discovering ourselves.   This is a book about us.

Commerce, industry, and agriculture flourish under the protective wings of the American eagle in this 1844 political banner.   The banner was painted by a signmaker from Auburn, New York.

New York State Historical Association

UNIT 1

The making of Americans

The history of the United States begins in Europe before an America was known there, and in America before the Europeans came.   In the Age of Columbus the peoples of Europe were discovering the world anew, reaching out to far and fabulous places.   Columbus's wonderful, puzzling find enticed other adventurers to risk their lives for riches and empire.

The America they found already held millions of people, but these were spread thin across two continents.   These Native Americans had neither the ships nor the science to reach out.   Europeans first put them in touch with the world. What for Europe spelled empire and success, for most Native Americans spelled a losing fight to keep their lands and ways of life.

The hopes that people brought from the Old World to the New were as varied as their nations.   Some came for gold or glory or adventure, some to worship in their own way, others to escape poverty, prison, or oppression.   Some came without hope—to serve as slaves on plantations, and in mines and mills.   Gradually life in America made them all into Americans.

THEMES IN AMERICAN HISTORY

- People leave Europe for the New World for a variety of reasons.

- The success of Europeans in the New World spells disaster for most Native Americans.

THEMES

- Shaped by their experiences in the New World, colonists begin to develop new ways of life.

On this beautiful map, drawn in 1459 by Fra Mauro, an Italian monk, Europe, Africa, and Asia fill the whole planet.   There is no room for America!

Art Resource, NY

1

What Europeans found: the American surprise

The discovery of America was the world's greatest surprise. When the first Europeans came, their maps of the world left no place for America. They knew only three continents—Europe, Asia, and Africa. These seemed to be merged together into one huge "Island of the Earth." That big island was indented by lakes, and a few seas like the Mediterranean and the Western Ocean. The planet seemed covered mostly by land, and there was no room for another continent.

Columbus was not looking for a new continent. He thought he was on his way to China and India. Europeans were disappointed to find unexpected lands in their way. Still they insisted on calling the natives here the "Indians." So America was discovered by accident.

As more Europeans came and explored the unknown lands, their disappointment became surprise. They had found a world for new beginnings.

1. Christopher Columbus: Who he was and why he came

The adventure that Columbus had in mind was exciting enough. He aimed to sail westward from the shores of Europe until he reached the shores of Asia. Asia was then Europe's treasure-house. It supplied peppers and spices and tea for the table, silks and gold brocade for the dresses of noble ladies and for draperies in palaces, diamonds and rubies for rings and bracelets and necklaces. Until then the main way to the Orient had been the slow, long trek overland. From Venice it might take a year to reach Peking. You would not arrive at all unless you survived the attacks of bandits, the high-mountain snows, and torrid desert heats. Even after you arrived in Asia, it was hard to bring your treasure back overland. For there were no wagon highways and you had to pack your treasure in caravans on the backs of donkeys, horses, and camels.

A direct westward voyage by sea would make all the difference. You could avoid bandits and mountains and deserts. The spacious hold of your ship would safely carry back your treasure. This was a simple and appealing idea. The wonder is why more people before Columbus did not try it.

Earlier in the 1400s a few sailors had tried. But they were not prepared for so long a voyage, and they did not know the winds. Some reached out into the Atlantic Ocean as far as the Azores and beyond. But the winds were against them and the seas rough. They all soon turned back for home.

As a determined young man Christopher Columbus decided that he would sail into the Western Ocean—to Asia and back. He had no doubt he could do it. He knew the sea, the winds, and the currents.

Early experiences. Columbus was born in 1451 in bustling Genoa, Italy, "that noble and powerful city by the sea." He was the son of a prosperous wool-weaver. For the first 22 years of his life he lived there. He saw ships bringing rich cargo from the eastern Mediterranean where the treasures of the Orient had been taken overland. When he went to sea, he sailed in all directions where ships went at the time. Once his cargo was wool and dried fish and wine carried from Iceland and northern Ireland to Lisbon and the islands of the Azores. Then he lived for a while in the Madeira Islands off the coast of Africa. He even sailed down the steaming African coast to distant Portuguese trading posts on the Gulf of Guinea.

When he left Genoa to settle in Lisbon, Portugal, that city was "the street corner of Europe." Its deep, sheltered harbor was the point of arrival and departure, a place of exchange, for the seaborne commerce of the whole western end of the continent. From there shipments went northward to the British Isles or the North Sea, southward for trade into Africa. And, why not westward—to Asia?

There in Lisbon the single-minded young Columbus laid his plans for his grand "Enterprise of the Indies." He called it an "enterprise" because he expected it to be not just a voyage of discovery but a money-making project. "The Indies" was the name for India and the other Asian lands of the Far East. Convinced that they had a great project to sell, Christopher and his brother Bartholomew made Lisbon their headquarters.

The "Enterprise of the Indies" would not be inexpensive. Ships would have to be bought or hired, crews found and paid. Food and other supplies had to be collected for the long voyage there and back. No ordinary merchant would have the wealth and the power needed. It would take a rich monarch. There was hope of great profit, but there was also great risk. Was there a ruler bold enough to take the big gamble?

No one knew exactly what the risks might be—or even how far it was from the coast of western Europe to the coasts of Asia. No one had ever made that trip before. The questions could not be answered from experience.

The learned men disagreed in their guesses. Some said it was about 2000 miles. Others said it was two or three times that long. The leading authority was the ancient Greek geographer Ptolemy. Columbus read the best geography books he could find. We still have some of them with his own marks. He underlined the passage that said, "this sea is navigable in a very few days if the wind be fair." He believed the writers who said the distance was short, and accordingly he made his plans.

Seeking support. Christopher and his brother traveled to the capitals of Europe trying to sell their project. The monarchs shunned Columbus's grand

Civico Museo Storico, G. Garibaldi, Como

No portraits of Christopher Columbus are known to have been painted during his lifetime. This picture by an unknown artist, painted some 30 years after Columbus died, is considered his earliest and best likeness.

Enterprise of the Indies. When in 1484 King John II of Portugal asked his committee of experts if Columbus could succeed, they said it was too far to Asia and told him not to take the risk. Instead King John sent daring sailors on the long way round Africa eastward to India. In 1488 Bartholomeu Dias succeeded in rounding the Cape of Good Hope, at the southern tip of Africa. Now the eastern route to India was open. Why risk the uncertain way west when there was a sea-path to the east?

Columbus then went next door to Spain, where Queen Isabella had a mind of her own. The bold mariner awakened her interest. To finance the trip she needed money from the royal treasury, but her committee of experts refused to approve the project. She kept the impatient Columbus waiting for six years. Finally, he gave up and prepared to take ship for France. At the last moment, the court treasurer convinced Isabella the gamble was worth

The astrolabe, first invented by the ancient Greeks, was used by mariners in the 15th, 16th, and even 17th centuries to try to find their latitude. This instrument was found off Ireland after the defeat of the Armada.

the risk. She now became so enthusiastic she was even prepared to pawn her jewels to help Columbus. But that was not necessary. She was told the royal treasury could pay the cost. So Queen Isabella sent Columbus a promise of royal support. She also granted all his demands for noble titles and a 10 percent share of whatever wealth came from land he might discover.

Columbus formed his enterprise in the small port of Palos, which had done something illegal. As a penalty the Queen fined it two caravels—light, swift sailboats—to go with Columbus. The caravels were the *Niña* and the *Pinta*. The third vessel of the expedition was the biggest, the *Santa Maria*, which Columbus chartered. The crew was mostly from Palos and nearby, and they were courageous and expert sailors.

The great voyage. With his three ships Columbus set sail from the coast of Spain on August 3, 1492. In the next weeks he proved that he was the greatest mariner of the age.

Still, it is hard to be at sea for weeks when you are not sure what—if anything—is ahead. So Columbus's men grew rebellious and reached the verge of mutiny. But Columbus was a true leader. A man taller than most, blue eyed and red haired, he was respected by his followers. He altered the records of distances they had covered so the crew would not think they had gone too far from home. He convinced them to go on. Still, on October 9, Columbus agreed that if they did not find land in three days, he would turn back. But by then there were more and more signs of land—birds in the air, leaves and flowers floating in the water.

It was not enough to know the sea. The winds were the engine that took you there and back. Others had failed because they did not know how to use the winds. They had tried going straight west from Spain. That was their mistake. Instead Columbus first had sailed south to the Canary Islands off the coast of Africa, then sailed west from there. That was where the winds blowing from the east would carry his ships straight on to his destination. Also the Canaries were on the same latitude as Japan, so if he went due west he thought he would arrive where he wanted to be.

The winds blew just as Columbus expected. This, the most important sea voyage in history, had good weather and clear sailing. At 2 o'clock in the

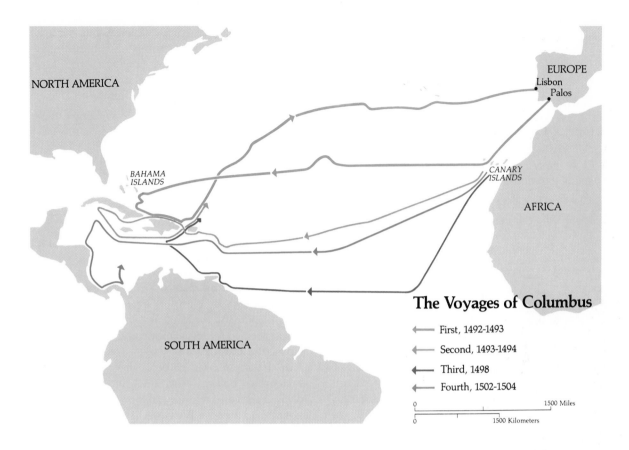

The Voyages of Columbus

← First, 1492-1493
← Second, 1493-1494
← Third, 1498
← Fourth, 1502-1504

morning on October 12, 1492, after thirty-three days at sea, a lookout sighted the white cliffs of an island in the Bahamas. The natives called it Guanahani, and Columbus named it San Salvador—Holy Savior. Columbus had discovered America—though he did not know it.

Columbus cruised about in the Caribbean Sea for several months. He landed on Cuba, which he thought and hoped might be Japan. After the *Santa Maria* was wrecked on a reef off Haiti, he built a fort on the island. They named the island Hispaniola (after Spain). He left about 40 men when he headed for home January 4, 1493. Columbus had found no great cities in his travels—but he had seen gold ornaments and found a little gold in a stream on Hispaniola. So he thought he had reached the outposts of the rich empire of Cathay (China).

By great luck Columbus did not try to sail back the way he had come. It would have been a mistake, for at that latitude the winds came from the east. Instead Columbus sailed north to about 35° north latitude. There the prevailing winds from the west blew him back to Spain.

When he arrived on March 15, 1493, he had accomplished much more then he knew. He had discovered a new world. The king and queen loaded him with honors and made his two sons pages at the court. Meanwhile he had shown sailors how to sail and where to sail so the winds would carry them to America *and back!* This made it possible for countless other ships to follow.

Columbus's other voyages. Three times on later voyages Columbus returned to the islands that he called the "Indies," or lands of the East. On these trips he established the first permanent settlement of Europeans in the Western Hemisphere, he skirted the shore of South America, and he explored the coast of Central America. He was always trying to prove that he had found the treasure lands of the East. But he finally reaped only misfortune and disgrace. When he returned to Spain in 1504 after his last voyage, he found Queen Isabella dying and his friends, his influence, and his reputation gone. Two years later Columbus died still believing that he had sailed to the coast of Asia.

1. Identify: Isabella, Enterprise of the Indies, Bartholomeu Dias, Cathay.

2. Locate: Peking, Genoa, Lisbon, Palos, San Salvador, Hispaniola.

3. Why did Columbus call the islands he found "The Indies"?

4. What important discovery did Columbus make about the winds?

5. What did Europeans want from the East?

6. **Identifying Central Issues.** What obstacles did Columbus face when seeking support from European monarchs?

2. Before discovery

If it hadn't been for Columbus, years might have passed before the people of Europe "discovered" America. But it was only for the people of Europe that America had to be "discovered." Millions of Native Americans were already here! For them, Columbus, and all the sailors, explorers, and settlers who came later, provided their "discovery" of Europe!

For Europeans the "discovery" of America offered vast lands, treasures of gold and silver and timber, places to build cities and places of refuge. For them this was a happy discovery. In the long run it would be a great discovery for the world. But for the millions of Native Americans already here their "discovery" of Europeans was not quite so happy. For some it meant the end of their Native American civilization. For some it meant slavery. For nearly all of them Europeans brought shock, disease, and change.

The first people to come to America were the ancestors of those who Columbus by mistake called Indians. No one knows when they came. A widely held theory is that sometime between 35,000 and 11,500 years ago during the last great ice age the first small groups arrived. They were people on the move. They had come from Northern China and Siberia.

So much of the sea had frozen into ice that it lowered the water in the Bering Strait. Then as they tracked wild game they could walk across the 56 miles from Siberia to Alaska. Without knowing it, they had discovered two large continents that were completely empty of people but were full of wild game—huge mastodons and mammoths, giant ground sloths, camels, antelopes, and great long-horned bison. In the thousands of years afterwards many other groups followed. These small bands spread all across North and South America.

The high mountains and broad rivers separated the communities. There were hundreds of languages and many different styles of life. Some small bands of people had no fixed homes. They followed their quarry and lived the wandering life of hunters. Others settled down and after centuries built vast kingdoms with flourishing cities, temples and palaces, and lively commerce.

Mayas, Incas, and Aztecs. The grandest of these Native American cultures astonished the Europeans. South of the present United States—from central Mexico to Peru—they found the Aztecs, the Mayas, and the Incas.

In the mountains, deserts, and rain forests of Guatemala, Belize, Honduras, and Mexico the Mayas had built temples and pyramids clustered about broad plazas. We can still climb them. The Mayas invented their own writing. Although they had no telescope, they built their own kind of observatory and made accurate calendars. Their "Indian corn" (maize) had never been seen in Europe. It was originally a wild grass, but would become a staple food for the world.

In Peru the Incas had constructed palaces surrounded by high walls, and had connected their mountain-towns with a network of roads. To farm their steep land they had built terraces. Where water was scarce, they had cut canals and erected stone aqueducts to irrigate their crops. The Incas gave us the potato and the tomato.

When European explorers came to Peru, they were amazed by the Incan government. They never expected to find such powerful rulers so well organized in the mountain wilderness. The Incas had succeeded even without a system of writing. No Americans were richer. In Cuzco, the mountain capital of the Incan empire, even the buildings were covered with gold!

The Aztecs were a warlike people who lived in central Mexico. They were clever architects. Like the Mayas, they too built grand temples and high pyramids. Their capital, where Mexico City is

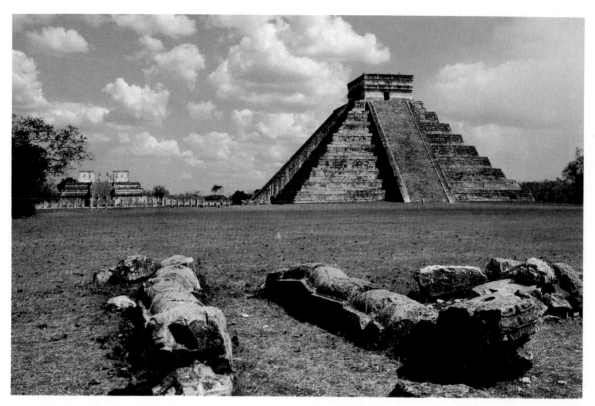

The great pyramid (above) at Chichen Itzá, Mexico, was part of a Mayan religious center. Machu Picchu (left) is located above the Urubamba River in Peru. This Incan center, with its terraces for farming, escaped destruction because of its inaccessible location. Pueblo Indians built these cliff dwellings (right) in Arizona.

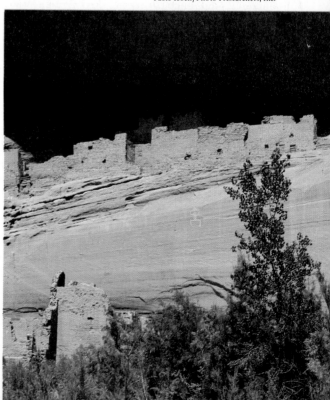

today, was a bustling metropolis. And they fashioned their gold into jewelry so ornate as to make European kings jealous.

These peoples had found their own ways of progress—different from the ways of Europe. They had never invented the wheel. They had no iron tools. Their beasts of burden were the dog and, in Peru, the llama. Unlike the peoples of Europe, they had not built ships to cross the oceans. They had not reached out to the world. In their isolation they found it hard to learn new ways. When the Spanish came, it seemed that the Incas, the Mayas, and the Aztecs had ceased to progress. They were ripe for conquest.

North American Indians. Of course there was no census of early America. But in 1500 the people in Mexico probably numbered about 12 million. Farther north in what is now the United States and Canada there were only some 4 million. The great empires of old America—of the Mayas, the Incas, and the Aztecs—were all in Mexico or south.

North of Mexico most of the people lived in wandering tribes and led a simple life. North American Indians were mainly hunters and gatherers of wild food. An exceptional few—in Arizona and New Mexico—settled in one place and became farmers.

The most advanced Indians of North America lived in the Southwest. The Anasazi came to be known as Pueblo Indians, after their style of building. A "pueblo" was a kind of apartment several stories tall, built of stone or adobe. The Anasazi also built cliff dwellings where they could defend themselves against enemy tribes. They and their descendants—the Hopi, Zuñi, and Acoma—made pottery, textiles, and baskets which we still admire.

When the Europeans came, the largest population of Indians north of Mexico was in California. They were a tenth of all the Indians in what is now the United States. They and the Indians of the Northwest lived by hunting and fishing and by gathering the plentiful nuts and berries.

Before Columbus and the Spanish came to America, there were not many Indians on the Great Plains. They walked for miles in pursuit of the herds of buffalo. The buffalo supplied them with skins to wear, meat to eat—and even (in dried buffalo chips) with fuel for their fires. Their only beast of burden was the dog. There were no horses in America until the Spanish brought them.

In the Eastern Woodlands the many tribes were mainly hunter-food gatherers, but they also did some farming. Some of them had joined in their own small version of a United Nations. Five tribes of Huron-Iroquois-speaking people—the Mohawk, Seneca, Oneida, Onondaga, and Cayuga—in upper New York State formed the Iroquois League. The council of chiefs who governed the league was chosen by certain women of high station. The council had no power to make war but planned defense. The powerful Chief Powhatan formed his own league (in Virginia), and there were others.

Down south in Mississippi the Natchez Indians seemed more like the Mexican Indians. Mainly farmers, they were divided into nobles and commoners, and were ruled by a man they called the Great Sun.

The Indians of North America were as varied as the peoples of Europe. There were countless tribes and hundreds of languages. Some tribes made elegant gold jewelry, but others were still in the Stone Age. Some wove handsome rugs and wore textiles of beautiful design. Others knew only skins and furs. Their meat depended on the place. Deer were nearly everywhere, and on the plains were herds of buffalo. The seashores and streams abounded in fish and shell food. The Indians planted corn, which made their bread, and beans, squashes, and many other crops. They knew where to find, and how to enjoy, the nuts and berries and mushrooms and other delights of the woods. They raised and smoked tobacco.

Because the Indians lived so close to nature, most of them had religions in which natural things played a major role. The Indians saw and worshiped Nature. They had learned to know the stones, the animals, and the plants. They were adept at using what they found for food, shelter, and clothing.

SECTION 2 REVIEW

1. Identify and locate: Mayas, Aztecs, Incas, Iroquois League, Pueblo Indians, Strait of Magellan.

2. **Identifying Alternatives.** How did the lifestyles of South and Central American Indians differ from those living north of Mexico?

ARCTIC OCEAN

ESKIMO

KOYUKON
INGALIK   KUTCHIN
        TANANA
ALEUT TANAINA
        HAN   ESKIMO
     NABESNA   HARE
  ATHENA   ESKIMO
                BEAR LAKE
     TUTCHONE
          MOUNTAIN   ESKIMO
               YELLOWKNIFE
        DOGRIB
TLINGIT   TAHLTAN   ESKIMO
        KASKA
             SLAVE
HAIDA   SEKANI
  TSIMSHIAN   CHIPEWYAN   ESKIMO
                                  HUDSON
          CARRIER   BAY
   BELLA COOLA
   KWAKIUTL
     CHILCOTIN   SARSI
        SHUSWAP KAIGANI (BLOOD)   CREE   MONTAGNAIS NASKAPI   BEOTHUK
NOOTKA LILOOET

        KUTENAI
SALISH   SIKSIKA   PLAINS CREE   MICMAC
PUYALLUP   (BLACKFOOT)
  SPOKANE COUER   ABNAKI   MALECITE
KLIKITAT   D'ALENE   ASSINIBOIN OJIBWA   PASSAMAQUODDY
     PALUS FLATHEAD   OJIBWA (CHIPPEWA)   OTTAWA HURON MOHICAN
CHINOOK YAKIMA NEZ PERCÉ CROW   HIDATSA   MOHAWK PENOBSCOT
COOS TILLAMOOK CAYUSE   MANDAN   MENOMINEE ONONDAGA PENNACOOK
   KLAMATH WALLA WALLA   ARIKARA   CAYUGA
SHASTA SHOSHONI—BANNOCK TETON DAKOTA SANTEE DAKOTA   SENECA MAHICAN MASSACHUSET
YUROK MODOC   NORTH CHEYENNE   SAUK FOX POTAWATOMI ONEIDA WAMPANOAG
YUKI NORTH PAIUTE   YANKTON   WINNEBAGO NEUTRAL WAPPINGER NARRAGANSET
YANA WASHO   SIOUX PONCA DAKOTA KICKAPOO   SUSQUEHANNA PEQUOT
HUPA MAIDU   OMAHA   WEA ERIE   DELAWARE
POMO MIWOK   PAWNEE   IOWA   PEORIA MIAMI
COSTANOAN   ILLINOIS   NANTICOKE
   YOKUTS   UTE   ARAPAHO OTO   POWHATAN
SALINAN SOUTH PAIUTE   KANSA MISSOURI   PAMUNKEY CHICKAHOMINY
CHUMASH   PUEBLO SOUTH CHEYENNE   SHAWNEE NOTTOWAY MATTAPONY
        MOHAVE HOPI JICARILLA KIOWA OSAGE PIANKASAW TUTELO ALGONQUIN
     HAVASUPAI ZUÑI APACHE   QUAPAW   CHEROKEE   PAMLICO
CAHUILLA   APACHE   KIOWA APACHE   CATAWBA
  YUMA   WICHITA   CHICKASAW   CREEK
  MARICOPA   CADDO   ALABAMA HICHITI
COCHIMI PAPAGO PIMA MESCALERO COMANCHE
     OPATA   APACHE   WACO NATCHEZ   CHOCTAW
     SERI   TONKAWA   BILOXI APALACHEE
   YAQUI CONCHO   LIPAN APACHE CHITIMACHA   TIMUCUA
   TARAHUMARA   ATAKAPA
           COAHUILTEC KARANKAWA
WAICURI   GULF OF MEXICO   SEMINOLE
                                                    CALUSA
   PERICU   ACAXEE   TAMAULIPEC
            HUICHOL
        TOLTEC   HUASTEC
     TLAXCALAN TOTONAC   YUCATAN
        TARASCAN AZTEC   MAYA
              MIXTEC
           ZAPOTEC   QUICHE MAYA

PACIFIC OCEAN

ATLANTIC OCEAN

Culture Areas
  Arctic
  Subarctic
  Northwest Coast
  California
  Plateau
  Great Basin
  Southwest
  Great Plains
  Northeast and Great Lakes
  Southeast
  Middle America

Major Indian Tribes
of North America
about 1500

0   1000 Miles
0   1000 Kilometers

Marco Polo leaves Venice on his journey to China in 1271. This illuminated manuscript shows colorful daily life when Venice was a center of commerce and culture for the Mediterranean.

3. Why Europeans went exploring

For centuries all these people and their cultures lay hidden from Europe: What happened to stir Europeans to reach out to this vast unknown?

The Renaissance, 1300–1600. Near the end of the Middle Ages, the Christians of western Europe launched crusades to take Jerusalem back from the Muslims. When thousands of Europeans traveled across the Mediterranean and reached the Holy Land, they discovered that they had much to learn from the East. Commerce grew and minds were opened. Scholars translated books of poetry, ad- venture, and science from Greek, Arabic, Hebrew, Persian, and other eastern languages. They revived the questioning spirit of the ancient Greeks. Am- bitious princes led new city-states in Italy. They built palaces and churches in the style of Greece and Rome. For the first time artists discovered the science of perspective. Leonardo da Vinci and Michelangelo painted their masterpieces and kept notebooks of all the wonders of the world.

Of course there were books before there was printing. But those early books were all copied by hand. It would take six months to make one copy of a long book. Books were costly and few people

Europe about 1500

SCALE: 0 — 500 Miles | 0 — 500 Kilometers

SWEDEN
NORWAY
Stockholm
NORTH SEA
SCOTLAND
Edinburgh
DENMARK
Copenhagen
BALTIC SEA
MUSCOVY (RUSSIA)
Moscow
Volga R.
TEUTONIC ORDER
LITHUANIA
IRELAND
ENGLAND
Hamburg
BRANDENBURG
Warsaw
POLAND
Dnieper R.
London
NETH.
Cologne
SAXONY
SILESIA
ATLANTIC OCEAN
LUX.
Paris
Rhine R.
HOLY ROMAN EMPIRE
BOHEMIA
Vienna
AUSTRIA
HUNGARY
FRANCE
Loire R.
Munich
SWISS CONFEDERATION
BAY OF BISCAY
Bordeaux
SAVOY
Rhône R.
MILAN
VENICE
GENOA
ADRIATIC SEA
Danube R.
BLACK SEA
Marseilles
CORSICA
PAPAL STATES
OTTOMAN
Constantinople
ARAGON
Barcelona
Rome
NAPLES (SPANISH)
EMPIRE
Lisbon
Tagus R.
Madrid
SPAIN
CASTILE
SARDINIA
Naples
AEGEAN SEA
Athens
PORTUGAL
MEDITERRANEAN SEA
SICILY
CYPRUS
AFRICA
MUSLIM STATES
CRETE

could read. Then Johann Gutenberg at Mainz in Germany invented movable type. Here was a way to make many copies of a book—and at much less cost. In 1456 he printed his first Bible and opened a new world for books. Within only fifty years 10 million copies of printed books appeared in Europe.

Modern astronomy was born. Copernicus showed that the earth revolved around the sun, and the word went everywhere in books.

The rise of nation states. At the same time, the modern nation state took shape. Strong kings conquered weak feudal lords. The nation's laws, taxes, armies, and courts replaced those of the local nobles. People began to glory in the power of their king. They were proud to be French, English, Spanish, or Portuguese. For "king and country" they sought glory in war, riches in commerce, honor in the arts. And the more adventurous went out to plant their country's flag abroad. The wealth of the nation commanded by the new monarchs would outfit the ships to explore the world.

The lure of the East. The fabled Orient had a wonderful charm for the people of Europe. In 1271 the Venetian merchants Maffeo and Nicolo Polo, and Nicolo's young son Marco, traveled to China. They spent seventeen years there in the service of the Khan. Upon the Polos' return, the people of Venice were astonished by the gold and silks and jewels they had brought back. Marco Polo's book about his adventures was printed two centuries later on the new presses. When Columbus read Marco Polo's book, it whetted his appetite for the East.

Meanwhile the rich people of Europe wanted more and more of the goods from the Orient. These had come partly overland by risky trails through mountain and desert and partly by sea. Much was lost to bandits or to shipwrecks. The rising monarchs began to think of finding a direct way to the East entirely by sea.

The techniques of discovery. In Columbus's time all educated people and most sailors believed that the earth was a sphere. They disagreed about the size of the globe, and about how much was land and how much water. The coast of Africa was only beginning to be explored.

Prince Henry "the Navigator" (1394–1460) had set up a school for explorers at Cape St. Vincent on the southwestern tip of Portugal. He began to push voyages of discovery along the coast of Africa. He trained the sailors and their captains, improved the design of ships, and gathered maps and charts. Within fifty years, his sailors made more progress exploring the west coast of Africa than Europeans had made in the thousand years before.

Since about 1200, sailors had had the compass to help them find their way. To figure latitude and see where they were on the map, they used other simple instruments—the astrolabe, the quadrant, and the cross-staff. They had no way to discover longitude. This meant that they could not figure exactly where they were east or west, or how wide was the Western Ocean.

During their African voyages of discovery the Portuguese designed a new kind of sailing ship—the "caravel." It was a lithe, but sturdy, three-masted or four-masted vessel that was excellent for exploration. Caravels had sails that could be set to catch the wind so if they sailed somewhere with the wind they could still sail back, even with the wind against them.

SECTION 3 REVIEW

1. Identify: Copernicus, Johann Gutenberg, Marco Polo, Prince Henry of Portugal, caravel.

2. Describe Portuguese explorers' contributions.

3. **Determining Relevance.** What developments set the stage for an age of discovery?

The lateen sail, invented by the Arabs, enabled Portuguese sailors to tack into the wind.

4. Spanish adventurers

All the forces at work in western Europe and all the new knowledge, equipment, and techniques gathered by the Portuguese came together, as we have seen, in the most important seafaring voyage in history. Columbus opened a half-century of Spanish exploration and conquest. For Europe the 1500s became the Age of Discovery and a time of grand adventure.

The Norse discoveries. In fact, Columbus was not the very first European to see America. From 800 to 1100 the best sailors in Europe came from Norway, Denmark, and Sweden. They sailed to Iceland by 870 and on to Greenland by about 985. They did not use the boats with big figureheads that we usually think of as "Viking," because those were warships. They crossed the ocean in heavy open boats without the aid of the compass.

The first Norseman to see America was probably Bjarni Herjulfson. He had set out for Greenland in

986, but missed it and came upon an unknown shore covered with woods. Bjarni did not land, but he saw Labrador and Baffin Island before sailing back to Greenland. His report of what he had seen led Leif Ericson in 1001 to sail across and put a temporary settlement in Newfoundland. The Norse sagas tell of others who came to America, including one of Leif's brothers and his bold but quarrelsome half-sister Freydis. When the Eskimos attacked one of these settlements, Freydis saved the day. Grabbing a sword, she rallied the frightened men and led them against the attackers. But the Norse people were too few, they did not know the frigid land, and they squabbled among themselves. They did not manage to stay.

The Norse voyages brought no feedback to Europe. Their tales were buried in the Norse sagas. Their actions led nowhere. Not until the first voyage of Columbus did Europe learn of America.

Amerigo Vespucci. Since Columbus discovered a New World, we might expect it to be called by his name. Instead, the name "America" comes from Amerigo Vespucci, an Italian navigator from Florence. Soon after Columbus, Vespucci made two voyages to the New World. Vespucci wrote a vivid account of the lands he saw. He called them a new continent—"what we may rightly call a New World."

Amerigo's name—America—first appeared on a map in 1507 because a French map-printer, Waldseemüller, had read his account of the New World and was impressed. So he called the new continent "America." The printer later changed his mind. He thought maybe some other name would be better. In his next maps he left off the word. But by then it was too late. Printing presses had spread hundreds of copies over Europe. The name "America" stuck because people liked it, and it has been used ever since.

The name "America" was first used on this map made by Martin Waldseemüller in 1507. These segments were designed to fit together into the sphere of the earth. The label "America" is to the right, on what represents South America. Waldseemüller left a gap between North and South America and avoided delineating the unknown west coast of North America.

The Treaty of Tordesillas.

The Christians in Europe believed that the Pope had the power to divide up all newly discovered "pagan" lands among the Christian monarchs. Columbus had sailed under the Spanish flag. When King John II of Portugal learned of Columbus's voyage, he protested to the Pope. He said that Columbus had sailed into lands reserved for Portugal. The Pope issued a series of new "bulls" (formal papal decrees) in 1493 that divided the world along a line drawn down the Atlantic Ocean. Luckily for Spain, Pope Alexander VI was a Spaniard who owed his election to Ferdinand and Isabella. The line he drew just happened to be in Spain's favor. All lands discovered west of the line (where most of the new lands were) would belong to Spain, all lands to the east (including mostly Atlantic Ocean) would go to Portugal.

Portugal was not pleased with this papal line. And Spain was not sure that it could enforce the line if Portugal did not agree. So in 1494 the two seafaring powers signed the Treaty of Tordesillas. This moved the line farther west. The two nations still thought the line would fall in the middle of the Atlantic. Instead it cut off most of what is now Brazil. This explains why today the Brazilians speak Portuguese. The lands of Brazil were discovered by accident by a Portuguese sailor in 1500. Portugal's claim to the area dates back to this treaty.

Balboa.

For Europeans wanting to sail west to Asia, the American continents were only an obstacle. How could they get through? In the first century after Columbus, explorers looked anxiously for a way through, around, or over America. Then they could reach the real Indies, where the treasure was!

At the time, nobody in Europe imagined there would be a Pacific Ocean. It, too, would be discovered by the good luck of courageous men. Vasco Núñez de Balboa, a Spaniard, had tried to be a planter on the island of Hispaniola in the Caribbean. When he failed, and was pursued by his creditors, he smuggled himself off the island in a cask. The ship he happened on was going to Panama, and Balboa joined the expedition.

In the new settlement in Panama the bold Balboa quickly rose to become governor. Darien (Santa Maria de l'Antigua) was the earliest permanent European settlement on the continent. Balboa married the daughter of an Indian chief. For Balboa's help in one of their wars, the Indians offered the Spaniards 4000 ounces of gold. The impatient Spaniards quarreled over the scales as the gold was weighed out. The Indian chief was disgusted. Since they seemed so greedy, he said, "I'll show you a region flowing with gold."

To find that fabulous land, Balboa set out across the Isthmus of Panama on September 1, 1513. With him were 190 Spaniards and several hundred Indians. There were 30 blacks with Balboa. He needed plenty of help, for the jungle was dense and dark. It took them four weeks to cover 45 miles. Finally, on September 29, Balboa, sword in hand, waded into the surf of the ocean that Europeans had never known. In the name of the king of Spain he claimed possession of the Sea of the South and all the coasts it touched.

Balboa's life ended in tragedy—the risk of every *conquistador* (Spanish for "conqueror"). When an enemy became governor of Darien, Balboa and four of his companions were falsely accused of treason. They were all beheaded in the Darien public square and their bodies thrown to the vultures.

Magellan.

The Pacific Ocean which Balboa had discovered was the largest ocean in the world. It was equal in area to all the lands of the planet. The man who unveiled the grandeur of the Pacific was Fernão de Magalhães, whom we call Ferdinand Magellan. A Portuguese noble and an expert sailor, he had already sailed eastward from Europe—even as far as the Spice Islands. Like Columbus, he believed that those islands could more easily be reached by sailing west. He proposed this round-the-world trip to his king, Manuel I. But by then King Manuel was more interested in the route around Africa which the Portuguese Vasco da Gama had already taken all the way to India.

So Magellan went on to Spain. The 18-year-old king, Charles I, snapped up the idea and put Magellan in charge of five ships carrying 265 officers and men.

In September 1519 Magellan set out on a trip around the world—the longest sea voyage in history. First, he had to find a way around America. That took him over a year, during which he put down a mutiny and lost one of his vessels in a shipwreck. By October 1520 he had entered what we now call the Strait of Magellan. It took him five

GREENLAND

Cabot

• Bristol

EUROPE

NORTH AMERICA

ATLANTIC OCEAN

Lisbon • • Palos
• Cadiz

ASIA

CHINA

PANAMA

INDIA

PHILIPPINE ISLANDS

Vespucci

Magellan

Calicut

✕ Magellan Died 1521

SOUTH AMERICA

AFRICA

Da Gama

INDIAN OCEAN

Magellan

PACIFIC OCEAN

Dias

MADAGASCAR

Magellan's Crew

AUSTRALIA

Strait of Magellan

TIERRA DEL FUEGO

Cape Horn

Cape of Good Hope

Line of Demarcation (As Adjusted, 1494)

Early Voyages of Discovery

⟵ Dias 1486-1488   ⟵ Vespucci 1499-1500

⟵ Da Gama 1497   ⟵ Magellan 1519-1521

⟵ Cabot 1497   ⟵-- Magellan's Crew 1522

0 ————————— 4000 Miles

0 ————————— 4000 Kilometers

See page 783 for map study skill exercises on this map.

weeks (as long as it had taken Columbus to cross the Atlantic) to make his way through the perilous, twisting, mountain-lined waterway at the southern end of South America. During this frightening passage the crew of one of his ships mutinied and sailed back to Spain.

On November 28, 1520, Magellan entered the Pacific with three ships and 150 crewmen. With no idea of its size, they started across the world's greatest ocean. The optimistic Magellan believed that it was only a few hundred miles from Panama to Japan.

Instead, the Pacific stretched 10,000 miles! For three months Magellan and his three ships sailed on. They had so much fair weather that they decided to call this the "Pacific" (peaceful) Ocean. But they had no fresh provisions or fresh water. After devouring their last moldy biscuits which swarmed with worms, they chewed the leather of

the rigging and they ate sawdust. They were glad to make a meal of the shipboard rats. Nineteen of the crew died of scurvy, caused by a lack of the vitamin C found in fresh fruit and vegetables. If they had been delayed by storms, they could not have survived. "Had not God and His blessed mother given us good weather," wrote Antonio Pigafetta, who accompanied Magellan, "we would all have died of hunger in that exceeding vast ocean."

On March 6, 1521, Magellan's fleet finally reached the island of Guam. There they resupplied for the next stage of their voyage—to the islands now called the Philippines (after King Philip of Spain). In the Philippines Magellan's slave Enrique, whom he had bought eleven years before at Malacca on the Malay peninsula, was able to communicate with the natives. Magellan made the fatal mistake of joining in the battles between the Philippine

This double-headed snake sculpture of turquoise mosaic was made by the Aztecs.

tribes. On the shore of a Philippine island in a petty skirmish over a cause he never understood, the great Magellan was hacked to death. He was denied the glory of completing that first trip around the world.

After his death in that trivial tribal fight, the remaining crew pushed on. One ship, no longer seaworthy, was left behind. Another was seized by the Portuguese. A further year of danger—completing three years at sea—at last brought one ship, the *Vittoria,* with eighteen sailors and three natives back home to Spain. Finally someone had circumnavigated the globe!

No other voyage has equaled Magellan's contribution to our knowledge of the earth. Now the notion that the world was round was no longer just a theory. Magellan fulfilled Columbus's dream of reaching the Indies by sailing west. The voyage began to show how much of the earth is covered by the sea. Even so, the extent of the Pacific would be underestimated for many years to come. Most important of all, Magellan's voyage—around America—revealed that the new lands were not part of Asia, not just a promontory of the Island of the Earth. The Americas were continents by themselves. The American continents would be called

the Western Hemisphere—which filled a half of the sphere that was the earth.

Spain and America. For more than 50 years after Columbus, the Spaniards had the New World mostly to themselves. Who dared challenge Spain—the richest and most powerful nation in Europe? In 1519 King Charles I of Spain was elected Holy Roman Emperor and became Emperor Charles V. In theory the Holy Roman Empire covered all of Christendom. The emperor was supposed to rule it all. The armies of Charles V defeated the French, then the only serious rival power on the continent of Europe. His fleets controlled the Mediterranean. And his Council of the Indies at Seville was supposed to run the affairs of the whole New World.

The Spanish court gave charters to one adventurer after another. Ferdinand and Isabella had made Columbus the "Admiral of the Ocean Sea." Some went without permission. Brave conquistadores led expeditions to the mainland of America. There they set themselves up as viceroys, or governors, of new provinces. Most spent their lives searching for treasure that never existed.

Some actually conquered native empires and fulfilled their dreams with the New World's treasure.

Hernando Cortes and the Aztecs. Perhaps the most courageous and successful conquistador was Hernando Cortes. In 1519, the same year Magellan set out on his voyage, the bold 34-year-old Cortes landed on the coast of Mexico with 550 soldiers, 16 horses, and 10 brass cannon. Within a year he had subdued the Aztec empire. He won by bravery, ruthlessness, skill, luck, and the help of imported European diseases which killed thousands of Indians. Cortes arrived in a ship larger than any seen there before. Riding on horses, the Spaniards seemed superhuman. Their guns killed at a distance with terrifying magic. No wonder the Aztecs thought they had been invaded by the gods!

From Mexico Cortes brought to the king of Spain the first rich cargoes from America. When the treasures of gold and silver reached the court of Charles V, Spaniards awoke to the fact that America was more than a mere obstacle to the Indies.

Pizarro and Peru. In Europe scores of other adventurers now hoped to find their fortune here. Early in 1531 another ambitious Spaniard, Francisco Pizarro, landed in Peru with a small force of 180 soldiers and 27 horses. In the splendid ancient city of Cajamarca he found the new Inca, or emperor, who had just won a civil war. The Inca greeted Pizarro as a friend. In return, Pizarro seized him. The Inca offered to fill a room with treasure to win his release, and Pizarro agreed. Soon the room was bulging with a glittering pile of gold, silver, and precious gems. When the gold was weighed, it totaled 13,265 pounds and the silver 26,000 pounds. Pizarro melted it down to divide between himself and his men. Each cavalryman received 90 pounds of gold and 180 of silver. Infantrymen received less, but everyone had enough to be rich for life.

The Spanish were afraid to release the Inca for fear he would lead an uprising against them. So they used treachery. They accused the Inca of crimes he had never committed and executed him. Then they took the Incan capital at Cuzco, which brought down the whole Incan empire.

When the treasure flowed back to Spain, countless adventurous young men laid plans for their own expeditions to America. To find another Mexico or Peru, was it not worth risking your life? Reckless,

Skilled Incan artisans fashioned these exquisite cups of solid gold to hold offerings to the gods during special ceremonies.

ruthless conquistadores crossed the ocean to face fever, starvation, shipwreck, and hostile Indians. They stumbled their way through pathless woods, swamps, jungles, and deserts—hoping to win their gamble for a fortune.

Exploration in the present-day United States. While some conquistadores explored southward from central Mexico, others were searching for gold—or something more precious—in North America. When Juan Ponce de León ventured to Florida in 1513, he was looking for an island named "Bimini." On that island there was said to be a fountain that would restore youth to all who bathed in it. Ponce de León named the mainland "Florida," either because of the flowers there or the fact that he arrived on or soon after Easter (Pascua Florida, or "Flowering Easter"). Unfortunately he never found the magic fountain.

HUDSON BAY

LABRADOR

Gilbert

Cartier

NEWFOUNDLAND

NORTH
AMERICA

GREAT LAKES

St. Lawrence R.

ROCKY MOUNTAINS

Colorado R.

GRAND
CANYON

Coronado

Missouri R.

Ohio R.

Arkansas R.

Red R.

Mississippi

De Soto

ATLANTIC

OCEAN

De Vaca

Rio Grande

Esteban

Conchos R.

Narváez

GULF OF MEXICO

FLORIDA

Ponce de León

Verrazano

Cortes

CUBA

Santiago

HISPANIOLA

San Juan

Tenochtitlán
(Mexico City)

Veracruz

CENTRAL
AMERICA

CARIBBEAN SEA

Santo Domingo

Balboa

PANAMA

Pizarro

Amazon R.

SOUTH
AMERICA

Cuzco

Early New World Explorations

Spanish

 Balboa 1513

Ponce de León 1513

Cortes 1519

Pizarro 1531–1533

Narváez 1528

De Vaca-Esteban 1528–1536

Coronado 1540–1542

De Soto 1539–1543

French

Verrazano 1524

Cartier 1534–1536

English

Gilbert 1583

Aztecs

Mayas

Incas

0   1500 Miles
0   1500 Kilometers

Florida, a beautiful tropic land, attracted many others who were no more lucky. Pánfilo de Narváez, the enemy and rival of Cortes, hoped to find in Florida (a name the Spanish applied to all America north of the Gulf of Mexico between the Rocky Mountains and the Atlantic) wealth like that Cortes had found in Mexico. In 1527 he landed with 400 men and 80 horses on the gulf coast.

Nothing was heard of the expedition until nine years later. Then remnants of Narváez's crew—Cabeza de Vaca, Alonso del Castillo, Andrés Dorantes, and Dorantes's black slave Esteban—met a Spanish party seeking Indian slaves in the western desert. The survivors told a hair-raising story of Indian battles, of building boats and trying to sail to Mexico, of the loss of their boats one by one, and then the deaths of all the other hundreds in their party. For years they had been held by Indians until they escaped and made their way toward Mexico. The Indians had learned to distrust the warlike strangers. Still the Indians did not kill these four because they were thought to be medicine men with powers to heal the sick.

When at last the four survivors reached Mexico, they reported the "hunchbacked cows" (the buffalo) that they had seen. And they repeated enticing rumors of cities with emerald-studded walls.

Esteban and Fray Marcos.

Having had their fill of exploring, three of these plucky adventurers—de Vaca, Castillo, and Dorantes—were glad to return to Spain. Esteban, no longer a slave, was hired in 1539 by Fray Marcos, a Franciscan monk, to help find the cities with emerald-studded walls—the fabulous "Seven Cities of Cibola." This new expedition found the pueblos of the Zuñi Indians, which can still be seen in New Mexico. Esteban was killed by the Indians. Father Marcos, who had only heard of the pueblos from Esteban, reported that he had located the fabulous Seven Cities.

Coronado.

On hearing Fray Marcos's report, Francisco de Coronado, with a well-equipped expedition, set out from Mexico to find the mythical treasures. With 300 Spaniards, 1000 Indians, and 1500 horses, mules, and beef cattle, the large party departed north in March 1540 to look for the Seven Cities. They also hoped to come upon the "Strait of Anian," the Northwest Passage which most people thought would lead through America and open the way to Asia. By amazing good luck the expedition discovered the Grand Canyon! Even this did not satisfy them. It would not make them rich. They saw the pueblos, and went all the way to central Kansas. But since he never found the fabled Seven Cities of Cibola, Coronado returned "in sadness" to report his failure to the governor of Mexico.

Hernando de Soto.

The most elaborate Spanish expedition in the New World was led by Hernando de Soto. He was already a wealthy man, since he had been a partner of Pizarro's in Peru. But he wanted to be even richer.

De Soto was in Spain when de Vaca returned there with his tall tales of the mysterious Seven Cities of Cibola. Upon hearing the news, de Soto thought this might be a chance to find another Incan empire. He went to Charles V for aid. The emperor agreed, since de Soto had lent him money. So Charles helped de Soto enlist hundreds of nobles and gentlemen along with carpenters, smiths, and priests.

De Soto's party of 570 men, 223 horses, a pack of dogs for hunting, and a herd of hogs for meat landed near the present Fort Myers, Florida, in May 1539. During the next four years the expedition wandered over what is now Georgia, Alabama, Mississippi, across Arkansas, and on to Oklahoma. Finally they gave up their fruitless quest for a new Incan empire. They made boats to sail down the Mississippi and cross the gulf to Mexico, where they arrived in September 1543. Over half the party had died during those four years, including de Soto, who was buried in the Mississippi River.

New Spain.

The Spanish settlers wanted gold. And at first they were not eager to settle in a land of disappointment. Still the Spanish actually claimed the entire North American continent. They settled only in the West Indies and Mexico. This realm, which they called New Spain, became a great overseas empire spreading into Central and South America. Not until the 1560s did they begin to plant permanent settlements in the present area of the United States. Then, when their settlements had pushed close to the Rio Grande, they conquered the Pueblo Indians and established the province of New Mexico. Santa Fe was founded in 1609, at about the same time as Jamestown.

1. Identify: Leif Ericson, Amerigo Vespucci, Vasco Núñez de Balboa, Ferdinand Magellan, Charles V, Hernando Cortes, Francisco Pizarro, Ponce de León, Pánfilo de Narváez, Cabeza de Vaca, Esteban, Francisco de Coronado.

2. Locate: Labrador, Greenland, Canary Islands, Panama, Newfoundland, Guam.

3. Why do we celebrate Columbus' discovery of America rather than the Vikings'?

4. What were the unexpected results of the Treaty of Tordesillas?

5. Why was Magellan's voyage important?

6. What effect did the conquest of the Aztecs have on Spain?

7. Why could the small armies of Cortes and Pizarro defeat the Aztecs and the Incas?

8. What is "the Northwest Passage"? Why did explorers want to find it?

9. **Drawing Conclusions.** How did the explorers' reports shape Europeans' views of the world?

5. French and English exploration

For many years the Spanish dominated the New World, but they did not have it all to themselves. Despite the Papal Bull dividing the New World between Spain and Portugal, other nations wanted their share. King Francis I of France joked at the Pope's division of the earth. The ancestor of all mankind was Adam. But where in Adam's will, Francis asked, was the provision cutting out all the other nations in the world? By now England, too, had become a great seafaring nation, ready to ignore the Pope's decision.

John Cabot. The first successful attempt to break the Spanish and Portuguese monopoly was made by England. The capable but cautious King Henry VII had actually refused to finance Columbus's voyage. Since he had missed that chance, he was ready to listen when John Cabot (who, like Columbus, had been born in Genoa) approached him. Since everyone still believed that Columbus had reached the Indies, Cabot now proposed to find a better way to get there. He thought that sailing northwest was the answer.

Cabot offered to make the trip at his own cost, but he wanted royal approval. He manned his one small vessel, the *Mathew,* with a crew of only eighteen. On May 20, 1497, he sailed into the North Atlantic. Except for one gale just before he reached America, he had an easy crossing. Shortly after sunrise on the morning of June 24 Cabot reached Newfoundland. He was probably only a few miles from where Leif Ericson had tried his settlement 500 years before.

Cabot—like Columbus before him—was looking for a way through to China. He turned south, probably because of ice. Then somewhere along the coast he entered a harbor (perhaps Griquet Harbor) and claimed the land for England. He coasted all along Newfoundland, but he did not stop again. Reaching the end of Newfoundland, Cabot sailed back to where he had first touched on the island and then headed for home. After an amazingly fast passage of fifteen days to Brittany he then sailed on to Bristol, where he had started. His whole trip had taken only eleven weeks. It would be nearly a century before anyone would make a faster round trip to America.

When Henry VII received Cabot's report, he was delighted. Stingy as usual, he handed Cabot only £10. Then, to show his pleasure, he gave Cabot a pension of £20 a year. Others were more enthusiastic. Londoners paid him "vast honor" and "ran after him like mad people."

In February 1498, King Henry gave Cabot the power to impress four good-sized ships into his service for a new expedition. King Henry even supplied one vessel himself. These ships were loaded with goods to start a trading post—in Japan! Cabot sailed again from Bristol in May 1498. One ship had to turn back, but the other four sailed away, never to return. Nothing was ever heard again of them, or of Cabot. But for the next two centuries John Cabot's first voyage remained the basis of England's claim to the whole mainland of North America.

Giovanni da Verrazano. The French also tried to find a passage through America toward the riches of the East. For the first half of the 1500s France was at war with Spain. In 1522, French corsairs seized a Spanish treasure ship that Cortes was sending home from Mexico. The riches on that ship must have encouraged Francis I.

Meanwhile, as early as 1503, French boats had started fishing on the Grand Banks of Newfoundland. In the next century French boats were active there and were drying their catch on the land.

At this time the geography of North America, between Newfoundland and Florida, was still a mystery. Why couldn't there be, somewhere along that coast, the long-sought water passage westward to Asia? Merchants in the French city of Lyon were eager for the profits of the China trade. With the approval of King Francis they hired the Italian explorer Giovanni da Verrazano from Florence to seek the way.

On January 17, 1524, Verrazano sailed for America. On March 1 he reached Cape Fear in what is now North Carolina. To avoid the Spaniards, he turned north. In the neighborhood of Cape Hatteras he looked across an isthmus only a mile wide. He thought he could see the Pacific Ocean. In fact, he was looking into Pamlico Sound. But he failed to find a way through the isthmus.

Verrazano then sailed still farther north. He missed Chesapeake and Delaware bays but discovered the beautiful bay of New York. He anchored near the site of the present-day Verrazano Bridge. He did not stay long. Instead he sailed east along Long Island, discovered Block Island, entered Narragansett Bay and anchored at Newport Harbor. Since the Indians there were friendly, he stayed two weeks before again heading east. He passed through Vineyard Sound, crossed the dangerous waters of Nantucket Sound with its many shoals, rounded Cape Cod, crossed to Maine, and sailed on to Newfoundland. Then, when he realized that he had reached the land discovered by Cabot, he turned for home.

Verrazano had done more than anyone before to fill in the map of east-coast North America. But he had not found the westward passage, and he had made no profits. The merchants of Lyon gave up, and King Francis turned to his endless wars with Spain.

Jacques Cartier.

Francis I's interest in America was accidentally reawakened on a pilgrimage to Mont-St.-Michel, the magnificent abbey which we can still visit on the northern coast of France. There the abbot told the king that in the nearby town of Saint-Malo lived a sailor who would discover lands

This delicately colored glazed terra cotta figure of Italian explorer Giovanni da Verrazano was made sometime around the 1520s.

for the king in the New World. The wealthy abbot even offered to share the cost of the expedition. With the help of the abbot, and a new Pope who now agreed to let Francis claim lands in the New World, the French returned to explore North America.

Jacques Cartier, the sailor from Saint-Malo, made three voyages to the New World for the king. On his first voyage in 1534, Cartier discovered and explored the Gulf of St. Lawrence. So he began to open the great passage to the continent's interior.

Cartier's voyage the following spring penetrated the continent. Entering the St. Lawrence River itself, he sailed all the way to the site of Montreal, where there was a large Indian village. Since his boat could not pass the rapids, he returned to the site of what is now Quebec. There he spent a long, hard winter. When his men came down with scurvy, they finally were saved by a friendly Indian who

Nicolas Vallard's map of Canada in 1547 showed the arrival of Cartier and his party, including the surprising presence of several women. Cartier is in front center wearing a short cloak. Vallard also portrayed several groups of Indians.

showed them how to cure the disease by eating the crushed and cooked bark of the evergreen arborvitae (tree of life).

When Cartier returned to France in July 1536, he brought back with him an Indian chief. The chief told the king tall tales about the riches of Canada. In May 1541 Cartier set out again with five ships, some colonists (many were convicts), and a variety of animals. This time he aimed to start a permanent French colony in America. Near modern Quebec they did build a settlement. Indian attacks killed off 35 of the colonists. The next spring, when no help had come from home, Cartier decided to take all the colonists back to France. Just as they were departing, at St. John's, Newfoundland, they met the expedition sent to their aid. It was too late. Cartier's patience was worn thin, and he led his people home. The new arrivals, after a hard winter ashore, also gave up.

Hardy French adventurers kept coming back to Canada to fish and trade for fur. They also tried to establish colonies in South Carolina and Florida. But decades would pass before there was a New France in America.

SECTION 5 REVIEW

1. Identify: John Cabot, Giovanni da Verrazano, Jacques Cartier, Henry VII, Francis I.

2. Locate: Newfoundland, Verrazano's route, Cartier's route, Florida, St. Lawrence River, Montreal, Quebec.

3. Why did Cartier fail to establish a successful permanent settlement in Canada?

4. **Making Comparisons.** How did France's and England's explorational aims compare to those of Spain and Portugal?

CHAPTER 1 REVIEW

FOCUSING ON IDEAS

1. Identify Columbus' most important navigational and geographic achievements and explain how they aided later explorations.

2. What political and cultural developments in Europe contributed to interest in and support for exploration?

3. What role did rivalries between European nations play in the discovery and exploration of the New World?

4. What lands in the Western Hemisphere did Spain, Portugal, England, and France claim? On what was each of these claims based?

TAKING A CRITICAL LOOK

1. **Recognizing Cause and Effect.** The story of the first European explorations of the Western Hemisphere is full of "accidents" and rumors. How did accidents and rumors affect where exploration took place?

2. **Recognizing Bias.** The first encounters Europeans had with the advanced Indian cultures of the New World, such as the Aztecs and Incas, left Europeans astonished. What elements of these Indian civilizations were most surprising to the Europeans? How is this astonishment an example of ethnocentrism, the feeling that one's own ethnic group or race is superior to all others?

3. **Making Comparisons.** Within a span of only 35 years, Dias rounded the Cape of Good Hope, Columbus made his voyage to the New World, Balboa discovered the Pacific Ocean, and Magellan and his crew sailed around the world. All of these events fit easily into an average lifetime. What major world events have occurred so far in your lifetime? During your parents' lifetimes? How do these events compare with those of the sixteenth century?

YOUR REGION IN HISTORY

1. **Geography.** What European nation first laid claim to your locality? What evidence can you identify as to their presence?

2. **Culture.** What Indian groups lived in your region about the year 1500? What sort of culture did they have? What, if any, artifacts did they leave behind?

3. **Economics.** In what ways did the early adventurers profit from the exploration of your region?

HISTORICAL FACTS AND FIGURES

Formulating Hypotheses. Study the graph below to help answer the following questions: (a)What happened to the Indian population of Central America during the period 1520–1610? (b) Formulate a hypothesis or educated guess explaining the impact of Spain's arrival in the New World.

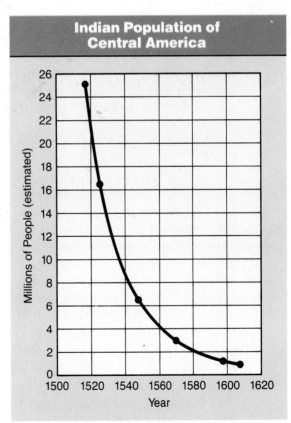

Source: Nicolas Sanchez-Albornoz, *The Population of Latin America*

CHAPTER 2

An assortment of colonies

The first Europeans to settle in America were the Spaniards. It was nearly 100 years before other Europeans joined them on the North American continent. The Spanish pioneers came for God, gold, and glory. They created an American empire that lasted 300 years.

The nearer the Indians were to centers of Spanish settlement like Mexico City or Lima, the more their own cultures were replaced by the language, the religion, and the politics imported from Spain. But there were remote areas that the Spaniards did not reach for a long time. Until 1700, in the jungles of northern Guatemala Mayan priests worshiped undisturbed! In the Amazon basin today there are Indians still untouched by Western civilization. But the Spanish wanted to convert all the Indians to their Spanish ways. And, on the whole, they were surprisingly successful.

When the English came, they never tried to make Englishmen out of Indians. Instead they saw the Indians as part of the wilderness that they aimed to clear away. The English came for many reasons. To them the American colonies were an assortment of dreams and hopes and fears. English settlers thought anything was possible here, and they were not far wrong. Some came with definite plans, others with troubled consciences. Some came as charity cases, owing everything to a few rich people in London. Some came simply for profit. Others came seeking refuge. All would become Americans.

Besides the Spanish and the English, the French, the Dutch, and the Swedes all founded colonies in North America. Each of these differed from the others. Whether a settlement died or lived and how it grew depended on many things. Much depended on the climate and the soil and the animals and the Indians. Much depended on government policies. Much depended on whether the settlers had planned, and what they had planned, and how quickly they could learn what the continent had to teach. And much depended on luck.

1. The Spanish Empire

Vast stretches of what is now the United States were explored by the Spaniards. Their forts and missions dotted the Spanish borderlands which stretched from Florida, Georgia, and the Carolinas westward along the Gulf Coast, across Arizona and New Mexico and on into California. The first traders and settlers from the United States arrived in New Mexico and California in the 1820s. There they found a Spanish-American society that had existed for 200 years. And there the Spanish settlements have left their mark to this day.

The control of the Indians. The settlers, the church, and the crown all competed for power in the Spanish colonies. At first the conquistadores who had come from Spain ruled them all. These men came to get rich quick. They enslaved the Indians, but both the church and the crown objected. So a new system was devised called the *encomienda* (from a Spanish word meaning to entrust). By the encomienda the king "entrusted" to a Spanish settler a group of Indian families. The Indians had to pay tribute to the Spanish settler. This tribute was either in the form of the crops they grew or in days of forced labor. Many times the encomienda was little better than slavery.

The kings of Spain feared that the lords of the encomiendas were becoming too rich and too independent. So over many years the crown slowly reduced the power of the encomiendas. Meanwhile diseases brought by the Europeans—smallpox, typhoid, and measles—were killing off the Indian population. At first there were about 50 million Indians in the areas the Spanish conquered. By 1700 this number fell to some 4 million Indians. The encomiendas naturally lost their value without Indians to work them.

As the encomienda system disappeared, its place was taken by another kind of forced labor on the large estates called *haciendas*. In theory, the Indians were not slaves, but they usually became indebted to the owner of the hacienda and were not allowed to leave. Still, the landowner had reason to keep the families well enough fed so they could do their work. The poor Indian farmer had become a "peon"—enslaved by debt.

Colonial government. The Spanish king thought of the colonies as his personal property. He ruled through the Supreme Council of the Indies, which remained in Spain. That Council had absolute power over colonial life. The head of the government in America was the viceroy.

This document which Indians sent to the Spanish court protested the burdens of the encomienda.

The Museum of Mankind

Spanish Borderlands about 1780

← Kino
← Serra
⚑ Mission and Fort
† Mission

0   500 Miles

0   500 Kilometers

Spanish policy aimed to make the colonies benefit the mother country. The colony was supposed to produce only what Spain needed and to buy everything that it needed from Spain. Thus the mother country profited both ways. This policy was called *mercantilism*. It was followed by all the countries that planted colonies in America. Unlike England, Spain strictly enforced this policy. The Council organized an elaborate system of control.

The Spanish king and Spanish churchmen believed it was their sacred duty to convert the Indians to the Roman Catholic church. To accomplish this, they organized missions. Each mission was a complete Indian settlement including a church, shops, farms, and livestock, all overseen by a few monks. Some missions, like the worst encomiendas, offered the Indians a kind of slavery. Others were sincere, saintly efforts to bring the Indians into a Christian community of brotherly love.

The church early declared itself against the enslavement of the Indians but did not oppose the use of black slaves. As the Indian population declined—and in some areas disappeared—black slaves from Africa took their place. At the end of the colonial period, in the 1820s, in Spanish America there were 750,000 blacks in a total population of 17 million.

Settling the Spanish borderlands. Since the Spanish feared that someone else would occupy the borderlands, they made it a point to settle there whenever it appeared another country might move in. They tried to hold the territory by setting up Catholic missions and army forts. The first Spanish settlement in the borderlands was built in 1565 at St. Augustine, Florida. At a fort there, a force of soldiers with their families was stationed. St. Augustine remained a Spanish settlement until 1821.

The Spanish moved into New Mexico mainly to convert the Indians. Missionaries were followed by the settlers who founded Santa Fe in 1609. When the Indians revolted in 1680, all the Europeans were forced to flee. They did not return until Spanish soldiers retook the area in the 1690s. Anglo-Americans, who came in the 1800s, remained a minority in New Mexico as late as 1928.

Missionaries, led by Father Eusebio Francisco Kino, entered Arizona in the late 1600s. In Texas, a mission was founded at El Paso in 1659. Six other missions and two forts were set up in Texas between 1712 and 1721. The Spanish advanced into California after Russian explorers and fur trappers began to show up there. Beginning in 1769 the Spanish built a string of missions and forts to protect California against the Russians.

The pioneer missionary was the brave and learned Father Junípero Serra. Born on the Spanish island of Mallorca, he became a Franciscan monk and was sent to Mexico City. He founded San Diego mission, the first of 21 missions on the California coast. Then he helped found missions at San Gabriel, San Luis Obispo, Santa Clara, and San Francisco. Father Serra was a living example of charity. He stood up for the Indians against the Spanish army commanders. He walked the long miles from one mission to another to counsel the missionaries and to protect the Indians.

The Spanish settler. Nearly all Spaniards who came to America were men. Unmarried girls in Spain were strictly supervised by their families and were not allowed to come to America alone. The young Spanish settlers here married Indian women. And there grew up in the Spanish lands an interesting racially mixed society.

These Spanish and mestizo (mixed blood) communities that arose before 1800 in New Mexico, California, and Arizona were small. Far from the chief Spanish settlements in Mexico, they had little contact with the outside world. They lived on what they could raise, grow, or catch. By 1810 in New Mexico there were 35,000 Spanish and mestizos raising corn, onions, peas, beans, wheat, red peppers, and sheep. Many of them had become peons like those in Mexico.

In California, too, there were a few thousand Spanish and mestizos. They raised horses, cows, and sheep, and grew grapes, figs, oranges, and olives near the missions and the forts. In the missions, the Indians were taught Spanish ways of building, farming, and worshiping. But they were not allowed to leave these mission "schools." They were forever students of the friars. The economic growth of California would come only after Mexico declared independence from Spain in 1821.

Results of the Spanish conquests. The Spanish cut off the development of the Indian civilizations.

The Spanish mission and presidio at San Francisco were founded in 1776. M. Louis Choris, a Frenchman, made this lithograph of Indians dancing outside the California mission of San Francisco in 1813. He may have based his work on an earlier painting that has now disappeared. The priests watch from the left in front of the mission, a characteristically low building made of sun-dried bricks covered with stucco.

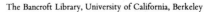

The Bancroft Library, University of California, Berkeley

In place of Mayan, Aztec, and Incan culture the Spanish built European-style cities. In Mexico City and Lima they set up universities and printing presses. They published learned books. They erected beautiful cathedrals. Spain's achievements and the wealth sent back to Spain led other countries to start their own colonies.

In the 1500s this overseas empire made Spain the most powerful nation in Europe. The riches pouring in from overseas tempted Spanish kings to extend their empire across Europe. Glutted with gold and silver from abroad, the Spanish rulers overlooked what their people needed at home. The growth of Spain's overseas empire became a cause of the decline of Spain.

SECTION 1 REVIEW

1. Identify or explain: encomienda, hacienda, Father Serra, Supreme Council of the Indies.

2. Locate: St. Augustine, the Spanish borderlands.

3. Describe the Spanish policy toward the Indians.

4. What was the aim of Spanish colonial policy? What was this policy called?

5. How did wealth from the empire affect Spain?

6. **Predicting Consequences.** If the Indian population had not declined, would the African slave trade have developed?

---

2. A great and victorious England

In the history of the United States the English colonies loomed larger than the colonies of other nations. Despite the early Spanish, Dutch, French, and Swedish settlements within the present borders of our nation, the English culture has dominated the land. Before England tried to rival Spain in America, England had to challenge Spain in Europe.

The Tudors transform England. A strong England needed a strong monarch. But until almost 1500 England was ruled by petty lords who fought with each other. The country was in a state of anarchy in 1485 when Henry Tudor (Henry VII) defeated Richard III in the battle at Bosworth. This began the reign of the Tudors, who unified the country and gave it great leaders. Tudor monarchs were intelligent, skillful, and ruthless. Henry VIII had many wives but a single love for England.

Wishing to run the church himself, he left the Roman Catholic church and made himself head of a new English (Episcopal) church. His brilliant daughter, Queen Elizabeth I, made England a leader of the Protestant states of Europe.

Queen Elizabeth was unusually learned for a monarch in those days. She read Latin and wrote poetry. But she never neglected the defense of her country. She never married, and so was called the Virgin Queen. She was afraid that if, as was the custom, her husband was the king of another country, England would be less independent. She saw that sea-power would build a strong nation. The navy would open the way to world-power. So she sent England's traders sailing to every corner of the globe. Elizabeth's "sea-dogs" looted the Spanish treasure ships. The boldest of her loyal pirates was Sir Francis Drake. On one voyage Drake took his ship around the world and returned laden with treasure. Elizabeth got her full share.

The grand test came when King Philip II of Spain decided to invade England. He was a proud and stubborn man. He worked hard at his job as ruler. He studied the products of his empire, and the weakening of his enemies. Philip was angered at the looting by English sea-dogs and by English support of a revolt against Spanish rule in the Netherlands. Since he had once been married to Mary Tudor, the Catholic queen of England, he believed that he and not Elizabeth should sit on the English throne. In 1587, when Philip was putting together his navy to invade England, Sir Francis Drake bravely sailed right into the harbor of Cadiz and burned a large part of the Spanish fleet. Philip still did not give up. He collected another fleet, and in 1588 the Spanish "Armada" (from the Spanish word for army or fleet), the largest ever assembled in Europe till then, set sail up the English Channel. Certain of success, the Spanish called it the "Invincible Armada."

England was ready and waiting. Every armed ship had been called into action. The British fleet fought the Spaniards as they moved through the channel and prevented them from reaching England. The Spanish sailors were well disciplined and well led. But they were far from home ports and could not get fresh supplies. The odds were against them. To cap it all, gale winds blew up to help the British defenders. The Armada was driven north and finally tried to reach home by sailing around

The "Armada Portrait" of Queen Elizabeth I, painted about 1588, emphasizes the power and wealth of the monarch whose navy has just gained supremacy on the sea. The English fleet sails by Elizabeth's right window. In the other window you can see the storm-tossed Spanish Armada.

Scotland and Ireland. In the end, only half the grand Spanish fleet limped home.

The defeat of the Spanish Armada in 1588 was one of the decisive battles of history. It marked the beginning of the decline of Spain and the rise of England. For only another century was Spain to remain a major power. In the last fifteen years of Elizabeth's reign, England still feared invasion. But England seized the opportunity to take the lead from Spain. England's trade was growing, and new industries (such as the manufacture of woolens) were prospering. Inspired by poets like William Shakespeare, the English set out to be heroes and pioneers—

This happy breed of men, this little world,
This precious stone set in the silver sea . . .

Gilbert, Raleigh, and Hakluyt. Patriots, dreamers, and adventurers, they went out to plant colonies overseas. Sir Humphrey Gilbert, like many Elizabethans, was not only a man of action, but a learned man as well. In 1566 he wrote *A Discourse of a Discoverie for a New Passage to Cataia* (Cathay) to persuade Queen Elizabeth to start settlements in the New World near the Northwest Passage to Asia. (They were sure the passage existed somewhere—but they never found it.) These settlements would extend England's trade

29

This portrait of Sir Walter Raleigh and his son Wat is dated 1602. A year later, on the death of Queen Elizabeth, Raleigh was imprisoned in the Tower of London.

Since he did not find a suitable place that summer, he decided to go home and try again the following year. But on the trip back to England his ship sank in a storm, and he and all the crew were lost. Gilbert had failed, but he was the pathfinder of the British Empire.

Gilbert's dream did not die with him. Others agreed that England must plant overseas colonies. And they found the ideal advertiser. A patriotic and industrious geographer, Richard Hakluyt, collected accounts of *The Principall Navigations, Voiages and Discoveries of the English Nation*. These three volumes told exciting tales of English heroes overseas. They encouraged others to serve their country by building an empire across the world.

Gilbert's half brother Walter Raleigh wanted to pursue the dream of a colony in America. The dashing, brilliant Raleigh was one of the most remarkable men of a remarkable generation. Educated at Oxford, he wrote good poetry and lively history. He even turned out a *History of the World*. And he too was a man of action if there ever was one. It is no wonder that he was a favorite of Queen Elizabeth's. In 1584 she granted him the right to start a settlement in America.

When Raleigh's men discovered Roanoke Island in Pamlico Sound, North Carolina, they said it was blessed with friendly Indians and fertile soil. It seemed perfect for an English colony. Raleigh then persuaded Hakluyt to write a *Discourse on Western Planting* to convince Queen Elizabeth to "plant" a royal colony there. The thrifty Elizabeth refused to risk her own money on the project, but she found less costly ways to please Raleigh. She knighted him and allowed him to name the settlement "Virginia" after her, the Virgin Queen.

In 1585 Sir Walter sent out his own expedition of about 100 men and boys to found his colony on Roanoke Island. After suffering through a terrible winter, the settlers gladly left when Sir Francis Drake with a fleet of 29 ships came by in the spring. Drake was on the way home after raids in the Spanish West Indies and at St. Augustine.

Still Raleigh did not give up. Having spent so much of his own fortune, now he had to enlist other people's money. He did this by the novel device of a "joint stock" company. He persuaded many people to buy "shares" of stock. In this way the risks in the venture could be divided. People without much money could still invest and have a

and give jobs to the unemployed. Gilbert himself would lead the way, and he would pay for the expedition.

In 1578 the queen gave him England's first colonial charter. An expedition in 1578–1579 failed to establish a colony. In June 1583 Gilbert set forth with five ships to try his luck once again.

share of the profit. Investors divided the profits (or losses) according to the number of shares they had bought.

With Hakluyt's help in advertising, Raleigh raised enough money to send out in 1587 a group of men, women, and children. Again they settled on Roanoke Island. The next year Raleigh and his fellow "adventurers" (as the investors were called) had a fleet of seven ships ready to take supplies to the colony. But they were stopped by the threat of the Spanish Armada. No supply ships went out in 1588, and none sailed the next year. Not until 1590 did help reach Roanoke. There they found an empty island and only the word CROATOAN written on a post and CRO on a tree. No one was sure what it meant. But the rescuers thought it was the name of the island to which the settlers had fled. Because of bad weather the relief expedition could not reach the island of Croatan. No one ever saw any of the Roanoke settlers again. They came to be called the "Lost Colony." Their true fate remained a mystery. But the Croatan Indians have a legend that the settlers became members of their tribe. Family names of 41 of the colonists survived within the tribe.

SECTION 2 REVIEW

1. Identify: the Tudors, Philip II, Humphrey Gilbert, Walter Raleigh, Richard Hakluyt, Croatoan, Lost Colony.
2. Locate: Cadiz, the Netherlands, London.
3. What was a joint stock company? Why was it used?
4. **Identifying Central Issues.** Why was the Spanish Armada's defeat important?

---

3. The planting of Virginia

Much had been learned from the failure of the Roanoke colony. Raleigh and Gilbert, helped by Hakluyt's advertising, had laid the groundwork for a British Empire in America.

At the end of Elizabeth's reign, England had the power and the will to found colonies in the New World. In a great burst of activity from 1606 to 1637, England planted Virginia, Maryland, and New England as well as colonies in Bermuda and the British West Indies.

Reasons for colonies. There were many reasons why England wanted to establish colonies. There was the lure of gold and silver. English sailors hoped at last to find a water passage through the North American continent to the rich trade of China and the Indies. And, of course, there was the chance to challenge Spain in North America!

The English hoped, too, that they would find in the New World the staple raw materials that they were spending their precious gold and silver to buy from other European countries. England was using up its own forests, and timber was needed for the navy. The settlers in America would be a market for British goods, especially for woolens. Commerce with the colonies would support a growing navy and merchant marine.

In England the rise in sheep farming had forced many men and women off the land. These jobless displaced people were flocking to the cities and increasing the crime there. If they were sent overseas, they could make their own way. And they could help convert the Indians to Protestant Christianity.

The unknown land. Even with all these motives, most people still did not want to emigrate. Why should they leave their familiar homeland for the dangers of an unknown America? Most of the facts they were told about the new country were wrong. Some of these imagined facts were printed because honest promoters did not know the truth. But much of what was printed was a sales pitch. The fantastic advertising brochures invented "facts" to help sell land in America. People who had invested in the American land knew that if nobody went out there it would remain a wilderness. And their land would be worthless.

So the promoters drew imaginary pictures, using ancient legends mixed with their wildest hopes and fondest dreams. The weather in America, they said, was always sunny. The oranges, lemons, apples, pears, peaches, and apricots were "so delicious that whoever tastes them will despise the insipid watery taste of those we have in England." The American venison was so juicy that English people would barely recognize it. The fish were large and easy to catch. In America there were no diseases—and no crowds. Everybody stayed young and everybody could live like a king. Come to this American paradise!

John Visscher's 1616 engraving of London Bridge shows a crowded city with no grass or trees. Promoters of the colonies emphasized the healthy life and open space to be found in America.

The real America was very different. Of course the Europeans heard rumors about the Indians, and what they heard was not encouraging. The "savages" of America, it was said, were not content merely to kill their victims. There were stories that they liked to torture their captives and even to eat them. Some Indian cruelties were supposed to be too horrible to tell.

It is surprising that English men and women dared to come to America at all. For in addition to all the real threats of a "hideous and desolate wilderness," they were haunted by horror stories and nightmares. Out there in Virginia the cheery advertising boasts were not much help. And it is still more surprising that, in spite of all their wrong "facts," the settlers in Virginia and elsewhere along the Atlantic Coast not only survived but managed to build lasting colonies.

Settling Jamestown. The first successful colony that these English people founded was in Virginia. A joint stock company named the Virginia Company of London (often called the London Company) was granted all the westward-stretching land between what is now the northern end of New Jersey and the middle of South Carolina.

In 1603 King James I succeeded Queen Elizabeth on the throne. He was the son of Mary Queen of Scots, who had been executed by Queen Elizabeth. With his passion for theories, he was as different as possible from the practical Virgin Queen. He could not get along with Parliament and was known as "the most learned fool in Christendom."

James I gave the Virginia Company its grant in 1606. The company quickly sent out three ships. This time the settlers avoided Roanoke Island and shallow Pamlico Sound and sailed instead into the broad, deep Chesapeake Bay. The settlers went up a river about 32 miles, landed on a peninsula, and began to build a town. Both the river and the town they named after their king.

In selecting the spot for Jamestown these settlers showed poor judgment. The site was low and swampy—just what the company had warned against. But the 104 men and boys who landed in this wilderness on May 23, 1607, somehow thought the site would be easy to defend against the Indians and the Spanish. From the swampy ground came mosquitoes carrying malaria, and from their well water came dysentery. They would have been better off if they had faced their enemies on dry and solid ground.

The council that governed the colony had no head. Members wasted time arguing, while no one had the power to make decisions. Disrupted by its squabbling council and weakened by disease, Jamestown was also menaced by Indian raids. These raids were brought on by rash acts of the colonists themselves.

Still, the colony was blessed with a remarkable leader, Captain John Smith. He had been a merchant's poor apprentice in England. But adventure was his middle name, so he had joined armies and fought in distant Hungary and Turkey. He had the bad luck to be made a slave in Turkey. But he escaped, returned to England, and joined the new Virginia Company.

Smith saved the settlers from themselves. With his courage and his wide experience he knew how to stop the settlers' quarreling. He worked to keep peace with the Indians. The Indians traded him the corn needed to feed the settlers till they could raise their own crops. Even then, more than half the colonists died of fever, starvation, or the arrows of Indians before the winter was over.

Fortunately, the company back in London was committed to make the colony succeed. In 1608 they sent out new recruits—men, women, and children—and supplies. In 1609 alone about 400 colonists arrived. But then the colony lost its leader when John Smith was injured by a gunpowder explosion and was forced to return home. The woods were full of game and the soil was fertile for growing corn. But without their leader the colonists proved unable to feed themselves. The bitter winter of 1609–1610 was called "the Starving Time." There were ghastly tales of cannibalism. Only 60 of the 500 settlers were left when spring arrived.

Over the next years the company still poured in settlers and supplies. But the colony could not be self-supporting unless they could produce something they could sell. What they found was quite a surprise. Earlier, the Spanish had brought tobacco to Europe from America, and the English had quickly taken to smoking. They smoked not only because they enjoyed it. Doctors at the time said it would cure almost any disease. In 1612 John Rolfe, who later married the Indian princess Pocahontas, learned how to grow a kind of tobacco in Virginia that English people especially liked. Because the English were eager to buy this crop, the colony now finally had found a solid economic base.

A Brief DESCRIPTION
OF
The Province
OF
CAROLINA
On the COASTS of FLOREDA.
AND
More perticularly of a New-Plantation
begun by the ENGLISH at Cape-Feare,
on that River now by them called Charles-River,
the 29th of May. 1664.

Wherein is set forth
The Healthfulness of the Air; the Fertility of
the Earth, and Waters; and the great Pleasure and
Profit will accrue to those that shall go thither to enjoy
the same.

Also,
Directions and advice to such as shall go thither whether
on their own accompts, or to serve under another.

Together with
A most accurate MAP of the whole PROVINCE.

London, Printed for Robert Horne in the first Court of Gresham-
Colledge neer Bishopsgate street. 1666.

Advertisements glowed with the wonders—real and imaginary—of the New World. Printers at this time often used a letter something like an "f" where we use an "s."

A colony established. By 1619 the Virginia colony was well on its way to success. The company was sending out hundreds of craftsmen and laborers. New directors in London then decided to give the settlers more freedom. Up to then the colonists had lived under strict martial law. For example, every man and woman had to attend church twice daily and could be fined a full day's pay for one absence, whipped for a second, and put in jail six months for a third. Strict discipline helped the colony survive the early years. But it would scare away new settlers. The company sent out a new governor with orders to let the people work for themselves as

THE INCONVENIENCIES
THAT HAVE HAPPENED TO SOME PER-
SONS WHICH HAVE TRANSPORTED THEMSELVES

from *England* to *Virginia*, vvithout prouifions neceffary to fuftaine themfelues, hath
greatly hindred the *Progreffe of that noble Plantation : For preuention of the like diforders*
heereafter, that no man fuffer, either through ignorance or mifinformation ; it is thought re-
quifite to publifh this fhort declaration : wherein is contained a particular of fuch necef-
faries, as either priuate families or fingle perfons fhall haue caufe to furnifh themfelues with, for their better
fupport at their firft landing in Virginia; whereby alfo greater numbers may receiue in part,
directions how to prouide themfelues.

Apparrell.

	li.	s.	d.
One Monmouth Cap	∞	01	10
Three falling bands	—	01	03
Three fhirts	—	07	06
One wafte-coate	—	02	02
One fuite of Canuafe	—	07	06
One fuite of Frize	—	10	00
One fuite of Cloth	—	15	00
Three paire of Irifh ftockins	—	04	—
Foure paire of fhooes	—	08	08
One paire of garters	—	00	10
One doozen of points	—	00	03
One paire of Canuafe fheets	—	08	00
Seuen ells of Canuafe, to make a bed and boulfter, to be filled in *Virginia* 8.s. One Rug for a bed 8.s. which with the bed feruing for two men, halfe is	—	08	00
Fiue ells coorfe Canuafe, to make a bed at Sea for two men, to be filled with ftraw, iiij.s. One coorfe Rug at Sea for two men, will coft vj.s. is for one	—	05	00
	04	00	00

Apparrell for one man, and fo after the rate for more.

Victuall.

	li.	s.	d.
Eight bufhels of Meale	02	00	00
Two bufhels of peafe at 3.s.	—	06	00
Two bufhels of Oatemeale 4.s. 6.d.	—	09	00
One gallon of *Aquauitæ*	—	02	06
One gallon of Oyle	—	03	06
Two gallons of Vineger 1.s.	—	02	00
	03	03	00

For a whole yeere for one man, and fo for more after the rate.

Armes.

	li.	s.	d.
One Armour compleat, light	—	17	00
One long Peece, fiue foot or fiue and a halfe, neere Musket bore	01	02	—
One fword	—	05	—
One belt	—	01	—
One bandaleere	—	01	06
Twenty pound of powder	—	18	00
Sixty pound of fhot or lead, Piftoll and Goofe fhot	—	05	00
	03	09	06

For one man, but if halfe of your men haue armour it is fufficient fo that all haue Peeces and fwords.

Tooles.

	li.	s.	d.
Fiue broad howes at 2.s. a piece	—	10	—
Fiue narrow howes at 16.d. a piece	—	06	08
Two broad Axes at 3.s. 8.d. a piece	—	07	04
Fiue felling Axes at 18.d. a piece	—	07	06
Two fteele hand fawes at 16.d. a piece	—	02	08
Two two-hand fawes at 5.s. a piece	—	10	—
One whip-faw, fet and filed with box, file, and wreft	—	10	—
Two hammers 12.d. a piece	—	02	00
Three fhouels 18.d. a piece	—	04	06
Two fpades at 18.d. a piece	—	03	—
Two augers 6.d. a piece	—	01	00
Sixe chiffels 6.d. a piece	—	03	00
Two percers ftocked 4.d. a piece	—	00	08
Three gimlets 2.d. a piece	—	00	06
Two hatchets 21.d. a piece	—	03	06
Two froues to cleaue pale 18.d.	—	03	00
Two hand-bills 20. a piece	—	03	04
One grindleftone 4.s.	—	04	00
Nailes of all forts to the value of	02	00	—
Two Pickaxes	—	03	—
	06	02	08

For a family of 6. perfons and fo after the rate for more.

Houfhold Implements.

	li.	s.	d.
One Iron Pot	—	00	07
One kettle	—	06	—
One large frying pan	—	02	06
One gridiron	—	01	06
Two skillets	—	05	—
One fpit	—	02	—
Platters, difhes, fpoones of wood	—	04	—
	01	08	00

For a family of 6. perfons, and fo for more or leffe After the rate.

For Suger, Spice, and fruit, and at Sea for 6. men — ∞ | 12 | 06

So the full charge of Apparrell, Victuall, Armes, Tooles,
and houfhold ftuffe, and after this rate for each perfon,
will amount vnto about the fumme of — 12 | 10 | —

The paffage of each man is — 06 | 00 | —

The fraight of thefe prouifions for a man, will bee about
halfe a Tun, which is — 01 | 10 | —

So the whole charge will amount to about — 20 | 00 | 00

*Nets, hookes, lines, and a tent muft be added, if the number of people be grea-
ter, as alfo fome kine.*

And this is the vfuall proportion that the Virginia *Company doe
beftow vpon their Tenants which they fend.*

Whofoeuer tranfports himfelfe or any other at his owne charge vnto *Virginia*, fhall for each perfon fo tranfported before Midfummer 1625.
haue to him and his heires for euer fifty Acres of Land vpon a firft, and fifty Acres vpon a fecond diuifion.

Imprinted at London by Felix Kyngston. 1622.

well as for the company. The governor allowed the colonists to elect an assembly to help make their own laws. The House of Burgesses, as Virginians called it, met at Jamestown on July 30, 1619. It was the first elected legislative assembly in America.

That same year saw the arrival of two groups who played a leading role in the colony's future. Jamestown was changed from a military outpost into a full community when the Virginia Company sent out from London a group of "respectable maidens" who soon married men of their choice. About the same time a Dutch ship arrived carrying twenty blacks. These were probably not slaves but indentured servants (like many of the white settlers). An indentured servant was a person who had signed an "indenture," an agreement to serve a master for a certain number of years. (It was called an "indenture" because the two parts of each agreement—one for master, one for servant—were indented to fit together.) Outright slavery probably did not appear in the English colonies until later.

In the next few years the company sent many more settlers to Virginia—often without the needed supplies. Some 5000 arrived between 1619 and 1624. And yet by 1624 the total population in the colony had increased by only 200. Sickness killed most of the newcomers, starvation took some, and others fell to the tomahawk. In 1622 the Indians attacked in an all-out try to drive the European invaders from their land. The colony lost 350 lives (including John Rolfe), and the settlers were pushed back close to Jamestown.

The men running the Virginia Company included some of King James's opponents in Parliament. He used the problems of the company to persuade his judges to annul the company charter. The settlement now became a *royal colony* with its governor appointed by the king. But after a brief pause the legislative assembly was allowed to continue.

The London Company had founded the first permanent English settlement in America. Tobacco—its staple crop—gave the colony a firm

This 1622 English handbill advises families leaving for America to take the necessary tools and supplies to avoid "inconveniencies."

This painting shows Pocahontas, also known as Matoaka, in English clothes. She married John Rolfe and died in England in 1617 just as she was about to return to America.

economic base. And the settlers in Virginia had set the pattern of representative government for future English colonies. All this had been done at fearful cost in money and lives. But the Virginia experience—the successes and the failures—would save lives and light the way for later settlers.

SECTION 3 REVIEW

1. Identify or explain: John Smith, John Rolfe, the Starving Time, indentured servant.

2. Locate: Jamestown, the Potomac River.

3. Why did England want colonies?

4. What problems faced the Jamestown settlers?

5. What significant events happened in Virginia in 1619? Why was each important?

6. **Making Comparisons.** Contrast Spain's and England's colonies.

4. The Puritans come to New England

The settlement of Virginia was mostly a business enterprise. Settlers of New England also hoped to make money. But their lives and their hopes were ruled by religion. The people who went there were called "Puritans" because they wanted to purify the Church of England. They wanted to do away with the colorful robes of priests, with prayer books, and even with altars. Some Puritans remained inside the Church of England and worked for reform there. Others were known as "Independents" or "Separatists." They went out of the church—separated from it.

The Pilgrims. Three centuries ago kings and queens believed that the religion of their people helped keep them loyal and obedient. Subjects who were allowed to make up their own minds about religion might also make up their own minds about politics—and even about whether to obey the king! James I began his reign by declaring that his subjects had to "conform" in religion or he would "harry them out of the land."

The Separatist congregations of some little villages in the east of England were harried until in 1608 they took refuge in Holland. That was the only country in Europe where complete religious freedom was allowed. But after they had lived there for a few years, they began to fear that their children would forget the customs and speech of England. These Separatists decided to move on to the new land of America. They were given permission by the London Company to settle in Virginia.

They went back to England, where they set out from Plymouth in the *Mayflower* on September 16, 1620, with 102 passengers. After a seven-week voyage in cramped quarters, they first sighted land in early November. They looked for a suitable place and finally landed on December 21, 1620. The winter was harsher than anything they had known in England.

Their pilot brought them by mistake to Cape Cod. They had no right to own the land there, for that required a *patent,* or land grant. They had no power either to establish a government, for that required a charter.

But they had something far better. They had a plan to build a purified society, and they had a guide in the Bible. This was important, for in the mysterious New World you would surely be lost unless you had some plans of your own. If you had goals, they would guide and encourage you while you were discovering what America was really like. Your plans had to be definite, but not too definite. You had to be willing to change your plans when you ran into trouble, or when the New World did not offer what you expected. You had to be prepared for disappointment. Yet you had to have self-confidence, faith in your mission and in yourself. The Pilgrims and other Puritans had all this. They were equipped, too, with just the right combination of hopes and fears, optimism and pessimism, self-confidence and humility to be successful settlers. And this was one of the most fortunate coincidences in our history.

The Mayflower Compact. When the Pilgrims reached Cape Cod, they were outside the boundaries where they had permission to settle. Some unruly passengers noticed this. They threatened "that when they came ashore they would use their own liberty, for none had power to command them, the patent they had being for Virginia." But the *Mayflower* leaders, anxious to land and begin their colony, could not tolerate a community without government. Why should their plans be spoiled by a few roughnecks?

So they decided on shipboard, then and there, to create a new government to serve their very special purposes. Their leaders included the steady William Bradford, who would be governor of Plymouth Colony for 31 years, and Captain Miles Standish, whom they had hired to head their militia. Like people making up rules for a club that already existed, they wrote out and signed an agreement, or covenant. This was the famous Mayflower Compact. In it they pledged allegiance to the king, combined themselves "into a civil body politic," and bound themselves to obey all the laws this new government might enact. They created an instant government. It worked surprisingly well for the infant colony, and later became the foundation for the state of Massachusetts.

Squanto to the rescue. The Pilgrims and other Puritans thought God was on their side when they settled in the wilderness. And often it seemed that He was. The Pilgrims might all have died if a remarkable Indian had not come to help them.

Squanto was an Indian kidnapped a few years before by an English sea captain, who had sold him into slavery in Spain. He escaped to England, where he learned some English, and then returned to New England in 1619. There he found that his whole village had died of disease. Now, in March 1621, it was Squanto—of all the thousands of Indians in America—who happened to turn up in Plymouth! He knew enough English to act as an interpreter. And he showed the Pilgrims how to plant corn (which was not known in England), how to fertilize the soil, where to catch fish, and how to trap beaver. No wonder the Pilgrims called him a "special instrument sent of God for their good beyond their expectation."

The Plymouth Colony never grew very large, and in 1691 it was absorbed into the Massachusetts Bay Colony. But we still revere the Pilgrim Fathers as the first successful settlers of the New England shore, who began an American custom—finding a way of self-government for every occasion.

The Massachusetts Bay Colony. Charles I's archbishop, William Laud, and other high officials within the established Church of England tried to force the Puritans to conform to the rules of the church. Many Puritans then made up their minds to leave England, and fortunately they had a place to go to. Some of them had received a charter from King James for a company that was allowed to create settlements in the Massachusetts Bay area in New England.

The most significant point about this charter was that it did not say where the company headquarters had to be. It did not say where the company should hold its meetings to admit new members, to select officers, or to make laws. This meant that if the company headquarters was transferred from England to Massachusetts, the stockholders in Massachusetts would be able to run the company. Since they were settlers, it also meant that settlers would be governing themselves.

In 1629 the company members voted to transfer the company to Massachusetts Bay. Certain strong Puritans, leaders like John Winthrop, were now willing to go there. From the start, Massachusetts Bay was a self-governing colony.

One thousand settlers went out in the summer of 1630 and planted settlements around Massachusetts Bay. By the end of the first decade, 20,000 settlers

American Antiquarian Society

John Winthrop, whose portrait was painted by an unknown artist in England, provided strong leadership as governor of the Massachusetts Bay Colony.

had arrived. Among these, right from the start, were more people of means and influence than in any other group of colonists. When the settlers arrived, they soon founded settlements at Boston, Charlestown, Watertown, Lynn, Medford, Dorchester, and Roxbury.

The Puritan religion was admirably suited for settling the wilderness. A church (by which the Puritans meant the members of a congregation) would receive a grant of land from the Great and General Court (a meeting of the company). Then it would move as a group to a spot already selected and surveyed. There a village would be built around a meetinghouse with the fields scattered outside the village.

Beautiful Touro Synagogue in Newport, Rhode Island, was designed by Peter Harrison.

Jack Spratt

A City upon a hill.

The Puritans had a grand purpose in America. John Winthrop, who was to be their governor for many years, spoke to them on the boat coming over:

> We shall be as a City upon a hill, the eyes of all people are upon us; so that if we shall deal falsely with our god in this work we have undertaken and so cause him to withdraw his present help from us, we shall be made a story and a by-word through the world.

Winthrop was saying what many Americans then and since have felt. The American example could help shape the lives of people everywhere.

With their beliefs, it would have been difficult for the Puritans to fail. Even the Devil, who was a lively presence for them, could not really defeat them. Sooner or later, they knew, God always won. He would see that His own people were not destroyed. The troubles of this world—New England blizzards, Indian arrows, the plottings of enemies in England, or the crimes of their own people—never overwhelmed them. The Puritans were ready for what wilderness America demanded.

Rhode Island.

The Puritans who settled Massachusetts Bay did not believe in religious freedom. They thought that they knew God's truth and that all reasonable men and women should be able to see that truth. If you disagreed with them, you had the right to go away but not to stay in Massachusetts.

Roger Williams, the young pastor of the church in Salem, would not agree to the Puritan version of the truth, so he was banished from Massachusetts Bay. He made his way, in 1636, to Narragansett Bay. There he purchased a tract of land from the Indians and began the settlement we know as Rhode Island.

Rhode Island was a haven for independent thinkers. One who went there was the bright, brave, freethinking Anne Hutchinson. She had held meetings at her house in Boston to discuss the preacher's Sunday sermons. Then she had begun to put forth her own ideas. Soon she was disagreeing with some of the accepted doctrines of the churches of the Bay Colony and criticizing many of its ministers. So Mrs. Hutchinson was banished. She moved to Rhode Island. Later she settled in New York where, in 1643, she and all but one of her household were massacred by Indians.

A MAP OF
NEW-ENGLAND,

Being the first that ever was here cut, and done by the best Pattern that could be had, which being in some places defective, it made the other less exact: yet doth it sufficiently shew the Scituation of the Country, and conveniently well the distance of Places.

The figures that are joyned with the Names of Places are to distinguish such as have been assaulted by the Indians from others.

This 1677 woodcut by John Foster is the first such map made in the colonies. West is at the top. The map shows Puritan settlements stretching from Maine to Connecticut. The Merrimack River (center) and the Connecticut River (top) are featured.

The scornful Puritans in Massachusetts called the Rhode Island people "the Lord's debris." They sneered that if any man had lost his religion he would be sure to find it in some Rhode Island village. Still, Rhode Island grew and prospered as a refuge for liberty.

In the 1650s, Quakers (considered in Massachusetts the most dangerous of all Separatists) and Jews began to appear in the colony. The Jews formed their first congregation there in 1658. In 1763 they built the beautiful Touro Synagogue, which still stands in Newport. But Catholics were not welcomed even in Rhode Island. They were allowed to settle there but were not allowed to vote.

Other New England settlements. In 1636, men and women from several Massachusetts towns were granted permission to "transport themselves and their estates" westward to the Connecticut Valley, noted for its rich farmland. They were the first wave of the mighty overland movement to the West that marked American history for 200 years. In Connecticut the first settlers founded Hartford, Windsor, and Wethersfield.

In 1639 the Connecticut settlers adopted their own "Fundamental Orders." This was a frame of self-government with a governor, a legislative assembly, and courts. Voting was restricted to male property owners, as was customary at that time. To vote in Massachusetts Bay, you still had to be a member of the church, but not here. Features of the Fundamental Orders remained the basis of Connecticut's government long after it became a state.

Another group of settlers who left Massachusetts Bay founded the New Haven Colony. They had no real quarrel with the Bay Colony—except that it was not quite strict enough! They had come from England to start commerce here, and they could find no harbor to their taste in Massachusetts Bay. At New Haven they had the harbor they needed. They settled there in 1638. This colony attracted many of the wealthiest settlers who had yet come to America. But the location they had chosen was not as good as they had thought. The harbor was too shallow. And hemmed in by Connecticut, they lacked lands to produce goods to export. The New Haven Colony was absorbed by Connecticut in 1664.

Settlers also went north from the Massachusetts Bay Colony. Some moved into New Hampshire, which became a royal province in 1679. Others traveled to Maine where Sir Ferdinando Gorges had tried in vain to plant a colony. He wanted one, unlike Massachusetts Bay, that would be faithful to the king and the Anglican church. But Maine remained a province of Massachusetts until 1820.

SECTION 4 REVIEW

1. Identify or explain: Separatists, Puritans, Pilgrims, James I, Squanto, John Winthrop, Roger Williams, Anne Hutchinson, Fundamental Orders of Connecticut.
2. Locate: Cape Cod, Plymouth, Rhode Island, Hartford, New Haven.
3. What was the Mayflower Compact? Why was it important?
4. Why did the Puritans make successful settlers?
5. Why was the Rhode Island Colony founded?
6. **Drawing Conclusions.** In which colonies were religious beliefs a central focus?

5. Other Europeans in North America

Three centuries ago the kings and queens of Europe regarded as their own private property any lands that ships flying their flag discovered. They granted these lands as they pleased to settlers or trading companies. Vast tracts of land in America were sold for cash or given away to favorites by the States-General (parliament) of the Netherlands and by the English, French, and Swedish kings.

New France. Samuel de Champlain—expert navigator, student of science, brave explorer, earnest missionary—became the founder of New France in America. At Quebec in 1608 he planted the first permanent French settlement in the New World.

For the French that was only a foothold. From Quebec, their explorers, missionaries, fur trappers, and settlers moved up the St. Lawrence River, through the Great Lakes, and down the Mississippi. In time, they claimed an empire that stretched over a great arc—behind the English. The French Empire reached from New Orleans on the Gulf of Mexico to the powerful Canadian fortress, Louisbourg, on the Atlantic Ocean.

But while New France was vast in area, it remained small in population. The reasons are not hard to find. Only French Roman Catholics were allowed in the colony. The fierce Iroquois were a constant menace. Farming was difficult in this cold northern land. Though those who did migrate found that by hard work they could become comfortable and relatively prosperous, most French people did not want to leave home for this rugged, far-distant colony.

All of this still might not have stopped settlers from coming. But the French crown, unlike the English, did not allow those who were discontented at home to go abroad. The English monarchs wisely let their dissenters leave. The French rulers insisted on keeping their Protestants, called Huguenots, at home where they could be watched and punished. As a result, by 1700 the English population along the Atlantic seaboard had grown to a quarter of a million. Meanwhile, the French population in Canada had barely reached 18,000.

The Dutch colony on the Hudson. The best place on the Atlantic Coast for a trading colony was at the present site of New York City. Its grand natural harbor invited commerce from the whole world. At the same time a broad river provided a superhighway for furs from the interior. Not the English but the Dutch took possession of this choice region. In September 1609 Henry Hudson, an English captain in the service of the Dutch, sailed up the river that now bears his name. Like countless other mariners in those days, Hudson was searching for the Northwest Passage from Europe to Cathay.

After Hudson's voyage, the Dutch set up a trading post on the river near the present site of Albany. Later, in 1623, they settled at Manhattan for their marketplace. They bought the island with trading goods valued at 60 Dutch guilders (about $24) from several Indian chiefs. Of course, in those days $24 was worth what several thousand dollars would be worth now. The Dutch called their colony New Netherland. But unlike the Puritans, the Dutch settlers were less interested in building "a City upon a hill," a model community as an example to the world, than in making money.

The Dutch were the merchants of the world. There on Manhattan Island they began the great American democracy of cash. If you had money or goods, the Dutch would trade with you. It didn't matter who you were or what you believed. The Dutch let in nearly everyone to New York—not so much because they believed in toleration, but simply because it meant profit.

The Dutch colony was a wedge between New England and the southern colonies. So in 1664, when England was on the verge of war with Holland, Charles II granted his brother James, Duke of York, all the land between the Connecticut and Delaware rivers, including New Netherland.

When a fleet sent out by the Duke of York arrived at the fort at the foot of Manhattan Island and called for the surrender of the colony, the stubborn Dutch Governor Peter Stuyvesant refused. But the leading citizens, hardheaded merchants, knew that resistance was hopeless. They finally persuaded Stuyvesant to yield, and New Netherland fell without a blow. The English flag now waved over an unbroken coast from Canada to the Carolinas.

New Sweden. When New Netherland fell to England, so did the land that had once been New Sweden. This was a colony first settled by Swedes and Finns in 1638 on the western shore of the Delaware River where Wilmington now stands. But since the settlement was small and weak, it was easily seized by the Dutch in 1655.

New Sweden gave America the log cabin. In the cold Swedish forests farmers had learned to use rough logs to build a cozy weather-tight house. Clever Swedish builders brought here their skill with logs. And the log cabin became standard housing on the western frontier.

SECTION 5 REVIEW

1. Identify: Samuel de Champlain, Peter Stuyvesant, Duke of York.
2. Locate: Louisbourg, New Orleans, Albany.
3. What was distinctive about New Netherland in American history?
4. **Recognizing Cause and Effect.** Why did the French colonies stay relatively small?

6. The proprietary colonies

Of the thirteen colonies that later united to form the American nation, all except Virginia and the New England settlements had been founded as *proprietorships*. This was halfway between a royal province and a self-governing colony. The king let control out of his hands, but he did not give it to a company or to the colonists. Instead it went to a man or a group of men, usually the king's personal friends. The "proprietors" then appointed the governor, set up law courts, and collected land tax ("quitrent") from the settlers. They also offered bonuses to lure settlers to their lands. They managed their provinces as business ventures, under whatever rules the king had put in their charters.

The proprietors were also limited by elected assemblies. All the proprietors except the Duke of York (who finally agreed in 1683) allowed the people some form of self-government. They could not attract settlers on any other terms. Even the royal provinces had to allow assemblies.

Starting with Maryland in 1634 a series of proprietary colonies was founded: the Carolinas in 1663, New Jersey in 1664, Pennsylvania in 1681, Delaware in 1702 (with the Penns as governors), and finally Georgia, first settled in 1733. Each colony faced its own problems, enjoyed its own successes, suffered its own failures.

Maryland, a colony founded for Catholics, like Rhode Island allowed religious freedom from the first. It passed an Act of Toleration in 1649. This permitted religious freedom only for all who believed in the Trinity—God the Father, Jesus Christ, and the Holy Ghost. It was the first legislative act of religious toleration in the colonies.

The Carolina proprietors tried to rule their colony by an elaborate constitution called the "Grand Model" drawn up by English philosopher John Locke. But the philosopher's theories proved unfit for the problems of government in the wilderness.

Pennsylvania.

Pennsylvania was founded by Quakers, who were a special kind of Puritan. They rejected all ceremonies of worship and the authority of all priests, ministers, or bishops. They obeyed only the "inner light," which they said came to them direct from God. The Quakers believed in equality so strongly that they refused to bow or remove their hats in the presence of officials. It is not surprising, then, that royal officials became impatient with them and persecuted the Quakers for any reason they could think up. The Quakers were not welcome in England.

William Penn, who had been jailed in England for his religious beliefs, decided to found an American colony for his fellow Quakers. Penn's father, a rich British Admiral who was not a Quaker, had loaned money to King Charles II. No doubt this helped young Penn, who was shrewd and persuasive, to secure a vast colonial grant from Charles. At the king's demand, the new land was called "Pennsylvania" in honor of Penn's father. There William Penn established religious toleration, and the colony soon became a haven for persecuted people from all over.

Back in England, the Quakers had been strict pacifists. They opposed war and refused to fight for any reason, even in self-defense. There they were nothing but a small group of peculiar people. If they refused to fight, the country could still be defended by others. It was quite different in Pennsylvania. Here at first they were the majority, but they ran the government until 1756, long after they had stopped being a majority. In Pennsylvania, if the Quakers refused to raise an army, the countryside was left defenseless. This is precisely what happened.

For some time, by various dodges, the Quakers did try to help defend the colony without violating their consciences. In one case they voted money "to feed and clothe the Indians" that they knew would go to defense instead. In another they voted "other grain" for a military garrison, even though they knew "other grain" really meant a not-very-nourishing grain called gunpowder.

But in 1755, dodges ceased to be enough. Total war broke out in western Pennsylvania. The Indians burned homes, ruined crops, and killed or captured men, women, and children. Panic gripped the land, and eastern towns were filled with refugees. The Quakers insisted on remaining pacifists even as western Pennsylvania ran red with blood.

At that time the Quakers, although numbering only one-quarter of the colony's population, still held over three-fourths of the seats in the legislature. And they would not vote funds for defense. They insisted they could not violate their consciences by helping to fight a war. Now, however, the non-Quakers had had enough. They forced the

That William Penn was more than just a visionary Quaker is apparent in this early portrait. The sternness, practicality, and pertinacity needed to found a successful colony all shine through.

Quakers to give up their control of the government. The Quakers never ruled the colony again.

After that the Quakers became the gadflies and prophets of America. They remained pacifists, and spoke out against slavery and other forms of oppression. They were the voices of everybody's conscience. That was their strength and their weakness. They were not meant for governing a colony.

Georgia. If Pennsylvania faced problems because of the beliefs of its settlers, Georgia suffered because of its English founders' ignorance and idealism. The 21 men in England who secured a charter for Georgia in 1732 thought they were very practical. The best known of them was James Oglethorpe. He was a tough-minded soldier who combined a passion for building the British Empire with a passion for reform. Oglethorpe and his friends had their eyes not so much on the Bible or on their own consciences as on the practical problems of their day. In London they worried over the growing unemployment and the increasing crime.

The land south of the Carolinas was rumored to be a new paradise. There they would settle some of London's criminals and the drunken, idle poor. That also happened to be right where the empire needed to block the Spaniards, who were trying to push their settlements northward. In Georgia, named after King George II, these unlucky people could serve as a human barricade. At the same time in that tropical climate they could provide the exotic products needed at home in England.

The founders even knew what the colony ought to produce—silk. At that time Britain was spending a fortune in gold and silver to buy silk. If the English could grow silk themselves, they would save their gold and silver and also provide work for the unemployed. The London promoters therefore ordered every settler in Georgia to grow mulberry trees so the leaves would be food for silkworms. Unfortunately, the black mulberry trees that grew in Georgia were not the kind the silkworms liked. This was a little fact that the London promoters had not bothered to notice.

Plans bred more plans. The ill-informed trustees of Georgia, sitting in their easy chairs in London, went on drawing their plans. Not only did they require mulberry trees to be planted, but they laid down rules on just where the people could live. They prohibited "Rum, Brandies, Spirits, or Strong

Methodist Collection of Drew University, Madison, New Jersey

This 1734 engraving by Pierre Fourdrinier was designed to attract settlers to Savannah, Georgia.

Waters." They would not let the settlers own or sell the land they worked. The settlers could use the land only according to company rules. No black slaves were to be allowed.

Georgia was intended to be a charity colony. It was the only English colony whose founders did not expect to make a profit. Because the people who were sent out were charity cases, they were not allowed to govern themselves. Almost as if they were in a Spanish colony, the inhabitants of Georgia had everything decided for them.

It is not surprising that colonial Georgia did not flourish. An empire builder's dream turned out to be a nightmare. The settlers rebelled, and the trustees who had founded the colony gave up. By the time of the American Revolution, Georgia—the spoiled child of charitable London—was the least prosperous and least populous of all the English colonies.

"The poor inhabitants of Georgia," a settler lamented, "are scattered over the face of the earth; her plantations a wild; her towns a desert; her villages in rubbish, her improvements a by-word, and her liberties a jest; an object of pity to friends, and of insult, contempt and ridicule to enemies."

SECTION 6 REVIEW

1. Identify: William Penn, John Locke, James Oglethorpe, Quakers.

2. Define a "proprietary" colony.

3. **Expressing Problems Clearly.** Why did both the Pennsylvania Quakers and Georgia's proprietors find it hard to rule their colonies?

43

FOCUSING ON IDEAS

1. Compare the Spanish and English colonies. Describe such things as the treatment of Indians; the population profile; slavery; and parent-country control.
2. What developments in the 1500s enabled England to challenge Spain in North America?
3. Both planning and luck were crucial to the success of the European settlements in America. Find two examples of good or bad planning and luck in the chapter.
4. Describe the key features of royal colonies and proprietary colonies.

TAKING A CRITICAL LOOK

1. **Recognizing Cause and Effect.** How did false advertising and rumors affect the settlement of the English colonies?
2. **Drawing Conclusions.** In what way did the founding of Connecticut and Rhode Island provide evidence of both religious intolerance and religious freedom in colonial America?

YOUR REGION IN HISTORY

1. **Culture.** How did the early settlers of your area carry on their Old World traditions? What evidence of Old World traditions can you find in foods, music, dance, speech, and other aspects of your region's culture?
2. **Economics.** How did the early settlers of your area earn a living? What environmental factors influenced their choices? What impact did the first settlers have on the environment?

HISTORICAL FACTS AND FIGURES

Synthesizing Information. Study the information on the chart below. Then write a brief paragraph summarizing the information presented in the chart about (a) the New England Colonies, (b) the Middle Colonies, or (c) the Southern Colonies.

	Colony	Date Founded	Reasons Founded
	Founding of the Colonies		
New England Colonies	Plymouth	1630	Escape religious persecution
	Massachusetts Bay	1630	Escape religious persecution
	New Hampshire	1622	Agriculture; trade; fishing
	Hartford	1636	Trade; escape religious/ political persecution
	New Haven	1639	Trade; escape religious/political persecution
	Rhode Island	1636	Escape religious persecution
Middle Colonies	New York	1624	Trade
	Delaware	1638	Trade
	New Jersey	1664	Land sales; escape religious/ political persecution
	Pennsylvania	1682	Land sales; trade; escape religious/ political persecution
Southern Colonies	Virginia	1607	Trade and farming
	Maryland	1632	Land sales; escape religious/ political persecution
	The Carolinas	1663	Trade; farming; religious freedom
	Georgia	1733	Land sales; home for debtors; buffer against Spanish Florida

CHAPTER 3

New ways in a New World

During these early colonial years, American ways of life began to appear. They emerged from how Americans defended themselves in war and governed themselves in peace. Challenged by a New World, they developed their own ideas about government, law, and politics. Still, the British colonists in America considered themselves loyal Britons. In 1763, at the end of the French and Indian War, few people anywhere would have predicted the break that was to come. The next twenty years were a time of surprising change. Before the colonists could realize it, they had made themselves into a new, self-governing nation.

How did that happen? To understand how this New World novelty was created, we must look at the relations of Americans to each other, to England, and to the wars that France and England exported to America.

1. Many kinds of Americans

During the seventeenth century the English settlements in America grew slowly. One hundred years after the landing at Jamestown the colonies still held only 250,000 people. Then the 1700s saw immigration and a high birthrate create the first American population explosion. The number of people more than doubled every 25 years. By 1765 they counted two and a quarter million. These were no longer just European emigrants, but a new breed of people, shaped by a New World.

A land of many peoples. The people who lived in the thirteen colonies at the end of the French and Indian War came from many lands. But the population was more English than it would ever be again. Since about 60 percent of all the white

settlers had come from England, it is not surprising that the English language, English customs, English law, and English ways of government dominated the land. Pennsylvania had the most mixed population of all, but even there the English stock made up at least half of the population.

What transformed Britons into Americans was that here they had the challenges of living with Africans, Scots, Scotch-Irish, Irish, Portuguese Jews, Swedes, Finns, Swiss, and even a few Austrians and Italians. This made life here much more interesting than life back home. Of course it made some new problems, but it created new opportunities.

These many peoples had come for many different reasons. Most came because they wanted to, some because they were forced. Some, like the Swedes, learned English and became Americans quickly.

Henrietta Johnson, an English artist, made this portrait in Charlestown in 1720.

Others, like the Germans, tried to hold on to their own language and their own customs, even in this New World. Still others, like the indentured servants and many of the blacks from Africa, might have wanted to become full-fledged Americans but were not yet allowed that chance.

Black Americans had been brought here against their will. Most were slaves, but at an early date there were a few who were free. In 1765 the colonies held 400,000 blacks scattered from Massachusetts Bay to Georgia. Over half worked on the tobacco plantations in Virginia and Maryland. Only 40,000 were found farther north.

Besides colonists of English or of African descent, the largest group consisted of the Scots, the Irish, and the Scotch-Irish (the Scots who had tried to settle in Ireland). These hard-bitten, intelligent people took naturally to the frontier. They could usually be found in the "back country." This was a new American expression for the unsettled lands that stretched from Pennsylvania down through the mountains into the Carolinas.

A smaller number were the Germans, industrious and thrifty, who settled mainly in Pennsylvania. So many came in the mid-eighteenth century that the English settlers there feared that the whole colony would become German.

The Germans worked large farms on the rich limestone soil. Some of their descendants are still working the same lands today. They are often mistakenly referred to as Pennsylvania Dutch (from *Deutsch*, meaning German). They were ingenious and willing to try new ways. For hunting they replaced the old-fashioned musket with the accurate long rifle of frontier fame. For travel they built the sturdy Conestoga wagon, which took many pioneers west. And to warm their houses in the winters, which were much colder than those in Europe, they developed and improved the iron stove.

The French Protestants, a small group, had an influence all out of proportion to their numbers. These Huguenots came to America after 1685 when the French government deprived them of their religious freedom and their right to take part in government. An older French law, the Edict of Nantes, which had once given them religious liberty, was repealed. Now they joined the stream of refugees who, over the centuries, came here to escape persecution. It was against the law for them to leave France, but they came anyway. Their intelligence and their skills enriched the colonies.

One famous descendant of the French Huguenots was Paul Revere, who made the celebrated ride in

Paul Revere's likeness was painted in 1765 by John Singleton Copley. It shows him in his silversmith's work clothes holding an elegant example of his craft.

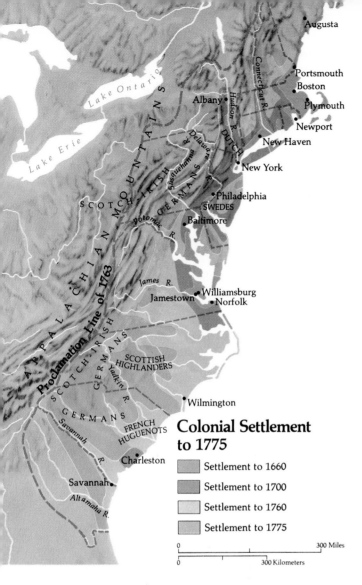

Colonial Settlement to 1775

Settlement to 1660

Settlement to 1700

Settlement to 1760

Settlement to 1775

0   300 Miles

0   300 Kilometers

they arrived in the colonies, hired themselves out as indentured servants—sometimes for as long as seven years—to someone already here. In a few cases indentured servants were treated no better than slaves. Some of them ran away. But if they worked out their full term, they usually received clothes and tools, and sometimes a little cash or even a piece of land to give them a new start in life. In America the shortage of labor and the abundance of land spelled opportunity—the chance to become a landowner.

Empty land creates slavery. To grow tobacco economically a planter needed a large estate and a sizable work force. It was easy to find the land, but hard to find the workers. Many indentured servants, once free, would go off and start their own farms. Why should they work for someone else?

Since the planters could not fill their labor needs with Europeans, they turned to slaves from Africa or the West Indies. The institution of slavery was ancient and familiar in western Europe and throughout Africa. People defeated in war, instead of being killed, were often enslaved. In Europe, with the passing centuries, slavery became reserved for people who were not Christians. They were called pagans. To justify the institution, slaveholders argued that they were helping pagans by making them into slaves so in time they could become Christians. When Jamestown was settled, slavery hardly existed in England. But English ships plied the slave trade between Africa and the Spanish colonies. And when the planters in the English colonies needed workers, they were supplied with African slaves.

Africans were not the only people who were brought to America by force. In England kidnappers seized unsuspecting poor people—children and adults—and then made a profit by selling them as indentured servants in the colonies. Political radicals, religious nonconformists—along with thieves and murderers—were "transported" to America as a punishment or simply to get them out of the way. When the term of their indenture was over, they were freed. But blacks, and sometimes Indians, were kept in slavery for life. Since Indians knew how to survive in the American wilderness, they could more easily run away. So southern planters turned more and more to using black slaves as their workers.

1775 to tell the people that British troops were on their way to Concord and Lexington. Revere made his living as a silversmith, and his elegant work can be seen in many museums today.

Empty land creates opportunity. Most colonists found here a greater dignity and a better life than they had had before. At long last they could buy their own tract of land and run their own farm. The vote in all colonies was restricted to male landowners, but most adult white males did own land and thus could vote.

Even poor people could eventually own land in America. Many immigrants, either before or after

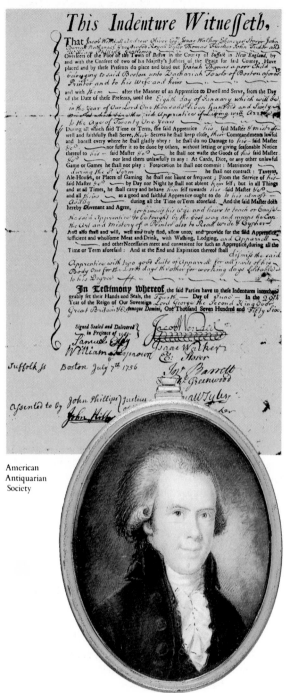

Worcester Art Museum

Isaiah Thomas's indenture papers apprenticed
him to a printer. During the Revolution
Thomas was the official printer for the
Massachusetts patriots. Later he became a
leading American publisher and founded the
American Antiquarian Society.

How the ocean tied some to England. The
southern colonies, stretching from Maryland and
Virginia down the seacoast to Georgia, were covered with plantations. In Maryland and Virginia
the planters grew tobacco, and in the Carolinas and
Georgia they grew rice and indigo (a blue dye used
by English textile manufacturers). In all these
colonies there were some small farmers growing
whatever they could.

The great plantations set the tone for these
southern colonies. To understand the plantation
South, we must understand Virginia.

Virginia was a land of riverways. Viewed from
Chesapeake Bay, Virginia had no solid seacoast but
was a half-dozen outreaching fingers of land separated by inreaching fingers of water. These were
the rich lowlands of "tidewater" Virginia, so called
because the ocean tides reach there. The land and
the sea seemed perfectly married. Deep navigable
rivers—the Potomac, the Rappahannock, the York,
and the James—divided Virginia into strips stretching southeastward. Each of these strips was nearly
an island. Each in turn was veined by smaller rivers,
many large enough to carry traffic to the ocean.

These riverways brought the whole world to the
door of every great plantation. From the ocean
came ships carrying slaves from Africa and the West
Indies, and carrying muskets, hoes, clothing, furniture, and books from London. Down to the ocean
went ships carrying large barrels (called hogsheads)
of tobacco from the broad plantations of the Lees,
the Carters, and the Byrds.

Every large plantation had its own dock. Goods
arrived there direct from London. Virginians felt
little need to have their own cities, for London was
their shopping center.

Planters with riverways running direct to London from their door felt close to Old England. In
those days before railroads, it was slow and expensive to carry anything across the land. It was easier
at that time for a Virginia family to get all the
way from London the products it needed than it was
for someone living five miles outside of London.
The ships that carried the large barrels of tobacco
back to England were happy to have a cargo to carry
to America. For very little cost they would bring
furniture and carriages from London to the wealthy
families of Virginia.

Planters could order from England almost everything they needed. Most purchases were made

Godfrey Meynall, an eyewitness, painted this watercolor of the hold of the slave ship *Albatross* in 1846. Similar conditions were the rule throughout the existence of the slave trade.

through an agent in London, generally the same man who helped sell the planter's tobacco there. The London agent ran a kind of mail-order shopping service. He supplied all sorts of things—a set of law books, a fancy bonnet, a case of wine, shoes for slaves. He arranged the English education of a planter's son or daughter. He reported this season's London styles and sent the latest market news. The London agent advised which recent books were worth reading, and he recounted court scandal or the latest trends in English politics. Sometimes he even helped a lonely bachelor-planter find a wife.

Virginia planters thought of themselves not so much as Americans, but as English country gentlemen who happened to live in America. They still relied on England for almost everything. The easiest way for them to send goods to Boston was to send the goods to London first, where they would be shipped out to Boston on an English vessel. Virginia Englishmen—including leaders of the American Revolution like George Washington and Thomas Jefferson—owed most of the furniture of their houses and of their minds to England.

The ocean that tied them to the English homeland helped them keep the habits and ideas of English gentry. With few exceptions they were moderate, sensible men and women. They would make no trouble and would stay loyal so long as they could prosper.

The colonies south of Chesapeake Bay also lived a tidewater life. This was true even though the Carolina and Georgia coast had shallow waterways which were harder to reach by ocean-going boat than the rivers in Virginia and Maryland. South Carolina's crops of rice and indigo were shipped to London from the deep harbor of the city of Charleston. Here many planters and their families would come to spend the summers away from the heat and malaria of their plantations. Charleston, one of the largest cities in America, had an active business life and more rich people for its size than any other city in the colonies. It was well known for its bustling, bubbling ways. It was a town full of people trying to rise, people trying to grow rich or richer. Most of Charleston's active trade was with England, so here too the ocean tied the people to the homeland.

Joshua Winsor was active in the mackerel and cod fishing industry. His house, built about 1768 in Duxbury, Massachusetts, was typical of seaside architecture. In the late 1700s Winsor's son-in-law, Dr. Rufus Hathaway, painted this picture showing the wharves, countinghouse, and fishing fleet. Winsor is in the foreground, on the right.

How the ocean led others out to the world. The same ocean that tied southern plantation owners to Mother England led the New Englanders elsewhere. The rough and rocky coast of New England offered few gateways to the interior. There were sheltered bays and deep harbors—Salem, Boston, Plymouth, and many others. But New England rivers, with few exceptions, ran steeply downhill. Although they were good for turning a millwheel, most of them were one-way streets tumbling to the ocean. In New England you could not take an ocean vessel very far inland.

New England bays became havens for big ships that traveled the oceans of the world. On the rocky New England soil, covered by snowy winters far colder than those of Old England, there grew no single staple crop. There was little tobacco, no sugar or indigo or rice. New England found its wealth in the sea.

"The abundance of sea-fish are almost beyond believing," Francis Higginson wrote in 1630, "and sure I would scarce have believed it with mine own eyes." There was seafood for every taste: mackerel, bass, salmon, lobster, herring, turbot, sturgeon, haddock, mullets, eels, crabs, mussels, clams, and oysters. A small quantity the New Englanders themselves ate. Most they dried, salted, and carried to far parts of the world. Some they sold to the Catholics of Europe, who ate much fish on Fridays. The scraps and leavings went to the Caribbean plantation owners as cheap food for their slaves.

Fishing became the main industry of Massachusetts Bay. In 1784 the Massachusetts House of Representatives voted "to hang up a representation

Colonial Trade about 1750

- ▨ English Colonies
- ⬅ The Triangular Trade
- ⬅ Manufactured Articles
- ⬅ Wine
- ⬅ Fruit, Salt
- ⬅ Tobacco, Rice, Indigo
- ⬅ Fish

of a codfish in the room where the House sit, as a memorial of the importance of the codfishery to the welfare of the Commonwealth." The codfish became the totem of the state. It hung over the Speaker's desk until the middle of the twentieth century.

The New England fisheries actually helped bring on the Revolution. Deep-sea fishermen need ships, and the New Englanders began building their own fishing ships in large numbers. This worried the English. They wanted to be sure the trade of the New Englanders benefited the mother country. And this was one of the reasons why the English clamped the Navigation Acts on the colonies, telling them where they could sail their ships and limiting where they could carry some of the produce of the colonies. Over the years the English went on to

tighten their senseless and unenforceable restrictions against colonial trading (p. 56). Faneuil Hall (which still stands in Boston), the meeting place of the Massachusetts rebels, was given to the city by Peter Faneuil, son of a French Huguenot immigrant and one of the many merchants who had become rich by shipping New England codfish to forbidden distant markets.

Why should bold and adventurous New England sailors obey boundaries marked off by a few English politicians? Even before the new United States was launched as a nation, New England sailors were showing their independence. They were shipping whatever they could find or make—and to wherever they were attracted by whim or profit.

New England ships roamed the world. Their sailors went to Portugal, Spain, France, Syria, the

West Indies, Brazil, Guinea, and Madagascar. They carried fish to trade for salt from Cadiz, wine from the Azores and Madeira, iron from Bilbao, grapes from Málaga, and oranges from Valencia to ports in England and the colonies. To get oil to burn in their lamps for light, whaling expeditions went out on long voyages from New Bedford and Nantucket south to the coast of Brazil and north to the Arctic Ocean. They took rum from New England ports to the west coast of Africa, where they traded it for slaves whom they then took to the Caribbean and sold for sugar, which was then taken north to be made into more rum. This was called "the triangular trade." They were willing to "trye all ports," as they said, with all kinds of freight. Nothing was too small or too big for their commerce or their imaginations.

In the days before independence when English laws still hemmed them in, enterprising New Englanders had to be smugglers. For them, American independence would be a great relief. It would make them honest, law-abiding traders. But long before the American Revolution, the minds and hearts and pocketbooks of bold New Englanders were attached to the whole world.

The Dutch, Germans, Swedes, and Finns who had settled in the Middle Colonies (New York, New Jersey, Pennsylvania, and Delaware) had no special ties with England. Their relatives were in their own homelands. For them the ocean was a highway to everywhere.

These Middle Colonies had the best-balanced economies of any of the English colonies. A wide variety of products came from the rich soil of their farms. Unlike the southern planters they did not depend on a single staple crop sold in England. They sold their produce to merchants in the thriving cities of Philadelphia and New York. The city merchants in turn sent the produce overseas wherever they could find the best market—no matter what the Navigation Acts said.

Family life. Life in colonial America put heavy demands on the family. On the farm, where most Americans lived, labor was in short supply. Every member of the farm family had work to do. Women took care of the cows, hogs, and chickens, and made the butter and cheese. In the fields they were expected to sow, hoe, and reap the corn. They also sewed the clothes, cooked the food, and kept the simple houses clean and neat. A woman had to be a combination farmer, chef, and tailor!

In addition to all this the women bore many children. Families with 10 or 12 children were common, and 22 or more were not unheard of. From poor nutrition and lack of medical care the mortality rate was high. Many of the children died young. For the children who survived, in the back country where there were no schools the mother was their only teacher.

What doctors prescribed was more likely to kill than to cure the patient. A sensible person would try to stay out of the hands of a doctor. George Washington died in 1799 after he was bled of two quarts of blood by leeches and then "dosed to nausea and blistered to rawness." Even Washington's sturdy constitution could not survive that sort of treatment.

There were few things women were not expected to do in America. Most women married, and usually they helped their husbands on the farm or in the shop. After their husbands died, the women kept the farms and plantations running. Women also showed their versatile talents as shopkeepers, shoemakers, printers, newspaper publishers, teachers, lawyers, and even as blacksmiths, gunsmiths, and shipwrights. Although women could not hold office and usually could not vote, they took an active interest in politics.

One of the most remarkable colonial women was Margaret Brent. A large landholder in Maryland, she ran her own plantation and actually led a force of men to put down a rebellion against the governor in 1646. And when the governor died, she was made executor of his will. She ran his estates and collected his rents. She was also attorney for the proprietor, Lord Baltimore, to take care of his affairs in Maryland. Naturally, she thought all this ought to give her the right to vote in the colonial assembly. When the new governor refused to let her have her rightful place in the colonial government, she moved to Virginia, where she made a new home and ran great estates until her death in 1671.

Few women were rich enough and willful enough to be as successful as Margaret Brent was in a man's world. The English common law which governed the colonies gave few legal rights to women. Husbands controlled the family property.

In those days, unlike ours, children were not allowed to make up their own minds. Parents decided whether a boy would be apprenticed to a shoemaker or a blacksmith, or be educated to become a minister or a lawyer. If not bound out as an indentured servant, the child worked for his parents, on the farm or in the shop.

Usually parents arranged marriages for their children. But in the New World things began to change. In New England more young people were beginning to be allowed to select their own mates.

The colonial family, of course, had no cars, no electric lights, no radios or television sets, no running water, no heat in winter except from the fireplace or, after around 1740, the iron stove. They had to take care of themselves and one another. They looked to other family members not only for love and advice, for food, shelter, and clothing, but they also needed them for their education and entertainment.

Education in the colonies. Compared to Europeans in their time, the American colonists were a well-educated people. Most were Protestants who believed that all Christians should be able to read the Bible. Massachusetts Bay Colony passed a law requiring every town of 50 families or more to maintain a school to teach the boys reading, writing, and arithmetic. Every town of 100 families or more was to have a "grammar school" where boys could prepare for college. Girls had little formal education. Instead they were expected to learn the household arts of sewing, cooking, housekeeping, and childrearing. Books were not for them.

In 1636, only six years after the first settlers of Massachusetts Bay arrived in the New England wilderness, the people founded Harvard College. In the Old World, colleges and universities were ancient and honored institutions. Would it be possible to establish such an institution in the wilderness? The colonists said they needed Harvard College "to advance *Learning* and perpetuate it to Posterity; dreading to leave an illiterate Ministry to the Churches." Many farmers' sons went to Harvard to learn to serve as ministers or lawyers, judges or governors—or simply to be well-educated.

These portraits of Boston merchant and lawyer John Freake and of his wife, Elizabeth, with their child Mary are the work of an unknown artist in the 1670s.

Worcester Art Museum, Sarah E. Garver Fund

Worcester Art Museum, Gift of Mr. and Mrs. Albert Rice (detail)

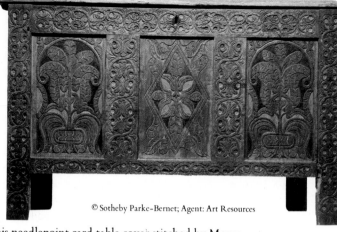

Colonial goods ranged from homemade items like this needlepoint card table cover stitched by Mercy Otis Warren to heavy carved and painted chests like this one made by the Pilgrims.

Outside New England the colonies were not so quick to establish schools. Teachers lived with families while they taught the boys living nearby to read and write. Women opened "dame schools" to teach reading to young boys and sometimes even to girls. Where there were no schools, parents had to teach their children at home. On large southern plantations, private teachers were hired to live on the estate and instruct the children. Then the boys sometimes went back to England to attend college at Oxford or Cambridge. A few went to London or Edinburgh to study law or medicine.

By the time Yale was founded in Connecticut in 1701, there were only two other colleges: Harvard (1636) and William and Mary (1693) in Virginia. But William and Mary remained little more than a grammar school for its first 35 years. Not until the 1740s were more colleges founded. Before that the colonies were too poor and the hardships and dangers of transportation too great. As the colonies flourished, new colleges appeared. Between 1746 and 1769, we see the founding of the College of New Jersey (Princeton), the University of Pennsylvania, King's College (Columbia) in New York, Rhode Island University (Brown), Queen's College (Rutgers) in New Jersey, and Dartmouth in New Hampshire. In 1784 Yale College, with its 270 students, had the largest student body. By the time of the American Revolution the colonies actually had a surprising number of institutions of higher learning. Of course they were not as well equipped—with libraries or scientific instruments—

as their English counterparts. But for the remote New World colonies these colleges were a wondrous beginning.

Journalism and the arts and sciences. Outside the cities, life in the colonies was simple. "Some few towns excepted," wrote John Dickinson on the eve of the Revolution, "we are all tillers of the soil from Nova Scotia to West Florida." The settlers, busy creating a new life in a New World, did not have much time for the arts or sciences.

The first successful newspaper did not appear until 1704, and as late as 1754 three of the colonies still had no newspaper. Despite their small numbers, American journalists pioneered in freedom. In 1733 a bold printer, John Peter Zenger, was arrested and tried for libel for printing articles critical of the governor of New York. But he went to court and won the right to print unpleasant political facts in his newspaper. This was a momentous step in establishing the freedom of the press in America. Gouverneur Morris later called the Zenger case "the morning star of that liberty which subsequently revolutionized America."

Colonial America, far from the Old World treasures of learning, produced a surprising number of original thinkers. Jonathan Edwards, though his writings are hard to understand, was a profound theologian who still has much to teach us. Benjamin Franklin won worldwide fame for his researches in electricity (he first suggested the lightning rod!) and his many practical inventions (he invented the Franklin stove). There were some others, too—other scientists, political philosophers, theologians, and historians.

Some colonists made their living as cabinetmakers and silversmiths. The desks designed by John Goddard of Newport, Rhode Island, were equal to the best made in Europe. Handsome silver bowls, beakers, and candlesticks by Paul Revere in Boston, Myer Myers in New York, and others in Newport, Philadelphia, and Charleston, adorned colonial tables and churches.

In those days before the camera, colonial painters traveled the countryside. They painted lifelike portraits for the family living room and for town halls. John Smibert, the Englishman who designed Faneuil Hall in Boston, preserved the faces of sturdy New England families. John Greenwood went to Surinam, where he portrayed the lonely sea captains away from home.

Most colonists, of course, could not afford fine furniture and silver or the price of a family portrait. At home they made what they needed. Their quilting, weaving, and needlework had a special simple charm. German gunsmiths in Pennsylvania turned out long rifles, which also were works of art.

American art reflected American lives. These were a practical people in search of a better life.

SECTION 1 REVIEW

1. Suppose Margaret Brent wanted to employ the following people: Paul Revere, John Smibert, John Peter Zenger, John Goddard, and Myer Myers. What products or services would each provide?

2. If you were to visit Salem and Charleston in colonial times, what kinds of products would you expect to see on the ships that sailed from these two ports?

3. How did the large amounts of open land affect those who came to America?

4. How did the ocean tie some colonies to England and others to the rest of the world?

5. **Predicting Consequences.** How would your life be different if you were a colonial man, woman, or child?

2. The colonists govern themselves

For 150 years after the founding of the first English colony, new colonies were settled, and the English empire grew, with little attention from England. In the seventeenth century the English people had problems enough at home. They were moving from the medieval world of monarchy into a modern world of representative government. In England Parliament was demanding the power to govern the nation.

England from civil war to Glorious Revolution. In the 1640s the English suffered through wars between the king and Parliament. After King Charles I was beheaded in January 1649, for a decade England was ruled by the obstinate and courageous Oliver Cromwell, who had led Parliament's army against the king. When Oliver Cromwell died, his son tried to rule, but failed dismally. Parliament called Charles II to the throne. Then Charles's brother, the foolish James II, who inherited the throne in 1685, soon alienated everyone.

The next explosion came with the "Glorious Revolution" in 1688. Then the king's opponents summoned William and Mary (daughter of James II) from Holland to take the throne as joint monarchs and preserve the power of Parliament. James II fled to France. When William and Mary came to the throne in 1689, they opened a new era of representative government. Parliament had shown that it was supreme. The monarch owed power to the people's representatives in the House of Commons. Never again would there be an absolute ruler in England.

William of Orange, who came to the throne with Mary, was also the leader of the Dutch. They had been fighting against France for their independence. The French under Louis XIV had replaced Spain as the dominant power on the continent. So in 1689, William brought England into the battle against France. From then until 1763, England fought four wars against the French on battlefields that stretched across the world—from Europe to India to Egypt to the West Indies to Canada. Meanwhile—when the government in London was too busy to notice—the American colonies were prospering. In 1763 England made peace with France. Then the government of England could turn its attention again to its colonies.

During these years of salutary (or helpful) neglect, the colonies developed their own institutions. These would make it difficult for England ever again to rule them. But now that peace had come, England intended to enforce the policy of mercantilism. This was the same policy that Spain had so long followed in its colonies (p. 26). Colonies were only servants of the mother country. It was the prosperity back home in England that was important. Colonists were not to be allowed to manufacture anything that competed with products at home. They must be encouraged to grow what England needed. They must not buy from anybody but the English; they must not ship their products to any country but England. To help the English shipbuilders, the colonists must use only English ships built in England or the colonies.

This was the theory. In fact, the policy was not enforced until after Cromwell took over. The Dutch had begun to trade with the colonists while England was embroiled in civil war. In this way the Dutch reaped profits that England wanted for itself. To bar the Dutch traders from America, Parliament passed a series of Navigation Acts. These laws, from the 1650s down to the 1770s, gave bounties to the colonists for growing certain crops and dictated what goods they could manufacture, in what ships they could transport their goods, where they could buy and sell.

Earlier laws listed only a few items that had to be bought directly from England. This list gradually grew longer. At first goods could be carried in any ships, provided these were *owned* by Englishmen, but by 1696, *all* trade between the colonies and England had to be carried in English-*built* (which included colonial-built) ships. *All* European goods for the colonies had to come from or through England. The principal colonial products could be exported only to England or to another British colony. Trade with the English or not at all!

It is not surprising that energetic people, who had crossed the ocean and were just beginning to explore the resources of a vast new world, would not let themselves be fenced in. They wanted to ship everywhere and buy everywhere.

Smugglers and pirates. But the Navigation Acts were not regularly enforced. In fact they couldn't be. The British navy, busy fighting France, had no time left for trying to catch smugglers.

Smuggling then became a wonderfully profitable business in the colonial period. Many famous old New England and New York families like the Cabots, the Hancocks, and the Livingstons built their fortunes on colonial smuggling. It was descendants of these same families who looked down their noses at later immigrants in the nineteenth century. They said that these new arrivals might not have enough respect for law and order.

A "privateer" was a legally licensed pirate. After the first Navigation Acts, the word came into use about 1664 to describe someone who had a "private" ship that he used for government purposes. The owner of a private vessel in time of war could get a license from his government (called a "letter of marque," after the old French word meaning *to seize*) allowing him to seize enemy ships. Since he helped the war effort by crippling the enemy, he was allowed by his own king to keep a share of the loot. But when a privateer with a letter of marque happened to find any ship carrying a rich cargo, he was tempted not to take too much trouble to find out its exact nationality.

Once a privateer (or "pirate," to use the less respectable name) had loaded his ship with treasure, he would hurry to an American port, such as New York. In port, he simply showed his letter of marque and explained that he had seized his rich cargo as a patriotic duty to help the war effort. New York merchants, who themselves found this trade profitable, did not want to know whether the goods were from enemy ships or whether they were actually stolen goods. They were only too glad to have the privateers deliver merchandise to them that they could not buy from England, and which they were forbidden to buy elsewhere.

The pirates found New York especially to their taste. His Majesty's governor and officers were pleased to have them around. The pirates paid handsome "protection money" to the governor. He issued their letters of marque, and he protected them while they sold their booty. There were few other places in the world where the market for pirates' booty was so good. Prosperous New Yorkers were ready to pay high prices for all the glittering items—heavily carved and inlaid tables and chairs, filigreed daggers, feathered fans, ornate porcelain, and gold-embroidered cloth—that the pirates had captured from "enemy" ships trading with the Orient. In this way the unenforceable

This painting from the 1750s shows British privateers and captured French ships in New York Harbor.

laws and the continuous wars of the British Empire transformed reckless pirates into respectable merchants.

The problems of governing.

Even if the American colonists had not already been independent minded and determined to govern themselves, the vast ocean would have made them so. In the days before the steamship or the transatlantic cable, the colonial office in London could not govern across three thousand miles of water. The ocean was the father of self-government.

When Charles II finally created the Lords of Trade in London in 1675 to manage colonial affairs, they had to do their business by mail. But in those days there was no regular mail service. Letters from London to Boston went by ships that depended on wind and weather and often took many weeks. If the mail-ship was captured by the French or Spanish, the letters were delivered to the bottom of the ocean.

Although each colony had its own representative assembly, the person who had the greatest power and the highest social prestige was the governor. In most colonies he came from England, but wherever he came from he received his orders from London. The Lords of Trade depended on him for information about his colony. But it was hard for him to get his messages across the ocean. If no ship was sailing, no message could go. The governor of North Carolina, for example, normally received his communciations by way of Virginia. In June 1745 the Board of Trade in London (successor to the Lords of Trade) wrote Governor Johnson of North Carolina complaining that it had had no letter from him in the past three years. A full year later he replied from North Carolina that their letter had only just reached him.

During the long New England winter when Boston Harbor was frozen or impassable, the whole colony received no word from the outside world. A letter that the governor of Massachusetts Bay wrote in late November was not likely to reach London before the following April or May. By that time the information it carried would be ancient history. Even if the mail actually reached an English port, there were more delays. It might take weeks or months for mail arriving at Bristol or Falmouth to be carried overland to London. Papers addressed to the Board of Trade were sometimes

57

lost in the customshouse, or they might lie there for a year before anyone bothered to deliver them.

Still, the king did try, from time to time, to control the situation so he might rule his distant subjects. Of all his domains, New England was one of the most troublesome. With its rocky soil, it could grow few crops that England needed, and so it did not fit well into the mercantile system. Its adventurous seamen were always daring to trade in prohibited areas.

The people of Massachusetts Bay, the richest and most populous of the New England colonies, found countless ways to irritate their king and express their rebellious spirit. Determined to "obey God rather than man," they went their own way. They coined their own money. They left the king's name off their legal forms. They ignored the Navigation Acts. They banned the Anglican church. They gave the vote only to their own church members. They even hanged Mary Dyer and three other Quakers on Boston Common.

Charles II had no love for these Puritan relatives of the fanatics who had beheaded his father. When Charles II sent commissioners to find out what was going on in the colony, they were insulted and ignored. Finally, in 1684, the king accused his unruly subjects of disobeying English laws. He managed to have his judges nullify the Massachusetts Bay Colony charter. The colony then became, like Virginia, a royal colony with a governor and council appointed by the king.

The Dominion of New England.

In 1685 James II succeeded his brother Charles II on the throne. James had been the proprietor of New York and New Jersey, so when he became king they automatically became royal provinces. From that start, on the advice of the Board of Trade, James decided to unite New York and New Jersey with all the New England colonies into one large Dominion of New England. It would be ruled by a single royal governor assisted by a council also appointed by the crown. Representative assemblies would be abolished. At last the king himself would really rule.

All of these changes were bad enough for the independent colonists. James II made matters worse by appointing as governor Edmund Andros, a faithful servant and honest man, who happened also to be harsh, narrow, and unbending. He quickly antagonized everyone. At first non-Puritans and some wealthy merchants who were tired of the "rule of the Saints" in Massachusetts welcomed Andros. But he soon lost their support, too, when he tried to stop their smuggling along with the privateering and the piracy that made them rich.

The colonists were saved from Andros and the Dominion of New England by the Glorious Revolution of 1688. Without even waiting to hear if it was a success, the people of Boston seized Governor Andros and threw him in jail. Then the separate colonies went back to running their own affairs.

England would not again try to combine colonies. It was just as well, because communication was too slow for the effective government of large areas from a single center. Anyway, each colony had become accustomed to governing itself.

William and Mary revise the colonial governments.

At first, William and Mary had too many problems in England and Holland to worry about the colonies. But by 1696 the English merchants saw that they were losing large profits because the colonial merchants were flouting the mercantile laws. They complained to the king and demanded that he turn his attention to America. He then formed a new Board of Trade (its full title was "the Lords Commissioners of Trade and Plantations") to oversee colonial affairs. For each colony he provided a regular customs service and special Admiralty Courts (which had no juries) to catch and punish New England smugglers.

He imposed "royal" government on one colony after another. This meant rule by governors appointed by the king. In 1682 there were only two royal provinces, Virginia and New Hampshire. By 1729 all the colonies except Connecticut, Rhode Island, and Georgia had governors either named by the crown or appointed by proprietors subject to the king's approval (Pennsylvania, Delaware, and Maryland). Georgia became a royal colony in 1752.

The colonists did not really suffer much from these new efforts to enforce the Navigation Acts. Customs officers were glad to be bribed. The Admiralty Courts became tangled in all sorts of legal technicalities. The royal governors found that they could not govern without the agreement of the colonial assemblies.

This "Old Colonial System," as the years of salutary neglect were called, turned out to be a "system" for not enforcing the Navigation Acts. It seemed to work as long as everybody agreed to leave well enough alone. And so during the many years while England's wars kept the government busy, the population of the colonies grew and their wealth accumulated. Between 1700 and 1760 the foreign trade of the thirteen mainland colonies increased fivefold.

SECTION 2 REVIEW

1. Identify or explain: letter of marque, Charles I, Oliver Cromwell, Charles II, James II, William and Mary, Edmund Andros.
2. What was the Dominion of New England, and why was it important?
3. Summarize the provisions of the Navigation Acts. Why were they not strictly enforced?
4. Why was it difficult for Britain to govern America?
5. What was the Old Colonial System?
6. **Drawing Conclusions.** What impact did the Glorious Revolution have on British citizens living in the American colonies?

3. Britain against France

The growth of the English colonies made a clash with France inevitable. From Louisbourg through Quebec, Montreal, Detroit, Sault Ste. Marie, Vincennes, and Natchez to New Orleans and Mobile a string of French forts tied together an immense, thinly settled empire.

For some time the French and English stayed far enough apart so that they did not bother each other. But the English were ever pushing westward. And after the Glorious Revolution when the energetic Dutch leader William of Orange and his popular wife, Mary, came to the English throne, it was not long before the two leading colonial powers of North America were at war.

America was a battlefield for European rivalries. A series of conflicts began as attacks by French soldiers and by their Indian allies upon outlying English settlements. King William's War (1689–1697), Queen Anne's War (1702–1713), and King George's War (1744–1748) climaxed in the French and Indian War proper (1754–1763). Life on the frontier became a nightmare. Unpredicted attacks by French regular troops and Indians were followed by massacres. Scalps were taken. Men, women, and children were kidnapped.

The Deerfield Massacre. One cold night in February 1704 the 300 inhabitants of the frontier village of Deerfield, Massachusetts, were sound asleep. Suddenly the silence was broken by French and Indian war cries. Within a few hours 50 settlers were dead and 17 of their houses burnt to the ground. One hundred and eleven settlers (including the town's minister, John Williams, his wife, Eunice, and one of his children) were taken prisoner. Eunice Williams, weakened by recent childbirth, could not keep up with the group as they were hastened north through the winter snow. She and others who fell behind were tomahawked and left to die.

Most of the tough New England settlers were more lucky. All but 17 of the 111 captives lived through the march to Canada. Finally, 60 of the Deerfield villagers, including John Williams himself, returned to the English colonies. Of those who did not go home, some died, some married Canadians, some converted to Catholicism, and a few, including Williams's own daughter, married Indians and made a new life with their captors.

The colonial reaction. English colonists reacted to these raids by attacking Quebec or some other stronghold in New France. Once, in 1745, they captured Louisbourg, France's Gibraltar in the New World. When the English government returned Louisbourg in exchange for Madras in India, New Englanders were outraged. Their interests seemed to count for nothing when the government back home saw a chance to add a distant piece to the empire.

By 1750, English colonists were beginning to make their way through the Allegheny barrier into the valleys that led down to the Ohio and the Mississippi rivers. The governors of the English colonies called for forts to protect them against the French. The French, at the same time, moved vigorously to bolster their defenses. In one of the backwoods clashes, at Great Meadows near the forks of the Ohio where Pittsburgh now stands, a Virginia militia force was commanded by 22-year-old George Washington. There he won his first skirmish, but was soon forced to retreat to Virginia.

The Albany Plan of Union.

The war that began at Great Meadows in 1754 was to continue until 1763. During these years battles were fought not only in America and in Europe, but even in India. This was truly a world war. Even before it had begun, American leaders had been calling for some union of the colonies. Now it seemed urgent against the bloody French and Indian menace.

In June 1754, just two weeks before Washington had to retreat from the French force, a colonial congress met at Albany, New York. Albany was then a small town on the Hudson River, sheltered from attack by a wooden stockade. The Iroquois in that area had long helped to protect the English from attacks down the Mohawk Valley because their traditional enemies, the Hurons, were allied with the French. The Albany meeting had been ordered by the British government to try to keep the Iroquois happy and firmly allied with the British.

The Albany Congress, attended by 150 Indians and representatives of seven colonies, renewed the alliance with the Iroquois. At the same time the colonial delegates voted to adopt a plan suggested by Benjamin Franklin for a new union of the colonies.

A Grand Council of 48 members (similar to that which the Iroquois used to govern their tribe) was to be chosen by the colonial legislatures. Meeting annually, this council would regulate Indian affairs, control a colonial army, manage the public lands, pass laws for the general good, and levy taxes for the common defense. A president-general appointed by the king would name the other high officials and could veto laws passed by the council.

But even the threats of war on their borders could not unite the colonies in this sensible common plan. The colonial legislatures turned it down. Each colony feared it would lose its power to govern itself. The king also rejected the plan because he feared that the union might give all the colonies together too much self-government.

The French and Indian War.

At first the war that opened with Washington's skirmish at Great Meadows went badly for the English. To strengthen the defense of the colonies, in the summer of 1755 the British General Edward Braddock set out with 1400 British regular troops and 450 colonials to try to take Fort Duquesne. The French had built this fort at the point called "the forks of the Ohio," where the Allegheny and Monongahela rivers meet.

Braddock had been warned by Benjamin Franklin, who was shrewd also in military matters, to watch out for surprise attacks by the Indians. But Braddock did not listen. He expected the Indians to behave like troops in the orderly wars in Europe. Over there, battles were usually fought only in good weather, when small professional armies faced each other on open fields. But the French and Indians did not follow the etiquette of Old World warfare. They caught Braddock off guard when they attacked his army from behind rocks and trees. The general was killed, and 976 of his men were killed or wounded.

In 1757, when the brilliant and self-confident William Pitt came to power as prime minister of England, he declared, "I am sure that I can save the country, and that no one else can." He put new life into the nation's armies and its fleets spread over the globe. He was the architect of the first British Empire. He removed weak commanders, jumped young men over older ones into positions of command, and gave colonial officers their due rank. Pitt realized that the British troops in America were fighting for a worldwide empire and not just defending American colonists. When he assured the colonies that England would pay the costs of raising and supporting their armies, the colonists offered the British their manpower and their cooperation.

In the campaigns of 1758, the British and Americans working together were victorious against the French all along the line. The cold and capable 41-year-old General Jeffrey Amherst and General James Wolfe, a bad-tempered upstart of 30, both of whom Pitt had promoted to command, recaptured the stronghold at Louisbourg. Another Pitt appointee, Lt. Col. John Bradstreet, led an expedition of 3000 men through miles of wilderness waterways to take Fort Frontenac on Lake Ontario. Since this cut the French line of communication between Canada and Fort Duquesne, the French troops there soon had to be withdrawn. The English occupied the fort and renamed it Fort Pitt (later Pittsburgh) in honor of England's great leader.

The fall of Quebec.

Pitt was now ready to carry out his grand strategy for the invasion of Canada. One army under General Amherst would go by the

New France and Louisiana before 1763

French

English

Spanish

0   400 Miles

0   400 Kilometers

natural valley through the mountains up the Hudson River-Lake George-Lake Champlain route to attack Montreal in the heart of French Canada. At the same time another force under General Wolfe would come by sea up the St. Lawrence to attack Quebec in the east. Wolfe's expedition reached Quebec in June 1759. But from then until September, while the British fleet lay in the river before the great rock of Quebec, Wolfe vainly sought an undefended landing place.

After a summer during which he was painfully weakened and often forced to keep to his bed by a mysterious disease, it seemed that Wolfe had failed. But he did not give up. Instead he devised an ingenious surprise tactic. He shifted his forces one way to fool the French and then under cover of darkness slipped his men ashore at a point upriver where they were not expected. When daylight came, the French commander, the Marquis de Montcalm, was astonished to see the English redcoats (who were so named because of the color of their uniforms) forming their lines of battle on the high Plains of Abraham west of the city.

In a battle in the classic European style the two sides drew up ranks and faced each other on an open field. Since Wolfe had trained his men in marksmanship (which was unusual at a time when muskets could be aimed only crudely), the powerful volleys of the English soon broke the French and gave Britain the victory. Both opposing generals—Wolfe and Montcalm—were mortally wounded.

The French tried but failed to retake Quebec that winter. The next summer when British General Amherst marched into Montreal, the French and Indian War in America was brought to an end. Elsewhere, war continued for two more years. Spain made the mistake of joining the conflict and lost Havana in Cuba and Manila in the Philippines. The French and Spanish empires in North America had begun to dissolve. Britain's navy now controlled the seas, and the British Empire reached from India west to the Mississippi River.

The Peace of Paris. A peace treaty between Britain and France was signed in Paris in 1763. In the part of the treaty dealing with America, France ceded to England all of Canada and all French lands between the Mississippi and the Appalachian Mountains. France retained only two small islands south of Newfoundland—St. Pierre and Miquelon. These were not to be fortified and were only to be used for drying fish. England gave back to France the sugar islands—Guadeloupe and Martinique—it had seized in the West Indies. To its ally Spain, France ceded New Orleans and all its country west of the Mississippi, the land called Louisiana (after the French King Louis XIV). England kept Florida, but gave Havana and Manila back to Spain.

Before they sat down at the peace table, the English leaders saw that if they really wanted France to stop fighting they could not keep all the French lands taken during the war. They had to choose. Canada was vast. But its cold climate resembled that of New England, and the land produced little

that the homeland needed. At the same time, the tiny Caribbean tropical island of Guadeloupe was rich in sugar, which England desperately wanted. Some argued, too, that if the French menace was removed from the colonial frontiers, it would be harder to keep the American colonies in line. According to the mercantile theory, Guadeloupe was clearly more valuable than Canada. But William Pitt had a wider vision. He saw that Canada might be the bulwark of a grand new empire.

Benjamin Franklin, who was in London at the time as a colonial agent, wrote a persuasive pamphlet on the subject in his usual simple style. He predicted that Canada would become a populous and prosperous agricultural community. Then Canadians would buy English goods and enrich the merchants of the homeland. American colonists who saw the English flag flying from the arctic seas to the Gulf of Mexico would be proud of their Englishness and doubly loyal to the homeland. The English, he said, need not fear that the colonists would ever unite against their own nation. If they had not been able to unite against the French and Indians, surely they would never combine against the land of their beloved ancestors.

Franklin won his point. England took Canada from France and gave back Guadeloupe. Thirteen years later the colonies declared their independence.

SECTION 3 REVIEW

1. Identify: Edward Braddock, James Wolfe, Montcalm, William Pitt, Jeffrey Amherst.

2. Locate: Sault Ste. Marie, Vincennes, Natchez, Great Meadows, Fort Pitt, Lake Champlain, Plains of Abraham, Guadeloupe.

3. Describe the Albany Plan of Union.

4. Summarize the terms of the Peace of Paris.

5. **Identifying Central Issues.** In what sense was America an "unwilling battlefield" for European rivalries?

CHAPTER 3 REVIEW

FOCUSING ON IDEAS

1. What problems did the colonists encounter in trying to govern themselves?

2. Why did plantation owners turn to using slaves to grow and harvest their crops?

3. How did conflict between France and England lead to the French and Indian War?

4. What was the goal of England's *mercantilist* policy?

5. By 1765 about 40 percent of the settlers in the English colonies were of non-English heritage. What were some effects of this mixture?

6. Describe Britain's "Old Colonial System."

7. Why did colonial artists specialize in painting portraits?

TAKING A CRITICAL LOOK

1. **Drawing Conclusions.** How did American colonial crafts reflect American lives?

2. **Testing Conclusions.** Do you think it is true that there was an "American Revolution under way long before fighting broke out"? What are your reasons?

3. **Recognizing Cause and Effect.** Britain's "Old Colonial System" worked best when it worked least. Why?

4. **Demonstrating Reasoned Judgment.** (a) To what extent was America involved in a "world war" from 1689 to 1763? (b) How did this war shape the future of the colonies?

YOUR REGION IN HISTORY

1. **Geography.** What countries had laid claim to your region by 1763?

2. **Culture.** What Indian or European settlements existed within 50 miles of your home by 1763? Describe how people lived in these settlements.

3. **Economics.** How, if at all, did the Peace of Paris affect the growth of the region where you live?

HISTORICAL FACTS AND FIGURES

Inferring Information. Some of the information in the graph below is very straightforward and can be gathered by simply reading the graph. Other information can be inferred. To *infer* means to draw a conclusion based on a careful analysis of the available data. Read the following questions and study the information in the graph. Then decide whether or not the answer can be inferred from the graph. If the answers need to be inferred, give the answer and explain how you derived it. (a) What percentage of the colonial population spoke English? (b) Were all Africans in the colonies slaves? (c) What is the largest percentage of the colonial population that could possibly have been Indians?

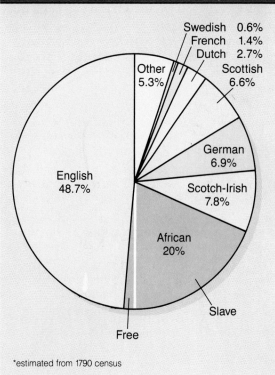

Ethnic Division of Colonial Population, 1775*

Swedish 0.6%
French 1.4%
Dutch 2.7%
Scottish 6.6%
Other 5.3%
German 6.9%
Scotch-Irish 7.8%
English 48.7%
African 20%
Slave
Free

*estimated from 1790 census

MAKING CONNECTIONS

THEMES

This unit began on page 1 with a brief but important observation:

In the Age of Columbus the peoples of Europe were discovering the world anew, reaching out to far and fabulous places.

This conclusion was supported by the three unit themes that are reprinted in **dark type** below. Use the time line and the information in Unit 1 to answer the questions that follow the unit themes.

1. **People leave Europe for the New World for a variety of reasons.**

   Evaluate the following opinion: "Immigration to America is the history of people trying to get *away* from some situations and trying to get *to* others."

2. **The success of Europeans in the New World spells disaster for most Native Americans.**

   Some people believe that Native Americans would be better off today if Europeans had never discovered the Americas. Do you agree or disagree? List facts that support your conclusions.

3. **Shaped by their experiences in the New World, colonists begin to develop new ways of life.**

   Many people in eighteenth-century Europe believed the American colonists to be rough and uncivilized farmers. What facts contradict this opinion?

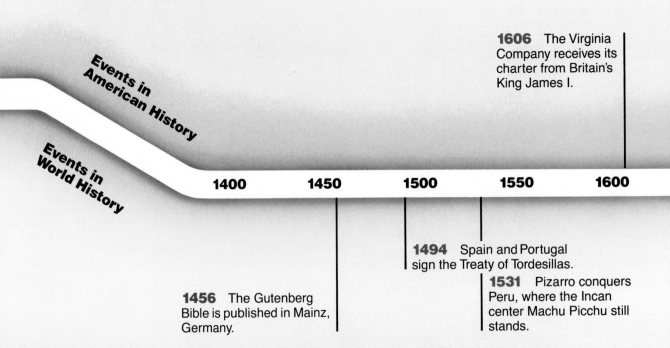

Events in American History

Events in World History

1400   **1450**   **1500**   **1550**   **1600**

1606 The Virginia Company receives its charter from Britain's King James I.

1494 Spain and Portugal sign the Treaty of Tordesillas.

1531 Pizarro conquers Peru, where the Incan center Machu Picchu still stands.

1456 The Gutenberg Bible is published in Mainz, Germany.

1616 Promoters of the colonies contrast overcrowded London with America's natural beauty.

1620 Separatist Puritans flee Britain for the New World.

1636 Harvard College is founded in Cambridge, Massachusetts.

1732 Georgia is established as a charity colony for London's outcasts.

1765 John Singleton Copley paints portrait of Paul Revere, silversmith.

1776 A Spanish mission is founded in San Francisco to convert Indians.

1776 Thomas Paine's *Common Sense,* urging American independence, is published.

1600 | 1650 | 1700 | 1750 | 1800 | 1850

1700 The Indian population of Central and South America has dropped from 50 million to 4 million.

UNIT 2

Forming a new nation 1763–1800

Winning the American Revolution, John Adams once said, was like trying to make thirteen clocks strike at once. The colonies were so different that they seldom had come to the same idea at the same time. Starting as colonies at different times and with different goals, they moved to independence in thirteen different ways. To bring the people of any single colony to agree was difficult enough. To lead thirteen different colonies to take common action seemed next to impossible. This was the main American problem in the War of Independence.

But the variety of the colonies turned out to be a secret weapon in the war. The colonies were like a monster with many heads. They could survive the loss of several of them. Nothing was more baffling to the British. Nothing did more to make it impossible for them to win the war. But after the war, this peculiarly American variety was a problem. Each new state wanted to act like an independent nation. They could not see that they ought to work together. During the early years, the Americans were still trying to find out what it meant to be the people of one nation.

THEMES IN AMERICAN HISTORY

- The British have trouble subduing the colonies because of the colonies' variety and lack of a critical center.

- The states' desire for self rule and their fear of tyranny result in a weak central government under the Articles of Confederation.

THEMES
- The drafting and the ratification of a new constitution begin the process of binding Americans together into one nation.

The American Revolution began on April 19, 1775, with the battles at Lexington and Concord. This engraving of the battle at the North Bridge in Concord was made by Amos Doolittle in 1775.

Print Collection, The New York Public Library, Astor, Lenox and Tilden Foundations

CHAPTER 4

The road to revolution and victory

In 1763 few people in Great Britain's American colonies would have foreseen that in little more than a decade the colonists would declare their independence. Fewer people, still, would have predicted that in a revolutionary war the thirteen former colonies, which had never been able to cooperate on anything, would be able to defeat the most powerful nation in the world. Yet strangely enough, against all belief, that is exactly what happened.

1. The British take a collision course

After its victory over the French in 1763 the British Empire was bigger than ever, which made the thirteen American colonies only a small part of the empire. To the north of the thirteen colonies the British had now added all of Canada, and to the west and south all the regions east of the Mississippi River, including Florida. The people living in these vast lands became new members of the British Empire.

The British situation in 1763. Between the Appalachian Mountains and the Mississippi River there lived 200,000 Indians who were now part of Britain's new empire. They had heard stories from the French that their new English masters were going to rob them of their hunting grounds. Indeed, in the spring of 1763 the Shawnee, Delaware, Seneca, and Ottawa were in the forefront leading the Indians of the West on the warpath.

By June the tribes had captured eight of the eleven British forts west of the mountains, and many settlers had died. Only Niagara, Fort Pitt, and Detroit remained, and Detroit was under siege by the Ottawa led by their able chieftain, Pontiac.

This garrison was of such strategic importance that the British came to call the whole war "Pontiac's Conspiracy."

The British were so desperate that they even resorted to sending blankets infected with smallpox to the tribes. Many Indians died of the disease. Illness and British troops broke most Indian resistance by 1764, but not until the following year were Pontiac and his followers put down.

The English government came to the conclusion that it would take a standing army of 10,000 men to control the western Indians and to protect all the American colonies. This task they could not entrust to the colonists. The French in Canada did not like their conquerors. The Americans could not even unite to defend themselves. In fact, some of them had even aided the enemy by carrying on forbidden trade with the French and Spanish West Indies. So the government would have to send over an army to America. And it was decided the colonists ought to be made to pay part of the costs of this army sent to protect them.

The Proclamation Line of 1763. The trouble really began when the well-meaning men running the government in London decided in 1763 to set this far-flung empire in order. Their plans were much too simple and old-fashioned to work on a continent that was nearly all wilderness. To prevent fighting among the colonies, and to avoid war with the Indians, the officials in London decided to try to keep the colonists confined where they already were. Settlement of the new lands would have to wait until Indian relations and a land policy were worked out.

The British thought that the Appalachian Mountains, which ran roughly parallel to the Atlantic coastline a few hundred miles inland, would be a useful barrier to keep the colonists separated from the Indians in the west. They proclaimed that for the time being the colonists should not settle on the western side of those mountains, and that the Indians should not go eastward.

This Proclamation Line of 1763 was a neat enough idea, but hardly designed to please Virginians. They were always looking for new tobacco land and were hoping also to make money from wilderness real estate. Virginians and other colonists wanted to go west now. Was not the continent theirs every bit as much as it was the Indians'?

The Sugar Act of 1764. At the same time George Grenville, who was in charge of the British treasury (his title was "Chancellor of the Exchequer"), was desperately looking for ways to pay the bills left over from a century of wars. He was aware of how much the American colonists had eventually benefited from the successful outcome of the British wars against the enemies of the empire. In the backwoods, colonists had seen their homes burned and their families killed by the French and Indians. On the sea, colonial merchants had lost ships and goods to marauding French and Spanish and Dutch privateers. The empire had come to their aid and ended all that. Why should not Americans now at last pay a fair share of the bills for keeping peace and defending the empire?

Before 1754

After 1763

Miquelon and St. Pierre (French)

PROCLAMATION LINE OF 1763

Results of the Peace of Paris

English   Spanish   Disputed

French   Russian

Grenville therefore persuaded Parliament to pass the Sugar Act in 1764. This act replaced the old Molasses Act of 1733, the only one of the Navigation Acts that might have caused real financial problems for the colonists. The Molasses Act had put a duty of sixpence per gallon on molasses imported from the French, Dutch, and Spanish islands of the West Indies into the ports of the American mainland. The molasses Americans imported was made into rum, which was sold in the colonies, used in the slave trade, and in trade with all the West Indies along with fish, lumber, horses, and wheat.

The Molasses Act would have made foreign molasses too expensive to buy. And the British West Indies, which the act was intended to help, did not produce enough molasses to supply the needs of New England merchants. New England's important rum trade would have been ruined. But the Molasses Act had not been enforced. Now, in the Sugar Act, Grenville lowered the duty on molasses to threepence a gallon, and he intended to collect it. Since the colonists had regularly paid a bribe of a penny and a half per gallon to the customs officers, Grenville reckoned they could afford to pay the duty. Grenville's purpose was not so much to regulate colonial trade as to extract American money. In addition to taxing sugar, new or higher duties were also put on coffee and wines imported into the colonies.

The Stamp Act. Then, on top of taxing colonial imports, in the Stamp Act of March 1765 the British imposed on the colonies a kind of tax that had long been used in England. The British now put taxes on all sorts of everyday things that the American colonists used, even if they were not imported. To show that you had paid the tax, you had to buy specially stamped paper. A stamp had to be put on nearly every piece of printed matter in daily use—on newspapers, magazines, calendars, receipts, legal papers for buying and selling land, on ships' papers, on insurance policies, and even on playing cards. If your papers did not have stamps on them, they would be seized and you would be tried without a jury in an Admiralty Court, and be fined or jailed.

It was bad enough for an uninformed Parliament three thousand miles away to control what came into the colonies. But many colonists still thought that might be a reasonable price to pay for preserv-

The hated Stamp Act of 1765 forced the colonists to buy paper bearing a stamp such as the above to show that they had paid the tax. After strong protests by the colonists, Parliament repealed the Stamp Act.

ing the empire and supporting the British navy. It was quite another matter—and far more serious—when the Parliament in London now started meddling inside the colonies. If Parliament taxed newspapers, then what couldn't they tax? If they could tax everything in the colonies, they could control all daily life. Where would it end?

In a new push to organize trade in the enlarged empire, and to improve business in England, Grenville now also decided to regulate the trade of the colonies more tightly than ever before. The old Navigation Acts restricting imports and exports had not been consistently enforced. Otherwise Americans would not have tolerated them. But Grenville intended that the new laws should be enforced. And to see that they were, he clarified the authority of the Admiralty Courts so they could try smugglers. These independent Americans would no longer be able to escape punishment by appealing to juries of their friends and neighbors, who seldom punished them.

The American reaction. If these new policies continued, Americans thought, they would no longer be American members of the British Empire with all the rights of freeborn Englishmen. They would simply be slaves of Parliament. Even in England, some people warned against the new policies.

The colonists quickly replied to what they considered British tyranny. They organized town meetings to protest. In order to punish British businessmen, colonists decided not to buy their goods. Some of the richest and most respectable Americans formed a secret society called the Sons of Liberty to terrorize the agents of the British who were trying to sell the hated tax stamps. They persuaded many of the British agents to resign. The Americans used all sorts of arguments, including brickbats and tar and feathers.

This broadside calls for a boycott of the import business of William Jackson by the Sons and Daughters of Liberty. He had refused to stop importing British goods.

WILLIAM JACKSON,

an IMPORTER; at the

BRAZEN HEAD,

North Side of the TOWN-HOUSE,

and Opposite the Town-Pump, i

Corn-hill, BOSTON.

It is desired that the Sons and Daughters of LIBERTY, would not buy any one thing of him, for in so doing they will bring Disgrace upon themselves, and their Posterity, for ever and ever, AMEN.

Hundreds of merchants in New York City, Philadelphia, and Boston agreed not to buy imported goods until the Stamp Act was repealed. Nine of the thirteen colonies sent official representatives from their colonial assemblies to a special Stamp Act Congress in New York City in October 1765, where they protested taxation by Parliament and the widening of the powers of the Admiralty Courts. They demanded the repeal of the Sugar and Stamp acts.

All this began to empty British pocketbooks. In a single year, 1765, British sales to America fell by £305,600, or more than 13 percent.

The London merchants began to worry. To save themselves, they demanded that Parliament repeal the Stamp Act. Benjamin Franklin, representing the colonies in London, went to the House of Commons and warned the British that they were on the road to ruin. If they did not change their policies, there would very likely be rebellion. The Americans, he explained, dearly loved their Mother England, but they loved their liberties even more.

The Declaratory Act. The rulers of Britain might still have saved the situation. If they had known the colonists better, they would have realized that Americans would not let their lives be run by others. A shrewder British government might have worked out a cooperative empire. Then there might never have been a War of Independence. But the rulers of Britain were shortsighted. They thought that government by Parliament had to be all-powerful or it would have no power at all. Unlike the Americans, they were not willing to compromise.

The colonists were practical people. They knew it was possible for Parliament to run their foreign relations and still permit Americans to have their own assemblies—in Massachusetts, in Virginia, and elsewhere—to govern inside the colonies.

The leaders in London did not see it that way. Even when they repealed the Stamp Act on March 18, 1766, they felt they had to pass a Declaratory Act that stated that Parliament still had power to make laws for the Americans "in all cases whatsoever." They did not realize that a new age had arrived. Two million people—one-fourth as many as in England—were now living in the thirteen colonies. And now they were beginning to be a new people—Americans.

Glorious News,

Juſt received from *Boſton*, brought by Meſſrs. *Jonathan Lowder*, and *Thomas Brackett*.

BOSTON, Friday 11 o'Clock, 16th May, 1766.
THIS Inſtant arrived here the Brig Harriſon, belonging to John Hancock, Eſq; Captain Shubael Coffin, in 6 Weeks and 2 Days from LONDON, with important News, as follows.

From the London Gazette.

Weſtminſter, March 18th, 1766.

THIS day his Majeſty came to the Houſe of Peers, and being in his royal robes ſeated on the Throne with the uſual ſolemnity, Sir Francis Molineux, Gentleman Uſher of the Black Rod, was ſent with a Meſſage from his Majeſty to the Houſe of Commons, commanding their attendance in the Houſe of Peers. The Commons being come thither accordingly, his Majeſty was pleaſed to give his royal aſſent to

An ACT to REPEAL an Act made in the laſt Seſſion of Parliament intituled, an Act for granting and applying certain Stamp-Duties and other Duties in the Britiſh Colonies and Plantations in America, towards further defraying the Expences of defending, protecting and ſecuring the ſame, and for amending ſuch parts of the ſeveral Acts of Parliament relating to the trade and revenues of the ſaid Colonies and Plantations, as direct the manner of determining and recovering the penalties and forfeitures therein mentioned.

Alſo ten public bills, and ſeventeen private ones.

Yeſterday there was a meeting of the principal Merchants concerned in the American trade, at the King's Arms tavern in Cornhill, to conſider of an Addreſs to his Majeſty on the beneficial Repeal of the late Stamp-Act.

Yeſterday morning about eleven o'clock a great number of North-American Merchants went in their coaches from the King's Arms tavern in Cornhill to the Houſe of Peers, to pay their duty to his Majeſty, and to expreſs their ſatisfaction at his ſigning the Bill for Repealing the American Stamp-Act, there was upwards of fifty coaches in the proceſſion.

Laſt night the ſaid gentlemen diſpatched an expreſs for Falmouth with fifteen copies of the act for repealing the Stamp-Act, to be forwarded immediately for New York.

Orders are given for ſeveral merchantmen in the river to proceed to ſea immediately on their reſpective voyages to North-America, ſome of whom have been cleared ſince the firſt of November laſt.

Yeſterday meſſengers were diſpatched to Birmingham, Sheffield, Mancheſter, and all the great manufacturing towns in England, with an account of the final deciſion of an auguſt aſſembly relating to the Stamp-Act.

When the KING went to the Houſe of Peers to give the Royal Aſſent, there was ſuch a vaſt Concourſe of People, huzzaing, clapping Hands, &c. that it was ſeveral Hours before his Majeſty reached the Houſe.

Immediately on his Majeſty's Signing the Royal Aſſent to the Repeal of the Stamp-Act the Merchants trading to America, diſpatched a Veſſel which had been waiting, to put into the firſt Port on the Continent with the Account.

There were the greateſt Rejoicings poſſible in the City of London, by all Ranks of People, on the TOTAL Repeal of the Stamp-Act,----the Ships in the River diſplayed all their Colours, Illuminations and Bonfires in many Parts. In ſhort, the Rejoicings were as great as was ever known on any Occaſion.

It is ſaid the Acts of Trade relating to America would be taken under Conſideration, and all Grievances removed. The Friends to America are very powerful, and diſpoſed to aſſiſt us to the utmoſt of their Ability.

It is impoſſible to expreſs the Joy the Town is now in, on receiving the above great, glorious and important News.----The Bells in all the Churches were immediately ſet a Ringing, and we hear the Day for a general Rejoicing will be the Beginning of next Week.

NEWPORT : Printed by *S. Hall*, for the Benefit of the Public in general, and his *good Cuſtomers* in particular.

Mr. Lowder and Mr. Brackett, have rode all Night, in order to bring the above glorious Tidings, and it is not doubted all Sons of Liberty will be generous in helping to defray their Expences.----All Donations are deſired to be left at the Printing-Office.

The New-York Historical Society

The news from London of the repeal of the Stamp Act was rushed to Boston. Then two men rode all night to deliver the message to Newport, Rhode Island, where the broadside shown here was printed. It notes that a ship owned by John Hancock had crossed the ocean with the report in six weeks and two days.

Museum of Fine Arts, Boston

Samuel Adams fanned the flames of the colonists' outrage over British abuses in Boston.

The Townshend Acts. The British government continued on its collision course. The government still wanted money from the colonists, and Charles Townshend, who was now Chancellor of the Exchequer, thought he saw a way to collect it. To get rid of the stamp tax, Benjamin Franklin had told Parliament that the colonists opposed it because it was an *internal tax* but that they would accept *external* taxes, like the import duties. Franklin said this to bring about the repeal of the Stamp Act; but he knew it was not so, and his deception would make trouble. For in fact the colonies had made it very clear that they opposed *any* tax placed on them by a Parliament in which they were not represented. *No taxation without representation!*

Townshend chose to take Franklin at his word. He proposed duties on many items Americans imported: lead, glass, paper, paint, and tea. He also suggested that the colonial customs service be reorganized. Furthermore, he wanted the governor of New York to veto every act of the provincial assembly until New York provided the full amount of supplies to British troops stationed there—as it (and every) colony was supposed to do under the Billeting Act of 1765.

This engraving by Paul Revere shows a monument that Bostonians put up on their Common to celebrate the repeal of the Stamp Act.

All these measures were contained in three acts passed by Parliament in 1767. The Townshend Acts, as they were called, created a fury of resistance in America. The act reorganizing the customs service was especially hated. The new officers who came to collect the various duties were little better than racketeers. Since they received one-third of the proceeds when a ship was seized and sold because it had broken the law, they used every trick possible to find an excuse to take possession of a vessel and its cargo.

The chief method adopted for opposing the duties was to refuse to import British goods. By the spring of 1769 non-importation agreements had been made by the merchants of New York, Philadelphia, and Charleston. Within a year the value of British exports to the colonies fell nearly 40 percent.

Sam Adams and the Boston Massacre. In response to colonial non-importation, smuggling, opposition to the customs racketeers, and to the colonists' denials of Parliament's right to tax America, the government sent British troops to Boston. That simply increased colonial resistance.

One of the ablest organizers of colonial rebellion was Sam Adams of Boston. He was a strange man who always had trouble managing his own affairs, but could persuade others how to run theirs. He came from a well-known family and went to Harvard College, where he studied Latin and Greek. When his father set him up in business, he soon lost his father's money. Then when he became tax collector for the town of Boston, he got into trouble when he failed to hand over all the taxes he collected. He was always in debt, and many

News of the Boston Massacre was spread by engravings like the one on the left which helped to arouse the colonists against British rule. The diagram showing the location of the bodies after the Massacre is thought to be the work of Paul Revere. The circles at the right represent British soldiers. Note the differences between the engraving and the diagram.

Bostonians considered him a shady character. But Adams made himself a master of propaganda and mob tactics. He was clever at creating a sensation out of every incident and blaming it all on the British. Two regiments of British troops sent to Boston in 1768 had been taunted for months by people there. Then late one March night in 1770 a small group of redcoats was jeered at and pelted with snowballs by a few restless unemployed workers. In their confusion, the British troops fired and killed five colonists. The first to die was Crispus Attucks, a black man of giant stature who was the leader of the throng.

Sam Adams advertised this event as the "Boston Massacre" where bloodthirsty British soldiers slaughtered innocent Americans. Later, Sam's cousin, John Adams, defended the soldiers in court and was able to get them acquitted of murder. But most Americans still believed Sam Adams's portrayal of the event.

Britain backs down. In the face of American opposition and the boycott, which was severely injuring British trade, a new English ministry led by Lord North retreated. All the Townshend duties were repealed, except for a small tax on tea, which King George III insisted should be kept in order to prove that Parliament had the right to tax the colonies.

When England backed down, the colonists' scheme of non-importation collapsed. And many Americans, though it went against their principles, paid the tea tax and the tax on molasses contained in the Sugar Act. They had won most of their points, and the threat of interference was much less. So the colonists traded and prospered.

Still, some energetic, freedom-loving colonists—including Sam Adams, Thomas Jefferson, and Patrick Henry—kept resistance alive. In 1772 Adams was the leader in organizing Committees of Correspondence in Massachusetts to consult on violations of the colonists' rights. The idea spread to other colonies, and in 1773 Virginia suggested that the committees in different states should work together.

The Boston Tea Party.

The colonists were now ready to act as one, and at this point Lord North made a bad mistake. The British East India Company was in financial trouble. It had large amounts of tea stored in England. But the company could not sell the tea there because it did not have enough money to pay the customs taxes due. To help this huge business, which not only controlled the trade of India but even governed that land, the government decided to let the company sell the tea directly to the colonies without paying any duty in England. In this way the company, even if it actually paid the customs charges in the colonies, could sell the tea for less than the colonists were then paying for tea smuggled in to avoid the customs duties. Everybody, it seemed, would benefit. The East India Company would sell its tea, the crown would get the American duty, and the colonists would pay less for tea.

The colonists did not see it that way. Colonial merchants, who stood to lose their profitable trade in smuggled tea, led the resistance. They cried "monopoly" against the East India Company. They insisted that as soon as they went out of business the East India Company would raise the price of tea. Most of the colonies refused to buy any of the tea, which quickly became a symbol of British tyranny.

Boston, where it was easy to collect a crowd, became a center of agitation. On the night of December 16, 1773, a group of townspeople, organized by Sam Adams, enjoyed the most famous tea party in history. It was also a costume party because they put on the disguise of Mohawk Indians before they boarded the tea ships in Boston Harbor and threw overboard 342 chests of tea.

The Intolerable Acts and the Quebec Act.

Still the British rulers of the empire refused to retreat or to compromise. Instead the "Boston Tea Party" made them decide to use force. In a series of acts in 1774, called the "Coercive Acts" in Britain and the "Intolerable Acts" in America, they tried to punish Boston. They closed its port. They undermined the independence of the colonial government by taking from the Assembly the power to appoint the Governor's Council and giving that power to the king. They interfered with local government by forbidding towns to hold the meetings in which New England towns normally conducted their affairs. They declared that government officials and soldiers accused of crimes punishable by death could be tried in England or Nova Scotia. They

Courtesy of the John Carter Brown Library at Brown University

This British view of patriot activity shows colonists forcing a tarred and feathered tax collector to drink some tea. In the background, other colonists dump tea from a ship into the ocean.

gave British troops in America the power to take over taverns, and even to live free of charge in private homes.

To these measures Parliament foolishly added the Quebec Act, which seemed one more attack on the colonists' freedom. From the British point of view the Quebec Act was only an innocent attempt to organize into the empire the area taken from France in the French and Indian War. But when the act extended the province of Quebec southward to the Ohio River, it cut off the claims of Massachusetts, Connecticut, Virginia, and New York to their western lands. For that area the act set up a government without a representative assembly and gave special privileges to the Catholic church. The irritated and suspicious colonists saw the Quebec Act as a signal of what might happen to the thirteen colonies.

SECTION 1 REVIEW

1. Identify or explain: Pontiac, Molasses Act of 1733, Sugar Act of 1764, Sons of Liberty, Declaratory Act, Townshend Acts, Boston Massacre, Committees of Correspondence.

2. What was the Proclamation Line of 1763?

3. Why did the Americans oppose the Stamp Act?

4. What were the Intolerable Acts? Why were they passed?

5. **Identifying Alternatives.** How could England have successfully re-established its authority over the colonies?

---

2. Declaring independence

Until the conflicts with the British government, the colonies had gone their separate ways. There had not been any congress or any central government where all thirteen colonies could meet and talk about their problems. Franklin and others had tried to persuade the colonies to join hands, but with very little success. Now within only a few years, the assertive politicians in London did more to push the colonies together than colonial statemen had accomplished in over a century.

The First Continental Congress. In response to a call from Massachusetts to stop all trade with Great Britain, twelve of the colonies—all except Geor-

gia—sent delegates (56 altogether) to Carpenters' Hall in Philadelphia on September 5, 1774. The meeting called itself the Continental Congress. It was not really the congress of any government, for there was no *American* government. It could be nothing more than a *continental* congress—a collection of delegates from the colonies that happened to be neighbors on the same continent.

At first each colony believed it had all the powers of a nation. Yet, because each had been part of the British Empire, many of the usual tasks of a national government—for example, building an army or navy, or conducting diplomacy—had been left to London. When the First Continental Congress met, then, it had to start from scratch.

The delegates to the Congress were men of widely varying views. Joseph Galloway, a conservative lawyer from Philadelphia, revived the Albany Plan that Benjamin Franklin had proposed twenty years before. Sam Adams and Patrick Henry desired outright independence. No one got his way entirely, but Sam Adams cleverly led the delegates along the radical path.

The Congress agreed to form a Non-Importation Association and cease all trade with Great Britain. Committees chosen in every county and town were to see that the boycott was obeyed.

The delegates also dealt with the difficult problem of the relationship of the colonies to Parliament. In a Declaration of Rights and Grievances written by John Adams, the Congress appealed to both the unchangeable "Laws of Nature" and the British constitution to deny any right of Parliament to tax the colonies. The colonists, they told the British government, could only be taxed by their own assemblies. To show that they were not unreasonable, however, they agreed to *allow* Parliament to regulate trade as it had in the Navigation Acts before 1763.

The battles of Lexington and Concord. Some Americans still hoped somehow to find their way back into the empire. But, in April 1775, within a few months after the First Continental Congress, dramatic events would put an end to their hopes. Massachusetts had been hardest hit by the British acts of force. And, without waiting for others, Massachusetts began to prepare for war by collecting military supplies in the little town of Concord, about twenty miles inland from Boston.

When the British Secretary of State for Colonies heard of this, he decided to act quickly to destroy that first supply base before the Americans were any better organized. Bostonians learned of the plan and on the night of April 18, 1775, sent Paul Revere and William Dawes on their celebrated ride to Lexington, which was on the road to Concord. They warned Americans to form ranks to stop the king's troops before they could reach and destroy the colony's Concord supply base.

Early the next morning when the 700 British troops reached Lexington, they found 70 American minutemen—militia who had agreed to be ready at a minute's warning—arrayed against them on the town common. The British killed eight and wounded ten Americans before hastening to Concord. As if by magic, the countryside sprang to arms. From nowhere appeared thousands of American militiamen. They harassed the British troops, who, before returning to their ships in Charlestown Harbor, suffered nearly 300 dead and wounded while the American losses were fewer than 100.

Now talk was at an end. War had begun. There was no turning back.

The Second Continental Congress.

When delegates from twelve colonies (all but Georgia's, who arrived late) met again in their Second Continental Congress in the Philadelphia State House in May 1775, they were no longer American children pleading for better treatment from their British parent country. Instead they were armed colonists demanding their rights. George Washington was chosen commander in chief of the "Continental Army," which was drawn up around Boston. It could not be called the Army of the United States, for there was yet no United States.

The Continental Congress quickly realized that they would need a navy. Following the old British example, the Congress, with their own letters of marque, began creating privateers. But now they were *American* privateers in hot pursuit of all British ships.

The Battle of Bunker Hill.

Sixteen thousand militiamen from New Hampshire, Connecticut, Rhode Island, and Massachusetts gathered around Boston after the battles of Lexington and Concord. Even before Washington could join his troops, these

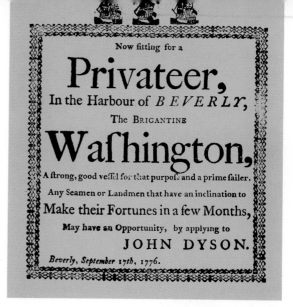

Broadsides or posters were used to recruit volunteers for privateers to attack British ships.

colonial militia met the English regulars in the bloodiest conflict that had ever taken place on the soil of British North America.

During the night of June 16, colonial militia under Colonel William Prescott were sent to fortify Bunker Hill across the water from Boston. By mistake, he and his men fortified Breed's Hill, and that was where a great battle was fought. But it was given the name of Bunker Hill—the hill where they should have been!

The next day the British decided to drive the Americans away from Breed's Hill. Twice the redcoats charged up the hill against Americans who were behind a rail fence stuffed with hay. Twice they were met with deadly fire and driven back with terrible losses. On the third attack the colonials, with powder gone, were forced from their position with bayonets.

But the American defeat in the Battle of Bunker Hill was a moral victory. It showed that the raw colonial troops could face regulars without flinching. When Washington heard of the battle, he said, "The country is safe." The British General Howe's loss of 1000 men was more than double that of the Americans. One-eighth of all the British officers killed in the Revolutionary War fell at Bunker Hill. "I wish we could sell them another hill at the same price," said one American officer.

The Americans offer peace and go to war. After Bunker Hill the Continental Congress sent a petition, called the Olive Branch Petition, to King George. It asked the king to stop the efforts of Parliament to enslave them and said that they wanted peace and harmony with England. The king refused to receive the petition. But even before that, on July 6, 1775, Congress issued a spirited declaration of war:

> We are reduced to the alternative of choosing an unconditional submission to the tyranny of irritated ministers, or resistance by force. The latter is our choice. We have counted the cost of this contest, and find nothing so dreadful as voluntary slavery. . . . Our cause is just. Our union is perfect. . . . In defense of the freedom that is our birthright . . . we have taken up arms. We shall lay them down when hostility shall cease on the part of the aggressors.

Though Congress still said that it did not want to separate from Great Britain, the breach between the two sides deepened. The king hired 30,000 mercenary troops from the German princes of Brunswick, Hesse, and Anhalt to help put down the rebels. In America, royal governors took refuge on warships. Their legislatures were refusing to obey them and were converting themselves into popular conventions controlled by the radical leaders. Congress was laboring to increase Washington's army and provide it with food, clothing, and money.

Brave captains of speedy privateers were attacking British supply ships and seizing barrels of flour and gunpowder. Eighty yoke of oxen were dragging cannons, captured in May at Fort Ticonderoga by Ethan Allen and the Green Mountain Boys, over the December snow to Boston. Richard Montgomery and Benedict Arnold were leading American troops to invade Canada. On the last day of 1775, in the midst of a blinding snowstorm, Montgomery was killed and Arnold severely wounded in a vain attempt to capture the town of Quebec. So ended the patriot effort to conquer Canada.

Common Sense **stirs the colonies.** On January 15, 1776, the most influential pamphlet ever to be published in America appeared. *Common Sense* was written by Thomas Paine, an Englishman who had come to America on Franklin's advice to help the cause of freedom. Paine urged that it was simply

This engraving of the Battle of Bunker Hill was made by Bernard Romans, an eyewitness, who was captain of a Pennsylvania artillery company. Later captured, he was taken to England.

COMMON SENSE;

ADDRESSED TO THE

INHABITANTS

OF

A M E R I C A,

On the following interesting

S U B J E C T S.

I. Of the Origin and Design of Government in general,
with concise Remarks on the English Constitution.

II. Of Monarchy and Hereditary Succession.

III. Thoughts on the present State of American Affairs.

IV. Of the present Ability of America, with some miscellaneous Reflections.

Man knows no Master save creating HEAVEN,
Or those whom choice and common good ordain.
                                                THOMSON.

PHILADELPHIA;

Printed, and Sold, by R. BELL, in Third-Street.

M DCC LXXVI.

American Antiquarian Society

National Portrait Gallery, Smithsonian Institution, Washington, D.C.; on loan from the National Gallery of Art; Gift of Marion B. Maurice

Thomas Paine's 47-page pamphlet *Common Sense* roused the colonies against British rule. The painting of Paine is by John Wesley Jarvis, one of the leading portraitists of the time.

"common sense" to stop recognizing the "royal brute," King George III. America should break all connection with Great Britain. This nation, he wrote, was destined to show the whole world how a people could rule themselves and be free of the tyranny of kings and nobles.

Common Sense swept the colonies. More than 100,000 copies were quickly sold. Many colonists agreed with George Washington that Paine's reasoning left no room for rebuttal. Edmund Randolph, a Virginia statesman, believed that, next to King George, Thomas Paine was the man most responsible for the declaration of our independence.

The British leave Boston. Washington brought the long siege of Boston to an end in March 1776 by seizing Dorchester Heights. There the cannon brought from Fort Ticonderoga over the snow looked down upon the town and the British fleet in the harbor. This forced the British general, William Howe, to sail away with his troops to Halifax, Nova Scotia. With Howe went 1100 Tory refugees

(Loyalists, the British called them) representing many of the "best families" of the colony.

Secret aid from France. What the Americans most needed was the aid of France with its great navy and, if possible, also the aid of Spain. So in March 1776 Silas Deane of Connecticut was sent to France to ask for help in men and money. To encourage this aid, the Continental Congress on April 6, 1776, at one stroke abolished a whole century's accumulation of Navigation Acts. They opened all American ports to all nations of the world, except Britain.

Meanwhile, fortunately for the Americans, the French were already conspiring with the Spanish to use this opportunity to tear apart the British Empire. The French King Louis XVI secretly arranged to supply gunpowder to the American rebels. From the French the American armies received nearly all the gunpowder they used during the first two years of war. But this was only the start of French aid.

79

The Declaration of Independence. In May the Congress advised all the colonies to form their own governments. American independence was rapidly becoming a fact. The Americans had set up their own Congress, they had organized their own army, they were beginning to organize a navy. They had already plainly declared commercial independence by abolishing all the British laws of navigation. Then, on July 2, 1776, the Continental Congress adopted a short resolution "that these United Colonies are, and of right ought to be, free and independent states," and that all political connection with Great Britain was now broken.

With the resolution on July 2, Americans *announced* their independence. They gave out the news that a new nation was born, but they had not yet given out the reasons. Strictly speaking, American independence was not yet *declared*. ("Declare" comes from the Latin word meaning *to make clear*.) It was not the mere announcement, but the "declaration"—the explanation—of independence that Americans would always celebrate. For Americans were proud of the reasons for the birth of their nation. These reasons gave the new nation a purpose that it would not forget.

One of the remarkable things about the United States, which made it different from the older nations of Europe, was that it could actually point to the reasons why it had become a separate nation. These reasons were listed in a Declaration of Independence prepared and approved by the very men who made the nation independent.

Three weeks before the Continental Congress adopted its brief resolution announcing independence, it had named a committee to prepare a longer Declaration of Independence. Virginia's brilliant Thomas Jefferson, then only 33 years of age, was appointed chairman. Also on the committee were John Adams and Benjamin Franklin, but Jefferson did the writing and the others only changed a word here and there.

Jefferson did not try to be original in the Declaration; he only tried to state clearly what everybody already believed. He tried to write the common sense of the subject. He was speaking to the whole world. It was no good trying to persuade the world unless you started from what lots of people everywhere already believed. That is precisely what Jefferson did.

The opening part of the Declaration, usually called the "preamble," was cribbed from various books and declarations that Englishmen had written a hundred years before when, at the time of the Glorious Revolution, they removed James II and replaced him with William and Mary. The British then could not possibly deny Jefferson's words in his Declaration—that governments derive "their just powers from the consent of the governed." Nor "that whenever any form of government shall become destructive of these ends"—life, liberty, and the pursuit of happiness—"it is the right of the people to alter or to abolish it, and to institute new government . . . in such form as to them shall seem most likely to effect their safety and happiness." Their own British government, as they were repeatedly saying after 1688, was made by precisely that formula. You could hardly call an idea radical if it was the basis of the very respectable government of England.

After the common sense in the preamble there came a long list—"a long train of abuses and usurpations." Every item showed how the British king, George III, had disobeyed his own laws. The king aimed to reduce the colonists to "absolute despotism," to establish "an absolute tyranny over these states." His many crimes included "cutting off our trade with all parts of the world," "imposing taxes on us without our consent," and "quartering large bodies of armed troops among us." They also included the king's crimes against the very special rights of Englishmen—for example, taking away the right of trial by jury and violating the legal charters given to the colonies.

The colonists, Jefferson explained, had shown great respect for their king and great love for their "British brethren." "In every stage of these oppressions we have petitioned for redress in the most humble terms: Our repeated petitions have been answered only by repeated injury." The king had proved himself a tyrant, "unfit to be the ruler of a free people." If the king would not respect the colonists' rights, the Americans had no choice. They had to set up their own government.

Jefferson's Declaration simply ignored the British Parliament. For, according to Jefferson, Parliament had no rights over the colonies. It was the king's duty to hold the empire together and to protect all his subjects. The Americans demanded nothing but

The Second Continental Congress approves the Declaration of Independence. Benjamin Franklin is seated in the center.

their simple rights as British subjects. The king had denied those traditional rights. The law was on the side of the Americans. If Americans wondered why they were fighting, here was their simple answer.

On July 4, 1776, Jefferson's Declaration of Independence was approved by the Second Continental Congress, signed by John Hancock, the president of the Congress, and certified by the secretary. Then copies were sent out to all the states. As new members arrived to represent colonies in Congress, they too signed the Declaration, even though they had not been there when Jefferson first presented it. One representative signed it as late as November (there were finally 56 signatures altogether). In this way, they showed that they believed in the Revolution.

Jefferson had written an eloquent birth certificate of the new United States, which would inspire people all over the world. A few years after the American Revolution was won, when the French people decided to defend their own rights against their king, they found inspiration in Jefferson's words. In the 1820s, when colonists in South America separated from Spain, they turned to the same source. Jefferson's Declaration of Independence, like other documents that live and shape history, has had the magical power to be filled with new ideas. In the twentieth century, when colonists in Asia and Africa tried to explain to the world why they were fighting for their independence, they still recalled the Declaration of Independence of the thirteen American colonies.

SECTION 2 REVIEW

1. Match each of the following with another in the list: Joseph Galloway, Paul Revere, *Common Sense,* William Howe, William Dawes, Tories, First Continental Congress, Thomas Paine. Why should each pair go together?

2. Could one soldier have fought at Lexington, Bunker Hill, and Ticonderoga? Why?

3. Name three tasks the First Continental Congress accomplished.

4. Although losing at Bunker Hill, the patriots considered the battle a victory. Why?

5. Why did America need French aid? Why was France willing to help?

6. Why did the Second Continental Congress adopt a Declaration of Independence?

7. **Distinguishing False from Accurate Images.** The first shot fired at Lexington has been called "the shot heard round the world." How does this image express the significance of the American Revolution?

3. How British power was overthrown

America produced a new style of warfare. Here the skirmish, not the battle, was important. Communications did not exist, the land was vast. There was no way of directing operations from a center. Every man for himself! Colonists had learned to hide behind rocks and tree trunks.

"In our first war with the Indians," the Puritan missionary John Eliot noted back in 1677, "God pleased to show us the vanity of our military skill, in managing our arms, after the European mode. Now we are glad to learn the skulking way of war."

War in Europe in the 1700s. In Europe it was the Age of Limited Warfare. Armies fought according to certain definite rules, which made a battle in many ways like a football match. Battles took place on open fields, in good weather. Each side set up its men in neat array. Each side knew what forces the other possessed, and each part of an army was expected to perform only certain maneuvers. To begin a battle before the heralds had sounded their fanfares, to use sneak tactics or unusual weapons, were generally frowned upon.

The only people who fought were the professionals out there on the battlefield. Officers came from the aristocracy. They knew the rules and were willing to abide by them. At nightfall, or when the weather was bad, officers from opposing armies would actually entertain one another at dinner parties, concerts, and balls. Then the next day they would take their places on the battlefield. The privates were human dregs who had been dragged out of jails and bars. The best-trained and most reliable soldiers often were mercenaries—like the Swiss or the Hessians—who made a living from hiring themselves out to the highest bidder.

Patriotism had very little to do with those battles. Armies were small. The men were seldom fighting to preserve their country, but more often for some secret purpose known only to the monarch and his few advisers. By modern standards, the casualties were few. Weapons were crude. The old-fashioned musket had a poor aim, was hard to reload, and would not fire at all in wet weather—so armies had the pleasant custom of going into winter quarters. Kings could have their battles, and yet interfere very little with the peaceful round of daily life. The people could leave the fighting to the professional soldiers.

The American soldier. In America, the Indian had never heard of the polite tradition of war-by-the-rules. The Indian conducted a primitive form of total war. And the colonists' only good protection was a primitive form of total defense. Colonists could not leave their defense to professional soldiers far away on some neat battlefield. Where everybody was a target, every man, woman, and child had to be a soldier. Here, then, grew a new and American kind of army. The colonists called it their "militia." The militia was not really an army at all, but only a name for all the men who bore arms. Regular membership in the militia usually began at about 16 years of age, and might last till a man was 60. There was no uniform, not much discipline, and little of the colorful ritual of the European battlefields.

Still, against a professional army like that of the British Empire, the militia had some grave disadvantages. American militiamen often ran away or just stopped fighting if they felt like it. The very idea of enlistment—which kept men in the army even when it was personally inconvenient—did not suit the militia. These were vexing problems for George Washington. His forces consisted largely of militiamen, but he could never be sure how many he could count on.

Militia were a home guard and not an imperial army. They did not like to travel far from home. But the American Revolution had to be fought wherever the battle required and against a large regular army. George Washington's first, and probably his greatest, achievement was somehow to create a Continental Army.

This Continental Army was made up of men who were enlisted and paid by the Continental Congress. It was a small regular army of the European sort, but it could always be helped by the militia. If it was hard to bring the militia together, that was because they were spread all over the continent. In vast and trackless America, that itself could be helpful. You did not have to transport all your soldiers. Wherever you were, or wherever the enemy was, the militia was always there.

The major problem with the militia was that you could not depend on them. Forces of militia melted away whenever the men decided to go home to help bring in the harvest, or to be present at the birth of a child, or sometimes simply because they were tired of fighting. When General Washington begged

I. N. Phelps Stokes Collection, Prints Division, New York Public Library. Astor, Lenox and Tilden Foundations

This engraving by Amos Doolittle shows how British soldiers fought out in the open in neat rows and bright uniforms. From the Indians Americans had learned a different way of fighting. Here minutemen hiding behind a stone wall harass the British retreating from Concord in 1775.

Congress for a regular army organized in the European way, he complained that he had never seen a single instance of militia "being fit for the real business of fighting. I have found them useful as light parties to skirmish in the woods, but incapable of making or sustaining a serious attack."

So the militia were useful and useless. They were everywhere and nowhere. They might by their very presence keep an enemy from winning, but could a militia ever *win*?

Washington creates, and saves, an army. After the evacuation of Boston by the British troops, the military history of the American Revolution falls into two stages. The first part was the critical period from 1776 to 1778, when fighting took place

in the North. During this time Washington's greatest tasks were to organize an army and then keep it in the field and prevent it from being destroyed by the British. The second stage of the war came in the years 1779 to 1781. Washington had proved in the first phase that he could not be easily defeated, so fighting moved to the South, where the British hoped the Loyalists would rise to help them. If the southern colonies surrendered, the British expected that it would be easier to reconquer the North.

In the beginning of the first phase, Washington had to create a Continental Army and also fight the British. After the British left Boston, Washington moved to New York City and Long Island, where he expected the next attack. The British did not

83

disappoint him. In July and August 1776, they poured men and equipment onto Staten Island until they had a force there of 32,000 soldiers. New York City in normal times contained only 25,000 people! Washington faced this great force with 23,000 men, most of whom were militia.

The British general, William Howe, crossed from Staten Island and landed 20,000 well-trained soldiers on Long Island during August 22–25, 1776. They attacked Washington's untrained troops on the 27th, inflicting heavy casualties. The American army retreated, and Colonel John Glover and his Massachusetts regiment of Marblehead fishermen ferried the army together with its horses, cannons, food, and equipment across the East River to Manhattan Island under the cover of fog. In this retreat, and again in the retreat from Manhattan Island that followed when Howe's redcoats crossed the river on September 15, the most important thing was for Washington to get his army away. Had Washington's army been trapped at that time, the rebellion might have been over. Cities the British could have, for there was no center in America whose loss would really matter. But if the American army was lost, all might be lost.

The British followed Washington out of New York and across the Hudson River. As he retreated through New Jersey in November 1776, the redcoats were close behind. This was the low point of the war for Washington and for the American cause. The militia drifted off to their homes. The regular troops were on one-year enlistments that would end on December 31. With the military situation looking so bleak, they would not re-enlist, and new men were unlikely to take their places. Washington's army would just fade away.

On December 7, 1776, Washington crossed the Delaware River into Pennsylvania. The last boatloads were just crossing from Trenton when the British entered that town. On December 18, Washington informed his brother, "If every nerve is not strained to recruit the new army, . . . I think the game is pretty near up." Thomas Paine called this *The Crisis* and wrote:

> These are the times that try men's souls. The summer soldier and the sunshine patriot will, in this crisis, shrink from the service of their country; but he that stands it *now*, deserves the love and thanks of man and woman.

Even after receiving reinforcements from other units, and 2000 militia from Pennsylvania, Washington had fewer than 8000 men. Nevertheless, he decided he must attack while he still had some soldiers. So on the night of December 25, John Glover and the Marblehead men ferried Washington and 2400 of his troops across the ice-filled Delaware River in a driving sleet storm. On the next day they struck Trenton, where Hessian mercenaries were sleeping off their holiday celebration. The surprise was complete. With a loss of only four men, the Americans took 900 prisoners.

The victory at Trenton, and Washington's persuasive powers, encouraged many of his soldiers to re-enlist for a little longer. Then he moved on the British again. He fooled General Charles Cornwallis and the main British army by marching away in the night from his burning campfires. Before Cornwallis had time to react, Washington had routed the British rear guard at Princeton.

After the battle at Princeton, the British evacuated New Jersey and returned to New York. Then both armies went into winter quarters. In a brilliant campaign of ten days Washington had saved the cause of independence. American morale shot up, enlistments increased, the war would go on. Lord George Germain, the new British Minister of War, sadly confessed that all his hopes "were blasted by the unhappy affair at Trenton."

Victory at Saratoga brings help from France.

The British drew up an elaborate plan for the military campaigns of the summer of 1777. Three armies were to invade New York and unite at Albany. By controlling the Hudson River they would shut off New England from the other colonies. Pleasure-loving "Gentleman Johnny" Burgoyne was to come down from Montreal by way of Lake Champlain and the upper Hudson. Lieutenant Colonel St. Leger was to move eastward from Lake Ontario through the Mohawk Valley, and General Howe was to come up the Hudson. So the plan said.

This scheme showed how little the British had learned from Braddock's defeat of twenty years earlier. For it totally disregarded the conditions of travel in northern and western New York. Had the forces succeeded in meeting at Albany, it is doubtful they could have held the land they had marched through. In addition the British had come up with

3. TURNING POINT OF THE WAR 1777
- Arnold
- St. Leger
- Burgoyne

NEW YORK

Crown Point
Ft. Ticonderoga
L. Champlain

Ft. Stanwix
Saratoga
Mohawk R.
Oriskany
Bennington
Albany

Quebec
Halifax
St. Lawrence R.
TO MASS.
Montreal
3. TURNING POINT OF THE WAR 1777
N.H.
Saratoga
Boston →**1. THE WAR BEGINS 1775**
N.Y.
L. Ontario
MASS.
Hudson R.
Newport
CONN. R.I.

L. Erie
Allegheny R.
Susquehanna R.
PA.
→**2. THE WAR IN THE MIDDLE COLONIES 1776-1778**
N.J.
Philadelphia
Delaware Bay
Baltimore
Annapolis
Potomac R.
MD. DEL.
Chesapeake Bay

Wabash R.
Vincennes ✕—**5. THE WAR IN THE WEST**
Cahokia
Kaskaskia
Ohio R.
VA.
Richmond
French Fleet
7. THE WAR ENDS 1781
Yorktown
Mississippi R.
Guilford Court House
N.C.
Cowpens
Kings Mtn.
Moores Creek Bridge
6. THE WAR IN THE SOUTH 1780-1781
Camden
S.C.
Charleston
GA.
4. CAPTURED BY THE BRITISH 1778 ✕ Savannah

1. THE WAR BEGINS 1775
Concord
Lexington
Medford
BUNKER HILL
Cambridge
Boston
Brookline
- Revere route
- Dawes route
- British

2. THE WAR IN THE MIDDLE COLONIES 1776-1778
Washington
- 1776-77
- 1777
- 1778
New York
Long Island
PENNSYLVANIA
Princeton
✕ Monmouth
Valley Forge
Trenton
✕ Germantown
NEW JERSEY
Brandywine
Philadelphia

The American Revolution
- ✕ American victory
- ✕ British victory
- ✕ Indecisive

a plan that favored the American militia. The British tactics were perfect for Europe, where the people from the neighboring countryside did not take part in the war and where by capturing a town it was possible to dominate an area. In America none of that was true, as the British were soon bitterly to learn.

St. Leger was defeated before he got halfway to Albany. Howe, perhaps because Lord Germain forgot to send his instructions, sailed off to Chesapeake Bay and then captured Philadelphia. Burgoyne proceeded to walk into a trap. The farther he moved into the forests, the more the militia from the countryside swarmed around him. Finally, at Saratoga, New York, he was brought to bay. He surrendered his outnumbered army on October 17, 1777.

The American victory at Saratoga was a turning point in history. The French, who were already secretly helping the Americans, now openly pro-

claimed themselves allies. On February 7, 1778, the French signed a treaty of alliance with the new American nation. Now American independence seemed assured. The Revolution could hardly fail with the help of the money, supplies, troops, and (most important of all) the navy of one of the world's great powers.

Washington heard the welcome news of the French alliance at Valley Forge, where he and his army had spent a terrible winter. Still he had kept his army together, and Baron von Steuben, who became Washington's right-hand man, had drilled it into a better fighting force.

Von Steuben had come, as had other European officers, to help the American cause. From France came the aristocratic young Marquis de Lafayette, who was commissioned a major general in the American army at the age of twenty! From Germany, in addition to von Steuben, came "Baron" de Kalb, also to be a major general. From

I. N. Phelps Stokes Collection, Prints Division, New York Public Library. Astor, Lenox and Tilden Foundations

This watercolor by a British officer shows Cornwallis's troops landing in New Jersey in 1776.

Poland came Count Casimir Pulaski (killed fighting in the South) and Thaddeus Kosciusko (who built the fortifications at West Point).

The nature of the war was about to change. The British had now decided to move the battle south, where they expected more help from the Loyalists. Also, the British army would then be closer to their colonies in the West Indies if the French attacked there.

With the decision to move south, General Clinton, who had succeeded Howe in the British command, abandoned Philadelphia. As Clinton marched back to New York, the British forces were attacked by Washington's army at Monmouth, New Jersey, on June 28, 1778. A fierce battle ensued, but the result was a draw. The British went on to New York and thereafter ventured out of that city only on raids. Monmouth was the last big battle of the war north of Virginia.

The pace of the war now slowed, and combat moved to the edges of the colonies. Out in the huge Ohio country west of the Appalachian Mountains in the summer of 1778, George Rogers Clark led a force of Kentucky frontiersmen across the trackless plains of southern Illinois to seize the British posts at Kaskaskia and Cahokia. And when, that winter, he heard that a British military unit had occupied Vincennes, he marched across icy swamps and flooded rivers to surprise the redcoats and force them to surrender in February 1779. That still did not end the British threat in the West, but Clark controlled the situation.

Defeat, then victory, in the South. The second—southern—phase of the Revolution now began. In December 1778, Savannah fell to the British, and swiftly they brought Georgia under their control. One year later, leaving a force to hold the city, Clinton sailed from New York with an army of 8500 men for the conquest of South Carolina. In May 1780, Charleston was captured with its entire defending American garrison. When the British defeated General Gates at Camden, South Carolina, on August 16, 1780, it seemed that the southern states were lost to the patriot cause.

But then on October 7, 1780, several regiments of backwoods militia caught a British force of 1200 Loyalists at King's Mountain, South Carolina, and killed or captured all of them in the bloodiest battle since Bunker Hill. The battle struck terror into the

Historical Society of Pennsylvania

The winter that Washington's army spent at Valley Forge was bleak. Food, clothing, and fuel were scarce. In this broadside, Washington orders local farmers to thresh their grain. Then the army could buy it. Grain not threshed would be seized, and the farmers would be paid only for straw.

British army and aroused the patriots throughout the Carolinas. Guerrilla bands under Sumter, Pickens, and the "Swamp Fox" Marion struck the British at every turn.

The Continental Army under Nathanael Greene and Daniel Morgan, everywhere assisted by backwoods militia, now proceeded to pick to pieces the British army, under Lord Cornwallis. Finally, the British general decided to head for Virginia. He believed that if he could link up with a British force under Benedict Arnold, who for pride and pelf had turned traitor, he could conquer Virginia and thereby hold the Carolinas.

Cornwallis, outmaneuvered by American forces under the young Marquis de Lafayette, moved to the coast and fortified a position at Yorktown, Virginia. Now Washington saw a chance to trap Cornwallis's army at Yorktown, especially when he learned that a French fleet under Admiral de Grasse was on its way there. Moving swiftly, Washington marched his troops, strengthened by a French force under General Rochambeau, to the head of Chesapeake Bay. There they met de Grasse, who ferried them to the Yorktown peninsula.

Cut off from the British fleet by the French ships, surrounded on the land side by Washington and Rochambeau whose troops outnumbered his two to one, Cornwallis was caught. As the siege lines drew closer, the British army could find no way out. On October 19, 1781, Cornwallis surrendered his entire army of 7750 regulars, together with 850 sailors, 244 cannon, and all his military stores. When news of Yorktown reached England, Prime Minister Lord North exclaimed, "My God! it is all over."

Wartime in America. The war affected every American in the thirteen colonies—patriot, loyalist, or indifferent; man, woman, or child; black, red, or white; slave, indentured, or free. Even in areas that never saw a redcoat, the war was felt, if in no other

Abigail Adams was a woman of many talents. Her vivid letters to her husband are some of the best sources for life in the age of the Revolution. This painting was made in 1800.

way than by inflation. To finance the war the Continental Congress and the state governments printed money as fast as they could. The phrase "not worth a continental" soon showed what people thought of this money.

The war brought prosperity to many. Farmers included 90 percent of all Americans, and many of them prospered by selling their crops to both the British and the American armies. They sold to whichever side paid more. Washington's men were starving at Valley Forge in the winter of 1777–1778, while the British, only a few miles away, were being well fed from the rich farms of Pennsylvania and New Jersey. Washington could never forget the irony of his army lacking food in a country filled with farms. One army officer, bitter about profiteering, wrote, "I despise my countrymen. I wish I could say I was not born in America."

Women at war. The departure of men for war forced women to take up many jobs. Like women who were widowed, they operated the farms, ran the printing presses, served as artisans and shopkeepers—doing whatever needed to be done. Some women gathered their children and followed their husbands to the army. They went with the army wherever it moved, and they helped to nurse the wounded, make camp, cook, do the laundry, carry out clerical tasks, and, in battle, carry water and bullets to the soldiers, even load and fire muskets and cannons.

Margaret Corbin followed her husband to war from their home in Pennsylvania. When he was killed while commanding a cannon at the Battle of Fort Washington, New York (November 16, 1776), she filled his place until she was severely wounded. More famous, though no more courageous, was Mary (Molly) McCauley, known as Molly Pitcher for the pitcher of water she carried back and forth during the hot weather and hot fighting of the Battle of Monmouth, June 28, 1778. When her husband fell in the battle, she too took his place at a cannon till the battle was over.

We know of at least one woman, and there were probably more, who passed as a man and fought as a soldier. Deborah Sampson enlisted in the 4th Massachusetts Regiment in 1782 and served for more than a year.

Abigail Adams, brilliant wife of John Adams, played another kind of role. She ran the farm and

Many women managed farms and other businesses while men were fighting. This detail from a commemorative handkerchief shows three southern women working the fields of their farm.

business while her husband was away at the Continental Congress. She kept him aware of what was going on at home. She told him of the profiteering, of how the people felt, and she discussed ways to recruit soldiers and finance the war. Abigail tried to improve the lot of women in the new country, but John was not impressed: "Depend on it," he wrote, "we know better than to repeal our masculine systems."

Blacks in the Revolution. Many blacks were involved in the war right from the start. They were present at the battles of Lexington and Concord. At the Battle of Bunker Hill, Peter Salem and Salem Poor stood out for their bravery.

After George Washington took over the army, however, it was decided not to have blacks in the service any more. But this policy did not last long because the British promised freedom to all blacks who came to them. Whenever British armies appeared in the South, large numbers of slaves, seeking to be as free as white Americans, joined them. At war's end 14,000 sailed away with the British.

As blacks flocked to the British, George Washington, Congress, and all the states except South Carolina and Georgia changed their minds. They enlisted blacks and promised slaves that they would receive their freedom after the war. Of course,

slaves could not join without their masters' permission, so of the 5000 blacks who fought in the war, most were from the North. In general, they served in mixed units and were present at almost all the military actions of the war.

The Loyalists. A substantial number of Americans opposed the war and wanted to stay with Great Britain. The Loyalists came from every occupation and were of every degree of wealth. Many kept quiet about how they felt and were not bothered by the patriots. Some went to Canada or England. A few, like Jedediah Smith and Phineas Lyman of New England, took their families from comfortable homes and headed west to try to establish a new life in the wilderness—far from the problems of empire and freedom. About 60,000 became soldiers and fought on the British side.

Loyalists who did not leave their homes, but whose sentiments were known, often found themselves shunned by their neighbors. Some were tarred and feathered, and many lost their property by state confiscation or patriot plundering. Others were treated as traitors and were imprisoned or exiled to towns far from home.

During the course of the war, and at its end, thousands of Loyalists left America never to return. Most went to Canada. There they added a strongly British element to the largely French population. They became useful citizens, serving in the assemblies and as judges and governors.

The Treaty of Paris. Even after the Battle of Yorktown, King George III showed his usual misunderstanding of the American situation when he wanted to keep fighting. But from the British point of view conditions were hopeless. The American phase of the war was over. In March 1782 a new government came to power in England with the sole condition that there would be "no veto to the independence of America." Peace negotiations began in Paris the next month.

The American delegates—Benjamin Franklin, John Adams, and John Jay—had been instructed by Congress to take no step "without the knowledge and agreements" of the French government. In spite of these instructions, thinking it more advantageous to act independently, they went ahead and concluded an agreement with the British without consulting Vergennes, the French minister of state.

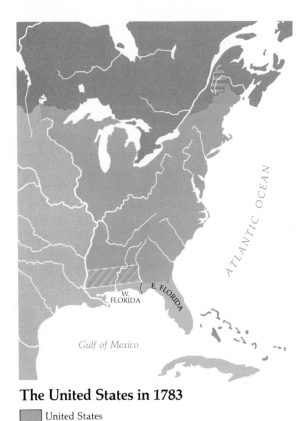

The United States in 1783

- United States
- English
- Spanish
- Claimed by U.S. and England
- Claimed by U.S. and Spain

In fact, Vergennes did not protest too much over American activities. After all, the treaty was only preliminary and would not go into effect until France had signed a treaty with England. This finally occurred on September 3, 1783, when peace treaties were signed between Great Britain and its enemies France, Spain, and the United States.

For America, the Treaty of Paris had the following provisions: England acknowledged the independence of the United States with approximately the present northern boundary, a western boundary set at the Mississippi River, and a southern border at Florida. The commissioners had tried to have Canada made part of the United States, but in this they failed. If Spain had had its way, however, America's western boundary would have been the Appalachian Mountains. The Mississippi River was to be open to the shipping of both America and Britain, and Americans were to be able to fish in England's Newfoundland fisheries. No legal ob-

stacles were to be placed in the way of British businessmen collecting debts owed them by American merchants.

Finally, there was the difficult problem of what to do about the Loyalists whose estates had been confiscated during the war. Feelings still ran too high for Congress to vote that their property should be returned to them. The treaty merely promised that Congress would "recommend" to the states to restore their property. Everybody took it for granted, however, that neither the nation nor the states, both burdened with a nearly worthless currency and heavy war debts, would do much about the Loyalists. Eventually Britain helped many of them with money and land in Canada.

French foreign minister Vergennes was astounded at England's generosity! "The English buy the peace rather than make it; their concessions as to boundaries, the fisheries, the Loyalists, exceed everything I had thought possible."

Why the British lost. At the end of the war, George Washington wrote that people in future years would hardly believe that the Americans could have won. "It will not be believed that such a force as Great Britain has employed for eight years in this country could be baffled in their plan of subjugating it by numbers infinitely less—composed of men sometimes half-starved, always in rags, without pay, and experiencing at times every species of distress which human nature is capable of undergoing." Even today it is not easy to understand how the Americans managed to win.

It is easier to explain why the British lost. The British were separated from their headquarters by a vast ocean. Their lines of communication were long. The British government was badly informed. They thought the Americans were much weaker than they really were. And they expected help from uprisings of thousands of Loyalists. But these uprisings never happened.

The most important explanation was that the British had set themselves an impossible task. Though they had an army that was large for that day, how could it ever be large enough to occupy and subjugate a continent? The British knew so little of America that they thought their capture of New York City would end the war. After the Battle of Long Island in August 1776, General Howe actually asked the Americans to send him a peace

Benjamin West began this painting of the negotiations that led to the Treaty of Paris in 1783. The Americans are (from left to right) John Jay, John Adams, Benjamin Franklin, Henry Laurens, and William Temple Franklin. West did not finish the painting because the British negotiators refused to pose.

commission, and cheerfully expected to receive the American surrender. But he was badly disappointed. For the colonies had no single capital that the British could capture to win the war.

American success was largely due to perseverance in keeping an army in the field throughout the long, hard years. George Washington was a man of great courage and good judgment. And Americans had the strengths of a New World—with a new kind of army fighting in new ways. Still, it is doubtful the Americans could have won without the aid of France.

Although many Americans opposed the Revolution, and some were lukewarm, it was a people's war. As many as half of all men of military age were in the army at one time or another. Each had the special power and the special courage that came from fighting for himself, for his family, and for his home.

SECTION 3 REVIEW

1. Identify or explain: mercenaries, Hessians, *The Crisis,* Cornwallis, Burgoyne, Lafayette, von Steuben, Morgan, de Grasse, Rochambeau.

2. Locate: Long Island, Trenton, Delaware River, Princeton, Saratoga, Valley Forge, Monmouth, Vincennes, King's Mountain, Yorktown.

3. How was war in America unlike war in Europe?

4. Point out how each of the following groups took part in the war or were affected by it: (a) farmers, (b) women, (c) blacks, (d) Loyalists.

5. How did the Treaty of Paris affect America?

6. **Testing Conclusions.** Some historians have said that the British were responsible for defeating themselves in the Revolutionary War. What evidence, if any, supports this conclusion?

CHAPTER 4 REVIEW

FOCUSING ON IDEAS

1. What were the results of the Peace of Paris?

2. How did the attitudes of the colonists change between the time that the first First Continental Congress met and the meeting of the Second Continental Congress?

3. Why did Thomas Paine write *Common Sense*?

4. What problems and difficulties did George Washington face when he set about creating the Continental Army?

5. Today, in many parts of the world, people who share a common language, history, or culture seek to set up independent nations. Were the American colonists motivated by a common language, history, or culture? Explain your answer.

TAKING A CRITICAL LOOK

1. **Testing Conclusions.** "The American Revolution took place because the British government, even with the best of intentions, did not understand what America and Americans had become." Challenge or defend this statement using evidence in the text.

2. **Distinguishing False from Accurate Images.** It has been said that the American Revolution was a people's war for the Americans and a "soldier's

war" for the British. How does the evidence presented in this chapter support or contradict this conclusion?

YOUR REGION IN HISTORY

1. **Geography.** What battles, if any, were fought in your region during the Revolutionary War?

2. **Culture.** What Revolutionary War heroes are honored by place names in your state?

3. **Economics.** Did Britain profit from your region before the Revolutionary War? Explain your answer.

HISTORICAL FACTS AND FIGURES

Testing Hypotheses. Historians often make hypotheses, or educated guesses, about the reasons past events occurred. Historians then test the hypothesis by examining the data and determining if it supports or contradicts the hypothesis. (a) Use the data on the chart below to test the hypothesis: "Colonial boycotts seriously affected trade with Great Britain." (Keep in mind that the colonists boycotted British goods in 1765, 1766, 1768, 1769, 1775, and 1776.) (b) Write a brief paragraph summarizing the data to see if it supports the results of your test.

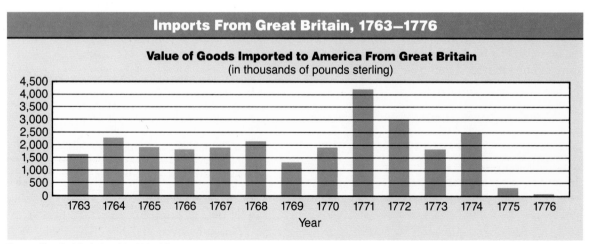

Imports From Great Britain, 1763–1776

Value of Goods Imported to America From Great Britain
(in thousands of pounds sterling)

Source: *Historical Statistics of the United States*

CHAPTER 5

From confederation to nation

When the assembled American colonies declared their independence on July 4, 1776, thirteen nations were created, not just one. The resolution that announced independence on July 2, 1776, had proclaimed "That these United Colonies are, and of right ought to be, free and independent *States.*" The first heading at the top of the Declaration of Independence called it "The Unanimous Declaration of the thirteen united States of America." They used a small "u" for united because it was only a hope.

Each state called itself "sovereign," which meant that now it had all the highest powers of government. Each state had all the powers to levy taxes, to raise an army and build a navy, to enter into treaties, and to make war and peace. When Franklin was in Paris as a representative for the Continental Congress, trying to persuade the French to give war aid, he found "ambassadors" from three separate American states.

The very same reasons that had made the colonists willing to revolt made them unwilling to unite. The people of Virginia were fighting to be free from a government in far-off London. Why should they submit to a government in far-off New York? The very same feelings that gave Americans strength, that explained why their scattered-everywhere army could not be defeated by a regular army of empire, also explained why it would be hard for them to become a nation. The task of making a nation had only begun.

1. New state governments

Even before the Second Continental Congress had worked out a frame of government for the united States, the individual states began to deal with the problem themselves. Of this process James Madison wrote:

Nothing has excited more admiration in the world than the manner in which free governments have been established in America; for it was the first instance, from the creation of the world . . . that free inhabitants have been seen deliberating on a form of government, and selecting such of their citizens as possessed their confidence, to determine upon and give effect to it.

Following old patterns. What the new states did, of course, was strongly influenced by their pasts. They did not return to the "state of nature" (when

93

National Archives

Charles Thomson sketched this design for the
Great Seal of the United States in 1789.

derive "their just powers from the consent of the
governed." Plainly, "the consent of the governed"
had to be secured in each colony and in the whole
new nation.

Ways of constitution making.

Beginning in 1776 the thirteen states (formerly the colonies) began creating new governments. In most states the existing assemblies drew up the new constitutions. In some, special elections were held for the assembly that was to draw up the constitution. But whether a special election was held or not, the legislators assumed that, because they had been elected, they had the "consent" of the people. So they drew up new constitutions and put them into operation.

In Massachusetts, the provisional assembly asked the local town meetings to consent to its drawing up a new government. Most towns agreed, and the assembly went to work. But then Concord objected. The Concord town meeting, in a series of resolutions that were circulated throughout the colony, challenged this procedure. The people of Concord pointed out that if the regular legislature wrote the constitution, it would be able to change it just as easily later on. To the people of Concord, that did not seem much protection for their liberties. Instead, Concord suggested that a special assembly should be elected that would have no other purpose than to draw up a new constitution. When it had finished its job, it would go out of existence.

The Massachusetts assembly paid no attention to Concord. But the independent-thinking townspeople of the state were listening. The assembly's new constitution was quickly rejected by the voters of the state when it was presented for their approval in 1778. The main reason was that they disapproved of the way it was drawn up.

The Massachusetts assembly finally followed the procedure demanded by the citizens of Concord. In 1779 a constitutional convention was called. The elected members drew up a new constitution, which was submitted to the people in March 1780 and approved by them in June.

A similar procedure was followed by other states when they revised their constitutions and, a few years later, when the whole new nation made a new frame of government.

Americans had found a way to make government by the consent of the governed into a living reality.

there were supposed to be no governments) that John Locke and other political writers had imagined once existed. In fact, the new states already had governments operating, since the provincial assemblies continued to meet after the Revolution broke out and the royal governors fled.

The colonists really had no desire or intention to form brand-new governments. They had been practicing a form of self-government for 150 years. They had nothing in particular against their colonial governments. Their main desire now was to change certain features so that government could never again become tyrannical.

How were they to go about forming—or "reforming"—these colonial governments? The Declaration of Independence said, and English and American experience agreed, that governments

Written constitutions. These new frames of government, no matter who drew them up, were all *written constitutions.* Like the constitutional convention, the written frame of government was an American institution that would be admired and imitated all over the world for centuries to come. Colonial charters themselves provided a handy framework for new written constitutions. In Connecticut and Rhode Island, for example, the colonial charters had been so liberal that all that was needed was to strike out mention of the king. Then these charters could become the new constitutions.

The British constitution was a plan of government that could not be picked up and read. It consisted of some basic documents like the Magna Carta and the English Bill of Rights. But much of it was a concoction of tradition, habit, and belief. Many Americans thought their rights to govern themselves would be safer if these were stated in plain language so that government officials could see them and citizens would never forget them.

The new state constitutions. The new state constitutions followed a pattern. Generally they began with a brief declaration of independence. Then came a section declaring the rights that the citizens reserved for themselves against any government. These included freedom of the press, the right to petition the government against abuses, freedom from unreasonable search of their homes, freedom from the burden of standing armies, and the right to trial by jury and other proper legal procedures.

Most state constitutions provided a framework similar to that of the old colonial governments. All but one state had a governor, an upper house, and a lower house of the legislature. But now all were elected directly by the people or by their elected representatives. Only in Pennsylvania did the constitution create a one-house legislature.

In all colonies there was an attempt to weaken the powers of the governor. He had represented the king in colonial days and had become a symbol of government from afar. Now most states deprived the governor of his power to veto legislation or to dismiss the legislature or suspend its meetings. In many states the governor was now elected by the legislature for a short term. The legislature could impeach the governor. The people of Pennsylvania were so fearful of the governor's powers that they abolished that position entirely.

Other posts that had been appointive in colonial times were made elective. Members of the upper houses and the judges—all formerly appointed by the crown—were selected by the voters.

Equality in the states. Although Jefferson, in the Declaration of Independence, asserted that "all men are created equal," there were many ways in which the colonial governments treated people as if they were unequal. Most Americans probably thought Jefferson's phrase meant that Americans were the equals of the English. But the statement itself, and the Revolution, led people to think more about the meaning of equality. In every colony in order to vote, a man had to own property or have a certain income. In no colony were women allowed to vote or hold public office. And then, of course, there were the slaves, who did not even have civil rights, much less political rights like the right to vote or hold office.

In most colonies from Pennsylvania south, settlers in the West had not been as well represented in their assemblies as were settlers in the East. The new state constitutions did give Westerners in those states somewhat better representation in the legislatures, but Easterners still continued to hold more than their share of the power. The amount of property needed to vote or to hold office was generally reduced. Most white American males did hold property and could vote.

The war helped to redistribute wealth. Loyalist estates were broken up and sold to other Americans. Wartime prosperity, especially on the farms, assisted more people to buy farms or enlarge their existing acreage.

First moves against slavery. As early as 1774, Rhode Island passed a law providing that "those who are desirous of enjoying all the advantages of liberty themselves should be willing to extend personal liberty to others." Any slave brought into the colony from that time on would be free.

Abigail Adams wrote to her husband, John, who was away attending the Congress, "It always appeared a most evil scheme to me to fight ourselves for what we are daily robbing and plundering from those who have as good a right to freedom as we have." That same year the Continental Congress passed a law that no slaves were to be imported after December 1, 1775.

When Jefferson tried to include the slave trade in the Declaration of Independence as one of the king's abuses, the southern colonies objected. Still, the War of Independence did lead to freedom for many blacks. Some, as we have seen, received their liberty for fighting in the American cause. When a slave in Massachusetts sued for his freedom because the new state constitution declared, "all men are created free and equal," the court agreed with him. With that decision in 1783, slavery ended in Massachusetts.

Pennsylvania began the gradual abolition of slavery in 1780. Connecticut and Rhode Island followed with their own gradual abolition plans in 1784. Virginia and North Carolina, which had long prohibited the practice, now passed laws that allowed owners to free their slaves.

SECTION 1 REVIEW

1. Why did the townspeople of Concord object to having the state legislature draw up a new constitution for Massachusetts?
2. Why did Americans want *written* constitutions?
3. Why did the new state constitutions reduce the power of the governor's office?
4. How did some states try to end slavery?
5. **Identifying Central Issues.** How did some state constitutions promote social equality?

---

2. The Continental Congress

When, on June 7, 1776, Congress declared war on Great Britain, it also called for a plan of confederation to help the states cooperate in the war effort. A committee of thirteen, with John Dickinson of Pennsylvania as chairman, prepared Articles of Confederation. These Articles, adopted by Congress in November 1777, were not ratified by the last of the thirteen states until March 1, 1781.

An illegal assembly. Because the Articles of Confederation were not ratified for so long, the Second Continental Congress, though still an "illegal" assembly, assumed the powers of government. The central governing was done for six years by the Continental Congress, which took the place of the British government. This Congress issued the Declaration of Independence, advised the states to form governments, and conducted the war against Great Britain nearly to its successful conclusion at Yorktown.

Young congressmen. At the beginning of the war, the Continental Congress was an assembly of talented men which included almost every leader of the Revolution. Jefferson, his teacher George Wythe, and Richard Henry Lee were there from Virginia. So was Washington, until he was sent off to lead the army. Sam and John Adams, Elbridge Gerry, and John Hancock came from Massachusetts. Ben Franklin and Robert Morris were delegates from Pennsylvania. Roger Sherman and Oliver Wolcott were there from Connecticut.

John Trumbull painted the Continental Congress signing the Declaration of Independence.

The members of Congress were young—most were just over 40, and Jefferson was only 33 in 1776. They generally stood to lose a good deal of property—and possibly their heads as well—if the Revolution was lost. Of the 56 men who signed the Declaration of Independence, 25 were lawyers, 8 were merchants, 6 were physicians, and 5 were farmers. The rest came from a variety of occupations. They were clearly not a rabble in arms.

During the war, the quality of the members of Congress declined. Many of the most talented men went back to their states as the state governments became more powerful. For the states kept their independence. They had their own armies and navies, competed with Congress for supplies, and some sent out their own "ambassadors." At the same time, Congress had to face the difficulties of

wartime. It had to avoid being captured by the British army. Sometimes it had too few members present to pass laws. Often its members were late arriving for meetings of Congress. Sometimes members went home when they were tired, when they did not like the weather, or just when they had something else to do. In these ways Congress was not unlike the militia.

Congress's successes and failures. Despite the difficulties of wartime, the lack of any legal grant of power, and the jealousy of the states, the achievements of the Second Continental Congress were substantial. It established the army, navy, and marines. It had the wisdom to appoint George Washington to lead the army—and to keep him there through bad times. It kept the army supplied

American Antiquarian Society

Congress could not keep its promise to redeem "continental currency" in gold or silver.

with ammunition. No battle after Bunker Hill was ever lost because of lack of gunpowder. Congress had more of a problem keeping Washington's troops fed, clothed, and paid.

Congress's greatest failure was in financing the war, and that was largely due to the states. They would not give Congress the right to tax, and when Congress asked for money, the states often failed to contribute. As a result, to obtain money Congress simply used the printing press. By the time the government under the Continental Congress was replaced by the new government under the Articles of Confederation, it was costing more to print the paper bills than they were worth as money.

The Continental Congress created a diplomatic corps, and won a great diplomatic victory when France recognized the United States as an independent nation and entered the war. In addition, it created a postal service and drew up the Articles of Confederation. For any assembly—legal or illegal—this was an impressive record.

SECTION 2 REVIEW

1. Characterize Continental Congress members.

2. Why did the quality of the members of Congress decline during the war?

3. **Drawing Conclusions.** Evaluate the successes and failures of the Continental Congress.

3. A weak confederation

When the Continental Congress turned to the problem of setting up an effective central government, they found it was easier to get rid of a government than to create a new and better one. Their new government would have to handle all the problems the empire had dealt with—regulating trade, making war and peace, and imposing taxes--yet none of the members of Congress had any experience in imperial administration.

The states and Congress. Congress also had to cope with the jealousy of the states. The states, having disposed of one tyranny, were wary not to put themselves under another. They had rid themselves of royal officials—governors, judges, and hated customs collectors. They had no desire to create a whole new set of officials to interfere in their affairs. They were happy to be able to levy their own taxes, to set up their own courts, and to regulate their own commerce, currency, and the right to vote.

The states wanted a new government strong enough to serve them but not so potent that it might dominate them. They feared the powers of a central government so far away that it would be beyond the people's control. Therefore the Articles of Confederation, which the Continental Congress now drew up, announced a "perpetual union" of the states and "firm league of friendship." But it preserved for each state "its sovereignty, freedom and independence, and every power and jurisdiction and right" that was not expressly delegated to the new Congress under the Articles of Confederation.

There was an argument over how the states were to vote in the Congress of the Confederation. It was finally decided—though the more populous states did not like it—to give each state just one vote. That would show that this was only a confederation of the thirteen sovereign states, and not a new government representing the people themselves. The agreement of nine states was required for important matters, and any change in the Articles had to receive the vote of every state. There was no provision for a President or other executive officers or for judges or courts.

The powers of Congress. Congress was given the sole power to deal with foreign countries, to settle disputes between the states, to decide admiralty cases (those involving ships at sea), to declare war, and to make peace. It could coin money, run the postal service, establish weights and measures, and trade with the Indians outside the states. It could borrow money, and it could request each state to contribute money in proportion to the value of the property in the state. Under this arrangement a large state, which had only one vote, was still supposed to donate more money than its less wealthy neighbors. Congress could only request financial support from the states. But if a state refused to help, there was nothing the Congress could do.

In fact, the Articles only outlined what the Continental Congress was already doing. But many people feared the powers of the new Congress and imagined that it might "swallow up the states." Despite these fears the Congress actually had no way to enforce its decisions. The Articles of Confederation provided, in the words of Gouverneur Morris of Pennsylvania, nothing but a "government by supplication"—a government by begging and pleading.

When the Articles of Confederation were sent to the states, the same questions that the Continental Congress had debated were now discussed all over again in town meetings and in the state legislatures. Most of the amendments suggested by the states would further limit the powers of Congress. Americans did not want to rush into a new government.

Western lands. Some of the smaller states were especially worried about the large areas of land that other states claimed in the West. Massachusetts, Connecticut, Virginia, North and South Carolina, and Georgia had claims from "sea to sea" based on their colonial charters. Virginia's claim was strengthened by George Rogers Clark's conquest of the Northwest, which had been carried out in the service of Virginia. New York claimed western lands, on the basis of treaties made with the Indians, but in 1780 voted to cede them to Congress.

The small states that had no western land claims were led by Maryland. They refused to agree to a general government until the other states gave up their claims to the land west of the Appalachians. The land-poor states thought that the land-rich states like Virginia and Massachusetts would be able to pay their war debts and the day-to-day costs of

state government with the income from the sale of their western lands. This would let those states keep their taxes low compared to the land-poor states. The small states feared their citizens would leave to go to the big land-rich states where taxes were lower.

Here an interesting, enterprising, and especially American kind of businessman came on the stage of history—the speculator. He would play a lively and leading role in developing the American continent. Land speculators had formed their companies and bought land from the Indians out west. The officials of Virginia had refused to recognize their claims. But the speculators thought the Congress might support their interests.

The small states and the speculators, both protecting their own self-interests, worked to have the Articles revised to give Congress control over the western lands. Most states, under wartime pressure, were willing to sign the Articles simply to get some kind of government going to conduct a successful struggle for independence. They planned to amend the Articles later. But land-poor Maryland refused to take the risk. The Articles could not go into effect until all the states—including Maryland—accepted them.

Virginia gives in. Finally the stalemate was broken when Virginia gave in. It was the largest state and the one with the best claim to the western lands. When the British army under Lord Cornwallis headed their way, Virginians needed little persuading that a strong, well-supported union of the states was required to help them win independence. On January 2, 1781, the state offered to cede its land to the central government. At the same time, Virginia insisted that as the land filled with people new states should be admitted with the same "rights of sovereignty, freedom, and independence as other States."

But Maryland—continuing to cooperate with the speculators—still refused to sign the Articles. As Marylanders felt British troops breathing down their necks, they asked the French naval forces to protect them. Then the French again aided the American cause. They refused to do anything to help Maryland until the state agreed to the Articles. In February 1781, Maryland finally signed, and on March 1 the Articles of Confederation became the law of the land.

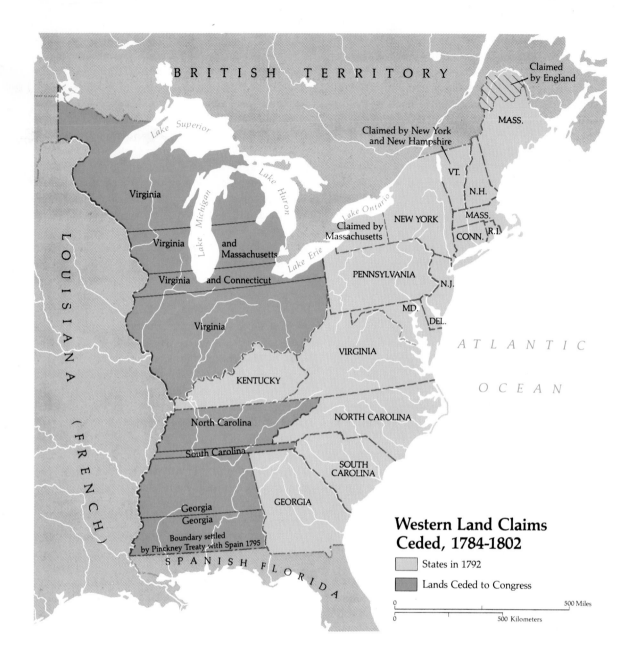

B R I T I S H   T E R R I T O R Y

Claimed by England

MASS.

Claimed by New York and New Hampshire

VT.

N.H.

Lake Superior

Virginia

Lake Michigan

Lake Huron

Lake Ontario

NEW YORK

MASS.

CONN.   R.I.

Virginia and Massachusetts

Lake Erie

Claimed by Massachusetts

Virginia   and Connecticut

PENNSYLVANIA

N.J.

Virginia

MD.

DEL.

VIRGINIA

ATLANTIC

KENTUCKY

OCEAN

North Carolina

NORTH CAROLINA

L O U I S I A N A   (F R E N C H)

South Carolina

SOUTH CAROLINA

Georgia

GEORGIA

Georgia

Boundary settled
by Pinckney Treaty with Spain 1795

S P A N I S H   F L O R I D A

Western Land Claims Ceded, 1784-1802

☐ States in 1792

■ Lands Ceded to Congress

0   500 Miles

0   500 Kilometers

The treasury of the nation. This new government had no power to enforce its will on the states, yet it had to finish the war and guide the country into peace. Despite its weakness, the new government would accomplish a great deal.

The western lands became the treasury of the new government. Since the Confederation had no power to tax and could only beg the states to donate money, lands took the place of taxes. These unsettled tracts (called the "public domain") were larger than all the settled states put together. By selling the land, the weak new government obtained the money that it could find in no other way.

The vast unsettled West would give the new government an important peacetime job. No nation, new or old, had been blessed with such a land-treasure in its own backyard. What should be done with it? This public domain, which belonged to all the states together, was far larger than France or England or Spain.

Unlike the sparsely settled lands controlled by those European nations, these lands would not become colonies. They would not be used by the thirteen original states to make themselves rich and strong.

Instead they would become (in Jefferson's phrase) an "Empire for Liberty." This Empire would be built by adding new states. Each new state would be the equal of all the older states. Nowadays this seems an obvious and sensible way for a nation to grow. But in those days it was quite a new idea.

Congress took the first step by passing the Land Ordinance of 1785. It provided that the land be carefully surveyed into townships—areas of land 6 miles square made up of 36 sections, each containing 640 acres. One section in each township was reserved for the support of public schools; four more were reserved for the central government. The rest were to be sold.

The Northwest Ordinance of 1787: an Add-a-State Plan.

For many years Thomas Jefferson, with his usual uncanny foresight, had been working on a plan for settlements in the western wilderness. The Northwest Ordinance of 1787 put his scheme into law. This American way of growing gave instructions for what we can call an Add-a-State Plan.

The plan was simple. Every part of the public domain would in time become a full-fledged state of the Union "on an equal footing with the original states in all respects whatsoever." This goal was reached by three simple stages described in the Northwest Ordinance. First, when there were still almost no people in a territory, it would have a governor, a secretary, and three judges named by Congress. Then, as soon as there were 5000 adult free men, there would be a legislature where the people of the territory could make laws for themselves. And finally, when the free population numbered 60,000, the people could apply for admission to the Union as a state.

How many new states should there be? It was anybody's guess. Congress had heard that the land out there was not good for much. It was said, for example, that there were vast areas that did not have even a single bush on them. Members of Congress did not realize that the treeless plains were some of the richest farmland in the world—and

The Northwest Territory

A TOWNSHIP

36	30	24	18	12	6
35	29	23	17	11	5
34	28	22	16	10	4
33	27	21	15	9	3
32	26	20	14	8	2
31	25	19	13	7	1

6 miles

A SECTION

Half Section 320 Acres

Quarter Section 160 Acres

Half Quarter Section 80 Acres

Quarter Quarter Section 40 Acres

AREA OF FIRST SURVEY
FIRST BASE LINE

were all the better for farming because they were not cluttered by trees. Since the rumors made western land seem so poor, it was decided that the new states would have to be big. The Northwest Ordinance of 1787 therefore said that in the whole area northwest of the Ohio River there should eventually be "not less than three nor more than five states."

The Ordinance also provided for religious freedom. And in a section probably inserted to attract

Town-building in the Northwest Territory began at Marietta and spread westward along the Ohio.

New Englanders to the Northwest Territory, slavery was prohibited there.

New Englanders settle along the Ohio.

The year after the Congress of the Confederation passed the Land Ordinance of 1785, a group of New Englanders formed the Ohio Company of Associates to promote the settlement of land along the north bank of the Ohio River. The first Ohio Company had been founded by Virginians in 1748 to explore the Ohio territory. But it was the company formed in 1786 that made the first organized settlements in Ohio—indeed in the Northwest Territory.

One of the leaders was General Rufus Putnam, who like his cousin General Israel Putnam served with distinction in the Revolution. Another leader

was the Reverend Manassah Cutler of Ipswich, Massachusetts. Cutler was a talented man with wide interests. He had practiced law and medicine, measured the distances of the stars, surveyed the altitude of Mt. Washington in New Hampshire, and made the first systematic account of the plant life of New England.

As soon as the Ohio Company was organized, Cutler went to New York City to persuade the Congress to give the company the right to buy up to 1.5 million Ohio acres at about 8 cents an acre. A government contract was signed on October 27, 1787. While in New York Cutler helped to draft the Northwest Ordinance.

Before the year's end, General Putnam was on his way west with an advance party. The 48 pioneers had set out in two units—one from Danvers, Massachusetts, and the other from Hartford, Connecticut. On April 2, 1788, they all embarked together from Sumrill's Ferry in western Pennsylvania for the trip down the Monongahela and then down the Ohio River. On April 7 the party landed on the east bank of the Muskingum where it joined the Ohio, just opposite Fort Harmar.

Under Putnam's direction the men quickly laid out their town on the compact New England model. Each settler was given a small "in-lot" within the town for a residence and an "out-lot" of eight acres for crops. On July 2, 1788, the agents and directors of the Ohio Company held their first meeting on the spot and named the town Marietta. Again following the New England example, they promptly provided a church and a school, both of which were operating before the end of July. Within a few months fifteen more families and many single men joined the town.

The Indians raided small parties that were tempted to go off and settle by themselves. This soon taught the Ohio pioneers to build garrison settlements of fifty or more people. One such raid in 1791 induced some settlers to build Fort Frye. It was a triangular palisade enclosing twenty families, ten single men, and eight or ten soldiers from Fort Harmar. Soon there was a string of such groups along the Ohio—at Farmers Castle, Belpre, Columbia, Losantiville, Ft. Washington (later called Cincinnati), North Bend, Gallipolis, Manchester, and many other places.

The heroic individual—like Daniel Boone, Meriwether Lewis and William Clark, Zebulon Pike—has held the spotlight of history. But in the settlement of the American continent the lone adventurer was rare. Early settlers, those who took one-way passage and became the backbone of new western communities, generally went together. People moving these great distances into an unknown landscape, threatened by numerous nameless dangers, banded together. They did so not because they especially loved their neighbors or had any ties to them, but because they needed one another.

Successes and failures of the Confederation.
Planning an Empire for Liberty—charting the settlement of the vast western public domain—was the greatest single achievement in domestic policy for the Confederation. In military matters, the Confederation brought the War of Independence to a successful end.

In foreign policy the Confederation's greatest achievement—really its only one—was the peace treaty with England. In other foreign affairs the Confederation was a failure. England did not even bother to send a minister to the United States until 1792. Though King George III graciously received John Adams as our first minister to England in 1785, Adams could not get the commercial treaty we badly needed. Even France did not take the United States seriously. Jefferson, our minister to France from 1785 to 1789, wrote home, "We are the lowest and most obscure of the whole diplomatic tribe."

Out beyond the mountains there were diplomatic problems, too. Great Britain held onto its fur trading posts on United States territory in the Northwest. Spain hoped to coop up the United States behind the Appalachians and even to make the settlers in Kentucky and Tennessee become part of the Spanish Empire. To encourage this move, Spain closed the mouth of the Mississippi to citizens of the young nation. Since that was the easiest way for western settlers to ship goods out, Spain hoped the settlers there would join the Spanish Empire in order to use the Mississippi.

When Spain closed the mouth of the Mississippi, it was bad enough for the Westerners. Then Congress was about to make a treaty with Spain giving up the right to use the Mississippi for 25 years in return for the right to use Spanish ports to sell American goods. This would have favored eastern merchants and hurt western settlers. Such an agreement would have permanently alienated the Westerners, but luckily the treaty was defeated in Congress.

Each state could keep out the farm produce and manufactured goods of its neighbors, much as the British Empire had kept out the products of the French. Instead of facing one large power across the ocean, each of the new states now found itself surrounded here in America by a lot of other annoying little states.

The great depression.
These problems were all bad enough, but with the end of the war there soon came a financial depression. As long as the war lasted there had been a business boom. When goods were scarce, anybody with something to sell found lots of buyers. After the peace in 1783,

Americans were still hungry for the things they could not buy during the war. Once again they began importing from Great Britain. But they bought a good deal more than they could pay for.

Each state issued its own paper money. Nobody knew just how much a New York dollar was worth compared to one from Pennsylvania or Rhode Island. The more money there was in circulation, the less a dollar bought. Then came the financial collapse. Paper money was refused as worthless. Gold and silver were hoarded by people who feared the future. For five long years after 1784 there was the worst business depression the colonies had ever suffered.

Shays's Rebellion. The depression hit people in debt especially hard. Their paper dollars were refused as payment. They had no gold or silver.

In the prosperous days of the war and its aftermath, many farmers had gone into debt to improve their farms, buy more land, or just to purchase luxuries they wanted. But the depression meant they could sell their crops only at very low prices. Thus it took many more bushels of corn or wheat than it once had to pay their debts and the taxes on their land. Farmers and debtors wanted their states to issue paper money with which they could pay their bills. Rhode Island passed a law that made it illegal for a person to refuse to accept that state's worthless dollars. Other states also tried to help the debtors by issuing paper money. But some states, including Massachusetts, refused to injure those who had loaned money just to help those who had borrowed it.

Debtors were often hauled into court where they had to pay high fees to lawyers and judges. And if they still failed to pay their bills, they could go to jail and be kept there until they finally did pay. The farmers of western Massachusetts were particularly upset about all this. In one year alone, 1784, there were more than 2000 suits for debt in Worcester County. Farmers there—and elsewhere—rioted to protest against the failure of the states to help them.

In western Massachusetts the popular Daniel Shays, a former captain in the Continental Army, led a rebellion. He demanded more paper money, tax relief, relief for debtors, and an end to imprisonment for debt. During the summer of 1786, these Shaysites traveled around the state preventing the collection of debts or the sale of property for debt. In January 1787, when Shays and his mob of farmers went to the Springfield armory to get more guns and ammunition, they were met by the state militia, which had been paid by wealthy merchants. Shays and his men were driven off, then pursued and captured in February 1787.

The effect of this rebellion was to swing many people over to demanding a change in the national government. In fact, things were not nearly as bad as they seemed. The depression was now coming to an end. The country was growing stronger.

Still, the central government lacked the power to deal with the states. As James Wilson pointed out in the summer of 1787, the states by their "jealousy and ambition" had reduced the Confederation to an "impotent condition." Men of property saw Shays's Rebellion as an attack on them. They considered cheap paper money as bad as taxation without representation.

SECTION 3 REVIEW

1. Name some powers of Congress under the Articles of Confederation. What important power did it lack?

2. Why did the land-poor states want western lands ceded to the central government?

3. Describe the provisions of the Northwest Ordinance of 1787.

4. What were the major achievements under the Articles of Confederation?

5. **Recognizing Cause and Effect.** How did Shays's demands lead to change in the national government?

4. Writing a nation's constitution

The thirteen new American governments had found it impossible to live with a strong London government. They now found it impossible to live without it. Yet nobody wanted to risk replacing the old British tyranny by a new American tyranny.

This was a decisive moment in history. Would America become another Europe? Would the New World become only a new battlefield for thirteen new little nations? Had they risked their "lives, their fortunes, and their sacred honor" only to turn the continent into a sea of anarchy?

The Constitutional Convention met in Philadelphia at the State House, later renamed Independence Hall. This 1790 engraving by William Birch shows a rear view of the hall.

Wise Americans dared not let this happen. Their children and their grandchildren, they said, would curse them if they threw away this opportunity to explore together and in peace the vast, mysterious, rich New World.

The Annapolis meeting.

In January 1786, Virginia sent an invitation to all the states to meet and discuss one of their major problems—the regulation of commerce. Nine states accepted the invitation, but only twelve men (representing five states) actually came to the meeting at Annapolis, Maryland, that September. By then farm workers could barely support themselves on their declining wages. Money lenders were seizing farms, and the Shaysites were rampaging through Massachusetts.

With fewer than half the states represented at Annapolis, there was not much they could do. Luckily, one of the twelve men there was the bold, young Alexander Hamilton. Born in the Virgin Islands of a family that had fallen on hard times, he had attended King's College (later Columbia University) in New York City. During the war General George Washington, recognizing Hamilton's brilliance, made him his close adviser and gave him the job of organizing military headquarters.

In 1786 when Hamilton was only 29 years of age, he saw that the thirteen states would never prosper until they formed a strong union. He demanded that the states send delegates at once to a larger meeting to see what could be done. The Congress of the Confederation issued the invitations. If Hamilton had never lived another day, his courage and vision at the Annapolis convention would entitle him to a place in American history.

The Philadelphia Convention.

The states responded to the call. Within a year 55 delegates from twelve states met in Independence Hall in

Philadelphia in the hot summer of 1787. They were only a block from Carpenters' Hall, where the First Continental Congress had met in 1774. The thirteenth state, little Rhode Island ("Rogue Island," a Boston newspaper called it), simply ignored the convention.

The invitation to this meeting was vague. It was not at all clear what the convention was supposed to do. The object was somehow to remodel the Articles of Confederation and "to take into consideration the situation of the United States."

The first of many questions that bewildered the delegates was this: What power did they really have? The wiser men did not worry about whether they had the right to do more than suggest amendments to the Articles of Confederation. Instead they thought about the job they had to do—to redesign the government to make life better in all the colonies.

Nothing was newer about the New World than the Constitutional Convention in Philadelphia. Never before had there been a meeting quite like this one. History gave the delegates very little to go on.

A federal or a national union? Despite the confusion, there was one fact on which nearly all the delegates agreed. Each of the states they represented was somehow "sovereign." That is, the people in each state believed they had *all* the powers to run *all* their own affairs. The American Revolution had been fought to prove it. This was not a mere technicality. It was everybody's starting point. And it was what made the job of the convention so hard.

What the delegates really had on their hands, then, was a kind of problem in international relations. This was precisely what they meant when they said they wanted to make a new plan for the "federal" union.

In those days "federal" meant something different from what it means today. It was still commonly spelled "foederal," because it came from the Latin word *foedus,* which means "treaty." A treaty was, of course, an agreement made by a sovereign state (or nation). And a "federal" union, then, would be a kind of international association held together by fully sovereign states that had made treaties with one another. Of course, that would be a very different kind of thing, and would

have much less power, than something like the government of England or of France. Could such a weak, loose international association of the thirteen new states do the job for America?

"No!" was the answer of many delegates to the Philadelphia Convention. Some of the most energetic men—like Alexander Hamilton of New York, James Madison of Virginia, and Gouverneur Morris of Pennsylvania—were sure that would not be good enough. To do the job, the government would have to be "national." That was the word they used, and by it they meant something more or less like the government of France or of England.

A "national" union would not be merely a collection of different states, each with its own government. It would be something much stronger. It would actually make laws, would have its own courts, would levy its own taxes, would control commerce, and exercise supreme power over all the people and all the states under it. To make that possible each of the "sovereign" states would have to give up some of its "sovereign" powers.

The need to compromise. It would not be easy to persuade people to do this. You would have to ask the people in each state to take powers away from their own Massachusetts, or New Jersey, or Maryland, which the people in that state loved and still called their "country." And you would have to give those powers to some imaginary new nation that did not even exist. There were good reasons to fear a powerful new government with its headquarters far outside your state. The best reason of all was the recent bitter experience with King George III and with the British Parliament. But there were other reasons.

The thirteen states—some large, some small— were very different from one another in other ways, too. What was good for seafaring New England might be bad for tobacco-raising Virginia. Even after giving up their western land claims, Virginia and New York were still large states, owning unmeasured stretches of wilderness. But Maryland and New Jersey and tiny Rhode Island felt themselves pushed up against the sea by these powerful neighbors.

If under the new plan for a government the states were all to be equal, then the small poor states, with very little to lose, could lord it over the large rich states and make them share their wealth. Or, if the states were all to be unequal, and each state had power in the central government proportioned to its own size or wealth, then what would happen to the little ones?

If any large number of delegates had stuck by their guns and demanded that everything go their way, there would never have been a Constitution. Luckily that did not happen. Although the convention was held in Philadelphia, which was the headquarters of the uncompromising Quakers, what prevailed in 1787 was the practical spirit of compromise.

Before the convention had any meetings it was plain that, if there was to be a new government at all, everybody would have to be satisfied with half a loaf. George Washington, the chairman of the convention, was used to bringing people together. With the glory of victory behind him, he had enough prestige to keep the delegates on the track. The good-humored Benjamin Franklin, already 81 years old, was able to keep them talking instead of fighting. Most of the convention members were wise enough to distrust their own wisdom.

The delegates in Philadelphia debated for the whole hot summer of 1787. We do not know exactly what they said. They had decided in advance to keep everything they said a secret. No complete record was made. We have to depend on the private notes taken by a few members, especially those of James Madison. But we do know what came out of their meetings. It was the same Constitution of the United States of America that (with only a few amendments) we live under today. (See pp. 822–855, for the text of the Constitution.)

They were able to make a Constitution only because they were ruled by the spirit of compromise. Everybody got something he wanted. Nobody got everything he wanted.

The Great Compromise.
The first question of major importance was the matter of representation. The large populous states naturally wanted the number of representatives in the new Congress to be based on population. Edmund Randolph of Virginia presented a plan to the convention that had been drawn up by James Madison. The Virginia Plan provided that there would be two houses of Congress and that in each one representation would be based on population. Then William Paterson of New Jersey replied with a plan more to the liking of the small states that had few people. The New Jersey Plan proposed that there would be only one house in which each state would have just one vote. At times the argument became heated.

Finally Roger Sherman, William Samuel Johnson, and Oliver Ellsworth of Connecticut suggested the Connecticut Compromise. Like many other ideas that have made history, it was remarkably simple. Why not divide the Congress into two houses? In one house (the Senate) each state, regardless of its population, would have the same number of representatives. In the other house (the House of Representatives) each member would represent nearly the same number of people. Quite appropriately this came to be called the Great Compromise. For it broke the deadlock and made it possible for the large states and the small states to work together.

The three-fifths compromise and the commercial compromise.
Other major compromises came on slavery and on the control of commerce. The southern states, where the slaves were really treated as property, still wanted the slaves counted as people for the purposes of representation in the new House of Representatives. Some delegates argued that if one kind of property was counted for representation, other kinds should be, too.

The issue was resolved when slavery and taxation were linked. It was assumed that Congress would need to raise some money by levying direct taxes on the basis of population. That would mean that if *all* slaves were counted for the purposes of representation, then *all* slaves would be counted for taxation. In that case, Southerners decided they were willing to lower their demands. By the three-fifths compromise it was agreed that three-fifths of the number of slaves would be counted *both* for representation and for levying direct taxes.

In other ways, too, there were forebodings that slavery, a great moral issue, would threaten the very existence of the nation. The northern states wanted to prohibit the slave trade. They also wanted to give the central government power to regulate commerce. The South feared that export duties might be placed on its tobacco, rice, and other crops. These two questions were compromised by stating that the slave trade could not be prohibited for twenty years and that Congress could regulate commerce but could never levy duties on exports.

A government "partly national and partly federal."

To satisfy those who wanted a union truly "national," the new government was given the power to tax, to control commerce, to make war, to raise an army and a navy, and to conduct foreign relations. To satisfy those who wanted a union merely "federal," the Constitution gave each state the power to make the laws controlling its daily life and all the powers not expressly given to the new central government.

This new government, as one member put it, was "partly national, partly federal." In the Constitution you will not find either the word "federal" or the word "national." The members of the convention knew that each of these words would be a

Oliver Ellsworth, who helped to work out the Great Compromise, and Abigail Wolcott Ellsworth are seen in their library. Painter Ralph Earl cleverly showed their house and yard in the window.

red flag to some members. They purposely left everybody to guess to what extent the new government was either federal or national. That way each side could think it had won a little more than the other.

If they did not call the new arrangement either "federal" or "national," what would they call it? Their answer was very wise and very simple. Every time they themselves mentioned the new government in the Constitution, they just called it "the United States."

The members of the convention were also wise enough to include in the Constitution itself instructions for changing it. Then, if the people in the future found they needed changes, they would not have to junk the whole Constitution and start all over again. They could keep the Constitution as a whole, while following the rules for making the few amendments they needed. This was a masterstroke, and was as new as anything else the convention did.

The final document repaired many of the weaknesses of the Articles of Confederation. The government under the Articles had no President and lacked the power to tax or to raise and maintain an army and a navy. The new government had three separate branches—executive, legislative, and judicial—each with its own special powers and duties. Spreading the powers and duties among the branches enabled them to check and balance each other. Then no one branch could become a danger to the freedom of the people.

The President was made Commander-in-Chief of all the nation's armed forces. He had the power to negotiate treaties, but the Senate had to approve them by a two-thirds majority of all senators present. The President was also given wide powers to appoint officials. But some of his choices, such as justices of the Supreme Court and ambassadors to foreign lands, had to be approved by the Senate.

Each house of Congress was given special powers. The House of Representatives, whose members represented the people rather than the states, had the sole power to initiate all bills for raising revenue. And only the Senate could approve treaties and certain appointments. Many specific powers were also granted to Congress. These included enacting taxes, providing for defense, declaring war, fixing tariffs, coining money, and setting up post offices. Surprisingly important in the long run was the power given to Congress to pass all laws "necessary and proper" to carry out its specifically assigned functions. This came to be called the "elastic clause," because it would be stretched in so many ways.

The Supreme Court was created to hear all cases raised under the Constitution and the laws of the United States, and certain others. Since the Constitution and the laws of the United States were "the supreme Law of the Land," the Supreme Court would wield great power to shape the new government. (The text of the Constitution and its amendments will be found in the Appendix on pp. 822–855. A detailed analysis also appears there, including information on why its major parts were included—"origins"—and what changes have occurred over time—"update.")

SECTION 4 REVIEW

1. Identify or explain: Annapolis meeting, Alexander Hamilton, James Madison, Edmund Randolph, Virginia Plan, William Paterson, New Jersey Plan, Connecticut Compromise.

2. Describe the Great Compromise. Why was it important?

3. What was the three-fifths compromise?

4. What powers that the Confederation lacked did the new government have under the Constitution?

5. **Making Comparisons.** Explain the difference between a federal union (as interpreted in 1700) and a national union.

---

5. The states ratify

It was not enough for the delegates to the Constitutional Convention to draft the document. It had to be ratified too. Here again the convention showed its wisdom—and its ability to go beyond the letter of the law.

Bypassing the states. The convention submitted the Constitution to Congress and asked that it be sent to state constitutional conventions for approval. This procedure would assure that it was ratified by the people themselves and not only by the state governments. Many believed that this

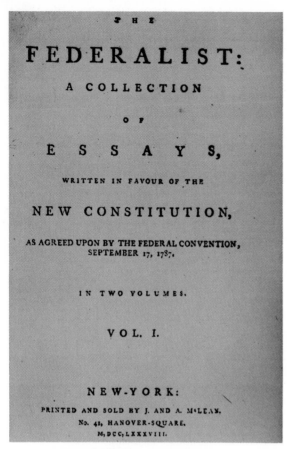

The *Federalist Papers,* written by Madison, Hamilton, and Jay, helped to persuade New York to vote for the Constitution.

would make it clear that the Constitution was superior to state laws. The state legislatures might not have made an impartial decision, because they were destined to lose powers under the new government. To go into effect the Constitution required the approval not of all thirteen but of only nine states. This would keep an obstinate few from sabotaging the work of the cooperative many.

The fight for approval. Since the convention had done its work in secret, there was great public interest both in what the new Constitution said—and in what it really meant. Those who supported the new Constitution were called *Federalists,* and their opponents were called *Anti-Federalists.* The Anti-Federalists feared that the new Constitution would create a super-government that might de-

stroy the very liberty that the Revolution was fought to win. The Constitution contained no bill of rights like that found in the state constitutions. And what would prevent the President from becoming a king?

The bitter struggle for ratification had intelligent, well-meaning people on both sides. The outcome was not certain until the very end. Only hard work and a number of political tricks by the Federalists brought about ratification of the document by the required number of states.

The process began easily enough. On December 7, 1787, Delaware by unanimous vote became the first state to give the new Constitution its approval. The Pennsylvania Federalists planned to rush through approval before the Anti-Federalists could muster their forces and reach the voters. They bought up newspapers to keep Anti-Federalist speeches from being printed. And their undemocratic strategy succeeded on December 12, when the Constitution won Pennsylvania's approval 46–23. New Jersey, Georgia, and Connecticut followed within a month.

Massachusetts, a key state. When the Massachusetts state convention met, the Anti-Federalists seemed to be in a majority. Luckily for the Federalists, the cleverest politicians were on their side. At first the ambitious John Hancock, the influential presiding officer of the convention, was opposed. But the Federalists persuaded him to change his mind. They promised to elect him governor of Massachusetts and hinted that he was the obvious choice for Vice-President of the new nation. When Hancock went before the convention to urge that it ratify the Constitution, he also proposed a series of amendments to the Constitution to guard citizens' rights. The convention accepted both of Hancock's suggestions. On February 6, 1788, Massachusetts ratified the Constitution by the close vote of 187–168.

What Massachusetts did suggested to other states that they too might approve the Constitution as it was and at the same time propose amendments to remove the objections and allay the fears of some of their citizens. Maryland ratified without conditions on April 26, 1788. South Carolina approved in May, but proposed amendments. New Hampshire ratified with amendments after a bitter struggle and a close vote on June 21.

Virginia and New York seal the victory. Now nine states had approved, and technically the government could go into operation. But, in fact, no central government could be effective without including Virginia and New York. Virginia was the largest state in the Union and had some of its best-known and ablest leaders—Washington, Jefferson, Madison, and many others. In Virginia there was a tough fight because Patrick Henry, George Mason, and so many who had been active in the Revolution feared the powers of the new government and became outspoken Anti-Federalists. But Washington's strong support for the Constitution was decisive. In a close vote Virginia finally approved, while suggesting amendments.

Still the crucial state of New York had not announced its decision. Luckily many voters there would be persuaded by a series of brilliant propaganda essays, called the *Federalist Papers*. Written by James Madison, Alexander Hamilton, and John Jay, these essays not only helped turn the tide in New York, but became (and remain) the classic statement of why freedom-loving people need a strong central government.

The news of Virginia's ratification, rushed north by an express rider, also helped New York to decide. On July 26, 1788, the delegates to the New York convention approved (though with many amendments) by a scary narrow margin (30 to 27). A change of only two votes would have meant the rejection of the Constitution by New York. Then perhaps the whole effort to frame an effective government for the new nation might have collapsed. Hamilton led the fight in New York and deserves much of the credit for ratification by that state.

Now the new government could go into action, despite the strong Anti-Federalists in two states. North Carolina did not ratify until November 21, 1789, after the Constitution was operating. When Rhode Island (which always went its own way) finally ratified on May 29, 1790, it had the distinction of being the last of the original colonies to approve the Constitution.

The Federalists promised that they would add to the Constitution a bill of rights—a series of amendments guaranteeing certain rights and liberties to the people. Without this promise the Constitution might never have been ratified. Had the Constitutional Convention included a bill of rights at the beginning, the struggle for adoption might have been far easier.

In 1788 the Massachusetts *Centinel* urged North Carolina and Rhode Island to complete the federal edifice by ratifying the Constitution. North Carolina did so the next year. Rhode Island, shown with a broken pillar but a firm foundation, followed in 1790.

The New-York Historical Society

After the long and bitter arguments in the state conventions, there was widespread rejoicing when the Constitution was adopted. Dinners, processions, and fireworks signaled the nation's new beginning.

A government in skeleton. Still, the Constitution provided only the skeleton for a government. The first President, the Congress, and the Supreme Court would have to put flesh on the skeleton. Why has this federal Constitution had such a long and successful life? How has a short document written nearly two centuries ago for thirteen struggling seaboard colonies been able to give strength and liberty to a vast, two-ocean nation of more than 200 million people?

Oddly enough, the shortness of the document itself is one explanation. The Constitution did not go into details. It left to future generations the right and the opportunity to apply the scheme, and so to grow in unpredictable ways. It is not surprising then that one of the shortest constitutions ever adopted by a nation was to become in time the oldest living written constitution.

SECTION 5 REVIEW

1. Why was it significant that voters rather than state legislatures ratified the Constitution?

2. Why did some people oppose the Constitution?

3. What did Massachusetts do that assisted in getting other states to ratify the Constitution?

4. What factors helped to win ratification in Virginia and New York?

5. **Testing Conclusions.** Is it true that the short length of the Constitution has contributed to its long life? Explain.

An express rider took eight days to carry the news to the New York ratifying convention in Poughkeepsie that Virginia had ratified the Constitution. This news helped sway the delegates at the New York State convention to ratify. Virginia's resolution, as we see, expressed hope for early amendments to correct the Constitution's imperfections.

POGHKEEPSIE,

July 2d, 1788.

JUST ARRIVED

BY EXPRESS,

The Ratification of the New Conftitution by the Convention of the State of Virginia, on Wednefday the 25th June, by a majority of 10 ; 88 agreeing, and 78 diffenting to its adoption.

"WE the Delegates of the People of Virginia, duly elected in Purfuance of a Recommendation of the General Affembly; and now met in Convention, having fully and fairly inveftigated and difcuffed the Proceedings of the Federal Convention, and being

With thefe Impreffions, with a folemn Appeal to the Searcher of Hearts for the Purity of our Intentions, and under the Conviction, that whatfoever Imperfections may exift in the Conftitution, ought rather to be examined in the Mode prefcribed therein, than to bring the Unt-

CHAPTER 5 REVIEW

FOCUSING ON IDEAS

1. Describe the process that authors of the state constitutions followed to make "consent of the governed" a living reality.

2. What type of new government had the states wanted to see created? Were their expectations realistic? Explain.

3. How did the framers of the Constitution plan for necessary future "repairs"?

4. Certain situations in the 1780s promoted separatism among the states, while others promoted greater unity. Give examples of these situations (or forces) and explain them.

TAKING A CRITICAL LOOK

1. **Demonstrating Reasoned Judgment.** The state constitutions were (and still are) longer and more detailed than the United States Constitution. Why might you expect this? What advantage, if any, do you see in a relatively short constitution?

2. **Determining Relevance.** What is the relationship between Shays's Rebellion and the Constitution?

3. **Making Comparisons.** How does the Constitution reflect the ideas contained in the Declaration of Independence?

YOUR REGION IN HISTORY

1. **Geography.** How was your state affected by the Northwest Ordinance?

2. **Government.** When was your state's constitution adopted? How was it drafted? If you live in one of the original thirteen states, investigate and report on the struggle for ratification of the federal Constitution in your state. When did your state ratify the Constitution?

3. **Economics.** How did the three-fifths compromise and the commercial compromise affect your state?

HISTORICAL FACTS AND FIGURES

Drawing Conclusions. Use information on the chart below to help answer the following questions. In each case explain how the information on the chart helped you draw your conclusion. (a) Did the writers of the Constitution feel that the national government or the state governments should deal with the governments of other countries? (b) Under what conditions or circumstances did the writers of the Constitution think that the federal government should become involved in business or private enterprise? (c) Is it more likely that there will be conflicting state and federal laws concerning copyrights and patents, taxes, or marriages?

System of Federalism

Examples of Delegated Powers	Examples of Concurrent Powers	Examples of Reserved Powers
Regulate immigration naturalization	Borrow money	Create corporation laws
Regulate interstate foreign commerce	Provide for health, safety, and welfare	Regulate intrastate commerce
Set standard weights and measures	Administer criminal justice	Establish and maintain schools
Create and maintain armed forces	Set minimum wage	Establish and maintain local governments
Make copyright and patent laws	Charter banks	Determine eligibility requirements for elected state officials
Establish postal system	Levy taxes	Determine and regulate laws of marriage, divorce, and professional licenses
Establish foreign policy		
Create lower courts		
Print money		
Declare war		

CHAPTER 6

The United States begins

The new Constitution stated that the President should be elected by "electors" from the states. Each state was to have as many electors as it had senators and representatives in Congress. These electors were to be chosen as the state legislatures saw fit. They were then to meet in their own states, and each elector was to cast one ballot on which he had written the names of his two choices for President. When all the votes were counted, the person with the highest number of electoral votes was to be President and the second highest was to be Vice-President.

Every elector wrote George Washington's name on his ballot. John Adams of Massachusetts received the next largest number of votes and became Vice-President. So to them would fall the difficult job of starting the new government on its way when they took office in April 1789.

1. The nation in the 1790s

The country George Washington was to lead as first President had changed only slightly from the land he had known as a boy. Of course, the population was larger. The first federal census in 1790 would reveal that there were nearly 4 million people in the country's 865,000 square miles. The nation occupied less than one-quarter the territory it was destined to fill by the late 1900s.

A rural land. The land was covered by a virgin forest of oak, chestnut, beech, sycamore, poplar, pine, and hemlock trees, which had been growing for centuries. Only in a few areas, such as southern New England and the Middle States, were there large stretches of cleared land.

Some sections of the country contained stands of dead trees. People starting farms in the great forest killed the trees by girdling (cutting all around the bark) and only removing them after they had fallen. In the meantime, they planted their crops in between.

Most people were farmers. Only a few Americans lived in cities. In 1789, there were just six cities with over 8000 people. Philadelphia with 42,000 people was by far the largest, cleanest, and most attractive. New York was second with 33,000, but it was dirty and smelly, though busy and rapidly growing. Much smaller were Boston, Charleston, Baltimore, and Salem. Only New York and Philadelphia had begun to install such modern conveniences as water pipes, curbs, and sidewalks.

Lake Superior

BRITISH

NORTH

AMERICA

Montreal

Norwich • Portland

Portsmouth

Salem

Boston

Lake Huron

Lake Michigan

Lake Ontario

Albany

Mohawk Trail

Ft. Niagara

Hartford • Providence

Boston Post Rd.

New Haven

Lake Erie

Ft. Detroit

New York

Ft. Sandusky

Trenton

Forbes

Rd.

NORTHWEST

Great

Trail

Ft. Duquesne
(Pittsburgh)

Philadelphia

Wilmington

Scioto

Lancaster

TERRITORY

Zane's Trace

Cumberland Fort

Cumberland Rd.

Trail

Braddock's

Baltimore

Ohio R.

Chillicothe

Alexandria

Great Valley Rd.

Fredericksburg

Sonioto

Warrior's Path

Williamsburg

Ohio R.

Richmond

Norfolk

St. Louis

Harrod's
Town

APPALACHIAN

Path

Western

Wilderness
Rd.

SPANISH

Cumberland Gap

Avery's Trace

Trading

Raleigh

LOUISIANA

Nashville

Cumberland R.

Virginia Rd.

Cape Fear Rd.

Nickajack
Trace

Great Trace

Charlotte

Wilmington

Mississippi R.

Chickasaw (Natchez) Trail

Tennessee R.

Trader's

Path

Charleston
Path

Post Rd.

Arkansas Post

Augusta

Savannah R.

Main

Charleston

Savannah

Natchez

Surveyed

WEST FLORIDA

Pensacola

Trail

St. Augustine

ATLANTIC OCEAN

New Orleans

SPANISH

FLORIDA

GULF   OF   MEXICO

Major Roads in 1800

——— Roads

– – – Paths

0   300 Miles

0   300 Kilometers

Philadelphia had many paved streets, but the rest had streets chiefly of dirt or cobblestone which were never cleaned. Not surprisingly, these cities were often plagued by disease.

Difficulties of travel and communication.

Transportation was little better than in the days of the French and Indian War. There had been few improvements in the road Washington had followed when he marched with General Braddock on the way to western Pennsylvania in 1755. "Road" was not quite the right word for the peculiar kind of obstacle course filled with rocks, stumps, and holes that extended from Maine to Georgia. In many sections it was just a wide track through the dense forest. In 1801 Abigail Adams took this road from the new capital city of Washington to her home in Massachusetts. By the time she arrived in Baltimore she reported to President Adams that she was beaten and bruised.

Even on the best roads travel was slow and expensive. It took two days for the stagecoach to go from New York City to Philadelphia. A ticket cost six dollars—not including the price of a night in an inn. In wet weather many sections of the road were impassable.

We cannot be surprised, then, that about two-thirds of the American people lived within fifty miles of the tidewater, where waterways provided a cheaper, more trouble-free passage. It was easier to travel several hundred miles by water than a much shorter distance by land, even though ships were still propelled only by oar, wind, and current.

In 1788 and again in 1790 the clever inventor John Fitch operated his steamboats on the river at Philadelphia. But he found most Americans uninterested and even suspicious of boats that belched smoke and carried fire that threatened to consume cargo and passengers.

In general, farmers who had crops to take to market waited until winter when the ground was hard and there was less to do on the farm. Then Southerners who did not live on the water's edge rolled their hogsheads (large barrels) of tobacco to the closest boat landing. But the rough roads made it hard work. One observer reported that he saw two slaves struggling with a team of horses that was having a hard time moving a single hogshead.

Out west, some farmers floated their crops all the way down the Mississippi to New Orleans, and then walked the dangerous way back home. Or they sailed on to Philadelphia and then returned to their homes by walking over the mountains. Others converted their grain into whiskey, a more compact and portable form in which to deliver it across the mountains. Still others fed the grain to their hogs and then drove the hogs to market.

Mail service was slow and uncertain. Twenty-nine days passed before news of the Declaration of Independence reached Charleston from Philadelphia. There was no regular mail service from Maine to Georgia until 1800, and even then a letter took three weeks to arrive.

All in all, the states remained as separate from each other as they were in colonial days. People still tended to think of their state as their country. Even worse—from the point of view of uniting the separate states—settlements had now grown up beyond the Appalachian Mountains. The nation was stretching west.

Daniel Boone and other bold frontier men and women began settling in Kentucky and Tennessee shortly before the Revolution. The path to those settlements across the mountains from the seaboard states was slow and hard. Even so, by 1790 there were 36,000 people in Tennessee and 74,000 in Kentucky. On June 1, 1792, Kentucky became a new state of the Union. But to trade and communicate with the world, the people who lived over the mountains depended on the broad Mississippi water-highway and its tributaries. These rivers provided a convenient network along the borders of Kentucky and the western territories and through their heartlands. Whether or not these lands could remain part of the Union would depend on who controlled the Mississippi River.

The American "aristocracy."

In 1789 England, the old mother country, was a land of rigid social classes. Here in America there were no kings and nobles. But there was an American kind of aristocracy marked off less by ancestry than by land and money. Of course, nobody could change his ancestors. But in so vast and so empty a continent there were many new opportunities for new businesses. An enterprising person—provided he was not a slave—had a good chance to move up the social ladder. Social classes were much more fluid than in the Old World. The American "aristocracy" of land and cash consisted of the rich merchants of

The painting above depicts the front door of George Washington's beloved home, Mt. Vernon. On the other side of the house is the large, columned porch, which overlooks the Potomac River. Washington said that no other estate in America was "as pleasantly situated."

New England, New York, and Pennsylvania, and the great planters of the South. Some of them went about wearing powdered hair, knee breeches, ruffles, and silver buckles on their shoes. They aped the fancy manners of English lords and ladies. But the frills of an aristocracy of birth really had no place in the new-world nation. As the careers of American Presidents would soon show, here a person might rise by hard work, intelligence, skill, and perhaps a little luck, from the lowest position to the highest.

By the early 1800s it had become difficult to acquire the large tract of land needed for a successful tobacco plantation. So it was harder to move into the aristocracy in the South than it was in New England. Still, the demand for cotton by the rapidly growing English cotton industry and the invention of the cotton gin in 1793 by Eli Whitney of Connecticut soon opened up chances to enter the American aristocracy even in the South.

SECTION 1 REVIEW

1. Use the map on page 115 to show two ways for New Englanders to reach the Ohio River.

2. Explain how the President was chosen in 1789.

3. In 1789 where were the largest stretches of cleared land? Which were the chief cities?

4. What problems did the government confront in the 1790s in trying to deal with transportation and communication difficulties?

5. **Making Comparisons.** In what ways were American "aristocrats" different from European aristocrats?

Yale University Art Gallery, Gift of the Associates in Fine Arts and Mrs. Henry F. Loomis in Memory of Henry Bradford Loomis, BA 1875

This portrait of Washington at the Battle of Princeton was painted three or four years after the fight by Charles Willson Peale, who served as an officer in the American army there. Although not a realistic battle scene, the painting shows Washington's self-confidence and poise. Peale set up one of the first museums in America.

2. George Washington sets the course

George Washington took office with a firm faith. The "sacred fire of liberty" as well as "the destiny of the republican model of government" depended on the outcome of the "experiment" the Americans had undertaken. No country in the world had ever tried this form of government. Washington knew that it was up to the first President and the first Congress to see that the experiment did not fail.

A strong executive. Washington believed that if the young nation was to survive in an envious, hostile world, the Chief Executive of the new government must lead. By showing the courage to be strong at a time when people accused him of trying to become a king, he earned a place too as an American peacetime hero. He had done more than anyone else to help the nation win independence. He now led the nation along the path to survival.

Washington's personal prestige gave the Presidency the dignity it needed. His physique and his stature helped. He was six feet, two inches tall, and his face appeared chiseled from granite. He looked every inch the national leader. But his commanding manner and his elegant way of life seemed to justify the suspicions of those who feared he wanted to seduce the nation to monarchy. He rented one of the finest houses in New York City, the nation's first capital, and staffed it with servants in uniform. He traveled in a canary-colored coach (drawn by six horses) on which was painted the Washington coat-of-arms. He held formal parties where he appeared in black velvet and silk stockings.

Washington wanted his office to seem dignified and important to all the world. He well knew, as he wrote, that "there is scarcely any part of my conduct that may not hereafter be drawn into precedent."

Creating a new government. The federal government, with no money, inherited numerous war debts to the French government, to Dutch bankers, and to its own citizens. To make the new nation respectable and trusted, Congress would have to raise money and begin to pay off those debts. Congress also had to provide for the national defense and deal with the Indian tribes. To fix the number of seats for each state in the House of Representatives, the Constitution said the federal government must take a national census each ten

Federal Hall, in the center of this engraving, was located in New York City on Wall Street at the head of Broad Street. Here George Washington took the oath of office as the first President.

years. Congress also needed to organize territories, establish federal courts, and regulate trade. Then there were diplomatic and commercial problems with England, France, and Spain. There were the executive departments to be set up—and a host of other tasks to accomplish.

The new House of Representatives, advised by Representative James Madison of Virginia, at once turned its attention to the first ten amendments— the Bill of Rights. These were drawn up by Madison based on the objections to the Constitution that had been raised by some of the states. The House also quickly passed a modest tariff bill to bring in some badly needed money.

Meanwhile, the Senate turned to creating the federal courts. The Judiciary Act of 1789 set up the Supreme Court, three circuit courts, and thirteen district courts (one in each state). To each district court it attached a United States Attorney to serve as a federal prosecutor and a United States Marshal to serve as the federal police. The act also set procedures for the federal courts. Disputes over the meaning of federal laws and treaties would, in the end, be settled by the United States Supreme Court as would conflicts between state law and federal law.

The Congress also set up the departments of Treasury, State, and War. These, with the Attorney General and the Postmaster General, were the only executive departments at the start.

For the important post of Secretary of the Treasury, Washington chose his brilliant young friend and onetime aide, Alexander Hamilton. Edmund Randolph of Virginia became Attorney General. The War Department was entrusted to General Henry Knox of Massachusetts. Thomas Jefferson was called home from Paris, where he had been minister since 1785, to become the first Secretary of State.

Roles are clarified. The relationship of the new departments and their Secretaries to the Congress or even to the President was not at all clear. Some people thought that the new departments should just carry out the laws and keep out of politics. The

Secretaries, then, would stay in office under successive Presidents. Hamilton saw the department heads as having a share in making policy. He thought that Secretaries, like English cabinet members, would go to Congress to speak in favor of bills that they wanted passed. But Congress refused to hear Hamilton when he tried to report, so the executive departments did not form close ties with Congress.

Some thought that the Senate, because it was to "advise and consent" on treaties, might become like the English Privy Council, which advised the king. One day Washington arrived at the Senate, sat down in the Vice-President's chair, and told the Senate that he and the Secretary of War had come to get their advice on an Indian treaty. But the Senate refused to debate the question in his presence. The Senate wanted to discuss the treaty without being overawed by the President. So Washington left without any advice and soon gave up trying to get the counsel of the Senate.

In domestic affairs, Washington believed it was the President's job to enforce the laws Congress made, not to lead the Congress in making laws. He allowed Hamilton to go his own way in handling the financial affairs of the country. But diplomatic problems were different. Washington often consulted with Jefferson, and he soon began to call in the Attorney General, and the Secretaries of State, War, and the Treasury for advice on complex problems in foreign affairs. Acting as an advisory group, the department heads slowly became the President's Cabinet.

Alexander Hamilton prepares financial plans.
During Washington's first term the great questions concerned finances. The disputes that arose produced the first significant arguments over the nature of the Constitution and drew the issues for our first political parties. Alexander Hamilton put the issues into focus. Though not tall (he was 5'6"), he was handsome and debonair. Intelligent and hard working, he had earned the full confidence of President Washington. But Hamilton's personal ambition and his lack of faith in the people sometimes tempted him to grand and clever schemes.

The House of Representatives, under Madison's leadership, directed the Secretary of the Treasury to prepare proposals for collecting the revenue and dealing with the public credit. Hamilton was told to present these plans to the House of Representatives—where, according to the Constitution, money bills had to originate.

In response to these directions Hamilton put together a design of breathtaking scope. He presented that program in three major reports: on the Public Credit (January 1790), on a National Bank (December 1790), and on Manufactures (December 1791). These reports were to help shape the future history of the United States.

The Report on the Public Credit.
Upon taking office, Hamilton found that the United States had debts amounting to $54 million. Of this sum, $10 million was owed to our wartime ally, France, and to Dutch bankers. The remainder was owed to United States citizens. In addition, many of the states had unpaid war debts amounting to $20 million.

Hamilton saw an ingenious way to use this heavy debt to strengthen the central government. His plan would provide capital for a national bank and even create wealth that could be invested in new private enterprises. He proposed that the United States should pay all these debts in full. But they would be paid in a way that would both stimulate business and give the wealthy classes good reason to support the new government.

Now everyone agreed that the United States must repay the French and the Dutch if the credit of the United States was to be any good in the outside world. Who would lend us money in the future if we failed to pay these debts?

There was opposition, however, to paying back American holders of the nation's debt. The reason for this dispute had to do with the history of the debt.

During the war Congress had issued paper certificates, or bonds, which promised to pay the holder at some point in the future the amount printed on the face of the paper plus interest at a certain rate. These bonds had been sold to people at their face value or given to soldiers to induce them to enlist. During the years of war and depression many of these original holders had been forced to sell their bonds for whatever they could. Speculators willing to gamble on the future bought up the bonds for as little as 15 or 20 cents on the dollar. Even as Secretary of the Treasury Hamilton made

The cartoonist here accuses Robert Morris, a prominent Federalist from Philadelphia, of some trickery in the moving of the capital from New York City to Philadelphia. Morris carries the Capitol (Federal Hall) on his shoulder, while the devil leads him on.

his proposal, some members of Congress, joining the other speculators, bought all the bonds they could find.

Madison tried to persuade Congress to accept a complicated proposal to pay bondholders differing amounts based upon when they had bought their bonds. Congress rejected this plan and followed Hamilton. And Congress was right—even if some of its members stood to make money by their votes. The whole point of Hamilton's bill was to restore national credit. That could only be done if all those who had bought the bonds, at any time and for whatever reason, were paid in full.

Before the vote was taken on the payment of the debt of the United States, the question of having the national government pay the debts of the states had to be settled. This was even more difficult than the problem of the national debt. Some states, such as Virginia and Maryland, had already paid a large part of their debts. Why should they have to help pay the debts of states like Massachusetts and South Carolina? Hamilton replied that since the war had

been fought for the benefit of *all* the states, the government which now represented all the states should pay the whole debt.

Madison had enough votes to defeat Hamilton's proposal to assume the state debts. But Madison believed that the United States should pay its own debts. The speculators warned him, however, that if he defeated assumption of the state debts by the national government, they would defeat the payment of the national debt.

At this point there was struck the most famous "deal" in American political history. The permanent site of the nation's capital had not yet been decided. Hamilton had a suggestion for Thomas Jefferson, who had just arrived from France to become Secretary of State. Hamilton would have his supporters in Congress vote to locate the capital at Philadelphia for the years 1790–1800, and then move it to a spot on the Potomac River favored by Virginia. In return, Madison and his friends should allow the federal government to assume the state debt. Madison and Jefferson accepted Hamilton's bargain, so the bill dealing with the debt was passed in July 1790.

The total debt of $75 million was then "funded." This meant exchanging the old bonds for new ones bearing interest, some at 6 percent, some at 3 percent. The new bonds went mainly to bankers, merchants, and wealthy speculators who owned most of the old bonds. As Hamilton had predicted, these influential people then became firm supporters of the national government. It had to survive in order to preserve the value of the new bonds. When the federal government assumed the state debts, it undercut the importance of the state governments to those who had once held the state bonds. And the national credit was now secure.

Hamilton's opponents accused him of creating a new wealthy class—those people who had bought the national and state bonds at low prices. But that was just what Hamilton intended. If the nation was to develop from a land of farms into a dynamic country of mines, factories, ships, and shops, it needed persons of wealth who were willing and able to invest large sums of money in new projects.

Hamilton's plan was both farsighted and daring. The opposition to it, however, disclosed a sectional split between the agrarian South and the mercantile North. That split, reinforced by the great moral issue of slavery, would endanger the future of the nation.

The Report on a National Bank.

Hamilton revealed the next phase of his plan in December 1790. He proposed that the United States create a new bank. The federal government would put in $2 million (one-fifth ownership) of the bank's $10 million capital and appoint one-fifth of the bank's directors. Private investors would supply the rest of the capital and elect the other directors. And they were even to be allowed to use their government bonds for part of their share.

What would the United States get for its money? Far more than just another commercial bank. This bank would serve as the government's financial agent—collecting taxes, providing a safe place to deposit the government's cash, and lending the government money when needed.

The bank could also provide a much-needed paper currency. Based on its capital, the bank would issue bank notes to supplement specie (gold and silver coin), which was in short supply. These bank notes could be used to pay taxes and import duties. They would keep the currents of commerce flowing.

The Bank of the United States, by lending its funds, would also help develop new businesses. This goal, too, was very much in Hamilton's view. For at that time, when the nation had only three banks, business leaders were in desperate need of capital.

"Broad" versus "strict" construction of the new Constitution.

The bank proposal at once ran into heated opposition. Thomas Jefferson voiced the belief of many Americans that farmers were "the chosen people of God." They did not want to see America become a land of cities, mills, mines, and factories. Instead they wanted a pastoral land where people tilled the soil and put their faith in the rewards of hard work and the produce of sun and rainfall. Only reluctantly had they gone along with Hamilton on paying the national and state debts. The new bank proposal was too much.

Jefferson, joined by Madison, told President Washington that since the Constitution did not give Congress the power to establish a bank, the bank should not be allowed. This kind of argument became known as a "strict construction" of the Constitution. They argued that the Congress or the President had no power to do anything unless the Constitution gave the federal government that power in so many words.

On the other side, Hamilton defended his bank by arguing that the government had the right to do everything necessary and proper to carry out any of the powers granted in the Constitution. The bank, he argued, was a necessary and proper way to borrow money and to regulate the currency, both of which powers the Constitution had plainly assigned to the Congress. This became known as a "broad" construction of the Constitution. Washington was never entirely convinced by Hamilton's theory. But seeing the nation's need for banks, he signed the bill into law on February 25, 1791.

The dispute that began over the first Bank of the United States between the "strict" and the "broad" interpretation of the Constitution still continues. But who takes which side never stays the same. In general, strict interpretation has been used by those out of power against those who hold the Presidency. As political parties began to emerge behind

Independence National Historical Park Collection   Independence National Historical Park Collection

Thomas Jefferson (above left) and Alexander Hamilton (above right) strongly disagreed over the question of establishing a national bank.   But both recognized the talents of Charles Willson Peale and commissioned him to paint their portraits.   The bank note below is similar to those issued by the first Bank of the United States.

Eric Newman/Numismatic Education Society

Jefferson and Madison opposing the followers of Hamilton, strict construction was advocated by the Jeffersonians. But when Jefferson came to power himself, he soon found he needed to follow the path of broad construction.

The Report on Manufactures. The capstone to Hamilton's economic policy was his Report on Manufactures of December 1791. Having provided capital and credit through the first two parts of his program, he now called for the development of American manufactures. The key feature of this report was a request for Congress to pass a protective tariff. This was a tariff high enough to keep out goods made in Europe even if they were cheaper. Then people would make them here, and the nation's factories would grow.

Planters and farmers opposed Hamilton's tariff plan because it meant they would have to pay higher prices for their manufactured goods. They were joined by northern merchants who made their living by importing tools, glassware, furniture, and other items that the farmers and planters purchased, and who saw that the protective tariffs would keep out their merchandise. So this part of his grand design did not pass Congress. For many years the tariff would be used only to raise money to pay the costs of government, not to promote manufacturing at home as Hamilton had wished.

The rise of political parties. Hamilton's program built a national economy. At the same time, it strengthened the central government over the states. But it divided the country into two camps— the new "political parties"—each shaping its politics according to a varying mix of economic interest, social position, and philosophical belief.

The followers of Hamilton, called Federalists, favored his economic program. Generally they supported a strong central government and had little faith in the mass of the people. They saw themselves as "the wise, the good, and the rich," or "the rich, the well-born, and the able." What they wanted was a government "of gentlemen, by gentlemen, for gentlemen." Some Federalists were even said to regret the separation from the empire. In the wars of that time between France and England they tended to support England. The French Revolution of 1789 frightened them, and they did not want it to happen here.

On the other side were the followers of Jefferson and Madison. Jefferson disliked cities and factories which, according to him, were sure to produce slums. His ideal was a nation of small farmers all of whom owned property and so had a stake in society. The Republicans (as the followers of Jefferson and Madison were called) opposed Hamilton's economic policies. They feared a strong central government here and did all they could to help the common people of France to overthrow the French nobility.

President Washington's support of Hamilton's economic policy seemed to make him a Federalist in the eyes of some Republicans. But actually Washington hated the whole idea of political parties. The infighting and compromises of politics did not appeal to him. He preferred the clear and simple principles of patriotism. What he really wanted was to go home to Virginia when his first term ended. But Madison, Jefferson, and Hamilton all told him that the nation needed him. Again obeying the call of duty, Washington reluctantly agreed to serve another term.

SECTION 2 REVIEW

1. Identify or explain: Henry Knox, debt assumption, "strict" and "broad" construction.

2. What is the Cabinet? How did it evolve?

3. Name Hamilton's famous reports. Tell what he hoped to achieve in each plan.

4. How did Washington, D.C., become our capital?

5. **Making Comparisons.** On what issues did Federalists and Republicans differ?

---

3. Foreign affairs for a new nation

The key to understanding George Washington's second term, which began on March 4, 1793, is found in foreign affairs, and especially in the turbulent events of the French Revolution. It was not, in fact, domestic divisions alone that had persuaded Washington to serve again. It was also, as he put it, "the delicate posture of our foreign affairs." The United States had difficult problems with the three largest nations of western Europe: Great Britain, France, and Spain.

Great Britain and the Indians in the Northwest.

The British refused to carry out the peace treaty of 1783. They still held fur-trading posts inside the United States. Their agents from Canada were giving arms and gunpowder to Indians who welcomed this support for their resistance to the invasion of their lands by the European settlers.

Full-scale combat with the Indians of the Northwest started in 1790 when General Josiah Harmar led a force from Fort Washington (Cincinnati) against Indian towns near what is now Fort Wayne. Harmar's troops failed and had to retreat. The following year a new force of 1400 men was sent out under General Arthur St. Clair. Badly trained and poorly equipped, it met disaster. It was ambushed while camped near the Wabash River, and 900 men—two-thirds of the army—were killed. This terrible defeat exposed the whole Northwest to the vengeance of the Indians.

Relations with Spain.

To the south, Spain also menaced United States interests. The Spanish still refused to allow our shipping to pass freely through New Orleans. In addition, they supported the Creeks and Cherokees against the settlers moving onto their lands. For Spain still wanted to hold the Southwest and perhaps even to detach Kentucky and Tennessee from the United States.

The United States dared not go to war over these differences with England and Spain. To have done so would have exhausted the strength of the new Republic and crippled the commerce that was now reviving. The weak new nation had to try to negotiate its differences.

Troubles with France.

France was the greatest problem of all. Having done so much to help the United States win its revolution, France had become our strongest ally. But when the French undertook their own very different kind of revolution, that nation's leadership and its direction changed from year to year, even from month to month. How, then, could the young United States fulfill its treaty obligations to satisfy the whims of the Paris mobs?

Only five days after Washington first took office in 1789, the revolutionary French Estates General (national assembly) met at Versailles. In the next two years it swept away age-old oppressive privileges of the king, the nobility, and the higher clergy.

The French revolutionaries first went to war against Austria and Prussia. Soon the French government fell into the hands of the extreme radicals, the Jacobins of Paris. Aristocrats and priests were massacred. The monarchy was overthrown for a republic. King Louis XVI and Queen Marie Antoinette were beheaded. When Washington was inaugurated for his second term, the Jacobins were preparing to crush the other factions. Their "reign of terror" was government by the guillotine. But the French people could not be silenced by terror. The opposition to the Jacobins simply multiplied and went underground.

Declaring a "world revolution," the French radicals announced their intention to assist any people who wished to overthrow their government. The menace of anarchy and rebellion thus led the governments of Britain, Spain, and Holland to join Austria and Prussia in war against the aggressive French Republic.

Federalists and Republicans clashed over the issue of the French Revolution. The beheading of the French king, Louis Capet, shocked the Federalists and prompted this broadside.

American Antiquarian Society

THE
TRAGEDY
OF
LOUIS CAPET:

Being a True and Authentic NARRATIVE, of the horrid and barbarous *EXECUTION* of the late unfortunate MONARCH, *LOUIS XVI* of France, who was beheaded, on the Twenty first of January, 1793, conformably to a Decree of the NATIONAL CONVENTION on Suspicion of TREASON.—Which bloody Transaction (it is thought by every true friend to American Revolution) will eternally disgrace the Annals of the French Nation : And may his Death be as sincerely lamented by every *honest* and *grateful* AMERICAN, as it is by the Majority of the Citizens of *France.*——This Narrative, with the Poetry annexed, is published in this Form at the Request of many true Republicans, and recommended to be preserved as a Memorial of that shocking and melancholy Event.

American Antiquarian Society

Americans were horrified that 20,000 people were beheaded on the guillotine or killed by mobs during the French Revolution.

"Citizen" Genêt's mission. Shortly after his second term began, Washington had to face the serious question of our relations with the slippery government of France. On April 8, 1793, the new French minister to the United States, "Citizen" Edmond Genêt, whose ship had been blown off course, landed at Charleston. He was greeted warmly everywhere on his four-week journey from Charleston to Philadelphia.

All this attention misled Genêt into thinking that the sympathies of the whole American people were on the side of the French radicals. But opinions here were, in fact, deeply divided. Hamilton, who was appalled by the bloodshed in France, was opposed to receiving Genêt at all. On the other hand, Jefferson had developed a deep affection for the French when he was American minister in Paris. He believed that Genêt should be received and that the new government should be recognized.

There was no denying that at a crucial moment France had furnished us with men and money to help us win our independence. By the treaty of alliance in 1778 we had promised to help France

defend its West Indian islands if they were attacked, as now seemed likely. We had also agreed to allow France to bring into our ports any ships it might capture in wartime.

Washington, despite his horror at the atrocities committed in Paris, sided with Secretary of State Jefferson. He agreed that the United States must recognize the new government. At the same time, however, he was determined that our weak young nation should stay out of war. That war was a by-product of the French Revolution and now was spreading all over Europe—and even to America and other continents. On April 22, 1793, the President issued a Proclamation of Neutrality, which declared that we would not take sides in the struggle.

Jefferson had opposed this decision. He had wanted first to extract some concessions from Britain. He wanted Washington to declare that we might become neutral if Great Britain would remove its troops from the Northwest and give the United States trading privileges throughout the British Empire. But the Proclamation gave away that bargaining position. Soon afterward, Jefferson announced that he would resign.

"Citizen" Genêt ignored the Proclamation of Neutrality and defied the rule of diplomacy that forbade interference in the politics of the host country. He appealed to the "true" republicans here to support their "sister republic" across the Atlantic. He enlisted sailors and fitted out privateers in United States ports to prey on British commerce in the West Indies. He tried to stir up the Canadians to revolt. He even prepared an expedition against Spanish New Orleans. His conduct was so outrageous that even Jefferson, despite his sympathy for the French, agreed that Genêt must go home.

Genêt's mission and the war between Great Britain and France brought a new bitterness into American party politics. Federalists and Republicans shrieked at each other with a new rudeness. Federalists were shocked by the bloodshed and violence of the French Revolution. In addition, they wished to preserve our valuable trade with the British Isles. They despised the Republican supporters of France as "filthy Jacobins" and "frog-eating, man-eating, blood-drinking cannibals." The Republicans replied by singing the "Marseillaise" (the battle hymn of the French Revolution) and by sneering at the Federalists as "aristocratic snobs," "Anglo-men," and "British boot-lickers."

Jay's Treaty.

In spite of Washington's Proclamation of Neutrality, the United States barely escaped war with Great Britain. In December 1793, Britain began to seize American ships trading with the French West Indies. Great Britain also stopped our ships, took off the sailors whom they claimed to be British citizens, and "impressed" them to serve in the British navy. War fever swept the country. People heard about a speech by the British governor-general of Canada to the Indians telling them to do their worst on the frontier. A bill cutting off all trade with England passed the House of Representatives. It was defeated in the Senate only by the tie-breaking vote of Vice-President Adams.

The Federalists, who liked England, still wanted to avoid war. Hamilton saw his whole financial plan on the edge of ruin, since the country's revenue depended on the duties received from British imports. Hamilton urged Washington to try to make peace.

In May 1794, the President sent Chief Justice John Jay to London to try to make a treaty. Unfortunately for Jay, Hamilton had let the British know that the United States would not join Denmark and Sweden in an alliance against the British seizure of neutral shipping. Knowing that, the British had no reason to give in to Jay.

After a year's labor Jay returned home with the best terms he could get. But when the treaty was seen in America it was greeted with cries of outrage. Nothing had been accomplished in the area of maritime rights—one of the main reasons for seeking a treaty. Britain would not stop searching our vessels at sea nor cease "impressing" sailors considered to be British subjects. Great Britain did open India and the West Indies to American trading vessels, but only under tight restrictions. Shippers remained dissatisfied. Not a word was said about compensation for the slaves England had carried off during the Revolution.

The one really positive point Jay had won was England's agreement to leave the frontier fur posts in American territory by June 1, 1796. Nothing at all was done about the disputed boundary between Canada and the United States, the damages for ships seized by the English, or the debts Americans still owed British merchants. These items were left to a joint commission in the future. Though no one knew it at the time, joint commissions would become the chief means to settle British and American differences. At this point, the mention of such a future commission seemed just one more failure of Jay's Treaty.

Washington hesitated to send the treaty to the Senate. But he finally concluded that the treaty with all its faults was the only way to keep peace with Great Britain. In the Senate it was barely approved by the necessary two-thirds vote—and probably would not have been ratified at all without the prestige of the President behind it.

Pinckney's Treaty with Spain.

Jay's Treaty had one important, if unexpected, result. It made Spain fear that an alliance between England and the United States might follow. Europe's problems now became America's opportunity. Spain had made a separate peace with France, while England remained at war. Now Spain feared that England might work with the United States to seize the Spanish possessions in North America—Florida and Louisiana. Our special envoy Thomas Pinckney went to Madrid to seek the freedom of American citizens to navigate the Mississippi. He found the Spanish minister, Godoy, surprisingly eager to please.

By a treaty concluded in October 1795, Spain granted every point that Americans had been demanding for a dozen years: (1) free navigation of the Mississippi, (2) acceptance of 31° north latitude as the southern boundary of the United States, and (3) "right of deposit." This was the right to transfer cargoes at New Orleans from riverboats to ocean-going vessels without paying duty.

The Treaty of Greenville.

Also in 1795, following the total victory of General "Mad Anthony" Wayne at the Battle of Fallen Timbers in northwestern Ohio the previous year, the United States made a treaty with the Indians of the Northwest. The chiefs of the Delaware, Shawnee, Wyandot, Miami Confederacy, and other tribes agreed to open up most of the Ohio territory to settlement.

These three treaties of 1795 were important in establishing the security of the new American Republic. They reduced, for a time, the fear that Kentucky and Tennessee would join Spain. They brought peace, if only temporarily, to the North-

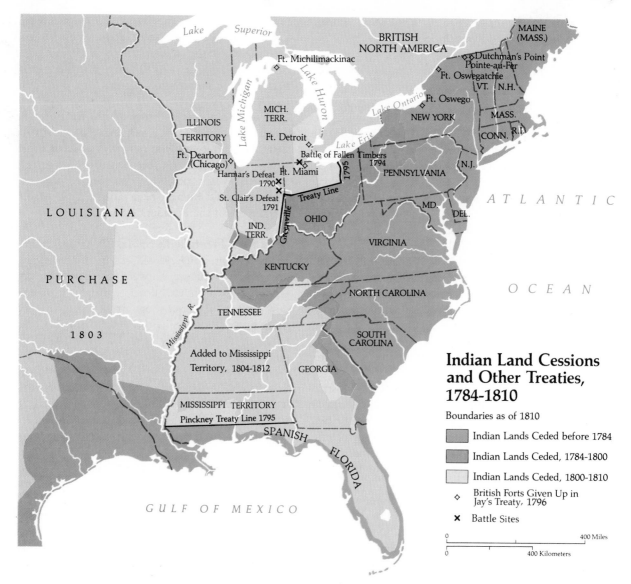

Indian Land Cessions and Other Treaties, 1784-1810

Boundaries as of 1810

	Indian Lands Ceded before 1784
	Indian Lands Ceded, 1784-1800
	Indian Lands Ceded, 1800-1810
◇	British Forts Given Up in Jay's Treaty, 1796
✕	Battle Sites

0   400 Miles
0   400 Kilometers

west. They gained recognition of the borders won from England in the Revolution. They enabled the United States for a few more years to stay out of the war that was raging in Europe. They allowed Washington to end his term with the nation at peace with the world.

The Whiskey Rebellion.

This busy—and success-ful—diplomacy strengthened the struggling young nation, and especially increased the influence of the Federalist party. So, too, had an event that oc-curred the previous year. In 1794 the farmers of western Pennsylvania protested against the whiskey

tax. This was an "excise" tax—an internal tax—passed a few years before to raise additional funds for the national government.

The whiskey tax angered farmers in the West because it was usual there to make grain (corn or wheat) into whiskey in order to carry it more easily across the mountains to market. Also, where specie and bank notes were in short supply, whiskey was used as a form of money. To the farmers Hamil-ton's excise tax on whiskey seemed to be a tax directed against them and their crops. They refused to pay the tax when the United States marshal tried to collect it, and in 1794 they staged a "rebellion." The governor of Pennsylvania thought the courts

After the Battle of Fallen Timbers, General Anthony Wayne negotiated the Treaty of Greenville, by which Indian tribes of the Northwest Territory ceded their lands to the United States. A member of Wayne's staff painted this picture, showing Wayne meeting with a group of Indians.

could handle the matter. But Washington, urged on by Hamilton, saw the "rebellion" as a direct attack on the authority of the government. Just as in the days of Daniel Shays, it seemed the state had become a victim of mob rule.

Fulfilling his duty under the Constitution to maintain a "republican form of government," Washington called out the militia. Fifteen thousand strong, it marched west to put down the farmers. In no mood to fight the militia, they returned to their homes. But the ringleaders were seized. Two of them were convicted of treason but were pardoned by the President, who wanted only to prove the strength of the new government. His decisive handling of this affair attracted supporters to the Federalist cause.

The Farewell Address.
In September 1796, in his "Farewell Address," Washington announced that he would not serve again. One of the most important statements ever made by an American President, it was largely written by Alexander Hamilton. Al-

though Washington never delivered it as a speech, it was published in the newspapers. Washington still called the United States an experiment. He urged his fellow citizens to remain loyal to the Union and to a republican form of government. He warned against sectionalism, foresaw the danger of secession, and cautioned against political partisanship. His most memorable warning was against "entangling alliances"—playing favorites in the community of nations.

The election of 1796.
The Federalist candidate for President in the election of 1796 was John Adams. His services to his country had put him far ahead of any other member of his party. The Republicans nominated Thomas Jefferson. In the electoral college, Adams won by a narrow margin—71 to 68.

Since he had the second largest number of votes, according to the Constitution Jefferson became Vice-President. Hamilton, who did not like the independent-minded Adams, had wanted someone in office who shared his belief in the virtues of the rich. That was not Adams. So Hamilton had tried to persuade the Federalist electors to leave Adams's name off their ballots and instead elect Adams's vice-presidential running mate, Thomas Pinckney, to the Presidency. But Adams's New England friends also knew how to use the electoral college. They simply left Pinckney's name off their ballots. The result was that the votes for Pinckney were fewer than those for Jefferson, so Jefferson became Vice-President.

Washington goes home. George Washington had led his country through its first difficult years. He had led the nation to victory in its battle for independence. A major influence in shaping the new Constitution, he had been the chief force in starting the new government. Now he had given the country time to grow by avoiding a needless war with England. Cold, practical, lacking the brilliance of Jefferson or Hamilton, he made up for his shortcomings by his unswerving devotion to his country. He deserved the country's gratitude. Still, some envious partisans accused him of kingly ambitions and rejoiced when he left public life.

SECTION 3 REVIEW

1. Identify or explain: Edmond Geñet, Jay's Treaty, Pickney's Treaty, Treaty of Greenville.

2. As Washington's second term opened, what problems did he face: (a) with England, (b) with Spain, (c) with France?

3. Why were some Americans upset by the French Revolution?

4. What dangers did Washington warn against in his Farewell Address?

5. **Identifying Central Issues.** What was the significance of the Whiskey Rebellion?

4. John Adams and the rise of parties

To John Adams now fell the difficult task of guiding a young nation divided by party strife at home and endangered by war in Europe. But Adams was no military hero. Short of stature, with an acid personality, he lacked Washington's enormous prestige.

Adams National Historic Site: photo by George Dow

John Adams was born in the house on the right. He and his wife, Abigail, later lived in the house on the left, and there John Quincy Adams was born. The two houses still stand in Quincy, Massachusetts, where the much larger family home may also be visited.

Sixty years of age when he became President, Adams was the descendant of a line of solid Massachusetts small farmers. He trusted neither the rich nor the poor, but only the wise and the able. And he had served his country well in the trying years of revolution. He had been in both the First and the Second Continental Congress. There he had helped write the petition to the king and the Declaration of Rights and Grievances, and had recommended Washington for commander of the army. Having served on the committee that wrote the Declaration of Independence, he then defended that document vigorously. His 80 committee assignments during the war (he chaired 25 of these committees!) included the crucial Board of War and Ordnance. Then he represented the new nation abroad—in England, France, and Holland. In his home state of Massachusetts, he was principal author of its new constitution of 1780. Working with Franklin and John Jay, he negotiated the peace treaty with Great Britain in 1783. Most recently he had filled the thankless position of Vice-President for eight years. There was no doubt of his patriotism, honesty, and courage.

Adams was, in fact, a great man. But he was also vain, willful, stubborn, prickly, and lacking in tact. Benjamin Franklin described him as "always an honest man, often a wise one, but sometimes and in some things, absolutely out of his senses." Confident of the rightness of his opinions, he made little attempt to harmonize conflicting views in his Cabinet, in the Congress, or in his party. He followed Washington in refusing to take account of political parties. But by his time party politics had already become fierce, and party demands could not be ignored.

The Cabinet.

Adams made his first, and one of his worst, mistakes when he retained the chief Cabinet officers of Washington's second term. These men, Secretary of State Timothy Pickering, Secretary of the Treasury Oliver Wolcott (Hamilton had resigned in 1795), Secretary of War James McHenry, and Attorney General Charles Lee were second-raters. Even worse, they were devoted friends of Adams's personal enemy, Alexander Hamilton, from whom they continued to take their orders. In Adams's defense, it might be said that, of course, there was still no tradition for Cabinet members to be replaced at the end of a President's term. This

was the first time the Presidency had changed. But even after he learned that these men were not really working for him, Adams waited too long to change his top command.

Renewed troubles with France.

Adams's administration was dominated by the problem of France. A new government of five men, called the Directory, had come into power in France in 1795. They had been angered by Jay's Treaty and by the recall of our minister, James Monroe. As a Republican, Monroe had been too friendly to the French for Federalist tastes. The French Directory began seizing our ships in their harbors, refused to receive C. C. Pinckney, Thomas Pinckney's brother, whom President Washington had sent to replace Monroe, and actually ordered Pinckney to leave France.

Angered by the treatment of our minister, Adams declared in a speech to Congress that we must convince France and the world that we were "not a degraded people, humiliated under a colonial spirit of fear." But since he was still determined to keep the nation at peace, he sent John Marshall and Elbridge Gerry to join Pinckney as a commission to deal with the French.

The XYZ Affair.

These envoys immediately ran into problems. The French foreign minister, Talleyrand, would not see them personally, but instead sent secret agents to meet them. The French agents told them that there could be no talks unless the United States apologized for President Adams's speech, promised to loan France $10 million, and paid a bribe of $250,000 to Talleyrand.

When they heard these insulting demands, the envoys answered, "No! no, not a sixpence." Marshall and Pinckney returned home at once. There they stirred the nation's patriotism and fervor against France by the story of their treatment. The whole incident was known as the "XYZ Affair," because the Secretary of State had substituted the letters X, Y, and Z for the names of the agents whom Talleyrand had sent to ask our commissioners for bribes.

Naval war with France.

Republicans and Federalists alike rallied to support Adams in his measures to compel respect for our envoys as "representatives of a great, free, powerful, and independent nation." For a rare moment in his life, the peppery

"Preparations for a War to Defend Commerce," William Birch entitled his 1800 engraving. It shows work on the frigate *Philadelphia,* which was not completed in time for the undeclared naval war with France.

John Adams was popular everywhere. Fellow citizens applauded his language of defiance. They bellowed the new national song, "Hail, Columbia." They adopted as a slogan (to serve again and again later in our history) the toast proposed at a banquet for the returning hero John Marshall: "Millions for defense, but not one cent for tribute!" Preparations for war were begun. Again Washington was called to lead the army, though it was agreed that he would not be expected to leave his home at Mt. Vernon unless there was open battle. Hamilton was to be second in command. A new Navy Department was created by Congress.

War was not formally declared, but Congress renounced the treaty with France that had been signed in 1778 and authorized our ships to prey upon French commerce. Actually, during the two years 1798–1800 a state of war at sea existed with France. More than 80 French ships were captured.

Talleyrand now saw that he could not threaten or bribe the United States. Not wanting war, he hastened to assure our minister to Holland that a new American commission would be received with due respect. At that moment President Adams, to his everlasting credit, resisted the demands of Hamilton and many other Americans (including his own Cabinet) that the nation should fight. That might have been a popular decision, but it would not have served the weak new nation. To the surprise of Federalist Hamiltonians, Adams sent a message to Congress simply nominating a new minister to France. He would send envoys to deal with this sly Talleyrand. Four days after the new envoys sailed, the upstart Napoleon Bonaparte overthrew the corrupt Directory.

Napoleon, intent on establishing his power in France and Europe, wanted no trouble with the United States. In September 1800, therefore, he signed an agreement that ended the treaty of alliance of 1778, thus freeing the United States from any obligation to help France in war. In return the United States gave up all claims against France for damages done to our shipping by French cruisers since 1793. This fair bargain enabled the United States to enter the 1800s at peace.

The Alien and Sedition Acts, 1798.

In 1798 when anger against the French had become the most violent, the Federalists took advantage of the situation. They passed a series of laws to suppress Republican opposition and insure power for their own party. But, in fact, they misjudged the temper of the nation. Their oppressive measures outraged many Americans and helped lead to the downfall of the Federalist party.

Leading Federalists believed—or pretended to believe—that most foreigners who came to the United States joined the Republicans. In the Naturalization Act, then, they extended the time it took to become a citizen from 5 to 14 years. In the Alien Act they gave the President at once the power to deport any alien he thought dangerous to the nation's security and then, in time of war, the power to deport or arrest all aliens who came from an enemy nation.

The Sedition Act was especially harsh. It provided a heavy fine and a jail term for any person found guilty of "combining and conspiring to oppose the execution of the laws, or publishing false, scandalous, or malicious writings against the President, Congress, or the government of the United States." These words were so vague and general that the Federalists could use the law to stop public criticism of the government by their opponents. This would spell the end of free representative government.

Some Federalist leaders, including Hamilton, actually disapproved of these laws that were pushed through Congress by extremist members of their party. John Adams had not promoted the mea-sures, but on the other hand he did not veto them or prevent their use against the Republicans.

The Virginia and Kentucky Resolutions.

The Sedition Act was used to silence Republican writers and newspaper editors who criticized President Adams. For example, Thomas Cooper, who later became president of South Carolina College, wrote a pamphlet in which he said Adams "was hardly in the infancy of political mistake" when he took office. Cooper admitted Adams had not yet interfered with a court of justice, though he implied Adams might still do so. For his writings, Cooper was fined $400 and spent six months in jail.

Only ten Republicans were convicted under the Sedition Act. Many other members of that party—but no Federalists—were tried. This attack on freedom of speech and the press outraged Republicans. Even some Federalists, most notably John Marshall, who was later to become Chief Justice, spoke out against it.

If the courts would not defend the people against the Alien and Sedition Acts or other tyrannical measures, who could do so? Madison and Jefferson believed that in this situation the only power able to oppose the federal government was the states. Resolutions passed by the Virginia legislature (and drafted by Madison) declared that each state had the right to judge the constitutionality of measures passed by Congress. The Kentucky Resolutions, which Jefferson wrote, went even further. He said that a state could declare acts of Congress "null and void" and that the rightful response to an unconstitutional act of Congress was *"nullification"* by the states.

The Constitution did not say who was to judge if Congress went beyond the powers granted in the Constitution. Madison and Jefferson believed the states had that right. The states' rights doctrine they championed would at last be carried so far that it would lead to civil war. Then it would be clear that the federal government, through its courts, had to be the judge of its own powers.

The election of 1800.

John Adams was proud of what he had accomplished as President. He had a right to be, even though his main achievement was to keep the nation out of war. He hoped, however, that in a second term he could make a more positive record.

But Adams was not reelected, in part because of the Alien and Sedition Acts, but mostly due to the enmity of Alexander Hamilton, who was a member of his own party. Republicans stumbled across Hamilton's bitter criticism of Adams and published it in their newspapers. At the same time Hamilton worked to defeat Adams in the electoral college in order to elect Adams's running mate, C. C. Pinckney. Hamilton's opposition took its toll. Meanwhile, of course, the Republicans had taken their own more careful steps to defeat Adams.

When all the electoral votes were counted, Adams had 65 votes, and Pinckney had 64. Then came the surprise. The Republicans had won a very close election, but their two candidates for President and Vice-President, Jefferson and Aaron Burr, each had 73 votes. The Republicans had made a serious mistake. Since the electors in the electoral college had to vote for two persons on their ballots without distinguishing between President and Vice-President, one Republican elector was supposed not to vote for Burr. That would have made Jefferson President and Burr Vice-President. Instead, they all voted for Burr. Since there was then a tie, according to the Constitution the election had to be decided in the House of Representatives.

As the country eagerly awaited the name of its next President, Congress gathered on Wednesday, February 11, 1801, in a partly completed Capitol in the raw new capital city of Washington. The House then voted on and off for several days. Some Federalists hoped to make Aaron Burr President. But Hamilton, despite his personal dislike for Jefferson, showed his patriotism and good judgment by opposing Burr. "Jefferson is to be preferred," he wrote his friends. "He is by far not so dangerous a man; and he has pretensions to character." Finally, on Monday, February 16, after receiving assurances that the public credit and the navy would be maintained, and that there would be no mass eviction of their fellow party members from office, the Federalists allowed Jefferson to be elected President.

After this election, the Twelfth Amendment to the Constitution was enacted in 1804. It provided for the naming of the President and the Vice-President separately on each elector's ballot.

The election of 1800 was the last time the Federalists came close to winning an election. But their Presidents—Washington and Adams—had served their country well. They put the nation on its way and set many useful precedents. They laid the foundation for a government based on broad construction of its powers. True enough, they failed to resolve the hard questions of the links between the executive and the legislature or between the central government and the states. That would take time—and in the end would cost the bloodshed of a civil war. Meanwhile they helped the nation grow strong by keeping the nation at peace during its critical early years.

John Adams, the last Federalist President, was a better man than history has often credited him with being. He sadly left the city of Washington early on the morning of Jefferson's inauguration and returned to Massachusetts. During the years that followed, he made up his differences with his former friend, Thomas Jefferson. They began a lively correspondence full of wit and wisdom that lasted the many years till their death. By an uncanny coincidence John Adams, then 90 years old, died in Massachusetts on the very same day that Jefferson, who was 83, died at Monticello in Virginia. That day was July 4, 1826, the fiftieth anniversary of the Declaration of Independence.

SECTION 4 REVIEW

1. How did it happen that Jefferson became Adams's Vice-President?

2. What was the XYZ Affair?

3. Why were the Alien and Sedition Acts passed?

4. Why was the Twelfth Amendment passed?

5. **Testing Conclusions.** Many people feel that President Adams's refusal to bow to any political party proved to be a foolish decision. Explain why you agree or disagree.

FOCUSING ON IDEAS

1. What lasting precedents did George Washington establish as President of the United States?

2. Why did the new government start out with a big national debt? How did paying the debt in full benefit the country?

3. Why did the Indians of the Northwest and Southeast form an alliance with the British and Spanish against the United States?

4. How did President John Adams avoid going to war with France between 1798 and 1800?

TAKING A CRITICAL LOOK

1. **Demonstrating Reasoned Judgment.** List in order of importance some of the Washington administration's major accomplishments. Justify your rankings.

2. **Making Comparisons.** How did Hamilton and Jefferson differ in their views of the ideal America? In which sections of the country were Hamilton's views most popular? Jefferson's? Why?

3. **Predicting Consequences.** The Whiskey Rebellion was a tax revolt. How do you think contemporary Americans would respond to what they considered unfair taxation?

YOUR REGION IN HISTORY

1. **Geography.** How large was the population of your state or region in 1790? What was its largest city?

2. **Culture.** The 1700s saw the rise of an American "aristocracy." Who would have fallen into this category in your region? Explain.

HISTORICAL FACTS AND FIGURES

Formulating Questions. Asking good questions is often the key to understanding a chart. Draw up a list of questions that will help people looking at the chart below understand Hamilton's grand plan for the Bank of the United States. Questions should draw forth information on the complex relationships that exist between the bank, the federal government, and private citizens in the United States.

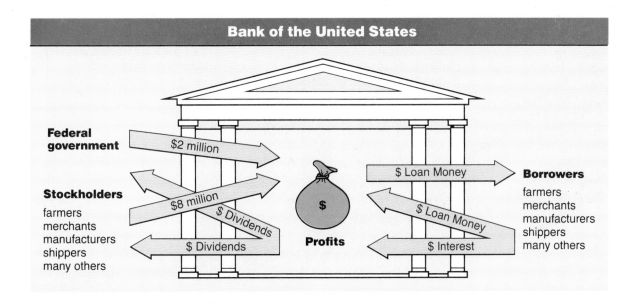

Bank of the United States

Federal government — $2 million
Stockholders: farmers, merchants, manufacturers, shippers, many others — $8 million — $ Dividends — $ Dividends — Profits
$ Loan Money — Borrowers: farmers, merchants, manufacturers, shippers, many others
$ Loan Money — $ Interest

MAKING CONNECTIONS

THEMES

This unit began on page 67 with the observation that winning the American Revolution and establishing a new nation was very much like trying to make thirteen clocks strike all at once:

> *To lead thirteen different colonies [or states] to take common action seemed next to impossible.*

This conclusion was supported by the three unit themes that are reprinted in **dark type** below. Use the time line and the information in Unit 2 to answer the questions that follow the unit themes.

1. **The British have trouble subduing the colonies because of the colonies' variety and lack of a critical center.**

   Why might the British have viewed the American colonies as "a monster with many heads" during the American Revolution?

2. **The states' desire for self rule and their fear of tyranny result in a weak central government under the Articles of Confederation.**

   Why did Americans eventually decide that a strong central government was necessary?

3. **The drafting and the ratification of a new constitution begin the process of binding Americans together into one nation.**

   How did the writing and ratification of the Constitution bring about not only a new government, but a change in the way Americans looked at themselves?

1765 Britain's Parliament passes the Stamp Act, a tax on goods the colonists used.

1775 Paul Revere warns Massachusetts residents that the British are planning to attack arms stored in Concord.

Events in American History

Events in World History

| 1760 | 1765 | 1770 | 1775 |

1788 Following New York's ratification, the Constitution is officially in effect.

1776 The Second Continental Congress issues the Declaration of Independence.

1777 The British plan to take control of the Hudson River, cutting off New England from the other colonies.

1780 An American militia captures 1200 British troops in a surprise attack in South Carolina.

1787 Daniel Shays leads a farmers' rebellion in western Massachusetts.

1787 The Federalist Papers argue for ratification of the United States Constitution.

1787 The Constitutional Convention begins in Philadelphia, Pennsylvania.

1784 An economic depression begins, burdening the young nation for the next five years.

1790 Alexander Hamilton proposes a plan for a National Bank.

1775 **1780** **1785** **1790** **1795** **1800**

1778 France enters the Revolutionary War on the side of the American colonists.

1789 The French Revolution begins, taking inspiration from the American Revolution.

1776 The British pour 32,000 troops into New York City, where 25,000 colonists live.

UNIT 3

E pluribus unum: One made from many
1800–1840

The Americans had won their independence and established a government. But they had not yet created a strong nation. The number of people was small and scattered over hundreds of square miles of wilderness. They had few roads and even fewer cities. The very vastness of the land—a source of pride and future power—was also a weakness. For the people tended to be more closely tied to their states and their regions than to the weak central government in its swampy forest clearing on the banks of the Potomac.

But the nation discovered new ways to grow. It fought a "second war of independence" with England. Its politics and political parties became ever more democratic. This created new traditions and fed national pride, which would begin to tie all the states and all the regions together. Americans were shaping a new kind of government.

THEMES IN AMERICAN HISTORY

- The nation discovers new ways to grow.
- The nation's growth is marked by the rise of two opposing forces: nationalism and sectionalism.
- The nation's political process becomes more democratic.

THEMES

This detail from Thomas Cole's "Sunny Morning on the Hudson" captures the wild grandeur of America the painter loved.

Museum of Fine Arts, Boston, M. and M. Karolik Collection

CHAPTER 7

Jefferson in power

Four of the first five Presidents of the United States were Virginia men. These were Washington, Jefferson, Madison, and Monroe. We usually call them the "Virginia dynasty." They had faith in the people.

Why did so many of our nation's first leaders come from a single state? An explanation lies in the special features of colonial Virginia. Young aristocrats like Washington and Jefferson and Madison and Monroe led a cozy life. A few families owned the largest tobacco plantations and most of the slaves. They not only ran the government, but members of these lucky families might hold more than one office. George Washington, for example, was at the same time a church vestryman, a justice of the peace, a commander of the militia, and a delegate to the House of Burgesses. This was aristocracy American-style.

For Virginia's representative government there had to be elections. But these were very different from today's rough-and-tumble contests. In our day, anybody can run for office and nearly every adult can vote. But not in colonial Virginia! There only property owners could vote, and only the well-to-do were eligible for high office. Virginia had no cities where unruly immigrants or discontented working people could secure a share in government. Is it any wonder that Virginia's aristocrats had faith in what *they* called representative government? The only kind of representative government they knew was safe and sane. Even the ownership of slaves helped to reinforce their belief in "representative" government. It meant that their poor workers had no hope of voting or sharing in the government.

When these Virginia aristocrats talked of "the people," they meant substantial property owners like themselves and other smaller property owners who respected their "betters." We can understand why they had a great deal less fear of "the people" and a great deal more confidence that "the people" would choose good representatives than did other thoughtful Americans of that age. But Northern leaders like John Adams and Alexander Hamilton knew the fickle big city mobs. They put their faith elsewhere.

1. The man and his policies

Thomas Jefferson became the President of a sharply divided country. The Federalists called him "godless" because he was no orthodox churchman, because he was so tolerant, and especially because he had supported the bloody French Revolution. They feared that this country too might soon be swept by a "reign of terror." But Thomas Jefferson's first term was to be one of the most successful presidencies in American history. A surprising number of Americans in all sections of the country were drawn into a united nation.

The new capital city. Jefferson was the first President of the United States to be inaugurated in the new capital, which his deal with Hamilton in 1790 had located on the Potomac River. The city had been laid out and surveyed in the following years. One of those who did this important job was Benjamin Banneker, a free black mathematician and scientist. Banneker was probably the first black civilian to work for the federal government.

The architect for the city had been a Frenchman, Major Pierre-Charles L'Enfant, who had served with the American army during the Revolutionary War. In 1801 the long vistas, grand avenues, and noble buildings he had envisioned for the wilderness were far from complete. Washington was only in its first stages of construction. The two wings of the new Capitol building, on a height overlooking the future city, were nearly finished, but the rotunda in the middle was still open to the skies. Since there were no hotels, the members of Congress stayed in nearby boardinghouses.

Between the Capitol and the President's house, one and a half miles away, lay swamp and woodland crossed only by a muddy track which was grandly named Pennsylvania Avenue.

L'Enfant's 1792 plan of Washington showed broad avenues crisscrossing the capital.

This portrait of Thomas Jefferson shows the Natural Bridge in Virginia, a spectacle which he much admired. His *Notes on Virginia* describes these natural wonders.

The President's "palace" was not yet known as the White House. It only got that name after it was burned by the British in the War of 1812. Then the Acquia Creek sandstone of which it was built was painted white to cover the scorch marks from the fire. The house was still unfinished in March 1801, but it had been lived in during the previous fall and winter by President Adams and his family. When the sharp-tongued Abigail Adams saw the new capital city for the first time, she described it as having "houses scattered over a space of ten miles, and trees and stumps in plenty." Mrs. Adams estimated it would take 30 servants to run the "castle of a house" when it would be completed. Meanwhile, she dried the family wash in the unplastered East Room during stormy weather.

"We need nothing here," one senator reported, "but men, women, and other little trifles of the kind to make our city perfect." In sober fact this new federal city had no shops, no theaters, no libraries—and few people. The legislators suffered the discomforts of monks living in a monastery, but they had taken no monastic vows.

Thomas Jefferson. On March 4, 1801, the day of his inauguration, Thomas Jefferson stepped out the door of the boardinghouse where he was staying and walked the short distance to the Capitol. He was escorted by a crowd of congressmen and other citizens.

Looking like a "tall, raw-boned farmer," he avoided the pomp that Washington and Adams had thought necessary for the President. Six feet tall, thin and angular, with light-colored hair tinged with red, Jefferson, unlike his predecessors, did not wear a wig. His clothing was—depending upon your point of view—either casual or just plain sloppy.

In place of the formal weekly receptions begun by Washington there were now informal gatherings. Citizens, with or without invitations, thronged to shake the President's hand. But life in the White House was far from simple, for Jefferson was still a southern aristocrat. He liked to live well, and during his years in Paris he had developed a taste for elegant French cooking. At his gracious dinner parties in the President's mansion, his lucky guests enjoyed a French chef's masterpieces. These were washed down by French wines of choice vintages. In a single year Jefferson's wine bill came to $2800.

Relaxed and easygoing in a small company, Jefferson was a charming conversationalist. But he disliked crowds. He was a halting public speaker, and he generally avoided formal public speeches. He did not follow the practice—begun by Washington and Adams—of addressing Congress in person. Jefferson said that he did not want to act like a king speaking to Parliament from a throne. But

Thomas Jefferson designed his home Monticello after an ancient Roman building that he saw in the south of France. The pencil and ink drawing below is done in Jefferson's own hand and reflects his attention to the smallest detail. It shows the first floor with the front hall where Jefferson displayed sculpture and curiosities of natural history. Today Monticello, near Charlottesville, Virginia, continues to impress visitors with its beauty and the ingenuity of its builder.

Jefferson's entry in his "Garden Book" notes an untimely killing frost on May 5 in 1774. Luckily some fruits and vegetables survived.

perhaps this was just an excuse to save himself from the public appearances which he never enjoyed.

Jefferson believed that slavery was a great moral evil. Still, he saw no easy way to abolish the institution that supported the southern plantation system. "We have the wolf by the ears," he once wrote, "and we can neither hold him, nor safely let him go. Justice is in one scale, and self-preservation in the other." He was himself the owner of large plantations and about 150 slaves. But unlike George Washington, he did not free his slaves upon his death.

A remarkably versatile man, Jefferson was also one of the best American architects of his age. He designed his own home in Virginia, and throughout his life he worked to improve it. We can still visit the delightful Monticello and can enjoy the gardens he planned and planted. We can admire his ingenious contraptions including a clock two stories high, designed to alert the household to the hours of their duties. To this house he brought his beloved wife, Martha Wayles Skelton, in 1772. She bore six children—four of whom died in childhood. When she herself died only ten years after her marriage,

Jefferson was plunged in grief. Partly to recover from this tragedy, he threw himself into an active public life.

Jefferson was also a surveyor, a philosopher, a scientist, and an inventor. At ease in French, Italian, and Spanish, as well as Latin and Greek, he corresponded with the eminent thinkers of his day wherever they were. He declared that they were all citizens of a worldwide "Republic of Letters."

The inaugural address. In his inaugural address Jefferson tried to play down the differences between himself and his opponents. He said they were "all Republicans, all Federalists" in their devotion to the Union. He promised (1) "equal and exact justice to all men" of every shade of political and religious opinion; (2) friendship with all nations but no alliances; (3) respect for the rights of the states while still preserving the "constitutional vigor" of the national government; (4) encouragement of agriculture and commerce; (5) freedom of speech, press, and elections; (6) economy and honesty in the management of the country's finances.

This was hardly a program to frighten the Federalists. Jefferson saw that many Federalists were unhappy with their leaders and were ready to become Republicans if he followed a moderate course. Elected by only a narrow margin, he had to widen the base of his public support if he was to govern successfully.

In later years Jefferson called his election "the revolution of 1800." He believed that election had turned the country away from militarism and monarchy. But he probably exaggerated those dangers. John Adams had already saved the nation from militarism by avoiding war with France, and there was never a real threat of monarchy.

Jefferson, unlike Hamilton, did not want to see an industrialized nation of cities. He hoped the country could remain a community of farmers who governed themselves in local assemblies. The government in Washington should confine itself, he thought, to managing the nation's dealings with foreign powers. Such a task could be performed by only a few public servants. Pursuing this policy, Jefferson aimed to reduce the army and navy and to apply the public revenue to paying off the public debt. No longer, Jefferson said, would the government "waste the labors of the people under the pretense of taking care of them."

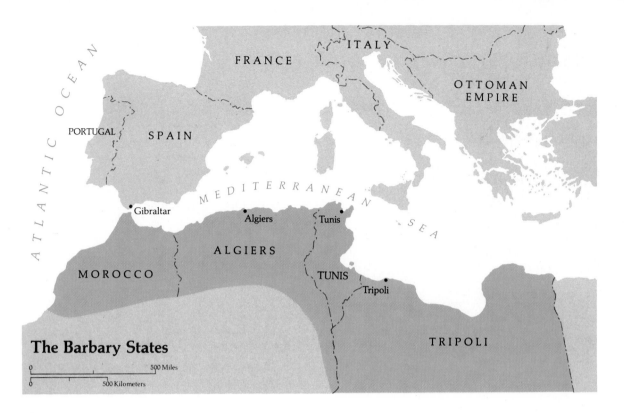

The Barbary States

0   500 Miles

0   500 Kilometers

For his Cabinet Jefferson selected the ablest men, including the architect of the Constitution, James Madison of Virginia, to be Secretary of State and Albert Gallatin, a brilliant Swiss-born financier from Pennsylvania, to be Secretary of the Treasury.

Following Jefferson's ideas Gallatin insisted on strict economy in government. He introduced a modern budget with specific sums for each item of national expense. The amount of money spent on the army and navy was reduced by half, and about 70 percent of the nation's revenue, more than $7 million a year, was used to pay off the national debt.

The Alien and Sedition Acts, which had expired at the end of the Adams administration, were not renewed. A new naturalization act was passed, restoring the short five-year waiting period for those who wanted to become citizens. The Bank of the United States was allowed to continue, as was the tariff. But the excise tax that had started the Whiskey Rebellion was repealed. There was not a great deal to distinguish Jefferson's policies from those of the Federalists.

The Barbary pirates. We remained at peace with the nations of Europe during Jefferson's first term. Our commerce and wealth increased rapidly. But one foreign problem grew more serious as our commerce expanded. For many years the Arab rulers of the Barbary States on the north coast of Africa (Morocco, Algiers, Tunis, and Tripoli) had sent out pirates to seize ships on the ocean, especially in the Mediterranean Sea, and hold their crews for ransom. The European nations paid tribute to these pirates and kidnappers as a cheap substitute for war. And we had done the same. In the decade 1790–1800 we gave them "presents" amounting to $2 million.

Jefferson was determined to put an end to the payments to these racketeers. So in spite of his devotion to peace and economy, he sent naval squadrons to punish the pirates. This was a costly business, and Congress had to impose an extra 2.5 percent tax on imports as a "Mediterranean Fund." But the results justified the sacrifice. The peace concluded with Tripoli in January 1805 discouraged the piratical raids.

The other Barbary States continued to ask for payments, though at a lower rate, and after the War of 1812 this problem had to be faced again. In 1815 Stephen Decatur, who had been a hero in the earlier

UNDER ☆ MY ☆ WINGS ☆ ☆ ☆ EVERY ☆ THING ☆ ☆ ☆ PROSPERS

In 1803 when this view was painted, New Orleans was small but bustling. The artist thought that as part of the United States the town would thrive.

war with Tripoli, was sent with a fleet to the Mediterranean. He promptly seized two Algerian frigates. He then forced the Algerian ruler to sign a treaty renouncing both raids and tribute. Decatur also received similar guarantees from Tunis and Tripoli. Although in 1804 and in 1815 our navy had performed an international service, leading the world toward freedom of the seas, the problem of the pirates was not entirely solved until France conquered Algiers in 1830.

SECTION 1 REVIEW

1. Identify or explain: Benjamin Banneker, Pierre-Charles L'Enfant, Monticello, "revolution of 1800," Albert Gallatin, Barbary States, Stephen Decatur.

2. Who were the "Virginia dynasty"? How did they gain experience in public affairs and faith in representative government?

3. Characterize Thomas Jefferson.

4. **Identifying Central Issues.** Name several accomplishments in Jefferson's first term.

2. Buying Louisiana

Jefferson's two basic political doctrines were strict adherence to the letter of the Constitution and severe economy in spending public money. He was a great leader because he could adapt his old beliefs to new needs without endangering the liberties of the people. Suddenly events in Europe caused him to stretch the Constitution as he had never thought would be necessary, and at one stroke to spend more money than any Federalist had ever dared.

The Mississippi River: artery for a continental nation. As more and more Americans settled between the Appalachian Mountains and the Mississippi River they floated their crops down many rivers—the Wisconsin, the Illinois, the Kaskaskia, the Wabash, the Miami, the Ohio, the Cumberland, the Yazoo, and still others. All these ran into what Americans called the "Father of Waters," the great Mississippi—down to the Gulf of Mexico, into the ocean, and out to the world. An enemy holding the mouth of the Mississippi could shut the Westerners off, destroy their trade, and make their crops useless.

President Jefferson understood this very well. His own state of Virginia was a land of many rivers. Jefferson wanted Americans to move out west over the mountains and start new farms, for he believed in the farmers' virtues. And the Mississippi River was the highway that made possible the life of the western farmer. When Jefferson became President, he began to worry over how to keep open the western Americans' highway to the world. It looked at first as though he would have to deal with Spain, which possessed the land on both sides of the mouth of the river.

Napoleon's dream. But suddenly everything changed. Napoleon, now dictator of France, had some grand and complex plans. He had a scheme to create a new French Empire in America. The former French lands west of the Mississippi had been named "Louisiana" after the French King Louis XIV. These lands had been ceded to Spain as a result of the wars of the eighteenth century. Napoleon, who had wonderful powers of persuasion (reinforced by his large French armies), actually got the Spanish to give him back all of "Louisiana." For reasons of his own, this had been accomplished in secret.

When word leaked out that the Mississippi River was no longer controlled by weak and decadent Spain, but by the clever, powerful, and ambitious Napoleon, Americans were more worried than ever. And they had good reason because the French soon showed that they knew how to use New Orleans. They shrewdly made this gateway to the Mississippi into a kind of tollgate. The French understood that they could extract whatever price they pleased for allowing Americans to pass through. To people who lived along the Mississippi River and its tributaries, the freedom to carry their produce out to the world was a matter of life and death.

When President Jefferson heard that France was taking control of the mouth of the Mississippi, he was upset. He wrote to Robert Livingston, the American minister at Paris, that though the United States had always looked upon France as her "natural friend" there was

> on the globe one single spot, the possessor of which is our natural and habitual enemy. It is New Orleans, through which the produce of three-eighths of our territory must pass to market. . . . France, placing herself in that door,

assumes to us the attitude of defiance. . . . The day that France takes possession of New Orleans . . . [we will be forced to] marry ourselves to the British fleet and nation.

Then Jefferson sent his friend James Monroe of Virginia as his special ambassador to France. Jefferson told Monroe and Livingston to buy from France the land at the mouth of the Mississippi or to find some other way to guarantee that western Americans could come in and out of their river. If there was no other way, they were to buy New Orleans and all the lands on the east bank of the river (then called West Florida). For this little piece Congress provided $2 million. But Congress told them they could pay up to $10 million if they had to.

Haiti upsets Napoleon's plans. Meanwhile, France was having trouble in the Caribbean. Before Napoleon could recapture the glories of the French Empire, he would have to retake the island of Haiti, then called Saint Dominique. Only the small western end of the island had been in the hands of the French before the French Revolution, yet it produced far more wealth for the empire than any other part.

Of the 600,000 people living on Haiti, 500,000 were slaves. They revolted during the French Revolution and slaughtered the whites. At that point, the French National Assembly abolished slavery and appointed the black genius Pierre Dominique Toussaint L'Ouverture as commander in chief of the armies on the island. Soon Toussaint ruled all of Haiti. But the French government got more than it bargained for. Toussaint had a mind of his own and would not be a lackey of the French. Napoleon, always mindful of military strategy, believed that he had to command the island if he was to build his grand new French Empire. Late in 1801 Napoleon sent out from France 25,000 crack troops under the command of his brother-in-law, General LeClerc, to conquer Toussaint and reduce the people of Haiti to slavery once again. At that point, the future of Louisiana, and perhaps of the United States, hinged on the actions of Toussaint L'Ouverture and his black followers.

As the second step in the revival of the French Empire, a great expedition was formed to sail for Louisiana in September 1802. But it never sailed because Haiti had not yet been reconquered. Toussaint was captured by treachery, but still the war went on. By January 1803 the French General LeClerc was dead of fever, Haiti was a ruin, and the French army had been destroyed by its black opponents and by yellow fever. Tons of expensive supplies had been lost. General Rochambeau, who succeeded LeClerc, wrote home that he must have 35,000 new troops to put down the blacks.

Napoleon decides to sell Louisiana.

Napoleon was a man who could make up his mind quickly. He could change his mind just as quickly. Since he could not control Haiti, he wondered how he could hold huge Louisiana. Without telling anyone, he suddenly decided to get what he could for his American empire. When the Americans in Paris offered to buy the small piece of land around the entrance to the Mississippi River, there was an amazing reply. Napoleon would *not* sell or even rent them that little piece. But he *would* sell them the whole of Louisiana!

Napoleon's offer to sell all of Louisiana was the last answer Monroe and Livingston had expected. They were not prepared for it. What should they do? Should they simply tell Napoleon they could give no answer till they had word from the President and Congress back in Washington? That would take weeks—or maybe even months—and by then the changeable Napoleon might very well say the deal was all off. Or should they, for the sake of their country, do what they really had no power to do? Should they snatch up this unexpected bargain and then pray that the people back home would support them?

This was one of the fateful moments of American history. It was not surprising that the French dictator had made a bold decision. But the young United States was a representative government under a Constitution that carefully described and limited the powers of the Congress. Could this self-governing nation match Napoleon's boldness? Or were the people of the Republic doomed to be slow and timid?

The American ministers in Paris, Livingston and Monroe, took the bold and dangerous way. They decided to take up Napoleon's offer. On their own judgment they offered $15 million for all Louisiana. And Napoleon accepted. As soon as the deal was closed, they began wondering whether what they would have to share was praise or blame. It was some years before either of them dared claim any credit for this move.

Jefferson makes a hard decision.

When the news finally reached the United States, it was greeted by shock, delight, and dismay. These two Americans, some complained, had been sent to Paris simply to buy a small piece of land in order to keep the riverways open in the West. Instead, they had allowed a whimsical dictator to trap them into buying half a billion acres of worthless wilderness!

This was perhaps the greatest test of statesmanship that Jefferson ever had to face. He was on the spot. The Constitution said nothing at all about whether or how Congress could buy land from a foreign country. Again and again, in many other cases, Jefferson had argued that Congress had only those powers that the Constitution had assigned in so many words. Maybe the power to buy land from foreign countries had been left out of the Constitution *on purpose*—to prevent the United States from playing the dangerous, old-fashioned game of empire. The people of the new United States had tried to escape from the ways of the Old World, where the rulers were in the habit of buying and selling, bartering and gambling faraway lands and unknown peoples.

Now would Jefferson go against everything he had been saying for years? If he had been weak, he would have been afraid to change his mind. But he decided to show the same courage that Livingston and Monroe had shown in Paris. It was harder for him, because he had to stand up and change his mind in public. All his enemies were there to hoot at him. Still, Jefferson decided to ask the members of Congress to vote the money to buy Louisiana. He asked them to forget technicalities—"metaphysical subtleties" is what he called them—and instead to think of the future of the nation. He asked the Congress to approve afterwards what it had not been foresighted enough to authorize in advance.

After long and bitter debate, the Congress agreed. In October 1803, when the Senate ratified the treaty with Napoleon, Louisiana became the property of the United States. Within a year, an American governor was sitting in New Orleans, where he could see that the Mississippi River would stay open. Western Americans would have their highway to the world.

The Mississippi River Basin

☐ Drainage Area of the Mississippi River

0   500 Miles

0   500 Kilometers

GULF OF MEXICO

A new world. The Louisiana Purchase was a triumph in more ways than we can count. It was one of the first modern proofs that in a battle of wits between a dictator and a government of the people the popular government does not need to lose. It showed that a people could have a Constitution to protect them against tyrants, and still make speedy decisions. If courageous leaders did what the nation needed, the people's representatives would approve.

And the Louisiana Purchase provided far more than a mere pathway from western America to the world. It helped make the new nation itself into a new world. The Louisiana Purchase *doubled* the area of the United States. It made it possible for Americans to keep going west—far across the

Mississippi River. It made it possible to carry the Add-a-State Plan westward to the Pacific. It made it possible to build a continent-wide Empire for Liberty. Some people from eastern states had opposed Jefferson's purchase of Louisiana because they feared that too many new states might be carved out of the West. Then the United States would no longer be an Atlantic-seacoast nation. The original thirteen would no longer run the Union.

In time, thirteen new states and parts of states, some of the richest land in the nation, would be formed from the Louisiana Purchase. The timid Easterners were wrong in imagining what the United States ought to be. The first thirteen states

OREGON COUNTRY
(U.S. and British)

BRITISH NORTH AMERICA

Astoria

Columbia R. 1805

Lewis and Clark 1806

Lewis Party 1806

Boundary Uncertain

Lake Superior

Missouri R.

Clark Party 1806

Ft. Mandan

Snake R.

Yellowstone R.

LOUISIANA

Pike 1805-1806

Lake Michigan

MICH. TERR

PURCHASE

Lewis and Clark 1804

Ft. Dearborn (Chicago)

North Platte R.

INDIANA TERRITORY

South Platte R.

Platte R.

Pikes Peak

1803

Missouri R.

St. Louis

Colorado R.

Pike 1806-1808

KENTUCKY

Santa Fe

TENNESSEE

Arkansas R.

PACIFIC OCEAN

SPANISH POSSESSIONS

Red R.

MISSISSIPPI TERRITORY

Natchitoches

Pike 1806-1808

WEST FLORIDA (Spanish)

**Lewis and Clark and Pike
Explore the West**

New Orleans

Chihuahua

San Antonio

← Route of Lewis and Clark

← Route of Pike

Rio Grande

GULF OF MEXICO

0 ——————— 500 Miles
0 ——————— 500 Kilometers

were nothing but a beginning: a starting line for the race across North America to the Pacific. There had been other one-ocean nations. Ours was to be a two-ocean nation.

The exact outlines of what we had bought in the Louisiana Purchase were uncertain. No one, not Jefferson or even Napoleon himself, knew exactly how far Louisiana reached up north or out west. But these vague boundaries would be gateways for new states of the great new American Union. Napoleon had provided Americans with expandable boundaries for their Empire for Liberty. The Louisiana Purchase freed Americans from the sharp, confining western boundary of the Mississippi River. The nation would no longer be imprisoned by the borders of the old British Empire.

The Lewis and Clark expedition. The Louisiana Territory roused widespread interest, for it occupied about half of the vast expanse stretching 1700 miles from the Mississippi to the Pacific coast. Jefferson was curious about the area. Indeed, even before the purchase, he had made secret plans to explore the lands beyond the Mississippi. Now Congress appropriated $2500 "to send intelligent officers with ten or twelve men, to explore even to the western ocean." They were to look for a water route to the Pacific, to study the Indian tribes, the rocks, the plants, and animals of the region. The expedition, after passing the Rockies, would be moving into territory beyond the western boundary of the United States. But this did not appear to trouble the President. He chose his private secretary, a captain in the army named Meriwether Lewis, to lead the expedition. William Clark, the younger brother of George Rogers Clark, was his lieutenant.

Lewis and Clark, with about 40 men, including Clark's black servant York, started westward from the mouth of the Missouri River in the spring of 1804. They spent the winter of 1804–1805 at Fort Mandan, a trading post in present-day North Dakota. There they hired Toussaint Charbonneau, a French-Canadian fur trapper, and his wife Sacajawea, a Shoshone Indian, as interpreters. Sacajawea, carrying her infant child, guided the expedition and persuaded the Shoshones to help them. Without her, it is doubtful the expedition could have been successful.

During the summer of 1805, the explorers crossed the "Great Divide" in the Rocky Mountains, and by November they had reached the Columbia River, where they began a turbulent descent. On December 3, 1805, in a fierce, cold rainstorm they reached the Pacific Ocean. There Clark carved on a tall yellow pine tree, "William Clark December 3rd 1805. By land from the U. States in 1804 and 1805."

This historic moment confirmed the claim of the United States to the whole Oregon region. The claim had been based on the discovery of the mouth of the Columbia River in 1792 by Robert Gray, captain of a fur-trading ship out of Boston. But the Lewis and Clark expedition did even more. It began to sketch in details of the vast heartland that the nation had purchased. The samples of rocks and plants and animals the explorers brought back revealed unsuspected natural treasures.

About the same time (1805–1807) the daring Captain Zebulon Pike, after exploring the upper Mississippi, ventured as far west as the Rockies. There he saw and described one of the continent's grandest mountains, which came to be called Pikes Peak. Then Pike turned southward. After he crossed into Spanish territory he was picked up by Spanish soldiers. They took him first to their settlement at Santa Fe and then on to Chihuahua. There they questioned him, took all his papers, and let him go. When Pike returned home, he gave the government valuable information on the number and types of troops that Spain had in the area.

Pike also wrote a description of the lands that he had crossed. From his report of wide sandy deserts came the misleading idea that these lands were not

In order to report on all they had seen, Lewis and Clark kept journals illustrated with drawings, such as this one of a wild fowl.

worth much—that the heart of the continent was "the Great American Desert."

The Federalist protest. The Louisiana Purchase relieved the economic fears of the western settlers and made Jefferson popular with them. But the Federalists saw the Purchase as a threat to their party and all they believed in. They feared that the settlers of the new lands would support the Jeffersonian Republicans. If those settlers were brought into the Union with all the rights of the earlier citizens of the United States, they would soon control Congress. Then the Federalist party would represent only a few states on the Atlantic fringe. The new states, they thought, would surely pass laws unfairly favoring farmers and debtors and damaging to the commercial and banking interests of the East.

In the spring of 1804 some New England Federalists, under the lead of Senator Timothy Pickering of Massachusetts, became desperate. They actually considered breaking up the Union and setting up a northern confederacy. When Hamilton opposed the idea, they turned to Aaron Burr and promised him the presidency of the new confederacy if he could bring in his state of New York.

Burr, who had not been renominated by his party for a second term as Vice-President, now ran as a Federalist for governor of New York. From this position, it was hoped, he could make the state part of the proposed confederacy. But Hamilton put his patriotism above his party loyalty. Distrusting Burr, he joined with the Republicans to keep the ambitious Vice-President out of a position where he might disrupt the Union.

Burr was badly beaten in the election. He blamed his loss on Hamilton, who had also helped to keep him from the Presidency in 1800. During the campaign, Burr claimed that Hamilton had expressed "a despicable opinion of him," and he used this as an excuse to challenge Hamilton to a duel. So it was that the two men faced one another with pistols on the banks of the Hudson River at Weehawken, New Jersey, early in the morning of July 11, 1804. After each had fired a shot, Hamilton fell mortally wounded. Washington's brilliant Secretary of the Treasury, the leader of the Federalist party, died the following day. Burr was forced to flee murder charges in both New Jersey and New York. The secessionist plans of the New England Federalists soon collapsed.

The Burr conspiracy. After this, the public career of the charming and talented, but erratic and ambitious, Aaron Burr went steadily downward. Since his duel with Hamilton had destroyed his political position in New York, he sought a new career out west.

What Burr really intended to do has never been clear. He may have hoped to seize New Orleans and then set up an independent country there. Perhaps he planned to conquer northern Mexico and carve an empire out of Spanish territory. Maybe his aim was quite innocent—simply to plant a colony of the United States west of the Mississippi. It is possible that he did not know what he was going to do but hoped to grasp the main chance. For some of his schemes he actually tried to secure aid from both the British and the Spanish.

Burr's trips to the West finally aroused suspicion in Washington. Then Burr was betrayed by the governor of Louisiana, General James Wilkinson, who had been involved with Burr's plots. To save himself, Wilkinson reported a part of Burr's plans to Jefferson, who ordered Burr to be arrested.

Burr was charged with treason and tried in Richmond, Virginia, in August 1807. Although Jefferson was eager to have Burr convicted, Chief Justice John Marshall defined treason in such a way that Burr was acquitted. Later, Burr returned to his prosperous law practice in New York, where he lived to a ripe age.

The trial of Aaron Burr is a landmark in the history of American liberties. President Jefferson disliked Burr and probably would have been glad to see him jailed for any reason. But, under the constitutional definition of treason, it had to be proved that Burr was guilty of "levying war on the United States." Chief Justice Marshall, insisting on the letter of the Constitution, instructed the jury that Burr must have made open war on the country and that there had to be two witnesses to his act. Respecting these requirements, the jury failed to convict Burr. Marshall's strict definition was at least partly due to his dislike of Jefferson. But, whatever his motives, the result was good for the nation. After the Burr precedent it would be difficult for the party in power to muzzle political opponents with a charge of treason. Ever since, trials for treason have been rare in the United States.

SECTION 2 REVIEW

1. Identify: Robert Livingston, James Monroe, Toussaint L'Ouverture, Sacajawea, Zebulon Pike, Aaron Burr, Timothy Pickering.

2. What was Napoleon's dream for Louisiana? How did events in Haiti upset his plans?

3. What were some of the major problems that Jefferson faced in asking Congress to approve the Louisiana Purchase?

4. How did the Louisiana Purchase change the United States?

5. What were the results of the Lewis and Clark expedition?

6. Why did some Federalists oppose the Louisiana Purchase?

7. **Drawing Conclusions.** What did Aaron Burr's trial accomplish?

3. Jefferson, Marshall, and the courts

During his first term Jefferson had tried to keep the Federalists happy. He had been moderate in his approach to most problems. He had even managed to help New England merchants (mainstay of the Federalist party) by his attack on the Barbary pirates who were menacing their commerce. New England fishermen were pleased that he supported a bounty on codfish.

The "midnight judges" and the patronage. At one point, however, Jefferson directly attacked the Federalists. After their loss of the Presidency and of Congress in the 1800 elections, the Federalists tried to keep control of the federal courts and of as many other offices as possible. In the Judiciary Act of 1801, passed just before they went out of power, they had actually increased the number of judges and added some minor judicial offices. They intended, of course, to fill these places with appointees from their own party before Jefferson and his Republicans took office on March 4. President Adams hastily nominated Federalists for the new positions, and they were quickly confirmed by the Senate. In order to put a small army of Federalists into these important permanent jobs, Adams signed some of their commissions on his final night in office. The last-minute appointees were sneeringly called "the midnight judges."

Adams had spent his last days seizing every chance to maintain Federalist influence by appointing many lesser officers: collectors of customs, consuls, postmasters, and clerks.

Jefferson was angered by this attempt of the defeated Federalists to keep "a dead clutch on the patronage." Once in office, he sent word to all those whose commissions had not yet been delivered to consider the appointments as never having been made. His first Congress then quickly repealed the Judiciary Act of 1801.

In this way began the first struggle between the political parties over the right to fill the offices of government with members of their own party. The struggle would never cease. The party going out of power always wanted to keep its supporters in office. Yet the victors in the election assumed that they had a right to appoint officials who supported their party. Jefferson naturally believed that he should have Republicans helping him in govern-

National Portrait Gallery, Smithsonian Institution

Keen-witted and persuasive, John Marshall was Chief Justice of the United States for 34 years.

ment offices if he was to do his best. Also this would help build a strong political party. After refusing to honor the commissions that Adams had signed at the end of his term, Jefferson picked Republicans for these posts. Whenever a job opened up due to a death or retirement, a Republican was appointed. In this way, by the end of his first term, Jefferson had named members of his own party to about half the highest positions in the government.

There was one position, however, that he had not been able to do anything about. The high office of

Chief Justice of the Supreme Court was held by his cousin and fellow Virginian, John Marshall. In his personality and his manners Marshall was much like Jefferson. He was sloppy in his dress and easygoing. Like Jefferson he had a brilliant and vigorous mind. And like Jefferson he insisted on seeing things his own way. But there were hardly any issues on which the two great men agreed. Before Marshall's appointment, it did not seem that the Supreme Court would play a major role in shaping the new nation. But under Marshall's leadership the Court became an active force protecting private property from state interference and building a strong central government.

Marbury *v.* Madison. When Jefferson refused to deliver the commissions signed by Adams, he gave Chief Justice Marshall the chance he had been looking for. One of Adams's "midnight" appointees, William Marbury, applied to the Supreme Court for a writ (a written court order) commanding Secretary of State James Madison to deliver his commission (already signed and sealed by President Adams) as justice of the peace. Marshall used the case to assert—even to create—crucial powers for the Supreme Court. The case of *Marbury* v. *Madison*, heard by the Supreme Court in February 1803, would become a landmark in American history.

Chief Justice Marshall said that Marbury had a right to his commission as a justice of the peace. But he did not let the matter rest there. If he had, Marbury's name would be unknown in American history. Instead, Marshall went on to declare that the section of the Judiciary Act of 1789 that gave the Supreme Court the right to issue writs in cases like Marbury's was unconstitutional, since no such right was granted in the Constitution. As a result, Marshall concluded there was no way for Marbury to get his commission from Madison.

The important question, of course, was not whether the unknown William Marbury should hold the lowly office of justice of the peace. Of the greatest significance to the nation was whether the Supreme Court had the power to declare a law of the land unconstitutional. In his brilliant, if devious, decision the strong-willed Chief Justice answered that question with a resounding, epoch-making Yes!

The Founding Fathers had, in fact, assumed that the Supreme Court would have the power to declare acts of Congress unconstitutional. But they had not put that power in so many words in the Constitution. So by a strict reading of the Constitution the Court had no such right. Nor had it ever used the right since the Supreme Court was created in 1789. Now in 1803 the Court suddenly assumed the right of *judicial review* in its role as guardian of the Constitution. The leading role ever since of the Supreme Court in American history has followed from this bold decision of Chief Justice Marshall.

The Supreme Court makes its decisions by a majority vote. In Marshall's day, when there were only six justices on the Supreme Court, any four of the justices had the power to overrule the President and the Congress on the meaning of the Constitution. Today, when there are nine justices on the Court, this power rests in the hands of five justices. In few other nations have the courts held such powers.

An attempt to change the courts by impeachment. Jefferson and the Republicans feared the power of judges. They were appointed for life, and there was no way for the Jeffersonians—or anybody else—to remove them except by the long impeachment process. What guarantee was there that these judges (who did not owe their positions to the voters) would show a proper respect for the will of the majority? Of course the Republicans feared the judges more because so many happened to be Federalists.

The Republicans started impeachment proceedings against several judges. Most important was their trial of Samuel Chase of the Supreme Court. Though a signer of the Declaration of Independence, Chase was open to attack. In his charges to juries in cases brought under the Sedition Act, he had gone out of his way to denounce Republicans. He called them "Jacobins" and "revolutionaries." The trial of Justice Chase before the Senate in January 1805 was especially dramatic. It was presided over by the flamboyant Vice-President Aaron Burr, who had only recently killed the famous patriot Alexander Hamilton. Burr took his role as judge seriously and conducted the trial with an even hand. All the while Jefferson, who felt his political prestige and power were at stake, was putting pressure on members of the Senate to convict Chase. Though the Republicans held a majority of seats in the Senate, Chase was acquitted.

This small ornate room in the Capitol is where the Supreme Court met until 1860.

The problem faced by the Senate was that the Constitution said (Art. III, sec. 1) that judges "shall hold their office during good behavior." But what did "good behavior" mean? Another section of the Constitution (Art. II, sec. 4) gave a clue. It declared that civil officers, meaning all government officers except those in the military, might not be impeached except for "treason, bribery, or other high crimes and misdemeanors." Fortunately, the Senate decided that Chase's behavior did not amount to an impeachable offense.

If Chase had been convicted, the next candidate for impeachment would probably have been Chief Justice John Marshall. And if Marshall had been impeached—simply because of an honest difference between him and the President over the meaning of the Constitution—the government of the United States might have been very unlike what it has become. Again and again, every party in power would have been tempted to use the tool of impeachment to destroy its political enemies. A system of two strong and freely disagreeing political parties might never have survived.

The election of 1804. Few administrations in our history have been as successful as Jefferson's first term. Our foreign trade had doubled. The customs' receipts far outran Gallatin's estimates. In fact, the national debt was reduced by $25 million, even after paying for the Louisiana Territory. The country between the Alleghenies and the Mississippi was filling rapidly. Mississippi had become a territory in 1798. Indiana had followed in 1800. Ohio had enough people to become a state in February 1803.

Except for what Jefferson called "bickerings" with Spain over West Florida, an area Jefferson still wanted to make part of the United States, our relations with European nations were friendly. Our commissioners under Jay's Treaty had satisfied the British merchants by awarding them more than $2.5 million in payment of long-standing debts from American citizens. We had compelled respect for the American flag by the Barbary pirates. We had acquired a vast domain west of the Mississippi.

The quarrelsome opposition of a few Federalists was drowned in the general chorus of approval. It was no wonder that in the next election Jefferson carried all but one state. Of the 176 electoral votes cast, Jefferson received 162. He won in a landslide over South Carolina's C. C. Pinckney, the Federalist candidate.

Here was a President whose election four years before had brought predictions of the ruin of our commerce, the end of efficient government, and the destruction of the social order. The happy result of Jefferson's first term had been quite the opposite. When Jefferson took the oath of office a second time, on March 4, 1805, he congratulated his fellow countrymen that "not a cloud appeared on the horizon."

SECTION 3 REVIEW

1. Identify or explain: "midnight judges," Judiciary Act of 1789, John Marshall.

2. How did the Federalists seek to retain influence in the government after their defeat in 1800?

3. Why is *Marbury* v. *Madison* a landmark case?

4. **Determining Relevance.** Why was Samuel Chase's impeachment trial important to the future of the Supreme Court?

4. Trouble on the seas

In the spring of 1803 war between England and France was renewed. In October 1805 Lord Nelson destroyed the combined French and Spanish fleets off Cape Trafalgar near the Strait of Gibraltar. A few weeks later Napoleon defeated the Russian and Austrian armies at Austerlitz. So, like the tiger and the shark, Napoleon was master of the continent of Europe, and England ruled the seas. What would this division of empires mean for the young United States?

British Orders and French decrees. Each of the two great powers now tried to damage the other by shutting off its commerce. The British issued *Orders in Council*, forbidding neutral ships to trade with ports under Napoleon's control on the continent. Napoleon replied with *imperial decrees* that authorized French seizure of all ships that traded with the British Isles or that allowed themselves to be searched by a British cruiser. Naturally, the British Orders were more damaging to America since Britain controlled the seas, but both orders and decrees cost Americans ships and cargoes.

The commerce of the United States was threatened with ruin. As a neutral nation willing to trade with all nations, we had profited from the wars in Europe by building up a prosperous foreign trade throughout the world. The sturdy American sailing ships were the favorite carriers for the merchandise of South America, the West Indies, and the Far East to all the ports of Europe. Our own exports too—the fish and lumber of New England, the cotton and rice of the South, the wheat and livestock of the trans-Allegheny country—had increased threefold since Washington took office.

Beginning in 1785, ships from the United States began to trade with China. Here the American flag flies with other flags over Canton, the only Chinese city open for foreign trade until 1842.

The Peabody Museum, Salem: photo by Mark Sexton

Napoleonic Europe

- French Empire
- Dependent on Napoleon
- Allied with Napoleon
- ✕ Battle Sites

0 — 500 Miles
0 — 500 Kilometers

Our merchant marine was growing at a rapid rate. So many new ships were added in 1805 that 4200 more sailors had to be hired. Sailors' wages rose from $8 to $24 a month. To share this prosperity, hundreds of foreign seamen, mostly British, became naturalized citizens of the United States. They wanted to escape the brutal discipline of the British navy. They wished to enjoy the higher pay, better food, and more humane treatment found on American vessels. But this brought some unexpected new problems.

The Chesapeake affair. The United States frigate *Chesapeake*, Captain Barron commanding, weighed anchor from Norfolk, Virginia, on June 22, 1807. She was bound on the long voyage to the Mediterranean, so her guns were still unmounted and her decks littered with tackle. Shortly after the *Chesapeake* reached the sea, the British warship *Leopard* overtook her. *Leopard* tricked *Chesapeake* into stopping by saying that they had dispatches for her. After the *Chesapeake* had heaved to, the *Leopard* demanded to be able to search the American ship for deserters from the British navy. Captain Barron refused and the British vessel thereupon poured three full broadsides into the *Chesapeake*, killing three men and wounding eighteen, before Captain Barron could reply. Unprepared to resist, Captain Barron struck his colors after firing a single gun. Then the British officers took four alleged deserters from the American frigate. They left her to limp back into Norfolk with her dead and wounded.

The impressment of American seamen. Napoleon showed no more respect than England had shown for American rights on the sea. But he did not have the cruisers to capture our ships on the high seas, to force them to France to pay duties, or to search them for departing sailors. All he could do was to seize our ships in his continental ports and sell their cargoes for the benefit of his treasury. Compared to the British, the French could do the American merchant marine very little damage.

In its desperate struggle with Napoleon, Great Britain needed every man who could be found to serve in the navy. It mattered little that the sailor had American naturalization papers. British law did not allow a British subject to switch his loyalty to another country. Furthermore, many of the naturalization papers were forged.

No one knows just how many legitimate American citizens were taken off United States ships by the British impressment officers. Shortly before the United States went to war with Great Britain in 1812, President Madison told Congress that more than 6000 American seamen had been "impressed and held in bondage" during the preceding years. And this was probably a good estimate.

Jefferson's difficulty. The British firing on the *Chesapeake* in June 1807 caused a storm of fury in the United States. Had he wished it, Jefferson could have had war in a minute. But Jefferson did not want war. Instead, he at once ordered British warships to stay out of our waters. He also sent orders to James Monroe, our minister in London, to demand an apology for the attack on the *Chesapeake* and an end to impressment.

The British were in no mood for the complete surrender that Jefferson demanded. Their government was determined to let nothing stand in the way of crushing Napoleon. "An insignificant and puny power," as one newspaper called the United States, certainly could not be allowed to interfere with Britain's control of the seas.

The reply of the British foreign secretary, George Canning, came in December 1807. Canning wished to avoid war and was eager to right the wrong done by the attack on the *Chesapeake*. Indeed, the admiral whose orders led to that attack had already been dismissed from his command. But on the crucial question of the right of search and impressment, the British ministry would not yield.

THE IMPRESSMENT OF AN

American Sailor Boy,

The New-York Historical Society

Americans sang songs like this (above) protesting impressment. British naval officers outraged Americans when they refused to honor seamen's citizenship certificates like this one (right).

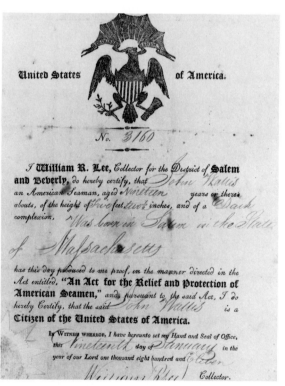

The Essex Institute, Salem, Massachusetts

158

The embargo. Cutbacks in the army and navy under Jefferson left them too weak to fight a war. Jefferson figured that our trade was so important to the nations of Europe that we would not need to fight for what we wanted. If we cut off our trade, they would be sure to do as we wished. Now he decided to try this form of "peaceful coercion" to bring both Britain and Napoleon to terms.

On December 17, 1807, Jefferson asked Congress for a law prohibiting any American vessel from sailing for any foreign port. Congress quickly passed the Embargo Act by large majorities.

The Embargo Act failed to scare Britain and France into a change of policy. It would take time for the British and the French merchants and workers to be hurt by the loss of our trade. But by that time, the embargo might then have destroyed the very American commerce it was designed to protect.

Soon there were signs that the merchants' worst fears were well founded. Ships were tied up at the wharves. Merchandise spoiled in warehouses. Thousands of people in the shipping ports were thrown out of work. Planters and farmers saw their exports of cotton, tobacco, rice, wheat, corn, and livestock fall off sharply. Our foreign trade during the "embargo year" of 1808 shrank to one-third of its value in 1807.

The farmers and the laborers, who had formed the chief support of the Republicans in the northern states, now began to desert the party. Shipowners disobeyed the embargo. Town meetings in New England passed resolutions of protest. Once again there was serious talk of New England leaving the Union.

But the increasing numbers of people on the frontier across the Appalachians had a different point of view. They thought the British were arming the Indians against them. Frightened and angry, they had little use for such soft measures as an embargo. They wanted war. They even talked of capturing Canada.

The embargo repealed. The year 1808 was an election year. Jefferson wanted his Secretary of State, James Madison, to succeed him. He persuaded the Republican members of Congress to pick Madison as the party's candidate. A congressional caucus (party meeting) was the usual nominating method at that time. But the election looked very doubtful. "The Federalists will turn us out by the 4th of March next," Albert Gallatin wrote in June. Yet these fears proved unfounded. True enough, as expected, Madison lost every New England state except Vermont. But the South and the West stood by him, and Madison defeated his Federalist opponent, again General C. C. Pinckney, by 122 electoral votes to 47.

In spite of their impressive victory, the Republicans could see that the embargo was destroying their broad support in the nation and was wrecking their party. On March 1, 1809, three days before Jefferson left office, the Republican Congress repealed the embargo. In its place they passed a Nonintercourse Act that forbade trade only with Great Britain and France. Furthermore, Congress authorized the President to reopen trade with either country should it cease to violate our neutral rights.

Jefferson continued to believe that, if the embargo had been kept in force, Great Britain and France would have come to respect American rights. He thought that the embargo had not been given a fair test. He hated war, for he thought that commerce was the proper weapon of civilized people.

SECTION 4 REVIEW

1. Identify or explain: Orders in Council, imperial decrees, *Chesapeake* affair, impressment, George Canning, embargo.

2. What British actions at sea angered Americans?

3. What was the Embargo Act? Describe its results. What law replaced it?

4. **Recognizing Cause and Effect.** How did war in Europe affect American commerce?

FOCUSING ON IDEAS

1. Why was control of the Mississippi vital to the western settlers? How did the Louisiana Purchase affect this situation?

2. Find examples in this chapter in which political leaders put their personal or party interests ahead of what seems to have been the national interest. Can you find an example in which someone put the national interest above personal or party advantage?

3. How did Jefferson's presidential victory in 1804 compare to his first election in 1800? What factors contributed to the change?

4. American Presidents have often shifted from the views they expressed before taking office. What turnabouts did Jefferson make and why did he make them?

TAKING A CRITICAL LOOK

1. **Predicting Consequences.** If the United States had not bought the Louisiana Territory, would it have been difficult for the United States to maintain good relations with a French neighbor on the western side of the Mississippi? Explain.

2. **Drawing Conclusions.** Would the United States have an effective system of checks-and-balances if the Supreme Court had never asserted its right to declare acts of Congress unconstitutional?

3. **Determining Relevance.** In 1962, a panel of 75 historians ranked Thomas Jefferson as one of five "great" Presidents of the United States. What achievements, in order of their importance, would merit such a rating? What failures or mistakes did Jefferson make that you would expect such a panel to consider in arriving at a fair judgment?

YOUR REGION IN HISTORY

1. **Geography.** If your state became part of the United States as a result of the Louisiana Purchase, what were some noteworthy features of the land and native population?

2. **Culture.** How was your state influenced by English culture? By French culture? By Spanish culture?

3. **Economics.** If your state is east of the Mississippi, how and to what extent was it probably affected by Jefferson's embargo?

HISTORICAL FACTS AND FIGURES

Determining Relevance. Using information in Chapter 7 and data from the graph, determine which of the events listed below seems to have had an impact on the volume of American exports and re-exports. Explain how this impact is reflected on the graph.

1803 The Louisiana Purchase
1806 Continent Acts and Orders in Council
1807 The Embargo Act
1808 James Madison becomes President
1809 Embargo Act Repealed
1811 Battle of Tippecanoe
1812 War of 1812

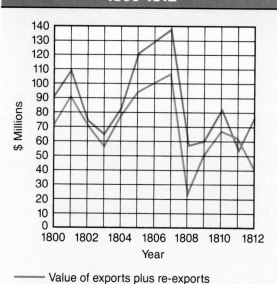

Source: *Historical Statistics of the United States*

CHAPTER **8**

Struggles of a young nation

The presidencies of Madison and Monroe were marked by the growth in American minds of two opposite sentiments. The first was *nationalism,* the sentiment that binds people to their country and makes them feel that from it all their blessings flow. But growing along with nationalism was the spirit of *sectionalism.* This was the belief that your section of the country, be it the North, the South, or the West, was where you actually owed your loyalty and your love. During the last years of the Virginia dynasty of Presidents, national enthusiasm—fed by war, foreign affairs, and visions of a great future for the United States—was growing rapidly. But lurking in the background, ready to leap out at any moment over everyday issues like roads and canals and banks and tariffs, were the forces of sectional interest.

1. The War of 1812

The War of 1812 was the most peculiar conflict in our history. It began after the cause for it had ceased to exist. It was not fought for the reason declared. The nation's main military victory came after the peace treaty had been signed. The peace itself gave Americans none of the things they had fought for. But despite all these failings, the United States emerged from the war a prouder, stronger, and more unified nation. It was ready at last to turn its back on the affairs of Europe and to build an American Empire for Liberty.

James Madison. The man who succeeded Thomas Jefferson came from a wealthy Virginia family and lived on a grand 2500-acre estate called Montpelier. James Madison was admirably trained to be a President. A leader in the Constitutional Convention, he kept the most complete records of what everybody said. His skillful arguments helped secure ratification. Then he served President Washington as adviser, and he did as much as anyone else to shape the new government. A disciple of Jefferson, he helped found the old Republican party and served loyally as Jefferson's Secretary of State.

The wrinkled little Madison was 58 years old when he became President. With friends he could be charming, brilliant, and entertaining, but he lacked the great leader's power to dominate. He was a man of ideas.

Macon's Bill No. 2. When Jefferson's embargo was lifted, it was replaced by a Nonintercourse Act that

National Gallery of Art, Washington. Ailsa Mellon Bruce Fund

This painting of James Madison by Gilbert Stuart was one of hundreds from his studio.

forbade trade only with Great Britain and France. This act was due to expire in 1810. As the deadline approached, Madison was hesitant and indecisive. The Congress, without guidance from the President, had to grope for its own policy. The result was a law that would cause trouble, Macon's Bill No. 2. Named for the chairman of the Senate foreign relations committee, it threw our commerce open to all the world. But it authorized the President, in case either Great Britain or France should withdraw its restrictions on our commerce, to cut off trade with the other power.

Now the wily Napoleon saw his chance. The French dictator quickly promised to lift his decrees if we would then stop trading with Great Britain. Madison fell into the trap. Though France in fact continued to seize our ships—and in spite of warnings from our ambassadors abroad that it was a trick—Madison agreed to Napoleon's terms. The President really wanted to believe that our diplomacy was working—that at last the French decrees

would be repealed and that a renewed threat of nonintercourse with Britain would bring about a change in the British Orders. So he accepted Napoleon's word and in February 1811 issued orders that forbade all trade with Great Britain and its colonies.

The rise of the War Hawks. When Congress met in November 1811, there were many new faces. These representatives championed a new spirit of expansive nationalism that had swept through the South and West. Tired of cautious diplomacy, they demanded a firm defense of our national rights. The leaders of this movement had little or no experience in public affairs, but they were bright, energetic, and young. Among them were men like Henry Clay of Kentucky and John C. Calhoun of the South Carolina hill country. They soon became known as the "War Hawks." Though not in a majority, they were so shrewd politically that they were able to elect Clay as Speaker of the House. Then these few young men pushed the nation into war.

Clay and his friends were not merchants or shippers. The frontier they cared about was not on the sea but in the American West. They wanted more land. In our day it seems strange that in a nation with millions of empty acres some people still called for more. The reason lay in the very abundance of the land and in the scarcity of people. The virgin western lands produced well enough for the first men, women, and children who farmed them. But after a few years the land could produce plentifully only with fertilizer, crop rotation, and careful cultivation. This meant lots of labor, which America had very little of. Here land was cheap, but labor was scarce. Instead of nursing the land, it was easier on the frontier to abandon old farms and make new farms in the wilderness.

But the way west was now blocked by Indians who would not let themselves be pushed around. The frontier people imagined that the Indians opposed their advancing settlements only because they were stirred up by outsiders—the British in Canada and the Spanish in Florida. Therefore, they argued, Great Britain and Spain must be driven out of America.

The Battle of Tippecanoe. Over the years, the most common way for the advancing settlers to acquire land from the Indians was for the government to purchase it. In this way, between 1795 and 1809, the Indians of the old Northwest gave up 48 million acres of land, and in general they obeyed their treaties. But white settlers squatted on the Indian lands, and then attacked the people they had dispossessed.

Finally some Indians, led by two able and intelligent Shawnee brothers, said they had had enough. Tecumseh, the politician and warrior, and Tenskwatawa, the religious leader known as the Prophet, decided to form all the Indian tribes from Canada to Florida into one large confederacy. They would sell no more land and would fight to keep the white people out. Settlers on the frontier were frightened.

Governor William Henry Harrison of Indiana Territory took action. He persuaded some other Indians to make a treaty that took away from Tecumseh and his people 3 million acres of their hunting grounds. This brought the frontier of settlement to within 50 miles of Tecumseh's village. Tecumseh went to the capital at Vincennes. There in a moving speech before armed white men and Indians and the governor himself, he demanded the lands back. He told the governor that if the United States agreed and also promised not to buy any more land except with the consent of all the Indian tribes, he would join them against the British.

Harrison did not accept this offer. Instead he waited until Tecumseh had gone south to persuade the Creeks, Cherokees, and Choctaws to join his confederacy. Then Harrison gathered a force of 900 men and marched to the Tippecanoe River, close to Tecumseh's village. Tecumseh had left strict orders to avoid war, but the Indians feared they were about to be attacked, so they struck first. In a brief encounter on November 7, 1811, Harrison's men defeated the Indians and then burned their village.

Most frontier people believed that British officials had been inciting the Indians. Harrison lent substance to their fears when he reported the capture at Tippecanoe of new guns and "ample supplies of the best British glazed powder." The British had, in fact, helped the Indians resist the invasion of their lands and had encouraged the formation of an Indian confederacy. But they had also opposed war. The Indians were happy to

Area of the Tecumseh Confederation

| 0 | | 300 Miles |
| 0 | | 300 Kilometers |

accept British help, though they needed no encouragement to defend their homelands.

After Harrison's attack, the Indians of the old Northwest went on the warpath. They killed settlers or drove them back to the few scattered towns and forts. The Battle of Tippecanoe became the first battle of the War of 1812, for it inflamed the West and stirred the War Hawks to cry for war. They could easily take Canada, they said, and that would end the Indian menace for good. John Randolph of Virginia complained that all he heard in Congress was "one eternal monotonous tone—Canada, Canada, Canada."

The declaration of war. During the winter of 1811–1812, the war spirit rose steadily in the West and South. Only those occupied with commerce in the East resisted it as a threat to their trade and prosperity. They also feared that an American victory in the war would strengthen the political power of the South and the West.

The War Hawks made fiery speeches. They predicted that a thousand Kentucky riflemen could easily take Canada. So they swept the nation toward a war for which it was unprepared. In April 1812, Congress imposed a 60-day embargo on American shipping in order to give our ships time to reach home before war was declared. In May, news arrived from England that the British ministry refused to change its Orders in Council until it was convinced that Napoleon had really repealed his decrees. This dispatch, Madison wrote many years later, was "the more immediate impulse to war." We had to choose, he said, between war and submission to shameful treatment.

On June 1, 1812, President Madison sent a message to Congress in which he reviewed "the injuries and indignities which had been heaped upon our country" by Great Britain: impressment, blockades, incitement of the Indians. A divided Congress, representing a divided country, responded to Madison's message by voting 79 to 49 in the House and 19 to 13 in the Senate to go to war. The states of the South and West, joined by Pennsylvania and Vermont, favored war. New York, New Jersey, and the seaside New England states were for peace.

This was expected to be a short war. Canada would fall quickly and then it would all be over. After declaring war, therefore, Congress adjourned without even voting the higher taxes needed to arm the nation.

The avoidable war. As the United States moved toward a declaration of war, its ban on trade with England was at last beginning to work. At the same time Napoleon, who was at the height of his power, prevented Great Britain from trading with western Europe. British factories closed, and British workers were thrown out of work because the warehouses were already full of goods that could not be sold. On top of that, a crop failure in 1811 led to a food shortage and high food prices in the following winter.

The British Prime Minister Spencer Perceval was seriously considering the repeal of the Orders in Council when he was assassinated by a madman on May 1, 1812. By the time his successor, Lord Castlereagh, acted and lifted the Orders, the United States had declared war. Jefferson's policy of peaceful persuasion had succeeded—but too late. A President who could not lead and a foolhardy Congress had already shoved the nation into a war it did not need and for which it was not ready.

False hopes of readiness to fight. The United States thought it could win easily. In the first place, we were now the unwitting ally of Napoleon, who invaded Russia just six days after our declaration of war. Our population was now more than 7 million. Canada had only 500,000 people, many of them French-Canadians who were less than eager to help the British.

The fighting forces of the two nations, however, were not so lopsided. Canada had 8500 regular troops—four British and four Canadian regiments. These would be helped by some 4000 militia and more than 3000 of Tecumseh's warriors. Against them the United States had fewer than 7000 men in its regular army. Congress had voted to increase this number to 15,000, but enlistments came in slowly. More than 400,000 militia, the home guard of all men who bore arms, were called up during the war. The militia still showed all the weaknesses they had revealed during the Revolution.

The United States Navy had only 16 sea-going vessels to face Britain's 97 vessels on this side of the ocean. The fast new American frigates were superior to the British ships, but they were greatly outnumbered.

The war in 1812–1813. The first summer of action saw a series of defeats on land. The grandiose plans to invade Canada ended in the loss of Fort Dearborn (Chicago) on August 15, 1812, and Detroit the following day. This left the British in control of a large part of the old Northwest.

The navy, however, helped relieve the gloomy picture. The *Constitution* ("Old Ironsides") defeated the *Guerrière* and the *Java* in 1812, while the *Wasp* was whipping the *Frolic*. The frigate *United States,* commanded by Stephen Decatur, even seized the British frigate *Macedonia* and brought her home as a prize. The British were stunned—just as the Americans were elated—by these naval victories. But their main result was to lift American morale. For soon most United States warships were blockaded in home ports.

Madison won a second term in the fall of 1812. Yet DeWitt Clinton of New York, supported by Federalists and Republicans who wanted peace, carried every eastern state north of the Potomac except Pennsylvania and Vermont.

The war might have ended in 1812 if the British had been willing to stop taking British sailors from

American ships and impressing them into their navy. They would not concede this point, so the war went on.

In 1813, United States military actions did not fare much better. In June the unlucky frigate *Chesapeake* accepted a challenge for a fight from Britain's *Shannon*. Outside Boston Harbor, Captain James Lawrence was killed and the *Chesapeake* was captured. Before he died, however, Lawrence spoke his memorable words, "Don't give up the ship."

Hundreds of miles away, those words were to fly on Commodore Oliver Hazard Perry's blue battle flag when he fought the British at Put-in-Bay on Lake Erie in September. Perry had built his fleet of small vessels during the winter of 1812–1813. Overcoming many difficulties, he was able to get his ships into Lake Erie and face the British fleet in September. There was a hot battle, during which the fleets fired away at each other at point blank range. Perry was able to report, "We have met the enemy and they are ours." He had worried about

Courtesy United States Naval Academy Museum

During the War of 1812, Thomas Birch painted "Engagement of the *Constitution* and the *Guerriere*," as well as other American naval victories.

The White House Historical Association

This painting shows "The President's House" after British troops burned it in 1814. When the building was repaired, the white-gray limestone was painted white and people started calling it the White House.

his new sailors, "blacks, soldiers, and boys," but they had fought bravely. Of the 50 blacks in his crew, he said, "they seemed absolutely insensible to danger."

Perry's success meant that the British at Detroit could be cut off from Canada. So they were forced to retreat. William Henry Harrison, now a general, led 10,000 Kentucky volunteers in pursuit. The Americans overtook the British at the Thames River on the Ontario peninsula and routed them. The British commander was almost captured, and the brave and visionary warrior Tecumseh—now a brigadier general in the British army—was killed.

Other American generals had less success in 1813. So, as winter closed in, the conquest of Canada was little nearer than it had been the year before. In the meantime, the British blockade grew tighter. Few ships were able to enter or leave our ports. Trade dropped to almost nothing.

Our swift-sailing privateers stayed abroad and successfully attacked the British merchant marine on all its worldwide lines of commerce. Even in the English Channel they were not safe from our raiders which, during the course of the war, captured some 1300 British ships and cargoes valued at $40 million.

Great Britain takes the offensive. During 1812 and 1813 the British were more concerned about fighting Napoleon in Europe than the United States in America. But the Russian winter would bring Napoleon's downfall. With his exile to Elba in April 1814, England was free to turn its full attention to the war with the United States. Some 14,000 of the Duke of Wellington's battle-seasoned regulars were now sent to America to bring about a quick British victory.

Offensive operations by the British began in August 1814 when a large fleet sailed into Chesapeake Bay and 4000 regulars landed on the banks of the Patuxent River. They brushed aside a militia force outside Washington and entered the capital on August 24. President Madison and his intelligent and attractive wife, Dolley, gathered a few valuables and fled to Virginia. Since an American force had burned York (Toronto) in 1813, the British now retaliated. After capturing the city, they set fire to the Capitol (with the Library of Congress), the White House, and some other public buildings.

The triumphant redcoats then sailed to Baltimore, where the citizens had been strengthening their defenses during the attack on Washington.

There the British troops were repulsed, and their commanding general was killed. But before they gave up and headed out of Chesapeake Bay, their fleet undertook an all-night bombardment of Fort McHenry, the American stronghold.

It was during that "perilous night" of shelling that a young Washington lawyer, Francis Scott Key, watched from an American ship "until dawn's early light" revealed to his relief that "our flag was still there." "The Star-Spangled Banner" was written under these painful circumstances.

In early September 1814 another large, well-trained British army containing some of Wellington's tough regulars was following Burgoyne's route along the shore of Lake Champlain. They were opposed by a much smaller force of American militia stationed behind strong fortifications at Plattsburg in upstate New York. The British put a strong fleet on the lake to support their attack. An American naval force on the lake was commanded by Commodore Thomas Macdonough. Although only 30 years old, he was already an experienced naval officer. His fleet was outgunned by the British vessels, but he handled his weaker force so skillfully that he gained a decisive victory. With the Americans in control of the lake, the British army turned back on September 12, 1814.

Macdonough's victory and the British departure from Baltimore at last lifted American spirits. Until then the nation's future had seemed dark. Our war vessels had been driven from the ocean, our coasts blockaded, and our commerce ruined. The Treasury was empty. The Capitol and the President's house lay in scorched ruins.

Andrew Jackson wins fame. There were other heartening events in 1814 that brightened the nation's future and created a new national hero. These were the deeds of the tall, rough-hewn Tennessean, General Andrew Jackson. Westerners were delighted when he invaded the lands of the Creek Indians and defeated them in the Battle of Horseshoe Bend. Then by the Treaty of Fort Jackson he forced them to give up two-thirds of their Alabama lands.

For his successes Jackson was promoted from the position of general of volunteers to the post of major general in the regular army. He invaded Spanish East Florida in November 1814 and captured a British force at Pensacola. Hastening to New

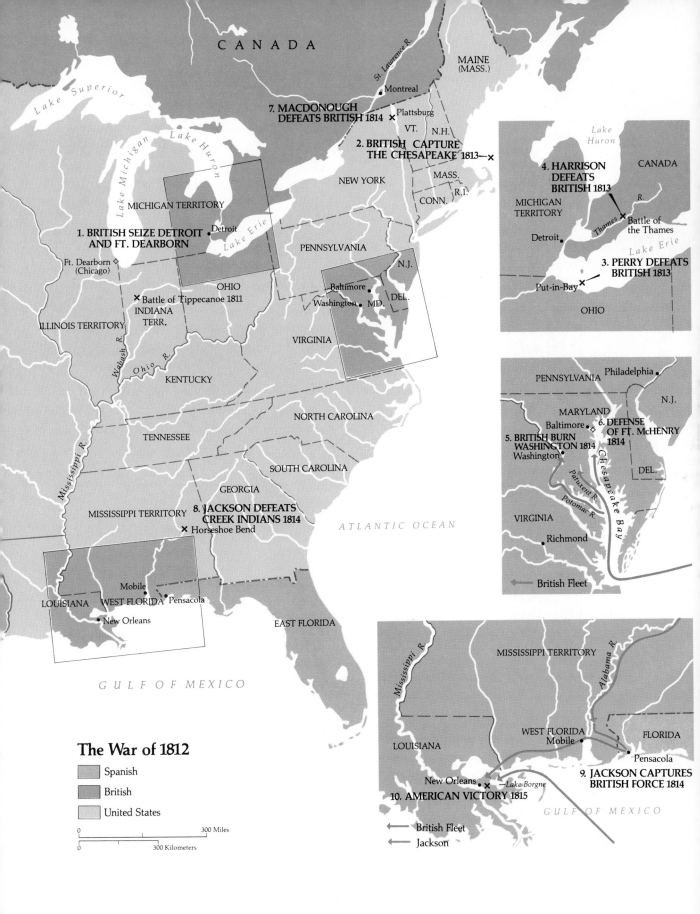

CANADA

Lake Superior

Lake Michigan

Lake Huron

**7. MACDONOUGH
DEFEATS BRITISH 1814** ✕ Plattsburg

MAINE
(MASS.)

St. Lawrence R.

• Montreal

VT.

N.H.

**2. BRITISH CAPTURE
THE CHESAPEAKE 1813**—✕

NEW YORK

MASS.

MICHIGAN TERRITORY

• Detroit

Lake Erie

CONN. R.I.

**1. BRITISH SEIZE DETROIT
AND FT. DEARBORN**

Ft. Dearborn ◇
(Chicago)

PENNSYLVANIA

N.J.

Baltimore •
Washington • MD.

DEL.

ILLINOIS TERRITORY

OHIO

✕ Battle of Tippecanoe 1811

INDIANA
TERR.

VIRGINIA

Wabash R.

Ohio R.

KENTUCKY

NORTH CAROLINA

Mississippi R.

TENNESSEE

SOUTH CAROLINA

GEORGIA

**8. JACKSON DEFEATS
CREEK INDIANS 1814**

MISSISSIPPI TERRITORY

✕ Horseshoe Bend

ATLANTIC OCEAN

Mobile •

LOUISIANA

WEST FLORIDA • Pensacola

• New Orleans

EAST FLORIDA

GULF OF MEXICO

Lake
Huron

**4. HARRISON
DEFEATS
BRITISH 1813**

CANADA

MICHIGAN
TERRITORY

Thames R.

Detroit •

✕ Battle of
the Thames

Lake Erie

**3. PERRY DEFEATS
BRITISH 1813**

Put-in-Bay ✕

OHIO

PENNSYLVANIA

Philadelphia •

MARYLAND

N.J.

Baltimore •

**6. DEFENSE
OF FT. McHENRY
1814**

**5. BRITISH BURN
WASHINGTON 1814**

Washington •

DEL.

Patuxent R.

Chesapeake Bay

Potomac R.

VIRGINIA

Richmond •

← British Fleet

The War of 1812

▨ Spanish

▨ British

▨ United States

0 ————————— 300 Miles

0 ————————— 300 Kilometers

MISSISSIPPI TERRITORY

Mississippi R.

Alabama R.

WEST FLORIDA
Mobile •

FLORIDA

LOUISIANA

Pensacola •

**9. JACKSON CAPTURES
BRITISH FORCE 1814**

New Orleans •
✕ —Lake Borgne

10. AMERICAN VICTORY 1815

GULF OF MEXICO

← British Fleet

← Jackson

167

"The Battle of New Orleans" was painted from sketches that the artist, an engineer with the American army, had made on the battlefield. The final battle was fought on plantations four miles south of the city. Note the strong American defensive positions.

Orleans in case the British should arrive there, he reached the city just in time.

Jackson quickly rounded up anyone who would fight to defend the city. Despite his preparations, before he knew it a British force of 2000 men landed and came within eight miles of New Orleans. He did not hesitate. On the night of December 23, Jackson's men struck in full force and stopped the British advance. If the British had been able to regroup and attack Jackson's forces right then, they probably would have defeated him. But they delayed to await reinforcements and gave his motley band of militia, blacks, and pirates time to throw up earthworks and bring in their artillery.

Twice the British—now 7500 strong—attacked and twice they were thrown back. The all-out charge, which came at dawn on January 8, 1815, was a disaster for the British. They suffered some 2000 killed and wounded and lost their commanding general. Incredibly, only 13 Americans died.

The redcoats then boarded their ships and sailed away. Jackson became "the hero of New Orleans." A future President—one of the nation's strongest leaders—had been created. Among the many oddities of the War of 1812 none was odder than the fact that its greatest victory, the Battle of New Orleans, was won after peace had already been negotiated in a distant European town.

The Treaty of Ghent. Peace discussions between American and British envoys had begun in Ghent, Belgium, in August 1814. The British demanded large tracts of land in their first proposals, but then Macdonough's victory on Lake Champlain made them realize that Britain could not win the war. The depletion of their treasury by the long Napoleonic Wars, together with many new problems in Europe, forced the English envoys to lower their demands. On December 24, 1814, a peace treaty was signed. If telegraph, telephone, or radio had existed, the Battle of New Orleans would probably not have been fought two weeks later. But, in fact, America did not learn of the treaty until the middle of February 1815.

The terms of the treaty made at Ghent simply provided for a return to the conditions that existed before the war. Lawyers called that the *status quo ante bellum.* It was agreed that certain issues would be settled later. Since neither side gained or lost anything, the treaty became the basis for a reconciliation between the parent country and its former thirteen colonies. Unlike most peace treaties, this one did not bear the seeds of future war. The peace was ratified unanimously by the Senate on February 14, 1815.

There is good reason to call the War of 1812 the Second War of Independence, for now at last the new American nation had stood up with its own army and navy in full-scale war against a major European power. And this was in spite of some dangerous quarrels at home.

Opposition in New England to the war.
As the war was drawing to a close, opposition in the North was rising rapidly. Every seaside state north of Maryland had voted against Madison (which meant against the war) in the election of 1812. New England, the richest section of the country, subscribed for less than $1 million of an $11 million loan authorized by Congress in 1812. "Organize a peace party," the Massachusetts legislature recommended a week after the war was declared. "Express your sentiments without fear and let the sound of your disapproval of this war be loud and deep. . . . Let there be no volunteering except for a defensive war." Some New Englanders were so disgusted with the war that they sold beef to the British army in Canada. The New England states and New York were unwilling to let their militias serve outside their home states.

The British blockade closed off the seaborne commerce of the United States. Exports and imports in 1814 were a mere 10 percent of what they had been in the peak year of 1807. One observer later reported, "Our ships were rotting in every creek and cove where they could find a place of security; our immense annual products were mouldering in our warehouses." Impoverished towns petitioned the Massachusetts legislature to take steps toward amending the Constitution of the United States to "secure them from further evils." Pessimists began to fear that the Union itself was in danger.

The Hartford Convention.
At the suggestion of the Massachusetts legislature, delegates from the five New England states met in a convention at Hartford, Connecticut, on December 15, 1814. These delegates, remnants of the old Federalist party, denounced the "ruinous war." They adopted resolutions, like those of Virginia and Kentucky in 1798, in which they proclaimed that when the Constitution was violated it was the duty of the states to "interpose their authority for the preservation of their liberties." They also proposed a number of amendments to the Constitution that were designed to lessen the power of the South and West, to secure the interests of commerce, and to check the seemingly endless succession of Presidents from Virginia.

By a lucky coincidence the messengers carrying these disruptive demands arrived in Washington just at the moment when events made their demands seem absurd. For the city was rejoicing over the news of Jackson's victory at New Orleans and

The Huntington Library, San Marino, California

The American and British flags both appear on this Cambridge, Massachusetts, invitation to a dance celebrating the end of the war.

The Huntington Library, San Marino, California

The cartoonist accuses four of the New England states present at the Hartford Convention of planning to rejoin England. George III seems eager to welcome back his "Yankey boys."

the tidings of the peace from Ghent, which reached Washington on the same day. The Republican triumph was complete, and the Federalist party was doomed.

There was nothing "treasonable" in the propositions of the Federalists at Hartford, for they were trying to amend the Constitution. But they made a bad mistake in their timing. As a party measure they were opposing a war at a time when it had become a struggle for the nation's very existence. Therefore there was reason enough for many Americans to call the Hartford Convention unpatriotic. The Federalists as a party put partisan or sectional interests above those of the whole country. For the last time, in the presidential election of 1816, the Federalists named a candidate. Rufus King of New York was easily defeated by the Republican James Monroe, Madison's Secretary of State. The Virginia dynasty would govern the nation for another eight years.

SECTION 1 REVIEW

1. Identify or explain: Macon's Bill No. 2, Henry Clay, John C. Calhoun, Tecumseh, the Prophet, Stephen Decatur, De Witt Clinton, James Lawrence, Oliver Hazard Perry.

2. Locate: Tippecanoe, Fort Dearborn, Thames River, Put-in-Bay, York, Fort McHenry.

3. Why did the War Hawks argue for war?

4. List some major land and sea battles in the War of 1812 and give their results.

5. Summarize the terms of the Treaty of Ghent.

6. Describe the opposition to the war of 1812.

7. **Distinguishing False from Accurate Images.** Was the War of 1812 the "most peculiar conflict in our history?" Explain your answer.

2. Madison and Monroe

The War of 1812 had hardly been a great American success story. It had revealed grave weaknesses in our government—especially in the nation's finances and in defense. At times during the conflict, the fate of the nation had hung in the balance.

Yet the war finally produced solid benefits. Never again would Great Britain believe that the United States could easily be defeated on the battlefield. Americans would no longer assume that Canada could be conquered by a thousand Kentucky riflemen. Both nations—the former homeland and the nation of former colonies—would be more willing to settle their differences at a conference table.

The other result was stranger. Out of a war in which the nation had attained none of its declared goals, the people emerged more united, more patriotic, and more filled with national pride than ever before.

"We have met the enemy and they are ours," "Don't give up the ship," and other fighting slogans became popular. "The Star-Spangled Banner" would become our national anthem. An energetic Jackson and his frontiersmen, blacks, and pirates were remembered trouncing the British at New Orleans. The near loss of much of the Northwest and the burning of Washington were almost forgotten.

The annual message of 1815. The new national spirit was revealed in President Madison's annual message to Congress in December 1815. This Republican President's program included: (1) funds for national defense, (2) frigates for the navy, (3) a standing army and federal control of the militia, (4) federal aid for building roads and canals, (5) a protective tariff to encourage manufactures, (6) re-establishing the national bank, and (7) federal assumption of some state debts. It seemed that Hamilton had replaced Jefferson as the idol of the old Republican party.

Henry Clay later referred to this program as the "American System," which would benefit every section of the country. The protective tariff would aid the manufacturers of the Northeast and create a large market for their products in the South and West. Internal improvements—roads and canals—would tie the country together and make it easier for Westerners and Southerners to get their crops to eastern markets. The national bank would provide the currency and the capital for the entire nation's economic growth. But each section found something in the package that it did not like.

The Tariff of 1816. American manufacturers wanted a protective tariff. After the British blockade had cut off our foreign commerce, large sums of capital were switched to manufacturing, in New England especially, so that we might make the items we had once imported. By the end of 1815 the cotton mills in New England had multiplied. Iron manufacturing was booming in Pennsylvania. Pioneer industries—in iron, wool, and cotton—had even appeared in the Ohio Valley between Pittsburgh and Cincinnati.

The British manufacturers who had supplied the rapidly growing American demand ever since colonial days did not wish to lose their market. Even before the Senate ratified the Treaty of Ghent, British ships were waiting off New York Harbor, loaded with goods that had been dammed up in English warehouses during the wars in Europe and America. These goods were to be sold even below cost in order to bankrupt America's new manufacturing plants.

The New-York Historical Society

The tariff of 1816 was designed to protect small industries like this one in West Point, New York.

To protect America's "infant industries" Congress enacted a tariff (April 1816) that continued the high duties that had been imposed as a war measure in 1812. South Carolina—later to lead the opposition—now strongly favored the tariff. Representative John C. Calhoun of South Carolina supported the measure because he believed the United States needed to build up its army, pay its national debt, and develop its new industries. Only in that way, he argued, could the United States be truly independent. The South as a whole, however, was not convinced. Southern members of Congress voted heavily against the tariff.

The second Bank of the United States.

The Bank of the United States, which had not been rechartered in 1811, had closed its doors. Without a national bank it was doubly difficult for the nation to pay for the war. Instead of being able to borrow from one central bank, the government had to deal with many. Without any Bank of the United States, state banks (private banks chartered by the states) had multiplied rapidly, each issuing its own paper money. There was no one national currency. In the dark days of the war, after the British burned Washington, many holders of these state bank notes tried to convert them to gold and silver (specie) as the banks had promised. But, lacking specie, the banks refused. As a result the value of the state bank notes declined. The bonds of the federal government sold below their face value, and the national debt soared.

To deal with these hard economic problems, the federal government decided to charter a bank similar to Hamilton's bank of 1791, but with a larger capital. Again the government would hold one-fifth of the stock and would name one-fifth of the directors. Southern statesmen who had argued against the constitutionality of the old bank now suddenly changed their tune. They favored the second Bank of the United States. Madison, who had called Hamilton's bank unconstitutional, signed the new bank bill on April 10, 1816.

Calhoun's Bonus Bill.

One of the lessons of the war was the need for better means of transporting goods and troops. All the sails, cannon, and cordage (ropes and lines) for Perry's fleet on Lake Erie and for Macdonough's on Lake Champlain had been laboriously carried overland. Supplies for the army were dragged over rough trails in the wilderness. Western farmers found it difficult and expensive to bring their crops and livestock to market.

John C. Calhoun, eloquent spokesman for the South, warned Congress that unless it found ways to tie the rapidly growing nation together there was a strong chance of "disunion." In December 1816, Calhoun introduced a bill to pay for roads and canals—what were called "internal improvements." The $1.5 million that the new Bank of the United States would pay for its charter (the so-called bonus) would support these new projects. In addition, the dividends that the United States would receive on its fifth of the bank's stock would help build roads and canals. The bill passed Congress in February 1817.

President Madison now suddenly returned to his old Republican beliefs. He had called for building roads and canals in his 1815 message. But now he decided that Congress had no such powers because they were not expressly given in the Constitution. So Madison vetoed the Bonus Bill.

It was unfortunate for his place in history that Madison chose to show constitutional scruples so near the close of his Presidency. The "American System" of the tariff, bank, and internal improvements was a package. Few liked all three items. Some Westerners were against the bank because they liked the easy money of the state banks. The South opposed the tariff. And New England disliked both the bank (now that it was a Republican measure) and internal improvements at government expense. Only the Middle States—New York, New Jersey, and Pennsylvania—voted for all three. When Madison vetoed the Bonus Bill, the "system" ceased to exist. Now the West, which most wanted roads and canals, felt left out.

A further problem with the veto was that the northern states had the money to spend for internal improvements while the South did not. When the North built roads and canals and, later, railroads to the West, the trade of the West naturally was drawn to the northern states. As a result the South remained agricultural, raising the staple crops of rice, tobacco, cotton, and sugar. With internal improvements at national expense, the economy of all the sections might have been different. And the South might have developed a mixed economy of farm and factory instead of becoming enslaved to slavery.

"First Harvest in the Wilderness," painted by Asher Durand in 1855, suggests the grueling effort needed to carve a farm out of forested highland. Durand was one of the painters known as the Hudson River School. They painted the wild and wonderful beauties of the American landscape.

The "Era of Good Feelings."

Madison's veto of the Bonus Bill was his last official act. The next day he saw his hand-picked successor, James Monroe, the last of the Virginia dynasty, take the oath of office.

The inauguration of President James Monroe began a curious period in American party politics. When the new President toured the North and the West, he was so well received that even a staunchly Federalist Boston newspaper called him the herald of an "era of good feelings."

President Monroe's term in office proved to be an era without political parties. The Federalist party died in 1816. The Jeffersonian Republicans had taken over their issues—banks, tariffs, and an active central government. When only New Englanders were found in the Federalist party, it had ceased to be national.

As the Federalists disappeared, so too did the Republicans. Without opposition there was no reason for them to stay together, and they fell apart into squabbling factions. With astonishing swiftness, the Era of Good Feelings became an era of bad feelings marked by the hot pursuit of the Presidency by several self-seeking so-called Republicans. Sectional bitterness boiled up, and a coherent national policy disappeared. Meanwhile, James Monroe avoided making domestic policy and drifted with the times.

Economic sectionalism.

In Monroe's day the United States was divided into geographic sections each as large as a European nation, each with its own economic interests. The East depended on commerce and industry. The South lived on an economy of large plantations. The West was a land of small farms. The differing economic interests of the sections produced conflicting ideas about the tariff, banks, internal improvements, slavery, the right to vote, and almost everything else.

For a time after the War of 1812 these sectional differences remained hidden. While the whole country prospered, national feelings overshadowed all others. But with the onset of a severe depression in 1819, people in each section looked for someone—elsewhere in the nation—to blame. Each section demanded new laws in its own special interest.

Adjustments with Great Britain.

Monroe's term of office began well, however, and a national spirit filled the air—a pride promoted by American diplomatic successes.

John Quincy Adams, Monroe's Secretary of State and the son of former President John Adams, was one of the ablest and most farsighted statesmen in our country's history. The agreement with Great Britain that he negotiated in 1817 (and which survives to this day) pledged each country not to keep warships on the Great Lakes. This policy was later expanded to a pledge not to arm the land borders between the United States and Canada. As a result, the northern border of the United States remains the longest unfortified international border in the world. The pact came to be known as the Rush-Bagot Agreement because it was contained in an exchange of notes between the acting Secretary of State, Richard Rush, and the British minister to the United States, Charles Bagot.

In the following year it was agreed that the 49th parallel would mark the boundary between Canada and the United States from Lake of the Woods in Minnesota to the Rocky Mountains. Also, for ten years Britain and the United States would jointly occupy the Oregon territory between the Rockies and the Pacific.

Spain cedes Florida.

The United States had long wanted all of Florida. Then in 1818, the federal government ordered General Jackson to protect southern and western settlers against Indian attacks from eastern Florida. He was told that he could follow Indian raiding parties back into Spanish Florida. Jackson—who was no Indian lover—responded to this assignment with enthusiasm. Supposedly chasing Indians, he swept across East Florida, capturing the Spanish strongholds of Pensacola and St. Marks on the way. During this campaign he executed two Englishmen who were suspected of supplying arms to the Indians. When Jackson went back to Tennessee in May 1818, he had turned Florida into a conquered province.

Jackson's deeds made him a hero in the West but seriously embarrassed the government. He might easily have caused a war with both Spain and England. The President's Cabinet was divided. Secretary of State John Quincy Adams supported the rash Jackson. But all the other Cabinet members wanted him to be censured and his acts disavowed.

Adams and Jackson prevailed, and the President sent Spain an ultimatum: either control the Indians or sell Florida to the United States.

The weak Spanish government, plagued by revolts in its other American colonies, had no way to control the Indians. So rather than have the United States take Florida for nothing, Spain decided to sell the land for what it could get. In the Adams-Onís Treaty of 1819, the United States received Florida. In return the United States government agreed to pay to its own citizens about $5 million—the damages American shippers claimed against Spain for Spanish interference with American commerce during the Napoleonic Wars.

The same treaty finally fixed the boundary between the Louisiana Territory and Spanish holdings to the west. This line had been in dispute ever since 1803. The United States gave up its claim to part of Texas, but in return Spain gave up its claim to the Pacific Northwest. The border of the United States now was drawn all the way to the Pacific!

John Marshall's decisions.

The rise of nationalism during these years was encouraged by a series of decisions of the Supreme Court under its strong Federalist Chief Justice John Marshall. When the Supreme Court decides a case, the justices write opinions giving the reasons for their decisions. Usually one justice will write an opinion for the majority. Marshall was noted both for the masterful opinions that he wrote and for his skill in winning other members of the Court to his views.

In Martin v. Hunter's Lessee (1816) and Cohens v. Virginia (1821) the Supreme Court insisted on its right to review decisions of state courts that dealt with matters arising under the federal Constitution.

In 1819 in the Dartmouth College Case, the Court protected private property from state interference. It annulled an act of the New Hampshire legislature that would have altered the college charter. States were forbidden by the Constitution to "pass any law impairing the obligation of contracts." A charter passed by a state legislature, Marshall said, was a "contract." Marshall was always willing to interpret the Constitution broadly when it increased the powers of the national government—or the Supreme Court. The decision in this case also encouraged business firms to invest their capital and to rely on the charters of their corporations without fearing the whimsies of state legislatures.

Marshall's most famous opinion came in *McCulloch* v. *Maryland* (1819). That decision became a bulwark of a strong central government in the United States. The state of Maryland had tried to force the Bank of the United States out of the state by taxing it. Marshall asserted that no state had the right to hinder or control any national institution established within its borders. "The power to tax," he said, "is the power to destroy."

Marshall seized the occasion to deal once again with the question whether the Constitution gave Congress the power to set up a national bank. Before signing the bill that had created the first Bank of the United States, President Washington had received conflicting advice on the issue from Thomas Jefferson and Alexander Hamilton (p. 122). But the power of Congress to create the bank had not been tested in the courts. Now Marshall had a chance to deal with the clause that gave Congress the right "to make all laws necessary and proper" for carrying out the powers granted it under the Constitution (Art. I, sec. 8).

Did these words mean "absolutely necessary and therefore proper"? Marshall said No! To carry out any of its direct powers, Congress could choose the appropriate means. Congress could create a bank as a convenient or useful means to carry out its direct powers to collect taxes and borrow money. It was only necessary that the means be within "the letter and spirit of the Constitution" and not prohibited by it. The decision therefore had the effect of broadening the powers of Congress and thereby the national government. The laws of the United States were "the supreme law of the land," and the states had no power to prevent the growth of a national government.

In *Gibbons* v. *Ogden* (1824), the famous "Steamboat Case," the Marshall Court drew some powerful conclusions from the clause in the Constitution that gives to Congress the power to regulate commerce with foreign nations, between the states, and with the Indian tribes (Art. 1, sec. 8). A monopoly of steamboat passenger service on the Hudson River that New York had granted to Robert Livingston and Robert Fulton could not be allowed to stand. Marshall now defined "commerce" so broadly that the champions of "states rights" accused him of trying to abolish the state governments altogether. Ultimately, Congress, by overseeing "interstate commerce," would regulate telephones, telegraphs,

New York State Historical Association, Cooperstown

After Fulton and Livingston's steamboat monopoly was broken, competition flourished.

and oil pipelines. Even manufacturing *within* a state would be regulated when the workers, the raw materials, or the products came from or went to other states. Henry Clay and other promoters of the "American System," advocates of a strong, unified nation, welcomed Marshall's words.

SECTION 2 REVIEW

1. Identify or explain: "American System," "infant industries," Bonus Bill, "Era of Good Feelings," Rush-Bagot Agreement, Adams-Onís Treaty.

2. How did Madison's annual message to Congress in 1815 express a spirit of nationalism?

3. What did the North, South, and West each like or dislike about (a) a protective tariff, (b) internal improvements, (c) the national bank?

4. Why did Madison veto the Bonus Bill?

5. What important agreements were made with Great Britain in 1817–1818?

6. What events led to the treaty with Spain in 1819? What were its chief provisions?

7. **Determining Relevance.** Why were the cases decided by the Supreme Court under John Marshall important to the growing power of the national government?

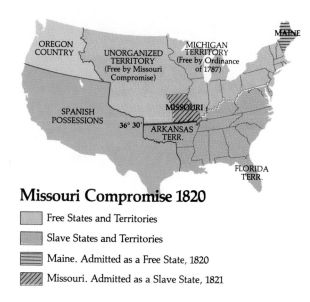

Missouri Compromise 1820

- Free States and Territories
- Slave States and Territories
- Maine. Admitted as a Free State, 1820
- Missouri. Admitted as a Slave State, 1821

3. The Missouri Compromise

One sectional interest in America was more sensitive and more explosive than all others—slavery. Unlike other economic issues, slavery was a great moral problem. In the early days of the Republic, it had appeared that slavery might die out. The price of tobacco was so low that many plantation owners were finding the use and care of slaves unprofitable. But then a single invention suddenly changed the picture.

Eli Whitney was a recent Yale College graduate who had gone south to be a tutor to the children of a plantation family. In those days there were few public schools in the South. The children of slaves were not sent to school, and the children of plantation owners were usually taught by a private tutor who came and lived in the mansion. The position of tutor was no longer vacant when Whitney reached Savannah in the fall of 1792, but he was invited to remain in Georgia for a time as the guest of Catherine Littlefield Greene, the widow of the Revolutionary War General Nathanael Greene.

While on Mrs. Greene's plantation, Whitney saw how well short-staple cotton grew in the southern uplands. He also saw that a slave had to labor a whole day to pick the seeds out of a pound of cotton in order to make the cotton usable for thread or for cloth. Whitney, who was handy with tools, was urged by Catherine Greene to try to find a better way to remove the seeds. He was a clever young

man. Within ten days he built a device that pushed the cotton through slots so narrow the seeds were left behind. By April 1793 he had a working machine that made it possible for one slave to clean 50 pounds of cotton of its seeds in a single day.

Whitney's cotton "gin" (for "engine") suddenly made the production of short-staple cotton highly profitable. Plantations would prosper if only they could find the workers to plant, to cultivate, to pick, and to "gin" the cotton. Black slaves seemed the obvious labor supply, and slavery began to seem "necessary" for southern prosperity. At the same time planters wanting more land to grow more cotton were moving rapidly westward.

The slavery question rises in the West. By 1818 some 60,000 settlers had crossed the Mississippi and were pushing up the valley of the Missouri River. St. Louis was a bustling city and the center of the western fur trade. Although most of the settlers in Missouri were from the states north of the Ohio, where the Northwest Ordinance prohibited slavery, there were some from slaveholding states like Kentucky and Tennessee. They had brought with them about 10,000 slaves.

Missouri's request for admission to the Union opened up a heated argument over the expansion of slavery. The question began as a matter of power. Up to this time when new states entered the Union, there had been an effort to keep an even balance between free and slave states. Slaveholding Alabama was about to come into the Union and then there would be 11 free states and 11 slave. That would mean that there would be an even vote between the two groups in the Senate. But there seemed to be no free state at that time that could be paired with Missouri to keep the balance even. And if Missouri was brought in alone, the slave states would have a two-vote majority in the Senate.

In 1819, the year when the issue came to a head, a deep economic depression split the country. The Bank of the United States was under attack as the villain that had created the depression to enrich a few greedy Northerners. Manufacturers in the Northeast called for higher protective tariffs, which would have raised the price of nearly everything Southerners bought. Whoever controlled the Senate, it was argued, would then be able to control government policy on the Bank, on tariffs, on federal outlays for roads and canals, and especially

This scene of the steamboat *Yellowstone* on its way down the Mississippi was painted by George Catlin, the Pennsylvania painter who portrayed the American West. Besides being a bustling river port, St. Louis in the background was a stagecoach center for those heading east or west.

on slavery. Slave-owning Southerners began to see a life-and-death struggle. How long could it be before Northerners would insist on abolishing slavery? And how could the South survive without the labor force that produced its cotton? A new bitterness entered the halls of Congress.

Achieving a compromise. The "Missouri Compromise," which Congress passed in 1820 after a whole year of debate, was not so much a compromise as a stalemate. Following the rules of the North-South tug-of-war, which had already been going on for at least twenty years, each side added one new state to its team. Missouri was added as a slave state, while Maine came in as a free state. At the same time the law drew a line through all the rest of the lands of the Louisiana Purchase excluding slavery "forever" from north of the parallel of 36°30' (the southern boundary of Missouri) except for the state of Missouri itself.

Although people at the time called it a compromise, it was not really like the compromises made by the framers of the Constitution in 1787. Those earlier compromises—for example, the one between the large and small states—were designed to give each side on every question part of what it wanted. Then everybody could consider the question settled and move on to other things. But slavery was a different kind of question. Both sides saw it as all-or-nothing. Both sides were simply biding their time.

Farsighted leaders realized that the Missouri Compromise was nothing more than a truce that announced the opening of a fight to the finish. The aged Thomas Jefferson, retired at Monticello on his Virginia mountaintop, was saddened. This was, he said, "a fire-bell in the night . . . the [death] knell of the Union." John Quincy Adams saw it as "a title page to a great tragic volume."

SECTION 3 REVIEW

1. What was the Missouri Compromise designed to settle? How was it supposed to do so?
2. **Recognizing Cause and Effect.** How did Eli Whitney influence (a) the growth of slavery and (b) its westward expansion?

4. The Monroe Doctrine

President Monroe played only a minor role in the crisis that finally produced the Missouri Compromise. In domestic affairs, he believed, it was the job of Congress to make the laws, and the President should only carry them out. But in foreign affairs, it was plainly the President's duty to lead the way in defining the nation's role. Monroe was assisted by his strong-minded Secretary of State, John Quincy Adams. Behind their determination to make the United States a leader in world affairs they had the support of the American people. Despite growing sectional differences, Americans of all regions shared a new national pride. The young nation's Second War of Independence, the War of 1812, had given them all a lift. The nation's growing self-confidence was revealed in the Monroe Doctrine.

Europe and America. During the Napoleonic Wars the Spanish-American colonies had begun to break away from Spain and to follow the example of the United States by declaring their independence. For those colonies it was a time of struggle—and an hour of decision. The United States feared that the continental European powers—Austria, Russia, Prussia, and France—would help Spain to reconquer its colonies.

At this point the British foreign secretary, George Canning, proposed that the United States and Great Britain make a public declaration against the attempt of European nations to use force to keep their former colonies in subjection. Monroe thought that we should accept Canning's offer. Madison and Jefferson agreed. But Secretary of State John Quincy Adams had misgivings. He knew the ins and outs of European diplomacy from his fourteen years as minister to the Netherlands, Prussia, Russia,

and Great Britain, and he had helped negotiate the treaty with Britain that ended the War of 1812. Adams distrusted the British government and thought the United States should make its own foreign policy. The United States, he told the Cabinet, should not "come in as a cockboat in the wake of the British man-of-war."

Monroe's message to Congress. Following Adams's advice, President Monroe announced a new policy to the world in his annual message to Congress on December 2, 1823. Though containing the ideas of John Quincy Adams, it came to be called the Monroe Doctrine: (1) The Western Hemisphere was no longer open to further colonization by European powers. (2) Any attempt of those powers to extend their political system (government by kings and not by elected representatives) to any portion of the American continents would be taken as a sign of unfriendliness toward the United States. (3) The United States would not meddle with European politics. (4) In return, Europe must not disturb the political status of the republics on this side of the ocean. In 1822 the United States had already recognized the independence of the new republics created from the old Spanish Empire. Now we proceeded to guarantee their independence against European interference.

The Monroe Doctrine was a defiant warning to strong and belligerent European powers. But like some later ringing American declarations it was a warning that the United States did not have the power to enforce. Then, as later, there were dangers in making threats if there was no strong army or navy behind them. At that time the only hope for enforcing the Monroe Doctrine was that it coincided with British foreign policy and that therefore it would be supported by the large British fleet. Whether European governments would pay attention to it in the future if it did not coincide with British policy would depend on the power of the young nation itself.

SECTION 4 REVIEW

1. What did the Monroe Doctrine proclaim?
2. **Testing Conclusions.** Is it true that the Monroe Doctrine was an outcome of revolutions in Latin America? Explain.

The Americas in 1823

- British Territory
- United Provinces of Central America
- Spanish Territory
- Territory Claimed by England and United States
- ▷ Protected by Monroe Doctrine

0   1500 Miles

0   1500 Kilometers

CANADA

OREGON

NEWFOUNDLAND

42°

EMPIRE OF MEXICO

UNITED STATES

CUBA

JAMAICA

REPUBLIC OF HAITI

PUERTO RICO

BRITISH HONDURAS

GUATEMALA

HONDURAS

EL SALVADOR

NICARAGUA

COSTA RICA

VENEZUELA

GREATER COLOMBIA

BRITISH GUIANA

DUTCH GUIANA

FRENCH GUIANA

ECUADOR

EMPIRE OF BRAZIL

PERU

UPPER PERU (BOLIVIA) Independent, 1825)

PARAGUAY

UNITED PROVINCES OF RIO DE LA PLATA

CHILE

URUGUAY (Independent, 1828)

5. A national spirit

In 1824 President Monroe invited the French hero of the American Revolution, the aged Marquis de Lafayette, then nearing 70, to visit the United States again. He arrived in August, and his triumphal tour through all parts of the country lasted a full year. The wild enthusiasm that greeted Lafayette everywhere showed that despite sectional differences a national spirit flourished.

Words, slogans, and symbols. Perhaps the chief symbol of the new American nationalism was the flag. On June 14, 1777, Congress had adopted the first flag, which had 13 alternate stripes of white and red, and a circle of 13 white stars on a blue field in the upper left-hand corner. Later the small stars were arranged in the form of a large star, but finally they were set in horizontal lines on the field of blue. An act of Congress of April 4, 1818, provided that a new star should be added for each new state.

Another symbol was the American bald eagle. Benjamin Franklin had jokingly suggested that the turkey should be our symbol. But instead the fierce eagle was chosen. It appeared on the official seal of the United States and on coins. It was a popular decorative device on walls, in pictures, on signs—wherever people could think to use it.

The Constitution itself, the nation's instrument of government, also became a revered symbol. After the Constitution was ratified, it was the custom to refer to the Constitution as if it had always existed. The Constitution became the nation's sacred document, the final arbiter of any discussion. Of course, people might differ over what the Constitution *meant,* but who dared question its authority?

"Liberty," "freedom," and "union" became national slogans. Although the nation was still young, it already had a history, with heroes and stirring mottoes. At the Battle of Bunker Hill, General Putnam ordered: "Don't fire until you see the whites of their eyes." When the British commanded John Paul Jones to surrender his ship, he retorted, "I have not yet begun to fight." With the War of 1812, "Don't give up the ship" entered the vocabulary of American patriotism. The sharpshooting Kentucky rifleman in his buckskins—who had fought at the Thames and New Orleans—now was hailed as a new, and peculiarly western, national hero.

Heroes of the Revolution. The American people were long reminded of their fight for independence by the inspiring presence of men who had actually fought in the Revolution. No Fourth of July parade was complete without a veteran of the war. Some of the best American artists like Gilbert Stuart and Charles Willson Peale made their reputations (in those days before photography) painting portraits of heroes of the Revolution. John Trumbull told the whole history of the Revolution in a series of panoramic paintings. The nation's leading museum, in Philadelphia, featured Peale's portraits of the leaders in the fight for freedom.

The grand hero of the Revolution, of course, was George Washington. Painting his portrait became an industry in itself. Gilbert Stuart copied his own first portrait of Washington 39 times. He painted the President twice thereafter and made more copies. Washington's birthday began to be celebrated by the nation even before his death. His Farewell Address became a classic of schoolroom oratory. It is still read in the Congress every February 22.

The cult of George Washington was further promoted by solemn biographies like that by John Marshall (in five large volumes!) and popular lives like that by Parson Weems, who invented the famous story about Washington cutting down the cherry tree.

A national education. After the Revolution numerous plans were proposed for a national system of education. Democracy surely could not succeed without an educated citizenry. This meant, of course, that everyone should go to school and learn to read. Elementary schools and high schools were left to the local communities. But there were many proposals for a national university. Every President from Washington through John Quincy Adams favored some kind of national university that would instill patriotism and prepare citizens to govern.

In the United States, unlike most other countries of the world, the public schools would not be run by the national government. But a national spirit would still stir the American schools through textbooks—like those of Noah Webster and Jedidiah Morse. Webster, beginning in 1782, wrote spelling and other books which he hoped would create a uniform and pure *American* (as opposed to English) language. With the same hope in 1828 he produced the first important *American* dictionary. It was so respected that in the United States the name "Webster" has become a synonym for our dictionary. Just as Webster bred pride in our language, Jedidiah Morse helped spread knowledge of our land and pride in our land by his popular American geographies.

Some enthusiastic patriots went off the deep end. "The United States was larger than all the universe beside," recalled a New Hampshire student of the 1820s. "We were taught every day and in every way that ours was the freest, the happiest, and soon to be the greatest and most powerful country in the world."

SECTION 5 REVIEW

1. Name some symbols and slogans that reflected the emerging national spirit of this period.

2. **Recognizing Ideologies.** How did the works of Gilbert Stuart, Charles Willson Peale, John Trumbull, and Noah Webster, reflect and promote nationalism?

The Reverend Jedidiah Morse, author of the first textbook on American geography, uses a globe for a family geography lesson. Samuel F. B. Morse, inventor of the telegraph, painted this watercolor of his parents' household in 1811 when he was only 20 years old.

National Museum of History and Technology, Smithsonian Institution.

181

FOCUSING ON IDEAS

1. Following the War of 1812, the United States was able to settle international disputes in 1817, 1818, and 1819 without going to war. Identify these three disputes. Why was each settled peaceably rather than by war?

2. One way to remember Presidents is to link them with the decisions they made on one or two major issues. What were two major issues facing Madison? Monroe? What important decisions did each make on these issues?

3. Tecumseh and the Prophet tried to organize Indian groups in defense of their rights. What was their strategy?

YOUR REGION IN HISTORY

1. **Geography.** Mexico won independence from Spain in 1821. If your state was once a part of Mexico, what Mexican settlements did it have in the early 1820s?

2. **Culture.** If your region was once a part of Mexico, how were feelings of pride in Mexican nationhood expressed? Are there still cultural ties to Mexico? If so, what are they?

3. **Economics.** How was your region affected by the Missouri Compromise? Identify economic activities that were affected because slavery was permitted or prohibited in your state after 1820.

TAKING A CRITICAL LOOK

1. **Drawing Conclusions.** How could a member of Congress opposed to slavery on moral grounds have voted for the Missouri Compromise? Explain.

2. **Recognizing Cause and Effect.** How do symbols and slogans help people in every state feel they are all Americans?

3. **Making Comparisons.** Compare the way Americans express their nationalism today with the ways they expressed it in the 1820s.

HISTORICAL FACTS AND FIGURES

Predicting Consequences. Use the data, or information, from the graph below to answer the following questions. (a) How did each region's population change between 1800 and 1830? (b) Describe two trends in the United States' population growth between 1800 and 1830. (c) Based on data in the graph, what predictions can be made about future population changes in each of the regions? (d) What other information about the United States during this period supports your prediction?

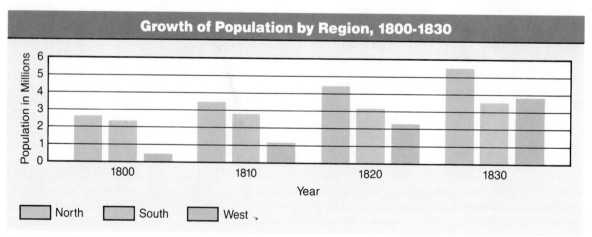

Growth of Population by Region, 1800-1830

North   South   West

Source: *Historical Statistics of the United States*

CHAPTER 9

The Jacksonian era

Gen. J.[ackson] will be here abt. 15 Feb.—Nobody knows
what he will do when he does come.... My opinion is That
when he comes he will bring a breeze with him. Which way
it will blow, I cannot tell.... My *fear* is stronger than my *hope.*

So wrote Senator Daniel Webster of Massachusetts as the nation waited
for the beginning of the Presidency of Andrew Jackson. For now the
people—the common folk of America—were to have their first President. He was an unknown, rawboned old man from Tennessee about
whom little more was known than that he was the hero of the Battle of
New Orleans. Wealthy merchants and bankers—the friends of Daniel
Webster—were worried. They would not like Andrew Jackson much
better when his Presidency was over. But by then there would be no
doubt that a fresh breeze had blown and that American political parties
and elections had been completely transformed since the dignified days
of the Virginia dynasty.

1. A second Adams in the White House

In 1824 as the second term of President Monroe was
coming to an end, candidates appeared on all sides to
try to succeed him. Each section of the country had
its favorite, but there was no opposition political
party. As a result, the Republicans were under no
pressure to unite behind a single candidate.

There was not yet anything like a national party
convention. Each party brought together its members of Congress in a "caucus," and they agreed on
their party's candidate for President. Now with so
many hoping to be candidates and with the lack of
an opposition party, this caucus system broke
down. Only about one-third of the Republican
congressmen attended their party caucus. They
nominated William H. Crawford of Georgia.

Additional candidates were nominated in other
ways—by mass meetings and state legislatures,
which added John Quincy Adams of Massachusetts,
Andrew Jackson of Tennessee, and Henry Clay of
Kentucky to the list.

Secretary of the Treasury Crawford, the favorite
of the old South, was supported by Madison,
Monroe, and Jefferson. But he had been stricken by
paralysis from which he had not yet recovered in
1824.

New England's candidate, the experienced Secretary of State John Quincy Adams, was the son of
former President John Adams. He was well
equipped for the Presidency, but his frigid manner
made him a poor vote-getter. Speaker of the
House Henry Clay, warm and charming "Harry of

the West," was an all-around good fellow who constantly promoted the "American System" of tariffs, internal improvements, and a national bank. No one had a more passionate desire to be President. His support came not only from his home state of Kentucky but also from Missouri, Illinois, Ohio, and Louisiana.

Tennessee nominated Andrew Jackson, "Old Hickory," the popular hero of the Battle of New Orleans. Since no one knew where he stood on the important issues, he had few enemies. His center of support was in the old Southwest.

South Carolina put forward its native son John C. Calhoun, Monroe's Secretary of War. He was an able administrator, a patriot, a gentleman with fine manners, "fascinating in conversation, kind and generous in his feelings, and a personality to look up to with reverence, admiration and confidence." When Calhoun withdrew from the race in order to run unopposed for Vice-President, he was only 42 years of age. There was still plenty of time, he thought, to become President.

The election. The bitter campaign became a contest of prejudice and name-calling. When the votes were counted, Jackson had the greatest number of popular votes, with strong support over all the Union except in New England. He led also in the electoral college with 99 votes. Adams, who carried New England and New York, followed with 84. Crawford received 41 from the Southeast, and Clay

had 37 from the old Northwest. Since no candidate had a majority of the electoral votes, for the second time a presidential election was thrown into the House of Representatives.

According to the Twelfth Amendment, the House had to choose between the three highest candidates. That put Clay out of the race. The paralyzed Crawford was no longer a serious contender. The competition then was between Jackson and Adams. The outcome lay in the hands of Henry Clay, who controlled the three states that he himself had carried. Clay, who felt threatened by Jackson as his political rival in the West, threw his support to John Quincy Adams. Only 7 states voted for Jackson and 4 for Crawford, while Adams received the votes of 13 states and so won on the first ballot. President Adams had been elected by the House of Representatives just as the Constitution prescribed, but there were grave disadvantages to not being a popularly elected President.

The "Corrupt Bargain." John Quincy Adams, like his father, was cold, tactless, and devoted to public service. He believed that the best men should hold office, and he did not suffer from excessive modesty. He had not the slightest doubt that he was more fit than Andrew Jackson to be President of the United States. Before his election by the House, Adams had met with Henry Clay to agree on their political futures. All the details of their discussion were never known. But when John

Supporters of John Quincy Adams in Cincinnati are called to a meeting to organize and win Ohio's electoral votes for Adams in the election of 1824. But the Ohio legislature was among those that nominated Henry Clay, who then carried the state in the election that fall.

JOHN QUINCY ADAMS.

The Citizens of Cincinnati, friendly to the elevation of this Gentleman to the Presidency of the United States, are requested to meet at the Presbyterian Church, on Walnut street, at 4 o'clock this afternoon, to adopt such measures as shall be deemed most advisable for the attainment of that object.

CINCINNATI, APRIL 24, 1824.

THE PEOPLE.

Quincy Adams named Henry Clay to be his Secretary of State, their enemies shouted "Corrupt Bargain." Adams, they said, was now paying off Clay for his support in the recent contest for the Presidency.

The two men were natural allies. They both distrusted and disliked Jackson. Also, to be a successful President and have his policies adopted by Congress, Adams needed the support of the West, which he hoped Clay could deliver. But Adams and Clay both misjudged human nature. The "Corrupt Bargain" charge disrupted Adams's Presidency from the start. It also sank Clay's chances to be President himself. The "Corrupt Bargain" kept coming back to haunt Clay. When it was known that he would be Secretary of State, one western newspaper that despised Adams called Clay "morally and politically a gambler, a blackleg and a traitor." Many voters would always believe so.

Jackson, thinking that he deserved to be President, attacked Clay as "the *Judas* of the West" for blocking his election. He resigned his seat in the Senate and began a four-year campaign to oust Adams and Clay and restore the government to "the people."

A national program. In his first annual message to Congress, John Quincy Adams called for a strongly national program. The laws he proposed might have passed in the era of national solidarity that followed the War of 1812. But now sectional feeling was on the rise. The realistic Henry Clay wanted Adams to tone down his demands. Adams would not retreat. He called for huge federal outlays—for roads and canals, for an enlarged navy, for new national institutions of learning. His proposals would touch every American. Yet most citizens still distrusted the federal government and were not ready for such a program.

Adams was a visionary. He preferred ideals and principles to the compromises of political parties. And he did not mend his political fences by keeping in touch with his supporters around the country. He ignored his followers—who were now called the *National* Republicans because of their nationalistic program. Thurlow Weed, a savvy New York politician who had delivered New York's vote to Adams in 1824, observed, "Mr. Adams during his administration failed to cherish, strengthen, or even recognize the party to which he owed his election;

When the old Hero hove in sight of the Capitol at Washington,

March 4, 1829,

he waved his hand and ordered all bargainers and billiard players, to leave the Cabinet. Old *Ebony* and *Rush* started one way, and *Clay* and *Peter R. Porter* another, all on horseback, Jehu-like, as will be seen above. The old General locked up the treasury, and directed that John Binns' salary should be stopped. A terrible rout followed. The whole air was rent with shouts of **Clear the Course! Clear the Course!** The old Hero's coming! *Farewell, a long farewell,* to the "**CORRUPT HOUSE OF BRAINTREE**"!

The New-York Historical Society

This gleeful Jacksonian broadside calls the defeated Adams and his Cabinet the "House of Braintree," after Adams's home town.

nor, so far as I am informed, with the great powers he possessed did he make a single influential friend."

The "Tariff of Abominations." Adams's tragic Presidency was a list of failures. The only major bill to pass was a tariff created by his opponents. The supporters of Andrew Jackson, who called themselves the *Democratic* Republican party (soon shortened to Democratic), controlled Congress. They posed as friends of industry and of the working class by favoring a higher tariff. At the same time they wanted to keep the friendship of the South by not actually passing any new bill that would increase the cost of living there. With these two contradictory purposes in mind, they created a bill with so many new duties and higher rates—so many "abominations"—that they expected even friends of the tariff to defeat it. Sarcastic John

When this watercolor was painted about 1826, Washington, D.C., was still a village. On the left is the White House. On the right in the background is the Capitol dome, which was completed in 1825.

Randolph of Virginia remarked of the new tariff bill that it "had nothing to do with manufactures except the manufacture of a President."

The trick did not work. Supporters of the tariff accepted the new bill, bad as it was, and the "Tariff of Abominations" became law in 1828, much to the surprise of the Jackson men. But the shrewd Andrew Jackson himself had said little about the tariff.

The election of 1828. The presidential campaign of 1828 turned out to be a contest of personalities. Of course Adams and Jackson differed over banks, the tariff, internal improvements, and other important matters. But the politicians tried to fuzzy up these issues.

For four years Jackson and his supporters had been working toward this moment. They received all the electoral votes of every state west of the Appalachians and south of the Potomac. In addition, they took Pennsylvania and won 20 of 36 votes in New York. Adams carried only New England, Delaware, and Maryland. The total electoral vote was 178 for Jackson to 83 for Adams. In popular votes, Jackson was given 647,286 to Adams's 508,064.

SECTION 1 REVIEW

1. Identify or explain: party caucus, William H. Crawford, Twelfth Amendment, National Republicans, Democratic Republicans.

2. How was the election of 1824 decided? What was the "Corrupt Bargain"?

3. What kinds of measures did John Quincy Adams ask Congress to pass? What was the outcome and why?

4. Describe the campaign and election of 1828.

5. **Identifying Central Problems.** Why did the system for nominating presidential candidates break down in 1824?

---

2. The new politics

On Inauguration Day, March 4, 1829, the tall and distinguished-looking Andrew Jackson walked from his boardinghouse to the Capitol. After taking the oath of office, he rode on horseback down the still-unpaved Pennsylvania Avenue to the White House. A motley crowd pursued him right into ·the building hoping to shake the hand of "their" President—and drink his orange punch. "One hundred and fifty dollar official chairs," one observer noted, were "profaned by the feet of clod-hoppers" in that hilarious, pushy mob. Exhausted, Jackson finally escaped back to his boardinghouse leaving the White House staff to get rid of the noisy guests by putting the punch bowl out on the lawn. The common people who had felt annoyed by an aristocrat—from Virginia or from New England—presiding from the "President's Palace" at last had their own President. He seemed to like them, to be one of them, and to have been elected by them.

Widening the suffrage. To understand how the suffrage (the right to vote) was widened so people felt the President represented them, we must re-

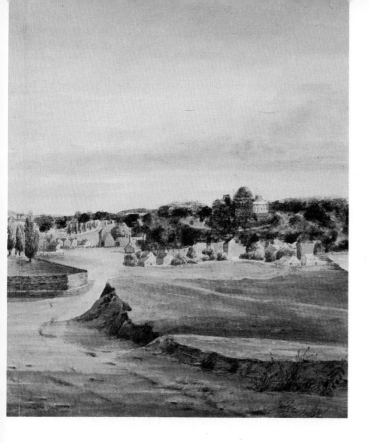

member that the Constitution allowed each state to decide for itself which of its citizens could vote. Early in the 1800s you might be a respectable farmer or a hardworking businessman, but you still could not vote unless the laws of your state included you among the voters. The chief qualification (other than being a male) was to own property—usually a certain amount of land. For it was believed that only by owning property would you have a "stake" in good government. That was necessary, it was felt, to make you a solid citizen with sound judgment about the candidates. If you were a woman, you could not vote. If you were black, you were probably a slave. But even if you were free, you could vote only in a few states.

In 1776 in most of the states, these laws did not keep many white men from being able to vote, since most Americans were farmers and owned land. But as the country grew, and with it the cities, there was always a body of men who could not vote. More and more people felt this was unfair. As the author James Fenimore Cooper wrote, "Every man who has wants, feelings, affections, and character has a stake in society." Therefore every man should vote whether he had property or not.

Early in the 1800s one state after another began to give the vote to adult white males even if they did not own property. Some of the first states to open up voting were in the newly occupied lands across the Appalachian Mountains. On that frontier there were no "old families," no long-established plantation or commercial aristocracy. For example, in Ohio, which in those days was still "West," the state constitution of 1802 gave the vote to almost all adult white men. And so did the constitutions in other new western states—Indiana (1816), Illinois (1818), and Alabama (1819)—and the new eastern state of Maine (1820).

The democratic influence of the frontier was echoed in the East by politicians looking for voters, by middle-class reformers, and by spokesmen for the propertyless worker. Many of the original thirteen states revised their constitutions. Connecticut (1818), Massachusetts (1821), and New York (1821) gave up their property requirement for voting. In some older states there was a bitter struggle. Former President John Adams—who had helped write the Declaration of Independence and had been a leader in the Revolution—was the chairman of the Massachusetts Constitutional Convention in 1820. He distrusted the common people, and he warned of anarchy and mob rule if Massachusetts gave the vote to men who had no property.

In aristocratic Virginia change was slow. Madison, Monroe, and Chief Justice Marshall—all members of the Virginia dynasty—wanted to keep the property qualification. Even after the new Virginia constitution of 1831, about one-third of the adult white men (some 80,000 people) and all the blacks still were not allowed to vote. It was 1851 before Virginia finally abolished the property requirement. But Virginia was an exception.

At the same time that the right to vote was widened, written ballots made it easier to vote, as we shall see. In addition, more people began to read about, hear about, and take part in politics through party newspapers, political conventions, and rallies. Candidates became (or were advertised as) just common men, not aristocrats like the Virginia dynasty. As a result more people began to go to the polls than ever before. Twice as many of the nation's adult white males voted in the election of 1828 as had voted in 1824. John Quincy Adams, the loser, actually received a larger popular vote in 1828 than *all* the candidates combined in 1824.

ued long into the 1800s. It was 1890 before Kentucky, the last state, finally gave up voice voting in presidential elections.

Gradually voice voting gave way to paper ballots. At first there were no printed ballots, and people had to write down their own votes. In the Pennsylvania election of 1796, for example, even if you had the right to vote, the only way you could vote for President of the United States was to write the names of fifteen different electors on your ballot. This was a great nuisance and increased the chance of making mistakes—especially for the people who were not used to writing at all.

The political parties soon recognized that they could help the voters—and win their votes—by printing ballots with the names of their party's candidates on them. Usually each party printed its ballot in a different color so they could be sure who was voting their party ticket.

The printed paper ballot made it easy to vote for all the electors and other candidates for office, but it was not so good for the timid voter whose landlord or boss might be watching. These ballots simplified the task of corrupt politicians. The color of the ballot showed whether a man voted the way he had been paid to vote. American elections became increasingly influenced by bribery, violence, and other forms of intimidation. It would not be until after the Civil War that voting became truly secret.

Nominating the candidates. A "party ticket" was the new name for the list of candidates supported by a political party. "Ticket-making" became a popular pastime. But who would make up the official party "ticket"? The old "caucus" where a few leaders got together and privately chose the candidates would no longer do. Everybody now wanted his say—not only about who was elected, but even about who was nominated.

To do this new job of ticket-making, the parties began to hold conventions. Members of the party in each county met to choose delegates to a state convention. There the delegates would meet to make up their party ticket. They listed their candidate for governor and for all the other state offices.

The state conventions were great fun. In the days before movies or radio or television, and when other public entertainment was scarce, farmers and villagers were delighted to have an excuse to visit

Library Company of Philadelphia

This unfinished etching and engraving of an exciting election day was done about 1815.

The process of voting. In early colonial times, voting was a kind of community ritual where a voter announced his choice aloud to the cheers (or jeers) of his neighbors. When the candidate received a vote, he would rise, bow, and personally thank the voter. "Mr. Buchanan, I shall treasure that vote in my memory. It will be regarded as a feather in my cap forever."

This vocal way of voting had been brought over from England. By the time the Constitution was ratified, it was still used in three states. Some of the new western states followed this procedure for voting when they entered the Union, so it continthe big city. A state convention was less like a solemn committee meeting than like a church picnic or a state fair. People exchanged jokes and gossip, and enjoyed plenty of refreshments. And, of course, delegates made speeches about their candidates, talked about party politics, and gave three cheers for the party. By the late 1820s and the 1830s state party conventions were being held all over the country. American politics was beginning to be a popular hobby. But it was not yet everybody's game. It would still be many years before blacks or women would be allowed to vote.

The next step, of course, was the national party convention. In the presidential election of 1832, for the first time, national nominating conventions were held by all the major parties.

Hotels serve convention delegates.
National conventions were now possible because of a new American institution—the hotel. Nearly everything about the American hotel was new. Even the word was new to the English language. "Hotel" was borrowed from the French language, where it meant a noble house or a city hall. The old English "inn" was a modest building with a few rooms where tired travelers could sleep. In England "tavern" was the name for the place where you could get food or drink. The American "hotel" combined the services of the inn and the tavern.

The architecture was new. The American hotel was often the biggest and most imposing building in a city. It looked more like a great church or a palace than like a modest English inn. The St. Charles Hotel in New Orleans struck English visitors in 1846 by its "large and elegant Corinthian portico and the lofty swelling dome." American hotels were impressive public buildings. They came to be called "Palaces of the Public" or "People's Palaces." And they deserved the name. For they were the social centers where a democratic people could meet, just as European nobles had met in the lobbies and courtyards of their ruling princes.

The spacious new American-style hotel was an ideal convention headquarters for candidates and for the party. One reason why so many early national conventions were held in Baltimore was that city-boosters there had built one of the grandest hotels in the country. Barnum's City Hotel was an elegant six-story building with 200 apartments. These national party conventions were even livelier and more festive than the smaller state conventions. Delegates could come from all over, enjoy their stay in a grand hotel, and go to the meeting hall to hear speeches by famous men. These large audiences whipped up enthusiasm for the party platform and for the party's candidates.

The new candidates.
The candidates changed, too. Now that nearly every adult white male could vote, almost everybody had an opinion about who should be President. As more and more people could vote, American politics became more and more democratic, and the personal appeal of the politician became more important.

The frosty, standoffish manner of an aristocrat from Virginia or Massachusetts could no longer attract votes. It was not enough to be a statesman. The successful candidate would have to be a popular politician. That meant shaking hands and kissing babies—and liking it!

Andrew Jackson, who was elected in 1828, was the first President of this new brand. He was a self-made man. His father was a poor immigrant from Ireland, and both his parents died before he was fifteen. He never went to high school or college, but he studied law and became a lawyer. Even before Tennessee was a state, Jackson had settled in the fast-growing western town of Nashville, and then he grew up with the place. Aggressive and outspoken, he helped write the first constitution of the state in 1796. He represented Tennessee as congressman and as senator, and became a judge of the state supreme court. In 1804, with an impressive public career behind him, he "retired" to private life at age 37.

Jackson was the owner of a plantation with many slaves. He was a gambler, a duelist, a cockfighter, and a horse racer. He bore a sabre scar on his head from being struck by a British officer whose boots he refused to polish. He had successfully led American troops against the Indians and the British. And, as we have seen, he was hailed as a hero when he defeated the British at New Orleans in 1815.

It was not quite clear how the talents of a military hero would make a successful President. Jackson did not have the learning or the eloquence or the experience of an Adams or a Jefferson. But in the new era of popular politics, that was not what the voters were looking for. To the voters he seemed one of the common people, although in fact he was a

This wooden figure of Andrew Jackson was
carved for the ship *Constitution* in 1834.

wealthy member of the Tennessee frontier upper
class.

Still, Jackson transformed American politics.
Unlike Jefferson, who was a man of learning and
who liked to speak of the international Republic of
Letters, Jackson was proud of not being literary. He
was not good at spelling, and once even said that he
had no respect for a man who could think of only
one way to spell a word!

Democracy in office-holding. Although he was a
wealthy plantation owner and slaveholder when he
became President, Andrew Jackson thought of
himself as one of the common people. After all, he
had not inherited his wealth but had earned it by his
own efforts. And couldn't other industrious
Americans do the same? Although the people
thought they had been robbed of their choice by the
"Corrupt Bargain" between Adams and Clay in the
election of 1824, now in 1828 they finally had their
man.

It was not enough, Jackson argued, for the
common people to have their own President. They
had the right to hold all the offices in their
government. According to Jackson this meant that
anybody would be about as well qualified as
anybody else—provided, of course, that they had
supported Jackson.

"The duties of all public officers are . . . so plain
and simple," he said, "that men of intelligence may
readily qualify themselves for their performance."
Instead of there being an office-holding class, the
government offices should be "passed around."
President Jackson was happy to use this persuasive
democratic argument to throw out of office the
followers of the hated Adams and Clay and make
way for his own henchmen.

This "spoils system" of rewarding political supporters with jobs was an old story in many states,
especially in New York. Jackson's bark was worse
than his bite, however, for in the eight years of his
Presidency only about one government employee in
six was removed from office. That was not much
different from what earlier Presidents had done.
But Jackson and his political friends actually boasted
of these removals as if they were a new kind of
public service. The Jacksonian motto (borrowed
from the battlefield)—"to the victors belong the
spoils"—became the guiding principle of the national political parties.

1. How did voter qualifications change between 1800 and the mid-1820s? What groups still could not vote in 1828?

2. How did the method of nominating political candidates change? How did the American hotel help to promote the change?

3. What was Andrew Jackson's special voter appeal?

4. What was the "spoils system"? Why is Jackson associated with it?

5. **Recognizing Cause and Effect.** How did the early printed paper ballots affect voter turnout and corruption at the ballot box?

3. Jackson takes command

Andrew Jackson believed in the southern code of honor, which required a gentleman to fight a duel against another gentleman who insulted him or his family. In 1806 Jackson faced a man who had insulted Mrs. Jackson. His opponent, Charles Dickinson, was a successful young lawyer who had learned his profession from Chief Justice John Marshall. He was a fine young southern gentleman—and a crack shot, too. When the two men aimed pistols at each other on the dueling grounds, Dickinson fired first, swiftly and surely. His shot hit Jackson near his heart but missed the fatal spot because Jackson's coat hung so loosely on his tall, thin frame. For a moment, Jackson believed he had been killed. But by force of his powerful will he held himself upright, waited for his eyes to clear, and then shot the man opposite him. His rival died the following day.

The incident clearly revealed several traits that marked Jackson as President—his fierce pride, his deep sense of honor, his unbending will.

The problem of Peggy Eaton. Andrew Jackson, at age 61 when he took office, felt sick and tired. His beloved wife, Rachel, had died only two months before. But, despite his grief, the gaunt, gray-haired old general radiated power.

It was his good luck, however, that in those days, although the President took office on March 4, the Congress did not assemble until the first Monday in December. So Jackson was able to spend his first nine months in office regaining his health, coping with the hordes of office seekers, and surveying the tasks of a President. One item that took much of his energy was nowhere listed in the laws or the Constitution. It was the troublesome problem of pretty Peggy O'Neale.

The daughter of a Washington tavernkeeper, Peggy was married to John Eaton, whom Jackson appointed Secretary of War. But she was not thought to be socially acceptable by Vice-President John C. Calhoun's wife, Floride, or by the wives of the other Cabinet members. This minor social problem would not be worth a line in a history book except that Andrew Jackson sided with the Eatons. He stopped meeting with his Cabinet and started taking advice from a group of friends, whom his enemies referred to as the "Kitchen Cabinet." Even more important, Secretary of State Martin Van Buren of New York used the problem to win the special favor of Andrew Jackson.

A blond, dapper little man, Van Buren liked to wear white trousers, a tan coat, a lace tie, and yellow gloves. He was a member of the new class of professional politicians, and he knew how to deal with people. He was always friendly, never angry, and never bothered to justify his actions with elaborate explanations. As an experienced New York politician he knew the spoils system and how to use it.

Van Buren, like Jackson, was a widower. So he could join Jackson without creating problems at home. His kindness to Peggy Eaton made Jackson grateful to him.

At last, the clever Martin Van Buren found a way to solve the problem of Peggy Eaton. He resigned as Secretary of State and engineered the resignations of Eaton and all but one of the other Cabinet members. For ridding him of the Eatons and the Cabinet members he could not work with, Jackson thought so highly of Martin Van Buren that Van Buren became his candidate for the next President of the United States.

At the same time, Calhoun had lost the President's confidence because his wife had been a leader in snubbing Peggy Eaton. This trivial incident checked, at least temporarily, Calhoun's march to the Presidency. Instead of Calhoun's rising as he had hoped from Vice-President to President with Jackson's support, Jackson now favored someone else. The South's most able spokesman would not

Webster replies to Robert Hayne (front, hands folded) in the chamber used by the Senate until 1860. Visitors crowd the galleries and pages sit at the front in this painting by G. P. A. Healy.

be President during the coming struggle between the sections for national power.

South Carolina and the tariff. Southerners opposed the protective tariff because it raised the prices of the manufactured goods they purchased. Since the higher prices went to northern manufacturers, they felt that they were being impoverished to enrich the businessmen in another section of the country. In South Carolina, a state that had been especially hard hit by the depression of 1819, the opposition was violent. Overproduction had made cotton prices plummet. The price of cotton fell from almost 31 cents a pound in 1818 to less than 10 cents in 1828. This caused great distress in South Carolina. There the worn-out fields produced fewer pounds per acre than did the new fields west of the mountains.

The slaveholding South Carolinians had other reasons, too, to be worried. In 1822 they had discovered what appeared to be a widespread slave conspiracy. It was headed by Denmark Vesey, a free black who lived in Charleston. Thirty-six blacks were executed, and many others were exiled. But since none of the plotters would talk, their exact plans were never discovered. Still, South Carolinians were terrified. They put the blame for the Vesey rebellion on the northern critics of slavery who had spoken out during the debates over the Missouri Compromise. They began to feel that slavery—the South's "peculiar institution"—must be treated as if it were a sacred institution. They would not consider any change, and they dreaded to discuss the issue. They also began to imagine that enemies of the South lurked everywhere.

So they became strong opponents of tariffs and internal improvements by the federal government. If a strong federal government could take money away from the South with a protective tariff to benefit the businessmen of another section (the North), if it could enter a state to build a road or canal, what would prevent it from entering a state to meddle with, or even abolish, slavery?

When the Tariff of Abominations was passed in 1828, flags were flown at half-mast in Charleston. South Carolina orators urged a boycott against the states that profited from the tariff. One excited journalist even announced that it was high time "to prepare for a secession from the Union."

The most influential protest came from the pen

of Vice-President Calhoun. He continued to think of himself as a nationalist, but he felt the Union could not be preserved if the rights of the states could be so infringed. In an unsigned essay, "The Exposition and Protest of South Carolina," he argued that a protective tariff was unconstitutional because it unfairly taxed one section of the country for the benefit of another. He reviewed the ideas of the Virginia and Kentucky Resolutions of 1798 that the Union was a compact of states. Each state, then, had the right to judge whether Congress was exceeding its powers. Within its borders, Calhoun argued, any state could nullify an act of Congress that it considered unconstitutional. For Congress to override that "nullification," it would then be necessary to use the long and clumsy amending process described in the Constitution. For that purpose the power asserted by the Congress, even if questioned by only one state, would have to be approved by three-fourths of the states.

The Webster-Hayne debate.
Soon this very question (and Calhoun's theory of "nullification") would be debated in Congress. The issue arose over the public lands. Many Easterners believed that the price of western land still owned by the government should be kept high. In that way the settlement of the West would proceed only slowly. Money and workers would not be drained away from the industrial East. But naturally enough, Westerners wanted all the land they could get. They wanted it fast, and they wanted it cheap!

At this point, southern planters saw their chance to create an alliance with the West. If they could join forces in Congress, the Westerners could get cheap land in return for their promise to help block any laws that touched slavery. On January 21, 1830, Senator Robert Y. Hayne of South Carolina moved in that direction. In his long speech that demanded the opening up of the public lands, he preached Calhoun's doctrine of nullification.

The reply to Hayne was delivered on January 26–27 by Senator Daniel Webster of Massachusetts. Someone said that no one could really be as great a man as Webster seemed to be. He was not only one of the nation's most skillful lawyers, but in the style of his time he was a tireless orator. He had a rich, deep voice and held his audience spellbound. His high forehead, thick eyebrows, burning eyes, and powerful form made him overwhelming and impressive in debate—a "great cannon loaded to the lips," Ralph Waldo Emerson called him. This particular speech, according to some listeners, was the most powerful ever given in the United States Congress.

Over the course of some six hours of oratory in two days, Webster made his case. He rejected the idea that the Union was only a league of sovereign states. According to Webster, not the states but the people had made the Union. "It is, sir, the people's Constitution, the people's government made for the people, made by the people, answerable to the people." Only the Supreme Court had the power to declare a law void. If Pennsylvania could annul one law, Alabama another, and Virginia a third, then Congress would soon become a mockery. The Constitution would be a mere "rope of sand." The Union would fall apart, and the states would return to anarchy. In his emotional ending, Webster prayed to God that he would never live to see the Union destroyed. He rejected the idea of "Liberty first and Union afterwards." Instead he called for "Liberty *and* Union, now and forever, one and inseparable."

Webster's speech swept the nation. For generations schoolchildren memorized its famous passages. He had caught the spirit of the United States in 1830 as Hayne and Calhoun had not. Few Americans were fearful any longer that a strong federal government would follow the example of King George III. The colonial experience was two generations in the past. Since the War of 1812 they had come to realize that their liberties could be preserved only by a strong Union. But John C. Calhoun, Robert Y. Hayne, and other Southerners believed that slavery was a sacred institution on which the prosperity of their region depended. They were not compromisers, and they had already set out on a collision course that could only lead to bloody civil war.

The Jefferson Day dinner.
President Jackson had not, of course, played any part in the great debate in the Senate. Some of Calhoun's supporters, however, hoped that the President from Tennessee could be enlisted on the southern side. In that same year of 1830 they arranged a banquet at Brown's Indian Queen Hotel in Washington to celebrate Jefferson's birthday (April 13). In that way they could call attention to the late Thomas Jefferson's Kentucky

George Catlin painted this scene of Winnebago Indians gathering wild rice in Wisconsin. During Jackson's Presidency, the Winnebagos and other Wisconsin tribes were forced to give up their lands and move west.

Resolutions, which they thought supported Calhoun's theory of "nullification."

When Jackson was invited to the celebration he realized that if the evening went off as Calhoun and his friends had planned, it might menace the stability of the Union. So he carefully prepared a toast to deliver at the dinner. When he was called on, he lifted his glass, looked at Calhoun, and proposed, "Our Union, it must be preserved." The Vice-President rose with the rest of the audience and drank the toast, but his hand trembled visibly.

Everybody knew that the President's words were a direct challenge to the Vice-President. "An order to arrest Calhoun where he sat," wrote one of the diners, "could not have come with more staggering, blinding force." After the shock had passed, it was the Vice-President's turn to toast. "The Union—next to our liberties, most dear!" he said. Then he added, "May we always remember that it can only be preserved by respecting the rights of the states and by distributing equally the benefits and burdens of the Union."

The issue was clear. In brevity as well as sentiment, Jackson had won the day. The news of the dinner and of Jackson's toast was soon out, and a wave of nationalism swept the country. Calhoun was observed in the Senate looking "crinkled and careworn."

A month later Calhoun was struck by another blow. He received a letter from the President asking if it was true that Calhoun had favored punishing Jackson for his Florida campaign back in 1818 (p. 172). The report was, in fact, correct. But Calhoun had been able to conceal his old attitude until now. When Calhoun was unable to explain himself, Jackson ceased speaking to him. At that point, Calhoun realized that his chance to become President was gone. Calhoun and his loyal southern followers knew as never before that their interests within the Union were in danger.

Indian policy. Like most frontiersmen and Indian fighters, Andrew Jackson felt that the best place for the Indians was somewhere else. He believed that the only way to handle the Indians who lived on the eastern side of the Mississippi was to move them all to the other side of the river. Settled on lands forbidden to the whites, they could be forever separated from the people of the United States. In that way, according to Jackson, there would be no more battles with the Indians. Presidents Monroe and Adams had proposed the same "solution" to the Indian problem. But it took President Jackson, who was no aristocrat from Virginia or Massachusetts but a rough man of the frontier, to carry out the brutal program to uproot the Indians from the land of their ancestors.

During his two terms in office, by fair means and foul, 94 Indian treaties were signed. Tribes agreed for varying amounts of compensation to give up their lands and go west. Some tribes went peaceably, though all went unhappily, to the lands west of the Mississippi. Other tribes dared to fight against superior forces of United States troops. In 1832 a few hundred Sauk and Fox Indians under Chief Black Hawk bravely tried to return to their homelands in Illinois and Wisconsin. Pursued by a United States force of regulars and militia, they were disastrously defeated on August 2, 1832, in the Battle of Bad Axe.

The courageous Seminole Chief Osceola in Florida led his people in the most successful Indian opposition the United States regulars ever had to face. The Seminoles hid their wives and children deep in the swamps. Helped by runaway slaves, but with meager supplies, they showed a surprising power to resist. Osceola was finally captured when the United States violated a flag of truce, and he died in Fort Moultrie at Charleston, South Carolina, in 1838. The Seminoles continued to defy the regulars into the 1840s. During these years many were captured and forcibly transported west of the Mississippi.

The Cherokees, more than any other Indian tribe, had adopted the ways of the white man. They were mostly settled in Georgia, where their farms, factories, and schools were not much different from any others. But they had no alphabet for their language until the brilliant Sequoya actually invented one. With this new alphabet the tribe

Self-trained George Catlin painted 600 portraits from life of Indian leaders like this one of the Seminole chief, Osceola.

printed its first newspaper. It was fitting that this Cherokee hero would later be commemorated in the great California redwoods, which are called "Sequoias."

The Cherokees went to court to retain their lands. In the case of *Worcester* v. *Georgia* (1832) the Supreme Court led by John Marshall ruled that the state of Georgia had no jurisdiction over Cherokee lands. But Georgia ignored the Court, and Jackson refused to intervene. "John Marshall has made his decision," Jackson was reputed to have said, "now let him enforce it." Jackson really hoped that the Indians would quietly leave Georgia as soon as possible. He feared that Georgia's clear resistance to the law of the land would encourage South Carolina's efforts to nullify the acts of Congress.

The Cherokees did not give in. Finally, in 1838, the army under General Winfield Scott rounded up those remaining in the East. During that October and November the soldiers drove 15,000 Indian men, women, and children westward. Through cold and rain the troops forced these innocent and bewildered Cherokees away from their homeland to the new "Indian Territory." This would later be called Oklahoma. The Cherokees called this path their "trail of tears." And it was the right name, for 1500 of their tribe died on the way.

The nullification controversy. In 1832 Congress enacted a new tariff to replace the Tariff of Abominations. Though the rates were lower than those of 1828, this was still a high protective tariff. The planters of South Carolina were outraged. They were especially frightened because this tariff had passed by big majorities, which meant that the government's tariff policy would not soon change.

Meanwhile in Virginia in August 1831 a black preacher named Nat Turner led a slave rebellion during which 60 white men, women, and children were killed. The terrified whites put down the rebellion by killing at least 100 blacks, many of whom had no part in the revolt. The situation was so serious that the Virginia Assembly in 1832 lengthily debated the issue of abolishing slavery (p. 240). South Carolinians too were in a mood to review the threatening past—the Missouri Compromise, the uprisings of Denmark Vesey and Nat Turner, the radical debates in the Virginia Assembly. In several southern states where the blacks outnumbered the whites, the whites saw no way to handle this situation except by keeping the blacks in slavery. Now this peculiar institution seemed especially vulnerable to hostile federal laws. The new tariff offered no hope that the federal government would cease tampering with property within the states. Would the next step be to free the slaves?

South Carolinian planters decided that they must protect their property—which to them meant their institution of slavery. They imagined that Calhoun's procedure for "nullifying" federal laws might be their salvation. That way not only could they get rid of the burdensome tariffs, but they would be prepared to void any federal laws that might interfere with slavery. A state convention was called to meet in November 1832, and delegates were elected. The nullifiers swept all before them.

The South Carolina convention voted by a margin of five to one that the tariff acts of 1828 and 1832 were unconstitutional and therefore null and void. They forbade South Carolinians to pay the duties required by these laws. The convention went even further and stated that any attempt by federal authorities to enforce tariff laws in South Carolina would be "a just cause for the secession of the state from the Union." Still the convention did leave one opportunity for compromise, for nullification was not to go into effect until February 1, 1833.

Jackson's response to nullification. Meanwhile, at the very time of that convention, the national presidential campaign was under way. On December 5, 1832, Andrew Jackson was reelected by an overwhelming majority. Jackson, always a nationalist, reacted immediately to the challenge from South Carolina. Within days of his reelection his words to the nation posed the issue loud and clear. "I consider the power to annul a law of the United States, assumed by one state, incompatible with the existence of the Union." Since the nation was supreme over the states, no state could refuse to obey any federal law. And, of course, no state had the power to secede from the Union. "I will meet treason at the threshold," he wrote to the customs collector of the port of Charleston. "In forty days I will have 50,000 men in South Carolina to enforce the law."

The people of the nation rallied around Jackson, who was now at the height of his power. His

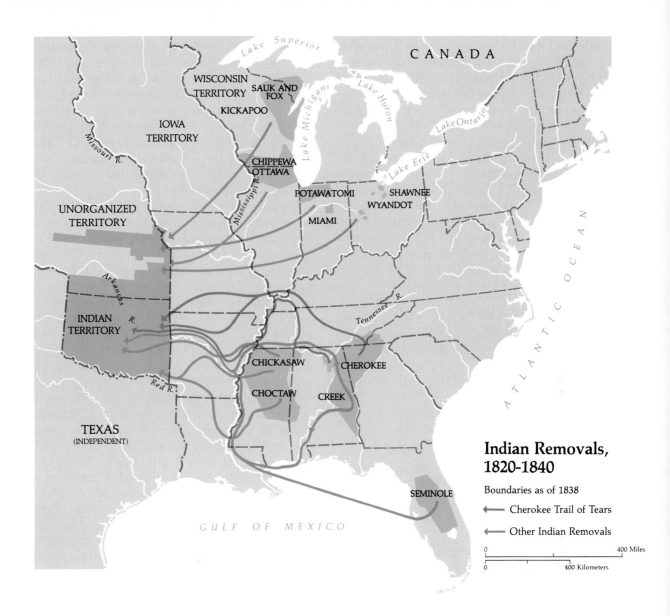

Indian Removals, 1820-1840

Boundaries as of 1838

← Cherokee Trail of Tears

← Other Indian Removals

| 0 | | 400 Miles |
| 0 | | 400 Kilometers |

unhesitating leadership had given new courage to all who loved the Union. Even Georgia, which was ignoring the Supreme Court's order concerning the Cherokees, supported the President. The uncompromising John C. Calhoun, who had resigned the Vice-Presidency in December in order to be elected to the Senate by South Carolina, now saw that his state must retreat. So he turned to Henry Clay — the man most responsible for the hated tariffs. Calhoun and Clay were united by their dislike of Jackson, and they shared a desire to avoid bloodshed. But Clay was also moved by his devotion to the Union.

Clay drew up a new bill that reduced the tariff rates but still preserved the protective system. Calhoun reluctantly went along with Clay's bill. Since it was offered as a compromise under pressure from South Carolina, it seemed to give Calhoun a way to save face, to stay in the Union, yet not give up his principles. The new bill reduced tariffs over a nine-year period until they finally were brought back down to the levels of 1816. It was signed into law by Jackson on March 2, 1833.

When the South Carolina convention met again a few days later, the domineering Calhoun advised the delegates to accept the new compromise tariff and rescind the nullification. This they did by an overwhelming vote. But then in a proud, if empty, gesture they turned around and nullified the "Force Bill" by which Congress had authorized the President "to employ the army and navy of the United States to collect duties in South Carolina."

Both sides now claimed victory. South Carolina planters felt they had compelled Congress to lower the tariff. Union supporters believed that Congress had forced South Carolina to back down and repeal nullification. Unfortunately this compromise bought time but offered no long-term solution. Since neither side had changed its principles, they had settled nothing. The day of battle was only postponed. The fighting language of nullification and secession would not be forgotten.

SECTION 3 REVIEW

1. Identify or explain: Peggy Eaton, "Kitchen Cabinet," Denmark Vesey, Robert Y. Hayne, Black Hawk, Osceola, Sequoya, *Worcester* v. *Georgia,* Winfield Scott, "trail of tears," Indian Territory, Nat Turner, Force Bill.

2. How did Martin Van Buren win Jackson's favor? Why did Calhoun fall out of favor?

3. Explain Calhoun's theory of nullification.

4. What was the *chief* issue in the Webster-Hayne debate? Where and how did Jackson take a stand on this issue?

5. Describe the treatment of the Indians under Jackson.

6. **Determining Relevance.** How did South Carolina's response to the 1832 tariff foreshadow secessionist sentiments?

---

4. Banks and money

A successful plantation owner and land speculator, Andrew Jackson was a practical, self-made man with strong prejudices. He distrusted banks. He disliked the cheap and sometimes worthless paper money they printed. The only money he trusted was hard money—gold and silver. He was especially bitter against the Bank of the United States, which with its monopoly of the government's business was a symbol of all hated special privilege. He thought it was evil as well as unconstitutional, and he loathed it.

The war on the Bank. The charter of the Bank of the United States was not due to expire until 1836. Its president, Nicholas Biddle, was aware of Jackson's feelings. So he felt that the Bank should lie low and try to arrange a truce with the President. The ambitious Henry Clay thought he saw in the Bank an issue that might defeat Jackson in the 1832 election. Clay was the unanimous choice of the National Republicans to oppose Jackson and the Democratic Republicans.

To bring the issue to a head, and reap the political benefit, Clay induced Biddle to apply for a new charter for the Bank early in 1832. He believed that if Jackson dared to veto the recharter bill, as he hoped he would, the President would lose enough votes in the East to cost him the election.

The recharter bill went to President Jackson on July 4, 1832. Jackson was sick in bed at the time, and he said to his running mate, "The Bank, Mr. Van Buren, is trying to kill me, but *I will kill it.*" Six days later he returned the bill to Congress with a veto which, in Nicholas Biddle's words, "had all the fury of a chained panther biting the bars of his cage."

Jackson could have sent Congress a brief message stating his objections to the bill. Instead he sent a long message that was shrewdly designed to garner votes. Jackson stressed that the Bank and its stockholders were claiming special privileges and wanted a democratic government to treat them like aristocrats. Of course in any human society there were some natural distinctions which God himself had made—"of talents, of education, or of wealth." But the government must not make laws that added to the "natural and just advantages artificial distinctions." When laws made "the rich richer, and the potent more powerful," the people had to protest.

Henry Clay and Nicholas Biddle thought that Jackson's demagogic appeal would have the opposite effect from that he intended. Jackson's words revealed how little he understood the Bank. Still he proved that he did understand what the people wanted. To the mass of voters it seemed that "Old Hickory" was the champion of all the little people against the money-kings. On election day Clay carried only six states with 49 electoral votes, while Jackson carried sixteen for a whopping 219.

The removal of the deposits. After this decisive victory over "the Monster," Jackson was impatient to kill the Bank at once. But its charter ran till

Jackson, armed with his veto, attacks the many-headed monster, the second Bank of the United States and its branch banks. Bank president Nicholas Biddle is the large, top-hatted head in the center. Helping Jackson is Major Jack Downing (right), the legendary backwoodsman in many Jacksonian cartoons. Martin Van Buren, piously declaiming that he dislikes dissension, eagerly congratulates those on both sides.

1836. He was determined not to wait four years until the charter expired. He decided to deposit no new funds in the Bank and to pay the nation's bills with the funds already on deposit there. These actions would rapidly remove all the government's money from the clutches of the hated Bank. It was not easy to find a Secretary of the Treasury who would help him murder the bank. After two unsuccessful tries he finally appointed his Attorney General, Roger B. Taney (pronounced Tawney), who agreed to do Jackson's bidding. On October 1, 1833, Taney began depositing government funds in certain "pet banks" around the country. The whole

nation would soon suffer from this vindictive act.

The Bank of the United States had been a wholesome influence on the nation's economy. Its officers had made sound loans that aided business. Now, using the vast government deposits, the imprudent "pet banks" lent their funds wildly and without counting the consequences. Reckless spending and uncontrolled economic growth followed. The government debt was paid off, and the surplus money that piled up in the "pet banks" spurred more and more growth. Sales of public land, which had been less than $2 million in 1830, rose to $24 million in 1836. The numerous new

Library of Congress

Jackson, dressed as "King Andrew the First," tramples with dainty shoes on bills passed by Congress and on the Constitution. The cartoonist makes clever use of the eagle as a leg for the table next to the throne.

banks that sprang up throughout the West fed the spending mania. They issued more money, which was used by land speculators to buy more land. Senator Thomas Hart Benton of Missouri had hated the Bank of the United States. But now he complained, "I did not join in putting down the Bank of the United States to put up a wilderness of local banks. I did not join in putting down the paper currency of a national bank to put up a paper currency of a thousand local banks."

The Specie Circular and the distribution of the Treasury surplus. Jackson, who shared Benton's distrust of paper money, was in a position to do something about it. On July 11, 1836, he issued his "Specie Circular," which forbade the Treasury to receive anything but gold or silver in payment for public lands. At once the land boom stopped. In that same year Congress voted to distribute to the states the surplus funds in the Treasury. Again the nation was to suffer from Jackson's ill-considered and hasty financial policies. But this time the results would not appear until his unfortunate successor had taken office.

Jackson's Presidency proved that the Chief Executive had the power to do more than simply execute the policies prescribed by Congress. He actually could make government policy and change that policy as he pleased. If the people supported him, there was little the opposition could do. His enemies were free, of course, to call him names, and they labeled him King Andrew I. To make it plain that he was a tyrant, the National Republicans renamed themselves the "Whigs," after the British party that had struggled against the king back in the 1700s.

The popular and energetic Jackson was still unshaken. One opponent confessed, "General Jackson may be President for life, if he wishes." When Jackson had enough of presidential power, he decided to retire to his beloved home, "The Hermitage," in Tennessee. As his successor he handpicked his favorite adviser, the dapper Martin Van Buren. In the election of 1836 the Whigs did not select a single candidate, but let each section choose its own in the hope of throwing the election into the House of Representatives. Still Martin Van Buren won easily over Senator Daniel Webster of Massachusetts, Senator Hugh L. White of Tennessee, and the military hero William Henry Harrison of Ohio.

The Presidency of Martin Van Buren. Martin Van Buren had been an adroit political manager. For some reason he proved unable to exercise that skill when he became President. To make matters worse, Jackson's reckless financial policies were coming home to roost. When Jackson had removed specie from the banks through the Specie Circular and the distribution of the surplus in the Treasury to the states, the banks began to restrict

By pulling a tab on the bottom of this Van Buren campaign curiosity, you could turn the bitter cup of William Henry Harrison into the sweet goblet of Martin Van Buren.

The Huntington Library, San Marino, California

AN UGLY *MUG* OF
LOG-CABIN HARD CIDER

their loans and to stop redeeming their bank notes in gold and silver. At the same time a financial crisis in Britain caused the Bank of England to reduce the flow of specie out of that country. It was this British gold and silver coming to the United States that had helped finance the boom during Jackson's second term. So, still another support to the American economy was lost. On top of that, farmers suffered a year of bad crops.

All these influences together brought on a financial panic in 1837. By 1839 the nation was suffering a severe depression. Land sales became a mere trickle. Banks failed and factories closed their doors. The surplus in the Treasury soon disappeared. States that counted on these funds to pay for the construction of elaborate systems of roads, canals, and railroads had to stop the projects. Thousands were thrown out of work. Van Buren's whole administration was blighted by this business depression.

Van Buren achieved only one lasting change during his Presidency. On March 31, 1840, he issued an executive order that no person could work more than ten hours a day on a federal project. For the first time government workers found that they no longer had to labor from dawn to dusk. Years later Michael Shiner, a free black who worked in the Washington Navy Yard, wrote in his diary that for establishing the ten-hour day Van Buren's name should be recorded in every workingman's heart.

The election of 1840. The Whigs spent these unhappy years of Van Buren's administration preparing to put their own candidate in the White House. Just as Andrew Jackson was the first new-style President, so the first rip-snorting modern presidential campaign took place in 1840. When the Whig party held its national nominating convention in Harrisburg, Pennsylvania, on December 4, 1839, it passed over the able Senator Henry Clay. He was too well known and had made too many enemies in his years in office.

A BEAUTIFUL GOBLET OF
WHITEHOUSE CHAMPAGNE.

HARD CIDER AND LOG CABIN ALMANAC FOR 18 41

HARRISON AND TYLER.

Hurah!! to HARRISON and TYLER.

I'll supply you all with true Hospitality

Do so Matty for by the Eternal its cursed Sour.

I shall Endeavor to stop the supply

NEW YORK:
TURNER & FISHER, 52 CHATHAM STREET,
AND No. 11 NORTH SIXTH STREET, PHILADELPHIA.
Of whom may be had all the Principal Almanacs now Published.

Boston Athenaeum

The Whigs used log cabins and hard cider to elect Harrison in 1840. Here a desperate Van Buren, encouraged by his mentor Andrew Jackson, tries to shut off the cider.

Instead the Whigs chose the old soldier William Henry Harrison, about whom most people knew little except that he had defeated the Indians at the Battle of Tippecanoe.

In order to pick up southern votes, the Whigs nominated John Tyler of Virginia for Vice-President. His only reason for being a Whig was that he shared their hatred for Andrew Jackson. The party drew up no platform (a list of what it stood for) because it could not agree on anything except the desire to defeat Van Buren, whom the Democratic party renominated.

This presidential campaign, like many to follow, did not center on key national issues, but resounded with empty slogans and name calling. When a Democratic newspaperman sneered that Harrison really did not care to be President but simply wanted a barrel of hard (alcoholic) cider to get drunk on and a log cabin to live in, the Whigs had their clue. They eagerly took up the cry: Hurrah for the log cabin and hard cider! Being an ordinary man who lived in a log cabin and liked to drink cider, they said, was no disgrace! On the contrary, that proved Harrison was a man of the people.

The log cabin idea had great appeal. General Harrison had really been born of an old, well-to-do Virginia family, and he lived in a mansion. But his supporters soon invented a log cabin that he was supposed to have been born in. The "aristocrat" Van Buren was pictured living in the White House enjoying fine foods and costly wines, indifferent to the suffering of the starving unemployed.

"Tippecanoe and Tyler too!" became the battle hymn of Harrison's supporters. At the Whig rallies, hard cider flowed freely from barrels on a stage-set of log cabins. The Whigs floated to victory on a sea of alcohol! "We were sung down, lied down, drunk down," a Democratic paper complained. Harrison and Tyler carried all but seven states, and against Van Buren's 60 electoral votes they won 234.

Harrison had proved himself the perfect new-style candidate. But it was one thing to be an appealing vote-getting candidate, and something else to be an effective President. As the Jacksonian era drew to a close, the nation was beginning to come apart at the seams. The country needed strong, farsighted leadership. The issues could not be washed away in hard cider. It would take more than songs and slogans to hold the young nation together.

SECTION 4 REVIEW

1. Identify or explain: Nicholas Biddle, bank recharter bill, Roger B. Taney, "pet banks," Specie Circular, Whigs, "Tippecanoe and Tyler too."

2. How did Henry Clay use the Bank issue to influence the election of 1832?

3. How did Van Buren make labor history?

4. Describe the election campaign of 1840.

5. **Determining Relevance.** What role did Jackson's financial policies play in the economic boom and financial panic?

FOCUSING ON IDEAS

1. John Quincy Adams was said to have made a bargain to become President, but his general unwillingness to bargain hurt his Presidency. Explain using evidence from the text.

2. What political factors contributed to the "choice of the common man" for President rather than the Virginia or New England aristocrat?

3. How was western land beyond the Appalachians involved in changes in suffrage qualifications? the Webster-Hayne debate? Jackson's Indian policy? Jackson's war on the Bank?

TAKING A CRITICAL LOOK

1. **Recognizing Ideologies.** Andrew Jackson was a man of "strong prejudices." What were some of his prejudices? How did they affect his personal relationships? his policies?

2. **Drawing Conclusions.** How did extending the right to vote reflect the growing influence of the "common man"?

YOUR REGION IN HISTORY

1. **Geography.** What percentage of the land in your state was taken from the Indians under the terms of Andrew Jackson's Indian removal policy? Where were the Indian groups in your state relocated?

2. **Culture.** When did your state grant voting rights to nearly all adult male citizens? To adult female citizens? What steps must you take to qualify to vote in your state?

3. **Economics.** How, if at all, did the Tariff of Abominations affect the economy of your state? Why did the tariff affect some industries more than others? Why were some industries not affected at all? How did people involved in industries especially hard-hit by the tariff respond? Cite specific examples to support your answer.

HISTORICAL FACTS AND FIGURES

Comparing graphs. Use the information in Chapter 9 and the two graphs below to answer the following questions: (a) Did the same candidate win the largest percentage of both the popular vote and the electoral vote? (b) Did the same candidate rank last in both the popular and the electoral votes? (c) How can you explain these results? (d) Which candidate had the largest difference between his percentage of the popular vote and his percentage of the electoral vote? (e) Which candidate won the election of 1824? (f) Do you think this was a fair election? Explain your answer.

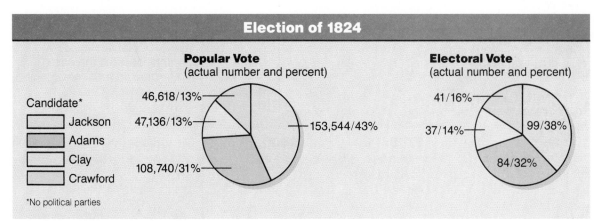

Election of 1824

Popular Vote
(actual number and percent)

Electoral Vote
(actual number and percent)

Candidate*
- Jackson
- Adams
- Clay
- Crawford

*No political parties

Popular Vote: 46,618/13%; 47,136/13%; 108,740/31%; 153,544/43%

Electoral Vote: 41/16%; 37/14%; 84/32%; 99/38%

Source: *Historical Statistics of the United States*

MAKING CONNECTIONS

This unit began on page 139 with the observation that the years 1800 to 1840 presented a great challenge to the people of the United States:

The Americans had won their independence and established a government. But they had not yet created a strong nation.

This conclusion was supported by the three unit themes that are reprinted in **dark type** below. Use the time line and the information in Unit 3 to answer the questions that follow the unit themes.

THEMES

1. **The nation discovers new ways to grow.**

   How did the nation develop both in terms of size and maturity during the years 1800–1840?

2. **The nation's growth is marked by the rise of two opposing forces: nationalism and sectionalism.**

   Do you agree that events and attitudes during this period acted like two large magnets on the nation, sometimes pulling it together, sometimes pulling it apart? Explain your answer.

3. **The nation's political process becomes more democratic.**

   What evidence would support the idea that the political process grew more responsive to the people between 1800 and 1840?

1800 Thomas Jefferson is elected President of the United States.

1804 Lewis and Clark begin to explore the area of the Louisiana Purchase.

1803 Chief Justice John Marshall decides the case of *Marbury* v. *Madison*.

Events in American History

Events in World History

| 1795 | 1800 | 1805 | 1810 |

1803 France sells Louisiana to the United States.

1830 The issue of nullification is raised in the Webster-Hayne debate.

1820s The printed paper ballot is introduced, making voting easier.

1828 Andrew Jackson is elected President of the United States.

1819 Chief Justice Marshall hands down a decision in *McCulloch* v. *Maryland*.

1832 President Jackson threatens to use federal troops to enforce tariffs in South Carolina.

1814 Representatives from the New England states meet at the Hartford Convention.

1832 President Jackson opposes rechartering the National Bank.

1810   1815   1820   1825   1830   1835

1817 The Rush-Bagot Agreement leads to the establishment of the U.S.-Canadian border.

1823 President Monroe outlines U.S. policy concerning European intervention in the Western Hemisphere.

1812 The United States goes to war against Britain.

UNIT 4

A nation growing and dividing
1800–1860

In 1831, Alexis de Tocqueville, a 26-year-old French aristocrat, arrived here to study the new nation.   By steamer, stagecoach, and horseback, he traveled for eight months over 7000 miles—as far west as Green Bay and Sault Ste. Marie and as far south as New Orleans.   He saw a great deal of the United States and talked to many Americans.   Back in France, Tocqueville wrote *Democracy in America,* one of the best books about our country.

"An attentive examination of what is going on in the United States," Tocqueville wrote, "will easily convince us that two opposite tendencies exist in that country, like two distinct currents flowing in contrary directions in the same channel."   These two opposite forces were nationalism and sectionalism.   As the nation grew, both forces would continue to grow.   In these next decades national leaders and sectional leaders worked hard to hold the country together.   They debated and passed laws of compromise.   We will see how strenuously they tried and how sadly they failed.   A divided nation was coasting down the road to civil war.

THEMES IN AMERICAN HISTORY

- The development of new transportation and communication systems draws Americans closer together.
- The growth of reform movements and a surge of western expansion forces the nation to face the slavery issue.

THEMES

This painting, "Geese in Flight," was done about 1850.   It reflects the interest of Americans in transportation.

Leila T. Bauman; National Gallery of Art, Washington; Gift of Edgar William and Bernice Chrysler Garbisch (detail)

The flourishing land

By the time of the Civil War there were distinct American ways of life. There were new ways of making houses, muskets, locks, and clocks—and nearly everything else. There were new ways of growing. The United States was the world's largest importer of people. And cities sprouted from raw western villages with a speed that startled Europeans.

But the sections did not grow all in the same way or at the same pace. Some regions were as different from others as, a century before, life in Great Britain had been different from life in the far-off American colonies. Thoughtful observers wondered if the Constitution that had been made to hold thirteen seaboard states together could really bind a continent.

1. Drawing the people together

At the time of the War of 1812 it took 75 days for a fully loaded wagon pulled by four horses to travel the 1000 miles from Worcester, Massachusetts, to Charleston, South Carolina. Letters and news traveled little faster. Could any union last if its people and their produce were so hard to bring together?

The age of roads and turnpikes. During the early years of the Republic, the land was gradually covered by a network of trails and roads. One of the most popular kinds of roads was the "turnpike." This was a road where the user had to pay a toll. It was named after a kind of revolving barrier with spikes on it that had been used on paths in England to prevent horses from passing through. The first turnpike in the United States was built during George Washington's second term to cover the 62 miles between Lancaster and Philadelphia in Pennsylvania.

The success of this Lancaster Turnpike began a wave of turnpike building in New England and the Middle States that lasted until about 1825. Most of the turnpikes were built by private companies. States and local governments sometimes helped. But the high toll-fees charged per ton discouraged their use for the farmers' bulky products.

Funds from the federal government would change the picture. In 1802 and 1803 Congress voted to use money received from the sale of the public lands for a National Road through the mountains and across Ohio. In 1806 Cumberland, Maryland, was selected as the road's starting point. This, the most important federal transportation project of the time, took a half-century. Work began in 1811. The road reached Wheeling, West Virginia, on the Ohio River in 1818 and did not

CANADA

Lake Superior

Lake Michigan

Lake Huron

Lake Ontario

Lake Erie

Mississippi R.

Portland

Boston

Providence

Albany

Buffalo

Mohawk Road

Catskill Turnpike

Boston Post Road

New York

Detroit

Seneca Road

Chicago Turnpike

Cleveland

Chicago

Pittsburgh

Harrisburg

(Cumberland Road)

Pennsylvania Road

Philadelphia

Columbus

Baltimore

Michigan Road

Northwestern Turnpike

Washington, D.C.

National Pike

Indianapolis

Maysville Turnpike

Traffic

Valley Turnpike

Vandalia

Boone's Lick Road

Maysville

Richmond

Norfolk

St. Louis

Louisville

Wilderness Road

Great Valley Road

Coastal

Harrodsburg

Cumberland Gap

APPALACHIAN MOUNTAINS

Nashville Road

Raleigh

Mississippi R.

Nashville

Wilmington

Chattanooga

Unicoy Road

Memphis

Augusta

Charleston

Natchez Trace

Jackson's Military Road

Savannah

ATLANTIC OCEAN

Natchez

General Jackson's Military Road

Major Roads about 1851

St. Augustine

New Orleans

GULF OF MEXICO

reach Vandalia, Illinois, until 1852. It became a vital wagon highway to the West.

Even after the turnpikes were built, the majority of roads were just bumpy trails, many with stumps a foot high in the middle. Most Americans lived on farms, and without a good cross-country road the farm family was isolated.

The canal-building boom.
The roads and turnpikes usually went to villages near the water where goods could be floated to their destination. In the West, streams and rivers led down to the broad Mississippi, which carried produce all the way to New Orleans, then out to the Gulf of Mexico and the world.

New Orleans flourished from the trade of the West which was drained into her harbors. Eastern cities wanted a larger share. New York's Governor DeWitt Clinton in 1816 came up with a daring scheme. Before becoming governor, Clinton had been five times elected mayor of New York City. Madison had defeated him for President in 1812.

Clinton was a battler for reforms. He was an abolitionist, he defended poor debtors, and he wanted Roman Catholics to have the right to vote. Now, to promote commerce he aimed to dig the longest canal ever seen in America. It would run 363 miles through the level Mohawk Valley from Buffalo on Lake Erie to Albany on the Hudson River. Western crops, instead of floating down the Mississippi to enrich the merchants of New Orleans, would go through the Great Lakes into the canal and down the Hudson River to New York City. This was a grand and startling idea. At the time there were only 100 miles of canals in the whole United States. And none was more than 2 miles long!

There was a fight in the state legislature. Some said it would be too expensive. Farmers along the Hudson River and on Long Island feared the competition of produce from western farmers. But Clinton won. In 1817 the lawmakers voted $7 million for the project. They took it for granted that clever men would find a way to dig the long ditch. And they were right. In 1825 when the canal finally opened, the whole state celebrated.

"Lockport on the Erie Canal" was painted in 1832. As horses pull the boat toward the locks, passengers on the roof enjoy the scenery.

Canals in the North about 1840

Clinton proudly took national leaders down the canal and the Hudson River from Buffalo to New York City and dumped a barrel of water from Lake Erie into the Atlantic Ocean.

At once the canal was a success. Its whole cost was repaid in nine years from the tolls charged the users. The cost per ton for sending shipments from Buffalo to New York dropped from 20 cents to less than 1 cent a mile. Farm products in western New York and the Ohio Valley doubled in value now that they could so easily reach the eastern market. Cities on the Great Lakes—Buffalo, Cleveland, Detroit, and Chicago, and many more—soon rivaled the older river cities of Pittsburgh, Cincinnati, and St. Louis. New York City became the nation's commercial metropolis.

The success of the Erie Canal sparked a canal-building boom. By 1840 more than $125 million had been spent all over the North and the West on a vast canal system of 3326 miles.

Most canal projects were halted by the Panic of 1837 and the depression that followed. Some states, like Pennsylvania and Indiana, which built canals in haste without figuring how to cover their cost, were near bankruptcy. Many states now amended their constitutions to forbid use of the state's credit for canals or other internal improvements. One result was that, when railroads were built in the 1840s and 1850s, though aided by state funds, they were built by private companies.

The age of the steamboat. For all human history, boats had been driven either by manpower or by windpower. There seemed to be no other way. Then, in 1807, Robert Fulton imported a steam engine from England, put it in his boat the *Clermont,* and astonished Americans. Fulton was clever and versatile. He was an expert gunsmith during the American Revolution, and then he became a painter. He had even designed underwater torpedoes and made a kind of submarine. Now he steamed upstream from New York to Albany in 32 hours. He proved to Americans that the steamboat could be used in commerce. Only four years later the first steamboat was launched west of the mountains on the Ohio River.

Travel by steamboat could be quite luxurious. The interiors were often full of carved wood panels and elegant velvet draperies. The exterior, as shown in this 1850s photograph of steamboats crowded at a small dock, was trimmed with carved wood.

For Westerners the steamboat solved many problems. They could still float their crops on rafts downriver to New Orleans. But now they could ride back upriver in comfort in a fast-traveling, luxurious side-wheeler. Soon western rivers were alive with the tall, colorful stacks of the crowded vessels.

The steamship on western waters was unlike anything seen before. It was driven by a new type of engine—the high-pressure engine, which was light. The pioneer maker of these engines was Oliver Evans, from the neighborhood of Philadelphia, who was a genius at labor-saving devices. He had made a flour mill that used chutes and moving belts in place of manpower. And he actually had a plan for a steam-driven carriage that might have been a pioneer automobile. At first, people said he was crazy. When the gadgets worked, people stopped laughing and began stealing his ideas.

The high-pressure engines were faster than anything known before. They burned lots of wood to keep up the steam pressure, but that was not serious in the virgin forests of the West. With a full head of steam their boilers sometimes exploded. But American pioneers were willing to risk anything to get there first. Their motto was "Go ahead anyhow."

Since these steamboats had to operate on shallow western rivers filled with snags, rocks, and sandbars, they were built with a shallow draft. The engine was set on deck inside a high superstructure. In 1838 there were twenty steamboats that could operate in only 30 inches of water. Some captains joked that their ships could run on a heavy dew!

Not only were these ships light and fast, but they were inexpensive to build. That was a good thing because with the American passion for speed the boats did not last very long.

On these western steamboats the accidents were shocking. Without safety valves on the crude boilers or with the valves tied down, unlimited speed meant unlimited disaster. Europeans were appalled.

"The democrats have never liked to remain behind one another," a traveling German nobleman reported from the West about 1840. "On the contrary each wants to get ahead of the rest. When two steamboats happen to get alongside each other, the passengers will encourage the captains to run a race. . . . The races are the cause of most of the explosions, and yet they are still constantly taking place. The life of an American is, indeed, only a constant *racing,* and why should he fear it so much on board the steamboats?"

These western racers, called "brag" boats, lived a short, exciting life. Of all the steamboats built before the mid-1800s, nearly a third were lost in accidents. The main cause was explosions, which killed scores of passengers by bursts of flying wreckage and floods of scalding steam. Some steamboat owners sent the passengers who had not yet paid their fares to the back part of the vessel. Then, in case of explosion, they were less likely to be killed, and the owner could still collect his fares from them.

The triumph of the railroads. The United States did not invent the railroad. But this country luckily was free from the artificial barriers of national boundaries that had grown up over the centuries in Europe. Here vast expanses of wilderness were filling up with people. Hordes of eager settlers wanted a speedy path to their new homes. Thousands of empty acres were suddenly populated by farmers and merchants who needed supplies brought in and who had to ship out their produce. Boston, Baltimore, and Charleston met the challenge of the Erie Canal. They built railroads to capture the commerce of the West.

It took time before everybody saw that the railroads would be the arteries that united the nation. Pennsylvania ignored the first successful railroads built in 1830. It chose instead to reach westward with a canal. But by 1840, in the country

State Historical Society of Wisconsin

News that the new railroad would pass through your town signaled prosperity: workers to lay the rails, new settlers, lower freight costs, and new business enterprises.

as a whole, there were as many miles of track as there were of canals.

The great wave of railroad building came in the vast American West in the 1850s. In a single decade the nation's tracks increased from 8879 miles to 30,626 miles—more than enough to circle the globe. Ohio and Illinois, then still called the "West," led the nation in their miles of track. Chicago, which did not become an incorporated city until 1833, within 30 years had grown to be the greatest railroad center in the world.

Railroad building in the United States. Cautious European railroad builders came over here in the 1840s and 1850s to see how Americans had managed to lay their tracks so fast over such vast distances. They were horrified. Just as the reckless Americans had pushed ahead on the rivers with

Railroads, 1850-1860

—— Railroads in 1850

—— Railroads Completed, 1850-1860

high-pressure engines on their steamboats, so now it seemed that railroading Americans were taking terrible risks. Instead of laying two sets of tracks—one for each direction—they saved time and money by laying only a single set of tracks. Of course, this increased the danger of collision. They did not trouble to level hills, to cut tunnels, or to lay their tracks in long, gentle curves. Sometimes they actually laid tracks on top of the snow—with disastrous results when the spring thaw came. No wonder the American trains so often went off the

rails as they came rocketing down the steep hills or failed to maneuver the sharp curves.

By 1850 railroad wrecks were as common as steamboat explosions. Experienced travelers rode in the middle cars, rather than at front or back. Fast American trains of the middle 1800s gave all the excitement of a roller coaster, but they were much less safe.

In their headlong pursuit of speed, Americans made some discoveries. Perhaps the most important was how to design light engines that put less strain on the track and still could hold the track around sharp curves. The heavy early engines were built with large wheels mounted rigidly on axles like those of the old horse carriage. John Bloomfield Jervis, a self-taught engineer from New York, saw another way. He made a separate little truck (called a "bogie") with four low wheels and put it under the front end of the locomotive. Since the bogie wheels were low, small, and could swivel, they were not so apt to derail, even on sharply curving track.

American railroads were built by private companies with both state and private funds. The companies were aided by the federal government with free surveys and lower tariffs on iron rails. After 1850 they were given thousands of acres of public land. In England, where railroads were also being built, they usually went from one big city to another. But in the United States, where people were only beginning to fill up the continent, things were different. Here, as an amused foreign editor remarked, the railroads often went "from nowhere in particular to nowhere at all."

Laying a railroad across the vast, empty stretches of the American West was a costly business. The tracks were expensive. Whole communities of laborers had to be moved out and provided for on the prairie, on a mountainside, or in the deep forests. There the teams surveyed the track, constructed roadbeds, laid rails, cut tunnels, and built bridges. Enormous capital was required, which private firms did not yet have. The states and the federal government provided large grants of land that could be sold to make up the difference.

By 1860 steam had transformed transportation over the land and on the lakes and rivers of the United States. The railroad had opened whole new areas to settlement, spurred the growth of factories, and turned the trade of the West from the South toward the East. Instead of floating most of their produce down to New Orleans or to the southern states, Westerners now shipped their goods by rail and canal to eastern cities. These same railroads and canals brought back to them the products of the East. The economic interests of western farmers and eastern factory workers were newly united. All this would have political consequences.

Letters in every mailbox. A workable national mail system was slow in coming to the nation. The

WANTED!
3,000 LABORERS
On the 12th Division of the
ILLINOIS CENTRAL RAILROAD
Wages, $1.25 per Day.

Fare, from New-York, only - $4 ½
By Railroad and Steamboat, to the work in the State of Illinois.

Constant employment for two years or more given. Good board can be obtained at two dollars per week.
This is a rare chance for persons to go West, being sure of permanent employment in a healthy climate, where land can be bought cheap, and for fertility is not surpassed in any part of the Union.
Men with families preferred.
For further information in regard to it, call at the Central Railroad Office,

173 BROADWAY,
CORNER OF COURTLANDT ST.
NEW-YORK.
R. B. MASON, Chief Engineer.
H. PHELPS, Agent.
JULY, 1853.

To get the tracks laid and the trains moving quickly, the railroads needed thousands of construction workers from the East Coast.

framers of the federal Constitution in 1787 had given Congress the power "to establish Post Offices and Post Roads." A post road was a main road with special stations ("posts") to provide fresh horses for the riders who carried the mail. For some years, almost all postal service was on one main post road along the Atlantic coast. People used the mail very little. When George Washington was President, the letters in the mail averaged less than one for every twelve Americans each year.

In those early years the postage on a letter was usually paid by the person who received it. If you did not want to pay the postage, you never got your letter. There was no home delivery. To get your mail you had to go to the post office.

Then in 1825 came the dim beginning of modern mail delivery. The postmaster in each town was allowed to give letters to mail carriers to deliver to people's homes. The carriers still were paid no government salary. They lived by collecting a small fee from the person to whom they delivered a letter. If you were not at home to pay, they would not leave your letters in your mailbox.

In the 1840s the growing country desperately needed a cheap and efficient postal system. The service was still so haphazard and expensive that there was widespread demand to abolish the Post Office. People called it an "odious monopoly" and said that private businesses could do better.

As a result, in 1845 Congress passed a law establishing cheap postage and tried to reform the whole system. At first each postmaster printed his own stamps, and there was chaos. Then, in 1847, the reformed Post Office Department issued the first national postage stamps—a 5-cent stamp showing the head of Benjamin Franklin and a 10-cent stamp with the head of George Washington.

Still, for most of the century, people outside of big cities had to go to the post office to pick up their mail. It was not until 1896 that Congress adopted "Rural Free Delivery"—RFD, for short. Then every family could have the mail brought to their own mailbox.

Morse and the telegraph. Some people dreamed of faster methods of communicating. But it was hard to imagine a system that did not depend on seeing signals or on sending written messages. Samuel F. B. Morse, an artist and a man of many talents, found a way to make an electric current do the job. The idea came to him on the sailing ship *Sully* coming back from a trip to Europe. After talking to a fellow passenger about electricity, he asked why it could not be used to send messages. Others before him had asked the same question—and got nowhere with their answer. But Morse did not know enough about the subject to be discouraged. He suddenly decided to make an electric "telegraph" (from the Greek words for "far writer").

On the next page is the cover for sheets of original music dedicated to Cyrus W. Field in honor of the transatlantic telegraph cable.

It took Morse five years to make a telegraph instrument that would work and six more years to convince Congress to build the first line. During that time he supported himself by giving painting lessons. Finally, in 1843, Congress appropriated $30,000. With this money Morse stretched a telegraph line from Baltimore to Washington. On May 24, 1844, he sent his famous message, "What hath God wrought?" from Washington to Baltimore.

By 1848, Morse and two partners had built a telegraphic network that stretched from Maine to South Carolina and westward to St. Louis, Chicago, and Milwaukee. Regular newspaper columns offered the latest bulletins under the heading, "By Magnetic Telegraph." Newspapermen boasted of the "mystic band" that now held the nation together.

Cyrus W. Field, a visionary New York businessman, thought there ought to be a telegraph line all the way to Europe. He formed a company to undertake the difficult task. After several years and many failures, the long line on the bottom of the ocean was finished in 1858, and telegraph messages began to pass between America and England. Within weeks the line failed, and then the Civil War prevented the laying of a new cable until 1866.

SECTION 1 REVIEW

1. Identify or explain: turnpike, DeWitt Clinton, Robert Fulton, "brag" boats.

2. Locate: Lancaster Turnpike, National Road, Mohawk Valley, Erie Canal.

3. Why were state and local governments willing to finance roads and canals?

4. What was the importance of the Erie Canal?

5. How did American railroads and engines differ from those built in Europe?

6. Name some significant developments in American communication in the 1840s.

7. **Expressing Problems Clearly.** Discuss the advantages and drawbacks of steamboat travel.

Smoke from the factories of Lazell, Perkins & Company was a daily reminder to Bridgewater, Massachusetts, that the Industrial Revolution had arrived. This late 1850s hand-colored lithograph advertised the firm's "Forgings . . . Casting and all Kinds of Machinery."

2. The Industrial Revolution

The Industrial Revolution is a name for the great changes brought by the modern factory system. It came first to Britain. The British government, hoping to keep its leadership, made it a crime to take out of the country the designs of its new factory machinery. It was a crime even for workmen from one of these advanced factories to go to work in another country. But people and ideas were on the move—and America was the place for an ambitious workman.

Samuel Slater, on his own, defeated Britain's shortsighted scheme of industrial secrecy. While he worked in one of the up-to-date English cotton textile mills, he memorized the design for the machinery. Then he came to the United States—with some of the most prized industrial secrets. Helped by two American businessmen in Pawtucket, Rhode Island, he set up the first American textile factory just like the most advanced factories in England. It opened in 1792 with 72 spindles and a work force of nine children.

The rise of the factory system. In 1850 the 7th Census of the United States reported a great change in American ways of making things that soon reshaped American ways of living. Eventually this would create an American Standard of Living. The Census noted that in earlier times "the bulk of general manufacturing done in the United States was carried on in the shop and the household by the labor of the family or individual proprietors who apprenticed assistants." But now most manufacturing was being done by a "system of factory labor, compensated by wages and assisted by power." This new factory system had begun to displace the old system of household manufacturing. Before, Americans had made the things they needed in their own homes and for their own use. Now goods were produced in factories and by machines for sale to anybody willing to pay for them.

This Industrial Revolution helped bring about a Transportation Revolution. The same steam power and new techniques that made factories possible also brought the steamboats and the railroads to carry products of farm and factory out to the wider world. The Transportation Revolution reached the thousands of new customers needed to buy the masses of goods now produced in the factories. Wherever canals, railroads, or steamboats went, they provided new customers for farmers, too.

The rise of a new economy. Now farmers began to buy factory-made clothing, furniture, kitchen utensils, and all the other output of industrial America. The pioneer family was no longer so isolated. A national economy began to emerge. Each region would specialize in what it could do best. The Northeast and the Middle States produced finished goods in their factories, the West grew wheat and corn, while the South specialized in cotton, tobacco, rice, and sugar. The produce of the South and West flowed to the Northeast, and from that region finished goods moved back to the South and West.

The United States, which only a century before was mostly an unsettled wilderness, surprised the world. Suddenly this nation became a strong competitor in the industrial marketplace. The country was lucky in its virgin forests, fertile fields, and untapped minerals. A stable government favored industry. The growing population was becoming ever more varied. People from everywhere who were persecuted, restless, or dissatisfied made the United States their mecca. They were enterprising and industrious, and they made the country stronger.

This was becoming a nation of nations. In Europe, national borders and jealous governments stopped the free flow of goods and of people over the land. But not here. The Founding Fathers had designed a great federal nation. They foresaw the need to let people and goods flow from state to state, back and forth across the whole country. "Everything new is quickly introduced here," one foreign observer remarked. "There is no clinging to old ways; the moment an American hears the word 'invention' he pricks up his ears."

The corporation. The cost of these new factories was usually beyond the means of any one person, or even a partnership of a few people. Vast sums had to be collected. For this purpose a new social invention was at hand. The "joint stock company" had not been invented here, but had already been used in England for just this purpose. "Joint stock" ventures had brought some of the first English settlers to America. Now, when a "joint stock" company was chartered by a state, it became a "corporation." This meant that it had a life of its own and would survive in legal theory even if the shareholders died. The corporation could sue in court and in other ways was like a real person.

Shares of stock were sold to numerous investors. Each then owned a "share" in the company. Of course they might lose whatever they had invested. But a clever legal arrangement provided that they could not be held responsible for the company's debts. This was called "limited liability." Hundreds of small investors put in a few dollars each. They could share the profits but still not risk losing large sums if the company was badly managed. In this way, funds were gathered to build a great industrial nation. And not only rich people but small investors, too, could have a share of the profits.

Waltham and the factory system. In 1813 Francis Cabot Lowell and his associates in the Boston Manufacturing Company in Waltham, Massachusetts, brought together under one roof, for the first time ever, all the processes for making cotton cloth. This required a large capital investment and a new kind of factory. It was risky business. Only bold organizers dared to take the lead—just as none but bold men would have built the Erie Canal.

Lowell came upon the idea for his factory on a trip to England during 1810–1812 when he visited the cotton textile factories. Soon after his return to the United States, the War of 1812 stopped his importing and exporting business. This gave him

The Boston Associates named their Lowell works the Merrimack Manufacturing Company after the river that powered the machines. The women in this label are weaving cloth. The worker on the right is printing calico—a light cotton cloth once imported from Calcutta in India.

time to make plans for his Waltham factory. The factory was such a success that the Boston Associates decided to expand. They found a site on the Merrimack River, where its 30-foot falls provided power to drive the machines. There in 1822 they built a new and bigger factory. They named the town "Lowell." Soon textile factories sprouted in Massachusetts, New Hampshire, and Maine. In hilly New England they could use the waterpower of the many streams that tumbled toward the ocean.

Foreign visitors noticed that the air of American factory towns was clear. The air of European cities was filling with smoke from the fuel that fired the steam engines. But New England factories used the streams. They were built in the pleasant countryside. An Englishwoman, Harriet Martineau, in 1836 saw the fortunate American workers in Lowell. There they "might catch as beautiful glimpses of Nature's face as western settlers."

The "Waltham" or "Lowell" labor system.

What impressed European visitors even more than the landscape was the work force. They were mostly young women! Francis Cabot Lowell had not wanted American workers to become like those he had seen in the English factories and their slums.

They were, he said, people "of the lowest character, for intelligence and morals." Did the workers in a factory have to be so degraded?

Lowell and his associates noticed that the Industrial Revolution was freeing young women from many of the farm chores. Why not let them make money by working in a factory? After a few years they would move on, marry, and raise a family. Then, perhaps their daughters, too, would return to the mill to work for a while. In this way, no permanent working class would ever spring up. And people would not be stuck in a slum.

Enlisting women solved another American problem—the scarcity of workers. This would be a reason also to bring children into the factories.

With this "Waltham" or "Lowell" labor system, there grew up communities with large numbers of women and children. At Waltham, Harriet Martineau was impressed by the houses the company built for its workers. Some of the women had built houses with their own earnings—"with piazzas and green venetian blinds, and all neat and sufficiently spacious." She was impressed by the church, the library, and the lecture hall, all provided by the company.

But not all New England factories were so pleasant. Even Waltham and Lowell did not remain idyllic for long. As his mill in Rhode Island grew, Samuel Slater followed the English system of employing entire families. Everyone in the family who was over seven years old went to work in the factory. This system became usual in Connecticut, Rhode Island, and southern Massachusetts. Here was a factory working class—like that in England.

Some Southerners defended their "peculiar institution" by saying that northern "wage slavery" was worse than their own plantation slavery. Southerners, they said, at least cared for their workers when they were old or sick. But northern factory owners discarded worn-out workers just like worn-out machines. The Southerners failed to note that, if northern workers lacked security, they were free to move. If they could save their money, they could go west to open land. Free American workers could change jobs and learn new jobs.

Eli Whitney's idea. In January 1798, the nation faced the danger of war with the French dictator Napoleon, and desperately needed guns. In those days a musket was made by one man who was called a "gunsmith." (The word "smith" came from an older word meaning to shape or cut.) Just as a goldsmith shaped pieces of gold into jewelry, so each gunsmith actually shaped all the pieces of a gun to make them fit together. Where could the United States find the thousands of gunsmiths it suddenly needed?

Eli Whitney, the inventor of the cotton gin, refused to see it that way. He had a different idea that was really very simple. Each musket was made of 50 different parts. For one man to make all these parts himself he had to be a skillful gunsmith and had to know a great deal about guns.

But suppose a worker had to make only *one* of these parts. Suppose you gave the worker a model of that one part and invented a machine to make lots of precise copies. That might be as simple as tracing out copies of a paper doll. Instead of tracing on paper, the worker would trace on sheets of iron. The worker would not need much skill at all. It might take years to train a full-fledged gunsmith. But in a single day you might be able to instruct a single worker to use a machine to make a hundred copies of that one part. Then suppose you found 49 other people and trained each one to make lots of copies of each of the other parts.

When all the workers had finished their day's work, you would have a hundred copies of each of the different parts in a musket. Of course, you would have to be very careful about your measurements. But if you could make each copy like every other copy of the same part, then any one part would fit together with any other. It would be easy to put the 50 parts of the musket together.

The test. In the wintry January of 1801 Eli Whitney went to Washington for the dramatic climax of his months of planning. Three years before, when he had first begun to figure out his new plan, he had promised the government to make 10,000 muskets. That was a fantastic number. Whitney was not a gunsmith and had never made even one gun before. Still, the government decided to finance his scheme. Even though it was a new way, it seemed quite logical. The nation was so much in need of arms—and quickly—that it seemed worth taking chances.

Before Whitney could make any muskets in his new way, he had to make the machinery for making the muskets. He spent more than two years inventing and perfecting the tools that would make precise copies of the single part that was used as a pattern. Since Whitney had spent so much time making the new machinery, he had been able to make very few muskets. Even his friends began to wonder whether his system was only a pipe dream. Would it work?

Now he had a chance to show. He had an appointment in the nation's capital with President John Adams, Vice-President Thomas Jefferson, the Secretary of War, the Secretary of the Treasury, and other members of the Cabinet. When they met, Whitney laid out separate piles of all the pieces needed to make ten muskets. The nervous Whitney watched while they followed his simple instructions: take any piece from each pile, fit them easily together, and you have a complete working musket! To do that you didn't have to be a gunsmith with years of experience behind you. Almost anybody could do it. To the astonishment of the nation's leaders in that room, the ten muskets took form in a few minutes. By this little drama the revolutionary system of interchangeable parts was proven to a doubting world.

On the battlefield there was another great advantage for guns made in this way. Since all their dimensions were uniform, if one part broke during combat it would not be necessary to send the whole gun back to the gunsmith. With a stock of standard parts you would do the job right then.

It was more difficult than Whitney had expected to make the machines to make the uniform parts of the guns. But by 1809 he had succeeded in delivering all the promised 10,000 muskets. Whitney's system soon was called the "Uniformity System" because each part in one gun was uniform (precisely the same in shape and size) with that same part in any other gun of the same design. Some called it the "Interchangeable System."

Mass production. Whitney's system came at just the right place and at the right moment. The growing United States had drawn an energetic, eager-to-learn population from all over. But there was a scarcity of immigrants who had been highly trained in the ancient skills (like gunsmithing). Oddly enough that proved to be an advantage. For if the United States had attracted thousands of gunsmiths, Whitney might never have been prodded to design his new way of manufacturing. Soon the Interchangeable System was used to make all sorts of things. Even before the Civil War, locks and watches were actually cheaper in the United States (where they were made by this system) than they were in countries blessed by many skilled locksmiths and watchmakers.

This is what we mean by "mass production." It means producing masses of items of exactly the same kind. It means, as Whitney explained, using the skill of the machine instead of the skill of the worker. In France, for example, a young man had to work for years as an apprentice before he finally became a master gunsmith. But in America the machine became specialized, not the worker. Here what you needed was general intelligence so you could handle complicated machinery. Here the worker had to be quick to learn new ways.

Since things produced in this way were cheaper, more people could afford to buy them. When there was a wider, more prosperous market, other people were encouraged to make still more inexpensive things to sell. Each worker's time was worth more, for now he could produce more of anything—guns or locks or watches—in a single day. The employer could afford to pay him more and still make a profit. Almost anything could (and would) be manufactured in this new way. Out of all this grew an American Standard of Living that astonished an envious world by giving more things to more people than ever before.

SECTION 2 REVIEW

1. Explain: limited liability, Waltham (or Lowell) labor system, "wage slavery," interchangeable parts, "Uniformity System."

2. How were the Industrial Revolution and the Transportation Revolution linked?

3. How did "limited liability" foster the growth of corporations?

4. What contributions did Lowell and his associates make to the development of the factory system?

5. What role did Eli Whitney play in the development of mass production?

6. **Drawing Conclusions.** How did the Industrial Revolution bring about a national economy?

3. America's leading import: people

To occupy the land, to build the roads, canals, turnpikes, and railroads, to staff the factories, the United States needed people. It was not surprising, then, that the United States became a nation of immigrants.

Reasons for coming to America. While Europe became more and more crowded, America offered open air and cheap land. When families in Europe could not find food or places for their children in school or as apprentices, they naturally thought of America. In Europe, too, it was an age of turmoil. Between the time of the American Revolution and the American Civil War, there were revolutions and dictatorships in France, Spain, Germany, Greece, Italy, and Belgium. And it was an age of floods and famines. There were lots of reasons why people in Europe might want to *get away* from their old world. The disasters of Europe made refugees by the millions.

And there were plenty of reasons why someone would want to come *to* America. Of course, the old legends started in the early advertising brochures had enticed people to the colonies. These still brought people to the new nation. Now there were lots of new legends—of rich land, undiscovered mines, and fast-growing cities. And there was the real-life romance of a new nation with its doors open and its people's eyes on the future.

When you had so little to lose, why not go to America?

During the 1820s only about 500,000 people migrated to the United States. But then the pace quickened. In the 1830s and 1840s, 2.5 million men, women, and children arrived, and in the 1850s, 2.7 million.

It was lucky that the United States had so much unfilled land. The overflow of the Old World could find a place in the New. Peoples who did not know one another or who had fought against one another could now live side by side. America would be called the "last best hope of earth." The story of European hopelessness is a story of American hope.

In the years between the American Revolution and the Civil War, the two great sources of new Americans were Ireland and Germany. Events in those countries far across the Atlantic Ocean helped make the United States a world nation.

The Irish and the potato famine. Potatoes were the main food of the Irish poor. But suddenly in the fall of 1845 a blight hit the potato crop and spoiled a third of it. In 1846 the blight destroyed the whole crop all over the country. The potato blight continued until 1850.

Tens of thousands died of starvation. Weakened by hunger, hundreds of thousands died of disease. Death haunted the land.

Even before the famine, the Irish had been coming to America by the thousands. Downtrodden by English rule, they had tried to revolt many times, but they were not able to throw off their English masters. So some Irish had come to America. The United States, in the phrase of the time, was "a sort of half-way stage to Heaven." To many Irish it seemed almost as hard to get here as to reach heaven, because the cost of a steerage ticket across the ocean (between $12.50 and $25) then seemed so high.

Letters written back to Ireland made everyone want to come. "This is the best country in the world," wrote one Irish girl from New York City in 1848. One new arrival wrote back with glee that the Irish here "eat the pig themselves, and have plenty of bread to their potatoes." "Every day is like a Christmas Day for meat."

And now the Irish came by the hundreds of thousands. Through the port of New York City alone, between 1847 and 1860, from Ireland there came over a million. That was nearly half of all the Europeans who landed in New York in those years.

The Irish in America. But once the Irish had landed in Boston or New York or some other port city, they had very little choice about where to go. Few had the money or the desire to move to a lonely western farm. The farming they knew in Ireland did not make them lovers of the land. So most of them stayed in the port cities of the eastern seaboard where they could enjoy the fellowship of others recently arrived from the old country.

Many of those who did move westward in the early years used their strong arms and sturdy backs to dig canals and build railroads. When the digging of the Erie Canal began in 1817, there were not many Irish around. But before it was completed eight years later, the Irish were arriving by the thousands. On the canal they were well known for their strength, courage, and willingness to work.

Many Irish immigrants helped to build the Erie Canal. This lithograph shows the excavation process at Lockport, New York. A horse drives the treadmill that powers the primitive crane.

Irish contractors organized teams of their fellow immigrants.

When the Erie Canal was finished in 1825, the enterprising and industrious Irish immigrants moved on to help build other canals and then the railroads. They helped bring life to many new western cities. Soon people could say that "of the several sorts of power working at the fabric of the Republic—water-power, steam-power, and Irish-power," none had worked harder than Irish-power.

The Germans emigrate. The other large group of new arrivals in the years before the Civil War was the Germans. Nobody planned it that way, but whenever and wherever the people of Europe suffered, the United States somehow gained. Over there, 1816 was the terrible "year without a summer." The Rhine River flooded, floating away barns and livestock. Autumn storms uprooted fruit trees. Hunger and misery cursed the farmer. We cannot be surprised then that during the following year about 8000 Germans arrived in American ports. Again in 1829–1830, the winter was one of the worst in the history of Europe. People froze because there was not enough wood to burn in fireplaces. Food was scarcer than ever, and prices went up.

By 1832, more than 10,000 Germans were coming to America in a single year. As suffering in the German countryside deepened, it became plain that their government was not going to help. Then Germans started coming to America by the tens of thousands. They continued to arrive in vast numbers till nearly the end of the 1800s. In 1854 alone (when Germans were half of all immigrants to the United States) they numbered nearly a quarter-million. The move to America became a craze. Overnight, people would decide to leave Germany, and they would depart the next morning. A 13-year-old boy with a pack on his back walked 300 miles to the French port of Le Havre in order to find passage to America.

The Germans revolt. Throughout these years, revolutions were brewing in Germany. In 1815 at the end of the Napoleonic Wars the rulers of Europe met at the Congress of Vienna to shuffle boundary lines and restore the old monarchies. Nearly 40

German states were organized into a loose German Confederation dominated by Austria. Wanting democratic rule and freedom from Austria, students formed secret societies and studied new constitutions. Peasants refused to pay taxes and roughed up tax officials.

In central Europe, Prince Metternich, the clever and calculating Austrian foreign minister, was in charge. He had seen the terror of the French Revolution of 1789, and he hated democracy, which he imagined was always government by a mob. He organized tyranny in Germany. But even Metternich could not prevent protests like that in May 1832 when 25,000 people gathered in a small German town to drink the health of Lafayette (the hero of the American Revolution) and to demand a republic.

Metternich's policies created a rising flood of refugees. By 1848 there was civil war and a full-fledged revolution in Germany. The land was in turmoil, and many had to flee when the rebellion collapsed.

The political refugees. These political refugees from Germany were not many—perhaps only a few thousand. But they included some, like the daring Carl Schurz, who became eminent here and helped to build in the United States the democracy they could not build in Germany. Back in Germany he had joined the rebel forces against the government. When the leader of his movement was put in prison, at the risk of his own life he helped his friend escape. When the German Revolution failed, Schurz came to the United States. His career covered the whole country. After becoming a lawyer in Milwaukee, he campaigned for Lincoln in 1860 and fought as a general on the northern side at Gettysburg. He was minister to Spain, senator from Missouri, and then served in the Cabinet as Secretary of the Interior.

As the career of Carl Schurz and many other liberty-loving Germans showed, Germany's loss was America's gain. New Americans from Germany built whole cities like Milwaukee, and helped make Milwaukee a brewing center for American beer. They spread all over the country, becoming farmers, teachers, professors, lawyers, doctors, and journalists. They built prosperous businesses. Many others besides Carl Schurz fought on the Union side in the Civil War.

The Huntington Library, San Marino, California

The flags of the United States and Germany decorate the menu cover for a party on March 2, 1899, honoring Carl Schurz.

The Germans brought with them some new ideas for schools. They believed in physical education, and many early physical education teachers were German. They persuaded Americans to build gymnasiums attached to schools. Until the Germans came, it was not usual to send children to school before they were old enough to read. The Germans brought over the *Kindergarten* (a German word meaning "garden for children") where children as young as four years old could learn by playing. The idea caught on, and soon there were American kindergartens everywhere.

The great migration. In the half-century before the Civil War, although the largest numbers came from Germany and Ireland, immigrants were coming from other places, too. Thousands came from the Scandinavian countries, from the Netherlands, Belgium, Switzerland, France, Italy, and elsewhere.

The nation was growing by a great migration. And these other new Americans, like the Irish and the Germans, worked in factories and on farms. They, too, helped dig the canals and build the railroads which transformed the United States from a land of farmers into an industrial giant, a leader of the world.

SECTION 3 REVIEW

1. Name some factors that led 5 million immigrants to enter the United States between 1820 and 1860.

2. What part did the Irish play in the Transportation Revolution?

3. **Recognizing Cause and Effect.** How was civil unrest in Europe related to immigration to the United States?

4. The rise of the West

Between 1815 and 1850 the lands west of the Appalachian Mountains became the nation's breadbasket. American workers would eat better than ever before. The farmers of the American West also fed the factory laborers of Europe. Though the South did not realize it, wheat—not cotton—was king.

The moving American. "In the United States," the young French traveler Alexis de Tocqueville noted during his visit in the 1830s, "a man builds a house in which to spend his old age, and he sells it before the roof is on." The people of the United States had become Americans by moving from other lands. They continued to move after they reached the New World. Over the next hill, round the next bend, in the next state, there they hoped to find the will-o-the-wisp "success."

In their constant movement these migratory people transformed half a continent. They cleared the forest and broke the thick turf of the prairies with the improved steel plows of the Industrial Revolution. They cut the grain with new mechanical harvesters.

In 1810 only one American in seven lived west of the Appalachians. By 1840 more than one in every three lived there. Most of these Westerners still lived on farms in the forest or on the prairies, where

State Historical Society of Wisconsin

Breckenridge, Minnesota, and Wahpeton, North Dakota, are at the river junction cited in this ad. Bois des Sioux remained only a dream.

they grew corn and wheat and raised meat for home and market. To serve them and handle their crops, new cities sprang up and began to dot the land.

Instant cities. In places where people still alive could remember the sound of the Indian war whoop and the shadow of the virgin forest, there sprouted cities. On riverways and the joining of rivers appeared Pittsburgh, Cincinnati, St. Louis, Louisville, Memphis, Minneapolis and St. Paul, Davenport, Des Moines, Omaha, and hundreds of others. On the Great Lakes and at the river entrances to the Lakes, men and women created Rochester, Buffalo, Cleveland, Toledo, Detroit, and Chicago. An astonishing crop of cities sprang up quickly in the lands west of the Appalachians.

When before had so many cities grown so fast? In the years between the Revolution and the Civil War, Americans went west to start new cities. Many hoped to make their living out of city-building. Some hoped to make money out of selling the land. The wilderness was worth very little, but once a city was there, land became valuable. Then some people would want to buy land for houses, others for farms to raise vegetables and chickens and eggs for the people of the nearby city.

The great cities of the Old World had been built on their rich past. People had come first, and then there followed newspapers to give them news, inns to house the travelers, theaters and opera houses to entertain the crowds, colleges and universities where learned men could gather and the young could be educated.

But that was much too slow and haphazard for impatient, purposeful Americans. Western city-builders wanted their city first. They wanted to see it even *before* the people were there. If they already had a newspaper, hotel, theater, and college, then surely people would come. But if they waited, then some other city might provide all those attractions first. People would then go on to Cleveland instead of staying in Pittsburgh, or they would move on from Kansas City to Omaha, or from Omaha to Denver.

The optimistic Americans were not always careful to distinguish between what had already happened and what they hoped (or felt sure) would happen. Foreigners complained that the cheery Americans did not always tell the truth. But the self-confident Americans replied that they were simply boosters. Why should they fail to report "facts" simply because they "had not yet gone through the formality of taking place"?

The families who went west in the early 1800s were often going to cities that did not yet really exist. To them a city was not just any place where lots of people happened to live. It was where people were building a community together. They built not only for their needs but also for their hopes.

For example, in Europe a city did not have a newspaper until it already had a large reading community. But in the American West, the city's own newspaper was actually founded *before* the city. Your place might never even become a city unless you *started* with a newspaper.

Hotels were constructed in the middle of nowhere. The large and elegant "Gayoso House" was built in the remote forest on the site of the future Memphis, Tennessee. It was three years before the city was even incorporated and ten years before there would be a railroad. Where were the guests? In the future, of course. When the English novelist Anthony Trollope traveled across America in the 1860s, he noted:

When the new hotel rises up in the wilderness it is presumed that people will come there with the express object of inhabiting it. The hotel itself will create a population—as the railways do. With us [in Europe] railways run to the towns; but in the States the towns run to the railways. It is the same thing with the hotels.

Every man his own carpenter. In their instant cities Americans needed houses. And they needed them quickly. There were no grandparents or other relatives to live with until you had a home of your own. There were no old houses to rent or to buy. And out in the West carpenters were scarce or nonexistent. If you wanted shelter, you had to provide it yourself. So Americans invented a new way of building.

In England, builders of houses had got into a rut. They believed there was only one right way to build a wooden house. You built it around a frame of heavy timbers. Each long timber was a foot square, and the timbers had to be carefully fitted together by a complicated technique called "mortise and tenon." You rested your floors on these heavy supports, and closed in the sides with mud, plaster, or wood. All this produced a sturdy building, but to make it required skilled carpenters clever with the crude tools of the day. In new western towns like Cincinnati, Chicago, and Omaha, carpenters were not to be found, and people themselves did not have the skill—much less the time—to build their own houses in the old style.

All these needs produced the "balloon frame." Probably the first was built in Chicago in 1833, but we do not know who invented this new American building. Old-fashioned builders ridiculed the light "balloon-frame house" and said it would blow away in a high wind.

What was the balloon frame? The idea is so simple that it is hard to believe it ever had to be invented. The first notion was to forget that you ever needed a frame of heavy timbers with their ends neatly carved for a mortise and tenon to fit into one another. Instead make the lightest possible frame! Get a supply of long pieces of lumber about two inches thick and four inches wide. Then buy some long heavy nails. Stand up some of the light two-by-fours—say, eighteen inches or two feet apart—and nail other boards across them to hold them together.

Once you have your frame up, cover it outside and in with thin wide clapboards or any other material you wish. Nothing could be simpler. About three-quarters of the wooden houses in the United States are now built this way.

Of course, to build a balloon frame you need plenty of nails. In the old days nails had been extremely expensive because each one was fashioned by hand. But here again the Industrial Revolution helped the West. By 1830 New England nail-making machines were turning out nails by the thousands, better and cheaper than ever before.

The new way of building was speedy. It took less than half the time to build a balloon-frame house than one of the same size built in the old style. In Chicago, within one week in April 1834, seven new buildings of this kind appeared. By mid-June there were 75 more. By October an additional 500 were in use.

The balloon frame proved to have other advantages that nobody had counted on. It turned out to be even stronger and more durable than the old heavy-timbered construction. On top of that it helped Americans on the move because it was easily taken apart and then could be quickly put together again in some other place. St. Mary's Church in Chicago, said to be the first balloon-frame building built anywhere, within ten years of its construction was taken down, moved away, and re-erected three times. Now finally Americans on the move had the kind of house they could knock down and take along.

SECTION 4 REVIEW

1. How were cities constructed in the West?
2. **Drawing Conclusions.** How did the "balloon-frame house" help western cities to grow?

5. The cotton kingdom

The South was a vast land of many different areas with different climates, different soils, different societies. It included tidewater Virginia with its dignified old families, the jungles and everglades of Florida where Seminole Indians still lived (along with many escaped slaves), and states west of the Appalachian Mountains that were more western than southern.

One thing drew all these states together. It was not so much that they were southern states, but that they were *slave* states.

The South on the defensive. Southerners opposed internal improvements because they feared that such federal projects would provide a precedent for "interfering" within a state in other ways, too. The federal government might start tampering with slavery.

Beginning in the 1830s their fears increased as the voices of northern reformers who demanded that this ancient evil be abolished sounded louder and louder. Before long, abolitionist literature covered the country. It awakened Northerners to the horrors of slavery. It made them despise slavery. It also made them lump together all people in the South as if all Southerners wanted slavery. More and more Northerners began to hate the South and to hate Southerners.

As the northern propagandists against slavery became more passionate, Southerners too became more unreasonable. Instead of worrying over how to get rid of slavery, Southerners began to worry over how to defend slavery, and the South and themselves, against all outside attack.

Leaders in the South stopped saying that slavery was only a "necessary evil." "Slavery is not an evil," declared the governor of South Carolina in 1829. "On the contrary, it is a national benefit." Soon no voice could be raised in the South to suggest that slavery might someday, somehow, end.

One of the strongest supporters of slavery was Senator John C. Calhoun of South Carolina. The former Secretary of War and Vice-President of the United States was now the leading southern thinker. "Many in the South," he said, "once believed that it [slavery] was a moral and political evil; that folly and delusion are gone; we see it now in its true light, and regard it as the most safe and stable basis for free institutions in the world."

Calhoun was supported by many others when he called slavery "a positive good." Southern ministers said the Bible required that the blacks be slaves. Southern "scientists" said the blacks were an inferior race—the product of a "separate creation" that God made in the beginning on the African continent. George Fitzhugh, a Virginia thinker and writer, even changed the defense into an attack. He claimed that the so-called equal rights of the North merely allowed the strong to oppress the weak. The strong in the North were masters without responsibilities. In the South, on the other hand, a master had to take care of the slaves for life. In this way the weak were protected. It was through slavery, Fitzhugh claimed, that Greece and Rome had achieved "their great prosperity and high civilization." Astonishing nonsense was written by otherwise sane people—all to show that slavery was the greatest thing that had ever happened to the human race.

The "middle passage."

Most people had come to America because they had wanted to come. But not the slaves. They had been brought in chains to America from Africa. In Africa, they had come from many different societies. Some were great empires, like Songhai and Melle. Some were complex cultures, like Benin and Yoruba. The Bantu and Bushmen came from societies that were more primitive. All these societies practiced slavery, as had all of Europe at one time. Some African chiefs captured members of other tribes and sold these slaves to black or white slave traders, who then marched them to the slave stations on the Atlantic coast. There the white men put them on ships to send to America. Of course, some of these terrified Africans tried to get away. And some preferred death to slavery. One slave trader reported, they were "so wilful and loth to leave their own country that they have often leap't out of the canoes, boat and ship, into the sea and kept under water till they were drowned."

The "middle passage," as the voyage to America was called, was a horrendous experience. Packed tightly below decks and chained together, frightened men, women, and children died in great numbers. Those who survived the torture of this long journey to the West Indian islands, Brazil, the United States, or wherever in America, were then sold at auction to the highest bidder.

The slave trade to the United States was legally abolished in 1807. But in later years slaves still were smuggled into the country and a flourishing domestic slave trade continued. Though many Southerners tried to avoid seeing the inhumanity of slavery— the purchase and sale of people as if they were things—the proof was often before their eyes.

From dawn to dusk.

To the slave owner, slavery was first and foremost a system of labor control. Just as cash wages were the system of control in the North, so slavery was the method in the South. Slavery was a way to use man-, woman-, and child-power to raise crops for sale. The largest of these crops was cotton, which the Southerners thought was "King" of all crops, but also important were tobacco, rice, hemp, and sugar.

It was the black slave, working from dawn to dusk, who planted, tended, and harvested these crops, as well as built fences, cut wood, and fed farm animals. Particularly at harvest time the work could be grueling. Under the eyes of the owner, an overseer, or a black "driver," the slaves would sometimes be pushed to exhaustion. And failure to perform up to expectations could lead to a whipping.

But the "peculiar institution," as Southerners came to call it, like all human institutions should not be oversimplified. While there were cruel masters who maimed or even killed their slaves (although killing and maiming were against the law in every state), there were also kind and generous owners. The institution was as complex as the people involved. Though most slaves were whipped at some point in their lives, a few never felt the lash. Nor did all slaves work in the fields. Some were house servants or skilled artisans. Many may not have even been terribly unhappy with their lot, for they knew no other. But certainly others were, as the Nat Turner revolt revealed. And there were many planned or rumored uprisings that were cut off before they happened. Though white Southerners claimed their slaves were happy, they lived in constant fear of slave revolts.

There were other ways to resist owners than by armed revolt. Slaves might just work slowly and carelessly. Sickness could be faked. When all else failed, some tried to run away—despite the certainty of severe punishment if they were caught. A number actually made it to freedom. And a few even risked being enslaved again by returning to help others escape. In the North they faced the trials of living in a society made for whites. Still, many thought that was better than slavery.

In the earlier days of slavery, some slaves were freed by their owners, or allowed to earn money to buy their own freedom and that of their wives and children. Under the attack of abolitionists, Southerners grew ever more defensive. Southern states passed laws making it harder and harder to free slaves. For this reason, there were a small number of black slaveholders in the South. They held slaves as a way to "free" friends or family.

Slaves and their families lived closely with owners and their families. They usually dwelt on isolated plantations where white and black depended on each other. About one-half of all slaves were owned in groups of 20 (about four families) or less. Sometimes a single slave worked on a family farm and managed to live much the same life as a white hired hand. There were only a few large plantations— where the other half of all slaves lived. No more than 10,000 Southerners had plantations with more than 50 slaves.

Not surprisingly in such a close-knit society, there were white Southerners who loved their slaves and who were loved by them in return. Usually the wives of plantation owners took care of slaves who were sick, saw that they had the proper clothes and food, and attended their weddings, funerals, and church services. Some even (against the law) taught a favored black child to read. While there were owners who killed their slaves, there were others like Rachel O'Connor of Louisiana, who wrote of a sick young black slave: "The poor little fellow is laying at my feet asleep. I wish I did not love him as I do, but it is so, and I cannot help it."

A world of their own. Whether an owner was kind or brutal, the slave was still considered by the law to be a chattel, just a piece of property to be bought and sold. Slaves were always at the mercy of their owners. It was in the interest of the owner to keep the slaves healthy and content enough to tend the crops that made the plantation thrive. But slaves could be whipped, beaten, confined, chained, and even sold away from family and friends at the whim of the owner. So whether happy or sad, well cared for or ill, the slaves could never feel the joy or the dignity of freedom.

Despite what laws may say, people remain human. Even under the most dreadful oppression they create a life for themselves. The churches and most owners recognized that blacks were human, with souls that could be saved by God. The slaves seized upon this awareness of their humanity to influence their owners to treat them better. Most masters seemed to believe that happy slaves did better work than unhappy ones. So the slaves used their owners' profit motive to get small benefits— the right to farm their own kitchen gardens or to sell a few products in town.

In their simple log huts in the slave quarters— huts often not much different from those occupied by poor Southern whites—they built their private world. There they married (though sometimes owners conducted these ceremonies), worshiped, celebrated the birth of a child, mourned the death of a friend, in their own way. In their new American homeland, as their owners wanted, the blacks became Christians. But they also combined this Christianity with some elements from Africa and made it special. They often went to the master's church on Sunday morning, where they sat in a separate section. But it was at their own service later in the day that they could freely practice their religion. There they heard the sermons of eloquent black preachers.

It was their own religious experience—their special mix of song, dance, prayer, call and response— that set them apart from the whites. Out of this experience blacks, even while they were slaves, were able to proclaim their moral worth. It was from their religion, perhaps more than in any other way, that black slaves who were separated from each other on scattered plantations were able to form a sense of their human unity. From their religious beliefs and practices and their past as slaves, black Americans formed the basis for their own culture— a culture which was to mix with and enrich the culture of the United States.

The effect of slavery on white Southerners. Most white Southerners were not slaveholders. In 1860 one-fourth of the white people in the South owned all the slaves. Still, even the non-slaveholders were generally convinced that slavery must continue. Some supported it because they saw no other way to control this "different" group in their midst. Even the poorest white people in the South liked to think of themselves as somehow superior to blacks. As one poor white farmer explained, "Now suppose they was free, you see they'd all think themselves as good as we."

The South paid a high price for slavery. All craftsmen and farmers received less for their labor because of the competition of slaves. Immigrants, unwilling to compete with slave labor, avoided the South. The money that might have gone into commerce or industry was tied up in slaves. As a result the South remained an agricultural community which exported crops and imported manufactured goods.

This made the whole South—white and black—a kind of colony of the North. "With us every branch and pursuit of life, every trade, profession, and occupation, is dependent upon the North," an Alabama newspaper complained. "In northern vessels [the Southerner's] products are carried to market, his cotton is ginned in northern gins, his sugar is crushed and preserved by northern machinery; his rivers are navigated by northern steamboats, . . . his land is cleared with a northern axe, and a Yankee clock sits upon his mantle-piece; his floor is swept by a northern broom, and is covered with a northern carpet; and his wife dresses herself in a northern looking-glass." This was only a slight exaggeration.

How had this come about? How had the home of Jefferson's small farmer become a backwater? No wonder that many Southerners, looking for someone to blame, decided to make Northerners the enemy. They began to think the backwardness of the South had been a product of a northern conspiracy. It seemed that somehow northern businessmen had been able to use the federal government for their own selfish purposes. The government subsidized northern shipbuilding. The tariff protected northern manufacturers so they could charge higher prices to southern planters.

Had not the southern states been pioneers in colonial days? They gave the nation its Washington, Jefferson, Madison, Monroe, and Jackson—its leaders in war and in peace. Now that the United States was prospering, must the South remain a colony within a nation?

SECTION 5 REVIEW

1. What was the "middle passage"?
2. Show how the treatment of slaves differed. How did some slaves resist their owners?
3. What were some effects of slavery on the South?
4. **Drawing Conclusions.** Why did Southerners turn from calling slavery a "necessary evil" to calling it a "positive good"?

This lively watercolor of slaves dancing on a festive occasion was found in Columbia, South Carolina. The artist is unknown, but the painting was made about 1800.

CHAPTER 10 REVIEW

FOCUSING ON IDEAS

1. Describe the role of federal, state, and local governments in the development of roads, canals, and railroads. Why did people seek such help from the government?

2. Identify at least three people who played major roles in the early stages of the American Industrial Revolution. Show how each contributed to the growth of industry.

3. What "favorable conditions" awaited immigrants to the United States?

4. What arguments would you expect an abolitionist to use in condemning slavery? What arguments did some white Southerners use to defend the institution of slavery?

TAKING A CRITICAL LOOK

1. **Identifying Central Issues.** Explain how the completion of the Erie Canal might have benefited each of the following: a wheat farmer in northern Ohio; a merchant in Buffalo; a Dutch immigrant family headed for Michigan Territory; an Albany hotel owner.

2. **Making Comparisons.** Compare pre-Civil War Irish and German immigration with regard to: motives for coming; dates; numbers; settlements; and contributions.

3. **Demonstrating Reasoned Judgment.** How was the birth of Western cities a testament to American optimism?

YOUR REGION IN HISTORY

1. **Geography.** Identify major roads, canals, and railroads built in your state or region between 1820 and 1860. How did these transportation developments affect where people in your state or region chose to settle?

2. **Culture.** What immigrant groups settled in your state or region between 1820 and 1860? When and where did they settle? What contributions did they make?

3. **Economics.** What kinds of manufacturing, if any, developed in your area in the period 1820–1860? Why did they develop there?

HISTORICAL FACTS AND FIGURES

Synthesizing Information. Look at the table below to help you complete the following exercises: (a) Summarize the overall immigration trend between 1820 and 1855. (b) Summarize the changes in the overall immigration trend that occurred between 1856 and 1860. (c) Using information from this chapter, write a hypothesis that explains the immigration trends between 1820 and 1860.

	Ireland	Scotland, England, Wales	Germany	All Other	TOTAL
		Origin of Immigrants to the United States, 1820-1860			
1821–25	16,540	11,300	2,362	18,686	48,888
1826–30	37,798	16,189	5,367	43,582	102,936
1831–35	72,257	32,182	45,593	102,462	252,494
1836–40	135,124	43,628	106,862	62,107	346,631
1841–45	187,095	80,186	105,188	57,867	430,336
1846–50	593,624	186,858	327,438	174,995	1,282,915
1851–55	645,056	235,981	647,273	220,114	1,748,424
1856–60	219,436	187,993	304,394	137,967	849,790

Source: U.S. Immigration and Naturalization Service

CHAPTER 11

Reforming and expanding

The half-century before the Civil War was a time of ferment in the United States. Factories were built, instant cities were created, immigrants poured in. From Missouri, long lines of wagons headed west to their promised lands—Texas, California, and Oregon. The Americans who stayed home looked for a more perfect society where they lived. These two movements of expansion and reform forced the nation to face an issue many Americans wished to avoid: What was the future of slavery in the United States?

1. An age of reform

In a land where even cities could appear overnight it was easy to believe that a perfect world could be created. Many Americans, like the first settlers, continued to feel that they were a "City upon a hill." For the whole world to see, they wanted to create a nation where there was no injustice, where all had an equal chance to succeed, and where citizens ruled themselves. They wanted to help the insane, the orphans, the prisoners, and the blind. Americans organized themselves into groups working for peace, for temperance in the use of alcohol, for improved education, for women's rights—and for the abolition of slavery.

A religious age. There was a Christian church to suit every taste and every temperament. Unitarians tried to bring together all men and women of goodwill without any dogma or sharp theology. Millerites proclaimed that the world would come to an end in the year 1843 and urged their fellow Americans to repent while there was still time. Shakers and Rappites and others each believed they had the one and only formula for an ideal community. Visitors from abroad came to think that there were as many denominations as there were Americans. A perceptive English lady, Mrs. Trollope, saw religious Americans "insisting upon having each a little separate banner, embroidered with a device of their own imagining."

The Protestant churches moved away from the old Puritan belief in a stern God who had decreed in advance the fate of each person for all time. Instead churches now emphasized how close each individual was to God and how much freedom each possessed to improve the world and make his or her own future. The world of Christians seemed more democratic, more self-governing than ever before.

These ideas were stressed between the 1820s and the 1850s in the religious revivals which constantly swept the land. Perhaps the greatest single force in this movement was Charles Grandison Finney. He used every means to excite his listeners to a sense of their sinfulness and to save their souls. His revival meetings and those of other preachers brought many Americans to support a wide variety of reforms.

Hancock Shaker Village, Hancock, Massachusetts

The Shakers, a religious sect founded by Mother Ann Lee, received their name from their dances during worship. The bright colors of their drawings, which the Shakers believed were divinely inspired, contrast with the simplicity of their architecture, furniture, and dress. This 1854 drawing shows the saints, including Christopher Columbus (top right), ranked in heaven.

The Transcendentalists.

One small group of intellectuals had an influence all out of proportion to their numbers. They called themselves "Transcendentalists." They believed that the most important truths of life could not be summed up in a clear and simple theology but actually "transcended" (went beyond) human understanding and brought together all people—high or low, rich or poor, educated or ignorant. For them God was an "oversoul" who was present showing everybody what was good or evil. It is not surprising then that Ralph Waldo Emerson, their most eloquent voice, declared:

> What is man born for but to be a Reformer, a Reformer of what man has made; a renouncer of lies; a restorer of truth and good. . . .

Since man was good, in time the whole world would become perfect. Then, of course, there would be no need for government.

Each person had to find his or her own path to heaven. Henry David Thoreau found his lonely way to the good life in a solitary cabin on the shores of Walden Pond near Concord, Massachusetts. While he stayed there by himself for two years, he earned his living making pencils and only went to town for groceries. He found his own way to protest against the policies of his government that he believed to be evil. When the nation waged war against Mexico—to add new slave states, he thought—he simply refused to pay his taxes. For this he spent only one night in jail, since to his irritation his aunt paid the tax for him. But his explanation for his protest—in his *Essay on the Duty of Civil Disobedience* (1849)—rang down the years and reached across the world. A century later when Mahatma Gandhi led the people of India in their struggle for independence, he declared himself a follower of Henry David Thoreau.

Theodore Parker, another member of the group, was a born reformer who joined movements and attacked slavery from pulpits and lecture platforms. Bronson Alcott was a mystic and a dreamer who worked for perfection but failed at everything. His educational ideas—which included physical exercises for students, attractive classrooms, and the pleasures of learning—seemed shocking to people of those times when schools were grim and discipline harsh. Alcott's school failed as did his attempt to build a new Eden at "Fruitlands."

Alcott was never able to earn enough to live comfortably until his practical and courageous daughter Louisa May made a great success with her book *Little Woman* (1868).

The Transcendentalists loved to tell what they thought. While Thoreau wrote and Parker and others preached, Emerson both wrote and lectured. Bronson Alcott talked. In his popular "conversations"—wandering monologues—Alcott entertained large audiences in the East and Northwest.

The "conversation" was also used by brilliant Margaret Fuller. She gathered a group of young Boston women around her and instructed them. From this experience came her influential book, *Women in the Nineteenth Century* (1845), which spurred on the women's rights movement. Fuller also edited the *Dial,* the Transcendentalist magazine, and worked as a literary critic for Horace Greeley on the *New York Tribune.*

Reform in education.

America—a new nation, full of open land and business challenges—was a wonderful laboratory for reformers. It is not surprising that the reformers focused on education. The ability to read and write, they argued, was the foundation of a democratic life.

The modern public school movement began in the 1830s in Massachusetts. This was quite natural because the Puritan founders of New England in the 1630s had believed in education. Now, 200 years later, the determined Horace Mann worked to fulfill the Puritan dream of an educated citizenry. He had hated the dull teaching he received as a boy, so he gave up a successful legal career to work for educational reform. Mann was appointed the first secretary of the new state board of education in 1837, and for the next twelve years he tried hard to better the training and pay of teachers, to erect new school buildings, to enlarge school libraries, and to improve textbooks. In other states crusaders followed Mann's example.

By 1860 the fruits of these efforts were impressive. The states were generally committed to providing free elementary education. Many pupils were still poorly taught, and laws did not yet require all children to attend school, but the nation had begun to realize that education was the foundation of a republic.

For students who wished more than a grammar school education, there were only 300 public high

State Historical Society of Wisconsin

Students in Milwaukee in 1846 did not have to wonder about how they should behave.

schools in the whole country and almost 100 of these were in Massachusetts. There were, however, an additional 6000 private academies, many of which charged only a small tuition to poor children. By 1860 many states were thinking of providing high schools open to all, but even by 1890 it was unusual to go to school beyond eighth grade.

Higher education. Colleges and universities were still small—few had over 100 students—and ill equipped, but their numbers had increased since colonial times. In fact, there had been a college-founding mania. Just as every instant city needed a newspaper and hotel even before it contained any people, so it needed what was loosely called a college. Usually the college was started by one of the many religious denominations, but the hopeful cities-of-the-future quickly joined in. Julian Sturtevant, founder in 1830 of Illinois College, said, "It was generally believed that one of the surest ways to promote the growth of a young city was to make it the seat of a college." So before the Civil War 516 colleges were founded—many little better than the private academies—but only 104 survived to the 1900s. These "colleges" were still chiefly concerned with educating young men for the professions and public life.

In many American cities, so-called mechanics' institutes were started for those who wished to learn the mechanical arts. And in 1824 a new kind of institution of higher learning, Rensselaer Polytechnic Institute, opened at Troy, New York, to instruct men "in the application of science to the common purposes of life."

Education for girls and women. In colonial days girls were taught the household arts but were not expected to learn to read and write. People

In some schools, students who behaved well could earn certificates of merit like this one for consistently good conduct.

American Antiquarian Society

A WINTER SCENE.

thought that "book learning" would put an undue stress on their delicate minds and bodies! It was a long while before women were allowed to show their full vigor. Progress came slowly and step by step. In Massachusetts girls began to attend summer sessions of the public grammar schools in the late 1700s. Still, in Revolutionary times only about half the women of New England could sign their names. By 1840 the efforts of reformers were showing results, and nearly all New England women could read and write.

But it was a while before women were given their chance at a college education. At first, small numbers of them were allowed to attend the boys' academies until secondary schools were set up especially for women. Finally in 1836 (200 years after Harvard College was founded for men) Wesleyan College in Georgia was chartered as the first college for women. Then the very next year Oberlin College in Ohio started the new era of coeducation. At last it was possible for at least some men and women to hear the same lectures and treat each other as intellectual equals.

The mentally ill and retarded.

For centuries people who were mentally ill or retarded had been treated like criminals and stigmatized as "insane." They were feared, imprisoned, and tortured. But the American reformers felt pity for them and took up their cause. Their heroic champion was Dorothea Dix, a young Boston schoolteacher who taught a Sunday School class in the women's department of a local prison. There she found people, whose only "crime" was their mental illness, being confined and punished.

In 1843, after two years spent investigating the jails and poorhouses in Massachusetts, she submitted her epoch-making report to the state legislature. She had seen the innocent insane confined "in cages, closets, cellars, stalls, pens! Chained, naked, beaten with rods, and lashed into obedience." She asked the legislature and all her fellow citizens to share her outrage. But old ways of thought and old fears were strong. Many would not believe the shocking truth, and others accused her of being softhearted. She stood her ground.

Finally Dorothea Dix succeeded in persuading the Massachusetts legislature to enlarge the state mental hospital. She began a new crusade—which lasts into our own time—to treat the mentally ill

with compassion and medical aid. She traveled in America and in Europe pleading her humane cause. Seldom has a reform owed so much to one person.

Women's rights.

Dorothea Dix always found it best to let men present her findings to legislatures. It was widely believed that there was something unladylike about a woman speaking in public. It was difficult for women to secure permission even to attend reform meetings.

The Industrial Revolution had freed many women—married and unmarried alike—from having to make many of the things necessary for the home and family. While in the early days thread had to be spun and cloth woven in each household, now cloth was mass-produced in factories. Crude, ready-made clothing could be bought in stores. At the same time, the role of the homemaker became more specialized. Now, as factory processes made the price of manufactured goods cheaper, more women could afford to buy many of the things they had once made for themselves. No longer did they have so many of the varied tasks of the frontier wife. Women found new work outside the home. The factories of Lowell and other New England towns were largely staffed by women. And the new public schools created jobs for women teachers.

This watercolor, probably painted in the first half of the 19th century, shows an evening school for girls. They are working by candlelight as their bonneted teachers watch.

By the rules of English law, brought here in colonial days, married women had no rights to property—in fact their only legal existence came through their husbands. All of a woman's property became her husband's when she married, including her wages if she worked. She could not even make a will without his approval!

The lowly position of women had long been obvious to some women. The strong-minded Abigail Adams, for example, had made the point again and again to her husband, President John Adams. But now in an era of reform, when women were eager to lead movements to improve education, to treat the insane more humanely, and to free the slaves, the rights of women seemed essential to a better America. A new status for women—their opportunity for an adequate education and the right to speak out in public—would mean a richer life for all.

Leaders of the women's rights movement. Two energetic and outspoken reformers, Lucretia Mott and Elizabeth Cady Stanton, organized a Women's Rights Convention that met at Seneca Falls, New

The women's rights movement included strong-minded leaders like Sojourner Truth (top), Susan B. Anthony (bottom right), and Elizabeth Cady Stanton (bottom left).

York, on July 19, 1848. The convention finally issued a clever statement based on the Declaration of Independence. The preamble stated that "all men and women are created equal." Their list of grievances was not against King George but against men, who had deprived women of their rights. They demanded that women "have immediate admission to all the rights and privileges which belong to them as citizens of the United States." They even went so far as to demand the right to vote, although many of the women delegates feared this was asking too much.

Similar conventions were held in other states. But there were plenty of people foolish enough to think that they could stop the movement by breaking up the meetings. In 1851, when the Ohio convention in Akron was disrupted, a careworn black woman of commanding stature rose and, to the surprise of all, began her eloquent appeal. The unexpected speaker, named Sojourner Truth, had been born a slave in New York. She replied to a minister's charge that women needed special assistance from men by pointing out that she had never received any help from men.

> I have ploughed and planted and gathered into barns. . . . And ain't I a woman? I could work as much and eat as much as a man—when I could get it—and bear de lash as well! And ain't I a woman? I have borne thirteen children and seen 'em mos' all sold off to slavery, and when I cried out with my mother's grief, none but Jesus heard me! And ain't I a woman?

It took a while, but within a generation Sojourner Truth's message about the equality of women began to spread across the land.

The reforming women, led by Susan B. Anthony and Elizabeth Cady Stanton, were, of course, widely ridiculed and accused of acting more like men than women. But they did make progress. New York led other states in giving women control over their own property, a share in the guardianship of their own children, and the right to sue. Divorce laws were liberalized.

But the right to vote still seemed far in the future. In 1853 a leading national journal, *Harper's New Monthly Magazine*, proclaimed that the very idea of women voting was "infidel . . . avowedly anti-Biblical . . . opposed to nature and the established order of society."

Elizabeth and Emily Blackwell braved male opposition and actually became qualified medical doctors. Maria Mitchell became an astronomer, a member of the American Academy of Arts and Sciences, and the first professor of astronomy at the new Vassar College for women when it opened in 1865. Sarah Josepha Hale edited the influential magazine *Godey's Lady's Book* for nearly 50 years, and in its interesting pages she recounted the progress of women and argued their rights to be free, fulfilled Americans.

SECTION 1 REVIEW

1. Identify: Ralph Waldo Emerson, Henry David Thoreau, Theodore Parker, Bronson Alcott, Louisa May Alcott, Margaret Fuller, Horace Mann, Dorothea Dix, Lucretia Mott, Elizabeth Cady Stanton, Sojourner Truth, Susan B. Anthony, the Blackwells, Maria Mitchell, Sarah Josepha Hale.

2. By 1860 what advances had been made in (a) public education? (b) the education of women?

3. What changes did Dorothea Dix seek in the treatment of the mentally handicapped?

4. How were women's rights restricted? What gains were made between 1828 and 1860?

5. **Identifying Central Issues.** What developments in religion were linked to the movements for social reform?

2. The abolition movement

The first moves to end slavery had come in the North at the time of the American Revolution (p. 95). But even in the South men like Washington and Jefferson were unhappy about slavery. Jefferson had actually inserted in the Declaration of Independence an item attacking George III for promoting the slave trade to America. It was finally taken out in deference to southern prejudices. Many other Southerners of goodwill who opposed slavery comforted themselves with the thought that it was a dying institution. Then the cotton gin led to a new demand for slaves to raise cotton. More than ever before, Southerners came to believe that slavery was the very foundation of the South.

The southern antislavery movement.

Still, some Southerners continued to look for a way to get rid of slavery. In 1816–1817 the South became the center of an antislavery movement built around the American Colonization Society. Since its members believed that the blacks could never be assimilated into American life, they raised money to send all the blacks back to Africa. The Society established a colony in Africa in what is now the nation of Liberia.

In its first twenty years the Society was able to send only 4000 blacks back to Africa—and many of those were not slaves. By 1830 there were 2 million slaves in the United States, and their number was increasing through new births at the rate of 500,000 every ten years.

Most blacks did not want to go back to Africa. In 1817 a group of free blacks in Philadelphia stated positively, "We have no wish to separate from our present homes for any purpose whatever."

As the attacks of northern abolitionists became more bitter, talk of freeing the slaves became more and more dangerous in the South. Southerners like James G. Birney of Kentucky and Sarah and Angelina Grimké of South Carolina who opposed slavery felt obliged to go north. The last debates over slavery in the South were those in Virginia. By 1831 many people in Virginia were worried about slavery. The new governor, who himself owned twelve slaves, tried to persuade the state legislature to make a plan for gradually abolishing slavery. The Virginia legislature held a great debate on slavery which lasted most of the month of January 1832. Then they voted 73 to 58 to keep slavery. The vote was a tragic mistake. It made it almost inevitable that if slavery was to be abolished in Virginia, it would have to be by force from the outside.

By 1833 no reform was welcome in the South. If one reforming "ism" (even pacifism) entered their section, Southerners feared that it might soon be followed by that worst "ism" of all—abolitionism. So the South turned inward and cut itself off from the outside world, keeping out northern books, checking the mails for abolitionist literature, and even preventing the discussion of slavery in Congress (p. 249).

The movement heats up.

The problem for Southerners was that the abolitionist attacks had become so strong. Many abolitionists were devout Christians. They believed that Jesus hated slavery. "Do unto others as you would have others do unto you." You do not want to be a slave yourself. What right, then, have you to enslave others? Christianity, they said, was the religion of love—love for everyone. The abolitionists wanted to preach love. But before very long they were also preaching hate.

It was easy enough to go from hating slavery to hating slaveholders. And easy enough, too, to go from hating slaveholding Southerners to hating all white Southerners. Since abolitionists were more interested in horror stories than in statistics, they did not advertise the fact that most white Southerners were not slaveholders. In their hatred of slavery they painted a picture of the South that had no bright spot in it. If there was any virtue in the South, why had not Southerners already abolished this monstrous evil for themselves?

The abolitionists were printing all the worst facts about slavery. Of course there were plenty of horrifying facts to be told about the mistreatment of individual slaves and the separation of black families.

Theodore Dwight Weld, a New England minister, started his career on a crusade against alcohol. Then, inspired by English abolitionists, he began to fight slavery. In 1839 he published *Slavery As It Is: Testimony of a Thousand Witnesses*, put together from items he had sifted from 20,000 copies of newspapers.

The book was a chamber of horrors. His purpose, Weld wrote, was to "see the inside of that horrible system. . . . In the advertisements for runaways we detect the cruel whippings and shootings and brandings, practiced on the helpless slaves. Heartsickening as the details are, I am thankful that God in his providence has put into our hands these weapons [these facts] prepared by the South herself, to destroy the fell monster."

Nearly everybody likes to read horror stories. The book spread through the North. Within the first four months it sold 22,000 copies, within a year more than 100,000. Northerners now began to get their picture of the South from Weld's lurid book and from others like it.

The abolition movement grew larger and more outspoken. William Lloyd Garrison, editor of the abolitionist newspaper *The Liberator* and one of the

Abolitionist editor Elijah Lovejoy was killed when a proslavery mob attacked his Alton, Illinois, printing plant in 1837.   A magazine of the day featured this illustration of the attack.

most angry of the abolitionists, actually burned a copy of the Constitution of the United States.   He called the Constitution a covenant with death and an agreement with Hell—because it allowed slavery.   Garrison's extreme attacks angered even his fellow Northerners.   They mobbed and nearly killed him several times.

Elijah Parish Lovejoy was a convinced reformer like many others.   He was against lots of things—including alcoholic drinks, the Catholic church, and slavery—all of which he attacked in his newspaper in Missouri.   But Missouri was a slave state.   So Lovejoy moved to Illinois, where slavery was not allowed, to find a safer place for his newspaper.   Even there the aggressive proslavery forces reached across the border.

His printing presses were destroyed by proslavery ruffians again and again.   Each time that he set up a new press the armed proslavery mob came back to destroy it.   Lovejoy's press was protected by 60 young abolitionists who begged him to leave town for his own safety.   But instead of fleeing he preferred to die for a just cause.   One night during an attack on the warehouse where Lovejoy was guarding his new press, the proslavery men set the warehouse on fire.   When Lovejoy leaped out, he was shot dead.

Elijah Parish Lovejoy thus became a martyr for abolitionists everywhere.

Both sides were collecting their heroes and martyrs.   It was becoming harder and harder to imagine that the people of the North and the South could be kept within a single nation.

SECTION 2 REVIEW

1. Identify or explain: James G. Birney, Grimké sisters, Theodore Dwight Weld, William Lloyd Garrison, Elijah Parish Lovejoy, American Colonization Society, *The Liberator.*

2. **Expressing Problems Clearly.**   As of 1833 the South tried to isolate itself from the rest of the nation. Explain.

3. Westward ho!

The national differences over slavery might not have come to a head so soon if the nation had not been growing and moving so fast. But Americans were pushing into Texas, into New Mexico, into California, and into the vast Oregon country north of California. The transplanted Americans out there naturally wanted their new homes to become part of the United States. In the East, stay-at-home Americans dreamed of a grand Empire for Liberty stretching from the Atlantic to the Pacific Ocean.

The push into Texas. In the Mexican province of Texas, Stephen F. Austin started an American settlement in 1821. A Virginia-born man only 27 years old, he had attended Transylvania University in Lexington, Kentucky, and did not look or act like a frontiersman. Seeking his fortune, he had lived for a while in Missouri before moving on to Arkansas and then to Louisiana. He had run a store, directed a bank, edited a newspaper, and served as an officer in a militia unit. Though only five feet, six inches tall, Stephen F. Austin had strong features and was a natural leader.

Austin's original grant from the government of Mexico allowed him to bring 300 families into Texas. Each family was to receive free of charge one *labor* of land (177 acres) for farming and one

league (4428 acres) for stock grazing. In return the settlers were expected to become Roman Catholics and to pay 12 1/2 cents per acre to Austin for his services. At this time the government of the United States was charging $1.25 per acre in cash, and the nation was still suffering the effects of the depression of 1819. No wonder that Texas was greeted as a land of opportunity!

It seemed not too hard to reach Texas from the eastern states. If you had enough money, you could travel comfortably on a boat around the Gulf of Mexico and up one of the broad rivers. Or if you lacked money and were hardy, once you had crossed the Mississippi River you could ride your horse or bring your wagon over the rolling open prairie.

Austin had no trouble finding people to join his new colony. He was a good-natured dictator and his people prospered. The number of immigrants to Texas from the United States grew rapidly until by 1830 there were nearly 8000. More than half of them lived on Stephen F. Austin's grants.

Traders and trappers in New Mexico. At the same time, other daring men were pushing into a more populated part of Mexico. In New Mexico an isolated Spanish-Mexican frontier community included some 35,000 people. They lived in large towns, like Santa Fe and Albuquerque, and in scores

This handcolored lithograph of Austin, Texas, in 1840 shows the capital only four years after Texans declared their independence (p. 247). The grand house on the hill belonged to Texan President Mirabeau Lamar.

of remote villages. They made their living by raising sheep and growing corn. From the 1600s to 1865 these Spanish and mestizo settlers were constantly at war with neighboring Indian tribes—Apache, Ute, Navaho, and Comanche. Like the Indians they fought, they came to think of their captives as prizes of war to be kept as slaves or exchanged in commerce.

In their midst the Pueblo Indians were living and farming in their own way. Often the Pueblos and New Mexicans fought side by side against the other Indians.

Under Spain this separate society had been barred from contact with the United States. Traders who made their way to Taos or Santa Fe were most likely to end in jail and lose their trading goods.

All of this changed, however, with the Mexican declaration of independence in 1821. Suddenly contact with New Mexico was allowed. That same year Captain William Becknell of Missouri, who had gone west to trade with the Indians, happened into New Mexico. There, much to his surprise, he was given a friendly reception. The next year Becknell put together a large expedition of wagons loaded with goods for trade in Santa Fe. On this trip Becknell established the famous Santa Fe Trail. For decades to come, it would be a frontier highway for wagon trains headed west.

American influence in New Mexico grew through an influx of traders like Charles Bent and fur trappers like Kit Carson. They settled in Taos, Santa Fe, and other New Mexican towns. These men often married Spanish-Mexican women and soon formed a growing "American" faction.

The mountain men.
The trappers who traveled through the West seeking furs discovered the hidden valleys and the easy passes across the mountains. They learned the language and the customs of the Indians, who often became their friends. The fur trade had drawn explorers to the West from early colonial times, but their great days were in the years after 1825. By 1840, however, the Rocky Mountains were nearly trapped out. As one mountain man remarked, so little was left that "lizards grow poor, and wolves lean against the sand banks to howl." Meanwhile the fur-trapping mountain men, who marked off and explored the cross-country trails, became the pathfinders for later generations of westward-moving pioneers.

On to Oregon.
On the Pacific Coast in the far Northwest, the pioneers were American sailors. Soon after the Revolution they had visited the Oregon ports to pick up furs with which they sailed to China to trade for tea and other exotic goods. The first attempt by an American to set up a permanent settlement in the Oregon country was made by John Jacob Astor, a hard-driving German immigrant. He had already made a small fortune in the fur trade and was to become the richest man in America before his death in 1848. The men of his Pacific Fur Company built Astoria on the Columbia River in 1811, but during the War of 1812 they sold the fort to the British.

In 1832 Nathaniel J. Wyeth of Massachusetts, a successful 30-year-old businessman and inventor, led a small group overland to trade in the Oregon country. His route became famous as the Oregon Trail—another grand pioneer-way to the promised lands of the West. The adventures of that trail were later vividly described by another young New Englander, Francis Parkman. His book, *The Oregon Trail* (1849), soon became an American classic.

Wyeth's attempts to make money in Oregon were failures, but he blazed the way for others. On his second trip, in 1834, he escorted a party of Methodist missionaries headed by mild, easygoing Jason Lee. When Lee arrived in Oregon at the fort of the Hudson's Bay Company, he and his party were welcomed by a huge, bearded Canadian, Dr. John McLoughlin, the director of the company's fur-trading operations in Oregon. McLoughlin helped Lee, as he was to assist many American settlers, and persuaded him to settle in the Willamette Valley.

The news of the success of the Methodists in establishing a mission encouraged other denominations to follow. In 1836 the Presbyterians sent out Dr. Marcus Whitman and Henry H. Spaulding, who founded a mission at Walla Walla. The missionaries' wives, Narcissa Prentice Whitman and Elizabeth Hart Spaulding, accompanied them. Their feat as the first white women to cross the Rockies inspired other families to make the long trip to Oregon.

Father Pierre de Smet, the friendly and learned Jesuit whom the Indians called "Blackrobe," went to Oregon in 1844. During the next few years he assisted in setting up a number of Catholic missions in the Oregon country.

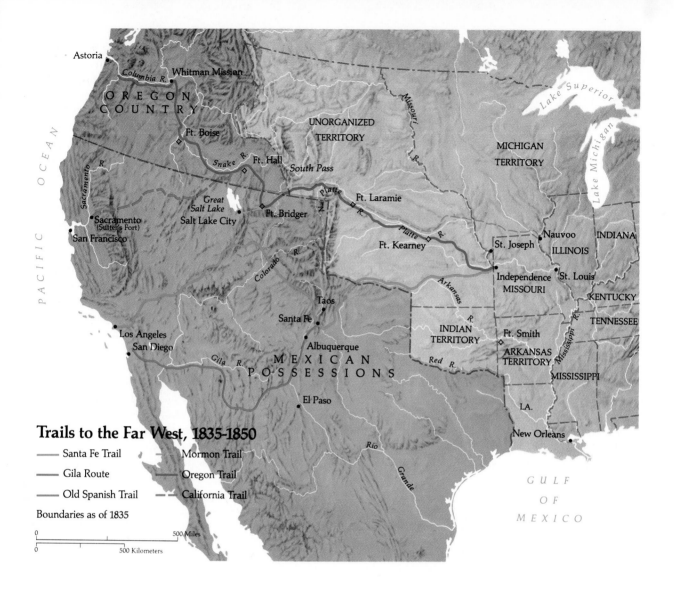

Trails to the Far West, 1835-1850

—— Santa Fe Trail

—— Gila Route

—— Old Spanish Trail

—— Mormon Trail

—— Oregon Trail

– – – California Trail

Boundaries as of 1835

0 ———— 500 Miles

0 ———— 500 Kilometers

By 1843 there were about 1000 American settlers in Oregon. They had come to this promised land because of the financial depression that had begun in 1837 (p. 201) and because they had heard tall tales that Oregon was a fertile country where it was always springtime.

Since Congress paid little attention to the small settlement, they followed the example of earlier pioneer communities and made their own government. In an old barn belonging to one of the missions, on July 5, 1843, they adopted a constitution "for the purposes of mutual protection and to secure peace and prosperity among ourselves . . . until such time as the United States of America extend their jurisdiction over us."

Nearly 1000 settlers came to Oregon during the course of 1843 in the first successful mass migration. The next year brought 1500 more settlers. And the following year an additional 3000 arrived. The government back in Washington could neglect the distant "republic" of Oregon no longer.

California in the 1830s. The first Americans to reach the Mexican province of California came by boat. They traded to the missions and the ranches all kinds of goods in exchange for the products of the cattle ranches—tallow for their candles and hides for shoes and saddle bags. This trade and the beauties of California, as well as the life of common sailors of those days, were described by Richard Henry Dana in *Two Years Before the Mast* (1840).

The Mexican government broke up the Christian missions in 1834. The lands were supposed to go to the Indian converts but instead were carved into huge ranches. American traders, who lost some of their most reliable customers, the Franciscan fathers of the missions, now appointed trading agents in California towns. These agents, who supervised dealings with the ranchers, later became important in the drive to make California part of the United States.

In the 1830s there were only about 4000 Mexicans scattered along the California coast between the two deep-water ports of San Francisco and San Diego. Americans from the crowded eastern seaboard thronged westward in long wagon trains to the magical country that sailors and traders had extolled. Most of these found their way to the West Coast by following the Oregon Trail to Great Salt Lake and then heading southwest to California. A thriving center sprang up in the Sacramento Valley. A focus of community life was the fort built by John Sutter. A wandering Swiss citizen who had arrived in California in 1839 from Hawaii, he received an enormous grant of land from the Mexican government.

Wagon towns moving west. From the very beginning of American history, the people who came here came in groups. And when Americans decided to move farther west in the years after the Revolution, they seldom went alone. Americans traveling to Oregon and California also moved in groups. You might start out alone with a few friends and family from the settled states. But you were not likely to reach very far into the unknown West unless you soon joined with 50 or 100 others.

Most of the West was still unknown except to the mountain men and the explorers. The few wagon ways that had been marked by the explorers were the only paths through the wilderness. The most important trails started from a little Missouri town called Independence 200 miles west of St. Louis.

At Elm Grove, just outside Independence, people from all over collected because they wanted to go west. Some had never seen one another before. Just as people in Chicago, Cincinnati, St. Louis, and a hundred other places were quickly coming together and forming their instant cities, so these people with wagons were forming their own kind of instant towns. These were wagon towns, towns made to move.

It was not safe to travel alone. Indians were apt to attack a small party, but a large group might

St. Ignatius Mission, founded by the Jesuits in Montana Territory in 1845, was painted in this watercolor by Peter Peterson Tofft, a Danish immigrant who also portrayed the Oregon country.

A pioneer headed for California made this sketch of his wagon train crossing the Platte River on July 20, 1849. The broad, empty plains stretch out endlessly before them.

frighten them off. And with enough wagons in your party, you could make a kind of fort every night. The wagons would be formed into a hollow circle or square, which was like a small walled town. People were protected while they cooked their meals. They could sing and dance, or hold meetings to talk about the problems of the trip. If the Indians attacked, women and children could be safe in the hollow center while the men and boys shot back at the Indians from behind the wall of wagons.

The covered wagon used for crossing the continent was about 10 feet long and 8 1/2 feet to the top of the canvas. It was usually drawn, not by horses, but by three pairs of oxen. Even if two oxen were lost, the four that remained could still pull the wagon. When fully loaded, it could carry a ton.

Getting this heavy wagon up a hill, across rivers, and down steep inclines was never easy. But it was much easier if you were in a large party. Then the whole party could help push or pull with their teams or their muscles.

The trip across the continent was long and slow. From Independence on the lower Missouri River to Sutter's Fort in California, it was about 2000 miles on the wagon trail. The normal speed for a wagon was only two miles an hour. Even with good luck, the wagon ride from Independence to the Pacific might take five months.

When so many people lived together for so long, they had to be organized. They had to make rules for health and safety. They had to appoint commanders and judges, select juries, and punish criminals. They had to keep order, arrange marriages, and perform funerals. They felt all the needs of people in Cincinnati or Chicago or St. Louis, and had additional problems, too. If the trip was not to take forever, the group had to see that everybody did a share of the work and risked a share of the danger.

What they did was very much like what the Pilgrims on the *Mayflower* had needed to do 200 years before. They made a government for themselves. Like the first pilgrims, each wagon train made its Mayflower Compact. Each had its own do-it-yourself government. They wrote out their own laws, which everybody signed. They elected a captain, who was like the captain of a ship. He had the difficult job of assigning tasks and settling quarrels. The fate of the whole wagon train might depend on his good humor and good judgment.

The Mormons move to Utah. The best organizers were the best captains of wagon trains. The Mormons were remarkably successful. With their new American religion they looked to the West for their promised land. They set up instant cities of their own in Missouri and Illinois. When the Mormons prospered, however, their envious neighbors believed all kinds of strange stories about them and persecuted them. In late June 1844 the founder of their religion and their leader Joseph Smith as well as his brother Hyrum were killed by an Illinois mob that feared and hated these distinctive people. The Mormons had to move on.

In February 1846 their new leader, the able Brigham Young, began taking them across Iowa toward the faraway land near Great Salt Lake. There they would be hundreds of miles from the nearest settlement. They traveled in carefully organized groups, building their own roads and bridges as they went. They even planted seeds along the trail so Mormon wagon trains the next season could harvest the crops for food as they came by. One wagon train that reached Utah in October 1847 brought 1540 Mormons in 540 wagons, together with 124 horses, 9 mules, 2213 oxen, 887 cows, 358 sheep, 24 hogs, and 716 chickens.

By cooperation, discipline, and hard work, the Mormons made the dry land bloom. They dug elaborate irrigation systems and laid out a city with broad avenues. In time they were to create many towns and cities in their distant, difficult land.

The Mormons were not the only ones who expected to find a promised land in the unknown West. Hundreds of other wagon towns were held together by their own vague hopes of a prosperous future.

SECTION 3 REVIEW

1. Identify: Stephen F. Austin, William Becknell, Charles Bent, John Jacob Astor, Jason Lee, the Whitmans, Francis Parkman, Pierre de Smet.

2. How did the Mormon migration differ from most of the other migrations?

3. **Making Comparisons.** How were wagon train parties similar to the earlier voyages of the Pilgrims across the Atlantic Ocean?

4. Texas and Oregon

The first opportunity for the flag to follow the American people into the new lands of the West came in Texas. But this question soon divided the nation. And it also led to war with Mexico.

The Lone Star Republic. By 1835 there were nearly 30,000 settlers from the United States living in the huge Mexican state of Coahuila-Texas. They had become Mexican citizens, but they had complaints about Mexican rule. Saltillo, the state capital, was 700 miles away from their settlements on the Brazos and Colorado rivers. These settlers from the eastern United States were in a majority in Texas proper. But they were only a small minority in the vast state of Coahuila-Texas. They had only a few representatives in the state legislature. They missed the Bill of Rights and all the guarantees of the United States Constitution, including especially the right to trial by jury.

These new Texans had come mostly from the southern United States. Since they had brought their slaves with them, they were outraged that the Mexican government tried to outlaw slavery. When that government imposed heavy customs taxes and stationed troops among the settlers, their thoughts naturally went back to the American Revolution. In 1835 they revolted and drove out the Mexican troops. Like the colonists who had revolted against George III 60 years before, the Texans declared their independence on March 2, 1836.

The convention that issued the declaration also elected a temporary government. David G. Burnet, an emigrant from Ohio who in his youth had fought for Venezuelan freedom from Spain, was elected president for the time being. Lorenzo de Zavala

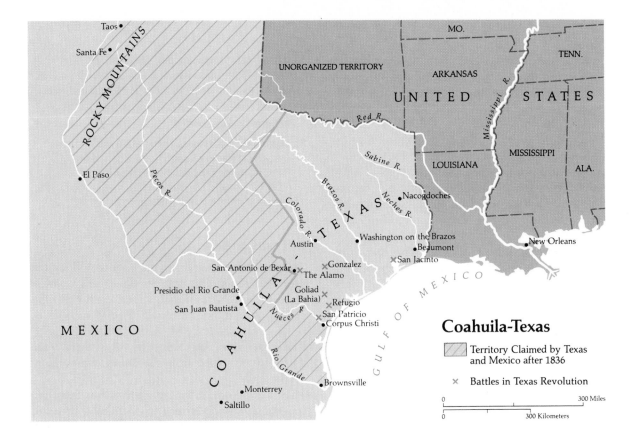

was made vice-president. He was an ardent republican who had been exiled from Spain. He had fought for Mexican independence and served that new nation as a state governor, cabinet minister, and ambassador to France. In 1834 when General Santa Anna took over the government and began to rule as dictator, de Zavala fled to Texas.

General Santa Anna led an army to crush the Texas rebellion. The first battle took place at San Antonio. The Texas defenders were led by William B. Travis, a 27-year-old lawyer, and James Bowie, reputed inventor of the bowie knife. The force included Davy Crockett, the famous frontiersman, two black slaves, and many Mexican Texans. Greatly outnumbered, they fortified themselves in an abandoned mission, the Alamo. In the end, 183 died in the siege, but they killed or wounded 600 of the 2400 Mexican soldiers. This bloody battle, which ended on March 6, 1836, was a military defeat. But it was also a kind of spiritual victory, for it provided the battle cry "Remember the Alamo," which Texans would never forget. The fury of the Texans was kept hot when three weeks later all the

defenders at Goliad were massacred after they had surrendered.

The Texan army was led by tall and magnetic Sam Houston, a veteran of the War of 1812, onetime governor of Tennessee, Indian trader, and adopted son of the Cherokees. Houston retreated with his small army until he felt the right moment had come to fight. Then he turned and attacked. In the Battle of San Jacinto on April 21, Houston's army routed the Mexican army, captured Santa Anna, and forced him to sign a treaty recognizing Texas independence. A republic was set up with Houston as the first president. A constitution modeled on those of the states of the Union was adopted. To reassure the settlers from the southern United States, the constitution of Texas forbade the Texas Congress from interfering with slavery. The new Republic of Texas offered the curious spectacle of people who had fought for their right to govern themselves—and for the right to keep thousands of their fellow Texans in slavery.

Texas at once asked for admission to the Union. But Texas was so big that there was no telling how many new states might be carved from its territory. Since all Texas was slave country, the northern states saw that the balance of North and South might be upset forever simply by creating numerous small slave states there. Some Northerners said that Texas was nothing but a slave owners' plot to smuggle a lot of new slave states into the Union.

The gag rule. Northerners were especially sensitive about slavery at this time because of the so-called gag rule in Congress. Faced with a flood of abolitionist petitions in 1836, the House of Representatives refused to discuss any further petitions against slavery. Northern opponents of slavery called this the "gag rule." Former President John Quincy Adams, now a representative from Massachusetts, protested that such a restriction of free speech in the Congress was "a direct violation of the Constitution of the United States, of the rules of the House, and of the rights of my constituents." "Old Man Eloquence," as Adams came to be called, angered members of the House with his lengthy orations against the gag resolution. He finally managed to secure its repeal in 1844 by convincing members that limiting free speech endangered the Union.

Southerners tried every measure—legal and illegal—to prevent the delivery of abolitionist literature into their states. When extremists in Charleston, South Carolina, seized and burned a sack full of abolitionist pamphlets, the Congress agreed with the Postmaster General that southern postmasters did not have to deliver such mail.

The passions of the slavery issue blazed high over Texas. It seemed that to placate the slavery forces by bringing Texas into the Union would incite war with Mexico and so cost American lives. Texas was kept out of the Union. The government of the United States recognized the Republic of Texas as a separate nation in 1837 and opened diplomatic relations with the new country. First Andrew Jackson and then Martin Van Buren refused to propose bringing Texas into the Union. The question played no part in the rowdy "log-cabin" campaign of 1840 when the Whig candidates, Harrison and Tyler, were elected.

The Texas question reopened. A surprising turn of events prevented the election of the Whig President William Henry Harrison from producing the results that voters intended. The aged Harrison caught a cold during his inauguration and died a few weeks later. Vice-President John Tyler, a states-rights Virginia Democrat, had been put on the Whig ticket with Harrison simply to attract votes. The Whig leaders expected that he, like Vice-Presidents before him, would be inactive. They never dreamed that he would do more than preside over the Senate. Now, to their shock and dismay, they had actually put him in the White House!

President Tyler left not a moment's doubt that he was a full-fledged President and would follow his own policies whether or not the Whigs liked it. He vetoed Whig bills to create a new Bank of the United States, and he opposed a higher tariff. The desperate Whig leaders could do nothing but read him out of the Whig party (to which he had never really belonged). They labeled him a "traitor" and a "President by accident." All of President Harrison's Cabinet resigned, except Secretary of State Daniel Webster. He waited until 1842 in order to complete negotiations for the Webster-Ashburton Treaty (p. 253).

Tyler as a Virginia Democrat naturally wanted to annex Texas. And of course he could expect no support from the Whigs, who by accident had put him in the White House. He was forced to look to the South. At first, he hoped to avoid a violent showdown over the slavery question. So he simply evaded the problem of Texas. But Great Britain soon made him face the issue.

Tyler learned that Texas was negotiating with Great Britain for aid and protection. The adept British diplomats saw that if they could make a firm alliance with Texas, they might block the south-westward expansion of the United States. At the same time they would secure a new source of cotton and a promising new market for manufacturers. The French government, too, supported an independent Republic of Texas.

Alarmed by this unexpected willingness of Texas to enlist the great powers of Europe, Tyler saw a new urgency in the issue. He quickly began negotiating with the government of Texas. In April 1844 John C. Calhoun, who was now Secretary of State, concluded a treaty that provided for the independent Republic of Texas to enter the United States as another state of the Union.

Unfortunately for the treaty's chances in the Senate, Calhoun used it as one more time to defend slavery. This merely confirmed Northerners in their belief that the annexation of Texas was a slave owners' plot. Over all brooded a fear that annexation would bring on war with Mexico. The treaty was rejected by the decisive vote of 16 to 35.

The election of 1844.

While Calhoun's treaty was being discussed in the Senate, the national conventions met to choose their candidates for President. To no one's surprise, at Baltimore on May 1 the Whigs ignored Tyler and named Henry Clay. At Clay's request, the Whig platform was silent on the subject of Texas. The Democrats also met at Baltimore, where it was expected that they would nominate their best-known leader, Martin Van Buren, who had already been President once. But Van Buren had committed himself against annexing Texas in order to gain the votes of the North. So he was passed over.

Then for the first time in American history a party nominated a "dark horse," a man who was not nationally known and who had not been thought of as a candidate. If there were few arguments in his favor, there was little to be said against him. Such a candidate, they thought, might have wider appeal than some famous man who had won loyal friends but also had made bitter enemies. The "dark horse" was James K. Polk, once governor of Tennessee and a loyal Democrat. The Whigs ridiculed the Democratic choice. Earlier that year the polka had become the most popular dance in Washington. "The *Polk*-a dance," they said, "will now be the order of the day. It means two steps *backward* for one step forward."

There was a surprise in store for the Whigs. The unknown Polk soon proved to be an adept politician. His formula for compromise was a single watchword: *Expansion!* To annex Texas all by itself expanded the slave area and seemed a menace to the North. But if at the same time you annexed the vast Oregon Territory, you had something to give the North in return. That was Polk's platform. Expand everywhere at once, and then there would be something for everybody. The very thought of stretching the nation all the way to the Pacific was exhilarating. Perhaps the nation could be united simply by marching westward together. In a divided nation, growth itself was a kind of compromise, something that everybody could agree on.

Henry Clay saw that Polk had found a popular issue. Clay had published a letter on April 27 (when he thought that Van Buren would be the Democratic candidate) opposing annexation. When he saw himself running against the expansionist Polk, he changed his tune. Clay was so anxious to be President that there were few things he would not do to smooth his path to the White House. Now he wrote that he "would be glad to see Texas admitted on fair terms" and that "slavery ought not to affect the question one way or another." But Clay misjudged the voters. His shifty behavior caused Conscience (antislavery) Whigs in New York to switch their votes to James G. Birney, the candidate of the small antislavery Liberty party. As a result Polk carried New York by a slim margin, which made it possible for him to win a close election. Henry Clay had outsmarted himself.

Ignoring the narrowness of Polk's victory, President Tyler, who had always wanted to annex Texas, called the election a "mandate" from the people. Not even waiting for Polk to come into office, in February 1845 he secured the passage of a resolution in both houses of Congress admitting Texas to the Union. The measure also provided that with the consent of Texas not more than four additional states might some time be carved from its territory, and that the Missouri Compromise line would extend westward above Texas. That was something for the South. Later that year, living up to his campaign promise, Polk claimed for the United States the whole vast Oregon Territory, which we had been sharing with Great Britain. That was something for the North.

Manifest destiny.

Americans were thrilled by the vision of their Empire for Liberty reaching to the Pacific. "Why not extend the 'area of freedom' by the annexation of California?" asked the usually conservative *American Whig Review.* "Why not plant the banner of liberty there?" Then there would be no question of Old World monarchies existing in America.

The catch phrase for this whole expansive movement was provided by a New York newspaperman, John L. O'Sullivan, who wrote that it was "our manifest destiny to overspread and to possess the whole continent which Providence has given us for the development of the great experiment of liberty and federated self-government entrusted to us." *Manifest destiny!* The idea that the American destiny was clear (or manifest) challenged, elated, and exhilarated. It was an up-to-date, expanded 1800s-version of an old American refrain. The Puritan City of God, their "City upon a hill," was transformed into a continental Empire for Liberty. Both would be beacons for the world.

Fifty-four forty or fight! Polk at first demanded a stretch of Oregon that reached all the way up to the borders of Alaska (then owned by Russia). "All Oregon or none!" shouted American champions of manifest destiny. "Fifty-four forty or fight!"—a reference to the latitude of the territory's northern border—became their slogan. But when the annexation of Texas brought on war with Mexico, Polk prudently decided not to risk war also with Great Britain. The two countries agreed in June 1846 to extend the 49th parallel as the border between the United States and Canada all the way to the Pacific. Western expansionists were outraged. They felt that Polk had broken his campaign promise and put the whole nation into the hands of the dreaded Slave Power.

SECTION 4 REVIEW

1. Identify or explain: Santa Anna, Sam Houston, gag rule, John Tyler, "dark horse," James K. Polk, Conscience Whigs, Liberty party.

2. Locate: Coahuila-Texas, the Alamo, Goliad, San Jacinto, the "fifty-four forty" line.

3. How was the annexation of Texas linked to the slavery issue?

4. How was the Oregon issue settled?

5. **Recognizing Ideologies.** How did the idea of "manifest destiny" echo the Puritains' belief in a "City upon a hill"?

---

5. War With Mexico

The nation's troubles with Mexico were far from settled. Mexico considered the annexation of Texas (which it said was still a part of Mexico) to be an act of war by the United States. It also disputed the boundary of Texas. Meanwhile, the American settlers in California were a new trouble spot. Following the example of Texas, they too wanted to join the United States. Polk was also eager to bring

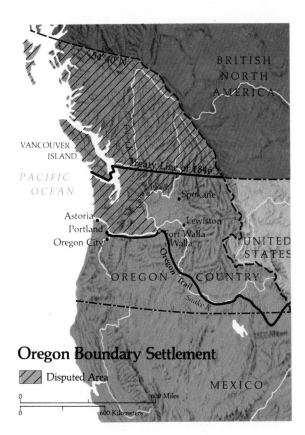

Oregon Boundary Settlement

///// Disputed Area

California into the Union. But he hoped to find a way that would avoid war.

The declaration of war. Polk sent an agent to Mexico to offer as much as $30 million for New Mexico and California. In addition the United States would assume all claims of its citizens against Mexico if Mexico would accept the Rio Grande instead of the Nueces River as the border of Texas. But Mexico was on the brink of a revolution. Feelings against the United States ran high. Both claimants for the presidency of Mexico played upon these feelings, even refusing to meet Polk's agent.

President Polk then decided on "aggressive measures." He sent General Zachary Taylor with 2000 regular troops to the Rio Grande. The Mexicans ordered Taylor to withdraw from the disputed territory. When he refused, a Mexican unit crossed the Rio Grande and ambushed a scouting party of Americans, killing or wounding sixteen men (April 25, 1846).

Polk had already drafted a message asking Congress for a declaration of war against Mexico. Upon receiving news of the attack upon Taylor's troops, he tore up his first draft and wrote a new one. Now he declared that, in spite of his efforts to keep the peace, the war had already begun "by the act of Mexico." He asked Congress to recognize that a state of war existed and then to provide funds and troops to fight it.

Northerners feared that victory over Mexico might add still more territory and lead to even more slave states in the Southwest. But once the fighting had begun, patriotic passions prevailed. The opposition proved weak, and Congress voted for war.

Northern fears proved to be well founded. After United States victories by General Taylor's army at Monterrey in northern Mexico (September 21-23, 1846) and at Buena Vista (February 22, 1847), Mexico City was captured by an army commanded by General Winfield Scott (September 14, 1847). The helpless Mexican government then gave up.

The conquest of New Mexico and California.

In June 1846, upon hearing of the war with Mexico, the explorer John C. Frémont and his band of frontiersmen helped American settlers in California to set up a republic under the famous "Bear Flag." But soon the navy arrived and the flag of the United States replaced the Bear Flag. Meanwhile, soldiers under General Stephen Kearny marched from Fort Leavenworth to Santa Fe and raised the United States flag over New Mexico. Then, with a small unit of cavalry, Kearny continued on his 1800-mile journey to California. When they came out of the mountains in December 1846, Kearny and his little force met brief but stiff resistance from Mexican Californians. With the aid of the navy, Kearny was able to put down this opposition and give the United States complete control of California.

The peace treaty and the Gadsden Purchase.

In the Treaty of Guadalupe Hidalgo (1848) Mexico dropped all its claims to Texas and agreed that Texas belonged to the United States. But that was only the beginning of Mexican losses. In addition it handed over all the lands between Texas and the Pacific. That included California, New Mexico, and most of the present states of Utah, Nevada, Arizona, and Colorado. In return, the United States paid Mexico $15 million and assumed claims of our citizens against Mexico of some $3 million.

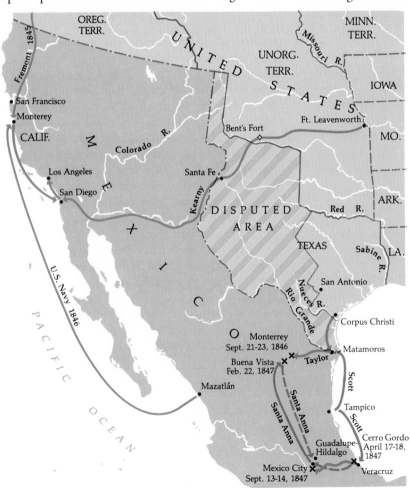

The Mexican War, 1846-1848

← U.S. Forces

← Mexican Forces

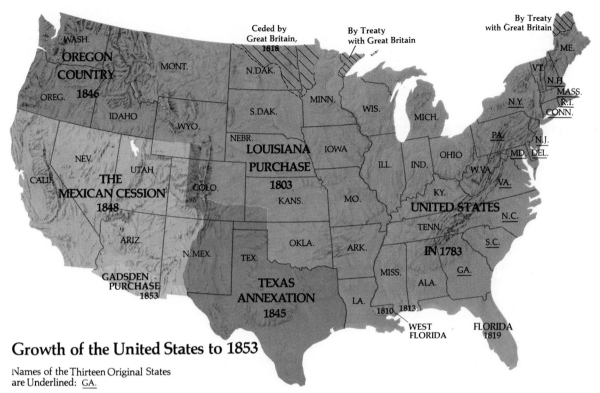

Growth of the United States to 1853

Names of the Thirteen Original States
are Underlined: GA.

After the Webster-Ashburton Treaty (1842) had finally resolved the long-disputed border between Maine and Canada, the Treaty of Guadalupe Hidalgo (1848) nearly filled in the outlines of the present United States except for Alaska and Hawaii. The final piece, a small strip of land south of the Gila River in Arizona and New Mexico, was bought from Mexico in 1853 for $10 million in the Gadsden Purchase (p. 262). This piece of land was believed to offer the best rail route across the southern Rockies to the Pacific.

The lands (including Texas) taken from Mexico after the war were larger than all the Louisiana Purchase or all the United States when the Constitution was adopted. This should have satisfied any American's yen for expansion. Yet when President Polk asked the Senate to approve the Treaty of Guadalupe Hidalgo, a dozen senators voted against it because they wanted to annex the *whole* of Mexico. "We believe it is a part of our destiny to civilize that beautiful country," the *New York Herald* proclaimed. Antislavery men also opposed the treaty, as did Whigs who envied Polk and the Democrats their success. So the treaty only squeaked through the Senate by 38 to 14, just 3 more votes than the necessary two-thirds.

It took no prophet to predict that more western lands spelled more trouble. Every new acre was a subject for debate, for a quarrel—or even for a battle. Southerners and Northerners alike thought of nothing but whether the new lands would spread the Slave Power.

In the bitterly divided nation, every stroke of national good luck struck a note of discontent. Each section somehow was afraid that the other would gain more. Ralph Waldo Emerson wrote in his journal as the United States invaded Mexico, "The United States will conquer Mexico, but it will be as the man swallows the arsenic, which brings him down in turn. Mexico will poison us."

SECTION 5 REVIEW

1. Identify or explain: Zachary Taylor, Winfield Scott, John C. Frémont, "Bear Flag."

2. Locate: Nueces River, Rio Grande, Monterrey, Buena Vista, Mexico City, Gadsden Purchase.

3. **Recognizing Cause and Effect.** How did the Treaty of Guadalupe Hidalgo change the geography of the United States?

CHAPTER 11 REVIEW

FOCUSING ON IDEAS

1. A chief feature of American Protestantism was its division into many denominations and sects. Identify some of these divisions.

2. Humanitarianism—concern for human welfare and human dignity—was at the heart of many reform movements. What were some of the most common violations of human welfare and dignity? What reforms were proposed to deal with these violations of people's most basic rights?

3. Individualism has long been regarded as an American trait, but it had to be limited on the western wagon trains. Why?

4. How did the Mexican War increase the land holdings of the United States?

5. Describe the kinds of people who helped to open the American West for settlement.

TAKING A CRITICAL LOOK

1. **Recognizing Cause and Effect.** Name some changes in American life between 1790 and the 1840s that led reformers to demand better schools. How were improvements in education linked to these changes in American society?

2. **Identifying Central Issues.** Why were people who defended slavery wary of social reformers?

3. **Drawing Conclusions.** How did the slavery issue complicate the idea of manifest destiny?

YOUR REGION IN HISTORY

1. **Geography.** From your locality, trace the route a family might have traveled in the 1830s or 1840s to reach Texas, California, or the Oregon country. If you live in Texas, California, Oregon, or Washington, pick a city on the east coast and trace the route a new settler might have followed in those years to reach your present home town.

2. **Culture.** Find out if the reform movements discussed in this chapter had any particular impact on your state. For example, what changes—if any—did your state make in public education, care of the mentally ill and retarded, women's rights?

3. **Economics.** How did the opening of the West affect business opportunities in your region?

HISTORICAL FACTS AND FIGURES

Developing Hypotheses. Study the chart below to help answer the following questions: (a) What happened to the total number of students between 1840 and 1870? (b) By what percentage did the school-age population increase from 1850 to 1879? (c) By what percentage did the number of students increase during the same period? (d) Write a hypothesis explaining why the number of students increased at a faster rate than the number of Americans age 5–19. (e) What facts can you find in this chapter to support your hypothesis?

School Enrollment Rates, 1840-1870				
	1840	**1850**	**1860**	**1870**
Total number of students: primary, secondary, and higher	2,025,636	3,642,694	5,477,037	7,209,938
Total population, 5 to 19 years of age	(not available)	8,661,689	11,253,475	13,641,490
White population, 5 to 19 years of age	5,275,479	7,234,973	9,494,432	11,799,212

CHAPTER 12

The failure of the politicians

The poison pill of the western lands soon began to do its work. The organization of every inch was disputed between the North and South. And the problem always was whether—and where—slavery should be allowed in the vast new West. Over this question Americans would kill each other in Kansas, political parties would collapse or split, and finally the nation itself would divide.

1. The Compromise of 1850

Emerson spoke for many Americans when he foresaw that the millions of acres acquired from Mexico—all raw material for new states—would produce strife and tragedy for the nation as a whole. The first act of this drama would end in a great "compromise." Many optimistic Americans, north and south, mistakenly believed this might settle the slavery question for good. But the moral issue of slavery was not a subject for compromise. The only question for a nation "conceived in liberty" was when and how slavery would be abolished.

The gold rush. By an astonishing coincidence, gold was discovered near Sutter's Mill in California in the very same year when Mexico handed over California to the United States. Gold rushers flocked to California.

Thousands went west by wagon train across the plains, through mountains and desert. Their trail was marked by broken wagons, dead animals, and human skeletons—relics of pioneers who had the spirit but lacked the strength or the equipment to carry them through. Others sailed to Panama and

walked across the malaria-ridden isthmus to battle for a place on a steamer going up the California coast. Some came all the way by sea, surviving an eight-month journey around Cape Horn. Often they formed companies to purchase old vessels. Then, like the members of the westward-going wagon towns, they drew up rules, elected officers, and sailed for the gold fields.

The clipper ships. Among the ships that sailed for California were some of the most splendid sailing vessels ever built. The swift clipper ships (so called because they could "clip" time off a passage) were built in New England, spurred by the need to speed to California. Huge profits rewarded the fastest ships. The grandest of the clippers were made by the master shipbuilder Donald McKay. As a young man he had emigrated from Nova Scotia. With a rare sense of design and a fine eye for detail, working in East Boston he turned out the speediest, most beautiful ships of the age. He became a hero for his generation, like the great designers of automobiles or airplanes for a later age. In April 1851 the Flying Cloud, the finest of McKay's many vessels, set a record of 89 days from New York to San Francisco.

Workers at Sutter's Mill were the first to discover gold in California.

This hopeful young prospector was one of those who traveled by land to California in 1849 to mine gold.

The advertisement for *Neptune's Car* boasts of the speedy 97-day sail to California.

Many clipper captains brought their wives. Mary Brown Patten took command of *Neptune's Car* when her husband became ill. At the age of 19, while caring for her sick husband, she navigated an 1800-ton clipper for the remaining 52 days on the way to California.

In the 1850s, after a railway was built across Panama, the day of the clipper ships was on the wane. British steamships, larger and more dependable than the clippers, brought the great age of sail to an end.

California asks for admission to the Union. People rushed to California from everywhere. Nantucket lost a quarter of its voting population in nine months. French soldiers and government officials deserted the Marquesas islands in the Pacific. Thousands came from the Mississippi Valley. Americans—north and south—sang

Oh Susannah, don't you cry for me.
I've gone to California with my wash-bowl on my knee.

During 1849 more than 80,000 people arrived in California. It was no surprise that these Americans wanted to join the Union as a new state. But in 1849 there were 30 states altogether, and the national score showed 15 slave and 15 free states. To admit California as a free state, as its people requested in 1849, would break the precarious tie.

The Wilmot Proviso. And what was to be done with all the rest of the newly acquired lands? How was slavery to be dealt with out there? That question had been raised early in the Mexican War when President Polk asked Congress for money to negotiate a Mexican boundary settlement. Antislavery congressmen knew that this would lead to demands for more territory from Mexico. So David Wilmot, a Democrat from Pennsylvania, offered an amendment to Polk's bill. Wilmot proposed that "neither slavery nor involuntary servitude shall ever exist in any part of the territory" acquired from Mexico. Antislavery men and Westerners who were bitter over the failure to take all of Oregon joined to support this amendment. It passed several times in the House in 1846–1847, but the Senate always voted it down. Americans were now divided by the problems of expansion.

The South through its leaders, John C. Calhoun of South Carolina and Jefferson Davis of Mississippi,

opposed the Wilmot Proviso. Congress, they said, had no right to interfere with slavery in the territories. More than that, they insisted that Congress had a positive duty, under the Constitution, to protect the property of Southerners in the territories. This meant their right to own slaves. Slavery might be forbidden only when a territory achieved statehood, and then only by act of the state itself.

Between the extremes—those who would bar slavery altogether and those who would protect slavery—many compromises were proposed. For example, some suggested that the Missouri Compromise line of 36°30' be extended all the way to the Pacific, dividing California and New Mexico into free and slave sections (map, p. 176). Others urged "popular sovereignty," which meant leaving the slavery question up to the settlers of each territory.

The election of 1848. As the election of 1848 approached, both political parties wanted to avoid all divisive questions. Since President Polk decided not to seek reelection, the Democrats nominated Governor Lewis Cass of Michigan. He was a strong expansionist, sympathetic to the South, and cared little about slavery one way or the other.

The Whigs, though they had opposed the war, nominated the hero of the Battle of Buena Vista, General Zachary Taylor. A professional soldier and a Louisiana sugar planter, he was the owner of 300 slaves. He had no experience in politics. This easygoing southern gentleman had not even voted for some years. The Whigs counted on his war record to sweep their "Old Rough and Ready" into office. To be doubly safe against the accusation that they really did stand for something, the Whigs had no party platform.

Voters who had strong feelings on the slavery issue were angered that the major parties offered them no real choice. As a result the "Free-Soil" Democrats combined with Conscience Whigs and abolitionists to form the new Free-Soil party. They nominated Martin Van Buren for President and Charles Francis Adams, the son of John Quincy Adams, for Vice-President. Their party supported the Wilmot Proviso and called for "Free Soil, Free Speech, Free Labor, and Free Men."

The Free-Soilers took away enough votes from Cass to give New York's 36 electoral votes to Taylor, who won a close election with 163 electoral votes to Cass's 127. The Free-Soilers won no state,

Free-Soilers organize in Massachusetts in 1848.

but 291,263 people voted for them, and they elected 13 members to the House of Representatives.

Clay has a plan. When the Senate met in December 1849 to decide the future of California and of the other lands taken from Mexico, the air was charged with fear and hate. For everyone at the time it was a moment of high drama. The nation's elder statesmen were still trying to resolve by words and by debate what would be settled only in blood and on the battlefield.

This was the last appearance in the congressional arena of three men who had played leading political roles ever since the War of 1812. All were giants on the national stage. Each was a hero to his part of the country. Henry Clay of the western state of Kentucky was there, 73 years old and in failing health. John C. Calhoun, relentless champion of the South, was at the end of his long senatorial career. Daniel Webster, shrewd New Englander at the height of his powers, never thundered more eloquently.

Senator Calhoun, sick and near death, had to have his speech read for him as he sat nearby and listened. He made impossible demands. He insisted that in order to "do justice" by giving the South "an equal right" in the new lands, the North

must admit slavery to California and New Mexico. Calhoun went even further and seriously proposed a fantastic constitutional amendment that provided for the election of two Presidents—one from the slave states and one from the free states.

On the other side, William H. Seward, a new antislavery Whig senator from New York, was just as uncompromising. Any concession to the slave cause, he declared, was "essentially vicious." On the issue of slavery he refused even to appeal to the Constitution. He preferred a "higher law."

Leading the forces of conciliation was Senator Clay, who had a plan. By nature a compromiser, he had the half-hearted support of many but the enthusiasm of very few. This legislative mix-master whom the nation had three times defeated for its President now offered the bundle of laws that was to become the "Compromise" of 1850. California was to be admitted as a free state (something for the North). A strong Fugitive Slave Act would protect the right of owners to recapture slaves who had escaped to the North (something for the South). The slave trade would be abolished in the District of Columbia (something for the North), but slavery would still be protected there (something for the South). He had offered something for everybody. But he had still left the main question unanswered.

What would become of all the rest of the vast new area taken from Mexico? Would it be free or slave? Clay's compromise simply postponed the answer. The people of those areas, he proposed, should in the future decide that for themselves. This arrangement was called "popular sovereignty" by those who admired it and "squatter sovereignty" by others.

Daniel Webster favors compromise. Finally, on March 7, 1850, Daniel Webster, the nation's most famous orator, rose to his feet to bring the lengthy debate to its climax. He was still an impressive and powerful figure. The galleries were crowded and the people listened patiently. For several hours the great Webster delivered one of his most carefully prepared orations. The audience did not hear what it expected.

Webster had put himself on record as being opposed to any extension of slavery. But now, sensing that the Union was truly in danger, he supported Clay's compromise at every point. He declared that slavery would never actually invade

Henry Clay posed for this daguerreotype in 1849. The photographer was Mathew Brady.

the deserts and plateaus of New Mexico. Why then insist on the Wilmot Proviso, which the South looked on as a "taunt and reproach"? He maintained there was a constitutional duty to return fugitive slaves. As to the abolitionists, he said they "had produced nothing good or valuable in their operations for twenty years."

Webster was bitterly denounced in the North for this speech. Longtime admirers deserted him. But northern businessmen who feared the loss of their valuable southern trade approved his stand and circulated 200,000 copies of his speech. To many, especially the abolitionists, it seemed the issue was more clearly posed than ever—between money and humanity. Webster was accused of being the heartless mouthpiece of people who valued their bank accounts more than the freedom of their fellow Americans.

Congress accepts the compromise. Still the debate went on. President Taylor wanted Congress at once to admit as free states both California and New Mexico. Taylor was so insistent that it was feared

he would veto Clay's compromise. But once again the course of history was shaped by a quite unexpected event. It was no eloquent oration nor any rational argument but the sudden death of President Taylor that saved Clay's compromise in 1850. After attending the Fourth of July ceremonies held at the base of the unfinished Washington Monument on one of the hottest days on record, President Taylor was stricken with a severe stomach ailment. Within five days he was dead, and in his place a professional politician, the compromising Vice-President Millard Fillmore, came to the White House.

As a result of the skilled political maneuvering of Senator Stephen A. Douglas of Illinois, who took over from an exhausted Clay, the several parts of Clay's compromise were passed separately. President Fillmore signed them into law in September 1850. Among them was the Fugitive Slave Act, which would become the special target of antislavery passion.

Shortsighted optimists hailed the Compromise of 1850 as a "final" settlement. But a second look showed that it only put off the day of reckoning. There had been no true compromise. Northerners had voted for particular bills that favored their section, while Southerners supported measures that helped their area. Only the fact that a few persons actually compromised their interests made passage of all the bills possible.

The great issue of slavery was far from settled. But the compromises of 1850 did give the North

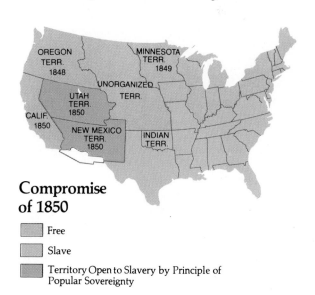

Compromise of 1850

- Free
- Slave
- Territory Open to Slavery by Principle of Popular Sovereignty

time to grow stronger—in manpower, railroads, and factories. For those who loved the Union, Clay and Douglas had performed a valuable service. They had bought time. When the evil day of armed conflict would come, that strength would help decide the issue for the North and for Union.

The revolt against the Fugitive Slave Act.
The Fugitive Slave Act of 1850 kept tempers hot in the North. It provided that state and city authorities and even plain citizens should assist in the capture and return of runaway slaves.

Harriet Tubman was called "Moses" by fugitives whom she led from slavery to freedom.

Library of Congress

State after state passed Personal Liberty laws. These forbade state officials or private citizens to assist federal courts in enforcing the Fugitive Slave Act. The laws also tried to guarantee protection and a fair trial to runaways.

Northerners showed their defiance of the Fugitive Slave Act dramatically and effectively by expanding their efforts to help slaves escape. The "Underground Railroad" was a well-organized series of routes and stopovers (stations) leading north to Canada for runaway slaves. By 1861 this scheme had helped some 75,000 slaves escape to freedom.

The most famous of all the "conductors" on the Underground Railroad was Harriet Tubman, herself an escaped slave. From 1849 to the Civil War she risked her life many times on trips into the South. During her long courageous career she helped spirit away to freedom her own elderly parents and some 300 other slaves.

The election of 1852.
There was no chance of preventing the two great national political parties from splitting into northern and southern factions unless the Compromise of 1850 was really "final" and somehow the discussion of slavery was itself abolished. But could so great an issue be simply wished away?

The Democrats, in their convention of 1852, pledged themselves to abide by the compromise measures. They nominated Franklin Pierce of New Hampshire. He was a pleasant man lacking force or decisiveness. But he had a good record as a politician and as a general in the Mexican War.

The Whigs were in a worse condition than the Democrats. President Fillmore had the backing of the southern wing of the party but was opposed by northern Whigs because he had supported the compromise. At the Whig convention it was not until the fifty-third ballot that they settled on a military hero, Virginia-born General Winfield Scott, who had captured Mexico City. The Whig platform also accepted the "finality" of the compromise measures.

But the Whigs failed to repeat the triumphs of General Harrison in 1840 and General Taylor in 1848 with this their third military hero. The Democrat Franklin Pierce won in a landslide carrying all but four states and receiving 254 electoral votes to Scott's 42. The bitter divisions in the nation were revealed in the fact that Pierce was the only President to win a popular majority between 1840 and 1864. With this defeat the Whig party began to fall apart.

Harmony was the key word of Franklin Pierce's inaugural address on March 4, 1853. The compromise measures of 1850, he said, were "strictly constitutional and to be unhesitatingly carried into effect." He sincerely hoped that no sectional ambition or radical excitement might again "threaten the durability of our institutions or obscure the light of our prosperity."

A book forces the issue. But an event had already occurred during 1852 that made Pierce's hope unlikely. It was the publication of a book, *Uncle Tom's Cabin,* by Harriet Beecher Stowe.

Mrs. Stowe found much of the ammunition for her antislavery novel in Theodore Dwight Weld's *Slavery As It Is.* In her book she tried to portray the

This advertisement for Uncle Tom's Cabin indicates some of the many different editions that were available as well as the wide variety of prices.

The Bettmann Archive

Brown Brothers

Harriet Beecher Stowe posed for this Mathew Brady daguerreotype in the 1840s. Brady, who learned the process from Samuel F. B. Morse, became the great photographer of the Civil War.

entire range of experiences a slave could have, from good owners to bad, from being bought and sold to attempts to escape to freedom. In the end, the hero of the story—the Christ-like black, Uncle Tom—is flogged to death by the brutal plantation owner, Simon Legree, because he will not give away the hiding place of two escaped slaves.

The book quickly sold more than 100,000 sets of an expensive two-volume edition. Then it was put out in a single cheap volume for 37 1/2 cents. Within a year it had sold a total of 300,000 copies. It was made into plays and musical comedies. Uncle Tom skits at fairs and circuses showed the escaping slave "Eliza Crossing the Ice" with her baby in her arms, and then Little Eva was yanked up to heaven by pulleys. "Uncle Tom's Cabin played here last night," said one newspaper. "The bloodhounds were good." The book sold enormously in England. It was quickly published in translation all over Europe. *Uncle Tom's Cabin* became America's all-time worldwide best-seller.

Mrs. Stowe gave one of the first copies to her congressman one day as he was about to board the train for Washington. He started reading the book on the train. The story was so sad that he began to cry. He attracted the attention of the other passengers as he wiped the tears from his face and blew his nose. To avoid embarrassment, he got off the train at the next stop, where he rented a hotel room and sat up all night finishing the book. There, in the privacy of his room, he could weep to his heart's content. Many other people, too, reported that the book had upset them. There must have been thousands of tear-stained copies of *Uncle Tom's Cabin*.

It is possible that, without this book, Lincoln never could have been elected President. During the Civil War, Mrs. Stowe went to see President Lincoln. "Is this the little woman," Lincoln asked her, "whose book made such a great war?"

SECTION 1 REVIEW

1. Identify or explain: Donald McKay, Wilmot Proviso, Lewis Cass, Zachary Taylor, William H. Seward, popular sovereignty, Millard Fillmore, Harriet Beecher Stowe.

2. How was the gold rush of 1849 linked to the slavery controversy?

3. How did the Free-Soil party affect the election of 1848?

4. Explain the Compromise of 1850 by (a) naming the chief issue it was supposed to settle, (b) giving its main provisions, and (c) describing the roles of Clay, Webster, and Douglas.

5. What was the Fugitive Slave Act and how did Northerners defy it?

6. **Drawing Conclusions.** What was the social and political significance of *Uncle Tom's Cabin*?

---

2. How the compromise collapsed

In his inaugural address President Pierce had boldly declared that his administration would not be controlled "by any timid forebodings of evil from expansion." This proved to be the understatement of the age. He went full speed ahead searching for new territories. He sent James Gadsden to buy the northern part of Mexico and all of Lower California. He sent Pierre Soulé as minister to Spain with orders to buy Cuba. He then reached out for Hawaii, sought a naval base in Santo Domingo, and explored the purchase of Alaska from the Russians.

Mexico had no interest in selling any large stretch of land. But Gadsden did succeed in arranging the purchase of a small tract south of the Gila River. Even then northern congressmen, wary of adding new territory for the slave power, were opposed. The Gadsden Purchase was approved only after 9000 extra acres Mexico was willing to sell were removed from the treaty. Expansion was no longer a means of compromise.

The Ostend Manifesto. The climax of aggressive nationalism came over Cuba. Southerners and their friends, including President Pierce, believed the island would add a large and profitable slave territory to the United States. But Spain did not want to sell.

In response to instructions from Secretary of State William L. Marcy, during the summer of 1854 the American ministers to Spain, England, and France met at Ostend in Belgium to shape the United States policy on Cuba.

The "Ostend Manifesto" which the ministers drew up was supposed to be a confidential dispatch to Marcy. But it soon reached the press and created an uproar. The possession of Cuba, the American ministers asserted, was essential to the welfare of the United States. And if Spain would not sell the island, they advised the United States to take Cuba by force. Pierce and Marcy said at once they had not had anything to do with the Manifesto. But that was no help. President Pierce was now branded as a proslavery man and a warlike expansionist. The Ostend Manifesto had now firmly identified slavery with expansion.

The Kansas-Nebraska Act. The only hope for the success of the Compromise of 1850 was to keep the question of slavery out of Congress. The advance of technology and the growth of industry and commerce soon made that impossible. By an ironic twist of fate the man who was destined to revive the slavery issue in Congress and so disturb the delicate balance was a main architect of the Compromise of 1850, Senator Stephen A. Douglas.

In the 1850s, of course, Americans had not yet begun to dream of reaching the moon. They had their own grand dream—to build a railroad all the way across the continent to unite East and West. No American city could want a greater prize than to be chosen as the eastern terminus of the nation's transcontinental railway. New Orleans, Memphis, St. Louis, Chicago, and many smaller towns all hoped they would be selected and so become the bustling headquarters for reaching the wealth and commerce of the West.

Douglas wanted his home city of Chicago to receive the prize. But a railroad through the empty land of the West could only be built with the aid of government land grants. And these land grants could be made only if the region the railroad passed through was already organized politically and surveyed. With this in mind, Senator Douglas introduced a bill to organize the lands west of Iowa and Missouri. In its final form the bill provided for a Kansas Territory and a Nebraska Territory. But Southerners would never vote for a railroad through land that was forever closed to slavery. And Douglas could not pass his bill without southern votes.

In order to win southern support, Senator Douglas, the wizard of compromise, concocted two special provisions. The Missouri Compromise of 1820 would be repealed and replaced by the Compromise of 1850. The decision whether Kansas and Nebraska should be free or slave would be made by popular sovereignty—the vote of the people living there. Douglas knew, as he said, that there would be "a hell of a storm" over the repeal of the 34-year-old Missouri Compromise. But he had to have the southern votes and that was the only way. He believed also that he could survive the storm and finally pass his bill with the help of the pro-South Pierce administration. Then, he imagined, the whole problem would quickly go away.

Douglas, an experienced politico who knew the ins and outs of Congress, actually managed to get his controversial Kansas-Nebraska bill passed in 1854, after nine months of debate. This was a great

American Antiquarian Society

Stephen A. Douglas, the "Little Giant," is shown carrying off the White House.

victory for Douglas, but it was an even greater victory for the South. For the whole Kansas-Nebraska territory was north of the old freedom-line of the Missouri Compromise. "Popular sovereignty" now might open those lands to slavery.

Angry rallies were held across the North in protest over the Kansas-Nebraska Act. The question of slavery in the United States had now been transformed into a battle over whether slavery should be allowed to spread into the territories.

Expansion and slavery.

There was one odd but significant truth about the bitter congressional battle over the spread of slavery into the territories. It was a battle over slavery where it did not exist and might never go. This did not make the struggle any less heated. Yet it did conceal an important fact. Many Northerners, of course, were against the expansion of slavery because they hated the "peculiar institution." But many others opposed its spread into the territories not so much because they disliked slavery as because they did not want to live near or compete with blacks. Several midwestern states such as Illinois and Indiana had even put in their constitutions a ban against blacks moving into their states. These restrictions were seldom enforced. Many Northerners would have been willing to guarantee slavery where it already existed in order to be sure they would never run into blacks—slave or free—in the western territories.

Southerners failed to recognize the extent to which the opposition to the spread of slavery was actually opposition to blacks. They saw it as an attempt to bar them and their property (slaves) from the territories. To them it appeared to be just one more way the power of the North was being used to injure the South and prevent it from growing.

John Brown led the vengeful abolitionist attack party that massacred five men in the proslavery town of Pottawatomie Creek, Kansas, in 1856.

Boston Athenaeum

The new Republican party.

The Kansas-Nebraska bill was greeted by anger in the North. Public meetings were held in many states. At one such meeting at Ripon, Wisconsin, the members decided to organize a new party to resist the *extension* of slavery. To show their connection to Jefferson's Democratic-Republican party, they now chose the name "Republicans," which had been dropped by the Democrats.

On July 6, 1854, the party was launched at a meeting in Jackson, Michigan. Its platform (1) declared that slavery was "a great moral, social, and political evil," (2) demanded the repeal of the Kansas-Nebraska Act and the Fugitive Slave Act, and (3) resolved to sink all political differences and unite in the battle against the extension of slavery until the fight was won. During the summer and fall of 1854, conventions in Maine, Vermont, Massachusetts, Ohio, and New York organized units of this new Republican or "Anti-Nebraska" party.

The congressional elections in November 1854 produced a revolution in American politics. The old Whig party—which in recent years had been held together by nothing but the desire for office—was shattered. Its northern members deserted and moved into the ranks of other parties. The Democratic party staggered but did not collapse. Of the 42 northern Democrats who had voted for the Kansas-Nebraska Act, only 7 were reelected to Congress in 1854. The Democrats had held a substantial majority in the 1852 Congress, but in 1854 there were only 83 Democrats to face 108 of these new Republicans and 43 representatives of another new party—the Know-Nothings.

The Know-Nothing party.

Numerous parties quickly appeared and as quickly disappeared during the active year of 1854. Only two of these new parties proved significant—the Republicans and the Know-Nothing party. The Know-Nothings were a reaction to the ever-increasing flood of immigrants into the country. The party grew out of the Order of the Star-Spangled Banner. This was a secret association formed in 1849 to combat the political influence of "foreigners," especially Roman Catholics. Its real name was the American party, but everyone called it the Know-Nothing party because its members evasively replied, "I don't know," when asked about the party's activities. Ever since then, "Know-Nothing" has been a name for people who refuse to face the real issues of their day and instead seek refuge in hate and prejudice.

In the election of 1854 the Republicans and the Know-Nothings together won enough seats to control Congress. It was not always clear, in fact, who was a Republican and who a Know-Nothing, since the Know-Nothings were still partly secret. It appears that nearly a majority of the members of the House were *both* Republican and Know-Nothing.

Bleeding Kansas. When the Kansas-Nebraska bill became law, Douglas boasted that "the struggle over slavery was forever banished from the halls of Congress to the western plains." He was wrong about the halls of Congress but right about the western plains. For the Kansas-Nebraska Act would bring bloodshed to Kansas.

The major problem with the doctrine of "popular sovereignty" was that it did not say *when* a territory could decide about slavery. As a result, there was a race for Kansas from South and North. The first to gain control, the first to create a majority—of Northerners or Southerners—would decide the fate of slavery in the territory.

Antislavery New Englanders organized and raised money to rush Free-Soil emigrants to Kansas. On the suggestion of the eminent minister Henry Ward Beecher, Mrs. Stowe's brother, these emigrants were supplied with rifles—"Beecher's Bibles." Armed proslavery men from neighboring Missouri and elsewhere in the South also flocked to the territory. "Popular sovereignty," it seemed, would be decided not by votes but by guns.

Acts of violence were inevitable in Kansas, but only twice did the situation become critical. In May 1856 a proslavery sheriff led a mob into antislavery Lawrence, sacking and burning the town. In revenge the self-proclaimed antislavery messiah John Brown led a party including his four sons to a proslavery settlement on Pottawatomie Creek. They dragged five men from their beds in the dead of night and murdered them by splitting their skulls with broadswords. Somehow Kansas avoided becoming a territory of total anarchy and civil war. Still, bands of armed men were killing each other over slavery.

Charles Sumner is attacked. The mounting violence reached even into Congress. Charles Sumner of Massachusetts—intelligent, vain, outspoken, and tactless—delivered a speech in the Senate that he called "The Crime Against Kansas." He attacked the South and several of its senators with every insulting word he could command. Representative Preston S. Brooks of South Carolina was the nephew of a senator from that state who had been insulted. In the southern tradition he avenged the "honor" of his uncle and the South—not with words but with a

During the 1850s Kansas was known as "Bleeding Kansas." In this lithograph, the Battle of Hickory Point, a village about 25 miles north of Lawrence, is shown. A band of proslavery men, armed with a cannon, are attacking the settlement of Free-Soilers.

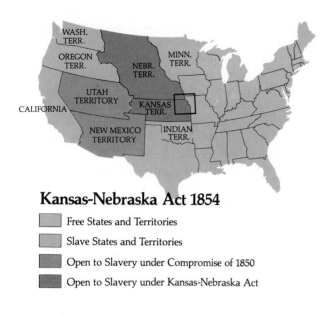

Kansas-Nebraska Act 1854

▢ Free States and Territories

▢ Slave States and Territories

▢ Open to Slavery under Compromise of 1850

▢ Open to Slavery under Kansas-Nebraska Act

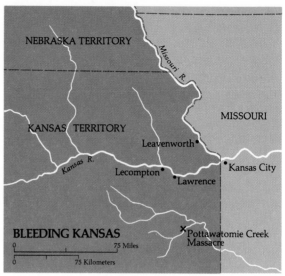

BLEEDING KANSAS

cane. On May 22, 1856, Brooks walked up to Senator Sumner, who was seated at his desk in the Senate Chamber, and beat him senseless. When Brooks was censured by the House, he resigned. He was then reelected by the people of his congressional district with only six dissenting votes. Brooks became a southern hero. Senator Sumner never completely regained his health and became a northern martyr. For several years before his return his empty seat in the Senate proclaimed that northern and southern leaders were no longer on speaking terms.

SECTION 2 REVIEW

1. Identify or explain: James Gadsden, Pierre Soulé, William L. Marcy, Ostend Manifesto, American party, "Beecher's Bibles," John Brown, Charles Sumner, Preston S. Brooks.

2. Locate: Lower California, Santo Domingo, Gila River, Kansas Territory, Nebraska Territory.

3. What moves did President Pierce and Secretary Marcy make to expand United States territory? How was the slavery issue involved?

4. What was the Kansas-Nebraska Act? Why did Douglas want it?

5. Name the events in May 1856 that further inflamed the slavery issue.

6. **Identifying Central Issues.** Why were the Republican and Know-Nothing parties formed? Were they successful? Explain.

3. The nation comes apart

The word of God could no longer hold Americans together. Even churches were dividing. In 1844 the Methodists had split into northern and southern wings, and the Baptists followed in 1845. One of the great national parties, the Whigs, had now nearly disappeared. In its place there stood a purely sectional party—the Republicans. They were looked upon with fear and loathing in the South.

The election of 1856. In the week following Brooks's attack on Sumner in the Senate, as violence convulsed Kansas, the Democratic national convention met at Cincinnati. The delegates were careful not to nominate any candidate who could be held responsible for what was happening in Kansas. They passed over both Pierce and Douglas. Instead, they chose James Buchanan, a dignified and conservative Pennsylvanian. He had had the good fortune to be out of the country during the past four years as the American minister in Great Britain. His "availability" consisted chiefly of two negative facts: He had no connection with Kansas and no abolitionist leanings that would offend the South.

The Republicans chose as their candidate John C. Frémont, the romantic "Pathfinder of the West" and "Conqueror of California." Their slogan was "Free speech, Free press, Free soil, Free men, Frémont." The Know-Nothing party split over the issue of slavery. Its southern wing nominated Millard Fillmore. But its northern wing, the

"North Americans," joined the Republican party in nominating John C. Frémont to keep from dividing the anti-Democratic vote.

The campaign then became not national but sectional. Buchanan ran against Fillmore in the South and against Frémont in the North. Buchanan's greatest strength was in the South where he carried every slave state except Maryland, which went for Fillmore. In the North and West he carried five free states to Frémont's eleven. Buchanan's electoral vote was 174 to 114 for Frémont.

Still the Republicans in this their first national campaign had made a remarkable fight and shown astonishing strength. They polled 1,339,932 votes to 1,832,955 for Buchanan. Fillmore had received 871,731. So Frémont could have been elected had he won some of the votes in the North that went to Fillmore. Frémont had received no electoral votes in the South, where the Republican party seemed the instrument of the devil. As one southern newspaper said, "If they should succeed in this contest . . . they would repeal the fugitive slave law . . . they could create insurrection and servile war in the South . . . they would put the torch to our dwellings and the knife to our throats." Some Southerners had counseled the South to secede from the Union if Frémont was elected.

Dred Scott v. Sanford, 1857. In his inaugural address President Buchanan expressed the ill-founded belief that the long agitation over slavery was now "approaching its end." And he expressed his hope that the Supreme Court would use its authority to settle the slavery issue for good. Two days later (March 6, 1857) the Supreme Court handed down one of the most momentous and most controversial decisions in its history. It dealt with the case of the slave Dred Scott. Some years before he had been taken by his master to Illinois, where the Northwest Ordinance of 1787 had forbidden slavery, and then to Minnesota, where slavery had been prohibited by the Missouri Compromise. Afterwards he had returned to Missouri. Now he sued for his freedom.

The case finally came up to the United States Supreme Court, which had to review the decision of the federal circuit court for Missouri. That court had declared that Scott remained a slave despite his travels and that, as he was not a citizen of Missouri, he did not even have the right to bring suit. To review this decision, the justices had to decide whether Scott was a citizen. That, of course, meant deciding whether he was free—which was what the case was all about. So the court decided to answer these two questions—was Scott a citizen and was he free?

The decision against Scott was 7 to 2. Its clarity was confused by the fact that each judge wrote his own opinion to support his vote. But the opinion of Roger B. Taney (pronounced Tawney) as the Chief Justice was the most important. Blacks, according to Taney, could not be citizens. The Constitution had been made by and for white men only. So Scott could not bring suit in court. And Scott was not free either. The Missouri Compromise (and by inference the Northwest Ordinance of 1787 and the Kansas-Nebraska Act as well) was unconstitutional. Why? (1) A slave was the property of his owner. (2) The Constitution nowhere gave Congress the right to deprive a citizen of the United States of his slaves in the territories, lands which were the common property of all the states.

What the Dred Scott decision meant was that Congress could do nothing about slavery in the territories. The people there had no power to restrict or abolish slavery until they applied for admission as a state.

Chief Justice Roger Taney created a storm of controversy with his decision in the Dred Scott case.

The South rejoiced that at last the highest court in the land had endorsed the proslavery doctrine of John C. Calhoun and Jefferson Davis. It now seemed that slavery would be able to spread into all the territories. The North was outraged. Some Northerners vowed to overturn the decision. Stephen A. Douglas and others who had hoped to bury the slavery issue through popular sovereignty were embarrassed. The Supreme Court, which was supposed to settle constitutional issues, had now deepened the nation's divisions and moved the nation's politics to the brink of war.

The Lecompton Constitution.

To make matters worse, the trouble in Kansas boiled up again. In November 1857 a convention met at the small town of Lecompton to draw up a constitution under which Kansas might come into the Union as a state. Most of the delegates favored slavery, since the Free-Soilers had refused to take part in the election of delegates. They had feared that proslavery men from Missouri would cross the border and vote illegally. The proslavery convention, realizing that the constitution they framed might be rejected in a popular vote, allowed a popular vote only on the question of whether the constitution would be adopted "with slavery" or "without slavery." If it was adopted with slavery, slaves might be brought into Kansas without limit. If without slavery, then no more slaves could be brought in. In either case the 200 slaves already in Kansas would remain slaves.

The Free-Soilers refused to go to the polls to vote on this tricky proposition. The result was that the Lecompton Constitution was adopted with slavery. It was clear, however, that the great majority of the people of Kansas did not want slavery. When a newly elected legislature submitted the Lecompton Constitution *as a whole* to the people, the Kansas voters (this time with the proslavery forces not voting) rejected it on January 4, 1858. The Free-Soil vote was much greater than the slavery vote had been.

Douglas breaks with Buchanan.

President Buchanan had pledged himself in his inaugural address "to secure to every resident inhabitant of Kansas the free and independent expression of his opinion" on the subject of slavery. But now, in spite of the fact that the voters had just rejected the Lecompton Constitution, he sent it to Congress. He asked that Kansas be admitted as a slave state. Despite the advice of the governor whom he had appointed for the Kansas Territory that the constitution was a "fraud," Buchanan called on party loyalists to support its adoption.

This was simply too much for Douglas, who had staked his political future on the doctrine of popular sovereignty. He immediately protested the Lecompton Constitution as a "travesty and mockery" of popular sovereignty. Douglas wanted a new constitution to be framed in Kansas and then submitted to an honest vote of the people there. The government had no right to force either slavery or freedom upon them. That was a question they should decide for themselves.

Buchanan used all the force of the Presidency to induce Congress to admit Kansas as a state with the Lecompton Constitution. He even withdrew all official patronage from Douglas. But the plucky Illinois senator fought back. He joined forces with the Free-Soil Republicans to defeat the admission of Kansas under the Lecompton Constitution. Kansas remained a territory until the withdrawal of the southern members of Congress on the eve of the Civil War. On January 29, 1861, Kansas was finally admitted as a free state.

Lincoln against Douglas.

Douglas's second term as senator was now about to expire. So he returned to Illinois in the summer of 1858 to seek reelection. His Republican rival was a self-educated lawyer from Springfield who had served four terms in the Illinois legislature, one term in the Congress, and had already been defeated once before in his try for the United States Senate. His name was Abraham Lincoln. A former Whig, Lincoln had joined the new Republican party on the Kansas-Nebraska issue and had risen to be their leading politician in Illinois. But he was still unknown to the nation. When Lincoln announced against the famous Douglas, who had caught the national spotlight during his fifteen continual years in the Congress, there was little doubt who would win. No one could predict that this campaign would set Lincoln on the path to his great career as hero and symbol of what was most American.

Douglas believed that the free and slave states could continue to live together in peace. He cared not at all whether slavery was "voted up or voted down." Lincoln was certain that slavery was a moral wrong. In his acceptance speech in June 1858, at the Illinois convention that nominated him as the Republican candidate for senator, Lincoln said:

"A house divided against itself cannot stand." I believe this government cannot endure permanently half slave and half free. I do not expect the Union to be dissolved—I do not expect the house to fall—but I do expect it will cease to be divided. It will become all one thing, or all the other.

The Lincoln-Douglas debates, 1858. On Lincoln's challenge, Douglas agreed to a series of debates. The difference between the candidates was striking. Douglas was scarcely five feet in height, thickset, quick, volcanic in speech and in gesture. Lincoln, six feet four, lank and awkward, was a superb stump speaker. Slow, hesitant, and thoughtful at first, he captured his audience and carried it with him to share his beliefs.

Douglas kept referring to Lincoln's "house divided" speech as an incitement to civil strife. He contrasted the fairness, the democracy, and the "Americanism" of his own policy of "popular sovereignty." Lincoln, on the other hand, insisted that the territories be kept free from slavery. He denounced the Dred Scott decision as a southern conspiracy. At the same time he made it clear that he did not want to interfere with slavery in those states where it was established.

The high point of the debates was reached at Freeport, Illinois, on August 27. There Lincoln asked Douglas whether the people of a territory could lawfully exclude slavery before they had become a state. Douglas was caught on the horns of a dilemma. If he answered "Yes," he would seem to defy the Dred Scott decision. If he answered "No," he would oppose his own doctrine of "popular sovereignty."

Douglas tried to find a way to support both. Even though the Supreme Court had decided that slavery was lawful in a territory, the institution "could not exist anywhere for a day or an hour," he said, without the support of "local police regulations."

This was Douglas's famous "Freeport Doctrine." It was his way of evading the central, moral

National Portrait Gallery, Smithsonian Institution

This miniature was painted of Abraham Lincoln in 1860. Lincoln said that the portrait was "an excellent one. To my unpracticed eye, it is without fault."

issue of slavery. By failing to pass laws for the protection of slavery, he said, the legislature of any territory could in fact exclude it. Lincoln challenged: "Then a thing may be legally driven away from a place where it has a legal right to be."

In those days senators were not elected by popular ballot. Douglas won by eight votes in the Illinois legislature. But his Freeport Doctrine had made him many enemies in the South. Southerners would oppose his nomination for President on the Democratic ticket. At the same time he had helped make a national reputation for Abraham Lincoln.

John Brown's raid, 1859. At this time a man made of the stuff of saints and martyrs produced a drama that underlined all the worst fears of the South. John Brown, who had led the Pottawatomie massacre in Kansas, now decided that he would invade the South, arm the slaves, and let them fight for their own freedom. The most famous of black abolitionists, the eloquent Frederick Douglass, gave Brown some advice but refused to join him. And when Brown talked to a colony of fugitive slaves in Chatham, Ontario, he could not persuade them to join him either.

But Brown pursued his wild plan. In October 1859 with his little band of 22 followers (17 white and 5 black) he seized the United States arsenal at Harpers Ferry, Virginia. Then, raiding the estates of a few nearby planters, the party forcibly "freed" about 30 slaves. Taking these reluctant people with them, Brown and his men retreated to the arsenal. Ironically, the first person to die in the affair—killed by John Brown and his men—was an already-free black gunned down by these "liberators."

The countryside immediately rose against the "invasion." Five of Brown's followers escaped, but the rest were trapped in the arsenal, surrounded as it was by rivers and mountains. A detachment of United States Marines commanded by Colonel Robert E. Lee arrived on the scene. After battering down the doors, they easily made captives of the seven surviving members of Brown's band. The remaining ten had been killed or mortally wounded in the raid. The survivors, including two blacks, were all hanged by the state of Virginia for their part in the raid.

Brown, who had been only slightly wounded, was promptly tried in a state court for treason to Virginia. That was his finest hour. After being sentenced to be hanged, he said, "Now if it is deemed necessary that I should forfeit my life for the furtherance of the ends of justice and mingle my blood . . . with the blood of millions in the slave country whose rights are disregarded by wicked, cruel, and unjust enactments, I say let it be done." One month later, John Brown was a corpse on the gallows. But his spirit marched on. Celebrated in song and legend, the impractical John Brown, who had not the force to hold a single arsenal, became a spirit leading thousands to risk their lives against slavery. Emerson compared him to Christ on the cross.

No other single event alarmed white Southerners more than Brown's deed. In their eyes his rash exploit at Harpers Ferry seemed part of a widespread abolitionist plot, supported by the "black" Republican party, to incite slave rebellion throughout the South.

SECTION 3 REVIEW

1. Identify or explain: Dred Scott, Roger B. Taney, Lecompton Constitution, Freeport Doctrine, Harpers Ferry.

2. How did the Dred Scott decision widen the split between North and South?

3. Why did Douglas break with Buchanan?

4. How did Lincoln and Douglas differ on the issue of the extension of slavery? How did his "Freeport Doctrine" hurt Douglas?

5. **Recognizing Cause and Effect.** What were the effects of John Brown's raid?

4. The election of 1860

As late as 1860, some people still thought the nation might avoid a civil war. Even if Americans could not agree on the issues, maybe they still could agree on a man. Perhaps the right American President—a man elected by all the people—could hold the Union together.

When the presidential election year of 1860 approached, the Democrats were still a national party. A tug-of-war was going on inside their party, but they still had support all over the country. If only the political battle could be fought out *inside* the party! Then perhaps there would be no more need for John Browns, no more Bleeding Kansas! Perhaps free debate—a battle of words—and friendly compromises at the party convention could settle matters. Perhaps the politicians from the North and South would stick together (as politicians often do) in order to be able eventually to share the rewards of a political victory. Could the good-natured game of politics take the place of the bloody game of war?

The Democrats divide. When the political parties met in their national conventions during the spring and summer of 1860, it quickly appeared that politics was not the road to reunion. By an evil fate the convention of the Democratic party was scheduled to meet at a traditional capital of the slave-holding South, Charleston, South Carolina. There the southern delegates demanded that the party declare its support for slavery in the territories. Douglas and other Northerners rejected this proposal. Bitter arguments followed. When Northerners finally refused to adopt the southern program, the delegates from eight southern states left the convention.

The great Democratic party was coming apart. The convention adjourned, and after a month it met again (without the delegates of the eight southern states). Then yet another group of Southerners withdrew. What was still left of the Democratic party, of course, was not a national party at all. As its candidate for President of the United States this northern remnant nominated Senator Stephen A. Douglas of Illinois.

The southern Democrats who had left the convention gathered at Richmond, Virginia. There they named their own candidate, John C. Breckinridge of Kentucky, who was then Vice-President of the United States. He believed in protecting slavery, and he thought states had a right to secede. The damage was done! Even the "national" political parties were no longer national.

Constitutional-Unionists and Republicans.

The Constitutional-Union party also appeared. It was made up chiefly of former Whigs and Know-Nothings, conservatives who feared the breakup of the Union if the Republican candidate was elected. This party sought to avoid the slavery issue entirely and ran on a single-plank platform for "the Constitution of the country, the Union of the states, and the enforcement of the laws." John Bell of Tennessee and Edward Everett of Massachusetts carried its standard.

The main opposition to the Democrats, however, was the six-year-old Republican party. The antislavery party of the West and the North, it had been founded for the very purpose of opposing the spread of slavery. Still vainly hoping for some national appeal, the Republicans named one of the most conservative men they could find in their party. He had not made any radical statements, and he sounded like the soul of easygoing common sense. Abraham Lincoln, nicknamed "The Rail-Splitter," came from Illinois.

"Honest Abe."

At the moment when the nation was coming apart, it was a stroke of rare good luck that Lincoln happened to be here. For there never was a better symbol of all America. Lincoln's own life was a capsule history of the whole nation. His restless family had come from England to New England and then to Pennsylvania. Lincoln's great-grandfather had lived in Virginia, where he had five sons. Four of them moved west. In 1786 Lincoln's grandfather, who had gone to Kentucky, was killed by Indians while clearing his farmland in the forest. There in Kentucky Abraham's father was raised, and there the future President was born in 1809.

Unlike other "log-cabin" candidates before him, Lincoln really was born in a log cabin. When he was only seven, his family moved again—on to Indiana. And when he was twenty-one, he moved with them once more, still farther west to Illinois. Working his way up in the world, he did a little of everything. He built a flatboat and navigated it down the Mississippi to New Orleans. For a while he worked as a surveyor, managed a mill, ran a country store, and served as a village postmaster. He was elected captain of the militia that chased Chief Black Hawk and his Indians back into the Wisconsin wilderness.

This oil painting showing a beardless Lincoln splitting rails was done about 1858.

Lincoln educated himself, and made himself into a lawyer. He was especially successful before juries. His political career had been brief and not impressive. After serving in the Illinois legislature, he had one term in Congress (1847–1849), where he opposed the Mexican War. Then in 1858 he was defeated for the United States Senate by the much better known Stephen A. Douglas.

Lincoln had magic in his speech. With his slow backwoods drawl, using the simple words of the Bible, he uttered the wisdom of a cracker-barrel philosopher. He sometimes told slightly vulgar jokes, and yet he had the uplift power of a first-class preacher. He spoke the way the average man could imagine himself speaking.

On the slavery issue Lincoln was firm, but he was no fire-eater. He was no abolitionist. In his debates against Douglas in 1858 he showed that he was about as conservative as an antislavery man could be. He tried to narrow down the whole slavery question into how to prevent slavery from spreading westward into the territories.

Himself of southern ancestry, and married to a Southerner, he did not hate the South. He believed in making every possible concession—short of allowing the spread of slavery. If anyone could have held the Union together, it would have been Lincoln. If an Abraham Lincoln—with Lincoln's shrewdness, with his charity, with his generous understanding of the South and its problems, with his feeling for compromise—could not do it, the Union was surely beyond the help of politics.

Lincoln is elected. The fateful presidential election of November 1860 confirmed fears that there were no longer any *national* parties. It convinced the South that their hope was not in words but in weapons. From ten southern states, Lincoln received not a single electoral vote. In the electoral college, Lincoln carried all eighteen free states, and Breckinridge carried eleven slave states. Douglas received many popular votes in the North, but carried only Missouri and a minority of New Jersey's split electoral vote. John Bell, the Constitutional-Union candidate from Tennessee, carried three border slave states.

Although Lincoln easily won in the electoral college (with 180 votes to 123 for all the others), he received only 39 percent of the popular vote. This was the smallest proportion ever for a successful candidate and far less even than many unsuccessful candidates had won. His opponents all together had received nearly a million votes more than Lincoln. But strangely, Lincoln would have won even if the votes for the other candidates had been combined, for he received his votes in just the right states.

When word of Lincoln's election reached South Carolina, that state seceded from the Union. It was quickly joined by five other states from the lower South: Mississippi, Florida, Alabama, Georgia, and Louisiana. Then their delegates met in Montgomery, Alabama, in February 1861, even before Lincoln was inaugurated. Soon they were joined by Texas. They wrote a new constitution and announced that a new nation, the Confederate States of America, was born.

Attempts to prevent war. Meanwhile confusion reigned in Washington. President Buchanan did not know what to do. He hoped that his term might come to an end before the storm broke. He believed secession was illegal. But he also thought the government had no right to compel a state to remain in the Union. Northern abolitionists such as William Lloyd Garrison were glad to see the "sinful" South separate itself from the Union. Pacifists like Horace Greeley, editor of the influential *New York Tribune,* would let the cotton states "go in peace" rather than engage in a war to "pin" them to the rest of the states "by bayonets."

In Congress even after the election, during December of 1860, desperate last-minute attempts were made to work out another compromise between the sections. Senator John J. Crittenden of Kentucky proposed a set of "unamendable amendments" to the Constitution. The most important of these would extend the Missouri Compromise line of 36°30′ to California as the dividing line between slavery and free soil. It would forbid the federal government ever to interfere with slavery in the states.

But the Republicans, on orders from President-elect Lincoln, held firmly to their refusal to allow slavery to go into any territories, even below 36°30′. Lincoln was convinced this would only lead to attempts to seize more territory south of the line in order to make more slave states. So the compromise—a compromise the South probably would have accepted—was defeated by the votes of

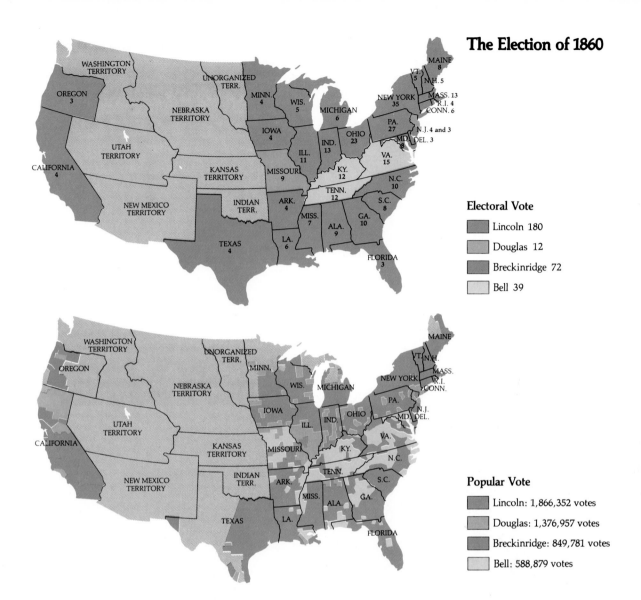

Electoral Vote

- Lincoln 180
- Douglas 12
- Breckinridge 72
- Bell 39

Popular Vote

- Lincoln: 1,866,352 votes
- Douglas: 1,376,957 votes
- Breckinridge: 849,781 votes
- Bell: 588,879 votes

the Republicans. They had heard the threats of the southern hotheads for so many years. They believed a confession of northern weakness would simply encourage the Southerners to make even bolder demands. The North must stand firm. If it did, they believed, many southern Unionists would flock to the Union banner and form common cause against the secessionists.

Lincoln faces a crisis. The Confederate States of America viewed the United States as a foreign nation. The seceded states therefore could no longer allow the United States to keep its arsenals and forts inside their borders. Using their own state troops, they at once began seizing federal posts. To avoid bloodshed, United States troops gave up all but a few strong positions. One of the strongest was a place right in Charleston Harbor called Fort Sumter.

As soon as Lincoln was inaugurated, on March 4, 1861, he had to make one of the great decisions in American history. He discovered that if Fort Sumter did not receive food soon, it would have to surrender. What should he do? Should he let the South have Fort Sumter and go its own way? That would mean no civil war. But it would also mean the end of the Union. Or should he send the needed supplies and risk a fight that might go on for years to keep all the states inside one great nation?

Lincoln decided to stand firm for the Union. He would not give up Fort Sumter. He would fight if necessary. But he would let the South fire the first shot. He notified South Carolina that he was sending supplies to Fort Sumter. South Carolina then decided to take the fort. At 4:20 A.M. on April 12, 1861, Confederate General P. G. T. Beauregard, a West Point graduate who had once fought for the Union in the Mexican War, began bombarding Fort Sumter from the Charleston shore batteries. At 2:30 the next afternoon Major Robert Anderson, also a West Point graduate who had fought alongside Beauregard in the Mexican War, surrendered the fort. No one had been wounded, but war had begun. The first, the quickest, and the most bloodless battle of the war was over. It was not a fair sample of what was to come.

SECTION 4 REVIEW

1. Identify: John C. Breckinridge, John Bell, Black Hawk, John J. Crittenden, Fort Sumter.

2. How did Lincoln manage to win in 1860 with only 39 percent of the popular vote?

3. Describe the founding of the Confederacy.

4. What attempts were made to prevent war?

5. How did Lincoln deal with Fort Sumter?

6. **Recognizing Ideologies.** How did Lincoln and his family typify the nation's history?

A Currier and Ives lithograph showed the shelling of Fort Sumter in 1861. Nathaniel Currier and James M. Ives became partners in 1857. Their lithographs were popular when photographs were rare and in black and white.

CHAPTER 12 REVIEW

FOCUSING ON IDEAS

1. Why did some Northerners who were not opposed to slavery in the South want to keep it out of northern states and territories?

2. Show the influence of the slavery issue on presidential elections from 1848 to 1860. Consider the choice of candidates, party platforms and slogans, and the rise of splinter parties.

3. How did each of the following further enflame the slavery issue: Mexican Cession, Wilmot Proviso, Ostend Manifest, raids in Kansas, attack on Charles Sumner, Dred Scott decision, Lecompton Constitution, and John Brown's raid on Harpers Ferry?

TAKING A CRITICAL LOOK

1. **Expressing Problems Clearly.** Some optimists saw the Compromise of 1850 as a "final solution" to the slavery issue. Name at least two features of the Compromise that would prevent it from being a solution.

2. **Determining Relevance.** How did the growth of political parties between the 1820s and 1860s reflect divisiveness of the country?

YOUR REGION IN HISTORY

1. **Geography.** What route would a person from your locality probably have traveled in order to reach California in 1849 to prospect for gold or other minerals?

2. **Culture.** What was the reaction to *Uncle Tom's Cabin* in your region? Consult local newspapers from the era for this information. Why do you think people responded as they did?

3. **Economics.** What were the principal businesses and/or industries in your region in the mid-nineteenth century. How might the abolition of slavery have affected the operation of those enterprises?

HISTORICAL FACTS AND FIGURES

Comparing Graphs. Use the information in the graphs below to derive answers to the following questions: (a) By what percentage did cotton production increase between 1800 and 1860? (b) By what percentage did the slave population increase during the same period? (c) Was the increase in cotton production a direct result of the increase in the slave population? Explain.

Cotton Production, 1800-1860	
1800	〖
1810	〖
1820	〖〖
1830	〖〖〖
1840	〖〖〖〖〖
1850	〖〖〖〖〖〖〖〖
1860	〖〖〖〖〖〖〖〖〖〖〖〖〖〖〖〖〖〖

〖 = 200,000 Bales of Cotton

Slave Population, 1800-1860	
1800	👤👤👤👤👤
1810	👤👤👤👤👤👤
1820	👤👤👤👤👤👤👤
1830	👤👤👤👤👤👤👤👤👤
1840	👤👤👤👤👤👤👤👤👤👤👤👤
1850	👤👤👤👤👤👤👤👤👤👤👤👤👤👤👤
1860	👤👤👤👤👤👤👤👤👤👤👤👤👤👤👤👤👤👤👤👤

👤 = 200,000 Slaves

MAKING CONNECTIONS

UNIT 4

THEMES

This unit began on page 207 with Alexis de Tocqueville's observation that two distinct trends, nationalism and sectionalism, were developing in the United States:

> "An attentive examination of what is going on in the United States will easily convince us that two opposite tendencies exist in that country, like two distinct currents flowing in contrary directions in the same channel."

This conclusion was supported by the two unit themes that are reprinted in **dark type** below. Use the time line and the information in Unit 4 to answer the questions that follow the unit themes.

1. **The development of new transportation and communication systems draws Americans closer together.**

   How did new forms of communication reveal the uniqueness and accent the differences between the regions of the United States?

2. **The growth of reform movements and a surge of western expansion forces the nation to face the slavery issue.**

   How did the American political tradition of compromise prolong slavery?

Events in American History

1813 The first full-fledged textile mill is opened in Waltham, Massachusetts.

1817 Construction begins on the Erie Canal, which will connect the Great Lakes and the Hudson River.

1803 Congress sets aside funds for building a road linking East and West.

1820 Congress passes the Missouri Compromise, declaring some states free from and others open to slavery.

Events in World History

1800   1810   1820   1830

1816 The Rhine River floods, destroying farmland in Germany and France.

135,000 SETS, 270,000 VOLUMES SOLD.

UNCLE TOM'S CABIN

FOR SALE HERE.

AN EDITION FOR THE MILLION, COMPLETE IN 1 Vol., PRICE 37 1-2 CENTS.
" " IN GERMAN, IN 1 Vol. 50 CENTS.
" " IN 2 Vols., CLOTH, 6 PLATES, PRICE $1.50.
SUPERB ILLUSTRATED EDITION, IN 1 Vol., WITH 153 ENGRAVINGS,
PRICES FROM $2.50 TO $5.00.

The Greatest Book of the Age.

1834 Cyrus McCormick receives a patent for his reaper, a labor-saving farm implement.

1838 Congress adopts the "gag rule," refusing to discuss abolition of slavery.

1852 Harriet Beecher Stowe's *Uncle Tom's Cabin* is published.

1844 Samuel Morse sends first message over telegraph lines from Washington, D.C., to Baltimore.

1860 There are 30,626 miles of railroad track crisscrossing the United States.

1830

1840

1850

1860

1870

1845 Ireland's potato crop is hit by blight, leaving thousands of Irish hungry.

1840 A total of 75,810 people have emigrated from England to the United States since 1830.

1833 Slavery is abolished in Great Britain, fueling the American abolitionist movement.

UNIT 5

The rocky road to Union
1860–1890

The Civil War began over the simple question of whether this was one nation, or whether any state or group of states could leave the Union and create a new nation. But soon, the North and the South were fighting over whether the institution of slavery should be allowed to exist. The North's triumph on the battlefield gave a decisive answer to both questions.

What was not decided with guns, however, was how the Southern states were to be treated after the war and the status of the newly freed blacks. In his second inaugural address, Abraham Lincoln expressed his hope that these problems could be solved "with malice toward none" and "with charity for all." But this was not to be.

To some Americans, the Civil War and Reconstruction were only far-off conflicts. During these years Northerners and Southerners alike were moving into the great American West. Pursuing the American dream, they hoped to conquer the wild West and open a new land of opportunity.

THEMES IN AMERICAN HISTORY

- The Civil War becomes a fight over the legitimacy of the institution of slavery.

- Lincoln's assassination dashes whatever chance the nation has of solving post–Civil War problems "with charity for all."

THEMES
- Increasing numbers of Americans seek new opportunities in the American West during and after the Civil War.

Winslow Homer's "A Rainy Day in Camp" shows Yankee soldiers cooking over a campfire while their horses are tethered nearby (detail).

Metropolitan Museum of Art, Gift of Mrs. William F. Milton (23.77.1)

CHAPTER **13**

The Civil War

The American Civil War was not quite like any war that had ever happened before. Half a nation fought against the other half over the freedom of a small minority. This itself was something new. It was as new, as strenuous, and as unpredictable as everything else in America. Leaving more than 600,000 dead, the Civil War would be the bloodiest in all American history—and the bloodiest war in the whole western world during the nineteenth century. Of every ten men who fought, four became casualties (killed or wounded). No other modern nation paid so high a price to hold itself together.

Southerners did not see themselves simply as slave owners fighting to preserve their property, or as rebels trying to tear the Union apart. Instead they imagined they were fighting the American Revolution all over again. White Southerners, they said, were oppressed by Yankee tyrants. The people of the South were now playing the role of the gallant American colonists. Northerners were the oppressive British, and Abraham Lincoln was another George III. If the British had no right to force American colonists to stay inside their empire, why did the United States government have any right to force Southern states to stay inside the Union?

Abraham Lincoln, in his first inaugural address, had tried to persuade Southerners that they had nothing to fear from his administration. But he told them there was no right under the Constitution for a state to leave the Union. And he declared, "In *your* hands, my dissatisfied fellow countrymen, and not in *mine,* is the momentous issue of civil war."

Southerners said they were fighting for self-government. One flaw in this argument was that it left out the whole question of slavery. Self-government—for *whom* and by *whom*? White Southerners who said they were fighting for their own right to govern themselves were also fighting *against* the right of millions of blacks to have any control over their own lives. Of course, Calhoun and other defenders of slavery had not seen it quite that way. Self-government, they said, was for white people only.

1. A new kind of war

Shocked by the fall of Fort Sumter, Northerners sprang into action. President Lincoln at once called for 75,000 militia to help put down what he termed an insurrection. With Lincoln's call for troops the states of the upper South seceded. They had hesitated to leave the Union, but they felt they could not fight against the other Southern states. The North and the South now hastened to prepare for war.

The sides compared. The two sides were vastly different from each other. If we ignore Maryland, Kentucky, and Missouri, which were still in doubt, the Union (the Northern states) had 20 million people. The Confederacy had 9 million, which included 3.6 million slaves. In other resources the North was way ahead, too. It had 22,000 miles of railroad tracks to the South's 9000. It had far more factories and factory workers, more money, more bank credit, more ships, more locomotives, more steel and iron, more farm machinery, more firearms. The North grew many kinds of crops, while the South was glutted with a few staples—tobacco, cotton, and rice—which it had to export in order to obtain all the things it lacked.

The North also had lots of labor-saving devices like the reaper to free men for the army, while the South depended for labor on its slaves. These slaves might at any moment turn out to be a "fifth column"—an enemy force behind the lines—because they had very good reasons for helping the North. Every third Southerner was black. White Southerners therefore lived in fear of a civil war all their own—if the blacks ever decided to take up arms.

Because Southerners did not see slaves as people, they also failed to use them well in the war. Even if it seemed too dangerous to give slaves arms, they might have helped in the army as a labor force and so have released whites to fight. The North, on the other hand, decided in December 1862 to use blacks in its armed forces. It was strengthened by more than 185,000 who fought on its side.

Worst of all for the South, it suffered from delusions which prevented it from seeing the facts. Southerners believed that the North was so divided that it would not be able to put up a strong fight. In fact, Southerners were astonished that any power on earth dared make war on the world's greatest producer of cotton. They had long told themselves "Cotton is King," and they believed Great Britain and France would break the Northern blockade and come to the South's aid just to get the cotton needed to keep their textile factories going. The South imagined too that only Southerners were civilized and that one Southerner "could whip a half-dozen Yankees and not half try." The South's grandiose dreams turned into nightmares.

In the end the substantial advantages of the North would produce victory. The South, unable to replace its losses of equipment, would finally die of economic strangulation. But it was a very near thing. The South came close to victory too many times for anyone to say that the leaders of the Confederacy should have foreseen the result.

The "short war." When Southerners said that they merely wanted to secede from the Union, they also gave themselves a military advantage. To win their point all they had to do was to declare their independence and go their own way. On the other hand, the North would have to *force* the Southern states to stay in the Union. The North would have to invade the South, occupy it, and subjugate it. The North had to attack.

At the beginning, many Northerners optimistically called it "the six months' war." They expected it to be over in short order. For the North seemed stronger in every way. Also the military men had been taught that the attacking army always had a great advantage. The textbooks used at West Point explained that the way to succeed was to mass your forces, invade the enemy's land, and win the war by a decisive battle or the decisive capture of the enemy's capital.

The rifle. The old-fashioned weapons had given almost no advantage to the defenders. For the old smoothbore flintlock musket (which was standard equipment in the British army during the Revolution and in European armies even later) was inaccurate. It had a short range, and it was slow to reload. That meant that the attacking forces could come very close before the defenders could shoot them down, and most of them would get through before they could be hit. If, as the Union generals at first imagined, the North could only keep the advantage of the attack, they could win a few decisive battles, capture the enemy capital at Richmond, Virginia, and then the war would be over.

These generals were wrong, though some never realized it. The war lasted four blood-soaked years. This new warfare would be as different from earlier American wars as an elephant is different from a mosquito.

A number of great changes made the difference. While the standard British weapon in the American Revolution was the flintlock musket, many American backwoodsmen had begun using the rifle. But it was not until the Civil War that the rifle became the standard American army weapon. All the textbooks that the Civil War generals had read at West Point came from the earlier age of the smoothbore flintlock.

The rifle was so called because the inside of its barrel was "rifled"—cut with spiral grooves. Then when the bullet was pushed out, it was set spinning. This gave it a longer range (500 yards instead of 50 yards) and a much more accurate aim. Another improvement was the "caplock," which used a new chemical (fulminate of mercury) enclosed in a cap to make the explosion that sent the bullet. The caplock was reliable even when the old flintlock—which struck a piece of flint against steel to make a spark—would not have worked because of wet weather. Also the old muskets had been "muzzle loaders," but some of the new rifles were "breech-loaders." This meant they loaded more quickly from the back near the trigger.

Virginia State Travel Service

The accurate long-range rifle made defensive positions all-important. Confederate troops defended this wall near Fredericksburg in some of the bloodiest fighting of the war in 1862. The elaborate fortifications below were erected near Atlanta in 1864.

Soldiers learn to dig in. Now, with their accurate long-range rifles, the defenders sat protected behind battlements in well-supplied positions. They could pick off the attackers before they even came close. They could fire again and again because of the range of their weapons. The attacking force then had to keep moving. If they stopped to reload, they were sitting ducks.

Library of Congress

In time the generals would learn that armies could no longer confront each other in solid ranks. Everyone had to take cover. Attackers had to spread out into small parties of skirmishers to make more dispersed targets. Now the "Indian" tactics, which Americans had used with success in the Revolution, would become common. Attacking soldiers had to make instant forts—of logs, bales of hay, rocks, anything in sight—so that they could get some of the advantages of defenders.

Most important, soldiers learned to make the earth itself into a fort by using the spade. This was the start of trench warfare. In the old days, generals thought it made soldiers cowardly to hide in a hole in the ground. Now the soldiers had no choice. When General Robert E. Lee ordered his men in the Army of Northern Virginia to work hard at digging trenches, at first they laughed at him as the "King of Spades." But they soon thanked him for giving them protection against enemy rifles. The spade was now as important as the gun.

The importance of railroads. The attacking army had to carry enormous supplies of ammunition, food, and bandages. It had to build its own fortifications as it advanced. The railroad, which had never been used much in wars before, was now a great help. But once the supplies left the rails, they still had to be carried by horse or mule over bumpy roads, through mud, and across streams.

In this kind of warfare, railroads were lifelines. They were slow and hard to build, but quick and easy to cut. If you could cut the rails, the enemy would eventually have to stop fighting. The Civil War therefore became more and more a war aimed at the enemy's communication lines. The first Battle of Bull Run (July 1861) was still very much like the old-fashioned warfare, with solid lines of soldiers standing up against each other to fight a "decisive" battle. By the time of the Battle of Petersburg three years later, the Union army was aiming at the Confederate railroads.

The war of exhaustion. This new kind of warfare was a war of exhaustion. It was not enough to cut off the enemy's supplies by railroad. You also had to stop supplies from coming in by water. The ocean and the Gulf of Mexico surrounded the Southern states. They had few deep-water ports, but there were many places on the 3500-mile coast where supplies could be landed. The South still had many highways to the world. The North therefore had to capture or blockade the Southern ports and coast if the South was to be strangled.

The South did wonders with small fast ships which constantly pierced the blockade at many points. Still the scores of Union ships offshore made it difficult for the South to export cotton and kept large merchant ships or Confederate naval vessels from reaching Southern ports.

The war of exhaustion hit everybody in the South, civilians as well as the military. The same ships that would have brought arms and ammunition to the armies also would have brought locomotives for the railroads, machinery for the factories, food and clothing and medical supplies for all. The Northern blockade against the South worked slowly but it worked surely. People called it the "Conda" after the anaconda, a huge snake that kills its prey by squeezing.

The war of exhaustion was slow. It was not won by a few knockout blows like the Battle of Waterloo, where Napoleon was defeated, but by slowly taking away everything the South needed. In this war all the enemy's resources had to be destroyed until the will to resist was gone. European experts, who had never seen this kind of war before, began to think it was not a war at all. One Prussian general in 1864 sneered that he would not even study the battles of the war because they were nothing but "the combats of two armed mobs." Another Old World critic compared the North and South to two lunatics playing chess—both knew a few moves, yet neither understood the game.

But this kind of war was no longer a game. The old rules of war which the generals had learned at West Point were not of much use. This was all-out war, with no holds barred. The winning generals turned out to be those, like U. S. Grant, who had never believed the old rules, or those, like William T. Sherman, who were good at forgetting them.

Everybody's war. The Civil War was everybody's war. In both the North and the South nearly every family lost a soldier. And in quite new ways the gore was brought into every home. For the first time in history, the battles were thoroughly covered by newspaper correspondents. They telegraphed back eyewitness accounts so that civilians could read the horrors next morning at breakfast.

The Union man-o-war (left) is shown overtaking a Confederate blockade runner in this oil painting. Rather than surrender, blockade runners sometimes ran their ships aground in the hope that part of the cargo might be carried ashore.

The *New York Herald* alone once had forty men in the field, and spent a half-million dollars on them. Northern reporters, who would have been shot as spies if discovered, smuggled themselves behind Southern lines disguised as women or as Confederate soldiers. When some generals objected that the newspapers were giving away valuable information to the enemy, the *New York World* protested that this was a "people's war."

The pioneer photographer Mathew Brady and his large crew took photographs at the risk of their lives and sent them back home to show everyone the battle action. Soldiers sometimes ran away from Brady's camera because they had never seen a camera before and imagined it to be a new kind of gun. Brady's photographic buggy, which soldiers called the "What-is-it?", was a conspicuous target. On several occasions, Brady barely escaped being killed.

Women at war. In the "people's war" women played a new and important part. Dorothea Dix, the courageous New Englander who had braved public opinion before (p. 237), arrived in Washington right behind the first troops. On June 10, 1861, she was appointed the first Superintendent of Women Nurses with the job of selecting and assigning women to hospitals. It took gumption to find any place for women in the army, and she was the pioneer.

Louisa May Alcott, later to make her name as the author of *Little Women*, came to Washington and worked in a hospital for Miss Dix until illness forced her to leave. She was appalled when the first group of dirty, injured soldiers appeared. But, she wrote, "I drowned my scruples in my washbowl, clutched my soap manfully, and, assuming a business-like air, made a dab at the first dirty specimen I saw." Luckily, he was a cheery Irishman, and with a good deal of laughter the job was done. Louisa May Alcott went more confidently on to her next patient.

Clara Barton, one of the first female clerks in Washington, left her job to help the injured troops. So began a career of caring for the sick and the wounded that lasted throughout the war. Clara Barton was never an official in the war effort. As a volunteer this brave woman brought food, bandages, and supplies to the wounded out on the battlefield. Then, for four years after the war, she was in charge of the search for missing Union soldiers. She identified thousands of graves at the Confederate prisoner-of-war camp at Andersonville, Georgia. In 1877 Clara Barton founded and became president of the American Red Cross. It would serve the nation and the world in later wars.

Women helped set up the voluntary United States Sanitary Commission. It assisted the military by creating hospitals, caring for the injured, promoting sanitation in military camps, and distributing all kinds of supplies "from currant wine to canton flannel underwear" to the troops. Supplies and money for this ambitious program were raised by women's groups throughout the Union.

Female clerks were rare in 1860, but that too changed with wartime. Soon there were large numbers of women in the Treasury Department, while others worked at the government printing plants or made cartridges in the arsenal and the navy yard. Women were usually paid less for this work than men, and several times groups of women went on strike for higher pay.

In the South, as well, women did many jobs in the government. They too made cartridges in munitions factories. They nursed the wounded in hospitals, and sewed soldiers' clothes or rolled bandages at home. "Ladies who never worked before," one Southern woman observed, "are hard at work making uniforms and tents."

In North and South, as the men went off to war, women had to take over businesses, farms, and plantations. Some women were so anxious to do their part in the war that several hundred of them pretended to be men and served in the ranks as soldiers wearing men's uniforms until they were discovered.

The border states. Like the generals, the political leaders of the opposing sides had to be able to forget

The Civil War pitted friend against friend and neighbor against neighbor. In this photograph, Union Lieutenant George A. Custer is shown with his friend, West Point classmate, and prisoner, Confederate Major James Washington.

peacetime rules. And here Lincoln was wiser than the Confederate president, Jefferson Davis. When the war began, Lincoln was not even sure who was on his side or whether Washington could be held. The city was surrounded on three sides by Maryland, a slave state. If Maryland seceded, Washington would be lost. When the first Union troops, the 6th Massachusetts militia regiment, passed through on their way to protect the capital, they were mobbed. Four soldiers were killed.

Lincoln now showed his instinctive grasp of the deeper meaning of the conflict for this nation. He felt that the Constitution could not contain the seeds of its own destruction. If he had to bend the Constitution in order to save the Constitution and the Union, he would do so. If he hesitated or retreated from the harsh words of Southern sympathizers in the North, the Union might be lost before a battle was fought.

So Lincoln moved swiftly. He imposed martial law in Maryland, suppressed newspapers, arrested civilians, and even refused to let them appear before

Women played an important role in nursing the wounded on both sides. Clara Barton (top) helped the injured on the battlefield and later founded the American Red Cross. Harriet Douglas Wheaton (bottom left) served on hospital ships sailing from New York and Philadelphia. Sallie Tompkins (right) received a commission as a captain in the Confederate army for her work.

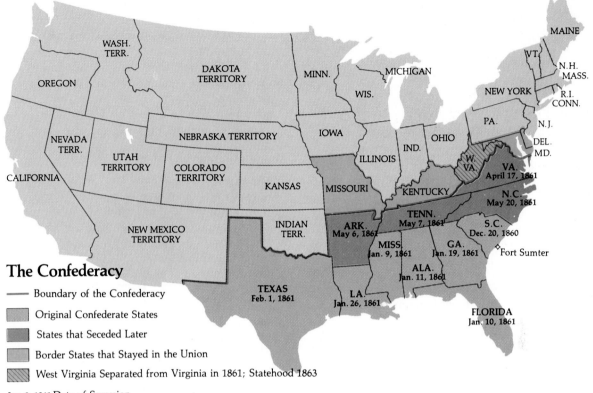

The Confederacy

— Boundary of the Confederacy

Original Confederate States

States that Seceded Later

Border States that Stayed in the Union

West Virginia Separated from Virginia in 1861; Statehood 1863

Jan. 9, 1861 Date of Secession

civilian judges to hear why they were being held. This is called suspending the *writ of habeas corpus.* This writ, or court order, gives a judge the power to free a person who is being held illegally or without just cause. It serves to keep people from being held in jail without a fair trial. When Chief Justice Taney issued a writ of habeas corpus for a secessionist named Merryman, the military commander of the area refused to free the man. Taney then issued an opinion that the President had no right to suspend the writ of habeas corpus, only Congress could do that. Lincoln believed that he must act to save the Union—even if he had to break the law to do so. So he ignored Taney's decision.

It was by actions such as these that Maryland was held in the Union and Washington was saved. Union sentiment within the state had time to grow. By June 1861, Maryland was filling its quota of enlistments in the United States Army.

Missouri and Kentucky were crucial too. If they seceded, the Confederate border would be pushed to the Ohio River, and then even southern Illinois might be lost. Lincoln handled each state dif-

ferently. In Missouri, he moved swiftly to seize control. In Kentucky, he moved slowly in order to allow Union sentiment to develop. The result was the same in both states—they were saved for the Union.

The question of emancipation. Lincoln was a strong leader. As a politician, he knew how important it was, in everybody's war, to keep everybody's support. At the beginning of the war, in order to keep in the Union the border slave states—Delaware, Maryland, Kentucky, and Missouri—he refused to emancipate the slaves. When General Frémont, commander of the Western Department, on August 30, 1861, freed the slaves of rebels in Missouri, Lincoln stepped in firmly and overruled him.

Lincoln's priorities were always clear. Much as he might have liked to free the slaves, his first job was to save the Union. When told that freeing the slaves would put God on the Union side, Lincoln replied, "We would like to have God on our side, but we must have Kentucky."

1. Identify or explain: "war of exhaustion," Mathew Brady, Dorothea Dix, Louisa May Alcott, Clara Barton, Sanitary Commission, writ of habeas corpus, border states, emancipation.

2. How did the rifle give defenders an advantage? How did it make the spade a tool of war?

3. What was the Union strategy with regard to Confederate railroads and seaports?

4. Describe the role of women in the war.

5. **Demonstrating Reasoned Judgment.** Why did Civil War soldiers view the war between the North and South as a new kind of conflict?

2. The first year: 1861–1862

The Civil War was fought mainly in three areas: (1) between Richmond and Washington, (2) in the valley of the Ohio, Cumberland, and Tennessee rivers, and (3) in the Mississippi River valley. The eyes of much of the world were on the classic battle in the East where two great armies maneuvered and fought in the small area between the Potomac and the James rivers and from the Atlantic to the Blue Ridge Mountains. Here the able Southern generals Robert E. Lee and "Stonewall" Jackson, though always outnumbered, faced and usually defeated the poorly led Northern Army of the Potomac in a series of titanic battles. The decisive war, however, took place beyond the Appalachians in the West.

The first Battle of Bull Run (Manassas). Northerners thought the war would be short and easy. They urged General Irvin McDowell to move with the main army of 30,000 men against the rebels, to seize Richmond, and so (they hoped) to end the war quickly. Since McDowell's volunteer troops and militia were not yet properly organized or drilled, and their three months' term of enlistment was about to expire, they had to be strengthened by some units of the regular army. But the Confederates were also untrained. So McDowell, thinking his forces stronger, asked to be allowed to attack.

General Winfield Scott, commander of the United States Army, protested. He outlined to the Cabinet another more long-term plan. He doubted that this war could be won in the lightning stroke of a single battle. Scott offered a plan to blockade the South, to seize New Orleans and the Mississippi River, and so "envelop the insurgent states." In this way, Scott thought, the South could be brought to terms with little bloodshed. He was wrong on the last point, and the strategy would take much longer than he expected. But at age 75, and having served in the army since Jefferson's time, "Old Fuss and Feathers" knew the realities of war. It was his plan, later called the "anaconda," reinforced by some bloody and brutal years of fighting, that would finally bring victory to the North.

The North was not yet ready to face the realities of the military situation. So Scott withdrew his opposition to McDowell's plan for a quick knockout blow to the Southern capital. Lincoln and the Cabinet then agreed to allow McDowell to move forward—"On to Richmond!"

McDowell's "grand army" met General Joseph E. Johnston's force of 22,000 on July 21, 1861, at Manassas Junction, a little town near Bull Run, a creek 35 miles from Washington. The untrained federal troops had the more difficult job of attacking, but they did well until mid-afternoon. Then fresh Confederate troops arrived by train and turned the tide of battle. Shouting loud "rebel yells," the Confederates broke the attack and sent the Federals fleeing in terror back toward Washington. Upon hearing the news of the retreat, hard-driving Southern General Thomas J. Jackson, who earned the name "Stonewall" for the firm stand of his men in the battle, shouted, "Give me 5000 fresh men and I will be in Washington tomorrow." But the disorganized Confederate forces were in no position to seize the strategic moment. Their President Jefferson Davis did not order an advance.

In the long run the South was actually hurt by this first victory. Now the Southerners made the mistake of believing that it would be easy to defeat the North. For the North, on the other hand, the defeat at Bull Run made people realize that the war could not be won in a few days. And they steeled themselves for the hard years ahead.

Command in the East was now turned over to red-haired General George B. McClellan, who was not yet 35 years old. Like most of the generals—North and South—he had gone to West Point and had fought in the Mexican War. He had then used his talents for discipline and organization to help survey the difficult route for the Northern Pacific Railroad through the Cascade Mountains. He had also been a railroad president in the Middle West. Returning to the army at the outbreak of the Civil War, his able command of Union troops in western Virginia had saved for the Union the area that two years later became the state of West Virginia. McClellan insisted on precision in drill and demanded ample supplies for his troops, who trusted and loved him for it. He spent the remainder of 1861 training the Army of the Potomac to meet his high standards of readiness for battle.

The Civil War, 1861-1865

United States

Border States (Slaveholding Union States)

Confederate States

✕ Union Victory

⨯ Confederate Victory

0   200 Miles

0   200 Kilometers

5. GETTYSBURG 1863
1. BATTLES OF BULL RUN 1861 AND 1862
4. FREDERICKSBURG 1862
9. FALL OF RICHMOND 1865
10. LEE SURRENDERS AT APPOMATTOX 1865
7. CHATTANOOGA 1863
2. SHILOH 1862
8. ATLANTA, SAVANNAH 1864
6. VICKSBURG 1863
3. NEW ORLEANS 1862

The Trent affair. In November 1861 a Union warship stopped the British steamer *Trent* bound for London. Two Confederate diplomats, James M. Mason and John Slidell who had boarded the ship in Cuba, were removed from the vessel. They were on their way to England and France to seek recognition of the Confederacy.

The British people were outraged at this violation by the United States of the freedom of the seas for neutral vessels. Many called for war, and 8000 British troops were rushed to Canada. It was a dangerous moment for the United States, since war with Britain would have made it impossible to conquer the South. Fortunately, President Lincoln and Secretary of State Seward recognized the danger. Mason and Slidell were freed and allowed to continue on their way, and the United States admitted it had acted wrongly. This ended the crisis.

The war in the West. The Tennessee and the Cumberland rivers pointed like pistols at the heart of the Confederacy, while the Mississippi River cut it in two. On these rivers the fate of the Confederate States of America would be decided.

The operations in the West brought to prominence the greatest Union general, Ulysses S. Grant. Also a West Point graduate who had served with credit in the Mexican War, he had resigned from the army in 1854 when he was accused of being a drunk. The outbreak of the Civil War had found him, at the age of 39, working as a clerk in his father's hardware and leather store in Galena, Illinois. Military success was to make him the hero of the Union and later President of the United States.

Grant soon revealed that he had the special talents needed to succeed as a general. He had a genius for seeing the whole scene—and then quickly deciding what needed to be done. He possessed a silent, grim, cool courage and persistence. General Sherman later wrote to Grant, "My only points of doubt [about you as a general] were as to your knowledge of grand strategy, and of books of science and history; but I confess your common sense seems to have supplied this." Perhaps because he was not a "book" soldier, but a man of supreme common sense, Grant recognized early that this was a new kind of war. "The art of war is simple enough," he said. "Find out where your enemy is. Get at him as soon as you can. Strike him as hard as you can, and keep moving on."

Henry, Donelson, and Shiloh. Grant's first successes came in Tennessee. There he showed that by a clever combination with naval forces he could make the riverways of the South serve as highways for Northern victory. Confederate forts guarded the lower Tennessee and Cumberland rivers. On February 6, 1862, with the vital aid of a fleet of ironclad gunboats under Flag Officer A. H. Foote, Grant captured Fort Henry and so opened the Tennessee River all the way to Alabama. Within ten days Foote had taken his gunboats back to the Ohio and up the Cumberland. In another joint military and naval operation, Grant compelled the

This vivid lithograph of the Union charge at Shiloh appeared on the title page of a song.

surrender of Fort Donelson with all its 14,000 defenders. Then defenseless Nashville fell without a blow to another Union army under General D. C. Buell.

Next Grant moved an army of 40,000 men up the Tennessee River to Pittsburg Landing near the Mississippi state border. They kept on moving inland as far as a country meetinghouse called Shiloh Church. Here his men, who had not yet learned to dig defensive positions, were surprised on April 6, 1862, by a Confederate army under the able and experienced General Albert Sidney Johnston, (not a relation of Joseph E. Johnston of Bull Run fame). The Union troops were driven back to the edge of the river, where they dug in and held. The Confederates had won the day, but at a heavy cost. When General Johnston was killed in that battle, they lost one of their boldest and most seasoned military leaders.

Grant was not so easily stopped. The very next day, strengthened by reinforcements, he attacked and drove the Confederate troops from the field. There were appalling losses on both sides—13,000 dead and wounded for the North and 11,000 for the South.

At Shiloh, Grant learned that he was in a war far different from what he had counted on in the beginning. He had thought at first that the rebellion would collapse "suddenly and soon, if a decisive victory could be gained over any of its armies." But he had actually won such victories at Fort Henry and Fort Donelson. Then instead of collapsing, the Southern forces turned around, took the offensive, and nearly defeated him. Now he knew that this would be a war to exhaustion. There would be no Northern victory unless his forces were allowed to "consume everything [in the South] that could be used to support or supply armies."

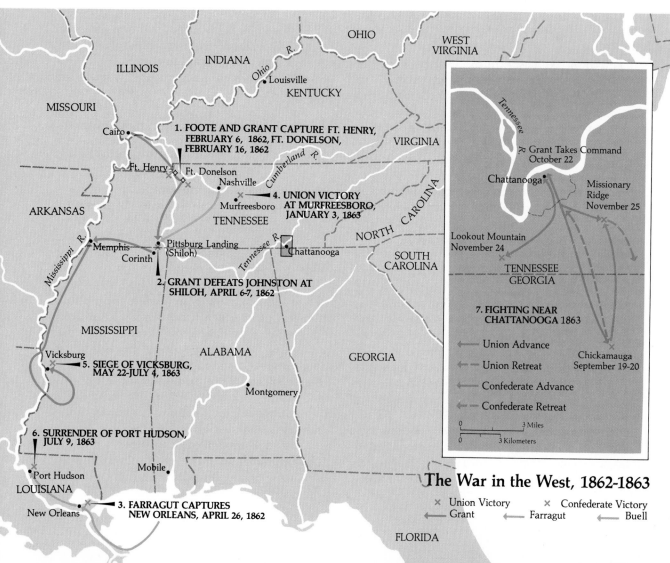

The War in the West, 1862-1863

1. FOOTE AND GRANT CAPTURE FT. HENRY, FEBRUARY 6, 1862, FT. DONELSON, FEBRUARY 16, 1862

4. UNION VICTORY AT MURFREESBORO, JANUARY 3, 1863

2. GRANT DEFEATS JOHNSTON AT SHILOH, APRIL 6-7, 1862

5. SIEGE OF VICKSBURG, MAY 22-JULY 4, 1863

6. SURRENDER OF PORT HUDSON, JULY 9, 1863

3. FARRAGUT CAPTURES NEW ORLEANS, APRIL 26, 1862

7. FIGHTING NEAR CHATTANOOGA 1863

Grant Takes Command October 22

Missionary Ridge November 25

Lookout Mountain November 24

Chickamauga September 19-20

Union Advance
Union Retreat
Confederate Advance
Confederate Retreat

× Union Victory   × Confederate Victory
← Grant   ← Farragut   ← Buell

New Orleans. Meanwhile Foote and General John Pope were working down the Mississippi River, opening it as far as the Confederate bastion at Vicksburg. At the other end of the river a bold move by the amazing David Glasgow Farragut captured New Orleans for the Union.

Farragut, the son of a naval officer, had been commissioned a midshipman at the age of nine. He had seen action in the War of 1812 when he was only eleven. His orders commanded him as he entered the river from the Gulf of Mexico first to capture the two forts at the mouth of the Mississippi that protected New Orleans. But disregarding orders he raced past the two forts (losing only three of his seventeen ships). He defeated an astounded Confederate fleet, sinking eleven of its ships. Then at one blow he seized the coveted prize—New Orleans, queen city of the South. Farragut took the city on April 26, 1862, almost before anyone knew he was in the neighborhood. Now the South could no longer support its troops in the West with supplies brought in from the Gulf of Mexico.

The war in the East. In the East, however, the prospects of the Federal forces were not nearly so rosy. Northern operations were paralyzed by the caution and indecision of General McClellan. He did not move forward. Although he actually commanded an army grown to 180,000 men, which was twice the size of the forces under General Joseph E. Johnston, he still believed he was outnumbered. And he blamed the "imbecile" administration at Washington for not sending him more reinforcements. General Johnston had his men well entrenched on the old Bull Run battlefield.

The Monitor and the Merrimac. While McClellan was hesitating, a historic sea battle was taking place. A new chapter in naval warfare was being opened. On March 8, 1862, a strange-looking ironclad vessel with sloping sides covered by four-inch iron plates and with a powerful iron ram on its bow came steaming out of Norfolk into Hampton Roads to attack the Federal blockading squadron there. This was the C.S.S. *Virginia,* usually known by its old name as the U.S. frigate *Merrimac.* To the astonishment and dismay of Northern sailors, their shots just bounced off her sides. She proceeded to destroy with ease the wooden sailing ships of the Federal fleet—including the 50-gun frigate *Cum-*

berland and the 30-gun sloop *Congress.* When the *Merrimac* returned to Norfolk, it seemed that the next day she would easily destroy the rest of the Federal fleet. Then what would prevent her from going right up the Potomac and shelling the Northern capital?

Before dawn on March 9, however, an even stranger craft steamed into Hampton Roads from the open sea. This was the *Monitor,* one of the small Union ironclads that the clever Secretary of the Navy, Gideon Welles, had ordered early in the war. From the deck of the *Monitor,* which was almost flush with the water, rose a revolving turret within which were two eleven-inch guns. This made the ship look like "a tin can on a shingle." When the seemingly "unbeatable" *Merrimac* appeared later that day, the *Monitor* was there ready for the challenge. A spectacular duel took place in which neither ironclad did much harm to the other. Then the *Merrimac* withdrew again to Norfolk.

The Union blockade of the South was not to be broken. The Confederacy's one day as ruler of the seas was over. And this first fight in history between ironclads marked the end of navies of wooden ships.

The peninsular campaign. After continual prodding by Lincoln, McClellan finally made up his mind to move. Following the West Point textbooks, he decided to try to take Richmond by a classic maneuver. He transported his large and well-equipped army by water to the peninsula between the James and the York rivers. Proceeding slowly, he worked his way to within a few miles of Richmond. The church towers of the town were visible from the Union front lines.

Then McClellan's weakness showed again. Instead of advancing swiftly to fulfill his plan before the enemy could get their bearings, he halted long enough to give the Confederates time to figure out how to beat him. In a series of battles, during which General Joseph E. Johnston was injured and General Robert E. Lee took command, McClellan saved his army from a near defeat. He finally ended up in a strong defensive position—protected by the Union navy and with his back to the James River, but surrounded by Confederate troops.

The Confederate Army of Northern Virginia was now in the command of the tactical genius of

PENNSYLVANIA

The War in the East 1862

Hagerstown

3. LEE AND McCLELLAN
CLASH AT ANTIETAM,
SEPTEMBER 17

Sharpsburg

Frederick

Harpers
Ferry

2. LEE AND JACKSON DEFEAT POPE,
SECOND BATTLE OF
BULL RUN, AUGUST 29-30

Shenandoah R.

Washington

Manassas
Junction

Cedar
Mt.

Fredericksburg

Rapidan R.

4. LEE DEFEATS BURNSIDE
AT FREDERICKSBURG,
DECEMBER 13

Rappahannock R.

Potomac R.

Chesapeake Bay

MARYLAND

DEL.

McClellan

Pope

Lee and Jackson

Burnside

Lee

Confederate Victory

Draw

0   40 Miles

0   40 Kilometers

Mechanicsville

1. McCLELLAN'S PENINSULA CAMPAIGN,
MARCH-JULY

Richmond

SEVEN DAYS' BATTLES
JUNE 25-JULY 1

Chickahominy R.

York R.

Appomattox R.

Petersburg

James R.

Yorktown

VIRGINIA

Norfolk

the Civil War—the man who has been called the greatest general of the age. A man of noble character, Lee felt his first love and first loyalty was for Virginia. But, oddly enough, he was no friend to secession or to slavery.

Robert E. Lee, a true Southern blue blood, was a descendant of one of Virginia's finest families and had married Martha Washington's great granddaughter. He had graduated second in his class from West Point and later served as superintendent there. In his character the honor and the loyalty of a soldier prevailed over everything else. He had commanded the Marines who captured John Brown at Harpers Ferry in 1859. When the Civil War broke out, Lieutenant Colonel Lee had been offered command of all the Union forces by his fellow Virginian, General Winfield Scott, under whom he had served brilliantly in the Mexican War. Lee felt that he could not fight against Virginia. When that state asked him in April 1861 to command its armies, he agreed. Then in June President Jefferson Davis called him into Confederate service to be his personal military adviser.

As commanding general of the Army of Northern Virginia, Lee knew that he must act promptly and with daring if the South was to win its independence. Since General Lee's talents were well known in the North, his name there inspired respect and fear.

The second Battle of Bull Run (Manassas).
General McClellan was now replaced. John Pope, who took over the command, had led an army that successfully cleared important points on the Mississippi. Lincoln hoped that this new brash and boastful leader would live up to his boasts and show a boldness that McClellan never had. Before Pope could march on Richmond and "end the war," he was attacked by Lee and Jackson at Bull Run (August 29–30, 1862). There his army was defeated. General Pope was speedily removed and his troops again placed under McClellan.

These reverses stirred resentment against Lincoln and his administration. Enlistments fell off, and desertions increased. People hesitated to buy Union war bonds. The congressional elections were in doubt. England considered recognizing the Confederacy. Southern hopes were high. The tide seemed to have turned for the South. Now perhaps Washington could be captured.

Antietam.
After Bull Run, Lee moved quickly. His army of 55,000 battle-hardened men crossed the Potomac into Maryland on September 4, 1862. Singing "Maryland, My Maryland," his troops expected soon to be joined by Southern friends. But somehow no one came to join them. When a Federal force at Harpers Ferry was not evacuated as expected, Lee divided his army and sent a unit to drive out the Union troops. Then a copy of Lee's orders, showing where his soldiers were located, fell into the hands of McClellan. If McClellan had moved rapidly, he might have destroyed Lee's army. But as usual, McClellan took his time and gave the enemy the chance to organize.

The two forces met at Sharpsburg, near Antietam Creek. Lee was heavily outnumbered, and the Potomac River was at his back.

All day long on September 17, in the bloodiest battle of an appallingly bloody war, the battle lines moved back and forth. At nightfall, Lee still held his position. The next day, although badly weakened, Lee's men faced McClellan's and dared them to attack. Once again, McClellan hesitated. That night Lee crossed the Potomac and returned to Virginia, leaving behind 2700 dead on the battlefield. The Union had lost 2100 killed. Each army had more than 9000 wounded. For both sides it was the worst single day of the war.

The battle, so far, was a draw, but Lee's invasion of the North had reached its farthest point. This was the high tide of the Confederacy. When news of Antietam reached England, the British decided to await further developments before taking any action. Never again would the Confederate States of America be so close to receiving the recognition from abroad that it desperately needed.

SECTION 2 REVIEW

1. Identify or explain: Irvin McDowell, Winfield Scott, anaconda policy, J. E. Johnston, Thomas J. Jackson, George B. McClellan.

2. Locate: Manassas Junction, Fort Henry, Fort Donelson, Shiloh, Vicksburg, Hampton Roads.

3. List six key military engagements in 1861–1862 and tell the outcome and significance of each.

4. **Expressing Problems Clearly.** General Grant realized that the Civil War would be a war of exhaustion if the North were to win. Explain.

3. The widening conflict

Abraham Lincoln had long been under pressure to make the war into a crusade against slavery. But he had resisted. To Horace Greeley, whose newspaper strongly criticized him for not freeing the slaves, Lincoln had written in August 1862:

> My paramount object in this struggle *is* to save the Union, and is *not* either to save or destroy Slavery. If I could save the Union without freeing *any* slave, I would do it; and if I could save it by freeing *all* the slaves, I would do it; and if I could do it by freeing some and leaving others alone, I would also do that. What I do about Slavery and the colored race, I do because I believe it helps to save this Union; and what I forbear, I forbear because I do *not* believe it would help to save the Union.

Abraham Lincoln and slavery. For putting the Union ahead of everything else, Lincoln has sometimes been criticized. But there is no doubt that Lincoln felt deeply that slavery was "a moral, social, and political wrong." He said:

> Let us discard all this quibbling about this man and the other man—this race and that race and the other race being inferior and therefore they must be placed in an inferior position. . . . Let us discard all these things and unite as one people throughout this land, until we shall once more stand up and declare that all men are created equal.

Abraham Lincoln was every inch a politician. He was not a crusader. The passionate reformers—the John Browns and William Lloyd Garrisons—also had their role. The nation needed them, too, if it was to fulfill its mission as "the last best hope of earth." Lincoln realized that his job was not to express his feelings but to shape the real world. The people of the North had entered the war mainly because of their love of the Union. Lincoln knew that if the South were allowed to secede and become a nation based on slavery, all would be lost. In the long run only if the Union was saved would the reformers in the North be able to abolish slavery in the South. While the result of the Civil War was still in doubt, Lincoln realized that people cared more deeply for morals than for politics. As the casualties increased, he saw that the North would

have to pay a high price in blood and tears. To pay that price they would have to be persuaded that this was a war against slavery.

The Emancipation Proclamation. Lincoln had, in fact, already drafted his *Preliminary* Emancipation Proclamation when he wrote to Horace Greeley in August 1862. But he was persuaded to wait for some kind of victory on the battlefield. Otherwise it might look, he later said, like "our last *shriek* on the retreat."

Antietam now gave him his chance. On September 23, 1862, Lincoln issued his Preliminary Emancipation Proclamation. He warned that on January 1, 1863, anyone held as a slave in any state or part of a state where the people were "in rebellion against the United States, shall be then, thenceforward, and forever free."

Neither in this early warning nor even in the Emancipation Proclamation itself, which was issued on January 1, 1863, did Lincoln free a single slave. That would only come with the success of the Union armies. The South viewed Lincoln's proclamation as a "fiend's" act that "destroyed $4 billion worth of property and bid the slaves rise in insurrection." Jefferson Davis said it made reunion "forever impossible."

The North was divided over the proclamation. Abolitionists were delighted—though they regretted that Lincoln had not freed the slaves everywhere. Many Northerners were displeased because they wanted to fight only for the Union. In Europe antislavery feeling was so strong that the Emancipation Proclamation helped to kill any chance of recognition of the Confederacy. Now this was not merely a war for a political Union, but a war against slavery, an evil that had afflicted the world.

Ending slavery. Early in the war Lincoln had attempted to persuade the Union states of Missouri, Kentucky, Maryland, and Delaware to free their slaves and be compensated for it by the federal government. To his great disappointment, he had failed. Congress had approved his plans, and in April 1862 it had abolished slavery in the District of Columbia and provided payments to the owners for the loss of their property. Two months later it had ended slavery in the territories without giving any compensation. But Congress could not do anything about slavery in the states.

A. A. Lamb; National Gallery of Art, Washington, Gift of Edgar William and Bernice Chrysler Garbisch

"The Emancipation Proclamation," an allegorical painting made about 1863, shows Lincoln holding his proclamation and following the goddess of liberty.

West Virginia entered the Union in 1863 with a constitution that provided for gradual emancipation. Maryland ended slavery in 1864, and a state convention in Missouri abolished it within that state in January 1865. But Delaware and Kentucky refused to act. The peculiar institution lingered in those states until the ratification of the Thirteenth Amendment was completed in December 1865.

Gloom in the North. For a while after Antietam the war did not go well for the North. A new general in the East, Ambrose Burnside, (whose name supplied the word "sideburns"!), showed that he had learned nothing about the new warfare. He attacked Lee's fortified position at Fredericksburg (December 13, 1862). The North suffered 10,000 dead and wounded to fewer than 5000 for the South. Out west, Grant and Sherman also suffered reverses. They had not yet found a way to take Vicksburg. Only in the middle theater, in central Tennessee, did a Union success at Murfreesboro lighten the gloom.

This was a bad time for Lincoln. There were demands that he reorganize his Cabinet. In the fall elections, the Democrats (who were no enthusiasts for the war) gained 32 seats in the House. Defeatism was widespread. Carloads of civilian clothing were being smuggled into the Union lines to aid deserters to escape. Voluntary enlistments fell so low that, in March 1863, the government was forced to pass its first draft law. It made all men between 20 and 45 liable for service in the national forces for a term of three years. But service could be avoided by payment of $300 or by finding a substitute to enlist for three years. The first drawing of names provoked four days of rioting in New York City in July.

The draft provided only a small proportion of total Union troops. More important were the bounties (as high as $1000) paid by federal, state, and local governments for voluntary enlistment. But this system suffered from "bounty jumping," enlisting and deserting again and again. The South had turned to conscription in 1862. But a clause

Union recruiters published posters in German to attract immigrants.   American Indians (top right) were photographed as they enlisted in the Union army.   The chromolithograph (below) was part of an advertisement published to urge blacks to volunteer for the Union army.

that exempted one slaveholder or overseer for every twenty slaves outraged many Southerners and brought desertions from their army.

Blacks in arms. The Emancipation Proclamation had provided another source of manpower for the Union army. It approved taking blacks into the armed services. They had, in fact, already fought in the war, and Congress had authorized the recruiting of blacks. But only with the Emancipation Proclamation were the gates really opened.

In time, more than 185,000 blacks were enlisted in the Northern armed forces. And some 38,000 were to die from sickness or wounds. During the Civil War black soldiers, for the first time in United States history, could join the militia and the regular army. The United States Colored Volunteers were pleased to be able to sing

> We look like men a'marching on
> We look like men o'war

They did all sorts of things—a small number were officers of black units, some were spies in the South, many were laborers or garrison troops. They showed their bravery in battle, for example in July 1863, when the 54th Massachusetts charged Fort Wagner outside Charleston, South Carolina. Black troops had the satisfaction of being present when the war came to an end at Appomattox Court House.

Banks, bonds, and currency. The needs of the war in 1863 brought about the creation of a new banking system. Up to now the United States had tried to pay the costs of the conflict by borrowing, by placing direct taxes on the states, by raising tariffs, by levying sales and other internal taxes, and by taxing incomes. The first income tax in our history had been passed in August 1861. All income over $800 a year was taxed at a rate of 3 percent.

In addition to these steps, beginning in 1862 a new type of currency, called *United States notes,* or *greenbacks,* was issued. This money was not based on gold or silver in the Treasury. It fluctuated widely in value depending upon the confidence of the people in the successful outcome of the war. By the end of the struggle $432 million of these notes had been issued.

Still it was clear as 1862 came to a close that even more needed to be done. So in February 1863, at the request of Secretary of the Treasury Salmon P. Chase, Congress passed a law that provided for national banks and national bank notes. The new banks were chartered by the national government. They were required to purchase at least $30,000 worth of national bonds (which would help pay for the war). Then they were allowed to issue national bank notes up to the value of 90 percent of the bonds. This would provide a more uniform and stable currency than the existing state bank notes or greenbacks. With only minor changes, the national bank system continued until it was replaced by the Federal Reserve Act of 1913 (p. 445).

The trans-Mississippi West, 1861–1865. During the Civil War, the westward movement of Americans continued. Some 300,000 men, women, and children made the long trek to California and Oregon, or moved into other western territories. Some went to farm. Others hoped to find gold or silver. And many wished to escape the draft.

The Far West kept up with news of events in the East by the telegraph. The first message from the East Coast to San Francisco was transmitted on October 24, 1861. All at once communication between the East and the West was instantaneous. Until then the fastest way to send word was by the Pony Express (which only lasted from April 1860 to October 1861). Spry young riders on relays of fast horses carried letters for $10 an ounce in ten days from St. Joseph, Missouri, to San Francisco.

When the Civil War broke out, the army units in the West were called east to fight the Confederates. Soon after they were gone, Indian war broke out in Minnesota, Colorado, and Montana. Untrained militia units were to try to put down some of the uprisings. But better fighting forces were the 1st through 6th Infantry Regiments, United States Volunteers, whose membership was made up of Confederate veterans enlisted from prisoner-of-war camps to fight the Indians. At one point fighting was so severe in Colorado that Denver was cut off from communication with the outside world.

Still the farmers and miners went west. By 1863 enough people had moved into Idaho for it to become a territory. There were 25,000 people in the Boise area alone. That same year Arizona was also made a territory. The next year Nevada came into the Union as a state, and Montana became a territory. The growth of the West seemed scarcely checked by the Civil War.

State Historical Society of Wisconsin

John Gaddis of the 12th Wisconsin painted this watercolor of his regiment in 1862. He showed the troops cheering as a train crossed a bridge they had built.

SECTION 3 REVIEW

1. What was Lincoln's chief reason for issuing the Emancipation Proclamation?
2. Describe the reaction to the Emancipation Proclamation in the South and the North.
3. What roles did blacks play in the war?
4. How did the North finance the war?
5. **Recognizing Cause and Effect.** What was the Civil War's effect on westward migration?

---

4. Gettysburg to Appomattox, 1863–1865

The war was now reaching its climax.

In the western theater, Grant led one of the most brilliant campaigns of the war. At the beginning of May 1863 he cut his army loose from its supply lines. While living off the land, the troops fought five battles in three weeks, isolated Vicksburg, and on May 22 began the siege of the South's last stronghold on the Mississippi River.

In the East, Lee defeated another Union general, "Fighting Joe" Hooker, in the Battle of Chancellorsville (May 2–4) in northeastern Virginia. But that victory could not balance Lee's loss of his most valued general, the powerhouse "Stonewall" Jackson, not yet 40 years old, by mistake shot and killed by his own men.

President Davis and General Lee now decided to move north. Lee hoped that by invading Pennsylvania he might demoralize the North and bring foreign recognition of the Confederacy.

The Battle of Gettysburg. Lee crossed the Potomac on June 15, 1863, leading an army of 70,000 men. The Union army under sound, steady George Gordon Meade followed the Confederates. Units of the two armies stumbled into each other at the sleepy little town of Gettysburg, Pennsylvania. Both armies then hastened to the spot. Here 165,000 men were to fight the greatest single battle ever to take place in the Western Hemisphere. Nearly twice as many Americans were to die at Gettysburg as were lost in the entire American Revolution.

Handsome General Robert E. Lee posed for his picture in 1864 in full-dress uniform. When the war ended, Grant generously let the Confederate officers keep their swords.

Lee had the advantage on the first day, before Meade had securely established his forces on high ground. Southern hesitation enabled the North to hold key points—Culp's Hill and Little Round Top—the loss of which might have led to a Northern defeat. If the bold "Stonewall" Jackson had been there, the result might have been quite different.

The South needed a victory, not another inconclusive battle. So on the third day, Lee made a desperate bid. He sent 15,000 infantry, including General George Pickett and his brave Virginians, against the middle of the Union line. But the artillery and the fire of Northerners protected by defensive works was too much. A hundred men reached the Union line, but they were all captured or killed. The Battle of Gettysburg was over.

On the afternoon of the next day, July 4, 1863, Lee began his retreat. He left behind 4000 dead.

The South divided. On that same day, though Lee did not know it, there was another critical defeat of the South. General Pemberton surrendered to Grant the great stronghold of Vicksburg—the key to control of the Mississippi. With the loss of that city went 170 cannon, 50,000 small arms, and 30,000 Southern soldiers as prisoners of war.

Five days later Port Hudson, the last Confederate post on the river, gave up. As Lincoln said, "The Father of Waters again goes unvexed to the sea." The Confederacy was cut in two between East and West. The supply line over which had come meat and munitions from Texas and Mexico was closed.

After Gettysburg and Vicksburg the death of the Confederacy was only a matter of time. But still the war went on. In fact, it would last for nearly two more years. Many thousands more would die so that (as Lincoln said at Gettysburg) "this nation under God shall have a new birth of freedom and that government of the people, by the people, for the people, shall not perish from the earth."

The North's victories at Gettysburg and Vicksburg were followed by Southern success at Chickamauga Creek near Chattanooga, Tennessee, in September 1863. The defeated Union troops then retreated into Chattanooga where they were trapped. At last, Grant's skill was recognized when he was made commander of all the Union forces in the West. At the end of November, assisted by reinforcements rushed 1200 miles by rail from the East, Grant defeated and pushed back the Southern

The War in the East 1863

← Hooker
←- Meade
← Lee
✗ Union Victory
✗ Confederate Victory

2. THE BATTLE OF
GETTYSBURG,
JULY 1-3

0 _____ 40 Miles
0 _____ 40 Kilometers

PENNSYLVANIA

Harrisburg
Wrightsville
Chambersburg
Gettysburg
Susquehanna R.

MARYLAND

DEL.

Hagerstown

WEST VIRGINIA

Sharpsburg
Frederick
Harpers Ferry
Monocacy R.

Shenandoah R.
Potomac R.
Washington
Front Royal
BLUE RIDGE MTS.
VIRGINIA
Manassas Junction
Rappahannock R.
Culpeper
Rapidan R.
Chancellorsville
Fredericksburg

1. LEE DEFEATS HOOKER,
MAY 2-4

THE BATTLE OF
GETTYSBURG, JULY 1-3

--- Union Line
← Confederate Attacks

Rock Creek
CULP'S HILL
CEMETERY HILL
Pickett's Charge
SEMINARY RIDGE
CEMETERY RIDGE
LITTLE ROUND TOP
DEVIL'S DEN
ROUND TOP

0 _____ 1 Mile
0 _____ 1 Kilometer

troops surrounding Chattanooga, in the battles of Lookout Mountain and Missionary Ridge. Now the North was in a position to strike for Atlanta and then to split off another large section of the South by driving for the sea.

The drives for Petersburg and Atlanta. On March 9, 1864, Lincoln promoted Grant to Lieutenant General—a rank last held by George Washington—and then gave him command of all the armies of the United States. Grant had finally figured out how this war had to be fought. Only if everybody attacked the South at the same time

could its ability to fight be destroyed. Lincoln immediately understood: "Those not skinning can hold a leg."

In May 1864 began the final, brutal, bloody battles of exhaustion. Grant's forces suffered enormous losses, but he knew that he could afford them while Lee could not. In 40 days Grant, constantly fighting, moved around Richmond until he reached the important railway junction of Petersburg. The carnage of these days was beyond belief. Grant lost 55,000 dead and wounded to Lee's 30,000. But these losses weakened the Confederacy far more than the Union. Now Lee was pinned down. He could not leave Petersburg without giving up Richmond.

For Northerners the months of July and August 1864 were to be the darkest days of the war. The lists of Northern dead grew ever longer, but they seemed to bring no great victories. Would this war never end? Lincoln feared that he would be defeated in the fall elections by the Democratic candidate, General George McClellan.

Just then the tide miraculously turned. The general responsible was the profound but unbending William Tecumseh Sherman, now in command of Union forces in the West. He understood that this really was everybody's war. When Sherman entered Atlanta on September 2, he told the mayor, "War is cruelty and you cannot refine it." Believing that the age of total war had come, he aimed to break the spirit of the civilian South.

In the Shenandoah Valley in Virginia the young and ruthless Philip Sheridan, whose victories had made him a Union general when he was barely 30, was following Sherman's theory of the new warfare to its logical conclusion. He burned mills and barns and whatever his men could not carry. He told his men to leave the people "nothing but their eyes to weep with."

These advances helped bring Lincoln a heavy soldiers' vote from the field, and he decisively won reelection. He carried every state but New Jersey, Delaware, and Kentucky for 212 electoral votes to 21 for McClellan.

Sherman's march to the sea. On November 14, while Grant still held Lee in Petersburg, Sherman abandoned his supply and communication lines (as Grant had done before striking Vicksburg). After he set fire to Atlanta and burnt down most of the city, he led his 60,000 men on a free-wheeling march of devastation "from Atlanta to the sea." His army traveled light. He told his men to carry only their arms, for he expected them to loot food, blankets, and whatever else they needed along the way. This would help exhaust the enemy at the same time that it solved his own problem of supply. He ordered them to move fast, without waiting to protect their rear.

For three weeks wild rumors spread through the North concerning Sherman's "lost army." In the meantime it was cutting a swath some 60 miles wide and 300 miles long through the breadbasket of the Confederacy. The newly gathered harvests were devoured or destroyed.

Soldiers in trenches outside Petersburg wait for the battle to begin.

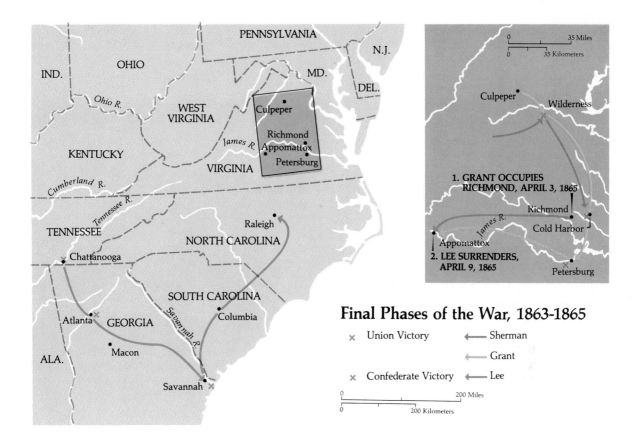

Final Phases of the War, 1863-1865

Inset map labels:
- 1. GRANT OCCUPIES RICHMOND, APRIL 3, 1865
- 2. LEE SURRENDERS, APRIL 9, 1865

Legend:
- ✕ Union Victory — Sherman
- — Grant
- ✕ Confederate Victory — Lee

Railroads were torn up. Barns, buildings, depots, machine shops, bridges, cotton gins, and stores of cotton were destroyed. Tens of thousands of horses and mules needed to pull the plows and wagons were taken. The civilian and military resources of the state were damaged beyond repair.

On December 10, after the 25-day march, Sherman reached Savannah. Two weeks later Lincoln received a telegram from him announcing "as a Christmas gift the city of Savannah, with 150 heavy guns, plenty of ammunition, and about 25,000 bales of cotton."

Sherman turns north. On January 16 Sherman and his men began to head north through South Carolina, the state that more than any other they blamed for starting the war. The state capital, Columbia, and other towns were left in ashes. It did not seem possible, but this march was even more cruel and devastating than the one through Georgia. Late in March, Grant renewed his attack on Petersburg. That stronghold fell on Sunday, April 2. Quickly, Jefferson Davis and other gov-

ernment officers left Richmond. Union troops entered the city the next day.

Lee tried to escape with his dwindling army to North Carolina, where he hoped to join forces with General Joseph E. Johnston, who was opposing Sherman. But Sheridan's cavalry headed him off. On April 7 Grant wrote to Lee, "General, the result of the last week must convince you of the hopelessness of further resistance."

The end—Appomattox Court House. On the afternoon of April 9, 1865, General Lee, accompanied only by his military secretary, rode his horse to a little white house in the town of Appomattox Court House in central Virginia. He went to arrange his surrender. There occurred one of the most remarkable and one of the most encouraging episodes in American history. It would show that, despite the monstrous indecencies of war, the respect of one American for another had not been destroyed.

Grant, who had just come in from the field, was dusty and even more unkempt than usual. Confronting him in the living room of the house that he

A Richmond flour mill in ruins was photographed by Mathew Brady at the end of the Civil War.

had taken for his headquarters was General Lee—handsome, erect, in a spotless uniform, and wearing his dress sword. The men sat down and then exchanged recollections of their fighting together twenty years before in the Mexican War. The two great generals talked to each other calmly, with courtesy and respect.

Now that the fighting was over, it seemed that humanity had suddenly returned. Lee heard Grant's terms of surrender. Grant was more generous than he needed to be. He allowed the Southern officers to keep their swords—the symbols of their honor—and he let the officers and men keep their horses so that they could go home and plant their crops. Lee was touched. "This," he said, "will have a very happy effect upon my army."

A renewed nation, fused in the fires of war, would now seek its destiny in peace.

SECTION 4 REVIEW

1. Identify: Joseph Hooker, George G. Meade, John Pemberton, Philip Sheridan.

2. Locate: Gettysburg, Port Hudson, Chattanooga, Petersburg, Shenandoah Valley, Appomattox.

3. What hopeful note for the future was struck in the surrender at Appomattox?

4. **Drawing Conclusions.** What did General Sherman expect to accomplish by his marches through Georgia and South Carolina?

FOCUSING ON IDEAS

1. List some aspects of the Civil War that would seem strange to an observer who was familiar with old-fashioned warfare.

2. Identify two women who played prominent roles in the Civil War and describe their contributions to the war effort.

3. Describe two developments that affected the lives of Americans west of the Mississippi during the Civil War.

4. What was the "anaconda" plan? Name some military and naval engagements that were designed to carry out the plan.

TAKING A CRITICAL LOOK

1. **Making Comparisons.** How did the North's General Grant and the South's General Lee compare as military leaders?

2. **Identifying Central Issues.** Why did Lincoln delay in issuing the Emancipation Proclamation? Why did he finally issue the proclamation freeing slaves? What limits were put on emancipation? Does Lincoln deserve to be called "the Great Emancipator"?

3. **Recognizing Cause and Effect.** How did industrial and technological developments such as the railroad and the rifle affect the course and outcome of the Civil War?

YOUR REGION IN HISTORY

1. **Geography.** Locate on a map and describe any Civil War battles or other military engagements that took place in your state or locality. What were the results?

2. **Culture.** What Civil War monuments, plaques, or other memorials can be seen in your area?

HISTORICAL FACTS AND FIGURES

Predicting Consequences. Study the chart below to help answer the following questions: (a) Which side—the Brown or the Tan—had the advantage in each resource category? (b) How would having a greater supply of each resource have been an advantage during the Civil War? (c) Which resources do you think were most important in determining the outcome of the conflict? (d) Which color do you think represents the Union? The Confederacy? Explain your answer.

Division of American Resources

Population Total: 31.5 million

Railroad Mileage Total: 31,000 miles

Factories Total: 130,000

Iron & Steel Output Total: 513,000 tons

Value of Exports Total: $316 million

Farmland Total: 162,667 acres

Value of Manufactured Goods Total: $1,949,969

Percent of National Total

CHAPTER **14**

To punish or to forgive?

The Civil War had cemented the Union that it was fought to preserve. Lee's surrender to Grant at Appomattox brought peace. But peace brought new problems. How to find jobs for the million men who left the Union and the Confederate armies? How to change factories from making cannons and rifles and bullets to making harvesters and sewing machines? How to rebuild the war-torn South?

When the South agreed to unconditional surrender, they put themselves at the mercy of the North. This gave the North a troublesome new problem—what to do with the conquered South. Now that the blacks were at last free, what was to be the relationship of the races to each other?

1. "With malice toward none"

There were wide differences of opinion in the North. Was it more important to punish the former rebels, to teach them a lesson they would never forget, so they would never again try to break up the Union? Or was it better to forgive, to welcome the rebels back into the Union, so they would feel at home and never again want to leave?

Of course the South had already been punished. A quarter of a million Southerners had died in the war. The Confederacy was a land of cinders and desolation—of charred plantation houses, broken bridges, twisted railways, and desecrated churches. An Englishman who traveled halfway across the South said he did not see a single smiling face. But the North also had suffered with its own one-third of a million dead. And for the Northerners who had lost fathers, sons, or husbands, no punishment of the South would be enough.

Yet this was not just a question of feelings. Unless the North wanted to feed and house millions

of Southerners, it was important to get the South back into working order. This meant getting crops planted, factories built, railroads running, and pupils and teachers into schools. It also meant getting the Southern states organized to govern themselves, to collect their own taxes, to keep the peace, and to protect life and property.

It was not easy to bring people to agree on how to revive the Southern states. There was wide disagreement over what the war had really meant. What the North called "The War of the Rebellion" in the South was called "The War between the States." The Southerners argued that their state governments had never been destroyed. Once a state always a state!

Lincoln against the Radicals. Lincoln himself almost agreed with the Southerners on this point. He also believed, once a state always a state! But for Lincoln this meant that the Southern states had no power to secede. And if these states had never

Mathew Brady made this touching photograph of Lincoln and his son Tad in 1864.

legally seceded, then after the Civil War they were still within the Union.

Of course, once the war was over, Southerners wanted to agree with Lincoln. As Lincoln said, they still had their states and therefore could still run their own affairs. The most, then, that the North could properly ask was that some Confederate leaders be barred from office.

Some Republicans and most Democrats agreed with Lincoln. But on the other side were Northern avengers and reformers. The most powerful of them were some Republican members in Congress called "Radicals." They were bitter against the Southern rebels. They wanted to punish white Southerners, and they also wanted to see that the newly freed slaves received fair treatment. To accomplish these ends, the Radical Republicans claimed that the Southern states had actually "committed suicide." By trying to rebel, they had actually destroyed their own states.

People who thought like this believed that after the war the Southern "states" could claim *no* rights under the Constitution. They had no right to govern themselves or to be represented in the Congress. They were nothing but so much territory—like parts of the sparsely settled West. And like those western territories, they could be governed in any way Congress decided.

Congress could treat them as "conquered provinces." They could be ruled by military governors—generals of the Union army. When, if ever, would they be allowed to govern themselves and take part in the national government? This would depend on how they behaved themselves and what the victorious Congress wanted. Such a view offered anything but a cheerful prospect for white Southerners.

Thaddeus Stevens and Charles Sumner. Two leaders of the Radical Republicans were Thaddeus Stevens and Charles Sumner. Thaddeus Stevens of Pennsylvania, a power in the House of Representatives, was one of the strangest men in American history. He was sometimes called "a humanitarian without humanity." He seemed to use up all his good feelings on large and noble causes, so that he had very little left for individuals. Born with a clubfoot, Stevens seemed to have a grudge against the world. Some said he had been raised on sour milk. He never showed charity to opponents in his speeches. Just as Lincoln inspired love and respect, Stevens inspired fear.

Very early in life Stevens took up the great cause of abolishing slavery. He never abandoned that cause. Nor did he ever forgive men who had held slaves or who had been entangled in the web of slavery. When the Confederate army invaded southern Pennsylvania in 1863, they destroyed Stevens's ironworks and burned the nearby city of Chambersburg. After Appomattox, Stevens made it his purpose in life to punish all "traitors." Old age never mellowed him. At the age of 75 he boasted that he would spend his remaining years inventing new ways to make the hated Southern rebels suffer.

In the Senate the leader of the Radicals was grim Charles Sumner of Massachusetts. Three and a half years after being brutally beaten by Brooks (p. 265), and still not fully recovered, Sumner had returned to his Senate seat. As early as 1862 he had begun to fight for equal rights for blacks. He was a proud, vain man, bitter against white Southerners and intolerant of all opposition. But in the Senate he was the conscience of the North. And he was just as bitter against the white South and just as concerned about black Southerners as Thaddeus Stevens. They formed an odd and awesome alliance.

Lincoln's plan for reunion. During the Civil War, Lincoln had shown his greatness—and his forgiving spirit—by his plan for bringing Southerners back to the Union. He was less interested in the past than in the future. Back on December 8, 1863, in his Proclamation of Amnesty and Reconstruction, he had explained his plan. He would pardon almost all Southerners, even if they had fought against the Union.

All that Lincoln asked was that Southerners take a solemn oath to support the Constitution of the United States in the future. As soon as enough citizens of a Southern state took the oath, Lincoln would recognize the government of that state and let the people rule themselves. Of course they must agree to abolish slavery. It would be enough, Lincoln said, if a number equal to only one-tenth of the voters in the 1860 presidential election took the oath of loyalty.

The Wade-Davis plan. Lincoln's plan did not satisfy the Radical Republicans. During the war they were busy in Congress concocting a plan of their own. Their Wade-Davis bill breathed quite another spirit. They could not take their eyes off the past. Under their plan each Southern state was to make a list of all its white men. The state could not be recognized until a *majority* of the people on that list took a new oath to support the Constitution. Then (since the Radicals believed that the old Southern states had committed suicide) there would have to be an election to call a convention to make a new constitution for each Southern state.

No one could even vote in that election, much less be a delegate to help make the new constitution, unless he took the "ironclad oath." This oath was not merely a promise of future loyalty but also an oath of past purity. You had to swear that you had never held office under the Confederacy or fought in the Confederate army. By the end of the war, most white men in the South could not honestly have taken such an oath.

Under the Radicals' scheme it would have been years before any Southern state could set up a majority government. It would have had to wait until the whole Civil War generation was dead. But that did not bother the Radical Republicans. They were quite willing to keep the Southern states under rule by Northern generals. The Radical Republicans said that they were in favor of liberty. But they were not willing to give it to hated white Southerners.

The Wade-Davis bill passed Congress on July 2, 1864. To become law it had to be signed by President Lincoln. What would Lincoln do?

Lincoln refused to sign. But he was shrewd. Instead of simply attacking the bill as a message of hate, he issued a new proclamation. He would not sign the Wade-Davis bill into law, he said, because he did not think it should be the only way a Southern state could get back into working order. Any "seceded" state that wanted to follow the Wade-Davis plan should feel free to do so.

But now, Lincoln said, there ought to be two possible paths. Any state ought to be allowed to choose between Lincoln's one-tenth plan and the Radicals' majority ironclad-oath plan. Lincoln was doing his best to avoid a head-on clash with Congress.

The assassination of Lincoln. Lincoln, cheerful and happy now that the long agony of war was over, called his Cabinet together on April 14, 1865, to discuss how to deal with Reconstruction. He urged them to use charity. He had already declared his generous spirit of "malice toward none." Now he begged them to put an end to the bitterness and hatred of war. His words helped calm the passions of four years of bloodshed. Still, it was hard to translate words of charity into acts of charity. Could President Lincoln have succeeded in that nearly impossible task?

We shall never know. For at this point there occurred one of those unexpected events that change the course of history. Now quite suddenly the South's hatred of Lincoln was focused in a single violent deed by a mad actor.

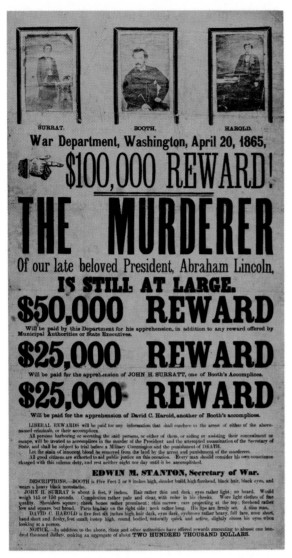

SURRAT.　　BOOTH.　　HAROLD.

War Department, Washington, April 20, 1865,

☞ $100,000 REWARD!

THE MURDERER

Of our late beloved President, Abraham Lincoln,

IS STILL AT LARGE.

$50,000 REWARD

Will be paid by this Department for his apprehension, in addition to any reward offered by Municipal Authorities or State Executives.

$25,000 REWARD

Will be paid for the apprehension of JOHN H. SURRATT, one of Booth's Accomplices.

$25,000 REWARD

Will be paid for the apprehension of David C. Harold, another of Booth's accomplices.

LIBERAL REWARDS will be paid for any information that shall conduce to the arrest of either of the above-named criminals, or their accomplices.

All persons harboring or secreting the said persons, or either of them, or aiding or assisting their concealment or escape, will be treated as accomplices in the murder of the President and the attempted assassination of the Secretary of State, and shall be subject to trial before a Military Commission and the punishment of DEATH.

Let the stain of innocent blood be removed from the land by the arrest and punishment of the murderers.

All good citizens are exhorted to aid public justice on this occasion. Every man should consider his own conscience charged with this solemn duty, and rest neither night nor day until it be accomplished.

EDWIN M. STANTON, Secretary of War.

DESCRIPTIONS.—BOOTH is Five Feet 7 or 8 inches high, slender build, high forehead, black hair, black eyes, and wears a heavy black moustache.

JOHN H. SURRAT is about 5 feet, 9 inches. Hair rather thin and dark; eyes rather light; no beard. Would weigh 145 or 150 pounds. Complexion rather pale and clear, with color in his cheeks. Wore light clothes of fine quality. Shoulders square; cheek bones rather prominent; chin narrow; ears projecting at the top; forehead rather low and square, but broad. Parts his hair on the right side; neck rather long. His lips are firmly set. A slim man.

DAVID C. HAROLD is five feet six inches high, hair dark, eyes dark, eyebrows rather heavy, full face, nose short, hand short and fleshy, feet small, instep high, round bodied, naturally quick and active, slightly closes his eyes when looking at a person.

NOTICE.—In addition to the above, State and other authorities have offered rewards amounting to almost one hundred thousand dollars, making an aggregate of about TWO HUNDRED THOUSAND DOLLARS.

Library of Congress

Four persons implicated in Booth's plot were hanged, and four more went to prison. John Surratt was arrested but not convicted. His mother, Mary E. Surratt, who harbored the gang, went to the gallows.

That very night President and Mrs. Lincoln went to Ford's Theater in Washington to attend a play. A far greater tragedy than had ever been performed on that stage was suddenly acted out in the President's box. It was one of the great tragedies of all American history. And it fulfilled an elaborate conspiracy which had been cooking for at least six months.

John Wilkes Booth, who planned it all, had a twisted feeling for drama. His father had made a great reputation on the London stage. Then he had come to settle in Maryland, where he had three sons. They all succeeded in the theater. Edwin, the oldest, became the most famous American actor of the age and was especially noted for portraying Shakespeare's tragic heroes. John Wilkes, though less successful, had also grown to be a well-known actor. A handsome, charming, and colossally conceited man, he was a passionate Confederate patriot. Having persuaded himself that slavery was the greatest thing that ever happened to humankind, he used his talents to enlist conspirators in a fantastic plot. His first idea was to kidnap Lincoln and so persuade the North to surrender or at least to give up its Southern prisoners.

When this plan failed, he organized a team to kill the President, Vice-President Johnson, and Secretary of State Seward in one fell swoop. It was less than a week after Appomattox. That night at the theater, Booth quietly entered the President's box, shot Lincoln, then leaped to the stage. "*Sic semper tyrannis!*" ("Thus ever to tyrants!") he screamed. Seward was seriously wounded, but the man assigned to kill Johnson lost his nerve.

Booth and his fellow conspirators were caught. He was killed, but legend said he still stalked the land. Now Lincoln, the martyr-President, was even larger in death than in life. He became a symbolic and heroic figure for all Americans and freedom-loving people everywhere.

SECTION 1 REVIEW

1. Identify or explain: Radical Republicans, Thaddeus Stevens, Charles Sumner, Proclamation of Amnesty and Reconstruction, "ironclad oath," John Wilkes Booth.

2. How did Lincoln and the Radical Republicans differ in their views on the legal status of the "seceded" states?

3. Describe Lincoln's plan for reunion.

4. What were the provisions of the Wade-Davis bill? How would this plan delay reunion?

5. **Drawing Conclusions.** Why was Lincoln's assassination "one of the greatest tragedies of all American history"?

American Antiquarian Society

Andrew Johnson, once a tailor, sews up the Union in this cartoon from about 1865.

2. Andrew Johnson and the Radicals

Andrew Johnson, the new President, was in some ways like Lincoln. Both had been born in the South to poor parents. Both had served in the state legislature and in Congress. With no schooling, Johnson began life as a poor tailor. His wife, Eliza, taught him to write. Though he came from Tennessee, he had stood against secession. As Democratic senator from Tennessee, he was the only Southern senator to support the Union after the Confederates fired on Fort Sumter.

Still, Johnson was no Lincoln. He lacked Lincoln's tact and warmth and wit. He did not know how to use a joke to make a serious point. Just as Lincoln was gentle, generous, and compromising, so Johnson was crude, stubborn, and argumentative. His weaknesses would not have been serious in an ordinary citizen. But in a President they were disastrous.

When Johnson became President in April 1865, Congress was not in session and was not due to meet again until December. Many Republicans distrusted Johnson because he had been a Democrat. In 1864 they had picked him for Vice-President on their "Union party" ticket, hoping that he would draw Democratic votes.

The Republicans wanted President Johnson to call Congress into special session to make new rules for the South, but he refused. Johnson declared his intention to follow the rules already announced by Lincoln. He alone—not the Congress!—would decide when the Southern states had satisfied Lincoln's requirements and so could govern themselves.

The Southern state conventions. Northerners were impatient to hear the South say "Uncle" and admit their defeat. The Southerners needed to be told what they had to do.

President Johnson now suggested that the Southern conventions gathered under his plan ought to repudiate (refuse to pay) their war debts, nullify their ordinances of secession, and adopt the Thirteenth Amendment freeing the slaves. These conditions were the least the North would accept as a signal that the South knew it was beaten.

But Johnson did not actually demand these terms. So South Carolina repealed rather than nullified its ordinance of secession. This implied that secession had been legal all along. Mississippi refused to adopt the Thirteenth Amendment. Instead, it announced that the slaves were free by the force of Northern arms. South Carolina and Mississippi refused to repudiate their wartime debts. Lacking firm direction from Andrew Johnson, those Southerners who were willing to give in and start life anew felt abandoned. Meanwhile the Southern fire-eaters—the extremists—were gaining strength.

The "Black Codes." Northerners were disturbed by the action of these Southern state conventions. They were even more shocked when the legislatures of the new state governments, at their first meetings, promptly adopted "Black Codes." These were based on old slave codes, Northern vagrancy laws, and laws passed in the British West Indies after emancipation was enacted there. These laws were supposed to provide for the new situation of the blacks now that they were no longer slaves. The laws strictly limited the freedom of the blacks. They could not vote. They were not allowed to

This store in Richmond, Virginia, was decorated to celebrate "Liberation Day," the anniversary of the Emancipation Proclamation.

marry whites. In some states they could be witnesses only in trials involving other blacks.

Many former slaves were using their newfound freedom to travel about and see something of the nation. This did not suit white planters who wanted to grow cotton again. So the Black Codes restricted the newly freed people to agricultural jobs or domestic service. And to keep them hard at work, harsh vagrancy laws were passed. Then they could not look for a new kind of job. In Mississippi, for example, if a black man was convicted of being a "vagrant"—a wandering person without a job—he could be fined $50. If he could not pay the fine, he could be hired out against his will to anybody who would pay the fine in return for his labor.

Northerners began to wonder if their young men had died in a Civil War merely to preserve slavery under a new name.

Confederates elected to office. On top of all this, the Southern states proceeded to elect important former Confederates to Congress. Instead of opposing this and warning the South of Northern reactions, President Johnson pardoned these men of the crime of rebellion after they had been elected to Congress.

By the time Congress met in December 1865, Andrew Johnson, a Democrat and a former slave owner, had been President for seven months. All the old Confederate states except Texas had formed new governments. In Washington, waiting to take their seats in Congress, were former leaders of the Confederacy. Among them were the Vice-President, six Cabinet members, 58 members of the Confederate Congress, and a number of high-ranking army officers. In no Southern state had steps been taken to give blacks the vote. Instead a new

311

Republican Thaddeus Stevens of Pennsylvania chaired the Joint Committee of Fifteen, which was set up by Congress to create a plan for re-admitting the Confederate states.

form for slavery—the Black Codes—had been instituted. To many Republicans it seemed that the South had learned nothing from the war.

To make matters worse, the Southern states would return to Congress with more members than when they had left the Union. For representation was now based on all the people in the South instead of counting the whites and only three-fifths of the slaves. If Southerners joined with Northern Democrats, the Republicans would lose control of Congress. The Republican programs for industrial growth, for railroads, and for protection of the blacks would soon be voted down.

When the congressmen from Johnson's "restored" states tried to take their seats in Congress, they were abruptly shut out. Moderate Republicans joined Radical Republicans to tell the Southerners that they were not really members of Congress at all—because the Southern states were not really states at all. Even if the Confederate

states had followed the President's rules, the Republicans said, the President had no power to make the rules. Only Congress (by which, of course, they meant the Republican majority) had that power.

Congress set up a Committee of Reconstruction made up of members of both houses—the Joint Committee of Fifteen—to draw up its own plan. It was led by the Radical avenger Thaddeus Stevens, but the Joint Committee was not yet an entirely Radical group. It began by trying to produce some bills that would take care of several matters of real concern to the North.

The Freedmen's Bureau. The first bill extended the life of the Freedmen's Bureau and enlarged its activities. The Bureau had been set up six weeks before Lincoln's death to help war refugees get Southern farms back in working order. It was also formed to help the recently freed blacks (who were called "freedmen," no matter what their sex) to start a new life.

The Freedmen's Bureau did a great deal of good work that nobody else could do. It handed out millions of free meals to black and white refugees. It built hospitals. It treated half a million cases of illness. And it brought thousands of white Southerners back onto farms where they could make a living again. The Bureau also helped freedmen to find jobs, and, in the new bill, it tried to protect them against the new slavery of the Black Codes.

The Bureau's most important work was in building schools and in providing teachers to give blacks the education they had been denied under slavery. The Bureau helped Howard University, Hampton Institute, Atlanta University, and Fisk University, which were set up for black students of college age. A quarter of a million black children were sent to school for the first time.

The moderate Republicans who drew up the new Freedmen's Bureau Bill thought President Johnson had told them he would sign it. But in February 1866 he vetoed it because it gave the Bureau the power, through military courts, to deal with any question concerning discrimination or infringement of civil rights. The local courts were open, Johnson said, and they were perfectly capable of dealing with such questions. Johnson even declared that Congress should pass no legislation at all before the Southern members had returned to their seats in Congress.

Students of many ages attended the primary
schools for freedmen in Richmond, Virginia.

Johnson's sabotage of their program angered
many Republican members of Congress. But they
did not yet have the votes to override his veto.
Instead they passed a resolution saying that no
congressman from a Southern state would be admitted until Congress had decided that the state was
entitled to representation.

The Civil Rights bill. Congress followed the
Freedmen's Bureau bill with a Civil Rights bill.
The idea behind this bill was to protect blacks in the
South. It allowed the federal government to
intervene in a state's affairs to protect the rights of all
United States citizens. Moderates urged Johnson to
accept this law, which had passed with large
majorities. But his background as an old-fashioned
states' rights Democrat kept him from doing so. He
vetoed the bill and insisted that the federal govern-

ment had no constitutional right to interfere within
a state to protect civil rights.

With this veto—and with his angry personal
attacks on the Radical leaders—Johnson drove away
the moderates and strengthened the Radicals. It is
difficult to imagine Lincoln in this same situation
failing to find a middle road.

Republican members of Congress who had tried
to work with the President now gave up. They
joined the Radicals and passed the Civil Rights Act
over the President's veto. Then they passed a new
Freedmen's Bureau bill, and when Johnson vetoed
it, they again overrode his veto.

The Fourteenth Amendment. Then Congress
drew up a new amendment to the Constitution—
the Fourteenth. It attempted to answer all Johnson's constitutional objections to the Civil Rights
Act. It defined United States citizenship and
forbade any state from depriving citizens of their
rights and privileges. It reduced the representation
of any state that did not allow its adult male citizens
to vote. It ruled that no state could choose to pay its
Confederate debt. And it said that no one who had
held state or federal office under the Union, and
then supported the Confederacy, could hold office
without being pardoned by a vote of two-thirds of
Congress.

Here at last were the North's clear terms to the
South. If they accepted this amendment, they could
enter the Union. No one knew what might happen
if they rejected it.

Tennessee promptly ratified the Fourteenth
Amendment and had its senators and representatives admitted to Congress. For Tennessee, Reconstruction was largely over. But the other states
followed Andrew Johnson's lead and refused to
adopt the amendment.

Now the Republicans and the President were
totally at odds. Johnson even decided to try to
form a new party of Democrats and moderate
Republicans to oppose the Republicans in the
autumn 1866 congressional elections. He became
the first President to travel the country and give
aggressive speeches in order to bring people to his
side. But since no President had ever done this
before, voters were shocked at such undignified,
"Un-Presidential" behavior. The result in the
elections was a landslide for the Republicans and an
increase in the power of the Radicals.

Neither Johnson (left) nor Stevens will give way on his plans for Reconstruction.

SECTION 2 REVIEW

1. Describe Southern action from April to December 1865 with respect to (a) writing new constitutions, (b) meeting Johnson's "suggestions" for reunion, (c) limiting the rights of black people, and (d) electing members of Congress.

2. What were the purposes of the Freedmen's Bureau and Civil Rights bills? What happened when Johnson vetoed the bills?

3. Why did Congress propose the Fourteenth Amendment? What were its provisions?

4. **Identifying Central Issues.** Cite examples of President Johnson's clashes with the Republican majority in Congress. Why were these clashes significant?

3. "Black Reconstruction"

When Congress met in December after the 1866 elections, it was ready to carry out its own Reconstruction of the South. Congressional Reconstruction would combine revenge, idealism, and political opportunism. Now the Joint Committee of Fifteen said the South was a "conquered province," and nobody would be allowed to forget it. Northern troops would be sent to occupy the South.

Military Reconstruction. Congress passed a law that divided the old Confederacy, excluding Tennessee, into five military districts. Each of the five districts would be ruled by a Northern general. The Radical Republicans in Congress laid down rules for building new Southern states. They wished to see the new states designed to keep political control in Republican hands. Some of the Radical demands, such as abolishing slavery and giving civil rights to blacks by ratifying the Fourteenth Amendment, were of course just and necessary. But others were not.

Worst of all was the Radical refusal to forgive or forget. They denied leading citizens of the Old South the right to vote or to hold any office in state or local government. Hungry for power, the Radicals wanted to rule the South through their own friends. Anxious to hold their Republican majority in Congress, they believed that freely elected Southern members might be against them. They said that they loved liberty, but really they were afraid of it. They were afraid to give political liberty to their old enemies.

Yet even now, Congress did not go as far as Thaddeus Stevens and the most ardent Radicals wanted. Stevens insisted that economic power was more important than political power. He wanted to seize rebel property and give every onetime slave 40 acres and a hut. But at this Congress balked. Unfortunately, few former slaves ever received any property after the war. Most remained dependent on white property owners for jobs and pay.

Although Johnson vetoed the vindictive act that turned the states into conquered provinces, it was passed over his veto. The South was stunned. Suddenly, two years after the war had ended, they were right back where they had started in April of 1865. Johnson had never warned them that this might happen. The Southerners' old fears of a slave rebellion seemed now to be coming true. They believed that they would be ruled by a mass of illiterate blacks.

The new military districts were quickly set up. They were to oversee elections for delegates to new constitutional conventions. The voters were to include all adult males regardless of color except those who were banned. And the banned persons included all the former leaders of the community— anybody who had once held any office in the state or the nation and who had then supported the Confederacy.

The impeachment of Andrew Johnson.

At the same time that the Radicals dealt with the troublesome South, they turned against the President. Under the Constitution he was supposed to enforce the laws of Congress. Though Johnson believed many of these laws were unwise, he still tried to enforce them. But now the Radicals were out to "get" Johnson. They could not bear the idea of a President who was not in their pocket. They passed laws taking away powers that the Constitution had given to the President. Even though the Constitution had made the President the Commander in Chief, the Radicals passed a Command of the Army Act taking away his power to command.

They were spoiling for a fight. They hoped to lure the President into violating even one law. Then they would have an excuse to oust him and seize his powers for themselves. Johnson watched his step. He was careful to obey the letter of the law and follow all the instructions of Congress.

Still, there was a limit to his patience. When the Radicals passed the Tenure of Office Act, which said the President could not dismiss any federal official without the consent of the Senate, that was too much. Secretary of War Stanton, whom Johnson had inherited in the Cabinet from Lincoln, had become Johnson's enemy and was actually plotting against him. So the President fired Stanton to test the Tenure of Office Act, which he believed to be against the Constitution. This was a small thing but enough to give the Radicals their chance. They took it.

The framers of the Constitution, being wise men, had provided a way to remove a criminal President. They had not made it too easy. The Constitution said (Article II, sec. 4) that the President could not be removed except "on impeachment for, and conviction of, treason, bribery, or other high crimes and misdemeanors." First the House of Representatives would have to "impeach" the President. This meant that a majority would have to vote to support a list of accusations. Then the President would actually be tried by the Senate. The Chief Justice of the United States would preside. But to remove a President a mere majority of the Senate was not enough. The framers showed their special wisdom when for such a drastic act they required the support of *two-thirds* of the members present.

When the Senate met on March 30, 1868, to try President Andrew Johnson on the impeachment brought by the House, the nation was in breathless suspense. Few really believed that Andrew Johnson had been guilty of "treason, bribery, or other high crimes and misdemeanors."

Johnson, like Lincoln, was a man of rock-ribbed honesty. No one could prove otherwise. Earnestly he had followed his oath "to preserve, protect, and

Johnson's impeachment trial drew large crowds to the gallery of the Senate. Visitors had to show tickets to be admitted.

defend the Constitution of the United States, against all enemies foreign and domestic." Perhaps he had sometimes lost his temper, or had shown bad judgment, or had used language that a President should not use. But these were not crimes. His only "crime" had been that he believed it his duty to obey the Constitution as he saw it.

On May 16, 1868, when the vote of the Senate was finally taken, 35 senators voted "guilty" and 19 voted "not guilty." This was a big majority against the President. But, luckily, it was *one* vote less than the two-thirds which the Founding Fathers required. The strength of the Constitution and the American system was upheld when even the President's bitter enemies accepted the result. Andrew Johnson remained President.

This was the first time American politicians came near to removing a President during his term of office. If they had succeeded, they would have opened the way for a new kind of dictatorship—a dictatorship of Congress.

The election of 1868. During the impeachment trial of Andrew Johnson, the Republican party met in Chicago and nominated General Ulysses S. Grant for President. Tough, silent, inscrutable Grant was the North's war hero. He knew nothing at all about politics, but many Northerners loved him.

General Grant's lack of concern with military neatness—a rumpled, unbuttoned uniform— was captured by photographer Mathew Brady.

To oppose Grant, the Democrats nominated the dignified and honest wartime governor of New York, Horatio Seymour. He had a reputation for being against both abolitionists and Southern extremists. Although he had opposed fighting to keep the South in the Union, he had raised troops to meet New York's quota in the army. He was a man of decency and moderation.

In the savage postwar campaign the Republicans "waved the bloody shirt" to remind people of how they had freed the slaves and saved the Union. Grant received 214 electoral votes to Seymour's 80, but Grant's popular majority was only 300,000 in a total of 5,700,000. Without 650,000 votes from blacks in the South, Grant would have lost the popular vote.

These figures made the Republicans more eager than ever to control the Southern governments and hold the black vote. With these political ambitions in mind they proposed the Fifteenth Amendment to the Constitution. It forbade the United States or any state to deny the right of voting to any citizen on account of "race, color, or previous condition of servitude." It became a part of the Constitution on March 30, 1870.

The new state constitutions. Meanwhile in the South new constitutions had been written and new governments set up. The constitutional conventions had white majorities in every state except South Carolina and Louisiana. Many of the black delegates were illiterate, but some were well educated and had experience in politics. Surprisingly, the blacks in the conventions showed no hatred toward their old masters. In many cases they even asked that the political rights of former Confederates be restored.

Naturally, the conventions did what Congress had commanded. They barred Confederates from state office and granted black suffrage. Beyond that, they provided a wide range of social welfare programs new to the Southern states. For the first time they called for free public schools. They made new provision for orphans and the handicapped.

The new state constitutions were bitterly criticized by white Southerners. It was difficult to get them approved, largely because blacks had played a role in framing them. But even after the Reconstruction governments were gone, these constitutions, largely unchanged, continued in use.

Black Reconstruction—myth and reality. The "myth" of Black, or Carpetbag, Reconstruction is that these governments were dominated by foolish blacks who were manipulated by a few evil whites, that the governments were corrupt and extravagant, and that the South suffered under them for a decade. The reality is quite different.

The governments that took office under the new constitutions were made up of what Southerners called "scalawags" (white Southerners), "carpetbaggers" (Northerners who had come South with no more belongings, it was said, than they could carry in a carpetbag), and blacks. The blacks dominated none of these governments. In South Carolina blacks controlled the lower house until 1874, but they never had a majority in the senate or held the post of governor.

It has been charged, with some truth, that these governments were extravagant. They had to rebuild the damaged South. They were also eager to repair and expand the railroads. They set up schools and offered other public services that had never been provided before. Of course, all this cost money, and as a result taxes rose. Naturally enough, planters complained. Many refused to pay the higher taxes. The result was that the tax receipts were less than expected. Southern states had to borrow, and their debts rose ever higher.

Another myth of Reconstruction is that these governments were always corrupt. Again, there is some truth to the charge. But in those days corruption was not peculiar to the South. The whole nation, including the governments of cities and states, was plagued by bribery, fraud, and outright theft. The stealing by Southern politicians was minor when compared with the activities of William M. Tweed, political boss of New York City, and his henchmen. Nor did corruption in the South cease when the Reconstruction governments were replaced by "conservative" governments. Good Confederates, it turned out, were just as apt to misuse the people's money as carpetbaggers, scalawags, and blacks.

For better or worse, in most of the old Confederacy the Reconstruction governments did not last long. In Tennessee, Virginia, and North Carolina they survived only until 1870. When Georgia moved out from Radical rule in 1871, the governor announced that the "long cheerless night of misrule" was over. That "long night" had lasted less than

Library of Congress

Four of the men shown in this 1870 poster with Frederick Douglass (center) served in Congress: Hiram Revels in the Senate and Benjamin Turner, Josiah T. Walls, and Joseph Rainey in the House. Also pictured are writer William Wells Brown and Bishop Richard Allen, founder of the African Methodist Episcopal Church.

two years. Texas went Democratic in 1873, Alabama and Arkansas in 1874, and Mississippi (which had an excellent Radical government) went Democratic in 1875. Only in Louisiana, Florida, and South Carolina did Republican rule last until 1877.

The South fights back. The Radical Republican governments were able to remain in power in the South only so long as blacks voted for them. Some Southern whites decided to make sure that blacks did *not* vote. The South was now at war with itself. Southerners said that they were only fighting against "outsiders." But they were really fighting against their fellow Southern blacks who wanted to be free and equal.

Before long, certain Old Confederates in the South had organized a secret army. Its purpose was to carry on the Civil War under another name. Although slavery was abolished by law, many Southerners still hoped to preserve as much as possible of their former way of life.

This secret army called itself the Ku Klux Klan—perhaps from the Greek word *kyklos,* meaning circle. Soon many branches, or circles, appeared all over the South. Klan members traveled the countryside flogging, maiming, and sometimes killing blacks who tried to vote or who in other ways presumed to be the white man's equal. The Klan uniform was a pointed hat with a white hood to conceal the face, and a long white or black robe.

Scores of other organizations joined in the bloody work—the Tennessee Pale Faces, the Louisiana

The viper Ku Klux Klan, about to devour the messenger dove sent by the goddess of Peace, destroys chances for reconciliation.

Knights of the White Camelia, the North Carolina White Brotherhood, the Mississippi Society of the White Rose, the Texas Knights of the Rising Sun, the Red Jackets, and the Knights of the Black Cross. In 1871 alone, in a single county in Florida, 163 blacks were murdered, and around New Orleans the murders came to over 300. These organizations kept the lists of their members secret to save them from punishment for their crimes. Thousands of blacks were driven from their homes, maimed, or tortured. Whole communities were terrorized by masked thugs on parade, by burning crosses, by kidnapping and tar-and-feathering.

Under pressure from Northern Radical Republicans, some Southern states passed laws against these outrages. On December 5, 1870, President U. S. Grant delivered a special message to Congress. "The free exercise of franchise," he warned, "has by violence and intimidation been denied to citizens of several of the States lately in rebellion." Congress then passed the Ku Klux Klan Acts to outlaw these organizations and to protect all citizens. But these laws had little effect. The state governments set up in the South by the Radical Republican Congress were replaced by old-fashioned Southern state governments. Confederate heroes were back in charge. Despite all the bloodshed of the Civil War, land and factories were still owned by white Southerners.

The work that first had been done by terrorists was now done "legally" by the state governments. Although the Southern states had approved the Civil War amendments (Thirteenth, Fourteenth, and Fifteenth) to the Constitution, although they had abolished slavery and their laws "guaranteed" the blacks their rights in the South, all these guarantees proved to be mere technicalities. Before long it was plain that slavery itself was just about the only thing the Civil War had abolished.

Thaddeus Stevens died in 1868, and soon enough his avenging spirit—along with his special concern for the rights of black people—was dead. Now more and more Northerners were anxious to "leave the South alone." In practice this meant putting the South back in the hands of white Southerners. And the South then remained divided into the same two nations—a "superior" race and an "inferior" race.

The South would not really become united with the rest of the United States until the South itself had become one. And this would take time.

1. Identify or explain: Joint Committee of Fifteen, Command of the Army Act, Tenure of Office Act, impeachment process, Grant, Seymour, scalawags, carpetbaggers, Ku Klux Klan, Civil War amendments.

2. What did the Southern states under military rule have to do to rejoin the Union?

3. What "illegal" act led to Johnson's impeachment? How did the trial turn out?

4. Describe the election of 1868.

5. **Recognizing Ideologies.** Why did some white Southerners fight back against Radical Republican rule in their states?

4. The North withdraws

In the election of 1872, Grant ran for a second term against Horace Greeley, the candidate of the Democrats and of a new Liberal Republican party. Greeley was the editor of the *New York Tribune*. He was best known for his advice, "Go West, young man, go West!" Right there in New York City, Greeley himself had found it possible to be a pioneer. He had organized the printers on his newspaper into a union. He had stood against slavery and championed women's rights.

But the nation was in no mood for reform. President Grant was easily reelected. Then his troubles began. Although Grant could pick the best lieutenants on the battlefield, in the world of politics he was as gullible as a child. He was an honest man himself, but he could not recognize crooks even when they appeared in his own Cabinet.

The Crédit Mobilier scandal. Soon after Grant's reelection, the first of a string of major government scandals broke. The transcontinental railroad had been authorized by Congress in 1862. The Union Pacific Railroad was to build westward from Omaha while the Central Pacific worked eastward from Sacramento. To build its part, the Union Pacific founded another company named the Crédit Mobilier of America. Using federal funds, the Union Pacific paid the Crédit Mobilier Company huge fees for work done—or not done. The Union Pacific officers, who were also the owners of Crédit Mobilier, made enormous sums from this swindle.

To persuade Congress not to look into the situation too closely, Vice-President Schuyler Colfax, Representative James A. Garfield (later to be President), and several other members of Congress were bribed with Crédit Mobilier stock. All this had taken place, in fact, before Grant became President. But Grant's administration was blackened by the exposures.

Other scandals. The same year of the Crédit Mobilier exposures, 1873, there occurred the notorious "salary grab." Greedy congressmen voted themselves a 50 percent increase in salary. On top of that they made it apply to the two preceding years. They also raised the pay of Supreme Court justices. The President, who signed the bill into law, had his salary doubled from $25,000 to $50,000. Under the Constitution a President's salary may not be increased during the term for which he has been elected. Grant avoided this provision by signing the bill the day before his second term began. The public outcry against the salary grab brought about its repeal—except for the increases for the President and the Supreme Court.

The following year brought the whiskey frauds. A large number of distillers conspired with Treasury officers to avoid the tax on whiskey. They cheated the government out of millions of dollars.

Scandal even reached into Grant's Cabinet. The Secretary of the Navy was shown to have received favors from men who stood to win government contracts. The Secretary of War, W. W. Belknap, was impeached by the House in 1876. He was accused of accepting bribes from a War Department agent charged with providing supplies to the Indians. He was saved from conviction in his trial by the Senate only because Grant was tricked into allowing him to resign.

The panic of 1873. Along with scandal and corruption, the country suffered a severe financial panic. After the war, the rapid growth of railroads and factories had strained the nation's financial resources. Two major fires—in Chicago in 1871 and in Boston the next year—cost insurance companies $273 million, and laid a colossal burden on these pillars of the financial community. The collapse of Jay Cooke's investment firm, which had put too much of its money in railroad construction, began the panic in 1873.

Soon a full-scale depression, one of the worst in the nation's history, was under way. It lasted for five years, shutting down mills and factories, bankrupting railroads, closing banks, bringing unemployment and starvation to thousands of workers, and spreading despair across the country.

The disputed election of 1876. Under this cloud of depression and scandal the Republicans were badly beaten in the congressional elections of 1874. A large majority of Democrats won seats in the House, giving them control for the first time since the Civil War. No longer could the Republicans win elections by "waving the bloody shirt" of war.

In their convention of 1876, the Republicans passed over their "Plumed Knight," the eloquent Speaker of the House James G. Blaine of Maine. He was suspected of granting illegal favors to a railroad, and in the climate of the times this made him an impossible choice. Instead, they picked a little-known Union general, Rutherford B. Hayes, who had built a solid reputation as a reform governor of Ohio. He was an honest man with moderate views on the Southern issue.

The Democrats named Governor Samuel J. Tilden of New York. He had an even more impressive reform record than Hayes, for it was his political courage and cleverness as a lawyer that had exposed the Tweed Ring. "Boss Tweed," a self-made, warmhearted man, had used Tammany Hall, a clique inside the Democratic party, to become the most powerful politician in New York City. He and his friends stole more than $45 million by having contractors on city jobs charge double what the work actually cost and then having the extra amount paid over to them. Tilden was helped to destroy the Tweed Ring by Thomas Nast, a clever German-born cartoonist. Nast stirred up outrage against Tweed by his drawings in *Harper's Weekly* showing Tweed as a vulture or a fat, rich thief. Nast kept up his attacks even after Tweed offered him $500,000 to stop.

The 1876 election campaign was one of the most bitter in United States history. The Democrats saw a good chance to gain the Presidency for the first time since 1860, and the Republicans fought to retain power. The finale was even more exciting because the electoral votes were so close. Late in the evening of election day it appeared that Tilden had been chosen. He had carried states with 184

Museum of the City of New York (detail)

The Boston Fire of 1872 was stopped near the State House, atop Beacon Hill, on the right of this Currier and Ives lithograph.

votes—only one less than a majority. Hayes had 165. Then came confusion. The three Southern states (South Carolina, Louisiana, and Florida) that were still ruled by Republicans sent in two sets of returns. The Republican set certified that Hayes electors had been chosen. The Democratic set said that a majority of the state votes had been cast for Tilden. Also Oregon had one disputed vote. In all, 20 electoral votes were in question.

There was no provision in the Constitution or any law of Congress for deciding which set of returns was legal. The Constitution simply says (Amendment XII), "The president of the Senate shall, in the presence of the Senate and the House of Representatives, open all the certificates, and the votes shall then be counted." The president of the Senate was a Republican. If he had the right to choose which set of votes he would *count,* as well as "open," he would naturally take the Hayes votes and declare him elected by a vote of 185 to 184. If, however, the disputed votes were thrown out, or even one of them counted for Tilden, he would be elected President.

The electoral commission. A few weeks before the date for inaugurating a new President, Congress created a commission of fifteen members—five representatives, five senators, and five members of the Supreme Court—to determine which of the disputed returns should be accepted. The commission included seven Republicans, seven Democrats, and one independent, Justice David Davis of Illinois. But then Davis was elected to the Senate, and a new justice had to be chosen. As there were only Republican members left on the Supreme Court to choose from, the commission was finally made up of eight Republicans and seven Democrats. It was no surprise, when the commission counted the

October 21, 1871

Boss Tweed's head is a moneybag in this Nast cartoon. Thomas Nast made Tweed's diamond tiepin famous.

disputed electoral votes, that it split along party lines and announced that Hayes had 185 to Tilden's 184.

The compromise of 1877. The crisis was not yet over. The nation seemed once again on the verge of civil war. Both houses of Congress had to approve the commission's report before a President could take office. Since the Democrats controlled the House of Representatives, they could prevent a Hayes victory. But a group of conservative Southern Democrats there, seeing the chance to use the crisis for their political advantage, had meanwhile been talking with spokesmen for Hayes. For the first time in many years, the politicians were trying the art of compromise.

The upshot was an agreement that these Southerners would break with their party and vote to accept the commission's report. In return, Hayes would grant four favors. (1) The last federal troops would leave the South. This would mean the end

of the Radical Republican state governments in Florida, Louisiana, and South Carolina. (2) At least one Southerner would get a post in the Cabinet. (3) Hayes would give conservative Southern Democrats control of part of the local patronage. (4) He would support generous spending for internal improvements in the South.

On March 2, only two days before Inauguration Day, the conservative Southern Democrats voted with the Republicans to approve the commission's report. The Republican Senate of course at once agreed, and the crisis at last was over.

In April 1877, after only a month in office, President Hayes withdrew the last of the federal troops from the South. In May he decorated the graves of the Confederate dead at Chattanooga. But "reconciliation" between the whites of the North and of the South—the end of Reconstruction—only occurred because the North no longer cared to protect the rights of black Southerners.

Tilden had actually won a large majority of the popular votes, and he knew that he had been cheated out of the nation's highest office. But he proved a good patriot and a good sport. He treated the whole matter as settled and retired from politics. When he died in 1886, he left his fortune to found the great New York Public Library.

SECTION 4 REVIEW

1. Identify or explain: Horace Greeley, Crédit Mobilier, "salary grab," W. W. Belknap, James G. Blaine, Rutherford B. Hayes, Samuel Tilden, Tweed Ring, Thomas Nast, electoral commission.

2. Describe the scandals of the Grant administration.

3. **Recognizing Cause and Effect.** What factors led to the panic of 1873? How did it and the scandals affect the 1874 elections?

5. The divided South

Peace and reunion had brought an end to slavery. But the roots of slavery ran deep. They reached into every nook and cranny of Southern life.

One of its roots was racism—the belief that one race was naturally better than another. This belief had helped keep slavery alive. At the same time slavery had kept racism alive. Under slavery, nearly all blacks in the South did lowly tasks. Therefore, it was easy for white people to believe that God had meant it that way.

Slavery could be abolished simply by changing laws. But it was much harder to abolish the belief that one race was better than another. Many generations of white Southerners had taught that to their children. After the war, it was still rooted in their minds and hearts.

And after the war it became clearer and clearer that the South was still split into two "nations." Much of the time these two "nations" lived at peace. Some of the time they lived in a nervous truce. Occasionally they were actually at war. Obviously the United States could not be truly united until the races ceased to be divided. And while this was a national problem, at first it belonged largely to the South because most blacks lived there.

Black voting. When Hayes withdrew the federal troops from South Carolina and Louisiana, the last of the Reconstruction governments finally collapsed. (Florida's had already fallen.) This did not mean that throughout the South blacks no longer voted or held office, or that segregation ("Jim Crow") laws suddenly appeared. It took time for the white South to come to a fixed conclusion about the place of blacks in Southern society.

Most white Southerners assumed that blacks were inferior. At the same time, many Old Confederates believed that they had a responsibility to the blacks. They believed that the "superior" white and the "inferior" black could work together to the advantage of both. So there were attempts by conservatives to bring blacks into the Democratic party. Blacks continued to hold political office in both state and nation. There were black members in every Congress but one from 1877 to 1900.

The rise of "Jim Crow" laws. Segregation was practiced in the new public schools of every Southern state except Mississippi and South Carolina from the beginning. But blacks and whites shared trains, hotels, and other public places. Then more and more in the 1880s informal segregation began to appear. At last, with the drive to remove blacks as a political force during the Populist period (p. 542), there also came new segregation laws.

The expression "Jim Crow" to describe the forced segregation of the races originated in a popular old minstrel song. Some white Southerners were shocked by the Jim Crow laws. One sensible South Carolina editor showed how absurd the whole idea was:

> If there must be Jim Crow cars on the railroads, there should be Jim Crow cars on the street railroads, also on passenger boats. . . . If there are to be Jim Crow cars, moreover, there should be Jim Crow waiting saloons at all stations, and Jim Crow eating houses. . . . There should be Jim Crow sections of the jury box, and a separate Jim Crow dock and witness stand in every court—and a separate Bible for every colored witness to kiss.

The Supreme Court approves "Jim Crow." What this editor ridiculed soon came to pass. And when "Jim Crow" became a reality, surprisingly few in the North or in the federal government spoke out against it. The Supreme Court, in 1896, in the case of *Plessy* v. *Ferguson* actually approved segregated facilities that were "separate but equal." The majority even argued that if blacks saw this as "a badge of inferiority" it was "solely because the colored race chooses to put that construction upon it." Justice John Marshall Harlan, a Kentuckian, spoke out in a bold dissent. He "regretted that this high tribunal . . . has reached the conclusion that it is competent for a state to regulate the enjoyment by citizens of their rights solely upon the basis of race."

The problem, of course, was that there really could never be such a thing as "separate but equal" facilities for the two races. When any race was kept apart from another, it was deprived of its equality— which meant its right to be treated like all other citizens. And the slogan became an excuse for providing inferior schools and washrooms and everything else for the race regarded as inferior.

Few blacks received any land after they were freed. Most had no choice but to go to work for whites. Since few whites had any cash after the war—or wanted to spend it if they had any—the system known as sharecropping soon appeared. A black or white family would be given a section of land to cultivate and then allowed to keep a share of whatever they grew while they paid the rest as rent. Ideally, this would have meant that in a good year the sharecropper would have received a share of the extra profits.

In fact, after the Civil War there were few good years. The price of cotton stayed low until 1900. Sharecroppers earned barely enough to stay alive. In bad years they could not even buy groceries. So to feed their families they borrowed from their landlord or from the local storekeeper. The landlord and the storekeeper, in turn, often had to borrow at high rates of interest. To repay their own debts, they made the sharecropper stop growing food and instead plant a crop that could be sold for cash. In practice this meant cotton. As a result landowner, storekeeper, and sharecropper were all kept in bondage to that piece of land and to that single crop.

The Reconstruction scorecard. Radical Reconstruction had increased white Southerners' fears of blacks. It had also helped to make the Two-Nation South into a One-Party South. When the Old Confederates once again took charge of the Southern states, they had no love for the Republican party. That was the party of Yankees, the party that had made war on the South and had then ruled the South with an army. By controlling the state governments, the Confederate heroes gave new strength to their old Democratic party.

The Radical Republicans had seen the evil of slavery. But they had not seen that the roots of slavery could not be pulled up in a year or two—nor perhaps even in a generation. Still, they had attempted to deal with the question of the place of blacks in the Southern states. The new, more liberal constitutions that Radical Reconstruction brought to the Southern states actually benefited the poor of both races. They laid the foundation of free public education for whites as well as blacks. Reconstruction gave the blacks a new role in political life—and valuable political experience. It was under Reconstruction that the Fourteenth and Fifteenth amendments were passed. And these would become the bulwark of equal rights.

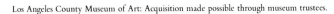

SECTION 5 REVIEW

1. What is racism? How did it continue to split the South into two "nations"?

2. Why was the *Plessy* v. *Ferguson* case important?

3. **Recognizing Cause and Effect.** What were *Jim Crow* laws? What effect did they have on Reconstruction-era attempts to protect blacks' rights?

"The Cotton Pickers," painted in oil by Winslow Homer in 1876, shows an endless field ready for harvesting. Homer tried to capture the true look of outdoor light.

FOCUSING ON IDEAS

1. Explain the term "Radical Reconstruction." How did Radical Reconstruction both harm and help Southerners?

2. How were the Reconstruction policies of Congress motivated by a desire for vengeance? How were they motivated by concerns for the rights and welfare of black Southerners? Which policies were motivated by political party ambitions?

3. What elements of Military Reconstruction resembled Lincoln's plan for reconstruction and the Wade-Davis Bill?

TAKING A CRITICAL LOOK

1. **Drawing Conclusions.** Was it reasonable for northern leaders to try to exclude the Old Confederate leaders from leadership positions during Reconstruction? Why? How might the exclusion of these formers leaders have affected the South?

2. **Making Comparisons.** How was the treatment of black Southerners in 1890 similar to and different from their treatment in 1850?

YOUR REGION IN HISTORY

1. **Geography.** If you live in a former Confederate state, use an outline map to locate and identify the military district to which your state was assigned.

2. **Culture.** If you live in a former Confederate state, make a time line of important events in Reconstruction history (1865–1877) in your state.

3. **Economics.** How did the panic of 1873 affect businesses in your region? What industries or businesses were especially hard-hit by the depression from 1873 to 1877? What industries or businesses, if any, prospered during these years? Check with your local, regional, or state's Chamber of Commerce.

HISTORICAL FACTS AND FIGURES

Distinguishing False from Accurate Images. Northerners proudly claimed that Reconstruction succeeded in incorporating blacks into the United States government. Decide whether or not this claim is justified. Write a paragraph explaining your decision, using data from the graph below and information in this chapter.

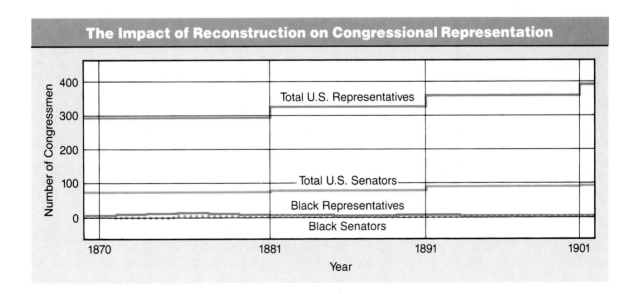

The Impact of Reconstruction on Congressional Representation

The passing of the frontier

By the time of the Civil War, more than two centuries after the first colonist arrived in New England, half the nation's land was still nearly empty. The frontier—a ragged line of settlements from the East—ran through part of Minnesota, along the border of Iowa, Missouri, and Arkansas and then swung westward into Texas. Reaching in from the West Coast there was also a thin line of settlement in California, Oregon, and Washington. Between these two frontiers there were only a few islands of settlers, such as the Mormons in Utah, the miners in Colorado, and the Mexican Americans in New Mexico. Even in the "settled" areas on the edge of the open land, it was often a long way between neighbors.

In that vast open space between the two frontiers there lay an empire. A land as large as all the rest of the occupied United States. A half-known land as large as all of western Europe. It had often been passed through by trappers hunting furs, miners seeking gold, and settlers hurrying on to California, Washington, and Oregon. But the highest mountains were still unclimbed, the swiftest rivers still unmapped.

During and after the Civil War, the American people pushed into the unknown. They settled the land even before it was discovered by the explorers, geographers, painters, and naturalists. And the fact of settlement before discovery allowed Americans to dream big dreams. It fostered an optimistic, competitive, booster spirit. It produced a new kind of American. The Go-Getter out there helped find and develop the riches of the new American empire. New American ways of life were invented by a wide assortment of Go-Getters—cattle ranchers and cowboys, miners, farmers and their families.

1. Indian wars and resettlement

Today the Old West is a place of romance—the scene for an exciting book, or movie, or TV program. But for a long time the West between California and the Missouri River was a place to avoid. Until just before the Civil War the area between the line of settlement in the East and the Rocky Mountains was marked on maps as the "Great American Desert." In 1856 the *North American Review* described the area of plains and

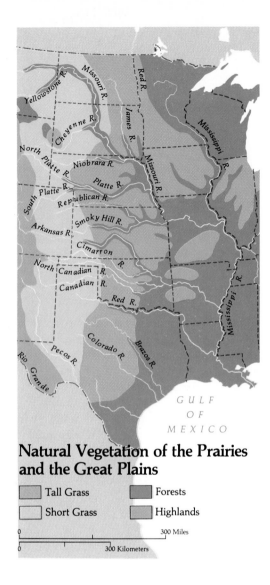

Natural Vegetation of the Prairies and the Great Plains

- Tall Grass
- Short Grass
- Forests
- Highlands

300 Miles

300 Kilometers

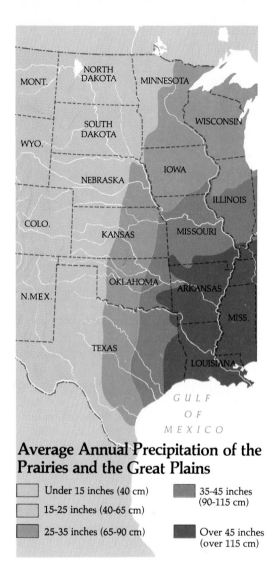

Average Annual Precipitation of the Prairies and the Great Plains

- Under 15 inches (40 cm)
- 15-25 inches (40-65 cm)
- 25-35 inches (65-90 cm)
- 35-45 inches (90-115 cm)
- Over 45 inches (over 115 cm)

mountains between California and Iowa as "a country destined to remain forever an uninhabited waste." Yet this area included some of the richest grasslands in the world. And it was not deserted. Thousands of Indians made their living off the land which was still the home of millions of buffalo.

In time, cattle ranchers, cowboys, miners, farm families, soldiers, and railroad construction crews would all begin to move into or through the Great Plains and the mountains. Then they would come face to face again with the land's first occupants—the Indians.

The Indians of the Great Plains. Spread over the whole inland empire between the frontiers were some 225,000 American Indians. Of these, perhaps half were the fierce occupants of the Great Plains. Seldom have people adapted more perfectly to their environment. The buffalo was the basis of the Indians' way of life. This was the American name for a shaggy kind of ox technically called the bison, which had also once roamed Europe but was no longer common there. It gave them food, clothing, shelter, and fuel.

When Europeans first reached the Great Plains, they had only single-shot long rifles. They were no match for the Plains Indians. Wonderfully at home on horseback, an Indian warrior could hold on by his heel and use the horse's body as a shield while he fired a barrage of arrows under his horse's neck.

Jules Tavernier, a French immigrant who was for many years an illustrator for *Harper's Weekly*, painted "Indian Camp at Dawn" while on a cross-country trip in the 1870s.

Carrying a short bow, he could shoot twenty arrows while galloping a distance equal to three football fields. His shield of buffalo hide was so hard that a bullet could pass through only if it hit straight on.

Not until Samuel Colt invented the six-shooter—a revolver designed to hold six bullets at a single loading—did the white invader have a weapon equal to the Indians'. Even then, according to General William Tecumseh Sherman, 3000 United States soldiers could be halted by 50 Indians.

The old Indian policy.
Beginning in the 1820s the government's policy was to push the eastern Indians westward across the Mississippi River. Let the Indians live on the "Great American Desert"! That would be their "one big reservation." If the land was not good enough for white settlers—or if white settlers did not have the skills to make their living there—leave it to the Indians!

In the 1850s (although they never planned it that way) white men, women, and children began to move into these areas once reserved for Indians. Some settled in Kansas and Nebraska, others moved on to Oregon, and still others went from place to place searching for gold. At first, the army in the West tried only to keep the trails open so that settlers, traders, trappers, and miners could travel across the land. Forts were built across the plains and treaties arranged with Indian tribes. Still the Indians, desperate to stop the invasion of their lands, organized deadly raids on the settlers and their wagon trains.

At the same time, numerous tribes who had lived for centuries on the edge of the plains were persuaded to give up their lands and move west. This stirred discontent among the tribes already there. Times were ripe for war.

Indian wars and a new policy.
Although there were some good government agents who wanted to help the Indians, many were inept and some were corrupt. Supplies promised the Indians were often slow to reach them. The Sioux went on the warpath in 1862 because they had not received the regular payments they expected and so were unable to buy food.

The many conflicts of the following years led the government to rethink its Indian policy. In 1865, when there were 25,000 soldiers armed against the Indians, a congressional investigation concluded that a new approach must be found. A Peace Commission sent out west held two large meetings and then signed treaties with the Indians in 1867 and 1868. There the Indians were told that they would be gathered together in large areas that would belong to them and where they were not to be bothered by the whites. Although the Indians did not realize it at the time, these treaties really announced the beginning of the end of the old Indian way of life.

New battles and smaller reservations.
The Indians naturally resisted. So for twenty years after the Civil War the American West was plagued by a quite different kind of war. In one sense it was

another kind of civil war—between two groups of Americans both trying to make their living off the North American continent, the earliest settlers against the latest settlers.

White Americans did not understand what the Indians had achieved. With their spears and bows and arrows and different manner of living, they had mastered the ways of the American wilderness. The Indians had learned to get along with nature by following in the footsteps of their forefathers. Most of them lived a wandering way of life because they needed large areas to support even a few people. Against them were the latecomers who had brought with them all the modern equipment of European civilization. In this unequal war it was not hard to predict who would win in the long run.

Before the issue was decided, thousands died and more thousands lived in fear while blood and tears were shed on both sides. The wild American West had become a battlefield. In 1864 a militia force under Colonel John M. Chivington slaughtered about 450 Cheyenne and Arapaho men, women, and children who had thought they were under the protection of the United States. Only a few years later, soldiers under Captain W. J. Fetterman were ambushed by a group of Sioux, and all 92 troopers were killed. It was all-out war.

These battles and many others led to a new policy of even smaller "reservations." Here the Indians were too confined and the lands too unfamiliar for them to carry on their hunting and foraging way of life. No longer could they roam the plains in pursuit of the buffalo or other wild game. Deprived of their ancient ways of making a living, the Indians were forced to look to the United States government. In 1871 the government even ceased dealing with the tribes as independent nations. No more treaties would be made. Now they were considered wards of the state, and they would be dealt with by acts of Congress.

Strangely, the same Congress that was trying to bring equality and integration to the blacks of the South approved the destruction of the Indians. General William T. Sherman, who had done much to free the slaves, now set about either killing the Indians or making them "beg for mercy."

The defeat of the Indians. The next years were marked by many battles until, in 1874, peace finally seemed to have arrived. Then unexpectedly in the Black Hills (an area which had been given to the Indians "forever") gold was discovered. Hordes of settlers rushed in from East and West. Once again the Indians were crowded out. The fearless Sioux under the leadership of Chief Crazy Horse and Chief Sitting Bull made another desperate effort to hold back the flood. This battle in June 1876 came to be called "Custer's Last Stand," because when General George A. Custer got himself trapped near the Little Big Horn River in Montana he and his 264 troopers from the 7th Cavalry were killed to the last man. But it might more accurately have been called the Sioux's Last Stand, for in other battles Crazy Horse was captured, Sitting Bull fled to Canada, and the desolate Sioux were left conquered and leaderless.

The reservation policy produced a saga of Indian courage in the face of overwhelming odds and certain defeat. As the Nez Percés in Oregon were about to go to a new reservation, some whites stole their horses. This provoked a group of young braves to go on the warpath. Chief Joseph, who had wished all along to avoid a fight, now tried to lead his people to safety in Canada.

There followed one of the great stories of the West. Chief Joseph led his tribe, defended only by

The sadness of a lost cause creases Chief Joseph's face in this old photograph.

Indian Reservations, 1875 and 1890

Little Big Horn 1876
Fetterman Massacre 1866
Sioux War 1862
Wounded Knee 1890
Chivington Massacre 1864

Reservations in 1875

Reservations in 1890

their 300 warriors against a well-equipped United States army, on a spectacular 1300-mile trek. On their way across Oregon, Idaho, and Montana the warriors fought a series of amazing battles, regularly defeating much larger army forces. Finally, after several months of marching and fighting, Chief Joseph and his depleted tribe reached a point only 30 miles from the Canadian border. Thinking they were already safe, they paused to rest. Then suddenly a United States army group galloped in from an unexpected direction. After suffering a five-day siege, it was plain to Chief Joseph and his courageous people that they had to surrender. Chief Joseph said,

> I am tired of fighting. Our chiefs are killed. Looking-Glass is dead. Too-hul-hut-sote is dead. The old men are all dead. It is the young men now who say "yes" or "no." He who led the young men is dead. It is cold and we have no blankets. The little children are freezing to death. My people, some of them, have run away to the hills and have no blankets, no food. No one knows where they are, perhaps freezing to death. I want to have time to look for my children and see how many of them I can find. Maybe I can find them among the dead. Hear me, my chiefs. My heart is sick and sad. From where the sun now stands I will fight no more, forever.

The final act in the tragedy of the Indian wars came on December 29, 1890, at Wounded Knee in South Dakota. There, shortly after the killing of their famous leader Chief Sitting Bull, a band of men, women, and children was arrested by the 7th Cavalry. Somehow a fight broke out. The soldiers opened fire upon the unarmed Indians and left more than 200 dead.

The buffalo slaughter. Whether the Plains Indians won or lost battles did not, in the long run, matter. They were doomed to defeat, not only by the guns of the army and the ever-increasing number of settlers who occupied their land, but most of all by the destruction of their food supply—the buffalo.

At the close of the Civil War the buffalo roaming the Great Plains numbered about 15 million. Sometimes a single herd would spread over 50 miles. The first force to endanger these clumsy, slow-moving beasts was the railroad. It split the herd into a northern and a southern group and at the same time brought hunters into their midst. The most famous of the buffalo hunters was William Cody, better known as "Buffalo Bill." At first he and the other hunters shot the buffalo for meat to feed the large crews of railroad workers. Later, city slickers who went west for adventure and for sport shot thousands from the safety of railroad cars. In 1871 a commercial method was found of treating the skins to make them usable as robes. The slaughter was on. Hunters roamed the range killing every buffalo in sight. The kill finally reached three million a year. The southern herd was gone by 1878, and the northern herd had disappeared by 1884. In 1889 all that was left of the millions of these noble animals was about one thousand.

With the animal that supplied their food, clothing, fuel, and shelter gone, the Plains Indians had to give up. These people who knew the plants and animals of the West better than any who came after them were condemned to reservations. Though wonderfully skillful and knowledgeable at wresting their living from the land, they now depended on the charity of the invaders.

Indian policy reform. In the West most settlers saw the Indians only as a menace. But many Americans, especially those raised back east away from the battles, were troubled by the sad plight of the Indians and wondered what they could do to help. Just as 30 years earlier Harriet Beecher Stowe had stirred the nation's conscience for the slave in her book *Uncle Tom's Cabin* (1852), now another eloquent woman awakened white Americans to the sufferings of the Native Americans. Helen Hunt Jackson, who came from Massachusetts before she moved to Colorado Springs, wrote *A Century of Dishonor* (1881) and *Ramona* (1884) to dramatize

Indians hunt buffalo on horseback in this 1832 painting of "The Buffalo Chase, Mouth of the Yellowstone" by George Catlin.

the crimes against the Indians. Another voice for decency was Sarah Winnemucca, daughter of a Paiute Indian chief. She had shown wonderful courage as "guide, messenger, and interpreter" to General O. O. Howard in the Bannock War of 1878. Now she pled the Indian cause in her popular *Life among the Paiutes, Their Wrongs and Claims* (1883), and drew large crowds to her lectures around the country.

These two women—and other champions of the underdog—demanded that the nation adopt a more humane policy toward the Indians. The Dawes Act of 1887 seemed to have this purpose. In an attempt to "Americanize" the Indians it divided up the reservation land and assigned each family a 160-acre farm. After 25 years these Indians were to receive title to this land and also become United States citizens. The act aimed to break up the tribes and make the Indians behave like all other Americans. Its very purpose was to destroy the Indians' culture. It was not surprising that somehow or other the best reservation lands ended up in the hands of whites. Between 1887 and 1934 the unlucky Indians lost more than half of all their lands.

Not until 1934 and the "Indian New Deal" did the United States government policy change. An attempt was made to rebuild the tribes and their tribal culture. The Native American population then grew rapidly. By 1980 the Indians numbered over 1.3 million—probably more than when Columbus came to America.

SECTION 1 REVIEW

1. Identify or explain: W. T. Sherman, George A. Custer, Samuel Colt, Crazy Horse, Sitting Bull, Chief Joseph, William Cody, Helen Hunt Jackson, Sarah Winnemucca, Dawes Act.

2. Locate: the Great Plains, Little Big Horn River.

3. Where were the two western frontiers in 1860?

4. What were the advantages of the Plains Indians as fighters?

5. What was the government's Indian policy in the 1820s? Around 1870? After 1887?

6. **Identifying Central Issues.** Why and how were the buffalo slaughtered? How did their disappearance affect the Plains Indians?

---

2. Seeking gold and silver

All the problems of Indian-white relations were complicated by the sudden appearance in the West of thousands of miners seeking their fortune from gold or silver. In much of the West the impatient, foot-loose miner arrived before the cattle rancher or the pioneer farmer.

The mining frontier was one of the most action-packed in our history. The very names of mining towns stir visions of adventure and violence: Tombstone, Deadwood (with Wild Bill Hickok and Calamity Jane), Last Chance Gulch, and Virginia City.

Today the West is covered with the sad remnants of once-booming communities. We call them ghost towns. First came the news that gold had been found. Then came the rush to the spot and the quick appearance of an entire city. Next, with the gradual petering out of the gold the people departed. They left behind a ghost town or one with only a few occupants. This cycle was often repeated.

From 1858 until about 1880 mining created new communities—all the way from the Sierra Nevada to the Rockies and into the Black Hills of South Dakota. It was mining that attracted the people who created the territories of Colorado (1861), Arizona (1863), Idaho (1863), Montana (1864), and Wyoming (1868). Mining focused the nation's attention—its hopes and its imagination—on the West.

"Pikes Peak or Bust." In 1858, news began to reach the East that gold had been found near what is now Denver. With careless enthusiasm, many workers threw down their tools, painted "Pikes Peak or Bust" on the sides of their wagons (though Pikes Peak was 80 miles south of the find), and headed west. General Sherman reported from Kansas that 25,000 people had left to go to the new mine fields even before there was any reliable news that there really was gold in Colorado. Many would return "Busted." But a few would make their fortune, though not always from gold.

William Larimer, born and raised in Pennsylvania, had tried his hand at various businesses before he heard that gold had been found at Cherry Creek, Colorado. Without hesitating he set out for the West. Larimer did not intend to make his own fortune by digging or panning for gold. He hoped

An unknown artist painted this watercolor about 1858 of Pundt & Koenig's general store in Omaha City, Nebraska. Two wagons heading west have stopped for provisions as the would-be prospectors stock up for the next leg of their journey across the Great Plains.

instead to get rich by laying out a city near the mine fields. Then he would be prepared to sell the land—or anything else—to the thousands who swarmed in from the East. He found the perfect site and claimed it. In February 1859 he was able to write, "I am Denver City."

Very few got rich in the Cherry Creek gold fields, for the gold soon ran out. At first the small miner might make good money—$50 or even a $100 a day—in those early diggings. There were many later gold discoveries in Colorado, but generally the Colorado gold was hard to get at. In the long run, there, as in most other mine sites in the West, only a

big company with large capital and elaborate machinery could extract the gold with much profit.

Virginia City. Rumors that there was gold around Virginia City in what is now Nevada began to be heard in 1859 during the "Pikes Peak" gold rush. Miners whose dreams had not come true in Colorado headed for Nevada. Arriving there, they were disappointed to find that the gold was hard to extract because it was mixed with "blue stuff." When someone took the trouble to analyze the blue stuff, each ton was found to contain $1595 in gold—and $4791 in silver! Now, to rival the

The Oakland Museum. Gift of Concours d'Antiques, Art Guild of the Oakland Museum Association

"Mountain Jack and a Wandering Miner" (top), painted in oil by E. Hall Martin in 1850, evokes the majestic grandeur of the Rocky Mountains.   The photograph below of Helena, Montana, shows that the day-to-day reality in a mining town was considerably less glamorous.

Montana Historical Society

Cherry Creek gold rush, Virginia City sprouted and prospered with its silver rush. Soon, where nothing had stood, according to Mark Twain, "Money was as plenty as dust." Newly rich citizens built showy houses where everything seemed to be silver plated. One man even had silver shoes made for his horses.

This rich silver find was called the Comstock Lode. Henry Comstock had not himself made the great discovery, but somehow he managed to claim the property. When he sold the mines, in bits and pieces, he received a total of only $11,000.

To extract great wealth from the mines required the energy and organizing ability that Comstock lacked. The person who had those talents, and was lucky enough to be on the spot, was John W. Mackay. He was a poor Irish boy whose parents had brought him to this country when he was nine. Eleven years later, in 1851, he decided to seek his fortune in the California gold fields. Mackay worked in various gold and silver fields, making little money but learning a lot about mining. He used his earnings to buy an old mine on the Comstock Lode. By ingenuity and new equipment he extracted more silver than anyone had thought possible. With these profits he bought other mines that were thought to be worked out. In 1873, using these new methods, he began to mine the amazing "Big Bonanza" from which he would take more than $100 million.

California State Library

Miners working the California rivers for gold hoped to get rich, but most were lucky if they found a little gold dust.

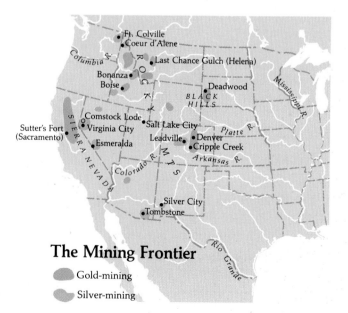

The Mining Frontier

 Gold-mining

 Silver-mining

Mackay made his millions from mines that others had given up. He was willing to invest more capital and dig deeper than others. Not many people were as lucky—or as enterprising—as John W. Mackay. Still, in the years after the Civil War thousands of impatient, ambitious, hopeful Americans on the move rushed out to new mines. Mackay's example lured them on. Behind them they left Last Chance Gulch and its Crab City (later Helena, Montana), Boise, Silver City, Centerville, Leadville, and finally, as the dead end of the miner's frontier, Deadwood, South Dakota.

335

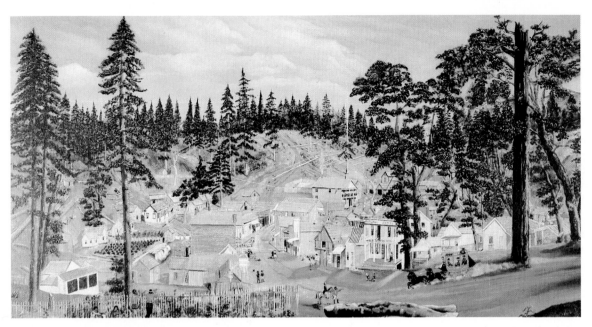

"One Sunday in July, Forbestown, California" was painted by an amateur artist about 1850.

Law in mining fields and towns. The mining towns were wild, but they were not without law. For the miners, like all the people who were on the front edge of America, made their own laws.

We have seen how the people on the *Mayflower* formed a community. And in the same way each wave of men and women who moved west into places that had no organized government had to make their own rules. In the mine fields and mining towns laws had to be made about the size, staking, and defense of mining claims. Where there was still no government, the first comers had to decide what was a crime and how it was to be punished.

These laws seemed so natural, following the traditions and customs of the mines, that many miners thought they actually did not have any law. When Congress passed its first major Mining Act in 1866, it enacted the rules that had been adopted by the miners themselves.

The significance of the mining frontier. The mining frontier, the first of the last frontiers, opened up the country from the Rocky Mountains to the Sierra Nevada. It taught Americans something of the natural wealth of this continental heartland. The finding and the getting of copper, iron ore, lead, zinc, coal, molybdenum, uranium, and oil were all still to come. The mines and the miners out there created new needs for railways. And by quickening the invasions of Indian lands they brought the Indian problem to a head. In some areas, especially in Idaho and Montana, the mining frontier opened up a new farming frontier because, when the gold ran out, miners remained to work the land. And, of course, mining towns demanded meat and so stimulated the cattle business.

Between 1860 and 1900 the mining frontier produced more than $2 billion in gold and silver. Much of this went into the pockets of people who had never before seen so much money. The quick-paced life of the mining West, so full of surprises, left a wonderful legacy of folklore—and the stories of Mark Twain and Bret Harte.

SECTION 2 REVIEW

1. Identify: William Larimer, Henry Comstock.

2. Locate: Pikes Peak, Black Hills, Cherry Creek, Virginia City, Last Chance Gulch, Deadwood.

3. How was the mining frontier significant?

4. **Making Comparisons.** How did later mining ventures differ from the earlier ones?

3. The cattle kingdom

While the miners were opening up the mountains and the land of the Great Basin between the Rockies and the Sierra Nevada, cattle ranchers were opening up the Great Plains. At the same time, the Indians were forced onto smaller and ever less desirable reservations and the buffalo were killed off.

The cattle frontier and the mining frontier mainly attracted men. Cowboys driving herds or riding the range, miners chasing from one spot to another after gold, soldiers pursuing Indians—all these were men on the move who had not the time or the opportunity to settle down to family life. A few hardy women did live on the lonely ranches, in the mining towns, or at the army forts, but they were far outnumbered by the migratory men.

Only as families began to settle the plains and cultivate farms did this situation change. The farming West, too, was a difficult and often frightening place for man, woman, and child. We can still share their troubles and their delights in the great novel *Giants in the Earth* by the Norwegian immigrant Ole Rölvaag, who helped build the Scandinavian community as a professor at St. Olaf College in Minnesota. Rölvaag described a new settler viewing the treeless plains where she must make her home: "How will human beings be able to endure this place, she thought. Why, there isn't even a thing that one can *hide behind.*"

To survive and build a family on the Great Plains, a woman had to be many things. She had to be a soldier holding off Indians, a farmer and a rancher, a parent and a teacher. Without women's courage and their efforts the vast open West might never have grown its permanent settlements. It is not surprising, then, that in 1869 Wyoming Territory became the first place in the nation to give women the vote and that western states were among the first to elect women governors.

Cattle and cowboys. About the time of the Civil War, the western cattle trade became big business. The men who made money from it were as different as possible from the European peasant who kept his few cattle at night in the room where he slept. The peasant could keep only a few because his house was small and he had to feed his animals by hand in winter.

By the 1890s, when this picture of women branding was taken on the Fritz Becker ranch in southeast Colorado, cattle ranching had become a family enterprise.

Colorado Historical Society

337

The western cattleman numbered his stock by the thousands. He did not have to give them a roof, for western cattle were tough enough to look after themselves on the range. And on the great western plains there grew "buffalo grass" which survived drought and provided free food right on the ground throughout the winter.

Raising cattle on the northern plains.

Western cattlemen were bold and adventurous, willing to take big risks in a wild country. One of the first and most energetic of these Go-Getters on horseback was John Wesley Iliff. Though his parents offered to set him up on a farm in Ohio, Iliff wanted to go west to seek his fortune. He did not find gold in the Colorado mountain streams. But he did find it in the cattle that came there with Americans pushing westward.

Iliff bought oxen from the people seeking gold who wanted to lighten their load before they headed up into the mountains. In Colorado he fed these cattle free on the open range that belonged to nobody and to everybody. He also bred more cattle. When his animals were fattened, Iliff sold them to butchers in the mining camps, to travelers returning east who needed oxen to pull their wagons, or to the government to feed the army and the Indians on the reservations.

When railroads—promoted by eastern Go-Getters—pushed west, they opened another new market. Now western beef could be shipped to the growing eastern cities. At the same time, hard-working crews building the railroads had to be well fed, and what they most wanted was meat. Iliff agreed to deliver cattle by the thousands to the Union Pacific Railroad construction gangs and to the United States troops guarding them against the Indians.

This was easier said than done. He had to find more beef than anyone had ever yet seen in one place. And he had to bring it to the middle of nowhere, where railroads were still to be built.

Iliff was helped by still another brand of Go-Getter, the western trailblazer. In 1868 a remarkable man with the unlikely name of Charles Goodnight agreed to deliver to Iliff's camp near Cheyenne, Wyoming, $40,000 worth of cattle from Texas.

To get the cattle from Texas to Wyoming, Goodnight had to find his own way over some of the driest and most unfriendly land in the whole continent—what maps before the Civil War called the "Great American Desert." It was a risky business, but it seemed worth trying when a steer, bought for $4 in Texas, sold for $40 in Wyoming. Multiply that by 3000 (the number of cattle Goodnight hoped to take on each trip), and it added up to a handsome profit. Goodnight succeeded because of the skills of Texas cowboys and the nature of long-horned cattle.

Texas longhorns.

When Americans had come to Texas in the 1820s, thousands of long-horned cattle were running wild. These were the descendants of a few animals brought over by Spanish explorers. The first cattle raising on the plains was started by Mexicans whose herds flourished on the rich grass. When later Americans arrived, they learned many things and borrowed much of their way of life from the Mexicans already there. These included the Mexican saddle, the lariat, along with the chaps, boots, spurs, and big hat, all suited for the rough life of the range. Many of the new words they used—"sombrero," "rodeo," "lariat," and "chaps" (*chaparajos*)—were borrowed from Mexico, too. The six-gun was also part of their outfit. All these things which made the cowboy picturesque to others were only his working weapons, clothes, and tools.

The cowboys' work was risky. The long-horned cattle of Texas, it was said, were "fifty times more dangerous than the fiercest buffalo." Armed with sharp horns which sometimes spread as much as eight feet from tip to tip, these bold beasts could not be managed by workers on foot. The long-horns made the Texas cowboy get on his horse, and they kept him there.

The long drive.

The Texas longhorns were well equipped for long trips. Their sense of smell, the cowboys said, was as much superior to that of an ordinary eastern cow as the bloodhound's was to that of a parlor poodle. Where water was hard to find, the longhorn's nose for water could make the difference between life and death.

The real problem was how to keep all those 3000 cattle together and moving at just the right speed. If they were allowed to stop or dawdle, they might never reach their goal. But if they were allowed to trot, they might get out of control or exercise off the weight that was worth money in Wyoming. Even with no problems and the cattle moving smoothly it would take from two to four months to reach their destination.

The crews who drove the cattle usually were made up of sixteen or eighteen cowboys for a herd of 3000. They were led by a trail captain. There was also a cook driving a chuck wagon and a boy to take care of the eight or ten horses needed for each man. Often a few of the cowboys were freed slaves.

Stationed at the front, or "point," of the herd were two of the most experienced men, called "pointers." They navigated for the whole herd, following the course set ahead by the foreman. Bringing up the rear were three steady cowboys whose job it was to look out for the weaker cattle—the "drags." To prevent the herd from straggling out for miles, the whole party moved no faster than the weakest "drags" at the rear. The rest of the cowboys were stationed along the sides to keep the herd compact and all the same width.

Communication between the front and rear of the herd was difficult. The rumbling of hoofs smothered words. The cowboys, then, borrowed a clever system of hand signals from the Plains Indians.

Apart from Indian raids, the greatest peril was a stampede. The cowboys sang to the herd at night to try to keep it calm. But suddenly a quietly dozing herd might rouse into a thundering mass. To stop a stampede, experienced cowboys on their horses drove the cattle in a circle, always round to the right. Then by tightening their circle they squeezed the stampeding cattle tighter and tighter together till they had no place to run. The milling herd was forced to halt.

If the encircling tactic failed, all was lost. The stampede would get out of control. Then the cattle would fly out like sparks into the night, and they might never be seen again.

The cow town. At the end of the long drive came the "cow town," which was as American as the cowboy. It was simply another smaller kind of "instant city" like those already dotted over the West. The cow town was where cowboys delivered their herd to the cattle dealers and the railroads. There, after long lonely weeks on the trail, cowboys enjoyed the company of strangers, bought liquor, and gambled away their money.

Go-Getting cattlemen made these instant towns prosper. One cattleman, Joseph G. McCoy, picked

Frederic Remington won fame for his paintings, illustrations, and sculptures of the "Wild West." He painted "The Stampede" in 1908.

Cattle Trails and Cow Towns

▨ Original Home Range of Texas Longhorn

▨ Range and Ranch Cattle Area

| 0 | | | | 500 Miles |
| 0 | | | | 500 Kilometers |

a place along the Kansas Pacific Railroad. In 1867, when he first made his plans for Abilene, it was a village of about a dozen log huts with sod roofs.

It was not much of a town, but there was open land around it and plenty of good grass and water for the cattle. So McCoy bought the whole town for $2400 and quickly built a shipping yard, a big barn, and a three-story hotel. It was all finished in 60 days, and by September 1867 the first shipment (twenty carloads of cattle) left Abilene for Chicago. Soon Abilene was sending thousands of cattle

east, and the town was booming. McCoy was offered more for a single city lot than he had paid for the whole town. And before the end of the second year the Kansas Pacific owed him $250,000 in commissions for the cattle shipped.

Other prosperous cow towns followed Abilene. There were Schuyler, Fort Kearney, North Platte, Ogallala, and Sidney in Nebraska. In Wyoming there were Pine Bluffs, Rock River, Rock Creek, Laramie, Hillsdale, and Cheyenne. Montana had Miles City, Glendive, and Helena.

The cow towns did not suffer from modesty. More than one boasted she was the "Queen of Cow Towns." Dodge City, in Kansas, and others competed for the title of the "Wickedest Little City in America."

Western cattlemen and cowboys were among the first and bravest of the Go-Getters. They tried the impossible and succeeded in making something from nothing. They captured wild cattle which belonged to nobody. Then they fed the cattle on the free open range on buffalo grass which nobody had even imagined could be food. And finally they transported the cattle on their very own feet for thousands of miles to places where they could become beef.

Who could have imagined that the "Great American Desert" would become the greatest beef factory in the world?

The end of the open range. The success of the ranchers was also their ruin. Everyone wanted to invest in cattle. As more and more ranches were started, more and more cattle were put out to feed on the range. In 1885, there came a hard winter, followed by a dry summer. This destroyed some of the grass and weakened the cattle. Then another bad winter in 1886 wiped out whole herds.

At the same time that cattle ranches were multiplying, farm families were pushing in, trying another way to make their living on the Great Plains. To protect their cattle the ranchers had been stretching miles of fence—even around land that they did not own. The newly arrived farmers had gone to great trouble to secure legal ownership of the lands they settled. Naturally enough they demanded government help against the high-handed ranchers.

All these forces—too many cattle, bad weather, farmers, and government intervention—would bring an end to the cattle kingdom of the open range. As farmers moved in, the ranchers could no longer graze their cattle free on the public lands. Now ranchers had to develop new methods. They actually had to buy their grazing land. Pastures were divided up and fenced. Better cattle were bred. Food was grown for winter feed. Water was supplied by well and windmill so that cattle would not have to walk far and lose weight. The cowboy became a cowhand working year-round and round the clock. No longer could he, as one recalled, "sit

around the fire the winter through" doing no work "except to chop a little wood to build a fire to keep warm by."

Some people specialized in breeding cattle, others in fattening them for market. Cattle raising became a scientific business. It was no longer the wild, romantic adventure it once had seemed. The day of the cattle kingdom was gone. The new era belonged to the ranch hand and the farmer.

SECTION 3 REVIEW

1. Identify or explain: Ole Rölvaag, John W. Iliff, Charles Goodnight, Joseph G. McCoy, long drive, open range.

2. Locate: Abilene, Dodge City, Cheyenne.

3. Why were women a small minority on the cattle and mining frontiers? What roles did women play in the development of the West?

4. How did Mexicans influence the cattle frontier?

5. **Drawing Conclusions.** What forces brought an end to cattle raising on the open range? How did cattle raising change thereafter?

---

4. The farmers' frontier

The American farmer and his family had avoided the Great Plains. It was a strange place, and at first they did not like it. They were accustomed to the wooded lands of the East. Some had become acquainted with the flat prairies that stretched from Illinois to Iowa and from Canada to Texas—land known for its rich soil, regular rainfall, and tall grass. But the Great Plains were different. Out there, trees were rare. The grass was short. Worst of all, there was very little rain. It is not surprising, then, that for a while the farmer had gladly left the West to others.

Problems on the farmers' frontier. When finally farmers decided to move onto the plains, they faced new problems. Since there was no wood for houses, they had to learn to make houses of sod. To their astonishment they found that sod houses could be warm and cozy in winter, cool in summer. These did not blow down in high winds. And they were wonderfully fireproof, which was welcome protection against the prairie fires that threatened the Great Plains. But these sod houses were dark, and

The Jerns family posed on their farm in Dry Valley, Nebraska, in 1886. By that time they had all the necessities for living on the plains. They had built several sod houses, erected a windmill, and strung barbed wire to keep their cattle from wandering away.

the ceilings dripped with rain. The old familiar wooden buildings had a lot to be said for them. Nearly every pioneer family looked forward to the day when it could build a frame house.

Whether in sod houses or frame houses, every farm family needed fuel for their fireplaces to cook food and to keep warm in the bitter winters. At first buffalo chips (dry manure) could be used, but soon the buffalo were gone. Then, at one time or another they tried everything in sight—cow manure, sunflower stalks, and hay. Until the railroads came carrying coal, nothing was quite satisfactory.

Then the weather offered new problems, for it brought only extremes. In the spring there were floods, in the summer searing heat, in the winter raging blizzards and sub-zero cold. And there were occasional prairie fires, started by lightning, which destroyed everything. Sometimes grasshoppers blackened the sky in countless numbers and in a few hours ate a whole year's crops. One very hot summer 30,000 people abandoned the Great Plains for places where life was easier. One refugee wrote on the side of his wagon that he was returning "From Kansas, where it rains grasshoppers, fire, and destruction."

Getting a farm. It has been said that civilization approached the Great Plains on three legs—water, wood, and land. But on the Great Plains only land could be found in abundance.

The railroads helped to make life easier by bringing in coal and other supplies and taking crops out to market. In addition, they encouraged settlers to come to the West. For the railroads had land sell. To persuade the railroad companies to lay their tracks across the empty lands of the West, the state and federal governments gave them wide strips of land along the tracks. So every time these companies sold a piece of land and brought out a new family of settlers, they created customers for their railroads.

At the same time, there was free land for the asking all over the West. In 1862 President Lincoln had signed the Homestead Act, which offered everybody who could get there the chance to be a landowner. To the European peasant it must have seemed a dream. The whole American West was begging for people. All you had to do was come. You only needed to be 21 years of age and to say that you intended to become a citizen. Then you picked a 160-acre plot of "homestead" land somewhere on the vast public domain which belonged to the United States government. If you simply lived on it and cultivated a part, then the whole 160 acres would be yours at the end of five years. You paid nothing but a small registration fee.

This was an Old World dream come true. Everyone a landowner!

It took lots of wood to build the balloon frame houses of the nation's fast-growing cities. This photograph was taken in 1892 of a special train loaded with lumber for Omaha, Nebraska.

The mess shanty of a lumber camp in Brill, Wisconsin, was photographed in 1902. Colorful posters, many of them advertising the play *Uncle Tom's Cabin,* decorate the walls.

But the "free" land was not really as free as it seemed. In the western plains, where most of the best homesteads were found, it cost labor and money to make wild land into a farm. Before anything could be planted, the ground had to be broken. The prairie grass had roots that grew in thick mats, unlike anything known in Europe. The familiar Old World plow would not cut through but was quickly twisted by the heavy sod. It was slow work to plow up enough land to support a family, and it was expensive to hire a worker with the right tools to do the job.

Then you needed to find water. Where streams and springs were rare, the only answer was to dig a well. And to pump up the water, you had to build a windmill. On the treeless plains you had to buy the lumber for your house. Posts and barbed wire for fencing had to be brought from great distances. All this added up. You needed about $1000 to make your homestead livable. That was a big fortune for a landless peasant.

Still, if you were healthy, and willing to work year-round, and not afraid to spend a few winters in a crude sod house, you might manage. The Homestead Act allowed you to be away from your land for six months each year without losing your claim. Some energetic homesteaders used this time to earn money by working as lumberjacks in the pine forests of Minnesota, Wisconsin, and Michigan. Others helped to build the short "feeder" railroads that branched off through the countryside. Or they worked as farm laborers.

The railroads, of course, tried to persuade people to come. They sent agents to Europe to tell them about the wonderful lands along their tracks. Their agents helped with information and loans. Sometimes the railroads actually provided newcomers with a house while they were getting settled.

Often the railroad builders were granted the best lands in the West. And, anyway, once the railroads were built, the land nearest the tracks—since there were no automobiles and few roads—would be the most valuable. While railroad lands sold at higher prices, they were usually much more attractive than the more remote lands left over for distribution under the Homestead Act. In addition, in the arid West 160 acres could not support a family, so more land had to be bought somehow.

Fencing the Great Plains. Neither the railroad nor the Homestead Act was enough to bring settlement. Pioneer farming could not really come to the Great Plains until the land could be fenced to keep out the cattle. There was no wood for fences, so various methods, such as the thorny, fast-growing "Osage orange" hedges, were tried to provide an inexpensive natural fence. But you had to wait some seasons till the hedges grew, and they were never quite tight enough. Then in the early 1870s, the answer was found in barbed wire. People tried all kinds of outlandish designs. There are still examples of at least 100 different kinds of barbed wire which show us how hard the inventors tried. As was true with other important discoveries, several people seem to have come up with the right idea at the same time. The most successful of these was an Illinois farmer, Joseph G. Glidden. He designed a wire that could be easily manufactured, was durable, and not too hard to string on posts. By 1875 he was making his fortune selling this new product. And by 1883 one company alone was turning out 600 miles of barbed wire a day!

Water and "dry farming." Of course fences did not solve all the farmers' problems. They still needed water. Even today the lack of water plagues farmers on the Great Plains.

The water under the plains could be reached only by deep wells. When drilling for oil, people learned to dig deep for water, too. To bring up the water that their steam engines needed, the railroad companies used windmills. The ranchers, and soon after them the farmers, followed their example.

The first windmills could supply only enough water for family use or for the stock. Irrigation of the fields was not possible. New methods of farming that preserved the scanty rainwater had to be developed to raise crops on the Great Plains.

"Dry farming," this was called. Developed by the Mormons in Utah, it was a way of keeping and using the moisture already in the soil. First the land was plowed deep to increase its ability to hold water. Then the topsoil was firmed so the moisture below could not escape. After every rain the farmer stirred the surface to keep a blanket of soil over the moisture in the ground.

This system needed a large area and big machines. It required the tractors, harrows, disks, and cultivators turned out in large numbers by factories

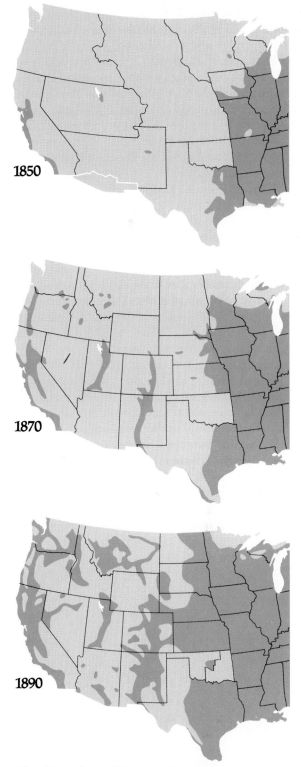

The Vanishing Western Frontier

Settled Area (2 or more people per square mile)

after the Industrial Revolution. Now farming, like mining and ranching, had become big business.

The growth of the West. Spurred by the discovery of gold, the open land, the Homestead Act, the railroads, and the flood of immigrants from Europe, the settlers in the West multiplied. Kansas had a population of 364,000 in 1870; it reached 1,428,000 by 1890. In those twenty years Nebraska grew from 123,000 to 1,063,000; Dakota Territory from 2000 to 540,000.

Senator Peffer of Kansas noted in the *Forum* of December 1889 that "a territory greater than the original area of the United States was peopled in half a dozen years." Kansas became a state in 1861, Nevada in 1864, and Nebraska in 1867. These were followed by Colorado in 1876, North and South Dakota, Montana, and Washington all in 1889, and Idaho and Wyoming in 1890. And new territories were established: Arizona in 1863 and Oklahoma in 1890. Each of these would become a new state before many decades had passed.

Oklahoma had been set aside for the Five Civilized Tribes. In 1834 these unfortunate Indians—the Cherokees, Chickasaws, Choctaws, Creeks, and Seminoles—had been forced to move there from their ancestral lands in the Southeast. At first when white "Boomers," as they were called, illegally entered Oklahoma Indian Territory, the army sent them away. When the pressure of new white settlers became too great, the government purchased some Indian lands and announced that on April 22, 1889, this land would be opened to homesteaders.

At noon a shot was fired, and thousands of hopeful homesteaders who had been held back by troopers rushed across the border for the new land. When they arrived, they were astonished and disappointed to find that the lands were already occupied by illegal settlers who were "Sooner." These had eluded the army guards and staked their claims ahead of time, leaving the law-abiding land seekers behind. Ever since then the people of Oklahoma have jokingly called themselves "Sooners." The sooner and later comers by the evening of that first day numbered 10,000 in Oklahoma City and 15,000 in Guthrie.

The next frontiers would be in cities, in factories, and in shops all over America.

SECTION 4 REVIEW

1. Identify or explain: Joseph Glidden, Homestead Act, public domain, dry farming, "Sooners."

2. Describe the hardships facing pioneer farm families on the Great Plains.

3. **Recognizing Cause and Effect.** How did each of the following influence the development of the farming frontier: railroads, the Homestead Act, barbed wire, windmills, mechanized farm equipment?

These campers are awaiting the signal to join the Oklahoma land rush in 1889.

CHAPTER **15** REVIEW

FOCUSING ON IDEAS

1. Why was the price of cattle in the 1860s ten times higher in eastern markets than in Texas? List the factors that influenced supply and demand in both markets.

2. How did railroad land grants benefit railroad stockholders? pioneer farmers and ranchers? the nation?

3. In what specific ways were the buffalo important to the Plains Indians?

4. Describe the laws necessary to maintain order in a mining town.

TAKING A CRITICAL LOOK

1. **Predicting Consequences.** Look at the map of Indian reservations on page 330. Suppose that five or ten times as much land had been set aside for Indians. In which decade—the 1830s or 1870s—would such a policy have been easier to adopt? Why? How might such an Indian-land policy have affected our national economic development? Social development?

2. **Making Comparisons.** Identify three mining boom towns in the 1870s and 1880s. As a traveler at that time, what differences would you see from towns of a similar size on the East Coast?

YOUR REGION IN HISTORY

1. **Geography.** Using an outline map of your region mark the cattle trails and/or wagon train trails that passed through your area. What cities do these trails pass through? Label them.

2. **Culture.** During what period of history was your locality a part of the American or Spanish frontier? How was frontier life in your locality similar to and different from life on one of the frontiers described in this chapter?

3. **Economics.** To what extent, if at all, has mining influenced the development of your state? What industries now use or have used the resources of these mines?

HISTORICAL FACTS AND FIGURES

Recognizing Cause and Effect. Study the chart below to help answer the following questions: (a) What was the overall trend of the Indian population between 1850 and 1900? (b) Which decade saw the smallest decline in the Indian population? (c) Which decade saw the largest decline in population? (d) What events and policies discussed in the chapter might have influenced these population shifts?

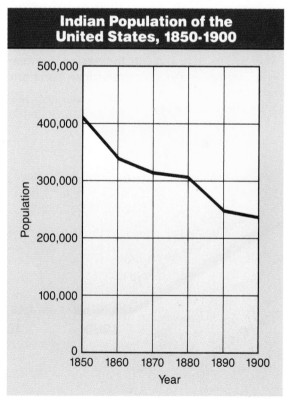

Source: Bureau of the Census

347

MAKING CONNECTIONS

THEMES

This unit began on page 279 with the observation that the mid-nineteenth century was an era of varied interests and conflict for the nation:

> *The Civil War began over the simple question of whether this was one nation, or whether any state or group of states could leave the Union and create a new nation.... To some Americans, the Civil War and Reconstruction were only far-off conflicts.*

These conclusions were supported by the three unit themes that are reprinted in **dark type** below. Use the time line and the information in Unit 5 to answer the questions that follow the unit themes.

1. **The Civil War becomes a fight over the legitimacy of the institution of slavery.**

   If the institution of slavery had not existed, would the issue of states' rights have emerged as a point of national debate in the mid-1800s?

2. **Lincoln's assassination dashes whatever chance the nation has of solving post–Civil War problems "with charity for all."**

   What factors contributed to the hostile relationship between President Andrew Johnson and Congress? Would these conflicts have developed had Lincoln not been assassinated?

3. **Increasing numbers of Americans seek new opportunities in the American West during and after the Civil War.**

   What skills and values prepared easterners and new immigrants to the United States for the opportunities and problems they faced in the West?

Events in American History

1860 South Carolina secedes from the Union, claiming states' rights.

1865 The Thirteenth Amendment, abolishing slavery, is ratified by the states.

1875 Joseph Glidden makes a fortune selling barbed wire to farmers.

1867 Congress passes the Reconstruction amendments against President Johnson's wishes.

| 1860 | 1865 | 1870 | 1875 | 1880 |

Events in World History

1873 Financial panic strikes Vienna in May, and New York in September.

1867 Russia sells Alaska to the United States for $7.2 million.

1863 Lincoln announces the Emancipation Proclamation, declaring all slaves free.

1858 News that gold had been discovered in Colorado reaches the East.

1889 The firing of a gun signals the opening of the Oklahoma Indian territory to white settlement.

1890 The population of Kansas reaches 1.4 million, up from 364,000 in 1870.

1885   1890   1895   1900

1880

1861 Lincoln resupplies Fort Sumter, in South Carolina, but the fort still falls.

1891 The Triple Alliance among Germany, Austria, and Italy is renewed for 12 years.

UNIT 6

The new industrial age 1865–1900

After the Civil War the United States was as large and varied as all western Europe. Immigrants from everywhere would find someplace to feel at home here—on lands not so different from where they had lived in the "Old Country." The English could settle on the rolling landscape of "New" England, the Swedes could farm the flat, snowy stretches of Minnesota and the Dakotas, and Italians could plant orchards and vineyards in sunny California. Imported people spread across the land. But how could these scattered people become a nation? They would have to invent ways to bring everybody closer together. The world was startled to see how Americans used railroads, telegraph wires, and bridges to bind a vast nation.

The continent did not yet seem overcrowded when Americans sent skyscrapers high in the air. For the first time in history, thousands came to live and work in a single towering building. In American cities, people would be close packed and piled up together as never before. Could so many varied city people still find national leaders to speak for them? And would the farm families who fed the nation also find champions? Could a nation where everything was becoming bigger still care for the little people?

THEMES

THEMES IN AMERICAN HISTORY

- Immigrants from across Europe pour into the United States.
- The rise of new cities and the growth of older cities give the nation an increasingly urban character.
- Urban industrialization and falling farm prices lead farmers and factory workers to protest the politics and big business of the Gilded Age.

New materials and new methods for using them transformed the nation during the Industrial Age. This detail from John Ferguson Weir's painting called "The Gun Foundry" shows molten metal being poured.

Bethlehem Steel Corporation

351

CHAPTER 16

The nation transformed

The everyday life of the American people was transformed in the generation after the Civil War. This nation would be not merely a democracy of people but also a democracy of things. It became easier for more and more Americans to share the good things of life. Farmers and ranchers found ways to make the American land yield more and better food. And many others played their parts in creating the American standard of living. A peculiarly American breed were the Go-Getters. These were men and women of all races and from all nations. The Go-Getters found new opportunities here, saw new ways to make a living for themselves, and at the same time helped build a better life for others. Without even intending it, they were bringing the whole nation together.

1. Railroads and big business

To make a profit from their land, farmers had to send their crops to market. To work their land, they needed tools from city factories. As factories grew to supply the nation's wants, the factories consumed more and more raw materials—iron, wood, and cotton. To keep the whole process going, the vast nation, spread across a continent, needed transportation. The nation was already served by its broad rivers, its many canals, and roadways. But there had to be easier, speedier ways.

Railroads gird the nation. To meet the demand, Go-Getters pushed railroads into every nook and cranny of the United States. As many miles of track were laid in the 1880s alone as in all the years from 1828 to 1870. By 1900 the nation had more miles of railroad track than all of Europe, including Russia.

When the first transcontinental railroad was completed in 1869, the time required to cross from ocean to ocean dropped from one month to one week. Within another 25 years four more transcontinental railroads were built. All but one of these railroads received generous land grants from the federal government to encourage them to build across the vacant West. Altogether, American railroads received 131 million acres from Congress and 49 million acres from the states. At the time they were given to the companies, the lands were worth little or nothing. They only became valuable after the railways were built. Then these lands would become prosperous farms and profitable sources for the nation's iron, copper, and oil.

Standard time. Americans loved speed. And railroads made it possible for them to race across the continent faster than ever before. The trains that

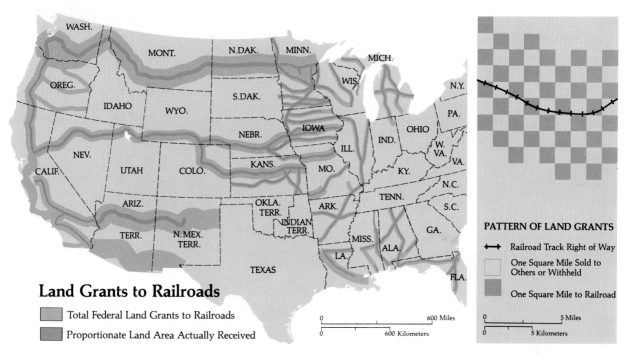

Land Grants to Railroads

▢ Total Federal Land Grants to Railroads

▢ Proportionate Land Area Actually Received

0 ———————— 600 Miles
0 ———————— 600 Kilometers

PATTERN OF LAND GRANTS

┼─┼ Railroad Track Right of Way

▢ One Square Mile Sold to Others or Withheld

▢ One Square Mile to Railroad

0 ——— 5 Miles
0 ——— 5 Kilometers

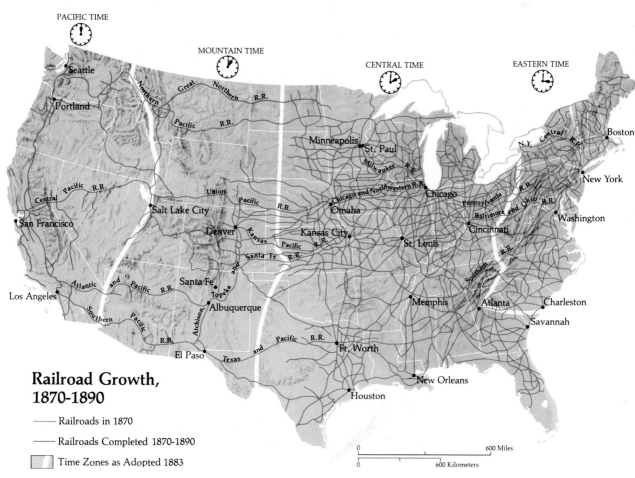

PACIFIC TIME

MOUNTAIN TIME

CENTRAL TIME

EASTERN TIME

Railroad Growth, 1870–1890

—— Railroads in 1870

—— Railroads Completed 1870–1890

▢ Time Zones as Adopted 1883

0 ———————— 600 Miles
0 ———————— 600 Kilometers

In their hurry to lay track, transcontinental railroads often built temporary wooden bridges. The permanent bridge over the Green River in Wyoming is already under construction (left) in this 1868 photograph. Citadel Rock is in the background.

sped from city to city brought strange new problems. One trouble which had not been noticed till then was that every town had its own clocks set to its own particular time. The astronomers said that it was "noon" when you saw the sun reach its zenith—the highest point in the heavens. Since the earth was constantly in motion, and since the sun rose sooner when you were more to the east, then whether it was yet noon obviously depended on *where* you were.

Imagine what this meant for a railroad! The Pennsylvania Railroad tried to use Philadelphia time on its eastern lines. But that was 5 minutes earlier than New York time and 5 minutes later than Baltimore time. In Indiana there were 23 different local times. In Illinois there were 27, and in Wisconsin 38.

Most railroads used the local time for their arrival in each station. In between cities there was the greatest confusion. Yet for speeding trains a few minutes could make the difference between a clear track and a fatal collision.

Finally it was suggested that instead of using "sun time" they should use a new kind of "railroad time"—which would be "standard time."

For the United States as a whole, you could mark off on a map a few conspicuous time belts—up and down the whole country. You would only need four—eastern time, central time, mountain time, and Pacific time—each several hundred miles wide. Standard time would be exactly the same for all the places within each zone. At the edge of each belt the time would change by a whole hour. These time zones would be marked on maps, and then everybody could know exactly what time it was everywhere.

In the oil painting above, Chinese workers cheer as a Central Pacific train heads into a snowshed built to protect it from heavy snow in the Sierras. The poster (right) shows how new railroad lines sprang up as demand grew.

This was a sensible plan, but it took a long time to convince everybody that they ought to tamper with "God's time." Finally, at noon on November 18, 1883, the plan for standard time was adopted, and people everywhere set their watches to the new time.

Standard gauge. Standard time helped to draw all the nation's railroads together. But other steps were needed too. In 1860 there were about 350 different railroad companies and about 30,000 miles of railroad tracks in the United States. Yet there was not really a national railroad network. The main reason was that the many railroad lines were not on the same "gauge." The gauge is the distance between the two rails measured from the inside of one rail to the inside of the other. There were many different gauges. Some railroad builders put their tracks six feet apart, but some put them closer together. There were at least eleven gauges in general use. A railroad car that would just fit one gauge would not run on narrower or wider gauges.

If you wanted to send a package any distance by railroad, it had to be taken out of the car that fitted one gauge and moved into a car to fit the gauge of the next railroad. In 1861 a package sent by railroad from Charleston, South Carolina, to Philadelphia had to change railroad cars eight times.

From the beginning, quite a few lines happened to have the same gauge. George Stephenson, the English railroad inventor, had designed his locomotive to measure 4 feet, 8 1/2 inches between the wheels—the usual distance between wheels on a wagon. When Stephenson locomotives were imported to the United States, they had this "standard gauge." And of course many early railroad lines built their tracks to fit the imported trains.

During the Civil War, in order to ship arms and troops quickly from place to place, many railroads changed to standard gauge. And then when the transcontinental railroad was completed with the standard gauge in 1869, that settled the question. Now if a railroad wanted to join the traffic across the continent, its rails had to be set 4 feet, 8 1/2 inches apart.

By 1880 about four-fifths of the tracks in the United States had been converted to standard gauge. Most of the other gauges were in the old Confederate South. Finally, in 1886, the southern railroads decided to change all their 13,000 miles of track to the national standard. A month in advance, crews went along loosening the old track. They measured the distance for the new standard gauge and put spikes along the wooden ties. On May 31 and June 1, the men worked frantically. One record-breaking crew on the Louisville and Nashville Railroad changed eleven miles of track in 4 1/2 hours. June 1, 1886, was a holiday along the southern tracks. By 4 P.M. the southern railroads had joined the Union.

Businesses compete. As the railroads crisscrossed the land, the nation's businesses grew in number and size because they could reach more people. These were challenging times for businessmen. Competition in certain fields—like oil, steel, and the railroads—was fierce. On top of that, thirteen of the years from 1873 to 1897 were years of recession or depression. John D. Rockefeller, who made a fortune in the oil business, once looked back on those years and marveled that he had managed to survive them.

> How often I had not an unbroken night's sleep, worrying about how it was all coming out. . . . Work by day and worry by night, week in and week out, month after month. If I had foreseen the future, I doubt whether I would have had the courage to go on.

Rockefeller did go on, and he prospered by devising ways to limit competition. He organized "pools" in which a group of companies agreed not really to compete but instead to keep their prices the same. The law often treated these agreements as a kind of conspiracy. Since there was no legal means to enforce the pools, they usually collapsed.

Then Rockefeller and some other big businessmen tried another device. They figured out a clever new way to use an old English institution. This was the "trust." In early times in England the "trust" was invented for charities. Money would

The front and back covers of this menu from the Santa Fe railroad reveal the change in transportation across the continent that took place between 1868 and 1888. The comfortable passengers in the dining car had a gourmet menu to choose from.

be given to "trustees" who invested it and gave the profits to the poor and the needy. The trustees controlled the money for the benefit of others. Now business firms set up "trusts"—not for charity, but to get around the laws against conspiracy. A group of companies would hand over all their stock to a board of "trustees" and receive trust certificates in return. The new trustees would then control all the companies, but the original owners—the holders of the trust certificates—would still get the profits. Still another ploy they used was the holding company. Its only purpose was to "hold" the stock, and so the control, of other companies.

For some years the trust proved to be an effective way to get around the law, to combine companies, limit competition, and increase profits. The first and most famous was Rockefeller's Standard Oil Trust, but there were also trusts in cottonseed oil, linseed oil, lead, whiskey, sugar, and other products. By 1890 Congress began to pass "antitrust" laws, and the courts decided that business combinations formed to limit competition were illegal. But many trusts continued to operate, and their powers lingered on.

J. Pierpont Morgan and Andrew Carnegie.

In the railroads, as well, combination became the answer to over-expansion and cutthroat competition. Here the main actor was the giant of finance J. Pierpont Morgan. Born to wealth, he was trained in the London office of his father's bank. His swashbuckling in the money world led people to call him a pirate. Actually he did not mind that. He had the look of a pirate, with his great frame, piercing eyes, and bulbous red nose. He named his luxury yacht (302 feet long!) the *Corsair,* which was the old French name for a pirate ship. Once, when Morgan was asked by a would-be yacht owner what it cost to run the *Corsair,* he replied, "If you have to ask, you can't afford it." But Morgan was also a man of culture. He built a great collection of rare books and works of art from all over the world, which he gave to the public.

Morgan was an amazing organizer. When hard times bankrupted many railroads during the late 1800s, Morgan put them back on their feet by reorganizing them. He often combined several weak companies to make a single strong one. In time he controlled eleven railway systems with 19,000 miles of track. He also organized the biggest

Culver Pictures

Brown Brothers

Sturdy J. P. Morgan, with his hawklike stare, was known as the financier extraordinary. Astute Andrew Carnegie (bottom) created the nation's largest steel company.

steel company of all. But to do so he had to take over Carnegie Steel.

Andrew Carnegie, controlling partner in Carnegie Steel, was a talkative, intelligent steel industrialist who had been born of a poor family in Scotland. His family came to the United States in 1848, and Andrew at age 13 went to work as a bobbin boy in a cotton factory for $1.25 a week. But instead of settling for that, he educated himself by reading books and rose rapidly to better jobs. By his energy and his power to enlist the talents of others, he built the Carnegie Steel Company and became one of the richest men in America. In 1900 alone he made $25 million. And since there was no income tax in those days, he kept it all! Meanwhile, he never forgot the power of books. He devoted much of his fortune to founding libraries all over the United States in order to give others the chance to educate themselves and rise in the world. More than any one person, Andrew Carnegie was responsible for the spread of the free public library. Along with the public school, it became a keystone of American democracy.

Now Morgan wanted to buy Carnegie's company and bring his own "system" to the steel industry. Carnegie asked almost half a billion dollars for his share—and Morgan paid. Carnegie Steel and several other steel companies then were merged to form the United States Steel Corporation. It soon produced 60 percent of the nation's steel. Morgan's banking house made money, too, by selling the stock and bonds of the company to the public for a billion and a half dollars.

The new mighty corporations alarmed many people. They were richer and more powerful than any state government. These huge impersonal concerns were run by managers who were quite separate from the thousands of stockholders who really owned the business. The stockholders, each of whom owned "shares" in the company, were spread across the land. Most never even saw the factories of which they were part owners. The factory workers, instead of working for a single human boss who owned the company, now felt that they were employed by an inhuman giant. It was these companies and many smaller ones that made the United States, by 1890, the greatest industrial nation in the world. Their products, as well as the wealth they created and the salaries they paid, transformed American life.

SECTION 1 REVIEW

1. Identify or explain: time zones, narrow gauge, John D. Rockefeller, pool, holding company, J. P. Morgan, Andrew Carnegie.

2. How did both the railroads and the public benefit from (a) the railroad land grants? (b) the switch to standard time? (c) the change to standard-gauge track?

3. Explain how a dozen big sugar companies might have formed a trust. Why would they want to do so?

4. **Expressing Problems Clearly.** In what sense did the giant corporations become more impersonal and inhuman?

2. Rock oil lights up the world

Americans before the Civil War, before anyone heard of an electric light, had to light their houses and their factories with oil lamps. People tried all sorts of mixtures hoping to find an oil that was cheap and safe, that burned well, and did not smell. They tried oils from the sap of trees, from vegetables, from fish, whales, or other animals. One oil called "camphene" was a mixture of turpentine (from pine trees) and alcohol. Another, invented in 1850 and made from coal, was called kerosene (from *keros,* the Greek word for wax). Camphene gave off good light but emitted an explosive gas. All except kerosene were smelly. Kerosene worked best, but it was expensive. So most homes were not lit at night. And people went to bed when the sun set.

Drilling for oil. In the mid-1850s George H. Bissell formed the Pennsylvania Rock Oil Company to buy lands in western Pennsylvania where oil was found floating in ponds. At that time rock oil (what we call "oil") was used mostly for medicine. Bissell found that he could not make enough money selling the oil for medicine to pay the expenses of collecting it. So he hired a famous Yale professor of chemistry, Benjamin Silliman, Jr., and agreed to pay him $500 to find out what else rock oil might be good for.

Professor Silliman's report opened a new age for rock oil. He found that rock oil—by now also called "petroleum" from *petrus,* Latin for rock, and *oleum* for oil—would make an excellent oil for lamps. His process was cheap. He simply distilled the rock oil—that is, heated it and collected the gas that came off. When the gas cooled down into a liquid, it formed a lamp oil that was just as good as kerosene made from coal. Kerosene made from rock oil gave a bright, white light, with almost no smoke, and would not explode.

The rock oil itself also had wonderful lubricating powers. It would keep the wheels and gears of machines from wearing out and would make them run quietly and smoothly.

Rock oil, with these valuable uses, could surely be sold in large quantities. But until then the only known way to collect it was to find it on the surface or by accident in a salt well. Sometimes people would dig a shallow ditch to increase the flow where it was already bubbling up.

Then one day, the story goes, Bissell saw an advertisement for rock oil from an old salt well. It was a sheet printed to look like paper money that featured the numeral 400. "A.D. 1848," it read. "Discovered in *boring* for salt water . . . about FOUR HUNDRED FEET below the Earth's surface." Boring! If oil could be obtained when you bored for salt water, why not simply bore for the oil?

"Oil coming out of the ground!" exclaimed a friend. "Pumping oil out of the earth the way you pump water? Nonsense! You're crazy."

But Bissell and other Go-Getting businessmen in the Pennsylvania Rock Oil Company decided to try. From New Haven, Connecticut, they sent Edwin L. Drake out to the oil fields. One reason they picked him was that since he had been a railroad conductor, he still had a free pass on the railroads. He could go out to western Pennsylvania without it costing anybody anything.

When Drake reached Titusville, the town closest to the biggest finds of surface oil, he decided to drill for oil. At first he could not find a driller willing to do the job. The drillers all thought that boring for oil was silly.

Then, luckily, he found an old salt driller, "Uncle Billy" Smith, who was also a skilled blacksmith and knew how to make drilling tools. Uncle Billy began drilling in June 1859, and on August 29 the hole still reached down less than 70 feet. When Drake and Smith came back two days later, the hole was full of oily black stuff.

"What's that?" Drake asked.

Uncle Billy replied, "That's your fortune!"

Soon there was an oil mania. Everybody wanted to get rich from oil. The map of northwestern Pennsylvania was dotted with such new names as Oil City, Oleopolis, and Petroleum Center.

John D. Rockefeller sets up the Standard Oil Company.

One of the most spectacular of all American Go-Getters was John D. Rockefeller. He was not an inventor or an explorer. Like J. P. Morgan and Andrew Carnegie, he was an organizer.

Young Rockefeller went to school in Cleveland, but he never went to college. His father, who traveled through the West selling patent medicines, left young John in charge of the family long before he was grown. John D. Rockefeller was ambitious. "I did not guess what it would be," he recalled. "But I was after something big."

This sheet music cover celebrates the Tarr Farm Oil Creek in Pennsylvania.

Even as a boy in Cleveland, young Rockefeller was systematic and well organized. While still struggling to make his way, he gave one-tenth of his income to the Baptist church and to charities. But when it came to organizing his oil business, he did not always use Sunday school methods.

Cleveland was a good place to organize "something big" in the oil business. At the receiving end of two railroads that came from the western Pennsylvania oil fields, Cleveland was on a lake big enough for large ships as well as on two major east-west railroads. Rockefeller determined to make Cleveland the center of the oil business and from there to command the biggest oil company in the world. Beginning with a small sum he had made in a grain-trading business, in 1865 he bought a Cleveland oil refinery. There crude oil from the fields was made into kerosene for lighting and oil for lubricating. Then he bought up other refineries in Cleveland and many oil wells in Pennsylvania.

As other oilmen went out of business, the railroads that carried the oil needed Rockefeller's freight more than ever. He was clever at making

Alarmed by the growth of large corporations, this 1881 cartoonist compares Standard Oil with an octopus.

the two big railroads passing through Cleveland compete for his business. He bargained with one railroad by threatening to give all his business to the other. And he finally forced them to charge him lower prices than they charged anybody else. By secret arrangements he pretended to pay the regular rates. Then the railroads gave him back a "rebate"—a refund on each barrel of his oil that they had hauled. Soon they even gave him rebates on what opposing oil companies shipped.

After he perfected these tactics, he went to the small refiners in other parts of the country and asked them to sell their companies to him. "If you don't sell your property," he would say, "it will be valueless, because we have advantages with the railroads." He would then offer a price far below what the owners thought their refineries were worth. But they usually sold because they knew that Rockefeller could drive them out of business.

When it became cheaper to pump oil through pipelines instead of carrying it in barrels, Rockefeller organized his own pipeline. Then, when a different kind of oil was found in Ohio, Rockefeller hired chemical engineers to invent new kinds of refineries.

Rockefeller's Go-Getting business reached around the world. To the Chinese, his Standard Oil Company sold inexpensive lamps by the millions—and then sold the oil to fill them. Before long, people on all continents were using lamp oil from American wells. Between the Civil War and 1900 over half the American output went abroad. In those years Rockefeller, the Giant Go-Getter, helped light up the world. Now Americans could afford a lamp in every room, and they did not have to go to bed at sunset.

In the 1900s, Rockefeller's business would grow in ways even he had never imagined. After the automobile was invented, petroleum was refined into gasoline—and rock oil made it possible for a whole nation to move on wheels.

SECTION 2 REVIEW

1. Identify or explain: rock oil, George H. Bissell, Benjamin Silliman, Jr., Titusville, rebates.

2. **Determining Relevance.** How did Rockefeller use the railroad to organize and build the giant Standard Oil Company?

3. City goods for country customers

During the colonial years, an American farm family made for themselves almost everything they needed. They built their own house (with the help of a few neighbors), and they made their own furniture. The wife and daughters spun the thread, wove the cloth, and then sewed the family's clothes. The pots and pans and metal tools which they could not make for themselves they would buy from a peddler. But they bought very few things. There were not many ready-made things for them to buy.

Then, in the years before the Civil War, American know-how drew upon ideas from Europe's Industrial Revolution to develop a new kind of manufacturing. Lots of new things were produced in vast new quantities. The new American System of Manufacture, which Eli Whitney and Samuel Colt had organized to make guns and revolvers, also turned out clocks and locks, and countless other items—both better and cheaper. Now farmers could afford to buy them.

But when farm families wanted any of these things, they had to go to the nearest village and visit the general store. Children loved the place because there you could buy candy and toys. Since the storekeeper kept a good fire in the stove, the store was where you could stay warm in winter. There you could meet friends and exchange ideas year-round.

But it was no place for bargains. The country storekeeper, who bought only a little bit of everything, could not command the best wholesale prices from the big-city manufacturers. Things would get dusty and out of date before they could be sold. And on top of that there were costly freight charges. Each item had to be hauled by wagon over bumpy backwoods roads.

Montgomery Ward. Soon after the Civil War an inventive young salesman, who had covered the West selling goods to the owners of general stores, began to think of a new plan. His name was A. Montgomery Ward. He had done all sorts of things, from working in a barrel factory and in a brickyard to selling dry goods. Often in his travels he had heard farmers complain about the small choice of goods and the high prices.

Young Ward's idea was to sell goods in an entirely new way. Instead of the old general store

Brown Brothers

The spread of mail delivery to the rural countryside enabled farm families to buy goods from mail-order firms in the cities.

which had stocked only a few of each item, Ward imagined a mail-order store. The storekeeper would stay in the big city where it was easier to collect a large stock of all sorts of goods. He would send out to farmers lists of his goods with descriptions and pictures. The farmer would not need to come to the store because the store—in the form of a catalog—would go to the farmer. And the farm family would order by mail, picking out whatever they wanted from the catalog. Then the storekeeper would mail the family the goods they had ordered.

If this new scheme worked, the storekeeper would be selling not only to the few customers in one village. He could sell all over America—to anyone within reach of a mailbox.

The possible customers of this new kind of store would not be just a few hundred, they might be millions! And then Ward could buy his goods from the manufacturer by the hundreds and thousands. The manufacturer could afford to give him a lower price.

For the customers, too, there were advantages. They had a much wider selection of goods. And they paid a lower price because the mail-order storekeeper, with so many more customers, could take a smaller profit on each item and yet would make more money in the long run.

"NOW I GUESS I'VE GOT THE BULGE ON THE MIDDLEMAN."

Ward's boasted that buying from them would save the customers money.

Young Montgomery Ward had lost nearly all his savings in the Chicago fire of 1871, but in the very next year he managed to scrape together enough to make a start with his new idea. He put in $1600 and a partner added $800. They rented a small room over a stable, and started modestly. Their single price-sheet listed the items for sale and told how to order. Within two years Ward was issuing a 72-page catalog with illustrations. By 1884 the catalog numbered 240 pages and listed nearly 10,000 items. Within another 30 years it was over 1000 pages and included just about anything a person could imagine for animals or people.

Trust was the most important thing for a mail-order store. If you bought in a general store, you were buying from a storekeeper you knew. You could see the goods and handle them to satisfy yourself. But when you bought from a mail-order store, you had to trust somebody you had never seen. You had to believe that the storekeeper would really send you the exact thing described in the catalog.

Ward was a spectacular success. The first secret of his success was not a secret at all. It was simply to be honest, give good value, and always let the customer be the judge. On everything Ward's gave an ironclad guarantee. "Satisfaction or your money back!" If you did not like the goods when they arrived, you could always return them. If something arrived damaged, you could send it back to Ward's to be replaced. The company paid the postage both ways.

Of course there had to be trust on the company's side, too. The company had to be willing to cash the customers' checks, to believe their complaints, and to replace damaged goods without a lot of investigating. Ward was willing to do this, and to take the risks.

The catalog showed pictures of Ward himself and of the men in charge of the different departments. This was to convince the customers that they were dealing with real people. Some customers wrote in to say how pleased they were to deal with such "fine looking men." Some even named babies after Ward, and said he would be an inspiration to their children.

Ward saw that their letters were promptly answered—even if they were not ordering goods but only asking advice. One customer asked how to find a baby to adopt. Parents asked how to handle disobedient children. Some wrote him simply because they were lonely and had nobody else to write to.

Just as the tobacco planter in colonial times had asked his London agent to send him whatever he needed, now the lonely farmer asked Ward's. One customer wrote asking them to send him "a good wife." Ward's answered that it was not a good idea to select a wife by mail. "After you get the wife and you find that she needs some wearing apparel or household goods," Ward's added, "we feel sure we could serve both you and her to good advantage."

Sears and his catalog. It is not surprising that the mail-order store was a roaring success. Of course, in an age of Go-Getters, Ward was not the only man who tried his hand at building a mail-order store. One of the most creative of these others was a young man named Richard Sears. He began selling jewelry by mail. He found a partner in Alvah Curtis Roebuck, a watchmaker who ran a print shop where they could turn out their catalogs.

Sears was a clever man, and a near-genius at selling by mail. He was always improving his catalog. He developed a new quick-drying ink, new systems of color printing, and thinner paper that would take color but was cheaper to mail. He found, for example, that four pages of advertisements in color would sell as much of the same goods as twelve pages in black and white. His improvements were widely copied by other advertisers and by publishers of newspapers and magazines.

As the mail-order catalog reached more and more people on remote farms and in small villages, it became more and more important in their daily lives. While the family kept the Bible in the living room, they kept the Sears or Ward catalog in the kitchen. That was where they really lived.

There were all sorts of stories about how much faith people put in this big book. When one little boy was asked by his Sunday school teacher where the Ten Commandments came from, he said he supposed they came from Sears.

Just as Puritan boys and girls in colonial times had studied the *New England Primer* with its stories about God and the Devil, now Americans on farms studied the Sears catalog. In country schoolhouses, where there were few textbooks, teachers made good use of the catalog. They used it to teach reading and spelling. For arithmetic, pupils filled out orders and added up items. And they learned geography from the catalog's postal-zone maps.

Nothing did more than the new mail-order stores to make rural life in America something new. Before the 1900s most Americans still lived on the farm. Now that the American farm family could order from Ward or Sears, their lives became even more different from that of European peasants. Their view of the good things in the world was no longer confined to the shelves of the little village store. The up-to-date catalogs brought news of all kinds of new machines, new gadgets, and new fashions. Now American farm families could buy big-city goods at prices they could afford and from someone they could trust.

SECTION 3 REVIEW

1. Identify: Montgomery Ward, Richard Sears.
2. **Making Comparisons.** What advantages did mail-order buying have over shopping at the rural general store?

---

4. Buyers' Palaces

Meanwhile other Go-Getters were inventing ways to attract the new millions of city customers. The big stores that now grew up in American cities were as different from the little London shops as the grand new American hotels were different from the modest Old World inns.

The new American hotels were People's Palaces. Anybody could meet friends in the elegant lobby or, if you had the money, entertain them in a dining room with a crystal chandelier. The new department stores were Buyers' Palaces. And they, too, were democratic.

In London, only people who looked like "gentlemen" or "ladies" were admitted to the elegant shops. Unless the shopkeepers knew who you were, they would not let you in. You had to be a "person of quality" (as the upper classes were called) to see "goods of quality."

Department stores changed all this. Suddenly there were vast Buyers' Palaces, some large enough to fill a whole city block—specially designed to display goods of every shape, price, and description. Anybody could walk in. Now everybody could look at stylish jewelry, clothing, and furniture of the kind once reserved for the eyes of the rich.

Stewart's department store in New York was one of the first of the new buyers' palaces. This 1876 engraving shows the Broadway front of the block-large cast-iron building.

Stewart's new store. This department-store revolution, which began shortly before the Civil War, changed the lives of American customers within a few decades. Stewart's Cast Iron Palace, completed in 1862 in New York City, was one of the first big department stores. It was the product of two different kinds of Go-Getters—a businessman and an inventor.

A. T. Stewart, the merchant who built up the business, came to the United States from Ireland at age 17. He started by selling the Irish laces he had brought with him. But he soon branched out into all kinds of goods. He was a bold, ambitious businessman. And he decided to spend a fortune on an enormous building in an entirely new style. To help him plan his grand new store, he picked an inventing genius who was sure to try something new.

James Bogardus, the man Stewart chose, had started as a watchmaker's apprentice in upstate New York. He first became famous by his design for an eight-day clock. Then he invented all kinds of new machines—for making cotton thread, for mixing lead paint, for grinding sugar, for metering gas, and for engraving postage stamps. He patented a metal-cased pencil with a lead that was "forever pointed."

His most important new idea was to construct buildings of cast iron. Bogardus's own five-story factory, built in 1850, was probably the first cast-iron building in America. The store he built for Stewart overwhelmed everybody at the time by its height—eight stories. It quickly became famous as the biggest store in the world.

Bogardus used cast iron to make an impressive Buyers' Palace. On the ground floor the outside walls no longer needed to be thick—as they had to be when a tall building was made of stone. Now there could be larger windows on every floor. Slender iron columns held up the high ceiling of display rooms a city-block wide. The ground floor was made even more palatial by a grand central staircase and a great rotunda reaching up the full height of the building, topped by a glass roof through which the sunlight streamed. You could enjoy long indoor vistas of appealing merchandise— gloves, umbrellas, suitcases, coats, furniture, all kinds of things in all shapes and sizes and colors. All the people busy looking, buying, and admiring helped make a splendid spectacle.

Naturally the Go-Getting department store-keepers wanted to display their goods to everybody who walked down the street. The thin cast-iron building frames made this easier, but it would not have been possible without a new kind of window. Before the age of the department store, glass was expensive. Windows had to be small. They were made to admit a little daylight or to look *out of.*

Then, not long before the Civil War, an Englishman invented an inexpensive way of rolling out glass in large sheets. These large sheets of glass now at last made possible the "show window." Americans invented this expression for the new kind of window that was made to look *into.* Now the goods could advertise themselves. The department store was a new, very American, and very democratic kind of entertainment where the admission was always free.

SECTION 4 REVIEW

1. Identify: A. T. Stewart, James Bogardus.
2. Why was Stewart's store so successful?
3. **Identifying Central Issues.** In what way were the new department stores "democratic"?

5. Things by the millions

On July 4, 1876, the nation celebrated its hundredth birthday with a Centennial Exposition held at Philadelphia. On the fairgrounds there were no rifle ranges or roller coasters or freak shows. There was no need for any. American products of all shapes and sizes—from shiny new bicycles to Alexander Graham Bell's strange machine that sent your voice over a wire—were themselves quite enough to entertain and amaze.

Visitors from Europe were astonished at how fast the United States had moved ahead. It was now threatening to take England's place as the leading manufacturing nation in the world. Machinery Hall, which drew the biggest crowds at the fair, was dominated by the gigantic Corliss steam engine. The largest ever, it was 40 feet high, weighed 700 tons, and produced over 2000 horsepower.

But it was not only size and quality that impressed visitors from the Old World. They were astonished by how cheaply Americans could make so many different things. Early in the 1800s one ingenious Connecticut manufacturer, Eli Terry, had already managed to turn out clocks that sold for so little it was not worth having an old one repaired. By the time of the Civil War good American clocks sold for less than 50 cents each, and New England factories were producing a half-million clocks each year.

Now in 1876, Europeans who saw the Philadelphia exhibits were convinced that Americans would change the world. The American machines, one Swiss engineer predicted, would "overwhelm all mankind with a quantity of products which, we hope, will bring them blessing."

Machine tools. To make things by the millions, Americans first had to create whole new industries and whole new ways of thinking. Newest and most essential was the industry for making machine tools. Machine tools were the parent machines— the machines for making the sewing machines, the gun-making machines, the clock-making machines, and all the rest. Since all these machines themselves were made of metal, machine tools were mostly metal-cutting tools.

One of the most remarkable of the American machine-tool makers was William Sellers of Philadelphia. By the time of the Centennial Exposition his work was already famous. He had invented machines that could measure and cut metal at the same time. These were essential for turning out standard-size screws and bolts.

And now these fasteners were more important than anyone could imagine before. They held together the millions of metal parts of the new machines. In the old days each bolt had been specially made for use at one place in one particular machine. If you took a piece of machinery apart, you had to label each bolt so you could put it back in the same place.

Now that would not do. What good was it to make guns or clocks with standard-size parts unless you could hold them together with standard-size fasteners?

In his *System of Screw Threads and Nuts* (1864), William Sellers offered his own standard designs for the tiny grooves. After that, if you said your machine used a "Sellers Number 6," then everybody knew exactly what you meant. The United States government adopted Sellers's system in 1868. Before the end of the century an international congress in Switzerland made it the standard for Europe, too.

Efficiency experts. While Sellers was pioneering in standard design, other Americans were inventing a whole new way of thinking about factories. In the old days, the individual craftsman in his shop would simply do things the way they had always been done before. This was called the "rule-of-thumb." You did the job in a rough, practical way, using your thumb instead of a precise measure.

But the new American factory could not be run that way. If the old gunsmith's handiwork was crude or inefficient, it meant simply that he made less money or that people stopped buying guns from him. But in a factory where hundreds of people labored elbow to elbow, everybody suffered if one worker blundered. If your work was not precise, your mistakes were carried all over the country in the thousands of misshapen parts that came off your machine.

Now there was need for a new science—a science of avoiding waste. "Efficiency" was another name for it. The Go-Getting engineer who invented it called it the "Science" of Management.

The efficiency pioneer, Frederick W. Taylor, was born in 1856 in Philadelphia. His mother, a fervent abolitionist, wanted to liberate men and women from slavery. Taylor hoped to liberate men and women from waste. He was astonished that people who worried about conserving forests and water-power and soil and minerals paid so little attention to conserving human effort.

He believed that there was one best way to do anything. But the one way that was least wasteful was not necessarily the way it had always been done.

Early in life he experimented to find the most efficient way to walk. He counted his steps and measured his stride. Then he figured out the best way to walk at different times and to different places. Taylor, who loved sports, even designed

This 1895 painting of "The Bessemer Converter" by S.B. Shiley shows foundry workers making steel at the Bethlehem Pennsylvania plant.

his own tennis racket, with a curved handle that made it look like a spoon. People laughed at him—until 1881 when Taylor and his partner (with Taylor using his spoon-handle racket) won the United States doubles championship.

The Bethlehem Iron Company hired Taylor to help make their huge plant more efficient. Every year millions of tons of coal and iron ore were shoveled into furnaces. Paying the men to shovel was one of the largest expenses of making iron. Each man brought his own shovel and shoveled any way he wanted. But wasn't it possible, Taylor asked, that there was actually only one best way to shovel?

Taylor and his crew went into the factory and wrote down exactly what the men were already doing. Each worker was using his one favorite shovel no matter what he was shoveling. A shovelful of "rice coal" weighed only 3 1/2 pounds, but a shovelful of iron ore weighed 38 pounds.

"Now," Taylor asked, "is 3 1/2 pounds the proper shovel load or is 38 pounds the proper shovel load? They cannot both be right. Under scientific management, the answer to the question is not a matter of anyone's opinion; it is a question for accurate, careful, scientific investigation."

Taylor experimented until he found the right-sized shovel for each job. Taylor had discovered a Science of Shoveling! He designed different shapes and sizes of shovels and then tested each one to see that it was best suited to the stuff it had to carry. His small flat shovel was for the heavy ore, and his immense scoop was for light rice coal. Soon there were fifteen kinds of shovels in the Bethlehem toolroom, and the number of men needed to do the work dropped from 600 to 140. Taylor had abolished the waste.

This system, said Taylor, made it possible to pay each shoveler 60 percent more in wages. The wages of workers did rise somewhat. But, naturally enough, many workers were afraid they would lose their jobs. Others were afraid that, even if they kept their jobs, they would have to work harder. Many were afraid they would be regimented. They liked their own shovels. They did not like anybody telling them how to do their simple job.

Still, all over the country, "Scientific Management" became more and more popular with employers. They discovered that by making a science of the simplest jobs, they usually could find a better way.

Edison and his invention factory.
Thomas A. Edison invented a new kind of factory—an "invention factory." Its purpose was to invent new kinds of things to make. In the 1870s Edison set up his first "invention factory" with $40,000 he received from his own early inventions.

Edison and the clever people he brought to his "invention factory" were tireless testers and imaginative mechanics. One of their first feats was to help make electric lighting possible. The hardest problem had been to find the right thread, or "filament," to put inside the bulb. It had to be one that would give light when electricity was sent through it and yet would not quickly burn out.

They tried all sorts of materials—carbon, bamboo, hair, platinum, copper, and scores of other substances. They finally discovered that a filament of carbonized thread served well if it was in a vacuum. This made possible in 1879 the commercial production of light bulbs, which soon replaced Rockefeller's oil lamps.

Edison and his fellow inventors, looking for a way to record the human voice, invented the phonograph. They worked on a way to use the new art of photography to show "moving" pictures. In 1891 Edison patented a "kinetoscope"—a kind of peep show which showed moving pictures inside a box.

Edison fired the imagination of the American people. He was nicknamed the "Wizard." When

This photo of bustling Herald Square in New York City was taken about 1910. Note the large advertisement for Edison's phonograph.

Congress awarded him a special gold medal in 1928, it was announced that his inventions had been worth $15,599,000,000 to humanity! But this was only to say that there really was no way of measuring his enormous contribution to American life. By the time of his death at the ripe age of 85, in 1931, he had become an American hero—a truly democratic hero because his work benefited every living American.

SECTION 5 REVIEW

1. Identify or explain: Centennial Exposition, Eli Terry, Frederick Taylor, assembly line.

2. What is "Scientific Management"? What fears did it arouse in workers?

3. **Identifying Assumptions.** What assumption underlies the opinion that Thomas Edison was a "democratic" hero?

---

6. Labor begins to organize

The growth of American business—the development of "scientific" ways of shoveling, of new kinds of stores, of bigger factories, of assembly lines, of huge corporations—transformed the lives of workers. They became cogs in a great machine. No longer were they skilled artisans, controllers of their tools. Instead they were becoming servants of the expensive tools of their employers. Workers no longer labored at home or in small groups alongside a boss who was both the owner of the business and their friend. Of course, even in those days they had worked from dawn to dark. But now they started and ended work when the factory whistle blew, and they worked twelve to sixteen hours a day in badly lighted and poorly ventilated buildings. Women and children made up more than half the work force. And the pleasant conditions of the early factories located in the countryside—in places like Waltham and Lowell—had disappeared under pressure of competition.

The rise of trade unions. Trade unions had existed for a long time. In the 1790s in New York, Philadelphia, and other cities, certain skilled workers such as shoemakers, printers, and carpenters organized to protect their interests. But the prospects for organizing more of the nation's workers were not good. At first the courts held that unions were illegal because they were conspiracies. Then the Massachusetts Supreme Court in *Commonwealth v. Hunt* (1842) opened the path for unions when it declared that they were just as legal as any other club organized to help members for a legitimate purpose. Some states followed, but many still treated strikes, the unions' weapon for survival, as illegal.

In a few cities the trade unions joined together in federations. But the largest of these, the National Trades Union, collapsed with the Panic of 1837.

By the time of the Civil War a small number of skilled trades—printers, iron molders, hat finishers, stonecutters, and cigarmakers, among others—had organized national unions to improve their wages and working conditions. But most American workers were not members of unions. It was harder here than in Great Britain, France, and other European countries to persuade workers to take the trouble and the risks of joining a union. For generally speaking, American workers were already better off than those abroad and had more hopes of rising in the world. Even with the arrival of large numbers of immigrants during the 1840s and 1850s and the increased competition for jobs, wages in the United States remained above those in other industrial nations.

Labor strife. As the size of factories increased and more and more businesses became large corporations, the gap between worker and employer grew wider. Especially in large cities, it became easier to think of labor as merely a commodity to be bought at the lowest possible cost. A big company with lots of money could afford to close its factory when times were bad and wait for conditions to improve. But a worker still had to eat every day—in good times or bad. If workers complained, or went off the job on strike, the company could bring in new workers—strikebreakers.

Of course, workers resented this treatment. The nation that had recently been a military battleground between North and South now became a scene of industrial battles between workers and their employers. Large numbers of workers (even many not organized into unions) were willing to go on strike. They were risking their jobs to improve their lives. Their aim was shorter hours and better wages. Workers also wanted more of a feeling of independence, of control over their own lives and working conditions. To win this, peaceful means were sometimes not enough.

Beginning in the 1870s labor battles became more frequent. In 1872 nearly 100,000 builders and mechanics in New York City went on strike. They refused to work longer than eight hours in one day. After several months, they won their point.

Miners in the eastern Pennsylvania coalfields organized a secret society called the "Molly Maguires." In 1875, on flimsy and possibly false evidence that private detectives had gathered for the employers, ten Molly Maguires were hanged for murder. Then in 1877 a railroad strike that began on the Baltimore and Ohio Railroad spread across the country bringing death and destruction in its wake (p. 393). The industrial battleground was becoming a place of bloodshed.

In 1886 came the so-called Haymarket Massacre in Chicago. A bomb killed 7 policemen and wounded 70 more after they tried to break up a meeting of workers called by anarchists and communists. In a fight at the steelworks at Homestead, Pennsylvania, in 1892, seven men were killed. The Pullman Strike in 1894 again tied up the railroads. In the Middle West, American troops, trying to keep the trains moving, were actually fighting American workers.

The Knights of Labor. Laborers tried a variety of ways of getting together to solve their problems. In 1869 the garment cutters of Philadelphia organized the Knights of Labor. Its idealistic aim was to bring all workers, skilled and unskilled, black and white, into one big union. They hoped that this union would give workers "a proper share of the wealth they create," more leisure time, more of all the benefits of society. They tried to set up companies owned by the workers themselves. They opposed child labor and demanded the eight-hour day.

The Knights were against strikes. But some of their radical members went on strike anyway when the railroads cut wages in 1884. After they won this fight for better wages, membership in the Knights boomed to 700,000. But then the Knights of Labor were involved in the Chicago strikes at the time of the Haymarket Massacre. Although they were not radical at all, a fearful public opinion lumped them together with anarchists and communists. Their membership then rapidly declined.

MOLLY MAGUIRE WARNING, No. 1

MOLLY MAGUIRE WARNING, No. 2

MOLLY MAGUIRE WARNING, No. 3

MOLLY MAGUIRE WARNING, No. 4

Brown Brothers

The Molly Maguires tried to help members by harassing the mine bosses.

Samuel Gompers and the AF of L. Labor leaders learned a good deal from the collapse of the Knights of Labor with its idealistic program and its attempt to combine all workers in one big union. One of them was a Go-Getter organizer named Samuel Gompers.

Born in London, Gompers left school at age 10 to begin work as a cigarmaker. He was 13 when his family came to the United States. Finding work in New York City, he became a member of the cigarmakers' union that took part in a strike that failed in 1877. Then he set about reorganizing the union on a nationwide basis. He charged high dues to build up cash reserves for strikes, and he strengthened discipline within the national union. Strikes were only allowed when the union had the money to support the workers so they could hold out long enough to succeed.

Gompers had developed a special American approach to the problems of labor. In those years many workers in Europe were organizing to make

The Longshoremen's membership card (top) bears several patriotic emblems and inspiring mottoes. The colorful poster (bottom) from the Locomotive Firemen's union honors English inventor George Stephenson, who is known as the "father" of the locomotive.

revolutions. Over there desperate workers were trying to abolish capitalism and take over the factories themselves. But Gompers was no revolutionary. A hardheaded, practical man, he believed that in the long run American workers would be better off if they organized swiftly for a larger share of the profits. They should be as businesslike as the employers themselves. This was "bread and butter" unionism—aimed at higher wages, shorter hours, and safer working conditions.

This approach was so successful that other trades followed the example. Gompers became the father of national unions in the United States. In 1881 he brought many unions together in the Federation of Organized Trades and Labor Unions. In 1886 this was reorganized as the American Federation of Labor. With Gompers as president, the AF of L grew steadily in size and power. By 1904 it had 1.75 million members.

Still, most workers remained unorganized. As late as 1923, steelworkers were laboring twelve hours a day, seven days a week. Labor had a long way to go. Unions would not come into their own until the days of the New Deal and World War II.

Practical and businesslike Samuel Gompers was the founder of the American Federation of Labor. This photograph was taken by a company detective as Gompers prepared to visit miners at a West Virginia coal mine.

AF of L-CIO

SECTION 6 REVIEW

1. Identify or explain: *Commonwealth* v. *Hunt,* National Trades Union, Molly Maguires, Haymarket Massacre, Homestead Strike, Pullman Strike, Samuel Gompers, AF of L.

2. What progress had labor unions made by the time of the Civil War?

3. Describe labor-management conflict after 1870.

4. What were the aims of the Knights of Labor? Why did their membership decline?

5. **Identifying Central Issues.** Explain Samuel Gompers' "bread and butter" unionism.

CHAPTER **16** REVIEW

FOCUSING ON IDEAS

1. How did each of the following developments help transform the United States between 1865 and 1900: railroad growth; trusts and other business combinations; new methods of merchandising; standardization in manufacturing; scientific management; labor unionism?

2. List some personal traits of the captains of industry and finance such as Rockefeller, Carnegie, and Morgan. Do you think the same traits characterize leaders of industry and finance today? Explain.

3. How did the technological developments of the late nineteenth century serve to democratize American life?

TAKING A CRITICAL LOOK

1. **Predicting Consequences.** Had Alexander Hamilton and Thomas Jefferson been able to see the United States in 1900, one of them probably would have celebrated and the other probably would have wept. Who would have celebrated? Who would have wept? Why?

2. **Identifying Central Issues.** The key to rapid industrialization of the United States was not so much the invention of machines and gadgets as it was standardization of parts. Discuss, giving examples.

YOUR REGION IN HISTORY

1. **Geography.** Using the maps on page 353 describe the growth of railroads in your region between 1870 and 1890. How was your area affected by standard time?

2. **Culture.** Use the newspaper archives at your local library to research the first department stores in your community. What types of goods and services did they offer? What impact did they have on the community at large? What happened to smaller stores that offered similar goods and services?

3. **Economics.** Identify and describe the achievements of some business or labor leaders in your state between 1870 and 1900. How was this person linked to developments described in this chapter?

HISTORICAL FACTS AND FIGURES

Predicting Consequences. Use the chart below to help answer the following questions: (a) How many barrels of oil were produced in 1870? In 1900? (b) Which decade saw the largest percentage increase in oil production? (c) What was the average percentage increase per decade between 1870 and 1900? (d) If oil production continued to increase at the same rate after 1900, how many barrels of oil would be produced today? (e) How do you think your estimate compares with the amount of oil actually produced in the United States today? Find out from the United States Department of Energy how much oil was produced last year. If this figure differs from your estimate explain what factors might account for the difference.

Production of Crude Petroleum, 1870-1900		
Year	Production (in barrels)	Value/Barrel
1870	▯	$3.86
1874	▯▯	$1.17
1880	▯▯▯▯▯▯	$.94
1886	▯▯▯▯▯▯	$.71
1890	▯▯▯▯▯▯▯▯▯	$.77
1892	▯▯▯▯▯▯▯▯▯▯	$.51
1900	▯▯▯▯▯▯▯▯▯▯▯	$1.19

▯ = 5 Million Barrels of Petroleum (210 Million Gallons)

Source: *Historical Statistics of the United States*

CHAPTER **17**

The challenge of the cities

In 1873, two years after the fire that had destroyed Chicago, architect Louis Sullivan visited the center of the city. He found it

> magnificent and wild; a crude extravaganza, an intoxicating rawness, a sense of big things to be done. For "big" was the word ... and "biggest in the world" was the braggart phrase on every tongue. ... [The men of Chicago] were the crudest, rawest, most savagely ambitious dreamers and would-be doers in the world ... but these men had vision. What they saw was real.

This, too, was the spirit of the years between the end of the Civil War and the turn of the century. It was called the "Gilded Age" to describe its vulgar, cheap, and gaudy aspects. But though it was sometimes ruthless, corrupt, and destructive, for the most part it was moving, building, expanding, reforming, and dreaming.

1. The growth of an urban nation

During the years after the Civil War there was not only a movement westward to settle the Great Plains, but also another great movement of people from the country to the cities. When the Civil War began, only one American in five was living in a city. By 1915, cities held half of all Americans. Between 1860 and 1915 the nation's rural population just about doubled, but the urban population grew more than 700 percent.

Farmers move to the city. The new cities grew mainly in the East, the Middle West, and the Far West, but they could be found wherever industry was developing. The new city-people came from everywhere.

Railroad builders sent salesmen overseas to boast the wonders of the American farms and persuade immigrants from European cities and farms to come settle along their tracks in the West. At the same time, many American farmers in the East and Midwest were moving away from the land to the city. Behind them in the countryside they left ghost villages. One such village in New England had a population of two inhabitants, one living on each side of the broad street. The abandoned church and the dilapidated schoolhouse were being taken apart for lumber and for kindling wood. Some of the farmers had gone west, but most had gone to the cities. By 1910 more than a third of the people living in American cities had moved in from American farms.

Maurice Prendergast's pen, ink, and watercolor, "Madison Square, New York," was done in 1901. His use of flecks of brilliant color reflects the influence of the French Impressionists.

Immigrants come to the cities. Of the 25 million immigrants who came to the United States between the Civil War and World War I, most settled in the cities. Outside of cities many of them would have felt lonely and lost. They loved the friendly bustle and wanted to be close to people like themselves. And some of them had no choice. They had spent everything to cross the ocean and had no money left for a trip west.

Within the big American cities there sprouted little immigrant cities. By 1890 New York City held as many Germans as Hamburg, twice as many Irish as Dublin, half as many Italians as Naples.

And besides, there were large numbers of Poles, Russians, Hungarians, Austrians, Norwegians, Swedes, and Chinese. Four out of five New Yorkers either were born abroad or were the children of foreign parents. The Germans and Irish who had come before 1880 were found nearly everywhere in the United States. There were also lots of Canadians in Boston and Detroit, Poles in Buffalo and Milwaukee, Austrians in Cleveland, and Italians in New Orleans.

The urban mixture. Cities were sometimes called the nation's "melting pots." Perhaps they should have been called "mixing bowls." The adult immigrant sometimes became Americanized only slowly. But very quickly a whole colony found its special place in American life. Just as the new United States had first been made from thirteen different colonies, now a great nation was being made from countless colonies of immigrants.

Wherever you came from, you could find a neighborhood in New York or in the other big cities where you could feel at home. Whether you were from Germany, Italy, Hungary, or Poland, you could shop in your own old-country language, buy familiar old-country foods, and attend a church offering your old-country services. By 1892 nearly a hundred newspapers in German were published in American cities. And there were dailies in French, Italian, Japanese, Polish, Yiddish, and a dozen other languages.

Although these immigrant colonies tried to keep separate, they could not stay separate forever. The people from different colonies became more and more alike. Children went to school and learned English. They stopped speaking their parents' language and sometimes stopped going to their parents' church. They were afraid to seem foreign. Then, too, a young man from the Italian colony might marry a young woman whose parents spoke German. In the city, people could not help feeling closer to one another.

City slums. If the crowds were the joy of the city, crowding was the curse. New York—the nation's biggest city and busiest seaport and the magnet for the world's immigrants—was where the problem was worst. And in New York, American know-how, which at the same time was building grand cast-iron palaces for department stores, produced another, but unlucky, American invention. This was the "tenement house."

New Yorkers, of course, did not invent the slum. European cities had their streets of ancient rickety buildings and evil-smelling hovels where the poor were tumbled together. But in the years after the Civil War, New York City produced a new kind of slum—the tenement-house slum.

Most newcomers to the city could not afford to pay much rent. Back in the early years of the 1800s the poorer people of New York had lived in shacks on the swamps at the edge of Manhattan Island. But as the island filled with people, specially

Immigrant women gather in the market square of a middlewestern town in the 1890s. One (far left) has adopted an American-style hat.

designed buildings went up for the city's new poor. Tenement houses were buildings six or seven stories high designed to hold the largest possible number of families. They were solid blocks of deep buildings whose inside rooms had no windows or ventilation. There were also helter-skelter buildings of many other kinds.

The dumbbell building. Then in 1878, to help find something better, *The Plumber and Sanitary Engineer,* a builders' magazine, announced a contest for architects. The editors offered a $500 prize for the best plan for tenement apartments for the poor.

The winning plan was the "dumbbell" tenement. It was called that because the whole building, looked at from above, was thin in the middle and bulged at both ends like the dumbbells used in gymnasiums. This plan had a good deal to be said for it compared with the plan of the flimsy firetraps that were common before. The dumbbell tenement, usually built of brick, was supposed to be fireproof.

It was designed to fit on a narrow lot. On each of the seven floors there were four sets of apartments—two in front and two in back. Since the stairway ran up the middle, the front and back rooms got some light and air from their windows on the street. Many people could be crammed into a small space.

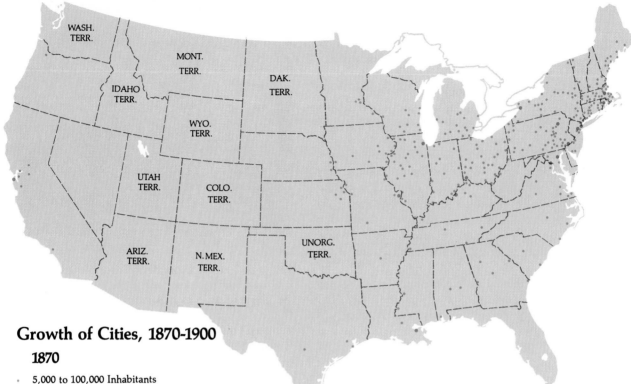

Growth of Cities, 1870-1900

1870

- 5,000 to 100,000 Inhabitants
- 100,000 Inhabitants and Over

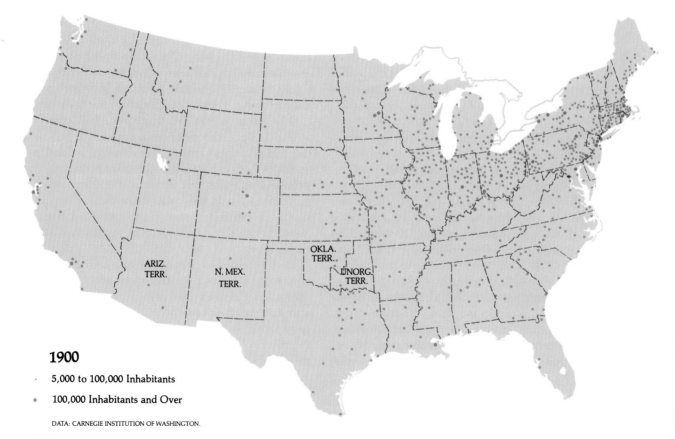

1900

- 5,000 to 100,000 Inhabitants
- 100,000 Inhabitants and Over

DATA: CARNEGIE INSTITUTION OF WASHINGTON.

Everett Shinn, who began his career as a newspaper artist, painted "Cross Streets of New York" in 1899. He was one of the group of painters known as the "ashcan school" because they chose scenes from everyday city life as subjects for their canvases.

What was new about the plan was that the inside rooms were also supposed to get some light and air. When another tenement like it was built alongside, between them there was a narrow air shaft on which each inside room had a window. This became the standard plan for tenements.

By 1900 on the island of Manhattan alone there were more than 40,000 buildings of this type, holding 1,500,000 people. A prizewinning plan had produced the world's prize slum!

The air shaft between the buildings was only 56 inches wide—so narrow that it did not really bring in light. Instead the foul air brought up smells from the garbage piling up at the bottom. If there was a fire, the air shafts became flues which quickly inflamed all the rooms around. Up the air shaft resounded the noise of quarreling neighbors. There was no privacy.

Dirt, disease, and crime. The primitive plumbing in the hallway on each floor was shared by four families. It bred flies and germs. Sometimes the toilets became so disgusting that the tenants would not use them but depended on the plumbing at work or at school. There were no bathtubs with running water. Nearly every one of these tenement houses had at least one sufferer from tuberculosis, and sometimes there were many more.

When Theodore Roosevelt was governor of New York, he appointed a commission in 1900 to report on the tenement-house slums. They were not at all surprised that these buildings festered with poverty, disease, and crime. But they were surprised that, in spite of it all, so many of the people raised there managed to become decent and self-respecting. And the commission reported that the slums were even worse than they had been 50 years before.

Slum neighborhoods were given names like "Misery Lane" and "Murderers' Alley." This was hardly the America that the thousands of hopeful immigrants were looking for.

On tenement back porches, like those shown in this photograph by Jacob Riis about 1900, clotheslines stretched from post to post and from porch to backyard alley. Notice the flowerpots and plant boxes on the railings.

The tenement kitchen was a multipurpose room. It was a second bedroom (top) for many poor families, and a workshop (bottom) for others. The sewing machine provided a livelihood for thousands of immigrant families.

Boss rule. Under the influx of people and the pressures of rapid growth, the governments of big cities broke down. Streets were unrepaired, sewers nonexistent, garbage uncollected. Big cities were described as the worst-governed units in this democratic nation. In New York City during the days of Boss Tweed between 1866 and 1871, the city was looted of some $100 million by the boss and his underlings. Other political groups, "rings" as they were called at the time, robbed Philadelphia, Pittsburgh, and other cities.

Many reformers blamed this state of affairs on the immigrant who, they said, was "a European peasant whose horizon has been narrow, whose moral and religious training has been meager and false, and whose ideas of life are low." But Philadelphia, where 47 percent of the population was native born of native-born parents, was as corrupt as New York, where 80 percent of the residents were of foreign birth or foreign parentage.

The immigrant and the politician. Immigrants did tend to vote for the boss and the followers of his political "machine." But this was because the machine members—often aldermen, or city councillors—provided friendly help. They supplied government jobs and money and advice. A new arrival who was arrested for a petty crime could turn to the alderman of his ward to find him a lawyer or to persuade the judge to let him off. The alderman organized benefit dances. The money paid for dance tickets would go to some worker who had been crippled at his work or to a widow who had no way of supporting her children. The alderman found doctors for the sick and brought groceries to the poor. He reached into his pocket to give a few dollars to needy orphans or to men wanting a new start in business. He was a one-man United Fund. No wonder immigrants voted for him and for the machine again and again.

The disappearing frontier. The problems of the Gilded Age—corruption in government and business, strikes, and labor violence—worried Americans. Why was it all happening? One bright young historian, Frederick Jackson Turner, who had been raised in the backwoods of Wisconsin, thought he knew the reason. The Census of 1890 had announced that the United States no longer had an unbroken line of wilderness frontier. Turner proposed the theory that this disappearance of the frontier explained many of the country's troubles.

According to Turner, what had made America the Land of Promise was not cities but the frontier. The free land out west, he said, had also been a safety valve. In earlier times if a family in an eastern city wanted a second chance, they could move out west. But now that the country was being filled up, it was no longer possible to find a second chance by going out to the edge of civilization. Now if you were an unlucky newcomer in a slum, there appeared to be no escape.

Oldcomers versus Newcomers. For a while it seemed that the country might be divided between Oldcomers and Newcomers. Oldcomers themselves, of course, had come from immigrant families, but their families had been here for a long time. Among them were the rich and famous. Few of them were crowded into slums.

In the older eastern states that still controlled Congress, the Oldcomers were in charge. They were most of those who had money and education and power. But the Oldcomers did not agree on how to cure the country's ills. Some tried to help the immigrant learn new ways, but some were

simply frightened. They wanted to keep the country the way it was. They blamed the troubles on the Newcomers. Their answer was to slam the door. Simply because *their* families had been here longer, they felt that the whole nation belonged to them.

At Harvard College a group of New England blue bloods thought that their world was coming to an end. Three young men in the class of 1889, Charles Warren, Robert DeCourcy Ward, and Prescott Farnsworth Hall, had been taught by their professors that there was an "Anglo-Saxon" race superior to all others. The race was supposed to be separated from other races not by color but by their homeland. The "superior" people were supposed to be from England and Germany. And that just happened to be where the families of Warren and Ward and Hall had come from!

These young men had been raised near Boston. Their parents were horrified by the hordes of "vulgar" immigrants and especially by those with unfamiliar ways—from Ireland and from southern and eastern Europe. These New England aristocrats said that the nation's problems could be solved by keeping out all people who were not like themselves.

Five years after their graduation, Warren and Ward and Hall formed the Immigration Restriction League to persuade Congress to pass laws to keep out all "undesirable" immigrants. In their League they enlisted famous professors and writers. Their real object was to keep out the "new" immigrants— the Newcomers. These "new" immigrants, they argued, were the main cause of the increasing crime, the strikes, and most of the troubles of the country.

The literacy test. To keep out "undesirables" they proposed a "literacy test." According to their proposed law persons over fourteen years of age who wanted to come into the United States would have to prove that they could read and write. They did not have to know English, provided they could read and write their own native language.

At first sight the test seemed harmless enough. Actually it was aimed against people from certain countries, such as Italy and Greece, where poor peasants had no chance to go to school. The Boston blue bloods believed that because Newcomers from such countries were not "Anglo-Saxons" they must be "inferior."

LOOKING BACKWARD.
THEY WOULD CLOSE TO THE NEW-COMER THE BRIDGE THAT CARRIED THEM AND THEIR FATHERS OVER.

Culver Pictures

Austrian-born J. Keppler's lithograph cartoon from the magazine *Puck* shows a group of well-to-do Americans barring the entry of a new immigrant. The Newcomer sees what the Oldcomers cannot-- the shadows looming behind them of their own immigrant fathers.

But in their proposed law they did not dare list particular countries. There already were many people in the United States from those countries. They would be insulted—and they, too, elected members of Congress.

Year after year the Immigration Restriction League tried to persuade Congress to pass a literacy test. But even when they finally pushed their bill through Congress, they did not manage to make it into a law. One President after another vetoed the bill. President Grover Cleveland called the law "underhanded," because it did not say what it really meant. President William Howard Taft said the United States needed the labor of all immigrants and should teach them to read. President Woodrow Wilson agreed.

All three Presidents said the law was un-American. The United States had always been "a nation of nations." It made no sense to keep out people simply because they had been oppressed. America was a haven for the oppressed. Here the starving could find bread, and the illiterate could learn to read.

In 1917, however, when the war in Europe was frightening Americans, the literacy test finally had enough votes in Congress to pass over President Wilson's veto.

Out on the West Coast, Oldcomers feared Newcomers from Asia. They worried about imaginary hordes that might come across the Pacific. And they had persuaded Congress to pass a Chinese Exclusion Act in 1882. Then, in 1907, President Theodore Roosevelt without the use of any law against the Japanese persuaded the Japanese government to stop their people from emigrating. This un-American agreement came to be called the

"Gentlemen's Agreement." And this became the slang expression for any agreement to discriminate against people when you were ashamed to admit what you were really doing.

SECTION 1 REVIEW

1. Identify or explain: "melting pots" and "mixing bowls," dumbbell building, Tweed Ring, political machines, aldermen, Turner's frontier thesis, Immigration Restriction League, Chinese Exclusion Act, Gentlemen's Agreement.

2. What movements accounted for the growth of cities after the Civil War?

3. Describe a typical tenement house.

4. Why and how was a start made on limiting immigration?

5. **Recognizing Cause and Effect.** Why did immigrant colonies form in the cities? Why did they lose their separateness?

Chinese immigrants, dressed in traditional clothes and with their hair in long pig-tails, walk down a street in San Francisco's crowded Chinatown about 1880.

Louis Stein Collection/California Historical Society

Culver Pictures

Jane Addams was a kind and gentle woman whose concern for needy newcomers led her to open Hull House settlement in Chicago. Many others were later to follow her example.

2. Reformers and self-helpers

Not all the Oldcomers were frightened. Some became reformers. If the country had too many strikes and too much crime, they said, that could not be blamed on those who had just arrived.

It was mainly the fault, they said, of the Americans who had been here longest and who had had the most chance to make the country better. Who had built the cities and the slums where the poor were condemned to live? Who were the members of Congress and the leaders of business and the police officers? It was not the immigrants' fault if the nation was not prepared to receive them.

Jane Addams. One of the most remarkable of the reformers and one of the most original Americans of the age was Jane Addams. She was born with a deformity of the spine which made her so sickly that after graduating from college in 1882 she had to spend two years in bed. When she was well enough to travel, her wealthy family sent her abroad to study art and architecture. What she really learned in Europe was something quite different.

Jacob Riis, a Danish immigrant, helped to improve the lot of New York City's poor with his books and striking photographs. This one showed Christmas Eve at a settlement house.

In June 1888, when she happened to visit the famous Toynbee Hall in London, she discovered her life's purpose. There in the poorest section of the city lived a group of Oxford and Cambridge graduates helping the people of the neighborhood. Why not try something like that in the United States?

Jane Addams's plan was simple. In the poorest, most miserable city slum she would settle a group of educated young men and women from well-to-do families. Like Toynbee Hall, the place would be called a "settlement house." The well-bred young men and women newly "settled" in the midst of a slum reminded her of the early colonial "settlers" who had left the comforts of English life to live in an American wilderness.

The young men and women who came to live in the slum, seeing the struggles of the poor, would learn things they could never learn from books. At the same time, the people of the slum would use the settlement house as a school, a club, and a refuge.

Hull House. Since she knew Chicago, she decided to do her work there. In the neediest neighborhood she persuaded the owner of a large old house to let her have it free. That became her settlement house—between an undertaker's parlor and a saloon. She called it "Hull House" after the man who had built it for his home years before.

In the neighborhood of Hull House there were Newcomers from all over Europe—Italians, Germans, Polish and Russian Jews, Bohemians, French Canadians, and others. For the young, Jane Addams set up a kindergarten and a boys' club. And she paid special attention to the very old people whom nobody else seemed to care about.

Jane Addams's work became famous. All sorts of unexpected projects started at Hull House. The Little Theater movement, of amateur actors putting on plays to entertain themselves and their friends, developed there and spread all over the country. She started a book bindery and a music school.

Settlement houses on the Hull House model appeared in big cities everywhere. Future playwrights, actors, composers, and musicians who had happened to be born into poor slum families now found their chance.

Thousands of lonely immigrants discovered that somebody else cared about them. Jane Addams—without the aid of governments or politicians—had helped make America the promised land.

Other reformers. In Hull House and other settlement houses the first social workers—many of them women—were trained, and they became a growing force for change. They moved beyond private charity to use the power of the state to improve conditions. Their first activities produced laws limiting child labor and governing the hours and conditions of labor for women.

Frances Willard was an Oldcomer who fought for reform in another way. In the Wisconsin wilderness, where she grew up, she became a good hunter. The only schooling she received came from her mother, but she learned enough to attend a college in Illinois and become a teacher. Then she was caught up by the temperance movement. Abstinence in the use of alcoholic beverages, she felt, would protect the home and Christian life. With her talent for organization and for oratory, in 1874 she was made president of the Women's Christian Temperance Union in Chicago and five years later was elected national president.

From that position Frances Willard worked also for women's right to vote. It was not surprising

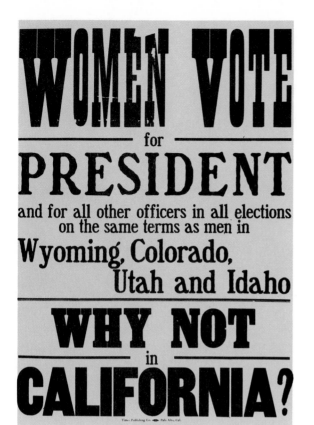

The Bancroft Library, University of California, Berkeley

A women's suffrage amendment was sent to a narrow defeat by California's voters in 1896 after a strenuous campaign.

that the first progress came on the western frontier. There it was plain that new communities depended on pioneer women. Why shouldn't they be allowed to vote? Wyoming came into the Union in 1890 with women's suffrage. Then other western states gave women the right to vote—Colorado (1893), Utah (1896), and Idaho (1896). But the movement stalled, and little progress was made for over a decade.

Out of the South, too, there came other women reformers. Ida B. Wells-Barnett, who had been born a slave in Mississippi, became a newspaper writer in Tennessee. But when she wrote fearless stories exposing the facts about a lynching, she was driven out of the state. Then she went to New York City where she helped set up black women's clubs which became the foundation of the National Association of Colored Women in 1896. In 1909 she helped to organize the National Association for the Advancement of Colored People. And in 1913 she established a settlement house in Chicago to help black newcomers from the South find jobs and homes in the big city.

SECTION 2 REVIEW

1. How did settlement houses help immigrants?
2. **Making Comparisons.** Compare the reform work of Frances Willard and Ida Wells-Barnett.

3. The spread of learning

In the city and on the countryside the public schools helped make Americans. They were free, and the states passed laws requiring all children to attend. There the children of Irish, German, Italian, and all sorts of other families learned and played—and sometimes fought—together. They came to know one another better than their parents knew people from other countries. And some of these young people went on to study at new colleges and learned to become leaders.

The schools make Americans. At home many families spoke Polish or Italian or some other language, but in school everybody spoke English. Even if the parents spoke English with a foreign accent, soon the children sounded like other Americans. At home the children taught their parents English and all kinds of American customs. One little girl in New York City who had learned to use a toothbrush brought it home from school. She showed it to her mother, who had been born in a peasant hut in Poland and had never seen such a thing. Her mother, too, was soon brushing her teeth in the American manner.

Now many children could go on to the free public high school, which was an American invention. After 1870 these new public high schools spread across the country. By 1900 there were 6000 high schools attended by nearly 520,000 students, more than two and a half times the number attending only ten years before.

The flourishing schools made the United States one of the world's first literate nations. Thousands of the peasants and poor city workers who arrived from Europe had never learned to read. But in the United States the proportion of people who could

Jacob Riis took this picture of immigrant children saluting the flag at the Moss Street Industrial School in New York City in the early 1900s. In rural areas the one-room schoolhouse was usual. The photograph (below) taken at the end of the 19th century shows pupils from a school near Black River Falls, Wisconsin, assembled with their teacher for their annual school picture.

read and write steadily increased after the Civil War. Unfortunately in the South the promising start made during Reconstruction was not followed by the Old Confederates when they took office.

Growth of the colleges. America had always been a land of help-yourself. But it was not easy for Newcomers to become leaders. So many respectable institutions remained in the hands of the Oldcomers whose families had been here for a century or more. For example, Harvard College—our oldest college, where young blue bloods had learned their ideas of Anglo-Saxon superiority—was run by Oldcomers. It was hard even to become a student there if you were not one of them.

New institutions offered the best chance for Newcomers who wanted to become leaders. Among the most remarkable and most American were the scores of new colleges and universities.

At the outbreak of the Civil War there were only seventeen state universities. Then, in 1862 an energetic Republican congressman, Justin S. Morrill

from rural Vermont, secured the passage of the Morrill Act. This act granted lands to the states from the public domain—30,000 acres for each of the states' senators and representatives in Congress—to support new state colleges. In these "land-grant" colleges students would be taught to be better farmers. The land-grant colleges also often offered solid courses in engineering, science, and literature. So here Newcomers, too, found an opportunity to learn.

After the Civil War, hundreds of other colleges and universities were founded. In the later years of the 1880s, some of the wealthiest Go-Getters gave millions of dollars to found and endow still more institutions of higher learning. In 1876 Johns Hopkins University was established from the fortune left by a Baltimore merchant. In 1885 a railroad builder, Leland Stanford, in memory of his son, set up Leland Stanford, Jr., University. In 1891 John D. Rockefeller, the Go-Getting oil millionaire, created the University of Chicago. And there were scores of others.

Many of these college founders had themselves never gone to college. But they shared the American faith in education. Even before the end of the 1800s, the United States had more colleges and universities than there were in all western Europe. And a larger proportion of the citizens could afford to go to college here than in any other country. The children of poor immigrants, along with millions of other Americans, now had a better chance to rise in the world.

Women's colleges multiplied rapidly in the years after the Civil War. In 1861 Matthew Vassar, who had been born in England and had made his fortune as a brewer and in whaling, founded Vassar College. When Vassar advertised to attract students to his college, he also publicized the importance of higher education for women. Before long there were more women's colleges, including Wellesley (1870), Smith (1875), and Bryn Mawr (1880). Many other new colleges, especially in the Middle West, were open to women as well as men. And the number of women in college grew from 9000 in 1869 to more than 20,000 in 1894.

Education for black Americans. Wealthy men and women, mostly from the North, also gave millions of dollars to help educate black people. By 1900 there were already about 30,000 black teachers. John D. Rockefeller, for example, had contributed over $50 million, most of it to train more teachers for black schools. The South spent less money than other parts of the country on education of all kinds. And blacks there had to attend separate, and inferior, schools. How then were they to get ahead? Black leaders could not agree.

One way was proposed by Booker T. Washington. Born a slave, Washington worked his own way upward until he was famous throughout the world. His own story of his life, *Up from Slavery* (1901), was read by millions.

In 1881 Washington founded Tuskegee Institute in Alabama. There he trained thousands of blacks to be better farmers and mechanics, to make a good living, and to help build their communities.

Frances Benjamin Johnston, a prominent turn-of-the-century photographer, caught this senior American history class at Booker T. Washington's Tuskegee Institute.

He believed in a step-by-step way "up from slavery." He did not want blacks to spend their efforts learning history and literature and foreign languages and science and mathematics. Instead, he said, they should train quickly for jobs—and mostly for jobs they could do with their hands. The vote, which had been taken away from them in the 1890s (p. 542), could wait. Self-respect, self-education, and self-help, he said, would bring blacks the opportunities they desired.

Many who admired Booker T. Washington still did not agree with him. Why should blacks have to wait for their rights? Twenty-five years after Booker T. Washington started his Tuskegee Institute in Alabama, a group met at Niagara Falls.

Their black leader was W. E. B. Du Bois. His life had been very different from that of Booker T. Washington. Born in Massachusetts after the Civil War, he studied at the University of Berlin in Germany and then received a Ph.D. degree from Harvard in 1895. Du Bois was a poet and a man of brilliant mind and vast learning. Why should anyone try to tell Du Bois and others like him to be satisfied to work with their hands?

In 1905 the declaration by Du Bois's Niagara Movement expressed outrage. It demanded for blacks *all* their human rights, all their rights as Americans, and *at once*. It opposed all laws and all customs that treated blacks as if they were different from other people. And of course, it demanded the right to vote.

SECTION 3 REVIEW

1. Identify or explain: Justin Morrill, Matthew Vassar, Tuskegee Institute, Niagara Movement.

2. How did public schools help to Americanize the immigrants?

3. What was the importance of the Morrill Act?

4. Trace the growth of colleges for women and for blacks.

5. **Recognizing Ideologies.** Contrast the views of Booker T. Washington and W.E.B. Du Bois.

---

4. Bridge-building heroes

Many of the fast-growing American cities were on the banks of rivers—the highways of the pioneers. As immigrant families and farm families pressed in, the cities had to expand. They had to find ways of carrying thousands of daily passengers out beyond the old city limits. This meant that in order to hold their citizens together they had to span the neighboring waterways. Go-Getting engineers transformed the ancient art of bridge building to reach out to the new city frontiers.

Bridging the Mississippi. Something about bridge building attracted and inspired the American inventive genius. James Buchanan Eads, the man who would build the bridge for St. Louis, had proven himself during the Civil War. In 1861, as an adviser to the Union navy, he proposed a fleet of ironclad gunboats to control the Mississippi River. Then, when the government took up his suggestions, he built the needed ships in 65 days.

After the war the people of St. Louis, which was on the west bank of the Mississippi, saw that they had to bring the railroad across the wide river and into their city if St. Louis was to grow. Many schemes were offered. But all were rejected until Eads appeared. As a boy he had worked on a river steamboat. When only 22 years old, he had invented a diving bell to salvage ships that had sunk in the river. And then he had done a lot of walking underwater on the very bottom of the Mississippi. He knew that river bottom almost as well as other men knew the city streets.

What Eads had learned was important. Building a bridge across the Mississippi depended first on finding solid support under the sandy river bottom. As Eads had moved along 65 feet below the surface of the water, he had seen the currents churning up the sands. He knew that the supports for his bridge would have to go far below those river sands—all the way down to bedrock.

In 1867, when Eads began construction, his first problem was to lay the foundations of the two stone towers that would hold up the arches of the bridge in midstream. The towers would rise 50 feet above water level. The foundation of one would have to go down 86 feet below water level, and the other, where bedrock was deeper, would have to go down 123 feet. But was this possible?

Working underwater. Eads's plan was to use his own diving bell together with some new caissons—watertight working chambers—that had recently been perfected in England. The 75-foot-wide caissons would keep out the water while the men dug beneath the river sands to reach solid rock.

When Eads's men finally reached bedrock, they were working ten stories below the surface of the water! Because of the great pressures at that depth, the men could stay down only 45 minutes at a time. They had to come up slowly, and they rested long periods between shifts. Despite all precautions thirteen men died of "caisson disease" (sometimes called "the bends") from too rapid change in air pressure.

The bridge completed. Steel had never been used in such a large structure, but Eads decided to use it for the three vast arches of the bridge. When the standard carbon steel did not meet his tests, he ordered large quantities of the new chromium steel, and then supervised its production. While chromium steel was more costly, it was rustproof and needed no covering.

It took Eads seven years to bridge the Mississippi. Finally in 1874 in a grand ceremony the former Union general, William T. Sherman, pounded the last spike of the double-track railroad crossing the bridge. Then fourteen locomotives, two by two, chugged triumphantly across the river. President Grant came to St. Louis to proclaim Eads an American hero.

A bridge to Brooklyn. And there were other heroic bridge builders who helped open ways to the suburban frontiers. Few cities were quite so hemmed in by water as New York. Manhattan Island, heart of the city, was surrounded by the East River, the Hudson River, and the Atlantic Ocean. For a half-century there had been proposals for a bridge across the East River, connecting lower Manhattan Island to Brooklyn. When the fierce winter of 1866–1867 stopped all ferry service and isolated Brooklyn from Manhattan for days, it was plain that something had to be done.

John Roebling was ready with a plan. When he came to the United States from Germany as a young man, he opened the first factory for making wire rope out of many strands of wire twisted together. This new material was wonderfully suited for reaching over wide rivers where it was difficult or impossible to build masonry towers in midstream. From high towers on both ends you could suspend the strong wire rope to hold up the bridge.

If the Niagara River, for example, was to be spanned near the Falls, it would have to be by such a "suspension" bridge. In 1855 Roebling completed a wire-supported bridge over the Niagara—strong enough to carry fully loaded trains. This feat made John Roebling famous. In 1860 he completed another suspension bridge, just outside Pittsburgh, reaching 1000 feet across the Allegheny River. And by 1867 he had completed still another outside Cincinnati across the Ohio River.

A bridge from Manhattan to Brooklyn would have to stay high above water level in order to allow the sails and smokestacks of large ocean-going vessels to pass underneath. Could a suspension bridge, Roebling-style, solve New York's problem? Roebling's ambitious plan in 1867 proposed towers at both ends 271 feet above water level, holding up a main suspension span of 1595 feet. That was far longer than any suspension bridge ever built before.

Washington Roebling carries on. During the very beginning of construction in 1868, a ferry crushed John Roebling's foot against the dock, and he died from tetanus infection in two weeks. John Roebling's son, Washington Roebling, was ready to carry on. He too was a man of courage and had proved himself on the Gettysburg battlefield.

On his father's death, Washington Roebling at once took over the building of the bridge. In 1872, when fire in the Brooklyn caisson threatened the whole project, Roebling stayed below for seven hours in the compressed-air chamber. As a result he acquired "caisson disease."

Washington Roebling never fully recovered. Too weak to supervise the bridge on the spot, he would sit in a wheelchair in his apartment and watch the work through field glasses. Then he would give instructions to his wife, Emily, who carried them down to the bridge. All his communications with the world were through her. Efforts were made to remove him from the job, but his mind remained active, and he would not give up the command.

The dedication of the bridge. At 1:30 on the afternoon of May 24, 1883, fourteen years after John Roebling had begun the job, President Chester A. Arthur and his Cabinet joined with Governor Grover Cleveland of New York for the formal

The grand opening of the Brooklyn Bridge on May 24, 1883, was celebrated with gun salutes and fireworks as this colorful Currier and Ives lithograph reveals.

opening of the Brooklyn Bridge. Six warships anchored below the bridge fired a resounding salute, and from the center of the bridge came a dazzling display of fireworks. The orator of the occasion declared that this, the world's greatest bridge, was a triumph of "the faith of the saint and the courage of the hero."

The "saint," Emily Warren Roebling, attended the celebrations. But Washington Roebling, the heroic bridge-building son of a heroic father, was too ill to leave the room from which he had overseen the work. The President of the United States went to Roebling's simple apartment at No. 110 Columbia Heights to give his congratulations.

SECTION 4 REVIEW

1. What contributions did Eads and Roeblings make to bridge construction?
2. **Identifying Central Issues.** How did bridge building contribute to the growth of cities?

5. Going up! elevators and skyscrapers

After the Civil War, Americans were not only stretching *out*. They began using their own know-how—together with materials and know-how from all over the world—to stretch their cities *up*.

Although some Americans were moving to the suburbs, more people than ever before wanted to live and work right in the center of the city. Businessmen wanted to be where the action was. And many people who could afford to live in the suburbs still preferred to live downtown.

Solving problems. With old kinds of construction the tallest buildings had seldom been over five or six stories high. There were two problems that had to be solved before buildings could go higher.

The first problem—how to get the people up and down—was beginning to be solved even before the Civil War. In a few luxury hotels, elevators already carried guests up to the fifth and sixth floors. And in some early department stores the elevator was an attractive curiosity. Still, people were afraid to use them. Elisha Graves Otis invented a brake that would automatically clamp the elevator cage to the sides if the rope broke. To calm people's fears, Otis staged a sensational demonstration. He rode the elevator to the top. Then while an attendant cut the rope, Otis waved nonchalantly to the astonished spectators. Otis's early steam-driven elevators were slow, but before 1880 the improved "hydraulic" elevators (pushed up by water pressure in a long vertical cylinder) were climbing at 600 feet a minute. By 1892 an electric motor was carrying passengers up so fast that it "stopped" their ears.

The second problem—how to hold up the building—began to be solved when James Bogardus and others used cast iron for their Buyers' Palaces. No longer was it necessary to build a tall building like a pyramid, with thick supporting walls on the lower floors.

From dreams to reality. The time was ripe for the "skyscraper." Of course Bogardus was only dreaming when he forecast buildings "ten miles high." But he was not far wrong when he told American builders that only the sky would be the limit.

Bogardus himself constructed one of the first buildings of true skyscraper design. Its frame was a tall iron cage. If the cage was strong and rigid, and solidly anchored at the bottom, then the building could go up high without needing thick walls at the bottom. This was "skeleton" construction. The building was held up, not by wide foundations but by its own rigid skeleton.

By the 1890s the new steel-framed skyscrapers were going up everywhere. Here is the Syndicate Building in New York City.

The first time Bogardus actually tried this, in 1855, he built a skeleton-framed tower eight stories high for a factory.

It was one thing to build a tower but quite another to trust the lives of hundreds to such a newfangled way of building. The first real try was in Chicago, where the pioneer was William Le Baron Jenney. An adventurous man of wide experience, he had helped build a railroad across Panama before there was any canal. In the Civil War he served on General Sherman's staff as an engineer.

In 1884 when the Home Insurance Company decided to construct a new office building in Chicago, they gave him the job. Jenney, who had probably heard of Bogardus's tower built 29 years before, decided himself to use an iron skeleton. In the next year his building was completed.

Steel and the age of the skyscraper. Even before Jenney's first skyscraper was completed, a better new material had been perfected. This new material, steel, like wrought iron, was made from iron ore, but was far superior. While wrought iron was easily shaped into beams, it bent too readily to be suitable for a skyscraper frame. Steel was the answer. And it was the material that made higher and higher American skyscrapers possible.

Though people had known how to make steel for centuries, the process had been difficult and time consuming. Steel was so expensive that it was used only for small objects. The swords used by knights in the Middle Ages were made by endlessly hammering and reheating and then again hammering the blades. Until the mid-1800s this was the usual way to harden iron to make it into steel.

Then an Englishman, Henry Bessemer, invented his new mass-production steel furnace. By blowing air through the molten iron mass, the carbon in it was burnt out much more quickly. Now it was possible to produce 100 tons of steel from a single furnace in twelve hours. Before the end of the nineteenth century, the United States—borrowing English methods, improved by American know-how—was producing about twice as much steel as Great Britain, and now led the world. Better, cheaper steel meant more tall buildings. The age of the skyscraper had arrived.

SECTION 5 REVIEW

1. Why did Americans build "up" as well as "out"?

2. **Determining Relevance.** How did the work of Otis and Bessemer affect cities?

---

6. New towns in the country

As the whole country became more citified, there grew up new kinds of instant cities. At first their aim was not to grow big, but to stay small—and so escape the troubles of the crowded metropolis.

Business firms were looking for new places to put their factories. Workers were anxious to escape the tenements and the darkened, crowded cities. Prosperous merchants and lawyers and doctors were eager to raise their families out in the open air.

Company towns. With the new railroad network there was less reason than ever for factories to stay in big cities. Almost any spot along a railroad line would do. Raw materials could be brought in from anywhere and finished products could be transported to any place.

If an industrialist built a factory away from a big city, the workers would not have to live in slums. Then why not build a "company town"? Out where land was less expensive, each worker could have a neat little house with a garden. The employer could provide parks and playgrounds, and workers might be more content. After the Civil War many energetic businessmen had this idea.

In 1881 Andrew Carnegie built a steel plant and a whole new town called Homestead seven miles up the Monongahela River from Pittsburgh. Besides small houses for the workers and their families, Carnegie provided a library and even bowling alleys. Homestead was not beautiful, but at least it lacked the crowds and the filth of the slums in the big cities.

George M. Pullman, inventor of the Pullman sleeping car for railroads, also decided to build a new town ten miles outside Chicago. In 1884 he bought a tract of land on the shores of Lake Calumet. He named it after himself and hoped it would be a model for other company towns. Pullman's architect designed the whole town, including a central square with town hall, churches, a library, and parks. All the buildings, including the small houses for the workers, were of dark-red brick.

In the company towns that sprang up all over the country, workers could escape the worst horrors of the big city. But they found some new horrors. Living in a company town was something like being a feudal serf in the Middle Ages. The company not only controlled your job but also decided where you would live and where (and at what price) you

The Carnegie Steel Company's enormous plant at Homestead, Pennsylvania, in the 1890s.

Library of Congress

could buy your food. The company controlled your schools and even hired your police.

Some of the most violent strikes were in these company towns. When the Carnegie Steel Company cut wages at its Homestead plant in 1892, the angry workers went on strike. In the resulting violence a dozen men were killed.

Garden cities. But the company town was not the only new-style city that grew up at the end of the 1800s. On the "suburban frontier" there appeared the garden city. The first of these had been started even before the Civil War when, in the 1850s, Llewellyn Park in New Jersey was created. It was followed in the 1860s by Riverside, Illinois, outside Chicago. There Frederick Law Olmsted and his partner Calvert Vaux laid out a planned, garden-like community along the winding Des Plaines River. Olmsted and Vaux had also helped bring the country to the city when they designed and created Central Park in New York during the 1850s.

Soon other towns followed the pioneer garden cities. Some rich families who owned summer houses in the country near cities began living out in the suburbs year-round. For example, some businessmen who worked in New York City preferred living in Old Greenwich, Connecticut, forty-five minutes away on the railroad. These rich suburban pioneers set up their own country clubs and tried to keep their communities "exclusive"—for Old-comers only and not for any of the Newcomer immigrants.

The push for new garden cities was encouraged by an English reformer. Ebenezer Howard had come to America as a young man and had spent five years around crowded Chicago. Then in his book, *Garden Cities of Tomorrow* (1898), he offered his blueprint for a suburban utopia. He urged people to group together to build garden cities—new small towns out in the country. These towns, he said, should be planned with a garden belt all around. Then, if the garden city was connected to the big city by a railroad, it gave its residents the best of both worlds.

Other Americans followed Howard's advice and built garden cities. These were no longer only for the very rich, but they were not yet for people of modest means. Lake Forest outside Chicago and Shaker Heights outside Cleveland tried to make the garden city more romantic than the big city. Instead of the monotonous parallel streets of checkerboard city blocks, the garden city streets wound across the countryside. Wide lawns separated the houses from the roads and from one another. Before long, garden cities like Radburn, New Jersey, were being specially planned for people of modest income. In 1910 a New York architect made a new design for space-saving "garden apartments" with "kitchenettes" (a new American word for a compact kitchen and pantry). Now you no longer needed to be rich to live out in a garden suburb.

SECTION 6 REVIEW

1. Identify some early suburbs.
2. **Identifying Central Issues.** What were good and bad aspects of company towns?

391

FOCUSING ON IDEAS

1. While some rural villages almost vanished in the farm-to-city movement, the number of rural towns and villages (places with fewer than 2500 residents) increased decade after decade until about 1930. How did the rural village serve the farm population? What additional services were provided in American towns and cities?

2. Rapid city growth required expansion of public services. What were some of these services? How was the expansion of such services linked to political corruption?

3. The "Gilded Age" of American history was a time when things appeared shiny and new from the outside, but a closer look at the under layers revealed decay and corruption. What are some examples of this paradoxical image?

TAKING A CRITICAL LOOK

1. **Expressing Problems Clearly.** Suppose that you were an Oldcomer in a big city in the 1890s. What changes taking place might upset you? Which of these changes might be easy to blame on the Newcomers?

2. **Recognizing Cause and Effect.** Between 1870 and 1910, total U.S. population increased about 230 percent, high school graduates per year rose 950 percent, and college enrollment jumped about 700 percent. How did the growth of cities help to bring about this rapid rise in educational attainment?

YOUR REGION IN HISTORY

1. **Geography.** To what big city or cities does your community have close ties? When did those cities grow most rapidly?

2. **Culture.** Identify a college or university in your area and research its origin. Who or what was it named after? Was it a product of the Morrill Act? What type of students would have attended this institution in 1900?

3. **Economics.** What economic developments after the Civil War led to the rapid growth of cities in your state?

HISTORICAL FACTS AND FIGURES

Testing Hypotheses. Use the graph below to answer the following questions: (1) Approximately what percentage of the population lived in cities in 1850? in 1880? in 1900? (b) How much did the total population grow between 1850 and 1900? (c) About how many immigrants came to the United States during this same period? (d) What hypothesis, or educated guess, can you make about where most immigrants chose to live during this period? (e) Does the information in this chapter support your hypothesis? Explain your answer.

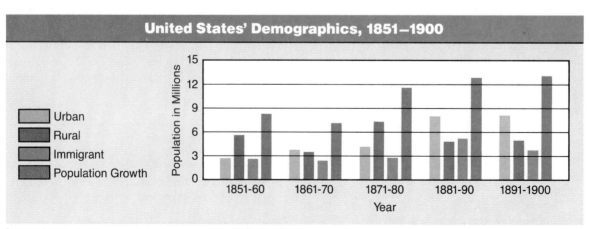

Sources: Bureau of the Census; U.S. Immigration and Naturalization Service

CHAPTER 18

Politics in the Gilded Age

In American history the years between 1865 and 1900 are known as the
Gilded Age. And for a good reason. Anything "gilded" is covered with a
thin layer of gold. It glitters on the surface. But what is underneath is
seldom so attractive. In this Gilded Age the surface of American life
shone with many kinds of new wealth, made by adventurous and enterprising Go-Getters. That glitter covered a multitude of sins. It was a
world of crowded cities, mammoth businesses, and extremes of wealth
and poverty.

1. Parties in balance

The two main political parties were nearly even in
strength between 1876 and 1892. In three of the
five presidential elections during those years the
difference in the popular vote between the Republican and the Democratic candidates was less than 1
percent. In 1876 the Democrats had a popular
majority of 3 percent but lost the election. And
again, in 1888, the Democrat Cleveland had 100,000
more votes than the Republican Harrison, but
Harrison won. Garfield in 1880 defeated Winfield
Scott Hancock by only 7000 votes in over 9 million
cast. Victory seemed almost an accident.

During these years Presidents seldom had their
own party in control of both houses of Congress.
This inability to win both houses, combined with
the closeness of the presidential vote, made an age of
timid Presidents. Any new step might lose the few
votes that meant a lost election and lost power.

Rutherford B. Hayes. Rutherford B. Hayes was
a cold, honest, and straightforward man whose
position as President was weakened by the way he
came to office. His enemies referred to him as "His

Fraudulency" or "Rutherfraud" B. Hayes. But
Hayes himself never doubted that by a fair count he
deserved to be President. Hayes further weakened
his position, however, by announcing that he would
serve only one term. This meant that his enemies
within the party were willing to oppose him, since
they knew that he would not be the party's
candidate in 1880.

The great railway strike. Hayes took office in
March 1877 during the deep depression that had
begun in 1873. Labor strife erupted almost at
once. The trouble began on the Baltimore and
Ohio Railroad where the workers had suffered a
series of pay cuts. In July the trainmen of the B & O
went on strike. They were soon followed by
railway workers in other states. Strikes, rioting, and
looting shook Baltimore, Pittsburgh, Chicago, St.
Louis, and many other cities. At the request of the
state governors, Hayes sent federal troops to Mar-
tinsburg, West Virginia, and to Pittsburgh to protect
property. He did not like using troops as strikebreakers, but he felt that he had no choice but to
agree to the governors' requests.

THE NEW LINE.

HAYES—"*That rail can't be laid on my track, Mr. Blaine!*"

This 1878 political cartoon shows upright and honest President Hayes pursuing a conservative course and building a solid new railroad line with civil service reform. He rejects James G. Blaine's rail of bloody-shirt radicalism.

The money question. The depression that brought the "year of violence" of 1877 brought demands for an increase in the amount of money in circulation. This demand would come time and time again in the Gilded Age. Between 1865 and 1896 prices were falling. It was a time of *deflation*, which meant that a dollar would buy more every year. So farmers and people in business who had borrowed money had to pay back their loans in dollars that were worth more than the dollars they had borrowed. For example, a debt that could have been paid off in 1890 with the sale of 1000 bushels of corn took 2320 bushels in 1896. As a result, farmers and others who borrowed money pushed for "cheaper money." Money became cheaper when there was more of it. So the "borrowing classes" demanded that the government either issue more "greenbacks"—paper money that had no backing in silver or gold—or coin silver in large quantities.

Increasing the supply of silver dollars was the favored approach. If the government was required to mint all the large supplies of silver then being mined in the West, the quantity of money would be much increased. A rise in the supply of money tends to lift the general level of prices. This is called *inflation.* If the price of wheat and cotton and corn went up, the farmers' problems might be solved. This proposal for minting silver was called "free silver" because it meant the "free"—that is, unlimited—coining of silver dollars.

The farmers were unable to persuade Congress to go that far. The most they could get was a bill for a limited coining of silver. In 1878 the Bland-Allison Act, named for its sponsors, Representative Richard "Silver Dick" Bland of Missouri and Senator William Allison of Iowa, passed both houses of Congress. It required the government to buy and coin at least $2 million worth of silver a month. Hayes vetoed the bill because he thought that coining silver dollars that were worth less than 90 cents in gold was dishonest. The bill passed over his veto. But it only partially satisfied the demand for a larger money supply. The question would return to haunt other Presidents.

The spoils system. Since Andrew Jackson's day, government jobs had been given to people who had worked hard to help the party win the election. "To the victors belong the spoils" was the motto of both parties. Every change of administration was marked by a wild scramble for government jobs. These were simply rewards for party loyalty. Thousands of offices were filled by people who had no other qualification. After they were on the government payroll, they were still expected to work for the party in election campaigns. They even had to hand over a part of their pay to support the party.

Some people believed that the problems of government might be solved if this system was changed. Their slogan was "Out with the party hacks." Only qualified people should hold government jobs. This program was called civil service reform. After the Civil War, influential citizens like Carl Schurz and George W. Curtis, the editor of *Harper's Weekly,* worked hard to abolish the "spoils system." Finally in 1871 Congress passed a law authorizing the President to make rules to reform the civil service. President Grant appointed a commission. But the "Stalwarts"—the old-fashioned Republican bosses—managed to prevent the commission from getting anything done. Their leader was the clever and knowledgeable Senator Roscoe Conkling, the New York State boss whose power was based on the spoils system.

The vain, handsome Conkling walked with "a turkey-gobbler strut" and was a master of ridicule. He called it "snivel" service reform. He sneered that the reformers "forget that parties are not built up by deportment or by ladies' magazines or by gush!"

Hayes and civil service reform. President Hayes did not agree. Wanting to abolish the spoils system, he revived the Civil Service Commission. He ordered that government employees must not work in political campaigns and must not be assessed for party "contributions."

In the opening battle of his war against the spoils system, President Hayes aimed to control the hiring in the New York customshouse. The 1000 people employed there collected two-thirds of all the nation's tariff revenue. First he asked Conkling's aides in New York, Collector of Customs Chester A. Arthur and Naval Officer Alonzo B. Cornell, to resign. But Conkling needed to control those jobs to keep himself and his party in power. So Conkling fought back.

Senator Roscoe Conkling appears still triumphant in 1878 during his fight with Hayes over the customshouse. But Conkling was soon to lose.

Culver Pictures

THE NEW OFFICIAL DOOR-KEEPER.

CONKLING—"Well, just at this moment, I feel as though I was a bigger man than old Hayes!"

Hayes won this battle of the customshouse, but he did not win the war for civil service reform. Cornell went on to become governor of New York, and Arthur, only a year later, was nominated for the Vice-Presidency. Now the professional politicians in his own party were Hayes's enemies, and Democrats controlled the House of Representatives. It is not surprising, then, that Hayes accomplished little during his last two years in office.

The Republicans name Garfield and Arthur. Hayes had been an honest, hardworking President who deserved the people's respect by his firm stands for what he believed was right. Although he had improved the Republican party's tarnished image from the days of Grant, he had made too many enemies among the leaders of his own party. They looked for a different kind of candidate to run in 1880.

The battle was between the Stalwarts led by Roscoe Conkling, who wanted a return to the "good old days" of President Grant when the bosses had their own way, and those whom the Stalwarts called the "Half-breeds." The party regulars sneered at these so-called "Half-breeds." Those people were only half loyal to the old-time Republican policies. They did firmly support the business interests, but they also were for civil service reform and took a hands-off policy toward the South. Their leader was the most magnetic politician of the age, James G. Blaine. He had the knack of making any cause seem a noble crusade, and so was called the "Plumed Knight."

The convention deadlocked between the Stalwart candidate U. S. Grant and the Half-breed Blaine. In the end it chose a "dark horse"—the popular James A. Garfield of Ohio. He had served gallantly in the Union army during the Civil War. Since then he had been a loyal Republican party leader in the Congress, but he had no particular program. In an attempt to please Roscoe Conkling and the disappointed Stalwarts, the convention named Chester A. Arthur for Vice-President. The angry Conkling tried to persuade Arthur to refuse the second-place nomination. Arthur accepted because, as he explained, "The office of the vice-presidency is a greater honor than I ever dreamed of attaining."

The party platform did plump for civil service reform but clearly avoided other issues. "What are we up here for?" a Texas delegate complained. "I mean that members of the Republican party are entitled to office, and if we are victorious we will have office."

Also aiming to win votes by avoiding the troublesome issues, the Democrats decided simply to prove their loyalty to the Union. They nominated General Winfield Scott Hancock, a professional army officer who had graduated from West Point. He was famous for fending off an attack by General Lee at Gettysburg but had no experience in politics.

Garfield is elected. The politicians fought a hard campaign without facing the nation's problems. By waving the "bloody shirt," Garfield managed to squeak into office—with a bare 7000-vote plurality out of more than 9 million votes cast. His electoral college vote was 214 to 155.

This campaign ribbon for Garfield and Arthur in 1880 was fittingly the color of the "bloody shirt" they waved during the campaign.

The southern states, now free of all federal interference for the first presidential election since 1860, cast a solid vote for the Democrat Hancock. The "solid South" became a new expression and a new institution in American politics. For the next years in every local, state, and national election the South was found solid in the Democratic column. Not until 1920 would a Republican candidate for President win a state of the former Confederacy.

Garfield was an intelligent, adaptable man. During his long career in the House of Representatives he had shown skill in party politics and parliamentary maneuver. But he had not escaped the taint of the Crédit Mobilier scandals. Many people did not believe him when he denied that he had been bribed with stock in the company.

His brief Presidency is remembered mainly for its violent end. The big issue right from the start was who would get what jobs. Garfield began by naming a Conkling rival to head the New York customshouse, and this move led to his death. On July 2, 1881, as the President entered the Washington railroad station for a trip to New England, Charles Guiteau, a crazed Chicago lawyer, shot him in the back. Guiteau was one of the thousands of party loyalists who had failed to get the government jobs they thought that they deserved. "I am a Stalwart," he shouted, "and Arthur is President now." For eleven weeks, Garfield lingered in pain before dying on September 19.

Arthur as President. Many people were shocked at the thought of Conkling's henchman, the Stalwart Arthur, in the White House. The dapper, wealthy Arthur was, in fact, an able organizer who had brought improved systems to the huge New York customshouse. But he also managed to take care of the party faithful. Even after his accidental rise to the White House, many voters continued to think of him as just another Stalwart, a high-class party hack.

The party regulars had a surprise in store for them. When President Arthur sent his first annual message to Congress, in an astonishing turnabout he called for civil service reform! The assassination of a President by a partisan office seeker outraged public opinion. Even Stalwart Republicans now had to go along. They feared defeat in the election of 1884 and saw "reform" as the only way to keep their own followers in office.

As a result, the Civil Service bill sponsored by Democrat George H. Pendleton of Ohio passed both houses of Congress in January 1883. Certain government jobs were "classified." This meant that they would be filled by the winners in competitive examinations to test "the fitness of applicants for the public service." A nonpartisan Civil Service Commission would do the examining and grade the candidates. The Pendleton Act forbade appointments to office for political reasons and made it illegal to assess jobholders to support the party.

Arthur named a strong head for the new Civil Service Commission and made strict rules to prevent evasion of the law. Fifteen thousand government employees (15 percent of the total) were put into the "classified" service.

President Arthur's whole administration showed that the office of President could actually lift a man above sordid party politics. He fought against wasteful "pork barrel" bills that would have spent the nation's money on unneeded river and harbor projects. He worked for tariff reform. He began the much-needed modernization of the navy. Before his term of office was over, he had surprised both his supporters and his opponents. But the people in both camps never stopped wondering how reliable he would be. They asked, "Can a leopard change his spots?" The eloquent perennial candidate, James G. Blaine, opposed Arthur for the Republican nomination in 1884 and was nominated on the fourth ballot.

SECTION 1 REVIEW

1. Identify or explain: Gilded Age, deflation, inflation, "cheap money," "free silver," "Stalwarts," Roscoe Conkling, Alonzo B. Cornell, "Half-breeds," James G. Blaine.

2. How did Hayes respond to the railway strike of 1877? Why?

3. Why did demands for "cheaper money" arise in the 1870s? What was Congress's response?

4. Who favored civil service reform? What steps toward it were made under Hayes? under Arthur?

5. **Recognizing Cause and Effect.** How did a tragedy hasten civil service reform?

2. The Democrats come and go

Blaine had been around for a long time, and he had made many enemies. So to oppose him the Democrats shrewdly chose a political newcomer, Governor Grover Cleveland of New York.

Grover Cleveland, the "reformer." Cleveland was the son of a poor Presbyterian minister, and his early life was spent in a small-town parsonage. There he learned the virtues of honesty, hard work, devotion to duty, and obedience to law. At the same time he was a jovial man. He weighed 250 pounds, which showed how much he loved good food and drink. He never went to college but became a self-trained lawyer. After serving as assistant district attorney and sheriff, in 1881 he was elected as a "reform" mayor of Buffalo. There he became known as the "veto mayor," for he opposed any measures that smacked of favoritism or waste.

In an age of shady political bosses, he stayed independent. He was just what honest Democrats wanted in their candidate for governor of New York. So they nominated Cleveland for governor in 1882, and he was elected in a landslide. He did not disappoint the reformers who supported him. For he lived up to his reputation as the sworn enemy of Tammany Hall—the organized bosses in his very own party. And he annoyed the bosses more than ever by his nonpartisan courage in the statehouse. There he supported the laws to clean up the government of New York City which were proposed by a bumptious 24-year-old Republican legislator named Theodore Roosevelt.

Blaine versus Cleveland. Grover Cleveland's political career was one of the speediest in American history. Only three years after being elected mayor of Buffalo, he was nominated for the Presidency. Suddenly this reforming upstart from New York was plunged into a mud-slinging national election campaign.

When the "Plumed Knight" Blaine was nominated by the Republicans, the Democrats advertised the bribe he had once received in Congress to favor an Arkansas railroad. This charge had kept him from being nominated in 1876 and 1880. The Republican machine bosses were against him, too. Some nasty remarks he once made against Boss Conkling had turned Conkling into his enemy. Although Blaine had helped make his party modern and responsible, many Republicans still considered Blaine himself to be little better than a Stalwart. He had a talent for inspiring intense personal dislike. Carl Schurz, George W. Curtis, and other reformers left the party and filled the newspapers with their onslaughts.

Now the Republican regulars answered with their own name-calling. They ridiculed the reformers for being pompous and self-important. So they cleverly picked up an old Algonquin Indian word for chief or high-muck-a-muck and called them "Mugwumps." This name was so appealing that no one could forget it. And they went on with personal attacks on Cleveland for being immoral and a drunkard.

The election on November 4, 1884, was another close one. Cleveland received 29,000 more votes than Blaine. A swing of only 600 votes in New York would have carried that state for Blaine and made him President.

Two trivial events during the campaign may have cost Blaine the election. In his presence a New York minister said that the Democrats were the party of "rum, Romanism, and rebellion." Blaine may not even have heard the remark, or perhaps he was just not paying attention. Anyway the unlucky Blaine did not disagree on the spot. The alert Democrats quickly advertised this insult to the religion and the drinking customs of thousands of Irish Catholic voters. Many of these were recent immigrants still struggling to make ends meet. On that same day, some of the city's richest men gave a dinner in Blaine's honor. The *New York World* portrayed Blaine feasting while "thousands of children in this great city whose fathers labor twelve hours a day, went to bed hungry and many supperless."

The Interstate Commerce Act of 1887.
Grover Cleveland accomplished little during his first two years in office—partly because the Senate remained Republican, but also because he did not believe a President should be very active. Without guidance from the President, Congress tried to get fair treatment from the railroads for the small customers. Senator Shelby M. Cullom had helped his home state of Illinois to pass legislation regulating the railroads. As governor he had strictly enforced those laws. But Cullom was convinced that only the national government could control the rail-

roads. Individual states were not strong enough to deal with the rich and powerful interstate railroads. So in 1887 Cullom oversaw the passage of the Interstate Commerce Act.

The railroads had given special low rates and also offered rebates to large companies like Standard Oil. They did not set their rates according to the distance the freight had to be carried. Where there was no competition, their rates were exorbitant. Since the railroads kept their rates secret, the small farmers could not know what it would cost to take their produce to market. And they could not count on the rates being fair. The new law banned rebates and the other favors given to powerful shippers. New rates would be proportional to distance. Rate schedules would be public and open to inspection by the new Interstate Commerce Commission.

This was the first of many attempts of Congress to solve the problems of the new industrial age by regulating "big business."

Pension vetoes.
President Cleveland, determined to reduce government spending, was at his best when he could oppose something. In 1886 he vetoed many Civil War pension bills for people who really did not deserve pensions. Then, in January 1887 Congress passed a bill awarding a pension to any needy veteran who had served in the ranks for more than 90 days. Refusing to let the pension list become an excuse for fraud, Cleveland vetoed the bill.

The issue of the tariff.
Finding that the United States Treasury was taking in $100 million a year more than it spent, President Cleveland aimed to stop the "unnecessary taxation" that produced this surplus money. In December 1887 he devoted his entire annual message to the need to reduce the tariffs—the customs duties that raised the price of goods that were imported. Both business and labor leaders had favored the high tariffs as a way to protect Americans against foreign competition.

With this message Cleveland threw down the gauntlet to the Republican party. Now, for the first time in many years, a presidential campaign would have a real issue. Many Republicans welcomed the challenge. James G. Blaine had long wanted his party to take a bold stand in favor of a high tariff.

A HYDRA THAT MUST BE CRUSHED—AND THE SOONER THE BETTER.

Joseph Keppler sided with Grover Cleveland on the tariff issue. In this imaginative cartoon of March 1888 Keppler showed the tariff as a "hydra"—a many-headed monster from Greek mythology. The heads were the trusts that supported the tariffs that made them thrive.

The presidential campaign of 1888. The tariff was debated in Congress for months. It became the "burning issue" of the day. The Democrats nominated Cleveland for another term and declared in their platform that "all unnecessary taxation is unjust taxation." When Blaine's poor health convinced him not to run again, the Republicans settled on Benjamin Harrison of Indiana. Their platform stressed the need for a high tariff to protect "the general business, the labor, the farming interests of the country."

The Republican candidate was the great-grandson of a signer of the Declaration of Independence and a grandson of President William Henry Harrison. He entered the Civil War as commander of a volunteer regiment from Indiana, then rose to become a general. He was an aloof, unfriendly man, unwilling to take the courageous positions that might have made outspoken enemies or firm allies.

After a career as lawyer for corporations, he had served one term as senator from Indiana.

The campaign was waged almost entirely over the tariff issue. Harrison wanted to avoid making mistakes that Blaine had made in New York by going out and mingling with the crowds. He stayed home and conducted a traditional "front porch" campaign. Delegations would come to see him, and he would make harmless short speeches promising to help them if they helped send him to the White House. Now at last the Republicans abandoned the old hatreds of the Civil War and stopped waving the "bloody shirt." Instead they tried appealing to everybody's pocketbook. This brought the Knights of Labor to their side. Wealthy businessmen, too, now gave millions of dollars to put the party back in power.

In one of the most corrupt campaigns in American history, the Republicans spent a fortune buying votes in the big doubtful states like New York and Indiana. Those states had gone for Cleveland in 1884. The Republicans did not succeed in buying a popular national majority, for Cleveland received almost 100,000 more votes than Harrison. But with the crucial support of those two states Harrison won the electoral vote by 233 to 168. The Republicans also carried both houses of Congress. Cleveland's strength was largely in the farm states. In the key industrial states, the Republicans convinced business people and laborers that the tariff really did work in their favor.

"Czar" Reed and Congress.

Harrison, unbending and abrupt, made enemies even when he tried to do the right thing. Senator Cullom said, "I suppose he treated me about as well in the patronage as he did any other senator, but whenever he did anything for me it was done so ungraciously that the concession tended to anger rather than please."

Oddly enough, the first session of Congress under Harrison produced more important legislation than any session since Reconstruction. This was due not so much to the man in the White House as to a powerful leader in the House of Representatives. The Republicans had only a thin margin of votes in the House, and this slight edge made the leader's role more important than ever. Representative Thomas B. Reed from Maine was an overpowering man in more ways than one. Standing six feet, three inches tall, he actually weighed 300 pounds. He ruled the House so firmly that he was nicknamed the "Czar." He forced the House to adopt the "Reed Rules." These prevented the minority from blocking bills and gave the Speaker and the majority the power to push through their program.

Electoral reform.

One of the first measures that the House considered was the electoral reform bill that Harrison had called for in his inaugural address. It was a pioneer civil rights bill. President Harrison was disturbed over the way Southerners often prevented blacks from voting. Since the blacks were usually Republicans, Republican Representative Henry Cabot Lodge of Massachusetts drew up a bill that allowed the federal government to see that there were fair elections.

The House passed the Lodge bill. But the rules of the Senate (unlike the House) allowed a senator to stop the regular business and prevent a vote by talking endlessly and refusing to "yield the floor." "Filibuster," the name for this practice, came from a Spanish word for the troublemakers who stirred up revolution in Latin America. Southern senators used the filibuster to block action on the tariff bill that many Republicans wanted to pass. So in order to get their tariff, the Republicans had to put aside the Lodge bill. When it was brought up later, Republican senators from the silver-producing states themselves helped to defeat it in return for southern support for a new silver coinage bill. The time for equal voting rights had not yet come.

A new tariff.

The McKinley tariff bill, named for Representative William McKinley of Ohio, raised the duty on almost every article produced outside the country that competed with American production. The list included food, clothing, furniture, carpets, fuel, tools, kitchenware, thread, and countless other items. Articles such as tea, coffee, spices, and drugs that were not produced in the United States were admitted free. Sugar also was put on the free list. But a bounty or subsidy of 2 cents a pound was to be paid to domestic producers of raw sugar. McKinley boasted that his bill, which passed the House in May 1890, was "protective in every paragraph and American in every line and word."

The senators from silver states were willing to help pass the tariff only if something was also done for silver. They said that under the Bland-Allison Act of 1878 the government still was not buying enough silver to inflate the currency or to keep the price of silver from falling. These Westerners wanted "free and unlimited" coinage of silver at the old ratio of 16 to 1 (that is, 16 ounces of silver was to be equal in value to 1 ounce of gold). Many Republicans wanted to avoid free silver, but at the same time they were determined to pass the McKinley tariff. So on July 4, 1890, the Sherman Silver Purchase Act (named after its author, Senator John Sherman of Ohio) provided that the government would purchase 4 1/2 million ounces of silver every month. This was more than double the amount required by the Bland-Allison Act. It equaled the whole current production of silver at the time. In addition, the bill provided for the issue of paper money (Treasury notes) to the full amount of the silver purchased. This would inflate the currency. And it would help farmers who wanted to pay off their mortgages in cheap money.

The bargain over silver won western votes for the McKinley tariff bill, which now finally passed the Senate. President Harrison signed the bill into law on October 1, 1890, only 35 days before the mid-term elections.

The Sherman Antitrust Act. Congress also faced the growing demand that they do something to help farmers and small businesses against trusts like the Standard Oil Company. Everywhere big companies seemed to be taking over. Bigness meant monopoly. And monopoly meant that a few people had the power to dictate to everybody else.

By 1880 the Standard Oil Company, by fair means and foul, had captured control of 90 percent of the lamp-oil refining in the United States. In the 1890s, if you wanted sugar for your table, you had to buy it from the E. C. Knight Company. Your tobacco was controlled by the American Tobacco Company.

How could small businesses and buyers in general be protected against these tyrants of "unlawful restraint and monopoly"? Many states passed laws outlawing trusts. Still the most powerful monopolies were organized in nationwide networks. This was a national problem.

In 1888 both major parties wrote antitrust planks into their platforms. President Harrison called for legislation in his annual message to Congress in 1889.

The result in July 1890 was the Sherman Antitrust Act (also named after John Sherman). This epoch-making law aimed to punish "restraint of trade or commerce." Now it was a crime for business firms to combine to prevent competition. But the language of the law was vague. And the law would not be effective at all unless the government worked hard to enforce it.

Yet any President who wanted to be reelected had to be careful not to offend powerful business leaders. It is not surprising that Presidents usually pretended that the law did not exist. If a President dared prosecute a trust, the Supreme Court often came to the rescue by technicalities. In 1895, for example, the Attorney General prosecuted the E. C. Knight Company, which controlled 98 percent of the nation's sugar refining. But the Supreme Court held the company *not* guilty under the Sherman Antitrust Act—because it was in "manufacturing" and not in "commerce." Only a fearless President

Cartoonist Edward Kemble saw the trusts as evil vultures feeding off the Senate. Seats were advertised for sale because senators were still chosen by the state legislatures.

like Theodore Roosevelt would be willing to use the act to smash monopolies (p. 431).

The billion-dollar Congress. This busy Republican Congress also passed many bills that were costly for the Treasury. They voted funds for river and harbor improvements, for steamship subsidies, and even to return the federal taxes paid by the northern states during the Civil War. Tight-fisted President Cleveland had vetoed the Dependent Pension Act, which old soldier Harrison now willingly signed into law. Pension outlays rose from $81 million in 1889 to $135 million in 1893. The "billion-dollar" Congress, as it came to be called, rapidly depleted the Treasury surplus which had worried President Cleveland. The surplus was gone by 1894, and there has never been one since.

In the congressional election campaign after this session the Republicans told the voters that they had accomplished a great deal. Many Americans did not agree. Once again farmers faced falling prices and rising mortgage payments. The Silver Purchase Act angered bankers and bondholders. At the same time, it did not go far enough to satisfy the silver interests and the farmers. Reformers felt that President Harrison had not lived up to his promise to abolish the spoils system, while party bosses felt that he had not given them enough patronage. Voters were troubled by Congress's spending spree. And now it seemed that the McKinley tariff might raise prices all over the land.

The election of 1890 was a landslide for the Democrats. They elected 235 members to the House, and the new Populist party surprised everybody by electing 9. The Republicans returned only 88—their smallest House delegation in 30 years. Even McKinley himself, after serving seven terms, was defeated. During the last two years of Harrison's term—with a President of one party and a House of Representatives of the other—no important laws were passed.

SECTION 2 REVIEW

1. Identify or explain: Mugwumps, Shelby M. Cullom, "front porch" campaign, "Czar" Reed, Henry Cabot Lodge, "billion-dollar" Congress.

2. What were the provisions of the Interstate Commerce Act? What abuses were they designed to stop?

3. How did Cleveland show his determination to keep a tight rein on government spending?

4. Why did the Republicans want a civil rights bill? Why did it fail to pass?

5. What effort was made to end business monopolies? Was it effective? Why?

6. What were the issues in the 1890 election campaign? What was the outcome?

7. **Recognizing Bias.** Whose interests did the tariff issue serve? Whose interests did the silver issue serve?

---

3. The farmers' revolt

During the Civil War, farmers—in both North and South—had prospered. While food was needed for the armies, there were fewer people working on the farms, and the prices of farm products went up.

Then, a few years after Appomattox, the farmers' troubles began. A bushel of wheat, which in 1873 still sold for $1.21, twelve years later went for 49 cents. A pound of cotton, in 1873 priced at 21 cents, in twenty years sank to 5 cents. Other prices that made up the farmers' income also fell. But western railroad rates remained high along with some items controlled by monopolies. Farmers constantly had to borrow to meet their mortgage payments, to buy the new machinery they needed, or to pay their help until they sold the next harvest. The heartless sheriff with a long mustache who threatened to "foreclose" the mortgage was no joke between 1870 and 1900. Thousands of poor families lost their farms.

The farmers organize. Farmers, like city workers, did not take their troubles lying down. In fact, the first national farm organization, the Patrons of Husbandry, entered the scene in 1867 at almost the same moment that the Knights of Labor was organized. The farmers' league was started by Oliver H. Kelley, a clerk in the Department of Agriculture at Washington. He had seen the loneliness and poverty of farm life, and he organized the Patrons as a social and educational society. Within ten years there were members all over the country in twenty thousand local lodges called "Granges."

Naturally enough, when the farmers gathered they began to discuss their troubles. More and more land was being owned by absentee landlords while more and more farmers became tenants. The burden of interest on their farm mortgages seemed to become heavier every year. The companies that owned the railroads and the grain elevators were always raising their rates. So, farmers in the Granges and later in Farmers' Alliances organized cooperatives to save money by buying seed and fertilizer in large quantities. They bought their own grain elevators and even set up factories to make farm machinery that members could buy for less.

The farmland under cultivation in the United States had increased enormously after the Civil War. At the same time new mechanical devices— reapers, binders, threshers—were invented and spread across the land. Production soared. Now the farmers fed the growing population with ease and still had large amounts of surplus crops to sell abroad. There they had to compete with produce from the newly opened lands of Argentina, Australia, and Canada. As the quantity of food produced went up, the prices the farmer received went down.

The "Granger laws."

Farmers did not understand the complex reasons for their plight. They blamed it on the greedy banks, railroads, and grain elevators. In about a dozen midwestern and southern states, new farmers' political parties appeared. They called for state control of corporations, particularly of railroads, for "cheap money," for economy in government, and for other reforms. Many Grangers joined the farmers' parties, and in the 1870s they managed to pass state laws regulating railroad and grain elevator rates. Unfortunately for the farmers, these "Granger laws" were not effective. The powerful railroads sometimes simply ignored the laws. Or they "persuaded" the legislatures to repeal them. In other cases the overawed courts nullified the laws by their decisions.

One important exception was the case of *Munn* v. *Illinois* (1876). Here the Supreme Court upheld the Illinois law that set maximum rates for grain storage. The "police power" of the state under the Constitution, they said, gave the state the right to regulate private property "affected with a public interest." This became a precedent for the right of the public to regulate large corporations in other ways.

The Farmers' Alliances.

When prosperity returned to the farms for a few years in the late 1870s and early '80s, farmers felt less need for the Grange and their own farmers' political parties. But when prices fell once again, the farmers suffered.

New organizations of farmers, called "Alliances," were formed in the 1880s and 1890s. They went actively into politics. In the western states they formed their own parties. In the South they worked among the Democrats who, for all practical purposes, were the only political party. The farmers' successes in the 1890 elections persuaded the western farm leaders to try to form a separate national party. They hoped that the southern farmers would join them in their effort to give a single loud voice to all the forces of discontent in the land.

Southern farmers of all races were ready for a change. So ready even that old racial prejudices began to soften. Some white farmers now were willing to work with blacks to gain the reforms that would bring all a better life.

The Populist party is formed.

Western and southern farmers along with an odd assortment of radicals and reformers met at Omaha, Nebraska, in early July 1892. They called themselves "Populists"—from the Latin word *populus*, meaning "the people." Their platform declared that they were meeting "in the midst of a nation brought to the verge of moral, political, and material ruin." Everywhere they saw corruption. They also saw

Haymaking in 1895 on the Fred Judas farm near Medford, Wisconsin, required the work of the entire family. This photograph was made for a handbook promoting farm opportunities in the state.

FOUNTAIN CITY SEEDER.

"THE "YANKEE" IS THE BEST RAKE IN THE WORLD"

FOUNTAIN CITY GRAIN DRILL.

THE YANKEE HORSE RAKE.

THE YANKEE RAKE HAS PROVED ITS SUPERIORITY OVER ALL COMPETITORS IN EVERY PUBLIC TRIAL IN WHICH IT HAS COMPETED.

MANUFACTURED BY WHEEL & SEEDER CO. FOND DU LAC, WIS.

Improved farm machinery of the sort advertised here helped farmers boost production.

"business prostrated, homes covered with mort-gages, labor impoverished, and the land concentrated in the hands of capitalists." The major parties seemed interested only in "power and plunder."

The Populists called for sweeping reform. They demanded the free coinage of silver and an increase in the money supply to $50 per person. They wanted an income tax to put a larger share of the burden on the wealthy. The government, they said, should take over ownership of railroads, telegraph, and telephone. The platform also called for a shorter working day for industrial laborers and the direct election of senators.

The farmers' leaders were not afraid to shock the rich and comfortable people. One of their best was the handsome, outspoken Mary Elizabeth Lease of Kansas, the mother of four. "What you farmers need," she urged, "is to raise less corn and more Hell!" She also went on:

Wall Street owns the country. It is no longer a government of the people, by the people, and for the people, but a government of Wall Street, by Wall Street, and for Wall Street. The great common people of this country are slaves, and monopoly is the master.

Then, also from Kansas, there was "Sockless Jerry" Simpson. Once when he ran for Congress, he accused his well-dressed opponent of wearing silk stockings. A reporter then sneered that Simpson was so crude that he wore no socks at all. Simpson made this into a boast. Always after that he was known as "Sockless Jerry."

Crusaders like the rabble-rousing Tom Watson of Georgia spoke for them in Congress and spoke loud and clear. "Before I will give up this fight," Watson warned, "I will stay here till the ants tote me out of the keyhole."

The election of 1892. The two major parties had held their conventions in June. The Republicans had picked Harrison again. The Democrats had chosen their strongest candidate, Grover Cleveland. He had the support of many business leaders because he opposed free silver and inflation and therefore was "sound" on the money question.

The Populists, with the eloquent and honest General James B. Weaver as their candidate, conducted a vigorous campaign. In the South they made common cause with all the poor, both white and black. Conservative southern Democrats, desperate to defend themselves against reform, raised the cry for white supremacy. They denounced all Populists as the enemies of law and order.

Fiery orator Mary Elizabeth Lease won many Kansas farmers over to the Populist cause.

General Weaver, an outspoken man of courage, declared:

> There is but one issue in the South. That is competition to see who can most hate the Negro. The man that wins gets the nomination. The whole thing is a dead-drag on the country. . . . Slavery must be the greatest of crimes. Here we are, all these years after it has been abolished, and we are still paying the penalty for it.

During the campaign summer of 1892 the nation was torn by labor strife. First came the bloody Homestead Strike (p. 369). When striking miners rioted in Coeur d'Alene, Idaho, President Harrison sent in federal troops at the governor's request. In these stormy times, people put their faith in Grover Cleveland. He had already proved once that he could be a competent, pacifying President. Cleveland received 373,000 more votes than Harrison and won with an electoral vote of 277 to Harrison's 145. The Democrats also won both houses of Congress. The Populist General Weaver actually received over a million popular votes, but he carried only four states—Colorado, Kansas, Nevada, and Idaho. The Populists elected three United States senators and eleven members of the House.

Cleveland's second term. Grover Cleveland's second term was as much a disaster as his first had been a success. It began with one of the nation's worst depressions, one that lasted his entire four years in office. Negative policies were no longer enough.

One major problem was that the Treasury was rapidly losing gold. Under the Sherman Silver Purchase Act, the Treasury notes issued to buy silver could be redeemed for gold. Since gold dollars were more valuable than silver dollars, people naturally turned in their silver Treasury notes for gold dollars. But the Treasury had to reissue the Treasury notes—which were then turned back in for gold again. It is not surprising that the Treasury was about to run out of gold.

Cleveland called a special session of Congress in August 1893 to demand repeal of the Sherman Silver Purchase Act. He wanted the government to stop spending $50 million a year taking in "cheap" silver for valuable gold. After some hard fighting that split both parties, his measure passed.

A new tariff and an income tax. President Cleveland now turned to the tariff, which the party platform had promised to revise. But the Wilson-Gorman tariff (named for Representative William Wilson in the House and Senator Albert Gorman in the Senate) was little different from the McKinley tariff. Cleveland was so disgusted by the bill that he refused to sign it. But since it did contain some reductions, he did not veto it. As long as Congress is in session, bills become laws after ten days even if the President neither vetoes nor signs them (Art. I, sec. 7). The President allowed this act to become law without his signature.

The Wilson-Gorman tariff did include one interesting feature. It provided for a tax of 2 percent on incomes above $4000. But before the tax was ever collected, the Supreme Court, in *Pollock v. Farmers' Loan and Trust Co.* (1895), declared the law unconstitutional. By a 5 to 4 vote they found an income tax to be a "direct tax." This settled the matter because the Constitution declared that any direct tax had to be levied in proportion to the population (Art. I, sec. 2, par. 3). The Sixteenth Amendment to the Constitution (1913) would

In 1894 Jacob Coxey, shown here on horseback, led a small "army" of protesters to Washington to make known the problems of the poor.

Library of Congress

have to be passed before Congress could levy an income tax.

Labor discontent. Meanwhile the depression was causing havoc. Millions were out of work. The winter of 1894 brought widespread suffering. In April a successful self-made businessman, reformer, and Populist, Jacob Coxey, led an "army" of 500 workers on a march from Ohio to Washington to publicize the plight of the poor. In May federal troops were fighting the Pullman strikers outside Chicago (p. 369). For the first time, and to many people's surprise, the Sherman Antitrust Act was turned against the workers. The act had been passed to control large corporations. But now a federal court declared that the striking union was a "conspiracy in restraint of trade," forbidden by the act. The court enforced its decision by issuing an order, called an "injunction," that told the union to stop the strike. This was a powerful new weapon. It made the strikers criminals if they refused to obey the court order and go back to work. The companies could now turn to the courts to stop a strike.

President Cleveland still seemed powerless against the depression. He had refused to give people "cheap money." He had used federal troops against starving workers. It is no wonder that he lost the voters' support. In the fall elections of 1894, the Populists' vote increased by 42 percent. And the Republicans, from being a minority in the House, jumped to a 141-seat majority. This was the largest congressional gain ever recorded. They also won control of the Senate.

Plugging the drain on gold. Grover Cleveland believed that a big part of the nation's economic trouble was public fear about the value of the American dollar. "Sound money"—not one dropping in value—would restore confidence and get the wheels of industry turning again. And sound money, it was widely believed, depended on the *gold standard.* A chief feature of the gold standard is that the government will, on demand, exchange its paper money for gold.

The repeal of the Sherman Silver Purchase Act in 1893 failed to stem the fall of the Treasury's gold reserves. Existing greenbacks and silver certificates could still be turned in for gold. How could the government stop the drain of gold? For a time, the sale of government bonds helped. But not for long. Cleveland was desperate to find a way to save the nation's credit by keeping a gold reserve in the Treasury. He turned to J. P. Morgan, the "organizer extraordinary"—the nation's most powerful banker. By organizing a group of bankers to sell United States bonds in Europe, Morgan brought in more than $65 million in gold. Of course Morgan reaped an enormous profit, though he never revealed how much.

Populists and Silverites were angered by President Cleveland's deals with the men of Wall Street. Within his own Democratic party his name became "a hissing and a byword." Ben Tillman, a Democrat, earned his nickname, "Pitchfork," when he told the people of South Carolina who had elected him senator, "[Cleveland] is an old bag of beef and I am going to Washington with a pitchfork and prod him in his old fat ribs."

Library of Congress

Silver-tongued William Jennings Bryan was a three-time Democratic candidate for President.

SECTION 3 REVIEW

1. Identify or explain: Patrons of Husbandry, *Munn* v. *Illinois,* farmers' alliances, Mary Elizabeth Lease, Jerry Simpson, Tom Watson, James B. Weaver, Jacob Coxey, Ben Tillman.

2. Identify problems faced by farmers in the years after 1870.

3. How was the election of 1892 affected by (a) the race issue? (b) labor strife?

4. In Cleveland's second term what action did the President and/or Congress take on (a) the money problem? (b) the tariff? (c) strikes?

5. How did the federal courts assist business managers during their struggles with labor?

6. **Determining Relevance.** Which planks in the 1892 Populist platform represented the demands of (a) farmers? (b) industrial workers? (c) both?

---

4. Our money: gold versus silver

In these times of troubles, the nation, and especially the farmers, wanted a cure-all. Many people came to believe that the cure-all might be free silver. There was something magical and mysterious about money. The amounts of money seemed to change the value of everything else. Money seemed a

medicine for everybody's ills. So money became the key to the election of 1896.

William Jennings Bryan. Inside the regular parties the most successful of the farm crusaders was William Jennings Bryan. Some called him the "Great Commoner" because he championed the common people. Others called him the "Prairie Avenger," or the "Boy Orator of the Platte"—after the river near his Nebraska home. Born in Salem, Illinois, he studied law in Chicago and then practiced law in small towns. He distrusted rich people and people of "good family."

A tall, handsome man of great energy, Bryan loved a political battle. And he had a talent for making issues seem very simple. After he had explained it, every political battle seemed to be between Bryan and God on one side, and his opponents and Satan on the other. His enemies said that Bryan did not really understand how complicated the problems were. Even his friends had to admit that what made him famous was not his sharp mind but his loud musical voice.

The "silver-tongued" William Jennings Bryan had decided that "free silver" would cure the

407

nation's ills. When Bryan arrived at the Democratic convention in Chicago on July 7, 1896, he was 36 years old—one year over the minimum age for a President. He had served only four years in Congress and was barely known outside of Nebraska. Unlike the other leading candidates, he did not have rich supporters.

As the convention met, it was still not decided whether the Democratic party would stay with the gold standard or whether they would join the farmers for free silver. Until Bryan came to the rostrum, the speakers at the Chicago convention had been dull and long-winded. Since there was no public-address system, most of the speakers could hardly be heard. Bryan was the final speaker for free silver.

This was young Bryan's great chance. The first sound of his ringing voice awakened the perspiring audience. They responded to his words with laughter and applause "like a trained choir," as he said, down to his last syllable. He spoke without hesitating, for he had given much the same speech many times before—to farm audiences all over Nebraska. "We will answer their demand for a Gold Standard," he ended, "by saying to them: You shall not press down upon the brow of labor this crown of thorns. You shall not crucify mankind upon a cross of gold."

The crowd went wild. Their yelling and cheering lasted for an hour. This one speech had transformed a Nebraska small-town lawyer into a front runner for President!

On the next day, the Democratic convention named him to lead their ticket. Then the Populists at their national convention also nominated him for President.

The campaign and election of 1896. The campaign offered one of the most spectacular contrasts in American history. The "Boy Orator of the Platte" hurried about the country by train, making speeches far into the night at every little town and often in between. On some days he made 36 speeches. Meanwhile, his conservative Republican opponent, William McKinley, remained calmly seated on his front porch in Canton, Ohio. McKinley made almost no speeches. When he did, he was careful to say nothing in particular—except that he was in favor of "sound money" (the gold standard) and "restoring confidence."

Mark Hanna, a clever Cleveland businessman and political boss who had secured the Republican nomination for McKinley, managed McKinley's campaign. Hanna counted on letting Bryan talk himself to defeat. And he used every trick to convince voters that Bryan was a dangerous radical. For example, he persuaded some factory owners, as a stunt, to pay their workers in Mexican dollars (worth only 50 United States cents). This was supposed to show the workers what their wages would really be worth if Bryan won. Employees in some factories were actually told that the businesses would shut down if Bryan won.

Hanna's tactics succeeded. McKinley overwhelmed Bryan by 600,000 votes, the greatest margin since 1872. The Republicans retained their control of both houses of Congress. Despite all this, Bryan's performance had really been spectacular. With little money or organization, deserted by the "gold wing" of his party, Bryan had polled some 6.5 million votes, more than had ever before been cast even for a winning candidate. The change of about 19,000 votes, distributed in six states, would have won him the election in the electoral college.

Bryan's fatal weakness was his inability to carry a single one of the urban-industrial states. He was a one-issue candidate, and his one issue—free silver—did not appeal to factory workers or city people. Still, he had attracted so many votes that the Democratic leaders could not ignore him. Twice again—in 1900 and 1908—he would be named the Democratic candidate for President. Bryan never won.

SECTION 4 REVIEW

1. Why did the Democrats and Populists choose Bryan as their candidate for President in 1896?

2. **Drawing Conclusions.** What tactics enabled McKinley to win the 1896 election?

FOCUSING ON IDEAS

1. In the 1880s and 1890s, what stand on the "cheap money" vs. "sound money" issue would you expect each of the following persons to take and why: An elderly city couple living on their savings? A Kansas wheat farmer? A factory worker? A merchant selling chiefly to farmers? A banker?

2. The Gilded Age was a period of governmental reforms. Describe three important reforms.

3. How did President Arthur's administration prove that the office of President can lift a person above narrow party politics?

TAKING A CRITICAL LOOK

1. **Expressing Problems Clearly.** Show that control of the national government was closely divided between the two major parties from 1876 to 1896. How did this situation make for "an age of timid Presidents"? How did it stimulate the rise of the Populist Party?

2. **Distinguishing Fact from Opinion.** Grover Cleveland has been criticized for being more concerned with managing the government and controlling spending than with facing the issues of the day. What evidence can you find for or against this criticism? Which is more important for a President—to be a good manager or to be a political leader?

YOUR REGION IN HISTORY

1. **Geography.** Which party's candidate received your state's electoral votes in the presidential elections of 1876, 1880, 1884, and 1888? Compare your state's election results to the returns in other states in your region. Did your region vote as a block?

2. **Culture.** What leaders from your state or region were active in national politics and the struggles of the Gilded Age? What were some of their accomplishments?

3. **Economics.** Can you identify a great-grandparent or other relative who lived during America's Gilded Age? How did he or she earn a living? What economic reforms would he or she have supported or opposed? Give reasons for your answer.

HISTORICAL FACTS AND FIGURES

Drawing Conclusions. Study the chart below to help answer the following questions: (a) In what year were the profits from the sale of wheat the highest? the lowest? (b) What was the relationship between the amount of wheat produced and the price farmers could obtain for their crop after 1870? (c) If you were a wheat farmer facing a wheat market in which that relationship between price and production existed, what would be your economic concerns? How would you protect your investment in farm land, livestock, crops, and equipment?

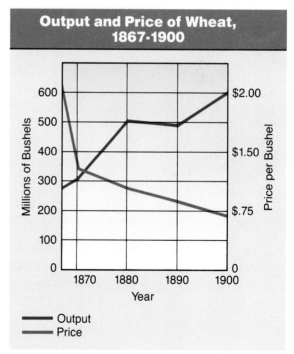

Output and Price of Wheat, 1867-1900

Source: *Historical Statistics of the United States*

MAKING CONNECTIONS

This unit began on page 351 with the observation that after the Civil War the United States was as large and diverse as western Europe. This raised the question:

Could a nation where everything was becoming bigger still care for the little people?

This question was explored by the three unit themes that are reprinted in **dark type** below. Use the time line and the information in Unit 6 to answer the questions that follow the unit themes.

1. **Immigrants from across Europe pour into the United States.**

   In what ways were American cities of the late nineteenth century "melting pots" and in what ways were they "mixing bowls"?

2. **The rise of new cities and the growth of older cities give the nation an increasingly urban character.**

   How did technology and science affect the character and growth of American cities?

3. **Urban industrialization and falling farm prices lead farmers and factory workers to protest the politics and big business of the Gilded Age.**

   How was the American spirit reflected in the political activism of its farmers and factory workers?

1870 Public high schools are established across the U.S., helping to educate and "Americanize" many immigrants.

1877 Wage reductions following the 1873 depression prompt the great railway strike.

Events in American History

Events in World History

| 1855 | 1860 | 1865 | 1870 | 1875 | 1880 |

1855 Bogardus builds the first skeleton-framed skyscraper, eight stories high.

1864 First International Workingmen's Association formed in London by Karl Marx.

1868 Construction begins on the Brooklyn Bridge, designed by John Roebling.

1881 Andrew Carnegie opens his steel plant in Homestead, Pennsylvania.

1889 Jane Addams founds Hull House in Chicago, in part to aid urban immigrants.

1892 Overproduction and falling crop prices lead disenchanted farmers to form the national Populist party.

1892 Nearly 100 German-language newspapers are published in American cities.

1900 In Manhattan, there are more than 40,000 tenements housing 1,500,000 people.

1894 The Immigration Restriction League is formed by Americans opposed to immigration.

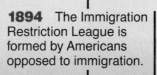

1880   **1885**   **1890**   **1895**   **1900**

1885 A new wave of immigrants begins to arrive in the U.S. from southern and eastern Europe.

1883 The World Exhibition opens in Amsterdam, highlighting new inventions.

1890 Twice as many Irish live in New York City as in Dublin, Ireland.

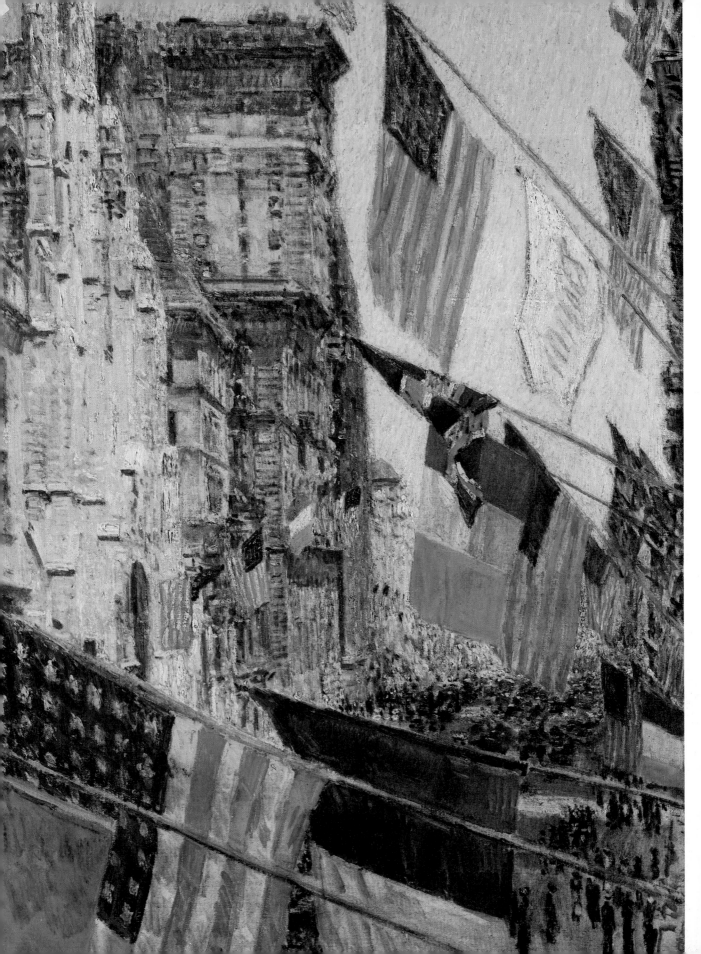

UNIT 7

Democratic reforms and world power
1890–1920

Until the Civil War the United States had seemed a world of its own. Almost every needed crop or animal or mineral was found somewhere within the nation and its territories. But after the war, the nation began to reach outward. There was still room to import people by the millions. American farmers and factory workers and business owners sought faraway customers. At the same time, American factories and homes wanted silk from Italy and China, rubber from Ceylon and Sumatra, coffee from Brazil, tin from the Malay peninsula, chrome from Rhodesia—and a thousand other items from across the oceans.

The years from 1890 to 1920 would test anew the belief of Americans in democracy. At home they worked to make government and business answer to the needs of the people. Abroad, how could the United States assist other nations to become democratic without choosing their governments for them?

Europe suffered from intrigue, tyranny, and old-fashioned monarchs. War was that continent's disease. Would our newly powerful nation be tempted to enter wars and try to run the affairs of people everywhere? How could Americans keep their ideals in this different kind of world? These years would offer many new challenges, and a few new answers.

THEMES IN AMERICAN HISTORY

■ The United States begins to reach outward as a result of rapid industrialization.

■ The United States becomes a world leader.

■ The Progressive Era produces significant reforms in American business and government.

THEMES

Childe Hassam's "Allies Day" captures the beauty of American, French, and English flags fluttering over 5th Avenue in New York City in May 1917.

National Gallery of Art, Washington, gift of Ethelyn McKinney in memory of her brother, Glenn Ford McKinney

413

CHAPTER 19

The United States and the world

During the Gilded Age, the United States filled its land with farms, factories, and cities. Busy in their vast nation, most Americans felt no need to go abroad. Protected by broad oceans, they paid little attention to events elsewhere. Then, in 1898, war with Spain suddenly thrust the United States upon the world stage. "The guns of Dewey at Manila have changed the destiny of the United States," the *Washington Post* observed. "We are face to face with a strange destiny and must accept its responsibilities. An imperial policy!"

1. Looking outward

From time to time, earlier in the 1800s, a few traders, whalers, missionaries, and diplomats did look outward. The expansion of other nations gave the United States the chance—and the excuse—to seek American advantages overseas.

Early expansion to the distant East. American merchants had been visiting Canton to trade with China since 1785. After the Opium War of 1839–1842, Great Britain secured special privileges in China. Then President Tyler sent out Caleb Cushing, the able champion of expansion, to secure the same privileges for Americans. In the Treaty of Wanghia (1844), Cushing won for the United States "most favored nation" status. This meant that in China the United States was to receive the best treatment offered any country. Four new Chinese ports in addition to Canton were opened to American merchants for the first time. Magnificent American clipper ships and other grand trading ves-

sels also went venturing out to the Philippines, Java, India, and other distant lands. In 1833 a commercial treaty was signed with faraway Siam.

The rulers of Japan, fearing corruption by foreign ways, kept out the foreigners. They allowed only a small colony of merchants of the Dutch East India Company to live on an island at Nagasaki. United States merchants wanted to trade with Japan, but this was not easy to arrange. It required a man of adventurous spirit and imagination. Luckily, in 1852, President Millard Fillmore found that man. He was Commodore Matthew C. Perry, a bold naval officer. He had an interest in ideas and the courage to risk danger. Perry tried to improve the education of midshipmen. He had fought pirates in the West Indies and had helped suppress the slave traffic from Africa. Now he would try to open trade with Japan. He awed the Japanese with his great "Black Ships"—bigger than any ever seen there before. When his ships arrived off the coast of Japan, he was firm and skillful in his diplomacy. He

This scene from a Japanese scroll shows the ceremonies upon Commodore Perry's arrival in Japan in 1854. The artist omitted the stripes and stars on most of the American flags flying from the longboats that had brought the delegation ashore.

refused to deal with minor officials. He demanded that the Japanese respect the Americans. And he secured the Treaty of Kanagawa (1854), opening two ports to ships from the United States.

Meanwhile, American traders had already arrived in Hawaii in the 1790s. They were followed in the 1820s by whalers and missionaries. As early as 1849, the United States declared that it could never allow the Hawaiian Islands to pass under the dominion of any other power.

When President Pierce had tried to annex Hawaii in 1854 (p. 262), the treaty was not even sent to the Senate. Every question was bedeviled by the issue of slavery. The same problem defeated his efforts to buy Cuba, Alaska, and all of Lower California. Now the slavery issue was out of the way. Expansion was no longer stopped by sectional rivalry. The whole nation's factories and farms hungered for new markets. Steamships and telegraph cables were drawing Americans out toward the world.

Seward pursues expansion. After the Civil War, Secretary of State William H. Seward became the champion of these expansionist hopes. When the Russians asked whether the United States might want to buy Alaska, he jumped at the chance. He could expel one more monarchy from the American continent. Seward also believed that a strong United States outpost on the other side of Canada would help to force the British out of Canada. Then Canada, too, could be added to the American Empire for Liberty!

But many sensible congressmen had their doubts. Was Alaska anything but a frozen wasteland? The eloquent Senator Charles Sumner of

Massachusetts shared Seward's hope to include Canada within the United States. He finally persuaded the Senate to approve the Alaska treaty (April 19, 1867). Opponents never ceased to call it "Seward's Folly." In order to secure approval by the House of Representatives of the $7.2 million purchase price, the Russian minister to the United States had to bribe some members of Congress.

When the federal government was still burdened by a Civil War debt of $3 billion, it did seem a wild extravagance to spend millions for "Seward's icebox." Few then imagined what a bargain they had made. The gold taken from the Yukon Valley since 1897 has paid for Alaska many times over. Besides, there would be North Slope oil. Best of all, this vast, untamed wilderness was a new frontier for all Americans.

The Caribbean, too, would offer its own kind of tropical frontier. Seward negotiated a treaty in 1867 to pay $7.5 million for the Danish West Indies (now the Virgin Islands). Since the Senate was slow to approve, the islands did not become part of the United States until they were purchased for $25 million in 1917.

The Alabama *claims*. Secretary of State Seward could not give all his efforts to the future. The Civil War had left him problems from the past. One of the knottiest concerned the so-called *Alabama* claims. These were claims for damages to Union shipping by a number of Confederate vessels that had been built in Great Britain. British law forbade anyone in the realm from arming a ship to be used by a foreign state against any nation at peace with Great Britain. The Confederate navy had evaded this law by having ships built in Great Britain and then taking them elsewhere to be armed.

By 1863 many of these commerce raiders were on the high seas menacing the Union. Our minister to Great Britain, Charles Francis Adams, objected in vain. Then the British government changed its policy, to favor the Union cause. Two powerful ironclad vessels, the "Laird Rams" (built for the South by the Laird shipyard in Liverpool), were not allowed to go to sea.

During the war the British-built ships already at sea destroyed 257 Union vessels. Union shipowners tried to escape this threat by a technicality. They "registered" their ships under foreign flags. More than 700 vessels were shifted to foreign registry. By 1865 only 26 percent of our foreign trade was carried in ships of United States registry.

The British-built *Alabama* alone destroyed more than 60 merchant ships. Finally in June 1864 the United States ship *Kearsarge* caught up with and sank the *Alabama* off the coast of France.

The United States demanded that Britain pay for the damages done by the *Alabama* and the other ships that had been made in Britain for the South. Seward claimed only $19 million. Charles Sumner, head of the Senate Foreign Relations Committee, had other ideas. He presented a much larger bill of damages against Great Britain. In an hour-long Senate speech he demanded $15 million for vessels destroyed and $110 million for driving our commerce from the ocean. This was only a beginning. Sumner asked $2 billion more for "indirect damages." That was half the Union's cost for the Civil War! The British owed so much, said Sumner, because the British-built vessels had made the war last twice as long. They could pay this enormous bill easily enough just by handing over Canada to the United States.

The Treaty of Washington. Of course, the British refused to take Senator Sumner's claim seriously. But many Americans approved. Finally in 1871, American and British commissioners signed a treaty at Washington. The *Alabama* claims would be submitted to an arbitration court at Geneva, Switzerland. In 1872 this panel of eminent judges from Switzerland, Italy, and Brazil found that during the Civil War Great Britain had violated the international laws of neutrality. They awarded $15.5 million in damages to the United States.

This peaceful way to settle differences was a happy precedent for later years.

Napoleon III's Mexican "empire." Another troublesome legacy of the Civil War was the many French troops in Mexico. Napoleon III, like his uncle Napoleon I, had dreamed of a French empire in North America. In 1863, when the United States was fighting the Civil War, Napoleon III sent an army to Mexico. He overthrew the Mexican government. On the Mexican throne he seated his puppet "emperor," the young Austrian archduke Maximilian.

The United States objected. But during the war it was in no position to use troops to put down this flimsy Mexican emperor. After Appomattox, the 50,000 federal troops in Texas could easily move into Mexico. They were President Johnson's and Secretary Seward's message that the French had better go home. In the summer of 1866 Napoleon III removed the French troops. But the foolish and romantic emperor actually thought he could hold onto his throne alone. Maximilian was the only one surprised when, in the summer of 1867, he was executed by a Mexican firing squad.

The United States and Samoa.
A wide variety of reasons led the nation to reach across the world. When steamships were powered by coal, coaling stations were needed everywhere. On the remote Samoan island of Tutuila, American sailors had long been interested in the fine harbor of Pago Pago. In the South Pacific Pago Pago had a strategic importance like that of Pearl Harbor in Hawaii in the North Pacific. The United States Navy tried, and failed, to set up a protectorate over the Samoan Islands. Germany also tried to seize control.

After narrowly evading war over Samoa, delegates from Germany, Great Britain, and the United States met in Berlin in 1889. They agreed to establish a joint protectorate. Ten years later Great Britain withdrew. The islands were divided between Germany and the United States. The tiny Samoan Islands enticed the United States onto the stage of world diplomacy.

The joint protectorate, our Secretary of State observed in 1894, was "the first departure from our . . . policy of avoiding entangling alliances with foreign powers in relation to objects remote from this hemisphere."

Problems with Chile.
But Latin America was in this hemisphere. And Secretary of State Blaine aimed to capture trade with our neighbors to the south. In 1889 at the 1st International American Conference in Washington the nations founded the International Bureau of American Republics—now called the Organization of American States. The idea was to encourage more cordial and more equal relations among these unequal countries.

The United States was an overpowering neighbor. It was not easy to enforce a neighborly spirit. In Chile, in October 1891, American sailors on shore leave from the cruiser *Baltimore* were attacked by a mob on the streets of Valparaiso. Two sailors were killed and eighteen injured. The Chilean government refused to apologize and put the blame on the Americans.

On January 25, 1892, President Harrison sent a special message to Congress that seemed to invite a declaration of war on Chile. When a squadron of eight United States cruisers was readied in the Pacific, the Chilean government yielded. They apologized and agreed to pay damages to the families of the killed and wounded sailors.

SECTION 1 REVIEW

1. Identify or explain: Caleb Cushing, Matthew Perry, Treaty of Kanagawa, Charles Sumner.

2. Locate: Canton, Siam, Nagasaki, Yukon Valley, Virgin Islands, Pago Pago, Valparaiso.

3. What kind of United States "expansion" to the Far East took place before the Civil War?

4. Explain the dispute that was settled by the Treaty of Washington.

5. What diplomatic problems arose in Samoa, Mexico, and Chile? How was each resolved?

6. **Recognizing Bias.** Why did some people continually refer to the purchase of Alaska as "Seward's Folly"?

---

2. Expanding on the seas

By 1900, without thinking of the consequences, the United States had become the third-ranking naval power in the world. This large navy was no solution to the problems of depression, farm revolt, labor unrest, free silver, and Populism. If the nation continued to build its costly navy, there must be some grand purpose. What was it?

Mahan and sea power.
Captain Alfred Thayer Mahan, a scholarly naval officer who helped set up the Naval War College in Newport, Rhode Island, had an answer. To be strong in the modern world, he said, the United States must sell its products on all continents. To secure and protect these foreign markets, the nation needed a powerful navy. Drawing on his study of ancient and modern times, he wrote *The Influence of Sea Power upon History* (1890). It was sea power "that made, and kept a nation great." Captain Mahan called for a strong

417

Culver Pictures

Captain Alfred Thayer Mahan, naval officer and eloquent historian, persuaded Theodore Roosevelt and others that the United States must become a great power.

navy, a canal across the Isthmus of Panama, United States dominance in the Caribbean, and control of Samoa and Hawaii.

Among the many who read and believed Mahan's message was Senator Henry Cabot Lodge of Massachusetts. He came from one of the oldest New England families and had inherited wealth. His upper-class background did not keep him from being a skillful politician. With a Harvard Ph.D. degree in history and a talent for writing history, he knew the American past and was fascinated by the struggle for power. During the 1890s again and again Lodge called for a bigger navy, annexation of Hawaii, a canal across the Isthmus of Panama, and the purchase of the Danish West Indies to protect the approaches to the canal. He also wanted to bring Greenland and Cuba under United States control and to dominate the Caribbean.

Lodge's colorful friend, Theodore Roosevelt of New York, was another follower of Mahan. He believed a nation should grow strong and be ready to fight. He shared Mahan's hopes and Lodge's plans for American expansion. As Assistant Secretary of the Navy under President McKinley, he worked for these goals.

Lodge and Roosevelt believed that a great nation must be strong. The world was full of weak nations. The American empire builders said that American power was only a force for good. Other nations should be glad to be ruled by us. And the American people would profit by reaching abroad. According to Senator Albert J. Beveridge of Indiana:

> American factories are making more than the American people can use; American soil is producing more than they can consume. Fate has written our policy for us; the trade of the world must and shall be ours. We will establish trading posts throughout the world as distributing points for American products. We will cover the ocean with our merchant marine. We will build a navy to the measure of our greatness. Great colonies governing themselves, flying our flag and trading with us, will grow about our posts of trade.

Renewed attempts to annex Hawaii. The people who lived in those potential "great colonies" did not all agree with Senator Beveridge. When Queen Liliuokalani came to the throne of Hawaii in 1891, she tried to shake off the control by American settlers. She wanted to restore the royal rights that her brother had given up. But she was frustrated in her struggle for freedom. In January 1893 the settlers, encouraged by the Harrison administration and assisted by United States Marines from the cruiser *Boston,* overthrew the queen. The new pro-America government drew up a treaty of annexation which President Harrison sent to the Senate for approval. The Democrats prevented Senate approval before Harrison left office.

Grover Cleveland, back in the White House again, was against expansion. Upon coming to office in 1893, he sent an agent to Hawaii to find out what had happened. The agent reported that the American minister to Hawaii had fomented the revolution. Cleveland withdrew the treaty to annex Hawaii. Instead he tried to restore "Queen Lil" to her throne. Not until after the Spanish-American War was Hawaii finally annexed by joint resolution of Congress (July 1898). Would the United States follow the European example and build an empire by conquest? Or could the Empire for Liberty in North America add states in the far Pacific?

The strong United States Navy, advocated by Mahan and supported by Lodge and Theodore Roosevelt, defeated the Spanish in the Philippines and in the Caribbean. Commodore Dewey commanded the American ships at Manila, so this painting is called "Dewey? We do!"

The Venezuelan boundary dispute. It was not easy for the growing United States to find its proper role. The new Latin American nations had only recently been colonies of European empires. The Venezuela-British Guiana boundary question was a test. President Cleveland thought the Monroe Doctrine (p. 178) was at stake. Great Britain claimed that 23,000 square miles of disputed borderland belonged to its colony of British Guiana (now the nation of Guyana). Venezuelans relied on the United States guarantees under the Monroe Doctrine. They begged the United States to defend them and save their land.

The United States urged arbitration of the dispute. But Britain refused. Then Cleveland's Secretary of State, Richard Olney, saw his chance to establish the right of the United States to intervene in Latin America. In a new version of the Monroe Doctrine he warned Great Britain. He said that the United States, "practically sovereign on this continent," would "resent and resist" any attempt by the British to take Venezuelan soil. The vast ocean between England and America, he said, made "political union between a European and American

state unnatural and inexpedient." Again he called for arbitration. The British Prime Minister, Lord Salisbury, replied that the Monroe Doctrine was no part of international law. This boundary dispute was no business of the United States.

President Cleveland responded with threats. He asked Congress to vote $100,000 for a boundary commission, which was only a start. He would defend his extension of the Monroe Doctrine—even if it meant war. Congress agreed.

But many Americans feared the consequences and rose in protest. The bellicose Theodore Roosevelt was disgusted. "The clamor of the peace faction," he wrote to his friend Senator Lodge, "has convinced me that this country needs a war."

Fortunately, calmer heads prevailed. The British already had enough troubles of their own, fighting for control of South Africa. Why turn the United States into an enemy over a petty border dispute? The British agreed to submit to arbitration. In October 1899 a tribunal in Paris (generally favoring Great Britain's claim) peacefully settled the boundary that had been debated for more than half a century.

The Venezuelan affair had expressed a more aggressive American spirit. "It indicates," Captain Mahan wrote, "the awakening of our countrymen to the fact that we must come out of our isolation . . . and take our share in the turmoil of the world."

SECTION 2 REVIEW

1. Identify: Alfred T. Mahan, Theodore Roosevelt, Albert Beveridge, Queen Liliuokalani.
2. What was Senator Beveridge's message?
3. What was the importance of the Venezuelan boundary dispute to the United States?
4. How did the United States obtain Hawaii?
5. **Recognizing Bias.** What was Captain Mahan's "message"? How did it influence Lodge and Roosevelt?

3. War with Spain

Many Americans who never read Captain Mahan's history books had their own reasons to reach out across the world. Some were crusaders who wanted to spread Christianity. Others wanted to teach the lessons of American democracy to faraway peoples. Still others thought that the nation would not be secure without bases in every ocean. And some wanted adventure—escape from economic hard times and the humdrum life at home.

Problems in Cuba. The United States had long been interested in Cuba. As early as 1823 John Quincy Adams called Cuba a natural appendage of the North American continent. Later Presidents, too, tried to acquire the island from Spain. In 1868, just after the Civil War, rebels in Cuba began agitating for independence.

In the United States many people felt sympathy for this latest American revolution. In February 1895 when Cuban rebels declared their independence, the Spanish government sent in troops. Their ruthless general was Valeriano "Butcher" Weyler. He ordered "all inhabitants of the country" to "concentrate themselves in the towns." Anyone found outside a town after February 10, 1896, would be shot. Cuban towns were made into "concentration camps." Cuban rebels were tortured. Innocent men, women, and children—including some United States citizens—were herded together, to die of disease and starvation.

The "Yellow Press." American newspapers splashed "Butcher" Weyler's atrocities on their front pages. The new speed presses flooded the cities with six editions each day. By 1896 rural free delivery of mail brought one of these editions daily even to remote farms. The larger a paper's "circulation"—the more copies it sold—the more it could charge for advertising.

Joseph Pulitzer, an adventurous Hungarian immigrant, had secured passage to America by enlisting in the Union army. His energy and enterprise made him a fortune in the newspaper business. He built circulation by championing the interests of his "American aristocracy"—the aristocracy of labor—and by printing sensational stories. If there was no startling news, he would invent some. He once sent Nelly Bly traveling around the world to beat the legendary record of 80 days.

To make his *New York World* interesting for readers of all ages, he invented the comic strip. He hired a clever cartoonist, Richard F. Outcault, to draw the adventures of a bad boy called the "Yellow Kid." Then when these comics appeared regularly in the Sunday *World*, Pulitzer's leading competitor, William Randolph Hearst, hired Outcault to do another Yellow Kid series for his own *New York Journal*. Because both of these sensational newspapers featured the Yellow Kid, they were soon called the "Yellow Press." And the Yellow Press was more interested in selling papers than in keeping peace.

The United States readies for war. American business firms had invested more than $50 million in Cuban sugar. Hoping to prod the United States to intervene, in 1895 the rebels destroyed these sugar plantations and their mills. Then, in 1896, William McKinley was elected President with his twin promises: Protect American business! Free the Cuban people!

When Spain began to negotiate with the United States about the freedom of the Cubans, it seemed that there would be no need to fight. But the Yellow Press now cleared the path to war. On February 9, 1898, the *New York Journal* printed a stolen letter. The Spanish ambassador, Dupuy de Lôme, had written that President McKinley was "weak and a bidder for the admiration of the crowd, besides being a would-be politician who tries to leave a door open behind himself while keeping on good terms with the jingoes of his party." Though de Lôme quickly resigned, Americans were angered by his insults. Before they could calm down, a more serious incident occurred.

To protect American lives and property, the United States battleship *Maine* had been sent to Havana Harbor. At 9:40 on the night of February 15, 1898, the *Maine* was shattered by an explosion, and 260 officers and men were killed. The Navy's court of inquiry reported that the cause was an underwater mine. (Later investigations seem to indicate it was an internal explosion.) Still they could not say for sure whether or not the Spanish were to blame. Anyway the Yellow Press called for war against Spain, and headlined the slogan, "Remember the *Maine!*"

On the day after the formal United States declaration of war on Spain, Hearst's *San Francisco Examiner* called "to arms" and ran the navy signal flags for "Remember the Maine" and "Commence Firing."

When the excitable Assistant Secretary of the Navy, Theodore Roosevelt, heard that McKinley was hesitating, he said the President "had no more backbone than a chocolate éclair." On February 25 the Secretary of the Navy made the mistake of taking the afternoon off. That left impatient Teddy as Acting Secretary—in charge of the whole United States Navy. Without consulting anyone, he cabled his friend Commodore George Dewey, who commanded the United States fleet in Asian waters. Make sure, he ordered, to have your ships ready for sea. In case of war attack the Spanish fleet in the Philippines.

When the Secretary of the Navy returned to his office next day, he was astonished. "Roosevelt," he wrote in his diary, "has come very near causing more of an explosion than happened to the *Maine*." But it was too late to change the order. So even *before* war had begun in nearby Cuba, Teddy had arrayed the United States fleet for war on the other side of the world.

The United States goes to war. If McKinley had been a stronger man, he would not have been afraid to keep the peace. The government of Spain now told him they would give Cuba its independence. But the Yellow Press was still demanding Spanish blood. The "jingoes"—the people who loved to see a fight—wanted war. Their name came from a line of British song of the 1870s, "We don't want to fight, yet by Jingo! if we do, We've got the ships, we've got the men, and got the money too." The jingoes had their way.

On April 11, the day *after* President McKinley learned that Spain would agree to do everything Americans said they wanted, he asked Congress to declare war.

The war lasted only a few months—but that was long enough to create the greatest confusion. At the training camp in Tampa, Florida, commanding officers could not find uniforms. Yet for weeks fifteen railroad cars full of uniforms remained on a siding 25 miles away. The commander of United States troops in Cuba, Major General W. R. Shafter, weighed 300 pounds and was therefore "too unwieldy to get to the front." Unprepared for combat, the Army committed every kind of foolishness.

The Navy was in better shape. On May 1, when Commodore George Dewey, following Roosevelt's

The Spanish-American War

impulsive orders, attacked the Spanish warships in the Philippines, he finished off the Spaniards in seven hours. The rest of the Spanish fleet, which was in North American waters, was bottled up in Santiago Harbor on the southeastern tip of Cuba.

Roosevelt and the Rough Riders. Meanwhile Teddy Roosevelt had himself named lieutenant colonel of a new regiment of cavalry. At a training camp in San Antonio, Texas, he gathered cowboys, sheriffs, and desperadoes from the West, and a sprinkling of playboy polo players and steeplechase riders from the East.

On June 22, Roosevelt's Rough Riders arrived in Cuba. In the battle to capture Santiago, they stormed both Kettle and San Juan hills. Without their horses, which had been left in Florida, the Rough Riders had to charge on foot. "I waved my hat and went up the hill with a rush," Roosevelt recalled. After bloody fighting they reached their goals.

Theodore Roosevelt never suffered from modesty. When Roosevelt published his book *The*

Rough Riders, the humorist "Mr. Dooley"—Finley Peter Dunne—said Teddy should have called it "Alone in Cuba."

The decisive naval battle occurred even before the Americans could place their big guns on San Juan Hill overlooking Santiago to bombard the enemy navy below. When the Spanish fleet tried to run for the open sea, the United States Navy sank every one of their warships. All over the United States, cheering Americans celebrated their victory.

The "splendid little war." By the standards of American history, this had not been a full-sized war. There were 385 battle deaths—less than one-tenth the deaths in the American Revolution, and only one-twentieth the deaths at the Battle of Gettysburg alone. While the American Revolution had lasted nearly eight years and the Civil War had lasted four years, the Spanish-American War lasted only four *months.* Future Secretary of State John Hay called it "a splendid little war." Even this "little" war cost a quarter-billion dollars and several thousand deaths from disease.

CELEBRATING JULY 4th, 1898 — "THE TRIUMPH OF THE AMERICAN BATTLE-SHIP."

The naval victories over Spain in 1898 showed that the United States was now a world power on the seas. Keppler's cartoon portrays all European powers but England as distressed by this development.

The little war marked a big change in the relationship of the United States to the world. The tides of history were turned.

The defeated Spain gave up to the United States an empire of islands. And this nation, born in a colonial revolution, would now have its own colonies. All were outside the continent; some were thousands of miles away. The United States acquired Puerto Rico at the gateway to the Caribbean along with Guam, important as a refueling station in the mid-Pacific. The Philippine Islands (all 7000 of them, of which more than 1000 were inhabitable!) off the coast of China were sold to the United States for a bargain price of $20 million.

These new American colonies added up to 100,000 square miles, holding nearly 10 million people. That was not much, compared to the vast empires of England, France, or Germany. But for the United States it was something quite new.

The meaning of this Spanish-American War in American history, then, was actually less in what it accomplished than in what it proclaimed. The American Revolution had been our War of Independence. Now the Spanish-American War at the threshold of the 1900s was our first War of Intervention. We had joined the old-fashioned race for empire.

Americans opposed to empire. Many Americans were worried. Some were saddened, and even angry. They called themselves "Anti-Imperialists," for they hated to see the United States become an empire. To be an empire, they said, meant lording it over people in faraway places. They also feared that seizing land in the Pacific might someday lead to war with Japan. Some felt Asians could never be part of a democracy. And most wondered how the United States could uphold the Declaration of Independence if it became an empire. Anti-Imperialists included Democrats and Republicans, of all

Territory Acquired by the United States, 1857-1899

United States Possessions

sections and classes—labor leader Samuel Gompers, industrialist Andrew Carnegie, President Charles W. Eliot of Harvard and President David Starr Jordan of Stanford, philosopher William James, social worker Jane Addams, and popular writer Mark Twain. William Jennings Bryan was also opposed to America's new imperialism.

The Anti-Imperialists were especially disturbed by the situation in the Philippines. The Filipinos did not want to be ruled by the United States any more than by Spain. Led by Emilio Aguinaldo they fought against the Americans. Guerrilla warfare went on for three years. The United States used more troops and spent more money than in the entire war against Spain. Many Americans were shocked by the brutal methods we used to put down the Filipinos.

It was not until April 1902 that the last rebel surrendered and the Philippines were officially declared "pacified." Even before then, however, in 1900 under the direction of William Howard Taft, first as head of the Philippine Commission and then

as civil governor, the large land holdings of the Catholic friars were distributed to the people. Under Taft's wise direction roads were built, harbors and sanitation improved, and the Philippines started on the path to self-government.

McKinley was renominated by the Republicans at Philadelphia in 1900 with a unanimous shout. Theodore Roosevelt, governor of New York and "Rough Rider" hero, was the vice-presidential candidate. Once nominated, Roosevelt threw himself into the campaign with his usual boyish vigor. Up and down the country he denounced the "mollycoddles" who would have us "scuttle" out of the Philippines.

The Democrats met at Kansas City on Independence Day and nominated William Jennings Bryan. Although Bryan insisted on a free-silver plank in the platform, the campaign was not fought on that dead issue. The Republican Congress had already passed an act making gold the only standard of currency. The issue was imperialism. A huge American flag hanging from the rafters of the

An expanding Uncle Sam turns down reducing medicine as McKinley fits him with larger clothes.

Democratic convention hall proclaimed, "The flag of the Republic forever, of an Empire never."

In 1900 that slogan was already too late. People did not like what they heard about the Filipinos fighting against American control, even though censorship kept them from hearing the worst. Still, the war had helped to return prosperity to the United States. McKinley, "the advance agent of prosperity," was easily reelected by 292 electoral votes to Bryan's 155.

The reorganization of Cuba.
For better or worse—and without much thought of what it all meant for the future—the United States was now running a colonial empire.

The administration had already begun setting up governments for the former Spanish islands. The Teller Amendment was attached to Congress's war resolution of April 20, 1898. It pledged that the United States would not exercise sovereignty over Cuba. We would leave government of the island to its people.

Still, United States troops did not leave. Under the military governor General Leonard Wood (1899–1902) the ruins wrought by the revolution were repaired. A school system was organized. The finances of the island were set in order. Peace lasted while the Cubans drew up a new constitution. But what use was a new constitution to people weakened and dying of the tropical disease of yellow fever? A commission headed by Major Walter Reed of the Army Medical Corps proved that yellow fever was carried by a mosquito (the female *Aëdes aegypti*) which bred in stagnant waters. Reed helped to stamp out the disease so Cuba could prosper.

The United States wanted certain assurances before it withdrew its army from Cuba. Cuba must make no treaties with foreign powers that would limit its independence. It should not permit any foreign power to acquire Cuban territory. Cuba should sell or lease to the United States land for coaling or naval stations. Cuba should not contract debts whose interest could not be met out of current revenues. And, finally, Cuba should allow the United States to step in whenever necessary "for the protection of life, property, and individual liberty."

The Platt Amendment, named for Senator Orville H. Platt of Connecticut, attached all these provisions to an army money bill. The provisions would have to appear in any constitution of the Cubans. And they would also be included in a treaty with the United States. Otherwise the United States would not withdraw its troops.

The Cubans protested these terms but finally wrote them into their constitution. American troops were then withdrawn. The Platt Amendment became a "permanent" treaty with Cuba in 1903.

A new status for Puerto Rico.
The island of Puerto Rico, with a population of almost a million, willingly came under the rule of the United States. The Foraker Act of April 1900 organized Puerto Rico as a compromise between a colony and a territory. The President would appoint a governor and a council of 11, including 5 Puerto Ricans. Puerto Ricans would elect a legislature of 35 members. The Spanish courts were swept away and replaced by a court system like that of the United States. Works of sanitation, education, road building, and agricultural development were begun. In 1901 Congress abolished customs duties between the island and the United States.

The "Open Door" in China.
On the other side of the world were more lands waiting to be occupied by the new imperial powers. After China had been defeated in a war with Japan, in 1894–1895, the country lay at the mercy of the great powers. China was cut up into "spheres of influ-ence." France, Germany, Japan, and Russia forced the Chinese government to grant them "leases" of great areas. Within each of these the lucky foreigners seized valuable railroad and mining rights and even abolished China's political rule.

The United States took Hawaii and the Philippines at the very moment when this piecemeal division of China was under way. The China trade was appealing to American merchants. Knowing that Great Britain wanted the same opportunities, McKinley's Secretary of State, John Hay, sent identical notes to enlist England, France, Germany, Japan, and Russia. They were not to interfere with the rights of any of the 22 ports in China, nor to disturb the regular collection of the Chinese duties. They were not to increase railroad rates or harbor dues or in any way to close their own "spheres of influence" to other nations. Every nation was to have equal commercial treatment throughout China.

When Hay addressed the Great Powers, they avoided giving a direct answer. Hay went ahead anyway. On March 20, 1900, he announced that their consent had been "final and definitive." In this very casual way, without realizing what the "Open Door" in China might mean, the United States plunged deeper into world affairs.

The Boxer Rebellion.
Meanwhile many Chinese would not let their country and themselves be treated like foreign property. They rushed to join a patriotic society called the "righteous Fists of Harmony" (shortened to "Boxers"). In May 1900 they rose up against the "foreign devils" hoping to drive them out of China. The Boxers killed missionaries and their families. They besieged the foreigners' neighborhood in Peking. It took seven weeks for a makeshift army of American, British, French, German, Russian, and Japanese troops to reach Peking and drive off the mob.

The foreign powers doing business in China wished to take their revenge and prevent this happening again. They wished to overthrow the government and divide China among themselves. Still, Secretary Hay stuck by his policy of the Open Door. He insisted that Chinese independence be preserved. Hay urged that, instead of overthrowing the shaky government of China, they only force the government to punish the ringleaders of the

Spheres of Influence in the Far East about 1900

Possessions

- ■ British
- ■ French
- ■ United States
- ■ Japanese

Spheres of Influence

- ▨ Russian
- ▨ Japanese
- ■ German
- ▨ British
- ▨ French

0   1200 Miles

0   1200 Kilometers

Boxer Rebellion and pay damages. The whole sum was finally fixed at a stiff $334 million. When it was found that less than half the $24 million allotted to the United States was enough to pay our military expenses, Congress returned the balance to China.

The Chinese government said that it was "profoundly impressed with the justice and great friendliness of the United States." It put the American money in a trust fund to send hundreds of young Chinese to colleges and universities in the United States.

The United States had not only acquired colonial outposts in the Far North, in the Caribbean, and the North and South Pacific. This nation had even committed itself to preserve the independence and the territorial integrity of China—a vast, half-understood country on the other side of the globe. These varied commitments, so casually undertaken, held a dangerous destiny. The New World was no longer simply a place of refuge for oppressed peoples from everywhere. Our nation had become one of the world's great powers.

SECTION 3 REVIEW

1. Identify or explain: Joseph Pulitzer, Richard Outcault, W. R. Hearst, Dupuy de Lôme, George Dewey, "jingoes," Rough Riders.

2. Locate: Havana, Philippines, Santiago, Guam, Puerto Rico, Peking.

3. Why did American Anti-Imperialists oppose expansion?

4. List the provisions of the Platt Amendment.

5. How did Secretary of State John Hay achieve the "Open Door" policy?

6. What was the Boxer Rebellion? How did it influence our relations with China?

7. **Determining Relevance.** What part did each of the following play in bringing on the Spanish-American War: (a) "Butcher" Weyler? (b) Cuban rebels? (c) the sinking of the *Maine*? (d) Theodore Roosevelt? (e) William McKinley? (f) the Yellow Press?

FOCUSING ON IDEAS

1. What groups of Americans opposed American overseas expansion? Why were they against imperialism?

2. How did the United States benefit politically, socially, and economically from expansion in the late nineteenth century?

3. Describe the territorial changes of the United States that occurred as a result of the Spanish-American War.

4. The value of the goods and services produced by Americans nearly doubled between 1870 and 1900. How was this economic growth linked to demands for overseas expansion?

TAKING A CRITICAL LOOK

1. **Determining Relevance.** What was the relevance of the Monroe Doctrine to the Maximilian affair? the Venezuelan boundary dispute? the Platt Amendment?

2. **Making Comparisons.** How did the overseas expansion of the United States differ from American westward expansion with regard to (a) settlement and (b) the way in which the new territories were governed?

YOUR REGION IN HISTORY

1. **Geography.** Was your state or locality involved in any special way in the overseas events described in this chapter? Investigate any events you discover and report to the class on the involvement.

2. **Culture.** Did any newspaper serving your community take a stand on the Spanish-American War? (Your public library or newspaper office may have a file or microfilm of back issues.) What stand did it take? What reasons did it give?

3. **Economics.** How did the vast increase in the value of goods and services produced in the United States affect the standard of living of residents in your region during the period 1870–1890?

HISTORICAL FACTS AND FIGURES

Summarizing Information. Study the graph below to help answer the following questions: (a) What was the value of foreign trade in 1865? In 1885? In 1915? (b) What caused the temporary decline between 1880 and 1890? (c) Write a hypothesis describing the trend in American foreign trade for the period 1865 to 1915. (d) What events in this chapter would support your hypothesis?

American Foreign Trade, 1865-1915

Source: *Historical Statistics of the United States*

CHAPTER 20

The Progressive Era

In the opening years of the 1900s, the reformers were so successful that the period came to be called the *Progressive Era*. American voters would have more to say than ever before in selecting their candidates. New laws would control big business. This was accomplished by no one leader or party but by a wonderfully varied crew—the aggressive Theodore Roosevelt, the genial William Howard Taft, and the ascetic Woodrow Wilson. Reformers appeared in Congress, statehouses, and city halls. Journalists and other social critics stirred public opinion and prodded officials to move forward. Within twenty years these forces of reform pushed the nation further into the world scene. There the United States would play a reluctant but decisive role.

1. Theodore Roosevelt's Square Deal

Fortune seemed to smile on President McKinley as he took the oath for his second term on March 4, 1901. The nation had sent him back to the White House with a solid vote of confidence. His early months in office were uneventful. In the spring he made a grand tour of the country. Then he spent a two-month summer vacation at his home in Canton, Ohio. In September he went to Buffalo, New York, to speak at the Pan-American Exposition. There at a brief public reception a man suddenly walked up to him and, without warning, shot the President twice. Just over a week later McKinley was dead.

The 28-year-old assassin, Leon Czolgosz, called himself an anarchist, which meant that he was against all government. But in a stroke of irony, Czolgosz unintentionally put the government of the United States under a strong and inspiring leader. "It's a dreadful thing to come into the Presidency this way," Roosevelt wrote a friend, "but it would be a far worse thing to be morbid about it." To the delight of the nation, "TR" would enjoy being President just as he seemed to enjoy everything else.

The Republican Roosevelt. No one who had visited Theodore Roosevelt as a child could have guessed that he would become a champion of the ordinary American. His father was a well-to-do New York banker who owned country houses and took his family to Europe for vacations. Among Teddy Roosevelt's early memories were seeing the Pope during a walk in Rome and visiting the tomb of Napoleon in Paris.

Young Teddy had no worries about money. But he had other worries. He suffered from asthma, which made it hard for him to exercise, and his eyesight was poor. He became interested in nature and began collecting specimens of plants and an-

Library of Congress

The ever-ebullient TR gives a rousing speech in New Castle, Wyoming, in 1903.

imals. When he was 12, his mother told a maid to throw away some dead mice that the boy had stored in a dresser drawer. "The Loss to Science," Teddy cried. "The Loss to Science!"

His father built a gym for the boy at home. There Teddy worked with a punching bag and did pull-ups on the horizontal bars. He also took boxing lessons. By age 17 he was expert in such track events as running, pole vaulting, and high jumping. On his grandfather's country estate at Oyster Bay on Long Island, he became an enthusiastic horseman and a crack shot. All his life Teddy Roosevelt felt that he had to make up for the childhood weakness of his body.

Roosevelt never lost his boyish excitement. He kept up his boxing. After he was hit in the eye while boxing with a young army officer, his left eye became blind. He managed to keep this a secret, and he devised ways to prevent people from knowing that he could see in only one eye. In spite of it, he became world famous as an explorer and big-game hunter in Africa and South America.

From the White House he preached "The Strenuous Life." Some genteel European diplomats dreaded being assigned to Washington when TR was in the White House. They could not do their diplomatic duty by sipping tea and making polite conversation. TR expected them—along with panting Cabinet members and generals—to join his exhausting tramps through the countryside. "You must always remember," a British ambassador once explained, "that the President is about six years old."

Dynamic energy was the key to Roosevelt's character. The variety of his interests and curiosities was enormous. His published works on history, politics, ethics, travel, and sport fill twenty volumes. Though born to wealth and an old family, he was no snob. Cowboys, ambassadors, social workers, labor leaders, senators, clergymen, writers, and prizefighters were his friends. They met one another in the reception room of the White House and sat down at his table together. He loved power. And he used it with confidence that his policies were right. He was certain that they would benefit the American people. He believed the President had all the powers not forbidden in the Constitution. He also saw the Presidency as a "bully pulpit" from which in his high-pitched, squeaky voice he spread his ideas. He was the first President since Lincoln to use fully the powers of the office.

TR believed the President should lead. And he liked a good fight—not only in the boxing ring, but also in politics. He had been shocked that earlier Presidents and the Supreme Court had not enforced the laws against monopolies. Their growing power worried him. "Of all forms of tyranny," he complained, "the least attractive and the most vulgar is the tyranny of mere wealth."

The coal strike. Hardly had TR moved into the White House when he had his first chance to show how a President should lead. The owners of the nation's anthracite (hard coal) mines were reckless of the safety of their men. Workers were dying needlessly each year. In 1901 alone, 441 men were killed in mining accidents in the anthracite fields of Illinois, Ohio, Pennsylvania, and West Virginia.

The men had received no raise in wages in twenty years. They were paid by the weight of the coal they dug, but the companies were not weighing honestly. A man might have to dig 4000 pounds before getting credit for a ton. Miners were sometimes paid in scrip that could only be used in "company stores" which charged high prices.

By 1902 the miners could endure no more. The union leaders decided to take action. John Mitchell, then the energetic young president of the United Mine Workers, was the son of a miner who had lost his life in the mines. Mitchell himself had begun mining at age 12. His union—150,000 strong—included thousands of immigrant newcomers who spoke over a dozen languages.

The coal miners went on strike in May 1902. But the mine owners refused to deal with the union. They tried to force the miners back to work. George F. Baer, the president of the Philadelphia and Reading Coal and Iron Company, was the chief spokesman for the owners. "The rights and interests of the laboring man," he declared, "will be protected and cared for not by the labor agitators, but by the Christian men to whom God in his wisdom has given the control of the property interests of the country."

By October with winter coming on, people feared that the railroads would have to stop running and that they would freeze without coal to heat their homes. Then the President came to the rescue. No matter who owned the mines, Roosevelt insisted that nobody owned the miners. He called the mine operators and John Mitchell to the White House. When the owners refused to arbitrate, he let them know he might send the army into the mines. At last on October 13 the owners gave in and agreed to deal with the union. The miners went back to work and later won most of their demands. When the strike ended, TR had shown how, in the new age of big business, it was possible for the federal government to help. He had proven himself a champion of the ordinary American. He had seen that the miners received a "square deal." That was what he wanted for all Americans.

The Northern Securities case. The coal strike was only the beginning of TR's flamboyant defense of the public interest against the trusts. His most famous target was the Northern Securities Company. It was a holding company, a corporation set up to hold a controlling part of the stock of other companies. It had been formed by railroad builder James J. Hill of the Great Northern, the Rockefellers, J. P. Morgan, and E. H. Harriman of the Union Pacific to control the four big railroads of the Northwest.

After a fierce battle over the control of the stock of one of the railroads, this holding company had brought peace between the competitors. But the people in the Northwest were now at the mercy of one big railroad combine. They depended on the railroad to bring in supplies and to take their produce to market. Now they would have to pay whatever rates the railroads wanted to charge.

The Northern Securities Company gave TR his perfect issue—and his chance to prove that he was a master of public relations. He used it skillfully to revive the Sherman Antitrust Act and to show the power of the federal government. These men of great wealth had plagued a whole region and disrupted the nation's stock market by their fight for

This 1903 cartoon called for new legislation to expose the activities of the trusts.

monopoly. So the President had the company sued under the Sherman Act.

J. P. Morgan was shocked. He went to the White House and told TR, "If we have done anything wrong, send your man [meaning the Attorney General] to my man [one of Morgan's lawyers] and they can fix it up." The President later remarked of this incident, "That is a most illuminating illustration of the Wall Street point of view. Mr. Morgan could not help regarding me as a big rival operator, who either intended to ruin all his interests or else could be induced to come to an agreement to ruin none."

But Roosevelt pushed the case, and in 1904 the Supreme Court, by a vote of 5 to 4, held that the Northern Securities Company did violate the Sherman Antitrust Act. The Court ordered the company to dissolve. After this first victory, TR moved against other unpopular trusts—the beef trust, the oil trust, and the tobacco trust.

In his own mind Roosevelt always made a distinction between "good" trusts and "bad" trusts. The law should be used to break up the bad trusts, those that were formed to gouge the public by trying to end competition. Good trusts should only be regulated. A good trust might simply beat its rivals because its prices were lower, its products better, or its management more efficient. By getting Congress to add a new Department of Commerce and Labor to the Cabinet, TR showed that he meant what he said. A Bureau of Corporations within the Department was formed to help judge which trusts were good and which were bad. The government, the President declared, must be "the senior partner in every business."

President in his own right.
Roosevelt's battles for labor and against the trusts made his first term a smashing success. He easily won the election of 1904 against the Democrats' dull and conservative candidate, Judge Alton B. Parker of New York. Roosevelt carried the entire North and West with 336 electoral votes. Parker was left with only 140 votes from the "solid South." For every two popular votes for Parker, Roosevelt collected three.

Now that Roosevelt was President in his own right, he moved swiftly for major reforms. His first goal was to strengthen the Interstate Commerce Commission so it could really regulate the railroads. But he had to be both inventive and persistent to overcome the opposition of the railroads and the big businesses that benefited from their rebates. Finally, in 1906, after a sixteen-month battle in the Senate during which he used all his skills as a leader, the Hepburn bill became law. It gave the ICC power over pipelines, express and sleeping car companies, bridges, ferries, and terminals. Railroad rebates and free passes were forbidden. If a shipper complained about any unfair rate, the Commission could reduce the rate until a federal court ruled on its fairness. To Roosevelt the Hepburn Act marked a major step on the path to effective federal regulation of business.

Other reform legislation.
Roosevelt went on to prove that a free society was not powerless against large corporations. The Meat Inspection Act gave federal officials the right to inspect all meat shipped in interstate commerce to see whether it came from healthy animals and was packed under sanitary conditions. Upton Sinclair had written a popular novel, *The Jungle,* showing the miseries of workers in the stockyards—and describing the rotten meat packed for sale. When the law passed in 1906, Sinclair said his book had tried to hit people in their heart, and instead had hit them in their stomach.

The year 1906 was a banner one for reform. A Pure Food and Drug Act was passed. The manufacture and sale of impure foods, drugs, and liquors was forbidden. Labels on patent medicines had to list the contents. The Employers' Liability Act provided accident insurance for workers in the District of Columbia and on interstate railroads.

Conservation of natural resources.
President Roosevelt gave a new meaning to "conservation"—the movement to conserve the nation's resources for future Americans. His own experience had shown him the need. As a young man out west he had enjoyed the open spaces. On his ranch in Dakota Territory he had ridden the range and explored the wilderness. He loved everything about the West—the cowboys, the life of the trail, fishing, and hunting. When he became President, he was shocked to see lumber companies wasting forests that had taken centuries to grow. He knew that the untouched wilderness could never be put back.

He saw some parts of the country troubled by floods while others lacked water. Saving rivers and streams and using their water wisely were just as important as protecting the land or the forests. In June 1902 his strong support helped to secure the

via the

Scenic Route

Denver & Rio Grande R'y

THE
ONLY LINE
THROUGH
SALT LAKE CITY
LEADVILLE
PUEBLO
COLORADO SPRINGS
& DENVER

GRANDEST MOUNTAIN SCENERY
IN THE WORLD.

E. A. MUDGETT, General Agent Passenger Department, Salt Lake, Utah.

The Huntington Library, San Marino, California

Photographer Carleton Watkins made an extensive record of life and development on the Pacific Coast. He was probably the first person to take pictures of Yosemite Valley. The one below was made in the 1860s. The works of painters and photographers sparked tourist interest in the Far West. In the 1880s the Denver & Rio Grande advertised the beauty of its route across the continent (left).

Stanford University Library, Special Collection

The wild American West gave painters exciting new subjects. Thomas Moran, an Englishman, painted this striking canvas of "The Grand Canyon of the Yellowstone" in 1871. Partly influenced by such inspiring landscapes, Congress established Yellowstone National Park in 1872.

National Museum of American Art, Smithsonian Institution, Washington, D.C. U.S. Department of the Interior, National Park Service

German-born Albert Bierstadt, who went west as early as 1858, was renowned for his heroic canvases of natural subjects. Here (left) he painted the giant redwoods and the native Indians. Author-naturalist John Muir (right) was a leader in the drive to make Yosemite a national park. He also helped to persuade Theodore Roosevelt of the importance of conserving forest land.

passage of the Newlands Reclamation Act. Money from the sale of public lands in sixteen western states and territories was to be used to build large dams and canal systems to conserve water for irrigation. Vast stretches of arid lands in the West were once worth just a cent or two an acre because they were good only for cattle grazing. Now they were worth hundreds of dollars an acre for growing crops.

In 1891 Congress had given the President power over "public lands wholly or in part covered with timber." He could set them apart as forest reserves. Presidents Harrison, Cleveland, and McKinley had set aside 50 million acres. Now Roosevelt increased the number of national forests to 149 totaling over 190 million acres, an area equal to Great Britain and France combined.

TR also withdrew from sale millions of acres of public land having waterpower sites and deposits of coal, oil, and phosphates. He took steps to prevent illegal use of the public lands by lumber companies and cattle raisers. He transferred forests from the Public Land Office to the United States Forest Service, headed by his enthusiastic supporter, Gifford Pinchot. For Pinchot, "conservation" meant scientific land management. So he planned "reforesting"—the planting of trees—to go along with the cutting of trees. He saw the nation's forests as a living resource that always had to be renewed.

The panic of 1907. In the summer of 1907, when prices fell sharply on Wall Street, a number of banks and businesses failed. Some newspapers blamed Roosevelt. Even many of his supporters urged him to "go slow" against the large corporations. Roosevelt did not relax his efforts for reform.

But he was willing to compromise. He agreed when J. P. Morgan explained the need for United States Steel to purchase its largest competitor. The

Tennessee Coal and Iron Company was near collapse. Without making "any binding promise" not to prosecute under the antitrust laws, TR told Morgan to go ahead.

Further efforts for reform. Prosperity soon returned. Then Roosevelt's messages to Congress in December 1907 and January 1908 called for still more reforms. On his list were income and inheritance taxes, federal rules for the stock market, limits on the use of labor injunctions, and more effective control of business. The panic, he insisted, had been caused not by enforcement of the law but by the corporations' refusal to obey the law.

Roosevelt's interest in social reform and his outspoken attacks on "predatory wealth" led conservatives to call him a socialist. But he really had no sympathy with socialist doctrine. He did not believe in public ownership of the means of production and distribution. His large purpose, he said, was to "avoid the extremes of swollen fortunes and grinding poverty." He believed in capitalism, but he wanted to make it benefit all the people. Always the reformer, he hoped to save the United States he knew by making capitalism work.

SECTION 1 REVIEW

1. Identify or explain: holding company, Alton B. Parker, Hepburn Act, Upton Sinclair.

2. What role did Theodore Roosevelt play in the coal strike of 1902?

3. What measures were passed to provide (a) improved transportation regulation, (b) consumer protection, (c) accident insurance, (d) conservation of resources?

4. **Checking Consistency.** Theodore Roosevelt believed that a President should lead. Were his actions consistent with his beliefs? Explain.

---

2. Middle-class reformers

The movement Theodore Roosevelt led was broad and deep. It reached out to states and cities across the nation.

The main centers were medium-sized cities and small towns. Support came from doctors, lawyers, ministers, small-business owners, merchants, white-collar workers, social critics, and intellectuals. Mostly Americans of old families, they had been disturbed by the strife and violence of the 1890s. They disliked the city political bosses and distrusted the great business corporations. They wanted to help the poor and the needy.

The Progressives no longer believed it was good enough for the government to be only an umpire. Even in a democracy, the powers of a citizen and a corporation were not equal. In the 1900s more and more Americans expected their government to be their guardian.

Reform in the cities. Beginning in 1889, reform mayors were elected in many cities. But bosses soon took over again. Still, some reformers managed to stay in office. Among them were some wealthy business leaders. For example, Hazen S. Pingree brought good government to Detroit. And there was Toledo's colorful Samuel M. "Golden Rule" Jones. He said, "I don't want to rule anybody, each individual must rule himself." Jones had already given his factory workers unusual benefits when he entered politics. Angered by his early reforms, the Republican machine dropped him as their candidate for mayor. But he easily won reelection as an independent.

In some cities the reform movements petered out. And then the old political machines would return to power. To prevent this, some reformers changed the form of city government. Under one plan, first used in 1900 in Galveston, Texas, the mayor and city council were replaced by a small commission usually elected on a nonpartisan ballot. Each of its members ran a city department. The commission passed laws and decided policies for the city. By 1912 more than 200 cities were using the commission plan.

Many more cities turned to a city manager. On the model of other large businesses, a trained manager was hired to run the city. A small council set the policies, and the manager carried them out. The manager was not a politician. The city manager system was most successful in small cities. It was harder to find skilled managers for big cities as well as more difficult to keep politics out. So, though city managers still run some large cities, among them the old mayor-council form of government is most common today.

State government reform. Reformers in the cities soon found that to reach their goals they had to reform the state governments, too. The earliest and ablest of the reform governors was Robert M. La Follette. In 1900 the people of Wisconsin elected "Battling Bob." After fierce fights he brought the state legislature under his control. And in his three terms it enacted a wide range of "Progressive" measures. The direct primary gave the voters the right to choose the candidates for public office. A commission was formed to control railroad rates. A competitive civil service was set up. Restrictions were put on lobbying. Laws were passed for conservation, for supervision of state banks, and for higher taxes on corporations. TR later called Wisconsin "a laboratory for democracy," and other states followed its lead.

By 1912 three-fourths of the states had passed child-labor laws barring the employment of young children and regulating the working hours of all young people. Workmen's compensation laws made the employer pay for injuries caused by defective machinery or dangerous tasks. In many states compulsory insurance systems created funds for the sick, the disabled, and the aged. In 1912 Massachusetts passed the first minimum-wage law

for women. Other states regulated women's hours and conditions of work. State after state outlawed intoxicating liquors. By the beginning of World War I, 26 states were "dry."

The reformers changed the tax laws to put a heavier burden on the rich. New charges were laid upon the profits of corporations, on the inheritance of fortunes, and on large incomes. At the same time most states formed railroad and public utility commissions to keep down rates and keep up the quality of services.

Direct democracy and women's suffrage. Time after time the efforts of the reformers were blocked by political bosses and "the special interests." So the Progressives looked for ways to break their power. If the people's representatives would not respond to the calls for reform, let the voters themselves play a more direct role.

The reformers started with the ballot. In most states voters were still using colored ballots printed by the parties (p. 188). Reformers felt that if voting was made truly secret, elections would be more honest, and better representatives would be elected. Political bosses would no longer be able to tell by the color of a ballot which way a person

"Battling Bob" La Follette (left) and his wife, Belle Case La Follette (right), were vigorous battlers for reform. She influenced many as a magazine editor, speaker, and organizer. He served as the progressive governor of Wisconsin, as a U. S. Senator, and ran for President in 1924.

voted. In 1888 Massachusetts became the first state to print and distribute ballots containing the names of all those running for office. The secret ballot was soon adopted by most of the states.

But the secret, or Australian, ballot (named for its place of origin) did not break the power of the political bosses. The Progressive reformers then tried to give the voters the right to choose the party candidates for public office. The *direct primary* might break the power of party bosses to dictate who would run. Mississippi in 1902 and Wisconsin the next year led the way. In some southern states, however, the Democrats said their party was a private club open only to white voters (p. 542). It would be many years before the Supreme Court outlawed this barrier to black voters.

A second reform was direct election of United States Senators. But the "rich man's club," as the Senate was called, blocked the proposal time after time. Oregon in 1904 began to allow voters to name their choice. Then the legislature "elected" the person so chosen. By 1910 more than enough states to ratify an amendment were electing their senators this way. So at last the Senate gave in. The Seventeenth Amendment, ratified in 1913, took the election of senators away from the state legislatures and gave it to the voters.

The reformers found two other ways to deal with balky lawmakers. The *initiative* allowed 5 to 8 percent of the voters to "initiate" or start a bill by petition. In some states the bill was then put on the ballot for the voters to pass or defeat in a *referendum*. In other states there would be a referendum only if the legislature failed to pass the bill by a certain time. South Dakota in 1898 was the first of about 20 states to adopt these two measures.

A dozen states and many cities and counties adopted the *recall*. By petition, voters could force an official to stand for reelection at any time.

Some Progressives took up the cause of women's suffrage. They thought women would be more inclined than men to support reform legislation. By 1896 four western states had granted women full voting rights (p. 383). Between 1910 and 1914 seven more states—all west of the Mississippi—granted women the ballot.

The muckrakers. With reform politicians came reform journalists and novelists. Roosevelt called them "muckrakers," and the name stuck. He compared them to the man in John Bunyan's *Pilgrim's Progress* who was so busy raking the filth on the ground that he never lifted his eyes to heaven.

The muckrakers looked everywhere—in government, in Wall Street, in labor unions, in the trusts—for crime and corruption. Where they couldn't find a crime they might invent one. The new speed presses and cheap paper carried their message in the new daily newspapers and mass magazines to millions in the cities. Rural free delivery of mail took the word to remote farms.

The great wave of muckraking began in October 1902 when *McClure's Magazine* carried "Tweed Days in St. Louis." The author of this exposé was the young Lincoln Steffens, one of the most fearless journalists of modern times. He was the pioneer investigating reporter. He wrote articles on misgovernment in the cities. Later he brought them together in his book *The Shame of the Cities* (1904).

The clever Ida Tarbell published her angry attack on the Standard Oil Company. Her father believed that Rockefeller had ruined him and had driven his partner to suicide. Since she had spent five years collecting materials for her articles, she was well armed with facts. Then she wrote about the Standard Oil Company not as a business enterprise but as Public Enemy Number One.

A new force—media power—had entered American politics. To read the shocking stories, true, half-true, and sometimes false, readers flocked to *McClure's*. Other mass magazines like *Munsey's, Cosmopolitan,* and *Everybody's* went into this profitable business of exposing evil. Finley Peter Dunne's witty and philosophical newspaper character "Mr. Dooley" complained that whatever magazine he picked up he always got this one message: "Ivrything has gone wrong."

But the muckrakers' message got through. Within six years after Steffens's *The Shame of the Cities,* reform movements appeared in Philadelphia, Chicago, Kansas City, Minneapolis, Los Angeles, and San Francisco.

The muckrakers wrote some sensational and persuasive novels, which we can still enjoy. Frank Norris wrote about the powerful railroads in California (*The Octopus,* 1901) and the wheat exchange in Chicago (*The Pit,* 1903). Theodore Dreiser used muckraking themes for novels which outlived the Progressive Era. His books were epics of wealth, power, success—and poverty. *The Financier* (1912),

Culver Pictures

This photograph of Ida Tarbell was taken in 1904, when her *History of the Standard Oil Company* caused a sensation. Her exposé had first appeared in nineteen installments in the popular *McClure's Magazine*.

Culver Pictures

The Titan (1914), and *An American Tragedy* (1925) became classics.

Painters, too, found a way to join the muckrakers. A new "ashcan school" of artists chose some unusual subjects. John Sloane, George Luks, Robert Henri, and others filled the respectable galleries with high-priced canvases showing alleys and tenements. The bold Danish immigrant photographer, Jacob Riis, published shocking pictures of starving children in garbage-ridden slums.

Social workers, sociologists, and historians also did their bit for reform. John Spargo described the horrors of child labor in *The Bitter Cry of the Children* (1906). Gustavus Myers made his *History of the Great American Fortunes* (1909) a rogues' gallery of crooks. Ray Stannard Baker told the story of racial discrimination in *Following the Color Line* (1908). Burton J. Hendrick's disclosures in *Story of Life Insurance* (1907) led to laws regulating New York's large insurance companies.

SECTION 2 REVIEW

1. Identify or explain: commission plan, Robert La Follette, direct primary, initiative, referendum, recall, Lincoln Steffens, Ida Tarbell, Frank Norris, "ashcan school," Jacob Riis.

2. How did reformers try to improve city government?

3. Why was Wisconsin called "a laboratory for democracy"?

4. Name some state reforms designed (a) to improve government, (b) to regulate business, (c) to aid workers, (d) to help the needy.

5. **Identifying Assumptions.** How did the "muckrakers' " attitudes about government affect their reform efforts?

3. Taft in the White House

Theodore Roosevelt had said that he would not run for a third term. His hand-picked successor was his Secretary of War—the jovial 300-pound William Howard Taft. The Republicans in Chicago in June 1908 chose Taft on the first ballot. The Democrats, meeting at Denver, decided to try again with William Jennings Bryan.

Taft won by over a million votes and an electoral vote of 321 to 162. But the election was more an

Lewis Hine was hired in 1908 by the National Child Labor Committee to travel the country to record the plight of child laborers. In 1911 he photographed (above) this young cotton mill spinner in Virginia. Jacob Riis made the shot (below) of New York waifs between 1880 and 1910.

endorsement for Roosevelt's candidate and policies than it was for the Republican party. The Democrats gained new strength from farmers and from workers organized in unions. Several states that voted for Taft elected Democratic governors. The Republicans also lost seats in the House, but they still retained control.

The new President. William Howard Taft took office on March 4, 1909. He was a comforting and comfortable man. But he was no cowboy and no crusader. He had served as United States Solicitor General and as a federal judge. As governor of the Philippines he had brought reforms without stirring up resentment. TR had appointed him Secretary of War, but he had never before been elected to office. Besides being a proven administrator, he was a learned and successful lawyer. By temperament

Theodore Roosevelt scores by getting rotund Taft the nomination in 1908. Notice that basketball was played with a closed basket.

and training he was deliberate and cautious. He was a huge man. And the movement of his mind was as sedate as his walk. He faced public issues like a judge weighing arguments. And he always preferred to postpone a decision rather than risk error or haste.

Naturally enough, Taft was troubled by the new schemes of "direct democracy" that were being pushed by the reformers. Wise legislation, he thought, should always be preceded by careful, time-consuming study. He favored the slow, dignified methods of courtrooms. He feared demagogues—lawmakers who would gratify popular prejudice to stay in office.

Taft disappoints the reformers. The tariff was a troublesome issue. A high tariff, which protected some American industries and their workers, raised prices for all consumers. The tariff issue had plagued many Presidents. Somehow it had been avoided by TR. In the Republican party platform of 1908 Taft and Roosevelt had inserted an ambig-

uous plank. It promised "substantial revision" of the existing Dingley tariff, which had stood unchanged for a dozen years.

Soon after taking the oath of office, Taft boldly called a special session of Congress to revise the tariff. People expected something dramatic. A bill that began in the House added items to the free list and lowered many duties. But the Senate, led by Nelson W. Aldrich of Rhode Island, revised the bill out of all recognition. What finally emerged hardly lowered duties below the level of the Dingley tariff.

This Payne-Aldrich tariff was a plain betrayal of party pledges. Yet Taft signed the bill without protest. To make matters worse, he soon called it the "best tariff ever passed by the Republican party." The press was filled with fiery editorials on the "hoax" of tariff revision. Progressives everywhere were beginning to wonder what kind of a President they had elected.

Taft lost what was left of Progressive support by a scandal in the sale of public land. During the summer of 1909 an argument arose between Gifford Pinchot, Chief of the Forest Service, and Richard A. Ballinger, Taft's Secretary of the Interior. In a sale

New York's docks were booming about 1900. Dockworkers and shipowners hoped lower tariffs would make ports even busier.

of government coal lands in Alaska to a group controlled by J. P. Morgan and Daniel Guggenheim, Ballinger was accused of favoritism. Taft stood by Ballinger. When Pinchot kept on fighting, Taft fired him—even though Taft knew this would anger conservationists and especially Theodore Roosevelt.

The "insurgent" revolt.

The Progressives sympathized with Pinchot. The Ballinger-Pinchot affair and the Payne-Aldrich tariff persuaded them that Taft was a "tool of the interests." They decided to become "insurgents" and strike out on their own. First they attacked the "stand pat" Speaker of the House, Joseph G. Cannon of Illinois. He appointed the Rules Committee where he was chairman. The committee decided whether a bill would be considered and even had the power to put bills "on the shelf." This made Cannon dictator of the House. Now the angry insurgents managed to strip him of his power. In the future, members of the Rules Committee would be elected by the House, and the Speaker would not be allowed to serve on the committee.

When Taft asked for a new act to increase the power of the Interstate Commerce Commission over railroads, the insurgents moved to make the act even stronger. By the Mann-Elkins Act (1910) they extended the ICC's powers to cover telephone, telegraph, cable, and wireless companies.

The royal progress of Theodore Roosevelt.

As soon as Taft took the oath of office, Roosevelt sailed for a long hunting trip in East Africa. He was now a private citizen for the first time in twenty years. He wanted to avoid any sign of his wishing to control Taft.

When Roosevelt "emerged from the jungle" in the spring of 1910, he held the spotlight of the whole Western world. His progress from Egypt through Italy, Austria, Germany, France, Holland, and England was a triumphal procession. When he landed at New York in June, he was welcomed by a huge cheering crowd.

Still only 51 years old, the vigorous TR was just not able to sit on the sidelines. And he did not like what was happening during Taft's Presidency. Pinchot had persuaded him that Taft was wrong in the Ballinger affair. Restless Roosevelt soon embarked on a nationwide speaking tour. He criticized Taft and praised the insurgents. In August,

at the Kansas home of John Brown, he called upon the memory of the old fanatic who had given his life for freedom.

He announced his own reform program, which he called the "New Nationalism." Listing the Progressive reforms (and adding some), he called for strict regulation of large corporations and a real tariff revision. He wanted federal income and inheritance taxes, nationwide workmen's compensation laws, and publicity for gifts to political campaigns. He asked for more protection of women and children in industry, for direct primaries, and for the initiative, referendum, and recall. It was a long list which included every one of Taft's hates.

The elections of 1910.

In the congressional elections of 1910, the splits within the Republican party produced an overwhelming Democratic victory. For the first time in eighteen years the Democrats were in control of the House. The Republican majority in the Senate was much reduced. With a dozen Progressive Republican insurgents in the Senate, Taft lacked effective support in either house of Congress. In the states, the Republicans lost eight governorships to the Democrats. In New Jersey the Democratic party elected the former president of Princeton University, Woodrow Wilson, as governor.

The Progressive Republican insurgents felt the time had come for them to take over the party. "Battling Bob" La Follette emerged as their strongest candidate for President in 1912. Some of TR's followers said they wanted him back in the White House again. Roosevelt said that he really did not want to run. But he loved a good fight. And Taft's policies had angered him—all the more because Taft had begun as TR's protégé. Taft had brought 45 indictments (criminal charges) against trusts. One was against U.S. Steel, during which Roosevelt's role in the company's takeover of Tennessee Coal and Iron came out. TR saw this as an attack on him. He still believed that the federal government should distinguish between bad and good trusts and should indict only the bad ones. Taft preferred to indict one and all, and then allow the courts to decide. Roosevelt was a man of strong dislikes, and for his own reasons, perhaps tinged with jealousy, he could not stand La Follette.

At first TR seemed to waver. But few people doubted that he really wanted to be President again. In February he announced that he would accept the nomination: "My hat is in the ring."

Taft versus Roosevelt. Taft's administration had its varied successes. More jobs came under the civil service. Over a million acres of forest in the Appalachian Mountains became part of the national reserves. In addition, Taft saw to it that the federal government would keep the coal, oil, and other minerals beneath the surface of public lands sold to private buyers. The new parcel post service and postal savings bank would help people in small towns. The Department of Commerce and Labor became two separate departments. New Mexico and Arizona were admitted as states in 1912. Taft also sponsored the income-tax amendment, which would become the Sixteenth Amendment in 1913.

President Taft controlled the 1912 Republican convention in Chicago, and he wanted to be nominated. From some states the badly divided party sent opposing conservative and Progressive delegations. But nearly all disputes were decided in favor of the Taft loyalists. TR was counted out, and the convention nominated Taft.

Many Progressives then walked out. Gathered in another hall, they condemned the convention as a "fraud." They urged TR to lead a new party. He did not need much persuading. The unreluctant TR plunged in with the slogan: "We stand at Armageddon, and we battle for the Lord."

A few weeks later the new Progressive party met again and nominated Roosevelt. With a crusading spirit, the delegates sang "The Battle Hymn of the Republic" and "Onward Christian Soldiers." TR

University of Hartford: Museum of American Political Life

TR and Hiram Johnson ran together in 1912.

was in his element. He loved the smell of battle. The platform declared that "the first task of the statesmanship of the day" was to destroy the "invisible government" of special privilege. Then they repeated the long list of Progressive demands. They favored more direct democracy, conservation, minimum wages for women, and an end to child labor. They demanded tariff revision and closer regulation of interstate commerce by expert commissions. When someone asked Roosevelt about his health, he said he was "strong as a Bull Moose." The Progressive party chose the Bull Moose for its symbol and set forth to "build a new and nobler commonwealth."

The election of 1912. The Democrats met at Baltimore. The split in the Republican ranks raised their hopes. But they faced a hard three-cornered fight for the nomination. Representative Oscar Underwood of Alabama had the support of the South. Champ Clark, the strong Speaker of the House, was backed by newspaper publisher William Randolph Hearst and other rich party members.

The third contender was a new face and an unlikely figure on the political scene. Scholarly Woodrow Wilson only two years before had been elected to his first political office, governor of New Jersey. His reform record there and his inspiring call for a moral revival of the nation had brought many delegates to his side. Clark had the most delegates when the convention began. Finally, with the support of William Jennings Bryan, Wilson won on the 46th ballot.

Like the Republicans, the Democrats called for conservation and banking and currency reform. The Republicans asked for mild revision of the tariff, while the Democrats wanted much lower duties. The Republicans would only regulate the trusts. The Democrats wanted to break up all monopolies.

The campaign was really a battle between Roosevelt and Wilson. Taft had little popular support. Also on the fringe, with no chance to win, was the self-educated Eugene V. Debs, the colorful (and perpetual) Socialist candidate. He had organized railroad workers into unions. He called for public ownership of natural resources and the major industries.

Roosevelt and Wilson were both Progressives, but there was a distinct difference between them.

Roosevelt called on the American people to realize that the country had entered a new age. Individualism and old-fashioned democracy, he said, would no longer work. An urban, industrial society needed a "New Nationalism." This meant a strong national government to regulate business and insure the well-being of the people. He offered a full program of social legislation—all the items in the Bull Moose platform.

Wilson had no such well-constructed program when he was nominated. During the campaign he worked out his own approach, which he called the "New Freedom." His program was more conservative and more traditional. He wanted the government to be only an umpire. He demanded that both business and labor be freed from control by monopolies. According to Wilson, Roosevelt's New Nationalism would put big business in control of the government. This would then enslave the ordinary worker. Wilson wanted to restore competition. He was for putting teeth into the Sherman Antitrust Act. He knew American history. With his preacherly eloquence, Wilson begged the nation to return to its traditions of individualism and open opportunity. The New Freedom, he hoped, would look after "the men on the make rather than the men who are already made."

When the votes were counted, it appeared that TR had split the Republican party. But he failed to divide the Democrats. Though Wilson received only 42 percent of the popular vote, he carried 40 of the 48 states. And he won four-fifths of the votes in the electoral college.

The election showed that an overwhelming majority of Americans really were Progressives in spirit. More than 10 million voted for Roosevelt and Wilson (who both favored Progressive reforms) while only 3.5 million voted for Taft. Debs received almost 1 million votes. Could Wilson now unite all Progressives behind his program?

Along with the Presidency, the Democrats won control of both houses of Congress. In all the decades since the election of James Buchanan, the Democrats had achieved such success only once before. They also elected governors in 21 of the 35 states where elections were held that year.

Taft cheerfully retired from the White House. A man of judicial temperament, he was more at home in a courtroom. What he really wanted was a seat on the Supreme Court. He finally reaped the

Culver Pictures

Campaigning by train in the days before air travel and television, Woodrow Wilson greeted the voters of Marion, Indiana, in 1912.

reward for his troubled years in the White House. In 1921 President Harding appointed him Chief Justice. He presided over the Court until his death in 1930. He is still the only man to have been both President and Chief Justice.

SECTION 3 REVIEW

1. Identify or explain: Payne-Aldrich tariff, Gifford Pinchot, Richard Ballinger, insurgents, Joseph Cannon, Mann-Elkins Act, Sixteenth Amendment, "Bull Moose" symbol, Eugene Debs.

2. How did Taft disappoint the reformers (a) on the tariff? (b) on conservation? What were some of his successes?

3. What steps led to the formation of the Progressive party? How did this party affect the election of 1912?

4. **Making Comparisons.** How did Wilson's "New Freedom" differ from Roosevelt's "New Nationalism"?

4. Woodrow Wilson and the New Freedom

Woodrow Wilson's father was a Presbyterian minister. Born in Staunton, Virginia, Woodrow absorbed from his parents a devout, unbending spirit. He decided against becoming a minister himself, but in some ways he always thought and talked like one.

Like Theodore Roosevelt, Wilson was a literary President, the author of many books. In almost every other way he was TR's opposite. While TR's first book was on sea power, young Wilson wrote about moral questions for the North Carolina *Presbyterian*. While TR adored "The Strenuous Life," Wilson lived in the world of ideas, "longing to do immortal work." At the age when TR was out west learning to ride broncos and was hunting with cowboys, Wilson was sitting in political science classes at Johns Hopkins University in Baltimore. Though Wilson wrote a book called *Congressional Government*, he had never even bothered to make the short trip to Washington to see Congress in session.

Wilson was an indoor sort of man. After a brief career as a professor, he was chosen president of Princeton University. His educational reforms there won him national fame. They also angered the alumni and some of the faculty, so he was glad to be asked to run for governor of New Jersey in 1910. It was his success as governor—his only political experience—that brought him the nomination for President in 1912. He could inspire people in large groups or from the printed page. But face to face he was stiff and standoffish. He had trouble making close friends.

While Wilson had some of William Jennings Bryan's religious appeal, his tone was very different. Bryan sounded like a preacher at a country tent meeting. Wilson could have been the minister of the richest church in town. Both could persuade voters that they were joining the Army of the Lord. Wilson, like Bryan, championed the struggling farmers and underpaid workers. As a more moderate kind of Bryan, Wilson had a wider appeal.

A new dedication. Woodrow Wilson set the tone for his Presidency on the day he took office. In his inaugural address he announced that he had come to Washington "to cleanse, to reconsider, to restore."

Certain new laws were needed—tariff revision, currency and banking reform, breaking up the trusts. Beyond that, however, he had come "to lift everything that concerns our life as a Nation to the light that shines from the hearthfire of every man's conscience and vision of the right." Arriving at the White House was his moment of high dedication. He allowed no inaugural ball.

Wilson's kind of leadership was useful at this moment in the nation's history. He could both describe what needed to be done and then had the eloquence to rally people to the job. While he was riding the wave of Progressive reform, he could also enlist the enthusiasm of loyal Democrats. Their party had been out of office so long that now the Democrats in Congress were glad to follow Wilson. He would help them build a stronger party.

Tariff reform. Wilson immediately called a special session of Congress to enact his urgent program. Laws must be passed to break down the barriers to individual enterprise. In the recent past, Presidents had sent a written message to open each session of Congress. The message was then droned out by a clerk. Instead, Wilson made a ceremony of this occasion. He went to the Capitol and became the first President since Washington and Adams to deliver his address in person.

In a brief and forceful speech Wilson dramatized his personal leadership. At the same time he focused the nation's attention on Congress. He made it clear that it was the duty of Congress to take action. Instead of scattering his shots, in this address he spoke only of the reform of the tariff. It was not "free trade" that he desired, but free opportunity for American business. The proposed duties would provide some revenue for the Treasury but would not enrich industries that no longer needed tariff protection.

Representative Oscar W. Underwood, who had spent his life studying the tariff, worked closely with Wilson. The new tariff bill reduced duties about 11 percent from the Payne-Aldrich Act. To make up for the lost revenue, an income tax with low rates was included. As usual, there was a bitter fight in the Senate. Then Wilson stepped in to denounce the "insidious lobby" at work in Washington. The Senate began its own inquiry that revealed how the business interests of some senators affected their attitude toward the tariff. An aroused public

Wilson and Taft rode together to Wilson's inauguration in 1913.

opinion now helped clear the road for major cuts in the tariff rates. After months of wrangling, the Underwood-Simmons bill was signed into law on October 3, 1913. It was the first real tariff reform since the Civil War.

Currency and banking reform.

Even before the tariff bill was passed, Wilson called for currency and banking reforms. There was wide agreement on the need to create a currency that would expand and contract as the economy required. Ever since the 1870s the money supply had failed to keep pace with the rising output of goods and services. And this had led to the calls for "cheap money."

The nation still had no banking system that could help a bank stop a "run" on its deposits. At the start of a business panic, most of the depositors might run to their bank to take out their money. But a bank keeps only a small cash reserve. For the bank to earn a profit, it must lend out most of its deposits. A "run" could force a bank to shut down in a few hours.

Bank "runs" in a number of places at the same time could start or worsen a panic. In addition to its small cash reserve, a bank would keep part of its required (legal) reserves in a big-city bank. And the big-city banks, in turn, kept part of their reserves in New York City banks. Thus much of the nation's deposit reserves tended to move to Wall Street, New York's financial district. The New York banks would lend large amounts "on call." This meant that the borrower had to repay the loan as soon as the bank called for its money. Many of the "on call" loans went to stock-market speculators. When small-city banks demanded their reserves, the big banks called in their loans. Then a wave of selling in the stock market—by the speculators to get money to repay their loans—caused further panic and "runs" on more banks.

The Progressive-Bryan faction wanted a system of reserve banks under federal control—that is, central banks that would hold part of the deposits (legal reserves) of the private banks. Conservative Democrats feared Bryan. To them Bryan always seemed radical. They also wanted a federal reserve system free from Wall Street control, but they wanted it to be owned and controlled by private interests. Wilson steered a middle course. Under his skillful prodding a compromise emerged.

The Federal Reserve Act.

The Federal Reserve Act was signed into law in December 1913. It divided the country into twelve districts, each with a Federal Reserve bank owned by the member banks. All were supervised by a Federal Reserve Board, whose members were appointed by the President. Every national bank had to become a member of the Federal Reserve System. Each subscribed some of its capital and surplus to form the capital of the reserve bank in its district.

These Federal Reserve banks were the central banks for their regions. They were the "bankers' banks." They held the member banks' reserves, lent money to a member bank when it was needed, and performed other services for the member banks. In case of a "run" on a bank, the member bank could pay its depositors by borrowing from the Federal Reserve bank. The "run" might not even start if the depositors believed that the bank could surely meet its obligations.

The Federal Reserve Act also created a flexible new national currency, *Federal Reserve notes.* These

In 1909, when Scott Joplin, a leading composer of ragtime, wrote this dance music, Wall Street was already the financial heart of the nation. Ragtime, a precursor of jazz, was popular until about 1915.

could be issued according to the needs of the business community.

This act provided a way to mobilize the banking reserves in time of panic. When bank withdrawals caused loans to be called in, threatening the closing of businesses and even of the banks themselves, the Federal Reserve banks could rush to the rescue. The Federal Reserve Act was a perfect example of the New Freedom. Private interests did the job, but the public supervised.

Regulating business. After the Federal Reserve Act became law in December, Wilson at last let the weary lawmakers go home for a month's recess. When they returned in January, he offered his program to regulate business. The Sherman Antitrust Act had been aimed at certain business practices that tended to limit competition. Wilson said that was not enough. He asked Congress for a law to break up monopolies.

"To supplement existing laws against unlawful restraints and monopolies," Congress passed the Clayton Antitrust Act of 1914. It prohibited one company from taking over the stock of another if it created a monopoly. It forbade anyone to serve as a director of two or more corporations when the effect was to lessen competition. This was to prevent "interlocking" directorates, like those used by J. P. Morgan & Co. The law exempted labor and farm groups from prosecution as combinations in restraint of trade. But later court decisions undercut this exemption.

No law could spell out in advance all the unfair practices that wily businessmen might dream up. Then what should the government do? A Boston lawyer, Louis D. Brandeis, had made a reputation for fighting what he called "the curse of bigness." He helped Wilson with an answer. The law should not just outlaw unfair trade practices in general. It should set up a Federal Trade Commission with powers to stop any unfair practices whenever they occurred. This was more like TR's "New Nationalism" than the "New Freedom," but Wilson now decided he had no other choice. After a hard fight the Federal Trade Commission Act was passed in September 1914, and the federal government was committed to regulate business.

The Federal Trade Commission (FTC) had five members. Advised by experts from different industries, they drew up fair trade rules. When the FTC found a company engaging in a practice that was unfair or in restraint of trade, it could issue a "cease and desist" order. And if the company disobeyed, it was punished. The main purpose of the commission was to help individual businesses obey the law.

More Progressive legislation. With these measures, Wilson's reforms were complete. For a moment, he turned against further reforms and even blocked a bill that forbade child labor. The mid-term elections of 1914 brought some gains for the Republicans. But the Democrats kept control

Teddy Roosevelt, portrayed here wearing his Rough Rider uniform with his Nobel Prize in his pocket and his big stick handy, had grand ideas about his place among Presidents.

of Congress. Wilson saw that he must continue Progressive reforms if he was to be reelected in 1916. So he offered a new program. Much of what he asked for came from Roosevelt's "New Nationalism." In 1915 the La Follette Seamen's Act improved the quarters, food, and wages in the merchant marine. The following year several important laws were passed. A Federal Farm Loan Act provided farmers long-term loans at low interest rates. A child-labor law finally limited employment of young children in factories, mines, and quarries. And an eight-hour day was enacted for workers on the railroads.

President Wilson's first term showed the most far-reaching legislative program ever passed in a single administration. The Democrats, he boasted, had not only carried out their own platform. They had "come very near to carrying out the platform of the Progressive party."

SECTION 4 REVIEW

1. Identify or explain: "bankers' banks," Federal Reserve notes, interlocking directorates, "cease and desist" orders, La Follette Seamen's Act, Federal Farm Loan Act.

2. How did the Underwood-Simmons bill reform the tariff?

3. What chief weakness of the banking system was the Federal Reserve Act designed to correct? How did the new law help solve the currency problem?

4. What kinds of business practices did the Clayton Act declare illegal?

5. How was the Federal Trade Commission supposed to promote fair business competition?

6. What other Progressive legislation did Congress enact in Wilson's first term?

7. **Making Comparisons.** How were Woodrow Wilson and Theodore Roosevelt alike? How were they different? Consider their backgrounds, experiences, and personal traits.

THE ART CRITIC.

Culver Pictures

5. Seeking a world role

Progressive leaders, who showed concern for the poor at home, sent the nation in search of power abroad. The United States played a new commanding part in Latin America.

TR and foreign affairs. Theodore Roosevelt had a clear view of the new role he wanted for the United States. Although he distrusted the power of large corporations, he loved power for the nation and for himself. He wanted the United States to hold the center of the world stage. For practical purposes he was his own Secretary of State. Though he never shrank from a good fight, he saw himself as a champion of peace. His motto was "Speak softly and carry a big stick." Still, he seemed to enjoy

447

bellowing while waving his big stick at home and abroad.

He wanted this two-ocean nation to become a power on the sea. An enthusiastic disciple of Admiral Mahan, he wanted the United States to have a great navy. In the Spanish-American War we had only 5 battleships and 2 armored cruisers. Before Roosevelt left the White House in 1909, we had 25 battleships and 10 heavy cruisers. We had become, next to the British, the strongest naval power in the world.

The United States and the Far East.

Events in the Far East offered TR a welcome chance to play the delicate game of power politics. Soon after he took office, the Russians began to move to control Manchuria. This was against our Open Door policy. But Roosevelt saw that there was little we could do to stop them.

In that part of the world Russia's great rival was Japan. When these two powers began to fight, Roosevelt drew the United States to the side of Japan. But Roosevelt did not want to see Russia driven out of the Far East, for Russia could keep the lid on Japan. Roosevelt aimed to insure a balance of power there. Only in that way, he thought, could China stay independent. So Roosevelt helped bring the Russo-Japanese War to a close before Japan could crush Russia. At Portsmouth, New Hampshire, the envoys of Russia and Japan met with him, and in August 1905 they announced the terms of peace. For this he was awarded the Nobel Peace Prize.

The peace had been won only by a bargain in which the United States, too, played a part. It was agreed that Japan would be allowed to annex Korea and to pursue its own interests in Manchuria. In return, Japan assured the United States that otherwise things would remain the same in the Pacific. Japan would not meddle with our colonies. The Root-Takahira Agreement of 1908 outlined these understandings.

Most Americans believed that all people should be allowed to govern themselves. They objected that in this pact we were bartering the independence of others. They recalled George Washington's warnings against "entangling alliances." In fact, the agreement only recognized the existing situation.

Theodore Roosevelt was a realist. He was in favor of the Open Door policy as long as it could be maintained by diplomacy. But in Manchuria the Japanese were willing to risk war to get their way. He believed that the United States should take a firm stand only when it was in our national interest to fight for our position.

Roosevelt thought the United States should stay on good terms with Japan. But we should not let the Japanese think we were weak. In 1907 he sent around the world our navy's "great white fleet" of 16 battleships—chiefly to impress Japan.

The Panama Canal.

In the Caribbean, TR would be more aggressive. For here he saw the vital interests of the United States. He thought that the United States should dominate the Caribbean. And he favored building an isthmian canal.

As a world power, the United States had to be able to move its navy speedily from one ocean to another. Besides the old reasons of commerce, this was an urgent new reason to cut a waterway through Central America.

For years Americans going westward had tried to find ways to shorten the voyage to California. When TR came to the White House, a French company had already been working on a canal for twenty years. They were plagued by tropical disease. And early in 1902 they agreed to sell their canal rights for $40 million. The United States still had to get a lease on the land for the canal route. It was in Colombia's province of Panama.

TR would let nothing stop him. First, Secretary of State John Hay drew up a treaty with an envoy from Colombia. We agreed to pay Colombia $10 million at once—and later, $250,000 a year. In 1903 the senate of Colombia balked. They wanted $20 million—and another $10 million from the French company.

Then suddenly a revolution broke out in Panama. A lucky coincidence for the United States! But there was evidence that the United States had helped start the revolt. And the United States Navy had prevented Colombian troops from landing to put it down. Quickly the new "independent" Republic of Panama made a treaty leasing the Canal Zone to the United States.

Work began in 1904 but halted the next year because the workers in the swamps came down with yellow fever. To build the canal, Americans first had to stop the sickness. Under the direction of Dr. William Gorgas, who had worked with Dr. Walter

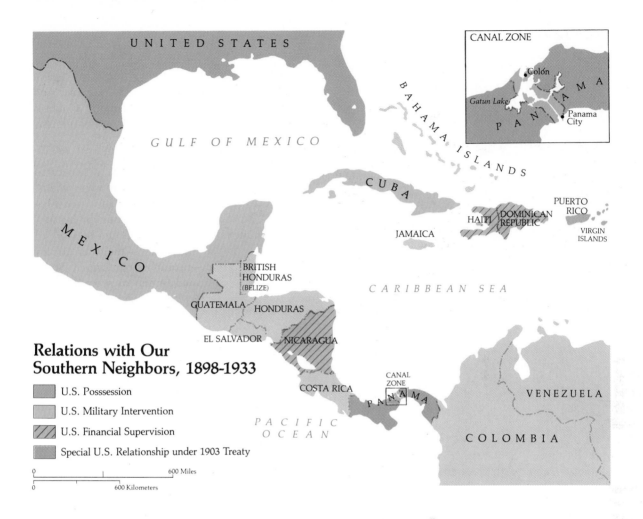

Relations with Our Southern Neighbors, 1898-1933

- U.S. Posssession
- U.S. Military Intervention
- U.S. Financial Supervision
- Special U.S. Relationship under 1903 Treaty

```
0                     600 Miles
0              600 Kilometers
```

Reed in Cuba to prevent yellow fever, the breeding places of the mosquitoes that carried the disease were destroyed. Once the mosquitoes were gone, the battle against the disease was won. Gorgas made the canal possible—and helped conquer yellow fever around the world.

Work resumed in 1906, and within eight years ships were passing through the canal. The Panama Canal had cost more than a half-billion dollars, but its benefits were beyond measure.

"I took the Canal Zone and let Congress debate," TR later declared, "and while the debate goes on the canal does also." Wilson's Secretary of State, William Jennings Bryan, negotiated a new treaty with Colombia. The United States agreed to pay $25 million for the loss of Panama, with "sincere regret that anything should have occurred to mar the candid friendship" between the two nations. Roosevelt denounced the treaty as "a crime against

the United States and an attack on its honor." The Senate rejected the treaty twice. In April 1921, after Roosevelt's death, the treaty was ratified by a Republican Senate with the expression of sincere regret left out!

The Roosevelt Corollary. After the Panama Canal was opened, the United States worried about the governments in that neighborhood. When the Dominican Republic (formerly Santo Domingo) went bankrupt, European creditors threatened to use force to collect their money. Roosevelt then declared a new American policy. In his message to Congress in December 1904, he explained what the United States would do in case of the "chronic wrongdoing or impotence" of a Latin American state. He said that we were bound to intervene, "however reluctantly," and to "exercise our international police power."

449

Library of Congress

Construction of the Panama Canal began in 1903, and the "Big Ditch" was opened to ships in 1914. Joseph Pennell sketched this view of the locks at Gatun as they neared completion.

With the consent of the president of the Dominican Republic, the United States took over the financial affairs of that country. Soon the debts were paid, and the creditors in Europe were then satisfied.

In the past the United States had told European powers not to interfere in the Americas. Now TR declared that the United States would police a whole continent. Though nobody else was allowed to, forces of the United States might intervene in Latin America. The nation that had inspired the world by its Declaration of Independence now shook the world with a new declaration of intervention! This was the "Roosevelt Corollary" to the Monroe Doctrine. TR meant what he said, and later Presidents agreed. Under this policy, the United States would intervene—sometimes more than once—in the Dominican Republic, Cuba, Panama, Haiti, and Nicaragua.

The Algeciras Conference.

It seemed unlikely that the restless, aggressive TR could stay out of the international politics of Europe. France and Germany were on the point of war over control of Morocco. At first TR hesitated to do anything.

Then "to keep matters on an even keel in Europe" he stepped in. He persuaded the two nations to attend a conference in 1906 at Algeciras, Spain. There United States delegates helped France and Germany come to a peaceful settlement. Could it be said anymore that America had a set of interests separate from those of Europe?

Foreign affairs under Taft.

TR never cared much about the economics of foreign affairs. Commerce was not nearly as dramatic as clashing navies or expanding boundaries. But for his successor, President Taft, money was the measure of diplomacy. "Dollar diplomacy"—the nickname for his foreign policies—meant using United States ambassadors (and armed forces) to promote business. Taft and his Secretary of State, Philander C. Knox, urged Americans to invest abroad to build American influence. Then our government would protect United States investors.

Taft pushed American bankers to invest in China. And there, as a response to Taft's dollar diplomacy, Japan and Russia enlarged their own spheres of interest.

"Dollar diplomacy" explained Taft's actions in Latin America, too. When civil war broke out in Nicaragua in 1912, United States Marines were sent in to protect American business interests. While there, the marines supervised the national elections. A small detachment stayed until 1925. Latin Americans began to wonder whether the people of the United States had forgotten their own Declaration of Independence.

A "moral" foreign policy.

President Wilson's first foreign policy test came in Mexico. Then and there he would set the moral tone that was to dominate his foreign policy.

Just before Wilson took office, a liberal government in Mexico, headed by Francisco Madero, had been overthrown by a cruel general, Victoriano Huerta. Madero was murdered while being taken to jail—probably on Huerta's orders.

Other Mexican revolutionaries opposed Huerta. But he controlled four-fifths of his country. Twenty foreign governments recognized Huerta as Mexico's president *de facto*. This meant that they did not judge whether Huerta's government was really legal. They only recognized that *in fact* he was in control.

Woodrow Wilson—the preacherly President—had other ideas. Formerly the United States had recognized *de facto* governments whenever they came to power. Now Wilson declared that he would not "extend the hand of welcome to anyone who obtains power in a sister republic by treachery and violence." He called upon Huerta to step down, and Huerta refused. Then Wilson turned to a policy of "watchful waiting."

Problems at Tampico and Veracruz. After a time Wilson plotted to force Huerta from power. He allowed arms to be sent to Huerta's chief rival, Venustiano Carranza. Soon a crisis arose. A shore party of American marines collecting supplies in Tampico, Mexico, was arrested and sent to jail. The marines were soon released and Huerta apologized, but he refused to fire a salute to the United States flag as we demanded.

On April 20, 1914, Wilson asked Congress to approve the use of armed force "to obtain from General Huerta the fullest recognition of the rights and dignity of the United States." The next day a wireless message came from the navy. It reported that a German steamer loaded with arms for Huerta was expected to dock at Veracruz in a few hours. So before Congress had even acted, the President ordered the seizure of the city to prevent their delivery. A detachment of marines was landed, and 19 Americans and 126 Mexicans were killed before the marines controlled the city. Mexicans—including Huerta's chief rival, Carranza—united against the United States, and it appeared that war was near.

The large republics of South America—Argentina, Brazil, and Chile, known as the ABC powers—now offered to mediate between the United States and Mexico. They recommended that Huerta give way to a provisional government. Huerta refused, but they had so undercut his position that he could no longer keep control. He stepped down in July, Carranza entered Mexico City in triumph, and in November Wilson withdrew American troops from Veracruz.

Chasing Pancho Villa. Still Wilson's Mexican troubles were not over. Carranza's most successful general was Pancho Villa, a former bandit and a brilliant cavalry leader. When Villa began a new revolt, civil war raged again. Villa's raiders killed people on both sides of the border. Finally, when he burned Columbus, New Mexico, in March 1916, many United States citizens were killed.

Wilson, with Carranza's reluctant permission, sent out General John J. Pershing and an expedition of 15,000 men to get Villa "dead or alive." The National Guard, 150,000 strong, was ordered to the border. A West Point graduate, Pershing had commanded cavalry against Chief Geronimo and had fought in the Spanish-American War and in the Philippines.

The pursuit of Villa and the mobilization of the National Guard soon showed how ill-prepared the United States was for war. Villa struck again in the United States, and another force of 8000 men was sent into Mexico in pursuit, only to end up in a clash with Carranza's forces. Once again war with Mexico seemed near. But by now the thunder of the great powers fighting in Europe put a bandit general in a new perspective. The United States might soon be drawn into a global conflict. Seeing this prospect, in January 1917 Wilson withdrew the forces from Mexico. With the entrance of the United States into World War I in April 1917, the Progressive Era would end.

SECTION 5 REVIEW

1. Identify or explain: Root-Takahira Agreement, "great white fleet," William Gorgas, Roosevelt Corollary, Algeciras Conference, Philander C. Knox, *de facto* recognition, Victoriano Huerta, Venustiano Carranza, Pancho Villa.

2. Locate: Manchuria, Panama Canal, Colombia, Dominican Republic, Morocco, Veracruz, ABC powers.

3. How did President Theodore Roosevelt try to advance the interests of the United States in the Far East?

4. Trace the steps leading to the construction of the Panama Canal and the political and economic settlement with Colombia.

5. Cite instances of Taft's "dollar diplomacy."

6. Why and how did the United States intervene in Mexican affairs in 1914 and 1916?

7. **Identifying Assumptions.** Why did President Roosevelt stretch the meaning of the Monroe Doctrine?

FOCUSING ON IDEAS

1. What traits in the young TR showed up in President Theodore Roosevelt? Explain.

2. The text names or implies many business abuses. Which chiefly affected workers? Consumers? Business competitors? Were there other victims? Explain.

3. How did Roosevelt "carry a big stick" in both domestic and foreign affairs? Cite examples. Did he observe the first part of his motto "Speak softly"?

4. Why do many historians refer to the early 1900s as "the Progressive Era"?

TAKING A CRITICAL LOOK

1. **Recognizing Cause and Effect.** Why would reforms have been less likely to occur without the "muckrakers"?

2. **Demonstrating Reasoned Judgment.** Assume that United States intervention in the Dominican Republic in 1904 and in Nicaragua in 1912 helped those countries straighten out their economic and/or political affairs. Would the "good result" justify the action taken? Explain.

3. **Predicting Consequences.** Would a business climate of more vigorous competition have led to less severe or extensive abuses? Explain.

YOUR REGION IN HISTORY

1. **Geography.** Did any big city in your state or region experience major reform in the early 1900s? What were the results?

2. **Culture.** Examine the literary and journalistic writings of the "muckrakers". How closely do they describe your locality during the Progressive Era?

3. **Economics.** List some Progressive measures aimed at reforming business that the legislature of your state passed between 1900 and 1914.

HISTORICAL FACTS AND FIGURES

Formulating Hypotheses. Use the map below to help answer the following questions: (a) In which region did women have equal suffrage in 1919? (b) In which region did they have partial suffrage? (c) In which region did women have no statewide suffrage? (d) Develop a hypothesis that explains this regional difference. (e) Does the information in this chapter support your hypothesis?

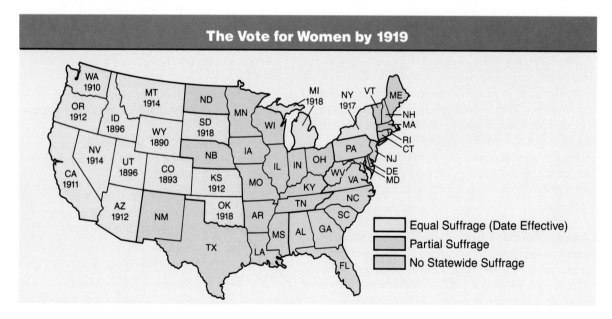

The Vote for Women by 1919

Equal Suffrage (Date Effective)
Partial Suffrage
No Statewide Suffrage

CHAPTER 21

The United States and World War I

The First World War began as an Old World war. Everything about it expressed the world that Americans hoped they had left behind. That Old World was a battlefield of national ambitions, religious persecutions, and language barriers. European armies had fought over whether a nation's boundary should be on one side or the other of a narrow river. Old World monarchs had transferred land from one flag to another, bartering people as if they were mere real estate.

In the 1800s the empires of Great Britain, France, and Germany had expanded over the whole world to the deserts and jungles of Africa, the high mountains of Asia, and the islands of the Pacific. Each empire sent out its own merchants and colonial settlers. Each built its strong navy to protect and police the ocean highways. Each built a vast army to guard the homeland and to suppress colonial uprisings anywhere on the globe.

At the same time in Europe national hopes had been growing and stirring up new conflicts. Ordinary citizens who had learned to read became proud of their own languages and their own national heroes. Daily newspapers now alerted citizens to their "national honor," awakened political hopes and ambitions, and nourished pride in the nation's exploits in faraway places. Kings and queens, princes and princesses, czars and czarinas—who were cousins and uncles and aunts—added their own family loves and hates to all the other reasons for peace or war.

1. A spark ignites Europe

By 1914, a world war might have begun almost anywhere. It happened to be sparked in the most confused part of Europe. In the mountainous Balkans of southeastern Europe, small nations jostled and offended one another with their ancient feuds and jealous princes. For centuries these mini-nations had been dominated by Turkey, Russia, Austria, and other major powers. The word "Balkan," in fact, came to describe any community that was broken up into small warring groups.

We cannot be surprised that this was where World War I began. It started in Sarajevo, the

Europe in 1914

- Allied Powers
- Central Powers
- Neutral

0 ___ 500 Miles
0 ___ 500 Kilometers

ATLANTIC OCEAN

NORWAY

SWEDEN

St. Petersburg

Moscow

NORTH SEA

BALTIC SEA

DENMARK

IRELAND

GREAT BRITAIN

London

NETH.

BELG.

LUX.

Paris

Berlin

GERMAN EMPIRE

RUSSIAN EMPIRE

FRANCE

SWITZERLAND

Vienna

AUSTRIA-HUNGARY

Belgrade

ROMANIA

BLACK SEA

PORTUGAL

SPAIN

CORSICA

Rome

ITALY

ADRIATIC SEA

Sarajevo

MONTENEGRO

ALBANIA

SERBIA

BULGARIA

Constantinople (Istanbul)

Ankara

MEDITERRANEAN SEA

SARDINIA

SICILY

GREECE

AEGEAN SEA

TURKISH EMPIRE

AFRICA

CRETE

CYPRUS (Br.)

capital of Bosnia, a small province of the old patchwork empire of Austria-Hungary. On June 28, 1914, Archduke Francis Ferdinand, heir to the Austro-Hungarian throne, and his wife were paying a state visit there. Suddenly they were shot down by a young Slavic nationalist from the little neighboring kingdom of Serbia. The Austro-Hungarian government blamed Serbia for not preventing the crime, and refused Serbia's offer to arbitrate the dispute. On July 28 Austria-Hungary declared war and bombarded Belgrade, the Serbian capital.

The powderkeg had exploded. Instantly Europe erupted into war. The elaborate system of alliances came into play. Russia, leader of the Slavic world, felt it must aid Serbia, so it began to mobilize. This brought Germany, allied with Austria-Hungary, onto the scene. Russia was allied with France. Germany had long feared that it might be squeezed by an attack from both Russia and France at the same time. So Germany decided to strike them first. On August 1, Germany declared war on Russia and two days later on France. Then

Germany moved swiftly to destroy France before the slow-moving giant, Russia, could get into action. Germany, ignoring its treaty that "guaranteed" Belgian neutrality, struck through Belgium into France. Now England, which had a defense agreement with France, plunged in against Germany. Then Bulgaria and Turkey joined the Central Powers—Germany and Austria-Hungary. Later, Japan and Italy came to the side of the Allies. By the time the war ended, in all of Europe only Norway, Sweden, Denmark, Holland, Spain, and Switzerland had remained neutral.

The United States struggles for neutrality. It is not surprising that Americans did not foresee the vast and tragic battle that would massacre millions, topple kings, and spark a half-dozen revolutions. They took it for granted that the bloody Civil War, fifty years in the past, was the last time many Americans would be called to battle. Americans of the Progressive Era tended to be optimistic and with good reason. The Spanish-American War had been only a mini-war. It made Theodore Roosevelt a hero but did not awaken the nation to the miseries of battle. The competition for markets waged by captains of industry seemed so much more sensible than shooting and killing. American leaders hoped that the United States would be a model for a world at peace.

At first Americans withdrew in shock when war broke out in the distant Balkans. What reason could there be for Americans to become involved? On August 4, 1914, President Wilson proclaimed the neutrality of the United States. Automaker Henry Ford chartered a Peace Ship. He sent it to the Scandinavian countries in a vain attempt to persuade them to mediate between the warring powers. Many Americans poked fun at what they thought was a foolish errand. The President called on all Americans to be impartial in thought as well as deed. That was not possible, even for Wilson.

Ties that bind. Most Americans, including the President, were drawn by powerful unseen forces toward the British cause. We spoke the English language and read the English classics. Our laws and customs were built on English foundations. We had fought an American Revolution to preserve our rights as Englishmen. Early in the war the British cut the transatlantic cable that brought news

In 1915 automobile manufacturer Henry Ford sent a "Peace Ship" to Scandinavia in the hope of ending the war by Christmas. Women made up a large part of the delegation. Here Jane Addams of Hull House (second from left) and others hold up a large peace banner. Despite their good intentions, the venture failed.

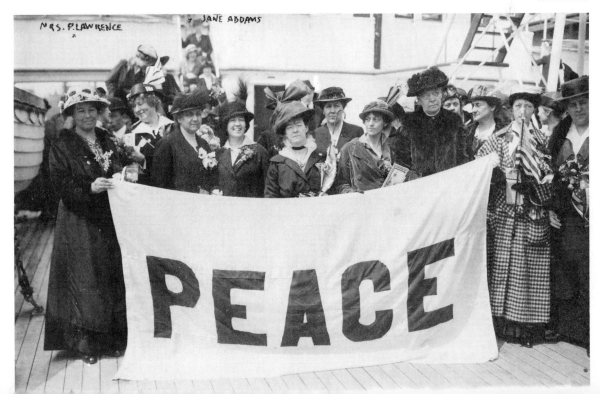

to the United States direct from Germany. After that, all news from Europe was channeled through England. This gave the British a great advantage that few Americans noticed.

There were millions of people in the United States who favored the Central Powers because they or their parents had been born in Germany, Austria, or Hungary. And there were more millions like the Irish who were glad to see anyone fight the British, because their own ancestors had suffered under British rule. But even some German Americans did not approve of Germany's actions. Kaiser Wilhelm had made so many warlike statements that many Americans saw Germany as a militaristic nation. Their feelings were confirmed when the kaiser's forces invaded Belgium and his prime minister called the German neutrality treaty with Belgium nothing but "a scrap of paper." The British circulated atrocity stories (some of them true) about how the invading German soldiers mistreated women and children in Belgium. Yet, until 1917 neither propaganda nor sentiment was strong enough to draw Americans to the battlefields of Europe.

The problem of neutral rights. There were great commercial advantages to staying out of the war. Over the years the nations of the world had agreed on a set of rules for the use of the seas. By these rules when a war broke out the neutral nations were still allowed to trade with both sides.

For more than a century the United States, far from Old World rivalries, had profited from being the great neutral commerce carrier of the world. In 1812 the nation had gone to war against Britain to protect its neutral rights on the sea. Again, in the 1900s, the United States would have to fight for the right to trade with the world.

Warring nations, by international law, were allowed to stop and inspect neutral vessels at sea. This was to make sure they were not ships of the enemy hiding under neutral flags. The warring nations were allowed to seize certain war materials ("contraband"—explosives, guns, and ammunition) even from a neutral ship. They were not supposed to seize other goods carried by neutrals. Before sinking a commercial ship, the attacker had to give warning, to see that the passengers were safe, and do everything else reasonable to save civilian lives.

Such rules as these were what people meant by *international law*. There was no court or police force to make nations obey. But the rules were still called "law" because so many people believed they ought to be obeyed. These special rights of neutrals were called the "freedom of the seas."

In 1914, when World War I broke out in Europe, these rules were still much the same as they had been for about 200 years. But the navies had changed. Most important was a new kind of ship—the submarine. Its great strength was the power to surprise. At the same time, however, it was thin-skinned and easy to sink. If it surfaced to warn a vessel, one shot from even a small "defensive" gun might send the submarine swiftly to the bottom.

To insist that all warring nations still had to follow the old rules would make the submarine useless. This would not have bothered Great Britain, who had the greatest navy in the world. But for Germany, with its smaller navy, submarines might make all the difference.

Great Britain intended to use its control of the seas to starve Germany into submission. The British government changed or interpreted the rules of war to suit its own needs. It enlarged the list of contraband to include all sorts of goods—even food!—that neutral ships had always been allowed to carry. The British insisted that all neutral ships go into British ports to be searched. They seized vessels bound for neutral countries, such as Holland or Denmark. This was to prevent the cargoes being resold to Germany. They declared the North Sea a military area and filled it with mines—underwater bombs that would explode when any ship came near. None of this was according to international law.

The United States protested. But since Wilson did not want war, he avoided making his language too strong. And when the language of the United States did become harsh, it was softened by our pro-British ambassador to London. Ambassador Walter Hines Page was convinced that the Allies must win to save Europe and the world from German domination. The British also wisely agreed to pay for all goods seized, so American merchants were not too concerned.

Germany unleashes its submarines. Germany could hardly sit still and allow itself to be strangled. Its submarines, however, could only do their deadly

World War I brought a new horror—submarine warfare. In 1915, when a German submarine like this torpedoed the British liner *Lusitania*, 1198 passengers died.

work if they, too, disobeyed international law. Germany therefore decided in 1915 to use its still-small fleet of 27 submarines for all they were worth and to let others worry about the rules.

On February 4, 1915, the Germans declared the waters around the British Isles a war zone. They warned neutral vessels against the danger of entering this zone in which their *Unterseeboote* (U-boats) would operate freely. The Germans advertised in American newspapers urging Americans not to travel on British ships. Secretary of State Bryan wanted to keep Americans from doing so. But Wilson insisted that under international law Americans had the right to sail on any ships—even those of Great Britain. He warned Germany that it would be held strictly accountable for any loss of American ships or lives.

Great Britain took this moment to announce another violation of international law, which they said was necessary for British victory. Blockades were supposed to be carried out only by vessels stationed near the enemy's ports. Now Britain said it would seize vessels carrying goods for Germany wherever they were found. "Germany is like a man throttled with a gag," First Lord of the Admiralty Winston Churchill declared. "You know the effect of such a gag. . . . The effort wears out the heart, and Germany knows it. This pressure shall not be relaxed until she gives in unconditionally."

Germany went ahead with its campaign of terror. On the afternoon of May 7, 1915, the British luxury liner *Lusitania* was torpedoed without warning off the coast of Ireland by the German submarine U-20. The ship went down in just 18 minutes taking with it 1198 men, women, and children including 128 Americans. The *Lusitania* tried to appear to be neutral by flying the American flag. Actually it was carrying 4200 cases of small-arms ammunition and 1250 shrapnel cases. Even so, according to international law that did not give Germany the right to sink the *Lusitania* without warning.

The *Arabic and* Sussex *pledges.*

President Wilson sent a strong protest to Germany. He insisted on neutral rights. And he said this meant the right of Americans to travel wherever they pleased—even on the ships of fighting nations and right into the war zone. Wilson said this was a matter of national honor.

Many Americans, including an increasingly belligerent Theodore Roosevelt, now called for war. But Wilson resisted. "There is such a thing," he declared, "as a nation being so right it does not need to convince others by force that it is right." Secretary of State Bryan feared that Wilson's insistence on the right of Americans to travel into the war zone would draw the nation into war. He resigned in protest and was replaced by Robert Lansing.

The sinking of another British liner, the *Arabic,* brought the loss of two more American lives. Now Germany was faced with the danger that the United States might join the war on the side of the Allies. Since the Germans did not yet have enough U-boats to defeat Great Britain, they backed down. On September 1, 1915, the German ambassador in Washington made the so-called *Arabic* pledge by which Germany promised not to sink unarmed liners.

Then in March 1916 a German submarine sank the French channel steamer *Sussex.* Now there was another crisis between the United States and Germany. Once more, fearing American intervention, the German government gave a pledge—the *Sussex* pledge of May 31, 1916. Again they agreed to abide by the rules of visit and search. Germany insisted that the United States should compel Great Britain also to observe international law.

The Germans were right, of course, to demand that both sides play by the same rules. But the Germans were at a disadvantage. Submarine warfare, their trump card, was spectacular and openly took neutral lives. Britain's blockade, on the other hand, quietly starved the civilians of Germany and Austria. It took only the property of neutrals, not their lives.

Trade with the Allies.

More and more the United States was drawn to the British side. Our trade with England and the Allies was enormous. We had become their storehouse—for munitions, food, and raw materials. And when the Allies could no longer pay for all the supplies, American bankers loaned them $2 billion. Secretary of State Bryan had protested that money was "the worst of all contrabands because it commands everything else." But if Bryan's policy of refusing loans to the Allies had been followed, the United States trade abroad would have ceased. This would have plunged the nation into a depression. President Wilson, who understood economics better than Bryan did, insisted on continuing our loans to the Allies.

During the early years of the war, in 1914–1916, American trade with Britain and its allies rocketed from $800 million to over $3 billion. At the same time, as a result of the British blockade, trade with Germany and its allies plummeted from nearly $170 million to about $1 million. It was plain where the nation's commercial interest lay.

Preparedness.

At first Wilson opposed "preparedness"—which meant arming and organizing for war. He intended that the United States be not a military but a moral force. But the Republicans, led by Theodore Roosevelt, demanded that the nation be prepared to fight. To avoid handing them a campaign issue in 1916, and to win votes himself, Wilson made preparedness his own cause.

In November 1915 the President called for a larger army and navy. Pacifists and farm-state Progressives like Bryan thought preparedness would only benefit big business and Wall Street. Wilson was forced to go to the people. Finally in the summer of 1916 part of his program was passed by Congress, and the United States was on the road to war.

Wilson knew that he could not win the coming election by the votes of Democrats alone. He needed support from at least some of the former Progressives. So in 1916 he garnered their votes by passing more reform legislation—much of it Roosevelt's New Nationalism (p. 443). "We are all Progressives," he now declared.

The campaign of 1916.

When the Democrats met in St. Louis, they nominated Wilson by

A campaign truck in 1916 urges the reelection of Woodrow Wilson and Thomas R. Marshall. A vote for Wilson was a vote for "Peace with Honor."

acclamation. Wilson was able to go to the country as a peace candidate. With a Progressive program enacted and "preparedness" under way, he offered something for nearly everybody. The party slogan was, "He kept us out of war."

The tireless TR made still another try for the Republican nomination. But the Republicans had had enough of the old Bull Moose. In a world at war his aggressive, boyish spirit seemed risky in a President. Instead the Republicans chose the safe and sane Charles Evans Hughes. As governor of New York he had sponsored far-reaching labor and welfare laws. Since 1910 he had served on the United States Supreme Court.

Wilson conducted his own kind of front-porch campaign from his New Jersey summer home. He pointed to all the reforms passed during his first term and to his firm defense of American rights at sea. Hughes toured the country. He denounced the administration for its Mexican policy, its bungling diplomacy abroad, and its lack of a program.

But the Republican candidate provided no clear-cut alternatives.

Before midnight of election day, it looked as though Hughes had been elected. He went to bed confident that he would move into the White House. He had carried almost all the northern states east of the Mississippi. The next day as the returns came in from the western states, the tide began to turn. When Wilson finally carried California by a slim margin, he was reelected by a small plurality and an electoral vote of 277 to 254. This was the closest race since the Hayes-Tilden campaign of 1876. This time the losing Republican candidate accepted the result without protest.

Still, the Republicans had increased their power in the Congress. They reduced the Democratic majorities in the Senate and in the House. Wilson's narrow victory had been made possible by the votes from the West of former Progressives. Except for Wilson's win, it was very much a Republican victory.

Wilson's efforts for peace. Taking his reelection as approval of his efforts for peace, Wilson again tried to stop the war. Twice before, in 1915 and 1916, he had sent his friend and adviser Colonel Edward House to Europe to try to arrange a peace. House became a mystery figure because no one knew how much power he really had. Anyway, he failed to persuade the warring nations to a compromise peace. And when Wilson tried once again in the winter of 1916–1917, he still found both sides bent on total victory. Wilson saw that the only hope for peace was for both sides to give up their dreams of conquest. On January 22, 1917, he called for "a peace without victory."

Nine days later Germany announced that it was starting unlimited submarine warfare. The kaiser had now decided that he had enough submarines to starve England into submission. He was confident that even if the United States finally came into the war, it would be too late to save the Allies.

Wilson broke off diplomatic relations with Germany. He still hoped that by some miracle he could avoid sending American soldiers to Europe.

The Zimmermann note. One thing after another now carried the United States down the road to war. The German foreign minister, Arthur Zimmermann, sent a foolish message to the German ambassador in Mexico. Zimmermann asked Mexico to join the German side. In return Germany promised to help the Mexicans recapture from the United States all of Texas, Arizona, and New Mexico. The message was intercepted and decoded by the British. Then they eagerly relayed it to Woodrow Wilson.

On February 26, Wilson asked Congress for the power to arm American merchant ships to protect them against the German submarines. He also asked for authority to take other measures to protect American commerce. Few people objected to his proposal to arm merchant ships in self-defense. But it was quite another matter to grant the President power to wage an undeclared naval war.

To persuade Congress to give him these wider powers, Wilson published the Zimmermann note. A wave of anger swept the country, and the Armed Ship bill passed the House by 403 to 13. Still, a small group of farm-state Progressives in the Senate, led by Robert La Follette of Wisconsin, refused to be stampeded. This "little group of willful men," as

Wilson called them, talked the bill to death in the closing days of the session.

The United States goes to war. Wilson did not wait for a new law to be passed. Instead he interpreted an old law so as to give him authority to arm American merchant ships. In his second inaugural address on March 4, 1917, he insisted that he was only preserving an "armed neutrality." The pace of events was now quickening. On March 15 a revolution in Russia drove Czar Nicholas from the throne. The very next day three American merchant vessels were sunk by German submarines with the loss of six lives.

Woodrow Wilson had won a second term with the slogan, "He kept us out of war." Now it seemed that, in spite of his hopes and promises, he could not insulate the nation from Old World rivalries. European conflicts had made the whole planet a single battlefield. On April 2, 1917, before a special session of Congress, he asked for a declaration of war against Germany. He no longer spoke merely about neutral rights. "The world," Wilson said, "must be made safe for democracy." Americans must fight "for the rights and liberties of small nations" and to "bring peace and safety to make the world itself at last free."

As usual, Wilson spoke eloquently of rights and liberties. He asked Americans to be soldiers of righteousness. But there was a good practical reason why the United States did not want to see the British lose. Americans had felt free to invest their nation's wealth in schools and factories and railroads, in a better life for all citizens. They had little need for large armies and navies like those that consumed the treasure of the warring nations of Europe. This had been possible because our two-ocean nation had the good luck to be protected by the great British navy.

As long as the friendly British ruled the waves, we could carry our cargoes and our people safely all over the world. The British, like the Americans, did not want to see other European nations build new empires in North and South America. The Monroe Doctrine had actually been enforced by the British navy. This arrangement was effective and economical. What would happen if imperial Germany drove the British from the sea? The United States would have to replace British sea power with a strong and costly navy of its own.

Wilson's dream. In January 1918, President Wilson went before Congress again—to explain the American program for the future of the world. He listed Fourteen Points. They were a noble list that applied to the 1900s the ideals of the nation's founders. Secret diplomacy was to be abolished. All treaties would be "open covenants openly arrived at." The bright light of publicity would make rulers ashamed to trade away other people's lives and liberties. Freedom of the seas would be restored. National borders would be adjusted to allow all people to govern themselves. And there would be a League of Nations to preserve peace and insure justice.

The Fourteen Points impressed the world. They were a kind of Declaration of Democracy for the planet. They stirred the world more than any other American statement since the Emancipation Proclamation or the Declaration of Independence. They reminded Americans of the principles that gave life to their New World nation. But could they reshape the whole world?

President Wilson proved himself one of the greatest preachers in modern history. He lifted the spirits of Europe's battle worn, and he expressed the hopes of millions everywhere. But to make his dreams come true the eloquence of a preacher was not enough.

SECTION 1 REVIEW

1. Identify or explain: Archduke Francis Ferdinand, Kaiser Wilhelm, U-boats, *Lusitania, Arabic* and *Sussex* pledges, Charles Evans Hughes, Fourteen Points.

2. Locate: Balkans, Sarajevo, Serbia, Belgrade, Belgium.

3. Trace the spread of World War I from Sarajevo to the entrance of Great Britain into the war.

4. How did each of the following draw the United States into the war: (a) overseas trade, (b) the preparedness program, (c) submarine warfare, (d) the Zimmermann note, (e) Wilson's idealism?

5. What were the rights of neutral ships under international law?

6. **Recognizing Bias.** How did Woodrow Wilson's religious upbringing influence his thinking about the war?

---

2. Helping to win the war

When the United States entered the war, few Americans realized that the Allies were desperate. Germany's submarine warfare had been so successful that the Allies needed everything. They suffered shortages of food, munitions, money, and men. The war was almost lost.

War on the western front. Trench warfare in Europe was like nothing ever seen before. When the war broke out in 1914, both German generals and French generals had their own plans for a knockout blow to end the war in a hurry. But the new machine guns and automatic rifles were deadly accurate against attack. Very soon *both* armies had to go on the defensive.

This was stationary warfare. Both armies dug their trenches, lived underground, and fired at each other from fixed positions. For three and a half years, the trenches stretched from the Swiss border to the North Sea. Month after month the battle lines hardly moved.

On both sides the trenches became elaborate systems. There was usually a line of front trenches, held as outposts. Behind were networks of supply and command trenches, some reaching back as far as five miles. These were connected by complicated tunnels and even by narrow railways. Soldiers became human moles, hiding by day and burrowing by night. As soon as darkness fell, they went to work, digging new trenches, stringing barbed wire, and connecting telephone lines.

Men in the front trenches had a terrible feeling of isolation. They were threatened not only by enemy gunfire, but by darkness, cold, and mud. Out of the filth and fatigue arose new ailments, which came to be called "trench fever," "trench foot," and "trench mouth." Poison gas blistered the skin, burned the eyes, and corroded the lungs. Soldiers wore gas masks which gave them the look of robots. The heavy, ceaseless artillery fire created a new mental disorder known as "shell shock."

In this kind of warfare, a "battle" meant that large numbers of men from one set of trenches rushed out and tried to break through the enemy's trenches. The hope was always to force a gap so that your troops could pour through and attack the whole enemy line from the rear. But advancing soldiers were tangled and torn apart in barbed wire, then mowed down by deadly machine-gun fire.

World War I, 1914-1917

Legend:
- Central Powers
- Allied Powers
- Neutral Nations
- German Submarine Zone
- Trench Warfare, 1915-1917
- Farthest Advances of Central Powers
- Eastern Front Armistice Line, December 1917
- Boundaries as of 1914

**Map labels:**

ATLANTIC OCEAN

NORWAY

SWEDEN

FINLAND

Petrograd (St. Petersburg)

5. RUSSIAN REVOLUTION, MARCH 1917; RUSSIANS SIGN ARMISTICE, DEC. 1917

IRELAND

GREAT BRITAIN

NORTH SEA

DENMARK

BALTIC SEA

EAST PRUSSIA

Minsk

RUSSIA

London

NETH.

Hamburg

Berlin

Tannenberg

3. RUSSIANS DEFEATED, AUG. 1914

1917

Ypres

GERMAN EMPIRE

Brest-Litovsk

Le Havre

The Somme

2. GERMAN ATTACK AUG. 1914

BELG.

LUX.

Dresden

Prague

POLAND

Kiev

The Marne

Paris

Verdun

Munich

AUSTRIA-HUNGARY

UKRAINE

FRANCE

Bern

The R.

SWITZ.

Vienna

Budapest

Odessa

Lyon

1. ARCHDUKE FERDINAND ASSASSINATED, JUNE 28, 1914

4. ITALY ENTERS THE WAR, MAY 1915

ROMANIA

Danube R.

BLACK SEA

Marseilles

SPAIN

CORSICA

ITALY

Rome

Sarajevo

MONTENEGRO

SERBIA

ALBANIA

BULGARIA

Sofia

Constantinople

SARDINIA

Naples

Gallipoli

GREECE

TURKEY

SICILY

Athens

AEGEAN SEA

Dardanelles

CRETE

CYPRUS

Early losses in the war. In the opening battles in 1914, even before the trenches were dug, each side lost a half-million men—more than there had been in the entire German army 50 years before. Then, during 1915, the British and French did not advance more than three miles at any point. Still the French lost a million and a half men in 1915 and a million in 1916. At the Battle of the Somme—which lasted for five months in 1916—the Germans lost more men than had been killed during the whole four years of the American Civil War. On one bloody day nearly 20,000 British soldiers were killed.

Never before had so many men been slaughtered so rapidly or so senselessly. Before the war was over, the soldiers killed on both sides would number 10 million, and another 10 million civilians would die from disease, starvation, and the revolutions that grew out of the war.

When the United States finally plunged in, both sides were weary and sick of the bloodshed. The Germans were near victory. They had made peace with the Russians and now could concentrate all their forces on the western front. In May 1918 the German trenches were within 50 miles of Paris.

Troops from the United States played a key role in the battles of 1918. Members of the all-black 369th Regiment fight from a trench in France (left.) Another group of Americans charges (above). Men of the 18th Infantry (below) march through the ruins of a small French town near St. Mihiel.

Art Resource, NY

There were many ways to help the war effort (top). The 1919 French poster (below) shows war-damaged Verdun.

State Historical Society of Wisconsin

Verdun

The Germans hoped that when they reached Paris they would force the Allies to surrender before American troops could make a difference.

The American Expeditionary Force. But the Americans came in time. At the end of May, the Second and Third divisions of the American Expeditionary Force (AEF) were sent into action. They fought bravely at Belleau Wood and Vaux near Château-Thierry. In July, 85,000 Americans were there to help save Paris. By August an American army of a half-million under General John J. Pershing advanced against the Germans on the southern front. Before the end of September a million and a quarter Americans were fighting in France.

After a bloody battle in October, the Americans advanced to Sedan, 50 miles behind the trenches that the Germans had held for three years. The Americans then cut the railroad that had supplied the German army in their sector. The German defense opposite them began to fall apart. At the same time, the French and the British were advancing all along the line.

The German generals and their emperor had made a bad mistake. They had not imagined that American help at the last moment could turn the tide. Though the Americans arrived late in the battle, they actually did make the difference that decided the war. The United States lost 50,280 men in action. But this was nothing compared to the 4 million lost by Russia, France, and Great Britain and the millions lost by the lesser powers. They had done the real dirty work.

The bloodiest war yet in history—a first "World War"—ended with the armistice on November 11, 1918. In New York, San Francisco, Dallas, Chicago, and Atlanta, Americans danced in the streets.

SECTION 2 REVIEW

1. Identify or explain: John J. Pershing, American Expeditionary Force, armistice.
2. In what ways was World War I different from earlier wars?
3. **Recognizing Cause and Effect.** How did the arrival of the AEF affect the Allies' war effort?

1. FIRST VICTORY FOR AMERICAN TROOPS, MAY 28

3. AMERICANS AT SEDAN CUT GERMAN SUPPLY LINE, OCTOBER-NOVEMBER

2. ALLIES REPULSE MARNE OFFENSIVE: TURNING POINT OF WAR, JULY-AUGUST

World War I, The Western Front 1918

——— Farthest German Advance, Sept. 1914

——— Stabilized Front, 1917-1918 (Spring 1918)

——— Farthest German Advance, June-July 1918

– – – Armistice Line, November 11, 1918

× Battles Involving American Troops

Boundaries of 1914

0   80 Miles

0   80 Kilometers

3. The home front

American troops had tipped the scale for the Allies. But it had been a near thing. The United States preparedness program had been inadequate. With the outbreak of the war the nation suddenly found that it had to mobilize men, money, machines, and minds to aid its struggling friends. To get this task done, the President was given new and sweeping powers. The government, acting through scores of boards, commissions, and committees, regulated daily life. It dictated what (and how much) people should eat. It rationed their sugar and their fuel, and discouraged their travel. It even tried to tell them what to think. The free enterprise system that business was accustomed to came to a halt. The government told industry what it could buy, what it could produce, even where it could build factories. This was the first experiment in total war. Never before had the nation been so organized for a single purpose.

Back our girls over there
Y.W.C.A.
United War Work Campaign

A YWCA poster (left) reminded Americans that women were "over there," too. Some women, like the Broadway chorus girls shown above, signed up for military training to serve in the Home Guard.

Mobilization of men and women. First of all the nation needed an army. The American tradition, expressed in the Constitution, distrusted a large standing army in peacetime. Experience since ancient times showed that ambitious rulers could use the army against the people. Congress passed a Selective Service Act on May 28, 1917, by a nearly unanimous vote in both houses. The law required all men between the ages of 21 and 31 to register for military service. During the Civil War, a person who was drafted could hire a substitute—if he could afford it. But not now.

Despite fears of draft riots like those during the Civil War, draftees were registered peaceably on June 5. Nearly 10 million men were listed. It was decided that a lottery would be the fairest way to choose whom to draft. Each man who had registered was given a number between 1 and 10,500. On July 20, 1917, these numbers were placed in a bowl, and blindfolded officials withdrew enough numbers to call 687,000 men into the army. Before the war was over 24 million men between the ages of 18 and 45 entered the Selective Service rolls.

Almost 3 million of these were called into service. The militia, now called the National Guard, was also brought into federal service. By the time of the armistice in 1918 nearly 4.8 million people—enlistees, draftees, and National Guard—were serving in the armed forces. Among them were women in the Nurses Corps of the army and navy. About 11,000 female yeomen enlisted for office jobs when the Navy Department decided that its right to enlist "persons" included women.

This vast army had to be fed, clothed, equipped, and armed. In the beginning, of course, there were shortages. Before many months American factories were supplying the needed pistols, rifles, machine guns, shells, and bullets. The heavy equipment—the artillery, the tanks, and the airplanes—was still provided by the French and the English.

The war at sea. To move American troops and supplies to Europe there had to be "a bridge of ships." German submarines were sinking ships faster than they could be replaced. "They will win," the British admiral Sir John Jellicoe warned, "unless we can stop these losses—and stop them soon."

Luckily, at the start the United States Navy was in better shape than the army. Fast destroyers were thrown into the battle against the U-boats. Rear Admiral Sims insisted that all ships headed across the Atlantic should travel in convoys. A convoy was an organized group of merchant and passenger ships surrounded and protected by naval vessels armed to ward off submarine attacks. This system worked so well that the German submarines did not kill a single member of the huge AEF on its way to France.

To provide the bridge of ships, the United States began a mammoth shipbuilding program. The government contracted for 10 million tons of ships and built shipyards to construct them. In fact, few of these vessels would be delivered in time to help the war effort. But by seizing the German vessels that happened to be in American waters in April 1917 and by impressing into service almost everything that could float, the government partly filled the gap. Meanwhile more than 1 million American soldiers and millions of tons of equipment were carried to France by the British merchant marine.

Mobilizing money. The expenses of the army and navy, and credit and materials for the Allies, ran into billions of dollars. Money, too, had to be mobilized for war. At least $23 billion was spent for the American war effort, and more than $10 billion went in war loans to the Allies.

In new shipyards like the one in the poster, the United States began an all-out shipbuilding program during World War I. Few ships were finished during the war, but by 1921 the United States had the world's largest merchant fleet.

ON THE JOB FOR VICTORY
· UNITED STATES SHIPPING BOARD ·   · EMERGENCY FLEET CORPORATION ·

The nation's effort in World War I was spurred on and supported by war bonds. Women sold them on the street (top left). A parade in New York City (top right) helped raise support for the fourth of the Liberty Loans. Below a poster asks support for the last, or Victory, Loan.

THEY KEPT THE
SEA LANES
OPEN

L. A. SHAFER

INVEST IN THE
VICTORY LIBERTY LOAN

The government used both taxes and loans to pay these huge expenses. Increased taxes brought in $10.5 billion. The rest was borrowed from the people through the sale of government bonds. Four Liberty Loans and a Victory Loan, "to finish the job," brought in $23 billion.

The government takes control. Of course, a nation geared to peace could not all at once meet the demands of war. Under the pressure of war, the government took over some private businesses. In December 1917, when the overburdened railroads were near collapse, the government took them over. Secretary of the Treasury William McAdoo became director-general of the railroads. He ran them as a single system but left day-to-day operations in the hands of the private managers. Half a billion dollars was invested in improvements and equipment. Soon the railway express companies and the inland waterway systems also came under McAdoo's control. Before the end of the war, government control was extended to telephone, telegraph, and cable companies.

To mobilize industry and agriculture, the preparedness legislation of 1916 had provided for a Council of Defense. In May 1917 this Council set up a national food-control program. It was headed by a hard-driving mining engineer who had run the Belgian War Relief program. His name was Herbert Hoover. Born a Quaker, he combined engineering efficiency and Quaker charity to bring help to the starving Belgians without offending their self-respect.

Hoover's board had no legal power to do its task. Wilson therefore asked Congress for broad powers over the production and distribution of food, fuel, fertilizer, and farm machinery. Hoover was named head of the new Food Administration. All sorts of measures were tried. There were voluntary "wheatless, meatless, heatless days." Hoover urged men and women to plant "war gardens." Prices on farm crops were set high enough to encourage farmers to raise more food and fiber. The use of grain to make beverage alcohol was banned. Coal was rationed for home use. Fuel and food output rose as home consumption went down.

While American "doughboys" were mired in trenches overseas, not all Americans were suffering equally from the war. The big rise in demand for

KEEP *it* COMING

"We must not only feed our Soldiers at the front but the millions of women & children behind our lines"

Gen. John J. Pershing

WASTE NOTHING

UNITED STATES FOOD ADMINISTRATION

The Food Administration, run by Herbert Hoover, urged Americans to waste no food.

food—for our soldiers and for the armies and the civilian population of the Allies—sent food prices skyrocketing. Farmers could pay off their mortgages, paint their barns, and buy new farm machinery. The price of land rose, too. But higher crop prices enabled farmers to extend their acreage. They began to plant marginal land that would not have paid off under ordinary conditions. When the war was over, and American farmers were no longer expected to feed European armies, food prices would plummet. Farmers would have to pay a peacetime price for their wartime prosperity.

The War Industries Board. The Council of National Defense set up in July 1917 to mobilize industry actually lacked the authority to do its job. As a result, by January 1918 the industrial war effort was on the verge of collapse. As heavy snows fell it seemed even the weather would not cooperate. The chairman of the Senate committee investigating the war effort saw "inefficiency in every bureau of the government." Republican senators called for a War Cabinet of three men. This would make President Wilson a mere figurehead.

Wilson fought to keep control and put the mobilization on track. He submitted a bill that gave him wide powers to reorganize the government and expend funds as he wished. Even before the Overman Act giving him these powers was passed in May 1918, Wilson created the War Industries Board. Bernard M. Baruch, a Wall Street financier of great energy and vision, was put in charge. He showed how a statesman of the business world could bring his wisdom to the national service.

The job of the War Industries Board was to decide what goods should be produced. It could also set prices for government purchases of supplies. For two years Bernard Baruch was the economic dictator of the country. But he seldom had to use force. He had other means of "persuasion." One day Baruch was having trouble getting the automakers to cut down on the output of automobiles. He had them listen in while he phoned the railroad office to stop train service to their plants. Next he called on the army to seize the auto firms' stockpiles of steel. The automakers promptly gave in. Under Baruch's direction the WIB soon gained control of the industrial war effort. Production went up, waste went down, and criticism lessened.

The labor force. The 4 million men enlisted in the armed forces were withdrawn from the nation's labor supply. A million women helped to fill the gap, doing jobs that they had never been allowed to do (nor known that they could do). The war helped them discover themselves as they streamed into mills and factories. They became furnace stokers, managed assembly lines, and wore the uniforms of railroad and streetcar conductors.

Some reformers announced that economic freedom for women had at last arrived. They were wrong. After the war, women were asked to leave their jobs as an act of "patriotism" so the men could return. By 1920 the proportion of women in the labor force had dropped below the level of 1910.

Blacks by the thousands moved north to take advantage of the new chances for jobs. After suffering in the South from wages that dropped to as low as 75 cents a day in 1914–1915, they saw the North as a promised land. Within a few years there were more than 75,000 blacks in the coal mines and 150,000 on the railroads.

The shortage of labor sent wages up as the government and private firms bid against each other. To fill essential jobs in vital industries, there was a United States Employment Service.

"This is labor's war," said AF of L president Samuel Gompers, and he pledged labor's support. In return for a promise not to strike, unions would get some direct support from the government. Early in April 1918, a National War Labor Board was created to arbitrate labor disputes. Some 1500 cases were submitted to this board. In the few instances in which labor refused to accept the decisions, the President used the pressure of public opinion to compel workers to return to their jobs. In extreme cases, he took over the plant.

Employers, on their part, were forbidden to discharge workers for union activities. Wherever possible, the government insisted on reducing the workday to eight hours. As a result of government support, the membership of labor unions doubled. In spite of a 50 percent rise in prices between 1914 and 1918, labor's *real* income rose 20 percent above the prewar level.

Mobilizing minds. The government also wanted to enlist the minds of the people in the war effort. Millions of Americans had opposed our entry into the war. Some German Americans, naturally enough, did not want to fight against the land of their ancestors. Some Irish Americans felt themselves traditional enemies of the English. Socialists declared that the war was only a capitalist dogfight. Midwest Progressives said the nation should devote itself to reform rather than war. And then there were the pacifists who said that war—only murder under another name—could never be justified.

How could the government convert these reluctant citizens? How could it whip up enthusiasm for our friends and hatred for our enemies? How could it sell war bonds and keep people hard at work? For these tasks President Wilson created the Committee on Public Information. George Creel, a journalist, was appointed chairman, assigned to "sell the war to America." In May 1917 the Creel Committee began publishing a daily *Official Bulletin* of the war news that the administration wished to make public. The committee hired professors, writers, artists, and lecturers by the thousands. Their job was to convince and to reassure Americans that the war was a crusade for freedom and democracy. The Germans were portrayed as hateful beasts, barbarous "Huns" out to dominate the Western world.

This effort helped create a war fever with sad aftereffects which long outlasted the war. It stirred up spy scares and a frantic hunt for traitors. Otherwise sensible Americans now refused to play Beethoven or Wagner. They dropped German courses from the schools. They turned "sauerkraut" into "liberty cabbage" and converted "hamburger" into "Salisbury steak." But this anti-German madness was really anti-American. For without the hundreds of thousands of immigrants from Germany the nation would have been much poorer. The United States—"a nation of nations"—had been created by people from everywhere and was enriched by all their languages and cultures.

The attack on civil liberties. The Espionage Act of 1917 gave the President powers of censorship. It enacted heavy penalties against anyone who handed out information about any place connected with the national defense. To urge resistance to the laws of the United States, to refuse to do military duty, or to hinder the draft now became crimes punishable by prison terms. The Trading with the Enemy Act of 1917 obliged any newspaper printed here in a foreign language to furnish the Postmaster General with English translations of everything it published about the war.

The Sedition Act of 1918 went even further than the infamous Sedition Act of 1798 against which Jefferson and Madison had protested. For the 1918 law imposed penalties on anyone who used "disloyal, profane, scurrilous, or abusive" language about the United States government, flag, or uniform. It empowered the Postmaster General to refuse to deliver mail to anyone who, in his opinion, was using the postal service in violation of the act.

With this barrage of propaganda and new laws, Americans who disagreed in any way with the activities of the government were hounded and harried. In 1917 more than 1100 striking copper miners who were members of the radical Industrial Workers of the World were taken forcibly from Arizona to New Mexico, where they were interned. IWW leaders were thrown into jail. Eugene V. Debs, the many-time Socialist candidate for President, was sentenced to jail for ten years for denouncing the war in 1918. While still in jail he ran for President in 1920. His sentence was finally commuted in 1921.

This was a strange way to fight a war for freedom and democracy. How could the nation improve its war effort if citizens were not allowed to criticize the government or the armed forces? In fact, opposition to the war was slight and scarcely hampered the war effort. But the mania of these times would last even after the war. The virus of witch-hunting and super-patriotism was not easy to cure.

SECTION 3 REVIEW

1. Identify or explain: Selective Service Act, Liberty Loans, War Industries Board, Bernard Baruch, Herbert Hoover, National War Labor Board, Committee on Public Information, George Creel, Espionage Act, Trading with the Enemy Act, Sedition Act, IWW.

2. How did the armed services grow? The merchant marine?

3. How was industry mobilized for war?

4. How did the war affect consumers? Farmers? Women workers? Organized labor?

5. Describe wartime attacks on civil liberties.

6. **Recognizing Cause and Effect.** How did the government encourage patriotism? What were some results?

4. Losing the peace

When the Germans agreed to the armistice in November 1918, they believed that the peace would be generous—and based on Wilson's high-minded Fourteen Points. They were in for a brutal shock.

The Versailles Treaty. President Wilson, announcing that he would go to the Peace Conference in Paris, gave ammunition to his critics. He said his only purpose was to help achieve the goals of his Fourteen Points. They said he was more anxious to be the Preacher to the World than to be the Protector of the United States. No President while in office had ever before gone to Europe.

ICELAND

ATLANTIC
OCEAN

NORTH
SEA

NORWAY

SWEDEN

FINLAND

Leningrad

ESTONIA

LATVIA

LITHU-
ANIA

SOVIET
UNION

IRISH
FREE
STATE

GREAT
BRITAIN

DENMARK

Danzig

EAST
PRUSSIA

London

BELG.

NETH.

Berlin

Warsaw

Brest-
Litovsk

Versailles
Paris

GERMANY

LUX.

Rhine

POLAND

FRANCE

CZECHOSLOVAKIA

AUSTRIA

HUNGARY

BESSARABIA

ROMANIA

SPAIN

ITALY

YUGOSLAVIA

Rome

ALBANIA

GREECE

BULGARIA

BLACK SEA

Constantinople
(Istanbul)

TURKEY

CASPIAN
SEA

PERSIA

**Europe and the Near East
after the Treaty of Versailles
and Other Peace Settlements**

MEDITERRANEAN
SEA

CYPRUS
(Br.)

SYRIA
(Fr. Mandate)

Baghdad

LEBANON
(Fr. Mandate)

IRAQ
(Br. Mandate)

PALESTINE
(Br. Mandate)

TRANS-JORDAN
(Br. Mandate)

Territory Lost by

Russia

Germany

Austria-Hungary

Turkish Empire

Boundaries as of 1926

0   600 Miles
0   600 Kilometers

LIBYA
(Ital.)

EGYPT

RED
SEA

HEJAZ AND NEJD

Riyadh

Medina

NETHERLANDS

Rhine

BELGIUM

RHINELAND

GERMANY

LUX.

SAAR

ALSACE-LORRAINE

FRANCE

SWITZ.

In Paris the three Allied leaders whom Wilson
had to bargain with were clever and tough. They
were Prime Minister David Lloyd George of Great
Britain, Premier Georges Clemenceau of France,
and Premier Vittorio Orlando of Italy. Each of
them remembered the enormous cost of the war to
his country. Each wanted to get as much as possible
in lands and wealth and power for his own
country. Each hoped to punish the enemies so that
they would never rise again.

Wilson irritated the other members of the "Big
Four." They saw him as a self-righteous leader

472

who always said he was worrying about "all mankind." They compared the Points that Wilson had announced from Washington with the Commandments given to Moses on Mount Sinai. "Mr. Wilson bores me with his *Fourteen* Points," Clemenceau sneered. "Why, God Almighty has only ten!"

The treaty that came out of the Paris Conference was not as selfish or as vengeful as the European leaders would have wished. Nor was it nearly as just and noble as President Wilson might have hoped. Each victor got land it had been promised in secret treaties. The German colonies were parceled out among the Allies. Yet, at the same time, some new smaller republics—like Czechoslovakia and Poland—were created so that at last these people could govern themselves.

The provisions most poisonous for the future of Europe had to do with "reparations." These were payments the Allies demanded from Germany to "repair" all the war damage. When the Germans signed the armistice, they knew they might have to pay for the damage to civilians.

The British and the French raised the damages to include the *total* cost of the whole war to all the Allies. This meant not only the homes and farms and factories destroyed, but also the cost of guns and ammunition, the uniforms and pay for soldiers, and even the pensions to wounded Allied soldiers and to their relatives. This sum was so vast and so hard to estimate that the Allies refused to name a figure—or even to name a time in the future when the Germans would be allowed to stop paying.

President Wilson did manage to put his own scheme for permanent peace—the League of Nations—in the very same package with all those things the other Allied powers really wanted. He believed that, even if the treaty was not perfect, his new League of Nations could correct the mistakes later.

The fight over the treaty begins.
When President Wilson returned to the United States, he was greeted like a hero. An escort of festive warships led him into New York Harbor. Ten thousand people welcomed Wilson at Union Station in Washington.

His triumph was short. Now his political mistakes came home to roost. When Wilson had chosen the American Peace Commissioners to go to Paris, he had snubbed both the Republican party and the Senate. Yet the Republicans held the majority in the Senate. And before any treaty became law, the Senate would have to approve it by a two-thirds majority.

President Wilson simply could not believe that there were reasons why sensible Americans might not want to approve his treaty. What frightened Americans most was the plan for a League of Nations—especially Article 10. Wilson, with typical obstinacy, said that Article 10 was the heart of the League, and that the League was the heart of the whole treaty.

Crowds cheered President Wilson on July 8, 1919, when he returned from the Paris Peace Conference. Watchful Secret Service men in white straw hats accompanied him.

In Article 10 each League member promised to respect and preserve all the other members of the League against "external aggression." At first sight that looked harmless enough. But the real purpose of the Article was to make each member of the League regard an attack on any other member as an attack on itself. In that case, each League member would be expected to prepare for war and then presumably fight to protect all the other members.

To agree to this would overturn one of the oldest American traditions. Should the United States let itself be *required* to plunge into some future European war?

Borah and Lodge lead the opposition. Two able, contrasting Republicans led a relentless battle against allowing the United States to join Wilson's League. One was Senator William E. Borah of Idaho. Borah, like Wilson himself, was the son of a Presbyterian minister who had wanted him also to go into the ministry. A graduate of the University of Kansas, he was as eloquent as Wilson but had more experience in politics. Although a Republican, he supported many Democratic measures when he happened to agree with them. He had worked for the income tax and had fought against the trusts.

Senator Borah's own rule in politics was to stay independent, and then support whatever measures seemed best. In the same way, he believed that the United States should not be dependent on other countries. He bitterly opposed our joining the League of Nations for fear it would take away our independence.

The other leader of the anti-League forces was the learned Senator Henry Cabot Lodge of Massachusetts. He, too, had had a long career as a politician. At the time of the World War he was chairman of the Senate Committee on Foreign Relations. That committee had the power to recommend to the Senate whether or not they should adopt the treaty. Unlike Senator Borah, Lodge was a man of strong personal hates. He distrusted Woodrow Wilson, and so he feared Wilson's League.

The failure to enter the League. Then President Wilson made his fatal decision to appeal directly to the American people. In early September 1919, though already in ill health, he traveled 8000 miles, visited 29 cities, and gave 40 speeches in 22 days. At Pueblo, Colorado, he collapsed and had to be taken back to the White House. There he suffered a stroke. For nearly eight months he could not even meet his Cabinet. Edith Wilson, his wife, carried messages back and forth from everybody else to the President. It was never quite clear which messages actually reached him.

Before the election of 1920 Wilson made another grave blunder. If he had been willing to work with Senator Lodge, he still might have found some compromise. Then he might have succeeded in steering the treaty and the League through the Senate. Instead Wilson once again became the preacher. "Shall we," he asked "or shall we not, redeem the great moral obligation of the United States?" He declared that the election of 1920 would be a "solemn national referendum" on the League of Nations.

The Democratic candidate for President, Governor James M. Cox of Ohio, stood up for the League. The weak, but likable Republican candidate, Senator Warren G. Harding of Ohio, opposed the League. He said vaguely that he favored some sort of "association of nations." Americans chose the Republican Harding by a resounding majority of 7 million votes.

The United States never joined President Wilson's League of Nations. Wilson was saddened that the American people chose a "barren independence." But he did not give up his hope that what a union of states had accomplished in North America, a union of nations might someday accomplish for the whole world.

SECTION 4 REVIEW

1. Identify or explain: David Lloyd George, Georges Clemenceau, Vittorio Orlando, "Big Four," reparations, William E. Borah, Henry Cabot Lodge, Warren G. Harding.

2. What mistake made it hard for Wilson to secure Republican support for the treaty?

3. What feature of the League of Nations was most opposed by Americans?

4. **Demonstrating Reasoned Judgment.** Which nations' interests were being served by the Treaty of Versailles? Explain.

FOCUSING ON IDEAS

1. Senator Norris of Nebraska was one of 56 members of Congress to vote against the declaration of war. He explained that the United States had violated its status as a neutral nation. What were some partisan actions of the United States prior to 1917? How did the government justify them?

2. Critics of the war pointed to huge gains made out of the war by Wall Street and big business. Who were other "winners" on the home front?

3. What kinds of freedoms were curtailed during the war? Explain.

TAKING A CRITICAL LOOK

1. **Identifying Assumptions.** In his War Message, President Wilson said that the German government's January 31, 1917, announcement of unrestricted submarine warfare was "in fact nothing less than war against the government and people of the United States." Then he spoke about a moral crusade to make the world "safe for democracy." Do you think he needed to make our entrance into the war a moral issue? Explain.

2. **Drawing Conclusions.** What are some important lessons that other Presidents might have learned from President Wilson's efforts to persuade the United States to take a leading role in world affairs?

YOUR REGION IN HISTORY

1. **Geography.** Was your area strategically located to support the war effort? Explain your answer, identifying military installations and/or factories involved in war production. If factories served the war effort, what products did they make?

2. **Culture.** What World War I memorials exist in or near your community? What contributions to the war effort do they commemorate?

3. **Economics.** How was the standard of living in your community affected by the war?

HISTORICAL FACTS AND FIGURES

Drawing Inferences. Study the graph below to help answer the following questions: (a) Which Allied power spent the most money during World War I? (b) Which nation suffered the most casualties? (c) How did the costs of war for the United States compare to those of its allies? (d) How were these costs reflected in the terms of the Treaty of Versailles?

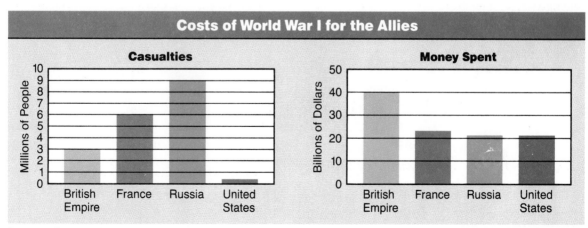

Source: V.J. Esposito, *A Concise History of World War I*

MAKING CONNECTIONS

THEMES

At the beginning of this unit, on page 413, several questions were raised concerning the United States's role in the world:

Would our newly powerful nation be tempted to enter wars and try to run the affairs of people everywhere? How could Americans keep their ideals in this different kind of world?

These questions were explored by the three unit themes that are reprinted in **dark type** below. Use the time line and the information in Unit 7 to answer the questions that follow the unit themes.

1. **The United States begins to reach outward as a result of rapid industrialization.**

   How was the United States's foreign policy in part a result of its economic and business interests?

2. **The United States becomes a world leader.**

   What political and social forces were at work in the country to bring the United States into the forefront of world leadership?

3. **The Progressive Era produces significant reforms in American business and government.**

   How did reformers attempt to make American business and government fairer and more democratic?

1898 The Yellow Press calls for war against Spain, with the headline "Remember the Maine."

1897 The Supreme Court applies Sherman Anti-Trust Act to railroad monopolies.

1900 Secretary of State John Hay announces the Open Door Policy for China.

Events in American History

Events in World History

| 1885 | 1890 | 1895 | 1900 |

1890 A. Mahan's *The Influence of Sea Power upon History* is published.

1900 The Boxers seize Peking, China, and attack foreigners.

1912 The U.S. Marines are sent to Nicaragua to protect American business interests during an uprising.

1902 The muckraker Ida Tarbell's exposé of Standard Oil is published.

1913 Congress enacts the Underwood-Simmons tariff reform bill.

1921 Shipbuilding during World War I gives the United States the world's largest merchant fleet.

1913 The Seventeenth Amendment provides for direct election of senators.

1906 Congress passes the Pure Food and Drug Act, responding to consumers' fears.

| 1900 | 1905 | 1910 | 1915 | 1920 | 1925 |

1914 Archduke Ferdinand is assassinated in Sarajevo, leading to World War I.

1919 The Treaty of Versailles is signed, ending World War I.

1918 Woodrow Wilson outlines his 14 Points in a message to Congress.

1904 T. Roosevelt establishes his corollary to the Monroe Doctrine.

UNIT **8**

From boom to bust
1918–1932

President Calvin Coolidge told Congress in December 1928 that the nation had never faced "a more pleasing prospect." At home, he declared, "there is tranquility and contentment...and the highest record of years of prosperity. In the foreign field there is peace...." The twenties, most Americans agreed, had been a wonderful decade.

Before the next year was out the stock market had crashed, and the ranks of the unemployed had begun to swell. The following years would see banks and factories close and find millions out of work. Most distressing of all to Americans, the government of the able engineer Herbert Hoover seemed unable to solve the nation's pressing problems. "In Hoover we trusted," placards read, "now we are busted." The President constantly made encouraging statements. He said that the crisis would soon pass. But it did not pass. From the euphoria of the booming "Jazz Age," Americans were plunged into the Great Depression. They no longer would wonder how high up women's skirts and the price of stocks on the market would go. Instead it seemed that the entire American system might collapse.

THEMES IN AMERICAN HISTORY

- The "Roaring Twenties" are characterized by experimentation, great changes in daily life, and booming economic growth.
- The stock market crash of 1929 signals the end of the "Roaring Twenties" and leads many Americans to grow disillusioned with the American economic system.

THEMES

Thomas Hart Benton's painting "Boomtown" with its oil wells evokes the spirit of the 1920s.

Memorial Art Gallery of the University of Rochester, New York; Marion Stratton Gould Fund (detail)

CHAPTER 22

Return to normalcy, 1918–1929

In the 1920s the sound of radios and phonographs began to fill the air. For the first time motion pictures opened fantastic vistas for the millions. Americans started their love affair with the automobile. Women's skirts—which had once been thought dangerously high when they revealed a glimpse of the ankle—now suddenly shot up to the knee. Long hair had been called a woman's "crowning glory." Now respectable women cut their hair short in a "boyish bob"—and actually wore lipstick. Some even smoked cigarettes in public!

At the same time there were still many old-fashioned Americans. They were shocked by what they saw. Women, they said, ought to be put on a pedestal, where they had neither the freedom nor the temptations of the rest of the human race. In this and other ways the twenties was an age of conflict, confusion, excitement, and experiment. Never was the nation more American. This was still a New World where people might try anything—at least once.

1. The postwar reaction

The cease-fire in Europe did not bring a quick end to the problems of war. The war itself had created new problems. It had left a trail of starvation and death and opened the floodgates of revolution. Peace on the battlefield brought another sort of warfare—in parliaments and factories. All over Europe, dissatisfied people seized the chance to turn their nations upside down. In the United States there was worry that the virus of revolt would infect Americans.

Allied intervention in Russia. In March 1917 a revolution in Russia toppled the government of Czar Nicholas II. Then the new liberal Provisional Government led by Alexander Kerensky had in turn fallen in November before radical Bolsheviks (Communists) led by V.I. Lenin. They promptly took Russia out of the war. Hoping to keep German troops from moving to the western front, the Allies stepped in. They said their purpose was to help Russia form a stable government. Some Western leaders, however, no doubt hoped that they could "strangle Bolshevism at its birth," as Winston Churchill later put it. Japan, for its part, hoped to secure control over eastern Siberia.

As a result, when the armistice came in 1918, many American troops stayed in Europe. They

This cover of a 1926 issue of the original *Life* magazine was done by John Held, Jr., whose drawings captured the flavor of the 1920s.

were fighting a new kind of war—a war against communism. Earlier that year the United States had joined Britain, France, and Japan in sending troops into northern and eastern Russia. The Allies lifted the hopes of the enemies of the Bolsheviks within Russia and so prolonged the "Great Russian Civil War" of 1918–1920. In the new Russia—now called the Union of Soviet Socialist Republics—the distrust of the Western powers would fester for many years.

During World War I, the Creel Committee had made the people of the United States suspicious of anything un-American. Now the mysterious Communists seemed to threaten to overturn the governments of Europe. They had even formed a party in the United States. It was small and harmless, but many Americans were still jittery, and other events in the country increased their fears.

Labor strife. Within the United States the truce between employers and workers came to an end as soon as the war was won. Workers were anxious to keep the wartime benefits they had gained and felt threatened by soaring prices. In 1919 some 4 million workers went out on strikes costing $2 billion in lost sales and wages. Union violence at home frightened the public.

In the autumn of that year, after the Boston police walked out in a labor dispute, looting and violence spread across the city. When the mayor asked for help, Governor Calvin Coolidge called out the National Guard to keep order. He declared that there was "no right to strike against the public safety by anybody, anywhere, anytime." This statement—and his prompt action against the striking policemen—brought him the Republican vice-presidential nomination in 1920.

A strike against United States Steel, during which eighteen workers were killed, failed. A coal strike, which President Wilson called "not only unjustifiable but unlawful," was broken by a court injunction. These defeats forecast the decline of the unions during the 1920s. Opposed by business, government, the courts, and popular opinion, union membership fell from 5 million in 1921 to 4.3 million in 1929. In these same years total nonfarm employment rose by nearly 7 million.

Urban riots. The end of the war was also marked by an increase in racial friction. Though blacks had served bravely on the battlefield and skillfully in the factories, anti-black feeling had increased. During the year after the armistice 70 blacks, including at least 10 soldiers in uniform, were lynched. "Lynching" was named after a Colonel Charles Lynch of Virginia. It was the barbarous act of a mob that hanged a person without a legal right to do so.

In the summer of 1919 there were more than 25 race riots. The worst occurred in Chicago, where a dispute at the beach set off six days and nights of rioting. Hundreds were injured, and 15 whites and 23 blacks were killed. The trigger-happy Attorney General A. Mitchell Palmer was haunted by Bolshevik ghosts whom he imagined to be everywhere. During that "Red Summer," without reason he accused the Chicago rioters—along with anybody else he disliked—of being Communist agitators.

Bomb scares. At the same time there really was an epidemic of terrorism that made many citizens nervous. In Seattle early in 1919 Mayor Ole Hanson had taken measures to break a general strike. Then on April 28, he received a bomb in the mail. It was discovered before anyone was hurt. The next day Senator Hardwick of Georgia received a package that was opened by his maid, who had both her hands blown off. Later, 36 similar packages were found that had not been delivered because they lacked sufficient postage. These were addressed to such people as Attorney General Palmer, the Postmaster General, the Secretary of Labor, J. P. Morgan, and John D. Rockefeller.

Only a month later other parts of the country were shaken by a series of explosions. One of these damaged the front of Attorney General Palmer's house and killed the person carrying the bomb. The bombings came to a climax at noon on September 16, 1920. On the corner of Broad and Wall streets in the heart of New York's financial district, the busy lunchtime crowds were blasted without warning. In that worst peacetime bombing in American history, 38 people were killed and hundreds injured.

A. Mitchell Palmer pursues the Bolsheviks. Attorney General Palmer lacked a sense of perspective. Instead of seeing the bombings as scattered acts by a few misguided terrorists, he imagined that the very existence of the nation was in peril. The strikes, race riots, and bombings seemed to him "the blaze of revolution." The whole country, he said, was infested by Bolsheviks and anarchists. Any alien, he screamed, might prove to be a bomb thrower. And if Palmer could make himself the nation's savior, he might eventually move into the White House.

In November 1919 he had 250 members of the Union of Russian Workers arrested. Most were guilty of no wrongdoing and later had to be released. In December 249 aliens, whose only crime in a majority of cases was that they were anarchists, were herded aboard the transport *Buford*, called the

This dramatic photograph shows the powerful effect of the bomb that exploded at lunchtime on Wall Street on September 16, 1920. The 38 dead and the hundreds of victims needing medical care had been removed by the time the picture was taken.

"Soviet Ark," and shipped to the Soviet Union. Palmer declared that there were thousands of "Reds" all over the country sworn and trained to tear the nation apart.

On January 2, 1920, he ordered raids on Communist meetings all over the country. Everyone who was present, Communist or not, was rounded up and more than 4000 people were thrown into jail. In all, 556 aliens were deported.

By now, however, criticism of Palmer was surfacing. His illegal arrests were doing more harm to American institutions than were the small groups of real "Reds" in the country. The ambitious and jittery Palmer was brewing trouble for millions of innocent and patriotic Americans. Following his example, excitable citizens were roused to vent their fears and their hates against any Americans who seemed "different." These included blacks, Jews, and Catholics, along with all reformers. Somehow, forgetting that the nation had been built by immigrants, Palmer and his followers aimed their blasts against all "foreigners."

The fear of foreigners. During the war the Immigration Restriction League had finally obtained passage of the law that every immigrant must be able to read to be admitted to the United States (p. 380). But they were not interested just in literacy. They had strong racial, religious, and ethnic prejudices. In fact, they wanted to cut down immigration from Russia, Poland, Italy, and the other countries of eastern and southern Europe. The nation had been enriched by the thousands who had come here from those countries between 1890 and 1910. But the restrictionists had an odd theory of their own about "superior" and "inferior" races. They pretended that it was a science. Really it was only a way of dressing up their prejudices. Their own ancestors happened to come from northern and western Europe. They liked to think, therefore, that all the best people came from there. The restrictionists included university presidents and were led by eminent New Englanders. It would take many years to remove the stain they left on our immigration laws.

The nation seemed to have forgotten its own origins! Free immigration had made the United States a free nation. Then in 1921 national quotas for immigrants were introduced. The National Origins Act of 1924 reduced quotas until, in 1929,

WHOSE COUNTRY IS THIS, ANYHOW?

Culver Pictures

A 1920 cartoon of an angry Uncle Sam reflects the hysterical fear of "Reds" and anarchists then sweeping the country.

only 150,000 immigrants were allowed to enter the United States each year. The quota from each country was based on the "national origins" of the people of the United States in 1920. This favored northern and western Europe, since the large immigration from other parts had come more recently.

The National Origins Act barred all Chinese, Japanese, and other Asians. It is not surprising that in Japan there were "hate America" meetings held on "Humiliation Day," July 1, 1924. On the other hand, Canadians and Latin Americans were exempt from the law's provisions. The 1920s saw the first large immigration to the United States of Mexican Americans.

The "new" Klan. While the Immigration Restriction League used the laws, another group was using terror and violence to enforce their prejudices. A new Ku Klux Klan appeared in the South and the West. It pretended to be in the old southern tradition to defend the rights of the "best" people. But in fact it was led by a collection of roughnecks and human dregs, with some respectable followers, who made a career of harassing blacks, Jews, Roman Catholics, and all "foreigners." Somehow they were able to enroll about 4.5 million "native born, white, gentile Americans." These included many who wanted someone to blame for lack of jobs and many who were worried by the turmoil of postwar Europe. Somehow the Klan came to dominate the politics of several states.

To enlist and keep its members, the Klan shrewdly used all sorts of hocus-pocus. They had passwords, marched about in white sheets, and held secret meetings. But they were no laughing matter. They whipped and killed innocent citizens. They burned buildings and brought terror to whole communities. Yet they seldom went to jail for their crimes, because they bullied sheriffs and judges into joining them.

The conviction in 1925 of the Indiana Grand Dragon for murdering his secretary marked the beginning of the end of the "new" Klan. The newspapers then began to expose the crimes of the Klan, and respectable Americans avoided it like the plague.

Sacco and Vanzetti. Every epoch of American history has had its martyrs. Their names enter the folklore. John Brown was a willing martyr of the fight against slavery. In this later age Nicola Sacco and Bartolomeo Vanzetti, two Italian-born immigrants, became unwilling martyrs in the struggle for equal justice to all.

In 1920 a holdup took place at a South Braintree, Massachusetts, shoe factory. A paymaster and guard were killed. Shortly afterward Sacco and Vanzetti were arrested. They were both gentle men with no criminal record. But they believed the philosophy of anarchy. They were tried, found guilty, and sentenced to die. There was no solid evidence against them. It was widely thought that they were really victims of the frenzied fear of radicals and aliens.

The belief in the innocence of Sacco and Vanzetti was so widespread that in 1927 the governor of Massachusetts finally had to appoint a committee to review the fairness of their trial. But the committee itself was loaded with prejudice. The author of its report was Harvard President A. Lawrence Lowell, long an officer of the Immigration Restriction League, who was well known for his belief in the "superiority" of the Anglo-Saxon peoples. It is not surprising that this committee reported that the trial had been fair.

When Sacco and Vanzetti were executed, millions of Americans mourned. They believed that the two gentle Italian immigrants were victims of fear and prejudice.

Ben Shahn's grim 1930s painting of Nicola Sacco and Bartolomeo Vanzetti shows them handcuffed together as they stoically await their fate.

Collection, The Museum of Modern Art, New York. Gift of Abby Aldrich Rockefeller.

The disillusioned writers. Some of the brightest American writers did not like what they saw. The brilliant H. L. Mencken, a Baltimore journalist, used his acid pen to ridicule American follies in phrases that would not be forgotten. He laughed at democracy and called the American people the "Booboisie." The American-born poet T. S. Eliot, who had moved to England, described the postwar world as *The Waste Land.*

Yet the age produced the greatest crop of writers ever to light up an American generation. Novelists Sinclair Lewis, Sherwood Anderson, F. Scott Fitzgerald, William Faulkner, and Ernest Hemingway, along with playwright Eugene O'Neill, made their criticism of their own age into enduring literature.

The nation goes dry. The temperance movement—to discourage the use of intoxicating liquors—was as old as the Republic. Ever since the 1830s it had won the support of some reformers and industrial leaders. As early as 1851, the state of Maine passed a model temperance law. More and more citizens believed that control of liquor was necessary to decrease gambling, organized crime, and political corruption. They were troubled to see workmen wasting their paychecks at saloons while their families went hungry. In the new industrial age, too, a drunk at a machine could injure himself and many others.

By World War I, half the states of the Union had passed laws banning the sale of alcoholic beverages. Then came the war, and all at once "Prohibition" became a national concern. It would conserve grain. It would strike at the German Americans who brewed beer. And it would insure sober, clearheaded workers and soldiers. The wartime Congress passed a Prohibition amendment to the Constitution and sent it to the states. It became the Eighteenth Amendment when it was ratified by three-fourths of the states by January 1919. The sale of beer, wine, and distilled liquors was to stop in January 1920.

In theory, the whole nation was now "dry." All but two states ratified the amendment, yet many Americans had no intention of giving up drinking. Millions of Americans who could see nothing "criminal" about enjoying a glass of beer or wine suddenly became lawbreakers. Only 1520 federal agents were hired to try to stop the flow of liquor. Prohibition could not be enforced. So it bred a disrespect for all law. Since law-abiding citizens could no longer deal in liquor, the trade became a source of wealth and power for gangsters. "Booze" became the plague of the nation.

Women's suffrage. A more successful by-product of World War I was women's suffrage. Like the temperance campaign, the move to give women the vote had long been a goal of reformers. The war finally brought them success. "The services of women during the supreme crisis have been of the most signal usefulness and distinction," Woodrow Wilson wrote. What good reason could there be for depriving half the nation's adults of the right to vote? President Wilson's support, in 1919, helped the suffrage amendment pass Congress with little opposition. Only fourteen months later, the thirty-sixth state ratified the Nineteenth Amendment. At last women became first-class citizens.

SECTION 1 REVIEW

1. Identify or explain: Bolsheviks, Calvin Coolidge, immigration quotas, Sacco and Vanzetti case, temperance movement, Eighteenth Amendment, Nineteenth Amendment.

2. What action in 1918 brought Russian distrust of the Western powers?

3. Describe the main developments in labor relations and race relations after World War I.

4. What events were troubling Americans in 1919–1920? How did Attorney General Palmer react?

5. Describe the goals and methods of the new Ku Klux Klan.

6. **Demonstrating Reasoned Judgment.** How and why was the Prohibition amendment approved? What were some of its results?

2. Searching for the good old days

The rash of postwar fears and headaches—bombs, Bolsheviks, riots, and strikes—made many Americans yearn for the "good old days." The nation was tired of their preacher-President. They wondered whether the United States should try to settle the problems of turbulent old Europe and the world. Their election of the Republicans' Warren G.

Harding and Calvin Coolidge showed the desire of Americans to turn inward. "America's present need," Harding explained, "is not heroics, but healing, not nostrums but normalcy, not revolution but restoration, not surgery but serenity."

Warren G. Harding. President Harding had started as the owner of a weekly paper in the small town of Marion, Ohio. His newspaper grew and prospered with the town, and he became a power in state politics. He had served in Ohio's senate and as lieutenant governor and had just completed a term as a United States Senator. When he was nominated for the nation's highest office, he had little training and even less capacity to be President of the United States. But he was friendly and likable. Silver haired and dignified, he looked so much like a President that voters easily imagined he had other qualifications, too. The Republicans picked him because the party was badly divided between its abler men—General Leonard Wood, Governor Frank Lowden of Illinois, and Herbert Hoover. The little-known Harding had few enemies.

Harding got off to a promising start. He seemed to know his own limitations and said he would choose some of the "best minds" to help him. And that he did. Charles Evans Hughes, one of the wisest Republicans in the country, was named Secretary of State. Herbert Hoover became Secretary of Commerce. Andrew W. Mellon, one of the nation's richest men and a wizard of finance, headed the Treasury. He would remain there for twelve years under three Presidents. Henry C. Wallace, widely known as the editor of a farm journal and a champion of conservation, became Secretary of Agriculture.

Some of Harding's other appointments were less wise, and a few were disastrous. Albert B. Fall of New Mexico, an old friend from Harding's Senate days, was named Secretary of the Interior. But he was opposed to conservation. That seemed an odd qualification for the head of a department founded to conserve the nation's resources. For Attorney General the President chose Harry Daugherty of Ohio. His only recommendation for the job was that he had "groomed" Harding for the Presidency and managed his campaign. It soon appeared that this would be a government by "cronies." The least able and more self-seeking officials seemed to be in charge. Harding's old friends, who spent more time

Brown Brothers

In 1923 Harding became the first President to address the American people over the radio.

playing cards together than planning the national welfare, came to be called the "Ohio Gang." They were not ashamed to use their offices to enrich themselves. Their crimes would make the weak Harding a synonym for incompetence, and their activities would help bring about his death.

Foreign affairs. As President, Harding was out of his depth. The affairs of the larger world were really too much for him, but he tried to seem decisive. In his inaugural address he declared that he wanted nothing to do with the League of Nations. "We seek no part in directing the destinies of the Old World," he said. "We asked the sons of this republic to defend our national rights, not to purge the Old World of the accumulated ills of rivalry and greed." As a result the Versailles Treaty was ignored, and the United States made a separate peace with Germany. It was signed by Harding on July 2, 1921.

The First World War had shown that when the world was at war no one could feel at peace. The great island-nations, Great Britain and Japan, needed strong navies—both for commerce and to protect their shores. And the United States was a two-ocean nation. After the war, each of these nations built up its navy. The world was supposed to be at peace, but these countries seemed to be preparing for war at sea. Where would it end?

Few Americans wanted to pay the cost of an arms race. At the call of President Harding, delegates from nine great powers with interests in the Far East met in Washington in the fall of 1921.

From their meetings three treaties emerged in 1922. In the *Five Power Treaty,* Great Britain, Japan, the United States, France, and Italy agreed to limit the number of their capital ships (vessels over 10,000 tons displacement). They would scrap 2 million tons of ships. The two biggest powers—Great Britain and the United States—each were allowed to keep 500,000 tons, Japan 300,000 tons, and France and Italy 175,000. In addition the powers agreed not to build any more forts or naval bases on their possessions in the Pacific—except for Hawaii.

Once the treaty was concluded, the Western powers feared that they had given Japan a free hand in the Pacific. They then managed to obtain the so-called *Nine Power Treaty.* This protected Western interests by binding all to observe the Open Door in China. They promised to respect China's integrity and not seek land or special privileges there.

To free Great Britain from its military alliance with Japan, a *Four Power Treaty* was signed between the United States, Great Britain, Japan, and France. They agreed to respect one another's possessions in the Pacific. Any issue that seemed likely to disturb the peace of the Far East would be sent to a joint conference. The Senate, though still fearing entangling alliances, accepted this treaty. But the senators did so with the reservation that the United States assumed "no commitment to armed force, no alliance, no obligation to join in any joint defense."

The Washington Conference was the first successful disarmament conference in modern history. But there was no way to enforce the agreements. Japan, with expanding industry and a growing population crowded onto its islands, was determined to become a great power. These treaties

provided a decade of peace. They also gave Japan the time to organize and to become a great Asian power without interference. Still, our nation's relations with Japan could not be happy so long as the Immigration Act of 1924 was in effect as an insult to the Japanese people.

Harding's domestic program. The way back to "normalcy," as Harding found, was a rocky road. A sharp decline in business began in 1920. To deal with the problems of depression and conversion to peacetime, the President called Congress into special session in April 1921. He asked for higher tariffs, lower taxes, less government spending, and aid to disabled soldiers and to farmers.

One of his proposals would open a new era in planning federal spending. He asked Congress to create a bureau to sift the money demands of each department. All requests would go into a single budget to be sent to Congress for its review and approval. For the first time, Congress and the people would be able to see all at one time and in one document how the government intended to spend the people's money. In response, Congress passed the Budget and Accounting Act. This set up the Bureau of the Budget. At the same time a General Accounting Office headed by a Comptroller General would check to see that the money was spent for the legal purposes and would recommend economies.

The President proposed new high tariffs to protect farmers from Canadian competition. An emergency tariff raised duties on 28 farm products. The next year the Fordney-McCumber tariff gave industrialists, too, the protection they wanted.

The effects of these trade barriers were not good. The Fordney-McCumber Act clogged the flow of foreign trade. Europeans needed to sell their goods here in order to get dollars to buy our products. To no one's surprise, then, European nations retaliated by raising their tariffs against goods from the United States. American business firms had trouble selling their products abroad. The tariff race, like the arms race, would be costly to everybody.

Secretary of the Treasury Mellon asked that the high wartime taxes (to support the armed forces) at once be reduced. Industry would not grow without more capital investment, which he believed the wartime taxes were preventing. In 1921 Congress repealed the wartime excess profits tax on industry. It also reduced the top level of taxes on the wealthy from 65 percent to 50 percent. (Mellon had wanted it to be 25 percent.) Congress also lowered taxes for middle- and lower-income people, which Mellon had not asked for. Mellon finally had his way in 1924 when a new tax bill reduced the top tax to 25 percent. In the next few years it was cut even more. During one tax debate someone observed that Mellon would receive a larger personal reduction than all the taxpayers in the state of Nebraska put together.

The bonus bill. When a war veteran was discharged, he received a "bonus" of $60. Disabled veterans could get hospital care and other special benefits. Veterans' organizations were demanding that those who had served in the armed forces in wartime deserved special treatment when the nation enjoyed the peace they had helped to bring. They asked for another and larger "bonus." Harding argued that the soldiers had never expected a bonus. He said that serving in the army was only their patriotic duty. He vetoed the "bonus" bill, and Congress failed to override his veto.

The veterans' groups kept up their pressure. In the spring of 1924, after Calvin Coolidge had become President, a new bonus bill (the Adjusted Compensation Act) was passed. This gave a veteran an insurance policy totaling in value $1.25 for every day spent overseas and $1 a day for service in the United States. Veterans could borrow up to 25 percent of the value of their policies. Coolidge vetoed the bill, but Congress easily passed it over his veto.

The war debts. The $9 billion in war debts owed to the United States by its former allies—Great Britain, France, and Italy—created a baffling problem. This money had been mostly spent in the United States to finance the war against Germany. The Allied powers argued that the United States should cancel the war debts because the money had been spent also in defense of the United States.

The Harding administration insisted that the war debts should not be canceled. So they were paid back in installments. The money came from the huge reparations the Versailles Treaty forced Germany to give the victorious European nations to repair the damage caused by the war. And the only way Germany could pay was by borrowing from the United States. With the depression of the 1930s, this whole merry-go-round stopped. Only Finland ever paid its entire debt.

The death of Harding. While the whole world was trying to find a way out of these vast and puzzling problems, Americans were plagued by corruption and by the bad judgment of their President. In 1923 Harding began to hear stories about what some of his "Ohio Gang" had been up to. He had made the mistake of appointing a chance acquaintance, Colonel Charles R. Forbes, head of the Veterans Bureau. This was a huge enterprise that had charge of the hospitals and all other forms of veterans' relief. In two years $250 million was wasted or stolen from these programs. Even after Attorney General Daugherty told Harding of the rumors about Forbes, the President, ever loyal to his friends, let Forbes leave the country. From Europe, Forbes resigned. When the Senate began a probe of the Forbes case, the Veterans Bureau's legal adviser, Charles F. Cramer, committed suicide.

Soon after hearing about Forbes, Harding learned that Jesse Smith, Daugherty's close friend and aide in the Justice Department, had been selling his influence. Smith himself committed suicide in May 1923.

The stories about Harding's "friends" revealed a scale of corruption not known since the days of President Grant. The pleasant, easygoing President was shocked. "I have no trouble with my enemies," Harding said. It was his friends who kept him "walking the floors at night."

The saddened President left Washington for a trip to the West Coast and Alaska in June 1923. During the trip he asked Secretary Hoover and others again and again what a man should do when he had been betrayed by his friends. During his travels Harding was taken ill. He died suddenly in the evening of August 2, 1923.

The Harding scandals. The nation mourned Harding's death. Soon the truth about his administration began to come out. At first the probes were called mere efforts at "character assassination" of Harding. But not for long. Forbes was sent to Leavenworth prison for two years. Thomas W. Miller, Alien Property Custodian, was also sent to

Jones, Brakeley & Rockwell, Inc. © *Life—The Humor Magazine*

The attempt of Harding's associates to enrich themselves by selling and leasing public property for their own profit brought this reaction from a cartoonist. Everything—from Cabinet members to the Mint—could be bought at bargain prices. Honor and ethics were "practically given away."

jail for selling for the profit of the Ohio Gang valuable property taken from the Germans during wartime. Attorney General Daugherty was tried, but he was not convicted.

The most sensational of the scandals was the attempted theft of the national oil reserves. Oil had taken the place of coal to power the ships of the navy. It had become a prime need for commerce and national defense. The government in 1912–1915 had set aside three promising oil fields as reserves for the nation's future. But Harding's Secretary of the Interior, Albert Fall, leased two of these—Teapot Dome in Wyoming, and Elk Hills in California—to private interests in return for $325,000 in gifts and "loans." Fall ended up with a year in prison, and the leases were later canceled by the Supreme Court.

SECTION 2 REVIEW

1. Identify or explain: Charles E. Hughes, Andrew Mellon, Henry C. Wallace, Albert B. Fall, Harry Daugherty, "Ohio Gang," Budget and Accounting Act, General Accounting Office.

2. What did the Harding administration accomplish in (a) control of spending? (b) tariff revision? (c) tax cutting?

3. What scandals took place during Harding's administration? Was Harding to blame?

4. **Identifying Central Issues.** Why was the Washington Conference historically significant even though the terms of the agreement were unenforceable?

3. "Keeping cool with Coolidge"

Vice-President Calvin Coolidge was spending his vacation at his father's home in the little village of Plymouth Notch, Vermont, when he was awakened with the news of Harding's death. By the light of a kerosene lamp his father, John Coolidge, a justice of the peace, administered the oath of office.

Coolidge had never even seen Washington, D.C., before he became Vice-President. He had hardly ventured beyond the borders of his native state of Vermont or neighboring Massachusetts, where he had built his political career. He had been mayor of Northampton, lieutenant governor, and then governor of Massachusetts. Home for Coolidge, his wife, Grace, and their two sons was half a double house in Northampton. This he rented for $27 a month.

President Coolidge. If a playwright had invented a character to contrast with Harding, he could not have done better. Harding was a genial, unbuttoned good fellow who liked to sit around the White House smoking cigars and playing cards with his cronies. This new President was reticent, plain, and thrifty. A man of few words, "Silent Cal" was not one to warm the cockles of your heart. He naturally tempted comedians to make jokes about his quiet manner and his immobile face. Once when a rumor started that he had died, a wit remarked, "How would you know?"

But Coolidge was like Harding in one way. He too was an admirer of American business. His best-known utterance was: "The business of America is business." Like Harding, he was anxious not to trouble business with government rules. In the 1900s Calvin Coolidge still shared Thomas Jefferson's belief that the government is best which governs least.

The election of 1924. This let-alone policy fit the temper of the times. Most Americans were tired of the rules and rationing of the war years. Coolidge followed the Harding policies. Only a year after Coolidge had been thrust into the White House, the Republicans meeting in Cleveland chose him to run for President in the next election. Charles G. Dawes, a banker who had served ably as Director of the Budget, was named for Vice-President.

When photographers began to follow Presidents everywhere, they took pictures of them in all sorts of situations. "Silent Cal," who never appeared comfortable in front of a camera, can be seen here posed stiffly in a hayfield. It seems doubtful that he intended to do any real work.

When the democrats met in their convention, the party was deeply divided. The split in the party mirrored a split in the nation. The Americans who still made their living on farms were troubled by the new ways of life in the growing cities. City dwellers believed they were the vanguard of progress. By a one-vote margin the convention actually refused to denounce the Ku Klux Klan (p. 483) by name. There were dozens of candidates who took advantage of the confusion.

Finally the main battle was between William G. McAdoo of California and Al Smith of New York. McAdoo, Woodrow Wilson's son-in-law, had served as Wilson's energetic and able Secretary of the Treasury and wartime director of the railroads. He was the candidate favored by the rural South and West. The colorful city politician Alfred E. Smith had left school at eleven. He had received his education on the sidewalks of New York, which was easy to tell because he spoke with a resounding New York accent. He was opposed to Prohibition, and he was a devout Roman Catholic.

Between Smith and McAdoo the convention deadlocked. After 102 ballots, the weary delegates settled on the safe and colorless John W. Davis. He was a conservative New York corporation lawyer. For Vice-President the Democrats chose William Jennings Bryan's brother, Governor Charles W. Bryan of Nebraska. At last the delegates could go home after sixteen days spent in the hot Madison Square Garden in New York City.

The Republicans, like the Democrats, would also suffer from the division between the city and the country. When the Republican convention adjourned, "Battling Bob" La Follette of Wisconsin broke with his party. Coolidge, he said, "had literally turned his back on the farmers." Senator La Follette himself then ran for President as the candidate of a new Progressive party. Both Republicans and Democrats attacked La Follette as a dangerous radical.

When the votes were counted, it was plain that most Americans preferred to "keep cool with Coolidge." He received 15 million votes to Davis's 8.5 million and La Follette's surprisingly large 4.8 million. During that election 123 women won seats in state legislatures. And two women, Miriam A. "Ma" Ferguson of Texas and Nellie T. Ross of Wyoming, wives of former governors, were elected governors of their states.

UPI/Bettmann Archive

The Democratic convention of 1924 took 103 ballots to nominate a presidential candidate. Among the delegates and alternates were many women, including this group from Missouri.

Government helps business. "If the federal government should go out of existence," President Coolidge once said, "the common run of the people would not detect the difference for a considerable length of time." That was the way he thought it ought to be. For him "free enterprise" simply meant the freedom of business from government rules. Regulation, he believed, would make business less profitable. And, according to Coolidge, it was profitable businesses that made the whole nation happy and prosperous. "The man who builds a factory builds a temple," he declared. "The man who works there worships there." Some people said the President was making business into a religion.

Regulatory agencies, like the Federal Trade Commission and the Federal Reserve Board, were put in the charge of men who would help the businesses they were supposed to regulate. The FTC urged whole industries to agree on trade policies. Some of these agreements tended to create monopolies. Secretary of Commerce Hoover also promoted these "fair practice" agreements so that industries could share information on products and markets. Hoover believed that the day of cutthroat competition was over. Now, he thought, the Department of Commerce should help them cooperate for better products and higher output.

The Supreme Court helped this process along. In 1920 the Court ruled that United States Steel was not a monopoly even though the company controlled 40 percent of the steel industry. This still did not, the Court said, "unreasonably restrain trade." With this green light—and with the help of Hoover and the regulatory agencies—companies all across the land merged to create larger units. By 1929, only 1289 firms produced three-fourths of all goods turned out by corporations. In many industries a few big firms were setting prices through trade associations. The Supreme Court still said that these industrial trade groups were not restraining trade.

And the country prospered. Most Americans were doing better. The price of shares on the stock market was going up rapidly. The economic picture looked promising.

The farm problem. There were a few areas that were slow to recover after the war. The textile, leather, and soft coal industries were weak. Blacks, Indians, and Mexican Americans still had little share in American prosperity. The obvious big problem was the distress on the farms. Now no one could ignore this problem, because the farmers had learned to speak up.

Farmers were growing poorer while much of the rest of the country was growing richer. It seemed that the more they produced, the less they were paid for their crops. At the same time their clothes, their farm implements, their fuel, and the other products they had to buy were going up. Their taxes were rising. When the farmers demanded help, they did get higher tariff protection. But this did little good. High tariffs on farm products could not keep prices up when there were surplus crops.

Now the farmers demanded more direct aid. Senator McNary of Oregon and Representative Haugen of Iowa devised a scheme to use government money to save the farmer from the free market. The idea behind their complex plan was to keep up the price of staple crops regardless of what happened to other prices. The federal government would buy the surpluses that would have driven down farm prices if they went on the open market. The government then would either hold the produce until the market for it improved or it would sell the produce abroad. The McNary-Haugen bill failed to pass Congress in 1924 and 1926. In the next two years it did pass, but Coolidge vetoed it each time. "Farmers have never made money," he said. "I don't believe we can do much about it."

The election of 1928. Near the end of his fourth year in office, Calvin Coolidge announced (in one of his *longer* speeches), "I do not choose to run for President in 1928." In his place the Republicans named the able and ambitious Secretary of Commerce, Herbert Hoover.

The Democrats nominated the "Happy Warrior," Alfred E. Smith. Smith had made a superb record as governor of New York. He had been opposed by many bigoted Democrats from the small towns and from the South who feared that a Catholic President would be only an agent of the Pope. But this time they were not strong enough to deny him the nomination he deserved.

Party platforms were not important in this election. Instead it was what the candidates seemed to stand for. Al Smith, with his New York East Side accent, his brown derby and cigar, and his Roman Catholic religion, was the image of the big city. City people liked his call for the repeal of Prohibition and the return of liquor control laws to the states. Hoover, on the other hand, seemed to stand for big business, for small town and rural America, and for Protestantism and Prohibition.

Prohibition and Smith's Catholic religion were the chief issues of the campaign. Smith met the religious issue squarely. He said that his devotion to his church meant as well devotion to the Constitution and the principle of separation of church and state. But his nomination stirred up much prejudice and fear, especially in the rural South and Middle West where the new Ku Klux Klan had been strongest.

The Bettmann Archive, Inc.

Herbert and Lou Hoover greet the crowd from their train at a "whistlestop" during the 1928 campaign.

Culver Pictures

Ever the "happy warrior," Al Smith waves to his enthusiastic supporters who line the streets of New York City in the midst of his race with Hoover.

Even without the Catholic issue Hoover could scarcely have failed to win in 1928. Although he lacked personality, his humanitarian record in the war and his policies in the Department of Commerce had made him popular. The country was prosperous, and most Americans were still Republicans. Few observers were surprised when Hoover trounced Smith. He received 21 million votes to Smith's 15 million and captured all but eight states. He even carried five states in the formerly solid South—the first Republican to do so since the days of Reconstruction.

Hoover's easy victory hid some trends that were important for the Democrats. Smith had attracted many new votes in the twelve largest cities, which had formerly been strongly Republican. For the first time since the Civil War, these population centers showed a net plurality for the Democrats. The key to future elections would be in these cities that could carry the big states with their large

electoral votes. But for now this crucial fact was hidden by the rosy glow of Republican prosperity.

SECTION 3 REVIEW

1. Identify or explain: Charles G. Dawes, William G. McAdoo, Al Smith, John W. Davis, Charles Bryan, Progressive party, Miriam Ferguson.

2. What were some unusual features of the campaign and the election of 1924?

3. In the 1920s how was business "helped" by (a) Coolidge's attitude toward business? (b) the regulatory agencies? (c) the Supreme Court?

4. Why were farmers in trouble in the 1920s? How did Congress propose to help them? What was Coolidge's response?

5. **Making Comparisons.** Who were the presidential candidates in 1928? How did they differ?

4. Life in the Jazz Age

During the 1920s the United States seemed a land of miracles. Never before were factories making so many new things. Never before had the daily life of a nation been so quickly transformed.

New products for living. At the opening of the 1900s the automobile was still such an oddity that in Vermont the law required a driver to send someone an eighth of a mile ahead with a red flag. By 1918 there were nearly 7 million cars on the road. Auto and truck production topped the 2 million mark in 1922 and climbed to more than 5 million in 1929. With the spread of automobiles came the building of new highways and the paving of the roads. Now Americans no longer had to live close together and near their jobs and shops. They could work and shop in places too far to walk to, and out of reach of a streetcar. The first "shopping center" for the newly mobile American was built in Kansas City in 1922.

Back in 1900 the closest thing to a movie was the crude "nickelodeon." In return for your nickel you looked into a box to see pictures move for a few minutes. In 1929 one hundred million tickets were being sold to the movies every week, and the movies could actually talk!

Until World War I most Americans had not even heard of the radio. The first broadcasting station—KDKA in Pittsburgh—did not open until 1920. Its first broadcast carried the Harding-Cox election returns. By 1929 the annual turnout of radio sets numbered 4 million. Television was still in the future. It seemed amazing enough that voices could be sent without wires.

The phonograph was a commercial success by 1905, and within ten years half a million phonograph records were being sold annually. By 1921 production had reached 100 million a year, and a music new to many Americans was sweeping the land. Blacks moving north during World War I brought with them their jazz and blues, and soon recording companies began making records of these surprising sounds. Blacks were now giving the United States a fresh kind of original American music. New heroes and heroines appeared on the scene—Louis Armstrong, "Duke" Ellington, "King" Oliver, Earl "Fatha'" Hines, Ferdinand Joseph La-Menthe Morton, known as "Jelly Roll," Bessie Smith, and many others.

During the 1920s everyone began to want a refrigerator to replace the inconvenient old ice box. At the beginning of the decade only about 5000 mechanical refrigerators were made each year. By 1931 over a million a year were being produced by the nation's factories. Now even city people could easily keep milk and fresh fruit and vegetables in all seasons.

Health and education. With advancing medical knowledge now at last the diseases that most threatened children—typhoid, diphtheria, and measles—were coming under control. Americans were healthier and were living longer than ever before. They were also making the highest wages in history—and working shorter hours.

Education in the United States was better and reached a larger proportion of the people than in any other country. By 1928 the money that Americans spent each year for education was more than that spent by all the rest of the world put together. In most European countries only a grade school education was free. But in the United States a free high school education was normal, and millions could hope to go to college.

"The Roaring Twenties." The 1920s have been called "the Roaring Twenties." And with good reason. There were the speakeasies (the illegal bars) and the flappers (young women with short hair and short skirts). There was the new music— jazz, ragtime, and blues suddenly blaring out of millions of phonographs and radios. For the first time in our history huge crowds gathered to watch sporting events. In a single ball park on many afternoons 50,000 fans cheered Babe Ruth as he was breaking all records with his home runs. One hundred forty-five thousand people paid $2.6 million to watch the second fight between Gene Tunney and Jack Dempsey. And a charming young southern gentleman from Georgia named Bobby Jones delighted the nation by defeating the world's best at golf.

The climax of national pride and excitement came May 21, 1927. That night the handsome Charles A. Lindbergh, "Lucky Lindy," landed in Paris. He had made the first solo nonstop flight from New York to Paris in 33 1/2 hours. The nation was inspired to see how courage and the airplane could shrink the Atlantic Ocean. Millions

COSMO HAMILTON'S *New Serial* "Daughters of Folly"

McCLURE'S

August   25 Cents

Culver Pictures

John Held, Jr., helped to create the image of "flappers" and "flaming youth" in the 1920s.

of New Yorkers roared their admiring welcome when he returned. As he was paraded through the streets, 1800 tons of shredded paper rained down from the surrounding skyscrapers. Americans admired Lindbergh's modesty as much as his bravery. He called his book *We* and always shared credit for his feat with his airplane, with those who built it, and with all the Americans who had made his adventure possible. The nation had a new hero—and a new kind of hero. He toured the nation to encourage the rise of air mail and to promote air travel.

The roar of the factory. More than the roar of music or crowds, the sounds that marked the twenties were the hum of the electric dynamo, the clatter of machines, the rhythm of the factory assembly line. The nation was finding and making new ways to manufacture radios, refrigerators, airplanes, automobiles, and all sorts of gadgets by the millions. Now a great new force—electric power—was added to the steam power that drove the first modern factories.

The ideas of Frederick W. Taylor on "scientific management" (p. 366) became more and more popular with employers. By making a science of the simplest jobs, they could find a better way to do them.

Charles Lindbergh was the first person to fly nonstop between New York and Paris and the first to fly across the Atlantic alone. He is shown here with his plane in which he made the flight. "The Spirit of St. Louis" can be seen at the National Air and Space Museum, Washington, D.C.

Culver Pictures

Henry Ford's assembly line introduced a new standard for efficiency in mass production. Instead of going from task to task, workers stayed in place and a moving belt brought their work to them.

In an astonishingly short time the American factory took on a different look. Scientific management engineers invented a whole new way of organizing a factory. Instead of having you walk around to pick up parts and bring them to your workbench, the management engineers designed a workbench that moved. Then you could stay in one place and keep your mind on your proper job. The bench (now a moving belt driven by electricity) would carry along the heavy parts from one worker to another.

This new kind of moving workbench was called an "assembly line" because on it the whole machine was put together or "assembled."

In April 1913 a bold mechanic named Henry Ford decided to try an assembly line for making automobiles. He wanted to make cars so cheaply that he could sell them by the millions. He made some improvements of his own in the assembly line. For example, he arranged the moving belt so that it would always be "man-high." Nobody had to waste energy bending down or reaching up.

Ford also varied the speed of the belt. He explained:

> The idea is that a man must not be hurried in his work—he must have every second necessary but not a single unnecessary second. . . . The man who puts in a bolt does not put on the nut; the man who puts on the nut does not tighten it. On operation number 34 the budding motor gets its gasoline. . . . On operation number 44 the radiator is filled with water, and on operation number 45 the car drives out.

Henry Ford opened his new plant with its electric-powered conveyor belt in 1914, and the time it took to put together a Model T dropped from 14 hours to 93 minutes. By 1925 the process was so perfect that one car rolled off the assembly line every 10 seconds. Machines that had not been imagined 50 years before now cost so little that they changed the lives of ordinary Americans.

Selling the products of the factories. There grew up a powerful American business to sell this outpouring of new products. Advertising had been around for a long time, but only about $1 billion a year was spent on it before World War I. By 1929 more than $3 billion a year was spent for advertising through newspapers, magazines, billboards, direct mail, and—fastest growing of all—the radio. Advertisements for consumer goods promised comfort, health, beauty, status.

Even more important in selling goods was buying on credit. Now you did not have to wait to buy what you wanted until you had saved enough money. "Buy Now, Pay Later," the ads screamed. By 1928 Americans owed more than $1 billion for the automobiles they had bought on the installment plan.

Buying "on time" can help keep business booming so long as people can afford to buy all that the factories produce. But in the 1920s wages did not rise as fast as output. The real wages of American workers rose 26 percent between 1918 and 1929 while their productivity was going up 40 percent. Without more money, workers could not buy—even "on time"—all the automobiles, refrigerators, radios, washing machines, vacuum cleaners, and other expensive items that fueled the economy.

Most Americans were unaware of any problems. They agreed with Herbert Hoover who caught the spirit of the time in his inaugural address in March 1929:

> Ours is a land rich in resources, stimulating in its glorious beauty, filled with millions of happy homes, blessed with comfort and opportunity. In no nation are the institutions of progress more advanced. In no nation are the fruits of accomplishment more secure. In no nation is the Government more worthy of respect. No country is more loved by its people. I have an abiding faith in their capacity, integrity, and high purpose. I have no fears for the future. . . . It is bright with hope.

Culver Pictures

Some automakers emphasized color and style. Henry Ford said his customers could have *any* color—so long as it was black!

SECTION 4 REVIEW

1. What kinds of new consumer goods and services became widespread in the 1920s?

2. What changes were making factory production more efficient?

3. **Drawing Conclusions.** Why was "roaring" an appropriate description of the decade of the 1920s?

CHAPTER 22 REVIEW

FOCUSING ON IDEAS

1. Identify some groups who suffered from the fears and hysteria of the early 1920s. How did they suffer? Why were they the targets of fear and government investigation?

2. The radicals in the 1920s included anarchists, socialists, and communists. What were the beliefs of each of these groups? Why were they considered dangerous by some Americans? Should all of these radical groups have been regarded as equally dangerous? Explain.

3. Many Americans in the early 1920s yearned for a return to the calmer prewar era. What postwar changes might they have found disturbing? What changes occurring later in the 1920s might most Americans have found agreeable? From your lists of the two kinds of changes, what conclusion can you draw about the kinds of social and cultural changes that Americans will be likely to resist and the kinds they will welcome in the future?

TAKING A CRITICAL LOOK

1. **Recognizing Cause and Effect.** How did governmental support help business to prosper?

2. **Making Comparisons.** Compare postwar corruption under Grant and under Harding. Consider the nature and extent of the fraud, the parties involved, and the President's role in it.

YOUR REGION IN HISTORY

1. **Culture.** Trace the migration of black Americans from or to your region, state, or locality during and after World War I. If substantial numbers of blacks moved to your region, what kinds of jobs did they find? How were they treated?

2. **Economics.** Trace the history of a local business in your area. How was it affected by government controls? What role did labor unions play in its development? How, if at all, did it use "scientific management"?

HISTORICAL FACTS AND FIGURES

Recognizing Cause and Effect. Study the graph below to help answer the following questions: (a) How many cars does each figure in the pictogram stand for? (b) In what year were the most cars sold? (c) In what year were the least sold? (d) By approximately what percentage did car sales increase during the decade of the 1920s? (e) What information in this chapter helps explain why more Americans were able to buy cars in 1929 than in 1920? (f) What other businesses or industries would have expanded as a consequence of increased car sales?

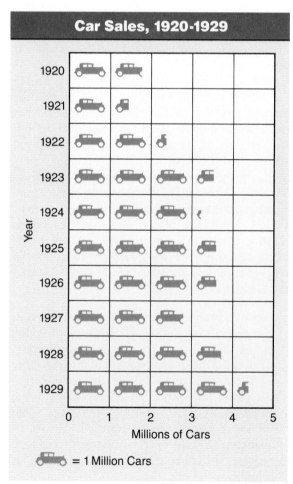

Source: *Historical Statistics of the United States*

498

The coming of the Great Depression

When Herbert Hoover took the oath of office in March 1929, trade was booming, industry was flourishing. Unemployment was low, wages were up, prices were steady, and corporations were making big profits and paying fat dividends. Some people had not felt this tide of prosperity, but even they seemed to take it for granted that their time would come.

Yet before the end of Hoover's first year in office, the stock market had collapsed. The nation was beginning to slide into the worst depression in its history. And by the time Hoover left office in 1933, many citizens had lost faith in their business leaders. Some had begun to question the American economic system and even democracy itself.

1. A prosperous nation

Most Americans were confident that with Hoover, the Great Engineer, at the helm, their country's growth and prosperity would never end. Progress, it seemed, must go on forever. Then, in late October 1929, came terrifying signs that the success story might have an unhappy ending.

Herbert Hoover, engineer. Herbert Hoover was a perfect symbol of the ideals and hopes of the American business community in the 1920s. He showed that to succeed in the United States and to be elected President you did not have to come from a rich, upper-class family. His life proved that in America character, intelligence, and hard work could make a national leader. Born of Quaker parents on a small farm in Iowa in 1874, he had been orphaned at the age of ten. He worked his way through Stanford University, where he studied engineering. Then he made his fortune as a mining

engineer—in Australia, Africa, China, Latin America, and Russia. He was a millionaire by the time he was 40.

When World War I broke out, Hoover was living in London. His Quaker heritage and his desire to soften the miseries of war drew him quickly into relief work. He did a speedy and spectacular job as head of the Commission for Relief, which fed 10 million starving people in Belgium and northeastern France. When we entered the war, he came home to lead the Food Administration. And at the war's end, Wilson put him in charge of economic relief for all Europe. Hoover and his team, as English economist John Maynard Keynes observed, "not only saved an immense amount of human suffering, but averted a widespread breakdown of the European system."

"The ungrateful governments of Europe," Keynes added, "owe much more to the statesmanship and insight of Mr. Hoover and his band of

The future of the country looked bright on March 4, 1929, as Calvin Coolidge (left) and Herbert Hoover posed for this picture just before going to Hoover's inauguration.

American workers than they have yet appreciated or will ever acknowledge."

In September 1919 when Hoover returned to the United States, he was a national figure—though it was not clear to what political party he belonged. "He is certainly a wonder," Assistant Secretary of the Navy Franklin D. Roosevelt then wrote, "and I wish we could make him President of the United States. There could not be a better one."

Had Hoover played his cards right, he might have been nominated—and elected—in 1920. Instead, he declared that he was a Republican, without lining up the support of that party. Now the Democrats could not nominate him. The Republican bosses could hold him in reserve, meanwhile naming a man they could control—Warren G. Harding.

If Hoover had become President in 1920, he might have established a reputation in the next eight years as one of our most successful Presidents in times of prosperity. Instead he became Secretary of Commerce under Harding and Coolidge. He made the young Department of Commerce an important new force in government. With the focus of an engineer, he formed an Office of Simplified Practice. The more efficient ways devised by this office saved business and government more money than the entire budget of the Department of Commerce.

Hoover's beliefs. Hoover believed in the American capitalist system. He had shared its success. And he had seen it become more responsible. He did not believe in big government, but he saw the federal government playing a larger role than imagined by Harding or Coolidge. He declared for the nation the credo of his own life:

> It is as if we set a race. We through free and universal education provide the training of the runners; we give to them an equal start; we provide in the government the umpire of fairness in the race. The winner is he who shows the most conscientious training, the greatest ability, and the greatest character.

The stock market boom. When Hoover took office, the country was in the grip of a speculative fever. The New York stock market was where people bought and sold stocks—"shares"—in the largest corporations. The owner of a share really owned part of the company. If the company grew and made a large profit, then the owner of the share would be paid a dividend as part of the profit. And if the dividends grew, the value of the share would go up. Naturally, everybody wanted to own shares in the most profitable companies.

Stock prices began to increase from 1921 on. But the stock market mania did not begin until 1927. Then many people started to buy shares hoping to make their profits not from the earnings of the company, but from the higher price that other stock market gamblers would pay them for their shares. More and more people began risking their money in the stock market. They expected to get rich when the price of their shares would suddenly go up. And with the money they made, they would buy other shares that they hoped would also go up.

Brokers at the Curb Market in New York buy and sell stock for their clients. During the 1920s speculating in stocks became a nationwide mania.

Margin loans. People borrowed on "margin" to buy stocks. When buying on margin, all you had to do was put down a small amount of cash to buy each share of stock. Then you could borrow the rest of the purchase price on the value of the stock itself. When the stock went up in price, you could make a great deal of money on a small investment. But if the price went down, you could lose all you had put in. For a time, stock prices appeared only to go up. Everyone seemed to know someone who had grown rich overnight.

Stock market gambling became a mania, a contagious disease. Americans who never would have thought of borrowing money to bet on the horse races now were borrowing to bet on stocks. The more the stock mania grew, the less connection there was between the real value of a company and the price people were paying for that company's shares on the stock market. Businesses found they could make more money with their cash by giving it to brokers to use for margin loans than by investing in new machines and factories.

Some people voiced concern over what was happening on the stock market, and especially over the size of brokers' margin loans. President Coolidge said it was only due to the "natural expansion of business." But later he told a reporter that "any loan made for gambling in stocks [is] 'excessive.'"

SECTION 1 REVIEW

1. What experiences qualified Herbert Hoover for the Presidency?

2. What are the two ways in which a person can make a gain by owning corporation stock?

3. **Recognizing Cause and Effect.** What was the effect of margin loans on the stock market boom?

2. The big crash

On September 3, 1929, the booming rise in the market came quietly to a halt. Even though a few stocks later reached new highs, the market began a slow decline. Soon the decline would become a collapse. It would wipe out the speculators, stop the economy, and lead to the greatest depression in United States history.

Black Thursday. During October the stock market had some bad days. Then, suddenly, on October 24 ("Black Thursday" it would be called) prices began to fall, and buyers on margin had to sell their stocks. The rush to sell made prices fall even faster.

On Black Thursday, New York's most powerful bankers met at the offices of J. P. Morgan & Co. They decided to pool their resources to the amount of $30 million to support the stock market. The action of the bankers was confirmed when Richard Whitney, the acting president of the Stock Exchange and a known agent of the Morgan firm, began placing orders above current prices. Prices at once began to move upward. At the end of the day the market had recovered much of its earlier losses. Some speculators had been wiped out during the course of the wild day, but the panic seemed over. On Friday and Saturday, prices remained steady. From Washington, President Hoover, who had never approved of the speculation, reassured the

This was the *New York Times* headline on the morning of October 29, 1929. Worse was still to come.

STOCK PRICES SLUMP $14,000,000,000 IN NATION-WIDE STAMPEDE TO UNLOAD; BANKERS TO SUPPORT MARKET TODAY

Sixteen Leading Issues Down $2,893,520,108; Tel. & Tel. and Steel Among Heaviest Losers

A shrinkage of $2,893,520,108 in the open market value of the shares of sixteen representative companies resulted from yesterday's sweeping decline on the New York Stock Exchange.

American Telephone and Telegraph was the heaviest loser, $448,905,162 having been lopped off of its total value. United States Steel common, traditional bellwether of the stock market, made its greatest nose-dive in recent years by falling from a high of 202½ to a low of 185. In a feeble last-minute rally it snapped back to 186, at which it closed, showing a net loss of 17½ points. This represented for the 8,131,055 shares of common stock outstanding a total loss in value of $142,293,446.

In the following table are shown the day's net depreciation in the outstanding shares of the sixteen companies referred to:

Issues.	Shares Listed.	Losses in Points.	Depreciation.
American Radiator	10,096,289	10⅜	$104,748,997
American Tel. & Tel.	13,203,09?	34	448,905,162
Commonwealth & Southern	30,764,468	3⅛	96,138,962
Columbia Gas & Electric	8,477,307	22	186,500,754
Consolidated Gas	11,451,188	20	229,023,760
DuPont E. I.	10,322,481	16⅜	169,030,625
Eastman Kodak	2,229,703	41⅞	93,368,813
General Electric	7,211,484	47½	342,545,490
General Motors	43,500,000	6¾	293,625,000
International Nickel	13,777,408	7⅞	108,497,088
New York Central	4,637,036	22⅝	104,914,071
Standard Oil of New Jersey	24,843,643	8	198,749,144
Union Carbide & Carbon	8,730,173	20	174,615,460
United States Steel	8,131,055	17½	142,293,446
United Gas Improvement	18,616,835	6	111,881,010
Westinghouse Elec. & Mfg.	2,589,265	34½	88,682,326
			$2,893,520,108

PREMIER ISSUES HARD HIT

Unexpected Torrent of Liquidation Again Rocks Markets.

DAY'S SALES 9,212,800

Nearly 3,000,000 Shares Are Traded In Final Hour—The Tickers Lag 167 Minutes.

NEW RALLY SOON BROKEN

Selling by Europeans and "Mob Psychology" Big Factors in Second Big Break.

The second hurricane of liquidation within four days hit the stock market yesterday. It came suddenly, nation. "The fundamental business of the country," he said, "that is, the production and distribution of goods and services—is on a sound and prosperous basis."

The Great Crash. But on Monday prices again dropped rapidly. The bankers, who were overcommitted in the market themselves, now decided that they could do nothing. Black Tuesday, October 29, 1929, was the worst day of all—the worst day in the history of the New York Stock Exchange. Some 16.5 million shares changed hands (a record-high volume for 39 years). Prices fell steeply. The next day prices recovered somewhat, only to fall again the following day. And that became the pattern.

In the weeks that followed, the prices of stocks sank lower and lower. A share in U. S. Steel, which on September 3 had sold for $262, by November 13 had fallen to $150. A share in Montgomery Ward, which had hit $138, dropped to $49. The average price of 50 leading stocks sank by half. In the last four months of 1929 the overall value of stocks plummeted by $40 billion. And their fall would continue. U. S. Steel would drop to $22. Montgomery Ward would reach $4. General Motors, once at $73, would fall to $8.

The unequal distribution of wealth. Why should it matter, in 1929, if gamblers on the stock market lost their money? The automobile factories and the people with the know-how were still there, just as good as ever. The wealth of the land and the energy of the people were still there. America was still a good investment. Wasn't Hoover right that "the fundamental business" of America was sound?

President Hoover was not quite right. There were serious weaknesses in the economy that had hardly been noticed up to then. As we have seen, while the output of American workers increased steadily during the twenties, their wages had not kept pace (p. 497). At the same time, business profits and the incomes of the wealthy had shot up. In 1929 the 36,000 wealthiest families in America had a combined income equal to that of the nearly 12 million families with incomes of less than $1500 per year. Yet the cost of necessities for a family was $2000 per year.

This meant that "prosperity"—the whole economy—depended on the spending and reinvestment of their money by the wealthy and by business firms. When the stock market panic frightened them, they stopped spending and investing. And the mass of the people could not pick up the slack. They had bought all they could on time, and they had no spare cash. Most consumers could no longer afford to buy the new cars and radios and refrigerators. Inventories piled up. Factories laid off more and more workers.

Other flaws in the economy. Another weakness in the economy lay in our relations with the rest of the world. As a result of the war, many nations owed the United States money. Yet our tariff walls kept them from trading with us. So we had to make loans and investments abroad if the foreign nations were to pay us. Once the flow of American money slowed down, these nations could not pay their debts. And they could no longer afford to buy American goods. This was another cause for factories to shut down, throwing still more Americans out of work.

The rise of "holding companies" had created some special problems that did not quickly meet the eye. During the 1920s more and more of these companies had been formed to hold the stock of other companies. Business power was being concentrated in fewer hands. Also, investment trusts were set up to sell their own stock and then invest the proceeds in the stock market. Naturally, the investment trusts and holding companies depended on the earnings of the companies they held. If anything happened to those, the holding companies and investment trusts would collapse. Then confidence in business throughout the nation would drop even more.

But the worst flaw in the economy of the late 1920s was the stock market itself. It provided a gambling arena where whims, unfounded fears, and unjustified hopes could trigger disaster. The stock market provided a stage where the whole nation could watch the price of Wall Street's stocks go *boom* and then *bust!* That made it hard for citizens to realize that what was roller-coastering was only the price and not the value of the nation's product. Doubt and fear spread across the nation.

Hoover takes action. It took a little time for the stock market crash to bring on a full-scale depression. Secretary of the Treasury Andrew Mellon adopted the traditional approach that the government should do nothing to end the depression or ease its effects. "Let the slump liquidate itself," he advised. "Liquidate labor, liquidate stocks, liquidate the farmers, liquidate real estate. . . . It will purge the rottenness out of the system."

When the collapse came, President Hoover did not sit still. He used all the familiar ways to relieve suffering. He called upon cities, states, and all private charities to help feed the hungry. He brought business and labor leaders to the White House, where they promised to keep up wages and keep the factories going. He actually cut his own presidential salary by one-fifth.

In November 1929 Hoover even took the daring step for those days of persuading Congress to cut income taxes. He hoped this would leave people some money to buy goods to keep the factories going. But for most people income taxes were still so low that the tax cut made little difference. A family with a $4000 income saw its tax decline from $5.63 to $1.88. The wealthy, of course, saved much more. But they were frightened of the future, and so did not dare to increase their spending.

Aid for the farmers and for business.

The farmers, who had not shared in the prosperity of the twenties, had just received some federal aid. During a special session of Congress in the spring of 1929, an Agricultural Marketing bill passed by large majorities. This created a Federal Farm Board with $500 million to lend to farm cooperatives to help them market their crops. The board was also told to use its funds to keep farm prices steady.

But the Farm Board had no control over production. Though its agencies bought huge amounts of wheat and cotton, it could not keep prices up. By the close of 1931 wheat had sunk from $1 to 61 cents a bushel and cotton from 16 cents to 6 cents a pound. On the purchases of wheat and cotton alone the government's loss was $185 million.

Hoover had also asked for a "limited revision" upward of the tariff to help the textile factories and a few other depressed industries. Instead, Congress gave him just what the country did not need. In 1930 the Hawley-Smoot Tariff Act actually boosted duties on a thousand items. Within seventeen months after President Hoover signed the law, United States exports and imports were cut almost in half.

The run on banks.

Hoover's "engineering statesmanship" was widely praised. The *Boston Globe* was pleased that the nation had "at the White House a man who believed not in the philosophy of drift, but in the dynamics of mastery."

Still the country plunged deeper into depression. If stocks could fall so fast, maybe nothing was worth as much as people thought.

People lost their faith in banks. In the Federal Reserve Act of 1913, Congress had tried to reduce public fears over bank failures (p. 445). Depositors would not be tempted to run to their bank to draw out their money when they heard about a bank failure here and there. If a run did start, the banks could get prompt help from their district's Federal Reserve bank. But this system could not stand up under the severe strains that came with the stock market crash. Foreign banks had large deposits in banks over here in order to carry on trade. These foreign bank deposits dropped sharply after 1930. Next, the whole rural credit system collapsed. Low prices for farm crops meant that farmers could not pay back their loans. Then rural banks could not pay their depositors.

So bank failures began to rise sharply. People everywhere seemed to want to draw out their money at the same time. When they could not produce the cash their depositors wanted, banks failed by the hundreds. The number reached 642 in 1929 and more than doubled the next year. In 1931 the 2298 banks that closed held deposits of $1.6 billion. People who had spent years saving to buy a house or to send their children to college had their hopes blasted. People who had scrimped for a lifetime to feel secure in their old age all at once were penniless.

The beginning of the Great Depression.

The Great Crash became the Great Depression. The factory owners who could not sell their products slowed down their factories and laid off workers. Jobless workers who had lost their savings could not afford to buy anything. Still more factories closed down. The collapse of the stock market had signaled the collapse of industry.

Before the end of 1932 there were 12 million able-bodied Americans (about one in every four workers) who were unemployed. Many who had jobs were working only part-time. When they could not afford to pay their rent, they had to

The aimlessness and despair of life during the Great Depression were caught by a number of talented photographers employed by the Farm Security Administration. One of the best of these was Dorothea Lange, who took the pictures above right and below.

squeeze in with friends or relatives. Thousands took to the roads, drifting from place to place, desperately hoping that somehow in the next town they would find a job. Respectable Americans who only a few months before had lived in decent houses now had to seek shelter in shantytowns of cartons and wood scraps on vacant lots. These were called Hoovervilles. The young people with no money, no job, and no prospects did not dare marry. Within three years, the number of marriages dropped by one-quarter. College enrollments sank.

Millions went hungry. Children cried for the food their parents could not give them. Two-thirds of the children in New York City suffered from malnutrition. Some parents went wandering through alleys, rooting in garbage pails for scraps to keep their families alive.

The unemployed strike back. Where were the bright hopes of the New World? It is not surprising that energetic Americans, whose lifeblood was optimism, would not take all this lying down.

Desperate unemployed people went on hunger marches. In Henryetta, Oklahoma, 300 men broke into food stores. In Iowa and Nebraska, farmers who could no longer pay their mortgages used their pitchforks to drive off the sheriffs who came to seize

Desperate for a little income, some of the unemployed sold apples at a nickel each as the man above is doing in sight of the nation's Capitol. When unemployment struck, a person's automobile was one of the first things that had to go for whatever price it would bring—even if the price was low.

their land. Between 1930 and 1934 one million families lost their farms.

In the spring of 1932 thousands of unemployed veterans formed a "Bonus Army." They demanded that the full cash value of their insurance policies should be paid them by the government at once. They marched on Washington. When they arrived in the capital, of course, they could not afford to stay in hotels. So they camped in empty government buildings and on government land waiting for their bonus. President Hoover called out the army to drive them away. "What a pitiful spectacle," the *Washington News* observed, "is that of the great American Government, mightiest in the world, chasing unarmed men, women, and children with Army tanks. . . . If the Army must be called out to make war on unarmed citizens, this is no longer America."

Where would it end?

Who had killed prosperity? In the panic many Americans lost their heads. Everybody wanted someone to blame. Crackpots offered fantastic cure-alls. Abolish banks! Print more money! Some even said that the end of the world was near.

Hoover tries to help. Never was there a more honest or more hard-working President. But Herbert Hoover was no politician. He did not like to persuade people. He did not enjoy the arts of compromise. As an engineer he felt that he saw problems clearly. After he had carefully prepared his solution, he thought people ought to follow his plan without arguing.

Wearing a high stiff collar, he was a stiff man who inspired respect but not love. He had none of William Jennings Bryan's eloquence, nor any of Theodore Roosevelt's pep. In ordinary times he might have been a good President to keep America on the familiar road to success. But these were not ordinary times. The skills of an engineer were not enough. The nation also needed in great measure the traditional American talents—for imagination and experiment.

Hoover used the Agricultural Marketing Act to try to keep up the prices of tobacco, cotton, corn, and wheat and help the farmers. In December 1930 he started a large program for the construction of public works. By the end of his term of office he would spend more than $2 billion on roads, buildings, and other public construction.

To save large corporations, banks, and insurance companies from bankruptcy, he asked Congress to create the Reconstruction Finance Corporation. The bill, to provide jobs by saving companies and to help "start the country forward all along the line," was enacted early in 1932. The RFC had $2 billion

Alexander Hogue's painting "The Dust Bowl," made in 1933, captured the bleakness of the land when drought came to the Great Plains and nothing would grow.

to lend to needy banks, railroads, insurance companies, and farm credit associations. Congress also passed at Hoover's request the Federal Home Loan Bank Act to help people with mortgages from losing their homes. As Hoover said, that was "one of the tragedies of this depression."

Hoover's limitations. Hoover did more than any other President before him had ever done to check a depression. But he refused to provide direct relief for individuals. He said it was dangerous to get people in the habit of receiving charity from the national government.

What Hoover did helped, but it was not enough. The disaster was more far-reaching than he realized. And it required remedies more novel than he could imagine.

Then to complicate his problem, one of the worst droughts in recent history hit the nation in 1930. On half a million farms in eighteen states from Virginia to Oklahoma crops withered and cattle died of thirst. Hoover went along when Congress voted $45 million to help farmers feed their livestock, but he opposed giving $25 million to feed the farmers and their families. Finally he allowed Congress to vote $20 million for loans. To give the money, the President said, "would have injured the spiritual response of the American people." But the times called for new measures. The American spirit would have to be lifted by a more adventurous American willing to try new ways.

SECTION 2 REVIEW

1. Identify or explain: Black Tuesday, Federal Farm Board, Hawley-Smoot Tariff Act, Agricultural Marketing Act, public works, Reconstruction Finance Corporation.
2. Who tried to stop the collapse of the stock market? How? What happened?
3. Why did it matter that the stock market crashed?
4. What steps did President Hoover and Congress take to stop the business decline? Why did these steps fail?
5. **Drawing Conclusions.** How did the Great Depression affect people's daily lives? How did some people react to hard times?

---

3. Foreign affairs in a gloomy world

The depression also left its mark on foreign affairs. American banks had made large loans to banks in Europe. As panic and depression spread, European banks also came under pressure from their depositors. In June 1931 Germany and Austria were on the verge of financial collapse. Hoover said that we would postpone for one year any payments on the war debts owed to us by our former allies. And he asked them to do the same on their debts to one another and on the German reparations.

Even this *debt moratorium* did not save the situation. Nation after nation was forced to give up the gold standard. They refused any longer to tie the value of their money to gold. Still, the President, supported by American business opinion, refused to allow the war debts to be canceled. Nations should follow the same rules as private individuals! President Coolidge had said, "They hired the money, didn't they?" Anyway, all the debtor nations except Finland ended up defaulting, or not paying. Many Europeans felt that their own depression and unemployment were caused by these war debts and by the high American tariffs against their goods. They expected the United States to be more charitable than other nations.

The Kellogg-Briand Pact. Not only the war debts but the memory of battlefield horrors haunted Americans. During the Coolidge years the United States along with Great Britain, France, Italy, Germany, Japan, and some 60 other nations had signed a peace pact. They had promised to "renounce war as an instrument of national policy in their relations with one another." They agreed to seek the solution of all disputes or conflicts, "of whatever nature," by peaceful means. This Kellogg-Briand Pact—named for Secretary of State Frank Kellogg and French Foreign Minister Aristide Briand—was signed in Paris in August 1928.

Some hardheaded Americans said that the Kellogg-Briand Pact did no more than express a pious hope. They warned that Americans should not feel secure simply because they hated war. Others had more confidence in the peace pact. They even thought it would now be safe to agree to reduce the size of the costly American navy.

In January 1930 a new naval conference of the United States, Great Britain, Japan, Italy, and France met in London. The United States, Great

MARRIED AGAIN

After World War I, according to this cartoon, the Kellogg Pact remarried Peace to the wicked world.

Britain, and Japan agreed to continue the limits on the number of large capital ships (p. 487). They also accepted fixed ratios for cruisers, destroyers, and submarines.

But new forces were rising in Europe. A few farsighted writers saw another world conflict brewing. The belligerent Mussolini had brought fascism to Italy in 1922. And it was the old tragedy—only with new villains—all over again. Fearing Italy, France refused to limit its naval power. Italy, openly warlike, refused to sign any agreement. Finally the whole purpose of the London naval treaty was frustrated by an "escalator" clause. This allowed any country to build more ships if another power threatened its "national security." Still, Secretary of State Henry L. Stimson said he looked forward to further conferences "confident that we shall obtain ever increasing security with ever decreasing armaments."

Coolidge and Latin America. United States relations with Latin America during the Coolidge years had been a strange mixture. At times we seemed interested only in "dollar diplomacy." Then again, we would seem to be a sincere "good neighbor." In 1916 the United States Marines were sent into the Dominican Republic to protect the sugar and fruit holdings of United States businesses. Then in 1924 these troops were pulled out. A treaty was agreed upon that ended our military rule there, and the troops were brought home.

The United States had long shown a special interest in Nicaragua. It was a possible site for a canal between the oceans. And American business had invested there in coffee, banana, and sugar plantations. But Nicaragua's main crop seemed to be revolutions. In 1912, marines were sent there to protect American interests. Hardly had they been withdrawn in 1925 when another revolution broke out. The United States sent back the marines, who put a friendly party in power. But the Nicaraguan guerrillas had their own ideas. The drama of civil war followed. The United States finally gave up armed intervention and withdrew the marines in 1933.

In Mexico it was oil that attracted special United States interests. The Mexican constitution of 1917 had declared that all oil deposits now belonged to the state. This was true even if they had been granted earlier to private companies. The name for this takeover was *expropriation*. Oil companies were supposed to apply for oil leases on land they thought they had already purchased. The United States protested, and it was not until 1925 that Mexico began to enforce its control over the oil. President Coolidge objected that Mexico was "confiscating property legally owned by American citizens."

In January 1927 Congress called for the peaceful settlement of the issues. Coolidge sent a former Amherst College classmate, the shrewd and able Dwight W. Morrow, as ambassador to Mexico. Morrow, a partner in J. P. Morgan's firm, showed what could be done by tact and sympathy. With his understanding of Mexico's problems he won the confidence of the government and the people.

When America's hero Charles A. Lindbergh made a nonstop goodwill flight of 2200 miles from Washington to Mexico City in December 1927, he too became an "ambassador of goodwill." There Lindbergh met Ambassador Morrow's brilliant and attractive daughter Anne. They married in 1929. Sharing a love of the airplane, they flew around the nation and the world exploring new air routes. They awakened enthusiasm for the Air Age. The Lindberghs also wrote popular books about their experiences and cheered the country by their romantic collaboration.

Hoover and Latin America. President Hoover and his Secretary of State Stimson were determined somehow to improve our relations with the countries of Latin America. For 30 years the United States had been intervening in their affairs, and now it was no easy matter to remove their suspicions. Before taking office, Hoover had shown that he meant business when he spent ten weeks on a goodwill trip. In Argentina he announced that the United States would no longer interfere in the domestic affairs of those nations.

By the Roosevelt Corollary to the Monroe Doctrine (p. 449), the domineering TR had declared the right of the United States to intervene in Latin America when United States interests were threatened. Now, it was announced, the Roosevelt Corollary was no longer our policy. "The Monroe Doctrine," Secretary Stimson said, "was a declaration of the United States versus Europe—not of the United States versus Latin America."

The Hoover administration declared that it would respect the facts of South American political life—whether we liked them or not. Any "de facto" government, that is, one that in fact controlled a country, would be recognized by the United States.

Japan ends the peace. On the other side of the world in 1931, the Japanese army seized Manchuria and the next year turned it into the puppet state of Manchukuo. Americans were shocked but could not be surprised. The firm agreements in the Nine Power Treaty and the high hopes of the Kellogg-Briand Pact were shattered. What could Americans do?

Secretary of State Stimson sent a note of protest. The United States, he said, would not recognize such changes made by force. The Council of the League of Nations, with an American "observer" present for the first time, invoked the Kellogg-Briand Pact to outlaw Japan. In January 1932, Japanese forces attacked Shanghai and bombed the city, killing thousands of civilians. But neither the League of Nations nor the people of the United States would risk war to restrain this aggression. Americans were more troubled by their depression than by the sufferings of the distant Chinese.

Stimson urged economic sanctions—a trade boycott—against Japan. Hoover refused, for he feared that sanctions would be the first step to war.

Meanwhile, war-loving leaders were rising to power in Italy and Germany. Later, Mussolini and Hitler would remember the timidity of the United States and other peaceful nations. If the high-sounding agreements had no power against an aggressive Japan, why should other aggressive powers hold back? Fascist Italy and Nazi Germany—the forces of tyranny and barbarism—saw their green light.

SECTION 3 REVIEW

1. Identify or explain: debt moratorium, Kellogg-Briand Pact, London Naval Conference, Henry Stimson, expropriation, Dwight Morrow.

2. Locate: Dominican Republic, Nicaragua, Manchuria, Shanghai.

3. How did Hoover try to ease financial stress in Europe?

4. **Checking Consistency.** Was the United States' Latin American policy consistent during the period 1920–1932? Explain.

4. The election of 1932

By 1932 industrial production in the United States was only half what it had been in 1929. Countless Americans were working only part-time, and 12 million more were out of work. President Hoover was the handiest person to blame, even though the depression had actually begun almost before he had moved into the White House. One folk song of the unemployed declared, "Hoover made a soup hound out of me." A man's empty pocket turned inside out was called a "Hoover flag." People looked forward to a change in the White House.

The conventions. Still, the Republicans felt they could not reject Hoover or his policies. When they met in the Coliseum at Chicago in June 1932, they renominated Hoover and Vice-President Curtis on the first ballot. The platform stood firmly on the merits of the Hoover administration. It warned against the dangers to business if the Democrats came to power. It supported Prohibition. In a word, it stood "pat"—hoping that natural forces would solve the nation's problems.

ALL FEES
ARE PAYABLE
Cash in advance

EMPLOYMENT
EXCHANGE
AGENCY

Isaac Soyer, the son of a Russian immigrant, knew from personal experience the trials of poverty in the big city. In realistic paintings, such as this one done in 1937, he tried to capture the despair of life during the depression years.

When the Democrats met in the same building a few days later, the leading candidate was Governor Franklin D. Roosevelt of New York. He had been Assistant Secretary of the Navy under Wilson and had run for Vice-President in 1920. His main rival was Al Smith, former governor of New York, who had the support of Tammany Hall. After a hard fight, the Roosevelt forces won the delegates of California and Texas, who had favored Speaker of the House John Nance Garner of Texas. Roosevelt won the nomination on the fifth ballot, and Garner was named for Vice-President.

FDR was no radical, but he loved to try new things. He was not afraid to break precedent by flying from Albany to Chicago to deliver his speech of acceptance. "Let it be from now on," he declared, "the task of our party to break foolish traditions."

The campaign. FDR loved campaigning. And his campaign delighted him with cheering crowds everywhere. The unlucky Hoover was often booed and heckled. "I've been traveling with Presidents since Theodore Roosevelt," one Secret Service agent remarked, "and never before have I seen one actually booed, with men running out into the streets to thumb their noses at him. It's not a pretty sight."

During the campaign Hoover argued that the real causes of the depression were world conditions

511

The urbane Franklin D. Roosevelt, here reaching to shake hands, and his running mate the homespun "Cactus Jack" Garner of Texas (right) were greeted with cheers and applause as they toured the nation during the 1932 campaign. Baltimore's mayor is in the middle.

that the United States could not control. He condemned Roosevelt's experimental ideas. He said they would destroy American free enterprise and the American system of government. If the Democrats were elected, he predicted, grass would grow in the streets of a hundred cities.

Roosevelt attacked the Republicans for encouraging the reckless stock market speculation that had brought on the panic. He was eloquent, persuasive, and smilingly confident. He promised a "New Deal" and a rapid recovery of prosperity for business and agriculture. But he did not produce a blueprint for recovery. He offered proposals that seemed to appeal to all the nation's varied groups. He supported many Progressive policies. He called for repeal of Prohibition, and he declared that everyone had a right to a comfortable living. The products of industry, he said, should be distributed more fairly. Except on a few issues, Roosevelt's speeches were so general that it was hard to disagree with them. Hoover thought FDR kept shifting his positions and called him "a chameleon on plaid." The usually wise commentator Walter Lippmann criticized FDR as "a pleasant man who, without any important qualifications for the office, would very much like to be President."

But it did not matter much what Roosevelt said. Almost anybody could have beaten Hoover. Who wanted to vote *for* the depression? To no one's surprise, the Democrats won a mighty victory. FDR received some 23 million votes and carried 42 states. Hoover, with fewer than 16 million votes, carried only 6 states. In the electoral college the count was 472 to 59. The Democrats won a majority of 191 in the House and 22 in the Senate. The American people had given their mandate to change the policies of government. Could FDR meet the challenge?

SECTION 4 REVIEW

1. What were the issues in the election campaign?
2. **Identifying Assumptions.** Why did people vote overwhelmingly for Franklin D. Roosevelt in the 1932 election?

CHAPTER 23 REVIEW

FOCUSING ON IDEAS

1. Buying stock in corporations always involves some risk. How does "buying on margin" increase the risk?

2. What were two experiences in Hoover's early life that helped shape his personal creed? Explain how each experience contributed to Hoover's world view.

3. A business recession has a "snowball effect"—growing in size and picking up speed as it rolls downhill. Show how the 1929 crash sent the economy spinning down hill. How did a collapse in one part of the economy lead to other business failures?

TAKING A CRITICAL LOOK

1. **Recognizing Cause and Effect.** How did the sagging economies of post-war Europe contribute to the depression?

2. **Identifying Alternatives.** Although peace was their goal, many post-World War I treaties and pacts carried the seeds of future violence. How might the agreements have been shaped to avoid future resentment and conflict?

YOUR REGION IN HISTORY

1. **Geography.** If your region was part of the dust bowl during the depression, prepare a map showing where the dust bowl struck. How did the dust bowl affect the population of your region? What is the condition of the land today?

2. **Culture.** Interview two or more persons who lived in your community or nearby between 1930 and 1932. How were their families affected by the depression? Find out as many details as you can about lay-offs, bank failures, mortgage foreclosures, and so on.

3. **Economics.** Find out how a particular business in your area fared in the early years of the Great Depression.

HISTORICAL FACTS AND FIGURES

Making Hypotheses. Use the information in the graph below to help answer the following questions:
(a) When was unemployment at its lowest point?
(b) How many Americans were out of work in 1933?
(c) This chapter began with the statement that when Herbert Hoover took office in 1929, "Unemployment was low, wages were up, prices were steady, and corporations were making big profits and paying fat dividends." Does the data on the graph support this point of view? Explain. (d) Formulate a hypothesis about the state of the nation's economy in 1933, when Franklin D. Roosevelt took office. Identify factors that contributed to those economic circumstances. Predict how President-elect Roosevelt would attempt to address the nation's economic difficulties. How would you have handled the situation FDR faced?

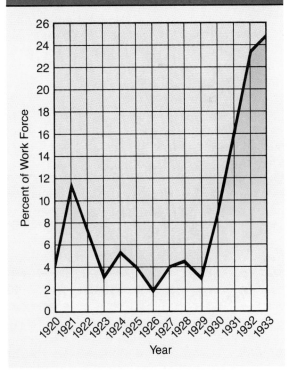

Unemployment, 1920-1933

Source: *Historical Statistics of the United States*

513

MAKING CONNECTIONS

THEMES

This unit began on page 479 with a description of a nation experiencing extremes during the years 1918 to 1932:

> *President Calvin Coolidge told Congress in 1928 that the nation had never faced "a more pleasing prospect," [declaring] "there is tranquility and contentment...and the highest record of years of prosperity...." Before the next year was out...[placards proclaimed] "In Hoover we trusted, now we are busted."*

This description was supported by the two unit themes that are reprinted in **dark type** below. Use the time line and the information in Unit 8 to answer the questions that follow the themes.

1. **The "Roaring Twenties" are characterized by experimentation, great changes in daily life, and booming economic growth.**

   How does the following poem, "First Fig," by Edna St. Vincent Millay, symbolize the extreme character of the 1920s?

   My candle burns at both ends; / It will not last the night; / But ah, my foes, and oh, my friends— / It gives a lovely light.

2. **The stock market crash of 1929 signals the end of the "Roaring Twenties" and leads many Americans to grow disillusioned with the American economic system.**

   How did Americans react to the "Black Thursday" stock market crash and the Great Depression that followed?

Events in American History

1920 Attorney General Palmer orders the arrests of thousands of suspected communists.

1919 The Eighteenth Amendment prohibits the sale of alcoholic beverages.

1920 The first radio broadcast in the United States—by KDKA in Pittsburgh—is heard.

Events in World History

| 1915 | 1917 | 1919 | 1921 | 1923 |

1920 The Nazi party is established in Germany.

1920s Musicians introduce the world to jazz, blues, and ragtime, and people dance.

1932 Congress creates the Reconstruction Finance Corporation to provide jobs for the unemployed.

1932 The veterans' "Bonus Army" marches on Washington and is dispersed by federal troops.

1925 One automobile rolls off the assembly line every ten seconds.

1931 2,298 banks close as Americans demand their savings from the banks.

1929 October 24— Black Thursday—the stock market crash begins.

1930 Congress enacts the Hawley-Smoot Tariff Act to restrict foreign imports.

1923 **1925** **1927** **1929** **1931** **1933**

1931 Austria suffers economic collapse, signaling financial failures across Europe.

1927 Charles Lindbergh flies alone across the Atlantic from New York to Paris.

UNIT 9

Depression at home and aggression abroad 1933–1945

On March 4, 1933, when Franklin Delano Roosevelt became the thirty-second President of the United States, the nation was in the deepest depression in its history. Poverty stalked the land. Some observers believed a revolution was at hand. But FDR was not discouraged. In his inaugural address he asserted his faith in democracy. He declared, "The people of the United States have not failed, . . . they want direct, vigorous action."

Roosevelt gave the nation action aplenty during the next twelve years. He did not always find solutions to problems, but he kept trying. The majority of voters never lost their faith in him or in their democracy.

In war, too, FDR would lead the nation with zest and confidence. Roosevelt had not expected war, but he organized the nation for its greatest defensive effort in history. His eloquent, strong leadership inspired his fellow Americans. He enlisted farmers and factory workers to overwhelm the forces of barbarism with American arms and supplies. As Commander in Chief he would send the armed forces to far corners of the earth. And he enlisted other world leaders in a grand strategy for victory.

THEMES

THEMES IN AMERICAN HISTORY

■ Franklin Roosevelt's strong leadership and New Deal programs ease the impact of the Great Depression on poverty-stricken Americans.

■ The rise of the dictators and fascism in Europe threatens the peace of the entire world.

■ The allied nations triumph in a world war on two fronts, but with victory comes a host of new fears and problems.

Max Weber's 1930s painting "Wayfarers" is a timeless rendering of the plight of those forced from their homes by poverty, prejudice, or war.

Photo Research International (detail)

CHAPTER 24

"Nothing to fear but fear itself"

Herbert Hoover had tried harder than any other President to save the nation from a depression. But it had been too little and too late. The crisis was too severe to be solved by the old ways—even under the leadership of the "Great Engineer." The American people wanted new directions from their new President. Franklin D. Roosevelt with his wonderful feeling for words had been precise when he promised a "New Deal." In most ways he was a conservative. He did not want to change all the rules of the American game. Instead he would try to use the government to deal out the cards so that everybody would have a better chance to win a good life.

1. Franklin D. Roosevelt's New Deal

Millions were out of work. Factories stood idle. Banks were tottering. In many states to keep the banks from collapsing the governors had ordered the banks to close for a "holiday." Farmers and homeowners, unable to make the regular payments on their mortgages, were losing the property they had bought with their life savings. Cities and states ran out of funds to feed the unemployed. While people in the cities were starving, farmers were burning their unsold corn simply to keep their families warm.

The homespun humorist and critic of American life Will Rogers observed:

> We got more wheat, more corn, more food, more cotton, more money in the banks, more everything in the world than any nation that ever lived ever had, yet we are starving to death. We are the first nation in the history of the world to go to the poorhouse in an automobile.

Franklin Delano Roosevelt. The Democrats had happened to pick one of the most winning men in American history. Franklin Delano Roosevelt was a distant cousin of Theodore Roosevelt's. And, like his cousin, he had a confident smile and a wonderfully winsome, cheerful personality.

Although few people in the country realized it at the time, FDR was a man of heroic character. The only child of wealthy, upper-class parents, he was brought up by tutors, governesses, and a doting mother. From his youth he had enjoyed sports. He had always loved politics and had been the Democratic candidate for Vice-President in 1920. One August day in 1921, while on vacation with his family in Canada, he was stricken with polio and was left paralyzed. This single, sudden thunderclap of bad luck reduced him from a bouncy, athletic, runabout politician to a bedridden invalid. A man of weaker character might have given up.

Instead, after his bad luck, he became more determined than ever to be active in politics. An

A genial Franklin D. Roosevelt chats with reporters in Warm Springs, Georgia. This jaunty FDR pose was used in hundreds of cartoons.

old friend who came on a sympathy visit to the hospital was surprised when FDR gave him a strong, good-natured wallop. "You thought you were coming to see an invalid," FDR laughed from his bed. "But I can knock you out in any bout."

People who went to cheer him up found that FDR gave them a lift instead. Sometimes he joked about his affliction. FDR wrote a friend that he had "renewed his youth" by "what was fortunately a rather mild case of *infantile* paralysis."

His case really was far from mild. He was never able to walk again. Only after long and painful exercises and by wearing heavy braces did he learn to use his hips so he could get around on crutches. He told his friends that he had an advantage. While they were running around, he could sit still and think. He used his long period of recovery in bed to write hundreds of letters to politicians all over the country. He wrote not about his own problems, but about politics and how to build a stronger Democratic party. All over the country the party's leaders valued his advice.

FDR made a fantastic comeback. When the Democratic convention in Chicago in 1932 chose him to head their ticket, it was not only because of his heroic personal qualities. For he had already proven himself a highly successful politician in New York. In 1928, only seven years after he had been stricken with polio, he managed to be elected governor of his state. He did so well as governor that when he ran again in 1930 he won by the biggest majority ever.

With his broad, contagious smile, Roosevelt was a wonderful persuader. He loved people, and he could make them love him. People cheered up when they saw his jaunty cigarette holder and felt his warm, firm handshake. He had all the human qualities that Herbert Hoover lacked. And these were what the nation wanted in that dangerous year of 1932.

519

FDR was no radical. In fact, during the campaign he was careful not to offend anybody. When he made speeches, he sounded more like William McKinley than like William Jennings Bryan. Some people who thought the nation needed stronger medicine criticized FDR. They said he was too eager to please everybody and had no real ideas about how to end the depression.

Those critics were wrong. FDR had courage in politics just as much as in his private life. And as soon as he took office on March 4, 1933, he showed both his courage and his imagination.

"A New Deal for the American people!" This was what FDR had announced in Chicago when he accepted the nomination. He promised to *experiment*. The nation and all its wealth were still there, he reminded people in his inaugural address. "We are stricken by no plague of locusts. Compared with the perils which our forefathers conquered because they believed and were not afraid, we have still much to be thankful for. Nature still offers her

bounty and human efforts have multiplied it. Plenty is at our doorstep." Franklin Roosevelt had faith that there really were lots of new ways that could be tried.

"The only thing we have to fear," he said, "is fear itself." His courage and his optimism, like his smile, were contagious. Americans were encouraged most of all because they believed that their new President really would experiment. He would try one thing, and then another—until ways would be found to put the country back on the track and to put people back to work.

The Brain Trust. To plan the measures that would bring *relief* to those in need, *recovery* to the economy, and *reform* so it would never happen again, Roosevelt assembled a varied group of advisers. That they were divided among themselves over what to do bothered the President not at all. He enjoyed the chance to be able to choose a course of action from a number of options.

Frances Perkins, Secretary of Labor, was the first woman Cabinet member. Here she stands with Representative Peyser (left) and Senator Wagner of New York as FDR signs a bill to combat the effects of unemployment in June 1933.

In his Cabinet he had the calm, conservative Cordell Hull as Secretary of State. Harold L. Ickes was Secretary of the Interior. A onetime Republican and Bull Moose, Ickes firmly believed in Progressive reform. Henry A. Wallace, another former Republican, became Secretary of Agriculture—the post his father had held under Harding and Coolidge. James A. Farley, a canny political manager who had directed Roosevelt's campaign, took over as Postmaster General. He could hand out hundreds of jobs to loyal party members. From 1934 to 1945 the Secretary of the Treasury was Henry Morgenthau, Jr., a close friend and New York neighbor of FDR's.

In one of FDR's striking departures from tradition, he chose capable and experienced Frances Perkins to be Secretary of Labor. She was the first woman Cabinet member. She had worked with Jane Addams at Hull House in Chicago. When she returned east, she became New York State Industrial Commissioner. Secretary Perkins would be important in shaping the New Deal legislation.

The Cabinet members were not Roosevelt's only advisers. When he found or heard of people anywhere in the country who he thought could help, he invited them to the White House and charmed them into the nation's service. He did not care whether they had government experience. What mattered was their imagination, their energy, and their ability to devise new experiments to save the nation. He consulted lawyer Samuel Rosenman, social worker Harry Hopkins, and many professors. Among these were Raymond Moley, Rexford Tugwell, Adolph A. Berle, Jr., and Felix Frankfurter. Each of these professors helped the President find and enlist their ablest graduates. Never had a President been so successful in seeking out and using the nation's best minds. This informal group of advisers made up what was called President Roosevelt's "Brain Trust." Scores of New Deal laws would bear the imprint of their thinking.

The "hundred days" begin.

Roosevelt had to wait four months before he became President. The election was held in early November, but the President was not sworn in until early March. During these intervening months when the people's choice was waiting in the wings, the "lame duck" President in the White House could accomplish very little. The Twentieth Amendment, ratified on January 23, 1933, changed this. Now January 3 is the date for the gathering of Congress, and the President takes the oath on January 20.

After he was elected and before he took office, FDR was asked by President Hoover to support his measures for dealing with the depression. But FDR wanted to make a fresh start. He did not want to be stuck with Hoover's policies.

On March 4, 1933, Roosevelt made his grand entrance. The need for leadership and experiment was so desperate that, for a time, he might have persuaded Congress to pass almost any law he asked for. "The whole country is with him, just so he does something," Will Rogers said. "If he burned down the capital we would cheer and say, 'Well, we at least got a fire started anyhow.'"

For the first time in history the whole nation was listening—to the radio. The voice they heard was warm, informal, and beautifully modulated. They felt closer to their President than ever before. And when FDR received half a million pieces of fan mail, he knew the people's response to his message of hope.

As soon as he arrived in the White House, there was a flurry of activity. He called a special session of Congress and declared a nationwide "bank holiday." Congress gathered on March 9 and received a hastily prepared emergency banking bill. Since there had not even been time to make enough copies to hand out, it had to be read aloud. "The house is burning down," the Republican floor leader announced, "and the President of the United States says this is the way to put out the fire." Within 40 minutes the House passed the bill. The Senate soon followed, and by 8:30 that night the President had signed it into law. So began the exciting first one hundred days of Franklin D. Roosevelt's first term.

Banking laws.

The Emergency Banking Act approved the President's closing of the banks. The law gave the Secretary of the Treasury the power to investigate all banks and then open them as he saw fit. On March 12, FDR went on the radio in the first of his many "fireside chats." In calm and friendly tones and in words that anyone could understand, the President explained the whole banking problem to the listening people. They were reassured.

The examination of the banks showed that four-fifths of them were in much better condition than the public had imagined. They were soon reopened, and confidence in them was restored. The run on the banks stopped. Within a month a billion dollars of deposits flowed back. By midsummer three-fourths of the nation's banks (holding 94 percent of all deposits) were in business again.

Within three months Congress passed a banking reform bill to help the people keep their confidence in their banks. The Glass-Steagall Act created the Federal Deposit Insurance Corporation, which protected depositors in insured banks up to $5000. All members of the Federal Reserve System had to belong to the FDIC, and others could join. The banking act added savings banks to the Federal Reserve System and widened the powers of the Federal Reserve Board. These new powers would enable the board to prevent the kind of wild speculation that had brought on the Great Crash.

There was a good deal of feeling in Congress in favor of government ownership of the whole banking system. But the President said that improved government supervision would be enough. "The policies which vanquished the bank crisis were thoroughly conservative policies," Brain Truster Raymond Moley later remarked. "The sole departure from convention lay in the swiftness and boldness with which they were carried out."

The currency crisis. The country was troubled, too, by *deflation.* Since there was so little demand for goods and so many people were looking for jobs, prices and wages sank (that is, were "deflated"). If the government printed more money and put it into circulation, it was argued, wages and prices would rise. Then it would be easier for wage earners and farmers to buy. It would be easier to pay debts, too. But how much inflation was needed? Some economists feared runaway price increases.

Again, as he had in the banking crisis, the President took a fairly conservative course. He put the country on a modified gold standard. There would still be a limit to how much money could be printed. Every dollar would still have to be secured by some gold in government vaults. People were ordered to deliver all their gold coins and gold certificates to the Federal Reserve banks and to accept Federal Reserve notes in exchange. From then on, anyone owing money could pay it back dollar for dollar in any coin or currency (legal tender) that the government declared was lawful at the time.

In the Gold Reserve Act of 1934, Congress gave the President power to reduce the gold backing of the dollar by as much as 50 percent. He then issued a proclamation fixing the gold value of the dollar at 59.06 cents. The main purposes of this "devaluation" of the dollar were to (1) provide more dollars for people to spend, (2) raise the prices of goods here at home, (3) boost exports, and (4) decrease the burden of debt. The move was especially popular among the nation's troubled debtors. Now they could pay back their debts with a cheaper dollar.

On the other hand, bondholders and other creditors called this devaluation "legalized robbery." They had loaned dollars worth 100 cents in gold but would be forced to accept repayment in dollars worth only 59.06 cents in gold. When they took their case to the courts in 1935, the Supreme Court upheld the law.

Securities regulation. One of the lessons of the stock market crash was the danger of dishonest and overblown advertising by people who sold securities—stocks and bonds. Men and women were being tempted to gamble what they thought they were only investing. In June 1934 Congress set up a Securities and Exchange Commission (SEC) to regulate the stock market and prevent these and other abuses. The SEC was given the power to (1) license and regulate stock exchanges, (2) require basic data on stocks and bonds offered for sale, (3) regulate activities of investment advisers, and (4) prosecute persons engaged in fraud. To reduce the temptation to gamble on the stock market, the Federal Reserve Board was given the power to fix margin requirements. Similar regulations were later applied to the commodity (wheat, sugar, cotton) exchanges.

Economy and beer. Balancing the budget was the traditional way for the government to cope with a depression. It was thought that the government must bring its income and spending into line and be conservative in its financial affairs. Then whatever had produced the downturn in the economy would disappear. Business leaders would regain their confidence in the system. They would resume

COME BACK!

BILLIONS OF GOVT. SPENDING

BILLIONS OF DEFICIT

BILLIONS OF DEBT

TAXPAYER

Herbert Johnson

The caption for this cartoon read "Nonsense! If it gets too deep, you can always pull me out." Some critics looked on New Deal spending as carefree and unconcerned about the taxpayer who they felt would drown in government debts and deficits.

spending on plants and equipment, and in time prosperity would return.

During the 1930s, however, a new solution was proposed. It was known as the Keynesian approach after its developer, the English economist John Maynard Keynes. He suggested that instead of cutting back on spending, the government should do just the reverse. It should lower taxes, spend money, and purposely run up large deficits. Public spending would put people to work and get money into circulation. This would promote private spending, and prosperity would return.

In between the extremes of balancing the budget and running large deficits as Keynes suggested, there were those who argued for letting the budget be unbalanced for a short time to "prime the pump." But then the government should step aside, cut expenses, and let private business take over.

During his campaign Roosevelt had promised to balance the budget. So one of the first measures he asked Congress to pass was an Economy Act. Within a week the bill was passed allowing FDR to cut government salaries and veterans' pensions and take other steps to reduce the deficit.

Roosevelt did not give up his hope of balancing the budget. But he found it impossible. The needs of the hour were too great. He was not willing to let citizens suffer simply to fulfill a campaign promise.

FDR showed what a clever politician he was as he worked for the passage of his Economy Bill. After the November election and the victory of the "wet" Democrats, Prohibition was on its way out. Even before FDR took office, Congress had passed and sent to the states a proposed Twenty-first Amendment to the Constitution repealing the Eighteenth (Prohibition) Amendment. Since it was clear that this amendment soon would be ratified, Roosevelt did not wait. Following his Economy Bill, he at once submitted a bill to legalize the sale of beer and light wines. Now, if the divided Congress paused too long to debate the Economy Bill, they would be keeping thirsty Americans from their beer. So both bills passed quickly, and the unhappy "noble experiment" of Prohibition finally came to an end.

Conserving the land and the people.

One of Roosevelt's most ingenious pet projects was a Civilian Conservation Corps. The idea was to provide 250,000 unemployed young men between the ages of 18 and 25 with useful work in the healthful outdoors. They would help conserve the nation's natural resources in the national parks and forests by planting trees, stocking fish in lakes and rivers, and building fire lanes and wilderness trails. The CCC would also restore the historic sites of Revolutionary and Civil War battles.

On an even larger scale he devised a plan to lift people's hopes, to improve the life and conserve the land of whole regions. Many of the 3.5 million people who lived in the mountains of western Kentucky, Tennessee, and Alabama, and in the valley of the Tennessee River were poorly off. Their land was exhausted. They could not afford to pay for electricity to light their houses or to operate their farms. Of course, factories would not move in without the electric power to run them.

FDR proposed building dams on the Tennessee and other rivers of the region. These dams would have a double purpose. They would protect against floods. And the water flowing through the dams would turn generators to make cheap electricity. With this power two old munitions plants left over from World War I could be converted into government factories to make fertilizer to improve the farms. All these purposes actually were accomplished by the Tennessee Valley Authority (TVA).

The Tennessee Valley was brightened in more ways than one! Doctors used this chance to rid the countryside of malaria. Librarians sent "bookmobiles" out to the farms. With better homes came better hospitals and better schools.

Of course, some people objected. They accused FDR of trying to be a dictator. Some owners of private electric and fertilizer companies complained that the government was competing unfairly.

The TVA naturally did not solve all the problems of the poor farmers in the Tennessee Valley. Yet the experiment was a success. It was an inspiring example of how imagination and government resources could improve people's lives and help them earn their own living.

Help for housing.

Owners of homes needed government help, too. Many were out of work or had lower earnings and could not meet their mortgage payments. This meant they might lose their homes and be forced out on the street. In June 1933, the Home Owners Loan Corporation was set up with the right to issue $2 billion in bonds to refinance mortgages. This was followed in 1934 by the National Housing Act, which established the Federal Housing Administration (FHA). It insured loans by banks, building and loan associations, and other private groups to homeowners for repair and to finance mortgages for new houses.

Under the Resettlement Administration, started in 1935, three entirely new towns, "greenbelt communities," were built. These were based on the ideas of Ebenezer Howard and the experiment at Radburn, New Jersey (p. 391). But not until 1937 was anything done about housing for the urban poor. Then the Wagner-Steagall Act was passed. It set up the United States Housing Authority to make loans to cities and states to clear away slums and to build low-cost housing. Under this law, some 350 projects were built or under way by 1940.

The Agricultural Adjustment Act.

Farmers all over the nation had their problems, too. They had never shared in the prosperity of the twenties. To help them now, the Agricultural Adjustment Act (AAA) was passed in May 1933. Its purpose was to raise the real income of farmers to "parity." That was a name for the higher price level that farmers had enjoyed before World War I (1910–1914). The act aimed to remove the chief cause of low prices by reducing the surplus of farm products. This would be accomplished by limiting the production of wheat, corn, cotton, hogs, tobacco, and milk. To pay the farmers for taking land out of production, the Treasury would issue cash bonuses. The money would come from a "processing tax" on the industries that made the raw products into finished goods. These were the industries that milled wheat into flour, that converted cotton into cloth, and made tobacco into cigarettes. The processor could pass the tax along to the consumer in the form of higher prices.

To deal with looming surpluses from crops already planted and young animals already born, the act provided that the cotton growers should "plow under" about 30 percent of their growing crop. Six million little pigs were slaughtered to keep them from growing into rotund, salable hogs.

At a time when people were hungry, it seemed foolish to hold down the production of food and to kill piglets that might have fed many families. But these were strange times. And the life of a great industrial nation was not simple. Secretary of Agriculture Wallace explained that farming was not a charitable enterprise. The farmers had to earn enough to live, and he said that this was a way to make sure that they did.

The AAA succeeded where Hoover's farm program had failed. For it managed to prevent the surpluses either before they were grown or before they could reach the market. The prices of farm products rose rapidly. Net farm income went up 240 percent between 1932 and 1935. Farm mortgages, many refinanced on better terms by another New Deal measure, the Farm Credit Act, dropped by $1.5 million. After the AAA, American farming would never again be the same. In exchange for the security of price supports, American farmers—Thomas Jefferson's ideal independent people—had bartered away their independence.

The fight for industrial recovery. Industrial workers were not much better off than the farmers. Millions were out of work. Industry alone seemed unable to absorb these jobless men and women, but perhaps the government could help. During World War I the government had mobilized factories for the war effort and then in the 1920s worked closely with trade associations. These were examples of a new kind of partnership between business and government. On this pattern FDR planned the National Industrial Recovery Act of June 16, 1933.

This act represented the thinking of business groups like the Chamber of Commerce, the National Association of Manufacturers, and the leading trade groups. It created a new National Recovery Administration (NRA), under which codes of fair dealing for each industry would be made by leaders of business and labor. These codes aimed to keep up prices and wages. They set maximum hours of work and minimum wages. They spelled out what goods should be made, how many of each thing, and

The New-York Historical Society

Government, labor, and business are shown united in the fight against the depression.

at what price. These were the very same kinds of deals that up to now big business had been punished for making. When business firms agreed on output and prices in this way, it had been called monopoly.

This new law said that the antitrust laws did not apply. To win support of the labor unions, section 7a was written into the NRA act giving workers the right to organize into unions.

The NRA came under the command of a profane and colorful general. Hugh Johnson was his name. In World War I he had shown his talents on the War Industries Board. Now he threw himself with the fury of a wildcat into the task of drawing up codes for all the nation's businesses. Industries large and small rapidly organized. These included steel and textiles—but also dog food and hair curlers! The energetic Johnson seemed to be everywhere. But he kept the spotlight on himself, constantly made statements to the press, and offended many people. Though his job was to get people to work together, he was a hard man to work with.

New Deal opponents thought that Roosevelt's programs tied up too many government resources.

Soon the NRA was being criticized from all angles. Owners of small firms said that it was helping the monopolies to swallow them up and that anyway it cost too much. Labor unions said that businesses were ignoring section 7a. Business leaders said that the codes gave unions an unfair advantage. Everybody seemed to consider the codes a means of self-protection.

Work relief. As another way to put people to work, a Public Works Administration (PWA) was set up by Congress with $3 billion to build roads, new government buildings, and other public projects. General Hugh Johnson had moved like a tornado, but Interior Secretary Ickes, the "old curmudgeon," pushed ahead with PWA projects only slowly and after careful planning. Some observers thought that Johnson and Ickes should have switched jobs. Still the PWA did manage, with very little waste, to build sewers, schools, post offices, hospitals, tunnels, housing projects, and even the aircraft carriers *Yorktown* and *Enterprise*.

The weakness of the PWA under Ickes was that it did not move fast enough. Roosevelt wanted as quickly as possible to put people to work. The Federal Emergency Relief Act of May 12, 1933, did exactly what President Hoover had refused to do—what he had said would destroy the American character. It provided $500 million for aid to the unemployed. Most of this was in the form of direct relief. Enemies of the program called it a "dole"—which meant that everyone who received it was a charity case. The New Dealers said this was unfair because really every citizen in need was entitled to help from the government. This program was directed by Harry Hopkins, a former social worker who became one of the President's closest advisers. The thin and sickly Hopkins proved fiercely energetic and surprised everybody by his effective leadership.

Roosevelt and Hopkins supported the dole only because it was the quickest way to help people in need. What they really wanted was to give people jobs. They believed people who could work should be paid only for working. Handouts to people who wanted to work would undercut their self-respect and self-reliance.

To avoid mere charity and really put people to work, the Civil Works Administration (CWA) was started in the fall of 1933. Again Hopkins was in charge, and he had $400 million to spend. This was not meant to be a permanent program, but only to help people until other jobs came along. The PWA had been set up to construct buildings and other large-scale public projects. In contrast the CWA was supposed to lay out as little as possible for bricks and mortar and to spend most of its money for wages.

In the one winter of 1934 "General" Hopkins managed to "mobilize" as many people as had served in the American armed forces in World War I. The CWA speedily put to work 4 million people in 180,000 programs improving and building roads, parks, playgrounds, and airports. It employed teachers in cities and rural areas. A billion dollars was pumped into the economy. But then the President and others began to fear that the CWA was creating a permanent class dependent on government grants. They were shocked at the huge cost. So Roosevelt ended the CWA that spring.

The election of 1934. Most of the New Deal programs alienated American business leaders. They asked if the great free enterprise nation could look forward only to "economic chaos with no end in sight." By June 1934 the New Deal spending—for relief, public works, home mortgages, benefit payments to farmers, and loans to business—had reached a staggering $5 billion. The national debt had nearly doubled since 1929. But the President insisted that the "human budget" must be balanced before the government's budget could be. He compared the war for economic survival to a war against invasion.

The immediate benefits of the New Deal programs were substantial. By the fall of 1934, two million people had been put to work, and national income was up 25 percent. Yet there was a long way to go to get the country back to normal. When the 1934 congressional elections came around, the unemployed still numbered 11 million. Full of their usual optimism, American voters were more impressed with what had been accomplished than with what remained to be done. The Demo-

crats won three-fourths of the seats in the House. In the Senate they gained ten seats, which gave them more than a two-thirds majority. When FDR made a campaign tour that fall, he said that he could see a remarkable change in the temper of the people from the time of his campaign two years before. "Now," he said, "they are a hopeful people." Much of the credit for that change was due to the vigorous and ebullient FDR himself.

SECTION 1 REVIEW

1. Identify or explain: "hundred days," Twentieth Amendment, "bank holiday," "fireside chats," modified gold standard, Securities and Exchange Commission, Twenty-first Amendment, Hugh Johnson, Harold Ickes, Harry Hopkins.

2. What personal traits helped Franklin Roosevelt succeed in politics?

3. Since 1933 we have had very few "runs" on banks. How did the Glass-Steagall Act help prevent such bank "runs"?

4. How did the CCC and TVA each promote conservation?

5. Describe measures passed to aid farmers.

6. How did the NRA seek to help industry? Labor unions?

7. What was the chief aim of both the PWA and CWA? How did the two programs differ?

8. **Determining Relevance.** How did FDR's "Brain Trust" illustrate his policy of bold experimentation?

---

2. From recovery to reform

Roosevelt won a resounding victory in the congressional elections of 1934. But now the great mass of New Deal laws provided a handy target for both conservatives and radicals. Before long, a conservative Supreme Court would strike down some of the New Deal laws that FDR believed to be the mainstays of his attack on the depression. As a result he would have to do much of his work all over again. He would need a Second New Deal.

Reorganizing relief. These problems lay in the future when Congress met in January 1935. In response to the President's request, Congress created

The Tennessee Valley Authority

Drainage Basin of the Tennessee River

〉 Major Dams

⚡ Major Steam-Electric Plants

0   100 Miles

0   100 Kilometers

still more enormous relief programs. The new $5 billion Works Progress Administration (WPA) would provide work for the able-bodied unemployed. Those who could not work were to be taken care of by cities and states.

The WPA, under Harry Hopkins, tried to enlist as many people as possible in building roads, bridges, public buildings, and other public works. Before it ended in 1943, the WPA would spend $11 billion and employ 8.5 million people. The National Youth Administration (NYA), a branch of the WPA, offered work to young people between 16 and 25. In one school year, for example, it aided 750,000 students in thousands of colleges and high schools. The WPA surprised and delighted many by helping people whom the government had never directly helped before. Writers, artists, actors, and musicians were put to work. They prepared guidebooks, decorated government buildings, wrote plays, and performed concerts to lift the nation's spirit. But some people worried that artists might be less free in the long run if the government ever became their main patron.

Thunder from the Right and Left. Conservatives were more and more troubled by FDR's programs. When the government helped business with the NRA, it seemed not too bad. The rest of the New Deal—especially the TVA—they called socialism. In 1934 some of these right-wing opponents of the New Deal—including even Democrats like John W. Davis and Al Smith, as well as some wealthy Republicans—formed the American Liberty League. Their purpose was "to combat radicalism, preserve property rights, and uphold and preserve the Constitution." In April 1935 the leaders of the Chamber of Commerce—which had earlier supported Roosevelt—joined their fight against FDR and the New Deal.

"Come along. We're going to the Trans-Lux to hiss Roosevelt."

Drawing by Peter Arno. Copyright © 1936, 1964 The New Yorker Magazine, Inc.

These wealthy opponents of FDR were headed for the Trans-Lux, a theater which showed newsreels and short features.

At the same time, FDR was being attacked from the Left. Senator Huey Long was a fast-talking, long-talking vote getter. He used the radio to sell himself to the people of Louisiana. As governor he had brought many reforms to his state. But he had also brought corruption and many wild hopes. Under his "Share the Wealth" program, he said, every man would be a king! There would be no more enormous fortunes and every family would have a guaranteed income. Of course, Ol' Huey would be "The Kingfish."

There were others who joined Long's attack on FDR. One of the most vicious and successful was the rabble-rousing Father Charles E. Coughlin. He called himself the radio priest, but he spread hate instead of love. He built a huge national following from his church in Royal Oak, Michigan. Money poured in from millions of listeners. At first he had supported the New Deal and called it "Christ's Deal." But when FDR did not follow Father Coughlin's own peculiar program—which increasingly turned toward fascism and anti-Semitism—he spoke out against the President. And he made himself a prophet of confusion and discord.

Another rabid critic of the New Deal was elderly Dr. Francis Townsend from Long Beach, California. He saw the extreme poverty of the aged and proposed a plan for old-age pensions that he said would solve the nation's problems. He wanted the government to give every man and woman 60 years old or older $200 a month—with the condition that they had to spend it each month. This would take care of old people and provide jobs for everyone else. Of course it would also have taken half the national income and turned it over to only 9 percent of the people. It is not surprising that many older people—but few others—became "Townsendites."

The early labor union support for FDR soon turned to opposition. Since section 7a had not fulfilled their hopes, union leaders were calling the NRA the "national run around." William Green, head of the AF of L, threatened that labor would oppose Roosevelt in the 1936 election.

Then a stroke of lightning hit the New Deal from an unexpected but most respectable source. The Supreme Court, in a series of shattering decisions, struck at the heart of FDR's program. In *Schechter* v. *United States* (May 1935), the Court declared the NRA unconstitutional. It also struck down laws passed to prevent foreclosures on farm mortgages and to provide pensions for railroad workers. Roosevelt was stunned. How could the nation solve its modern problems if Congress could not experiment with modern remedies? He declared that the justices of the Supreme Court were trying to push the country back to the days of the "horse and buggy."

The second one hundred days. When the NRA was declared unconstitutional, Congress was preparing to go home. They had done little since January. Now the President sprang into action. He kept Congress in session for another one hundred days, during the hot Washington summer. He insisted that they pass a law that would provide income for the elderly and for laid-off workers. He wanted a law that would boost labor's bargaining power. He called for a "soak the rich" tax and the breakup of certain holding companies. The First New Deal had been directed mainly toward recovery from the depression. This Second New Deal aimed at reform.

Social Security. The United States was far behind the industrial nations of Europe in protecting citizens against the risks of unemployment and old age. Under prodding from Dr. Townsend and his followers, from the AF of L, as well as some members of Congress, Roosevelt in January 1935 asked for an insurance plan. But until the *Schechter* decision, Congress had failed to act. Now the President pushed hard for his new idea of social insurance. While people were working, each of them would pay a small amount every month, with their employers paying the same amount, into a national Social Security fund in the Treasury. Then when a worker was too old to work, he or she would receive a monthly payment. The pay-outs would not start until 1940, since workers would have to build up some credits in their Social Security account. And only workers in trade and industry were covered at first. So the law also had a plan to take care of those in need.

This second part of the Social Security Act came to be known as *public assistance.* It was not social insurance, since the persons getting the monthly welfare checks did not pay into an insurance fund. Public assistance was a federal-state program. Any state that accepted the plan would get federal funds covering about half of the costs. The money would come from general state and federal revenues. The aged, the blind, and the dependent children covered by public assistance would have to prove their need for aid.

Unemployment insurance was a third part of the new law. It was also a joint federal-state program. The plan was to give laid-off workers some income for a number of weeks while they were hunting for a new job or waiting to be rehired. The money would come from a payroll tax paid by employers of eight or more persons. Each state would set up its own system under standards set by federal law.

The Social Security Act meant that millions of people would not have to live in fear of starving. And since persons getting old-age insurance would have put some of their own hard-earned money into the fund, they would not have to feel like charity cases. "Social Security" was a good name for the plan. It made millions feel more secure.

Moving against concentrated wealth and power. The Social Security Act took the wind out of the sails of Dr. Townsend. The President's series of "soak the rich" taxes helped him win away followers of "Kingfish" Long. FDR asked for higher estate and gift taxes, higher income taxes on the largest incomes, and a corporate income tax graduated to the size of the profits of businesses. The President said the bill would help "to prevent an unjust concentration of wealth and economic power" and reduce "social unrest and a deepening sense of unfairness." These measures were passed in a Revenue Act in August 1935.

Roosevelt also moved against the powerful utility companies that provided the nation's gas and electricity. Just thirteen holding companies controlled 75 percent of all the country's electric power. The Public Utility Holding Company Act was designed to restrict each company to operating a single system in a single area. A "death sentence" clause—enacted only after a bitter fight—empowered the SEC after January 1, 1940, to dissolve any utility holding company that could not prove that it was saving the consumers money. Under this law most of these great holding companies were broken up within the next three years. The law also gave federal agencies the power to regulate companies that sold natural gas or electric power across state lines.

Helping labor. FDR was the greatest friend of organized labor who had ever lived in the White House. His Second New Deal included the National Labor Relations Act. Senator Robert Wagner of New York had first proposed this act as early as 1934, but then FDR thought that section 7a of the NRA would give labor all the help it needed. After the Supreme Court killed the NRA, the President threw his support to Wagner's labor bill.

The new Wagner Act guaranteed the right of workers to join unions and to bargain collectively. It set up the National Labor Relations Board (NLRB) to oversee elections by which workers would decide which union, if any, would bargain for them. The Board could also stop unfair practices by employers against unions. Since the law put no obligations at all on the unions, it is not surprising that many employers thought the act was unfair and one-sided. Passed in July 1935, the law was upheld by the Supreme Court in 1937. The unions called it "Labor's Magna Carta."

By the time the second hundred days of the New Deal came to an end, in August 1935, the President found that most business leaders and wealthy people were against him. But he saw his reform program as nearly complete. Now, he said, there would be a "breathing spell."

More trouble with the Supreme Court.

During 1936 the Supreme Court struck down the AAA. The judges declared that the so-called "processing tax" could not be collected because it was not really a tax at all. Instead, they said, it was an unconstitutional way to limit farm output. Did this mean that the federal government could do nothing at all to solve the problem of farm surpluses? To get around the Court's objections, Roosevelt had Congress pass a Soil Conservation and Adjustment Act (February 1936) that restricted production under the name of conservation. The government paid farmers to plant soil-conserving crops on part of their land.

In April the Supreme Court limited the powers of the SEC. It also struck down the Guffey-Snyder Coal Act of 1935, which had tried to set up a "little NRA" by enacting the NRA coal code into law.

The President was concerned to find a constitutional way to protect workers by setting minimum wages. But the conservative Court ruled (5–4) against a New York state law that had set minimum wages for women. The majority argued that the Fourteenth Amendment left the state "without power by any form of legislation to prohibit, change, or nullify contracts between employers and women workers as to the amount of wages to be paid." In 1923 the Court had already struck down a federal wage law for women in the District of Columbia. Now the Court seemed to be saying that neither the states nor the federal government could set minimum wages. Still, FDR did not give up. He asked Congress for a law that he hoped the Court might accept. In the Government Contracts Act of June 1936, Congress gave the Secretary of Labor power to set minimum wages and maximum hours for workers in firms doing business with the federal government. It also prohibited them from employing boys under 16 or girls under 18. Since thousands of firms wanted to sell part of their output to the government, the new law improved the lot of many workers.

The election of 1936.

In early 1936, of course, FDR focused his attention on the coming presidential election. He believed that his New Deal had already proven itself a substantial success and that he deserved to be reelected. By June industrial production had returned to the level of 1923–1925. Factory employment was up. Farm income and weekly wages for workers had risen. The unemployed, who numbered more than 10 million in the winter of 1934–1935, had now dropped to 7 million. National income had increased 60 percent over 1933. Although the depression was far from over, Franklin D. Roosevelt was the most popular President since his cousin Teddy.

When the Republicans met at Cleveland in June, they had the impossible task of naming someone who could defeat the attractive "miracle worker" in the White House. To be named the Republican candidate that year was like being handed a lottery ticket that was sure to lose. On the first ballot they chose Governor "Alf" Landon of Kansas, a liberal Republican and onetime Bull Moose progressive. Despite the opposition of conservative Republicans to the New Deal, he ran on a surprisingly liberal platform. The Republicans seemed to have little choice but to endorse most of the New Deal programs. It was difficult to attack old-age and unemployment benefits, the right of labor to organize and bargain collectively, minimum-wage and maximum-hour laws for women and children, and soil conservation. The depression, FDR, and the New Deal had somehow changed the point of view of a whole nation. And despite lingering suspicions of "big government," the Republican party, too, came right along.

It was no surprise when the Democrats nominated Roosevelt and Garner again. FDR used his acceptance speech to set the tone of the campaign. He considered much of the criticism of business leaders to be mindless. And he directed all his considerable talents of wit and irony against them. He called them "economic royalists." He said they were anxious to build their personal dynasties, to control the government, and to exploit the workers—rather than to serve the nation's interests.

Shoppers on Main Street in 1936 saw campaign banners like these. The cartoon below was drawn after Harry Hopkins said that the needy numbered "one person out of every ten."

"They denied the Government could do anything to protect the citizen in his right to work and his right to live." It was time, he said, to destroy their anti-democratic power. "This generation," he proclaimed, "has a rendezvous with destiny."

The Democratic platform spelled out the far-reaching duties it believed the government should fulfill. Among these were to protect the family and the home, establish a democracy of opportunity for all, and aid those overtaken by disaster.

To the left of Roosevelt there were other candidates. The mild-mannered intellectual Norman Thomas, who had led the Socialists in 1928 and 1932, was again their candidate. The Communist party also entered the race. A new "Union party" drew together several unhappy groups—the followers of Father Coughlin, of Dr. Townsend, and of Huey Long. (Senator Long had been assassinated on the steps of the Louisiana state capitol in September 1935.) Their candidate was Representative William Lemke of North Dakota.

But it was Roosevelt all the way. His margin of 11 million votes over "Alf" Landon was the largest in history until that time. He carried every state but Maine and Vermont. "I knew I should have

ONE PERSON OUT OF EVERY TEN

532

gone to Maine and Vermont," he joked. "But Jim Farley wouldn't let me." All together the Socialists, Communists, and Unionists polled only about 1 million votes.

The new majority party. The election of 1936 revealed that, for the first time since the Civil War, Roosevelt had succeeded in making the Democrats the party of the majority. The party's enlarged support came mostly from those whom the New Deal had been able to help. FDR would be spokesman for "the Forgotten Man." This meant the immigrants and their children, the farmers and the laborers—Americans who somehow had not won the race for money and success. Teachers, social workers, and reformers of many sorts felt that FDR was their leader. Blacks were swinging to the Democrats in ever larger numbers.

Many of these "forgotten people" lived in the big cities, and they provided him a solid following.

Their votes could carry the largest states, which themselves had nearly enough electoral votes to win the election for President.

A new kind of Presidency. Roosevelt's success was not all due to his programs. Now his personal charm and his warm resonant voice could reach the whole nation. FDR was our first radio President. In his fireside chats over the radio, he came right into everybody's living room. He explained what he was doing in simple language that anybody could understand. Even his paralysis somehow became an advantage. He had to sit down while he talked. This meant that when he spoke to the nation he did not sound like a politician making a speech but like a member of the family in friendly conversation. When he began a radio talk, he did not say "Fellow citizens," but "My friends."

He also held many press conferences, which pleased the newspaper reporters. In all his four

FDR was our first President to use the radio effectively. His friendly, mellifluous voice was able to reach right into the homes of the three out of four families who owned radio receivers in 1936.

years President Hoover had offered only 66 press conferences. FDR met the press 337 times during his first term. He made the reporters his friends. This was plain in the stories they wrote about their President.

SECTION 2 REVIEW

1. Identify or explain: WPA, NYA, American Liberty League, Huey Long, Father Coughlin, Francis Townsend, William Green, *Schechter* v. *United States,* social insurance, NLRB, Government Contracts Act, "Alf" Landon, Union party.

2. Explain the importance of the WPA.

3. Describe the three main programs set up by the Social Security Act.

4. Why would the tax law, the holding company law, and the labor law in 1935 displease business leaders?

5. How were laws to aid farmers and wage earners written to avoid Supreme Court objections?

6. **Recognizing Bias.** Who were the critics of the New Deal? How did their complaints reflect their own prejudices?

3. The end of the New Deal

When FDR began his second term, everything pointed to more success in his effort to give the nation a New Deal. His inaugural address on January 20, 1937, admitted that much still remained to be done: "I see one-third of a nation ill-housed, ill-clad, ill-nourished." He promised to do something to help them. But soon he was involved in a struggle that wasted his energies and undercut his influence with Congress.

The attack on the Supreme Court. On February 5, 1937, without consulting his Cabinet or the Democratic party leaders, Roosevelt sent to Congress a plan to reorganize the federal courts. Although he did not say so, nobody doubted that his target was the Supreme Court. FDR proposed that the President should have the power to increase the number of justices on the Supreme Court from nine to fifteen if the justices refused to retire at the age of 70.

What he offered as a plan to "reform" the Court really was a way to make the Supreme Court approve the New Deal laws. If he had come out and declared his purpose, he would have lost much support. So he pretended that the nation needed his "reforms" because the courts were behind in their work. His plan came to be called a scheme for "court packing." And the name was not unfair.

Roosevelt's "court packing" message split the Democratic party and the nation. He had grown overconfident because of his great victory at the polls. He made the mistake of thinking that the nation would follow wherever he pointed.

Chief Justice Charles Evans Hughes was adroit in his opposition. He pointed out that the Court was up to date in its work and that a larger Court would be inefficient. He even timed a Court decision to help his cause. The Court upheld a Washington state minimum-wage law, reversing its decision of just ten months before, and showing that the Court did not always strike down reform legislation. One headline proclaimed, "A Switch in Time Saves Nine." Then the Court upheld the Wagner Act and the Social Security Act.

The Senate rejected Roosevelt's plan to pack the Court. In its place, Congress passed a law that allowed federal judges to retire at age 70 with full pay. One conservative justice retired while the debate was going on. Another retired the next year. FDR claimed that he had really gained what he wanted. It was more accurate to say that he won his battle but he lost the war. To win that battle he had lost much of the goodwill of Congress.

The Roosevelt recession. During 1937 the President learned a harsh lesson in economics. Business was booming. There were still 7 million unemployed, but some of his advisers feared a runaway inflation. In his first election campaign Roosevelt had promised to balance the budget. He now took the necessary steps. The Federal Reserve Board began to put the brakes on credit. Then the government cut the WPA by 1.5 million people. Now, when Social Security taxes were collected for the first time, still more money was drained out of the economy. At the end of 1937, business had slumped, and the number of unemployed had risen to 10 million. To stimulate the economy the President saw that he would have to resume his large-scale spending.

In April 1938 Roosevelt sent to Congress a message asking for an increase of the WPA work force—this time by 1.5 million, the same number who were cut in 1937. He said he would need $3 billion more for recovery and relief. The act was passed in June. Only by these means did the Roosevelt recession come to an end.

New farm and labor reforms. In 1938 the President also asked Congress for new measures to help the farmer and to control wages and hours in industry. The second Agricultural Adjustment Act (which Secretary of Agriculture Wallace called the best program of farm relief ever enacted) provided an "ever-normal granary." This meant putting farm products in storage in years of surplus and then releasing them in years of scarcity. Prices could then be stabilized around the "parity" level of 1910–1914. The second AAA continued giving to farmers the benefits of the Soil Conservation Act. And it allowed growers of certain crops to set marketing quotas if two-thirds of them agreed. A new Federal Crop Insurance Corporation insured wheat crops against natural disasters like drought, flood, and plant disease. Wheat itself could be used to pay the insurance premium.

Congress also passed a Fair Labor Standards Act. In all industries involved in interstate commerce, the length of the work week would gradually be reduced to 40 hours. The minimum wages (first set at 25 cents an hour) would increase over eight years to 40 cents an hour. Time and a half was to be paid for overtime. The law also forbade labor by children under 16.

The purpose of this Fair Labor Standards Act was to boost the buying power of wage earners. Also, the cut in the work week, along with the overtime pay rule, would induce employers to hire more workers. People were astonished when they learned that 750,000 workers had to receive raises to bring their wages up to 25 cents an hour.

The attempted "purge." FDR's fight over the Court had soured his relations with Congress. At the same time, the demands of the unions (p. 530) and the new government-spending policy upset the conservatives in both parties. Roosevelt's pet measures—such as his proposal for six regional projects similar to the TVA—were defeated by an alliance of Republicans and conservative Democrats.

The "ever-normal granary" program helped to fill huge grain elevators like these shown in 1941 by FSA photographer John Vachon.

535

Then the angry President decided to try to "purge" his party of his conservative opponents. Most of these were from the South. In 1938 he made the mistake of intervening in primary elections by writing letters, attending conferences, and making speeches. This effort boomeranged. In nearly every case where he interfered, the conservative candidate won.

Republicans saw their chance to take advantage of the splits in the Democratic party. And they profited from the rising tide of conservatism. They gained 75 seats in the House and 7 seats in the Senate. They elected 11 governors and polled 51.5 percent of the vote outside the "solid South."

The election of 1938 really marked the end of the New Deal. Republicans and conservative Democrats now had enough votes in Congress to block any more New Deal laws. And the President turned to problems abroad. Fascist Italy, Nazi Germany, and Imperialist Japan were on the march.

The New Deal—an appraisal. So the New Deal came quietly to a close. What had it accomplished? Many Americans were not sure. Millions were still out of work. Prosperity would not return until the nation was forced to try the Keynesian approach in a big way by World War II. Then massive government spending would put all the factories back to work.

Still the experimental Franklin D. Roosevelt had magically lifted the nation's spirit. "It was this administration," he said, "which saved the system of private profit and free enterprise after it had been dragged to the brink of ruin." The President had avoided the extremes. He had taken a middle course. Rejecting the dogmas of socialism, he yet increased government control over the economy— over banking, agriculture, and public utilities. The federal government played a new role in setting standards for wages and hours of work and in providing some income support for farmers, the aged, and the unemployed.

Americans discovered new strength. On the whole, the federal Constitution proved remarkably adaptable to the needs of a new age. Americans had survived their worst peacetime disaster—without spreading hate, without inciting civil war or abridging liberties. And they had not been seduced by a dictator. Freedom had proved the best atmosphere in which to keep freedom alive.

SECTION 3 REVIEW

1. Identify or explain: Charles E. Hughes, Roosevelt recession, second AAA, ever-normal granary, crop insurance, Fair Labor Standards Act.

2. Name some government actions that helped to bring about a recession in 1937–1938. What steps were taken to end the recession?

3. Describe additional measures that were enacted by Congress in 1938 to help farmers and industrial workers.

4. **Making Comparisons.** What was Roosevelt's plan to "reform" the Supreme Court? How did it compare with his other New Deal reforms?

CHAPTER 24 REVIEW

FOCUSING ON IDEAS

1. Compile a list of New Deal laws and programs described in this chapter. Which of these laws and programs were "experimental," or represented new or greatly broadened areas of federal activity?

2. Identify and describe New Deal measures designed to help workers, consumers, and owners of businesses.

3. Why was there increasing congressional opposition to President Roosevelt's proposals during his second term?

4. What United States Supreme Court decisions disrupted President Roosevelt's New Deal program? Explain.

TAKING A CRITICAL LOOK

1. **Checking Consistency.** What did John Maynard Keynes believe a nation should do to lift itself out of a depression? How did Roosevelt respond to this idea?

2. **Making Comparisons.** How did the first "hundred days" of the New Deal compare to the second "hundred days"?

YOUR REGION IN HISTORY

1. **Culture.** Identify buildings, roads, parks, or other projects in your locality that were built or improved under the Public Works Administration, Works Progress Administration, or other work-relief programs of the New Deal. Are the works of any artists or writers employed by the WPA on display in your community or in your local archives?

2. **Economics.** Name some New Deal measures that you think would have received wide support in your community in the 1930s and explain why. Which measures would probably have had little support? Why do you think many people would have opposed these programs?

HISTORICAL FACTS AND FIGURES

Using Evidence. Using the information provided in the graph define (a) a budget deficit, (b) a budget surplus. (c) In what year was the budget surplus the greatest? (d) In what year did deficit-spending begin? (e) In what year was the deficit largest? (f) What information in this chapter helps explain the origins and growth of the budget deficit between 1930 and 1940?

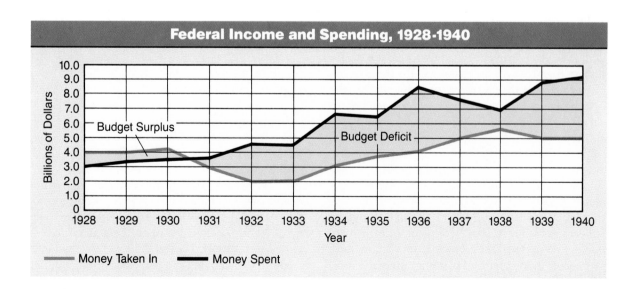

Federal Income and Spending, 1928-1940

CHAPTER 25

Reshaping American life

In 1933 another Bonus Army descended on Washington. This time, instead of being driven away, they were housed and fed by the government. Their leaders talked to the President. Then one day these veterans were startled to meet a tall, gawky woman with appealing eyes and a wide, toothy smile trudging through the mud to the old army barracks where they were housed. The visitor was Eleanor Roosevelt, wife of the President of the United States. She sat and talked with them, listened to their troubles, and joined in their singing. And she carried her sympathy back to the White House.

Eleanor Roosevelt personified the change in the government. Her humane spirit represented to many groups—blacks, immigrants, migrant workers, the aged, and the unemployed—the hope that through the New Deal they, too, might somehow someday enjoy the plenty of American life.

1. Problems on the farm

But it was far easier for Eleanor Roosevelt to sing with the Bonus Army or for FDR to speak warmly to "my friends" over the radio than for the government to change the daily lives of people in trouble. The problems of the farmers, for example, were varied and complicated. No single law could give all they needed. Some farmers needed electricity. Some were fighting dust storms. Others, working as tenants, were not getting a square deal from their landlords and had no way to share in the government's bounty. Many could not afford to buy the tractors or combines to make their land profitable. Still others, who lived on worn-out land, had no money to buy fertilizer. Nor did they know how to renew their land by planting diverse crops.

Their problems seemed as overwhelming and unmanageable as nature itself.

The dust storms. In the 1930s the Great Plains began to blow away. Bountiful rains in the 1920s had encouraged farmers to plow the fragile grasslands without worrying about the future. Then the rains ceased. Drought cursed the whole mid-continent from Canada to Mexico.

The sun baked the land into a brittle, powdery crust. Nineteen states in the heart of the nation became one enormous "Dust Bowl." Crops shriveled. Cattle died. When the wind blew, the topsoil—with no living roots to hold it in place—swirled into the air. Great, dark, yellowish clouds filled the sky, choking the nose and throat, blotting

William C. Palmer's 1934 painting "Dust, Drought, and Destruction" shows the ravages wrought by the great dust storms of the 1930s. The farm has been abandoned, the windmill has fallen, the tree has died, and the wind swirls the soil away through the air.

out the sun and causing street lights to be turned on at midday. The precious soil of the Great Plains blew all the way to the East Coast—even sifting into the White House—and on out into the Atlantic Ocean.

Many families whose fields grew only dust gave up. They loaded their old cars with what they could carry and left the land where they had been raised. The "flivver" that Henry Ford had invented no longer carried them to a holiday in town. Now instead it took them on their desperate quest for a better life—anywhere. They moved in all directions, without a clear destination and with no real plan. The "Okies" from Oklahoma and the "Arkies" from Arkansas headed west. A third of a million people from those states and from Texas, the Dakotas, Kansas, and Nebraska hit the road. Thousands ended up in California as migrant laborers picking fruit and vegetables and living in squalid camps. Their hard journeys and their frustrated lives can never be forgotten, for they became the long-suffering heroes of John Steinbeck's powerful novel, *The Grapes of Wrath*.

The mild climate and the legend of its golden land made California the number one goal of the migrants. In 1939 that state tried to stem the tide by passing a law forbidding poor migrants to enter. But two years later the Supreme Court declared the law unconstitutional.

A quarter-million Mexicans seeking work went to California during the 1930s. Other Mexicans, along with Filipinos, Okies, Arkies, and other migrants—at least another 100,000—moved north into Colorado, Wyoming, and Montana to work in the sugar beet fields. But, unlike the Okies, they had no Steinbeck to tell their story.

The depression forced many families to go on the road in search of work. A large number headed for the West Coast, where they hoped to find jobs in the orchards and vineyards. In this photograph by Dorothea Lange in November 1936 a family in California uses their car for a home.

Conserving the land. FDR's own experience had shown him the need for soil conservation. The land on his ancestral estate at Hyde Park, New York, had been worn out by centuries of unscientific farming. He renewed that land by planting thousands of trees "in the hope that my great grandchildren will be able to try raising corn again—just one century from now." Trees would help stop the dust storms on the Great Plains. Farmers across the nation followed their President's example. With seedlings from the government they planted 200 million trees across the expanse extending from the Dakotas to Texas. For years experts had said no trees would grow on the western plains. But these trees took root. Their growth surprised the experts and helped other farmers, too, by making new "shelterbelts," conserving water and holding in place the precious topsoil.

The New Deal, from its start, tried new ways to help the farmer. As early as 1933 a Soil Erosion Service was set up to preserve the farmer's most valuable resource. Farmers and CCC boys were taught terracing and contour farming. Then the Soil Conservation Act of 1936 aimed to reduce surpluses and also to promote soil conservation (p. 531). Today we still profit from the New Deal experiments—the TVA, the great dams in the West, reforestation, and grazing control—all ways to preserve and renew the American land.

The lot of farm tenants. After the Civil War, there were no longer slaves to till the soil in the South. Their place was taken by a new class, the *sharecroppers* (p. 324). These farmers—white and black—did not own the land they lived on, and they were not paid wages for their work. Instead they received a share of the crops, and the owner of the land got the rest.

Sharecroppers were not legally slaves, but they were tied to their plot of land by the bonds of debt and despair. Since they had no capital, the only way they could secure the seed for the next year—and the food and clothing for their family— was to pledge their share in advance. One year of bad crops was enough to drown them in debt. They could not survive on their land, yet they dared not leave.

Although it was not planned that way, the condition of the sharecroppers was made even worse by the first AAA. The law paid landowners to take some acres out of production, and this was often the marginal land the sharecroppers farmed.

To help the poor sharecroppers and other tenants who still could work their land, Harry Hopkins under the Federal Emergency Relief Act loaned them money and gave them seeds and equipment. When their land was too poor to support them, he tried to resettle them on better lands. In 1935 FDR moved these activities to the Resettlement Administration under Rexford Tugwell.

But all these efforts hardly made a dent in the problem. Senator John Bankhead of Alabama proposed a new approach. The Bankhead-Jones Farm Tenant Act of 1937 provided long-term loans to help tenants buy the farms they worked. Blacks and whites were treated alike. And the unfortunate Okies and the Arkies who became migratory farm laborers, following the ripening crops, were at least

"Roasting Ears" was painted by Thomas Hart Benton of Missouri in the 1930s.

The Metropolitan Museum of Art, The Arthur H. Hearn Fund, 1939 provided with clean camps. The Farm Security Administration replaced Tugwell's agency to carry out these programs.

The problems of American farmers—of the poor tenants, sharecroppers, and migrants—were as broad and as varied as the continent. These were not to be solved in a few years, nor by a single farm program in Washington. Still, the New Deal efforts could give them hope and cheer them with the news that they were not forgotten.

Rural electrification. By the mid-1930s electricity had reshaped the daily lives of Americans in cities. It was lighting their homes at night, running their radios, cooling their refrigerators. But not for farmers. They fed an electrified nation, but they themselves had not yet entered the electric age. Only one farm family in ten had electricity.

On May 11, 1935, President Roosevelt set up the Rural Electrification Administration to help bring electric power to the farms of America. The REA could loan money at low interest to help private companies or farmers' cooperatives build their own generators and install power lines. This produced an electrical revolution. By 1941, four out of five American farms were enjoying the comforts that only electricity could bring. More than any other transformation, this showed that their government, which now remembered them, could draw them into the mainstream of modern America.

SECTION 1 REVIEW

1. Identify or explain: Eleanor Roosevelt, "Dust Bowl," John Steinbeck, sharecroppers, Rexford Tugwell, Bankhead-Jones Farm Tenant Act, Farm Security Administration.

2. How did the New Deal try to help poor tenant farmers?

3. How did the REA help most farm families?

4. **Recognizing Cause and Effect.** What was the effect of dust storms on farmers in the Great Plains?

---

2. The problems of black Americans

In 1930 around 80 percent of all black Americans were still living within the borders of the old Confederacy. There they were not allowed to vote. Little money was spent on their education, and they went to separate and inferior schools. They found it hard to borrow money to buy houses or farms. In some southern states the blacks made up more than half the population. Yet the paths to wealth and political power were closed to these black citizens.

It was no wonder then that, in 1938, President Roosevelt called the South "the nation's No. 1 economic problem." By almost any measure—health, housing, schools, auto ownership, farm equipment, or family income—the South was the worst-off section of the whole United States. And in the impoverished South, the blacks were the poorest of all.

Yet new forces were at work in America. Among them were black leaders themselves. Even under slavery there had been brave rebels like Nat Turner and Denmark Vesey. The persuasive Frederick Douglass had been a leader in the abolition movement. During the Civil War he had helped recruit blacks for two regiments in the Union army. After the war he became marshal of the District of Columbia and United States consul general in Haiti. In the early 1900s, too, there were many kinds of black leaders who offered different views of American life and the doors to opportunity. Booker T. Washington and W. E. B. Du Bois, each in his own way, pointed in new directions for black Americans (p. 385).

Black Southerners lose the right to vote. When the Populists had tried to unite all the poor—black and white—behind economic reforms in the South (p. 405), they provoked an extreme reaction. White Democrats defeated the Populists by pointing with alarm to the fact that they worked with blacks. And soon white Populists admitted they could never win elections if the race question was used against them. Southern whites combined their energy and ingenuity to find ways to keep blacks out of the polling booths. This was no easy task. The Fifteenth Amendment, adopted during Reconstruction, had plainly declared that the right of citizens to vote should not be denied "by the United States or by any state on account of race, color, or previous condition of servitude."

Southerners tried using the "grandfather clause." A state would simply pass a law giving the right to vote to those persons who did have the right to vote on January 1, 1867 (before the Fifteenth Amendment) and to those persons' descendants. Anyone else who wanted to vote had to pass all sorts of impossible tests. Of course that included blacks. They would not be allowed to vote simply because their grandfathers did not have the right to vote! Beginning in 1895 seven southern states passed "grandfather" laws. Not until 1915 did the United States Supreme Court declare that these laws violated the Constitution.

Another trick was the so-called literacy test. It pretended to limit the vote to people who could read. But when blacks came to vote, the white election judges gave tests that they themselves probably could not have passed. They would ask a black to explain the most difficult part of the Constitution. A white person only had to read out a simple sentence.

Some southern states also used the poll tax. That was a tax that everybody had to pay before going to the polls to vote. Most blacks in the South were so poor that they really could not afford the few dollars for the tax. And even if a black person paid the tax, the election judge could always find some mistake in the tax receipt, and so keep the black person from voting.

The craftiness of some white Southerners seemed endless. They even went so far as to pretend that the great political parties in the South were not political parties at all, but only private clubs. Therefore, they said, nobody except white "members" had a right to vote in the primary election when their "club" picked its candidates for public office.

Since the Democratic party was in complete control in most of the South, winners in that party's primary would win the offices. By keeping black people from voting in the primary, then you would take away their votes.

Working for rights for blacks.
Thoughtful citizens all over the country became ashamed that the nation had been so slow to give all Americans their simple rights. The Niagara Movement, sparked by W. E. B. Du Bois, grew stronger (p. 386). The National Association for the Advancement of Colored People (NAACP) was founded in 1909 on Lincoln's birthday. It was formed in response to shocking race riots like the one in 1908 in Springfield, Illinois, Lincoln's burial place. Du Bois became the impassioned editor of the NAACP magazine, *The Crisis.*

Americans of all races and religions, from all parts of the country, joined hands. People like Jane Addams, who already were working for the poor of all races in the northern city slums, gave money to pay for lawyers to help blacks secure their rights in the South. The president of the NAACP, Boston lawyer Moorfield Storey, argued the case when the Supreme Court in 1915 set aside the "grandfather" laws. The NAACP also won other important cases. One of these declared that no trial of a black could be a fair trial (as the Constitution required) if blacks were kept off the jury. During the next years the NAACP was the most important group trying to awaken all Americans to the rights of blacks.

Things were getting better for blacks. But the progress was painfully slow—and there was a long way to go.

Failures of the New Deal.
For millions of black Americans—especially in the South and in the big city slums in the North—there still seemed almost no change. Black workers were the last hired and the first fired. Black children still had less money spent on their education. Blacks were not allowed to live wherever they could afford, but had to live in special neighborhoods. Even under the New Deal, blacks were not always given their fair share. For example, they were not allowed to live in the model towns built with government money in the Tennessee Valley.

Most of those blacks whom Du Bois called the "Talented Tenth" still had to take lowly jobs. When the NRA codes allowed blacks to be paid less than whites, blacks began to say that NRA just meant "Negroes Ruined Again." *The Crisis* said in 1935 that blacks "ought to realize by now that the powers-that-be in the Roosevelt administration have nothing for them."

Yet more and more blacks voted for FDR and the New Deal. In Chicago, for example, where in 1932 only 23 percent had voted for Roosevelt, 49 percent favored him in 1936, and 56 percent in 1940. But the New Deal had done nothing to remove the poll tax. In most of its programs, blacks were still treated unequally. And when an anti-lynching bill was introduced to Congress, FDR refused to support it. "If I come out for the anti-lynching bill now," Roosevelt told

In spite of the high unemployment in the nation's cities in the 1930s, black families from the rural South continued their farm-to-city migration. In Chicago they had no choice but to live in the black belt on the South Side—often in houses like the one in this 1930s' photograph.

Walter White of the NAACP, "they [southern senators] will block every bill I ask Congress to pass to keep America from collapsing. I just can't take that risk."

Blacks in government. Despite the failings of the New Deal, Roosevelt did convince most blacks that he sided with them in their fight for equal treatment. He spoke out against lynching as "collective murder." Under Woodrow Wilson and his Re-

publican successors, blacks in government jobs were segregated. Now those who were brought into the growing bureaucracy were given their rightful place with other Americans. A "Black Cabinet" or "Black Brain Trust" became close advisers of the President. Among the persons in the large and ever-shifting group were William H. Hastie, Assistant Solicitor in the Department of the Interior, and Mary McLeod Bethune, the forceful director of the Division of Negro Affairs of the National Youth

Administration. Mrs. Bethune channeled large amounts of aid to thousands of black youngsters, helping them stay in school or learn new trades.

As usual, Eleanor Roosevelt helped blacks to feel that the administration cared about them. She was known to be a good friend of Mary McLeod Bethune's. She invited the National Council of Negro Women to tea at the White House. She was seen, and photographed, visiting black schools and other projects useful to black citizens.

A "Black Renaissance." After World War I a movement called the "Black Renaissance" or the "New Negro Movement" began in Harlem. This neighborhood in New York City became a gathering place for black poets, writers, scholars, painters, and musicians. Poets like Langston Hughes and Countee Cullen revealed whole new vistas of American experience. Also in Harlem then was Du Bois, who told the exciting story of the renaissance in *Black Manhattan* and *Along This Way*.

The Harlem Renaissance ended about 1930, but its influence spread outward. In cities across the nation there were small but active groups of poets, writers, painters, and actors. The movement was helped along by the New Deal's Federal Writers' Project.

The rights for black Americans would come gradually—but not fast enough for W.E.B. Du Bois. He lost faith in America and in democracy. He joined the Communist party and then renounced his United States citizenship. In 1961, at the age of 93, he moved to the new African country of Ghana. But, as we shall see, others of stronger faith—the Rev. Martin Luther King, Jr., for example—continued their struggle in and for America. They would bring historic victories of justice and equality, not only for blacks, but for all Americans.

SECTION 2 REVIEW

1. Identify: W.E.B. Du Bois, NAACP, Mary M. Bethune, "Black Renaissance."

2. Name and explain devices used in southern states to keep blacks from voting.

3. **Expressing Problems Clearly.** How did the New Deal fail to help black Americans? In what ways did it help them?

---

3. The New Deal and women

Many Americans had thought that winning the right to vote would allow women to become an independent force in politics. This had not happened. Many women failed to go to the polls. And because they did not vote, politicians had little reason to respect their special demands. It would take more than the Nineteenth Amendment to bring women into the mainstream of American political life. It would take a long program of education and the slow discovery that women were not shaped by nature only for roles as wives and mothers. They were just as qualified as men for leadership and service in government, business, and the arts. In the experimental spirit of the New Deal era millions of Americans—women and men—were awakened to these opportunities.

Eleanor Roosevelt. The person best placed to help them was the President's wife. Eleanor Roosevelt's mother had died when she was eight, and her father, just before her tenth birthday. Raised by her grandmother, she had lived a lonely life. Perhaps her own unhappiness as a girl had made her sympathetic to the needs of others who felt alone and abandoned. She adopted all the nation's unhappy and neglected people as her foster children. And she dared to speak up for them in her regular press conferences. She wrote a newspaper column and gave radio talks. She traveled everywhere. In 1933 alone she covered 40,000 miles. One newspaper headlined on its society page, "Mrs. Roosevelt Spends Night at White House." FDR, in his wheelchair, could not move about as she did. She became the conscience of the New Deal and the eyes of the President. It was not unusual for him to tell the Cabinet that something needed to be done because "My Missus told me so and so."

Women in government and politics. With Eleanor Roosevelt in the White House, women for the first time gained substantial political influence and positions of power on the national scene. Women reformers came to Washington in large numbers to work for the government. Mary (Molly) Dewson, a friend of the Roosevelts', took over the direction of women's work in the Democratic party. In 1936 the Democratic convention ruled that each member of the Platform Committee had to have an alternate of the opposite sex. The

New York Times called this "the biggest coup for women in years."

Eleanor Roosevelt and Mary Dewson fought hard to get women into the government and to see that New Deal programs helped women. In 1930, women held only 17.6 percent of the postmaster positions, but six years later their share had gone up to 26 percent. The Civil Works Administration employed 100,000 women by the end of 1933.

Some of the most important positions in FDR's administration were given to women. Frances Perkins was Secretary of Labor. Florence Allen became a judge of the Circuit Court of Appeals. Other women became ambassadors and top officers of the WPA and other agencies. Formerly all the women executives in the federal government could

Among the most active supporters of a larger role for women in the government and the Democratic party during the New Deal were Eleanor Roosevelt (below) and Mary Dewson. Because FDR was unable to walk, Mrs. Roosevelt traveled everywhere, becoming his eyes and ears outside the White House.

meet for dinner in a small clubroom. Now they needed a large hall.

Eleanor Roosevelt thought that women could help humanize government. The aim of the New Deal, as she saw it, was to promote "the general happiness of the working man and woman and their families." Women had something special to offer.

The economic inequality of women. Still, during these years women were usually given jobs that were considered "women's work"—as teachers, typists, clerks, nurses, and textile workers. They were seldom put in supervisory positions. Though 80 percent of the schoolteachers of the nation were women, in superintendent positions they were only 1.5 percent. One-third of all graduate degrees were awarded to women, yet they made up only 4 percent of the college professors. Even when they did the very same work, women often were paid less than men.

In those depression days of widespread unemployment, many Americans—including leading women—feared that women would take jobs from men. This would increase the unemployment of the traditional family "breadwinners." Florence Kahn, congresswoman from California, declared, "Women's place is not out in the business world competing with men who have families to support." Secretary of Labor Frances Perkins agreed.

While women were heartened by the examples of Eleanor Roosevelt, Frances Perkins, Mary McLeod Bethune, Mary Dewson, and others like them on the national scene, they still had a long road to travel toward economic equality.

SECTION 3 REVIEW

1. Identify: Mary Dewson, Frances Perkins.
2. How did Eleanor Roosevelt help women achieve political influence?
3. **Drawing Conclusions.** How did the depression affect women's job prospects?

4. The struggles of labor

The New Deal hoped to enlist the help of organized labor to improve the lot of "forgotten Americans"—blacks, women, immigrants, the poor. Through section 7a of the NRA, and then by the Wagner Act and its National Labor Relations Board, the government lent its support to the attempts of workers to organize.

The growth of the AF of L. Loss of jobs had cut union membership after the Great Crash. Then the unions began to recover in 1934. But they were still unable to organize the great mass-production industries—steel, autos, rubber, textiles. The AF of L was a federation of craft unions and so was better suited to the past than to the future. Its ways of thinking were not adapted to a world of vast factories, of power-driven machinery, and mass production.

The Carpenters' Union, for example, had grown by moving from the construction trades into any industry that dealt with things made of wood and finally anything "that ever was made of wood." In this way—and by expanding into many new and smaller fields—the AF of L had reached a membership of 3.5 million by 1936.

The birth of the CIO. Some union leaders were not happy with the craft approach. They felt that the age of crafts had gone out with the horse and buggy. John L. Lewis, the massive, shaggy-browed leader of the United Mine Workers, believed that the industrial world of the 1900s required a new kind of labor organization. The American Federation of Labor, led by Samuel Gompers and William Green, had organized the aristocracy of American labor. They believed that the skilled workers in the old crafts—carpenters, plumbers, and bricklayers—could only lose if they threw in their lot with the millions of unskilled workers in factories and mines.

Lewis had begun working in the mines when he was 16. Even after he became a high union official he never forgot that he was a miner. And he was confident that if labor was to become a great power and defend its interests it would have to organize in a new way. Unions would never get into the steel mills or auto plants if the company had to deal with a dozen craft unions. Each union would want what was best for its own members. Lewis said that a single union should bargain for all the workers—skilled and unskilled—in a giant industry. There should be one industrial union for steel, not a dozen or more craft unions.

The AF of L had never organized the steel industry. For it did not fit into the old craft pattern. Now Lewis wanted to unionize the

Wide World Photos

John L. Lewis, shown here after a trip down into a mine, was the tough and charismatic leader of the CIO in the 1930s.

steelworkers because steel mills were the largest single users of coal. Their owners also owned coal mines.

In 1935 the Committee for Industrial Organization (later the Congress of Industrial Organizations) was formed by Lewis. He was joined by other labor leaders who agreed that American labor needed a new approach—Sidney Hillman of the Amalgamated Clothing Workers, Charles Howard of the Typographical Union, and Thomas McMahon of the Textile Workers. This "CIO" quickly changed the direction of American labor organization. At first the founders said they only wanted to advise the AF of L on how to organize the giant industries. But the conservative leaders of the AF of L resisted these efforts. In 1937 when the CIO

leaders and their members were expelled from the AF of L, the CIO declared its independence and became an important new force in American life.

The CIO quickly stepped up its efforts. In 1937 alone production was halted by 4740 strikes. That winter the workers themselves invented an ingenious new weapon that worked for a short while. When they went on strike, instead of leaving the factory they simply stayed there and sat down at their machines. They refused to work or let others work. They had food brought in and slept on the factory floor. They said that since it was their work that made the factory valuable, the factory really partly belonged to them. But the Supreme Court disagreed, and in 1939 "sit-down strikes" were banned.

Of course, the strikers did not always simply sit down. And employers sometimes hired private police who were reckless of the rights and the lives of workers. Outside the Republic Steel plant in Chicago ten striking workers were killed. From these struggles came a new era for labor unions in the United States. During 1937, General Motors, Chrysler, U.S. Steel, and many smaller steel companies as well as Firestone Rubber, General Electric, and some major textile firms signed CIO contracts. Unions would play a strong new role in American industrial life. As never before, workers would look to them to hear their grievances and protect their rights. The power of factory owners over their workers was much reduced. Through the NLRB, the federal government supported the unions.

Challenged by the success of the CIO, the AF of L swung into action to expand its membership. Between 1936 and 1938 membership in all unions increased from 4 million to 6 million. Soon big labor would face big business.

New union members. The membership of the old-line craft unions of the AF of L had been mostly Americans of the older immigration—English, Scots, Germans, Irish, and Scandinavians. Out of fear and from prejudice these unions commonly excluded the later comers from southern and eastern Europe in addition to blacks and women. The new CIO unions welcomed all these groups with their theme song, "Solidarity Forever."

Women found new openings in the factory because the CIO began to recruit workers without

Employees at a General Motors Corporation plant in Flint, Michigan, sat down by their machines in 1937 in the nation's first sit-down strike. They were seeking recognition of their new CIO union, the United Automobile Workers, and their tactic prevented the company from running the plant with strikebreakers. They won their demands, but the sit-down strike was soon declared illegal.

regard to sex. Within a few years nearly a million women joined the unions. But even in the unions women were not yet quite equal. For example, the liberal Amalgamated Clothing Workers still allowed women to be paid less than men for the same work.

The unions themselves showed dramatic changes. The International Ladies Garment Workers Union, whose members had been largely Jewish at the end of World War I, now in the mid-1930s was nearly half Italian. Before 1940 many of its members were Puerto Ricans. By opening their doors the unions had the power to open opportunity for new immigrants and the children of immigrants.

The labor movement continued to harbor large pockets of prejudice. Despite the example of the CIO, certain unions—especially in building trades—continued to exclude blacks, Puerto Ricans, Mexicans, and others whom they considered "different." Farm laborers, migratory workers, and domestic servants remained outside the ranks of organized labor.

Neither the unions nor the New Deal could bring an end to unemployment. Even after the mobilization for war in 1940 had provided thousands of new jobs, there were still 6 million out of work in 1941. Not until 1943 would the nation reach full employment.

SECTION 4 REVIEW

1. Identify: John L. Lewis, Samuel Gompers, William Green, CIO.

2. How did some employers try to break strikes?

3. What gains did American labor unions make in the years 1936–1938?

4. What groups formerly left out of unions made big gains through the efforts of the CIO?

5. **Making Comparisons.** How did an industrial union differ from a craft union?

FOCUSING ON IDEAS

1. What economic problems were sharecroppers facing in the 1930s? Did the New Deal benefit these farmers?

2. What New Deal laws or other actions of the Roosevelt administration helped black Americans of the 1930s? Explain how these laws and actions improved black people's lives.

3. What tactics did labor use to improve its position in the 1930s? Which tactics were the most successful? Why?

4. How did Eleanor Roosevelt represent the "spirit" of the New Deal?

TAKING A CRITICAL LOOK

1. **Recognizing Bias.** How would you expect a leader for women's rights in 1940 to assess the decade of the 1930s—the progress and setbacks for women?

2. **Making Comparisons.** Who were the "forgotten Americans" of the 1930s? What groups, if any, would you call "forgotten Americans" today? What are the similarities and differences between the two groups?

YOUR REGION IN HISTORY

1. **Geography.** Using a state map, locate the areas of your state that benefited from the Rural Electrification Administration during the New Deal. How did electricity change the way people in your state lived?

2. **Culture.** The 1930s was rich with musical diversions for those suffering from the Depression. Interview people in your community to learn the titles and lyrics of songs made popular during the period. Ask them whether the music of the period made it easier to bear the difficult conditions of the Depression.

3. **Economics.** Some older women in your community probably obtained their first jobs in the

1930s. Find out from them—and from other sources—what kinds of jobs were available for women in the 1930s. Ask women who did find their first job during these years how employment outside the home changed their lives? Report your findings to the class.

HISTORICAL FACTS AND FIGURES

Synthesizing Information. Study the graph below to help answer the following questions: (a) How many American workers were members of labor unions in 1900? In 1920? In 1940? (b) By what percentage did the number of union members increase during the period 1900–1940? (c) If the 8,500,000 union members in 1940 represented 15.5% of all workers, what was the approximate size of the total labor force? (d) What information in the chapter helps explain why the number of union members increased so dramatically during this period?

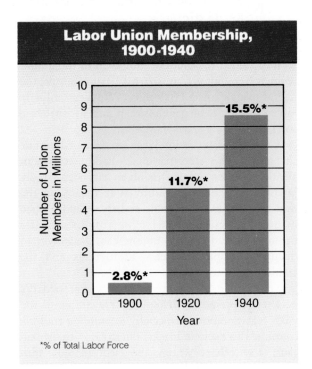

Labor Union Membership, 1900-1940

*% of Total Labor Force

Sources: *Historical Statistics of the United States*
Statistical Abstract of the United States

CHAPTER 26

Clouds of war

While Americans were trying the New Deal experiments in democracy, desperate and hungry people in Europe were handing over their lives and liberties to ruthless dictators. Some of the most civilized peoples of Europe had returned to an age of barbarism. In Italy, only ten years before FDR entered the White House, Benito Mussolini and his Fascists (as his party was called) marched on Rome. They seized the government, abolished democracy, destroyed the liberties of the Italian people—all on the promise of jobs and glory. In Germany, too, in the very month when FDR took his oath of office, Adolf Hitler, with his gang of Nazis, was made dictator.

1. Foreign affairs, 1933–1939

When Franklin D. Roosevelt moved into the White House in March 1933, the world prospects were grim. The outlook for civilization was darker than at any earlier time in American history. Two decades before, when President Wilson was elected, European nations were battling for empire and for the world's treasure. Now the threats to peace came from national leaders who screamed their hatred of democracy and modern civilization. They declared war on the ideals of equality and representative government on which the United States was founded.

The rise of Hitler. During the next years, European diplomacy would be dominated by Adolf Hitler, the most destructive dictator of modern times. He was not really a German, because he was born in Austria. A high school dropout, he wanted to be an artist, but twice failed the admission examination for the art academy in Vienna. He

lived on charity and by selling copies that he made of picture postcards. In World War I he joined the German army. He was gassed and wounded, and never reached a higher rank than corporal. After the war he began to organize his own political party, aiming to seize the government and lead Germany to world power. Driven by a passionate, senseless anti-Semitism, he was determined to exterminate the Jews—whom he blamed for Germany's defeat.

In 1923, after his Nazi thugs failed to take over in the southern German state of Bavaria, where they surrounded the leading officials in a beer hall, he was sent to prison. There he wrote his 800-page *Mein Kampf* (My Struggle), which became the bible of the Nazis, and then of all Germany. He declared that the Germans were the "Master Race," entitled to rule the world. Democracy, he said, was a fraud, and the only good government was a dictatorship. The dictator should rule not by truth but by the "Big Lie." Christianity, according to him, was also a fraud, invented by the Jews to make cowards of

Adolf Hitler (center) marches in a November 1938 Munich parade commemorating early Nazi struggles in Bavaria.

the Master Race. Hitler's plans for a "Third Reich" to last a thousand years were so simple-minded and so immoral that few people outside Germany took them seriously.

But inside Germany, thousands, and then millions were joining his National Socialist (Nazi) party. They resented the Versailles Peace Treaty after World War I and the reparations that had been imposed on the German people. Partly as a result of these heavy payments, the economy fell apart and inflation ran wild. A loaf of bread that cost ten marks one week would be priced at one thousand marks the next week, and then would quickly skyrocket to a billion marks. Money lost its value so fast that salaries and wages had to be paid every 24 hours. Life savings became worthless.

Hitler comes to power. The democratic government within Germany after the war was weak. The German parliament, split into a dozen political parties, was unable to organize the nation's economy. Millions were unemployed, and goods were scarce. The world depression that in the United States had led Americans to try their New Deal left the Germans leaderless, hungry, and hopeless.

Who could help them? Whom should they blame?

At this moment Hitler, with his mad vision of world power, came on the scene. He gave them their scapegoat—the Jews—upon whom they could blame everything. But he was not so mad that he could not organize spectacular meetings with swastika flags flying for thousands to hear his hour-long orations of hate and glory. And he was a master of the radio. He appealed to the unemployed and the rabble made up of both the ambitious and the disappointed.

Reasonable leaders in other countries found his schemes so outrageous that they would not believe they were real. Yet respectable Germans sat by watching while his thugs beat up opponents, assassinated enemies, sent innocent millions to concentration camps, and filled the newspapers with their Big Lies. Hitler showed that people were more timid than was ever before imagined.

The Germans made Hitler their God. When they greeted each other, they no longer said "Grüss Gott" (God be with you!) but "Heil Hitler!" And anyone who used the old greeting was suspected of treason. They set up their German Christian church to make Christianity serve the Master Race.

The photograph above shows guards rounding up women and children to be sent to concentration camps where Adolf Hitler (below) and his followers tortured and murdered millions.

The main new institution they invented was the concentration camp. To these places of torture they sent millions of Jews and countless other anti-Nazi Protestants and Catholics. There they used gas chambers to kill children, women, and men whom they considered their enemies. They extracted the gold from the teeth of the corpses to buy armaments and used human ashes to fertilize their fields. And one of the most difficult tasks facing FDR and his supporters was to persuade Americans that this was not just a nightmare.

Communist Russia, as the same time, was in the grip of the wily and vicious Josef Stalin. There, too, people who spoke up were tortured and sent to labor camps in remote Siberia. In Japan the expansion-minded army leaders were shaping the nation's policies. And the Italians under Mussolini were planning to create a new Roman Empire.

The looming threat of war. Italy, Russia, and Japan had all been American allies in the First World War. President Wilson had called that a war "to make the world safe for democracy." Now these same countries had become threats both to democracy and to peace. Germany, risen from defeat, was building an enormous new army, making weapons at frightening speed, and menacing its neighbors. Any one of the new military powers had a better-equipped army than the old democracies had.

In 1935, pursuing its dreams of empire, Italy invaded Ethiopia and bombed innocent villages from the air. In 1936 Germany moved its army back into the Rhineland, which had been demilitarized after World War I. Seeking a base for their aggressions in western Europe, Hitler and Mussolini slipped arms and men into Spain to support the Fascist General Francisco Franco. Spain became the world's battlefield in a bloody civil war. Fascist forces from everywhere fought against the republican government, which was aided by Communist Russia and supporters from France, England, and the United States.

Except to the cheeriest optimists, it was plain that another world war was brewing. Should the United States sit by and see the forces of savagery dominate the world?

The Good Neighbor policy. Roosevelt came into office in 1933 pledging that the United States would be "the good neighbor" in world affairs. We would be "the neighbor who resolutely respects himself and, because he does so, respects the rights of others." He meant his statement to apply to all the world, but the "Good Neighbor policy" became a label for his Latin American policy.

Roosevelt intended to continue the policies of Herbert Hoover toward our southern neighbors. We would not try to run their governments. To prove his point, FDR withdrew our marines from Haiti. But when Cuba was torn by another revolution, our pressure brought the conservatives to power. Some Latin Americans wondered then whether the United States had really changed. FDR tried to reassure them. At a Pan-American conference at Montevideo, Uruguay, in 1933, Secretary of State Cordell Hull joined in a declaration that "no state has the right to intervene in the internal or external affairs of another."

The United States gave solid evidence of the new policy. Back in 1901 our Congress had forced the Cubans to add the Platt Amendment (p. 426) to their constitution as a condition for the withdrawal of American troops from the island. Cuba promised to provide the United States with naval and coaling stations. They also gave the United States the right to intervene to preserve order and maintain Cuban independence. It amounted to a Cuban declaration of dependence on the United States. Now, in May 1934, by a new treaty the United States gave up its right to intervene. At last Cuba would be treated like a sovereign nation.

The real test of the Good Neighbor policy came in Mexico. In 1938 President Lázaro Cárdenas suddenly announced that the Mexican government was taking over all foreign oil properties. The holdings of the seventeen British and American companies were valued at nearly half a billion dollars. The British broke off diplomatic relations with Mexico. Some Americans urged us to send in our troops, but Secretary Hull was patient. He preferred to negotiate and reached a settlement in 1941. Mexico agreed to pay the oil companies for their properties and also settled other claims of United States citizens. The Roosevelt administration began to persuade our Latin American neighbors that the United States was ready to treat them as equals.

Japanese-American relations. On the other side of the world, a military clique in control of Japan reached across the narrow Sea of Japan to conquer an empire. When the Japanese seized Manchuria in 1931, the League of Nations condemned Japan as an aggressor. The Japanese withdrew from the League and in 1937 attacked weak China. The democracies of western Europe uttered bold, brave words against the Japanese, but they were afraid to act. They preferred to let Japan enslave Asian millions rather than risk war themselves.

On December 12, 1937, the United States gunboat *Panay* on the Yangtze River in China was sunk by Japanese bombs. Two American sailors died. The United States protested. A prompt apology from Japan, with an indemnity of $2 million, closed the incident, but left Americans worried.

FDR and neutrality. President Roosevelt warned that if aggression continued in Asia, Africa, and Europe, the whole world would be engulfed in war. The United States could not remain a mere spectator. If the democracies of Europe were conquered by the Nazis and their allies, the United States would be next on their list. He called for a "quarantine" of the aggressor nations. But for the moment he could do little more to help the free nations of Europe. Americans had not forgotten the senseless slaughter in the First World War. More and more Americans said, "Never Again!" Some were becoming pacifists, saying they would never go to war for any reason. Still others became "isolationists," hoping to fence off the New World. Naturally enough, Americans who had come from Italy or Germany did not like the idea of fighting against their old homeland. Americans of Irish descent remembered the English tyranny over their island. A few people even became American Nazis.

Some historians argued that if the United States had really been neutral during World War I, our nation would not have had to go to war at all. Might the world have been better, they asked, if the United States had remained at peace? The seeds of the world's problems, they said, were planted in World War I. Perhaps a neutral United States might have prevented the follies of the Treaty of Versailles. Some sensational hearings presided over by Senator Gerald P. Nye of North Dakota seemed to show that arms manufacturers and bankers had led us into the war for their own profit.

The obvious answer seemed to be to pass a law. If Congress had the power to declare war—why could not Congress simply declare peace? Why could not strong, clear "Neutrality Acts" keep us neutral? Some thought that the United States occupation of the Philippines might involve us with Japan in the Pacific. In 1934 the Tydings-McDuffie Act provided for the independence of the Philippines in twelve years. Early the next year, Roosevelt recommended to the Senate that we join the World Court, which had been set up by the League of Nations. But isolationists feared that even the "advisory opinions" given by the Court might draw us onto the battlefields of Europe.

As war clouds gathered, Americans' fond hopes for neutrality grew ever stronger—and more futile. Acts were passed in 1935 and again in 1936 to prevent Americans from sending arms to the nations at war. Americans were warned that they traveled at their own risk on the ships of nations at war. When the Spanish civil war broke out in 1936, the neutrality laws were extended to bar shipments of arms to either side. But this hurt only the Spanish republicans. Franco was already receiving all the arms he needed from Hitler and Mussolini.

WAKE UP! WAKE UP, UNCLE!

Daniel Bishop, *St. Louis Star-Times*

As world war approaches, Uncle Sam sleeps and is tied down by opponents of involvement.

The isolationists came up with still another "neutrality" law in 1937. This permitted sales to belligerents, but only "cash-and-carry." A country at war had to pay cash for its goods before the goods left our shores. And the country at war had to carry the goods in its own ships. The law embargoed munitions and also allowed the President to extend the embargo to other exports. The isolationists believed that at last they had passed a law that would keep the United States out of war.

Still, some isolationists sought an amendment to the Constitution that would prevent Congress from declaring war without first submitting the question to a popular vote. A poll of the American people in 1937 showed that 75 percent favored such an amendment. President Roosevelt was strongly opposed. He warned that "it would encourage other nations to believe that they could violate American rights with impunity." And the House refused to submit the amendment to the states.

Neither President Roosevelt nor a dozen acts of Congress could block the world's drift toward war. In January 1938, FDR suggested a world conference to reduce armaments and promote national economic security, but the British Prime Minister Neville Chamberlain said no.

Hitler on the march. One of Hitler's goals was to bring into the "Third Reich" all the millions of people of "German blood" in Austria, Czechoslovakia, and Poland. Of course, there was no such thing as "German blood," but some German professors supported him, and the millions of German people went along.

In March 1938 Germany invaded and annexed Austria. Hitler's next target was the strategic Sudetenland on the Czech border with Germany. It contained 3 million people of German ancestry. The Czechs mobilized, expecting aid from Great Britain, France, and Russia. But those countries would not risk war to save the Czechoslovak republic.

Prime Minister Chamberlain of Britain and Premier Daladier of France met Hitler and Mussolini at Munich, Germany, on September 28, 1938. There, in an attempt to appease Hitler, they agreed to dismember Czechoslovakia—the one democracy in Europe that survived east of the Rhine—and give a piece to Germany. As Hitler occupied the Sudetenland, Chamberlain reported to Parliament that the Munich Pact guaranteed "peace in our time."

We know today that if Britain and France had resisted at this moment, German generals were planning to remove Hitler. But Hitler was riding high. He and his German people began to think he was unbeatable. Could anything prevent a world war?

"There can be no peace," Roosevelt warned, "if national policy adopts as a deliberate instrument the threat of war." In November 1938 when Hitler increased his brutal persecution of the Jews, Americans were more horrified than ever. Now FDR demanded that the arms embargo be removed from the neutrality law so the United States could help the victims of aggression. Still most Americans were optimists. And many others were isolationists hoping that we could remain an island of peace and prosperity in a world of war and misery.

On March 15, 1939, Hitler seized the rest of Czechoslovakia. The policy of appeasement was now exposed as a failure. Great Britain pledged aid to Poland in case its independence was threatened.

United Press International Photo

A German motorized detachment rides through a Polish town already destroyed by bombs.

When Mussolini invaded little Albania on April 7, Britain gave a similar guarantee to neighboring Greece and Romania.

In a desperate effort to keep all Europe from catching fire, President Roosevelt asked Mussolini and Hitler to promise to refrain for ten years from attacking a list of 31 nations. In return these nations would promise not to attack Italy or Germany. But Hitler replied with sarcasm. In his shrieking, abusive speech before the German Reichstag (legislature) he ridiculed FDR. He knew that the democracies were not prepared for war. He was determined to have his own way and dominate the world before the democracies dared stand against him.

President Roosevelt asked Congress to repeal or modify the arms embargo because it was helping the aggressor nations, who were well supplied with

United Press International Photo

Hoping to start life anew, a family returns to its farm near Bromberg, Poland, in November 1939 after Nazi bombings have left it in ruins.

arms from their own factories. By a vote of 12–11, the isolationists in the Senate Foreign Relations Committee put off any changes in the law until the next session of Congress, which was to meet in January 1940.

Continuing problems with Japan. Meanwhile, on July 26, 1939, the State Department moved against the Japanese war machine. Japan was told that in six months we would end the Japanese-American Commercial Treaty of 1911. This freed Congress to stop the sale of war materials to Japan. The Japanese had been invading China with arms bought in the United States. And the Japanese were disturbed by news that their new ally Nazi Germany had made a sudden alliance with Japan's old enemy Russia. For a time Japanese expansion in Asia was slowed.

War comes to Europe. In Europe the attempts to appease Hitler seemed only to whet his appetite for more conquests. He had risen to power by telling the German people that Communist Russia was their prime enemy. Now he shocked the whole world when he announced a nonaggression pact with Stalin in 1939. The secret terms gave Germany western Poland, while the Soviet Union was free to take Finland, Estonia, Latvia, eastern Poland, Bessarabia (in Romania), and Lithuania. The Nazis believed that in this way they would protect themselves against war on two fronts. In return Russia would gain a buffer zone against Germany— and a temporary assurance against attack.

Throughout the summer of 1939 Hitler demanded that Poland return to Germany certain districts containing people of "German blood." Poland, bolstered by Britain and France, stood its ground. Then on September 1, without warning, Hitler invaded Poland. Two days later England and France declared war on Germany. Then Stalin's armies marched into Poland from the east on September 17. Within two weeks, on September 29, brave, long-suffering Poland was divided between the two tyrants.

German and Italian Aggression, 1935-1939

- Germany and German Possessions
- Italy and Italian Possessions
- Areas of German Expansion
- Areas of Italian Expansion

Boundaries as of 1935

The United States reacts. Unlike President Wilson 25 years before, Roosevelt did not ask the American people to be neutral in thought as well as deed. He invoked the Neutrality Act of 1937 when war broke out. But in a fireside chat, he reminded the American people, "Even a neutral cannot be asked to close his mind or his conscience."

President Roosevelt called Congress into special session on September 21, 1939. He asked them to change the "cash and carry" Neutrality Act of 1937

and repeal the embargo on selling or shipping arms to the belligerents. He believed it was urgent for the United States to find ways at once to help the Allies against Hitler. If the United States waited, the barbaric forces might win, and then it would be too late. Many voices were raised against his attempt to break out of our isolation. Among them were Senator William E. Borah of Idaho and the nation's hero, Colonel Charles Lindbergh. "Preparedness" Republicans like Henry Stimson and

Frank Knox supported the President. After a bitter debate Congress voted the Neutrality Act of 1939. It helped the forces of democracy by repealing the arms embargo.

SECTION 1 REVIEW

1. Identify or explain: Adolf Hitler, *Mein Kampf*, National Socialist party, Nazis, concentration camps, Josef Stalin, Benito Mussolini, Francisco Franco, Lázaro Cárdenas, *Panay*, Tydings-McDuffie Act, neutrality laws, Neville Chamberlain, appeasement.

2. Locate: Ethiopia, Rhineland, Montevideo, Manchuria, Yangtze River, Sudetenland, Albania, Estonia, Latvia, Lithuania.

3. What conditions in Germany led the people to accept a dictator?

4. Cite instances where the government followed Roosevelt's Good Neighbor policy.

5. What was the outcome of the Munich Pact?

6. What events in the summer of 1939 led to the outbreak of World War II?

7. **Recognizing Cause and Effect.** What factors contributed to the isolationist stance of many Americans? How did these Americans try to isolate the United States?

2. The battlefield is everywhere

For six months, while Germany was moving its armies back from Poland, there was no fighting in western Europe. The British were busy moving their forces to France. The French sat smugly behind their Maginot line along the border of Germany. They thought that no enemy could pierce this 350-mile line of tunnels, concrete forts, and anti-tank fields. The headlines spoke of a "phony war." In November the giant Soviet Union attacked its tiny neighbor, Finland. The bravery of the Finns against hopeless odds stirred the admiration of the free world. But part of Finland came under the Communist heel. Then, in April 1940, Hitler launched a stunning new kind of war.

The new warfare. *Blitzkrieg* (lightning war) was Adolf Hitler's surprising strategy. This depended on air power. And it was nothing like the battles that generals had read about in their textbooks. The idea was to strike with lightning speed. Using the fastest new vehicles (airplanes, tanks, trucks, and even motorcycles), the Nazis would thrust rapidly into the very heart of enemy territory. Their sluggish enemies would be overwhelmed.

Blitzkrieg also meant war that struck like lightning—from the sky. Air power made it possible. Leaping over "standing" armies, over water barriers

The German "Stuka" dive bombers, shown here flying in formation in 1941, served the Nazi "blitzkrieg." Swooping out of the sky, they devastated all below.

Wide World Photos

and coastal fortifications, the Nazi air force would strike at the heart of the defenseless nations.

On April 9, 1940, Hitler ended the "phony war" and shocked the world by invading Denmark and Norway. One month later he rushed into the Netherlands, Belgium, and Luxembourg. From there he quickly bypassed the "impregnable" Maginot line and lunged deep into France. On June 14 his Nazis marched into Paris. Thousands of weeping men and women lined the streets, helpless against this lightning invasion. France surrendered by the end of June. Meanwhile in England pugnacious Winston Churchill had replaced the ineffective Neville Chamberlain as Prime Minister.

The battlefront was now everywhere. The airplane had transformed warfare. What the submarine had done to the freedom of the seas, the airplane was doing to almost all the other rules of warfare.

Billy Mitchell advertises air power. Just as Admiral Mahan had alerted Americans to the influence of sea power on history, so during World War I the bold and outspoken Billy Mitchell had begun to advertise air power.

Air power was then so new that few took it seriously. In the Civil War and the Spanish-American War, light observation balloons had been used. But "military ballooning," as it was called, was still thought of mostly as a sport or a hobby. In 1913 when Mitchell was a young officer in the Signal Corps, he began to be intrigued by the airplane's military uses. Then, during World War I, as General Pershing's Chief of Air Services, he was impressed by what warplanes could do.

At the end of the war, American generals and admirals still considered the airplane as merely another weapon. Like a new machine gun, it was to be used by either the army or the navy in their own regular operations.

Billy Mitchell had other ideas. He was convinced that airplanes really ought to be put into an entirely new military unit, under a command all their own. So long as Americans thought of airplanes only as helpers for the army and navy, he argued, we were sure to be left behind. We would lose the next war to nations who saw that air power was something new and world-shaking.

Air power, Mitchell said, had shifted the main targets. No longer were they the enemy *armies.*

The charm of Billy Mitchell, champion of U. S. air power, shows in this early picture.

Now the targets would be the "vital centers"—the centers of industry, the centers of supply, and the centers of the enemy's will to resist. "Armies themselves can be disregarded by air power," he explained, "if a rapid strike is made against the opposing centers."

Americans could not bear the thought of a new warfare that was so horrible. They hated to believe that whole cities might have to be destroyed.

Mitchell was an expert at getting publicity. He made speeches and wrote magazine articles and books to alert all citizens to the importance of air power. Many of his fellow officers disliked him for it. Some called him "General of the 'Hot Air' Force."

Mitchell gives a demonstration. But Mitchell was not to be put off. Battleships were supposed to be "unsinkable." To prove that airplanes were effective against battleships, he planned a spectacular show. He arranged to have the German battleship *Ostfriesland,* which had been surrendered at the end of World War I, hauled to a position 60 miles off the Virginia coast. It was a ghost ship, with not a soul on board.

560

Just before noon on July 21, 1921, a flight of Mitchell's army bombers left Langley Field 85 miles away. As they arrived over the battleship, they dropped six 2000-pound bombs. Within twenty minutes the "unsinkable" battleship was at the bottom of the ocean. It was the first time a battleship had ever been sunk by planes.

When admirals and generals still refused to grasp the full meaning of air power, Mitchell tried other tactics. He publicly denounced the conduct of our defense by the War and Navy departments as incompetent, criminally negligent, and "almost treasonable." This was the sure road to court martial—and that seemed to be his purpose. On December 17, 1925, a panel of generals found General Billy Mitchell guilty of "conduct which brought discredit upon the military service." They sentenced him to a five-year suspension from active duty.

Building air power.

Mitchell's campaign had already forced President Calvin Coolidge to take some action. The committee he appointed did not support all Mitchell's demands, but they did urge the buildup of an American air force.

Then, on May 21, 1927, Charles Lindbergh made his famous nonstop flight from New York to Paris. As the military meaning of Lindbergh's feat sank in, Americans began to realize that some of Billy Mitchell's "wild" ideas were not so wild. Now it seemed quite possible that some day the United States might be attacked by airplanes that came nonstop across the ocean. The nation began to take Mitchell, and air power, seriously.

In 1935 the new American long-range B-17 bomber (soon called the "Flying Fortress" and equipped with the super-accurate Norden bombsight) first went into the air. Now it was hard to doubt that air power would change the meaning of war. Air war against "vital centers" would be as different as possible from the old trench warfare.

The United States Navy also had its champion of air power. He was as different from Billy Mitchell as night from day. Admiral William A. Moffett, a pilot and aviation enthusiast, was quiet and diplomatic, just as Mitchell was noisy and brash. Each in his own way served the cause of air power.

Moffett became head of the Navy's newly created Bureau of Aeronautics in 1921. He worked steadily for the development of aircraft carriers and for catapult-launched airplanes on battleships and cruisers. His farsighted work would help to make possible the United States victory over Japan in World War II.

The United States prepares for war.

President Roosevelt had long recognized the Nazi menace. Even before the Germans had overrun France, he had sent a special message to Congress warning the nation to rearm. He announced a bold plan to turn out 50,000 planes in the next year, 1941, and every year until the Nazis were beaten. And he asked for billions of dollars to create a two-ocean navy. In one of his most effective fireside chats over the radio, he alerted the nation:

> The Nazi masters have made it clear that they intend not only to dominate all life and thought in their own country, but also to enslave the rest of the world. . . . We cannot escape danger, or the fear of danger, by crawling into a bed and pulling the covers over our heads. . . . No nation can appease the Nazis. No man can tame a tiger into a kitten by stroking it. . . . Let not the defeatists tell us that it is too late. It will never be earlier.

Still there were those who believed they could ward off the Nazi menace by the old-fashioned magic word "Neutrality!"

The isolationists hoped the Neutrality Act of 1939 would keep us out of war. But Roosevelt saw during 1940 that if Great Britain was not to fall, it would have to receive more help from the United States. Could he convince the country in time?

The Battle of Britain.

Great Britain now stood alone against Hitler and Mussolini. "The battle of France is over," the eloquent Prime Minister Winston Churchill told the House of Commons. "I expect that the Battle of Britain is about to begin." He warned that on its outcome depended the future of the world. "Let us therefore brace ourselves to our duties, and so bear ourselves that, if the British Empire and its Commonwealth last for a thousand years, men will say 'This was their finest hour.'"

Hitler sent hundreds of bombers to rain devastation and death upon London and other British cities during the summer and fall of 1940. He was determined to force the British to surrender before a rearmed America could come to their aid.

The cheerful fortitude of the English during the Battle of Britain became legendary. Here Londoners
sleep between the rails or on the platform of a subway station to escape German bombs.

A key factor in the Battle of Britain—and in the entire war against Germany—was that the British had figured out how to read Germany's most secret coded messages. These intercepted messages were referred to by the British as "Ultra," from Ultra Secret. Through Ultra and helped by "radar"—a word made up of *ra*(dio) *d*(etecting) *a*(nd) *r*(anging)—the British often knew when the German bombers were coming and where they were headed. In this way they were able to move the small fleet of Royal Air Force (RAF) fighter planes from place to place to intercept the incoming bombers.

But even Ultra was not enough to save Great Britain from terrible losses. About 3:00 P.M. on November 14, 1940, the Ultra signals revealed that the city of Coventry was to be attacked that evening. It was too late to evacuate the city, but its officials were alerted and enabled to prepare for the attack. The warning from Ultra also gave time for the RAF to station fighter planes over the city. But many German bombers got through. Hundreds of people died as thousands of houses and Coventry's grand old cathedral were destroyed in the raid.

With the help of Ultra the British defense against German bombers was increasingly successful. That fall Hitler decided that he had to postpone "Sea Lion," his plan to invade England across the channel. But throughout the winter the Germans continued the bombing of British cities.

World affairs and the presidential campaign of 1940. As the Battle of Britain raged, the United States held an election campaign. The Republican convention at Philadelphia in June surprised nearly everybody. Thomas E. Dewey, the racket-busting young district attorney of New York, had been the leading candidate. But an eleventh-hour drive brought to the front a man who was no politician and had never run for office.

Wendell L. Willkie was the bright, dynamic president of Commonwealth and Southern, a large public utilities corporation. Born in Indiana, where he attended the state university, he practiced law in Ohio before becoming a man of wealth and a powerful corporation lawyer in New York City. He had a warm, boyish appeal, and his trademark was a floppy lock of hair which marked his informal approach to life. He was persuasive in a very different way from FDR. Instead of FDR's cultivated Harvard accent, he spoke with the voice of the Middle West and for the values of self-made America. He so much disliked the New Deal emphasis on government aid that, though he had been a Democrat all his life, he finally became an outspoken Republican in 1940. He had made a name for himself fighting against the TVA, which he said unfairly competed with his company. Willkie was nominated on the sixth ballot. The convention chose Senator McNary of Oregon, known as a friend of farmers, to run for Vice-President.

In mid-July 1940 in Chicago, the Democrats did not surprise many when they chose FDR. But no one in American history had ever run for a third term as President. Secretary of Agriculture Henry A. Wallace of Iowa was picked as his running mate.

Although Willkie opposed FDR's New Deal policies, he shared the President's determination to aid Great Britain and to arm the United States against the aggressor. Foreign policy was not as much an issue in the election as the isolationists had hoped. Willkie also favored conscription, which Roosevelt had asked for in June. His support helped the measure to pass in September. This draft law provided for the registration of men between the ages of 21 and 35. No more than 900,000 were to be called into the service at any one time during peace, and the act was to expire on May 15, 1945.

The destroyer deal. Roosevelt tried every legal device to help the Allies secure supplies. To get around the law, he approved selling American military equipment to private companies that were buying for the British. But offering the goods on American shores was not enough. Italian and German submarines were sending these supplies to the bottom of the sea before they reached Britain. Winston Churchill asked for American destroyers to convoy these essential supplies, to hunt down and ward off the enemy submarines. "I must tell you," the British prime minister cabled to FDR in July 1940, "that in the long history of the world this is a thing to do now."

If he did as Churchill asked, Roosevelt feared that the isolationists would accuse him of bringing the United States into the war without the approval of Congress. Candidate Willkie assured him that he would not make the transfer of destroyers an issue in the campaign. Still, to protect himself against isolationist attacks, the President shrewdly devised a "Destroyer for Bases" deal. In September the President, as Commander in Chief of the Navy, transferred 50 old, but still useful destroyers to Great Britain. In exchange, we received the use of eight British naval bases all along the Atlantic coast from Newfoundland to British Guiana (Guyana). Great Britain promised that, if conquered, it would not surrender its fleet to Hitler.

The end of the campaign. As the election campaign wore on, Willkie, desperate for a winning issue, accused FDR of leading the nation into war. When Willkie became reckless in his attacks, Roosevelt became reckless in his responses. "I have said this before," he told American parents, "but I shall say it again and again and again: Your boys are not going to be sent into any foreign wars."

FDR won handily—though not as easily as in 1936. Willkie polled 45 percent of the popular vote, but he carried only ten states with 82 electoral votes to Roosevelt's 449. The precedent-breaking FDR had broken another precedent. He was the first person to be elected President for a third term.

Helping the British. Soon after the election, Roosevelt was faced with a dilemma. The British had run out of cash and were running out of ships. If the neutrality law was not quickly changed, the United States might not be able to get help to the British before they were defeated by the Nazis.

FDR showed his usual genius for compromise and for persuasion. He offered a clever plan called "Lend-Lease." We would "lend" or "lease" to the British—or any other country whose defense the President considered vital to the defense of the

United States—whatever war supplies we could make. In that way the British would not need cash, and the hesitating members of Congress might be persuaded that we were getting value in return.

At the same time, in January 1941, in his annual message to Congress, President Roosevelt proclaimed the Four Freedoms. After the war he hoped for "a world founded upon four essential human freedoms"—freedom of speech, freedom of religion, freedom from want, and freedom from fear. Later that year, after a secret meeting with Churchill on a warship off the coast of Newfoundland, the two men issued the Atlantic Charter. This was an up-to-date version of Woodrow Wilson's Fourteen Points (p. 461).

SECTION 2 REVIEW

1. Identify or explain: Maginot line, "phony war," Winston Churchill, Thomas E. Dewey, Wendell Willkie, "Destroyer for Bases" deal.

2. Why was the Nazi advance called a blitzkrieg?

3. Discuss Billy Mitchell's ideas on air power.

4. What steps did FDR take to rearm the nation?

5. How did "Ultra" help defeat Hitler?

6. **Demonstrating Reasoned Judgment.** How was Roosevelt able to supply the Allies while remaining an isolationist?

---

3. War comes to the United States

Step by step the United States moved closer to war. Of course Americans did not want to send our troops into battle. But how could that be avoided? The aggressor nations were everywhere triumphant. Could we let them succeed?

The war spreads. President Roosevelt extended the zone "necessary to the defense of the United States" far out into the North Atlantic. Our troops occupied the island of Greenland in April 1941 and Iceland in July. On May 7 Congress authorized our government to seize 92 ships in our ports. These ships belonged to Germany and Italy and to countries like France, Holland, and Norway, which Hitler had conquered. German and Italian property in the country was "frozen" on June 14.

Eight days later Hitler made his great blunder. In his crazy belief that all battlefields were alike, and that blitzkrieg could conquer all, on June 22, 1941, only a year after conquering France, he suddenly invaded Russia. If he had studied history, he might have learned that more than a hundred years before, Napoleon had lost his empire in the same desperate gamble. Vast, frigid Russia embraced and paralyzed invaders. At first it seemed that Hitler might conquer Russia as quickly as France. But when the Germans were deep into Russia—only fifteen miles from Moscow—the Russian winter arrived. The fingers of Nazi soldiers became numb. Frozen oil crippled the motors of tanks. The Nazis had to stop to await the return of warm weather.

Meanwhile the German navy stepped up its submarine warfare in the Atlantic. The United States was already convoying American merchant ships. On September 1, 1940, we began to convoy British ships, too. Then on September 4, 1941, the United States destroyer *Greer* was attacked by a submarine. The President issued new orders for our ships to shoot German subs on sight. He had not told the American people that the *Greer* had been following the Nazi sub and reporting its position to the British. FDR now ordered our merchant ships to be armed. He let them sail to the ports of the countries at war.

On October 17 the destroyer *Kearny* was hit and badly damaged with the loss of eleven lives. Then on October 31 the destroyer *Reuben James* was sunk by a German submarine with the loss of half its crew. In the Atlantic Ocean the United States had entered an undeclared war.

Trouble in the Pacific. Still, it was not Germany but Japan that plunged the United States into World War II. In 1940 Japan had become a partner of Nazi Germany and Fascist Italy. Japanese aggression was building what they called the Greater East Asia Co-Prosperity Sphere. This was a fancy name for Japanese domination of the Far East. German victories in Europe had encouraged the Japanese to try to seize all the poorly protected French and Dutch lands in Asia. Perhaps they could also take the British colonies. And China, too, was on their list.

To prepare for all this, the Japanese planned to seal off the Burma Road—the Allied supply route

ICELAND

ATLANTIC
OCEAN

NORWAY
SWEDEN
FINLAND

NORTH

SEA

BALTIC SEA

Oslo
Stockholm
Helsinki
Leningrad

ESTONIA

LATVIA

Moscow

USSR

NORTHERN
IRELAND

IRELAND
GREAT
BRITAIN

DENMARK

Copenhagen

Memel

Smolensk

Coventry
London
Dunkirk
Brussels
NETHERLANDS
BELGIUM
RHINELAND
LUXEMBOURG
Paris
FRANCE

Danzig
EAST
PRUSSIA

LITHUANIA

Berlin

GERMANY

SUDETENLAND

Warsaw

POLAND

Kiev

UKRAINE

Voronezh

Stalingrad

Rostov

Prague
CZECHOSLOVAKIA
Vienna
AUSTRIA

Vichy
VICHY FRANCE

SWITZERLAND
Bern

Budapest

HUNGARY

BESSARABIA

Odessa

Kerch

ROMANIA

Yalta

Lisbon

PORTUGAL

Madrid

SPAIN

CORSICA

ITALY

Rome

SARDINIA

YUGOSLAVIA

ALBANIA

Belgrade

Bucharest

BULGARIA

BLACK SEA

Istanbul

TURKEY

GREECE

Athens

SYRIA

IRAQ

MEDITERRANEAN

SEA

SICILY

Tunis

CRETE

CYPRUS
(BRITAIN)

LEBANON

SPANISH
MOROCCO
Oran
Algiers

MOROCCO-
(VICHY)

ALGERIA-
(VICHY)

TUNISIA-
(VICHY)
MALTA
(BRITAIN)

Axis Nations

Farthest German Advance,
December 1941

Axis-Controlled Territory,
November 1942

Vichy-Controlled Territory

Maginot Line

Boundaries of 1937

0   600 Miles

0   600 Kilometers

for China. Then China could not receive aid when the Japanese attacked. The Japanese managed to occupy bases in the north of French Indochina. And in July 1941 they took the bases in the south. The United States responded with an embargo on all trade with Japan.

In the discussions that followed between Japan and the United States, the one sticking point was China. The Japanese demanded that the United States cut off aid to the Chinese Generalissimo Chiang Kai-shek. Secretary Hull not only refused to abandon the Chinese but demanded that the Japanese withdraw from China at once. Faced with the choice of giving up their dreams of empire or

going to war, the Japanese militarists chose war. In mid-October a more warlike government under General Hideki Tojo came to power in Japan.

The United States had broken Japan's diplomatic and naval codes. We called the intelligence we received this way "Magic." Having read their dispatches, we knew that the Japanese would attack, but not where. It appeared that they were aiming at Thailand, the Malay peninsula, and the Dutch East Indies (Indonesia)—perhaps even the Philippines. United States forces there were alerted to expect attack. But the Navy did not know that on November 26 a Japanese aircraft carrier force had left Japan headed for Pearl Harbor in Hawaii.

The attack on Pearl Harbor. Just before 8 o'clock on Sunday morning, December 7, 1941, while Japanese diplomats were pretending to discuss peace at the White House, a fleet of 191 Japanese warplanes attacked American airfields at Pearl Harbor. Then they dropped bombs on the ships of the United States Navy anchored in the harbor. An hour later came a second fleet of 170 Japanese warplanes.

The attack was a perfect surprise—and the greatest military disaster in American history. One hundred and fifty American warplanes—the bulk of our air force in the Pacific—were destroyed on the ground. It was a better demonstration than Billy Mitchell could have imagined, and the fulfillment of his most dire prophecies. Of the 94 American ships in Pearl Harbor at the time, all the most powerful—the 8 battleships—were put out of action, together with 3 cruisers and 3 destroyers. More than 70 civilians and 2300 servicemen were killed.

The next day President Roosevelt appeared before Congress to announce that Japan's "Day of Infamy" had plunged us into war. Three days later Germany and Italy declared war on the United States.

SECTION 3 REVIEW

1. Identify or explain: Greater East Asia Co-Prosperity Sphere, Chiang Kai-shek, Hideki Tojo, "Magic."
2. Locate: Burma Road, French Indochina, Thailand, Dutch East Indies, Pearl Harbor.
3. What were the Japanese war goals in the Far East in 1941?
4. **Predicting Consequences.** If Japan had not attacked Pearl Harbor, would the United States have ever entered World War II? Explain.

On December 7, 1941, the majority of the United States Navy's Pacific fleet was caught unawares by the Japanese attack on Pearl Harbor. This photograph was taken when the destroyer *Shaw* exploded.

FOCUSING ON IDEAS

1. How did Franklin D. Roosevelt's policies toward Latin America differ from those of Theodore Roosevelt?

2. Cite actions by the world democracies in 1933–1938 that tended to encourage aggressive acts by Germany, Italy, and Japan.

3. How did the United States shift from a position of strict neutrality in 1935 to one of active help for the Allies by October 1941? Cite specific actions by FDR and Congress.

4. Why did Adolph Hitler and Josef Stalin sign a nonaggression pact in 1939? Why did it surprise the world?

TAKING A CRITICAL LOOK

1. **Recognizing Ideologies.** Some Americans praised the European dictators for putting the jobless back to work and getting the "trains to run on time." What values were they overlooking in their praise of the dictators?

2. **Making Comparisons.** How did new technology affect the way World War II was fought? Compare this to what you have learned about the effects of new technology in earlier wars.

YOUR REGION IN HISTORY

1. **Geography.** What was the ethnic composition of your area at the outbreak of World War II. On a world map, plot the countries that were represented in your community. How would this ethnic distribution have affected attitudes about our involvement in World War II?

2. **Culture.** Through interviews with older residents and research of local papers published in the 1930s, try to determine the extent of isolationist sentiment in your community in the late 1930s.

3. **Economics.** How did your region benefit from the sale of arms during World War II?

HISTORICAL FACTS AND FIGURES

Drawing Inferences. Study the graph below to help answer the following questions: (a) In 1939 which nation, the United States, Germany, France, or Britain, had the most naval vessels? (b) Which nation had the most airplanes? (c) Which had the most tanks? (d) Which nation had the largest number of armed forces? (e) What geographic facts help explain why Britain had a large navy? Why France had a large number of troops? (f) What does the information in the graph suggest about the relative military preparation of these nations prior to World War II?

Comparative Military Strengths, 1939				
United States	✪✪	✈	⛴	⚓⚓⚓⚓
Britain	✪	✈✈✈	*	⚓⚓⚓⚓⚓
France	✪✪✪✪	✈✈✈	⛴⛴⛴⛴⛴⛴⛴⛴⛴⛴⛴⛴	⚓⚓
Germany	✪✪✪✪✪✪✪✪✪✪	✈✈✈✈	⛴⛴⛴⛴⛴⛴⛴⛴⛴⛴⛴	⚓⚓

*Data not available

✪ = 200,000 Soldiers   ✈ = 1,000 Planes   ⛴ = 200 Tanks   ⚓ = 100 Ships

Source: *The Crucial Years*, Hanson W. Baldwin

CHAPTER 27

A world conflict

The United States now faced war on two fronts. For the first time in our history, this two-ocean nation was threatened by enemies on both oceans. And the enemies were winning everywhere. In the Pacific, Japan followed the Pearl Harbor surprise with attacks on the Philippines, Wake Island, Guam, the Dutch East Indies, Malaya, and Hong Kong. In the Atlantic, German submarines were disrupting our vital supply lines. The Nazis controlled western Europe from the Norwegian Sea to the Aegean. They had overrun the Balkans and stood at the gates of Moscow. Russia seemed ready to fall. The Italians had taken Libya. In southern Russia German forces were poised to cut through the Caucasus to Iran and Iraq, hoping to meet the Japanese army in India. For the Allies it would be a long road back.

1. Mobilizing for defense

The United States was not prepared for World War II, but it was in much better shape than in 1917. The draft had been started in 1940, and by the time of the attack on Pearl Harbor the army had grown to 1.6 million. A mammoth defense program had been launched to produce a torrent of guns, planes, tanks, and ships.

Converting to wartime. Before Pearl Harbor many industries, just emerging from the depression, were not eager to convert to wartime production. Labor expected a larger share of the new prosperity. In 1941 strikes multiplied fivefold.

With the United States entry into the war, the nation turned to the urgent task of becoming the "arsenal of democracy." Again, as in World War I, government agencies were created to focus the nation's life—the work of factories, farms, and mines, the research of industries and universities—on this great purpose.

Rationing was needed to be sure that everyone had a fair share, enough but not too much, of scarce items like heating oil, shoes, meat, sugar, and coffee. Every man, woman, and child received coupons for a share of rationed items. Gasoline, too, was rationed, not because it was in short supply, but to conserve rubber in tires, which was dangerously scarce. Americans were not used to this sort of regulation. Still, daily life in the United States was less regulated than in most other countries at war. Our own armed forces and those of our allies suddenly demanded all that the country could produce. Full employment replaced unemployment. Prosperity returned on the home front.

By 1942 American production equaled that of Germany, Italy, and Japan combined. And by 1944 it was *double* theirs. Even in ships, where the

United States had failed badly in World War I, production was enormous. From July 1940 to August 1945, United States shipyards produced a tonnage equal to two-thirds the merchant marines of all the Allied nations combined. Before the war was over, American factories turned out 250,000 planes, 100,000 armored cars, 75,000 tanks, 650,000 pieces of artillery, and millions of tons of bombs, shells, and bullets.

Women in the armed forces. To fight the war it was necessary to build a huge army. Ultimately 15 million men and women served—10 million through the draft and 5 million as volunteers. Now all the services began to enlist women to perform all sorts of duties except those of combatants. In 1945 there were 258,000 women serving as Army WACS, Navy WAVES, Coast Guard SPARS, and women marines. Over 1000 women flew as civilians in the Women's Air Forces Service. They performed the hazardous job of ferrying military planes to Great Britain and other theaters of war. In 1979 the Air Force belatedly recognized these women pilots as war veterans who were entitled to all veterans' benefits.

Racial segregation and the war. Of the 15 million in the armed forces, about 1 million were blacks. They suffered less discrimination than in World War I. During World War II, the Marine Corps no longer kept them out, and before the war was over there were 17,000 black "Leathernecks." It became easier for qualified blacks to become officers. The Air Force trained black officers and pilots, and more than 80 won the Distinguished Flying Cross. Even the Navy, which before had taken blacks only for kitchen work and as waiters, began to open up. The example of Dorie Miller at Pearl Harbor may have helped. Even though only an untrained messman, he grabbed a machine gun during the attack and shot down four Japanese planes. For his heroism Dorie Miller received the Navy Cross.

Blacks served in every theater of the war. After the Japanese captured the Burma Road lifeline to China, black engineering battalions helped perform the incredible feat of building the Ledo Road. They pushed this new supply line through the steaming jungles and mountainous terrain of northern Burma.

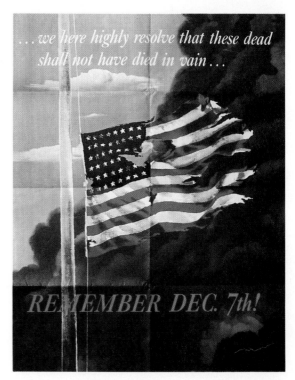

...we here highly resolve that these dead shall not have died in vain...

REMEMBER DEC. 7th!

Brown Brothers

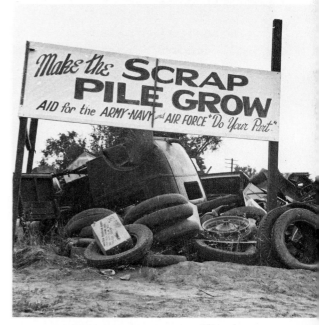

Library of Congress

Stunned by Pearl Harbor, the most crushing disaster in our history, Americans vowed not to forget. They saved rubber, metal, and paper to be made into armaments and war supplies.

During World War II, blue stars were hung in windows to indicate that family members were away in the armed forces. Gold stars were shown for those who died in the war. This woman had three sons in the service.

One black doctor made a major contribution to the war effort that helped save countless lives of soldiers of all colors. Charles Drew developed the blood bank for collecting and storing the blood plasma which injured fighting men so badly needed. Ironically, over the strong objection of Dr. Drew, the blood plasma of whites and blacks—for no scientific reason—was kept segregated.

The long shadow of the divided South remained. At first, most blacks, once more fighting for democracy, were still segregated in the services. Some progress was made during the course of the war in breaking down segregation. All shared equally the risks of battle. Death was no racist.

Newspaper correspondents noted that there was no color line in the foxholes. After the war, President Harry S Truman appointed a national committee to recommend action to bring racial equality into the armed services. By 1949 the army, navy, and air force had abolished racial quotas. They finally realized, as *The Crisis* had said during World War II, "A jim crow army cannot fight for a free world." In the Korean War of 1950–1953 Americans of all races fought side by side.

Black Americans and the home front. One of the most effective fighters for racial equality at home was the black labor leader, A. Philip Randolph. Born in Florida, he attended the City College of New York, founded a magazine, and became active in the Socialist party. He created the Brotherhood of Sleeping Car Porters in 1925 and after a bitter fight won recognition from the Pullman Company, which manufactured and ran the sleeping cars on American railroads. The march on Washington that Randolph organized in 1941 threatened to bring 100,000 blacks to the capital to protest against racial discrimination in wartime hiring.

Under this pressure, even before the march could take place, President Roosevelt issued his historic Executive Order 8802. This outlawed any discrimination on the basis of race, creed, color, or national origin in the federal government or in defense factories. A Fair Employment Practices Committee (FEPC) was appointed to enforce this policy. Roosevelt's order did not end discrimination. But substantial progress was made in both industry and government.

As in World War I the flood of blacks from the South to northern cities for jobs in the booming war factories increased racial tensions. In 1943 there were race riots in a number of cities. The worst of them, in Detroit, left 25 blacks and 9 whites dead.

After World War I about 80 percent of all blacks in the United States still lived in the South. But by 1950 nearly half of them lived in other parts of the country. During the war, black Americans, like other Americans, were becoming more and more citified. Outside the South nearly all of them were living in cities. And in the South they too were moving off the farm. Along with other Americans, they were churning quickly and easily around the country. It was harder than ever for the old South to keep its old ways.

Japanese Americans are interned. Japanese and Americans of Japanese ancestry had long faced discrimination on the West Coast. After Pearl Harbor their situation became much worse. For no good reason, other citizens blamed them for what the Japanese militarists had done and even began to suspect that they might be helping the enemy across the Pacific. Western politicians and frightened military men pressured FDR to remove them from the coastal states. President Roosevelt gave in. Early in 1942, under the excuse of national security, 110,000 Japanese Americans were rounded up. There was no evidence that these Americans were disloyal. They were forced to sell their homes and businesses on short notice and at sacrifice prices. They then were confined in camps, watched by armed guards, and treated as if they were dangerous. Not until after the presidential election of 1944 did the government change its policy and begin to release these innocent citizens.

Despite this humiliating treatment, 1200 men volunteered from the camps to serve in the United States armed forces. In a segregated unit these soldiers in the 442nd Regimental Combat Team fought heroically in Italy. Another Japanese American battalion was recruited from Hawaii, where there was no internment because there were so many Japanese.

In time of war it is harder than ever for a free nation to preserve its freedoms. Defending the country becomes a matter of life and death. Dissenters are open to the charge of being traitors. This is a true testing time of democracy. In World War II, except for the disgraceful treatment of Japanese Americans, the nation's record was far better than it had been in World War I.

Women and the war effort. The need for workers opened economic opportunities for women. Now, instead of being dissuaded from taking jobs as they had been during the depression, they were urged to go to work. Six million women joined the 12 million already in the labor force. They took on a wide variety of jobs and surprised the men who had said they were too weak and delicate to be lumberjacks, blast furnace operators, stevedores, or blacksmiths. They proved that they could handle all these jobs. And they also operated complex

Ordered to leave their homes and businesses on short notice by order of the United States government, bewildered Japanese Americans wait in Los Angeles for a train to take them to an internment camp.

Library of Congress

For some, the war opened new opportunities. These two women welders worked in a Connecticut factory in 1943.

machines in shipyards and airplane factories. Many for the first time could show their talents as doctors, dentists, chemists, and lawyers. "Rosie the Riveter" became an inspiration for all Americans.

Black women benefited, too. Before the war a greater percentage of black women worked than white. But they were generally restricted to low-paying jobs as domestic servants or farm laborers. When war came, they found more interesting and better-paying jobs. Nearly half a million black women who had worked as domestics left that work during the war to take positions in factories.

When World War II ended, it seemed that once again women might be forced to leave their jobs to make places for returning servicemen. But this time a much larger proportion was offered work in peacetime production. Prodded by war, the nation discovered its women and helped women discover themselves.

Raising money. War was expensive. From 1941 to 1945 the federal government spent $321 billion—twice as much as was spent during all the years from 1789 to 1941! Even during the depression, when people were alarmed by the size of the federal budget, the government had paid out only $8 billion each year.

Americans were paying the highest taxes in the nation's history. To prevent great fortunes from being made from the war, the federal income tax reached 94 percent for the highest incomes. Still, taxes brought in only 41 percent of the cost of the war. The rest was borrowed from banks, corporations, and individuals.

When everyone was employed, when wages were high but there were few goods to buy, prices went up rapidly. This was wartime inflation. But if people loaned their money to the government for war bonds, they would have less to spend on goods. So prices might be kept down. The government therefore ran a massive campaign and sold $100 billion in war bonds.

To prevent prices going sky-high, wages and prices were frozen by the government in 1942. In spite of these efforts, in the course of the war the cost of living went up 29 percent. Manufacturing wages went up more than 50 percent. Farmers earned more than ever before. The depression now seemed ancient history. The needs of a world at war had brought prosperity to Americans at home.

SECTION 1 REVIEW

1. Identify or explain: rationing, WACS, WAVES, SPARS, Dorie Miller, Charles Drew.

2. In what ways did each of the following contribute to the war effort: (a) industry, (b) women, (c) blacks?

3. How were West Coast Japanese Americans treated during the war?

4. How did the federal government (a) raise money to pay for the war? (b) try to control inflation?

5. **Making Comparisons.** How did the gains of women and black Americans during World War II compare with gains made during World War I?

World War II, The Mediterranean, 1942-1944

←— Allied Forces

× Allied Victories

Axis Nations

Axis-Controlled Territory, 1942

Vichy-Controlled Territory, 1942

Allied Nations

0   500 Miles

0   500 Kilometers

2. "The end of the beginning"—1942

Soon after the United States entered the war, the Allies agreed that the first goal was to defeat the Germans. It was clear that if the Germans won in Europe, the United States would be left to face the aggressor nations all alone. So the United States postponed the offensive in the Pacific. There we would have to be satisfied with "active defense" until we had disposed of Mussolini and Hitler.

The battle of the Atlantic. The battle of the Atlantic was being lost to the "wolf packs" of German submarines. Month after month they

were sending thousands of tons of Allied supplies to the bottom of the ocean. In May 1942, for example, 120 ships were sunk. Unless the submarines were beaten soon, Allied forces would be left without food or weapons, and the war would be lost. These critical months of the battle of the Atlantic were between mid-1942 and mid-1943. By good research (and good luck) the Allies invented radar and sonar in the nick of time. Airplanes using radar could locate and destroy submarines or direct armed ships to the attack. Navy ships using sonar—*so*(und) *na*(vigation) *r*(anging)—could hear distant propeller noises from subs. They could also locate their targets by echo-ranging. Sharp-sounding "pings" were sent out from a submarine destroyer, which found the enemy when these sounds rebounded off the submarine hulls.

Success in North Africa. While the battle of the Atlantic was being fought, the Allies began their first offensive moves in North Africa. German and Italian forces there were commanded by the "Desert

Fox," General Erwin Rommel, one of the most shrewd, daring, and resourceful commanders of the century. His forces had reached El Alamein, only 70 miles west of Alexandria, Egypt. They now threatened the Suez Canal and the oil fields of the Middle East. At this moment of danger the British were again aided by Ultra, their secret decoding machine. It revealed Rommel's plans for his crack *Afrika Korps*. With great sacrifices of men and weapons, the British managed to hold their lines and then began to build up for a counteroffensive.

Meanwhile the Russians were pressing the Allies to open a "Second Front" in Europe with a new invasion of the continent into lands held by the Axis powers. This would divert the enemy from their attack on the Russians. Instead the Allies decided in July 1942 to use their forces to clear Africa of the Germans and Italians. They would try to divert Rommel by invading and attacking North Africa from the west.

To strengthen Allied forces in Africa, British troops were withdrawn from other fronts and sent to Egypt. Using Ultra, the British were able to destroy German supply vessels. On October 23, General Bernard Montgomery led the British Eighth Army in the attack. At first Rommel's lines held. Then, on November 4, Montgomery's army broke through. They began chasing Rommel's Afrika Korps, which had a reputation for being unbeatable. Within a week Hitler had the news that his precious Afrika Korps was in disarray. Rommel's failure to take Egypt had cost him 500 tanks, 400 guns, and 60,000 men.

At this strategic moment, United States and British forces struck their stunning surprise blow. On November 8, 1942, a huge Allied force, guarded by 350 warships, landed from 500 transports onto the west and north coasts of Africa. Most of these had come from Great Britain, but 101 ships carrying 35,000 soldiers had crossed the ocean from the United States. This gigantic operation had been planned and launched in only four months.

The Allied landing was an immediate success. At the time, that area was ruled by the "Vichy" French, who had been conquered and were helping the Nazis. They had that name because the town of Vichy in central France was the new capital of their puppet government. But now the Vichy French in North Africa quickly sided with the Allies. Within three days all of North Africa to the borders of

Robert Capa/Magnum

Robert Capa, one of the top photographers of World War II, caught this picture of a United States paratrooper in full battle dress preparing for a jump into Germany.

Tunisia was in Allied hands. The Germans fleeing from the west had managed ahead of the Allies to reach Tunisia, where they met the remnants of Rommel's Afrika Korps. There the Nazis gathered and regrouped their forces hoping to counterattack.

When Montgomery's army arrived at the borders of Tunisia, the two Allied forces united to surround the Germans. So 1942 ended with Tunisia firmly held by a still-dangerous Axis force and the land around them held by the Allies.

In November 1942 the Russians had gone on the counteroffensive. After some of the bloodiest fighting of the war, they broke the siege of Stalingrad and surrounded an entire German army. After that army was captured in February 1943, the Russians swept rapidly westward. Meanwhile in January the siege of Leningrad had ended. The tide was beginning to turn.

World War II and Latin America. The "Good Neighbor policy" paid dividends in World War II. In 1939, by the Declaration of Panama, an Inter-American Conference drew a 300-mile offshore defense zone around the whole hemisphere south of Canada. The warring nations were warned to avoid combat within this zone. At a conference of foreign ministers of the Latin American countries in January 1942, twenty-one of them agreed to break off diplomatic relations with Nazi Germany and its Fascist allies.

Some of them went further. Nine Caribbean republics declared war on the German-Italian-Japanese Axis in December 1941. Mexico and Brazil joined them in 1942. All the New World nations finally declared war on the Axis. Pro-Fascist Argentina did not join the Allies until almost the end of the war.

The Latin American nations provided vital war materials—rubber, quinine, tin—along with naval and air bases. Brazil sent troops to Europe, and Mexico had an air squadron in the Pacific. The Mexican and Cuban navies patrolled the Caribbean for German subs. In return, the United States gave military equipment and loans.

Active defense in the Pacific. In the Pacific for months after Pearl Harbor the Japanese knew nothing but success. By March 1942 they controlled all the waters from the Gilbert and Solomon islands to the mainland of Asia, a distance of 4500 miles. They held every island within that area except for the southern part of New Guinea and the Bataan peninsula of Luzon in the Philippines where a doomed American force bravely fought on until May 1942. The Japanese were masters of the Malay peninsula, the British bastion of Singapore, and Thailand. They had invaded Burma. During all this fighting, the Japanese destroyed their enemies' navies while they themselves lost no ship larger than a destroyer.

The Allies had to take steps at once to prevent their being knocked out of the Pacific before they

UPI/Bettmann Newsphotos

Japanese tanks cross a makeshift bridge over a stream during their campaign against Burma early in 1942.

could finish off the Nazis. They decided on a policy of more active defense. They had to hold what little remained to them in the Pacific. Otherwise they would not have bases to start from when they finally went on the offensive. They had to be sure of course they [...] from the United [...] Australia. Fortu- [...] submarines than the [...] se them against warships, [...] s were seldom attacked.

[...] kyo. By great good luck the [...] raft carriers had happened to be at [...] Japanese hit Pearl Harbor. During [...] of active defense the Navy used them for [...] e raids on Wake and other Japanese-held [...] s. Then, on April 18, 1942, General James B. [...] Doolittle led B-25s launched from a carrier to attack Tokyo. This first raid on the Japanese capital did little real damage to the city. But it gave the Japanese people a hint of what was to come. And it lifted American morale.

After Doolittle's raid, the Japanese decided to establish a new line—a "defensive perimeter"—run-ning from the Aleutian Islands in the north, through Midway, Wake, the Marshalls, the Gilberts, Fiji, and Samoa to Port Moresby in New Guinea and to Tulagi in the Solomons. At this line they hoped to stop air raids like the one on Tokyo. They also planned to disrupt the sea transport between the United States and Australia. Planes would patrol the waters between the scattered islands. The Japanese navy would be stationed near the center, ready to be rushed wherever needed. This would help them "save face." It was also a symptom of what a Japanese admiral later called the "victory disease."

The Battle of the Coral Sea. The skilled Japanese Admiral Yamamoto hoped to bring on a major sea battle with the Allied Pacific Fleet in 1942. Unless that fleet was destroyed, he feared that by the next year the Allies would be strong enough to launch an offensive against Japan.

Japanese Conquests in Far East to August 1942

Japanese-Controlled Territory

× Allied Victories

The first collision between the two fleets occurred in the Battle of the Coral Sea, May 7 and 8, 1942. This historic naval battle showed how modern science had changed war. For the first time in history in a great naval encounter, no ship on either side was within sight of an opposing ship. Now it was aircraft carrier against aircraft carrier.

During the battle both sides made mistakes, and both suffered heavy losses. The Japanese sank the United States carrier *Lexington*. For them this made it a "tactical" victory. "Tactics" had to do with winning the box score in a particular battle. But it was a "strategic" success for the United States. "Strategy" (from the Greek word for "general") had to do with the big picture and the war as a whole. To gain their advantage in the Coral Sea, the Japanese had to recall their invasion force headed for Port Moresby. So they were forced to stop their drive toward Australia.

The Battle of Midway.
From the Japanese point of view the island of Midway was the key to the whole perimeter scheme. From there they could bomb Pearl Harbor and make it useless as an offensive base for our Pacific Fleet.

Admiral Yamamoto intended to force a showdown at Midway with the American Pacific Fleet of Admiral Nimitz, which was still suffering from the disaster inflicted by the Japanese on December 7. But the United States had the advantage of the "Magic" decoder. Our forces knew where the Japanese were going. So they were ready and waiting when the Japanese struck at Midway on June 4, 1942. During the battle that followed, United States carrier planes sank four of Japan's best carriers and destroyed some of their most skilled air groups. The United States lost one carrier, but handed Japan its first great naval defeat.

For the first time in World War II, the balance of naval power in the Pacific had now shifted to the United States. In this one decisive battle the whole strategic situation in the Pacific was transformed. The Japanese had to abandon their plans for taking Midway, Fiji, and Samoa.

The battle for Guadalcanal.
The Japanese decided to risk one more try to take Port Moresby in New Guinea. To protect that gamble they seized Guadalcanal, one of the nearby Solomon Islands, and established an air base there. Under the Allied policy of active defense, this could not be allowed. Guadalcanal was the stepping stone that the Allies needed for returning to the Philippines and finally for invading Japan itself.

The Allied attack on the position the Japanese were building on Guadalcanal was nicknamed "Shoestring." It had to be undertaken with very little in the way of men or equipment because at that same moment forces and supplies were being gathered for the invasion of North Africa. On August 7, 1942, some 20,000 marines were landed on Guadalcanal and the neighboring island of Tulagi. These landings were followed, in the early morning hours of August 9, by the Battle of Savo Island. There a Japanese cruiser force sank four out of the five United States and Australian heavy cruisers that were protecting our transports unloading on Guadalcanal. This terrible defeat forced the withdrawal of the transports, which left the marines short of supplies.

War in the steaming jungles of Guadalcanal was old-fashioned hand-to-hand fighting. There the alert dodging of an enemy's knife could mean life instead of death. The marines had been trained for this sort of combat. They never were put to a harder test. The Allied marines lived up to their reputation for heroism. On land, this may have been the only time the Japanese were ever outfought by an enemy they met on equal terms. Finally the beaten Japanese evacuated the island on February 9, 1943. At heavy cost of pain and life, it was there at Guadalcanal that the Japanese advance was finally stopped.

The end of the beginning.
Early in January 1943 President Roosevelt and Prime Minister Churchill met at Casablanca in Morocco to plan future operations. There had been a striking improvement in the military outlook since their last meeting a year before. The Soviets had won the Battle of Stalingrad and were beginning to turn the tide in Russia. Egypt had been saved and Morocco, Libya, and Algeria taken for the Allies. Guadalcanal would soon be taken from Japan. The RAF and the United States Eighth Air Force were bombing Germany with deadly accuracy and increasing frequency.

"Now, this is not the end," Churchill said. "It is not even the beginning of the end. But it is, perhaps, the end of the beginning."

3. Victory in Europe

The Allies were divided on where they should go after they seized Tunisia, as they confidently expected to do. At Casablanca the Americans argued for an invasion of France in 1943, but again the British resisted. They wanted first to free the Mediterranean completely by taking Sicily and then knocking Italy out of the war. The British view finally prevailed. The Allies also agreed that they could now begin to take the offensive in the Pacific. Most important, the Allies announced that they would not stop fighting until they had won "unconditional surrender" from all their enemies. Some people thought this was a strategic error and might prolong the war.

The fall of Tunisia. The Axis army in Tunisia was now trapped. They tried to fly out their best troops, and some did escape that way. But then the Allied bombers caught their transport planes on the ground and destroyed them. On March 7, 1943, Rommel was recalled to Germany, where Hitler confessed that Africa was lost. When Rommel asked him if he still believed that total victory was possible, Hitler replied, "I know it is necessary to make peace with one side or the other [Russia or the Western powers], but no one will make peace with me."

On May 7, 1943, General von Arnim surrendered the Axis forces in Tunisia. He and sixteen other generals were taken prisoner along with a quarter-million Axis troops, including some of Germany's best-trained and best-armed soldiers. This victory was as dramatic and as decisive as Stalingrad. Italian morale was destroyed, and Great Britain's Mediterranean lifeline was opened again. Now the way was prepared to act on the Allies' secret decision to invade Italy from the south.

The battle in Italy. On the morning of July 10, 1943, swiftly and suddenly 250,000 American and British troops landed along 150 miles of Sicilian coastline. It was the greatest amphibious operation of all time. Never before had so many troops been landed at once for a single attack. Unfortunately, because the plan was faulty, the German and Italian forces were allowed to escape from the island of Sicily to the mainland of Italy.

But the Italians had now had enough of war. Mussolini was forced to resign, and a new government was installed. At the end of July the Italians began to put out peace feelers to the Allies. After much bargaining, an armistice was signed on September 3 with Italian forces. But during those long negotiations the Nazis rushed reinforcements to Italy to hold the country till the bitter end.

When British and American troops landed on the toe of Italy, they ran into fierce German resistance. Not until June 4, 1944, did the Allies finally enter Rome. Still the Germans held on. For the United States this invasion of Italy was one of the deadliest campaigns in the war. Seventy thousand Americans were killed. By their courage and that of the British, Poles, and other Allied troops, they tied up 23 German divisions and weakened the Nazis everywhere else.

The air war. While the Allies were making their slow way toward the invasion of France in 1944, Germany was already being invaded by air.

The lightning strike of air power at Pearl Harbor had shocked Americans into seeing that the world faced a new kind of war. Now the battlefield was everywhere. There was no place where civilians could hide from the airborne terror. Warplanes sometimes flew so high they could not be seen and could barely be heard, to strike at homes and factories.

Robert Capa took this picture of the jubilant citizens of a small Sicilian town in 1943 welcoming the American troops who have liberated them. Capa was killed covering the Vietnam War.

The British began bombing Germany in 1941 when the RAF dropped 46,000 tons of bombs on enemy targets. British bombers flew over Germany at night and "saturation" bombed whole areas. Incendiary bombs set fire to entire cities. Since these attacking bombers could not be seen from the ground, British losses were not heavy. They hoped that by destroying cities, disorganizing labor, and shattering civilian morale, they could force the Nazis to surrender even before the Nazi armies were conquered.

The United States Army Air Force made its first raid on Germany in August 1942. It pursued another plan—"pinpoint" attacks in daylight. When bombers could see their targets, they could focus their bombs on the crucial factories and could report whether they had hit their targets. At the same time the Germans could see the approaching planes. The Americans thought their B-17 bombers—called "Flying Fortresses" because they bristled with so many machine guns—were so heavily defended that the Germans could not deal with them. But soon German fighters were downing American bombers in disastrous numbers. In response, the United States developed new long-range fighter planes to protect the bombers and so continued their precision bombing. Soon the skies of Germany were raining bombs day and night.

This American B-17 "Flying Fortress" bomber has just made a direct hit on a huge aircraft plant in East Prussia where the Germans had thought they were outside the Allied bombing range.

The Germans responded with their V-1 flying bombs and their even more terrifying V-2 rockets, which dropped suddenly and silently from the sky carrying death-dealing one-ton bombs. Never before in the history of warfare was there so much suffering by civilians. But bombing did not end the war. German factories continued to produce airplanes and other war machines in large numbers. The military effect of Allied bombing was to force the Nazis to use up their energies on fighter planes and antiaircraft weapons for their own defense. And this drained away the Nazi power to attack.

Allied planes killed nearly a third of a million Germans and destroyed 5 million homes. Still, bombing did not have a substantial effect on the German war effort until 1944. Then the bombs were concentrated on specific war industries— airplane, tank, truck, and ball-bearing factories, oil and gas production. Since Germany had dispersed its factories to defend against air attack, the Allied attack on railroads and highways helped paralyze Nazi war production.

D-Day in France. The United States and Great Britain secretly agreed that in June 1944 they would invade France by landings across the English Channel. This was the most important—and the best-kept—secret of the war. The invasion would be directed by the American General Dwight D. Eisenhower, who became Supreme Commander of the Allied Forces in Western Europe. The Allies intended at the same time to keep maximum pressure on Italy and to invade the south of France.

The cross-channel invasion was a dangerous maneuver, for the Germans had been building up their forces to meet an expected attack. They had had four years to construct their coastal fortifications. They had brought 58 divisions to France. But the Allies could pick the time and place to attack. Allied bombings had already brought chaos to the Nazi transportation system. And the Allied invaders could count on aid from the French Resistance, men and women who at great risk gave secret help to the Allies.

To mislead the Nazis, the Allies skillfully led the Germans to believe that the attack would come in the area of Calais at the narrowest part of the English Channel. By radio broadcasts, arranged so that the Nazis would get the message, they gave the Germans the impression that a great invasion force was prepared to land there.

During the night of June 5 on the orders of General Eisenhower, a mighty force of 600 warships and 4000 supporting craft carrying 176,000 men moved toward the coast of Normandy. They were protected by an air cover of 11,000 planes. At 5:30 A.M. the navy began its bombardment of the coast of Normandy. At 6:30 A.M. the first troops hit the beach between the mouth of the Seine River and Cherbourg. The Allies had achieved tactical surprise, and despite some trouble spots the initial landings were a success.

The German generals now wanted to throw all their armored forces—the German name was "Panzer," meaning armor—against the invaders in one great counter stroke. But Hitler, who thought that he was wiser than his generals, overruled them. He still was sure that the main invasion would come at Calais. So Rommel, the army group commander on the spot, was forced to hold

General "Ike" Eisenhower gives a pep talk to a group of paratroopers about to be dropped into France on D-Day. The men's faces are darkened to lessen their chances of being seen.

United Press International Photo

back the Panzer divisions. The Allied men, armor, and supplies managed to reach shore and establish a secure beachhead. After the first few days the invading force was out of danger. It was one of the greatest Allied achievements of the war. In a single week the Allies had landed 326,000 men, 50,000 vehicles, and 100,000 tons of supplies.

The Allies on the move. The battle of the Normandy invasion lasted from June 6 to July 24, 1944. At the end of that time, the Allies had landed more than a million men and controlled 1500 square miles of Normandy and Brittany. The breakthrough and the beginning of the battle for France came on July 25 when General George Patton's Third Army struck hard at the Germans. Soon thousands of Patton's tanks were pouring through. The FFI (French Forces of the Interior—the Resistance) now came out into the open to aid the Allies. Up from the Mediterranean came the United States Seventh Army under General A. M. Patch to join the eastward-moving Allied troops. Paris was liberated on August 25, Brussels and Antwerp a few days later. Within six weeks after the breakthrough all France had been cleared of Germans. And the Germans had lost nearly half a million men and untold amounts of machinery and material.

Units of General Courtney Hodges's First Army moved onto the "sacred soil" of Hitler's "unbeatable" Thousand Year Reich on September 12, 1944. Soon six Allied armies with 3 million men were facing the powerful Siegfried line of fortifications that extended the whole length of Germany's western border.

Meanwhile from the east, huge Soviet armies were hastening toward the German border. A great Russian offensive had speedily swept 460 miles across the Ukraine and Poland to the gates of Warsaw. There, unfortunately, the Russians stopped. This gave the Germans time to crush a heroic revolt of the Polish underground in the city.

When the Russians moved toward the south, Romania and Bulgaria surrendered quickly. On October 20 the Russians reached Belgrade. In December at Budapest the Germans dug in and put up stubborn resistance.

On the western front, meanwhile, the Allies were once again divided over their strategy. Should they strike straight for Berlin, or instead advance on a broad front? One try at the sudden-thrust strategy

Imperial War Museum, London

Trucks, guns, tons of equipment and thousands of men are unloaded on the beachhead at Normandy as barrage balloons float overhead.

was an attempt to jump the river-barriers of the Meuse, the Waal, and the lower Rhine with three airborne divisions. One British officer called it "a bridge too far." And so it proved. When this failed, the Allies settled for the slower strategy.

The election of 1944. In the United States, despite the war-to-the-death against totalitarian powers, politics continued as usual. During the summer that saw the liberation of France, Franklin D. Roosevelt was unanimously nominated for his fourth term as President. He said he only wanted to go home to Hyde Park, "But as a good soldier . . . I will accept and serve." The strains of

On November 7 the nation gave President Roosevelt a decisive victory. He won by 3.6 million votes and by 432 to 99 in the electoral college. The Democrats also won substantial majorities in both houses of Congress. Just as during the Civil War, when Abraham Lincoln was re-elected, the nation had decided "not to change horses in the middle of the stream."

The Battle of the Bulge. On December 16, 1944, the Germans made a final desperate bid to break the Allies. With two armies they struck a weakly held front in the Ardennes district of France intending to sweep through and seize Antwerp, the main Allied base. This would have cut the Allied army in two and left the northern half without access to its supply harbor. The German attack was favored by foul weather, which grounded Allied planes. Heavily wooded terrain screened the Nazi movements and gave them the advantage of surprise over the unwary Allies.

The German attack got off to a good start. Spearheaded by Panzer divisions of heavily armored vehicles, they penetrated 60 miles, almost to the Meuse River, creating a large "bulge" in the Allied lines. Finally they were stopped by the armies of Patton and Montgomery. There at the vital rail junction and road center of Bastogne, the 101st Airborne Division under General McAuliffe made its heroic stand. When he was surrounded by the Germans and asked to surrender, McAuliffe made his historic one-word reply—"Nuts!" McAuliffe's 101st disrupted the German timetable, halted the attack, and held out until relieved by the Third Army. By the end of January the Bulge was "pinched off" and the Germans were forced back to their Siegfried line. United States losses were heavy, but the "Battle of the Bulge" had cost the dwindling Nazis 120,000 of their best remaining men.

the Presidency in wartime had taken their toll on FDR. How long could he bear up?

The Vice-Presidency was more important than ever before. At the Democratic convention the real battle was over FDR's running mate. In the end the convention named Senator Harry S Truman of Missouri. He had begun his career as a machine-politician in Kansas City. But he made a name for himself in the Senate as the head of a committee looking into defense contracts.

Wendell Willkie hoped once again to win the nomination of the Republican party. Now his liberal international views troubled many of the party leaders. Governor Thomas E. Dewey of New York soundly defeated him in the Wisconsin primary. Then Willkie withdrew from the race, and Dewey was nominated as the Republican candidate. Willkie was to die in October after a series of heart attacks.

Conferring at Yalta. In February 1945, when the defeat of the Nazis appeared to be in sight, President Roosevelt met with the other Allied leaders, British Prime Minister Churchill and Russian dictator Josef Stalin. At Yalta, a Russian summer resort on the Black Sea, they would agree on their plans for the Nazi surrender. Germany was to be taken apart. Once again, the Germans would have to pay enormous "reparations."

Churchill, Roosevelt, and Stalin, the leaders of "the Big Three," pose for photographers in a courtyard during their important meetings at the Russian summer resort of Yalta. FDR, tired and haggard, was to die only two months later.

Stalin was a tough and clever bargainer. At first he demanded that Poland be put under a Communist puppet government. When Roosevelt and Churchill objected, Stalin promised to let the Polish people choose their government by free elections. Then, arguing that the Soviet Union had been the most devastated of the Allies, he made them agree to give Russia half of all the German reparations.

Stalin promised to declare war against Japan soon after the defeat of Germany and said that when the new United Nations was organized, the Soviets would join. In return the Soviets gained some strategic Japanese islands. Stalin would also be allowed to conquer Outer Mongolia—a vast area twice the size of Texas—on the Russian border in central Asia. At the same time, Stalin solemnly promised not to interfere in the countries along the Russian border in Eastern Europe. He said he would let the people of Poland, Czechoslovakia, Hungary, Romania, and Bulgaria elect their own governments.

Too soon the democratic leaders would discover what Stalin's promises were worth. Looking back, some historians say that Roosevelt and Churchill should have known better than to believe anything Stalin said. Again and again the Communist leaders had called democracy a fraud. But at the time, the British and American leaders did not have much choice. The Soviet armies still had unrivaled power in Eastern Europe. The Western powers thought they desperately needed the help of those armies to finish off the Nazis and Japanese. All they were able to demand from their Russian ally was promises. They felt lucky even to get those! For the next twenty years the free world would pay the price for Stalin's lies.

The failure to take Berlin. Now the Allies closed in for the kill. On March 7, 1945, the First Army crossed the Rhine bridge at Remagen. Crossings were also soon made at other locations, and by the first week of April all the Allied armies were across the river. Caught between the Russian Communist armies speeding westward and the Anglo-Americans speeding eastward, German resistance was now rapidly collapsing.

5. GERMANS SIGN SURRENDER AT REIMS, MAY 7, 1945

World War II, European Theater, 1944-1945

☐ Axis-Controlled Territory 1942

→ Allied Forces

✗ Allied Victories

400 Miles

400 Kilometers

1. D-DAY, JUNE 6, 1944

3. BATTLE OF THE BULGE, DEC 16-26, 1944

2. PARIS LIBERATED, AUG. 25, 1944

150 Miles

150 Kilometers

General Dwight D. "Ike" Eisenhower, who had successfully directed the invasion of Europe, now faced a decision that would shape the future of Europe. If he wanted, he could quickly move his forces into Berlin, the capital of Germany, and also into Prague, the capital of Czechoslovakia. In Anglo-American hands, these capitals would be strongholds to help the democracies enforce Stalin's promise to let the people of Eastern Europe choose their own governments.

Or, General Eisenhower could wait to mop up the German troops behind his own lines—

meanwhile letting the Russians overrun more of Eastern Europe and consolidate their positions in Berlin and Prague. But in Communist hands, those capitals would help the Russians to foist their dictatorship on all the surrounding peoples. The Russians could then make the border countries—Poland, Czechoslovakia, Hungary, Romania, and Bulgaria—into a group of "satellites" revolving around Moscow.

The farsighted Winston Churchill saw this threat. "I deem it highly important," he warned General Eisenhower, "that we should shake hands with the Russians as far to the east as possible." But Eisenhower was anxious to avoid the loss of more American soldiers, and FDR did not interfere. Instead of rushing the democratic forces eastward, Ike decided to stop 50 miles west of Berlin at the River Elbe. Stalin applauded this fateful decision, for now both Berlin and Prague were left to the Russians.

Until the last minute, Churchill kept trying to persuade President Roosevelt to push speedily on to Berlin and Prague. The new "mortal danger to the free world," he said, was our so-called "ally," Russia. How tragic, after the long struggle against the Nazi tyranny, to hand over half of Europe to a Communist tyranny!

The death of Roosevelt. Before Churchill's wisdom could prevail in Washington, President Roosevelt was dead. Worn down by wartime burdens, he had gone for a rest to Warm Springs, Georgia, where he often went for treatment of his paralyzed legs. On April 12, 1945, he complained of a headache, and within minutes a blood vessel had burst in his brain. The valiant, cheerful leader, who had helped raise his fellow Americans from the depth of the Great Depression and who had organized their battle against Nazi barbarism, did not live to have the satisfaction of receiving the Nazi surrender.

The nation grieved as it had grieved for few Americans since Lincoln. Men and women wept in their offices, at home, and in the streets. They felt that they had lost not only a national leader but a personal friend.

Germany surrenders. Russian and American troops met at the Elbe on April 25. Other Russian troops were fighting their way from house to house through the heaps of rubble of Berlin. Hitler committed suicide in Berlin. Meanwhile his old henchman Mussolini had been captured by Italian partisans and executed. To show their contempt for the strutting dictator who had brought their beautiful land to ruins, they hung up Mussolini's body by the heels for all to see. On May 8, 1945, the Germans signed terms of unconditional surrender at General Eisenhower's headquarters in the French city of Reims. The day was celebrated joyously in the victorious countries as V-E (Victory in Europe) Day.

Elie Wiesel, winner of the 1986 Nobel Peace Prize, was among the slave laborers liberated by American troops at Buchenwald. Wiesel is second to the right of the man with the bandaged head.

1. Identify: Flying Fortresses, V-1 and V-2 missiles, Dwight Eisenhower, George Patton, FFI, A. M. Patch, Courtney Hodges, Siegfried line, Harry Truman, Thomas Dewey, A. C. McAuliffe, V-E Day.

2. Locate: Sicily, Calais, Normandy, Cherbourg, Brittany, Ardennes, Bastogne, Yalta, Remagen.

3. What were the chief results of (a) the Allied victory in North Africa? (b) the Italian campaign?

4. How did the British air attacks on Germany differ from those by the American planes?

5. How did Germany's situation change between June and November 1944?

6. Why was the Battle of the Bulge important?

7. Where did the Anglo-American and Russian armies meet? Why was this meeting line significant?

8. **Drawing Conclusions.** What agreements were made at Yalta? Why did it seem necessary at the time to make them?

United Press International Photo

4. The war in the Pacific

"The victory is but half won," President Truman warned. "The West is free but the East is still in bondage. When the last Japanese division has surrendered unconditionally, only then will our fighting job be done."

The struggle for the islands. After the fall of Guadalcanal in February 1943, a two-year struggle began to regain other islands and to prepare for the final attack on the Japanese homeland. General Douglas MacArthur and his troops would advance through the islands of the western Pacific from New Guinea to Mindanao in the Philippines. At the same time the navy and marines would have to cross the central Pacific in a series of amphibious operations by way of the Gilbert, Marshall, and Mariana islands. So long as the Japanese held these central Pacific islands, their airplanes could attack anything that moved along the New Guinea-Mindanao path of General MacArthur. Both advances had to succeed together.

General MacArthur, brilliant leader of the army in the Pacific, was generous in victory.

Japan fiercely resisted every landing and stubbornly contested every inch of ground. Our losses were high in the capture of Tarawa in the Gilberts in November 1943, and of Kwajalein and other islands in the Marshalls and of Saipan in the Marianas in February 1944. The tiny island of Iwo Jima was the scene of some of our heaviest losses and some of the most memorable American heroism. After a month of desperate fighting (February-March 1945), at the frightful cost of 5000 dead, the marines planted the American flag there on Mount Suribachi. With the capture of Iwo Jima and Okinawa (April-June 1945), where 11,000 more troops died, we were within striking distance of the Japanese homeland. Victory was in sight.

The return to the Philippines. Meanwhile in the southwest Pacific in a series of brilliant campaigns,

587

General MacArthur's forces were leap-frogging toward the Philippines. Two years before, when MacArthur had left the Philippines and Allied prospects were dim, he had promised, "I shall return!" Now, on October 20, 1944, he fulfilled his promise when the Americans swarmed ashore at Leyte Island on the southeast tip of the archipelago. Again and again the Japanese vainly tried to land reinforcements on Leyte.

Before the Allies could clinch their victory in the Pacific, they would have to fight the greatest sea battle of all time. They would have to end, once and for all, the Japanese navy's ability to keep the Allies off their home islands. In the Battle of Leyte Gulf on October 23–25, the Japanese were so badly defeated that their navy was knocked out of the war.

American troops were now free to land on the main Philippine island of Luzon. The first troops went ashore on January 9, 1945, and were followed by later waves. They fought toward Manila from the north and the south. When they reached the city, the Japanese stood firm. Each house became a fortress for a few Japanese soldiers who gave their lives to delay the American advance. Finally on March 9, after fierce street fighting the last Japanese soldier in the city gave up. During the battle for Manila, MacArthur declared the Commonwealth of the Philippines to be reestablished. "My country has kept the faith," he said; "your capital city, cruelly punished though it be, has regained its rightful place—citadel of democracy in the East."

On July 4, 1946, (fulfilling the promise made by the McDuffie Act back in 1934) the Republic of the Philippines was proclaimed independent. In the following March, a 99-year agreement was signed, giving the United States military and naval bases in the islands.

Splitting the atom. Upon the death of President Roosevelt in April 1945, the tremendous task of finishing the war and planning the peace suddenly fell to the courageous, peppery new President Harry S Truman. He was a man of decision

American infantry wade ashore from amphibious landing craft onto Leyte Island in the Philippines. The jungle still smolders from the pre-attack naval and air bombardment.

destined to make some of the most fateful decisions in modern history. And he was prepared for great decisions. Ever since he was a young man, he had been reading books of history. He especially admired President Jackson and President Lincoln. He knew how earlier American Presidents had shaped the future. When he took his oath of office, he felt overwhelmed, and he asked the nation to pray for him.

His first great decision was on a subject so secret that even as Vice-President he had not heard of it. It concerned the colossal American project that had already nearly succeeded—to build an atomic bomb. "Atom" was a word of Greek origin that meant something unbreakable. It was believed to be the smallest possible unit of matter. To create a bomb by the splitting of tiny atoms would be the most gigantic, most costly single scientific effort of the war. This startling achievement would change the relations between all nations, possibly for the rest of human history.

Those who made the American bomb possible were (in addition to many American scientists) a "Who's Who" of world science. From Germany came the greatest physicist of the age, Albert Einstein. Because he was a Jew, the Nazis had taken away his German citizenship and seized his property. From Italy, as a refugee from Mussolini, came the brilliant Enrico Fermi, who was one of the first to propose an atomic bomb as a practical possibility. Scientists, engineers, and mathematicians came also from Hungary, Austria, Denmark, and Czechoslovakia—refugees from all the enslaved parts of Europe. The barbarism of the enemies had brought together in the United States the greatest scientific minds of the age.

To build an atomic bomb certain theoretical questions first had to be answered. Was it really possible to achieve "the controlled release of atomic energy"? If it was possible to break the atom, and create a "chain reaction," then an enormous amount of energy would be released even from one atom. If a chain reaction could be started, then when one atom was split it would split the other atoms touching it, and a fantastic blast of energy would suddenly explode. But could it be done? And if a chain reaction was started, could it be controlled so that one exploding atom would not destroy the world? These were the two great practical questions.

The answer came at 3:25 on the afternoon of December 2, 1942, in a secret laboratory that had been a squash court on the campus of the University of Chicago. Professor Enrico Fermi supervised the experiment. When everything was prepared, he gave the signal to pull out the control rod. Suddenly the Geiger counters resounded with tell-tale clicks from the radiation made by the successful breaking up of uranium atoms. The dignified scientists let out a cheer. They had produced a chain reaction that transformed matter into energy. And they had been able to prevent it from blowing them up! The Atomic Age had begun.

One of the physicists hurried to the telephone and gave the code message to be relayed to the President of the United States.

"You'll be interested to know," he reported with mock casualness, "that the Italian navigator has just landed in the New World. The earth was not as large as he had estimated, and he arrived in the New World sooner than he had expected."

"Is that so?" he was asked. "Were the natives friendly?"

"Everyone landed safe and happy." This meant that Professor Fermi (the "Italian navigator") had succeeded even ahead of schedule. The "New World" was, of course, the uncharted world of atomic power.

The atomic bomb. In May 1942, only seven months before the Fermi experiment succeeded, President Roosevelt had set up the super-secret Manhattan Project to prepare to build a bomb. But it took another three years and a cost of $2 billion for the Manhattan Project to do the job.

At 5:30 on the morning of July 16, 1945, on a remote desert near Alamogordo, New Mexico, the moment came to prove that the bold thinking of the scientists could be matched by the practical know-how of engineers. The answer required no delicate Geiger counter to detect it. The world's first atomic bomb exploded—with a blinding flash and a towering mushroom cloud such as had never been seen before.

By the time the bomb was perfected, the Germans and Italians had already surrendered. Of the enemies now only Japan remained. On July 26 the Allied leaders gave the Japanese a solemn warning that "the alternative to surrender is prompt and utter destruction." Still they did not surrender.

ON TO JAPAN!

SEVEK

After the victory over Germany, this dramatic poster, with a map of the world as background, symbolically showed the full force of the Allies being directed at Japan.

Should the United States use the atomic bomb? No one knew how long Japan would hold out. Despite the terrifying fire raid of March 10, 1945, when more than 100,000 people died and much of Tokyo was destroyed, the Japanese militarists appeared determined to resist. If the war dragged on and Americans had to invade Japan, it might cost a million lives. The atomic bomb, President Truman knew, might kill many thousands of innocent Japanese. But life for life, the odds were that it would cost less.

On August 6, 1945, three weeks after that first blinding blast on the New Mexico desert, a single American B-29 dropped an atomic bomb on Hiroshima. About 75,000 people were killed outright. Tens of thousands more perished later from wounds or radiation. The Japanese still held on. A few days later another plane dropped an atomic bomb on Nagasaki. Then the Japanese finally caved in. They announced their surrender on August 14, 1945.

The cost of World War II. The human cost of World War II can never be finally known. The United States lost 292,000 lives in combat, over five times the toll of World War I. Without the brilliant medical advances of the war—the blood banks and wonder drugs, the skilled doctors and

In 1945 Nagasaki, Japan, like Hiroshima, was obliterated by an atomic bomb. Only reinforced concrete buildings remained standing after the blast. Everything else was blown away.

World War II, Pacific Theater, 1942–1945

⬅ MacArthur

⬅ Nimitz

✕ Allied Victory

▨ Japanese-Controlled Territory 1942

0   1200 Miles
0   1200 Kilometers

5. UNITED STATES DROPS ATOMIC BOMBS ON HIROSHIMA AND NAGASAKI, AUGUST 6 AND 9, 1945

4. ALLIES TAKE IWO JIMA AND OKINAWA, FEBRUARY–JUNE, 1945

3. BATTLE OF LEYTE GULF, OCTOBER 23–25, 1944

2. ALLIED FORCES CAPTURE TARAWA, 1943

1. BATTLE FOR GUADALCANAL, AUGUST 7, 1942 – FEBRUARY 3, 1943

nurses—the number of combat deaths would have been far higher. Still, the cost for the United States was small compared to the rest of the world, where perhaps 60 million died—18 million Russians, 4 million Germans, 2 million Japanese, possibly 22 million Chinese, and millions of others. Most horrible of all was the Nazis' gigantic crime, the Holocaust (from the Greek *holo*, "whole," and *kaustos*, "burnt"). This was their attempt to kill all European Jews. Six million Jews were exterminated in gas chambers and concentration camps.

At last World War II was over. The menace from Germany and Japan was destroyed. But the world was haunted by a host of new fears. These had been created by the war itself.

SECTION 4 REVIEW

1. Identify or explain: Douglas MacArthur, Albert Einstein, Enrico Fermi, chain reaction.

2. Locate: New Guinea, Mindanao, Tarawa, Kwajalein, Saipan, Iwo Jima, Okinawa, Leyte Gulf, Luzon, Hiroshima, Nagasaki.

3. What was the Allied strategy in the Pacific in 1943–1944? Name the major battles.

4. What were some costs of World War II?

5. **Predicting Consequences.** How did Truman's decision to use the atomic bomb, forever change the nature of warfare?

FOCUSING ON IDEAS

1. From 1939 to 1943 the number of workers in nonfarm jobs jumped from 30 million to 42 million. How was the rapid expansion of the labor force achieved at a time when the armed forces were growing by more than 8 million people?

2. How did technological advances change warfare in World War II from what it had been in World War I? Give examples.

3. How did "the tide turn" in late 1942 and early 1943?

4. How did the "Good Neighbor policy" pay dividends in World War II?

TAKING A CRITICAL LOOK

1. **Making Comparisons.** For the civilian population, how did wartime hardships compare with the depression hardships a few years earlier?

2. **Checking Consistency.** What were some major differences between the war against Germany and the war against Japan?

YOUR REGION IN HISTORY

1. **Geography.** Identify any military camps or other armed forces facilities in your state that served the war effort between 1940 and 1945.

2. **Culture.** Find out how high school students in your area helped on the home front.

3. **Economics.** What kinds of goods were produced in your community or state to aid the war effort in World War II?

HISTORICAL FACTS AND FIGURES

Predicting Consequences. Study the graph below to help answer the following questions: (a) What percentage of all the soldiers who died in World War II were citizens of the Soviet Union? Of Britain? (b) What percentage of wounded soldiers were German citizens? Americans? (c) What nation suffered the most civilian deaths during World War II? (d) Why were there so few American civilian deaths? (e) How might the overall number of casualties experienced by the Soviets have affected Soviet society and their attitudes toward war?

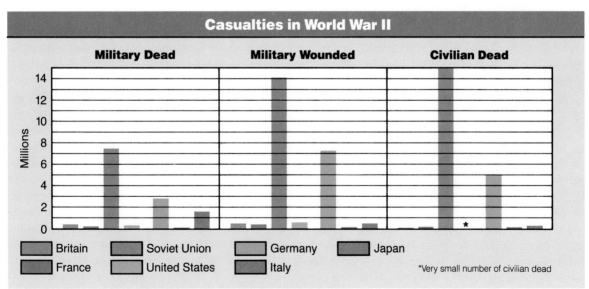

Casualties in World War II

Source: Henri Michel, *The Second World War*

593

MAKING CONNECTIONS

THEMES

This unit began on page 517 with Franklin D. Roosevelt's observation that strong leadership and decisive action would guide America's future:

"The people of the United States have not failed, . . . they want direct, vigorous action."

This conclusion was supported by the three unit themes that are reprinted in **dark type** below. Use the time line and the information in Unit 9 to answer the questions that follow the themes.

1. **Franklin Roosevelt's strong leadership and New Deal programs ease the impact of the Great Depression on poverty-stricken Americans.**

   What elements of Franklin Roosevelt's New Deal were a radical departure from earlier government programs?

2. **The rise of the dictators and fascism in Europe threatens the peace of the entire world.**

   What conditions in the world made it possible for nazism and fascism to take root and spread throughout Europe?

3. **The allied nations triumph in a world war on two fronts, but with victory comes a host of new fears and problems.**

   What lessons for the future might world leaders have learned from World War II?

1936 Congress passes neutrality laws preventing the United States from arming either side in the Spanish Civil War.

Events in American History

1930s Keynes proposes the idea of increased government spending to expand the economy.

1934 The Securities and Exchange Commission is set up to regulate the stock market.

Events in World History

1930   1932   1934   1936   1938

1935 Attempting to create an empire, Italian troops invade Ethiopia.

1930s Depression and reparations required by Versailles Treaty leave German economic and political system unstable.

1936 The Spanish Civil War begins as the Fascists and republicans fight for control.

1943 The Works Progress Administration has spent $11 billion to employ 8.5 million people.

1945 Churchill, Roosevelt, and Stalin meet in Yalta and plan for the Nazi surrender.

1941 The Japanese attack Pearl Harbor, and the United States enters World War II.

1945 The United States reveals a devastating new weapon in dropping the atomic bomb on Hiroshima and Nagasaki.

| 1940 | 1942 | 1944 | 1946 | 1948 |

1938

1939 Stalin and Hitler sign a nonaggression pact and agree to divide Poland.

1938 Neville Chamberlain rejects FDR's proposed international conference on armaments and economic security.

Postwar problems
1945–1960

With the explosion of the first atomic bomb in New Mexico on July 16, 1945, a new era in the history of the world had begun. Under the menacing shadow of the atomic bomb, war between great powers could never again be the same. Isolation was no longer possible. Could the United States shape a foreign policy for survival in this frightening world?

In the postwar age, the American ways of living, thinking, and doing would be transformed. Magic machines would change the meaning of space and time. Faraway events would be seen in everybody's living room. Now millions, in their two-week vacations, could jet to Paris or Rome or Tokyo and see the world for themselves. Computers took over old jobs and created new jobs. Suburbs and highways changed the places where people lived and worked, went to school and shopped. The nation was ruled by machines that no one had imagined a few years before. Could Americans still preserve the self-government of the simpler days of the Republic? Could a machine-America keep alive the spirit of adventure that had conquered a continent?

THEMES IN AMERICAN HISTORY

- Tensions between the United States and the Soviet Union, and the shadow of atomic weapons produce an era of "cold war."

- Growing demands for racial equality produce new leadership and new government policies.

THEMES
- Technological advances transform American ways of living, thinking, and doing during the Truman and Eisenhower years.

The smallest air current moves the parts of Alexander Calder's hanging sculptures, creating ever-changing patterns. Mobile and technically refined, they reflect qualities of the United States in the post-World War II era.

Whitney Museum Exhibit. Photo Researchers, Inc. © Farrel Grehen 1976

CHAPTER 28

Truman: neither war nor peace

At the end of World War II, the United States faced a world in ashes. The old order was burnt out, and nothing had arisen to take its place. Some Americans yearned to return to the former isolation of the Western Hemisphere. But world trade was more important than ever before. To prosper, the United States had to exchange goods with the nations of Europe, Asia, and Africa. Now, with airplanes and atomic weapons, the battlefield was everywhere. On this new-fashioned planet, Americans could not withdraw. The end of the war did not break our ties with Europe. And before long we would be drawn into the battles of Asia.

1. Beginnings of the cold war

The United States and Great Britain had been the allies of Soviet Russia for only one reason—to defeat Adolf Hitler. Since the two Western powers had never trusted Stalin, they had not even told him about the atomic bomb. The Communist leaders feared the capitalist nations but expected the whole world to become Communist. They hoped for the collapse of the democracies.

Still, American leaders thought that these differences would not have to bring on another war. Perhaps the Soviets could be persuaded to join a new and stronger League of Nations, where capitalists and Communists might talk to each other instead of shoot at each other. Before long, Americans would discover that the Soviet leaders had a very different view of the future.

Harry S Truman. The day after taking the oath of office, President Truman held a press conference. "Last night," he told the reporters in his midwestern twang, "the moon, the stars, and all the planets fell on me." To the surprise of many (including, perhaps, the new President himself), Harry S Truman proved equal to all his great decisions.

Harry Truman was born in Lamar, Missouri, in 1884. After high school, he worked as a bank clerk and then ran the family farm. In World War I, he served in the field artillery and rose to the rank of major. When the war was over, he started a clothing business, which failed during the postwar recession. Between 1922 and 1934 he was the elected County Judge (county commissioner) in Jackson County, Missouri. He studied law in night school.

In 1934, with the help of the political machine run by Kansas City's boss, Tom Pendergast, Truman was elected to the United States Senate. At that point he was considered only a routine machine politician. But Truman soon became known for his hard work, his intelligence, and his fairness. As

Department of Energy

Postwar leaders faced the task of controlling the fearsome power of the atom bomb.

head of the Senate Committee Investigating the National Defense Program during World War II, he held the national spotlight.

Building a new world organization. In 1943 Britain, the United States, and Russia had agreed to set up a new organization to replace the League of Nations. At the beautiful Dumbarton Oaks estate in Washington in 1944, China joined these three to make detailed plans. Then, on April 12 the next year, 200 delegates from 50 nations met in San Francisco to form the United Nations (UN). This was not a peace conference, for the war was still being fought on all fronts.

The Soviet Union and the United States disagreed over the use of the veto in the Security Council. They both thought there should be a veto so the great powers could protect themselves from unfavorable United Nations decisions. But on matters not concerning themselves directly, Russia and the

United States parted company. The Soviets thought that any action should be able to be vetoed. The United States disagreed, fearing that this would paralyze the new organization. Despite these differences, a charter emerged for the United Nations. After World War I the Senate had rejected the League of Nations. But now, on July 28, 1945, the Senate ratified the United Nations charter by the decisive vote of 82–2.

The UN aimed to preserve the peace and provide a better life for all. The General Assembly included delegates from every member nation. There each nation had one vote, except for the USSR, which had three votes—one for itself and one each for the Ukraine and Belorussia. This concession to Russia had been offered at Yalta to persuade the Soviets to join the UN. The General Assembly could discuss any subject within the scope of the charter. And it made recommendations to the small and powerful Security Council. The Assembly fixed the UN budget, admitted new members approved by the Security Council, and elected member nations to the many UN agencies.

The Security Council had eleven (later fifteen) members. Of these the Big Five (United States, Britain, the Soviet Union, France, and China) had permanent seats and the right to a veto. The six other members were elected for two-year terms but had no veto. This Security Council had the power to look into disputes and to act against any nation that threatened the peace.

The Secretariat, headed by a Secretary-General, would handle the UN's day-to-day affairs. Trygve Lie of Norway was the first person to head this office. An American, Dr. Ralph Bunche, the grandson of a former slave, served for many years as Under Secretary.

The International Court of Justice was the court for the UN. It could deal with legal questions that arose between members. Many other agencies were set up under the Economic and Social Council (UNESCO) to build the world community. The United Nations Relief and Rehabilitation Administration (UNRRA) was financed mainly by the United States. It supplied food and clothing to nations devastated by the war.

Controlling the atom. What could the UN do to control the menacing new power of the atom? In June 1946 Bernard Baruch, for the United States, proposed a world agency with control over atomic energy and the right to inspect atomic-energy plants anywhere. If the inspection system was set up, the United States said it would destroy its atomic bombs. Under Baruch's scheme no vetoes would be allowed. But Russia once again sabotaged the plan by insisting on its right to veto. The Soviets demanded that the United States destroy its weapons even before the new controls were created. As a result, there was no progress.

Problems with the Russians. The dispute over the atom was only one signal of the widening gulf between the United States and Russia. Time after time the Soviets refused to live up to their promises. At Yalta Stalin had pledged to hold free elections in Poland for the formation of a new government. Instead he forced a Communist government on the Poles. The Soviets also retained their hold on the former Baltic republics (Latvia, Lithuania, and Estonia). And they supported Communist forces in Hungary, Bulgaria, and Romania. Russia's goal was to keep "friendly" states all along its borders. If those people would not vote for a Communist government, Stalin was ready to fasten it on them with guns and tanks. And if communism was crammed down the throats of the people of Eastern Europe, what about the lands that bordered those nations? Now a Communist tyranny threatened Europe.

To broadcast the new danger, Truman sponsored a speech by Winston Churchill at Westminster College in Fulton, Missouri. There on March 5, 1946, the eloquent Churchill sounded the alarm. "From Stettin in the Baltic to Trieste in the Adriatic an iron curtain has descended across the Continent," he warned. "I do not believe that Soviet Russia desires war. What they desire is the fruits of war and the indefinite expansion of their power and doctrines." Churchill's words were reinforced by Russia's failure to keep its promise to remove its troops from Iran. The Soviets were also squeezing Turkey to give them military bases and control of the straits leading from the Black Sea bordering southern Russia to the Mediterranean. Then the Russian navy could move freely back and forth.

In Greece, civil war erupted in the fall of 1946. The right-wing government was under attack by Communist insurgents supported from the neighboring Communist countries. Would the Soviets

try to force their ways on the world? A Soviet spy ring in Canada (including a member of the Canadian parliament) was exposed. Atomic secrets, it was learned, had been sent to Russia.

Warnings about Russia. Meanwhile some thoughtful American leaders were alarmed by the Soviet threat to the free world. One was the learned George F. Kennan, our minister-counselor in Moscow. Another was our Under Secretary of State, the suave and cultivated Dean Acheson. They believed that the Russian Communists intended to conquer the world. As Kennan warned in a long telegram to the State Department from Moscow in February 1946, Russia must be "contained" within its present limits. Soviet communism would then either collapse from within or the Russian people would force a change in policy.

Kennan and Acheson—and President Truman himself—believed that if Hitler had been stopped at Munich instead of being "appeased," World War II might never have happened. Now, to prevent a third world war, the United States must stand up to Russia. And they were encouraged in this belief by events in Iran. After a strong warning from Britain and the United States (and the threat of force), Russia withdrew its troops from Iran in May 1946.

The Greek civil war. By the beginning of 1947 the situation in Greece was serious. Great Britain had been sending troops and money to the Greek government. Still the British had problems enough of their own at home. They could no longer afford to support the anti-Communist cause in Greece. Without that support the right-wing government would probably fall and the Communists would take over. Americans feared that this would put the USSR in control. "A highly possible Soviet break-through might open three continents to Soviet penetration," Acheson warned. "Like apples in a barrel infected by one rotten one, the corruption of Greece would infect" Asia, Africa, and Europe.

The Truman Doctrine. Acheson's appraisal of the situation was probably overdrawn. In 1948 Yugoslavia's ruling Communists, under Marshal Tito, would break with Moscow. Like the Yugoslavs, the Greek leftists were not just another wing of Soviet Russia. But Acheson did not know that. From his view the withdrawal of British support

Shown next to President Truman in 1950 are Dean Acheson (left) and George Marshall (right), the main architects and managers of foreign policy in the Truman years.

meant the Communists would take command and Stalin would be in charge.

To prevent this, Secretary of State George Marshall, working with Acheson, quickly devised a program of military and economic aid for Greece. Marshall had been Chief of Staff of the Army during World War II. Truman sent the program to a special session of Congress in March 1947. He asked $300 million for military and economic aid to Greece and $100 million for aid to Turkey. He also asked Congress to allow him to send civilian and military personnel to Greece and Turkey to oversee the use of our aid and to train their people. "It must be the policy of the United States," Truman declared, "to support free peoples who are resisting attempted subjugation by armed minorities or by outside pressure. . . . We must assist free people to work out their own destinies in their own way." This was called "the Truman Doctrine."

The Greek-Turkish Aid bill became law in May 1947. Congress and the President declared that the United States was threatened wherever Communists challenged. To oppose Communist expansion, peacetime military aid to other countries would be a regular tool of our diplomacy. The Truman Doctrine would guide the foreign policy of the United States for a generation.

The Russians denounced the aid bill as an invitation to war. Critics at home (led by former Vice-President and now Secretary of Commerce Henry Wallace) did not share President Truman's distrust of the Soviets. For opposing his "get tough" policy, Truman fired Wallace. Meanwhile United States aid—especially military advisers and equipment—helped defeat Communist and other guerrilla forces in Greece and Turkey. This weakened Soviet influence there.

Marshall proposes a plan. In May 1947, while Congress was debating the Truman Doctrine, Winston Churchill described Europe as "a rubble heap, a charnel house, a breeding ground of pestilence and hate." The homegrown Communist parties of France and Italy (supported by the Soviets) became ever stronger. It seemed that nothing could prevent the Communist conquest of Europe.

The Policy Planning Staff of the State Department set itself a difficult task. Was there some way, short of war, to stop the Communist advance and "contain" the Russians? Could a new plan of economic aid somehow preserve free governments? Poverty and unemployment made people desperate and brought dictators to power. Prosperity and jobs could save democracy. But how could war-torn Europe be healed? The Truman Doctrine was a way to stop the advance of communism. But how could we advance freedom?

In his memorable speech at Harvard University on June 5, 1947, Secretary of State Marshall proposed a plan. During the next three or four years the United States ought to help Europe with substantial gifts to prevent "economic, social, and political deterioration of a very serious character." This would not be military aid but would be directed "against hunger, poverty, desperation, and chaos."

Russia was invited to join, but the Soviets refused to take part. And they kept Poland and Czechoslovakia (which was still attempting to keep free of Soviet domination) along with the other East European "satellite" nations from accepting American aid. By staying out, the Russians made it easier to persuade Congress to pass the plan.

The European Recovery Program. For ten months Congress debated the pros and cons. Supporters of Marshall's European Recovery Program (ERP) explained that it was necessary for our own defense and economic survival. Opponents, led by Senator Robert Taft of Ohio, charged that it would cost far too much. It would also expose us to new dangers abroad, which might lead to another world war. On the left, Henry Wallace denounced the plan as an attack on Russia—a "Martial Plan."

A bloodless Communist coup d'etat in Czechoslovakia in February 1948 helped the supporters of ERP. Senator Taft himself voted for the bill, and the measure was passed by large majorities in both houses of Congress. The Marshall Plan, signed into law by President Truman on April 3, 1948, provided $5.3 billion for European recovery over the follow-

After the Second World War the people of Europe carried on their lives among the ruins. This woman created a flourishing garden within bombed-out walls.

David Seymour/Magnum

ing year. The United States was now committed to save Western Europe. "Containing" Soviet Russia, as Ambassador Kennan had urged, would not only strengthen American defense. It would also create new markets for our goods.

At it turned out, ERP was a brilliant success. Of the $12 billion spent in Marshall aid, more than half went to Britain, France, and West Germany. By 1950 these nations of Europe had increased their output by 25 percent over prewar levels. As European nations became more prosperous, they could buy more of our goods. This in turn would help keep our economy booming.

The Point Four program. The Marshall Plan was later followed by another generous program of aid, also intended to fight communism by promoting economic growth. This, too, would create new markets for American farms and factories. "Point Four," it was called, because it was the fourth point in President Truman's 1949 inaugural address. This program would give economic and technical aid to the poor free nations of Asia, Africa, and Latin America. For these purposes billions of dollars were—and still are—being spent abroad.

SECTION 1 REVIEW

1. Identify or explain: Security Council veto, "iron curtain," George Kennan, Dean Acheson, President Tito, George C. Marshall, containment policy, "satellite" nations.

2. Locate: Dumbarton Oaks, Baltic republics, Trieste, Iran, Black Sea.

3. Name the chief United Nations agencies and describe their functions.

4. What was the Baruch plan for atomic energy? Why was it not put into effect?

5. Name some early signs of the widening gulf between the Soviet Union and the United States.

6. What warnings about the Soviet Union were sounded by (a) Churchill and (b) Kennan?

7. Describe the Marshall Plan by giving the reason for it, its provisions, and its results.

8. **Recognizing Cause and Effect.** Why was the Truman Doctrine proclaimed in 1947?

---

2. Dealing with a new world

The nation had to shift somehow to a peacetime way of life when World War II ended. How could we combat the threats of inflation and unemployment? How could we meet the pent-up demands of business and labor? How could we help men and women change over from the armed forces to civilian life? All this and more had to be accomplished under a new and untried President.

Bringing the boys home. As soon as the war ended, Truman faced extreme pressure to "bring the boys home." At first the plan was to decrease the size of the armed forces only slowly and stay alert to any new threats abroad. But when there were riots by troops who wanted to go home, the President gave in and suddenly reduced the army. By midsummer 1946 the armed forces had been cut back from 12 million to 3 million. Truman warned that this was "disintegration" rather than demobilization. Still the United States—the sole possessor of the atomic bomb—remained the most powerful nation on earth.

Fortunately, Congress had prepared for the return of the veterans. In June 1944 it had passed a Servicemen's Readjustment Act—usually called the "GI Bill of Rights." This provided hospitals for the sick and wounded and clinics to help the disabled. It offered payments to veterans without jobs. It gave them preference for jobs in the federal civil service. Money was earmarked to help them buy homes, farms, and businesses. Free tuition, books, and expenses for job training, college, or other advanced education were given to those who wanted them. Eight million veterans of World War II used this educational program at a cost of $14.5 billion.

The Atomic Energy Act. How could a nation at peace use the newfound power in the atom? Both political parties agreed that the federal government had to keep control of the raw materials of atomic power. These rare metals—uranium and plutonium—were called "fissionable materials" because their atoms could be split. But the two parties disagreed on whether control should be put in the hands of civilians or of the army.

A compromise, the Atomic Energy Act, was signed by President Truman on August 1, 1946. It preserved the government monopoly of fissionable materials. A five-member civilian Atomic Energy Commission (AEC) was put in control. It was to encourage private and government research and development in both military and peaceful uses of atomic energy. In less than a decade the commission would employ 7000 workers and spend $2.5 billion a year.

Converting to peacetime. To help provide peacetime jobs, Congress passed the Employment Act in February 1946. A new Council of Economic Advisers would advise the President and Congress on how to create jobs and national prosperity. In fact, the nation adjusted swiftly to peace. There was no lack of jobs.

Instead, the nation was troubled by shortages of materials, by strikes, and by inflation. With the end of the war, labor, whose wages had been held down by government controls, was keen on seeking wage increases. A nationwide railroad strike threatened to tie up transportation, and the coal miners also went on strike. On President Truman's order the government seized both the railroads and the coal mines. The coal strike was soon settled, but the Engineers and Trainmen refused the compromise accepted by eighteen other railroad unions.

The angry President then asked Congress for power to declare a state of national emergency whenever a strike in a vital industry endangered the national safety. Workers who continued to strike would lose all benefits of employment and seniority and be drafted into the army. The House passed this extreme measure. But the Senate had not yet acted when the strikers returned to work.

Consumer goods—refrigerators, stoves, and cars, for example—were scarce until factories could shift to peacetime production. The new prosperity gave money to people who had waited years to buy these products. Truman wanted to continue price controls to prevent runaway inflation. But Congress refused to extend wartime controls. Between 1946 and 1947, the wholesale prices of food, clothing, and fuel went up 25 percent.

The attitude of the 80th Congress. In the midst of the strikes and shortages, inflation at home and challenges from abroad, elections for Congress took place in the fall of 1946. The Republicans campaigned on the slogan, "Had Enough?" They won control of both houses of Congress for the first time since 1928.

The 80th Congress, elected in 1946, expressed the desire of many Americans to turn back the clock to

War veterans picket a mine in 1946 claiming that they should have back the jobs filled by "outsiders" who were hired during the war.

Wide World Photos

the simpler days before World War II. They hoped to cut government spending and to undo much of the New Deal. The leading speaker for this yearning was Senator Robert A. Taft of Ohio, the son of President William Howard Taft. He was a man of sharp intelligence, high principles, and utter honesty, although he lacked a sense of humor and was not a good mixer. Senator Taft wanted to limit United States commitments abroad and to free the individual at home. He wanted, as he said, "to break with the idea that we can legislate prosperity, legislate equality, legislate opportunity. All of these good things came in the past from free Americans working out their destiny."

The Taft-Hartley Act.

The most important single piece of domestic legislation passed by this Congress was the Taft-Hartley Act of 1947. Fed up with strikes and disturbed by corruption and communism in some unions, Congress hoped to curb union power. The bill did not go as far as either Senator Taft or Congressman Hartley had wanted. But it aimed to achieve a better balance between labor and management. It outlawed the "closed shop," which had allowed only dues-paying members of a union to be hired. It did not ban the "union shop," which required workers to join a union after they had been hired. Instead the law permitted a state to enact what came to be called a "right-to-work" law. This would forbid the union shop in that state.

An interesting clause of the Taft-Hartley Act was the "cooling off" period. If the President saw that a strike might endanger the public safety, he could require the parties to "cool off" for 60 days. During this period there could be no strike or lockout, while labor and management tried to agree. The law forbade unions to make political contributions. Union officers had to sign statements that they were not Communists if they wished to bring cases before the NLRB. The law was passed over Truman's veto.

The unions bitterly attacked the Taft-Hartley Act. They called it a "slave labor" law meant to destroy their unions. But in fact the law worked quite well. In spite of the fears of union leaders, the unions continued to grow. Between 1945 and 1952 their members increased from 14.6 million to 17 million. Big labor now began to oppose big business.

An active Congress.

Republican members of Congress believed that the income tax was unfair to people with higher incomes. They argued that the "soak-the-rich" taxes would destroy the profit motive. So in 1948 Congress lowered taxes all along the line, but most of all for the wealthy. When Truman vetoed the bill, it was passed over his veto. To economize, Congress cut aid to farmers and refused the President's requests to help public housing, to expand Social Security, and to aid education.

The 80th Congress was fighting an old battle. It was really attacking the New Deal and the four-term President, FDR. Congress passed the Twenty-second Amendment to limit any President after Harry Truman to two terms. This amendment was ratified by the required three-fourths of the states by February 1951.

In 1947 Congress also passed the Presidential Succession Act. Seven times in our history until then, American Presidents had died in office. In each case the Vice-President had been sworn in as Chief Executive. The next officer in line for the Presidency after the Vice-President was the Secretary of State and then on through the Cabinet in the order in which their positions were created. Cabinet members, of course, are appointed by the President. But Truman believed that the President should always be someone who had run for office and been elected by the people. The 1947 act made the succession pass from the Vice-President to the Speaker of the House and then to the presiding officer of the Senate. Cabinet members were to follow these three officials in the same order as before.

Truman tries to extend the New Deal.

In the anti-New Deal 80th Congress Harry Truman found a perfect foil for his own election campaign. During 1947 and 1948 he sent to Congress bill after bill for his "Fair Deal." Most were extensions of the New Deal, but in 1948 he also asked for far-reaching civil rights laws.

Truman had long been worried by discrimination against blacks. In 1924 he had been defeated in an election because he opposed the Ku Klux Klan. In 1946 he had set up a Committee on Civil Rights to find better ways to protect the civil rights of all the people. Their report showed the evil effects of segregation, and in February 1948 Truman called

Europe after World War II

- U.S. Zone
- British Zone
- French Zone
- Russian Zone
- Annexed by U.S.S.R.
- Annexed by Poland

0   600 Miles
0   600 Kilometers

NORWAY   FINLAND

SWEDEN

U S S R

NORTH SEA

Stockholm

ESTONIA

LATVIA

Moscow

LITHUANIA

BALTIC SEA

NORTHERN IRELAND

GREAT BRITAIN

IRELAND

DENMARK

Gdansk

EAST PRUSSIA

NETH.

London

Berlin

Warsaw

POLAND

ATLANTIC OCEAN

BELG.

GERMANY

LUX.

Rhine

Paris

Nuremberg

Prague

CZECHOSLOVAKIA

Kiev

FRANCE

SWITZ.

AUSTRIA

Budapest

HUNGARY

Belgrade

ROMANIA

PORTUGAL

SPAIN

Madrid

Lisbon

CORSICA

ITALY

Rome

YUGOSLAVIA

Danube R.

BULGARIA

BLACK SEA

ALBANIA

GREECE

Istanbul

SARDINIA

MEDITERRANEAN

SICILY

SEA

TURKEY

SPANISH MOROCCO

MOROCCO (FRENCH)

ALGERIA (FRENCH)

TUNISIA (FRENCH)

BERLIN

— Wall Built 1961

0   15 Miles
0   15 Kilometers

WEST   EAST BERLIN

BERLIN

---

upon Congress to act to end racial injustice. He asked for anti-lynching and anti-poll tax laws and a permanent Fair Employment Practices Committee, along with stronger and better-enforced laws for civil rights.

When southern senators threatened to filibuster, Congress refused to act on his proposals. Still the President did what he could on his own. In 1948 he began the desegregation of the armed forces (p. 584). He appointed the first black governor of the Virgin Islands and the first black judge in the federal courts. He strengthened the Civil Rights Section of the Justice Department. And he ordered the Department to assist blacks in their own civil rights cases.

The decisive Congress. Because Congress had failed to enact much of his Fair Deal, during the election of 1948 Truman called the 80th Congress the "Do-Nothing" Congress.

Yet this was actually one of the most effective Congresses in United States history. It put the Truman Doctrine and the Marshall Plan into effect. It passed the National Security Act, which placed all the armed forces under a new Cabinet department with a civilian Secretary of Defense. The Secretaries of the Army, Navy, and Air Force now served under him and were without Cabinet rank. The act also placed military leadership in the Joint Chiefs of Staff. It created the National Security Council, a super-Cabinet to plan and coordinate defense. This Council included the President and Vice-President, the Secretaries of State and of Defense, and the Director of the Office of Emergency Planning. The act also set up the Central Intelligence Agency (CIA)—the first permanent, worldwide intelligence agency in United States history.

The problem of Germany. After Germany surrendered, it was split up into zones of occupation among France, Great Britain, Russia, and the United States. Berlin also had been divided among all four victorious powers, but it was surrounded by Soviet-controlled territory. The leaders of the Big Three wartime powers—Stalin, Truman, and Churchill—met at the Berlin suburb of Potsdam in July 1945 to discuss ending the war against Japan and solving postwar problems in Europe. They decided that the future of Germany should be worked out by the foreign ministers of the United States, Great Britain, Russia, and France.

At Potsdam the Big Three leaders confirmed that "war criminals" would be brought to justice swiftly. In October a four-power tribunal meeting at Nuremberg, Germany, began to try Nazi leaders for crimes committed during the war. Ten of these Nazis were executed. Hundreds of German soldiers were also sentenced to death by the Allies' military courts, and 500,000 other Germans were punished for their Nazi activities. Later, Japanese leaders were also tried in Japan, and Premier Tojo and six others were executed. Four thousand Japanese were sent to jail, and 400 Japanese officers were sentenced to death for committing atrocities.

The Allies could not agree on what to do with Germany. So in March 1948, the United States, England, France, and the Benelux nations (Belgium, the Netherlands, and Luxembourg) announced plans to make the Western Zone of Germany a single unit. A federal government would be set up there. And West Germany would come into the European Recovery Program.

When the Russians blockaded West Berlin in 1948–1949, the Western powers responded with a gigantic airlift which brought thousands of tons of supplies to Berlin each day.

ARCTIC
OCEAN

North Pole

SOVIET UNION

CANADA

UNITED STATES

GREENLAND
(DENMARK)

ICELAND

NORWAY

TURKEY 1952

DEN.
WEST
GERMANY
1954
NETH.
GREAT
BRITAIN   BELG.
LUX.
FRANCE
ITALY
GREECE
1952

ATLANTIC

OCEAN

PORTUGAL

NATO

North Atlantic Treaty Organization Nations 1949

Soviet Union and Satellite Countries

0   1500 Miles

0   1500 Kilometers

The Berlin blockade. Hoping to prevent the Western powers from setting up a separate West German government and to keep Germany from helping European recovery, the Russians put pressure on West Berlin. On June 24, 1948, they banned all traffic between the Western Zone and Berlin by railroad, highway, or canal. This combat without open fighting came to be called the "cold war."

Harry Truman never considered giving in. "We are going to stay, period," the feisty President said. There would be no backing down to the Russians as long as Truman was in the White House. The United States, England, and France began to supply the city by air. Food, coal, clothing—all kinds of things the people of the city needed—were flown in. Four thousand tons of supplies reached Berlin each day.

On May 12, 1949, the Western powers approved the Basic Law for the German Federated Republic (West Germany). On the same day Stalin recognized his defeat and ended the blockade. Then in September the West Germans began to rule themselves. In military and foreign affairs they were still controlled by the occupying powers. One month later the Russians responded by setting up their German Democratic Republic in East Germany. West Germany formally was given full sovereignty in 1955. East Germany remained a Russian satellite. Hitler's "Thousand Year Reich" had become a divided nation. Could Germany ever be reunited without threatening the peace of Europe?

The creation of NATO.

Out of the Berlin blockade came the North Atlantic Treaty Organization (NATO). The Atlantic Pact that established NATO allied the United States and Canada with ten Western European nations extending from Norway to Portugal. Later, when Greece, Turkey, and West Germany joined, the membership numbered fifteen. The Atlantic Pact was signed by the foreign ministers on April 4, 1949.

Under Article 5 of this pact an attack on any one of the parties would be treated as an attack on them all. Some senators argued that this committed the United States to go to war without a declaration by Congress. This same fear had defeated the League of Nations in the Senate in 1919. But now the senators approved the Atlantic Pact in July 1949 by a vote of 82 to 13. The Senate followed our long tradition by avoiding calling this an "alliance." And Congress actually did retain the right to declare war. Yet there was no doubt in anyone's mind that whatever NATO was called, the United States had made a major shift. We had joined the first peacetime alliance in our history. General Eisenhower was named commander of the NATO forces. He set up Supreme Headquarters, Allied Powers in Europe (SHAPE) at Paris early in 1951.

The Republicans scent victory in 1948.

In the midst of the Berlin blockade, the United States held a presidential election. The Republicans, after taking control of Congress in 1946, thought they would easily win. Now shortages and strikes, though less worrisome than they had been, remained a nuisance. The world still seemed on the brink of war. No wonder plain little Harry Truman seemed an easy man to bring down.

Many Republicans wanted the chance to run against Truman. Among the hopefuls were Senator Robert A. Taft, called "Mr. Republican," Governor Harold Stassen of Minnesota, Governor Earl Warren of California, and the 1944 candidate Governor Thomas E. Dewey of New York. Some leaders in both parties hoped to draft the war hero General Dwight Eisenhower. But he refused to be a candidate.

The Republicans, meeting at Philadelphia, feared that an outspoken anti-New Dealer like Taft could not win. They turned again to the moderate Tom Dewey and chose Earl Warren as his running mate. New York and California! That seemed an unbeatable team. The Republican platform approved many popular New Deal reforms. It also accepted the "bipartisan" foreign policy—the policy agreed on by both parties—that had been followed ever since Pearl Harbor. There were, in fact, real questions about the policy of containment that deserved public discussion. Yet these important issues were not debated by the candidates because foreign policy was supposed to be bipartisan. In the campaign the Republicans simply insisted that they could run the country better. Their slogan said, "Time for a change."

The Democrats divide.

The Democrats also met in Philadelphia. And many party leaders wanted to dump Truman. They were sure he would lose. But he was self-confident—and he loved a fight. Using his powerful position in the White House, he was able to win on the first ballot. His friend, Alben W. Barkley of Kentucky, the Democratic leader in the Senate for eleven years, took the second spot on the ticket.

The Democratic platform favored repeal of the Taft-Hartley Act. It pledged recognition of the new state of Israel, which was struggling to be born in Palestine. It came out for strong civil rights legislation—abolition of poll taxes in federal elections, a national anti-lynching law, fair employment legislation, and the end of segregation in the armed forces. The Democrats were bidding for the continued support of the black voters who now held the balance of power in the big northern cities. Their votes might well swing their states into the Democratic column.

The adoption of the civil rights plank split the party wide open. Thirty-five members of the Mississippi and Alabama delegations walked out of the building. Only two days after the Democratic convention adjourned, delegates from thirteen southern states held their own convention in Birmingham, Alabama. In a hall flanked with Confederate flags and resounding with rebel yells, they nominated Governor J. Strom Thurmond of South Carolina for President. Governor Fielding Wright of Mississippi was named his running mate.

They called themselves States Rights Democrats or "Dixiecrats." Their platform asserted the doctrine of states' rights. It condemned the civil rights plank of the Democratic convention and insisted on the segregation of blacks.

It appeared even more certain that Truman would lose when Henry A. Wallace and his followers also left the party to create a party of their own. Calling themselves "Progressives," his supporters chanted, "One, two, three, four—we don't want another war." Wallace was convinced that both at home and abroad Communists and liberals should work together. The Communist party endorsed his candidacy. The Progressive platform called for the repeal of the draft, strong civil rights laws, cooperation with Russia, banning atomic bombs (and destroying all American bombs), and freedom of speech and political action for Communists. Senator Glenn H. Taylor of Idaho, the self-styled "Singing Cowboy," was the Progressive nominee for Vice-President.

The election of 1948. People remembered that the election of 1946 had already shown a swing to the Republicans. Now the Progressives and the Dixiecrats split the Democratic vote. Public opinion polls showed strong support for Dewey. The Republicans considered their victory certain. Many Democrats privately agreed with them, and most big-city newspapers predicted that Truman was a sure loser.

Truman gleefully displays the headline that too hastily announced his defeat in 1948.

Wide World Photos

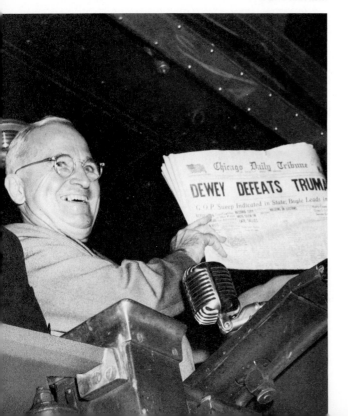

Meanwhile, Truman was not sitting still. He called the 80th Congress back into special session and challenged them to enact the platform the Republicans had issued at their convention. When they failed, the President scorned them as the "Do-Nothing" Congress throughout the election.

Truman now shrewdly could run against the Republican 80th Congress instead of against Governor Dewey. He convinced people that the Congress had done nothing but serve the powerful corporations. Through the Taft-Hartley law, he said, Congress had tried to enslave the workers. By keeping America's doors closed against the displaced persons of Europe, Congress had struck a blow against all immigrants. He continued to appeal to blacks by calling for civil rights laws.

Truman conducted a rough-and-tumble, whirlwind campaign. He traveled on a special train that made countless quick whistle-stops—just long enough for his speech and some friendly greetings from the townspeople. He gave 356 speeches, covered 30,000 miles by train, and met 12 million people. On the other hand Dewey, a reserved and dignified man, acted coolly and quietly as he thought befit the next President of the United States. One reporter quipped, "How long is Dewey going to tolerate Truman's interference in the government?"

In the 1948 campaign, for the first time, television was important. On TV and on the road, President Truman seemed relaxed and homey. Critics said that Governor Dewey appeared stiff and formal like the bridegroom on a wedding cake. Television offered a vivid new chance for American voters to size up their candidates.

On the morning after election day, based on the early returns the *Chicago Tribune* headlined that Dewey had won. In fact, the spunky Harry Truman—who never gave up—had turned defeat into victory. President Truman's favorite picture of himself showed him holding up a copy of that *Chicago Tribune.* When the later returns from the farm belt turned the tide, Truman's popular vote was 24 million to nearly 22 million for Dewey and over 1 million each for Thurmond and Wallace. In the electoral college Truman had 303, Dewey 189, Thurmond 39, and Wallace 0. In addition the Democrats won a majority of 93 seats in the House and 12 in the Senate. Nearly everybody was surprised—except Harry Truman.

1. Identify or explain: GI Bill of Rights, Atomic Energy Commission, Employment Act of 1946, Twenty-second Amendment, Presidential Succession Act, "Fair Deal," National Security Act, CIA, Nuremberg trials, Berlin blockade, NATO, Atlantic Pact, Harold Stassen, Earl Warren, Alben Barkley, Strom Thurmond.

2. Describe demobilization in 1946. How were the war veterans helped?

3. How did Truman respond to the strikes and inflation in 1946? What was the result?

4. List some purposes and provisions of the Taft-Hartley Act.

5. On what measures did the 80th Congress support Truman? Oppose him?

6. Describe Truman's stand on civil rights.

7. Why was Germany divided in 1948–1949?

8. Describe the candidates, the issues, and the outcome of the 1948 presidential election.

9. **Checking Consistency.** How did the creation of NATO depart from American tradition?

3. President in his own right

Harry Truman's second four years in office were momentous. They would be marked by hysterical spy hunts, by the "loss" of China, by Russia's explosion of an atomic bomb, by defensive alliances, and by an undeclared war in Korea. Through it all Harry Truman was courageous and decisive. But many Americans did not agree with his decisions.

Truman asks for a Fair Deal for all. President Truman interpreted his victory in 1948 as a signal that the nation approved his "Fair Deal." Instead when he tried to persuade Congress to pass his Fair Deal laws, he ran into strong opposition from both Republicans and Democrats. Still, during the next four years he did manage to persuade Congress to raise the minimum hourly wage from 40 to 75 cents and to extend Social Security to an additional 10 million Americans. He signed laws to clear slums, to renew cities, and to provide low-income housing. Congress voted more funds for the TVA, for bringing in electricity to rural areas, and for the expansion of hydroelectric, water-control, and irrigation projects. But Truman suffered defeats on civil rights, on national health insurance, on the repeal of the Taft-Hartley Act, on federal aid to education, and on his plan to keep up farm incomes.

The second red scare. The stresses of the cold war with Russia, along with the 1946 reports of spying in Canada, frightened Americans. On very little evidence, they began to suspect that there was a strong Communist conspiracy to take over the United States. Truman, who had some reasons of his own to distrust the Russians, joined the crowd. On March 22, 1947, the President issued an Executive Order for the FBI and the Civil Service Commission to check on the loyalty of all federal employees. The honest, hardworking government workers were made miserable. The order made it seem that they were guilty of disloyalty until they proved they were innocent.

Within the next four years 3 million employees were cleared, 2900 resigned, and 300 were dismissed as being of doubtful loyalty. The criteria for suspicion were so broad that it may well be that none of these people was ever a Communist or else had only been a Communist before the war. In December 1947 Attorney General Tom Clark listed 90 organizations said to be disloyal to the United States. The listed groups were not allowed to prove that they were not disloyal. Membership in one of these groups at once became cause for suspicion that the person was a Communist.

Meanwhile, the 80th Congress breathed new life into the House Un-American Activities Committee (HUAC). One of its most active members was a young congressman from California, Richard M. Nixon. The committee held numerous public hearings and treated those who refused to answer its questions as guilty. Its free-swinging actions led to many ruined reputations and produced blacklists in the movies, radio, and TV.

The most famous case to come out of the HUAC was that of the charming and successful Alger Hiss. He had served in the government since 1933, had been an adviser to the President at Yalta, and then temporary secretary at the San Francisco conference to set up the United Nations. In 1946 he was elected president of the Carnegie Endowment for International Peace. In 1948 Alger Hiss was accused by Whittaker Chambers, a confessed former Soviet courier. Chambers said that Hiss had provided him with classified documents, which then had been photographed by Communist agents and returned to government files.

Hiss sued Chambers for libel. He denied Chambers's charges before a New York grand jury. In one trial the jury could not agree. After a second trial Hiss was convicted of perjury in January 1950. High-ranking Democrats were among the character witnesses for Hiss. And President Truman made the mistake of saying that the Hiss case was a "red herring" put out by the 80th Congress to prove that it was actually doing something. Many Americans, already upset by the crisis with Russia, now believed that the Democrats were "soft on communism."

The world situation worsens. In September 1949, several years earlier than expected, the Soviet Union exploded an atomic bomb. No longer did the United States have its monopoly. Then in February 1950, Klaus Fuchs, a scientist who had helped to make the first atomic bomb, was arrested by the British as a spy. He confessed that from 1943 to 1947 he had given the Russians important secrets about the bomb.

Our former ally Chiang Kai-shek was driven from the vast mainland of China to the small island of Taiwan (Formosa). By October 1949 the Chinese Communists, led by Mao Zedong, were in control of the Chinese mainland. At first the United States had given Chiang large amounts of aid. We had tried to mediate between him and

Chinese Communist troops had just taken Nanjing from the forces of Chiang Kai-shek in 1949 when famed French photographer Henri Cartier-Bresson took this picture.

Mao to form a single government. But neither of them had been willing to compromise. When fighting broke out between them, the United States had backed Chiang. Many Americans who did not want to see communism come to China still were only lukewarm supporters of Chiang. They saw him as another dictator and disliked the corruption in his government. But his fall and the loss of mainland China to the Communists seemed one more defeat for the United States.

The rise of McCarthy. At this moment a clever and unscrupulous politician began to play upon the fear and helplessness felt by Americans. It was hard to explain how the strongest nation in the world had reached such a pass. Was this the fault of traitors inside the United States? Joseph R. McCarthy, Republican senator from Wisconsin, gave them the answer they wanted to hear. On February 9, 1950, in a speech in West Virginia he charged that the State Department was infested with Communist agents. He waved a piece of paper on which he said were listed their names. His charge, repeated over and over, increased the alarm. Even after McCarthy was unable to find a single Communist in the State Department, many troubled Americans still listened to him. McCarthy became the strongest political power in the country outside of the major party leaders. Even Presidents feared to cross him.

Protecting the United States. Members of Congress, too, seemed panicked by the internal threat for which there was so little proof. But most of all they wanted to prove that they were not soft on communism. In 1950 Congress passed the McCarran Internal Security Act. It required Communist or "Communist-front" organizations to register with the Attorney General. These included groups that were not Communist at all but which, it was suspected, might harbor some Communists. Of course, it was impossible in practice for any large organization to prove that it had no Communists. The suspect groups had to provide membership lists and financial statements. Membership in the Communist party itself was not made a crime, but employment of Communists in defense plants was forbidden. In case of an internal security emergency, the act gave the President sweeping powers to round up and detain anyone who might even

possibly commit espionage or sabotage. President Truman vetoed the McCarran Act. He said that it was worse than the Sedition Act of 1798 (p. 133) and that it took a "long step toward totalitarianism." But the law was passed over his veto.

Using the excuse of "internal security," in 1952 Congress passed a new immigration law, the McCarran-Walter Act. Again Truman vetoed the bill, but again it was passed over his veto. The law kept the quota system, which favored immigrants from northern and western Europe. It provided a complicated and insulting system of loyalty checks for foreigners who wished to visit the United States. It also gave the Attorney General the power to deport immigrants for being members of Communist and Communist-front groups even after they had become citizens. The law did include one small victory for the American tradition. It finally allowed Asians living in the United States to become citizens and set a quota permitting about 2000 to enter the country each year.

The fears of Communist subversion were heightened by the arrest of Julius and Ethel Rosenberg and Morton Sobell, on the report of Klaus Fuchs that they had passed key secrets about the atomic bomb to the Russians. In March 1951 the Rosenbergs, after a lengthy trial, were sentenced to death for a crime "worse than murder." Sobell was sentenced to 30 years. The Rosenbergs were executed in 1953. As with Sacco and Vanzetti back in the 1920s, many citizens doubted that the Rosenbergs were guilty. Or they believed that even if they were guilty, the nation was not well served by inflicting this drastic penalty in peacetime.

Civil war in Korea. Troubled by these problems at home, Americans soon discovered that from the other side of the globe the Soviets could find ways to threaten the American peace of mind. Civil war exploded in Korea in June 1950. Korea was an ancient country (the size of Mississippi and Indiana together) on a peninsula in East Asia, opposite Japan. Its borders touched Communist China and the Soviet Union. It had been annexed by Japan in 1910 and was surrendered to the Allies in 1945. At the end of the war Russian troops had moved into the country as far as the 38th parallel. American troops had freed the country south of that line.

Korea was supposed to be united under a government chosen by free elections ordered by the

Korea, 1950–1953

—— 38th Parallel
– – Pusan Perimeter, September 1950
– – Farthest UN Advance, November 1950
– – UN Retreat, January 1951
– – Cease-fire Line, July 1953

0   200 Miles
0   200 Kilometers

MANCHURIA

CHINA

USSR
Vladivostok

Yalu R.

NORTH KOREA

Wonsan

Pyongyang

SEA OF JAPAN

Panmunjom

Inchon

Seoul

YELLOW SEA

REPUBLIC OF SOUTH KOREA

Pusan

Korea Strait

JAPAN

USSR

CANADA

KOREA

CHINA

JAPAN

UNITED STATES

0   3000 Miles
0   3000 Kilometers

UN in 1947. But the Soviet Union prevented the vote from taking place. Instead the Soviets set up a separate puppet government in the North. Elections were held in the South for a national assembly, which adopted a constitution and chose Syngman Rhee as the president. Rhee had been struggling for Korean freedom for 50 years. The Japanese had imprisoned him. He had then come to the United States where he studied at Harvard and Princeton.

After the United States removed its troops from Korea in June 1949, both sides of the divided country threatened war. Skirmishes took place along the 38th parallel. Early in 1950 South Korea mobilized its army. In March Syngman Rhee boldly announced that his troops would liberate North Korea. Suddenly on June 25 from North Korea a strong force of 60,000, armed and organized by the Soviets, plunged south into the Republic of Korea. They came without warning and seemed headed for quick victory.

The United States helps South Korea. When news of the invasion reached President Truman, he reacted speedily and with vigor. He asked Secretary of State Dean Acheson, who had succeeded Marshall in 1949, to bring the issue before an emergency meeting of the Security Council of the UN. Six months before, the Soviet Union had stalked out of the Council when the UN refused to seat a Chinese Communist delegate. Now, free from the Russian veto, the Council lost no time in adopting (9–0) a resolution that condemned the invasion as "a breach of the peace." The UN called for an end to the fighting. The invaders were ordered to withdraw to north of the 38th parallel. All UN members were asked to help see that its resolution was obeyed.

That evening and the next, Truman met with his advisers in Washington. He ordered the Seventh Fleet to protect Taiwan, where Chiang Kai-shek and the remnants of a non-Communist China were in charge. General MacArthur, who was in command of our occupation forces in Japan, was now told to furnish arms and naval and air support to the South Koreans. This seemed to go beyond the UN resolution. But both Democrats and Republicans praised Truman for his strong decision. Members of the House stood and cheered the news of his actions.

The United Nations enters the war.

On June 27, 1950, the Security Council called on member nations to aid the Republic of Korea. The UN had no ready military forces of its own. Russian vetoes had prevented that. But now the UN established a United Nations Command and invited the United States to name the general to lead it. In time, nineteen member nations contributed arms or troops. Still, Americans made up four-fifths of the UN forces. MacArthur was put in command.

Truman thought that as Commander in Chief under the Constitution he could order United States troops into battle in Korea. So he did not ask for congressional approval. Congress might well have supported his decision at the time. Still there was, in fact, little discussion of the legality of Truman's action.

The early days of the war in Korea were nip-and-tuck. South Korean and United Nations forces were driven into an ever-smaller area around Pusan at the southern end of the Korean peninsula. Then General MacArthur, who had carefully built up his forces, went on the offensive. On September 15, 1950, in a daring flank movement, MacArthur landed his forces from the sea at Inchon. His brilliant gamble worked. The South Korean capital of Seoul was soon retaken, and half the invaders south of the 38th parallel were killed or captured.

China attacks.

Now the question became whether the UN forces should stop at the 38th parallel or move on to attempt to conquer the North and then unify Korea. On October 7 the UN General Assembly created a committee on unification and declared that the UN aimed to create "a unified, independent and democratic government." The next day UN forces passed beyond the 38th parallel. The Chinese Communists now warned that "if the U.S. or UN forces crossed the 38th parallel, China would send troops to the Korean frontier to defend North Korea." This threat was not taken seriously. Soon UN forces were above the 38th parallel driving the North Koreans toward the Yalu River boundary of Manchuria.

Here the Chinese had massed a million "volun-

teers." For weeks MacArthur seemed to ignore the appearance of more and more "volunteers" in the battle. Then on Thanksgiving Day, 1950, he launched a great attack designed to drive the enemy beyond the Yalu and end the war before Christmas. The Chinese Communists lived up to their threat. They crossed the river and swept down upon the UN troops. World War III seemed at hand. The retreating UN forces lost Seoul to the Chinese. It required several weeks of desperate fighting before the UN troops were finally able to stabilize a defense line 60 miles below the 38th parallel.

The brand new war.

General MacArthur now declared that this was "an entirely new war." He urged that the United States blockade the Chinese coast, bomb the mainland, and help Chiang Kai-shek invade China from Taiwan. The Joint Chiefs of Staff refused to give him the order he requested. Their chairman, General Omar Bradley, stated flatly that a war with China would be "the wrong war, at the wrong place, at the wrong time, and with the wrong enemy."

In January 1951 the Joint Chiefs of Staff ordered General MacArthur and General Matthew B. Ridgway, in command of the Eighth Army in Korea, to restrict their activities to the Republic of Korea. They warned the American generals not to

Despite the snowy winter, UN forces in January 1951 were once more pushing forward in Korea.

provoke a general war with China. Slowly the UN forces worked their way back up toward the 38th parallel, at the same time taking a heavy toll of enemy lives.

The President fires MacArthur. MacArthur spoke out angrily against the strategy of a limited war. Merely to free South Korea, he said, would leave the Koreans at the mercy of their Communist neighbors. But Truman had not forgotten his powers as President. The Constitution said that the President was Commander in Chief of all the United States armed forces. Now MacArthur was openly challenging Truman's orders to keep the war inside Korea. President Truman called a surprise press conference at one o'clock in the morning on April 11, 1951. He announced that General MacArthur had been removed.

MacArthur was a true American hero. His generalship in the Pacific during World War II had been brilliant, and as Supreme Commander in Japan after the war his economic and political reforms had transformed that nation into a modern democracy. Huge crowds greeted him on his return to the United States. On April 19, he gave an oration to Congress. "In war," he urged in his deep baritone voice, "there can be no substitute for victory."

But even as the sound of the general's voice died away, more and more Americans saw that Truman was talking sense. You could no longer talk about "victory" as the general did. Communist Russia now had its own atomic bomb. If there was another world war, both "winners" and "losers" would go up in atomic blasts. The only hope for mankind, said President Truman, was to keep the fighting limited. Now even "little" wars carried big risks.

The United States builds its defense. While the United States was fighting in Korea, it was also building up defenses in Europe. Military supplies in ever-growing amounts were shipped to our allies there. Four American divisions were sent to General Eisenhower's new NATO command. A vast system of air bases was set up in England, France, Italy, North Africa, and Turkey within easy striking distance of key Soviet centers. Russia had been targeted as the main enemy.

At the same time, the United States was working to create a system of security pacts in the Pacific. A mutual defense treaty with the Philippines was concluded on August 30, 1951. Two days later Australia, New Zealand, and the United States signed the Tripartite Security Treaty, which came to be known as the ANZUS pact.

Then at San Francisco on September 8, 1951, a "peace of reconciliation" was signed between Japan and 48 other nations, not including Russia. It was largely the work of John Foster Dulles, adviser to the State Department, who wanted to make Japan a bastion against communism. Japan was made to give up its overseas empire, but there were no punishing reparations. Full sovereignty was restored to the Japanese people. On the same day, the United States concluded a security treaty with Japan that granted the United States land, sea, and air bases on Japanese soil. Japan—which only recently had been the leading Asian enemy—had now become the cornerstone of the United States security in the Far East. Across the world, an armed United States and its allies faced a hostile Soviet Russia and its satellites.

SECTION 3 REVIEW

1. Identify or explain: HUAC, Richard Nixon, Alger Hiss, Whittaker Chambers, Chiang Kai-shek, Mao Zedong, Joseph McCarthy, McCarran Act, McCarran-Walter Act, the Rosenbergs, Syngman Rhee, Omar Bradley, Matthew Ridgway, ANZUS pact, John Foster Dulles.

2. Locate: Taiwan, Korea, Pusan, Inchon, Yalu River, Seoul.

3. In 1949–1952 what parts of Truman's Fair Deal program were passed, and which parts were defeated, by Congress?

4. Describe and evaluate the loyalty programs carried out by the Truman administration and the House of Representatives in 1947–1948.

5. How did Congress respond to the alarms sounded by Joseph McCarthy?

6. What were the causes of the Korean War? How did Truman respond?

7. Describe the course of the Korean War in 1950–1951. Why did President Truman dismiss General MacArthur?

8. **Recognizing Cause and Effect.** How did the fall of China lead to the "second red scare"?

FOCUSING ON IDEAS

1. Why could the United States not return to an isolationist foreign policy at the end of World War II?

2. Identify actions that increased Western distrust of the Soviet Union.

3. How did American leaders expect our economic aid to foreign countries to halt the spread of Communism? Promote prosperity in the United States?

4. Fear of Communist influence in the United States pervaded the Truman years. How did government officials respond to this fear? Cite as many examples as possible.

TAKING A CRITICAL LOOK

1. **Recognizing Bias.** As an employer, what provisions of the Taft-Hartley Act would you most favor? Why? As a union leader, what provisions would you most oppose? Why?

2. **Distinguishing Fact from Opinion.** In 1962 a panel of historians ranked Harry Truman as one of our "near great" Presidents. What accomplishments—and failures—would you expect historians to consider in arriving at this judgment of President Truman?

YOUR REGION IN HISTORY

1. **Geography.** What products from your region might have been sold to buyers in countries receiving American economic aid in the Truman years?

2. **Culture.** Interview older people in your community about their experiences and/or impressions of the "red scare." Ask them to describe the political climate during the McCarthy hearings.

3. **Economics.** Interview World War II or Korean War veterans to find out how they benefited from the "GI Bill." Report your findings to the class.

HISTORICAL FACTS AND FIGURES

Understanding Geography. Following World War II, the territory of Germany was divided among the victorious Allies. (a) What nation controlled the southwestern part of the country? The southeast? The northwest? The northeast? (b) In what part of Germany is divided Berlin situated? (c) What are the boundaries of present-day East and West Germany? (d) What information in the chapter helps explain why Germany was finally divided into two nations?

Germany Divided

SWEDEN
DENMARK
North Sea
Baltic Sea
SOVIET UNION
NETH.
BRITISH
Berlin
POLAND
BELG.
SOVIET
LUX.
CZECH.
FRANCE
AMERICAN
FRENCH
AUSTRIA
SWITZ.

```
0      100      300      500 Miles
       200    400
0      200    400
  100    300    500 Kilometers
```

N
W   E
S

- American Zone
- British Zone
- French Zone
- Soviet Zone
- West Germany
- East Germany

CHAPTER 29

Eisenhower, moderate Republican

The end of the Truman years found the United States locked in a hot war in Asia and a cold war in the rest of the world. The declared American purpose was to "contain" international communism. "Containing" meant to box in communism where it already was and keep it from expanding. Fear of Communists within the United States was running rampant, fanned most of all by Senator Joseph R. McCarthy.

In fact, the threats at home and abroad were nowhere near as serious as many Americans feared. Communism was not a single, solid force. It was found in many nations, and everywhere was the declared enemy of the democracies. But each country had its own history. People had their patriotism as well as their communism. Where the Soviets ruled nations from the outside, they had trouble keeping their forced allies under control.

The secretive, insecure Soviets were at least as afraid of the United States as Americans were of them. Communists were taught that in the long run, out of war and confusion, the capitalist democracies were sure to lose. But they were impressed by the power of the United States, by our technology and our comfortable way of life. Many of them realized that all peoples of the world would be losers in a third world war. Somehow in the years ahead the United States and the Soviet Union had to exist together.

1. The Republicans return

For twenty years our Presidents had been Democrats. They had led the United States through a depression, hot war and cold, and now into a "police action" in Korea. What would happen to the domestic and foreign policies forged during these years when a Republican again became President?

Ike and Adlai. The Republican National Convention met at Chicago on July 7, 1952. The party's chances of winning the election in the fall looked good. The war in Korea was at a stalemate. The country was plagued by inflation. China was lost to communism. And some petty corruption had surfaced in Washington—even touching friends of the President. The main competition for the nomination was between Senator Taft of Ohio with his conservative followers, and the liberal international wing of the party, which had persuaded General Dwight D. Eisenhower to enter the race.

Eisenhower won on the first ballot after skillful early convention moves by his supporters. His running mate was the eager anti-Communist Senator Richard M. Nixon of California. He had been elected to the Senate in 1950 in a mud-slinging campaign when he recklessly accused his opponent of links to the Communists. The Republican platform attacked Democrats for their foreign policy, blaming them for the loss of China and the war in Korea. The Republicans were not satisfied merely to "contain" communism. Instead they intended to free the captive peoples behind the iron curtain. At home, they wanted to balance the budget, lower the national debt, and "return honesty to government."

When the Democrats arrived in Chicago for their convention, they had no leading candidate. President Truman had declined to run again but had urged the urbane Adlai E. Stevenson, governor of Illinois, to be the nominee. The wellborn Stevenson was as different as possible from the rough-hewn, self-made Truman. The grandson of a former Vice-President, he was a graduate of Princeton, a prosperous lawyer, and a full-fledged intellectual. Stevenson refused Truman's suggestion. The chance of beating the nation's war hero

Eisenhower fought a hard battle for the Republican nomination in 1952. But in 1956, after four years as President, he was renominated by the wildly cheering crowd.

Wide World Photos

looked slim. But Stevenson roused the interest of the delegates with his wise and witty speech that opened the convention. When no candidate received a majority on the first two ballots, the delegates drafted Stevenson.

The election of 1952. Governor Stevenson declared that it was time to "talk sense to the American people." They were faced with "a long, patient, costly struggle which alone can assure triumph over the great enemies of man—war, poverty, and tyranny—and the assaults upon human dignity which are the most grievous consequences of each."

Stevenson waged one of the most eloquent campaigns in United States history. Still it was hard to beat the friendly and attractive war hero everyone knew as "Ike." "I like Ike," the buttons read. With earnest charm, Ike promised to go to Korea to end the war. He pounded at Communists and corruption in government. Eisenhower had found the formula for victory.

Ike's broad grin and impressive military record had wide appeal.

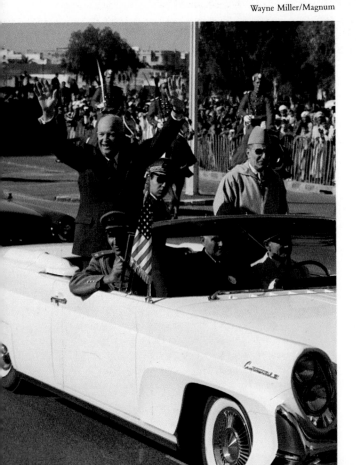

Sixty-one million Americans went to the polls. On the evening of November 4, millions watched the returns on television as Eisenhower swept to victory. He carried thirty-nine states, including the usually Democratic southern states of Virginia, Tennessee, Florida, and Texas, piling up a total of 442 electoral votes. Stevenson's 89 votes came from the other nine southern states. The popular vote was 33.6 million to 26.6 million.

The victory was more a nationwide approval of the famous war hero than an endorsement of the program of the "GOP"—the Grand Old Party, as the Republicans liked to call themselves. In sharp contrast to the Eisenhower landslide, the Republicans won Congress by only the slim margin of one vote in the Senate and eight in the House. The popular "Ike" had ended twenty years of Democratic Presidents.

Dwight David Eisenhower. "He has the power of drawing the hearts of men toward him as a magnet attracts the bits of metal," British General Montgomery said of Eisenhower. "He merely has to smile at you, and you trust him at once." This was what attracted people to Ike—even more than his successful leadership of the Allied invasion of Europe.

Ike was a career soldier. Born in Texas in 1890, he moved with his family to Abilene, Kansas. After high school, he went to the United States Military Academy at West Point. When he graduated in 1915, he began his army career. He served under MacArthur in the Philippines (1935–1940), then speedily rose in rank to command the huge Allied Expeditionary Force that was to win victory over Germany.

Ike's great skill as a general was not in leading armies in the field but in persuading other generals to cooperate. He had a quick temper, but he kept it under control. He was good at smoothing over the differences between the talented but touchy commanders from many nations. All these men had to work together if Hitler was to be defeated.

After the war he remained in the army as Chief of Staff. In 1948 he became president of Columbia University. Three years later he was called back to serve as the first Supreme Commander of NATO forces in Europe. That was his job when he resigned in June 1952 to return home and campaign for the GOP nomination for President.

Achieving peace in Korea.

Ike had promised that if elected he would go to Korea to end the war. He kept his promise and went to Korea one month after his election. There was no simple way to end the conflict. Talks had collapsed in October 1952. Now, in 1953 when the United States threatened to bomb China and use atomic bombs in Korea itself, the negotiations were reopened at Panmunjon. Neither side gained much in the armistice signed between North Korea and the United Nations on July 27, 1953. The border, protected by a demilitarized zone, was put back near the 38th parallel.

The Korean peace was no "victory" for the United States. The American dead had numbered 35,000. But at least the immediate threat of an atomic war was removed. This was a kind of victory for humanity.

A new foreign policy.

For his Secretary of State Ike chose John Foster Dulles, a leading Washington lawyer. The chief Republican spokesman on foreign policy, Dulles had negotiated the United States–Japanese peace treaty. Now, with the end of the Korean War, Eisenhower and Dulles could turn to reshaping the nation's foreign policy. Ike believed in balancing the budget, and this meant spending less money on defense. The result was a "New Look" for the armed forces, which reduced their size. Many units were brought back to the United States to serve as a "mobile strategic reserve."

Because of these cutbacks, the national defense depended more on the atomic bomb. In 1952 the United States had successfully tested a new kind of atomic bomb—the hydrogen bomb (H-bomb). This was 500 times more powerful than the bomb exploded over Hiroshima. Russia followed with its own H-bomb in 1953. Secretary of State Dulles now threatened "massive retaliation" against the Soviet Union or Communist China if they attacked any country. It was necessary, he warned, to go "to the brink of war" to preserve the peace of the world. "Brinkmanship," his critics called this policy.

At first Dulles wanted not only to "contain" communism but also to turn back the tide. He said we were going to remove the Seventh Fleet from the Formosa Strait. This would "unleash" Chiang to attack the Communist Chinese mainland from Taiwan. We would also free all the "captive peoples" still under Soviet rule. In time, when Dulles saw the facts of life, he would give up these grandiose visions.

War in Indochina.

But before that time there would be some dangerous moments. The first came on another, larger peninsula that, like Korea, also bordered on Communist China. This peninsula, in Southeast Asia, was known as Indochina. In the part called Vietnam, there was a fierce struggle. At the fall of Japan in 1945, Vietnam had been liberated from the Japanese empire by forces led by a Vietnamese Communist named Ho Chi Minh. Even France had recognized him as head of an independent state—the Democratic Republic of Vietnam. To win that recognition, Ho had allowed the French to send in 15,000 soldiers. Then the French began to become difficult. Like other old imperial powers after World War II, France, even including its Communists, wanted to hold onto its former colonies. Now the French moved to bring down Ho and replace him with their own puppet. In 1947 Ho and his Viet Minh troops took to the hills.

After the fall of China to the Communists, the United States began to view Vietnam as a bulwark needed to "contain" the Communists. The French resistance to Communist forces in Vietnam, it seemed, was part of the large battle against Communist advances that we were then fighting in Korea. In 1950 the United States began helping the French with money and arms. In 1953 Eisenhower asked $60 million for such aid. And by 1954 the United States was bearing 80 percent of the cost of the war between the French and the Communists in Vietnam.

But the struggle was going badly. As the end of the Korean War approached, the Chinese Communists increased their help to the Communist Viet Minh troops. In a great push to defeat the French, these troops trapped a large French force at Dienbienphu.

Many in the United States government wanted to assist the French by an air strike around Dienbienphu. Ike disagreed. He wanted some sort of joint move with other nations so that the United States would not seem to be fighting to put back the old colonial system. The British government warned that it would not support such an action because it might lead to general war in the Far East. Leaders in Congress, also fearing a larger war, were cool to the idea. For the moment, plans to use American forces in Indochina were abandoned.

On May 8, 1954, the day after the fall of Dienbienphu, a conference opened in Geneva, Switzerland, to settle the Indochina question. The great powers—France, Great Britain, the Soviet Union, China, and the United States—attended along with delegates from Vietnam, Cambodia, and Laos. There it was decided to temporarily divide Vietnam in two. The northern half would become a Communist state, and the southern half would be a "free" government under the former emperor of Vietnam, Bao-Dai.

"Pactomania." With the division of Vietnam, Secretary of State Dulles feared that all Asia might fall to the Communists. He pushed for a treaty organization similar to NATO to protect the Pacific area. At a meeting held in Manila, there were delegates from Australia, Britain, France, New Zealand, Pakistan, the Philippines, Thailand, and the United States. On September 8, 1954, they signed a pact creating the Southeast Asia Treaty Organization (SEATO). They pledged joint action in case of aggression against any member. Cambodia, Laos, and South Vietnam—the non-Communist nations that had once been part of

French Indochina—were to get special protection.

This was the beginning of what critics called Dulles's "pactomania"—the attempt to encircle the Communists by treaties. In December 1954 Dulles took his next step when he signed a mutual defense treaty with the Chinese Nationalists on Taiwan. This committed the United States to the defense of that island. A similar treaty with South Korea in October 1953 had committed us also to their defense.

These pacts were capped by the Baghdad Pact of 1955, which was also promoted by Dulles. This group, known as METO (the Middle East Treaty Organization), included Great Britain, Turkey, Iraq, Iran, and Pakistan. To the Western powers—especially Britain—the oil of the Middle East was vital. In the struggle against the Soviets it seemed important to cut them out of that area. But to avoid provoking the Communists, the United States did not join this pact.

The European Defense Community. A further step to isolate the Soviets was the Paris Pact of October 1954. In this treaty the Western powers agreed to full sovereignty for the Federal Republic of Germany. This was the part of Germany that the Russians had not taken over and forced to become

Secretary of State John Foster Dulles signs the SEATO pact in Manila on September 8, 1954.

Communist. West Germany was admitted to NATO and was allowed an army of 500,000 men to serve under NATO command. The United States and Great Britain promised to keep large forces on the European continent so long as they were wanted by the Western European nations—another bulwark against the spread of the Communists.

Undercover operations. Meanwhile, the United States was also working under cover, through the Central Intelligence Agency. In 1952 it may have helped Gamal Abdel Nasser and other young army officers to depose the decadent and corrupt playboy King Farouk of Egypt. In 1953 in Iran the CIA also helped topple the government of Premier Mossadegh, who had tried to nationalize the British-controlled oil industry. The Shah of Iran was returned to his throne. This new, friendly government gave the United States valuable oil concessions. On our side of the world, in the following year, the CIA helped an opposition group in Guatemala to overturn a government there that seemed too friendly to the Communists.

Meeting at the summit. Stalin, the cruel Soviet dictator, had filled Siberian prison camps with his opponents. He would stop at nothing to stay in power. Yet he could not live forever. When he died in 1953, a new clique headed finally by Nikita Khrushchev came to power. Inside Russia there was a struggle to control the government. The insecure leaders sought to ease world tensions. They called for "peaceful coexistence." On his side Eisenhower, ever since he came to office in 1953, had offered to negotiate all issues. To show that they were now serious, the Soviet Union at last agreed to make peace with Austria and remove its troops from the zone they occupied. On May 15, 1955, a peace treaty was signed between Austria, the United States, France, Great Britain, and the Soviet Union. The occupying troops of all four countries were withdrawn. Austria now became a neutral country—free of the fear of becoming a Soviet satellite. Then the Soviets proposed a "summit" conference. Each country would send its chief of state to discuss the issues between Russia and the West. Dulles opposed this, but the President overrode him.

The heads of government of the United States, the USSR, Britain, and France met in Geneva, Switzerland, in July 1955. President Eisenhower proposed that there should be "open skies" so that each nation could inspect the other by aerial photography. This was to protect each nation from the chance—and the fear—of massive surprise attack. But the Russians turned down any kind of inspection. In fact, the conference brought no solid results. Still, the optimistic Ike hoped that it might be a beginning of a better understanding between East and West. Anyway, even without Soviet permission, the United States soon began spy flights over Russia by the new model U-2, which could fly 13 1/2 miles in the air, higher than any plane before.

SECTION 1 REVIEW

1. Identify or explain: Adlai Stevenson, John Sparkman, H-bombs, Ho Chi Minh, SEATO, Baghdad Pact, Paris Pact of 1954, King Farouk, Premier Mossadegh, Nikita Khrushchev, U-2.

2. Locate: Korean demilitarized zone, Indochina, Vietnam, Dienbienphu, Cambodia, Laos, Iran.

3. Describe the candidates, issues, and results of the presidential election of 1952.

4. How did the Korean War end?

5. What kind of foreign policy did Dulles first call for? What strategy did he later adopt?

6. How was the United States involved in the French-Vietnamese war?

7. Why was a summit conference held in 1955?

8. **Identifying Assumptions.** Trace the career of Dwight David Eisenhower. Why did this record make many Americans think Eisenhower would be a good President?

2. Everybody's New Deal

Many Democrats feared that the return of Republican rule would mean the end of New Deal and Fair Deal measures and a retreat to the 1920s. In some ways the Republicans gave them cause for alarm. Douglas McKay, Eisenhower's Secretary of the Interior, proclaimed, "We're here in the saddle as an administration representing business and industry." But before very long, the New Deal was safe. The Republican President even began to expand some of these measures, describing his program as "dynamic conservatism."

Reducing government activity.

At first Ike sounded as if he intended to undo the New Deal. He aimed to cut back on government—on the size of the budget, on taxes, and on regulation of the nation's business. As one step to lessen government control of business, Ike ended the price and wage controls imposed during the Korean War. Congress gave him the authority to sell to private industry government-owned factories for making synthetic rubber. The Atomic Energy Act was amended to give private companies a larger role in atomic research and the making of atomic power.

The President had to face the question whether the federal government or the states owned the vast oil deposits thought to exist under the seas lapping the nation's shores. Twice, in 1946 and 1952, Congress passed bills giving title to the states. On both occasions President Truman blocked the action. With stern vetoes, he said that the offshore oil belonged to all the people. But Eisenhower wanted to reduce the activities of the federal government. He denied such sweeping national claims. He gladly signed a compromise in May 1953. Title to submerged coastal lands went to the states, but only within their historic boundaries. The Supreme Court in May 1960 set these boundaries at the usual three-mile limit except for Texas and Florida. Their historic boundaries were said to extend 10 1/2 miles out into the sea.

Public vs. private power.

The President also had to face another issue between private industry and government ownership. In 1953 there began a bitter battle over whether dams on the Snake River in Idaho should be built by a private power company or the federal government. No one was surprised when the President supported private ownership.

Eisenhower had another chance to oppose government ownership of public power in dealing with the TVA. In 1953 he referred to the Authority as "creeping socialism." But when asked if he would sell the TVA, the President admitted that it probably was not possible without wrecking the whole enterprise. Still, he attempted to keep it from growing any larger and favored private power companies instead.

The farm problem.

While people in many other countries were starving, in the United States the basic farm problem was *over*production. The number of Americans on farms continued to decline. Still, food output went on climbing. New machinery, better seeds, more powerful fertilizers and pesticides, and more efficient marketing made the difference. Farmers were alarmed at their declining numbers. They feared that they would lose their political influence. They wanted the federal government to continue to guarantee the prices of their produce. They wanted at least the 90 percent parity payments which they were receiving under the Agricultural Act of 1949. ("Parity" was defined as the relation of farm to nonfarm prices during the period 1910 to 1914.) The surpluses, they said, could be used to fight hunger throughout the world. But Secretary Benson called for lower and more flexible price supports. He said that the government could never solve the problem of mounting surpluses until it stopped paying farmers to overproduce.

In 1954 Congress passed Benson's Agricultural Act. This replaced rigid supports with flexible supports. Now Benson could lower the parity payments in order to discourage overproduction. Farmers were outraged. Since Ike did not want to lose the votes of farmers, Benson did not make much use of his power.

In the election year of 1956, to make farmers happy the administration asked Congress for a "Soil Bank" plan. This was a way of paying farmers for *not* planting their land. The theory was that this saved the nation's soil for the future. Congress provided a billion dollars for farmers who took land out of production and used it instead as pasturage or forest. Still farm surpluses mounted, and farm income continued to decline.

The Republicans become more moderate.

Although Eisenhower had come to office wanting to turn back the clock, he was always a practical man. He soon saw that the New Deal measures were popular. Most Americans had come to believe that a more active government served the general welfare. In 1954 Ike stated his new view. The administration had to be "liberal when it was talking about the relationship between government and the individual, and conservative when talking about the national economy and the individual's pocket book." As one White House aide noted, "The President's changed, we've all changed since we came here."

As a result, in 1954 and 1956 Social Security

American farmers were so productive that sometimes they had to store their output in the streets.

benefits were increased. The system was broadened to make eligible 10 million more workers. In 1955 Congress and the President compromised on a law lifting the minimum wage from 75 cents to one dollar an hour.

New programs were voted for urban slum clearance and public housing. Congress also was asked to provide federal support for private health insurance plans—but refused. Instead money was voted for medical research and hospitals. On April 1, 1953, President Eisenhower signed a bill (first proposed by President Truman) creating a Cabinet Department of Health, Education, and Welfare. HEW was to oversee Social Security, health programs, food and drug acts, welfare legislation, and educational programs. Mrs. Oveta Culp Hobby of Texas, who had been the successful commander of the WACs in World War II, became the first Secretary of the department.

The search for Communists. Senator Joseph McCarthy of Wisconsin, now the chairman of the Government Operations Committee, was in full cry against Communists in government. He accused the Democrats of "twenty years of treason" and claimed that they had let Communists take many government positions. Ike, the brave military leader, did not show his usual courage in dealing with the senator. And McCarthy would soon discredit the President's party. Ike's approach was to avoid a head-on collision with McCarthy. As one of his aides said, he did not want "to offend anyone in Congress."

To beat McCarthy to the punch, Ike issued his own security order on April 27, 1953. This widened the area of behavior that might make anyone a "security risk." If any charge—no matter how foolish or unsupported by facts—was brought against a government employee, he or she would be suspended until proved innocent. This reversed the American tradition that in a free country a person is presumed to be innocent until proved guilty. Government officials were no longer treated with the respect shown to other citizens. The morale in

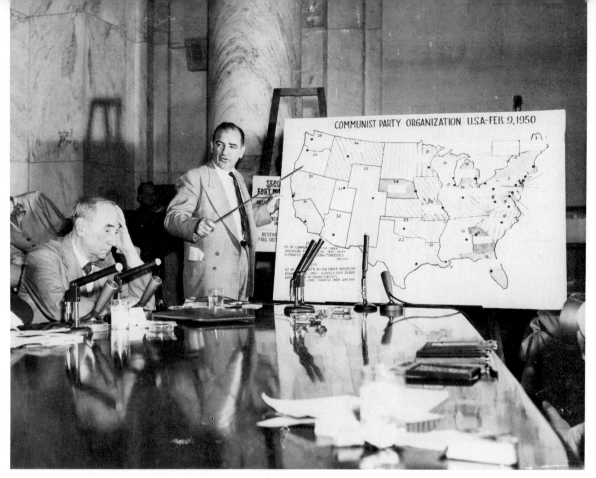

Senator Joe McCarthy, during the Army-McCarthy hearings, uses a map for the locations of Communists. Joseph Welch, the chief counsel for the Army, listens in dismay. The day before, June 9, 1954, Welch had called McCarthy a "cruelly reckless character assassin."

the government service sank to the lowest point in our history. The administration actually boasted that a thousand "security risks" had been fired. In time it appeared that only a small number of individuals had been removed under the security procedures. But the damage was done.

The fall of McCarthy. Still none of this satisfied McCarthy. He admitted that the Eisenhower administration was doing well in some areas by ridding the government of Communists. But he said that they were batting "zero" in other areas. And he broadened his wild attacks. He forced the removal of "Communist" books (books that he did not agree with) from United States libraries overseas. In 1954 he accused the Secretary of the Army of concealing evidence of espionage activities at Fort Monmouth, New Jersey. In February he accused

Brigadier General Ralph Zwicker of shielding Communists and called him a disgrace to his uniform. At long last the White House supported the Army when it struck back. The Army charged that McCarthy had sought privileged treatment for an aide who had been drafted.

Televised hearings were held over the charges and counter-charges. Hardly had the first session opened than McCarthy interrupted the chairman. "A point of order, Mr. Chairman. May I raise a point of order?" And over the following months as 20 million watched, McCarthy interrupted constantly with his made-up points of order. He treated witnesses rudely and showed himself an unscrupulous bully. Television exposed and defeated McCarthy, though his fellow senators could not and the President would not. His influence rapidly declined. Only a few months later, in

December 1954, he was condemned by the Senate for conduct "contrary to senatorial traditions." McCarthy's reign of terror was over.

The election of 1956. President Eisenhower was renominated along with his Vice-President Richard M. Nixon at the Republican convention in San Francisco in August. His fellow party members were not troubled by Ike's health problems—which included a serious heart attack. Adlai Stevenson had conducted a spirited and successful fight in the presidential primaries. He was renominated when the Democrats had met in Chicago a week before the Republicans. Senator Estes Kefauver of Tennessee, Stevenson's chief rival in the pre-convention campaign, was named for the Vice-Presidency.

Both parties ran short campaigns, and both relied heavily on television. The Republicans had the advantage of the nation's prosperity and Ike's continuing popularity. Stevenson somehow lacked the verve he had shown in his first campaign. Eisenhower swept the country, winning 35.5 million votes and carrying 41 states to Stevenson's 26 million votes and 7 states. But while they "liked Ike," the voters still favored Democratic domestic policies. In both houses of Congress the Democrats increased the majorities they had won in 1954. Not since 1848 had the party that won the Presidency lost both houses of Congress.

SECTION 2 REVIEW

1. Identify or explain: offshore oil rights, Dixon-Yates contract, Oveta Culp Hobby, HEW.

2. How did flexible price supports and the "Soil Bank" seek to reduce farm surpluses? Were these measures successful?

3. Cite some New-Deal-type programs adopted between 1953 and 1956.

4. How did the Eisenhower administration react to Joseph McCarthy's anti-Communist campaign of the early 1950s?

5. Trace the events leading to McCarthy's fall.

6. **Recognizing Ideologies.** Why was President Dwight Eisenhower in favor of "less government" in business?

---

3. The fight for equality

After World War II, all around the globe there was a new struggle by poor people and colonial peoples for freedom and a better life. As old empires fell, former colonies everywhere suddenly became independent nations. A new republic appeared in Africa in 1957 when Ghana became independent from Britain. By 1965 there were 30 new African member-states in the United Nations.

In the United States, too, black people struggled to be equal. Soldiers who had fought for democracy, and workers who had helped bring victory, refused to be second-class citizens. They objected to segregation and every other kind of inequality.

The Supreme Court rules for equality. Back in 1896 in *Plessy* v. *Ferguson* (p. 323) the Supreme Court had declared that laws requiring blacks to use separate washrooms, schools, and railroad cars did not violate the Fourteenth Amendment. It was all right, the Court had said, for services to be separate so long as they were "equal."

Who had the power to complain if the schools were not really equal? Most blacks were kept from voting in the South, so they had no way of forcing government officials to listen. The Supreme Court had okayed the two-nation South.

In the South, blacks continued to have the worst of everything. In any case, people who are forced to use washrooms and water fountains and schools not used by other Americans are not being allowed to be equal. Simply because they were separate, the schools for blacks could not possibly be equal.

Finally in a series of decisions the United States Supreme Court began to outlaw southern practices and laws that had taken from blacks their full rights as Americans. In three separate decisions—in 1944, 1947, and 1953—the Court declared that the laws that kept blacks from voting in Democratic primaries violated the Fourteenth Amendment. Beginning in 1938 the Court had started to narrow the "separate but equal" doctrine. It began to insist that what was separate had to be really equal. It outlawed segregation in interstate commerce. And in 1950, after hearing a case argued by persuasive Thurgood Marshall for the NAACP, the Court declared that the black law school in Texas could not possibly be made equal to the prestigious University of Texas Law School.

In 1953, President Eisenhower appointed former

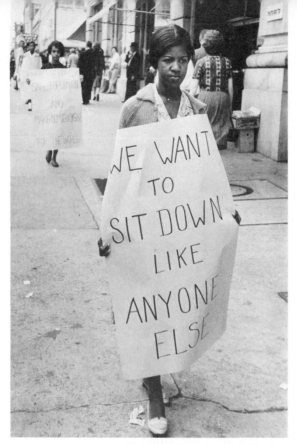

Don Uhrbrock/Life Magazine © Time, Inc.

Georgia students picket a southern lunch counter where they were not allowed to sit down.

Governor Earl Warren of California as the Supreme Court's new Chief Justice. Warren, more politician than lawyer, was to preside over the Court until 1969. He was to be deeply influenced by two of the Court's most forceful justices, Hugo Black and William O. Douglas. During the Warren years the Supreme Court would make many far-reaching decisions on segregation, the rights of criminals, and legislative apportionment within the states (pp. 698-699).

Perhaps no decision of the Warren Court was more significant than *Brown* v. *Board of Education of Topeka, Kansas* in 1954. This case too had been argued by Thurgood Marshall, who would become the first black to sit on the Supreme Court when he was appointed by President Johnson. A unanimous Court ordered that, under the Constitution, public schools could not be separated by race. Americans had a right to go to school with all other Americans of their age and grade. This was a part of their education. No American should be deprived of that right. The opposite of separation was "integration" —bringing together into one. And the Supreme Court now seemed to say that all public schools in the United States had to be "integrated."

The South resists. The South, however, resisted integration. In 1955 the Supreme Court ordered that the integration of schools was to go forward "with all deliberate speed." While progress was made in Washington, D.C., and in many border states, the lower South held out. And they were encouraged to resist when, in March 1956, more than 100 southern members of Congress signed the "Southern Manifesto." They bitterly attacked the Supreme Court decision and promised "to use all lawful means to bring about the reversal of this decision which is contrary to the Constitution." In the Senate only three southern senators—Lyndon Baines Johnson of Texas and the two senators from Tennessee, Estes Kefauver and Albert Gore—did not sign the manifesto. The South was now launched on its policy of "massive resistance" to the order of the Supreme Court.

The first serious incident occurred in the fall of 1957 when the Little Rock, Arkansas, school board moved to integrate its high schools. Governor Orval Faubus suddenly declared that there was a danger of violence in Little Rock and sent in the National Guard. The National Guard prevented the black children from attending school. Then a federal judge forced the National Guard to be removed. On September 23, when the black children again tried to attend school, a white mob forced them to leave.

The government intervenes. President Eisenhower hesitated to involve himself in the integration of the schools. He later said he believed that the Supreme Court decision in *Brown* was correct, but at the time he was silent. He thought that a President should not approve or disapprove of court decisions. Southerners, he said, should be given a chance to adjust to this great change. The process would have to go ahead slowly, Eisenhower said, because "we have got to have reason and sense and education, and a lot of other developments that go hand in hand in this process—if this process is going to have any real acceptance in the United States."

One thousand paratroopers insured that the integration of Little Rock High School would be peaceful.

Bert Glinn/ Magnum

But the mob violence was too much. The President finally acted. He ordered the Arkansas National Guard into the federal service so that Governor Faubus could not use them to stop integration. Then he sent in 1000 paratroopers and opened the schools. Still the story had only begun. The paratroopers stayed, but in the fall of 1958 Governor Faubus ordered the high schools closed to prevent integration. They were closed the entire school year. Virginia also closed some schools that same year to prevent them from being integrated. The battle for integration would be long and hard.

Martin Luther King and Mrs. Rosa Parks. In the 1950s the nation was ready for the work of Martin Luther King, Jr. He began in a small way and in one place. Within a few years his message had carried out to the world.

Born in Atlanta in 1929, the son of a minister, he attended Morehouse College and received a doctor's degree in theology from Boston University. He was a natural leader, American to the core. He combined the common sense of a Booker T.

Washington with the impatient visions of a Du Bois.

On December 1, 1955, Rosa Parks, a tired black seamstress returning from work, boarded a crowded bus in Montgomery, Alabama. She took a seat in the front row of the section of the bus reserved for black passengers. When she was told to give up her seat to a white man and move farther back in the bus, she refused. The police arrested her for violating the law.

Martin Luther King, who was then a Baptist minister in Montgomery, agreed with Mrs. Parks that it was time for action. It was time to stop any Americans from being degraded.

The nonviolent way. Although King was indignant and saddened, he was not angry. He was a thoughtful man, and a Christian, and he decided to try another way. He called it the only true Christian way. It was the way of Thoreau and Mahatma Gandhi. It was the way of massive and nonviolent opposition to unjust laws.

He did not tell people to burn the buses or fight

629

the police. No, he said. All people need to be educated in the ways of peace and decency. If you fight your enemies with violence, you will be using their weapons and brutalizing yourself. But if you are peaceful and simply do not go along with them, you will eventually prevail. And if you win this way, your victory will not merely be the truce in a running battle. It will actually be peace. Your enemies will understand, and they will begin to be decent, too.

So he preached to the blacks in Montgomery. He told them to stop using the buses until the buses gave them their place as Americans. Of course many blacks were angry. But Martin Luther King begged and pleaded with them to keep their heads, and to keep love in their hearts, even while they joined the bus boycott.

For 381 days the blacks of Montgomery refused to ride the buses. It was difficult. Some formed car

Martin Luther King stands beneath a picture of Mahatma Gandhi, the Indian leader who taught the way of nonviolence.

Bob Fitch/Black Star

pools. Some were given rides by friendly white neighbors. Many walked miles to work. Others simply did not get to their jobs and had to lose their wages. And the bus company was about to go bankrupt.

In the end the Supreme Court ruled that segregation on buses was illegal. The blacks and all the decent people of Montgomery had won. They had brought an end to another form of injustice. When the buses ran again, every passenger was treated like all the others. Martin Luther King, Jr., called this a "Stride Toward Freedom."

It was a step along a new path. Many Americans were encouraged to walk along that path in the years that followed. By 1960 many blacks in the South were using this new way to fight segregation. They sat down at lunch counters where they had not been allowed to sit. They swam in swimming pools that had been denied to blacks. And they worshiped in churches that had kept out blacks. They did not fight the police or strike out at anyone. Quietly and peacefully, they simply acted like decent Americans who knew their rights.

Civil rights laws. Now the federal government moved, too. In August 1957 the Eisenhower administration finally won the first Civil Rights Act since the days of Reconstruction. It was not an earthshaking law. The main thing that it did was to give the Justice Department the right to bring suits on behalf of blacks who were denied the right to vote. The real significance of the measure was that it passed and that it was a truly bipartisan measure. Republicans and Democrats working together overcame the resistance and the filibusters of the southern members to pass this bill. One of the leaders in its passage was a Texas senator named Lyndon B. Johnson, the Democratic leader of the Senate.

This was followed in 1960 by another Civil Rights Act, again passed with bipartisan support. It gave even more aid to blacks who wanted to vote. When the Republicans and the Democrats met in their conventions to draw up platforms and select candidates for the Presidency in 1960, both parties supported desegregation. At last the nation was turning back to the unsolved problems of the Civil War. And blacks themselves were in the vanguard bringing about that change.

1. Identify or explain: *Plessy* v. *Ferguson,* "Southern Manifesto," Lyndon Johnson, Estes Kefauver, Orval Faubus, Rosa Parks.

2. Locate: Ghana, Topeka, Little Rock, Montgomery.

3. How did World War II influence the struggle for racial equality?

4. What did the Supreme Court decide in *Brown* v. *Board of Education?*

5. Describe southern resistance to the *Brown* desegregation decision. How did President Eisenhower respond?

6. How did enactment of the Civil Rights Acts of 1957 and 1960 help in the movement for racial equality?

7. **Drawing Conclusions.** What role did Martin Luther King, Jr., play in the struggle for racial equality? What was his strategy?

4. Difficulties abroad

Eisenhower could claim no great diplomatic victories during his first years. He had, in fact, slowly retreated from aggressive anti-communism. Now Chiang Kai-shek was discouraged from starting a new war to drive communism from mainland China. The United States talked less of "massive retaliation." The policy was simply to contain communism and "coexist."

A difficult year. The year 1956 made clear that the world's problems were fearfully complex. Secretary of State Dulles's hope to liberate the people behind the iron curtain had been dealt a blow in 1953. A workers' revolt in East Berlin and other East German cities was harshly put down by the Communists. There was little protest from the West. At the end of October 1956 a people's uprising against Communist rule in Hungary was ruthlessly crushed by Soviet tanks and troops. Without going to war, the United States could do little to aid these enslaved neighbors of Russia in their fight for freedom against the great invader. But afterwards the American people (as they had done again and again) could and did offer refuge to those who fled from tyranny.

In that same year, the Middle East also blew up. Egypt had long been a colonial puppet of the Western powers—especially of the British and the French. Gamal Abdel Nasser, the able young officer who had led the army coup to dethrone King Farouk, was the new leader of Egypt. With the other Arab leaders, Nasser refused to recognize Israel.

Israel had emerged after World War II in the land of Palestine. The British ruled Palestine between the World Wars and during these years many Jews were allowed to emigrate to their ancient homeland. Great Britain tried to establish a Jewish-Arab state, but the Arabs would have none of it. After World War II, the United Nations tried to solve the problem by dividing the country between the Palestinian Arabs and the Jews. Following the UN decision, the Jews announced their new state of Israel on May 14, 1948, and were immediately recognized by the U.S. and the USSR. The next day Israel was invaded by armed forces from a number of Arab states—Transjordan (Jordan), Egypt, Syria, Lebanon, and Iraq. But the poorly trained and ill-equipped Arabs were no match for the Israelis. Israel quickly seized most of Palestine. Transjordan took the area of Palestine called the West Bank (because it was on the west bank of the Jordan River). Hundreds of thousands of Palestinians fled. These refugees were to create problems for decades to come.

As leader of Egypt, Nasser armed and assisted raiding parties of Palestinians to attack Israel from the Egyptian-occupied Gaza strip. Israel's powerful raids in response showed how militarily weak Egypt was. So Nasser made an arms deal with the Soviet Union (by way of Czechoslovakia) and began importing large quantities of new weapons. Nasser also wanted to build a vast and costly dam at Aswan to control the flooding of the Nile River and use the water for irrigation. At first the United States had offered to help. But Nasser's new friendliness with the Soviet Union led the United States to withdraw in July 1956. Nasser then seized and nationalized the Suez Canal, which was run by an Anglo-French company. He said he would use the revenue from its operation to pay for the dam.

Goaded by the border raids and fearful that Egypt's new arms would be used to destroy them, the Israelis attacked Egypt on October 29, 1956. Two days later Britain and France amazed the world by joining the attack. The British feared their loss

Eric Lessing/Magnum

Hungarians burn Stalin's picture in 1956.

of control of the Suez Canal, while the French were angered by Egyptian aid to the rebellion against their rule in Algeria. British and French forces seized the northern third of the canal while Israel struck across Egypt's Sinai peninsula. The Egyptian air force was quickly destroyed.

All this was convenient for the Soviets. It helped the Russians turn world attention from their slaughter of the rebels against their rule in Hungary. Premier Khrushchev screamed that England, France, and Israel were aggressors in Egypt. Posing as a friend of the Arabs, he threatened to send air and naval forces to Egypt and then even launch missiles against London and Paris. Once again a third world war seemed at hand.

The United States did not rush to the defense of its allies. Eisenhower and Dulles had not been consulted before the British and the French took military action. They were angry. And they feared another world conflict. Ike joined Khrushchev to support a UN resolution demanding a cease-fire and quick withdrawals from Egyptian territory. Britain, France, and Israel had no choice but to comply, since they were threatened by the Soviet Union and opposed by the United States. In March 1957 a UN Emergency Force made up of troops from Colombia, Denmark, India, Norway, and Sweden arrived in Gaza to patrol the shaky peace. Meanwhile, the Soviets ignored a UN resolution calling upon them to withdraw their troops from Hungary.

Developing missiles. During this crisis in the Middle East, there was the threat of a menacing new weapon—the long-distance rocket. This weapon was designed to rise high into the air, even beyond the earth's atmosphere. Such a weapon could go farther than any other, and it was hard to detect. But it was extremely difficult to design. Out beyond the atmosphere, of course, airplanes would not work. Every airplane engine then known was driven either by an internal combustion engine (like that in an automobile) that used gasoline to turn a propeller, or by a jet engine that pushed ahead by burning gases. Both required oxygen. Up over 250 miles, beyond the atmosphere, there is no oxygen. A very special kind of engine was required.

To solve these and other problems of space travel, we needed a twentieth-century Columbus. The exploring spirit that had inspired the first settlers was still alive. A young American physicist, Robert H. Goddard, dreamt of traveling in space. When people first heard him, they laughed, just as they had laughed at Columbus. His idea was to use rockets to push through outer space. A rocket carries its own fuel and also carries its own "air." This is usually in the form of liquid oxygen to keep the fuel exploding. The rockets exploding behind push the spacecraft forward.

In 1914 the 32-year-old Goddard received a patent for his liquid-fuel rocket engine. In his technical report for the Smithsonian Institution in Washington, he explained his rocket engine. He said this engine would make it possible someday to reach the moon. The *New York Times* and other respectable newspapers wrote editorials ridiculing his idea. For the rest of his life Goddard distrusted newspapers. Unlike Billy Mitchell, who had used

632

the newspapers to promote the new airplane, Goddard hated publicity and kept his work secret. He went ahead perfecting his rocket engine and finally secured 214 patents on the improvements that made space travel possible.

When Goddard died in 1945, few Americans yet believed that human beings would ever travel through space.

The V-2 rocket. The people of England, however, already had reasons enough to know that rockets could work. Raining down from the skies in 1944 came more than a thousand German V-2 rockets. Aimed from launching pads 200 miles away in Holland, they did not carry pilots but still reached their English targets. Traveling far faster than the speed of sound, they fell silently from a height of 60 or 70 miles. Each held a ton of explosives.

The V-2 rockets were the work of German scientists who had been experimenting since 1932. When the Nazis came to power and plunged the world into war, the Nazis had provided these scientists with a secret new laboratory in Peenemünde, a little German fishing village on the Baltic Sea.

By 1944 some 12,000 Germans were making V-2 rockets. These were pouring death and destruction on English cities every day. The name "V-2" came from German words meaning "vengeance Weapon, No. 2." It was, next to the atom bomb, the most terrifying weapon of the war because it struck without warning and no defense against it could be found.

The race for rockets. At that very moment the Russians were speeding westward across Europe in their final triumphal march. They hastened to Peenemünde to capture the German rocket factory—for their own future use. When they arrived they found, to their dismay, that the most valuable resource, the rocket scientists themselves, had already fled to the West.

"This is absolutely intolerable," Dictator Stalin raged. "We defeated the Nazi armies; we occupied Berlin and Peenemünde; but the Americans got the rocket engineers!" Stalin was especially angered because the Russian Communists lacked big bombing planes. Their only weapons, then, for a future long-distance attack on the United States would be long-distance rockets.

Some farsighted American generals had orga-

nized the project to rescue the German rocket engineers, the V-2 equipment, and 14 tons of documents for the West under the code name "Operation Paperclip." They collected 127 of the best German rocket scientists (including their chief, Wernher Von Braun), and signed them up to work on rockets and space travel for the United States. The brilliant Von Braun later became head of the United States Army rocket research. In time, the Russians also captured German rocket scientists who went to work on rocket research for them.

The United States and Communist Russia began a terrifying new arms competition. This time it was rockets. By 1956 the chief of the Russian Communist party, Nikita Khrushchev, boasted that Soviet military rockets soon would be able to hit any target on earth.

Then, on October 4, 1957, the Russians sent up the first man-made earth satellite. It was a package of instruments weighing 184 pounds. They called it *Sputnik*, which in Russian meant "fellow traveler" (of the earth). One month later they launched a much heavier satellite, *Sputnik II*, which weighed 1120 pounds. This satellite carried a dog, called Laika, to see how a living creature would react to life in outer space. Could an animal from earth live out there where everything floated and nothing had any weight? Laika survived.

The space race was on! The Soviets had exploded a hydrogen bomb in 1953. If they had rockets powerful enough to launch satellites, what would prevent them from bombarding the United States with nuclear weapons? Now it seemed that Khrushchev's boasts were true.

The early American efforts to make rockets were not always successful. The White House announced that on December 6, 1957, the United States would launch its own satellite with a Vanguard rocket. While the whole nation watched on television, this much-advertised rocket collapsed on the wet sand. The next try did succeed. Two months later *Explorer I*, the first American satellite, went into orbit.

The United States reacts to Sputnik. Americans were still frightened to see the Russians so far ahead in the space race. According to Senator Henry Jackson of Washington, *Sputnik* was a "devastating blow to the prestige of the United States." Americans now began to fear that the

Wide World Photos

Muscovites gaze at a model of *Sputnik I*, the satellite that opened the Space Age.

Soviet educational system which had trained the scientists who produced the satellites was better than ours. In a series of articles, *Life* magazine proclaimed a "Crisis in Education." Congress voted the National Defense Education Act in 1958. Its $1 billion program was intended to produce more scientists and teachers of science. It made available money for loans to high school and college graduates to enable them to continue their scientific education. Funds were also provided for laboratories and scientific equipment for schools and colleges.

Shortly after *Sputnik* the President appointed James R. Killian, Jr., the president of the Massachusetts Institute of Technology, as his Special Assistant for Science and Technology. He was, Ike said, "to have the active responsibility for helping me to follow through on the scientific improvement of our defense."

In 1958 Ike's already large defense budget was increased by another $4 billion for rocket and missile research and development and for the conquest of outer space. The new National Aeronautics and Space Administration (NASA) would coordinate these space efforts.

Problems in the Middle East. Meanwhile, during 1957, the United States was losing influence in the Middle East as Egypt's Nasser fanned anti-Western feelings and promoted Arab nationalism. Nasser's ties to the Soviets made his actions especially worrisome. The oil from this region was vital to the economies of the Western nations. They could not just watch the area fall to the Communists.

To combat this new threat, the President announced the Eisenhower Doctrine, which was adopted by Congress in a joint resolution in March 1957. The United States would help any Middle East country that requested aid to resist military aggression from any Communist-controlled country. Still, the main threat to American influence in the Middle East came from the weakness of the existing governments. So the policy was soon modified to include American help for pro-Western governments against Communist-supported attempts to overthrow them.

Still, the situation worsened. Syria and Egypt joined hands in the United Arab Republic. Violence threatened the friendly government of King Hussein in Jordan. In May 1958 civil war broke out between Christians, who favored keeping Lebanon independent and pro-Western, and Moslems, who supported an alliance with Egypt and Syria. Finally in July the king and the prime minister of Iraq were murdered by pro-Nasser army officers and another friendly government seemed lost to the West.

After this change of the government in Iraq, Jordan and Lebanon asked for help under the Eisenhower Doctrine. Britain supported King Hussein of Jordan with paratroopers, and the United States landed 14,000 marines in Lebanon. The large United States force also served as a warning to the new Iraqi government not to nationalize its oil fields. British and American forces were soon withdrawn. They had, at least for a time, helped to stabilize the situation in the Middle East and proved to Nasser that there were limits on what he could do to promote Arab nationalism and anti-Western feeling. They also showed him that there were limits to the support he could expect from the USSR. That nation had voiced disapproval of the troop movements, but had taken no other action.

More crises. Even as the United States struggled to preserve its position in the Middle East, war

Trouble Spots of the Cold War, 1950s

Communist Bloc

Map labels:

UNITED STATES

ATLANTIC OCEAN

PACIFIC OCEAN

GUATEMALA 1954

SOVIET UNION

BERLIN 1953, 1958
POLAND
HUNGARY 1956

IRAN 1953

KOREA 1950-1953
MATSU 1958
TAIWAN
QUEMOY 1958
VIETNAM 1953-1954

INDIAN OCEAN

AUSTRALIA

THE SUEZ CRISIS 1956

TURKEY

CYPRUS
LEBANON 1958
Beirut
ISRAEL
Tel Aviv
Alexandria
Suez Canal
Cairo
SINAI PEN.
EGYPT
Aswan Dam
RED SEA
SYRIA
Baghdad
IRAQ
JORDAN 1958
SAUDI ARABIA
IRAN

threatened on the other side of the globe. In August 1958 the Chinese Communists began to shell the Nationalist Chinese islands of Quemoy and Matsu off the mainland. President Eisenhower declared that the United States would join the fighting if the Communists seized the offshore islands as part of a campaign against Taiwan, seat of the Republican Chinese government of Chiang Kai-shek. Ike sent the powerful Seventh Fleet into the Formosa Strait off Taiwan to back up his warning.

Reeling from crises in Suez, Lebanon, and the Formosa Strait, the United States suddenly faced a stern new test from Russia. On November 27, 1958, the Soviet government called on the Western powers to leave West Berlin and make Berlin a "free" city. The Russians threatened that if the Western powers did not pull out of Berlin within six months, Russia would withdraw from East Berlin and sign a peace treaty with the East German regime, which then might cut off Western access to West Berlin. The Western powers rejected the Soviet proposal, but neither side forced a showdown.

Relaxing the cold war. To ease tensions, in the summer of 1959 Vice-President Nixon went on a goodwill tour of the Soviet Union and Poland, while the veteran Soviet leader Anastas Mikoyan came to the United States. Nixon and Khrushchev, in front of television cameras, debated the merits of the two nations' economic systems while inspecting a kitchen display at an American exhibit in Moscow. A war of words was better than any other kind! Vice-President Nixon thought that Khrushchev really ought to see the United States.

In August President Eisenhower announced that he and Khrushchev would exchange visits. Then in mid-September the President received the Russian leader. While traveling to the West Coast, Khrushchev said he wanted to visit Disneyland. He was infuriated when, for security reasons, his request was refused. The spirit was better when he conferred with the President at Camp David in the Catoctin Mountains of Maryland. That good feeling came to be called the "spirit of Camp David." The two leaders agreed to settle the Berlin issue by negotiation, and the Soviets withdrew their six-month time

Tempers rose during Khrushchev and Nixon's famous "debate" that took place at a model American kitchen display in Moscow in 1959.

limit. They also agreed to continue their talks at a later summit meeting.

"At this wondrous moment," British Prime Minister Macmillan said, "we seem on the threshold of genuine practical steps toward peace." The next meeting was set for May 16, 1960, at Paris.

Collapse of the conference.
The spirit of Camp David was shattered on May 5, 1960. Khrushchev announced that Soviet forces had shot down an American U-2 plane engaged in aerial reconnaissance over the Soviet Union. Thinking the pilot had died in the crash or committed suicide as ordered, the United States flatly denied the charge of spying. Then Khrushchev revealed that the pilot had been captured and had confessed.

Americans were surprised when the President in a television address accepted personal responsibility for the aerial spying and defended it. Since

Khrushchev was already facing opposition within the Soviet Union and was being criticized by the Chinese for not being tough enough on the imperialist Americans, he angrily demanded an apology. Eisenhower refused.

The heads of state gathered in Paris, but they never conferred. Khrushchev bitterly attacked Eisenhower and the United States. He withdrew his invitation to the President to visit the Soviet Union. He said he would have no more meetings with Eisenhower until he apologized. The President again refused. The thaw between the superpowers ended and relations iced over again.

Troubles in Latin America.
The United States faced critical new problems even with our neighbors in the Western Hemisphere. Since the days of the Good Neighbor policy and World War II, the nation's attention had been directed mainly to the large challenges farther away.

The United States had tried to prevent the spread of communism by supporting governments that proclaimed their anti-communism. But this policy sometimes backfired. We often ended up helping repressive governments. We found ourselves bolstering dictatorships—merely because they were anti-Communist. This lost us friends among freedom-loving people. In many parts of the world, where free institutions were weak, we had no easy choice.

United States weakness in Latin America was exposed by the rapid movement of events in Cuba. In 1958 the longtime dictator of that country, the corrupt Fulgencio Batista, was overthrown by a young lawyer, Fidel Castro. For three years Castro had led guerrilla forces operating from the Cuban hills. Castro seized the large foreign (mainly United States) holdings in Cuba. He collectivized the farms. He freed the country from its dependence on the United States. But he tied himself to the Soviets and set up a new police state. "Cuba, sí, Yanqui no!" was Castro's popular rallying cry. An eloquent and long-winded speaker, he soon became a folk hero. He was famous for his big Havana cigars and his friendly manner with Cuban peasants. He outlawed all parties except the Communists and set up prison camps for his enemies. With Soviet aid, Castro built up one of the strongest military forces in Latin America. This loaded pistol was only 90 miles off the coast of the United States.

Eisenhower steps down. If it had not been for the Twenty-second Amendment, Ike could probably have run for and won a third term. Unlike TR or FDR, he had not been a strong President. But his calm and friendly way and his good-humored honesty helped ease the bad temper and quiet the jumpy nerves that troubled the nation when he took office. In addition, he had consolidated the New Deal economic and social programs. He made them all-American institutions when he adopted them for the Republicans. And most important of all, the nation was no longer involved in any foreign wars.

Outgoing President Eisenhower cheerfully posed with his young successor at the White House before Kennedy's inauguration.

Elliot Erwitt/Magnum

Before leaving office, Eisenhower followed the example of another General-President, George Washington, more than a century and a half earlier. Like Washington, Eisenhower turned his farewell address into a warning against the dangers hidden in the future. He cautioned against the "military-industrial complex" that was making its influence "felt in every city, every state house, every office of the federal government." In the future, he admitted, our nation would certainly need vast military forces and enormous factories. What troubled him was "the potential for the disastrous rise of misplaced power. . . . We must never let the weight of this combination endanger our liberties or democratic processes." Still beloved by the mass of Americans, Ike retired to his farm in Gettysburg, Pennsylvania. He left the many unsolved problems of the nation and the world to a promising young President, John F. Kennedy.

SECTION 4 REVIEW

1. Identify or explain: Aswan Dam, UN Emergency Force, *Sputnik, Explorer I,* National Defense Education Act, NASA, King Hussein, Anastas Mikoyan, Camp David, Fidel Castro.

2. Locate: Suez Canal, Sinai peninsula, Gaza, Syria, Jordan, Lebanon, Iraq, Quemoy, Matsu.

3. Summarize the crises in Hungary and Egypt under these headings: (a) causes, (b) participants, (c) results.

4. What part did each of the following play in the development of rockets, missiles, and earth satellites: (a) Robert Goddard, (b) German scientists, (c) "Operation Paperclip," (d) Wernher Von Braun, (e) Russian scientists?

5. How did the United States react to *Sputnik?*

6. What was the Eisenhower Doctrine? Where was it applied? What were the results?

7. Describe the crises centering at Taiwan, Berlin, and Cuba.

8. What efforts were made in 1959–1960 to relax the cold war? How did they turn out?

9. **Recognizing Bias.** Why was it surprising that Eisenhower warned Americans about the dangers of a "military industrial complex" in his farewell address?

FOCUSING ON IDEAS

1. The President needs to be a policymaker, administrator, diplomat, and leader. How did Eisenhower's career up to 1952 provide experience in these roles?

2. Cite instances when the Eisenhower administration made a *forceful response* (use of military force or threat of force) to troublesome events in foreign affairs. On what occasions did the United States use diplomacy or make other non-threatening responses to tension-filled overseas events?

3. What events in the 1950s gave Eisenhower chances to exert leadership for human rights. How did he respond?

TAKING A CRITICAL LOOK

1. **Recognizing Cause and Effect.** During six years of his eight-year presidency, Eisenhower had to work with a Democratic majority in Congress. How might this have influenced his move to "moderate Republicanism"?

2. **Distinguishing False from Accurate Images.** Some observers see the Eisenhower years as a period of relaxation for the United States—after the turbulent years of depression, world war, and postwar adjustment. Is this an accurate image of the postwar period? Explain. Does the nation need a "breathing spell" after a period of rapid change?

YOUR REGION IN HISTORY

1. **Geography.** Describe your locality along racial and ethnic lines in the 1950s. Develop a demographic map of the population of your area for this time period. How has this population distribution changed over time?

2. **Culture.** How were schools in your state affected by the Supreme Court's 1954 school desegregation decision? If change had to take place, how was the matter handled?

3. **Economic.** Identify changes that took place in your city or county during the Eisenhower years focusing on such areas as housing, other construction, industry, and population. Were any of these changes stimulated by federal laws enacted in these years?

HISTORICAL FACTS AND FIGURES

Formulating Questions. Study the graph below to help answer the following questions: (a) What was the median income for white families in 1940? For non-whites? (b) What was the trend in family income for white families from 1940 to 1980? For non-white families? (c) Was there a clear difference in the economic conditions of the two groups during this period? Explain. (d) What questions would a historian need to ask to determine the reasons for the differences you noted? Make a list of the questions you have identified.

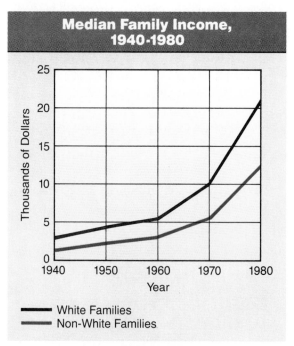

Median Family Income, 1940-1980

— White Families
— Non-White Families

Source: *Historical Statistics of the United States*
Statistical Abstract of the United States

CHAPTER 30

Mobile people and magic machines

In every war, besides the killing and the misery, large changes are at work. Wars set people on the move. There are not only the men and women serving in the armed forces. Thousands move to the factories in distant cities making arms and tanks and planes. Wars change the way the nation grows. Families are separated. Young people cannot settle down and raise new families.

Wars also produce new machines. The nation's scientists and engineers must invent new devices to defeat the enemy. They have to find new ways to send information across great distances, to move troops, to feed and shelter people at home and at the front. Out of the machines of war eventually come machines of peace. The radio and the airplane, which were tried and proven in World War I, changed American life in the years that followed. And so from World War II came new medicines like penicillin and electronic machines like television.

The forces of mobile people and magic machines have a "momentum" —a power to keep themselves going. In this chapter we will see how the forces that gathered strength during World War II (and had started even before) gained momentum. They transformed the country during the eras of Truman and Eisenhower. And these forces still continue to shape the nation today.

1. A changing people

After World War II dramatic changes took place in the population—in the rate of growth and length of life—as well as in the occupations people held and the places where they lived. All this had far-reaching effects on the lives of every American.

Studying the population. The study of population is called "demography." This comes from the Greek words *demos* (people) and *graphein* (to write or record). Demographers point out that, at

different times and places, the population grows in different ways. For example, during wartime when young men and women are away from home in the armed forces, families have fewer children. The "birthrate" normally goes down. After wars, husbands and wives are reunited, more young people marry, and the birthrate goes up. So it was after World War II.

Demographers analyze statistics about population. Such statistics are important for planning by government and business. The framers of the

Constitution back in 1787 knew that the growing nation would need up-to-date facts about the moving population. So they established the federal census (Art. I, sec. 2), requiring the national government to count the population every ten years. Then the members of the House of Representatives could be reapportioned according to the changes.

As the census became more detailed, the public could use this information to plan the water supply and roads and schools. Businesses could build factories where workers would be living. They could predict the size of the market for their product. The Bureau of the Census (now in the Department of Commerce) became an American institution. It has gathered all sorts of facts about our people. And demographers even invented ways to estimate the changes occurring between the regular decennial (every ten years) census.

The nation grows. After World War II the United States experienced a "population explosion." When the Great Depression finally ended, people had more money to support a family. And then when veterans returned home at the war's end, the birthrate increased. But this was not just the normal increase after any war. The population soared so fast that even expert demographers were astonished.

In 1940 there were 132 million people in the United States. During the decade of the 1930s our population had increased just 7.2 percent—the smallest proportionate increase in the nation's history. By 1950 there were 151 million, an increase of 14.5 percent over 1940. Between 1950 and 1960 the number of people went up even faster—by 18.5 percent—to a total of over 179 million. This was mainly due to the high birthrate. At the same time, refugees from war and nazism and communism swelled the number of immigrants coming to the United States from 1 million during the decade of the 1940s to 2.5 million in the 1950s.

By the end of 1950 one person was being added to the nation every twelve seconds. This explosive growth was equal then to another Richmond, Virginia, every month and a whole Maryland every year. It put strains on cities and states, which were forced to build bigger hospitals, to hire more police and firefighters, and especially to add new schools to cope with the large numbers of children.

Paolo Koch/Photo Researchers

During the 1950s, our population increased so rapidly that experts said we were in the midst of a "baby boom."

Slowing the boom. During the 1960s the population boom began to slow down. Still the nation grew by 13.5 percent, which meant adding nearly 24 million people to make a population of 203 million by 1970. The nation now had twice the number of people it had only 50 years before.

By the end of 1972 the baby boom was over. The Census Bureau reported then that American women were not having quite enough babies to keep the population steady. But the many male and female babies born during those years of population explosion would grow up and in time have their own children.

Moving west, north, and south. Even while the rate of growth of the American population changed, same time, one of every three Americans lived on a farm. In 1970 only one American in every 22 still lived on a farm. Each year farms held a smaller and smaller proportion of the people. The number of farms had fallen from a peak of 6.8 million in 1935 to under 3 million in 1970, and it was continuing to fall rapidly. Of course, at the same time, the farms that remained grew much larger in size. Farmers still spoke with a powerful voice in national politics. The 4.5 million American farm workers in 1970 were more numerous than all the workers in the steel, automobile, and transportation industries combined.

Back in 1820 the average farm worker could produce only enough to feed four people. Now, modern farm machinery, improved seeds, better fertilizers, and scientific methods had enormously increased what each farmer could produce. By 1950 one farm worker could feed 15, and by 1970 each one could produce enough for 45! American farmers helped feed people in Russia, India, and all over the world.

For those who remained on the farm, life became less isolated during the postwar years. The spread of telephones and automobiles meant that farm families could see or talk to their neighbors more easily. Television brought to the farmhouse the same news broadcasts, sports programs, and other entertainment seen by apartment dwellers in the big cities. Some American farmers drove large tractors equipped with air conditioning, citizens' band (CB) radios, TV sets, and high fidelity sound systems. The experiences of all Americans were becoming more and more alike.

The move to the suburbs. Meanwhile, the city people did not sit still in the centers of their growing metropolises. After 1950 they moved in large numbers out of the central cities to the nearby suburbs. In 1950, 35 percent of the nation's people lived in the central cities and almost as many—27 percent—in the suburbs. By 1970 the suburbs were winning, for 31 percent lived in the central cities and 37 percent in the suburbs. This gave many Americans a new opportunity to enjoy fresh air, to mow their lawns, to watch birds, and plant gardens of flowers and vegetables. But it also produced "suburban sprawl" and new traffic jams! Homes and factories and shopping centers were jumbled together in ugly mixes.

the people never ceased to move. After World War II, the lure of the West drew millions all the way to the shores of the Pacific. By 1964 California, with 10 percent of the nation's people, had become the most populous state in the Union.

At the same time there were new north-south movements. Between 1920 and 1960 many blacks left the South heading north, hoping for better jobs, more equality, more opportunity. In 1940 three-quarters of all blacks still lived in the South. But by 1970 half of all black Americans lived in the North. After 1960 a new migration of whites from North to South more than made up in numbers for the departing blacks. The "Sunbelt," as the states in the South and Southwest were called, was now growing faster than any other section.

Moving off the farms. All across the nation there was another great and speedy migration—from the countryside to the city. In 1920 the nation's rural and urban populations were equal in size. At the

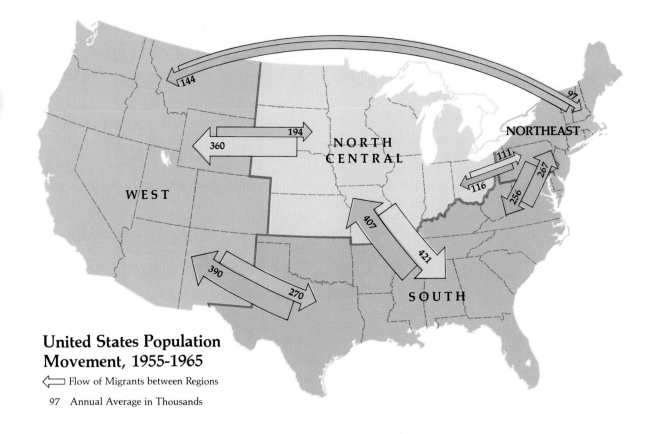

United States Population Movement, 1955-1965

Flow of Migrants between Regions

97 Annual Average in Thousands

After World War II, suburban tract housing like Levittown, Pennsylvania, shown here, was rapidly built to hold the growing population.

Van Bucher/Photo Researchers

To describe this America, it was no longer possible to talk simply of "cities." Americans were spread across the country in new clusters. The Office of Management and Budget called these clusters Standard Metropolitan Statistical Areas (SMSAs). Until the 1980s each SMSA was supposed to be a dense population (including suburbs) surrounding a central city of 50,000. But then it was found that population often flowed to smaller towns or groups of towns and that these too were becoming metropolitan areas—though without any major central city. To describe these new areas better the government dropped its requirement of a large central city and created three different classes of Metropolitan Statistical Areas. Now all that was needed was a central town or group of towns and a dense metropolitan area. Benton Harbor, Michigan, for example—with a population in 1980 of 14,707—was defined as metropolitan because it was the heart of an area with over 170,000 people.

The most striking population change of the 1970s, however, was the discovery that "rural" areas were growing faster than metropolitan areas for the first time since the decade from 1810 to 1820. These were not farms, but new communities in the countryside. Many businesses, factories, workers and their families were moving into the remote fringes of the big metropolitan areas. Still, by the 1980s three-fourths of the American people lived in cities or their surrounding suburbs—with the larger part in the suburbs.

The metropolitan areas were often so close together that it was hard to know where one ended and another began. Looking down from an airplane flying northward from Norfolk, Virginia, to Bangor, Maine, what you saw looked like one big super-city. This needed a new name, and people began calling it a "megalopolis" (from the Greek words for "giant" and for "city"). Sprawling giant-cities grew also in Texas, Florida, California, and on the edge of the Great Lakes.

One surprising fact was that—although the heart of the continent had been filling up for two centuries—more than half of all Americans now lived within 50 miles of the oceans, the Gulf of Mexico, or the Great Lakes.

A mobile people. Even when they reached California or Florida or arrived in their chosen city, Americans did not settle down. Every year after 1948 one American in five moved to a new place—down the street, to a nearby town, or on to another state. The census found that in a single year in the 1970s more than 36 million people had changed houses. Of course, most of them had just moved within the same city or county. Still, they had to get used to a new neighborhood with different stores and schools. In 1970 a quarter of all the people in the United States were living in a different state from where they had been born.

This moving around made problems—and opportunities—for all Americans. For example, most black Americans were transformed from rural to urban citizens. In 1940 one-third of all employed blacks worked on farms. By 1970 fewer than 4 percent were farm workers, and four-fifths of the black population lived in urban areas. Most were still prevented from moving to the suburbs by their own poverty or by white prejudice. In the half-century after the Civil War the proportion of blacks in the whole population of the United States declined from 13 to 11 percent. That proportion has remained about the same ever since.

In a fast-moving America—of Americans living close together—it was easier for blacks to demand their rights. The first successes of Martin Luther King, Jr., and Rosa Parks were in crowded Montgomery and on the buses that carried people to work (p. 630).

The concentration of this 11 percent in the cities also gave blacks an increased political power. They were a voting bloc that could be easily identified and (because of segregation) easily found. Now at last, even in the South, they were allowed to vote. Their support for Kennedy in 1960 and for Carter in 1976 helped provide the narrow margins for victory. In the cities, where they lived closer together, it was easier for them to support their candidate. Their votes brought Atlanta, Georgia, its first black mayor in 1973. By then there were black mayors in Los Angeles and Detroit and in 90 other cities.

In 1964 there were only four blacks in Congress, but by 1972 there were fifteen, including Edward Brooke, Republican senator from Massachusetts. Black influence at the polls would have been even greater if more blacks had voted. In the late 1970s only one-third of the 15 million blacks eligible to vote had registered, and only one-third of those registered bothered to cast their ballots.

As the barriers were slowly broken down, during

Standard Metropolitan Statistical Areas

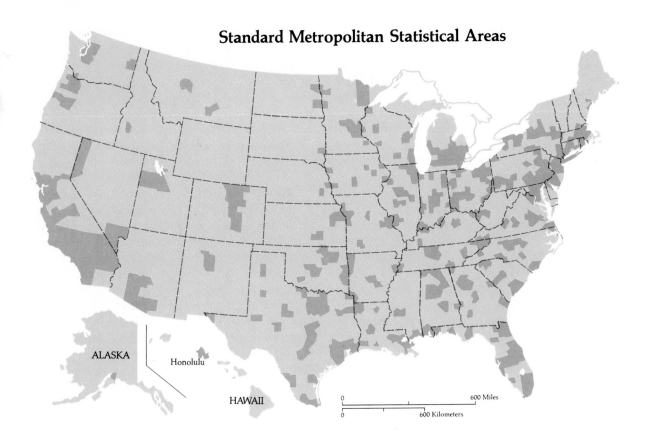

ALASKA

Honolulu

HAWAII

0   600 Miles

0   600 Kilometers

the 1960s an increasing number of blacks began to join fellow Americans in the suburbs. There they rose from 2.5 percent to 4.2 percent, still far below their 11 percent in the total population. Political power now lay with the suburbs because more voters lived there than in either the cities or the rural areas.

An aging population. The nation was reshaped—not only by how the population moved but by how the population grew. After World War II, there was a striking increase in the number of Americans over 65. People were living longer because of better diet, advances in medicine and surgery, and the invention of "miracle drugs" (like sulfa and penicillin), which cured diseases that had often been fatal. In 1900 the average life expectancy of all Americans at birth was only 47, and people over 65 represented only 4 percent of the population. By the 1940s the average life expectancy reached 65. By 1970 it had climbed to 71.

The census showed that men generally did not live as long as women. In the 1970s men at birth had a life expectancy of 67 while for women it was nearly 75. By 1970 the number of people over 65 had grown to 20 million—10 percent of the whole population. They outnumbered the people in all the twenty smallest states combined. And they had their own special hopes. They were another new group whom the successful politician had to please. American youth usually looked for adventure and opportunity. "Senior citizens" cared more for security and leisure. In the 1960s and 1970s, could these different hopes be matched?

SECTION 1 REVIEW

1. Explain: demography, SMSA, megalopolis.

2. Point out major trends in population growth and movement from 1945 to 1970.

3. **Drawing Conclusions.** How was population mobility beneficial?

644

2. Everyday life transformed

The new world of adventure was the world of science and of machines. Ever since the colonists had "invented" their nation, and devised a new kind of written constitution, Americans had loved to experiment. They also liked to buy new things. Visitors from abroad noticed that Americans were machine minded.

The famous cartoonist Rube Goldberg said the American motto ought to be, "Do it the hard way!" Americans loved complicated ways of simplifying everyday life. Why walk if you could ride? Why use a wooden pencil if you could use a metal pencil with retractable lead—including many colors that you really did not need? Why write with a pencil or pen if you could use a typewriter? Or why use a simple hand-operated typewriter when there was a much more complex electric machine? Why write it yourself at all if you could first dictate it into a machine that recorded your voice on a tape, which would be put into another machine to be played back to someone who would transcribe the words on an electric typewriter? In the machine-rich United States, everyday life was full of fantastic surprises.

A growing economy. All these machines helped create the American standard of living. They helped make life more interesting, as well as more complicated. They opened opportunities for investors to put their money into new ventures in hopes of profit, for business leaders to build factories, for skilled workers to make the machines—and for salespeople and advertising experts to sell these machines by the millions. After the war the economy expanded and prospered.

The quarter-century from the end of World War II until about 1970 brought the nation its longest period of prosperity. There were brief recessions, but the statistics of economic growth were astonishing. The Gross National Product (GNP)—the total value of all goods and services produced in the nation—measured in 1958 dollars rose from $355.2 billion in 1945 to $722.5 billion in 1970. In the same period, per capita income before taxes increased (in 1958 dollars) from $1870 to $3050. Most Americans prospered as they shared one of the highest per capita incomes in the world.

Reasons for prosperity. Immediately after World War II, there was a large, pent-up demand

Stores encouraged their customers to "Charge it!" and the nation's economy boomed.

for housing and for all peacetime products, such as automobiles and kitchen appliances, that were hard to get during the war. This demand, backed by wartime savings, gave a big boost to sales. Government spending did not decline and kept the economy booming. American export trade, supported by the billions of dollars the United States government paid out for foreign aid, flourished.

All sorts of new machines—radios, high fi's, television sets, washing and drying machines, deep freezes, power lawnmowers, and countless others—kept factories busy and customers eager to buy. None was more important than the automobile. Fewer than 1 million new automobiles were produced during World War II. By 1970, 8 million a year were being turned out. These consumed one-fifth of the nation's new steel, half its malleable iron, and two-thirds of its rubber and lead.

All these cars needed highways. In 1956, then, the nation began the largest road construction program in its history. Under President Eisenhower, Congress voted $33 billion (later increased) for a ten-year program to build a whole 42,500-mile network of interstate superhighways. By 1975, because of inflation, it would cost $39 billion just to finish the last 5500 miles of the system. In 1978 President Carter signed a highway bill that

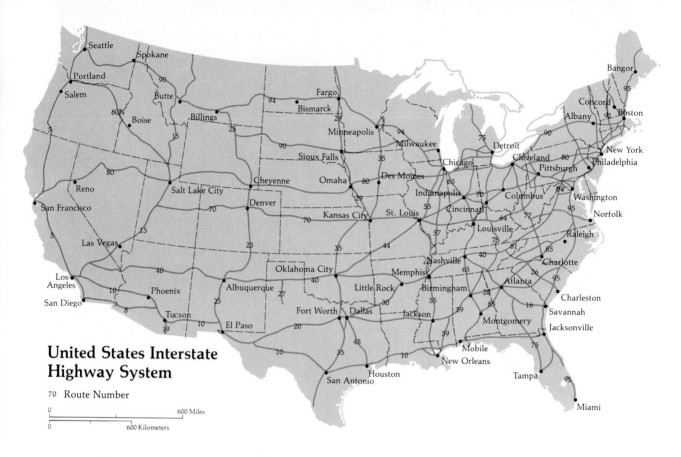

United States Interstate Highway System

70 Route Number

0 ——————— 600 Miles

0 ——————— 600 Kilometers

provided $9.3 billion a year for three years. Many more billions were spent by states and localities.

The automobile and the suburbs. In earlier days cities had grown up near waterways. Then railroads went to the cities, and new cities grew along the railroads. Even before the automobile, streetcars took people out to the suburbs to live and back into the center of the city to work and to shop. The automobile gave its owner a new freedom. Of course, railroads and streetcars had to stay on their special tracks. But the car would take Americans of the twentieth century anywhere there were roads. Factories, stores, and movie theaters moved out to shopping centers in the suburbs. The "downtown" of a big city was no longer the center of people's lives.

Americans had fallen in love with their automobiles. In 1971 alone, they spent the staggering sum of $180 billion to buy new and used cars. This was more than four times what they spent for their public elementary and high schools. From their homes in the suburbs Americans could drive to work every day. Life in the suburbs—shopping, going to school, visiting friends—required a car.

Living with the automobile. The automobile brought strange by-products. One of these was the "credit card." The first credit cards were offered by the large gasoline companies to attract customers. They gave out these identifying cards so that people could charge gasoline purchases anywhere on the road at one of their hundreds of stations. After 1950, other businesses picked up the credit card idea.

The parking problem was also new. To attract customers to the central city, huge parking garages were built in choice locations. So automobile traffic increased. Then the poor pedestrians had to risk their lives when they crossed the street. Cars ruled the surface of the earth. Millions of automobiles polluted the atmosphere with carbon monoxide and hydrocarbons. It was hard to live *without* automobiles, but could Americans learn to live *with* them?

Machines to do everything. Of course, the automobiles needed accessories—windshield wipers, turn

Even the large-scale construction of superhighways like this could not prevent traffic jams when the nation's automobiles multiplied after World War II.

signals, car radios. This created new industries by the hundreds. Also Americans wanted, made, and bought new electric appliances for the home, for the factory, and for the office. These included air conditioners, dehumidifiers, electric blankets, electric knives and toothbrushes, automatic washing machines and dryers, dishwashers, garbage disposals, pencil sharpeners, typewriters, cash registers, and countless other items. The factories to make these products, and the factories to make the machines that went into the factories, created new jobs by the thousands.

To produce the electricity to run these homes and factories, the nation burned the old reliable coal, which had driven the factories in the preceding century. The factories also were powered by oil and natural gas brought in by giant pipelines from the West and Southwest to the cities of the South, Midwest, and East.

Light metals like aluminum, magnesium, and titanium were combined with chromium into sparkling, rust-free new alloys. Aluminum production leaped from 287,000 tons in 1940 to 2 million tons in 1960 and over 4 million in 1970. Industrial chemists invented "plastics"—which were cheaper than wood or metal, easier to shape into the new tools and toys and gadgets. There were man-made wash-and-wear textiles like nylon and Dacron, which never lost their press. And countless other "synthetics" were used for detergents, drugs, insecticides, and fertilizers.

All these products had to be put in packages. The packaging was as new as the product. In the 1800s, people had taken their own containers to the general store to carry home their milk or coffee or crackers. Then, after World War I, the rise of advertising, national brands, and supermarkets created a whole new "packaging" industry. As customers walked through the aisles of supermarkets to serve themselves, they bought their groceries in familiar packages. Sometimes even when they didn't really need something, they bought it simply because they were attracted by the colorful, much-advertised package.

The spread of television. Advertising these packaged products became still another big industry. This advertising supported broadcasting on radio

647

and television while it filled every American living room with "commercials."

Television, one of the most magical of American machines, conquered the nation with astounding speed. In 1948 there were only 200,000 television sets in all the United States, and of every hundred families only one owned a set. But by 1970 nearly every American home (95.5 percent) had at least one television set. After the first commercial communications satellite, *Early Bird*, was put into space in 1965, live broadcasts could be sent from Europe to the United States. In the 1970s satellites brought events from all over the world—even President Nixon's visit to far-off China—into the nation's homes.

Now Americans could see and hear events as they happened. The war in Vietnam, civil rights marches, riots in the streets—along with entertaining series, cartoons, old movies, and sports events—all appeared on the TV screen. The magic of television brought a new kind of confusion. The wonderful box in everybody's living room created the Instant Everywhere. You could stay wherever you were and see what was happening at that instant all over the United States—and all over the world. Americans felt magically close to events in Vietnam, on the civil rights battlegrounds of Alabama and Mississippi, even on the moon! They sometimes forgot how far away those fearful and exciting events really were.

"Network" programs, which cost a fortune to produce, made celebrities out of the newscasters. Citizens all over the nation could see and hear their President and watch events in Washington. There was a new danger that they would pay less attention to their mayor or their governor or the real neighbors in their own town.

Americans, for the first time, could see events "replayed." They forgot that this, too, was a modern miracle. Before photography or radio or television, an event happened only once. Then it was gone forever unless an artist painted it in a picture or a writer told the story. In the age of television, by the 1960s when you watched a sporting event, you could not only see the game played once. You could see the most thrilling moments played again and again on instant replay. With your tape recorder, also developed after World War II, you could reproduce music from radios, records, and live groups to be played again

Here the distant Statue of Liberty is bracketed by a new feature of the American landscape.

whenever you wanted. You could record your family gatherings at Christmas or Thanksgiving. Members of the family could send each other greetings in their own voices.

New-style pioneers. There were many American pioneers on these new machine-frontiers. The age of the Go-Getter was not over. Instead of clearing the land and building cities in the wilderness, the modern pioneer built machines no one else had imagined, to satisfy needs never before felt. One clever inventor, Edwin H. Land, devised an instant camera and film that not only took pictures, but developed them on the spot. Imaginative Chester F. Carlson, who had worked his way through the California Institute of Technology, invented a new copying system. Bold businessmen in Rochester, New York, supported his research and invested in his machine to make an image on paper. They renamed his process "xerography" (from the Greek words *xeros*, "dry," and *graphein*, "to write"). Soon Xerox machines were everywhere. Offices and libraries all over the country were reproducing letters and books. It was easier than ever before to make a copy of anything.

More machines, and more machines to make machines! All these required energy, which meant more electricity. Between 1940 and 1970 the production of electricity in the United States increased over sevenfold. We used far more energy than any other nation. As a result of improved machines and better working methods, between 1947 and 1970 the output of factories per working hour more than doubled!

Machines to run machines. There seemed no end to the powers of machine magic. The next step was to invent machines to run the machines. In the years after World War II, that actually happened. About 1946, Americans began to use another new word, "automation." The fantastic new machine was the "computer." Its main inventor was a brilliant Hungarian immigrant, John von Neumann, who had helped plan the atomic bomb and now was a professor at Princeton. In a few seconds the electronic computer would count and calculate what once had busied a hundred workers for days. High-speed computers could count, sort, remember, and select information—then use it to run factories or oil refineries.

In the 1960s and 1970s computers found thousands of new uses—to monitor patients in hospitals, to process checks in banks, to handle credit-card bills, and to keep track of library books. They solved problems for scientists, mathematicians, educators, engineers, and business leaders. The computer even moved into supermarkets and provided a machine that could read the lines on packages, then add up the price. The take-it-for-granted customer instantly had a neat shopping list with the name and price of each item.

In all sorts of factories, the work was transformed. In automobile factories, for example, welding machines with electronic memories made some of the decisions live workers once had to make. After a "live" welder guided the computers once through their jobs, the machines were then "programed" to remember what to weld and then they would repeat it over and over again as each car came by.

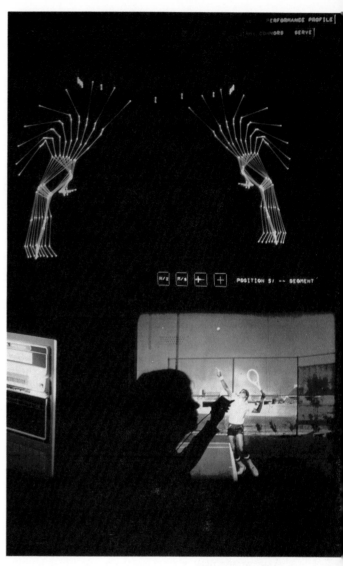

Dan McCoy/Black Star

An athlete working to improve his tennis stroke uses a computer to analyze his movements and help him do better.

The advantages of these miraculous machines were obvious. They took the place of a great deal of drudgery. But, like all other machines, they had their price. They put people out of work. And until those people could be trained for new jobs created by the new machines, they might feel lost and useless. This was the kind of price that other new machines had always extracted. Here was another challenge to American enterprise, education, and government.

Planning for the new. Whenever someone invented something, most Americans asked, "Why not try it?" And they did. They were anxious to have a new gadget or a new model even if they weren't sure that it was better. Wasn't it better just *because* it was new?

But this made problems, too. New machines made old machines obsolete. The changes in assembly-line factories had to be carefully planned. On the assembly line one piece after another was added to the car's chassis as it moved along. Each piece had to be fitted into all the others. To make a new model car was complicated and required long-range planning.

Henry Ford thought his Model T was the best car that could be made. For many years he refused to change the design. Then General Motors and other manufacturers invented the idea of an "annual model"—changing the design every year. Customers now had a reason to sell their old car—even if it still worked—so they could buy another car of this year's stylish design.

Customers liked the idea. But car manufacturers had to plan the new models years in advance so the factory machinery would be ready. Every fall Americans waited for that year's models to appear. In Europe the car manufacturers changed their designs only slowly and over many years. Some American car makers in the 1960s even began to change their models twice a year. Change was becoming ever more rapid. Was the new model really new?

The hidden frontiers: research and development. The many new products—from the life-changing computer to the electric toothbrush—did not appear just by accident. Electronics had developed rapidly because of the World War II research to make more accurate weapons and better ways to track enemy aircraft, ships, and submarines. In peacetime, too, scientists, engineers, and technicians worked together on hidden frontiers in laboratories all over the country. Supported by universities, by businesses, by government, or by their own hopes and savings, they went in search of answers to all sorts of questions. Could they make a camera that would photograph under water, an inexpensive highway cement that would dry quickly and not crack in summer or winter? In 1970, $27 billion was spent on *research* and *development* (R&D)—more even

than the nation's total expenditure of $23 billion on higher education. Two-thirds of this came from federal funds and the rest from private industry.

The industrial research laboratory had not been invented in the United States, but in Germany. Americans followed the lead. Ever since Thomas A. Edison built his invention factory in Menlo Park, New Jersey, in 1876, research and development had shaped American life. Large corporations like General Electric (GE), American Telephone & Telegraph (AT&T), and International Business Machines (IBM) would invest millions asking a new question or finding new answers to old questions. By the 1950s the nation had over 200 large laboratories and 2000 smaller ones. Out of them came the tiny transistor for pocket radios and portable TV sets, photovoltaic cells that change sunlight into electricity, the new form of light known as the laser (which can cut through steel and reach to the moon), microprocessors (tiny chips of silicon that hold thousands of pieces of information), and hosts of other inventions that made dreams come true.

A changing work force. Machines created by experts and technicians needed a world of experts and technicians to keep them alive and in good working order. Automation made jobs in new industries and changed the jobs that people did. A strong arm, a sturdy back, the power to handle a shovel and lift heavy weights—these were no longer so useful.

Fewer jobs could be done by those who had no skills. At the end of World War II, one-third of all jobs could still be handled by untrained people. By 1970 only half as many jobs could be performed by the unskilled. As a result, in the late 1970s untrained teenagers suffered twice the rate of unemployment of the older, skilled workers.

SECTION 2 REVIEW

1. Why did the nation prosper during the period 1945–1970?

2. What part did "research and development" play in the postwar prosperity?

3. **Predicting Consequences.** What would American life be like if the television had never been invented?

3. Education and religion

These were difficult times. To find jobs, young Americans needed skills. To enjoy their life, to understand the complex world, to explore history and science—they needed a "liberal" education. This meant an education to "liberate" them—to lift them out of their hometown and open the wide world of books. And to find peace and try to cope with the stresses of the postwar world, most Americans turned to their houses of worship and their religious leaders.

The spread of high school education. The free public high school was an American invention—a foundation of democracy and opportunity. It was needed to provide students for the multiplying American colleges and universities. In 1900 only about 10 percent of young people between 14 and 17 years of age were in high schools or private secondary schools. Among young people of college age, only 1 person in 25 went on to college. Then the change was rapid and spectacular. By 1930 half of all Americans aged 14 to 17 were in high school. By 1950 high school enrollment had reached three-quarters of that age group, and by 1970 it was 90 percent. In that same year college enrollment, which was only 10 percent in 1930, had reached 50 percent of all college-age Americans.

Veterans of World War II, Korea, and Vietnam were rewarded by the "G.I. bills." These laws paid the veterans' way to college or technical training. Millions were qualified because they had graduated from high school.

Were schools mainly to prepare those who were going on to a "higher" learning in college? Or should they be designed for everyone? One answer came from John Dewey, whose writings on education during his long life (1859–1952) shaped the philosophy of thousands of teachers. Brought up on a Vermont farm, he knew from his own experience raising chickens and planting vegetables how children learned by actually doing. Dewey noticed that as more families moved into the city, fewer children had his experience. He believed that schools could take its place. "Education," Dewey said, "is a process of living and not a preparation for future living." He planned schools where children would learn by doing. They made things as they worked together.

Other educators, like President Robert Maynard Hutchins of the University of Chicago, disagreed. They believed it was more important for schools to teach people to learn by reading. Students should read and discuss the great books of the past. In school, Hutchins said, students should be taught about science and history and geography, because later on they would have plenty of time to learn by doing.

When *Sputnik* suddenly appeared in the sky in 1957 (p. 633), many Americans began to fear that the Russian achievement was produced by better schools. James Bryant Conant, who had recently retired as president of Harvard University, in his influential book *The American High School Today* (1959) called for changes in the high schools. He proposed a minimum size for high schools, higher standards, and greater emphasis on courses in English, foreign languages, mathematics, science, and social studies. Still, the philosophy of Dewey and his followers in the "Progressive Education" movement permeated the schools. Grammar schools and high schools would continue to accommodate "all the youth of a community."

Religion in postwar America. Just as education took new forms, so did religion. In America religion always seems to be either in the doldrums or booming. After World War II, the Catholic, Jewish, and Protestant religions in the United States all experienced revivals. Millions of dollars were spent to build new churches and synagogues, and Americans in ever larger numbers flocked to religious services.

The years from 1945 to 1960 were an "Age of Affluence" as goods poured from American factories, unemployment and inflation remained low, and wages rose. But they were also an "Age of Anxiety" as communism spread, war came to Korea, and the United States and the Soviet Union built and tested more and more nuclear weapons. Perhaps their anxiety was one reason many Americans returned to their churches.

They also read books by religious leaders and listened to them on radio and TV. One of the first to publish a best-seller was Rabbi Joshua Loth Lieberman, who in 1946 showed how the discoveries of the great Austrian psychoanalyst Sigmund Freud could lead to *Peace of Mind,* as his book was titled. In the 1940s and 1950s, through radio and television and in his book *Peace of Soul,* Monsignor

Fulton J. Sheen reached millions of people and brought many converts into the Catholic church.

The Protestant minister Norman Vincent Peale's *Guide to Confident Living* (1948) and *The Power of Positive Thinking* (1952) were read by millions who found in them a road to inner peace. Millions more listened to Peale on radio and records, read his articles, and watched him on TV. One of the most persuasive preachers of the 1950s and after was Billy Graham. Graham was in the grand old American tradition of the evangelical revival. (Evangelical comes from the word *evangel*, which comes from a Greek word meaning "bringer of good news.") His revival meetings drew hundreds of thousands to make "decisions for Christ" while vast audiences listened on radio and watched on television.

Still, by the end of the 1950s, the American revival was losing force and attendance at churches was dropping off. Some theologians began to say that religion had lost its power in the United States. "God is dead," they mourned.

The 1960s were a troublesome time for churches as they were for all Americans. The civil rights movement and the war in Vietnam revealed the gap between American ideals and American reality. They sharpened the great moral issues that would haunt the nation in the years to come.

Some ministers began to fear that somehow the churches were not really speaking to the problems that most worried Americans. They tried new ways to attract people to their churches with rock music, guitars, and new seating arrangements. Many ministers marched for civil rights and in protest against the Vietnam War. Black ministers, and most especially Martin Luther King, Jr., were in the forefront of the fight for civil rights. And King early raised his eloquent voice against the war in Vietnam.

In the confusion and chaos of the 1960s some people turned away from traditional Western religions and sought their answers in Hinduism and Zen Buddhism. Among the young, some turned to nihilism ("nothing"-ism, the total rejection of law and institutions) and violence, while others withdrew into communes where they could invent their own customs and traditions.

These troubles of the 1960s stirred the Fundamentalist Protestants. While some people were turning away from old values, Fundamentalists spoke out for them. About a third of all Protestants in the 1980s were Fundamentalists. They believed in the literal truth of the Bible and the need to be "born again" in Christ. Organized in groups like the Moral Majority they could bring strong political support to candidates who shared their beliefs.

Despite the vigor of the Fundamentalists, some historians noted a turning point in American history. The Protestant values that had dominated American life from the beginning no longer seemed supreme. American religion had entered a new age.

SECTION 3 REVIEW

1. Identify: John Dewey, James B. Conant, Fulton J. Sheen, Billy Graham, Norman Vincent Peale.

2. Explain some events occurring outside the United States that affected American education.

3. **Recognizing Cause and Effect.** How did technology affect religion in the United States?

4. Art and the machine

Meanwhile the machines and new ways of life left their mark on the arts. After the camera was invented, anybody with a camera could make a picture exactly like what he saw. It was no trick anymore to make a "likeness" of a person or a landscape. So the artists, too, tried to make something different. They experimented with new ways to paint and new kinds of statues. These were no longer pretty figures of men and women, trees or flowers. Instead they were abstract patterns showing the artist's private vision.

Adventurous artists. The most famous of these was Jackson Pollock (1912–1956), who had been born in Cody, Wyoming, and was trained to paint in the traditional style. He invented his own kind of Abstract Expressionism called "action painting." He would put his large canvas on the floor and then (he explained) paint with "sticks, trowels, knives, and dripping fluid paint or a heavy impasto with sand, broken glass and other foreign matter added." Along with Pollock came Willem de Kooning, Helen Frankenthaler, Franz Kline, Adolph Gottlieb, Mark Rothko, Barnett Newman, and Robert Motherwell, each with another new vision of how to paint. Some people wondered whether what they produced was really "art." But many more enjoyed what they saw. They believed

Americans should experiment with art, just as they did with everything else.

Collectors, museums, and galleries began snatching up "minimal art" at high prices. This art did little or nothing to change an object, and simply considered the object as art. Andy Warhol's "pop art" offered larger-than-life paintings of Campbell soup cans and Brillo boxes. Claes Oldenburg's pop art produced a huge statue of a lipstick or a canvas of a *Hamburger with Pickle and Tomato Attached.*

Rock 'n' Roll. Popular music, too, was transformed during the 1950s and 1960s and would never be the same again. The new music, growing out of black rhythm and blues, was given a different form by country and western singers. Finally it emerged as "Rock 'n' Roll." Rock was deeply influenced by modern machines—electric guitars, loudspeaker systems, and the magic created in recording studios by audio tapes, mixers, and other complex devices.

The first great popular star of Rock 'n' Roll was Elvis Presley. From the small town of Tupelo, Mississippi, Presley burst upon the music scene in the 1950s and swept all before him. Across the Atlantic, four young singer-musicians in the English port city of Liverpool picked up this new sound. During the 1960s the music of the Beatles, as they called themselves, would conquer the world.

The Beatles were far more original and more talented than Presley. They created their own distinctive sounds. And the Beatles' influence on the young went beyond music. Their long hair, their casual clothes and manners, their irreverent humor, and their flirtations with drugs excited and captivated young people around the world. Rock 'n' Roll groups both reflected and shaped the outlook of young people in the turbulent 1960s (pp. 688–689).

"Blue Territory" (above) by Helen Frankenthaler. Jackson Pollock's "Autumn Rhythm" (below), one of the artist's "action paintings."

Writers in a complex world. Writers also had trouble casting the new world of speedy change and all-powerful machines in the old patterns. Herman Wouk's *The Caine Mutiny* (1952) told about the problems of command in the modern Navy. James Jones's World War II novel, *From Here to Eternity* (1951), showed characters who were lonely and lost. J. D. Salinger's *Catcher in the Rye* (1951) was a story of an adolescent trying to escape hypocrisy. In *Invisible Man* (1952), Ralph Ellison's black hero gradually saw that he was powerless and that the world was out of his reach. Ellison made the black man in a white world a symbol of everyone's puzzling experience in the industrial age. Joseph Heller's *Catch-22* (1969), a hilarious tale of wartime red tape, became a name for all the no-win situations in modern America. Carson McCullers portrayed the silent world of two mutes in *The Heart Is a Lonely Hunter* (1940) and the loneliness of a young girl in *The Member of the Wedding* (1946). Eudora Welty in *Delta Wedding* (1948) and *Losing Battles* (1970) described the intimate ties that bind families together. Katherine Anne Porter described us all in *Ship of Fools* (1962).

William Faulkner wrote about how the South (and America) lost the simple ideals of the farming past. In a mythical county in Mississippi in *The Hamlet* (1940), *The Town* (1957), and *The Mansion* (1959) he told the long story of the greedy and unpleasant Snopes clan. Faulkner won the Nobel Prize for literature in 1950.

Still other writers, like Saul Bellow, who also won the Nobel Prize, described the problems that thoughtful men and women faced inside themselves. Norman Mailer, after writing *The Naked and the Dead* (1948), his action-novel about World War II, turned to writing about himself. His "new journalism" report on the anti-Vietnam march on Washington in 1967 was called *The Armies of the Night.*

In spite of all the hi-fi's and television sets and the other entertainment machines, Americans bought and read more books than ever before. Each year's new titles numbered more than 40,000. Inexpensive paperback books, hardly known in this country before the war, flooded the market. Readers could find them everywhere—not only in bookstores, but now also in drugstores, supermarkets, and airports. Millions joined book clubs. Best-selling books often went on to become movies or television shows. And sometimes movies were turned into novels.

To help it use all sources of knowledge, back in 1800 the Congress had set up its own library. By the late twentieth century the Library of Congress was the largest in the world—with about 20 million books (in 468 languages!) and about 80 million other items. Besides books, magazines, and newspapers, there were photographs, motion picture films, musical recordings, art prints, maps and globes, the manuscripts of famous men and women, and braille books and "talking books" for the blind. It served all other libraries, along with writers, scholars, and all the people. Like the Congress itself, it was a symbol of democratic America that everybody could visit on Capitol Hill in Washington. And it, too, was using the magic of the computer to control its millions of items and offer them to Congress and the nation.

Americans were delighted and bewildered, frustrated and challenged by the kaleidoscope-world of new machines. Books, the movie screen and the TV tube, the works of painters and sculptors helped make sense of their world. Political leaders, the men and women whom Americans elected to represent them and to manage their government, were still the most conspicuous shapers of American life. In the next generation, could these elected leaders offer the uplift and the direction the nation needed?

The forces of mobile people and magic machines, unlike the terms of Presidents, did not end on a particular day. These forces came to a climax under Presidents Truman and Eisenhower. But the forces were rooted in World War II, and even earlier, and did not end with any President's term. The forces we have described would become stronger with the passing years. They help explain the new problems and new opportunities that the nation would face in the turbulent 1960s and after.

SECTION 4 REVIEW

1. How did painters break with tradition in the postwar era?

2. **Recognizing Cause and Effect.** What effect did television and movies have on the book publishing industry?

CHAPTER 30 REVIEW

FOCUSING ON IDEAS

1. What is "demography"? What general trends have demographers noticed concerning the population of the post–World War II United States?

2. How have farming and farm life in the United States changed since 1950?

3. Identify ways in which computers and other forms of automation affect you and your family.

4. What evidence do you see that religion continues to have a significant influence on American life?

TAKING A CRITICAL LOOK

1. **Predicting Consequences.** What social changes would you expect to see in the United States as the proportion of young people declines and the proportion of elderly people rises?

2. **Identifying Central Issues.** What are some "learning by doing" school experiences that you have had in the past ten years? How else do you learn history besides reading history books?

YOUR REGION IN HISTORY

1. **Geography.** Study the "Flow of Migrants" map on page 642. Did your region have an overall gain or loss of population from the migration? Which other region, if any, received the heaviest flow of migrants from your region? What particular attractions might have brought people to relocate to your region during the period 1955 to 1965?

2. **Culture.** Interview leaders of a local church or synagogue about changes that have occurred in their local or national institutions since 1950. Ask them what changes in American life have contributed to changes in their religious institutions.

3. **Economics.** To what extent have blacks or Hispanics gained political office and government jobs in your locality in recent years? Other minorities? To what factors do you attribute these social and political changes?

HISTORICAL FACTS AND FIGURES

Determining Relevance. Study the graphs below to help answer the following questions: (a) How many Americans owned television sets in 1948? In 1960? (b) What percentage of Americans owned televisions in 1948? In 1960? (c) What economic or cultural changes occurred in the United States as a result of the invention and widespread sale of the television? Find evidence in the chapter to support your conclusions.

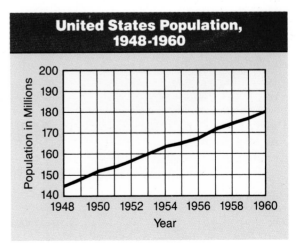

Homes With Television Sets

Year	
1948	(0)
1950	(1)
1952	(3)
1954	(6)
1956	(7)
1958	(9)
1960	(10)

📺 = 5 Million Homes with Television Sets

Source: *Statistical Abstract of the United States*

United States Population, 1948-1960

Source: *Statistical Abstract of the United States*

MAKING CONNECTIONS

THEMES

This unit began on page 597 with the observation that a new era of history had begun in the years between 1945 and 1960:

> *Under the menacing shadow of the atomic bomb, war between great powers could never again be the same. Isolation was no longer possible, . . . [and] in the postwar age, the American ways of living, thinking, and doing would be transformed.*

This conclusion was supported by the three unit themes that are reprinted in **dark type** below. Use the time line and the information in Unit 10 to answer the questions that follow the unit themes.

1. **Tensions between the United States and the Soviet Union, and the shadow of atomic weapons produce an era of "cold war."**

   How did the Soviet Union's actions after World War I fuel America's fear of communism? Was this fear well-founded?

2. **Growing demands for racial equality produce new leadership and new government policies.**

   How did the Supreme Court's decision in *Brown* v. *Board of Education* change the way in which civil rights issues were confronted?

3. **Technological advances transform American ways of living, thinking, and doing during the Truman and Eisenhower years.**

   How did technological advances realized between 1945 and 1960 change American life?

Events in American History

Events in World History

| 1935 | 1940 | 1945 | 1950 |

1947 The Truman Doctrine—granting military aid to governments opposed to communism—is introduced.

1946 George Kennan warns that the Soviets must be contained to prevent a third world war.

1945 The United Nations is formed, with its headquarters in New York City.

1948 The United States air-lifts food to West Berlin, following the Soviet blockade.

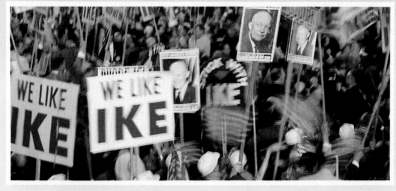

1952 General Eisenhower is elected President of the United States.

1954 The Supreme Court declares "separate but equal" doctrine unconstitutional in *Brown v. Board of Education*.

1955 Martin Luther King, Jr., leads Montgomery, Alabama bus boycott.

1957 Congress passes first civil rights legislation since Reconstruction.

1970 95% of American homes have at least one television set.

1953 McCarthy launches his campaign to rid the country of suspected communists.

1960 More Americans live in suburbs than in cities as a result of the automobile.

1955   **1960**   **1965**   **1970**

1950

1955 The countries of eastern Europe form the Warsaw Pact as a NATO equivalent.

1953 Nikita Khrushchev replaces Stalin as leader of the Soviet Union.

UNIT 11

Turbulent times
1961–1974

"Let the word go forth from this time and place, to friend and foe alike, that the torch has been passed to a new generation of Americans, born in this century, tempered by war, disciplined by a hard and bitter peace, proud of our ancient heritage. . . ."

So John F. Kennedy introduced his Presidency, and so began a turbulent era for the United States. During the following thirteen years one President would be assassinated. Another would decline to run again because of opposition to his foreign policy. And a third, facing impeachment, would resign. During these years, which had begun with so much hope, Americans would be distressed and divided by the actions of their government and their Presidents.

The United States not only survived. The Republic drew new strength by discovering that the people could control their government. They would not wage war without understanding the reasons. They could even replace their President. Never before had Americans seen so clearly how the Constitution had given power to the people.

THEMES IN AMERICAN HISTORY

- John F. Kennedy's 1000 days in office bring optimism to the nation.

- Lyndon Johnson's strong leadership expands opportunities for all Americans while deeply dividing the country over the war in Vietnam.

THEMES
- The Watergate scandal tests the nation's constitutional system of government and leads to President Nixon's resignation.

"Blues" by Adolph Gottlieb seethes with energy contained and released. It foreshadows the turbulence of the new era.

National Museum of American Art, Smithsonian Institution, Gift of the Woodward Foundation

CHAPTER 31

Years of hope and promise

The White House took on a new tone when John F. Kennedy, his beautiful wife, Jacqueline, and their vigorous little children moved in. To many people the Kennedys, with their youth, good looks, charm, and culture, created in Washington something like a fairy tale with all its magic. Camelot, they called it, after King Arthur's palace and the idyllic happiness of the time. This Camelot was to last only a brief 1000 days. Then Americans would awaken again to the real, hard world.

1. John F. Kennedy wins

The 1960 campaign would be the first fought mainly on television. Both candidates were carefully "packaged" for sale to the American public. For the first time, all who wished to watch could see them face each other on TV in "great debates."

Nominating the candidates. Before the national convention there were two serious Republican contenders. The energetic Nelson A. Rockefeller, who had been elected governor of New York in 1958, represented the liberal wing. But in December 1959, finding that the party leaders would not support him, he withdrew from the race. When the Republicans met in Chicago in July 1960, the road was cleared for Vice-President Richard M. Nixon of California. He was nominated for President. Then Henry Cabot Lodge, Jr., a former senator from Massachusetts and now ambassador to the UN, was chosen for second place because of his experience in foreign affairs.

The Democrats faced a heated contest. The main candidates were all senators—John F. Kennedy of Massachusetts, Hubert H. Humphrey of Minnesota, Lyndon B. Johnson of Texas, and Stuart Symington of Missouri. Adlai Stevenson, although not active in the race, waited in the wings hoping that the nod would come his way once more. The most important early fight was between Humphrey and Kennedy. Hubert Humphrey hoped to rally all the old Roosevelt and Truman liberals. The 42-year-old Kennedy was a proven vote-getter and had a conservative record in the House and Senate. His chief handicap was that he was a Roman Catholic. Many party leaders wondered whether a Catholic could be elected President.

The first test of this question came in the primary in West Virginia, where the voters were 95 percent Protestant. The Democrats there would choose whether their delegates to the Democratic convention would support Kennedy or Humphrey. Kennedy won a smashing victory. This knocked Humphrey out of the race and did much to quiet the religious issue. Then Kennedy went on to other victories. When the delegates gathered at the convention in Los Angeles, a last-minute push by

John Kennedy's performance on television in the "great debates" swung many voters to his side.

Lyndon Johnson failed, and Kennedy was nominated on the first ballot.

Kennedy, wanting to make peace with his strong rival and to unify the party, chose Johnson for his running mate. The powerful majority leader of the Senate surprised everyone by accepting. Since LBJ came from Texas, he would help "balance" the ticket and attract votes in the South and Southwest.

The "great debates."   Kennedy argued that, under the Republicans, the nation was stagnating and not moving ahead. During the 1950s, he said, the Gross National Product (the total of all the goods and services produced) had not been growing as it should. He warned of a recession. According to him, the government had neglected all those who needed special help—the young and old, the poor and minorities. Our cities were plagued by slums. Our schools were not doing their job. The general in the White House, he said, had not improved our defense. The nation was behind Soviet Russia in nuclear missiles, and our other arms could not deal with the small "brushfire wars." His slogan was, "Let's get the country moving again." He pointed the way toward a "New Frontier." "Mr. Nixon says, 'We never had it so good.' I say we can do better."

The two candidates appeared together on television in a series of four one-hour programs. People called these the "great debates." But they were not like the old-fashioned Lincoln-Douglas debates a century earlier. In those debates one man spoke for an hour, his opponent replied for an hour and a half. Then the first speaker had another half hour to reply. Now the candidates would only speak for 8 minutes in the first and last debates. All the rest of the time reporters would ask them questions. Each candidate had only 2 1/2 minutes to give his answer.

These "great debates" reached the largest audience that had ever watched a political discussion. Seventy million citizens saw each program. In earlier times the only people who could hear a candidate were those he could reach with his own voice—outdoors or in a meeting hall. Now a whole nation could see and hear both candidates at once. Kennedy seemed to gain more from the debates than Nixon. Though he was less well known, now his charm, poise, and good looks came into everybody's home. His adept handling of questions undercut criticism of his youth and inexperience.

The United States had become a television democracy. And there were new dangers. The man who showed up best on TV was bound to be the best "performer." He could give the cleverest response in 2 1/2 minutes to questions that he had just heard—and look the best doing it. But was that a good test for a President?

The election of 1960 was a cliffhanger. The final count showed the narrowest popular edge (3/10th of 1 percent of all votes cast) since 1880. Alaska had entered the Union in January 1959 and Hawaii followed in August, so there were now 50 states. In the electoral college, Kennedy carried, sometimes by razor-thin margins, enough states to give him 303 votes to Nixon's 219.

There were enough disputed ballots in key states so that Nixon might have challenged the result. But like most other losers of close presidential races, Nixon decided for the good of the nation not to contest the numbers.

John F. Kennedy. Kennedy was the youngest man ever *elected* President, although not the youngest ever to hold the office. That distinction belonged to Theodore Roosevelt. Kennedy, who had been born in Brookline, Massachusetts, on May 29, 1917, was still only 43 when he took office. He came from a large Irish Catholic family. His grandfathers on both sides had been leaders in Democratic politics in Boston. His father, Joseph P. Kennedy, made a fortune in business and finance, and supported FDR for election. FDR appointed him to the Securities and Exchange Commission and then sent him as ambassador to Great Britain. The young Jack Kennedy inherited a love of politics and of the Democratic party.

The year when Jack graduated from Harvard, 1940, was a time of crisis for the free world. The young Kennedy felt the crisis. He revised his student thesis and made it into a book called *Why England Slept.* He told how English statesmen had appeased the Nazis and let them become the menace to the peace of Europe. Then during World War II Jack Kennedy served as a naval officer for four years and won Navy and Marine Corps medals for heroism. He had risked his life to rescue the crew of his PT boat when it was cut in two by a Japanese destroyer. After the war no one was surprised to see another Kennedy enter Massachusetts politics. Of course he was a Democrat. He was elected to the

United States House of Representatives in 1946 and then was elected to the Senate in 1952 and 1958. But Jack Kennedy did not leave an impressive record as a lawmaker.

Like FDR he turned bad luck into an opportunity. He had injured his back in college playing football, and the crash of his PT boat made it worse. After a back operation in 1954 he could not leave his bed for six months. During his slow and painful recovery he wrote another book, *Profiles in Courage.* This story of brave choices by American statesmen won the Pulitzer Prize for biography in 1957.

While Kennedy was writing his book about courage, the Senate was deciding whether to censure Senator Joseph R. McCarthy for his reckless attacks on government servants. Kennedy now kept silent. He did not cast his vote on the McCarthy condemnation because he was recovering from his operation. And he never revealed how he might have voted had he been present on the Senate floor. His critics wondered whether he really understood the meaning of courage.

When Kennedy became President, he brought to the White House youth, vigor, broad culture, and a quick mind. His ability as a speed reader became a legend. He loved to sail, and people were pleased to see that their President was energetic enough to enjoy touch football.

But before he became President, Jack Kennedy had run nothing larger than his Senate office. The nation had not shown great enthusiasm for him. He had won election by the smallest of margins. Could this attractive but inexperienced young man really lead the country to a "New Frontier"?

The inaugural address. On January 20, 1961, a bright sunny day in snow-covered Washington, John F. Kennedy was inaugurated. After the New England poet Robert Frost recited a poem, JFK took the oath of office. His inaugural address was short and eloquent. Since his slim victory might make it difficult for him to get major bills through Congress, Kennedy spoke chiefly on foreign affairs. The first President born in this century, he announced that a "new generation of Americans" had taken control. "Defending freedom in its hour of maximum danger," his generation, too, would hold the line against communism. "Let every nation know, whether it wishes us well or ill, that we shall pay any price, bear any burden, meet any hardship, support any friend, oppose any foe to assure the survival and success of liberty." He called on his fellow citizens to "ask not what your country can do for you—ask what you can do for your country."

Many Americans were ready for Kennedy's call after the quiet, steady General Eisenhower. But some remembered the ringing, world-resounding words of Woodrow Wilson. And some feared that Kennedy's brave words, too, might lead us into a world conflict.

The new administration. Kennedy brought into office a whole new team. The President himself clearly planned to play a leading role in foreign affairs. For his Secretary of State he appointed a calm, quiet Georgian, Dean Rusk, who was president of the Rockefeller Foundation. For Secretary of Defense he chose Robert S. McNamara, who was only a year older than Kennedy. As president of the Ford Motor Company, McNamara had earned a national reputation for finding new ways of running a vast organization. McNamara's slick hair showed his concern for neatness and precise control. Kennedy asked C. Douglas Dillon, a Republican and a wealthy New York investment banker, to become Secretary of the Treasury. This appointment, the new President hoped, would quiet fears that he might be "unsound" in economic matters.

Family feeling was strong among the Kennedys. Now President Jack appointed his brother Robert as Attorney General. Robert Kennedy had only served a brief stint as a lawyer in the Justice Department and then as counsel for Senator Joe McCarthy, before the senator was condemned, and for other congressional committees. He had managed his brother's campaign with skill and ruthlessness. "I see nothing wrong," JFK joked, "with giving Bobby some legal experience before he goes out to practice law." Robert Kennedy remained

John and Jacqueline Kennedy brought youth and glamor to the White House. Beside them at the Inaugural Ball are John's parents, Joseph and Rose Kennedy, and Lyndon and Lady Bird Johnson.

his brother's closest adviser and turned out to be a forceful Attorney General.

SECTION 1 REVIEW

1. Describe the Kennedy-Nixon television debates. What were the dangers in such debates?

2. What qualifications did Kennedy have for the presidency?

3. **Checking Consistency.** How did Kennedy's inaugural address deal with issues of which he had been critical during the "great debates"?

2. Learning hard lessons

The new Kennedy team came to power believing that they could solve all problems. They would soon discover that both at home and abroad some issues were too complex for their hopeful, youthful energies. The first blows to their self-confidence came in foreign affairs.

Trouble in Laos. One of the nations created from French Indochina was Laos. A pro-Western faction was put into power there with the secret help of the CIA. The Communists, and those who wished to remain neutral between Russia and the United States, tried to overturn this regime. "You might have to go in there and fight it out," Ike told JFK. On March 23, 1961, Kennedy publicly warned that the United States would use armed force to prevent a Communist takeover of Laos.

Kennedy was urged by some of his advisers to send in American troops. But to avoid war he agreed to compromise. The British helped persuade the Soviets to come to a conference to set up a new government that would be neutral.

A truce was then arranged. Finally, in June 1962, the three warring factions in Laos came together. They formed a "coalition" government—in which each had a part. Then at Geneva in July, the United States, Russia, Great Britain, and eleven other countries signed a treaty promising to keep the country neutral. Without the use of American

At a March 1961 conference President Kennedy makes a point about the Laotian situation.

Wide World Photos

forces, it did prevent—or at least postpone—a Communist takeover. Two years later, to nobody's surprise, the Communist faction (the "Pathet Lao") backed out of the coalition. Laos was still a battleground.

The Bay of Pigs. President Kennedy had good reason to be cautious in Laos. For meanwhile close to home—only 90 miles off the Florida coast—the United States suffered a shocking setback. In September 1960 President Eisenhower had approved a plan proposed by Allen Dulles (brother of Secretary of State Dulles), director of the CIA. The United States would supply money and arms in Guatemala for a force of anti-Castro Cubans. This force was trained and ready to go by April 1961. Kennedy and his advisers expected that when the small invasion force landed, the Cuban people would seize the chance to overthrow Castro. So the President gave the signal for the invasion to proceed.

Some 1500 Cuban refugee fighters landed at the Bay of Pigs (Bahía de Cochinos) on the south coast of Cuba on April 17. They were not greeted by the popular uprising they expected. Instead, within hours their attack had bogged down, and they were in trouble. On April 18 Khrushchev threatened that the Soviet Union would go to Cuba's assistance if the United States did not "call a halt to the aggression against the Republic of Cuba." Soon the fighting was over, and 1200 of the anti-Castro troops were captured. In December 1962 after American companies and individuals paid Castro a ransom of $50 million in food and drugs and $3 million in cash, the unlucky refugee troops were freed.

Conference at Vienna. The Bay of Pigs disaster shook President Kennedy and his advisers. It dismayed our European allies and made further problems with the Soviets. At the peace settlement in Potsdam after World War II, the democracies had made the mistake of dividing the great capital city of Berlin and allowing the Soviets to surround it with their troops. Now once again Khrushchev called for the evacuation of West Berlin before the end of 1961 by France, Britain, and the United States and the creation there of a "free city."

Prosperous West Berlin was an outpost of democracy and free enterprise in the very heart of Communist East Germany. It was a living adver-tisement for freedom, which Russia and the Communist dictators of East Germany feared. The East German leaders would not allow their people to escape to the free world. Still some of their desperate and courageous citizens risked their lives to slip through to West Berlin. The democratic powers were supplying West Berlin by highways controlled by the Communists. Khrushchev again threatened to sign a peace treaty with East Germany. This would allow the East German Communists to starve West Berlin by cutting off all the food that came by land.

At the same time, the unpredictable Khrushchev also made some friendly gestures. He released some American airmen whose RB-47 plane had recently been shot down over Russia. And he told the American ambassador in Moscow that he would like to meet Kennedy. So in June 1961 JFK flew to Vienna, Austria. It was not expected that this would be a full-fledged "summit" meeting, where important treaties would be signed. Instead this was supposed to be merely a chance for discussion.

The talks did not go well. Made even bolder by the Bay of Pigs fiasco, Khrushchev stormed and threatened. But Kennedy was not adept at handling the Russian leader. Still, he did get a Soviet promise to work for peace in Laos, and he stood fast on Berlin. At the end he said to the Soviet premier, "I see it's going to be a very cold winter."

The Berlin wall. In a somber speech to the American people soon after his return, President Kennedy made it clear that, if necessary, the United States would stand and fight for Berlin. Now he increased the draft quotas. He called up reserve and National Guard units. And he asked Congress for $3.2 billion to enlarge our armed forces. At the same time Kennedy made it clear that the United States was ready "to search for peace."

In August 1961 the Russians suddenly sealed off East Berlin from West Berlin, first by erecting a fence and then by building a grim, high wall. No longer could Easterners escape to freedom through West Berlin. Kennedy responded by sending a force of 1500 men to the city as a signal that the United States would act.

The firm refusal of the Western powers to give in led Khrushchev to back down. In October he withdrew his year-end deadline. In 1963 Kennedy encouraged the free world when he went to Berlin

M. Scheler/Black Star

The Brandenburg gate is seen here from the West Berlin side of the wall built by the Soviets. The sign warns: "Attention! You are now leaving West Berlin."

and stated "I am a Berliner." This was an American President declaring that the United States would not allow free people to be strangled.

"Flexible response." During these crises spread across three continents—in Laos, Cuba, and Berlin—President Kennedy was trying to make over American foreign policy. He had been impressed by a speech of Khrushchev's in January 1961 that promised Soviet aid for "wars of national liberation." Khrushchev would use these wars by people to throw off the yoke of colonial rule as a way to spread communism. Kennedy wanted to oppose this threat. But as McNamara put it, the United States ought to be able to use "a flyswatter where a flyswatter is a proper weapon, instead of using a sledgehammer." The President did not want to choose only between doing nothing or threatening "massive retaliation." He thought we should have armed forces capable of a "flexible response"—based on the size and the danger of the challenges.

The large purpose of our foreign policy would remain the same—to stop the growth of communism. Still, as JFK showed in Laos, when United States interests were not directly threatened, we would not use force against governments that were neutral. Kennedy believed that we should support progressive governments. Removing poverty and injustice would discourage Communist revolutions. He was friendly to the new nations of Africa. Sékou Touré, Guinea's leader, once called him "my only true friend in the outside world."

The Alliance for Progress. Kennedy proposed that we join the nations of Latin America in an Alliance for Progress. Similar to the Marshall Plan for Europe, this promised to Latin American nations $20 billion in economic aid over ten years. In August 1961 an Inter-American Conference in Uruguay accepted the plan. To receive economic aid the Latin American nations would improve their farms, reduce poverty, and promote industry.

666

They promised to invest $80 billion. In fact, few of these reforms were ever undertaken. Wherever possible, they avoided spending their own money. And the Kennedy administration did not insist that they live up to their promises. The United States tended to aid any government that was anti-Communist, that worked with the Alliance, and that had some popular support.

The Alliance made some friends—but it also made enemies. Critics in Latin America saw us using the Alliance to keep dictators in power. They said that the United States was more interested in stopping communism than in promoting freedom.

The Peace Corps. A favorite new program of JFK's—the Peace Corps—was designed to answer those arguments. This would show that the United States wanted to help all the poverty-stricken people in the world.

The plan was to train thousands of young Americans to work in underdeveloped countries. They would have all their expenses paid and receive some "severance pay" at the end of their two-year term. But they would not get a salary. They would be "volunteers"—like volunteers for the army in wartime—but their job would be peace. They would serve as teachers, nurses, doctors, engineers, and carpenters. Wherever they were sent, they would help the needy people raise better crops or build roads and bridges or improve their water supply. The President began the program even before Congress provided funds. By 1965 the project was costing $115 million a year.

Unfortunately, the Peace Corps was not the complete success all hoped it would be. Curing the ills of needy people was not so simple. Every country had its own large problems. To solve these you had to understand its language, its religion, and its history. Intelligent young Americans with high ideals seldom had enough of the knowledge or the skills required. Most of them had never before lived outside the United States. Some were lonely. It was hard to learn the customs of a remote country. Some countries even asked the Americans to leave. Yet many members of the Peace Corps helped people in ways they could not help themselves. And nearly all the volunteers learned more about the world. When it began, the program lifted the nation's spirit and helped bring a new patriotism in peacetime.

SECTION 2 REVIEW

1. Identify or explain: Pathet Lao, Allen Dulles, Potsdam Conference, Berlin Wall, wars of national liberation, Sékou Touré.
2. What problems did Kennedy face in Laos?
3. Explain the purpose and the outcome of the landing at the Bay of Pigs.
4. Why did the Communists want the Western powers to leave Berlin?
5. What was the policy of "flexible response"?
6. **Making Comparisons.** How did the goals of the Alliance for Progress differ from those of the Peace Corps?

3. Facing Communist challenges

Wherever they looked around the world, JFK and his advisers saw tests of America's determination to stand for peace and freedom. Responding to these challenges would call upon all the young President's will and resourcefulness.

The "missile gap." During the election campaign the candidates had disagreed over the nation's power to wage war. Were we trailing the Soviet Union in nuclear missiles? Kennedy declared that we were. Nixon, who knew because of secret information from the U-2 flights, said we were not. But the Vice-President could not reveal how he knew, so the argument continued. Upon entering office JFK found that there was no gap. Anyway, the Kennedy team decided to build more missiles. This was partly to satisfy Congress. And it was partly to have extra strength. Then we could survive a "first-strike" attack by the Soviet Union and still be able to hit back. If we had that strength, perhaps the USSR would never dare launch a surprise attack.

This policy was called "assured destruction" or "*m*utual *a*ssured *d*estruction" (MAD). The aim was to deter the Soviet Union from attacking the United States or any of our allies by having enough nuclear weapons—in silos, airplanes, or submarines—to assure the destruction of the USSR even if they mounted a nuclear attack first. Deterrence through "assured destruction" has been the U.S. defense policy ever since.

With this purpose Congress voted new funds for the ICBMs (*intercontinental ballistic missiles*). Known as Minutemen, they were stored in concrete silos buried deep in the ground.

In addition there was the Polaris SLBM (*submarine-launched ballistic missile*), carried by nuclear submarines. Unlike earlier subs, those driven by atomic power could circle the globe without ever surfacing for fuel, supplies, or air. They carried missiles underwater. The first nuclear-powered sub, the *Nautilus*, had been launched in 1954. Then in July 1960 the first Polaris missile—weighing 14 tons with its deadly nuclear warhead—had been tested. It landed 1150 miles away right on target.

By 1964 the stepped-up Kennedy defense program had provided the United States with 1100 intercontinental bombers, 800 land-based ICBMs, and 250 Polaris missiles under the sea. In every class the Soviets were far outnumbered.

Putting a man on the moon. But we were still behind the Russians in outer space. On April 12, 1961, they had sent up the first man in space. Yuri Gagarin went whirling around the earth in a satellite and made nearly a full orbit—in 89 minutes. The best the United States could do was a flight 115 miles into the sky by Alan B. Shepard on May 5. Some Americans feared that the Russians might use their lead in outer space to launch weapons against the United States. President Kennedy took up the challenge.

Sending a man into outer space was much more risky than exploring the arctic or another continent on earth. Could a human being survive out beyond the earth's atmosphere? Since humans needed oxygen to live and there was none in outer space, they would have to carry their oxygen with them. Could they carry enough? Also the President remembered that when we had first tried to put an object in space the missile had collapsed on the sand. The United States should not risk another fiasco.

Some Americans said that the $40 billion needed to reach the moon might be better spent. But the persuasive Vice-President Lyndon B. Johnson was a space enthusiast. And President Kennedy decided to take the grand risk. After the Russians sent Yuri Gagarin into orbit and after Shepard had made his successful flight, JFK promised that the United States would land a man on the moon before 1970.

This spectacular success would make America the pioneer once more—this time out to another New World. Although Kennedy would not live to see it, his promise would be kept.

Working for disarmament and a test-ban. If the United States led the way to outer space, what would the Russians do? Wouldn't they be tempted to build up their arsenal? President Kennedy still hoped somehow to stop the costly arms race. To halt the testing of nuclear weapons would be a first step. Beginning in the 1950s, people began to learn more about radiation. This was the deadly cancer-causing side effect of testing nuclear weapons.

In November 1958, Russia, Great Britain, and the United States—the only nations that at that time had nuclear bombs—had met in Geneva to discuss the problem. The United States promised that it would do no more testing so long as the Soviets did none. During the next two years the talks dragged on. Meanwhile Khrushchev was pushed by his own scientists and by Chinese criticism that he was "soft" toward the United States. In September 1961 he allowed testing in the atmosphere to begin again. Khrushchev boasted to a Communist party congress that Russia had exploded a 50-megaton bomb. This meant a bomb equal to 50 million tons of TNT, a bomb 2500 times bigger than the one that had killed instantly 75,000 people at Hiroshima!

JFK answered by ordering the United States to begin testing underground. The dangers of radiation there were much less. Then at the United Nations he called for complete disarmament. "Mankind must put an end to war," he told the delegates, "or war will put an end to mankind."

When Kennedy received no reply from Russia, in March 1962 he ordered new tests in the atmosphere. In fact, JFK did not believe these tests were really necessary. But he did not want the Russians to think the United States was weak or afraid.

The Cuban missile crisis. During the summer of 1962, the Soviets stepped up the cold war. They began to move ballistic missiles into nearby Cuba. On October 14, 1962, clear pictures of Soviet missile sites under construction were obtained by one of our U-2 spy planes. How should President Kennedy act against this threat of enemy weapons right on our doorstep? The policy of deterrence seemed to depend on making the Soviet Union

5 TRUCKS UNDER CAMOUFLAGE NETTING   CABLE   THEODOLITE STATION

5 TRUCKS UNDER CAMOUFLAGE NETT

MISSILE SHELTER TENTS

This sharp photograph from a high-flying U-2 shows one of the medium-range missile sites under construction by the Soviets in Cuba. It was released by the Defense Department on October 28, 1962, the same day that Khrushchev announced that the missile sites would be dismantled.

really believe the United States would fight if it was pushed too far.

The Joint Chiefs of Staff recommended an invasion to seize the missiles and bring down Castro. At the very least, they wanted a general air strike—at targets all over the island. Kennedy wisely rejected this advice. Still, he did risk a showdown. In a dramatic television address on Monday, October 22, he denounced this "secret, swift, and extraordinary build-up of Communist missiles." He stated that he had ordered the Navy to begin "a strict quarantine [blockade] on all offensive military equipment under shipment to Cuba."

War now seemed to hang in the balance. Would the Soviet ships that were on their way to Cuba turn back? What would Khrushchev do? Of course, the Soviets denied there were any missiles on the island. Then at an emergency meeting of the

UN Security Council, our Ambassador Adlai Stevenson proved with photographs that the missiles were there. On Wednesday, five Soviet ships stopped short of the quarantine zone. On Friday, the Russians began to signal that maybe the question could be negotiated. Then Kennedy received two letters from Khrushchev. He decided, on the advice of his brother Robert, to answer the one that held out some hope of peace.

On Sunday Khrushchev broadcast that he had ordered the missiles to be dismantled and removed from Cuba in return for an American pledge not to invade the island. "We should like to continue the exchange of views," he added, "on the prohibition of atomic and thermonuclear weapons, general disarmament, and other problems relating to the relaxation of international tension." To the relief of the world, the superpowers had drawn back from the brink of nuclear war.

JFK consulted Ike a number of times during his Presidency. This photograph was made after the Bay of Pigs fiasco in 1961.

The weakening alliances. Still, the world could see that the war of words could easily become a war of missiles. The allies of the United States in NATO feared someone's bad guess or a miscalculation. The proud president of France, Charles de Gaulle, had disliked following the lead of the United States. Now, he said, the missile crisis showed how a single member of the NATO alliance could drag the other countries into war against their will.

To draw all the NATO nations closer together, President Kennedy had proposed his *Grand Design* for Western Europe in 1962 before the missile crisis. The United States would join the European Common Market in lowering tariffs. Congress approved this plan by the Trade Expansion Act of 1962. The President was permitted to reduce tariffs 50 percent and remove the tariffs entirely on articles heavily traded by the United States and Western Europe. But Congress said Kennedy could not remove the tariffs entirely unless Great Britain was admitted to the Common Market.

De Gaulle said that Kennedy's Grand Design was simply a plan for control of Western Europe by Great Britain and the United States. In January 1963 France vetoed Britain's application to join the Common Market. De Gaulle hoped to create a new power bloc—a Third Force—led by France, which was building its own nuclear weapons. In 1966 de Gaulle took France out of NATO and ordered American forces to leave his country. In 1967 NATO headquarters was moved from Paris to Brussels, Belgium.

The Communist alliance had its own problems. Satellites like Poland and Romania struggled to show at least a little independence. The great split in the Communist world was between China and the Soviet Union. In 1960, after a series of quarrels, the Russians withdrew their technical experts from Communist China. Then when China attacked India in a border dispute in 1962, the Soviets supported India. After Khrushchev's retreat in the Cuban missile crisis, Mao's Chinese Communists sneered at the Soviets. They said that the USSR was only a "paper tiger." And the Soviet leaders answered that war would not turn the world to communism.

A test-ban treaty. Once again in June 1963 President Kennedy called for an end to the arms race. Nearly fifty years earlier, Woodrow Wilson had wanted "to make the world safe for democracy." Now Kennedy expressed a more modest hope. "If we cannot end now all our differences, at least we can help make the world safe for diversity." He revived the test-ban talks. In July, Great Britain, the United States, and the Soviet Union agreed to outlaw nuclear tests in the atmosphere, in outer space, and underwater. The treaty did not touch the vast arsenal of nuclear weapons still held by the Big Three. And it allowed underground testing to continue. The treaty was signed and approved by the Senate 80 to 19 on September 4, 1963.

More than 100 nations agreed to the test-ban treaty. No one was much surprised when the French, who had recently exploded their own atomic bomb, and the Communist Chinese, who soon would have a bomb of their own, refused to sign.

Problems in Vietnam. His success with the missile crisis and the test-ban treaty encouraged JFK to think that bold diplomacy might save the world from atomic war. The civil war in South Vietnam proved a tougher problem. The Geneva peace conference of 1954 had decided that elections to unify all Vietnam would be held by July 1956. But Ngo Dinh Diem, who was now leading South Vietnam, refused to go along. He was sure that he would lose to the Communist North. The United States agreed with Diem. Neither South Vietnam nor the United States had signed the Geneva accords.

After South Vietnam refused to take part in elections, guerrilla warfare against Diem's government broke out. The war was led by former members of the Communist Viet Minh. Enormous amounts of money and supplies were already pouring into the country from the United States. Now we began to send in "advisers" to train the South Vietnamese army. In 1960, opponents to Diem—including Communists and others—created the National Liberation Front (NLF). Their goal was to overthrow Diem and reunify the country. Diem named them the "Viet Cong," meaning Vietnamese Communists.

President Kennedy continued the support of Diem begun by Eisenhower. As NLF victories increased, he resisted advice from Vice-President Johnson and others to send in many more troops. Still, the number of American "advisers" slowly grew.

These advisers urged Diem to carry out reforms to strengthen his support in the country. Instead of making reforms, Diem brutally put down all opposition. When Buddhists staged demonstrations against him, his troops opened fire on them. Several Buddhist monks—in desperate protest—burned themselves to death in public. Kennedy now began to see that outsiders could not solve the problems of the South Vietnamese. "It is their war," he declared. "They are the only ones who have to win it or lose it."

At that time the American military advisers in South Vietnam came to 16,000. The United States military leaders wanted to send more. On November 2, 1963, Diem was overthrown, with American knowledge and approval, by a military junta. Diem was murdered. The military outlook for the anti-Communists became worse and worse. But President Kennedy would not live to make the next move.

SECTION 3 REVIEW

1. Identify or explain: missile gap, ICBM, Polaris missile, *Nautilus,* Yuri Gagarin, Alan B. Shepard, Charles de Gaulle, Trade Expansion Act of 1962, Ngo Dinh Diem, NLF, Viet Cong.

2. How and why did the Kennedy administration step up the defense program?

3. How did Kennedy challenge the Russians in the space race?

4. How were problems concerning the testing of nuclear weapons resolved in 1963?

5. How did the Cuban missile crisis turn out?

6. What splits appeared in the Communist bloc?

7. How did Kennedy respond to the problem in Vietnam?

8. **Expressing Problems Clearly.**   How did France disrupt efforts to strengthen NATO?

4. A New Frontier

President Kennedy found that domestic affairs were just as tricky as foreign affairs. Since he had been elected by only a hair's breadth, he had no clear "mandate" for any policy. In Congress he faced an unfriendly coalition of Republicans and conservative southern Democrats.

The domestic program that JFK outlined in 1961 was mostly an extension of the New Deal. He aimed to stop the business recession, to spur the nation's growth rate, and to "get the country moving again." There were few bold new proposals in what Kennedy called the "New Frontier."

Congress refuses to act. The hardest blow was when Congress refused to pass Kennedy's ambitious bill for federal aid to education. He hoped to help make education more equal in the different states. Of the $5.6 billion he requested, the states would receive $2.3 billion for public school construction and teachers' salaries. The rest would go to needy college students. The bill passed the Senate easily enough. Then Roman Catholic leaders insisted that it be amended to provide aid to parochial schools. Though President Kennedy was himself a Catholic, he would not yield. Enough Roman Catholic Democrats joined the Republicans to defeat the bill in the House of Representatives. A similar bill failed again in 1962.

Kennedy offered an equally ambitious plan to use the Social Security system to provide medical care for the aged. But his proposal did not receive serious consideration from Congress. The powerful American Medical Association called it "socialized medicine." JFK did not push the measure, since he knew he could not win.

Some successes. All was not disappointment and defeat. The Housing Act of 1961 provided $4.9 billion for urban renewal. The minimum wage went up from $1 to $1.25 an hour. In order to get the increase, JFK agreed to exclude 700,000 workers in laundries and small intra-state businesses. An Area Redevelopment Act offered $300 million to create new industries and retrain workers in "distressed areas" suffering from unemployment. Federal insurance under Social Security (p. 530) was extended to more of the unemployed, and federal funds were provided.

Congress also approved the Twenty-fourth Amendment to outlaw the poll tax. This tax was still being used in five southern states to discourage poor people—chiefly blacks—from voting. This amendment became part of the Constitution in January 1964.

Controlling the economy. These measures, together with the large sums spent for defense and for space programs, helped end the recession that had started in 1960. But unemployment remained high. Kennedy also worried about inflation caused by rising government spending.

To control inflation, JFK proposed "wage-price guideposts." These tied any increase in wages to an increase in output. If a firm making 1000 items for $10,000 could boost output to 1100 for the same $10,000 cost, the productivity increase would be 10 percent. Wages could then rise by that amount while the company could still sell the items to its customers for the same price. There would be no price inflation.

A conflict with the steelmakers. At the large United States Steel company, the employers and the workers signed a new labor contract on March 31, 1962. To avoid inflation, the union accepted a modest wage increase well within the President's guidelines. The workers took it for granted that the company would not raise prices. Then on April 10, the president of United States Steel announced a large increase in the price of steel. Other steel companies followed.

Since steel was used in so many products, the rise in its price would push other prices up. An enraged President Kennedy denounced the company and demanded that they roll back their prices. They soon gave in. The whole business community, which had been unsure of the President's attitude toward business from the start, was shaken by his anger. In May 1962, partly as a result, the stock market suffered its sharpest decline since the Great Crash of 1929.

As it turned out, the President's quarrel with business was not deep or lasting. His first friendly gesture was a Revenue Act in September 1962. It granted $1 billion a year in special investment tax credits for business firms making new outlays for machines and equipment. He did not object when some steel companies announced price increases early in 1963. Wall Street was encouraged, and prosperity seemed on its way.

Getting the economy moving. President Kennedy still thought that the gross national product was not growing fast enough. Russia's GNP was growing more rapidly, and he feared that in time we might lose our lead.

From the start of Kennedy's term, his Council of Economic Advisers had urged a big cut in taxes. The government was already running into debt, spending more on arms and services than it brought in through taxes. Still they argued that cutting taxes would be a good idea. If people had to spend less on their taxes, they would have more to spend on other things. Business would prosper, and in the long run more taxes would come in to help balance the budget. JFK did not manage to convince Congress to make the cut.

The problem of poverty. The economy was growing during most of the postwar years. Yet certain areas of poverty seemed never to be touched by private business or government programs. There had always been some poverty in the United States. But as the nation became ever richer, some people hoped that ours might be the first country where nobody was poor.

In his popular book, the author Michael Harrington called the nation's poor *The Other America* (1962). These were "the unskilled workers, the migrant farm workers, the aged, the minorities, and all the others who live in the economic underworld of American life." Even in the United States, he wrote, there were millions "maimed in body and spirit, existing at levels beneath those necessary for human decency. If these people are not starving, they are hungry. . . . They are without adequate housing and education and medical care." President Kennedy began to worry as much about these people as about the nation's business. He began to plan a war on poverty.

The problem of civil rights. "Civil rights" described the rights of all Americans to vote and to have a fair trial. It also meant the right to have an equal chance at any job they could handle and to live and play wherever they could afford. President Kennedy believed that the federal government should pass laws to guarantee these rights to all Americans everywhere in the country.

During the election campaign of 1960, he had criticized Eisenhower for not doing enough. Now he himself moved only slowly. He was afraid that if he demanded these reforms, he would lose the support of southern members of Congress for his "New Frontier" bills. Finally, in 1962, he signed his name to an order to desegregate public housing projects supported with federal funds.

Just as Ike had done, he appointed a Committee on Equal Employment Opportunity. It was to see that companies that worked for the government gave everybody an equal opportunity. He directed his brother Robert at the Department of Justice to support the efforts of blacks to vote in the Deep South.

JFK encouraged blacks by his appointments. He named Carl Rowan ambassador to Finland and Andrew Hacker as associate press secretary. He appointed a number of blacks as United States district judges and Thurgood Marshall as judge of a United States Court of Appeals. He tried to set up a Cabinet Department of Urban Affairs and put Robert Weaver at its head. But conservative Democrats and Republicans defeated the bill. On the other hand, to keep on the right side of southern Democrats, he named several segregationist judges to federal district courts.

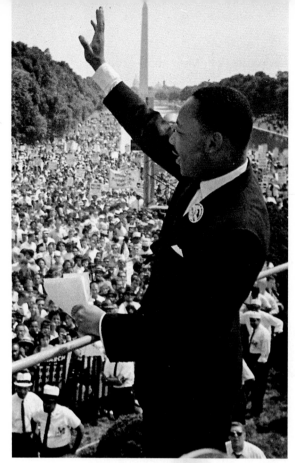

Thousands gathered at the Lincoln Memorial to listen to Martin Luther King, Jr., during the 1963 March on Washington.

The black revolt. The pressures to do more were building rapidly. In 1961 "freedom riders," blacks and whites from North and South, took buses south to protest segregation of the races in bus stations. They were greeted by riots and beatings. Their buses were burned. On May 29, 1961, Attorney General Robert Kennedy called on the Interstate Commerce Commission to ban segregation in interstate bus terminals. That was finally done in September.

In the fall of 1962, a black Air Force veteran, James Meredith, tried to enroll in the all-white University of Mississippi. A court ordered that he be admitted. Still, Governor Ross Barnett personally prevented him from registering. When Meredith finally did enroll, riots followed that caused two deaths and injuries to hundreds. President Kennedy ordered 5000 federal troops to the scene to restore quiet. Meredith remained at the

University of Mississippi—protected by federal troops.

All this violence to prevent one young black man from going to college! It was seen by millions on TV across the country. Now the civil rights struggle came into everybody's living room. Television was bringing the nation together. Civil rights was the whole nation's problem.

The pressure for an end to segregation—in schools, colleges, hotels, restaurants, employment, and all American life—grew enormously in 1963. Sit-ins and demonstrations forced the desegregation of lunch counters, hotels, and theaters in 300 cities in the South. Slowly the hated signs telling people what could be used by "white" and what by "colored" were coming down.

In April 1963 Martin Luther King, Jr., and his Southern Christian Leadership Conference (SCLC) began a drive to end segregation in Birmingham, Alabama. There segregation was enforced by local laws. King insisted that the struggle should be peaceful. He and his demonstrators were opposed by Chief "Bull" Connor's police with electric cattle prods, snarling dogs, and fire hoses. Birmingham exploded with rioting and fire bombing. And all this, too, was seen on television.

In June Governor George Wallace prevented two blacks from enrolling in the University of Alabama. He promised segregation in the state of Alabama "today, tomorrow, and forever." But strong pressure from JFK finally made Wallace give in, and he allowed the blacks to register.

A new civil rights law. By now, one hundred years after the Emancipation Proclamation, it was clear that if blacks were to be treated equally with whites, new federal laws were needed. On June 11, 1963, Kennedy addressed the nation on television. "Are we," he asked, "to say to the world and, much more importantly, to each other that this is a land of the free except for Negroes; that we have no second-class citizens except Negroes; that we have no class or caste system, no ghettos, no master race except with respect to Negroes?" Later that same night Medgar Evers, head of the Mississippi NAACP, was murdered outside his home.

A week later Kennedy sent a new civil rights bill to Congress. It was not nearly as strong as many people wanted. Still, it went far beyond any civil rights law ever requested before.

The march on Washington. To put pressure on Congress to pass Kennedy's bill, supporters staged a mammoth march on Washington. It was organized by Bayard Rustin, who had helped A. Philip Randolph organize an earlier march on Washington, back in 1941. Kennedy tried to discourage the march because he feared a backlash in Congress. But on August 28, 1963, there was one of the largest demonstrations in American history. More than 200,000 black and white "Freedom Marchers" gathered in Washington before the Lincoln Memorial. The eloquent Reverend Martin Luther King, Jr., stirred the audience—and the nation watching on television—with his dream of a United States where all people are equal. A place "where all of God's children, black men and white men, Jews and Gentiles, Protestants and Catholics, will be able to join hands and sing in the words of the old Negro spiritual, 'Free at last! free at last! thank God almighty, we are free at last!'" And, led by Mahalia Jackson, they all sang the old Baptist hymn that had become the anthem of the civil rights movement, "We Shall Overcome."

But the nation was large, and prejudice had deep roots in history. In September Americans received another lesson of how far away lay the fulfillment of the Reverend King's dream. A bomb exploded at a Birmingham church, and four little black girls were killed.

SECTION 4 REVIEW

1. Identify or explain: Housing Act of 1961, Area Redevelopment Act, 24th Amendment, "wage-price guideposts," investment tax credits, Thurgood Marshall, "freedom riders," James Meredith, George Wallace, Medgar Evers.

2. What major Kennedy proposals did the House of Representatives and the Senate reject? What were his successes?

3. How did President Kennedy propose to hasten economic growth? How did both houses of Congress respond?

4. List successes and failures in JFK's civil rights record.

5. **Recognizing Cause and Effect.** What was the effect of television on the American civil rights movement?

5. The tragic end

In November 1963 President Kennedy took time out to mend his political fences. He thought of the presidential election coming in 1964. And he wanted to arouse support for himself and "New Frontier" bills that still had not been passed. Like many Presidents before him, he went out on the road. He traveled to the two southern states he hoped to carry in 1964, to Florida and then to Texas. The crowds were large and enthusiastic.

Death in Dallas. JFK had been warned that there was bitter feeling against him in Dallas. Only a month before, an angry crowd had pushed and spat upon Adlai Stevenson when he went there to speak on United Nations day. Yet if the President visited Texas, he could not skip the state's second largest city. So he scheduled a three-hour visit for November 22, 1963.

The presidential party included Jacqueline Kennedy, Vice-President and Mrs. Lyndon B. Johnson, and Governor and Mrs. John B. Connally of Texas. Their motorcade passed through cheering crowds on its way to the Trade Mart, where the President was to deliver a luncheon address. As the President's car passed through Dealey Plaza, rifle shots were heard. One bullet ripped through Kennedy's neck and another through his brain. Governor Connally was wounded. The President was dead by the time his car reached a hospital. The dream of Camelot had ended in nightmare.

Lee Harvey Oswald, a solitary, neurotic young man, was seized for the crime. Only two days later the nation watching television saw Oswald, escorted by police, being taken to the Dallas county jail. Before the nation's eyes Oswald was gunned down by a nightclub owner named Jack Ruby.

The first reaction to all of this was disbelief. Had the youngest elected President really been murdered at the height of his powers? America was stunned and could find no ready explanation. Who had killed the President, and why? One of the great tragedies of American history would also remain one of the mysteries.

The Warren Commission. A commission headed by Chief Justice Earl Warren would spend nine months trying to get to the bottom of the matter. They called scores of witnesses, took the advice of ballistic experts, and interviewed hundreds. They concluded that Lee Harvey Oswald had acted alone and so had Jack Ruby. Still the commission failed to pursue many leads and left many questions unanswered.

In 1979 a committee of the House of Representatives reported the results of their own year-long study. They used a new kind of sound analysis to tell how many shots had been fired and from where. And they concluded that more than one rifle had been fired at JFK. They also suggested that when he killed Oswald, Ruby might have been acting for others. But who held the second rifle, if there was one, and why had Oswald and Ruby fired their deadly shots? These questions were never fully answered.

The people's reaction. The shocked American people watched the tragedy played again and again on television. On their screens, in their living rooms, they mourned at the President's funeral.

John F. Kennedy was the fourth President in 100 years to die at the hands of an assassin. Was it no longer safe for an American President to move among the people?

Even JFK's political opponents were overwhelmed by the tragedy. Everyone was reminded how unpredictable was history. People who had not voted for JFK still wept at the wasted talents of a brilliant leader. After his death, his friends naturally inflated what he had accomplished in his 1000 days. "Robbed of his years," one journalist wrote, "he is being rewarded and honored in death as he never was in life. Deprived of the place he sought in history, he has been given . . . a place in legend."

The Kennedy years: An appraisal. JFK's months in office are less important for the laws that were passed than for a new uplifting spirit. The young President was still growing and learning his job. No one could say whether he would have done better in a second term. There was always the chance. His untimely death left him a President noted more for his promise than for his achievement.

In foreign affairs, he led the cold war. He believed that the United States had to remain stronger than the Russians. He was also worried that we should not even seem to be weak. But the force of events, the power of the Russians, and the creeping spread of communism gradually changed his hopes. Whether we liked it or not, Kennedy concluded, we must accept a world that was not all free. "No one can doubt," he said, "that the wave of the future is not the conquest of the world by a single dogmatic creed but the liberation of the diverse energies of free nations and free men."

JFK always disliked "experts." He felt that they had led him into the Bay of Pigs disaster. Yet when he moved away from "massive retaliation" to "flexible response," he created new experts. The RAND (Research *and* Development) Corporation was set up by the Air Force to plan for air and space needs. And there were other new "think tanks." More than ever before, universities were drawn into research for the Defense Department and the CIA.

What remained from John F. Kennedy's brief Presidency was a lively and cheerful, but not substantial, inheritance. Humor, charm, vigor, and excitement were his trademarks. After his administration it was hard for people anywhere to think that the United States was a tired old nation. And the New World nation would not lack new young leaders.

SECTION 5 REVIEW

1. Identify or explain: John Connally, Lee Harvey Oswald, Jack Ruby, Warren Commission.

2. **Predicting Consequences.** How might society be different had JFK not been assassinated?

As millions watched on television, the funeral cortege of John F. Kennedy moved grimly towards Arlington Cemetery. The riderless horse symbolized the loss of a leader.

Dan McCoy/Black Star

FOCUSING ON IDEAS

1. What were some of the successes and failures of the Peace Corps?

2. What factors contributed to the nomination and election of John Kennedy in 1960?

3. How did Kennedy attempt to stimulate the economy while at the same time controlling inflation?

4. What were Kennedy's most significant achievements in foreign affairs? In domestic affairs?

TAKING A CRITICAL LOOK

1. **Testing Conclusions.** Evaluate the following opinion: "It is critically important to elect a President who has great personal charm and the ability to attract supporters." What information in the chapter supports or contradicts this viewpoint?

2. **Making Comparisons.** How did the Vietnam conflict differ from the earlier war in Korea? Consider both the nature of the problems and the responses of the United States government.

YOUR REGION IN HISTORY

1. **Geography.** Freedom marches punctuated the civil rights movement during the Kennedy years. Trace the routes followed by civil rights marchers in your region.

2. **Culture.** Interview people who participated in or observed the civil rights movement in your area during the Kennedy years. Find out how these people reacted to the civil rights movement and/or the effect that their participation had on the community.

3. **Economics.** How, if at all, has the economic position of black people in your state or locality changed since 1960? What factors have contributed to this change?

HISTORICAL FACTS AND FIGURES

Distinguishing False from Accurate Images. Study the graphs below to help answer the following questions: (a) How many blacks lived below the poverty level in 1965? in 1975? in 1985? (b) How many whites lived below the poverty level in those same years? (c) What percentage of blacks lived in poverty in 1960? In 1980? (d) What percentage of whites lived in poverty in 1960? In 1980? (e) How does the presentation of the information in the two graphs affect the conclusions you draw about people living in poverty? Would either graph shown by itself present a biased picture? (f) Write a paragraph that combines your conclusions into one statement about poverty in the United States.

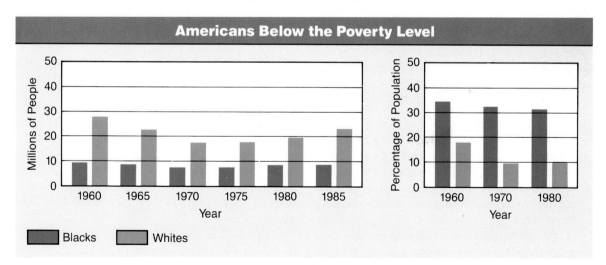

Americans Below the Poverty Level

Blacks   Whites

CHAPTER 32

Lyndon B. Johnson— from success to failure

This would be a time of triumphs and troubles. Led by a strong President, Lyndon B. Johnson, the Congress found new ways to protect the rights of some citizens and to widen the opportunities for all. At home it was an age of fulfillment. The injustices of centuries would begin to be righted. Yet this would take time. Impatient Americans turned to violence. Meanwhile, an undeclared war on the other side of the world, in a place most Americans had never heard of, would cost thousands of American lives. There, too, the President said, Americans were defending freedom. But the nation was unconvinced. He did not persuade Americans that they needed to be fighting there—nor did he tell them all they wanted to know. One of the best-qualified, strongest Presidents became the leading figure in an American tragedy. People would forget his successes at home because of his failures abroad.

1. Taking the reins

The nation, stunned by the loss of its young President, wanted to hear a clear, commanding voice. Lyndon B. Johnson, the new man in the White House, saw what the times needed. As he later explained:

Everything was in chaos. We were all spinning around and around trying to come to grips with what had happened, but the more we tried to understand it, the more confused we got. We were like a bunch of cattle caught in the swamp, unable to move in either direction, simply circling 'round and 'round. I understood that; I knew what had to be done. There is but one way to get the cattle out of the swamp. And that is for the man on the horse to take the lead, to

assume command, to provide direction. In the period of confusion after the assassination, I was that man.

Lyndon Baines Johnson. Johnson was perfectly trained to take charge. He was not as young or as witty as JFK. But he stood a commanding six feet three—as tall as Texans are supposed to be. And he spoke with a Texas drawl that carried a charm all his own. He had spent most of his life in the House of Representatives and the Senate. He knew the members of Congress by their first names. He respected them and they respected him. Better than any other man alive, he knew how to put laws through Congress.

LBJ's life had centered upon politics. His father had been a state legislator in Texas, and the young

Lyndon loved to go to the statehouse to watch and listen. Even more, he enjoyed traveling around with his father, visiting the voters of their district during election campaigns. "Sometimes," he recalled, "I wished it would go on forever."

While still a student at Southwest Texas State College, Johnson worked as campaign manager in the successful reelection of a state senator. After graduating from college in 1930, Johnson taught for a year in a high school in Houston. His political skills were already recognized, and he was asked to be the aide of a Texas congressman. In 1932, at the age of 24, he arrived in Washington, where he would spend most of the remaining 41 years of his life.

One brief break came from 1935 to 1937 when he returned to Texas as state director of the National Youth Administration. Even then his sympathy for the downtrodden was clear. Years later an aged black leader recalled how "we began to get word up here that there was one NYA director who wasn't like the others. He was looking after Negroes and poor folks, and most NYA people weren't doing that."

Johnson was elected as a Democrat to the House of Representatives in 1939. In 1941 he was the first member of Congress to enlist in the armed forces. His navy career was cut short a year later when FDR ordered all senators and representatives back to Washington. He remained in the House until 1948, when he was elected to the Senate.

The Senate was the perfect stage for a man of LBJ's character and talent. Since there were only 96 senators, and each served for six years, it was a kind of club. All the members of the House of Representatives were elected every two years, and there were more than 400 of them. The Senate was a more intimate place. LBJ was a careful student of both people and issues. And he was always doing favors for others.

He earned a reputation as a superb "horse trader." Johnson used to roam the halls seeking senators whose help he needed on some bill. When he "accidentally" met one of them, he would give him "The Treatment." In his colorful Texas slang, the overpowering LBJ would plead, threaten, accuse, cry, laugh, complain—until his fellow senator agreed. "The Treatment" might last minutes or hours. A senator who knew called it "an almost hypnotic experience that rendered the target

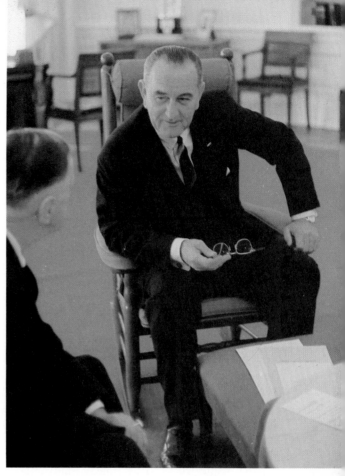

Fred Ward/Black Star

LBJ here exerts his famous powers of persuasion in the Oval Office in 1964.

stunned and helpless." But Johnson was not just acting. "What convinces is conviction," he said. "You simply *have* to believe in the argument you are advancing. If you don't, you are as good as dead."

When he was majority leader of the Senate from 1955 to 1961, LBJ ran the place as if he owned it. Then when John F. Kennedy asked him to join his ticket as candidate for Vice-President, LBJ accepted. The tall Texan wanted to use the office to become a national figure.

He hoped it might be a stepping stone to the White House. Since the inauguration of Lincoln a century earlier, five Vice-Presidents had become President. Still, for an energetic and ambitious politician, being Vice-President was frustrating. The Vice-President had to support the President's policies, yet he had no executive powers of his own. And Presidents had seldom consulted their Vice-Presidents.

Suddenly fate thrust LBJ into the post he wanted most of all. It was the perfect moment for the man who knew how to manage Congress. Goals had been set by President Kennedy. But the laws had not been passed. Now LBJ—the great wheeler-dealer—could work his magic.

A new civil rights law. Five days after the assassination, Johnson addressed the Congress. He called for national unity. He asked Congress to complete the programs begun by JFK, and he stressed civil rights. "No memorial oration or eulogy," he told Congress, "could more eloquently honor President Kennedy's memory than the earliest possible passage of the civil rights bill for which he fought so long. We have talked long enough in this country about equal rights. We have talked for one hundred years or more. It is time now to write the next chapter—and to write it in the books of law."

Johnson was determined to be more than just a southern President. He wanted to be President of all the people. For him, civil rights was the nation's problem. To swing the liberals of his party to his side, he would try to pass Kennedy's bill without any of the weakening changes that are usual in the process of enacting laws.

Ordinarily Johnson tried to reach his ends by compromise. This time there was to be no compromise. The bill ran into a record filibuster by southern senators who tried to talk the civil rights bill to death. They talked for 83 days. Meanwhile, Johnson, the adroit veteran of the Senate, worked ceaselessly to put together a winning alliance of Republicans and Democrats. Finally the Senate, under the floor leadership of Senator Hubert Humphrey, adopted *cloture.* This rule, then requiring a two-thirds majority vote by those present and voting, restricted further debate to one hour per person. In this way the Senate in a few days would be forced to vote on the issue. The Senate passed the bill on June 20, and the House accepted the Senate version on July 2, 1964. President Johnson signed the bill that same day.

The Civil Rights Act of 1964 forbade racial discrimination in the use of federal funds and in places of public resort, such as hotels, amusement parks, and other public facilities. It tried to protect the right of blacks to vote. It sought to protect their right to jobs by setting up an Equal Employment Opportunity Commission. It empowered the Attorney General to start court cases to speed the desegregation of schools. And it created a Community Relations Service to assist individuals and officials with racial problems at the local level.

LBJ pushes Congress onward: A blizzard of laws. Congress also passed the tax cut asked by Kennedy. This lowered taxes by $11.5 billion, left more money in people's pockets, and so began to stimulate the economy.

At the President's urging, Congress passed a billion-dollar Economic Opportunity Act for a war on poverty. It contained a Community Action Program to let the people of an area decide what they thought needed to be done. It set up job- and work-training programs. Funds were provided for loans to college students and for small businesses to hire the unemployed. It also established VISTA (Volunteers in Service to America), a domestic Peace Corps to provide a chance for people to help the poor.

Karl Hubenthal

President Johnson so "played upon" Congress that it produced any tune he wished.

LBJ also encouraged Congress to pass the National Defense Education Act for expanded aid to schools and colleges. And Congress increased the food stamp program for people on welfare and granted $1.4 billion to the states for hospitals and health centers. A $375 million program helped cities with their mass-transit systems.

Expanding cities and extending highways meant there were more people who wanted and needed to get close to nature. But where would they go? The very businesses that gave Americans a better life had transformed wilderness into farm and factory. For years Congress had debated laws to protect millions of acres of public land as wilderness forever. This meant keeping out dams, buildings, roads, automobiles, and other motorized vehicles. The lands could be used only for camping, hiking, or horseback riding. Naturally enough, ranchers who grazed cattle and sheep on the public lands and the companies that cut and sold timber, that mined coal or oil or copper—under federal permits and leases—objected. They said that the nation needed to use these resources now. Conserving wilderness, they said, was simply a way of "locking up" the rich American lands.

The nature lovers replied that conserving the wilderness was "now or never." You could mine or cut timber elsewhere, they said, but you could never "put back" the wilderness. They wanted to keep intact 60 million acres. The Wilderness Act of 1964 set aside 9 million acres of national forest and national park land as "wilderness." There Americans could continue to use and enjoy the wilderness that once was all America.

Seldom has Congress passed so many important laws in such a brief time. It was a stunning performance. In a few months LBJ showed that he really deserved his reputation as a wizard at handling Congress. JFK had outlined the program, and his death set the stage. But LBJ's congressional magic had made the hopes into laws. Since it seemed certain that LBJ would be the Democratic candidate in the coming election, many Democratic members of Congress voted with him to earn his support for their own reelection.

Choosing the candidates. The Republicans were caught up in a bitter fight for control of their party. Conservatives, led by the earnest Senator Barry Goldwater of Arizona, were resolved to oust the

Bill Strode/Black Star

Appalachia was a main target of the War on Poverty. Amid great natural beauty, millions lived there in extreme poverty.

liberal eastern wing of the party, which had named the candidate at every convention since 1940. They wanted to get away from what they called "me-too" Republicans. They would offer the nation "a choice, not an echo."

The liberal Republicans did not realize what was happening until it was too late. At the Republican convention in San Francisco, Goldwater was nominated easily on the first ballot. He did nothing to make himself more palatable to the liberals. In his acceptance speech he proclaimed, "Extremism in the defense of liberty is no vice." This seemed to seek support from the most right-wing elements in the party. And he made no effort to "balance" the ticket. Instead, his choice for Vice-President was Congressman William Miller, a little-known conservative from New York State. This did not help to heal the breach in the party ranks. Seasoned observers were surprised. They expected that Senator Goldwater, once he became a candidate for President, would try to appeal to all the voters. Instead he stuck by his guns and ran on the principles of Barry Goldwater. Many Americans admired his personal honesty, but not so many shared his dogmas of American life. He lost the votes of millions of Republicans.

President Johnson was in full control when the Democrats met at Atlantic City, New Jersey, in August. The only drama LBJ could create was over who would be his running mate. He kept the delegates guessing until nearly the last moment, when he named ebullient, talkative Senator Hubert H. Humphrey of Minnesota. Humphrey had a record that would appeal to the more liberal wing of the Democratic party.

LBJ triumphant. Not since 1936 had there been a presidential campaign where the candidates were so unevenly matched. Johnson was masterful. He tried to please nearly everyone. On foreign affairs, he showed wise restraint—even while he was secretly discussing plans for deeper moves into Vietnam. On domestic policy he stood for the Civil Rights Act of 1964, the war against poverty, and federal aid to education. Johnson dominated the middle-of-the-road.

Goldwater, on the other hand, promised voters a clear-cut choice. He had voted against the Civil Rights Act, the Test Ban Treaty, and most of the Kennedy-Johnson welfare measures. During the campaign he opposed the government programs that had already become popular. He suggested the sale of the TVA, and he questioned the Social Security system. He gave the impression that he believed violent conflict with the Soviet Union was inevitable. For that reason he proposed giving control of tactical atomic weapons to NATO commanders in the field. Sometimes he said things he did not really mean and then he tried to take them back. "Don't print what he *says*," one of his aides told reporters, "print what he *means*."

Goldwater's campaign went steadily downhill. On election day Lyndon B. Johnson received 61 percent of the vote, the largest majority in history until that time. His popular vote was 43 million to Goldwater's 27 million. He captured 486 electoral votes to Goldwater's 52.

The message seemed clear. Most Americans really wanted the federal government to do something for them. They expected new programs to help them meet new problems.

SECTION 1 REVIEW

1. Identify or explain: Hubert Humphrey, cloture, "war on poverty," VISTA, National Defense Education Act, Wilderness Act, Barry Goldwater.

2. Explain the significance of the Civil Rights Act of 1964.

3. How was the Economic Opportunity Act supposed to conquer poverty?

4. Give the highlights of the campaign and election of 1964.

5. **Demonstrating Reasoned Judgment.** What experiences in Johnson's political career qualified him to be President?

---

2. The Great Society

In a speech at the University of Michigan in May 1964, LBJ had put a name on the program he wanted for America. This was to be the "Great Society." During the past century, he said, Americans had been settling and subduing a continent. "The challenge of the next half century," he declared, "is whether we have the wisdom to use that wealth to enrich and elevate our national life, and to advance the quality of our American civilization." Nearly all Americans shared his dreams. But, he would find, many doubted that LBJ had staked out the path to make them real.

The fruits of victory. LBJ's great election victory gave the President for the first time since 1938 a firm working majority in both houses of Congress. Now his party's majority was so large that to enact his program he would not really need the votes of conservative southern Democrats.

Nobody understood this better than LBJ. And he moved quickly. As a seasoned politician he knew that he must act while his support was still strong. All during 1964 he had put task forces to work on bills to send to Congress. The two at the top of his list were medical care for the aged and federal aid to elementary and high school education. He put them there because he knew it would be hard to get them passed. Perhaps he could push them through in the afterglow of his triumph at the polls. And he did!

Medical insurance and aid to education. The Medicare bill, which he signed into law in July 1965, had been changed by Congress. It provided even wider protection than LBJ had asked. Citizens over 65 received low-cost hospital insurance financed by an increase in the Social Security payroll tax. If they wished, they could have medical insurance for doctors' bills and other out-of-hospital expenses with the government paying half the cost of the insurance premium. Another part of the law, called *Medicaid,* offered federal grants to states that wanted to set up their own plans to help needy people below the age of 65. The first limited program of medical aid for the needy aged had been enacted in 1950. It helped only those who were not receiving Social Security payments. It had been greatly expanded in 1960 to cover all older people who were not able to meet their medical expenses. These earlier medical aid plans were now superseded by Medicare and Medicaid.

The President's next message to Congress asked $1.3 billion for aid to education, "the key which can unlock the door to the Great Society." Past attempts to give federal aid to education had been stopped by the religious issue. The Constitution (First Amendment) forbade Congress to make any law "respecting an establishment of religion." If Congress gave federal funds to "parochial schools"—those supported by a particular church— did this violate the Constitution? President Johnson sidestepped the issue. He offered aid to a school chiefly according to the number of its students whose families had annual incomes below poverty level. No school could receive aid unless it obeyed the laws against segregation.

To sign the Elementary and Secondary Education Act, LBJ went back to the one-room schoolhouse in Stonewall, a mile from his birthplace in Texas, where he had gone as a boy. He knew how to make the ceremony into a warm human drama. Present there were his first teacher and also seven Mexican Americans who had attended the school in Cotulla, Texas, where he had taught before graduating from college.

A flood of bills. President Johnson had chosen the right strategy. After these two controversial bills passed so easily, his others found clear sailing. The list of important laws passed by the 89th Congress was eye-popping. It covered the nation. There were laws to beautify the highways (supported by his wife, Lady Bird) and laws for clean air. There was a law to insure truth in packaging. The Appalachian Regional Development Act gave to the poverty-stricken mountainous region stretching from Pennsylvania to Alabama and Georgia $1.1 billion for highways, health centers, and industrial development.

The cities, too, received their share. The Housing and Urban Development Act of 1965 aided construction of a quarter-million units of low-rent public housing. "Urban Renewal"—the clearing of slums and rebuilding of cities—received $2.9 billion. The rents of low- and moderate-income families were subsidized. Congress created a Department of Housing and Urban Development. To head the department Johnson named Robert C. Weaver, the first black in the Cabinet. The following year, Congress established the Department of Transportation.

The Immigration Act of 1965 abolished the quota system. Each year 120,000 persons could come from Western Hemisphere lands. Another 170,000 could be admitted from all other nations, but not more than 20,000 of these could come from any one country. Families of people already in the country, skilled workers, and refugees had priority. Congress voted billions for the war on poverty—and for exploring outer space. LBJ's program offered something for nearly everybody.

The power of books. Presidents had great power. But so did authors. Rachel Carson, a slight, modest woman, graduated from Johns Hopkins University and became a famous marine biologist. Her poetic books about the oceans and the seashore introduced Americans to the wonders of life in the unpolluted sea. Then in 1962 she published *Silent Spring*—a block-busting book on a most unlikely subject. She showed that pesticides—especially DDT—were damaging the environment more than anyone suspected. The poisonous new chemicals used to wipe out destructive insects were passing through the food chain—from the insects to the birds who ate the insects. Birds were dying from the poisons

Here we see a price for the nation's spectacular industry and high standard of living. Highways crisscross the landscape and smog darkens the sky.

meant for insects. One day, she warned, we might awaken to a "silent spring." No birds would be left to sing.

Rachel Carson alerted Americans to "ecology." This was the science of the relation between organisms and their environment. President Kennedy had set up a commission to study the questions raised by Rachel Carson.

Just as the pesticides aimed at insects were killing birds, so the exhaust fumes of automobiles could pollute the air that everybody breathed. Now President Johnson persuaded Congress to pass laws to reduce pollution from the exhaust pipes of cars and trucks and from factory chimneys.

The waters of our lakes and rivers were polluted by chemicals dumped from mines and factories.

Junkyards and cemeteries for dead automobiles made a mess of the wild and beautiful American countryside. People called this "visual pollution." New laws were passed requiring fences around these eyesores. The number of billboards was limited. Pesticides were controlled.

The wonderful power of books was proved again in 1965 when Ralph Nader, a bright 31-year-old lawyer, stirred the nation with his *Unsafe at Any Speed*. In that year alone, he wrote, nearly 50,000 Americans would die in automobile accidents and more than 4 million would be injured. He argued that many of these deaths and injuries would be the fault of the automakers. He accused them of being more interested in selling cars than in saving lives. They cared too much, he said, about car styling and sales gimmicks and too little about safety features. Bumpers were not even strong enough to resist an impact of over three miles an hour, and car bodies were not much stronger. Nader's campaign helped spur Congress to pass the Highway Safety Act of 1966. It set safety standards for new cars and for tires.

LBJ and administration. Never before in American history had Congress produced so many social programs so speedily. Between 1965 and 1968 the reform laws came to 500. It was much easier to pass a law than to change the way people behaved. LBJ was a wizard in the Congress. But making all the new laws work was quite another matter. The restless President Johnson had a way of asking for more new laws even before old laws on the same subject had been tried out. For example, the standards for the Water Quality Act of 1965 had not yet been set when the Clean Water Restoration Act was passed calling for the setting of still more standards.

Administering all these new programs, finding the good people to run them, was itself a colossal job. Meanwhile the President was being distracted by some other colossal problems, thousands of miles away, in Vietnam.

"Wartime" inflation in peacetime. Just like earlier wars, the undeclared war in Vietnam suddenly increased the demand for goods. After the tax cut of 1965, citizens had more money, and the government was now spending billions on defense. Though the nation had not actually declared war, wartime inflation was here again! Prices began to shoot up. The Consumer Price Index had risen by an average of only 1 percent a year during the Kennedy years. Then it went up 3 percent in 1967 and 5 percent in 1968. The government's wage and price guidelines collapsed.

To slow down inflation and pay the ever-higher costs of the Vietnam War, LBJ asked Congress for a temporary 10 percent surcharge on income taxes in 1967. (Taxpayers would figure their regular tax and then add 10 percent to it.) But by that time Congress was becoming less cooperative. They asked whether a tax increase was really necessary. To pay for the war, President Johnson was forced to cut back on non-defense spending. "Great Society" programs suffered. Still, every year the federal

government went deeper into debt. From $3.8 billion in 1966, the deficit rose to $8.7 billion in 1967, and $25.2 billion in 1968. In June 1968, when the tax surcharge finally became law, inflation was on the rise.

SECTION 2 REVIEW

1. Identify or explain: "Great Society," Medicare, Medicaid, Elementary and Secondary Education Act, Truth-in-Packaging, Appalachia.

2. What important laws were passed under President Johnson on (a) health care, (b) education, (c) pollution, (d) consumer protection, (e) regional development, (f) housing and rents?

3. Why did inflation speed up in the late 1960s? How did Johnson try to deal with it?

4. **Recognizing Cause and Effect.** How did Rachel Carson and Ralph Nader influence "Great Society" legislation?

---

3. Black revolt and youth rebellion

President Kennedy and President Johnson had raised high the hopes of many Americans that injustice, inequality, and poverty could be erased. The failure to achieve quickly the difficult goals they proclaimed may have been inevitable. But among certain groups—blacks and the middle-class young especially—the result was frustration and anger and ultimately violence.

The beginnings of black revolt. Centuries of discrimination could not be wiped out in a few years. Black Americans were disappointed that the eloquent speeches and beautiful promises were not all fulfilled overnight. Disappointment became frustration. And frustration led to revolt. In the northern states that had fought to free the slaves, the discontent was most acute. There segregation continued not by law, as it did in the South, but in everyday fact.

Civil rights laws could do little for the 50 percent of the black Americans in the North. They had to live by themselves in special neighborhoods. They were not admitted to some of the best schools and clubs. Even if they were bright and well trained, they could not get jobs in the building trades, or as executives in businesses or banks, or in the best law firms. Since laws had helped so little, they flailed

Both black and white leaders joined Martin Luther King, Jr., and Coretta Scott King in the march from Selma to Montgomery in March 1965.

about trying to find ways to awaken their fellow Americans. They staged a "stall-in" of autos to disrupt the opening of the New York World's Fair in 1964. And riots erupted in Rochester and New York City.

The Summer Freedom Project in Mississippi in 1964 aimed to register blacks so they could vote. Civil rights workers (white and black) came down from the North. Three of them were murdered and became martyrs to the cause of equality. Many of the civil rights missionaries were beaten or wounded. Black homes and churches were burned. Because of these violent tactics, blacks feared to demand their rights, and only 1200 new voters were registered.

The murders in Mississippi had their effect. But it was not what the plotters expected. The national outrage helped to push the stronger Civil Rights Act of 1964 through Congress in July. Then, even in Mississippi, public places—such as restaurants— began to serve both races. When schools opened there in September, a few white and black children of Mississippi began going to school together. The last strongholds of segregation started to fall.

The Voting Rights Act. In 1964 the Rev. Martin Luther King, Jr., received the Nobel Peace Prize. The Nobel Prizes had a strange history. They were founded by Alfred Nobel, a Swedish manufacturer of arms who invented dynamite (both the chemical

and the name). He was worried that his products were used mainly by people at war to kill one another. His guilty conscience led him to leave his huge fortune to create a foundation that would give prizes in science, literature, and peacemaking. All people in the world were eligible, and there was no greater honor awarded anywhere.

Upon his return from Sweden, early in 1965, King announced his drive to register 3 million voters in the South. He began his push in Selma, Alabama, a city with 15,000 blacks, but almost no black voters. Once again black Americans were clubbed, shocked with electric cattle prods, and arrested— only for trying to exercise their rights. The horrified nation saw it all on TV screens in their living rooms.

Then King announced that he would lead a march for freedom from Selma to the Alabama capitol in Montgomery. On March 7 the freedom marchers were attacked by the police and turned back. Two days later they tried again, and again they were turned back. Governor George Wallace did everything he could to stop the march. He went to court. He told President Johnson that Alabama could not afford to protect the marchers. On March 15, LBJ called units of the Alabama National Guard into federal service and ordered federal marshals and the FBI to Alabama.

That same day President Johnson went before Congress—while the nation watched on television.

He denounced the denial of constitutional rights to the black citizens of Mississippi. He demanded a law to provide federal registrars at the polls wherever blacks were not already voting in normal numbers. These registrars would have the power to enroll new voters so that no person could be denied the right to vote on account of race. LBJ compared the battle of Selma to the battles of Lexington and Concord in the American Revolution. He repeated the slogan of the civil rights forces—"We *Shall* Overcome."

On March 21 the great march from Selma to Montgomery began under the protection of federal marshals, the FBI, and the Alabama National Guard. Ministers, priests, and rabbis from all over the country went to Selma to join Martin Luther King in the march. Four days later the demonstrators peacefully entered Montgomery. But that night a white woman civil rights worker was shot and killed.

For the first time in history all American citizens at the same time could see their fellow citizens in another part of the country demanding their rights. It was before their eyes on television. No wonder, then, that Congress now passed the Voting Rights Act. President Johnson signed it into law on August 6, 1965. Only one year later the number of blacks registered to vote had gone up 50 percent, from 870,000 to 1,289,000. Soon black officials began to be elected in communities throughout the South. At last it appeared that the dreams of Radical Republicans after the Civil War might finally be achieved.

Burn, baby, burn. Hardly had the Voting Rights Act of 1965 passed than Watts, a black ghetto in Los Angeles, exploded in violence. This was only the first of more than 100 riots that would rage in many cities across the nation during the long, hot summers of the next three years.

LBJ was stunned by Watts. He had just signed his great Voting Rights Act into law—and now this. "How is it possible," he asked, "after all we've accomplished?" Johnson was understandably bitter. For the riots hurt his Great Society programs. They seemed so aimless and only served to destroy, when what was needed was to build. They created a backlash among many whites who already felt blacks were receiving too much from the government. This was less a revolution than an explo-

sion. The President tried to understand. "God knows how little we've really moved on this issue," he said, "despite all the fanfare. As I see it I've moved the Negro from D+ to C-. He's still nowhere. He knows it. And that's why he's out in the streets."

The riots drew attention to the more radical black leaders. The handsome Malcolm X was an ex-convict who had become a member of Elijah Muhammad's Nation of Islam—usually called the Black Muslims. Muhammad rejected integration. He called all whites "devils." He thought whites and blacks should be separate and that blacks should have a nation of their own. Malcolm's eloquent voice carried a message of hate. "When I speak," he said, "I speak as a *victim* of America's so-called democracy."

Malcolm X split off from Elijah Muhammad's Black Muslims and formed his own group. He did not follow Martin Luther King's Christian gospel of nonviolence. But after a pilgrimage to Mecca, where all true Muslims were supposed to go once in their lives, he began to change his view that all whites were born evil. For true Muslims believed that all races were equal. Malcolm X's career ended in a blaze of gunfire from several of his many black opponents in February 1965. His powerful *Autobiography*, which came out after his death in 1965, fanned both black anger and black pride.

Black Power. The summer of 1966 was a season of riots in northern cities. In the South, James Meredith, the first black to attend the University of Mississippi, tried to walk from Memphis, Tennessee, to Jackson, Mississippi, to encourage black people not to be afraid. He was shot and wounded. This provoked some black leaders to think that maybe Malcolm X was right. Stokely Carmichael, a young black radical, began to preach "Black Power." Martin Luther King had preached love and human brotherhood. Now the angry champions of "Black Power" mainly wanted to be able to "get even." They wanted their chance to lord it over others.

By the fall of 1966 the civil rights movement was divided and in disarray. White backlash grew stronger. For the first time in recent years, a civil rights measure failed to pass Congress. The summer of 1967 saw the worst rioting in United States history. Blacks went on the rampage, destroying

Massive rioting in Detroit in 1967 brought death and destruction. Federal troops and the Michigan National Guard were sent into the city to restore order.

their own neighborhoods and leaving smoking rubble in Newark and Detroit. In Detroit alone 43 died and 5000 were left homeless. The Soviet newspaper *Pravda* gleefully printed a picture of army tanks on the streets of Detroit.

Again during 1967, LBJ asked for new civil rights laws, but Congress was no longer sympathetic. About all that LBJ could do that year was to appoint Thurgood Marshall to the Supreme Court. A graduate of the Howard University Law School, he had headed the legal staff of the National Association for the Advancement of Colored People, and he had successfully argued the case against segregation in 1954. Now he was the first black ever to serve on the highest court in the land.

A new generation. This was a time of troubles and struggles. The nation's young people had been the source of hope and optimism. But now, in the 1960s, many acted as if they had been raised on sour milk. They were the product of the "baby boom"—born during and soon after World War II. Between 1960 and 1970 the number of Americans aged 15 to 24 grew by 50 percent—from 24 million to 36 million. This was more than they had increased in all the last seven decades.

This new generation was different. They were the first generation to have lived all their lives under the shadow of nuclear weapons. They were the first TV generation. Their parents were sobered by knowledge of the Great Depression. But the society that these young people knew had enjoyed almost continuous prosperity since their childhood.

They had been surrounded with countless new things—TV, high-fidelity records, stereo, FM radio, wide-screen movies with wrap-around sound, large cars dappled with chrome, superhighways and supermarkets. At the same time they heard the dire warnings of Rachel Carson, Ralph Nader, and other prophets of doom. They could see that all the many wonderful things in American life still did not solve the ancient problems of justice and equality. And on TV they would see their young President assassinated, their cities smoldering in riots, their generation dying on the distant battlefield of Vietnam—and people of scores of new nations starving in Africa and Asia. The world seemed confusing and frustrating as never before. Where was the new frontier?

Hippies and the New Left. Different young people reacted in different ways. Most went about their business. They attended classes, read their textbooks, and prepared themselves to make a living. But some joined in the so-called "counterculture," which was opposed to the culture accepted by most Americans. They used drugs, they let their hair grow long, they wore beads, fringe jackets, army and navy surplus clothes, and long dresses. They wanted to look as different as possible from other Americans. They called themselves "hippies" (from the slang expression "hip," meaning knowledgeable, worldly-wise, "with it").

Hippies often reacted to American life by "dropping out"—by refusing to be a part of it. Other students organized in a New Left to transform America. The first active New Left group was the Student Nonviolent Coordinating Committee (SNCC). This was a small group mainly of southern black students. It was founded in 1960 to coordinate student activities, especially sit-ins (p. 630), for civil rights. SNCC was soon joined in its efforts by members of Students for a Democratic Society. SDS was an arm of an old social-democratic organization named the League for Industrial Democracy. Early in the 1960s SDS broke away from its parent to present a more radical reform program for America. Both SNCC and SDS were born as reform movements, but both soon were to reject reform and turn to anarchism and disruption.

For SDS the center of opposition became the university. Its members thought that by attacking the universities—their rules and regulations, their research contracts to help with the war in Vietnam, and their support of a supposedly unjust American society—they could make students radical and turn them into revolutionaries. But their revolutionary aims were vague and negative. Soon colleges and universities from Berkeley in California to Harvard in Massachusetts were in disarray. Daily the TV screen showed students picketing, occupying buildings, shouting obscenities, and stopping all classes. They demanded "Student Power." Across the country, people outside universities wondered what had happened to the American love of learning and the Jeffersonian tradition of free debate.

Still, most students seemed less concerned with "revolution" than with the war in Vietnam. The New Left became more and more frustrated as the 1960s wore on. SNCC turned to a racial movement for "Black Power" and so lost funds and members. SDS collapsed and a few of the most

Charles Moore/Black Star

Hippies tried to show that they rejected the values of most Americans.

embittered activists went off to make bombs against the society they despised.

SECTION 3 REVIEW

1. Identify or explain: Nobel Prizes, freedom march, George Wallace, Watts, Malcolm X, Black Muslims, Stokely Carmichael, "Black Power," Thurgood Marshall, hippies, SDS.

2. What kinds of discrimination were northern blacks facing in the early 1960s?

3. What was the Summer Freedom Project of 1964? What was its unexpected effect?

4. How did the Voting Rights Act help to assure the voting rights of southern blacks?

5. Describe some responses by young people to the troublesome 1960s.

6. **Recognizing Cause and Effect.** What were some causes of the riots between 1965 and 1967?

4. "The most unpopular war"

During 1964 the United States sank deeper and deeper into the war in Vietnam. In the course of the campaign for President, Senator Barry Goldwater had asked LBJ to send more American troops. But the President resisted. He had promised during the campaign, "We are not about to send American boys nine or ten thousand miles from home to do what Asian boys ought to be doing for themselves." Still, Johnson would not negotiate with North Vietnam. "We do not believe in

conferences to ratify terror," he declared. Secretary of State Dean Rusk said that just as our duties to the free world required us to stay in Berlin—so now we must defend freedom in Vietnam.

The Tonkin Gulf Resolution. Off North Vietnam in the Tonkin Gulf on August 2 and 4, 1964, two United States destroyers were attacked by North Vietnamese gunboats. This brought matters to a head. President Johnson said they were attacked without cause. (Later it appeared that they had been protecting South Vietnamese gunboats making raids on the North.) He went on television to announce "that repeated acts of violence against the United States" must be answered. At that moment, he revealed, United States planes were attacking targets in the North.

The next day, August 5, he asked Congress for a joint resolution to empower "the President, as Commander in Chief, to take all necessary measures to repel any armed attack against the forces of the United States and to prevent further aggression." It passed without a single negative vote in the House. In the Senate there was debate only because the independent Senator Wayne Morse of Oregon threatened a filibuster if there was no discussion. Morse said the resolution violated the Constitution by giving the President powers that belonged to Congress. Senator Ernest Gruening of Alaska called it "a predated declaration of war." But only these two voted No.

In fact, President Johnson did not believe that he really needed the resolution. He believed that as Commander in Chief he had the right to send armed forces wherever necessary. He said that this meant even sending troops to Vietnam. He followed the example of Truman in Korea, Eisenhower in Lebanon, and Kennedy in the Cuban missile crisis, who had not asked Congress for permission to use armed force. But LBJ wanted a resolution to protect himself from later congressional criticism. Americans agreed that the President must use troops to defend the United States. It was not so clear that he should send Americans into a civil war on the other side of the globe.

The widening Asian commitment: Vietnamese Communists. In January 1965 Johnson's advisers warned him that the United States would have to increase its aid if South Vietnam was to be saved

Vietnam

—— Demarcation Line of 1954

SOUTHEAST ASIA 1945

A desperate refugee in Vietnam carrying household goods trudges past United States troops.

from the Communists. In February there was a Communist attack on a United States military unit, and 7 Americans were killed and 100 wounded. To retaliate, LBJ ordered the bombing of North Vietnam. Still, he hesitated to order all-out bombing or to commit more troops. "If there is one thing that the American people will not take," he said, "it is another shooting war in Asia." Despite his worst fears, that was exactly what Americans were in.

Could the United States now afford to "lose" South Vietnam? That was the unwelcome question. To avoid defeat more and more American power was needed. In March American planes were bombing regularly. On April 1, 1965, against his own promises, LBJ sent American troops against the Viet Cong. A few days later, with no public announcement, he added another 20,000 men to help the 27,000 already in Vietnam. American troops were sinking into the quicksand and disappearing into the jungles of Southeast Asia.

Why we were in Vietnam. It was not easy to make clear to the American people why we were in Vietnam at all. The simplest explanation was offered by President Eisenhower (who, in fact, carefully stayed out of Vietnam). This was the "domino theory." Vietnam, he said, was like the first in a row of standing dominoes. If you toppled it over, the other dominoes (the neighboring countries) would fall, too. All Southeast Asia would quickly be taken over by the Communists.

Another reason was to stop aggression. Early in 1965 there were still only a small number of North Vietnamese soldiers in South Vietnam. But American military leaders remembered how Europe had fallen to the Nazis because Britain and France had not acted soon enough.

A third reason for going into Vietnam was to protect our reputation. We wanted other free countries to believe that we would stand by them if they were attacked by Communists. This was called our "credibility." If we did not protect South Vietnam, we feared other nations would not believe we would help them. Then our whole worldwide system of defense and deterrence against the Communists might collapse.

For all these reasons in July 1965 President Johnson committed the United States to victory in Vietnam. By the year's end the American troops there numbered 185,000. Were we in so deep that it no longer mattered why we were there? The urgent task now, a State Department spokesman explained, was "to avoid humiliation." While this was seen as a patriotic duty, it was not inspiring.

The Dominican Republic. The Communist issue was still very much alive in the Caribbean—on our own doorstep. In the Dominican Republic a revolution had overthrown the government on April 24, 1965. No one could tell who would take power. When civil war broke out, the American ambassador in Santo Domingo panicked. He feared that Juan Bosch, the last popularly elected president, was winning and that he supported the Communists. The ambassador asked Washington for troops to protect American lives and "prevent another Cuba." LBJ sent in American forces. By May 5, when a truce was arranged, the United States had 22,000 men in the Dominican Republic.

Johnson defended this intervention. "The American nation," he said, "cannot, must not, will not, permit the establishment of another Communist government in the Western Hemisphere." Later, it became plain that the situation in the Dominican Republic had not been as bad as we had thought. The Communists had not been about to take over after all.

Widening the "credibility gap." Even after LBJ decided to commit troops to the fighting in Vietnam, he refused to admit that there had been any shift in United States policy. In July 1965, when he decided to build up our forces in Vietnam, he chose not to reveal to Congress or the people what he intended to do. He announced that he was sending 50,000 men right away, and he asked for more money to pay for that commitment. But he did not let Congress know what the full cost would be.

President Johnson later explained that he feared if he told the whole truth he would not be able to pass his Great Society legislation. He was on the verge of achieving his dream "of improving life for more people than any other political leader, including FDR." If Congress began to debate foreign policy, that might be the end of the Great Society. "I was determined to be a leader of war *and* a leader of peace."

LBJ had not fully shared his intentions or fears about Vietnam or the Dominican Republic with the American people. And in domestic affairs, when news leaked out of what he was going to do, he would sometimes change his plans and do something else. Soon there developed a "credibility gap." This was a gap between what the President wanted people to believe and what was credible

(really believable). As the months of the Vietnam War went on, that gap widened. The American people began to doubt what Johnson told them about Vietnam—or anything else.

A "peace offensive." During 1965 all across the nation there appeared signs of growing opposition to the war in Vietnam. The influential Senator J. William Fulbright of Arkansas, chairman of the Senate Foreign Relations Committee, had voted for the Tonkin Gulf Resolution. Now he argued that we were in too deep and should withdraw. At the University of Michigan students and professors staged a new kind of demonstration. Part study group, part political rally, this was the first antiwar "teach-in." In October a few young men burned their draft cards. The climax came in November 1965 when 30,000 antiwar protesters marched on Washington.

Ever since July, Secretary McNamara had been urging a halt in the bombing of North Vietnam. He said this would be a goodwill gesture to encourage the Communists to negotiate. As opposition to the war grew, Secretary of State Rusk moved to that position, too. So on December 23, 1965, LBJ announced a halt in the bombing and a "peace offensive." The President explored many diplomatic avenues. Still there was no reply from North Vietnam. Early in 1966, after a 37-day pause, the B-52s resumed bombing North Vietnam.

Johnson loses support. Even while public opposition to the war increased, the United States commitment in Vietnam was also growing. By the end of 1966 there were 400,000 American men and women there. The casualties (killed, wounded, missing) were rising rapidly. There were 2500 in 1965 and 33,000 in 1966. Yet the war seemed to make no progress, and no end was in sight. All this provided opponents of the war with new arguments. Students, led by a small but loud group who called themselves the New Left, sabotaged public meetings and refused to allow debate. Many others who opposed the war were disgusted by their violence and bad manners. By late 1966 President Johnson had to restrict his public appearances.

Still a considerable number of Americans believed that, even though the war might never be "won," the United States dared not walk away from Vietnam. They feared that if the Communists from the North occupied South Vietnam they would kill thousands of innocent Vietnamese who had opposed the Communists.

As 1966 drew to a close, Secretary of Defense McNamara was becoming more and more gloomy about the war. Since the continued heavy bombing of the North did not seem to be forcing the enemy to give in, he advised that the bombing be stopped. He urged LBJ to make stronger efforts for a negotiated peace. He even suggested that we offer "a role for the Viet Cong in negotiations, postwar life, and government of the nation." But no such plans were made, and the war dragged on.

In November 1965 the opinion polls showed that 66 percent of the American people approved of the way Johnson was running the country. By October 1966 only 44 percent thought he was doing well. In elections that fall the Republicans gained in both the House and the Senate. The main reason was the voters' unhappiness over the war in distant Vietnam. The nation, puzzled over why we were there at all, was still more puzzled over why we stayed.

Mounting opposition to the war. In May 1967 Secretary McNamara expressed the rising discontent. "The picture of the world's greatest superpower," he wrote to LBJ, "killing or seriously injuring 1000 noncombatants a week, while trying to pound a tiny backward nation into submission on an issue whose merits are hotly disputed, is not a pretty one." The United States was dropping more bombs each month on little Vietnam, which is the size of New Mexico, than had been dropped in total on Nazi Germany during all the months of heaviest bombing in World War II.

In June 1967 McNamara commissioned a study of the role of the United States in Vietnam since World War II. The study showed that the American people had been deceived about the real situation. That fall McNamara resigned. In 1971 this report, called the Pentagon Papers, was finally leaked to the press (p. 706).

Throughout 1967 the number of United States troops in Vietnam continued to increase. They reached 475,000, and casualties that year climbed to 80,000. Opposition to the war became ever more shrill. In New York 300,000 marched in protest, and a crowd of 100,000 tried to close the Pentagon in the nation's capital. The bitter cry, "Hey, hey, hey, LBJ, How many kids did you kill today!"

These Americans marched in the streets proclaiming opposition to the war in Vietnam.

was heard at demonstrations in colleges across the land.

The Tet offensive. All this was just a prelude to 1968. In January, General William Westmoreland, the American commander in Vietnam, issued another optimistic report telling how the war was being won. Four days later, on the Vietnamese New Year's holiday called "Tet," the Viet Cong and North Vietnamese suddenly launched their strongest offensive. They struck at cities throughout South Vietnam, even penetrating the heavily guarded grounds of the United States embassy in Saigon. Within a few days, most of the fierce fighting was over. Only in the city of Hué, which had fallen to the Viet Cong, and a few other spots did fighting continue. General Westmoreland claimed correctly that the Tet episode was actually a victory for the United States and South Vietnam. The Communists had suffered enormous losses. It would take them years to rebuild their strength. But the Communists had seized the offensive and in this, the first war shown on TV, the American public had witnessed the horrors. When General Westmoreland called for 206,000 more troops and more fighter squadrons, it seemed that we had not won, but lost, during the Tet offensive.

Shortly after Tet, the American public was shocked to hear that United States troops had killed some 300 civilians, mostly women and children, in the little village of My Lai. The fact that the Viet Cong had murdered many hundreds of civilians during their month-long occupation of Hué was lost in the American distress over the atrocity committed by U.S. troops in My Lai.

Clark Clifford, a trusted personal adviser of LBJ, now replaced McNamara as Secretary of Defense. He was a "hard-liner" (a "hawk") on the war. This meant that he believed we should continue fighting in Vietnam even at great cost. But when he studied the detailed military reports, Clifford himself began to have doubts. Soon he, too, began to work for "winding down"—removing our troops and moving out.

The fall of LBJ. After Tet, at the very moment when the fighting in Vietnam was heaviest, the presidential campaign in the United States was getting under way. Senator Eugene McCarthy of Minnesota, a gentle man of poetic temperament who had enlisted some college students and other opponents of the war, challenged Johnson for the party's nomination. He called for a negotiated settlement and a prompt withdrawal of all American forces.

The first primary contest was held in New Hampshire in mid-March 1968. As the unknown McCarthy toured New Hampshire, LBJ's rating in the opinion polls continued to fall. By March the polls reported that only 36 percent of the people approved of his Presidency, and a mere 26 percent thought he was handling the war well. McCarthy made a surprisingly strong finish in the New Hampshire race against LBJ—with 42 percent of the votes. This was not a victory, but it was as good as one. A President in office was supposed to win easily.

The vote for McCarthy was, in fact, a protest against LBJ. Many who voted for McCarthy actually favored the war—but they thought it was being badly handled. When McCarthy's success showed that Johnson might be beaten, on March 16 Senator Robert F. Kennedy, a younger brother of

President Kennedy's, entered the race.

Secretary of Defense Clifford, LBJ's old friend, reported that he had consulted leaders around the country. Once they had been for the war. Now they thought we ought to get out. When Johnson himself consulted his advisory group of former and present government officials, they agreed with Clifford.

On March 31, 1968, LBJ announced on television that he had ordered sharp restrictions in the bombing. He called for peace talks. Then he stunned his listeners. He declared at the end that in order to keep his actions on Vietnam from being thought of as just playing politics, "I shall not seek, and I will not accept the nomination of my party for another term as your President."

Three days later, the North Vietnamese agreed to begin talks to end the war. The next day in Memphis, Tennessee, Martin Luther King, Jr., was assassinated. Blacks in cities across the nation exploded. They burned, looted, and rioted in 100 cities. In Washington, the flames of smoldering buildings in black neighborhoods, fired by blacks themselves, could be seen from the White House. The problems of the United States on the battlefields of Vietnam, halfway around the world, seemed on the way to solution. But in the nation's own front yard the challenges remained.

Peace talks began in Paris in May and dragged on throughout the months of the presidential campaign. On June 23, 1968—with the count starting from December 22, 1961, when the first American serviceman had died in Vietnam—the war became the longest in United States history.

SECTION 4 REVIEW

1. Identify or explain: Dean Rusk, Wayne Morse, "domino theory," "credibility gap," J. William Fulbright, Robert McNamara, Pentagon Papers, Tet offensive, Eugene McCarthy.

2. Why did President Johnson intervene in the Dominican Republic?

3. Trace the decline of support for the war in Vietnam and for President Johnson.

4. **Drawing Conclusions.** How did the Tonkin Gulf incident lead to our increased involvement in Vietnam?

FOCUSING ON IDEAS

1. What legislation was John Kennedy unable to convince Congress to pass? Why was President Johnson able to gain congressional approval for the same legislation?

2. How did the Civil Rights Act of 1964 change the lives of blacks living in the Deep South?

3. How did legislation enacted between 1964 and 1966 seek to promote greater equality? A better environment? Consumer protection?

4. Summarize the philosophies of Martin Luther King, Malcolm X, and Stokely Carmichael—the three principal black leaders of the 1960s. Which leader had the most lasting influence on the civil rights movement?

TAKING A CRITICAL LOOK

1. **Demonstrating Reasoned Judgment.** Which of the reasons cited for the United States' involvement in Vietnam do you consider the most compelling? The least compelling? Why?

2. **Recognizing Bias.** What reasons would you expect an antiwar activist in the 1960s to give when explaining why the United States should withdraw from Vietnam?

YOUR REGION IN HISTORY

1. **Geography.** Locate wilderness areas in your region that were preserved by the Wilderness Act of 1964.

2. **Culture.** Did any political demonstrations or urban riots in the 1960s take place near where you live? What brought them on? What happened? If your locality remained calm, how do you account for this?

3. **Economics.** How was your region directly affected by "Great Society" programs?

HISTORICAL FACTS AND FIGURES

Predicting Consequences. Study the graph below to help answer the following questions: (a) How many whites voted in 1964? How many blacks? How many Hispanics? (b) By approximately what percentage did white voter turnout increase from 1964 to 1984? Black voter turnout? Hispanic voter turnout? (c) Summarize the trends in voter turnout depicted by the graph. (d) What information in this chapter helps explain these trends? (e) How might these figures have differed had the civil rights legislation proposed by the Johnson administration not been enacted?

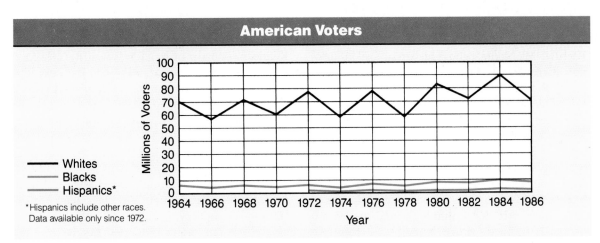

American Voters

Whites
Blacks
Hispanics*

*Hispanics include other races.
Data available only since 1972.

Millions of Voters

Year

Source: Bureau of the Census, Department of Commerce

CHAPTER **33**

The rise and fall of Richard Nixon

The Presidency of Richard M. Nixon produced a crisis in the life of the nation. In 1972 he and Vice-President Agnew won a second term with a popular majority of 18 million votes, the greatest number in history. Yet within two years, Agnew had resigned to avoid trial for bribery and income-tax evasion, and Nixon himself had left office to avoid impeachment. The ordeal of the nation was without precedent. But it also offered a unique opportunity for the representatives of a free people to show that the President was not above the law.

1. Electing the President, 1968

The election campaign of 1968 brought into the open many of the hopes and fears of the American people. In its course the short, blazing political career of Robert F. Kennedy would be snuffed out. It would see armed guards, barbed wire, and rioting in the streets of Chicago during the Democratic National Convention. And its end would find Richard M. Nixon, who had barely lost in 1960, now narrowly achieving his consuming ambition to be the President of the United States.

The race for the Democratic nomination. The Vietnam War ended the long political career of Lyndon B. Johnson. It also pushed Robert F. Kennedy into the presidential race. He campaigned across the country in the primaries against Senator Eugene McCarthy of Minnesota. Campaigning in the critical race for California's 174 convention delegates, Kennedy drove himself to exhaustion. And he won that state's support in the coming

Democratic convention. On the same day, June 5, he also won in South Dakota.

RFK went to the ballroom of the Ambassador Hotel in Los Angeles to thank the workers who had made his California victory possible. After his brief speech, he suddenly decided to leave the hall by the kitchen to avoid the crush of his well-wishers. There Sirhan Sirhan, a Jordanian who disliked Kennedy's support of Israel, was waiting. He fired three shots at the senator, who died the next day.

The nation had not yet recovered from the shock of the assassination in April of Martin Luther King. Now, only two months later, another prominent leader was murdered. The people who mourned their loss were also lamenting the rise of violence in American life.

When Lyndon Johnson stepped aside in March 1968, his buoyant, voluble Vice-President, Hubert Horatio Humphrey, decided to enter the race. Humphrey ran in no primaries, but he had the support of the leaders of the Democratic party.

When he arrived in Chicago for the party convention, he had enough votes to win the nomination on the first ballot.

Chaos in Chicago. The events that occurred in Chicago during the Democratic convention of 1968 were played out on television. What people saw damaged Hubert Humphrey's chances to win the Presidency.

Inside the convention hall, protected by guards and barbed wire, there was a nasty name-calling fight over the platform plank on the Vietnam War. One side, the followers of Eugene McCarthy and the late Robert Kennedy, demanded an immediate end to the bombing and the quick withdrawal of United States and North Vietnamese troops. They called for a coalition government of all South Vietnamese parties. The other side, followers of Johnson and Humphrey, supported peace talks. But they opposed withdrawing unless North Vietnam also withdrew. They wanted to stop the bombing of North Vietnam only when it "would not endanger the lives of our troops." Finally the Johnson-Humphrey resolution won. New York State's antiwar delegates pinned on black armbands of mourning.

In most cases, national party conventions in the United States had been good-humored. Festive delegates wore colorful hats, sang, joked, and cheered. At those times the nation could see each convention end in happy unity. Now the dark shadow of the Vietnam War had turned a circus into a funeral. The bitterness and violence of European and Latin American politics had somehow infected American life.

Outside, on the streets and in the parks of downtown Chicago, thousands of opponents of the war swarmed. Most conspicuous were the "Yippies"—the Youth International Party—who made fun of the whole affair. They nominated a pig, Pigasus, for President. But the fun soon ceased as fierce fighting broke out between the police and those who hated the war. The hot weather did not help. The result was an unpleasant spectacle, seen by millions on television just as Hubert Humphrey was nominated for President.

Humphrey would never escape the scenes of Chicago. They seemed to reflect the worst side of the United States of recent years—the war, the angry young people, the rioting in cities and on

Fred Ward/Black Star

The 1968 Democratic nomination was won by Hubert Humphrey after a bitter contest inside the convention hall in Chicago.

college campuses. The divided, wrangling Democrats did not look like a party that was prepared to solve the nation's problems.

The Republicans choose Nixon. The Republican fight for the nomination was, as usual, a far more gentlemanly affair. Richard Nixon had led the race all the way. Though challenges were made by Governor Rockefeller of New York and Governor Ronald Reagan of California, Nixon won easily at Miami, Florida. For his vice-presidential nominee, he chose Governor Spiro T. Agnew of Maryland. Agnew had begun as a liberal Republican, but after a riot in Baltimore following the death of Martin Luther King, he had emerged as a strong spokesman for law and order.

In his acceptance speech, Nixon called for the

During the Democratic convention in Chicago, streets teemed with youthful demonstrators: Yippies, members of SDS, and McCarthy supporters. Police, demonstrators, and bystanders finally met in a bloody clash which thousands of Americans watched on television.

support of the "silent majority." These Americans were "the non-shouters, the non-demonstrators, that are not racist or sick, that are not guilty of the crime that plagues our land." And on the war he made it clear that he would bring peace. "Those who have had a chance for four years and could not produce peace," he declared, "should not be given another chance."

The American Independent party. A third candidate, former Governor George C. Wallace of Alabama, opposed the federal push to integrate the schools, and he spoke out against the courts that "coddled criminals." He protested the attempts of the government to halt segregation in the sale or rental of all housing. He wanted to "win" in Vietnam. "I think we've got to pour it on there," he said. Wallace hoped to appeal to enough discontented voters to keep either of the major candidates from winning. Then the election would be thrown into the House of Representatives. There his supporters could use their votes for trading purposes to achieve Wallace's goals.

The issue of the courts. The main issue of the campaign was clearly the war in Vietnam. Nearly as important was the question of law and order. This issue touched everyone—especially people living in the slums of the cities, where the crime rate had soared. In the country as a whole during the 1960s, while the population went up only 13 percent, violent crimes climbed 148 percent.

Some people blamed this on the Supreme Court. Under Chief Justice Earl Warren, who had been appointed by President Eisenhower, the Court seemed to be overturning old standards and interfering everywhere.

It was constantly intruding within the states. In the *Brown* case it had decided for school integration. Then it began to lay down new rules for elections. In 1962 the Court declared that federal courts could step in to guarantee equal representation to all citizens in all states. For some years Americans had swarmed from farms into cities and their suburbs. Still many states had not changed their laws that apportioned representatives in the state legislatures. City voters did not have enough representatives, while farmers were over-represented. In 1964 the Court required all state legislatures to reapportion both their houses and their congressional districts on the principle of "one man, one vote." The people who lost their over-representation naturally did not like it.

The Supreme Court also decided some hard cases involving the separation of church and state. In 1962 the use of a prayer composed by the New York Board of Regents in public school classrooms was found to violate the First Amendment, which prohibited the establishment of religion. The next year the Court outlawed Bible readings in public school classrooms for the same reason. These decisions provoked outcries from some citizens. They denounced the Court for undermining the religious faith of American young people. They recalled that in the 1950s "under God" had been added to the Pledge of Allegiance and "In God We Trust" printed on all our currency. But others applauded the Supreme Court's defense of the First Amendment and said that religion was strong in the United States because it was not enforced by the government.

Many more Americans were troubled by the decisions of the Supreme Court which, they said, showed too much sympathy for persons accused of crime. They did not like the Court's rule in *Gideon* v. *Wainwright* (1963) that the state had to furnish legal counsel to poor defendants even in minor criminal cases. They objected when the Court decided in *Escobedo* v. *Illinois* (1964) and *Miranda* v. *Arizona* (1966) that a conviction would not stand unless the police had informed the accused of the right to remain silent and to have an attorney present when questioned. Suspects also had to be warned that any statement they made could be used against them in court. And in 1968 the Court ruled that in capital crimes (punishable by death) a person who opposed the death penalty could not for that reason be kept off the jury. This meant that many of the 435 persons awaiting execution on death row would have to be retried.

To many Americans these attempts of the Court to safeguard the constitutional rights of the individual against the power of the state just seemed another way of "pampering" criminals. In July 1968 a Gallup poll revealed that three Americans out of every five were unhappy over the Supreme Court's decisions. Candidate Nixon promised that

when there were openings on the Court, he would appoint "strict constructionists"—judges who would interpret the Constitution strictly.

Nixon wins. The election turned out to be closer than anyone had expected. Humphrey's campaign, which started slowly, began to pick up steam toward the end. And Wallace's drive, though weaker than he had hoped, won 10 million voters. Thirteen percent of the total cast their ballots for George Wallace and gave him five southern states. Nixon defeated Humphrey by only 510,000 votes out of the 73 million cast, and he received only 43.4 percent of the total vote. This gave him the lowest winning majority since Woodrow Wilson in 1912. The Democrats retained their control of both houses of Congress.

SECTION 1 REVIEW

1. Identify or explain: Eugene McCarthy, Sirhan Sirhan, "Yippies," Edmund Muskie, Ronald Reagan, Spiro Agnew, "silent majority," American Independent party, Earl Warren, *Gideon* v. *Wainwright*, *Escobedo* and *Miranda* cases.

2. How did violence affect the 1968 election campaign? Give examples.

3. What stand did the Warren Court take on (a) equality of representation? (b) school religious exercises? (c) criminal rights? Why did the Court's decisions arouse criticism?

4. **Predicting Consequences.** Would the outcome of the 1968 election have been different if George Wallace had not run? Explain your answer.

2. Nixon's first term

On election night Nixon declared that the theme of his Presidency would be to bring the American people together again. He said that he would try to calm the conflicts that were tearing the nation apart. But by nature he was a fighter and not a conciliator. He had battled his way—to the Congress, to the Vice-Presidency, and now to the White House—by attacking Communists and others whom he called enemies of the people. He was at home in the rough and tumble of politics. He was not well qualified to unite a troubled and divided nation.

After taking the oath of office, President
Nixon received the congratulations of LBJ.
Vice-President Agnew looks on (right).

Richard M. Nixon. Richard Nixon had been
born in California to Quaker parents. As a boy he
had worked hard in their grocery store. After
attending Whittier College in his hometown, he
went to Duke University Law School in North
Carolina. He practiced law in Whittier. Then
during World War II he worked for the Office of
Price Administration in Washington before going
into the navy. After he was discharged in 1946, he
ran for Congress as a Republican and was elected to
the House of Representatives.

Nixon made his reputation as the relentless
pursuer of Communists on the House Un-American
Activities Committee. There he won national
attention in the Alger Hiss case (p. 611). With the
personality of a prosecuting attorney, he made
many bitter enemies and many lukewarm friends.
The Hiss case helped elect him to the Senate from
California in 1950. Two years later he was nominated to run for Vice-President with General
Eisenhower.

When he ran for President against John F.
Kennedy in 1960, he lost by the smallest of
margins. Then in 1962 he ran for governor of
California, and again he lost. When Nixon's
political career seemed over, he moved to New
York City to join an important law firm. But he
never really gave up politics. And he stayed in the
public eye by his travels to foreign countries and his
speeches for Republican candidates. In 1968 he ran
again for President, and this time he won.

Although Richard Nixon had spent many years
in the national political spotlight, few people felt
that they knew the "real" Nixon. He was the
most private of men. Even his supporters wondered whether they knew the sort of man he
really was.

The Nixon White House. President Nixon proclaimed that he was going to keep the most open
White House in history. He would appoint only
the ablest people to his Cabinet, and they would
help him make policy. The President's staff, he
said, would merely collect information. The decisions would be made by others. But soon Nixon's
White House staff became the governing force in
the country.

He organized his staff with the military neatness
and chain of command that General Eisenhower
had brought to the Presidency. As chief of staff to
guard the President's time and arrange his calendar,
Nixon enlisted H. R. Haldeman, an efficient advertising man who had been a leader in Nixon's
election campaign. As his assistant on foreign affairs
he named Henry Kissinger, a witty and scholarly
Harvard professor. John D. Ehrlichman, a 44-
year-old Seattle lawyer and campaign aide, became
assistant to the President for domestic affairs.

Soon President Nixon had set up a presidential
staff of 48 personal assistants and hundreds of
secretaries and other employees—the largest in
history. In firm command and with these many
assistants, he hoped to secure effective control of the
huge and sprawling federal government. The
people working in the nation's bureaucracy now
numbered over 3 million—more than the country's
whole population at the signing of the Declaration
of Independence. Was it possible for any President
to direct so enormous an enterprise?

President Nixon was never satisfied with his
plan. Again and again he reorganized his staff and
rearranged his Cabinet. Oddly enough, the result
always seemed to be that power flowed into fewer
and fewer hands. The President seemed to become
isolated from the vast army of government workers—and the people who directed them.

The adventures in space. Nixon had been in the White House only six months when the great adventure of the century climaxed in success. The moon-landing project had been started by President Kennedy and pushed by President Johnson.

The enormous and costly project needed all the support it could find from the Presidents, the Congress, and the people. For there were great risks to life, and the costs ran to billions of dollars. When a fire exploded in 1967 during tests of a spaceship, three of the most experienced astronauts were killed. The final price tag on the moon shot came to $25 to $35 billion. Still, there were incalculable benefits—new industries, new products, and employment in new jobs for a third of a million people all over the country. And, most important, it gave a boost to the nation's courage and confidence along with new breath for the exploring spirit.

"We work in a place," boasted someone at the Manned Spacecraft Center in Houston, Texas, "where 13,000 men can feel like Columbus."

Finally, after nine years of preparing and two trial voyages around the moon and back, on July 16, 1969, Americans set out to land on the moon. Neil Armstrong headed the mission, Michael Collins piloted the command ship *Apollo 11,* and Edwin E. Aldrin, Jr., was to work with Armstrong during the landing.

None of these astronauts was a great scientist. None came from a family that was rich or famous. But they shared a passion for flying. All three were athletes in top physical condition. They were modest men who had practiced working together.

The dangerous voyage. The moon trip was unlike earlier explorations of unknown lands. For this voyage was watched on television by the whole world—including the explorers' own families. Hundreds of millions of people could share the adventure and the suspense.

The three astronauts shot up in the command ship *Apollo 11,* which took them orbiting around the earth. Then, after 2 1/2 orbits, they steered *Apollo 11* off toward the moon, more than 200,000 miles away. After the three-day journey through interplanetary space, they arrived in their moon orbit. Armstrong and Aldrin climbed into a small "lunar module" attached at the nose of *Apollo 11.* They called this little ship *Eagle.*

They separated *Eagle* from the command ship.

After orbiting the moon to the agreed position, they landed *Eagle* on the moon at 4:17 P.M. eastern daylight time on July 20, 1969.

There were risks till the last instant of the landing. As the computer guided them down, Armstrong noticed that they were about to settle in a deep crater about the size of a football field, filled with large boulders. He seized the controls and guided *Eagle* to a safe, smoother site.

Footsteps on the moon. Six and a half hours after landing, the first man, an American, stepped out on a heavenly body. For that moment the whole world, except those whose dictators forbade them to know, watched proudly together.

Surrounded by the footprints of the first earthlings on the moon, there remains to this day the launching stand from which Armstrong and Aldrin took off from the moon in their lunar module. And on it is a plaque that may last forever. For on the moon there is no atmosphere, there is no wind to blow, no oxygen to rust, and no water to erode. The message on the plaque does not boast an American achievement but proclaims the hope of the world. "Here men from the planet earth first set foot upon the moon, July 1969, A.D. We came in peace for all mankind."

Winding down the war. The nation had been reunited in these exhilarating moments. Watching together, people knew that this was another triumph of Americans working together—sharing resources with the whole world of science.

But when the day of success in outer space was past, Americans still remained divided by the miseries of the no-win war in Vietnam. President Nixon had promised to end that war. He told the nation again in May 1969 that he intended to keep that pledge. But he "ruled out either a one-sided withdrawal . . . or the acceptance of terms that would amount to a disguised American defeat." To make his message doubly clear to North Vietnam, in March he had actually taken the risk of widening the war. He then began secret large-scale bombing of suspected North Vietnamese and Viet Cong bases in Cambodia. To avoid antiwar protests, Nixon did not tell Congress or the American public. In fact, this operation was so hush-hush that even the Secretary of the Air Force was kept from knowing about it.

The first human beings to step on the desolate surface of the moon were two United States astronauts. Neil Armstrong took this dramatic photograph of Edwin E. Aldrin, Jr.

While Nixon secretly enlarged the war, he began publicly to withdraw from it. When he took office, there were half a million American troops in Vietnam. In June he announced that 25,000 American soldiers would be coming home. And in September he announced that another 35,000 would be withdrawn during the following months.

Opposition to the war. Still the President's actions did not satisfy those who wanted the United States out of the war. In October and November 1969 they held antiwar rallies in Washington and elsewhere. Opposition to the war now included large numbers from all parts of American society. The Senate, too, was making it clear that it intended to play a more active role in foreign affairs. In June a "Sense of the Senate" resolution, passed by the overwhelming majority of 70–16, told the President not to commit men or funds to any country without the express approval of Congress.

Nixon's policy, as he explained to the nation during 1969, was to decrease American involvement while at the same time letting the South Vietnamese take over the struggle. On April 20, 1970, he informed the country that over the next year he would remove 150,000 more United States troops from Vietnam. This decision, he said, "means that we finally have in sight the just peace we are seeking."

Ten days later the nation was staggered to learn that United States troops had entered Cambodia, a small country that shared a long border with Vietnam. This was called an "incursion," to make clear that it was just a brief raid—to strike at supplies and the "headquarters for the entire Communist military operation in South Vietnam."

The Cambodian "incursion" was greeted by a storm of opposition, especially in colleges and universities across the United States. At Kent State University in Ohio students became so violent that the governor called out the National Guard. And then, on May 4, a frightened Guard unit opened fire on the students, killing four. Soon more than 80 colleges and universities suspended classes, seething with opposition to the war. Thousands of demonstrators, including college presidents, professors, and students, gathered in Washington.

All this impressed and persuaded the Congress. On June 24, 1970, the Senate voted 81–10 to repeal the Tonkin Gulf Resolution (p. 690).

Peace at last. Even as the United States wound down American involvement and brought fighting men home, the conflict in Indochina continued to spread. This war seemed to have its own terrible momentum. In February 1971 South Vietnamese troops, aided by American helicopters and bombers, invaded Laos. Later the State Department explained that this was only an attempt to protect the withdrawal of United States forces. That November, Congress was still disturbed by Nixon's failure to end the war. An amendment was tacked on a military procurement bill calling for the withdrawal of the United States by a "date certain" after the release of United States prisoners of war. The President signed the bill but said he would ignore the amendment.

In March 1972, thousands of North Vietnamese troops openly invaded South Vietnam. The United States replied by unleashing the largest and most powerful air force in history in bombing raids all across Indochina. Two months later there was still no word from North Vietnam. The President increased the pressure by allowing mines to be dropped into Haiphong Harbor, even though Russian ships there might be endangered. Still, in late August he announced that by December 1972 there would be only 27,000 American fighting men left in Vietnam.

Within months after Nixon took office, secret peace talks between the United States and North Vietnam had begun. Finally, in the fall of 1972, terms for a cease-fire were reached. But the South Vietnamese had not been informed of the talks and they refused to agree. Still, the United States presented the South Vietnamese demands to the North Vietnamese. With that, the agreement collapsed. Then, on December 18, United States planes began the fiercest bombing attacks of the war on North Vietnam. They were meant to force the North to accept the agreement with the United States. They were also intended to persuade the South Vietnamese to go along by showing that the United States would support them if North Vietnam ever violated the cease-fire. The United States, without any public explanation, halted the attacks on December 30.

On January 15, 1973, Nixon announced that so much progress had been made in the peace talks that he was calling a halt to all United States offensive action in Vietnam. Then on January 27 a cease-fire accord was finally reached in Paris. All fighting was to stop in Vietnam, and the North Vietnamese were to release the American prisoners of war. The United States was to withdraw completely from Vietnam.

After losing 46,104 men in the war and with 1200 missing, the United States was doing exactly what President Nixon had said we never would do. This was both "a one-sided withdrawal" and "the acceptance of terms that would amount to a one-sided defeat." American troops withdrew while North Vietnamese troops remained. When the United States had entered the war in a big way in 1965 there were, according to the State Department, 20,000 North Vietnamese in South Vietnam. When we left there were 145,000. But American soldiers were no longer fighting in South Asia.

Moscow and Peking. The world had become smaller than most Americans imagined. The jet airplane had brought the continents close together.

In the middle of July 1971 Nixon startled the American people when he announced that he intended to fly to Communist China. The People's Republic of China, with its 800 million people, had become a leading power in the world. Still, after 22 years, the United States had not recognized the government or exchanged ambassadors. Early in August, the President declared that the United States would reverse its position and support Red China's membership in the UN. Nixon was able to make these moves because no one could challenge his credentials as a fighter against communism.

On February 21, 1972, President Nixon landed in Peking. There, aided by Secretary of State Kissinger, he began to bring the relations of the two countries back to normal. This was the boldest diplomatic move by an American President since Jefferson bought Louisiana.

The Chinese and the Russians, though both had Communist governments, were bitter rivals. A clever American diplomacy required that the

One of the highlights of President and Mrs. Nixon's visit to the People's Republic of China was a formal Chinese banquet hosted by Zhou Enlai, the Chinese premier (second from left). Under the flags of both nations, Nixon and Zhou toasted the newly opened communications between their two countries.

United States balance its new friendliness to China with a new gesture to the Soviets. A few months later, therefore, President Nixon went to Russia for a summit meeting with Soviet leader Leonid Brezhnev. The two men were to sign a series of agreements on the environment, space, health, and science. But the main document was the *Strategic Arms Limitation Treaty* (SALT). The two countries had been working on it since 1969. That treaty, signed on May 26, 1972, aimed to slow down the dangerous and expensive nuclear arms race. Each country agreed to set up only two antiballistic missile (ABM) defense sites. Both agreed to build no more ICBMs or SLBMs.

The Peking and Moscow trips were successful steps in Nixon's plan to ease tensions and reduce risks of war with the Communist powers. The new expression for this was détente (from the French word meaning to ease or relax). Truman had aimed at "containment"—to keep the Communists boxed in. But Nixon's main hope was to prevent open conflict.

Nixon and domestic affairs. At home, too, the President said he wanted to reduce conflict. He criticized the Supreme Court for giving the "green light" to criminals and for failing to slow down the integration of the schools. During his election campaign he had promised to appoint more conservative justices to the Court. In May 1969 he nominated, and the Senate confirmed, Judge Warren Burger of Minnesota as the Chief Justice in place of Earl Warren, who was retiring. But in its first decision the Burger Court unanimously ruled that segregation in Mississippi schools—and also, this meant, throughout the nation—must end "at once." The Nixon administration had joined the state of Mississippi in asking for a delay.

President Nixon had the opportunity to name three more members of the Supreme Court. But the Senate was suspicious of his nominees. They refused to confirm two of them, saying they were not qualified. With the new appointees whom the Senate did approve, the Supreme Court changed. It did continue to press for school integration. But it was less active than the Warren Court (pp. 698-699), and it tended to interpret the Constitution so as to narrow somewhat the rights of those accused of crimes.

Richard Nixon was mainly interested in foreign affairs. He had no grand dream for a new domestic policy to remake the face of the nation. Like President Eisenhower, he wanted to cut the cost of government and turn over more activities to the states. He wanted to balance the budget and bring inflation under control. But since the Democrats controlled Congress throughout his time in office, he had trouble reaching his goals.

A troubled economy. Inflation was becoming familiar. It had begun under LBJ and was Nixon's gravest domestic problem. During the election he had promised to end inflation. He hoped to do this by balancing the budget (then about $200 billion) and, if possible, by producing a surplus. Still, inflation kept rising. Congress continued to pass expensive programs. And a tax reform act in 1969 ended President Johnson's income-tax surcharge. Meanwhile, the unhappy war in Vietnam increased the demand for everything and kept the spiral of prices going up. Even so, the country went into its first business recession since 1961.

During 1969 and 1970, Nixon avoided setting wage-price guidelines. He hoped that the mild business recession of 1969-1970 and his economic policies would slow the upward rise of prices. Instead, between January 1969 and August 1971, prices went up 14.5 percent. This rapid rise forced Nixon to change his policies. On August 15, 1971, he announced a 90-day wage-price freeze. He was the first President ever to use mandatory wage-price controls in peacetime.

At the same time, he cut the dollar loose from gold. This meant that the United States would no longer let foreign governments turn in their dollars for our gold. He also asked foreign nations to let their own money become more valuable in dollars. And he put a 10 percent surcharge on foreign imports. President Nixon hoped in this way to promote the sale of American goods abroad and also discourage Americans from buying foreign products.

After these policies were adopted, inflation fell in 1972 to 3.5 percent. With a budget that in 1971 showed a $22.3 billion deficit and with an even larger deficit projected for 1972, the economy began to thrive and unemployment dropped from 5.9 percent of the work force in 1971 to 5.6 percent in 1972. For President Nixon—and the nation—these were welcome facts as he planned for reelection.

1. Identify or explain: H. R. Haldeman, John Ehrlichman, Henry Kissinger, Neil Armstrong, Michael Collins, Edwin E. Aldrin, Jr., *Apollo 11,* Cambodian incursion, Kent State incident, Leonid Brezhnev, SALT Warren Burger.

2. Summarize Nixon's career up until 1968.

3. Make a time line showing key events in the Vietnam War, including responses to the war at home, from 1969 to 1973.

4. What were Nixon's goals for (a) the Supreme Court, (b) the economy, (c) foreign policy? To what extent was he successful in achieving those goals?

5. **Making Comparisons.** In what ways was the moon-landing project different from previous explorations of the unknown?

3. The fall

The election of 1972 was to see Richard Nixon win the greatest popular majority in the history of the United States. Yet less than two years after his great victory he would become the first President ever to resign from office.

The Nixon outlook. The destruction of Richard Nixon began long before the campaign. Perhaps it began as far back as 1960 when he lost to Kennedy by such a narrow margin. For that convinced Nixon that he must never again leave anything undone in an election campaign—no matter how certain victory might appear.

His trouble was rooted in his view of himself and his opponents. Nixon the fighter never failed to see politics as a battleground—where you used whatever tactics were needed to win. "His use of football analogies was so revealing," Cabinet member Elliot Richardson explained. "Anything was OK except what the referee sees and blows the whistle on."

Pursuing enemies. It was not surprising that Nixon had a passion for secrecy. Those who opposed him he called his enemies. His special targets were people in the antiwar movement and his newspaper and TV critics. Against them he believed that he had the right to wield all the powers of the President. To spy on them and harass them he used government agencies such as the CIA, FBI, IRS, and FCC. Even when these activities were not technically illegal, they were an abuse of his presidential powers.

Nixon was determined to find out how the news of the secret bombing of Cambodia had reached the newspapers. In 1969, then, he ordered the FBI to place wiretaps (without the court orders required by law) on certain government employees and reporters. Believing that the antiwar protesters were actually tied to the Communists, in 1970 he tried to create his own super-secret intelligence group. This group would open mail, tap telephones, and even break into private homes and offices to get evidence to prove that his political opponents—his "enemies"—were really traitors. If his personal spies were caught, the answer would be that it was all for "national security"—to protect the nation. This plan was dropped, however, because J. Edgar Hoover, the man who had built up the FBI and was the nation's chief spy-catcher, refused to go along. "The risks are too great," he warned.

In June 1971 the *New York Times* began to publish the "Pentagon Papers." This was the secret study of United States involvement in Vietnam that Secretary McNamara had ordered in 1967 (p. 693). The document had been given to the *Times* by Daniel Ellsberg, who had worked on the report. The government said the report would reveal secret information damaging to the national security and therefore sued to stop the *Times.* When the case went to the Supreme Court, the Court refused to intervene and allowed the papers to be printed.

The Department of Justice then indicted Daniel Ellsberg for theft, conspiracy, and espionage. President Nixon remained deeply disturbed. He was determined to track down his enemies—even if he had to set up his own system of counterespionage!

Within the White House, Nixon now formed a secret special unit. Since the job of this unit was to "stop leaks" of information, it was called the "Plumbers." Their first assignment was to find some way to ruin the reputation of Daniel Ellsberg. But the Plumbers were inept. Hoping to uncover some embarrassing information, they broke into the Los Angeles office of Ellsberg's psychiatrist. They found nothing. This was only one in a series of illegal acts that would destroy Nixon and his closest aides. For the Plumbers would soon turn from "national security" to party politics. And they would finally bring down the President, whom they were supposed to protect.

McGovern wins the Democratic nomination. One part of the Nixon campaign strategy for reelection in 1972 was to divide the Democrats against themselves. Then the Nixon group would promote the candidate who was the easiest to defeat. This scheme included giving financial support to George Wallace of Alabama, opposing middle-of-the-road Edmund Muskie of Maine, and favoring the candidacy of George McGovern of South Dakota. It also included a variety of "dirty tricks." False letters were sent out attacking one candidate under the name of another. "The idea," one of the Nixon managers explained, "was to get the candidates backbiting each other."

George Wallace's push for the Democratic nomination was cut short by a shocking act of violence. While delivering a campaign speech in Laurel, Maryland, he was shot by an angry listener. Three bystanders were also shot. At first it seemed that Wallace might not survive. He lived but became paralyzed from the waist down and was no longer a serious contender.

Muskie's campaign faltered early, and George McGovern took the lead. He had helped to reform the party rules after 1968. More women, blacks, and young people would be delegates at the convention in 1972. He made a special effort to appeal to each of these groups.

When the party met in Miami Beach early in July, Senator McGovern won the nomination easily on the first ballot. As his running mate he chose Senator Thomas F. Eagleton of Missouri. But soon it came out that Eagleton had been hospitalized for psychiatric problems. McGovern asked Eagleton to step down. As a replacement the Democratic National Committee named Sargent Shriver, a brother-in-law of John and Robert Kennedy's. McGovern's judgment and his stability were called into question by his handling of this problem. At first he had said that he was behind Eagleton "1000 percent." Then suddenly he turned around and dropped him.

The 1972 campaign. The Republicans also met in Miami Beach and quickly renominated Nixon and

Lawrence Fried/Magnum

Despite some enthusiastic support, George McGovern was badly defeated in 1972.

Agnew. They had an easy campaign. President Nixon seldom left the White House. He took a strong stand against busing and for the local control of schools. He also opposed abortion. He was against legalizing the smoking of marijuana and against welfare payments for those who would not work. He kept the bitter Vietnam issue alive by opposing amnesty for those who had avoided fighting in the war by deserting from the armed forces or by dodging the draft. At the same time the news in late October that peace seemed to be at hand in Vietnam was a boost for Richard Nixon's campaign.

McGovern was openly against the war in Vietnam. He favored allowing the states to permit abortions, and making the smoking of marijuana a noncriminal offense. He was for cutting defense spending and changing the welfare system. Some of his proposals were not well thought out and were easy to attack. The Republicans called him a far-left candidate with far-out ideas.

On election day Nixon won a resounding victory. With 60.2 percent of the vote, he carried 49

James H. Pickerell

H. R. Haldeman testifies before the Senate Committee probing the Watergate break-in.

of the 50 states. McGovern had hoped for strong support from the new young voters. In 1971 the Twenty-sixth Amendment had been passed allowing any citizen 18 or over to vote. But many of these 11.5 million new voters failed to vote at all, and of those who did, many voted for Nixon. Only 55.7 percent of all Americans old enough to vote went to the polls—the lowest number since 1948.

Spying on the Democrats. The result showed that the Republicans had such an easy win that they really could have played by all the rules and still gained a large majority. Yet, for some reason they would not leave well enough alone. The nervous Nixon team, to make their victory doubly sure, had turned to underhanded tactics. As early as January 1972 Attorney General John Mitchell, who was soon to resign to devote full time to heading Nixon's campaign, heard one of the Plumbers present a program of secret, illegal campaign activities. A $1 million program of kidnapping, wiretapping, and "dirty tricks" to hurt the Democrats was suggested. Mitchell rejected the plan as too expensive.

Though he was the nation's chief law-enforcement official, the Attorney General said nothing about the idea being wrong.

Finally, the campaign managers agreed to spend $250,000 on a new kind of political intelligence-gathering plan. None of them really liked it. In fact, one later said, "We feared that it might be a waste of money and also that it might be dangerous." But the White House wanted to know what its political opponents were up to. John Mitchell and the others approved an elaborate criminal plan, which included "bugging" the office of Lawrence O'Brien, head of the Democratic National Committee.

The first wiretap on O'Brien's phones did not work. Then, on the night of June 16, the Plumbers once again broke into the Democratic National Committee offices in the Watergate office building. And this time they were caught! They carried evidence that might link them to the White House and so open the President to the charge of being a criminal conspirator.

Nixon orders a cover-up. President Nixon did not know about the Watergate break-in until after it happened. But then easily, almost carelessly, he moved to cover up the crime. As soon as he and his aides did that, they were committing a crime themselves.

First the President ordered his staff to tell the CIA to stop the FBI from investigating the case. They were to say that "national security" was involved. Richard Helms, Director of Central Intelligence, refused to have the CIA involved. So Nixon saw that money was paid to the Plumbers to keep them quiet about their connection to the White House. By September 1972 these men had received $220,000 in hush money.

Somehow the Watergate affair did not really catch the public's attention when it took place. Still, newspaper reporters Robert Woodward and Carl Bernstein kept probing the strange events surrounding Watergate. Their reports, published in the *Washington Post,* kept the time bomb of Watergate ticking. It would go off, however, only after Nixon was safely reelected. Watergate would prove to be one of the oddest—and most unnecessary—crimes in American history.

Investigating the campaign. Soon after the Senate convened in 1973, it voted 77–0 to set up a committee to look into any "illegal, improper, or unethical activities" in the 1972 election. Senator Sam Ervin of North Carolina was to head the committee.

When the Ervin Committee began its hearings, President Nixon and his aides felt pressure from three sides. If anyone involved in the burglary told the truth to a judge or to the Department of Justice or to the Ervin Committee, the White House link to the Plumbers would be revealed. So the President and his aides tried to devise still more ways to cover up their connection to the crime.

Nixon sank deeper and deeper into a new crime—the crime of the cover-up. The American people might have excused a President for making mistakes. But they would not tolerate a President who did not take seriously his sworn duty to obey and enforce the law.

Nixon under pressure. Hoping to lift some of the pressure, on April 17, 1973, the President issued a statement that because of "major developments in the case" he had ordered "intensive new inquiries." He said that he had not learned until March 21, 1973, that there were attempts to cover up the scandal. This was a lie, for he had known ever since late June 1972. Nixon now heard that some of the people involved in the cover-up were beginning to talk. He was desperately trying to save himself. He had been informed by Attorney General Richard Kleindienst that the Department of Justice had enough information to indict Haldeman, Ehrlichman, and John Mitchell. He knew, too, that he could be impeached. So he began to thrash about, talking of using "a million dollars" and "clemency" to end this disaster.

On April 29, Nixon told his chief aides, Ehrlichman and Haldeman, who were in deep trouble, that they were fired. The following day, he told the nation on TV that he was naming a new Attorney General, Elliot Richardson, who was empowered to appoint a special prosecutor to investigate the Watergate case.

The discovery of the tapes. "The Greatest Show on Earth," as the Ervin Committee hearings soon were called, opened its televised proceedings on May 17, 1973. They went on for three months. Millions watched fascinated by all the strange doings of the Nixon men—"enemies lists," money drops,

dirty tricks, millions raised illegally from corporations, and attempts to use the IRS to harass enemies.

Then, late in the hearings, the news came out that since February 1971 there had been tape recording machines in the White House and Executive Office Building. Unknown to all but a few, these machines had been taping everything said there by the President and his aides. Nixon had been anxious that the events of his Presidency should be amply recorded for future historians. The tapes would make history in a way he never imagined. They would finally destroy Richard Nixon.

As soon as the existence of the tapes was known, both the Ervin Committee and the new special prosecutor, Harvard professor Archibald Cox, wanted to hear certain key conversations. Nixon refused to hand over the tapes. He insisted that the President could not do his job if his records were not kept confidential. So the matter went to the courts. On October 12, the Court of Appeals ruled, 5–2, against the President. "Though the President is elected by nationwide ballot," the court declared, "and is often said to represent all the people, he . . . is not above the law's commands." Nixon had a week to decide whether to appeal the decision, to turn over the tapes, or to take some other action.

Agnew resigns. At this moment when the net was closing ever more tightly around the struggling President, Vice-President Agnew—who had risen to power by preaching law and order—was accused of serious crimes. On August 1, 1973, he was told by the Department of Justice that he was being investigated for income-tax evasion, conspiracy, bribery, and extortion. There was evidence that he had accepted kickbacks from Maryland state contractors as governor and even as Vice-President.

At first Agnew protested his innocence. Then, after bargaining with the prosecution, he decided to resign as Vice-President and to plead "no contest" to tax evasion. This meant that he would not try to prove his innocence in court and that he would accept the penalties of being guilty. In return, the government was willing to drop the other charges against him. The prosecution also asked the court for leniency "out of compassion for the man, out of respect for the office he has held, and out of appreciation for the fact that by his resignation he has spared the nation the prolonged agony that

During the Watergate hearings, a cartoonist showed the White House as a giant tape recorder.

would have attended upon his trial." The court fined him $10,000 and placed him on probation for three years. The government then released in detail the evidence against him.

Fortunately, in 1967 the Twenty-fifth Amendment to the Constitution had been adopted. It came from the time of President Eisenhower's illness and was mainly intended for a situation when the President was not physically able to carry on the duties of his office. In case of a vacancy in the office of the Vice-President, the President would nominate someone who was to be confirmed by both houses of Congress. President Nixon now made the first use of the amendment. For the new Vice-President he chose Gerald R. Ford of Grand Rapids, Michigan, the Republican floor leader in the House of Representatives. Well known and respected in Congress, he was quickly confirmed.

War in the Middle East. To add to Nixon's troubles, on October 6, 1973, war broke out anew in the Middle East. Egypt and Syria attacked Israel on Yom Kippur, the holiest day of the Jewish year. Then, on October 12, the President decided to go all out to aid the Israelis and offset the supplies the Arabs were receiving from Russia. He ordered a massive airlift from the United States all the 6450 miles to Israel—including helicopters, howitzers, and even 50-ton tanks. In response, the Arabs

embargoed oil shipments to the United States. The winter of 1973–1974 found the United States faced with its first gasoline shortage.

The Saturday Night Massacre. President Nixon now made a move that was to lose him much of whatever support he had left in the country. First, he announced on Friday, October 20, that Watergate was sapping the strength of the nation. To resolve the crisis, he said he would compromise on the issue of the tapes. He would offer summaries of their contents. He also revealed that he had ordered Special Prosecutor Cox to stop trying to get the tapes.

The following day Cox refused to accept the President's order. He demanded the actual tapes. Nixon then told Attorney General Richardson to fire Cox. But Richardson had promised both Cox and the Senate that he would not interfere with the Special Prosecutor, so he resigned. Then Nixon asked the Deputy Attorney General to fire Cox. But he, too, resigned rather than carry out the order. Finally, Robert Bork, the Solicitor General, who believed that the President had the right to fire Cox, whatever might be the wisdom of the act, discharged the Special Prosecutor.

This was called "the Saturday Night Massacre." Elliot Richardson later said that by firing Cox, President Nixon wanted to show the world that he was still in charge of the government. "It was like the 1970 action in Cambodia," he said. "He wanted to show Moscow and Peking his determination, and to do that he would pay the necessary domestic price."

But Nixon had misjudged the American people. To them his actions seemed an admission of guilt. *Time* magazine, which had never before run an editorial in all its 50 years, now said, "The President Should Resign."

The President's troubles mount. At this point the House Judiciary Committee began hearings to decide whether the President should be impeached. Nixon finally gave in. He agreed to give up to the court the tapes that had been subpoenaed and to appoint a new Special Prosecutor.

As if Nixon did not have enough problems at this point, his personal finances were also being investigated. A House committee revealed that he had paid less than $1000 in taxes in both 1971 and 1972 even though he had earned $200,000 each year. His low taxes were based on a questionable gift of his vice-presidential papers (which he valued at $570,000) to the National Archives in 1969. This had saved him $235,000 in taxes. It also came out that $10 million in federal funds had been spent on his properties at Key Biscayne in Florida and San Clemente in California and on his daughters' houses. Even though the money was said to be for security for the President and his family, the amounts seemed to be way out of line.

By early 1974 President Nixon was under such pressure that he was no longer able to govern effectively. But still he held on, although he spent as little time as possible in Washington.

On March 1, 1974, Mitchell, Haldeman, Ehrlichman, and five others were indicted by a grand jury for conspiring to cover up the Watergate break-in, for obstructing justice, and for perjury. In a secret report the grand jury also named Nixon as a co-conspirator. He was not indicted because the new Special Prosecutor, Leon Jaworski, argued that a President could not be indicted until he had been impeached and removed from office.

Nixon made one last desperate attempt to escape his problems. On April 29, 1974, he went on television. He was seated before a tall stack of blue notebooks, which he described as the transcripts of more tapes that he had recently been asked for—and which he had refused to hand over. These, he said, contained everything about Watergate "and what I did about it."

The transcripts astounded the country. They revealed the President and his aides as petty men, speaking in vulgar expletives. They were constantly scheming about how to "get" their enemies. Senator Hugh Scott of Pennsylvania, leader of the Republicans in the Senate, called the tapes "a shabby, disgusting, immoral performance."

Still the Judiciary Committee and Jaworski continued to press Nixon for the actual tapes themselves. When he refused, the question went on its way to the Supreme Court.

The House committee favors impeachment. Under the Constitution, the House of Representatives has to vote the articles of impeachment against a President. Then the President is tried by the whole Senate, with the Chief Justice presiding.

On July 24, after nearly three months of private hearings, the House Judiciary Committee began its public televised debate over the articles of impeachment. On July 27 the committee voted 27 to 11 in favor of Article 1—that the President had followed a "course of conduct or plan" to obstruct

President Nixon sits before a stack of notebooks containing what he claimed to be the full transcripts of the Watergate tapes.

justice in the cover-up of the Watergate break-in. Six Republicans had joined the 21 Democrats to vote against their President. Two days later, the committee voted a second article of impeachment— that the President had abused his power when he used the Plumbers, the IRS, FBI, CIA, and other government agencies in violation of the constitutional rights of citizens. Finally, on July 30, it voted 21 to 17 to impeach the President also for failing to abide by legal House subpoenas. The committee voted against attempting to impeach the President for the secret bombing of Cambodia or for evading taxes or for using government funds on his homes.

The whole nation watched in sadness—but also in awe and admiration—as they saw the men and women of the committee show such judicial fairness. The committee as a whole seemed to rise above the bitterness of partisan politics. The nation was inspired to see its representatives take such pains to cleanse the White House. As it became plain that the committee would have to vote to impeach the President, some committee members of both parties were in tears. They, too, were saddened at what they had to do.

The President resigns. Even at this point, it seemed possible that the House of Representatives might vote not to approve the committee's report. Or, even if they did approve the three articles of impeachment, perhaps the President would not be convicted by the Senate. Some members of Congress still felt that the committee had not found the "smoking gun"—the clear, unmistakable evidence of a presidential act to cover up the break-in. Without such evidence, should a few hundred representatives in Congress vote to remove from office a Chief Executive who had been voted into office by a majority of millions of Americans? Some of the members of Congress still feared that they would set a precedent. Would some future Congress remove a President simply because they did not like him or disagreed with his policy?

The tapes (which the President himself had ordered to insure his place in history!) proved Richard Nixon's final undoing. The Supreme Court decided on July 24 that he had to hand them over. Then the President could hide no longer. On August 5, 1974, he confessed that portions of the tape for June 23, 1972, were "at variance with certain of my previous statements." That tape clearly recorded the President in his own voice ordering Haldeman to get the CIA to stop the FBI investigation of the break-in. This showed that Nixon had lied all along about when he knew of the cover-up and that he had, in fact, personally ordered the cover-up.

That night, as the fall of the President seemed certain, Secretary of Defense James R. Schlesinger took the unheard-of action of ordering all United States military commanders to refuse to accept orders from the White House unless they were countersigned by him. The President could no longer be trusted. The following day Nixon informed the Cabinet that he still would not resign. Congress would have to impeach him. But on August 7 three of the most respected Republican leaders—Senator Hugh Scott, Senator Barry Goldwater, and Representative John Rhodes—called on President Nixon and made it clear that he had no support. If he tried to stand and fight, they said, he would be impeached by the House, and then he would be convicted by the Senate.

The next day Nixon, on television to the nation, announced his decision to resign. On August 9, 1974, he signed the official letter of resignation. He was the first President ever forced to leave office before the end of his term.

While the tearful former President was flying across the nation to his home in San Clemente, California, back in Washington Gerald Ford was being sworn in as the thirty-eighth President of the United States.

SECTION 3 REVIEW

1. Identify or explain: wiretaps, Daniel Ellsberg, "Plumbers," George McGovern, Sargent Shriver, Lawrence O'Brien, Woodward and Bernstein, Ervin Committee, Elliot Richardson, Archibald Cox, 25th Amendment, Gerald Ford, oil embargo, "Saturday Night Massacre," Leon Jaworski.

2. Account for President Nixon's easy victory in the 1972 election.

3. Recount the highlights of the Watergate affair from the break-ins to Nixon's resignation.

4. **Recognizing Ideologies.** How was Nixon's preoccupation with "national security" reflected in his pursuit of his "enemies"?

FOCUSING ON IDEAS

1. Why have modern Presidents required a large White House staff? What problems arise from this arrangement?

2. Why did President Nixon undertake to establish relations with the People's Republic of China? Why was Nixon well-suited to bring about this change of policy?

3. In May 1969 what conditions did Nixon rule out in the Vietnam peace negotiations? Were those conditions met? Explain.

4. How did two resignations bring Gerald Ford to the Presidency?

TAKING A CRITICAL LOOK

1. **Drawing Conclusions.** How did the "Sense of the Senate" resolution in 1969 reflect popular opposition to the Vietnam War?

2. **Recognizing Cause and Effect.** Opinion polls taken in 1973 and 1976 showed a sharp drop in people's "trust in government". What may have been some other side-effects of Watergate?

YOUR REGION IN HISTORY

1. **Geography.** Was your state legislature reapportioned as a result of the 1964 Supreme Court decision in *Reynolds* v. *Sims*? If so, how has your county or other election district been affected by reapportionment?

2. **Culture.** Was your school district affected by the 1962 and 1963 Supreme Court decisions on religious exercises? Explain. How do those decisions affect your school today?

3. **Economics.** Collect data on the cost of living, rate of unemployment, and average salary earned for your region during the Nixon era. How does this information relate to major Nixon Administration economic policies? Did Nixon win a majority of votes in your region in his bid for reelection?

HISTORICAL FACTS AND FIGURES

Synthesizing Information. Study the graph below to help answer the following questions: (a) Approximately how many American soldiers were in Vietnam in 1968? In 1970? In 1973? (b) Contrast the following list of events with the information presented in the graph:

1970 American troops sent into Cambodia to attack enemy bases. Secret bombings of Cambodia begin.

1971 American helicopters and bombers help South Vietnamese invade Laos.

1972 United States resumes bombings over North Vietnam.

1973 Peace agreement and cease-fire begin.

What information in the chapter helps explain why the United States was reducing troop strength at the time that our involvement in the Indochina war was expanding?

Troops in Vietnam, 1968-1973

1973	Fewer than 250
1972	
1971	
1970	
1969	
1968	

= 100,000 Troops

Source: Department of Defense

MAKING CONNECTIONS

THEMES

This unit began on page 659 with the observation that the 1960s would herald the beginning of a turbulent era for the United States, punctuated by the convictions of a new generation:

"Let the word go forth from this time and place, to friend and foe alike, that the torch has been passed to a new generation of Americans..."

This declaration was supported by the three unit themes that are reprinted in **dark type** below. Use the time line and the information in Unit 11 to answer the questions that follow the unit themes.

1. **John F. Kennedy's 1000 days in office bring optimism to the nation.**

   How did John F. Kennedy lift American spirits? What did he accomplish?

2. **Lyndon Johnson's strong leadership expands opportunities for all Americans while deeply dividing the country over the war in Vietnam.**

   What questions did President Johnson's domestic and foreign policies raise concerning American values?

3. **The Watergate scandal tests the nation's constitutional system of government and leads to President Nixon's resignation.**

   How did President Nixon's beliefs about the powers of the presidency create an atmosphere in which the Watergate affair occurred?

Events in American History

1963 200,000 black and white freedom marchers gather at the Lincoln Memorial to demand civil rights reform.

1967 Race riots erupt in Cleveland, Detroit, Boston, Newark, and other cities.

1964 Congress passes the Tonkin Gulf Resolution, expanding U.S. involvement in Vietnam.

Events in World History

1961   1963   1965   1967

1963 Ngo Dinh Diem, South Vietnam's president, is overthrown in a military coup.

1961 The Soviet Union builds the Berlin Wall, sealing off East Berlin.

1961 President Kennedy proposes the Peace Corps and the Alliance for Progress.

1965 The Voting Rights Act aids black voter registration.

1971 President Nixon announces a 90-day wage-price freeze.

1972 The United States establishes relations with the People's Republic of China.

1974 Richard Nixon becomes the first United States President to resign.

1973 Congress begins hearings into the Watergate affair.

1967 **1969** **1971** **1973** **1975** **1977**

1968 North Vietnam launches the Tet offensive, surrounding American troops.

1971 The United Nations votes to admit the People's Republic of China and to expel Taiwan.

UNIT 12

The United States looks ahead

When the United States had its two-hundredth birthday in 1976, it was already the oldest of the new nations. And when in 1987 Americans celebrated the two-hundredth anniversary of the framing of the Constitution, the nation was living by the world's oldest written constitution still in use.

Since the Civil War, Americans had been seeking ways to keep their country young in spirit. The nation had been kept young by always asking what it meant to be an American.

In these next years the nation, more anxiously than ever before, would seek equality of opportunity for all Americans. Congress passed laws, and citizens organized, to bring women, as well as black, brown, and red Americans, and handicapped Americans into the mainstream of national life.

Competition—within the nation and between nations—was still strenuous and demanding. The unusual American opportunities and needs to compete had made the nation strong and would keep the nation strong.

The millions of immigrants, their children and their children's children, would still seek new opportunities for themselves and all other Americans to show what they could do. "We can no longer say there is nothing new under the sun," Thomas Jefferson had written back in 1801. As the twentieth century neared its close, the United States remained a nation of experiments.

THEMES IN AMERICAN HISTORY

- Congress passes legislation intended to extend equality of opportunity to all Americans.

- Conflicts with other nations create new problems for the United States during the Ford and Carter administrations.

- Ronald Reagan's two terms as President reflect the American people's conservative mood.

THEMES

Michael Hayden's 744-foot-long light sculpture "The Sky's the Limit" illuminates this tunnel at O'Hare Airport in Chicago.

P. Pearson Click/Chicago

717

CHAPTER 34

A new world of competition

The late twentieth century was a time of climax. Never before had Americans cared so much for the ideal of equality. Never before had they worked so hard to keep Americans free—to choose their President, to decide on their laws, to know their government. It was not surprising, then, that this was a difficult time.

It was difficult, too, because the nation was built not only on the ideal of equality, but also on the ideal of freedom. Equality and freedom were twin ideals. Equality meant the right to be equal at the ballot box and in the courts. Freedom meant the right to have your say, to believe and worship as you pleased, to grow and be educated according to your talents, to choose your job, and to compete for the best things in life. In the two centuries of the nation's life both these ideals had grown. And it had combined the two quests—for equality and for freedom—more successfully than any other nation.

Equality meant opportunity, freedom meant competition. Although the twin ideals—equality and freedom—both came from the American Revolution, as the years went on the two ideals had not always worked together.

1. The two ideals

We can understand why equality and freedom sometimes conflicted if we think of life in America as a kind of game. Of course everyone wanted to be a winner. But to keep the factories and the farms going, and to keep life decent and pleasant, the game had to be played by certain rules. That meant, of course, that there would be winners and losers. The nation would be strong and keep its place in the world only if the rules made it possible

for everybody to have a chance to play—and then let the best person win. This meant that there could be no rules to keep anyone out because of race, sex, religion, or where their family came from. This meant, too, that to keep the chances fair, everybody was entitled to education, health, and decent housing. This was the American idea of equality.

Still, everybody knows that some people are stronger than others, some are brighter, some work

718

After the famous physicist Albert Einstein came to the United States in 1933 to escape Nazi anti-Semitism, Ben Shahn made this painting of him arriving carrying his violin. Among the other immigrants portrayed is the Lithuanian-born Shahn himself. He is the man wearing number 76.

harder. Freedom meant the opportunity for everyone to show the ability to try to win in the competition. In communist countries and other tyrannies people are assigned their jobs by the government, which also tells them where they have to work, and what they can earn. The winners are named by the government. But freedom is a chancy world. It means keeping the market open for ideas to compete against one another. It means keeping the nation open for everybody to try to become a winner. Extra rewards then ought to go to anyone who is especially able.

Naturally everyone wants a fair chance, and the ideal of equality aims to guarantee that chance. Still everybody cannot be an equal winner. The ideal of freedom aims to guarantee everybody's right to be as successful as that person can be—even more successful than somebody else.

This tradition of the two ideals goes back to the nation's very beginning. Every age must find new ways to live these ideals. The great drama of American life in our time has been the struggle to make the two ideals work happily together.

The Declaration of Independence. Back in 1776 the Declaration of Independence declared the right of Americans "to assume among the powers of the earth, the separate and equal station to which the Laws of Nature and of Nature's God entitle them." The British government had not allowed Americans their equal rights to govern themselves and vote on their own taxes. It had not given them the freedom to trade where they wanted and to produce what they wished. The American Revolution, then, was fought to give this new nation both equality and freedom in the world of nations.

Within the nation, too, these ideals of equality and freedom would rule. "We hold these truths to be self-evident, that all men are created equal, that they are endowed by their Creator with certain

Thomas Jefferson wrote the Declaration of Independence in Philadelphia on this lap desk. Jefferson's proclamation of human equality and unalienable rights would guide Americans through many challenging years.

unalienable Rights, that among these are Life, Liberty, and the pursuit of Happiness." According to Jefferson, the bulwark of rights was education. He preached a "crusade against ignorance." "Diffusion of knowledge among the people" was the only "sure foundation . . . for the preservation of freedom and happiness."

The "natural aristocracy." Every generation, Jefferson believed, had enough of its own bright and able people to run the government and preserve freedom. While all men were "created equal," with equal rights before the law, Jefferson did not believe that every individual person was just as clever and as talented as everybody else. He said there was a "natural aristocracy." This was nothing like the Old World aristocracy. Over there certain lucky people had high-sounding titles and power in the government only because their parents and grandparents were rich, owned lots of land, or were friends of the king or queen. No one had elected them, and they had not earned their wealth or their high position.

The "natural aristocracy"—a democratic aristocracy—in this country would be a different breed. They would be the ablest, most industrious, and best educated. And they would be elected to government positions because of their very own talents and knowledge.

Jefferson outlined a system of education to train these people and prepare them to lead. All would compete, and then the people who did best in the examinations would move up to the next level of schools. In this way, he hoped, the nation would be well supplied with the kind of "aristocrats" needed in a free republic.

This was a grand idea. If it was perfected to include everyone, it would save this new nation from the prejudices and the unfair advantages that had ruled the older nations of Europe. On the whole, in the long run the United States did not do too badly in working toward the ideal. But there were some serious problems that plainly got in the way of the system, even in Jefferson's day.

The difficult dream. Thomas Jefferson himself was a wealthy Virginia aristocrat in the Old World sense of the word. From his father he had inherited a plantation of several thousand acres and slaves to work the land. His mother came from a family with high social position. He had the advantage of an excellent education at the College of William and Mary. He became a lawyer, and then was easily elected to the Virginia House of Burgesses. If he had been born in the slave-quarters, we might never have heard of him. He might never have had the opportunity to use his great abilities. Jefferson himself believed that slavery was a curse that violated the will of God. But he lived on a plantation in Virginia where nearly all the blacks were slaves.

To make Jefferson's dream of a full-fledged "natural aristocracy" come true, many changes would have to be made in the life of that Virginia. In his time, no person would even have a chance to take the examinations for higher education without the good luck to be a son born into a white family that could send him to grammar school to learn to read and write. Jefferson did not believe that women should be taught the same difficult subjects that were taught to men.

In this book we have traced the progress, over the centuries of American history, of efforts to widen opportunity. We have seen the rise of the American public school, the free public high school, the wonderful growth of American private schools,

A neat one-room schoolhouse about 1900 was caught in this watercolor made by Perkins Harnly. The month was February, when Valentine's Day sentiments mingled with patriotic feelings on the birthdays of Washington and Lincoln. Students of the different grades sat together.

private colleges, and state and land-grant public universities.

It would take a long time to make opportunity equal for all Americans. There would never be perfectly equal opportunity, even with a whole system of free education for all. There would always be differences between families. Naturally some parents would be more anxious than others for their children to go on with their education. And, of course, better-educated parents in homes where there were lots of books would be able to give their children a head start in the competition.

Still, a great deal could be done to make opportunities more equal. In the southern states where slavery had flourished and where blacks continued to be treated as second-class citizens, the public schools were often not equal at all. And in big cities in the North, segregated black neighborhoods tended to leave their children at a real disadvantage.

When the Supreme Court of the United States in 1954 outlawed segregation in the public schools, it took a big step to insure that educational opportunities would be more equal. The 1962 law against segregation in federally funded public housing helped. After the anti-poll tax amendment to the Constitution (Twenty-fourth Amendment) was finally adopted in 1964 and the Voting Rights Act was passed in 1965, blacks in the South were able to use their votes to elect officials who would protect their rights and improve their opportunities. The years after World War II saw these and other strenuous efforts to fulfill the American dream of equal opportunity.

Immigrant problems and immigrant inequality. The blacks were not the only Americans whose opportunities had not been equal. Every immigrant group except the English had suffered discrimination when it arrived on these shores. They all had

721

Many young people were among the new wave of immigrants that came from Asia. They took quickly to the ways of their new country. This group obviously enjoys being Boy Scouts.

their painful problems. They had been kept out of the best schools, the best colleges, the best neighborhoods, and the best jobs. With only a few exceptions, there had been no civil rights laws or constitutional amendments to protect them. In fact, as we have seen (p. 379), some of the most respectable, richest, and best-educated Americans actually formed organizations purposely to discriminate against new immigrants.

When the Irish came here in the 1840s as refugees from the potato famine and from religious persecution, they were treated as intruders by some of New England's oldest residents. Factories and offices needing employees displayed the sign saying, "No Irish Need Apply." The Know-Nothing party, beginning as a secret society in New York City in 1849, organized discrimination against Catholics and immigrants. Its special targets were the new Irish Americans and the many German

Americans who had been moving into the Middle West. Hatred against Catholics was again organized in 1887 in a group that called itself the American Protective Association. Its members poured slanders on the thousands of recent Italian and Polish immigrants. In 1894, when the flood of immigrants came from central, eastern, and southern Europe, many leading Bostonians (whose parents had immigrated some time before) joined with professors and university presidents from Harvard, Wisconsin, and California to form the powerful Immigration Restriction League.

Among the groups most discriminated against were the Jews. Seeking refuge from ghettos and persecution in Germany, Poland, and Russia, Jews brought with them a tradition of learning and a reverence for books and education. Many were eager to pursue their studies in the best universities and medical schools. But the best universities, like

Harvard and Yale, set up shameful restrictive quotas, which deprived Jews of their equal chances.

Chinese, Japanese, and Korean immigrants, too, suffered more than their share of discrimination—simply because they also wanted their full opportunities as Americans. The school board in San Francisco even tried to force their segregation in the public schools until President Theodore Roosevelt made them stop.

At the dawning of the twentieth century there were 76 million people in the United States. Of these, more than 10 million had themselves been born outside the country, and more than one-third of all Americans—26 million—had at least one foreign-born parent. Although people boasted that this was a nation of immigrants, nearly every kind of immigrant at some time had suffered some sort of discrimination!

The social disease of discrimination, as we have seen, lasted violently into the modern century. In the 1920s the Ku Klux Klan, along with its hocus-pocus and its costume of white sheets, dared to target its terror against Catholics, Jews, and blacks in the South and the Midwest. During World War II, FDR gave in to panic and put thousands of innocent Japanese and Japanese Americans into concentration camps. When the able Al Smith ran for President in 1928, he lost votes merely because he was a Catholic. And when John F. Kennedy was nominated for President in 1960, political leaders wondered whether the time had yet come when a Catholic could be elected.

Prejudice and discrimination, then, were not the monopoly of any one part of the country or of any one period. Perhaps they would never be entirely cured. But the United States had made a good start. The traditional American open door policy at home gave refuge to oppressed people from the whole world. The Civil War against slavery, the Emancipation Proclamation, and the Thirteenth, Fourteenth, and Fifteenth amendments to the Constitution were long-overdue steps. In World War II the United States had fought the discrimination, barbarism, and racial superstitions of the Nazis. Now Americans were ready again to move ahead. Civil rights laws, supported by Presidents of both parties beginning with Truman, declared that the American conscience had been newly awakened. In our land the twentieth century would be another century of progress for human equality.

SECTION 1 REVIEW

1. How did Jefferson's "natural aristocracy" differ from the Old World aristocracy?

2. What makes discrimination a "social disease"?

3. How is a system of free education, open to all, related to the ideal of equality?

4. **Expressing Problems Clearly.** Why do the twin American ideals of freedom and equality sometimes lead to social conflict?

2. Dealing with racism

Righting past wrongs was not easy. Americans loved speed. They expected to accomplish in a few years what elsewhere had required centuries—or had never been tried. And Americans, too, had a faith that laws could cure almost anything. By the Eighteenth Amendment and the laws against alcoholic beverages, Americans showed that they believed laws could cure the social ills of drunkenness. In that they were disappointed. But could laws speedily cure discrimination?

Congress and the states passed new laws and set up new commissions. Still the problem was more complicated and deeper rooted than it seemed at first. Programs to cure past ills also created new problems.

Trying to integrate the schools. The Supreme Court decision in 1954 outlawed racial segregation. Southerners fought a long, losing battle against the law of the land, but by the late 1970s legal segregation in the South had ceased. The age-old system of separate public schools and colleges for the races came to an end. But racism survived in the form of private schools that white parents set up to avoid integration. Large numbers of white students attended these schools throughout the South. In some areas, schools which had been integrated after the Supreme Court decision came to be attended largely by blacks as increasing numbers of white students went to private schools or moved to other school districts where there were fewer blacks.

In northern cities neighborhoods were often racially segregated. Sometimes, too, school boards tried to prevent integration. They built new schools and drew the lines of school districts to keep

Alex Webb/Magnum

To bring about racial balance in northern schools, students were sometimes bused from one neighborhood to another.

the races separate. The courts held this kind of segregation just as unconstitutional as the separate schools in the South.

To prevent segregation the courts took control in some cities. But the courts had no experience in running public schools. They ordered that students be bused to schools in other neighborhoods to provide a racial balance. Violence erupted in communities where white parents tried to stop the buses. Boston was scarred by the struggle. A judge there ran the school system for over ten years. But Buffalo, New York, set the nation an example. Aided by federal money and the patient help of parents, the schools there were peacefully integrated. Buffalo showed how "magnet" schools

with special programs could bring white students back to the public schools.

In 1987 a judge found segregation again in Little Rock, Arkansas, just 30 years after federal troops had overseen the admission of black students to Central High. During those years, whites had moved to the suburbs and whole neighborhoods had become segregated. To counteract this resegregation in the schools, the court ordered the merger of the city's school district with two neighboring white school districts. Students were to be bused to schools within this large district.

Busing was one method of counteracting segregation. But it brought many new problems. Some children had to waste long hours riding on buses. It was hard for parents to stay in touch with teachers who were no longer in their neighborhood. To avoid busing, many whites moved away and soon the schools were segregated again. All across the country parents disagreed. Some felt that the benefits of mixed schools outweighed all the problems. Others—white and black—missed their neighborhood schools.

"Affirmative action" and "reverse discrimination." Another new kind of problem was created by what were called "affirmative action" programs. Affirmative action grew out of the civil rights movement of the 1960s. It was designed first for blacks, and then for other minority groups and for women, to do something positive to correct past injustices. It gave preference to women, blacks, and other minority persons for particular jobs or for college and professional school admissions even though they were not better qualified than other applicants. This tended to produce "quota" systems. The programs meant, of course, that all equally qualified persons did not have an equal chance for these jobs or schools.

The purpose of affirmative action, which many Americans approved, was to give new advantages to groups that had suffered from discrimination. It tried to make up for past injustices. But people who were not in the "minority" groups now felt they were being discriminated against. They thought it was not their fault that women, blacks, Latinos, Native Americans, or Asians had suffered in the past. "Backlash" described a new kind of prejudice created by the efforts to remove old prejudices. Some white male workers and students

New opportunities for jobs and education, which became increasingly available from the 1960s on, allowed some black families to join other Americans in the move from the cities to the suburbs.

could not understand why others were receiving special preference. They called this "reverse discrimination," and brought lawsuits to secure their equal rights.

The Supreme Court was unsure how to deal with affirmative action. For example, at the University of California at Davis, Allan Bakke, a white applicant, was rejected for the medical school, which received federal funds. The university said that he was better qualified than certain minority applicants whom they admitted. But they had set a quota of 16 minority students out of every 100. In its decision in 1978, the Supreme Court ruled 5 to 4 that setting a specific quota for minority students in each class at a medical school that received federal funds was unconstitutional. But the Court said a more flexible program might be legal.

The next year in 1979, a white worker, Brian Weber, went to court because the Kaiser Aluminum and Chemical Corporation, where he was employed, had set up a special program to train skilled workers for better jobs. In order to make the racial proportion in the plant like that of the surrounding area the company reserved half the places for blacks. Weber said this discriminated against him. In this case the Court approved the training program. They said that it did not deprive other citizens of their equal rights, but was only an attempt to overcome past "patterns of social segregation and hierarchy" by reflecting the racial characteristics of the area surrounding the plant.

Under President Reagan, the Justice Department tried to stop affirmative action plans. Officials of the department said they wanted a "color-blind, gender-neutral society" where all paths were open and no special help was given to anyone. They were heartened when the Supreme Court ruled that the Memphis Fire Department could not ignore its seniority system to keep newly hired blacks while it laid off longer-serving whites. The Court said that the Memphis blacks could not show that they personally were victims of discrimination.

But then, as the Justice Department pushed to overturn goals and quotas, the Supreme Court supported affirmative action plans. In 1987 in

California, under an affirmative action plan, Santa Clara County promoted a woman over a man who had received a higher score in the job interview. The Court upheld the county's "moderate and flexible" plan. This was the Court's first decision on an affirmative action plan to help women.

Deep-seated problems. In education, and in the better jobs opened up by education, there was real progress for black Americans. By the 1980s blacks spent almost as many years in school as whites. Far more blacks were finishing high school and going on to college. But there was a troubling sign. The percentage of blacks, Hispanics, and Native Americans enrolled in colleges and universities peaked in the 1970s and then began to decline.

The percentage of blacks in skilled jobs rose in the 1960s by about 50 percent. Between 1960 and 1980, the number holding professional, technical, and managerial jobs skyrocketed. Law schools and medical schools desperately searched for qualified students. Special scholarships were offered to black students, and colleges, finally, tried to find black professors for their faculties. Now there were many more blacks in political office, in the courts, in banks and businesses. In the early 1980s, blacks gained places on the highest courts of ten states. President Johnson appointed the first black, Thurgood Marshall, to the Supreme Court. He also brought the first black into the Cabinet, when he named Robert C. Weaver as Secretary of the new Department of Housing and Urban Development. President Carter named a black woman, Patricia Roberts Harris, to that position in his Cabinet. Later she became head of the huge Department of Health, Education, and Welfare.

The difference between the wages paid to black and to white workers narrowed significantly. But the gap among blacks themselves widened. Successful blacks tended to move to the suburbs, leaving the poor and uneducated behind in the crowded cities. There they faced a host of problems. By 1983 over one-half of all black children were born to unwed mothers. Many of these mothers were teenagers. The black families who had no father at home rose from 21 percent in 1960 to 50 percent in the 1980s. Blacks suffered more than twice the rate of unemployment of whites.

Still, much had changed for the better over the past 30 years. No longer satisfied to ride in the back of the bus, blacks set their sights higher. Now when a young black boy or girl was told the heroic story of Rosa Parks, Martin Luther King, Jr., and the Montgomery bus boycott (pp. 629-630), there was a new response. "I don't want to ride that bus, anyhow. I want a car of my own."

But it has remained harder for blacks than for whites to fulfill their American dreams. Federal aid, called "welfare," desperately needed to take care of poor black families who lacked jobs, created new problems. Welfare families were tempted to expect too much from the federal government. Of course, the government could help, but they would also have to help themselves. Black leaders urged them to put their hope in themselves, in their churches, and in education. In the long run, their problems belonged to the whole country. For the nation had grown and prospered on the American ideal of equal opportunity.

SECTION 2 REVIEW

1. Identify or explain: racism, segregation, desegregation.

2. How and why did school segregation continue after legal segregation ended?

3. Did the civil rights movement bring the nation closer to the ideal of equality? Explain.

4. **Recognizing Bias.** What is "affirmative action"? Why do some people call affirmative action "reverse discrimination"?

---

3. Women seek equality

But blacks were not the only Americans who had not enjoyed full equality. Since women were more than half the American population, technically they were not a minority. During these years of awakening conscience, new voices called women the forgotten majority.

Women were among the earliest champions for all the suffering and disadvantaged. Dorothea Dix, as we have seen, took the side of the mentally ill who had been treated as criminals and prisoners. The pioneer American abolitionists Elizabeth Cady Stanton and Lucretia Mott had been refused seats in

Western states granted women the right to vote much earlier than did eastern states or the Constitution. These women were photographed at the polls in Colorado.

the antislavery convention in London because they were women. Then, in 1848, they assembled their own convention in Seneca Falls, New York. If it was unjust to discriminate against people because of the color of their skin, was it any better to discriminate against them because of their sex? They demanded the right to vote and equal rights for women to education and to jobs. In 1869 the National Woman Suffrage Association was founded, and in that year Wyoming Territory was the first to grant women the right to vote. Utah, Colorado, and Idaho—other western states that pioneer women had helped to build—gave women the vote by 1896.

The women's rights movement in the new century was based on the hope that if women only had the right to vote, they could then remove their other inequalities. This was the belief of Progressive leaders, too. Still, even after the Nineteenth Amendment was ratified in 1920 insuring women the right to vote, they stayed unequal in countless other ways. Then, along with the civil rights movement for blacks, a new women's movement gained momentum in the 1960s.

The women's rights movement reawakens. The new feminist movement, too, showed the power of a book. Betty Friedan, who had been born in Peoria, Illinois, and graduated from Smith College, wrote *The Feminine Mystique,* which was published in 1963. She denied the popular notion that women could be fulfilled only by bearing children and doing housework. Women, she said, were just as able as men (maybe more able) to do every kind of job. They, too, should be allowed to lead the world in science, politics, and business. Modern advertising, in newspapers and magazines and on television, had reinforced the old-fashioned idea that women were the "weaker sex." This mistaken notion she called "the Feminine Mystique." It had kept women frustrated and unfulfilled, confined at home in their "comfortable concentration camp." In that same year a Commission on the Status of Women, appointed by President Kennedy and headed by Eleanor Roosevelt, had found discrimination against women in every part of American life. In 1966 eloquent Betty Friedan founded the National Organization for Women (NOW) and in 1970 she organized a nationwide Women's Strike for Equality. She urged women to march, to picket, and to speak up for their equal rights.

Many conservative Americans—men and women—were irritated by these demands and by the ideas in *The Feminine Mystique.* They found the new feminists to be raucous, unladylike, and "unfeminine." In a way their objections proved the point the new feminists were trying to make. Why, the feminists asked, shouldn't women have the same rights as men to speak up? It was considered manly for men to stand up for their rights—and why shouldn't that also be womanly?

Others were puzzled because it seemed that in the United States women already had more freedom to go where they pleased and do what they pleased than women anywhere else. In fact, there were few formal or legal barriers. Instead, the style of American life stood in the way. Women (unlike men) were always expected to put home and family first. This kept them from reaching the top in business and the professions. It also discouraged employers from giving women the high positions for which they really were qualified. If a woman had another child, or if her husband's job was moved to another city, then she was expected to give up her own job—in order to care for her child or go with her husband. Even if a woman was single, employers feared she might marry and then they would lose her. As famed anthropologist Margaret Mead observed, "The very fact that the formal barriers are down reduces women to battling with feather-soft barriers that never really yield but instead smother the attacker."

The status of women. Statistics confirmed the arguments of the new feminists. In 1971, for example, full-time working women were paid only 59 percent as much as men. Women with college degrees earned only half as much as men with similar education. In the 1970s women made up 40 percent of the labor force and the proportion was still rising. The number of working wives and mothers was also increasing. Among the reasons for this were inflation, the better education of women, and the rising American standard of living. Many women wanted jobs that gave them new challenges. Still, one-third of all female workers were employed in clerical tasks—as secretaries, file clerks, and telephone operators. Few were executives or managers. In the early 1970s women accounted for only 7 percent of the physicians and only 3 percent of the lawyers. But during these years the number of women in medical and law schools increased rapidly. By 1980 they made up one-fifth of the medical students and one-third of the law students.

Still many women were not yet in the positions that their talents deserved. But the American tradition of free speech and the right to organize made sure that they would be heard. The rising level of education helped. In 1960 only 35 percent of American college students were women, but by 1978 the figure had risen to 48 percent. And in the late 1960s some formerly all-male colleges like Yale and Princeton began to admit women.

Women now demanded their full share of the American tradition of equal opportunity. The pioneer and the immigrant traditions also played a part. When a family first came to America or moved into the unfamiliar West, women had to make important decisions. They had to find new ways to keep the family well fed, well schooled, and happy together. Ever since colonial times, foreign visitors to this country had noticed the power of American women and sometimes made fun of it. But the opportunities for women had not yet been

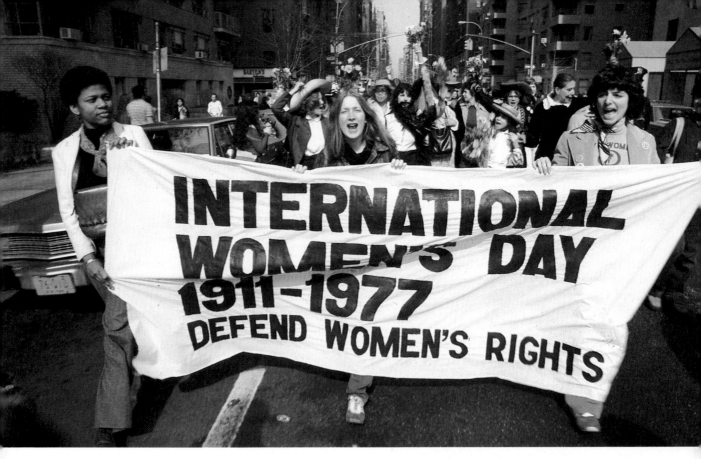

American women in 1977 joined in International Women's Day to demonstrate for their equal rights.

brought into an urban age of technology and large industry.

The drive for equal rights.
The new feminist movement took many forms. Betty Friedan's National Organization for Women demanded changes to bring women into "the mainstream of American society . . . in fully equal partnership with men." Small militant groups even called for female separation, the end of the family, and the end of separate masculine and feminine roles.

The first national success of the women's rights movement came by accident. When the House of Representatives was debating the Civil Rights Act of 1964, Congressman Howard Smith of Virginia offered an amendment to Title VII to bar job discrimination on the basis of sex as well as race. He did this not to assist women, but because he thought this would help defeat the entire measure. Instead, the bill with his amendment became law.

This ban against sexual discrimination would be used in businesses, schools, and colleges.

As the movement gained momentum, Congress added its support. In 1972, two-thirds of the members of both houses of Congress approved an "Equal Rights" Amendment and sent it to the states. A similar amendment had been proposed in 1923 but had repeatedly failed to get approval by Congress. The proposed amendment now read: "Equality of rights under the law shall not be denied or abridged by the United States or any state on account of sex." It was quickly ratified by 22 states. Then it ran into strong opposition.

The feminist movement and the Equal Rights Amendment were opposed by critics such as forceful, articulate Phyllis Schlafly and others. They valued the privileges more than the rights of women. They believed in the old tradition. There was no more important work, they insisted, than bearing and raising children. They thought that nature intended women for different roles than men. Reformers in the Progressive Era had demanded special laws to protect women in factories. "Equal rights" might mean the end of such special protection for women. It might also mean the end of "alimony," the money awarded by courts to support mothers and their children in case of divorce.

To adopt the Equal Rights Amendment, the Constitution required ratification by three-quarters of the states. In 1979, when the amendment was still three states short of the needed number, Congress extended the deadline for ratification to June 30, 1982. Still even that was not enough. The amendment failed to receive enough votes and died. A number of states included its principles in their own constitutions.

Aid from the government and the courts.
Meanwhile the federal government found new ways to use its power to end discrimination. In 1972, President Nixon's Secretary of Labor ordered companies that contracted with the government to set goals and timetables for hiring women and minorities. The Justice Department started suits under Title VII of the 1964 Civil Rights Act to force large business firms to end job discrimination. Colleges and universities that received federal aid were investigated to see if they discriminated against women. The Equal Employment Opportunity Act passed in 1972 required employers to pay equal wages for equal work. Other laws barred discrimination against women when they applied for credit.

And again the Supreme Court played a role. In 1971 the Court ruled that unequal treatment based only on sex violated the Fourteenth Amendment. In one of its most controversial decisions, the Court held in 1973 that, except in the later stages of pregnancy, states could not make it illegal for women to have abortions. The new feminists hailed this as a victory. They said that a woman's most important right was to control her own body. But their passionate "Right-to-Life" opponents said that the unborn child had rights of its own and that abortion was murder.

Women moving ahead.
By the 1980s, women were beginning to be active in nearly every occupation. The avenues of choice were widening. Women now worked as truck drivers, car mechanics, business leaders, architects, computer scientists, and even as astronauts. By 1986, 20 percent of all lawyers were women and 18 percent of all doctors. In the other professions counted by the Department of Labor—scientists, teachers, librarians, engineers, psychiatrists, social workers, and many others—women held half of all the jobs compared to only one-third as recently as 1983. Now women were also governors, mayors, and Cabinet officers, as well as members of the Senate and the House of Representatives. There were 1168 women in 1987 in state legislatures and holding statewide office, compared to just 301 in 1969.

Women now took a full 50 percent of all the bachelors degrees given by colleges and universities. Yet a woman college graduate was paid only slightly better than a male high school dropout. If a woman wanted to work after having a baby, she needed a good child-care center. Many unions

Women who worked needed good day-care centers for their children.

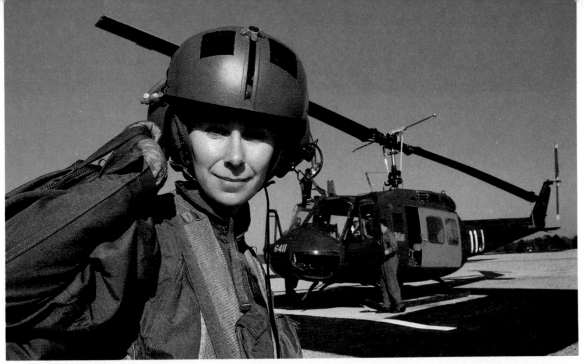

In the years after World War II women entered new and exciting fields that once would have been closed to them (above). Nancy Landon Kassebaum was reelected to a second Senate term in 1985.

made child care an issue, because one-third of all union members were women. Some large companies like Ford and General Motors now agreed to help with child care.

Although they had come a long way, women still had a long way to go. In 1979, for the first time an American silver dollar had appeared with the likeness of a real woman–Susan B. Anthony (p. 239), the courageous leader who fought all her long life for women's rights. Her face on the coin bore an important new message. "For the first time in modern history," a woman journalist observed, "a woman is born into a society which has acknowledged her right to the freedom to choose the role she wants."

SECTION 3 REVIEW

1. If there were few legal barriers to the advancement of women by the 1960s, what factors held back their efforts to achieve equality?

2. **Distinguishing Fact from Opinion.** Cite evidence showing (a) gains by women by the 1970s and (b) continued male-female inequality.

4. Spanish-speaking peoples

During these years of civil rights movements, other groups organized for equal rights. After women and blacks, Spanish-speaking people were the largest such group. The census bureau called all Spanish-speaking groups Hispanics. Their population was growing at a rate five times faster than non-Hispanics. Demographers predicted that they would be the largest minority in the United States by the year 2000.

They had come from many places and at many times. Some of their ancestors came to America with the Spanish conquerors in the century after Columbus, and their families had lived here for more than 400 years. Others emigrated to the mainland United States from Spain, Cuba, Puerto Rico, and other Caribbean islands, as well as from Latin American countries.

The Mexican Americans. Nearly two-thirds of all Spanish-speaking people in the United States are Mexican Americans. They are both the newest of the new immigrants and the oldest of the old. The ancestors of many of them settled in the Southwest and California in the 1600s and 1700s (p. 26). Those early settlers were followed by millions of others. By the late 1980s there were over 11 million Mexican Americans in the United States and thousands more were entering the country every year. By far the largest number of them have continued to settle where their first settlements lay—in California, Arizona, New Mexico, Colorado, and Texas. Their language and their culture give a special rich flavor to the food and shape the music, the architecture, and the literature of the whole region.

Many Mexican Americans are descended from the intermarriage of Spanish and Indian peoples. They proudly trace their heritage all the way back to the great Aztec and Mayan civilizations. They generally call themselves by a variety of names: Mexican or *Mexicano,* Mexican American, Chicano (a form of *Mexicano*), Hispano, Latino, mestizo, and sometimes just *La Raza* (meaning "the people"). Conservative and hardworking, the Mexican Americans are almost entirely Roman Catholic in religion, with strong family ties, and they cling to the Spanish language.

Although originally a rural people, now, like the whole nation, they are largely urban. Fully 80 percent have settled together in city neighborhoods, which they call *barrios.*

From the very beginning the differences of religion, language, skin color, and culture between the Mexican Americans and other Americans (whom they call "Anglos") created conflicts. Each group tended to think its own way of doing things was better. But in most areas Anglos were the majority, in control of government, courts, and schools. Mexican Americans were often discriminated against. Great numbers of them ended up in low paying jobs where no training was needed.

The rise of a "Brown Power" movement. The Mexican Americans organized their own groups to voice their needs. For example, the thousands of veterans who had fought in World War II formed the Mexican G.I. Forum. Then, in the tumultuous 1960s, Mexicans began to speak out more loudly.

During the 1960s there developed a Chicano or "Brown Power" movement. Among its most outspoken leaders was the feisty Reies Lopez Tijerina, or *El Tigre.* Born in Texas, he led a fight in New Mexico for the return of the lands he said the Anglos had stolen from the first Spanish-speaking settlers. But many of the conservative Mexican Americans, like Senator Joseph Montoya of New Mexico, disapproved of Tijerina's radical program. And instead of "Chicano," which some of the young had begun to use as a symbol of pride, they preferred to be simply Americans.

Another high-spirited leader was Rodolfo "Corky" Gonzales of Colorado. He was a former prizefighter and once director of a war-on-poverty youth program. In 1965 his Crusade for Justice in Denver began to build Chicano pride by giving them jobs and providing social services in their own communities.

Organizing farm laborers. Many Mexicans and Mexican Americans worked as poorly paid farm laborers. Some of these *braceros* (a Spanish word meaning laborers) came north under contracts to work in the fields. Others entered the country illegally by slipping across the long and difficult-to-patrol border between Mexico and the United States. They were called "wetbacks" because some of them swam or waded across the Rio Grande.

Farm workers had always been the most difficult laborers to organize into a union. Since they came

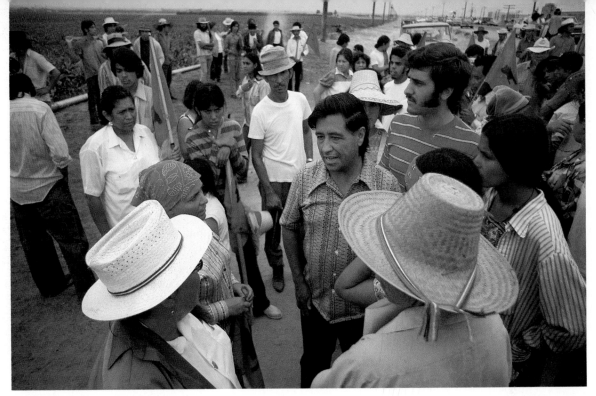

Cesar Chavez organized migrant workers in California into a union and led them in a long and finally successful strike against vineyard owners. He then tried to help other farm workers.

to work only for a season, and were spread across the countryside, it was hard to bring them together for meetings. But the shrewd and eloquent Cesar Chavez decided to try, and he had remarkable success. He had worked as a farm laborer himself. In 1962 he began to organize the migrant laborers—brown, white, and black—into a union. In 1965, when 900 Filipino grape pickers in another union went out on strike, Chavez's union decided to go out, too. The following year, the two unions merged to form the United Farm Workers Organizing Committee.

Chavez, like Martin Luther King, Jr., believed in nonviolence. He stuck to his principles through the long painful years of the strike against the owners of the vineyards in Delano, California. This won him public support from church groups, from other unions, and from political leaders like Robert F. Kennedy.

A brilliant publicist, Chavez organized an effective nationwide boycott of California grapes. When some of his followers resorted to violence, he protested by fasting for 25 days—and badly injured

his health. But nonviolence prevailed. Finally, the opposition of the vineyard owners started to crumble. In 1970, after five years, many of them signed with Chavez's union. He had actually organized farm laborers into a union and won better pay and working conditions. Chavez had done what seemed impossible.

Chavez himself stayed out of politics, but other Mexican Americans won high office. Both New Mexico and Arizona have elected Mexican American governors. Other Mexican Americans have been chosen for the Senate and the House, or to be mayors of large cities, like Henry Cisneros of San Antonio, Texas, and Federico Peña in Denver, Colorado. A Mexican American woman, Romana A. Bañuelos, was named by President Nixon to be Treasurer of the United States. She was later followed by Katherine Davalos Ortega, who was appointed by President Reagan. And President Carter made Leonel Castillo his Commissioner of the Immigration and Naturalization service. Mexican Americans were playing an ever-larger role in state and national politics in the 1980s.

Puerto Rican Day is a time for parades and celebration in New York City.

Puerto Rico and the Puerto Ricans. The Puerto Ricans were different from most other Hispanics because all of them were citizens of the United States before they arrived on the mainland. The special relation between Puerto Rico and the rest of the United States allowed them to go back and forth to their home island at will.

The island of Puerto Rico had been visited by Columbus in 1493, even before any Spaniards had come to mainland America. When Columbus arrived, the Arawak Indians were already there. During the colonial period the island was settled by Spaniards and by black slaves imported from Africa. The land and the climate were ideal for raising sugar cane. And from the sugar was made the famous Puerto Rican rum. In 1898, after the Spanish-American War, the United States took over the island.

One of FDR's braintrusters, Rexford G. Tugwell, was sent to Puerto Rico as governor in 1941. There he and Luis Muñoz Marín, a poetic and inspiring Puerto Rican political leader, produced "Operation Bootstrap." This was a program to improve agriculture and attract industry to the island. In 1948 Muñoz Marín became the island's

first popularly elected governor. He led the way toward a special "Commonwealth" status for Puerto Rico within the United States. The Commonwealth of Puerto Rico was proclaimed on July 25, 1952. The following years showed how the resourcefulness and intelligence of people might make up for the lack of other natural resources.

Under the ingenious "Commonwealth" plan, Puerto Rico became an independent self-governing state in voluntary association with the United States. Puerto Rico is represented in Congress by a resident commissioner who can speak but has no vote, except in committees. Puerto Ricans do not pay federal income tax on money earned in Puerto Rico, and they do not vote in national elections. By 1970, with the aid of "Operation Bootstrap," Puerto Rico had the highest per capita income and the best standard of living in Latin America. Still, Puerto Rican incomes were low compared to those in mainland United States.

After World War II, when the population grew rapidly, producing widespread unemployment, thousands of Puerto Ricans moved to the mainland. The emigration slowed in the 1970s, but by the late 1980s more than 2 million Puerto Ricans were living in the continental United States. About one-half lived in New York City, where many worked in the garment trades. The city now held more than twice as many Puerto Ricans as the island capital of San Juan. They were citizens, but in other ways they suffered many of the problems of earlier immigrants. Since they spoke another language, they felt strange and they formed their own neighborhoods where the signs were in Spanish. Strangers, without the advantages of money or education, they, too, joined the American quest for equal opportunity.

Many Puerto Ricans were not satisfied. Some agitated and used violence to try to win independence so that Puerto Rico could be a separate nation. Others wanted Puerto Rico to become a state in the Union. Still, in election after election the majority of Puerto Ricans voted to keep the unusual Commonwealth status. Meanwhile, Puerto Rico, with its delightful tropical beaches and its Spanish-American flavor, became a favorite vacation spot for thousands from the mainland. And Puerto Ricans were enriching the culture of the United States, through such figures as opera singers, Martina Arroyo and Justino Diaz, guitarist José Feliciano, violinist José Figueroa, and actors and actresses like José Ferrer, Rita Moreno, Chita Rivera, Raul Julia, and Hector Elizondo.

The flight from Cuba. Throughout its history the United States has been a refuge for people fleeing turmoil and repression. After Fidel Castro seized power in Cuba in 1959 and began to create a communist state, over half a million islanders fled to the United States. Some went on to settle in other lands, but nearly 400,000 chose to remain here. Many stayed in Florida, especially around Miami.

Some of these newcomers dreamed and planned only for the day when they could return to their Cuban homeland. But others became Americans and began a new life.

The Cubans who came to the United States in the first years after Castro's takeover were generally well educated, and over two-thirds were trained for white-collar jobs. Hardworking and ambitious, some of them soon rose to head banks and businesses. Among the most successful was Yale-educated Roberto Goizueta. He became head of one of the nation's largest businesses, the Coca-Cola Company, in 1981.

By 1988, 700,000 Cubans were living in Miami, and large sections were as Cuban as Havana itself. A Cuban-born American, Xavier Suarez, was elected mayor of Miami in 1985. The young, Harvard-trained lawyer was reelected in 1987, defeating once again Maurice Ferre, a Puerto Rican who had been the city's mayor from 1973 to 1985.

This first wave of refugees was joined in 1980 by more than 100,000 Cubans who fled when Castro suddenly allowed dissatisfied citizens to leave. These new migrants were called "Marielitos" because they had come to the United States in a massive flotilla of boats that shuttled between the Cuban harbor of Mariel and Key West in Florida. Once again the United States was a haven and a land of new opportunity.

Among the Marielitos was a small number of criminals and mentally ill. These, along with several thousand more who committed crimes (often minor ones) after they arrived, were sent to American camps and prisons. Many remained in the prisons even after they had served their sentences because the United States government declared that they had never entered the country legally. Therefore they could be deported.

In 1985 the United States and Cuba reached an agreement to allow up to 20,000 Cubans a year to migrate to the United States. It included a provision permitting the United States to deport to Cuba several thousand of its Cuban prisoners. But the agreement was suspended by Castro after the Voice of America began broadcasting to Cuba over a new station called Radio Martí, named after the famous Cuban writer and patriot, José Martí, who was killed in 1895 fighting for his homeland's independence from Spain. Radio Martí aimed to bring Cubans the facts of life from the free world. In the late fall of 1987 the agreement was suddenly

In 1980 Fidel Castro suddenly allowed dissatisfied Cubans to sail from the port of Mariel for Florida. In a brief period 100,000 went by small boats across the dangerous waters to Key West.

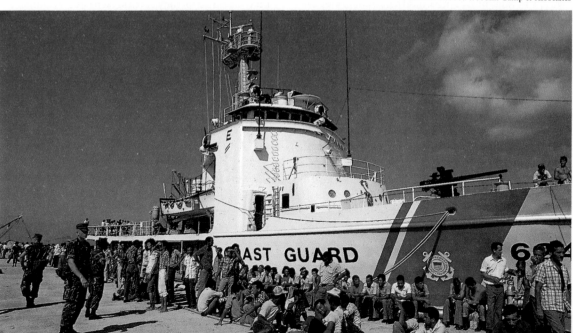

reinstated. Cubans held in prisons in Atlanta, Georgia, and Oakdale, Louisiana, feared that they would be sent back to Cuba. They swiftly seized control of their prisons, took hostages, and burned buildings.

Negotiations, with the help of Cuban-born Roman Catholic Auxiliary Bishop Agustin A. Roman of Miami, finally ended the takeovers. Government officials promised that no prisoners would be returned to Cuba without a fair hearing.

SECTION 4 REVIEW

1. Identify or explain: *La Raza, barrios,* Joseph Montoya, Rodolfo Gonzales, Luis Muñoz Marín, Operation Bootstrap.

2. What are the chief groups that make up the Spanish-speaking peoples of the United States? Locate their major areas of settlement.

3. How does the legal status of Puerto Ricans differ from that of other Hispanic immigrants to the United States?

4. **Drawing Conclusions.** How did the work of Cesar Chavez help bring about greater equality for all Mexican Americans?

---

5. New waves of immigration

The United States was still the land of opportunity for oppressed people from everywhere in the late twentieth century. Refugees from war, revolution, persecution, and poverty, and tens of thousands simply seeking a better life—all flocked to what they considered the New-World promised land. They, too, sought equality and freedom. They enriched the nation with their hopes and their efforts, but they added problems.

Asians from many nations. The fall of South Vietnam, Laos, and Cambodia to the Communists in 1975 set off a massive emigration by land, sea, and air. Refugees fled to Thailand, Malaysia, Hong Kong, the Philippines, and China. From those lands many hoped to come to the United States. To help those who had aided the United States during the Vietnam War, 125,000 Vietnamese were allowed to enter the country right away. It seemed that this was enough relief at the time.

But more thousands continued to flee. They filled the refugee camps in Southeast Asia and over-

flowed to the United States and other nations. By 1985, 728,000 had come to the United States. These new immigrants from distant lands did well. They were eager to become Americans. They worked hard and added a delightful new Asian spice to the life (and food) of the United States. Many Asian young people overcame the language handicap and did exceedingly well in school. President Reagan in his State of the Union message to Congress in 1985 pointed to Jean Nguyen, who was seated in the balcony beside Mrs. Reagan. She symbolized the amazing progress of these newest immigrants. Just ten years before she had fled Vietnam with her family, and now she was about to graduate from the United States Military Academy at West Point. In 1988, in New York City, eleven of the fourteen finalists in a nationwide science competition were Asians.

From other parts of Asia—from India, Taiwan, Korea, and the Philippines—they came by the tens of thousands. In the 1970s and 1980s Asian Americans were the nation's fastest growing minority.

Refugees from the Caribbean and Latin America. The poverty-stricken and turbulent islands of the Caribbean sent another wave of immigrants. From Haiti, they were fleeing the brutal dictatorship of the Duvaliers, "Papa Doc" and his son, "Baby Doc." Half the people had no jobs in that island of hunger. Even after the long Duvalier rule (1957–1986) ended, they still came.

A third wave of unhappy people arrived from troubled Central America, from strife-torn Guatemala, Nicaragua, and El Salvador. Many came in haste and terror without passports or visas. How were we to help these people without flooding our border cities with a new wave of the unemployed? To check the flow from Haiti, the government in the 1980s began to return those who came without permits. Other refugees were detained in prisons and camps while the courts decided whether they should be granted political asylum. Still the government found ways to allow many refugees from the centers of poverty and violence around the world to stay.

Offering sanctuary. In 1986, as the United States celebrated the 100th anniversary of the building of the Statue of Liberty, refugees from tyranny and poverty around the world were being held in camps and prisons here because they had entered

Bart Bartholomew/Black Star

With the rapid rise in the number of Asians in the United States, new Asian shops and restaurants catered to the tastes not only of the new immigrants but also of native-born Americans.

the country without the proper papers. Religious groups started a "sanctuary movement" dedicated to helping refugees from Central America. This was a new "underground railroad," like the one that helped escaping slaves before the Civil War (p. 260). Some 300 churches, synagogues, and meetinghouses ignored the law to guide these immigrants to homes and jobs.

At first, the United States government paid no attention. Then in 1985 it prosecuted 16 sanctuary workers for aiding illegal aliens. Still, the movement grew. It was encouraged by a Supreme Court ruling that refugees could claim asylum here even if they could not prove that they were sure to be persecuted in their homeland.

Immigration reform. Immigrants came from trouble-spots on all continents—from Afghanistan, South Africa, the Soviet Union, Ethiopia, and Ireland. They came for a job and for a better life. Even if they had entered illegally they often found work. They were willing to take jobs that other Americans shunned, and they worked hard. Any of their children born here were citizens of the United States, according to the Constitution. And if they became legal residents, their relatives would be admitted to join them.

President Carter proposed a law in 1977 to make legal all the illegal aliens who had been here since 1970. Had the law passed, employers were to be fined for hiring illegal aliens. President Reagan asked for a similar law. But Congress refused to act. By 1986 the whole nation was troubled. The United States had been built by those seeking asylum from poverty and tyranny. How were we to adjust this tradition to the late twentieth century?

In 1986 there were millions of illegal aliens in the United States. And more were entering every day. Unemployment and inflation in neighboring Mexico drove thousands across our southern border. In late 1986, the Immigration and Naturalization Service reported that in just one year it had caught a record 1.8 million people, most from Mexico, who were trying to slip in. Thousands of others never became statistics.

Finally Congress passed the Immigration Reform and Control Act in 1986. Illegal aliens who could prove that they had been in the United States since January 1, 1982, were allowed to become legal residents. For the first time, anyone hiring illegal immigrants would be fined. And our borders were to be more closely patroled.

Not everyone was happy with the law, but it was generally welcome. Until then there really was no clear policy. Laws on the books were sometimes enforced, sometimes ignored. Hispanics, especially those here for a long time, were glad. They no longer lived in the shadow of uncertainty.

The United States had not opened the door wide to all comers. But it had not slammed its door. For many, this nation of immigrants remained a haven.

SECTION 5 REVIEW

1. What major immigrant groups sought refuge in the United States in the 1970s and 1980s? Why did they leave their homes?

2. Why were many Americans in favor of reforming immigration laws in the 1970s and 1980s?

3. **Making Comparisons.** In what ways is the "sanctuary movement" of the 1980s like the "underground railroad" of the mid-1800s? In what ways does it differ?

6. The American Indians

After World War II when Americans tried once again to make opportunities equal, injustices of the American past came home to roost. It was one thing to give all Americans an equal chance for education and for jobs today. That was difficult, but not impossible. It was quite another thing to try to undo history.

This problem arose in regard to the very first Americans. They were here, of course, centuries before the first Europeans or Africans. As the United States grew, their own cultures had not prospered. American Indians were not immigrants, were not settled in big cities, and for many years could not vote. They had little appeal for politicians. In colonial times, and for much of the 1800s, newer Americans considered them simply part of the wilderness to be cleared away. Later they were treated as "wards" of the government and put on reservations (p. 329). These

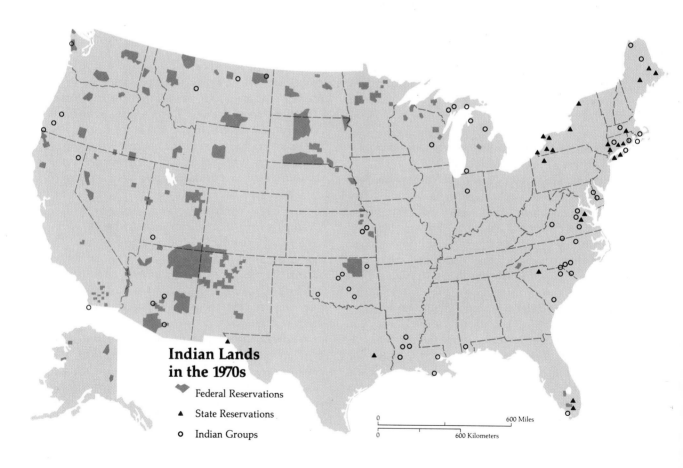

Indian Lands in the 1970s

◆ Federal Reservations

▲ State Reservations

○ Indian Groups

0   600 Miles

0   600 Kilometers

were usually on land that nobody else wanted. Then during the twentieth century their numbers grew. Though in 1900 they totaled less than a quarter-million, by the 1980 census they numbered over 1.3 million. Not until the Snyder Act of 1924 were all Indians born in the United States admitted to full citizenship.

The Indians had been the victims of varying whims of United States officials. Under FDR there was an Indian "New Deal," which aimed to halt the sale of Indian land, to restore tribal land-holding, to rebuild the tribes, and to promote tribal culture. In a bold move FDR appointed outspoken and combative John Collier, the executive director of the American Indian Defense Association, as head of the Bureau of Indian Affairs. Between 1933 and 1945, Collier fought to enable the Indians both to preserve their old ways and to participate fully in American life.

During World War II, 25,000 American Indians served in the armed forces. They felt they had earned their right to be full-fledged American citizens, with fully equal opportunities. But after World War II, the Native Americans still had the least education, the lowest incomes, the highest unemployment, the worst health, the shortest life expectancy, and the highest suicide rate of any large group in the country.

Termination and relocation.

In the 1950s, under President Eisenhower, the federal government's policy toward the Indians changed once again. Congress enacted laws for a new program called "termination." The idea was to end all federal involvement with the Indians and leave the states to deal with them. But most states would not provide the health, education, and welfare services that the Indians needed.

Another new program called "relocation" offered jobs to induce Indians to relocate in cities. There, it was hoped, they would earn a better living and fit into the larger society. This program, too, was a disaster, precisely because many Indians were persuaded to relocate. The proportion of American Indians living in urban areas increased from 10 percent in 1930 to 45 percent in 1970. But the effects were not what was planned. Urban Indians generally had higher incomes and were better educated than reservation Indians. Yet in the cities many of them felt displaced and unhappy.

John Running

Peter McDonald is the leader of the Navahos. Scattered across Arizona, New Mexico, and Utah, the Navahos are the largest Indian group in the United States.

They created new urban Indian ghettos. In 1972 the program was finally dropped.

New help for Indians.

President Lyndon Johnson, in a special message to Congress in 1968, called the Indian "The Forgotten American." He pointed to their poor housing, their alarming 40 percent unemployment, and the fact that only half of the young Indians completed high school. He asked Congress to enact a program to give Indians a standard of living equal to that of other Americans. Congress replied by voting $510 million for Indian aid programs—the highest amount ever.

President Nixon, too, tried to find new ways to help the Indians. He called for the end of the "termination" program. He also proposed that federal programs on the old Indian reservations be run by the Indians themselves. Indians were appointed to twenty top positions in the Bureau of Indian Affairs (BIA). And the Office of Education, after a two-year study, recommended that tribal history, culture, and languages be stressed in Indian education and that Indians be given a larger role in running their schools.

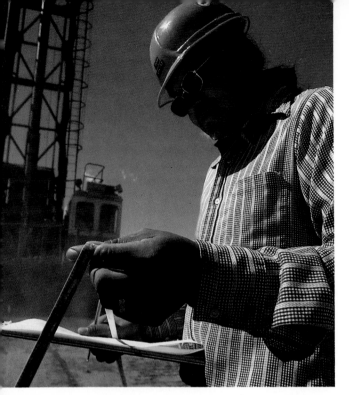

Native Americans work at many jobs, from farming to the professions to steelworking on skyscrapers. This Navaho Indian is a geologist.

Indian Power. Some Indians began to take violent action to call attention to their wants. During 1969 an angry group of 78 Indians seized Alcatraz Island with its deserted prison in San Francisco Bay. They demanded that it be made an Indian cultural center. Finally, they were evicted by United States marshals in 1971.

In 1972 the militant American Indian Movement occupied the offices of the BIA in Washington. They demanded all the rights and the property that they said had been guaranteed to the Indians over many past years by their treaties with the United States government. After a week of talks—and damage estimated at a half-million dollars—the Indians finally left the building.

More than 200 armed members of the American Indian Movement during 1973 took over the village of Wounded Knee on the Oglala Sioux Pine Ridge Reservation in South Dakota. They opposed the local tribal government and demanded other reforms. This town near the site of the last battle of the Indian wars—the massacre at Wounded Knee Creek in 1890 (p. 330)—was a symbol of Indian suffering. The occupation continued for two months. The Roman Catholic church, the trading post, and other buildings were destroyed. Two Indians were killed in the shooting between the Indians and the government agents.

The Indians themselves were sharply divided. The militants at the BIA and at Wounded Knee wanted to oust from authority all Indians who did not follow their orders. Many other Indians rejected violence. They preferred to seek their rights through the courts.

The Indian Self-Determination and Education Act of 1975 assured the Indians of more say on their own reservations and on their education. To advance Indian interests, in 1977 President Carter created a new post of Assistant Secretary of the Interior for Indian Affairs. He named knowledgeable Forrest J. Gerrard, a Blackfoot Indian, to the position.

Secretary of the Interior James Watt made the position of the Reagan administration clear. He called Indian reservations examples of "the failures of socialism." Government interference, Watt said, was the cause of all the Indians' problems. As with other government programs, funds for Indians were cut back under Reagan.

Still, in 1987, Interior Secretary Donald P. Hodel estimated that $3 billion a year was spent on Indian programs. With his Assistant Secretary for Indian Affairs, Ross Swimmer, a former chief of the Cherokee Nation of Oklahoma, Hodel recommended that the tribes should be allowed to decide how to spend government funds.

Indians turn to the courts. Indians from Maine to California went to court during the 1970s and 1980s to win the return of lands taken from their ancestors centuries or decades before. They also demanded the right to raise their children on reservations, to hunt and fish when they wished, and to control mineral, water, and grazing rights on the reservations.

In the mid-1970s the Department of Interior, which the Indians long had regarded as their enemy, began to side with them. Time after time the Indians won in the courts. The state of Rhode Island returned 1800 acres taken illegally from the Narragansets many years before. The Penobscot and Passamaquoddy Indians of Maine were granted thousands of acres and millions of dollars to settle their claims. The Sioux of the Black Hills won a ruling that 7 million acres of their land had been taken from them illegally and the Federal Indian Claims Commission awarded them $105 million. But the Indians rejected the offer. They wanted the land. A bill in Congress which proposed to give them 1.3 million acres never came to a vote. Members of Congress believed it was impossible for the government to right all the wrongs of history.

The White Earth Indian Reservation in Minnesota illustrated the problems. Scattered across northern Minnesota, it contained 844,000 acres when it was set aside for the Chippewa in 1867. Over the years, the Indians lost much of their land—through theft, trickery, ignorance, or for failing to pay taxes that were, in fact, illegal. The Indians felt all the land had been stolen from them. By 1975 when they had only 58,000 acres left, they filed claims with the government for the return of 100,000 acres. But this made trouble for the innocent farmers who had bought the land many years before and were living on it. Because of the Indian claims, the banks would not lend them money to work the land and buy machinery. But nobody else would purchase their land. Bad feeling grew between the whites and the Indians. Here was just another example of how efforts to right old wrongs could make new ones.

When Indians won control of their land and resources, they had new power. It came from their inherited wealth, for their reservations contained about 16 percent of the nation's valuable coal, uranium, and oil.

SECTION 6 REVIEW

1. Identify or explain: Snyder Act of 1924, Wounded Knee, Forrest Gerrard.

2. What were the "termination" and "relocation" policies? What were their results?

3. How did Federal policy toward the Indians change under Presidents Johnson and Nixon?

4. Describe gains made by Indians in the 1970s.

5. **Identifying Alternatives.** What action did members of the American Indian Movement take to win Indian rights? What other strategy did Indians use?

---

7. New vistas of equality

Americans discovered new opportunities and new problems as they attempted to deal with the meaning of the word equality. They discovered new groups that now sought equal treatment.

Equal rights for the physically handicapped. The postwar American crusade against inequalities responded to the demands of another group. This "minority" was not an immigrant group. It included Americans of all races, all religions, and both sexes. It was found in every state and every city of the nation. These were the physically handicapped—people who were disadvantaged by a disability that made it difficult for them to compete on an equal basis with other Americans. They included all those whose hearing or vision were impaired, and persons who lacked the use of one or more of their limbs, or suffered from an illness like epilepsy. Some were veterans. Their numbers were large. In 1988 it was estimated that 35 million Americans—more than all the blacks, Latinos, and Indians taken together—were physically or mentally handicapped.

The Rehabilitation Act of 1973 forbade discrimination against the physically disabled in any of the programs, activities, and facilities that were supported by federal funds. Other laws aimed to prevent job discrimination against handicapped persons. The new federal regulations for equal opportunity in some conspicuous ways eased the everyday lives of the handicapped. In 1977 federal regulations required that public sidewalks must not have a slope greater than 5 percent and could not be interrupted by steps. Every public building had to have at least one main entrance designed for wheelchairs. In public places, too, some telephone booths and toilets had to be provided for use by the handicapped. In 1978 federal specifications required that new buses have a facility for boarding passengers in wheelchairs.

To help those whose vision was impaired, the signs in public buildings had to be made with raised letters or numbers. Doorknobs leading to rooms not intended for public use had to have special ridges to make them identifiable to the touch. Wherever warning signals were given by sounds, there also had to be visual signals to warn the hearing-impaired. On TV, many programs were "closed-captioned" for them. This meant that a

New laws to prevent discrimination against the handicapped have assisted many skilled individuals like this receptionist to find productive jobs and take their rightful place in the work force.

special decoder would let them see the program accompanied by printed captions.

Even in 1978, when Congress was cutting other costs, it authorized $5.2 billion to be spent over the next four years to provide equal opportunities and legal protection for the handicapped.

Mainstreaming. Other kinds of handicapped persons—the mentally ill and the mentally retarded—also gained. In 1965, community health centers were virtually unknown. Only ten years later they numbered more than a thousand. During these years, too, education of the mentally retarded was improved. By 1979 ten states had declared that their handicapped students had a right to equal protection with the non-handicapped.

Everywhere there were signs of concern. By a series of laws and court decisions during the 1970s the federal government insisted that education in the nation's schools and colleges should be opened to all qualified mentally and physically handicapped. This was called "mainstreaming"—taking the handicapped out of special institutions and bringing them into the mainstream of American life.

But not all programs were successful. One approach had some unhappy results. This was the effort to take mentally ill persons out of state mental hospitals and return them to their communities. In the late 1960s and 1970s many people who were not dangerous were being locked away for years and yet receiving little treatment. The tragedy of their lives was dramatically presented by Ken Kesey in his novel and the engrossing movie *One Flew Over the Cuckoo's Nest.* But when they were sent out without help they created new problems for themselves and the community.

The change was hastened when the Supreme Court ruled in 1975 that the mentally ill who were not dangerous to themselves or others could not be confined against their will. Meanwhile new medicines and federal aid through Medicare and Medicaid seemed to provide support for the mentally ill if they were released from state hospitals.

But often it did not work that way. Few local communities had planned for this new responsibility. Many of those released became homeless. They lacked skills and could not find jobs. Who would look after them? The result, as the American Psychiatric Institute noted in 1984, was a major tragedy for society.

The mentally ill really needed "halfway houses." There—just halfway back into the community—they could be trained for jobs, while they had medical help. Then when they were ready they would try to return to a normal life. Halfway houses were already helping convicts, alcoholics, and drug addicts. But few communities would pay for the urgently needed services. By the late 1980s the homeless, on the streets of the nation's cities, were the new Forgotten Americans.

Gay and lesbian rights. In the late 1960s another group began to push more openly for equal treatment. With the increased concern for the civil rights first of blacks and then of other groups, it became easier for homosexuals to demand equal treatment.

Many Americans were shocked by the calls for gay and lesbian rights. They believed that the Bible clearly condemned homosexuality, that it was unnatural and even evil. But the homosexuals of both sexes argued that they, too, should have the right to live their lives without facing discrimination. Instead of the familiar word homosexual, men preferred to call themselves "gay." Women homosexuals called themselves "lesbian." Some churches came to the aid of homosexuals, and they also formed their own churches.

Their battle was not easy. While certain cities, like San Francisco and New York, passed anti-discrimination laws, they were bitterly opposed in others. In 1977, the Miami, Florida, Metro Commission barred discrimination against homosexuals in employment, housing, and public places and transportation. A citizens' group strongly protested and the ordinance was then put to a public referendum, where it was defeated by a large vote. Many of the critics of gay rights' legislation in Miami and elsewhere argued that even without new laws homosexuals could find ample housing, jobs, and education. In Massachusetts, Cardinal Law of the Roman Catholic church, while saying it was "unjust" to discriminate against homosexuals, said that no additional laws were needed to protect them.

The AIDS crisis. In the fall of 1987, 200,000 homosexuals and their defenders gathered in Washington, D.C. They called for an amendment to the Civil Rights Act of 1964 to bar discrimination on the basis of "affectional and sexual orientation." The marchers also demanded more federal funds for research and treatment of the dread disease

Homelessness is rapidly becoming a national problem. An increasing number of the homeless today are young children.

known as AIDS. *Acquired Immune Deficiency Syndrome* is a disease for which no cure has been found. It is caused by a virus that destroys the body's immune system—which protects us against disease. People who get AIDS then die from other diseases, infections, and cancers from which their bodies can no longer protect them.

AIDS was most often transmitted through physical sexual relations and through the needles of drug users. Those most at risk from the disease were homosexuals and certain drug addicts. Scientists feared that it might break out of these groups and spread through the whole population. Suddenly, sexual promiscuity was found to be dangerous to the health of all. Since there was no known cure, education became the only way to slow the spread of the disease. The Surgeon General of the United States, Dr. C. Everett Koop, urged that grade school students be taught about the disease. AIDS, a shocking discovery of the 1980s, was a worldwide human catastrophe. It was estimated that in the United States alone, by 1991—just ten years after the disease was first discovered—180,000 Americans would have died of it.

How many languages? Never before had a nation tried so strenuously to give all its people pride in themselves. In Europe, Asia, and Africa, people had fought wars and killed each other over what language they would use in school. But the United States was a nation of nations. Here people from everywhere found that they could all learn to speak the same language. They would not lose their dignity but actually would be drawn closer to all people. Immigrant parents who knew only German or Polish or Italian learned English from their children who went to American public schools.

Gradually one language helped to make one nation. The languages from the old homeland lived on, in churches, in clubs, and in special newspapers and magazines. But English was the language of the public schools. The English language took on a wonderful new life here.

In the new quest for equality some groups began to demand that their children should use their own language as well as English in the public schools. Bilingual education, they said, would make the Spanish-speaking, the Indians, and other Americans proud of their heritage. Of course, it was important that Americans of all groups should know their heritage and not forget the language of their parents. This would enrich the whole nation. Still, there was a danger. If all Americans were not required also to learn and speak the English language well, they might lose their equal opportunity to compete for the best jobs. The one nation might be broken into small groups that could not speak to one another, could not read the same books, or understand the same TV programs.

And there were other problems, too. In the crusade for equality some people objected to all examinations. They argued that it was unfair to give tests for entrance to colleges or to find the most qualified people for jobs. They wanted "open-admissions"—which meant admission for all whether or not they could pass a test. Others, who followed the tradition of Thomas Jefferson, continued to believe in a "natural aristocracy." They argued that all Americans must be given the opportunity to become prepared. Then the examinations would find those who could benefit most from the education or could do the job best. Equal opportunity had to begin with equal kindergartens and elementary schools and high schools for all. In the long run everybody would profit if all Americans could show their true abilities, could be tested impartially, and compete fairly.

Equality among nations: ministates and microstates. Abroad, too, in the community of nations, Americans faced the challenge of equality. President Kennedy noted "a worldwide declaration of independence," which within 30 years had broken up a few old empires into 90 new nations. Each became a member of the United Nations. There in the Assembly they would have an equal vote and an equal voice. This had become a strange community of unequals. A few of these nations had populations of more than 200 million people spread across continents. Many others were tiny islands with populations of less than 100,000. Half the nations who are members of the United Nations have less population than the single state of North Carolina. And four out of every five states in the United States have a larger territory than 30 of these newly independent countries.

By the mid-1980s, there were 159 member nations in the United Nations. The United States Department of State expected that there soon might be created another 50 nations. Nearly every one of the new nations would have a population of less than 100,000.

This would make new problems for the community of nations. International law declared that all nations of the earth were entitled to equal treatment. That meant one thing when the community of nations was dominated by a few big nations. These nations usually had languages of their own, and long and separate histories. In those times the voices of the smallest nations were hardly heard.

Now nations were being created with dizzying speed. It was hard even to remember how many there were. A small nation with an atomic bomb was the equal in terror to any other. Now large nations had to show a new self-restraint. Small nations, too, would have to learn the ways of the world and show new respect for others.

SECTION 7 REVIEW

1. Describe efforts in the 1970s to provide equality for the handicapped.

2. What is "mainstreaming"?

3. **Identifying Assumptions.** Why do some groups want bilingual education in the public schools?

FOCUSING ON IDEAS

1. How does a society benefit when its people engage in lively competition for income and social status? What are the "costs" of such competition?

2. Why did the Old World aristocracy not become firmly established in most of colonial America? In which region here did a landed aristocracy thrive? Why?

3. List kinds of United States laws and government programs that are designed to promote the ideal of equality. List laws and programs designed to promote competition. Are these efforts too much, too little, or about right? Explain.

TAKING A CRITICAL LOOK

1. **Recognizing Cause and Effect.** Analyze several recent federal laws or major bills now in Congress and show how they will promote or restrain competition; and advance or retard equality.

2. **Drawing Conclusions.** How is political equality linked to social, economic, or other kinds of equality?

3. **Making Comparisons.** How has United States government policy regarding American Indians changed, if at all, since President Lyndon Johnson referred to the American Indian as the "Forgotten American"? Why has this change taken place?

YOUR REGION IN HISTORY

1. **Economics.** Does your school district have an affirmative action program? What changes has it produced? How have people in the community responded to these programs?

2. **Government.** Have any Indian groups in your state or region begun legal action to obtain land, special fishing or hunting rights, or other compensation? What settlements or proposed settlements have been reached?

3. **Culture.** How has the drive for equality affected your community? Consider both costs and benefits.

HISTORICAL FACTS AND FIGURES

Predicting Consequences. Study the graph below to help answer the following questions: (a) What percentage of women worked outside the home in 1950? In 1965? In 1985? (b) What events or trends discussed in this chapter are related to this increasing percentage? (c) If the rate of increase remains constant, estimate the percentage of women who will be working outside the home in 1990. In 1995. In 2000. (d) Do you think this trend will continue over the next 25 years? Explain your answer.

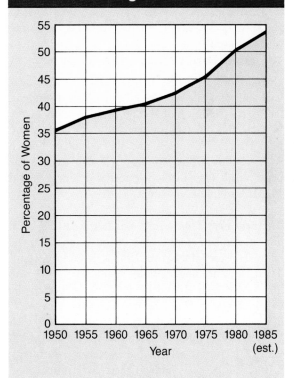

Source: *Statistical Abstract of the United States*

CHAPTER 35

Changing leaders in Washington

The American people had proven their power to remove their President. But it was much easier to change the nation's President than to solve the nation's long-term problems. How could the United States profit from the lessons of Vietnam and Watergate and still give the President the power to lead? Inflation, the energy crisis, and difficulties with Communist and other nations were not the fault of either political party or of any one President. Now new leaders would have to face these hard problems.

1. Gerald Ford becomes President

Gerald Ford, the first man to become President without being elected President or Vice-President, faced an awesome task. The people's faith in the honesty and integrity of their political leaders had been shaken. Congress and the executive branch were at odds. The economy was in tatters as the nation sank into the worst recession since World War II, and inflation soared.

The new President. Ford was not a dashing man nor an eloquent speaker, but at this moment in the nation's history he was something more important. There was nothing devious about him. He was honest and open. And his long experience in the Congress gave him much knowledge and some wisdom about how Washington functioned.

When he became President in August 1974, Ford wanted to put an end to the Watergate problems, restore the people's faith in their government, and cure the nation's economic ills—especially inflation.

He promised to run an open administration and to work with Congress. As he took the oath of office on television, Ford reminded the nation's voters that, since they had not chosen him, he had a special duty to earn their confidence.

Selecting a Vice-President. Now that the Vice-Presidency was vacant, under the Twenty-fifth Amendment Ford had to name a new Vice-President, who would take office if confirmed by both houses of Congress. He chose Nelson A. Rockefeller, a grandson of John D. Rockefeller and a leading liberal Republican who had served Presidents of both parties from FDR to Eisenhower. He had also been the highly effective governor of New York from 1958 to 1973.

Because of Rockefeller's enormous wealth, Congress spent an unprecedented three months looking into his life and character. Finally in December 1974 both houses of Congress confirmed his selection. The cheerful and dynamic Nelson Rockefeller, who had sought the Presidency himself in 1964 and 1968, was one of the most experienced Americans ever to become Vice-President.

Pardon and clemency. Soon after taking office, Ford revealed that he was thinking of moderating any punishment for former President Nixon. At first he said that he would not do anything until the courts had acted.

Then, less than two weeks later, he went on television to announce that he was granting Nixon a full pardon for *any* crimes he might have committed during his time as President. Ford said he feared that unless the people and the government put Nixon and Watergate behind them, it would be impossible for him to govern effectively. The nation would continue to be torn apart by the troubles of the past.

Nixon accepted the pardon. Although he admitted that he had handled the Watergate question badly, he still failed to say that he had done anything wrong. But President Ford had been trained as a lawyer. As Ford himself later explained, before granting the pardon he had discovered what a pardon really meant. The Supreme Court had decided that in accepting a pardon a person was confessing guilt.

Pardoning Nixon lost Ford much public support. Some people felt that the former President should have been tried in the courts for his acts. Many thought that Nixon should at least have been made to admit that he had done something wrong.

As another way to bury the past, Ford announced a program of clemency for those who had deserted from the armed forces or evaded the draft during the Vietnam War. They would not be punished if they took the oath of allegiance to the United States and then did up to two years of alternative service in jobs that would "promote the national health, safety, or interest." Since this was not an outright pardon, only about 22,500 of the 124,000 draft evaders and deserters accepted Ford's offer. Some Americans felt that these men had shirked their duty and deserved to be punished. President Carter later pardoned nearly all the draft evaders. But this provoked less comment because by then the passions of war had begun to cool.

Controlling the CIA and the FBI. The Watergate and impeachment hearings had led to serious charges against the Central Intelligence Agency and the Federal Bureau of Investigation. Soon President Ford appointed a commission under Vice-President Rockefeller to study the CIA. Committees in the House and Senate began their own probes of the CIA and FBI.

These studies showed that under six Presidents, from Franklin D. Roosevelt to Richard Nixon, the FBI had abused its powers. Without legal permits its agents had tapped telephones, read private mail, broken into buildings, placed listening devices in homes and offices, and kept records on thousands of innocent citizens.

The CIA also had been spying on Americans and opening their mail. It had even experimented on unsuspecting people with dangerous mind-control drugs. Abroad the CIA had worked secretly to bring down a Marxist regime in Chile and then had denied doing so to Congress. It was accused of having plotted to assassinate unfriendly foreign leaders.

Clearly the nation needed to gather every kind of information from every part of the world. This

Energetic Nelson Rockefeller (left) was Ford's choice for Vice-President.

was the job of the CIA. Also, to enforce federal laws and to convict criminals there had to be an FBI. Still, Congress wanted to oversee both agencies. In Communist countries and in dictatorships citizens were at the mercy of the police. But in a free country innocent citizens had to be protected from harassment and from snoopers.

Was it possible to devise a system of oversight that would neither give away our secrets nor hamstring our intelligence operations at home and abroad? President Ford set up an Intelligence Oversight Board made up of three private citizens to monitor the CIA. Both the House and Senate appointed their own committees. At the FBI, a new director promised to take firm control of the bureau's agents and activities. Congress worked on laws to define more strictly the activities of the two agencies.

Opening up government and protecting elections.
Watergate also created a strong feeling in Congress that the activities of all the hundreds of government agencies had to be opened up so people could know what their government was doing. A little-used Freedom of Information Act, passed in 1966, was strengthened by a series of amendments in 1974 and 1976. Government departments and agencies now had to give copies of documents in their files to anyone—even Soviet officials—who asked for them. Only a few exceptions for national defense, foreign policy, and law enforcement were allowed. A Privacy Act, also passed in 1974, gave citizens the right to see the information collected about them and to correct it.

By these laws, the United States government became the most open in the world. Now there was a danger that officials might spend so much of their time and energy answering the public's questions—and trying to please the newspapers—that they would have little left for the business of government.

The Watergate hearings had also revealed large-scale illegal gifts to the Nixon reelection campaign. To limit the size of political contributions—and reduce temptations—a Federal Election Campaign-funding Reform Act was passed in 1974. It also provided federal funds for candidates in presidential primaries and elections.

Congress strengthens its hand.
Congress moved on other fronts as well to assert its power. While Nixon was still President, Congress had tried to reclaim its right under the Constitution to declare war. Senators and representatives felt that Presidents since World War II had bypassed the Constitution—especially during the fighting in Korea and Vietnam. In November 1973, over Nixon's veto, Congress had passed the War Powers Act. This declared that the President must inform the House and Senate within 48 hours of putting American troops where they might be involved in fighting. The President had to bring the troops home within 90 days unless both houses voted to let them stay.

On the domestic front, Congress also acted to hold its powers. In the Budget and Impoundment Act of 1974 it declared that a President could not "impound" funds—that is, refuse to spend money Congress had voted. Nixon had done this late in his Presidency. This law also created a new Congressional Budget Office (CBO) to provide Congress with its own income and expense figures. Previously, legislators had received the budget figures from the President and had no way to check their accuracy. A bright professional economist, Alice Mitchell Rivlin, was appointed the director of this important new office.

Problems with the economy.
While President Nixon was distracted by the long agony of Watergate, he had not managed to bring inflation under control. By 1973 inflation was running annually at 8.5 percent. In 1974 it had increased to 12 percent and a recession had begun. By raising prices and so decreasing the amount a dollar could buy, inflation hurt every American.

When Gerald Ford came to the White House, he viewed inflation as the nation's number one problem. Government spending poured more and more money into the marketplace and kept prices going up. Again and again he tried to cut government spending. He used his veto 66 times to try to check Congress. But Congress continued to vote costly programs.

Oil and the economy.
A large factor in inflation was the price of oil. Until 1953, the United States produced more oil than it could use, and regularly exported petroleum and petroleum products. But as the economy expanded and everybody used machines for everything, we came to use more oil than we produced. Homes and automobiles, farms and

factories needed the energy made from oil. To keep the air clean, the nation cut back on burning coal. For reasons of safety, it slowed the development of nuclear power plants. At the same time, existing tax and price policies actually hindered the search for new sources of oil and natural gas. The nation needed more and more imported oil.

As the 1970s began, there were substantial reserves of oil throughout the world. These large reserves, combined with government support of the major American oil companies, should have been enough to keep the price of oil from rising. In fact, it appeared the price might drop to below one dollar a barrel (it cost only 25 cents a barrel to produce). But then in 1971 the revolutionary government of Colonel Muammar el-Qaddafi of Libya demanded higher prices for Libyan oil. The United States government failed to help the oil companies resist the demand—and even suggested that Libya's request was fair. So Libya raised the price of its oil. Other oil-producing countries quickly followed Libya's example. Now prices began to rise rapidly. By the fall of 1973 they had quintupled.

Then came the 1973 Yom Kippur War (p. 710). In anger at Nixon's very public aid to Israel, the Arab nations of the Middle East cut off their oil shipments to the United States. The Netherlands, another supporter of Israel, was refused oil, too. By purchases from other nations, especially Canada, Iran, and Indonesia, the United States kept its shortage down to 7 percent. But American drivers panicked. For the first time in American history they waited in long lines to fill their tanks. Gas stations became a scene of bad-tempered scuffling for a few more gallons.

As the demand increased worldwide, governments and dealers bid up the price for some oil to an astonishing $17.40 per barrel in December 1973.

OPEC. Some of the oil-producing countries, led by Venezuela, had begun to organize back in 1960. But their Organization of Petroleum Exporting Countries (OPEC) had never been strong. Each oil-producing country wanted all it could get for its oil and feared higher prices would decrease its sales and income. But the price rises that had begun in 1971 had made the OPEC nations rich. Now they could afford to ask for even more, and the high prices received for some oil in December 1973 re-

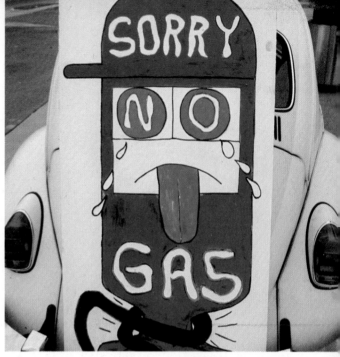

Dennis Brack/Black Star

Filling-station managers found amusing ways to say "No Gas Today" during the Arab oil embargo of 1973–1974.

vealed that the world could be made to pay. Meeting in Teheran, Iran, at the end of the month, they set the price for all of their oil at nearly $12 per barrel. Then they limited production to force customers to pay this high price. The Western world and the developing nations were hit hard. The high cost of oil brought on recession and inflation.

Despite warnings of our growing dependence on imported oil, the Nixon administration had made no provision for dealing with an oil cutoff or high prices. Now Nixon proposed a number of short-term measures, such as increased taxes on oil and a 55-mile-per-hour speed limit. For long-term measures he proposed more nuclear plants and greater use of coal. At last we would push ahead with a pipeline across Alaska to the vast oil deposits on the edge of the Arctic Ocean. This oil had been discovered early in 1968. Had the pipeline been completed in 1973, the United States would easily have replaced the lost Arab oil from its own sources.

When Gerald Ford became President, the worst of the oil shortage brought on by the Arab nations was past. But because of high energy prices, the United States was still in the worst recession since World War II. Ford now tried urgent measures to get the economy moving again. Taxes were cut

OPEC, 1975

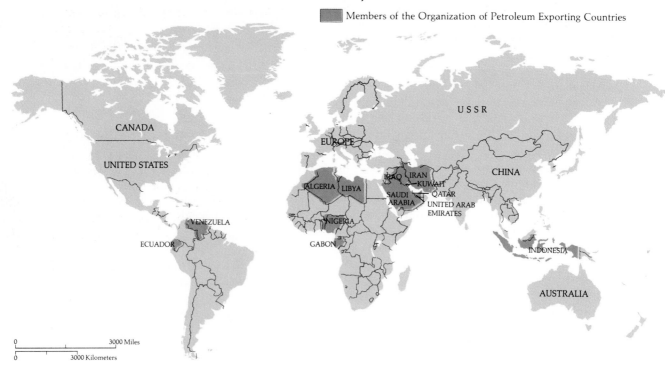

Members of the Organization of Petroleum Exporting Countries

and large government deficits, running over $50 billion, pumped new money into the economy. The economy did recover and, due to the lingering effects of the recession, inflation in 1976 fell to below 5 percent.

Running for President. The presidential campaign of 1976 was one of the longest in our history. Gerald Ford announced in July 1975 that he wanted to be President in his own right. His main opponent for the Republican nomination was Ronald Reagan, a former movie star and a persuasive public speaker, who had served two terms as governor of California. He represented the conservative wing of his party. An outspoken anti-Communist, he criticized the policy of détente with Russia. He wanted the Republican party to take strong conservative positions—on limiting government activity, on taxes, and on all public issues. Ford favored more moderate positions to broaden the party's appeal. After a series of primaries early in 1976, the two candidates were neck and neck when the party gathered in Kansas City, Missouri, for its convention. Ford narrowly won the nomination on the first ballot with 1187 votes against 1070 for Reagan.

The Democratic campaign was even longer than the Republicans'. As early as September 1973, Governor Jimmy Carter of Georgia, a man little known outside his state, told his mother that he was going to run for President in 1976, "and I'm going to win."

Carter's term as governor ended in January 1975. Since state law barred him from succeeding himself, he began to spend all his time campaigning for the Democratic nomination for President. As late as October of that year, however, few people considered him a serious contender.

But this was soon to change. He showed a single-minded devotion to his purpose. A "born again" Christian and a member of the Baptist church, he impressed people with his simple manner, his honesty, and his sincerity. He was also helped by the fact that he had had nothing to do with Vietnam or Watergate. In 1976 he began to win primary after primary over the many other Democratic hopefuls. When the party met in New York City for its convention, Carter was clearly in the lead. He was chosen on the first ballot and named Walter F. Mondale, an attractive liberal senator from Minnesota, to run for Vice-President.

The election of 1976. In the campaign, President Ford pushed hard to sell the country on his achievements. He pointed out how he had cut federal spending, lowered the rate of inflation, and decreased unemployment. For the first time in years, Ford stressed, no United States soldiers were in combat anywhere in the world. Carter said he would bring honesty and integrity back to the government and bring government back to the people.

Carter was far ahead in the opinion polls when the campaign began, but Ford pulled up rapidly. The two candidates met in three television debates, the first since 1960. Never before had a President in office agreed to debate. Ford appeared to win the first debate on domestic affairs. But he was badly hurt in the second debate when he seemed to say that Eastern Europe was not under Communist domination.

Still, the result was very close. Carter won just over 50 percent of the popular vote to Ford's 48 percent. The electoral margin was the narrowest since 1916, as Carter received 297 to Ford's 240. Again the number of people who bothered to vote at all declined—only 53 percent went to the polls.

In his inaugural address Jimmy Carter declared, "For myself and for our nation I want to thank my predecessor for all he has done to heal our land." The first unelected President, Gerald Ford, had served his nation well.

SECTION 1 REVIEW

1. Identify or explain: clemency programs, Freedom of Information Act, Privacy Act, Federal Election Campaign-funding Reform Act, War Powers Act, Alice M. Rivlin, Muammar el-Qaddafi, OPEC, Ronald Reagan, Walter Mondale.

2. How did Gerald Ford's training and experience fit him for the Presidency?

3. How did Nelson Rockefeller become Vice-President?

4. According to Ford, why did he pardon Nixon?

5. What new controls were placed on the CIA and the FBI? Why?

6. Why was there an energy crisis in 1973 and 1974?

7. **Identifying Alternatives.** What were some proposed solutions to the energy problem?

---

2. Carter: a campaigner as President

Jimmy Carter had run against the government in Washington during his bid for office. He profited from the disrespect for government and for politicians that spread after Vietnam and Watergate. Now he had to prove that an "outsider" actually could make the government efficient and responsive to the needs of the people.

A peanut-farmer in the White House. During the campaign, supporters of Jimmy Carter wore buttons in the shape of a peanut. They said they were working to elect a peanut-farmer as President. When they succeeded, their symbol proved appropriate. The new President showed both the special virtues and the limitations of a farmer rooted in his own part of the country.

James Earl Carter, or Jimmy Carter, as he officially signed his name, had been born and raised in the small towns of Plains and Archery, Georgia. After high school, Carter was appointed to the United States Naval Academy. He graduated from Annapolis in 1946, and that same year he married Rosalynn Smith of Plains.

Carter spent the next seven years in the navy, first on battleships and then on the early nuclear submarines. At that time he served under hard-driving Captain Hyman Rickover, the "father" of the nuclear-powered navy. Carter believed that, except for his parents, Rickover had the greatest influence on him. "The standards that he set for one's effort, and the need for an executive to know the details of circumstances before a decision is made" were the education he received from Rickover.

In 1953 when his father died Carter returned to Plains to run the family peanut farm and warehouse. From there he went on to become a state senator in 1964 and governor of Georgia in 1970. He was outspoken in his opposition to racial discrimination. And his supporters applauded his reorganization of the state government.

Carter came to Washington with a burning desire to get things done. Unfortunately, he suffered the disadvantage of not knowing the leaders of Congress or the way things worked in Washington. He picked a capable Cabinet, but as his closest staff aides he kept the young and inexperienced Georgians who had helped in his campaign. His most trusted adviser was the bright Rosalynn Carter, who, more than most Presidents' wives, shared in his highest decisions on people and policies. To keep up with what was being planned, she sometimes sat in on Cabinet meetings—the first "First Lady" to do so.

Proposals and pitfalls. On the domestic scene Carter offered a wide variety of goals. His ambitious and miscellaneous plans included an energy program, tax reform, electoral reform (the direct election of the President and Vice-President), Social Security legislation, control of inflation, a balanced budget by 1980, a strong environmental program, a national health plan, reorganization of the executive branch, and a new welfare system.

He immediately ran into trouble with Congress. Though he was a Democratic President and his own party dominated Congress, he failed to work closely with congressional leaders. After Watergate, Congress was understandably sensitive about its own role in government, and this caused problems. Carter's tendency to set deadlines that his aides found hard to meet also created difficulties. When he sent his energy program to Congress in April 1977, it was found that some of his figures were wrong. He raised high hopes when he grandly announced this program to Congress as "the moral equivalent of war." But then he proceeded to ask for legislation on many other matters. Congress and the nation wondered what his priorities were.

Jimmy and Rosalynn Carter brought a relaxed air and informal clothes to the White House. During the four years of Carter's Presidency, his wife was his most trusted adviser.

Dennis Brack/Black Star

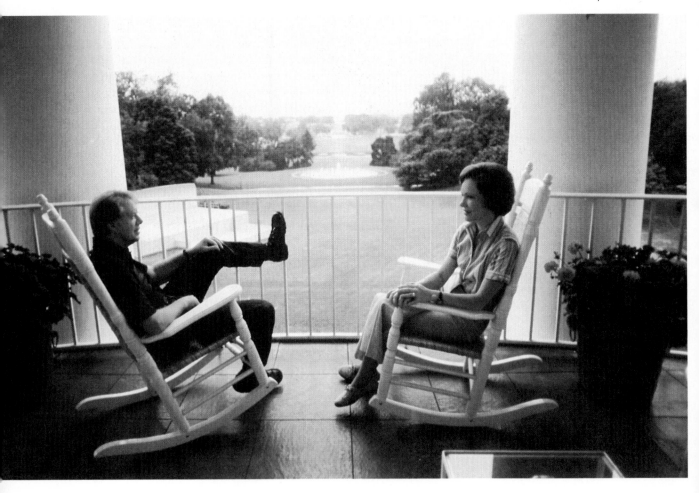

The issues Carter was trying to deal with were all worthy of the nation's attention. But they were complex and more difficult to solve by laws than his Georgia experience had led him to believe. The problem was not with *what* he was trying to do, but with his hesitant leadership. By October 1977, the leaders of Congress were pleading with the President to stop sending his proposals. Congress was swamped.

Successes and failures. The Social Security system was in trouble. It was paying out more money than it was taking in. In a few years the whole system would be bankrupt. Then, unless the federal government voted funds, the disabled and the elderly would no longer receive their pensions. The law that President Carter signed in December 1977 raising Social Security taxes was the largest peacetime tax increase in American history.

Carter did not submit his promised major tax reform. Instead, he offered a law simply to reduce taxes to stimulate the economy. Pursuing his campaign promises against big government, he abolished some 480 advisory committees in the government, but his idea of making 200 super-agencies out of 1900 existing agencies was dropped. His programs for energy, for electoral reform, and for a sweeping change in the welfare system were all stymied. An effective President, Carter now found, would have to be effective in Congress.

His failures *with* Congress were partly due to changes *in* Congress brought on by Watergate. The new members elected in 1974 and 1976 tended to view every presidential act with suspicion. Members of Congress themselves now had larger staffs to give them information, which made them more independent of the President and the House and Senate leaders. The seniority power of long-term members was reduced and dispersed to many committee and subcommittee heads. All these developments made it much harder to pass the laws a President wanted.

The rise of the special-interest state. Party loyalty had also declined. The major political parties had been forces for moderation, compromise, and discipline in a large and diverse nation. To elect a President or a member of Congress or to pass a law, people with different goals had to come together. And the parties had helped.

A great change was in the making. In late twentieth-century America citizens were organizing less around their political parties than around their own particular interests. Environmentalists, poor people, pro- and anti-gun forces, blacks, Hispanics, businesses, labor unions, truckers, farmers, ship owners, mayors, governors, consumers, pro- and anti-abortion groups, and many others pushed for their own special programs. Many of these groups had their own Political Action Committees (PACs), which contributed large sums to elect their favorite candidates. These special interests naturally wielded great influence in Congress.

With the power of these groups growing greater all the time, the broad issues of national concern were lost. The rise of television, opinion polls, and public relations helped the groups attract attention. Politicians were attacked or supported not for their general political outlook, but for their stand on a single issue. In Congress, under such pressures, party loyalty declined. Members of Congress were less apt to follow the President's lead or pass measures for the good of the party.

Presidential weaknesses. Carter's own lack of experience made his problems worse. He was clumsy in his dealings with Congress. Soon after taking office, he attempted to deny some members their share of the "pork barrel"—local improvement projects, such as dams, canals, and highways, that made members of Congress popular in their own districts. Carter infuriated several members whose pet water projects he opposed. Then he enraged others who had supported him by quickly backing down without giving them warning. It was expected that he would have to do some compromising to push his program through Congress. But his hasty retreats on the water projects, on a tax rebate, and on other matters left his supporters on Capitol Hill feeling deserted.

Part of Carter's problem lay in his own character. He did not make friends easily. The men around him, the Georgians, were mostly much younger than he and had even less experience in national problems. The only one about his age was Georgia banker Bert Lance, who became Carter's director of the key Office of Management and Budget. But soon after Lance took office, serious charges were made over his handling of his own personal finances as well as his management of the banks he had headed. Though later cleared by the courts, in September 1977 Lance was forced to resign.

Once in the White House, the friendly campaigner became remote and hard to reach. He failed to seek the advice of older and more experienced heads who might have steered him through the thickets of Washington. And while he immersed himself in details, the government lacked a strong leader.

The problem of inflation. By 1979 inflation even overshadowed the energy crisis. While Carter urged voluntary restraints and set government wage-price guidelines, the rate of inflation soared, reaching 1 percent a month during the first half of 1979.

The problem of inflation was deep-seated and complex. It was produced by the rising cost of oil, a higher minimum wage enacted in 1977, the increased Social Security taxes, costly environmental and safety regulations, and ever-higher wages as workers sought to keep their standard of living in the face of ever-rising inflation. The many welfare programs to aid the sick, the poor, the aged, and the unemployed played their part, too. The government's constant attempts to stimulate the economy to provide more jobs also made the problem worse. The nation saw a baffling new phenomenon: stagnation of the economy and inflation of prices. People called this "stagflation."

The energy problem. The United States was the most profligate energy user in the world. With only 6 percent of the world's population, the United States used 33 percent of all the world's energy! Even with our own rich oil fields, by the late 1970s we still had to import more than 30 percent of the oil we used. As OPEC constantly raised prices the cost of foreign oil soared. During the 1970s our annual bill went from $1.5 billion to $60 billion. Of course this pushed up the price of electricity, of gas for cars and trucks and buses, heating oil for homes, and fuel to run factories.

As these prices rose, so did the price of everything produced on the farms and in the factories. As American dollars poured out of the country to pay for oil, our "trade deficit" mounted. This was the amount of goods we sold abroad compared to what we bought abroad. So the purchasing power of the dollar overseas declined.

Environmental action. Efforts to clean up the environment and conserve the American wilderness made the energy problem more complicated. When President Nixon signed the National Environmental Policy Act on January 1, 1970, he announced a "now or never" fight on pollution by a new Council on Environmental Quality. Almost unnoticed, the law also stated that all projects involving federal funds, property, or permits would have to be accompanied by environmental impact statements—reports on just how the project would affect the environment. This clause did help to protect wildlife and our land and water, but it also brought costly delays and expensive lawsuits.

Nixon signed other laws to clean up our air and water and to protect federal lands in the West. In December 1970 the new Environmental Protection Agency (EPA) brought together the agencies dealing with water quality, air pollution, and the disposal of the millions of tons of bottles, paper, and other solid waste that Americans throw away every week. It also set standards for the disposal of nuclear waste and regulated the use of pesticides.

When President Carter took office, he announced his strong support for this movement to protect the environment. But these efforts quickly collided with the need to conserve oil. Which was more important?

The problem with coal. The United States had more coal than any other nation in the world—enough to supply our needs for hundreds of years. But burning coal fouled the air with sulfur dioxide, which helped to create still another problem. When mixed with moisture high in the sky, the oxides of sulfur and nitrogen that came from burning coal and from car exhausts produced "acid rain." Containing sulfuric and nitric acid, this rain killed fish in lakes and threatened forests. To keep the air clean, factories and power plants had been urged to switch from coal to oil. Then, with the oil shortage, President Nixon urged the electric power companies to switch back again to coal. But the equipment needed to reduce the pollution from burning coal was expensive. These efforts to save the environment added still more to inflation.

Strip mining was one of the commonest and cheapest ways to dig coal. Large strips of the earth's surface were cut away to get at the coal just below. Each strip mine left an ugly gash on the landscape where sod and trees had been torn up and great seams of coal removed. Putting the land back was costly and not always possible.

President Ford had vetoed laws forcing the strip miners to restore the land. He said it was so expensive that it would discourage the coal mining the nation badly needed. President Carter, however, endorsed these laws and tried to make them even more strict. He thought restoring the land was worth the higher price for coal.

Energy vs. the environment. Another cause of air pollution was the automobile. The exhaust pipes of cars emit carbon monoxide and other pollutants that can irritate the eyes and lungs. In big cities like Los Angeles, New York, and Chicago, thousands of cars fill the air with pollutants, which leave a blue-grey pall hovering in the heavens. "Smog" (*smoke* and *fog*) was the new word for it. Devices added to car engines reduced these dangerous emissions. But the devices themselves added to inflation by increasing the cost of the car.

Efforts to preserve land for national parks and wilderness ran into the energy problem. Some members of Congress bitterly opposed attempts to keep millions of acres in Alaska untouched instead of encouraging efforts to explore it for oil and use its resources by mining and timbering. President Carter worked to preserve the land as wilderness. In December 1980, the Alaska National Interest Lands Conservation Act set aside 103 million acres in Alaska—an area larger than all of California.

The question of nuclear power. Nuclear power, which many thought was the likely supply for our new energy needs, was plagued by problems of pollution, safety, and cost. No one had found a safe way to dispose of the used-up uranium. Even after the uranium no longer had the energy to run a nuclear reactor, it remained dangerously radioactive and could cause cancer. The government stored it in temporary holding places until a solution could be found.

There were other fears about nuclear reactors. If something went awry in the plant, radioactive material might be released in the air, endangering the lives of people for miles around. This threat appeared remote during the first twenty years of nuclear power. Then suddenly, in the spring of 1979, something went wrong at the Three Mile

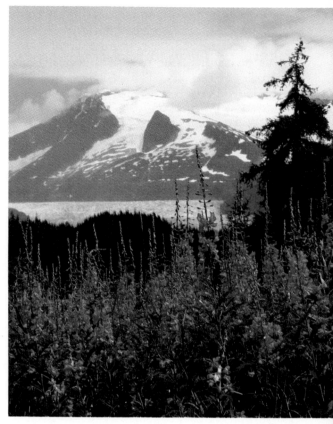

Harald Sund

The Alaska National Interest Lands Conservation Act of 1980 preserved millions of acres of unspoiled wilderness.

Island nuclear plant near Harrisburg, Pennsylvania. For several days there seemed to be a danger of a massive escape of radiation. Though the immediate problem was brought under control by the end of a week, the full cleanup would take years. This incident advertised the problems of the whole nuclear power industry—which already supplied 12 percent of the nation's electricity.

Complex and ever-changing safety regulations, soaring construction costs, and rising interest rates put heavy obstacles in the way of the new nuclear electric industry. Meanwhile, the rising cost of electricity brought a decline in demand. In the 1980s these problems resulted in the cancellation of all new nuclear plants ordered after 1973. To many observers, it appeared that energy from coal, small plants producing electricity from streams and rivers, and such new alternative sources as solar power might be the wave of the future.

A weak energy program. During 1977, President Carter's main accomplishment in his energy program was to create a new Department of Energy. The department took over most federal energy agencies.

The following year, eighteen months after Carter had asked for it, Congress finally passed a weak energy bill. It was far different from what he wanted. It began to free newfound natural gas from government price regulation, but it failed to remove price controls on old gas and all domestic oil. It required most electric power plants to burn coal. New taxes and tax credits would encourage conservation, as did government laws that demanded improved gasoline mileage for new cars.

Energy crisis. In 1979, a revolution in Iran toppled the friendly government of Shah Mohammad Reza Pahlavi. This stopped the flow of oil from Iran, which had provided 10 percent of the oil for the non-Communist world. The government of the fanatic Ayatollah Khomeini (p. 763) produced chaos, along with a hate campaign against the United States. Iran's oil production sank. Then OPEC, reckless of the world economy and the well-being of the developing countries, again increased its oil prices. During this "second oil shock" some prices reached a staggering $41 a barrel.

Despite all the warnings, the United States and other Western nations had failed to prepare for another oil crisis. Delegates of the seven leading industrial nations, including President Carter, met in June 1979 in Tokyo, Japan. All the nations agreed to cut their use of oil. Carter hastened home to find that lines at gas stations had been growing, and American tempers were rising.

He announced that he was going to Camp David to prepare a new energy program. His speech about it, scheduled for July 5, was suddenly canceled without explanation. Advisers urged that something more substantial was needed than another speech on energy. To Camp David Carter called more than 100 American leaders—from government, business, religion, journalism, and many other fields. They discussed the energy crisis, the state of the nation, and how to improve Jimmy Carter's "image" so that he could be reelected President in 1980.

An accident at the Three Mile Island nuclear power plant in 1979 sparked fears about the safety of such plants.

Robin Moyer/Black Star

Finally, ten days after the speech had first been planned, Carter spoke to the people on television. He attacked the growing cynicism, selfishness, and lack of goals in the American people. He was critical of his own leadership, and he said there was a "crisis of confidence." Then he briefly outlined his energy plan. Reporters were reminded of the campaigning Jimmy Carter, who spoke in sermons.

The following day he announced the details of his program—"the most massive peacetime commitment of funds and resources in the nation's history." He aimed to cut oil imports in half by 1990. He proposed ways for the nation to produce synthetic fuels in large amounts, to develop solar and nuclear power, and to conserve energy.

Hardly had Carter announced these sweeping proposals when he distracted attention from the energy problem by a major shake-up of his Cabinet. The press and the public were puzzled that the President congratulated Secretary of HEW Joseph Califano for a fine job—and then said he was fired. Altogether, five Cabinet members resigned or were fired.

The Cabinet changes were part of Carter's attempt to prepare for the 1980 campaign for President. He was trying to return to the role of "outsider" that he had played in 1976. He attacked the "isolated world of Washington" and pledged to go out to speak to the people. But his Presidency was in serious trouble. Public opinion polls showed only 25 percent of the people approving his Presidency—lower than Nixon's rating at any time.

Marvin Newman/Woodfin Camp & Associates

Henry Kissinger arrives in Israel on one of his "shuttle diplomacy" missions.

SECTION 2 REVIEW

1. Identify or explain: Hyman Rickover, "the moral equivalent of war," "pork barrel," Bert Lance, wage-price guidelines, EPA, acid rain, strip mining, Three Mile Island, Shah Mohammad Reza Pahlavi, Joseph Califano.

2. What were some of the causes of Jimmy Carter's inability to get his programs passed by Congress?

3. What caused the steep inflation of the late 1970s? How did Carter try to halt it?

4. **Recognizing Ideologies.** Show how environmental and energy concerns collided.

3. The United States and the world

Despite the sudden turns of domestic politics and the rapid changes in the outside world, the foreign policy of the United States remained surprisingly consistent. The war in Vietnam still left its mark. But the nation continued to pursue the goals of national security and détente. The aim was to keep old friends and try to avoid making new enemies. If we could help relax world tensions and reduce the dangers of war anywhere, our nation, with others, might hope for a generation of peace. This could be achieved not by sudden moves, but only by slow and steady diplomacy.

Henry Kissinger and foreign affairs. During the long months while the nation struggled over Watergate and the possible impeachment of President Nixon, our foreign policy did not falter. Nor was it inactive. This was largely due to the talents of Henry Kissinger and to Nixon's willingness to

757

put confidence in him. In 1969 Nixon had chosen Kissinger, then a professor of government at Harvard, to be his special assistant for national security affairs. In 1973 Nixon had named him Secretary of State.

Kissinger had been born in Germany. When he was fifteen years old, his family fled to the United States to escape Hitler's persecution of the Jews. He became a citizen in 1943, served three years in the United States Army, then attended Harvard, where he received his A.B. *summa cum laude* and his Ph.D. A brilliant and profound student of history, he was the author of books on the relation between national power and world diplomacy. He never entirely lost his German accent, and he joked about that, as he did about much else. Unlike the solemn diplomats, he was witty and outspoken about himself and other world figures. But he was good at keeping diplomatic secrets and was constantly surprising the press and the public by turning up in unexpected places. He had made a secret trip to China to prepare for President Nixon's history-making visit. Newspaper reporters and his staff were exhausted trying to match his endless energy as he shuttled around the world.

Kissinger's personal brand of "shuttle diplomacy" produced results. He finally negotiated an end to American involvement in the war in Vietnam, and he helped to open the way for United States relations with Communist China. He promoted détente with Soviet Russia. And he led the way toward peace between Egypt and Israel. When President Ford came to office, he kept Kissinger as Secretary of State and so preserved the continuity of American foreign policy.

During the early 1970s some old problems were resolved. The struggle between the "two Germanys"—a Communist east and a democratic west—had threatened European peace ever since the end of World War II. In 1972 East Germany and West Germany finally signed a treaty of mutual recognition. Both nations joined the UN in 1973.

In 1975, the European Security Conference, made up of 35 nations including the United States, met in Helsinki, Finland. It settled some more of the remaining issues of World War II. Among the many terms of the Helsinki Agreements were recognition of the new national borders drawn after the war, and an agreement by all the nations—including the Soviet Union and its East European satellites—to respect human rights. As usual, it turned out that the Communist dictatorships did not share the democratic nations' belief in human rights. When some Soviet citizens tried to monitor Soviet compliance with the treaties, they were harassed, imprisoned, or forced into exile.

A pause in the Middle East. After the Yom Kippur War in the Middle East between the Arabs and Israel in 1973 (p. 710), the United States and the Soviet Union pushed a cease-fire resolution through the UN Security Council. United Nations troops were sent in to separate the opposing forces. Then Kissinger's "shuttle diplomacy" served a very practical purpose. Since the two sides would not speak to each other, Kissinger shuttled between them. He made it possible for them to communicate and finally to come to some sort of agreement. The result was a pullback of the troops of both sides. Buffer zones between Egypt and Israel and between Israel and Syria were patrolled by UN forces.

By another exercise in shuttle diplomacy in 1975, Kissinger persuaded Egypt and Israel to renounce the use of force to settle their differences. They both agreed to move farther back and create a much larger buffer zone. The 1975 agreement was made possible because the United States agreed to station 200 American civilian technicians at two main passes on the Sinai peninsula. They would monitor the cease-fire to give an early warning in case either side moved to attack.

The fall of Cambodia. The long United States presence in the former lands of French Indochina came to an end in 1975. Even after the signing of a cease-fire for Vietnam early in 1973 and the withdrawal of United States armed forces, the fighting had never stopped. As Communist troops in South Vietnam, Cambodia, and Laos advanced, President Ford asked Congress to increase military aid to the non-Communist governments. But Congress had had enough. It refused to act.

Nixon had widened the war in Vietnam by attacking North Vietnamese troops that were illegally using Cambodia as a refuge from American and South Vietnamese forces. The Cambodians, who hated the Vietnamese, had allowed them to use these sanctuaries because they were not strong enough to push them out. In March 1970 Prince Norodom Sihanouk, the wily neutralist leader who had carefully kept Cambodia out of the war, was toppled by General Lon Nol, a right-wing nationalist. He believed it would be easy to drive out Cambodia's ancient enemy. With the American bombings and the "incursion" by U.S. troops (p. 701), the Cambodians thought they saw their chance and attacked the North Vietnamese. Then the North Vietnamese quickly overran half the country and worked hard to arm and train the Khmer Rouge (Red, or Communist, Cambodians).

The Khmer Rouge in Cambodia were a violent, deadly force that had no desire for peace or compromise. They moved forward steadily against the nationalist forces. The United States, whose interest remained centered on Vietnam, did little to stop them. On April 12, 1975, Phnom Penh, the capital of Cambodia, fell to the Khmer Rouge. Then they showed the world just how ruthless they were. They emptied the city of its people—even driving the sick and wounded from the hospitals—and forced them back to the countryside. Phnom Penh and other Cambodian cities became silent as tombs. Millions died. In 1978 even so strong an opponent of the Vietnam War as George McGovern called for an international force to invade Cambodia to save the people from their own government.

The victory of North Vietnam.
The end in South Vietnam also came with stunning swiftness. All along, both sides there had violated the cease-fire. At first President Thieu tried to hold or seize every position, instead of concentrating his forces for defense. When he finally decided on a retreat in the face of ever-stronger attacks by North Vietnamese and Viet Cong forces, his army suddenly collapsed. The retreat turned into a rout. North Vietnamese soldiers escorted by tanks entered Saigon on April 30, 1975.

As the war came to its rapid close, the bitterness and divisions it had produced in the United States were still much in evidence. When President Ford asked Congress to allow him to use military force to help evacuate Vietnamese who had aided the United States during the war, Congress failed to act. These were the people most in danger from the Communists, but many members of Congress feared the request was an excuse for more American in-

As the North Vietnamese swept toward Saigon, thousands of South Vietnamese fled in terror.

Aventurier/Gamma-Liaison

volvement. In the end, although some 100,000 did escape one way or another before the Communist takeover, thousands of Vietnamese who had thought we would help them were left behind—as others had been in Cambodia.

The end in Indochina. In Laos, the country north of Cambodia and bordering North Vietnam, during the Vietnam War the government had slowly become weaker and the Communist Pathet Lao ("Land of the Lao") had become stronger. Less than a month after the cease-fire agreement was reached in Paris between North and South Vietnam (p. 704), a peace agreement was signed in Laos. A coalition government with members from both the left and right was set up in April 1975. But it did not last long. Soon after the fall of South Vietnam, the Pathet Lao took full control. And in December 1975 they deposed the king of Laos and proclaimed a People's Democratic Government.

Now the last of the "dominoes" (p. 691) seemed to have fallen. But instead of putting up a united front against the world, the new Communist governments began to fight each other. Vietnam invaded Cambodia in December 1978 and installed a puppet government. Communist China then briefly attacked North Vietnam to punish it for its Cambodian venture. The Khmer Rouge and other opponents of the puppet regime in Cambodia continued to fight. Indochina still lacked peace.

Many had feared a bloodbath in South Vietnam if the Communists triumphed. It did not happen. But many thousands were imprisoned, thousands more were resettled, and over 500,000 fled, often in flimsy boats. How many of these "boat people" died at sea will never be known. In all, during 30 years of fighting, at least 2 million people had died in Vietnam.

From the debacle in Indochina the United States emerged chastened, bewildered, and divided. It would take time for the passions aroused by the war to fade and for all Americans to learn its hard lessons. What those lessons were remained in dispute. But it was clear to nearly everybody that the United States could not withdraw from the world to lick its wounds. Still a superpower, the United States could not avoid some responsibility for peace in the world. Since the American Revolution the nation had served as a beacon of hope for people who wanted to govern themselves.

SECTION 3 REVIEW

1. Identify or explain: shuttle diplomacy, Helsinki Agreements, Prince Norodom Sihanouk, Khmer Rouge, Pathet Lao.

2. **Identifying Central Issues.** What happened in Southeast Asia after United States forces withdrew from Vietnam?

4. New initiatives by Carter

With the election of Jimmy Carter, Cyrus Vance, a calm and cool New York lawyer who had served as Kennedy's Secretary of the Army and Johnson's Deputy Secretary of Defense, took office as Secretary of State. Abroad, friends now hoped that a President whose party held a majority in Congress could chart a clearer, firmer American foreign policy with the united support of the nation. Their hopes were short-lived.

The issue of human rights. President Carter's first initiative in foreign affairs was to make a bold stand for human rights. He angered the Russians by praising their dissident citizens. He cut off military aid to Argentina, Brazil, and Ethiopia, which had been guilty of political repression.

Some of Carter's critics felt that his stand for human rights should be backed by quiet, behind-the-scenes pressure rather than public speeches. They noted that only friendly nations were apt to heed our advice, and that others could be persuaded not by words but by deeds. The Communist nations were likely to reduce their repression in particular cases only if we somehow made it worthwhile. Still, victims of tyranny across the world admired the American President as a needed voice for freedom.

Dealing with Russia. Relations with the Soviet Union, already strained by Carter's outspoken stand for human rights, now became even worse. Instead of pursuing the slow, step-by-step diplomacy of Nixon and Ford toward a second Strategic Arms Limitation Treaty (SALT II) agreement, President Carter suddenly proposed a broad new plan for arms limitation. The Soviets objected that his proposals were one-sided and unfairly favored the United

States. They quickly rejected Carter's plan. Since SALT I was soon to expire, détente seemed about to come to an end. Without a new agreement the arms race would begin again.

In July 1977, President Carter made an effort to improve relations with the Soviets. He admitted that the Russians had reason to fear the new American arms. These included a low-flying "cruise" missile that was like a small airplane and was hard to see on radar because it flew so close to the ground. He became less outspoken about Soviet violations of human rights. The USSR, too, became more conciliatory. Détente seemed back on the track.

This change by both sides made it possible for the SALT talks to go forward. And in June 1979 Carter and Brezhnev met in Vienna to sign the SALT II agreement. It was intended to slow the arms race because both sides agreed to limit the number of their missiles and long-range bombers. The Senate scheduled lengthy hearings. Under the Constitution, a two-thirds majority of the Senators present must vote for any treaty for it to become official. But before the Senate could approve this treaty, new aggression by the Soviets (p. 763) increased American suspicions. SALT II would never become law.

The Panama Canal treaties. President Carter inherited the problem of the Panama Canal. Inside the Republic of Panama was a Canal Zone controlled "in perpetuity"—that is, forever—by the United States under the old treaty of 1903. Against this, the irritation of the Panamanians and other Latin Americans was festering. In 1964 bloody riots in Panama led President Johnson to begin talks about a new treaty, which were still continuing when Carter took office.

President Carter believed the Treaty of 1903 was an old wrong that had to be righted. He feared angry Panamanians might sabotage the canal. And he wanted to improve our relations with all Latin America. Finally in August 1977, after hard negotiations, two treaties emerged. In one treaty the United States agreed to hand over the canal to the Republic of Panama at noon on December 31, 1999. Meanwhile, the canal would be run jointly by the United States and Panama. The second treaty made the canal a neutral waterway open to all shipping after 1999. The United States was given the permanent right to protect and defend that neutrality.

Bill Arnold/The Picture Group

The Panama Canal treaties turned over control of the canal to Panama while assuring that all nations would still be able to use it.

The Panama Canal treaties helped our relations with the Latin American nations. But many Americans were disturbed. Without looking too closely at how we had acquired the canal in the first place (p. 448), they simply said that the canal was ours. We had built it and paid for it. Why, they asked, should we give it away? For our two-ocean nation they believed a free and open path between the oceans was vital. And they feared putting so vital a national interest at the mercy of a small, unstable Central American government.

Having at last achieved agreement with Panama, President Carter now had to see the treaties through the Senate. Their defeat would be a sign of weakness in his administration and would make it hard for him to shape foreign policy elsewhere. During a long hard fight in the Senate, the President had to lobby with all his bargaining power. The Senate finally ratified the treaties by just one vote more than the necessary two-thirds margin in March and April 1978.

A changing world. For most of the years since World War II, the United States had tended to see world events as dominated by Soviet-American relations. Between the Communist Soviet Union and its satellites on one side and the capitalist United States and its allies on the other, there was suspicion and fear. But now besides these two "worlds" of East and West, there was a "Third World." These were nations in Europe, Latin America, Asia, and Africa who felt no strong attachment either to the Soviets or the United States.

The world was also split between the so-called "developed" or industrial nations and the "underdeveloped" or "developing" nations. The poorer nations looked for aid from both the East and the West. Meanwhile the two superpowers competed for their goodwill. These developing nations covered much of the planet and had two-thirds of the world's population. They were useful military allies, sources of needed raw materials, and profitable customers. How could they be won over?

For these reasons the relations between the United States and the Soviets were not so simple anymore. The whole world was a scene of their

After the signing of the peace treaty between Egypt and Israel, President Sadat (left) and Prime Minister Begin shake hands.

Wally MacNamee/Woodfin Camp and Associates

struggle. The government of mainland China, though Communist, feared and hated the Soviet Union, which threatened its borders. The Chinese were a new balancing force. Japan, which had surprised the world by becoming again one of the world's great industrial powers, was going its own way. Ten of the nations of Western Europe had become another new force. They were working together in a Common Market and a European Parliament. Their mixed economy equaled in strength that of the United States.

The Middle East. The Middle East remained a tinderbox. A fire started there might ignite a world war. The region was divided by many conflicts, old and new. There were religious conflicts—between Muslims, Christians, and Jews, and even between different Muslim sects. There were political divisions between moderate and radical Arab states. No Arab country had yet recognized Israel's right to exist. And they were constantly threatening Israel's existence by war or terrorism. The problem of the Palestinians was still unsolved.

The Palestinians had once lived in the land that was now Israel and still considered it theirs. Many were refugees in makeshift camps in other countries. Arab states, using Palestinians as pawns against Israel, refused to give them a homeland. And Israel would not agree to a Palestinian state carved from within the various boundaries it claimed for itself. The Palestine Liberation Organization (PLO) tried to abolish Israel with a restless campaign of terrorism. Israel survived, but so did the problem of self-government and a homeland for the Palestinians.

In November 1977 President Anwar el-Sadat of Egypt took a courageous initiative. He was the first leader of an Arab country to visit the state of Israel. In Jerusalem, while the world watched on television, he delivered a moving plea for peace.

President Carter seized the opportunity to make his own bold move. He invited Sadat and Israeli Prime Minister Menachem Begin to the President's mountain hideaway at Camp David. In that friendly informal atmosphere, away from newspaper reporters and the glare of television lights, Carter hoped to persuade them to work out their differences. For thirteen days he moved back and forth between the two leaders. Until the very end, it seemed that he would fail. But at last, on September 17, 1978, Sadat and Begin astonished and pleased the world by agreeing to peace between Egypt and Israel. Even then it took another trip by Carter to Egypt and Israel to produce a peace treaty in 1979.

Other Arab nations objected. Their leaders said that Egypt should not have acted alone. Although the treaty did deal with the Palestinian problem, they said that it did not do enough. In anger, they imposed an economic boycott on Egypt.

Iran and the United States.
For the United States 1979 was a year of crises. In Iran, early in the year, the Shah was overthrown. He had been helped to regain his throne by the United States (p. 623). His government had improved education and public health and given new opportunities to women. But he had used dictatorship, corruption, and torture to hasten the country into the industrial era, and his "Westernization" of Iran had been deeply resented by many of his people.

The dictator of Iran who replaced the Shah was Ayatollah (the title for a major religious leader) Ruhollah Khomeini, a fanatical Muslim who tried to return the country to the Middle Ages. Khomeini and his fellow religious leaders (mullahs) detested both the United States and the Soviet Union. The United States wanted a friendly Iran as a source of oil for industry and defense. Iran also bordered the Persian Gulf, through which much Middle Eastern oil was shipped from other countries. From bases in Iran, American spy planes and listening posts had surveyed Soviet missile sites to see that SALT agreements were not violated.

In October 1979 the Shah of Iran, suffering from cancer, was allowed to enter the United States for medical treatment. Carter had been warned that this action might endanger the Americans in our embassy in Iran. Still he was shocked when on November 4 a raging mob invaded the United States embassy in Teheran and seized the Americans there. According to the customs of civilized nations, diplomats are considered sacred. The mob, with the secret support of some members of the Iranian government, made the embassy building into a jail, and blindfolded and taunted the innocent diplomats and their staffs. By this venture in international kidnapping they said they would force the United States to send the Shah back to Iran to be tried—and executed—for his crimes. President Carter refused the Iranian demand.

The United States was outraged but helpless. Fearing the hostages would be killed, Carter opposed military action. Since Khomeini had put his nation outside the pale of civilized diplomacy, diplomatic efforts and economic pressure accomplished little. So Carter finally agreed to a daring plan. In April 1980, a small American commando force in helicopters tried to rescue the hostages by a surprise midnight raid. The effort ended in tragedy. Eight American servicemen died when two rescue planes collided in the dark at a landing strip deep inside Iran. Secretary of State Vance resigned to register his protest over the attempt. By July, when the Shah died of cancer, the kidnappers still had not freed the hostages.

Nicaragua.
In July 1979 in Nicaragua, the largest country in Central America, dictator Anastasio Somoza was toppled by Marxist and other rebels. Somoza's father had been helped to power in 1933 by United States Marines (p. 509), and his family had run the country as if it were their private property. The United States quickly recognized the rebel government and hoped by working with it to keep Nicaragua from becoming another base for Communist expansion. But soon the leftists were in full control. They were called Sandinistas after César Augusto Sandino, one of the leaders of the rebellion against the United States Marines from 1927 to 1933.

The Soviets invade Afghanistan.
On Christmas Day 1979, the Soviet Union gave the world another shock. It poured invading troops into Afghanistan, which borders the Soviet Union and Iran. The Soviets aimed to prop up a friendly puppet government there. The Afghan people, at home in their rugged mountains, fought back bravely with primitive weapons.

The United Nations General Assembly called for the Soviet Union to withdraw. To protest the Soviet move, the United States placed an embargo on the sale of grain to the Soviets, and with 61 other nations boycotted the 1980 summer Olympic games in Moscow. Still the Soviet invaders stayed on. They were unable to pacify the Afghans. But now Soviet troops and airfields stretched along a large part of the Iranian border, and Soviet planes were several hundred miles closer to the vital oil sources on the Persian Gulf.

_{UPI/Bettmann Archive}

A mob seized the United States embassy in Teheran and held 52 Americans hostage in Iran for more than a year.

Carter vs. Reagan. Jimmy Carter's inability to solve the hostage problem, the energy crisis, and inflation haunted him in the election of 1980. In midsummer, the Gallup poll found that only 21 percent of the people approved of his handling of the Presidency—the lowest rating in the 45-year history of the poll. Still, using the great powers of the Presidency, he was able to win the Democratic party nomination over his chief rival, Senator Edward M. Kennedy of Massachusetts, the youngest brother of President John F. Kennedy.

Carter's main opponent was the personable Ronald Reagan, whom the Republicans had nearly nominated in 1976 (p. 750). Reagan's conservative message remained much the same. He wanted to get tough with the Soviet Union, end inflation, stimulate economic growth, and reduce the size, cost, and regulatory role of the federal government. Only for defense did he want to see increased government expenses. This time Reagan's party and the American people were ready to listen.

As the campaign began in September, Carter had rebounded in the polls and was reported to be running neck and neck with Reagan. John Anderson, a Republican congressman from Illinois running as an independent, trailed far behind. When Reagan and Carter debated less than a week before election day, Reagan gained. TV was his element, and he charmed the audience (estimated as half the American people) with his easy manner, confidence, and good humor. "There you go again," Reagan responded with a smile to Carter's tense debating points. But perhaps Reagan's most telling question

was, "Are you better off than you were four years ago?"

During 1983 it was learned that before the debate Reagan's aides had somehow acquired a copy of the material Carter was using to prepare for their meeting. Still, few observers thought that Reagan would have lost the debate even if his staff had not had Carter's briefing book.

Up to the very end of the campaign, it seemed that either of the major candidates might win. But on election day, Ronald Reagan swept to victory with 8 million more votes than Jimmy Carter. He took all but seven states and, for the first time since 1952, the Republican party carried the Senate.

SECTION 4 REVIEW

1. Identify or explain: Salt II, Third World, Anwar el-Sadat, Menachem Begin, Ayatollah Khomeini, Anastasio Somoza, Sandinistas.

2. Why was our government willing to make new treaties on the Panama Canal? What did the treaties provide?

3. How did the United States government respond to revolutions in Iran and Nicaragua?

4. What contribution did Jimmy Carter make to the peace treaty between Egypt and Israel?

5. **Recognizing Cause and Effect.** What was the purpose of President Carter's bold stand for human rights? What was its effect on U.S. foreign policy?

FOCUSING ON IDEAS

1. For many years both major political parties have allowed their presidential nominees to pick the candidate for Vice-President to be their running mate. Under the Twenty-Fifth Amendment the President also nominates a Vice-President when the office is vacant. Should the President or the candidate for President have such a strong voice in the selection of the Vice-President? Why?

2. In the 1976 election campaign Jimmy Carter made many promises—far more than presidential candidates customarily had made. How did this strategy hurt him after he became President?

3. Like slavery in the 1850s, some of today's issues that concern special-interest groups do not lend themselves to compromise. What are some of these hard-to-compromise issues? How did the major political parties approach them in the 1970s?

4. Support or attack the proposition that the advancement of "human rights" around the world should be a cornerstone of American foreign policy.

TAKING A CRITICAL LOOK

1. **Recognizing Bias.** What arguments would you expect people to give for or against President Ford's clemency plan for Vietnam War deserters and draft evaders?

2. **Making Comparisons.** John F. Kennedy served as President for 34 months and Gerald Ford for 29 months. Compare their problems and their successes as President.

YOUR REGION IN HISTORY

1. **Geography.** How have antipollution laws and regulations of the Environmental Protection Agency affected industries in your area? What have been the effects on your family or neighborhood?

2. **Economics.** What measures were taken by your state to deal with the energy crisis.

3. **Government.** Identify organizations in your community that engage in political action.

HISTORICAL FACTS AND FIGURES

Synthesizing Information. Study the graph below to help answer the following questions: (a) What general trend concerning government expenditure of tax dollars is evident during the period 1965–1987? (b) What program has received the most funds throughout this period? The least? (c) When did education experience the greatest percentage increase in government funding? (d) When did the defense budget grow the most? (e) What was the one area of government spending to suffer a drop in funds between 1980 and 1987? (f) What information in this chapter helps explain these trends?

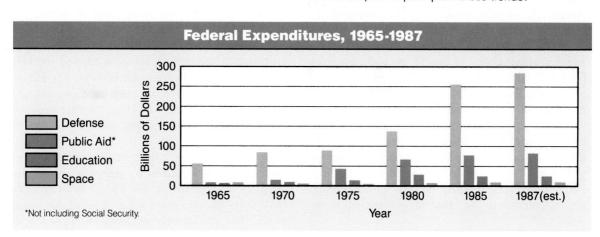

Federal Expenditures, 1965-1987

- Defense
- Public Aid*
- Education
- Space

Billions of Dollars

300 / 250 / 200 / 150 / 100 / 50 / 0

1965   1970   1975   1980   1985   1987(est.)

Year

*Not including Social Security.

CHAPTER 36

New directions

As the nation prepared to inaugurate a new President, it was plagued by problems at home and abroad. Inflation seemed to be soaring out of bounds. The economy had stopped growing. Fifty-two of our citizens were held hostage in Iran. Many Americans were afraid that it was no longer possible for any President to control Congress and the huge executive department or assert our dignity in the world.

1. Reagan takes charge

At 69, Ronald Reagan was the oldest man ever elected President. But his lively manner, ruddy complexion, and full head of brown hair made him seem much younger. His years in the movies, on radio and television, as governor of California, and on the lecture circuit had made him easy to listen to, polished and persuasive. He had developed a firm and clear-cut conservative philosophy that was opposed to many of the ideas that had influenced government since the days of Franklin D. Roosevelt. Now he would try to turn the government in new directions.

Inauguration Day. Reagan's inauguration was held, for the first time, at the West Front—instead of the East Front—of the Capitol. The new location seemed to symbolize his intention to reverse the direction of the government. His message of change was clear: America's first problem was inflation. A major cause, he said, was the enormous government spending that produced massive deficits. "In the present crisis," he said, "government is not the solution to our problem; government is the problem."

Only moments after Reagan had taken the oath of office, after months of negotiations by President Carter and his aides, the 52 hostages were released by the Iranians. They had been held 444 days. President Reagan tactfully sent Jimmy Carter to meet them.

Reagan and the economy. The new President moved quickly after taking office. He sent to Congress a package of cuts in domestic programs, reductions in personal and corporate taxes, and large increases in spending for defense. He spoke of his hope to stir private citizens and businesses toward active competition and new initiative.

After Jimmy Carter's troubles in trying to put his program through Congress, it seemed unlikely that Ronald Reagan could get his way. But Reagan telephoned many members of Congress and brought them to the White House to ask their support. He went on television and was dazzlingly persuasive.

He was also lucky. In gaining popular support for his program, President Reagan was actually assisted by an attempt on his life. On March 30, 1981, a 25-year-old man, whom a jury later found insane, shot and severely wounded the President as

Ronald Reagan's friendly and relaxed manner on the campaign trail helped to persuade the American people to vote for him. He easily defeated Jimmy Carter in 1980.

he left a Washington hotel. The bullet came within an inch of his heart. Reagan's jaunty good humor and courage in the hospital charmed the nation and kept people behind him. Within a month he was standing before a cheering Congress and asking support for his economic program. In July, Congress passed the President's tax cuts and the new budget, which shrank social programs and slowed the growth of the budget even as it began large increases in defense spending.

Supply-side economics. The Reagan program was based on an economic theory called "supply-side economics." This differed from the ideas of the brilliant British economist John Maynard Keynes (p. 523), which had been followed by the government since the late 1930s. Keynesians thought that government policies could smooth out the booms and busts of a free enterprise economy. In a time of recession or depression, for example, the Keynesians thought the government should run large deficits and start programs that would put money in the hands of the people. With this money people would buy what they wanted and the economy would revive. This was called influencing "demand" because people would be able to buy (or demand) more goods and services. Then industry would work to supply them.

The "supply-siders" reversed the equation. They said the ideas of Keynes were not working to end stagflation. They wanted to try a new way. They said government ought to influence not "demand" but "supply." If the government cut taxes on businesses and individuals—especially those with large incomes—then this money, they thought, would be reinvested in more businesses. These new and improved businesses would employ more people, produce more goods and services, and help the economy grow. As business boomed, more people would work and pay taxes, and government income would go up. Even with lower tax rates, more money would come to the government from the new workers and businesses. The deficit would disappear.

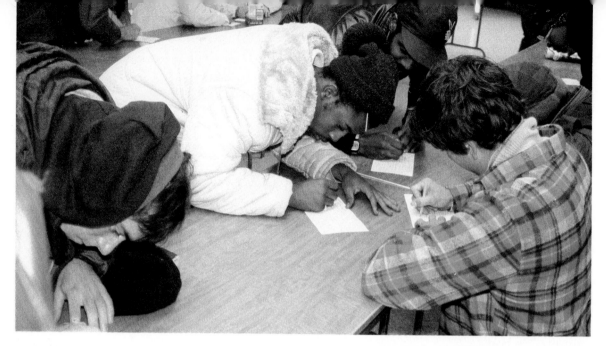

In the recession of 1981, unemployment rose dramatically and many jobs disappeared for good. Here unemployed carpenters in New York City sign up for a retraining program at their union's headquarters.

A troubled economy. The Republicans controlled the Senate, but the Democrats enjoyed a majority in the House. To achieve his program Reagan, like all successful Presidents, had to compromise. But as the Reagan tax proposals went through Congress many additional tax cuts and "loopholes" (ways to avoid or decrease taxes) were added. As a result, the final bill reduced tax revenue far more than Reagan had wanted.

The Reagan program was also hard hit when the economy went into a recession even deeper than the one inherited by Gerald Ford in 1974. By 1982 it turned out to be the worst since the Great Depression of the 1930s. This recession was largely a result not of Reagan's programs, but of those of the Federal Reserve System.

The "Fed," the nation's central bank, has a strong influence on the nation's economy. It controls the amount of money in the system, the financing of the national debt, the amount of reserves banks must hold, and the interest on money it loans to banks.

In 1979, the Federal Reserve Board, led by the newly appointed chairman, tall, cigar-smoking Paul Volcker, had concluded that a major cause of inflation was Federal Reserve policy. The board decided to restrict the money supply (which included checking and savings accounts) and let interest rates go where they wanted. "Tight money" caused interest rates to soar. Since borrowing for home building, automobiles, and other things became increasingly expensive, the country went into a recession. The recession helped control inflation, but it caused new problems for the budget.

In a recession, government revenues fall because people out of work pay less in taxes. But government expenses increase because more money has to be spent in unemployment payments, food stamps, and other welfare programs.

As inflation fell and the recession worsened, the projected deficits grew. By late fall 1981, the estimate for 1984 predicted an enormous deficit of $162 billion.

Reducing the government. Another cause of rising government deficits was Reagan's insistence that the United States increase its defense spending. In 1981 he proposed that the United States spend $1.64 trillion (1640 billion) over the next five years for defense. Reagan and his Secretary of Defense,

Caspar Weinberger, argued that the safety of the nation depended on defense. So they fought every effort to cut defense spending. Except for defense, Ronald Reagan really did want to cut back on federal activities. The number and complexity of government regulations were reduced. The budget of the Environmental Protection Agency was cut and the agency became less active in protecting the air and water.

Reagan insisted that many welfare programs needed to be reduced, although those that served as a "safety net" for the poor, the old, the unemployed, and the handicapped would be kept. Still, many of these programs were reduced. Government statistics soon revealed that more people were counted as poor than at any time since the days before Lyndon Johnson's Great Society programs (pp. 682–683).

Reagan did slow the growth of the welfare budget, but a more complicated problem was how to deal with a subject new to most Americans. "Entitlements" were payments such as Social Security, Medicare, and veterans' benefits to which many people were legally entitled because of age, unemployment, illness, or having served in the armed forces. These benefits went to a wide variety of Americans who firmly opposed any tampering with their claims.

SECTION 1 REVIEW

1. Identify or explain: Paul Volcker, tax loopholes, Federal Reserve, "supply-side economics," John Maynard Keynes.

2. How does "supply-side economics" work in theory? How does it differ from the economic theories of Keynes?

3. How did the actions of the Federal Reserve Board contribute to the recession of 1981–1982?

4. **Recognizing Ideologies.** How was Ronald Reagan's view of government a change from Jimmy Carter's? From FDR's?

---

2. The changing economy

The economy began to improve by the end of 1982. At the peak of the recession more than 11 million Americans were unemployed. But the nation was learning some valuable lessons. American businesses were losing the battle against foreign competition. Americans bought their cars, TVs, VCRs, and even shoes and clothes from other nations. And American companies purchased steel, machine tools, and many other things they used, from abroad. Steel and automobile makers here complained that since foreign governments gave special aid to their own industries the United States should use tariffs to keep out foreign competition.

The decline of the smokestack industries. American industry had been one of the wonders of the world. But in the late 1960s the productivity of American workers was no longer increasing. Industry had been hit by inflation, ever-changing government regulations, and increased foreign competition from new factories built in the countries devastated in World War II. Now the "smokestack industries,"—the old factories with tall smokestacks that made steel, textiles, and automobiles—were closing down whole plants and laying off millions of workers. This threatened industries and the communities, like Detroit and Pittsburgh, that depended on them.

Some economists thought the nation needed a long-term plan to "reindustrialize" America. It would have to be drawn up by government, business, and labor, all working together.

As the nation's people and companies bought more and more from abroad, the United States's balance of trade—the amount in dollars that all its companies sold abroad balanced against the amount that Americans bought from abroad—grew steadily worse. Even the surprising fall in the price of oil, brought about by the huge surpluses created when the world quickly turned to conservation after the oil shocks of the 1970s (pp. 749, 754), was not able to solve the problem of the trade deficit. In 1986 the United States bought $170 billion more from abroad than it sold. Millions of American jobs were being lost to other nations.

The unfavorable balance of trade was matched by an enormous federal deficit. This was the amount the government was spending over what it was receiving in taxes. The government was deeply in debt and had to borrow to keep going. It did this by issuing bonds and notes that paid interest to the holders. Large quantities of these issues were bought by foreigners who liked their safety and high interest rates.

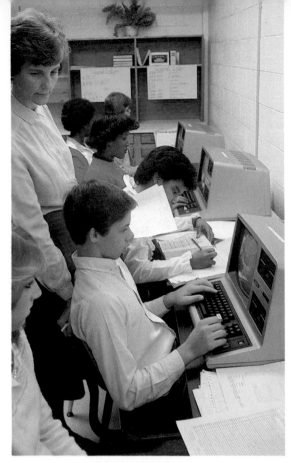

Billy Barnes/Click/Chicago

Many schools used computers to teach their students new skills.

These foreigners bought dollars in order to buy United States bonds. And this forced up the price they paid for dollars in other currencies. The American dollar became more expensive abroad. This made American products more expensive for foreigners. Naturally they bought less, and our trade deficit increased.

In only a few years the United States went from being the world's richest creditor nation to being the world's greatest debtor. Economists thought that if the American dollar could be made cheaper for foreigners the situation would improve. Our government and other industrial nations allowed the value of the dollar to fall steeply in 1986 and 1987. This did help to reduce the trade deficit. But it also brought down the American standard of living. Now that the dollar was worth less abroad, Americans could afford to buy fewer imported products, and foreign travel was more expensive.

The world of the future. During these years, with dizzying speed the computer was changing American ways of working, learning, and playing. Computers were becoming steadily smaller, smarter, and quicker. They appeared everywhere—in libraries for cataloguing books and storing information, in hospitals to help doctors diagnose diseases, in banks, factories, stores, and homes. There seemed no end to the new uses for these clever machines.

Computers started a new "information" industry. Information in huge amounts could be stored in computers, analyzed with lightning speed, and instantly sent over thousands of miles to other computers. Computers were now beginning to "see" and even learning to "read" written text.

The computer also opened up opportunities for daring and enterprise. In California, the area called "Silicon Valley" (after the wafer-thin silicon chips that make computers work) became a boomtown for young Go-Getters of the age of computers. There they created new programs and new devices to make computers "friendlier" (easier to use). Whole regions of the country were transformed. After New England lost its textile and shoe factories, computer companies moved in and provided jobs.

The new Computer Revolution, like the earlier Industrial Revolution, brought its own problems. In the automobile industry, for example, computer-run robots could now be programmed to do several different, complicated operations. And computer-run robots worked more cheaply than human workers. Some experts predicted that by the end of the twentieth century most factory jobs would be done by these new robots.

On other frontiers, biologists were plumbing the mysteries of the gene. In the heart of each cell, genes carry the blueprint of heredity. Understanding the gene could help grow new and better crops, improve animals, and even control some diseases, perhaps cancer itself.

Doctors were using new techniques to implant organs such as livers, kidneys, and even hearts. Since the first human heart transplant in 1967, the operation had been done many times. Twenty years later it was estimated that 4000 Americans were alive with replaced hearts. Wonderful vaccines had been found against polio, mumps, and measles. On the new frontiers, scientists were creating whole new industries—making jobs and saving lives.

One of the most exciting scientific breakthroughs of the 1980s was the discovery in 1987 of new materials that made it possible to achieve superconductivity at higher temperatures than ever before. Superconductivity (the transmission of electricity with almost no resistance) could be used to increase the speed of computers, to improve telephone cables, and even to develop high-speed trains. The Japanese had already built a train that used superconductivity in magnets to allow it to float on air and shoot smoothly along at over 300 miles an hour. With the newly discovered materials, such trains were no longer just expensive experiments but a real possibility for high speed travel.

Across the country in the 1980s new businesses appeared by the thousands. Women were in the forefront of this boom, starting new companies at an even faster rate than men.

The spirit of the times—the search for adventure and the attempt to solve old problems in new ways—did not always seem practical. One dreamer was Paul MacCready, Jr., who in his forties founded a company to study energy and environmental problems. He built an airplane, powered like a bicycle by the passenger, which flew across the English Channel. He made another plane that ran by solar energy.

European observers were astonished at the way the American economy continued year after year to create millions of new jobs. Most of these jobs were in services and small businesses. Some experts thought the United States might actually have a labor shortage in the 1990s.

Deregulation. Ever since the Interstate Commerce Commission had been created in 1887 to oversee the railroads (p. 398), the government had been adding more regulatory agencies. Airlines, banks, telephone companies, and interstate trucks, buses, and moving companies were told where they could operate and what they could charge. They often were protected from the competition of new companies and new techniques.

Deregulation had begun in the late 1960s, but the big shift came under Jimmy Carter. He brought about the deregulation of airlines, trucks,

Deregulation allowed airlines to fly where and when they wanted. The new competition helped passengers by lowering fares, but sometimes it led to crowded conditions and long delays on the ground.

Ian Berry/Magnum

railroads, and some banking. Airlines still had to live up to safety rules, but they faced more competition from the new businesses that could now enter the market.

New low-cost airlines appeared and fare wars broke out. Passengers profited from lower fares. But when the government no longer told airlines where they should fly, people in smaller cities lost their airplane service. The result was not always what was predicted. The purpose was to increase competition, but after a decade of deregulation, only eight major airlines existed where there had been twelve before deregulation. Then it was feared they might not compete as much as they had before and fares might rise again.

In 1974, the Department of Justice brought suit under the antitrust laws against the American Telephone & Telegraph Company (AT&T), which owned and ran the Bell telephone system. They charged that the company, which controlled telephone service across the country, was the kind of monopoly that had to be broken up. Finally in 1983 AT&T and the government reached a settlement. AT&T would sell all of its local telephone companies. But it would continue to compete against smaller companies with long-distance calls. Now AT&T was allowed to enter the computer industry. Competition did lead to lower long-distance prices. But many Americans were confused and unhappy when they lost their old reliable "Ma Bell." And they were astonished that the best telephone service in the world could be disrupted by antitrust laws.

Labor in difficult times. During the years after World War II the number of workers in unions went from 35 percent of the work force to half that. The unions were hurt by the decline of the smokestack industries, deregulation, and foreign imports. Some companies went bankrupt. Others found they had to lower prices to compete with new companies. Often this meant they had to reduce their labor costs. Naturally, workers did not want to see their pay go down or lose their places to robots. The results were strikes and changes in the relations of business and labor.

President Reagan gave an early indication of his stand on labor issues. In August 1981 the air traffic controllers went on strike for higher pay and shorter hours. The controllers were employed by the Federal Aviation Administration to see that planes flew in and out of airports safely and did not run into each other in the skies. They were working under a contract that barred them from striking. Reagan ordered them to return to work or be fired. When they continued their strike, he fired all 11,500 strikers. By a variety of means, most airline flights continued while new controllers were trained to replace the members of the union.

For many years, businesses had given labor unions much of what they had asked for. The increased costs were passed along to the consumer in higher prices. But when competition from abroad increased, high costs for labor could no longer be passed along.

As a result, there were some new features in labor contracts. In "give-backs," the workers gave up some of the benefits they had won in better times. To keep their firms out of bankruptcy and their jobs alive, workers accepted temporary wage freezes, or fewer vacations, and allowed companies to hire new workers at lower wages. In return, workers received job security and sometimes bonuses from the companies' profits.

In these and other ways, companies cut their costs so they could compete better. As one airline official explained, they were building a new, more efficient company inside an old one.

The farmers. Some Americans had problems because of their success. American farmers were the most productive in the world. In 1953, one farmer could feed 17.2 people. Today that same farmer can produce enough food to feed 75!

Consequently food prices fell, and soon farmers could not make enough money to meet their expenses and pay off the loans they had taken out to buy land and equipment. In the early 1980s, they too were hurt by the worldwide recession. Farm foreclosures, rare since the Great Depression, were now in the news again.

Farmers, too, were in a new world of competition. The "green revolution" of fertilizers, better seeds, and modern-farming techniques helped India, the Philippines, and other countries to produce enough wheat and rice to feed themselves. Even more surprising, in 1986 the United States began to import more food than it exported. Fruit and vegetables came from Mexico, oranges from Brazil, beef from Costa Rica, and even wheat from

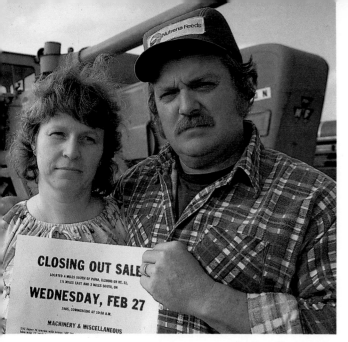
Roy Roper/Gamma-Liaison

Economic conditions for farmers in the 1980s were the worst since the Great Depression. Many farmers, like the couple above, were forced to sell everything to pay off their debts.

Canada. Suddenly it seemed that every nation had a crop to sell here. Now the world was feeding Americans. This nation, once the world's largest food exporter, suddenly became the world's second largest food importer.

In these ways the progress of farmers across the world made problems for the American farmer. Some farm families went hungry. The banks that loaned money to the farmers and the businesses that sold to them also suffered.

The first Reagan farm program, Payment-in-Kind (PIK), paid farmers in surplus crops from government storage bins for not planting their land. So many farmers took part that it cost far more than Reagan had expected. A new law, the Food Security Act of 1985, reduced the amount the government would loan farmers on their crops and allowed farmers to sell certain crops, like rice and cotton, for whatever they could. It was hoped this would lower the price of American farm products so exports would increase and food costs for American consumers would go down. Farmers who participated in the program by limiting production and not planting part of their land were guaranteed direct payments from the government to protect

them from loss. The program seemed to help farmers, but it, too, was more expensive than the program's supporters expected. By 1987, the farm crisis seemed to be ending. Farmers were doing much better, as were the businesses and banks that dealt with them.

SECTION 2 REVIEW

1. Identify or explain: "smokestack industries," Silicon Valley, AT&T, air traffic controllers, Payment-in-Kind (PIK) program, deregulation.

2. What were some of the causes of the decline of America's "smokestack industries"?

3. List some uses of the computer in the 1980s.

4. Why did Reagan fire the striking air traffic controllers?

5. **Recognizing Cause and Effect.** Why was AT&T's monopoly broken up? What were some of the effects of this breakup?

3. Foreign affairs

Few of President Reagan's associates came into the government with experience in foreign affairs. They would find world problems even more difficult to solve than those of a changing economy.

El Salvador and Nicaragua. In Nicaragua, in Central America, the Marxist Sandinistas had taken control in 1979 and were forging close ties with Cuba and the Soviet Union. That same year, in El Salvador—a tiny country about the size of Massachusetts and the most densely populated in Central America—guerrillas, some of them Marxists, began to try to topple the government. They said the government helped only the interests of the few very rich, who owned most of the nation's land. The Reagan administration feared Marxist governments in Central America. As allies of the Soviet Union they might threaten our very borders. To prevent this, the United States aided the government in El Salvador and pressured Nicaragua to become democratic.

The United States, through the Central Intelligence Agency (CIA), armed rebels to oppose the Sandinistas. The "contras" (a shortened form of the Spanish for counter-revolutionaries) attacked Nicaragua from bases in Honduras and Costa Rica. Some of these were former followers of the deposed dictator Somoza (p. 763). President Reagan hoped by helping the contras to stop the Soviet Union and Cuba from shipping arms through Nicaragua to the guerrillas in El Salvador. But Congress thought he also wanted to topple the Sandinistas. To an appropriations bill in 1982, Congress attached an amendment that became famous. This was the first Boland amendment, named for Congressman Edward P. Boland of Massachusetts. It forbade using government funds to overthrow the Sandinistas.

In April 1984, it was learned that the CIA had helped the contras to plant mines in the harbors of Nicaragua. The CIA had also given the contras a war manual which told them how to use blackmail and assassinations. Congress was troubled by what seemed a violation of the law. They voted the contras only non-military aid—food, clothing, and medicine. Military aid was barred for two years.

In another Boland amendment, in October 1984, Congress barred the CIA and any other government agency involved in intelligence from giving military aid to the contras "directly or indirectly."

Israel, Lebanon, and the Middle East. Meanwhile, the Middle East festered with religious hatred and political chaos. The assassination in 1981 of peace-loving Anwar el-Sadat of Egypt by Muslim fundamentalists kept the pot boiling. And Israel took new steps to defend itself against those Arabs who said it had no right to exist. It bombed a nuclear reactor in Iraq and annexed the Golan Heights, which it had seized from Syria in 1967. This too, Israel argued, was in self-defense.

To complicate matters even more, Iraq and Iran were locked in a bloody war. It had begun in September 1980 when Iraq invaded Iran hoping to seize a contested piece of land, but the Iraqis soon bogged down and tried to withdraw. Iran refused to make peace and the war dragged on.

The Nations of Central America

Still, the worst problem in the Middle East was Lebanon. For a time it was a haven of peace and prosperity. But it had begun to slide toward chaos in 1970 after the PLO, driven out of Jordan by King Hussein, moved in. Soon one-tenth of the population was Palestinian. They would set off the explosion that would blow the country into anarchy.

Lebanon was a mix of ethnic groups and warring sects of Christians and Muslims. It could remain a nation only as long as they were willing to work together. But the Palestine Liberation Organization had seized control and was using Lebanese territory as a military base against Israel. The PLO was not interested in building a unified, independent Lebanon.

In June 1982, Israeli troops invaded Lebanon in an attempt to end its use as a base for attacks on Israel. Thousands died as Israeli tanks and troops, under cover of their strong air force, swept halfway up the country. They entered West Beirut in August, trapping the PLO.

Philip Habib, President Reagan's patient envoy, shuttled between Lebanon, Israel, and Syria. He worked out an agreement for the PLO guerrillas to leave Beirut for other countries. Under the protection of a peacekeeping force from the United States, Italy, and France, the PLO departed. After they had left, the peacekeeping force, which had promised to protect the Palestinian refugees still in Beirut, went home.

With the guerrillas gone, it seemed that peace might return. But then the newly elected Christian president of Lebanon, Bashir Gemayel, was assassinated even before he could be inaugurated. In revenge, his Christian Lebanese followers entered the Palestinian refugee camps in Israeli-occupied West Beirut. There they massacred over a thousand men, women, and children.

Trying to bring peace to Lebanon.

In desperation, the international peacekeeping force of United States, French, and Italian troops returned to Lebanon. They were later joined by British troops. This force hoped to prop up the government of new President Amin Gemayel, Bashir's brother, and stop the fighting between the warring Christian and Muslim groups. But the deep religious hatreds in Lebanon seemed incurable. The peacekeepers themselves became a target. On Sep-

M. Milner/Sygma

Palestinian young people attacked Israeli troops early in 1988.

tember 1, 1983, after the 800 American marines in Lebanon came under attack, Reagan sent in 2000 more to help protect them.

In April 1983, the people of the United States had been sickened when a truck full of explosives was used to blow up the American embassy in Beirut. Forty-seven people in our embassy died. Iranian radicals took credit for the crime. The unseen force of fanatical terrorists was more frightening than the bullets from soldiers in uniform.

Then on Sunday morning, October 23, another truck packed with explosives raced past marine guards and hit the main marine building near the Beirut airport. The explosion killed the driver of the truck and 241 marines asleep in their barracks. This act marked the beginning of the end of American involvement in Lebanon. Though President Reagan had said he would not withdraw our troops in response to terrorism, he had to face the fact that the peacekeeping force was a failure. Finally, at the end of February 1984, all the marines were pulled out.

Argentina vs. Great Britain. Our troubled relations with our Latin American neighbors were suddenly made more difficult by an unexpected conflict far away in the South Atlantic. Few Americans had heard of the Falkland Islands. Even fewer thought their fortunes should affect our foreign policy. These islands stood 250 miles out in the Atlantic Ocean, off the tip of South America. They had been held by Britain since 1771. Their 1800 inhabitants were almost all of British descent. Argentina, however, called these islands the Malvinas, and since 1820 had claimed to own them.

On April 2, 1982, the Argentinians, led by military dictators, tried to settle the matter by invading and seizing the islands. The British refused to give in and a war for the Falklands followed. The United States failed in the effort to make peace. On April 30, the United States publicly supported the British and offered military supplies. The Argentine dictators said they were fighting against colonialism. And they said too that the United States had known they were planning their invasion, but did not try to discourage them. Other Latin American countries supported Argentina. On June 4, 13,000 Argentinian troops surrendered to the British forces and the war came to an end.

The Argentinian defeat brought the collapse of the murderous military junta that had ruled Argentina since 1976. They had tortured and assassinated their opponents. Thousands of dissidents had "disappeared" because the dictators had seized them and refused to bring them to trial or report on their whereabouts. In 1983 new elections ended the repression and returned Argentina to democracy. But no one knew how long the new government would last.

Grenada. In October 1983, just two days after the marine headquarters in Lebanon was blown up, 1900 United States marines and airborne troops invaded the small Caribbean island nation of Grenada. With them were 300 troops from the Organization of Eastern Caribbean States. The leftist government of Grenada had been overthrown and

President and Mrs. Reagan greeted wounded marines at a memorial service for the 241 marines who were killed when terrorists attacked the peacekeeping forces in Beirut.

its leaders murdered by an even more radical group. The United States and several of Grenada's neighbors said they feared that the island would become a base for exporting communism to nearby countries. There was also concern that the 1000 Americans on Grenada, many of them young medical students, might be held hostage by the unpredictable new government. Reagan did not want to face another Iran. The military occupation of Grenada took several days longer than expected, and ultimately 6000 U.S. soldiers and marines landed on the island.

The Reagan administration hoped the Grenada attack would show that the United States would stand by its friends. It also wanted to prove to friend and foe—and especially to Nicaragua—that our nation had not been paralyzed by Vietnam. We still could and would use force, if needed.

Opinion polls showed that a majority of the American people applauded the United States's invasion of Grenada. It appeared, too, that most Grenadians agreed. But some Americans doubted that any government in Grenada posed a real threat to the United States. Other Americans argued that even if it is, the United States should set the example of not invading another country. They asked how the United States could condemn the Soviet use of force in Afghanistan, and still use force in the Caribbean.

The problem of Third World debts.
Argentina, Mexico, Brazil, and other Third World countries faced severe economic problems. During the prosperous years after World War II they had financed their development by borrowing large sums from banks in the industrial nations. Especially during the years of high inflation in the 1970s it had seemed cheap to borrow. The debt could be paid back with money worth much less than it had been when it was borrowed.

By 1983 Third World countries and others had run up debts totalling $700 billion. They could not even pay the interest. Their problems had been created by high oil prices and by the worldwide recession of the early 1980s, which made it difficult for them to sell their products abroad. This debt crisis fueled the disputes between the industrial nations and the developing countries. It threatened the banking systems and the economies of the entire world.

The United States and the USSR.
Relations between the United States and the Soviet Union worsened during Reagan's first years in office. The President and his aides viewed the problems of the world as chiefly the results of the aggressive and expansionist policies of the Soviet Union. President Reagan called the USSR the "evil empire."

Events in Poland brought further strains. A new unofficial labor union called "Solidarity" had appeared there in 1980. For a time it seemed to force the Polish government to be more open. But the Soviet Union would not allow it. Military maneuvers on the Polish border helped to put new Soviet puppets in power. In December 1981, they imposed martial law and the movement for freedom was crushed.

Discussions between the United States and the USSR on arms control stopped. Still both countries continued to abide by the SALT agreements. SALT II had been condemned by Reagan during the presidential campaign, and because of the Soviet invasion of Afghanistan the Senate had never acted on it. But President Reagan found that the United States actually did benefit by the treaty, so for a time we continued to observe it.

The major crisis came over the decision of the United States and its NATO allies to place intermediate-range Pershing II missiles and cruise missiles in Western Europe. The cruise missiles were so called because they flew (cruised) to their targets at low altitudes instead of arching high into the sky like other missiles. These weapons not only could hit Eastern Europe, but could reach to the Soviet Union. President Carter and our NATO allies had decided to put these new intermediate-range missiles in Europe as a response to the Soviet Union's placement of its own new missiles in Eastern Europe, aimed at Western Europe.

Reagan offered not to deploy the new missiles if the Soviet Union would remove all its rockets from Eastern Europe. The Soviet Union refused because, they said, both Britain and France had missiles aimed at them.

The Soviets threatened to break off all arms talks if the new missiles were deployed. The president of France, François Mitterand, called the crisis the most dangerous since the Berlin blockade of 1948 and the Cuban missile crisis of 1962. An official of the English government stated that the Soviet missiles had created "an imbalance of terror."

Mitterand and other European leaders argued that in response the NATO alliance must show strength and unity.

In Europe and the United States, hundreds of thousands of people marched and demonstrated. Some called for a "freeze" on the building of nuclear weapons, or even one-sided disarmament by the West.

Even before the new missiles arrived in Europe in December 1983, relations between the Soviet Union and the West had worsened. On September 1, a Soviet fighter plane shot down a South Korean airliner, killing all 269 people aboard. The civilian plane, on its regularly scheduled flight, had wandered over Soviet territory and close to missile and naval bases. The free world was outraged by what appeared to be the cold-blooded slaughter of innocent civilians.

Dealing with the Soviets was further complicated by changes in the leadership of the Soviet Union. The Soviet leaders were not elected by the people. They were chosen by a few insiders. Their choice was mysterious and unpredictable to the outside world. Leonid Brezhnev, who had led the nation since 1964, died in November 1982. A former head of the KGB, the infamous Soviet security police, Yuri V. Andropov, was named in his place. But Andropov was a sick man, and he died in February 1984. He was replaced by 72-year-old Konstantin U. Chernenko, a run-of-the-mill Communist official and the oldest man to run the country since the Russian Revolution. Americans could not expect new friendly proposals from him. They were not surprised when the Soviet Union and its satellites paid the United States back for boycotting the 1980 Olympics in Moscow by refusing to come to the Olympic Games that were held in Los Angeles in the summer of 1984.

Memories of Vietnam. Despite the passage of years, the war in Vietnam remained a burning memory. In November 1982, a monument to the 58,132 Americans who died in the war was dedicated in Washington, D.C. The name of every one of them was inscribed on a black marble wall. Then, on Memorial Day 1984, an unknown serviceman who had died in Vietnam was buried in the Tomb of the Unknowns in Arlington National Cemetery. Americans were honoring the many Americans who had died fighting for their country.

A stark, beautiful new memorial in Washington, D.C., listed all 58,132 Americans who had died in the war in Vietnam.

Peter Marlow/Magnum

But, as President Reagan said, we could "write no last chapters" on the war in Vietnam. The United States continued to demand a report from the Vietnamese on what had happened to the nearly 2500 American servicemen and civilians who still were missing in Vietnam.

Paul Fusco/Magnum

Ronald and Nancy Reagan campaigned vigorously in 1984.

SECTION 3 REVIEW

1. Identify or explain: El Salvador, PLO, Amin Gemayel, Grenada, Falkland Islands, Malvinas, Solidarity, François Mitterand, Yuri V. Andropov, Konstantin U. Chernenko.

2. What events in Lebanon since 1970 led to the stationing of an international peacekeeping force there in 1982 and 1983? What happened to the peacekeeping force?

3. Why did Third World countries go heavily into debt to foreign banks in the developed nations? What effects did this have on the economies of both?

4. How did Reagan approach relations with the Soviet Union? How did the Soviets respond?

5. **Identifying Assumptions.** Why did Reagan and his advisers want to stop the rebels in El Salvador and help the rebels in Nicaragua?

4. Successes and failures

The millions who watched on television while Ronald Reagan delivered the annual State of the Union message to Congress on January 25, 1984, were not surprised at his superb performance. This speech opened his campaign for reelection. "America is back," he said, "standing tall, looking to the 80's with courage, confidence, and hope."

Reagan's program. He called for programs to insure steady economic growth. He said he wanted a constitutional amendment to require a balanced budget. He repeated his support for allowing prayer in the public schools and his opposition to legal abortion. And he offered to work for peace with the Soviet Union and in the Middle East and Central America.

To aid the nation's effort to conquer "our next frontier" he called for a costly new program to establish a manned space station. There scientists could live weightless in space and do research on metals, medicines, and communications that would be impossible on earth.

A basis for this was the space shuttle begun by his predecessors, which had now achieved success. The shuttle was the first space vehicle designed to rocket into space and then return to land like an airplane. It could shuttle back and forth between the space station and earth. The long-planned first flight by the *Columbia* had gone into space in 1981 and then returned to land gently on earth. The *Columbia* became the first reusable space vehicle when it went back into space a few months later.

The fight for the Democratic nomination. Seven Democrats made a serious start in the race for their party's nomination for President, but the field narrowed rapidly to three. There were two former Senators, the experienced Walter Mondale of Minnesota, who had been Vice-President under Jimmy Carter, and young Senator Gary Hart of Colorado.

779

Democratic nominee Walter Mondale chose Representative Geraldine Ferraro as his vice-presidential running mate. She became the first woman to run on a major party's national ticket.

The Reverend Jesse Jackson, a black minister who had worked with Martin Luther King, Jr., also continued the contest. He was a passionate speaker and made a special appeal to his fellow blacks.

After a bitter struggle, Mondale gathered just enough delegates to claim a majority and the nomination. Shortly before the convention met, he announced his choice for Vice-President. After a highly public search, he selected Geraldine Ferraro, the daughter of Roman Catholic Italian immigrants and a third-term member of Congress from Queens in New York City. She became the first woman to be nominated for the Vice-Presidency by a major party. Quick and intelligent, Representative Ferraro was to add zest to the campaign of the more reserved Walter Mondale.

The race for the election. The team of Ronald Reagan and George Bush was renominated by acclamation in Dallas, Texas. All the opinion polls showed them well ahead of Mondale-Ferraro.

During the campaign the continuing dangers of terrorism appeared. Terrorists were savage and unpredictable. Once again the United States embassy in Beirut was bombed. In England, an attempt was made on the life of Prime Minister Thatcher. And finally, on the last day of October, Indira Gandhi, the powerful prime minister of India, was assassinated by two of her own bodyguards. How should the United States fight terrorism? None of the candidates had a good answer.

On election day, some 92 million people, only 53 percent of the voting-age population, went to the polls. The result was a Reagan landslide. He took 59 percent of the popular vote and swept the electoral vote with the highest number in history, 525 to 13. Mondale carried merely his home state of Minnesota and the District of Columbia. Still there was some solace for the Democrats. They continued to control the House and the Republican margin in the Senate declined.

Many people who voted for Reagan disagreed with him on particular issues—such as a nuclear

President Reagan and General Secretary Gorbachev held a summit meeting in Washington, D.C., in 1987, during which they signed a treaty removing their intermediate range missiles from Europe.

freeze, the budget deficits, and the Soviet Union. But they liked Reagan's personality and admired his ability to lead the nation. No President had served two full terms since Dwight D. Eisenhower in the 1950s.

After the successes of his first term, President Reagan faced hard problems as he began his final four years. Could he reduce the enormous budget deficits, improve relations with the Soviet Union, slow down the nuclear arms race, and keep support for his anti-Communist programs in Central America?

Signs of trouble. To mark 40 years of reconciliation, President Reagan made an official trip to West Germany in May 1985. He visited a cemetery in the small town of Bitburg where two thousand German soldiers of World War II were buried. Among them were 49 members of the SS, the Nazis' ruthless troops of terror and persecution. They had been Hitler's bodyguard, had served as the barbarous secret police (Gestapo), and were the sadists who guarded concentration camps. Hoping to emphasize the spirit of forgiveness, the President had gone there despite public outcry and the opposition of Congress. But the visit, as his aides confessed, was a political fiasco.

Reagan then was troubled by health problems. In July 1985 doctors removed a small cancerous growth from his colon. The operation was a success, and the nation again admired his cheerful courage.

A new leader in the Kremlin. Reagan's hopes for progress in reducing nuclear arms were boosted in March 1985 when after only 13 months in office Chernenko, the ailing, aged Soviet leader, died. Within hours the Soviets' secret and mysterious process produced his successor. He was the dynamic, tough, and intelligent Mikhail S. Gorbachev. At 54 he was the youngest leader of the USSR since Josef Stalin. The world wondered where the new Soviet dictator would lead the Communist world.

At first Gorbachev seemed as hard-line as his predecessors. But he soon agreed to meet President Reagan. A "summit" meeting in Geneva,

The crew of the *Challenger* makes its way to the shuttle shortly before lift-off.

Switzerland, in November 1985 was the first between the leaders of the Soviet Union and the United States since 1979 (p. 761). At least, it was hoped, Reagan and Gorbachev would get to know each other. And when the talks ended both men expressed high hopes for better relations between their two countries.

Nuclear disaster. Mikhail Gorbachev swiftly showed a new style of Soviet leadership. He went out and talked to the people on the streets and in the factories. Two Russian words became his slogan. *Glasnost* meant a more open society. *Perestroika* meant restructuring of the economy, the party, and the government. They were supposed to carry a new message of "new thinking" about old problems.

Gorbachev was only beginning to entrench himself in power when he was shaken by a catastrophe inside the Soviet Union. A nuclear reactor at Chernobyl, near Kiev, exploded and burned in April 1986. Radioactive waste spewed into the air and spread radioactive terror across Europe. The radiation released was equal to all that had ever come from the explosion and tests of nuclear bombs. At Chernobyl 31 people were killed and several hundred injured. Experts estimated that as many as 6000 to 24,000 more would die from radiation exposure over the next 70 years.

What would the Chernobyl disaster mean for Gorbachev who had just begun to take charge? The mysterious workings of the Kremlin were impossible to predict. His predecessor Nikita Khrushchev said that the U-2 affair with the United States (p. 636) had driven him from power. No one believed that Chernobyl would force Gorbachev from power. But his old-guard opponents took advantage of the disaster to discredit his "new politics."

Challenger. Even before the Chernobyl disaster, the United States had suffered its own tragedy. In 1986, on January 28, a day much colder than normal in Florida, the space shuttle *Challenger* lifted off from Cape Canaveral. One member of its crew of seven was a sprightly young schoolteacher, Christa McAuliffe, who had been selected from many competitors to be the first "citizen observer" to go into space. A Senator and a Congressman had gone on earlier missions. Only 74 seconds into the flight, the millions watching on television were horrified to see the *Challenger* disappear in an enormous explosion. Americans were reminded that the space adventure carried mortal risks. Astronauts were soldiers staking their lives for the nation's progress.

President Reagan appointed a committee of experts to investigate the disaster in public, find the causes, and help avoid such tragedies in the future. The whole nation would share the brutal facts. This publicity was in stark contrast to the secrecy and delay with which the Soviets would at first shroud Chernobyl. The investigation showed that rubber insulation weakened by the cold weather had burned through and caused the external fuel tank to collapse and explode. The President's Commission criticized both NASA and the manufacturers for failing to deal with a problem they had known about and for ignoring warnings to postpone the mission because of cold weather.

The *Challenger* tragedy led to the grounding of the shuttle fleet. But it was hoped that the nation's space program could continue with unmanned rockets. This hope, too, was suddenly shattered by a series of mishaps. In April 1986 a Titan 34D rocket, which was probably carrying a secret spy satellite, exploded on lift-off. All Titan rockets were grounded. Then in May, a Delta rocket carrying a weather satellite went out of control and had to be destroyed. The United States space program was at a standstill.

The United States finally returned to space on October 27, 1987, when it launched another Titan 34D. Although the payload was not announced, it was assumed to have been a KH-11 spy satellite— the best of the United States spy satellites. This launch was important. The United States then had only one KH-11 spy satellite left in space (instead of the usual two) and the remaining KH-11 would last only two months. These satellites were essential for monitoring the Soviets and making sure they carried out any arms agreements.

An age of terrorism.
Terrorism had no end. It was the work of scattered barbarians who respected no civilized law. It was dangerous to negotiate and hopeless to exterminate the leading criminals. In Lebanon, American citizens continued to be kidnapped. Then in June 1985, a TWA flight was hijacked by Shiite Muslims and, after trips to Lebanon and to Algiers, finally landed back at Beirut. A United States Navy man was killed by the hijackers, and 39 passengers and crew members were held hostage for the release of 700 Shiite Muslim prisoners held by Israel. When Israel let them go, the hostages were freed after being held more than two weeks.

An Italian cruise ship, the *Achille Lauro,* was hijacked off the shores of Egypt with 400 passengers and crew aboard in October 1985. A number of the passengers were Americans and an elderly man in a wheelchair was slaughtered by the Palestinian terrorists. Before his death was discovered, the PLO had persuaded the hijackers to surrender the ship in return for their safe passage out of Egypt. The United States denounced the deal. President Reagan ordered U.S. Navy planes in a daring maneuver to intercept the airliner carrying the Palestinians. They forced it to land in Italy. The Italian government then held the hijackers for trial but it freed two Palestinian negotiators who were with them. The United States had evidence that one of them had acutally planned the seizure of the ship.

On December 27, 1985, terrorists set off bombs at the airports in Vienna and Rome. Nineteen holiday travelers including five Americans were killed. One hundred and ten innocent people were injured. The United States government said it had "irrefutable evidence" that Libya was guilty of these (and other) terrorist crimes.

To punish terrorists the United States severed economic ties with Libya. In March 1986, President Reagan ordered the U.S. Mediterranean fleet into the Gulf of Sidra along the Libyan coast. Most of the world believed these were international waters, but Libya claimed them. When Libya fired missiles at United States Navy planes, the United States attacked two of its patrol boats and a missile site.

In April 1986, a bomb exploded at a Berlin discotheque frequented by members of the United States armed forces. Two people were killed, one an American, and 230 were injured. The United States claimed it had evidence Libya was behind this bombing, too. President Reagan ordered American planes from England and the U.S. fleet in the Mediterranean to attack targets in Libya.

They struck on the night of April 14–15, attacking military targets as well as Qaddafi's home and the tent where he often worked. Qaddafi was not hurt, but one of his eight children, a young adopted daughter, was killed. The attack seemed to discourage Libya from terrorist crime.

The growing federal debt.
The federal deficit was hurtling out of control. The national debt was expected to go over $2 trillion in 1986. This more than doubled what it had been when Reagan took office. Just paying interest on this enormous debt would use up almost 25 percent of the entire budget.

At last, in December 1985, Congress took drastic action. The new Balanced Budget and Emergency Deficit Control Act was usually called the Gramm-Rudman Act after its sponsors, Congressman Gramm of Texas and Senator Rudman of New Hampshire. It set budget goals that would reduce the deficit each year until a balanced budget was achieved in 1991. This date was later changed to 1993. Some people called this the "meat axe" approach to the problem. Instead of selecting unnecessary projects to be cut, the law was entirely automatic. If Congress appropriated more than the goals allowed, "across the board" cuts came into action and all federal programs were slashed by the same proportion. Only a few exceptions (like Social Security and pensions) were allowed. The act showed that Congress was unwilling to take political risks to save important programs. Instead they abdicated to the world of numbers. Programs were measured only in dollars and not by the nation's need.

A new tax law. The year 1986 was not to end well for President Reagan. But before his troubles began, two important laws were passed—one for immigration reform (p. 737) and another for tax reform. Reagan had argued that tax reform was needed to keep the free-enterprise system prosperous. He had used his charm and persuasive powers on television in May 1985 to call for sweeping tax reform. The old tax laws had become so complicated that filling out the forms had become a puzzle and a headache for all citizens. And the rates were so high for people with large incomes that Reagan said they were being discouraged from starting new enterprises. The Tax Reform Act of 1986 did not make the laws any simpler, but it did make a big cut in the tax rates. Two basic rates would replace the 15 earlier brackets. The new law was not supposed to increase or decrease the government's total revenue. But it was expected that 60 percent of individual taxpayers would pay less and corporations would pay more. Some critics complained that poor people would have to pay more while the rich would pay less. But others actually called this the most important antipoverty legislation since the days of Lyndon Johnson. It completely freed six million people with the lowest incomes from having to pay any income tax.

Reykjavik. Reagan had great faith in the personal approach to problems. He met again with Gorbachev on October 11 and 12, 1986, this time at Reykjavik, Iceland. Some hoped that by frank discussion the two leaders might make progress on nuclear arms reduction. They even talked of abolishing all strategic (long-range) nuclear weapons. But our allies in Western Europe were afraid of this proposal. They feared these weapons were needed to keep the Soviets from conquering westward.

The short talks ended suddenly with no decisions. Gorbachev objected to Reagan's Strategic Defense Initiative (SDI). This was a system of ad-vanced defensive weapons often referred to as "Star Wars." The Soviets demanded that for the next ten years Americans should only test it in the laboratory. But many Americans believed—as the Soviets later confessed—that the Soviets already were working on their own SDI. Why should they let Americans match it?

The Strategic Defense Initiative. Reagan had first proposed the Strategic Defense Initiative in a speech in 1983. He hoped to build a defensive shield of advanced weapons, some operating in outer space, to make the United States safe from nuclear attack. To reassure the Soviets, Reagan even said that we would share the technology with them. Critics, including some scientists, objected that the system was too expensive, and might not work anyway. Since new weapons had to be perfected, no one knew how many billions of dollars it might cost. Then perhaps the money would be wasted when the Soviets built new weapons to beat the system. Meanwhile new fears bred by the SDI debate could worsen the "imbalance of terror" between the two countries.

Still everyone knew that Gorbachev wanted to improve the standard of living of the Soviet people. This meant spending less on weapons. So he had an interest in slowing down the arms race. If he could only stop American progress on SDI, the Soviets might be able to cut back on their own arms budget. As it turned out, Reagan's unbuilt SDI proved to be a powerful bargaining chip against the Soviets.

SECTION 4 REVIEW

1. Identify or explain: balanced budget amendment, Indira Gandhi, Bitburg, Mikhail S. Gorbachev, *perestroika, glasnost.*

2. What controversial stands did President Reagan take during his 1984 reelection campaign?

3. What was the importance of the Strategic Defense Initiative (SDI) during the Reykjavik superpower summit?

4. **Checking Consistency.** Was the doubling of the national debt during Ronald Reagan's Presidency consistent with his strong stand for a balanced budget? Why or why not? List factors to support your answer.

---

5. New problems for "the Teflon President"

A witty critic once called Ronald Reagan "the Teflon President." Teflon was a patented new material for pans which never let anything stick to it. So it always looked clean. President Reagan was not only lucky. Somehow failures or criticisms never seemed to stick to him. But in the fall of 1986, the Teflon stopped working. A series of problems plagued the Reagan administration.

A string of setbacks. On October 2, the *Washington Post* revealed that the administration had used a "disinformation program" to plant untrue stories in the press against the Libyan leader Muammar el-Qaddafi. The aim was to make Qaddafi fear he might soon be overthrown. The State Department spokesman, Bernard Kalb, resigned in protest. "Faith in the word of America," he said, "is the pulsebeat of our democracy."

Soon afterwards a cargo plane carrying supplies to the contra rebels in Nicaragua was shot down, two American crew members were killed and an American cargo handler, Eugene Hasenfus, was captured. Hasenfus told the Nicaraguans that he was working for the Central Intelligence Agency (CIA). The United States vehemently denied this confession. The Boland amendment had banned military aid to the contras. Many people did not believe the administration's denial. They wondered where else the contras could be getting their arms.

Then on November 3, Reagan was rebuffed in the fall mid-term elections. He had campaigned for Republican candidates in 22 states. He attacked the Democrats as big-spenders and asked for the election of a Republican Senate to achieve an arms pact with the Soviet Union. But the voters favored the Democrats. That party kept control of the House of Representatives. And when the Senate met again in the 100th Congress, the Democrats had achieved a solid majority (55 to 45) there, too. It was an unhappy prospect for President Reagan. During his last two years in office he would have to deal with a Congress run by the opposite party. Presidents before him (like Eisenhower) had the same problem. But it made the President's work more difficult.

Worse was still to come. On November 3, a Lebanese magazine reported that the United States

After Oliver North was sworn in, his testimony shocked committee members.

had been supplying arms to Iran. Robert MacFarlane, President Reagan's former National Security adviser, they said, had visited Iran for that purpose. But the United States had been trying to stop other countries from supplying arms to Iran. And the President was known for his attacks on all who dealt with terrorists. Friends of the President could not believe the story. Then, to their astonishment and dismay, they heard the President admit that for 18 months the United States had been dealing with Iran. He listed four reasons: to renew relations with Iran; to try to end the war between Iran and Iraq; to end terrorism by Iran; and to bring the American hostages held in Lebanon safely home. He puzzled the nation when he said, "We did not, repeat, *did not* trade weapons or anything else for hostages—nor will we."

Two weeks later, the President confessed that he had "not been fully informed" about the Iran policy. An investigation by Attorney General Edwin Meese, he said, now disclosed that millions of dollars from the Iranian arms deals had been diverted to the Nicaraguan contras. He also said that his

National Security Adviser, Admiral John Poindexter, and an aide, Colonel Oliver North, would leave the White House.

"Iranscam"—The Iran-contra affair.

The President appointed a commission headed by former Senator John Tower of Texas, to untangle the story. Their report criticized the President for not being fully informed. Their analysis as well as lengthy public hearings held by the House and Senate committees, made it clear that despite President Reagan's denials the United States had traded arms for hostages. Antitank and antiaircraft missiles had been sold to Iran in 1985 and 1986 with the understanding that the American hostages held by Iranian-backed groups in Lebanon would be released. Three hostages were freed, but three more Americans were seized to take their places.

The whole story was bizarre, bordering on the unbelievable. While Iran was fooling the United States government, the United States was profiting from the deal with Iran. Israel, who played the middleman in these transactions, was charging more for the weapons than they cost the Defense Department. So after Israel paid the Defense Department what the weapons cost, there was money left over.

These excess funds, $48 million, were hidden in secret bank accounts in Switzerland. The money then was used by a mysterious organization called "the enterprise" to aid the contras and support other covert activities. This shady outfit owned a ship, a warehouse, airplanes, and a whole airfield. It was this organization, it appeared, that had run the supply operation to Nicaragua and employed Eugene Hasenfus.

The enterprise was managed by private citizens who did not have to report to the United States government, but instead were personally directed by the swashbuckling Lieutenant Colonel Oliver North, who was just a staff member of the National Security Council. Admiral Poindexter and William Casey, director of the CIA, had known about and approved this secret organization. Since Casey died in May 1987 he never revealed the full story.

North brazenly told Congress that this organization outside the law was to be self-financing and would go on indefinitely. It could be used for covert action outside the normal channels of government and not authorized by Congress. Its activities were so secret that not even the Secretary of State or the Secretary of Defense knew about them.

The nation was treated to a new version of an old American institution. Congressional hearings, now on television, gave the whole nation a chance to see the heroic posturing of the handsome Colonel North. Millions heard his self-righteous preachments on how he was saving the continent from communism by running his personal foreign policy with a private army. The hearings successfully competed with other TV soap operas when North's attractive and devoted secretary, who had made him her hero, testified. Other countries had been entangled in the web of intrigue. Saudi Arabia and the Sultan of Brunei had contributed millions for the contras at the request of government officials. Private citizens in the United States had also given money to the cause.

The committees were never able to find out exactly what the President knew or how the money was spent. Reagan admitted authorizing the sale of arms to Iran, but he said he did not know of the diversion of funds to the contras. Poindexter shocked the nation when he said that he never told the President about it in order to give him "deniability," in case the project turned sour.

The majority report of the committees, signed by both Republicans and Democrats, was disastrous for the President. They said if he did not know what was happening it was just as bad, for it was his duty to know. "The ultimate responsibility for the events in the Iran-contra affair," the majority wrote, "must rest with the President." The President, they said, had failed in his constitutional duty to "take care that the laws be faithfully executed." The committees' report ended with a 50-year-old quotation from Supreme Court Justice Louis Brandeis: "If the government becomes a law-breaker, it breeds contempt for law, it invites every man to become a law unto himself, it invites anarchy."

The report of the congressional committees did not end the Iran-contra affair. A special prosecutor was appointed to see what laws had been broken. It seemed likely that some people, including the sanctimonious Colonel North, might be indicted. Impeaching the President was mentioned. But there seemed little desire in Congress to pursue the disruptive course that followed the Watergate

Wide World Photos, Inc.

Presidents can never be sure how their appointees to the Supreme Court will vote. But Reagan hoped the justices he selected would be more conservative than their immediate predecessors.

scandals. The Reagan Presidency had only a little over a year to go.

Conflict in Nicaragua. Before anyone knew about the Iran-contra affair, in August 1986 Reagan finally convinced Congress to vote $100 million for military aid for the contras. This was a major victory for the President.

The best solution would be for the people of Nicaragua and other Central American countries to solve their own problems. In February 1987, President Oscar Arias Sanchez of Costa Rica proposed a peace plan for all Central America. The presidents of Guatemala, El Salvador, Honduras, Nicaragua, and Costa Rica signed an accord in August based on those proposals. The plan called for an end to all outside aid to guerrilla groups, for restoration of freedom of the press and political activity, and for free elections. Arias's plan was given a boost when he was awarded the Nobel Peace Prize.

Nicaragua could not survive forever torn by civil war. The Sandinistas made token efforts to abide by the accord. They allowed a radio station and a newspaper critical of the government to reopen. A limited political opposition was permitted, but the Sandinistas harassed their meetings. President Reagan, believing the Arias plan did not go far enough, sought more military aid for the contras. But Congress put its hopes on Arias's plan and only voted short-term nonmilitary support.

When the Central American presidents met in Costa Rica in January, 1988, they finally persuaded President Daniel Ortega to suspend the state of emergency in Nicaragua. He also agreed to start direct talks with the contras.

The Supreme Court. Since justices of the Supreme Court serve until they retire or die, their influence on the nation reaches far beyond the term of any one President. Therefore President Reagan was especially concerned to appoint conservative justices. His first appointment was Sandra Day O'Connor. A conservative Republican, she had earned respect on the Arizona Supreme Court as a skilled, hard-working judge. Easily approved by the Senate, she became the first woman to sit on the United States Supreme Court.

Justice O'Connor joined the Court in 1981. Not until 1986 was Reagan given the opportunity for another appointment. Chief Justice Warren E. Burger stepped down in June and the President nominated the brilliant William H. Rehnquist, a conservative Associate Justice, to take his place. After a hard fight, he was approved by the Senate.

To fill Rehnquist's seat on the Court, the President named Antonin Scalia, an intelligent, scholarly, and witty appeals court judge, who was also conservative. The son of an Italian immigrant, he was speedily and unanimously approved by the Senate. He symbolized American opportunity as he became the first American of Italian descent to sit on the Supreme Court.

The President's future choices for the Court would not have such smooth sailing. The next opening was made when Justice Lewis F. Powell, Jr., decided to step down in 1987. Now it was not just a question of another justice. Justice Powell had been an important "swing" vote providing the crucial fifth vote on important issues. He had been nominated by President Nixon, and was himself a conservative. But he was conspicuously open-minded, and his vote was often unpredictable.

To replace Powell, President Reagan named Judge Robert Bork of the United States Court of Appeals for the District of Columbia. Bork was a bearded, learned, and especially outspoken conservative. He had been a professor at the Yale Law School. For 30 years he had taught, written, and spoken against Supreme Court decisions on abortion, privacy, and civil rights. As Solicitor General of the United States under Nixon, Bork had carried out Nixon's order to fire special prosecutor Archibald Cox (p. 710).

The Constitution requires that the Senate confirm the President's choices for the Supreme Court. The fight over the Bork nomination was one of the bitterest in American history. Bork's champions defended him as a brilliant and courageous conservative. His opponents, led by Senator Edward Kennedy of Massachusetts, attacked him for being insensitive to the rights of minorities and standing outside the mainstream of American social progress. After three weeks of televised public hearings, the Senate Judiciary Committee voted 9 to 5 against the nomination. It was defeated in the full Senate 58 to 42, the largest margin by which a Court nominee had ever been rejected.

In haste and anger, President Reagan then nominated the young and little-known Douglas H. Ginsburg, who had only recently been named to the United States Court of Appeals. Then, to everyone's surprise it was revealed that Ginsburg had smoked marijuana while he was a professor at Harvard Law School. This embarrassed an administration that was so strongly for "law and order" and on an anti-drug crusade.

Judge Ginsburg speedily withdrew his name from consideration. President Reagan, retreating from his fight with the Senate, finally made a choice that was not controversial. He named Judge Anthony M. Kennedy of the United States Court of Appeals. A moderate and pragmatic conservative, Kennedy was confirmed without a dissenting vote early in 1988.

Creation science. Meanwhile, the Supreme Court was the scene of a final encounter in an old battle. Ever since Darwin wrote *The Origin of Species* in 1859, fundamentalist Christians had fought against the idea of evolution. They thought the Book of Genesis in the Bible told the whole story.

Back in 1925, a bright young schoolteacher, John T. Scopes, had been convicted of teaching evolution in Tennessee when that state's law forbade it. The trial in the heat of summer made headlines because the prosecuting attorney was the crusading William Jennings Bryan (pp. 407–408), the three-time Democratic candidate for President, and the defense attorney was the homey Clarence Darrow, famous champion of unpopular opinions and the underdog. Many people thought the perspiring, stout Bryan cooling himself with a fan looked and sounded ridiculous. But the local jury had no sympathy with "newfangled" scientific ideas.

In June 1987, the question finally reached the Supreme Court in the case of *Edwards* v. *Aguillard*. It tested a Louisiana law that required public schools that taught evolution also to teach what they called "creation science," which was really only the Bible story. Justice Brennan, writing for the majority, declared that the state law was clearly intended "to advance the religious viewpoint that a supernatural being created humankind." Therefore the law violated the First Amendment to the Constitution which prohibited any law "respecting an establishment of religion" (p. 699).

Fundamentalist Christians vowed not to give up the fight. They were encouraged when the television preacher, Pat Robertson, who shared their views, entered the race for the 1988 Republican presidential nomination.

In 1987, United States Navy ships began escorting Kuwaiti tankers, flying the American flag, through the dangerous waters of the Persian Gulf.

Troubles in the Persian Gulf. On the other side of the world, the long war between Iran and Iraq added to the President's problems. In 1987, attacks increased on the tankers that carried much-needed oil from the area to Europe, Japan, and the United States. As the ships came through the Persian Gulf they were subject to attack by either side. On May 17, an Iraqi plane mistook a U.S. Navy frigate for an enemy ship. Since the officers of the *Stark* considered the Iraqis to be friendly, they did not prepare for defense. The Iraqis hit the ship with two missiles that killed 37 crew members.

Despite this disaster, the administration decided to allow Kuwait to put eleven of its tankers under the American flag. Then United States Navy vessels would escort them through the Persian Gulf. In the first convoy of escorted Kuwaiti ships flying the American flag, one tanker struck a mine. This was an omen of more trouble to come.

The Iran-Iraq war drew world attention away from Israel and the problem of the Palestinians. But protesting Palestinian youth captured the news when they took to the streets in Gaza and the Israeli-occupied West Bank. They attacked Israeli soldiers with stones. Israeli troops responded with rifle fire and almost daily young Palestinians died. The Palestinian problem apparently was not going to go away until the Palestinians, too, had their own homeland.

SECTION 5 REVIEW

1. Identify or explain: "The Teflon President," "Iranscam," *USS Stark,* Oscar Arias Sanchez.

2. Why did the Supreme Court rule that laws requiring public schools to teach "creation science" were unconstitutional?

3. Why were Judges Robert Bork and Douglas Ginsburg rejected as nominees to the U.S. Supreme Court? Why did the Senate then confirm Anthony Kennedy?

4. **Expressing Problems Clearly.** Explain the meaning of this quote from the late Justice Louis Brandeis cited in the Congressional report on the Iran-contra affair: "If the government becomes a lawbreaker, it breeds contempt for law, it invites every man to become a law unto himself, it invites anarchy."

6. The end of the Reagan years

As Ronald Reagan approached the end of his Presidency, he no longer dominated the scene as he had for so much of his two terms. The American people became increasingly interested in the race to select his successor. Still, much was going on at home and abroad that would influence the nation and the world the next President would have to face.

World changes. While the United States confronted many challenging situations around the world, there were also encouraging signs. In China, Mao Zedong who had been almost worshiped as a god, had died in 1976. A new leader, clever and resilient Deng Xiaoping, had emerged. He seemed more interested in accomplishment than in ideology. To invigorate China's economy, he moved away from strict Marxist-Leninism and even tried small experiments in free enterprise. Contacts and trade between the United States and China increased.

In Latin America, while the troubles in Central America continued, there were signs of a swing toward democracy. Military rule seemed to be losing out in Argentina, Bolivia, Brazil, Guatemala, Honduras, Peru, and Uruguay. But the new governments faced daunting problems. Their populations were exploding. Their economies were troubled. And their troubles became headaches for the whole world when their large foreign debts, which they could not pay, began to endanger the world's banking system.

In the Far East, Ferdinand Marcos was toppled from power in the Philippines after the chief of the opposition party was murdered and Marcos was suspected of plotting the kill. His successor was the spirited Corazon Aquino, wife of the murdered party chief. She had little experience as a politician. The world wondered whether she could handle the many problems of the Philippines. The Communists were a powerful threat and a Muslim minority, which disliked both the Communists and the government, wanted to secede. After the long

New leaders appeared around the world in the 1980s. In the Philippines, Corazon Aquino (right) replaced Ferdinand Marcos. Archbishop Desmond Tutu (left) spoke out for black South Africans.

Neil Victor/Sygma

Sygma

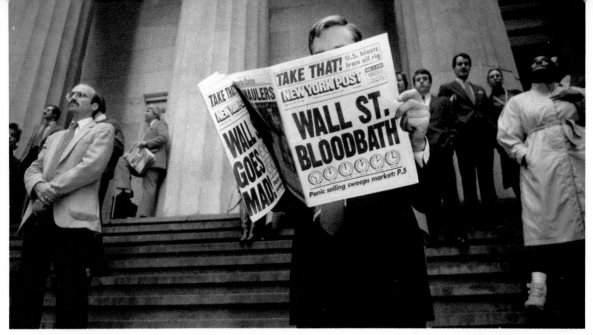

In October 1987 the stock market suddenly plunged. This man is reading all about it as he stands on the steps of the New York Stock Exchange.

years of corrupt Marcos rule, could she bring the country back to democracy?

Because Marcos had been friendly to the United States, he was given asylum in Hawaii. President Reagan wanted to save him from being treated as rudely as President Carter had treated the Shah of Iran, another friend of the United States, when he had to leave his country (p. 763). The Shah had been kept out of the United States and only admitted for surgery.

Americans were distressed by South Africa's system of "apartheid." This was a scheme by the small white minority to control and exploit the black majority. The word in Afrikaans meant, literally, "apart-hood," but it really was racism at its worst. After 1984, violence was increasing there and the world was isolating and ostracizing South Africa. Bishop Desmond Tutu, a brave, black Anglican priest in South Africa and a leader of the peaceful struggle against apartheid, was awarded the Nobel Peace Prize.

In 1986, Congress voted stronger economic sanctions against South Africa. President Reagan vetoed the bill. He said that he believed it would hurt the people it was supposed to help. But Congress passed the bill over his veto. It was hoped that these measures and the departure of American companies from South Africa would encourage South Africans to abandon apartheid. But the white government of South Africa did not respond.

The world was measled with danger-spots. The war in Afghanistan dragged on. It had begun in 1979 when the Soviet Union sent in troops to support a Communist government which was facing growing guerrilla opposition (p. 763). But the Soviets found themselves mired in their own Vietnam. The rebels, with weapons supplied mainly by the United States, Saudi Arabia, and China, were able to control most of the country outside the main cities. On April 14, 1988, the Soviets seemed to admit that the cost of the conflict was too great when they agreed to remove their troops. Afghanistan, where perhaps 1 million people had died in the fighting, was to be allowed to settle its own affairs.

The crash of 1987. One of the most unpleasant domestic surprises of the decade came in October 1987. It surfaced where the nation least expected it—in the stock market. Encouraged by an improving economy, the price of stocks had begun climbing in August 1982. Five years later, the Dow Jones stock average, which was a barometer of the financial weather, had gone up 230 percent.

The rising market was called a "bull market," for the buyers were charging ahead. This was the third best bull market in American history.

Then in August 1987 the stock market began slowly to go down. After the government reported a trade deficit $1.5 billion higher than expected on October 14, the Dow Jones average suddenly fell a record 95 points.

Modern communications, speeded by the computer, had linked the world. This shocking decline in New York was registered far away during the night in Tokyo and London. The next day the New York market fell another 57 points and on Friday it was down still another 108 points. On Monday the collapse came—an astonishing drop of 508 points! In just one day stocks had lost over 20 percent of their market value. This drop, even deeper than the Great Crash of October 1929 (p. 502), was the worst in American history. President Reagan appointed a committee to find the causes. They reported that the main cause was the huge new computer trading programs. The computers could instantly generate large sell orders even as the market was only beginning to fall. This meant that the tendency of prices to fall was self-accelerating. The more prices fell, the faster they fell.

Would the crash of 1987 trigger another great depression (pp. 504–506)? Economists thought it was most unlikely. During the 1930s, as a result of the crash of 1929 many laws had been passed to protect the nation's savers and investors. These included federal insurance on bank accounts and the Securities and Exchange Commission to police the stock market and protect and inform the small investor. The revised Federal Reserve System was unlikely to repeat the mistakes that had helped bring on the Great Depression.

Reducing nuclear arms. A bright spot in this dark picture was renewed hope for arms control agreements with the Soviet Union. Despite the impasse at Reykjavik in 1986, talks went on in Vienna, Austria. In February 1987, General Secretary Gorbachev suddenly offered to sign an agreement for eliminating both Soviet and U.S. medium-range missiles. These were missiles that could not cross the ocean, but with them both the Soviet Union and Western Europe could hit each other. Tough verifying procedures would allow each country to

station representatives outside the other country's plants that had manufactured these weapons. This would actually place Americans at a plant in Sverdlovsk, the very city where the U-2 had been shot down in 1960 (p. 636).

On December 7, 1987, a smiling, handshaking Gorbachev arrived in the United States. He had schooled himself in American techniques of public relations. On the following day General Secretary Gorbachev and President Reagan signed the new Intermediate Nuclear Force (INF) Treaty. This would remove all missiles with ranges of 300 to 3400 miles from Eastern and Western Europe. All 2611 missiles of this type would be destroyed—859 by the United States and 1752 by the Soviet Union.

For the first time in history, the INF treaty aimed to reduce the size of nuclear forces. It did not really make the world safer, because both nations still had enough long-range missiles and nuclear warheads to destroy each other. Some Americans and American allies actually believed it would make the world less safe. They feared that the treaty would leave Western Europe exposed to the much stronger regular armed forces of the Soviet Union. Still it was a way of testing the willingness of the world's greatest adversaries to come together. And it might be a first step away from the world's atomic self-destruction.

The election of 1988. As Ronald Reagan entered the last year of his Presidency, he could at least be pleased with his efforts for peace. But he was plagued by the bad faith of his former aides who had tried to use their connections with the Reagan administration for personal profit. In 1987 Michael Deaver, a longtime associate from California, was convicted of lying about his use of his White House influence for his public relations company. Another, Lyn Nofziger, was convicted of violating the Ethics in Government Act by lobbying his former government associates soon after leaving office. Unfriendly critics said there had been a shocking number of cases of questionable or illegal activities by officials or nominees of President Reagan's administration.

These problems were not helpful to the President's loyal Vice-President, George Bush, who hoped to succeed President Reagan in the White House. But the question that caused candidate Bush the most trouble was what he knew about the

Iran-contra affair and what he had said to the President. Bush said his advice was confidential. Still, the Democrats mocked him with calls of "Where was George?"

Many candidates entered the races for the Republican and Democratic presidential nominations. But before either convention met, voters in the primaries had chosen Vice-President Bush for the Republicans and Massachusetts Governor Michael Dukakis for the Democrats. The choice of running mates then became the center of interest.

Governor Dukakis surprised the nation when he selected Senator Lloyd Bentsen, a 67-year-old Texan who had once beaten George Bush in the race for Senator and who had been successful in business and politics. While Bentsen had disagreed with Dukakis on some issues, he was widely respected and might help to carry Texas.

George Bush's choice was far more controversial. He astonished voters when he named a young (41), wealthy, good-looking, and little-known right-wing Republican Senator from Indiana, Dan Quayle. The press accused Quayle of using family influence to avoid military service in Vietnam. Many people questioned Bush's judgment in selecting such a person to stand only a heartbeat away from the White House.

Steve Liss/Gamma-Liaison

The Reverend Jesse Jackson (above) won many votes in the Democratic primaries. Governor Michael Dukakis (below) and Senator Lloyd Bentsen were defeated after a hard fight.

UPI/Bettmann Newsphotos

UPI/Bettmann Newsphotos

Vice-President George Bush and his running mate Senator Dan Quayle, helped by the continuing popularity of Ronald Reagan, were elected after a long campaign.

Michael Dukakis had a different kind of problem, not of his own making. How would he handle the Reverend Jesse Jackson, who had the second highest number of delegates? The handsome Jackson had skillfully used his pulpit voice and gestures to secure the solid support of fellow blacks and of an unexpectedly large number of discontented whites. He naturally wanted respect and an offer of the Vice-Presidency. But Dukakis simply saluted him with enthusiasm at the convention and promised him a role in the campaign.

Both presidential candidates had long political experience, but of different sorts. Bush knew the national and international scene, as Vice-President for eight years, as Congressman, as envoy to the United Nations and to China, and as head of the CIA. Dukakis, son of Greek immigrants, had been an energetic three-term governor of Massachusetts. On the campaign trail, the tall Bush had a preppy look and sound, while Dukakis, slight of build, was stiff and intense.

Bush could hold on to President Reagan's coattails, and promise more years of Reagan peace and prosperity. But Dukakis had to make it on his own. Could he convince voters of the need for a change? The campaign became a slug-fest of personal attacks. Both candidates shrouded the great issues in a fog of slogans and generalities, while each advertised the weaknesses of his opponent. This was not an inspiring contest.

In the end, on November 8, 1988, the voters chose to stay with the policies of Ronald Reagan, and George Bush was elected President. Now it would be his task to lead the nation toward fulfilling the ideals of the Declaration of Independence and the Constitution.

SECTION 6 REVIEW

1. Identify or explain: Deng Xiaoping, Ferdinand Marcos, Corazon Aquino, apartheid, Desmond Tutu, medium-range missiles.

2. What did Reagan's committee think caused the stock market crash of 1987?

3. What were the terms of the Intermediate Nuclear Forces (INF) Treaty signed by President Reagan and Soviet General Secretary Gorbachev?

4. **Making Comparisons.** What are the similarities and differences between the Soviet invasion of Afghanistan and the U.S. involvement in the Vietnam War?

CHAPTER 36 REVIEW

FOCUSING ON IDEAS

1. During Reagan's first term, inflation was brought under control and the dollar gained value in foreign markets. Unemployment and interest rates rose also. Identify groups who would benefit from each of these economic trends, and groups who would be hurt by them.

2. The memory of the Vietnam War continued to influence American policy into the 1980s. Name two different "lessons of Vietnam" that people remembered when they saw U.S. involvement increasing in Central America and the Middle East. What conclusions did people who remembered each lesson reach? How did the two groups reach such different conclusions from the same information?

TAKING A CRITICAL LOOK

1. **Recognizing Ideology.** The Reagan Administration viewed government as a "necessary evil," while the previous few administrations had tended to see government as a positive force for improving society. How would Ronald Reagan and Lyndon Johnson have responded to each of the following questions: Why does government exist? How much government should there be? What should government do for people?

2. **Recognizing Cause and Effect.** In recent years the role of unions has begun to change from challenger of management to occasional partner of management. What caused this change? What effects did it have?

YOUR REGION IN HISTORY

Government. The nomination of Geraldine Ferraro as the Democratic party's 1984 vice-presidential candidate and Jesse Jackson's serious drive for the Presidency in both 1984 and 1988 represent major changes in the American political tradition. What groups in your community are attempting to have their voices heard or are running for local office for the first time?

HISTORICAL FACTS AND FIGURES

Predicting Consequences. Study the chart below to help answer the following questions: (a) Which two five-year periods showed the sharpest increase in the federal deficit? (b) Did the deficit ever decrease during the period 1961–1986? If so, when? (c) What information in the chapter helps explain the enormous increases in recent years? (d) The total amount of money that the United States government owes to various creditors exceeds $2 trillion. The interest payments on this amount totaled $195 billion in 1987. What effect will these interest payments have on attempts to solve or even control the deficit problem? (e) Given current trends, predict what the federal deficit will be for the year 2000.

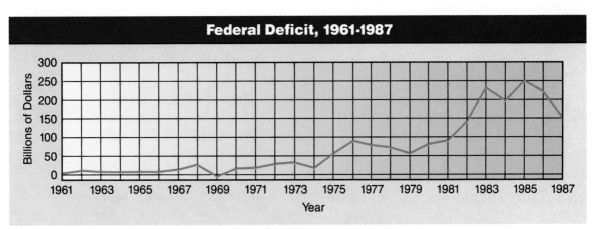

Source: U.S. Office of Management and Budget, *Historical Tables, Budget of the United States Government*

MAKING CONNECTIONS

UNIT 12

THEMES

This unit began on page 717 with the observation that although Americans have the oldest written constitution still in use, the nation remains young in spirit:

> *As the twentieth century neared its close, the United States remained a nation of experiments.*

This conclusion was supported by the three unit themes that are reprinted in **dark type** below. Use the time line and the information in Unit 12 to answer the questions that follow the unit themes.

1. **Congress passes legislation intended to extend equality of opportunity to all Americans.**

   How have laws enacted by Congress since 1950 supplemented Thomas Jefferson's belief in a "natural aristocracy"?

2. **Conflicts with other nations create new problems for the United States during the Ford and Carter administrations.**

   In what ways did President Carter's foreign policy break with the foreign policy of previous administrations?

3. **Ronald Reagan's two terms as President reflect the American people's conservative mood.**

   How was the growth of conservatism in the United States reflected in President Reagan's economic policies?

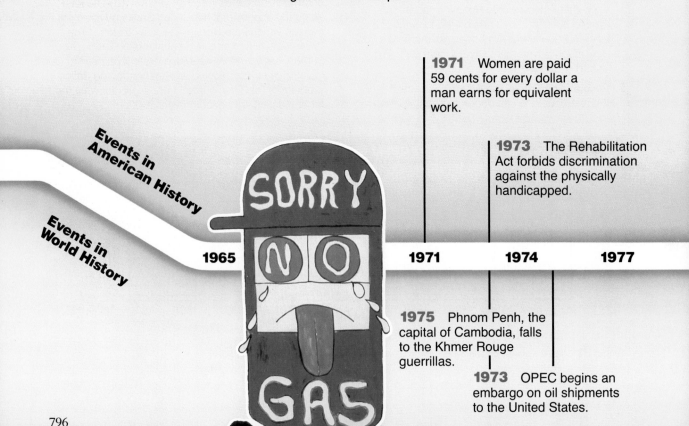

1971 Women are paid 59 cents for every dollar a man earns for equivalent work.

1973 The Rehabilitation Act forbids discrimination against the physically handicapped.

Events in American History

Events in World History

1965   1971   1974   1977

1975 Phnom Penh, the capital of Cambodia, falls to the Khmer Rouge guerrillas.

1973 OPEC begins an embargo on oil shipments to the United States.

1972 Congress passes the Equal Employment Opportunity Act— guaranteeing equal pay for equal work.

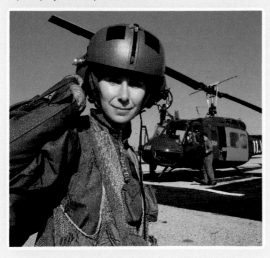

1977 President Carter makes human rights a cornerstone of his foreign policy.

1979 President Carter and Brezhnev meet to sign the SALT II agreement.

1981 President Reagan rallies public support for his economics package.

1982 President Reagan and Congress agree to $30 billion in budget cuts and a tax increase mostly for business.

1977   1980   1983   1986   1989

1979 Ayatollah Khomeini, a fundamentalist Moslem, deposes the Shah of Iran.

1979 Nicaragua's Sandinista guerrillas overthrow the dictator Anastasio Somoza.

1987 Tensions rise as Palestinians protest Israeli occupation of the West Bank and Gaza Strip.

1988 President Reagan and General Secretary Gorbachev meet in Moscow for their fourth summit.

1977 Egyptian president Anwar el-Sadat makes an unprecedented trip to Israel.

Epilogue:
the mysterious future

When we look back on the story of America, we feel very wise. In some ways we really are even wiser than William Bradford or Benjamin Franklin or George Washington or Abraham Lincoln.

We know what they did not know. What for us is history, for them would have been prophecy. For we know how it turned out. They had to guess.

We can see how right it was for the Pilgrims to risk the long voyage across the wild ocean. We see how lucky it was that the thirteen little colonies somehow united for independence. We can see how much better the American Revolution would have been fought with a stronger, more unified Continental Army.

We can see how futile were all the "compromises" on slavery before the Civil War. We can see, too, the Civil War toll in blood and hate. We can see that while the Civil War abolished slavery and saved the Union, it cost more than 600,000 lives and created new hates that would not quickly die.

From American history we can learn that the future is always full of surprising secrets. This New World has been such an exciting place because it has been so new. The great achievements of America are mostly things that never before seemed possible.

Which signers of the Declaration of Independence in 1776 could have imagined that their feeble little confederation, in two centuries, would be the world's greatest democracy—a continent-nation of more than 200 million people, the refuge of the world, the strongest nation on earth?

Georgia O'Keeffe suggests the mysterious promise of the land in her 1960 painting "It Was Blue and Green," inspired by her view from a high-flying airplane.

Collection of Whitney Museum of American Art. Lawrence H. Bloedel Bequest.

Of those 55 men in Philadelphia struggling in the hot summer of 1787 to agree on how to prevent the colonies from falling apart—how many would have believed that their work would become the longest-lived written constitution in history?

Who would have imagined that a nation of immigrants, the most miscellaneous people on earth, would someday be the most powerful? Or that men and women from the Western Hemisphere, from all over Europe, from Africa and Asia—of many races and religions and traditions—would adopt one language, and become loyal builders of one new nation?

Who would have guessed that out of the American wilderness (still only half explored in 1850) so soon would come men to explore the moon, and then to send marvelously complicated machines into space to photograph and study the planets of our solar system? Or that modern science, which brings us from the whole universe the boundless vistas of the radio-telescope, would discover strange new kinds of knowledge, and keep us ever faithful to the motto, "Toward the Unknown!"

These were some of the happy surprises. But there were others not quite so happy, and to the founders of our nation just as secret.

Who would have guessed that, within less than 200 years, a trackless, half-mapped continent could be crisscrossed by superhighways, defaced by billboards and tin cans? Who would have guessed that Americans would perfect horseless carriages to go a hundred miles an hour—and yet be stuck in traffic jams where they could not even move as fast as a walking horse? Or that ten times as many would be killed by these horseless carriages every year as were killed in all the battles of the American Revolution?

Who would have imagined that the fresh air of a New World would begin to be smoke-filled? Or that the sparkling waters of lakes and rivers would become so darkened and dirtied by factory sewage that even the fish found them unlivable and the birds no longer enjoyed their shores?

Who would have believed that the wonderful American silences—once broken by Indian chants or the songs of birds or the call of the coyote—would be shattered by the roar of speeding jets, lumbering trucks, and ear-jarring motorcycles? Who would have believed that a continent, once frightening by its emptiness, would now terrify people by crowding them together?

Who would have believed that a nation of nations, created by people of all races from everywhere, which had suffered through a bloody war for union and freedom, would see new forms of racism?

Who would have believed that a nation designed to be a refuge for all people from the violence of the Old World could ever be plagued by reckless violence within?

Who would have foreseen that a nation rich in natural resources—in coal, oil, uranium, natural gas, and flowing water—would fear that it might be crippled by a lack of enough energy to run its cars and factories and to warm its houses?

But Americans have always faced hard problems. We, even more than other people, love the adventure of the unexpected. Ours has always been a story of dealing with the unknown, a story of movement and discovery—to America, within America, from America. The future is just as much a mystery story as it ever was.

Americans have been planters in this faraway land, builders of cities in the wilderness, Go-Getters. Americans—makers of something out of nothing—have delivered a new way of life to far corners of the world.

If the future is a mystery story, then, that does not frighten Americans. For we Americans have always lived in the world's greatest treasure house of the unexpected.

BERING
SEA

ARCTIC OCEAN

ICELAND

GREENLAND

60°N

70°N

180°

160°W

140°W

120°W

100°W

80°W

60°W

40°W

20°W

10°W

20°E

30°E

Bering Strait

Point Barrow

BEAUFORT SEA

BAFFIN BAY

Yukon R.

BROOKS RANGE

Mt. McKinley △

Mackenzie R.

YUKON

Mt. Logan △

ROCKY MOUNTAINS

ALEXANDER ARCHIPELAGO

Great Bear Lake

ARCTIC CIRCLE

50°N

C A N A D A

Great Slave Lake

HUDSON BAY

UNGAVA PEN.

Ungava Bay

50°W

PACIFIC OCEAN

40°N

COAST RANGE

SELKIRK MTS.

Columbia R.

CASCADE RANGE

GREAT BASIN

SIERRA NEVADA

Great Salt Lake

L A U R E N T I A N   U P L A N D

Lake Manitoba

Lake Winnipeg

G R E A T   P L A I N S

Missouri R.

Great Lakes

GULF OF ST. LAWRENCE

St. Lawrence R.

APPALACHIAN UPLANDS

ATLANTIC OCEAN

30°N

COAST RANGE

Mt. Whitney △

Colorado R.

U N I T E D   S T A T E S

ROCKY MOUNTAINS

Ozark Plateau

Arkansas R.

OZARK PLATEAU

Ohio R.

Mississippi R.

Red R.

ALLEGHENY MOUNTAINS

APPALACHIAN

BLUE RIDGE

Chesapeake Bay

TROPIC OF CANCER

GULF OF CALIFORNIA

M E X I C O

SIERRA MADRE ORIENTAL

SIERRA MADRE OCCIDENTAL

Rio Grande

20°N

GULF OF MEXICO

Straits of Florida

OCEAN

CENTRAL PLATEAU

Mt. Orizaba △

BAY OF CAMPECHE

YUCATAN PEN.

North America
Physical

CARIBBEAN SEA

10°N

0   1200 Miles

0   1200 Kilometers

120°W

110°W

100°W

90°W

80°W

70°W

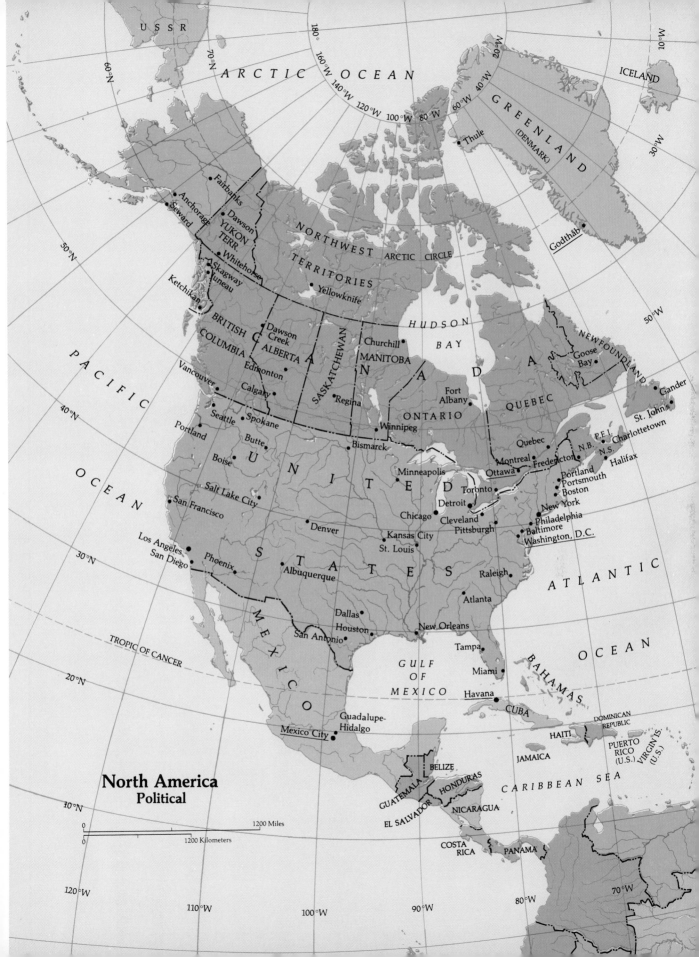

USSR

ARCTIC OCEAN

ICELAND

180°
170°W
160°W
140°W
120°W
100°W
80°W
70°W
60°W
40°W
30°W
10°W

70°N
60°N
50°N

GREENLAND
(DENMARK)

Thule

• Fairbanks

• Anchorage
Seward
Dawson
YUKON
TERR.

NORTHWEST

ARCTIC CIRCLE

Godthåb

50°W

Whitehorse

TERRITORIES

• Yellowknife

50°N

Skagway
Juneau

Ketchikan

BRITISH
COLUMBIA
Dawson
Creek
ALBERTA

Edmonton

A

SASKATCHEWAN

MANITOBA

N

Churchill

HUDSON

BAY

A

D

NEWFOUNDLAND

Goose
Bay

Gander

Vancouver
Calgary

Regina

ONTARIO

Fort
Albany

QUEBEC

St. John's

PACIFIC

40°N

Portland
Seattle
Spokane
Butte

Boise

U

N

I

Winnipeg

Bismarck

T

E

Minneapolis

D

Quebec
Montreal
Ottawa

Fredericton
N.B.
Toronto

P.E.I.
Charlottetown
N.S.

Portland
Portsmouth
Boston

Halifax

OCEAN

Salt Lake City

San Francisco

Denver

Chicago

Detroit
Cleveland
Pittsburgh

New York
Philadelphia
Baltimore
Washington, D.C.

30°N

Los Angeles
San Diego

Phoenix

S

Albuquerque

T

Kansas City
St. Louis

A

T

E

S

Raleigh

ATLANTIC

Atlanta

TROPIC OF CANCER

MEXICO

Dallas
Houston
San Antonio

New Orleans

Tampa

Miami

OCEAN

20°N

GULF

OF

MEXICO

Havana

BAHAMAS

CUBA

Guadalupe-
Hidalgo

Mexico City

DOMINICAN
REPUBLIC

HAITI

PUERTO
RICO
(U.S.)

VIRGIN IS.
(U.S.)

JAMAICA

North America
Political

10°N

BELIZE

GUATEMALA

HONDURAS

CARIBBEAN SEA

EL SALVADOR
NICARAGUA

0   1200 Miles

0   1200 Kilometers

COSTA
RICA

PANAMA

120°W
110°W
100°W
90°W
80°W
70°W

Europe

Eurasia

ATLANTIC OCEAN

GREENLAND (DEN.)

60°W
40°W
20°W

0°

20°E
40°E
60°E

NORT

ICELAND

ARCTIC

NOVAYA ZEMLYA

KARA SEA

Reykjavik

ARCTIC CIRCLE

SVALBARD (NOR.)

BARENTS SEA

AZORES (PORT.)

IRELAND
Dublin
London
UNITED KINGDOM

NORTH SEA

NORWAY
SWEDEN
FINLAND

Murmansk

Arkhangelsk

WHITE SEA

S O V I

MADEIRA IS. (PORT.)

CANARY IS. (SP.)

Lisbon
PORTUGAL
SPAIN
Madrid

Paris
FRANCE

4
5
3
6
7
8
9
10
12

Stockholm
BALTIC SEA
Helsinki
Leningrad
Lake Ladoga
Novgorod
Warsaw
POLAND

Moscow

Gorki
Kuybyshev
Sverdlovsk

U R A L M t s.

Magnitogorsk

Strait of Gibraltar

ITALY
Rome

MEDITERRANEAN SEA

11
Dnestr R.
Kiev
Dnepr R.
Odessa
Sevastopol
Yalta
Rostov
Astrakhan
Volgograd (Stalingrad)
Volga R.

ARAL SEA

15
14
13

BLACK SEA

CAUCASUS Mts.

CASPIAN SEA

Tashkent

TURKEY
Ankara

22
19 21
18
20

IRAQ
Baghdad

Teheran
IRAN

Kabul
AFGHANISTAN

PAKIST

Kuwait

PERSIAN GULF

Riyadh
25
OMAN
QATAR
Doha
24
Muscat
Karachi
Indus R.

TROPIC OF CANCER

RED SEA

SAUDI ARABIA

Mecca

ARABIAN SEA

YEMEN
Sana
23
OMAN

SOCOTRA
(P.D.R. OF YEMEN)

GULF OF ADEN

1600 Miles

1600 Kilometers

INDIAN

KEY TO THE NUMBERS ON THE MAP

NAME OF COUNTRY AND ITS CAPITAL

1 NETHERLANDS-Amsterdam
2 BELGIUM-Brussels
3 LUXEMBOURG-Luxembourg
4 DENMARK-Copenhagen
5 FEDERAL REPUBLIC OF GERMANY-Bonn
6 DEMOCRATIC REPUBLIC OF GERMANY-Berlin
7 SWITZERLAND-Bern
8 CZECHOSLOVAKIA-Prague
9 AUSTRIA-Vienna
10 HUNGARY-Budapest
11 ROMANIA-Bucharest
12 YUGOSLAVIA-Belgrade
13 BULGARIA-Sofia

14 GREECE-Athens
15 ALBANIA-Tiranë
16 NEPAL-Kathmandu
17 BHUTAN-Thimphu
18 ISRAEL-Jerusalem
19 LEBANON-Beirut
20 JORDAN-Amman
21 SYRIA-Damascus
22 CYPRUS-Nicosia
23 PEOPLE'S DEMOCRATIC REPUBLIC
  OF YEMEN -Aden
24 UNITED ARAB EMIRATES-Abu Dhabi
25 BAHRAIN-Manama

60°E

80°N

BERING SEA

CHUKCHI SEA

WRANGEL I.

180°

160°E

140°E

120°E

100°E

80°E

POLE OCEAN

EAST SIBERIAN SEA

LAPTEV SEA

80°N

ET UNION

Lena R.

KAMCHATKA PEN.

SEA OF OKHOTSK

50°N

KURIL IS.

40°N

SAKHALIN

30°N

Yenisey R.

Omsk

Novosibirsk

Irkutsk

Ulan Bator

MONGOLIA

Lake Baikal

MANCHURIA

Amur R.

Khabarovsk

Harbin

Shenyang

SEA OF JAPAN

JAPAN

20°N

Tokyo

Irtysh R.

N. KOREA

Pyongyang

S. KOREA

Kyoto

Hiroshima

Lake Balkhash

A L T A I   M T S.

THE G O B I

Beijing
(Peking)

Lüda

Seoul

Pusan

Nagasaki

IWO JIMA (JAP.)

10°N

Alma-Ata

T I E N   S H A N

Tarim R.

Huang He

Xi'an

Nanjing

Shanghai

EAST CHINA SEA

RYUKYU IS.

OKINAWA (JAP.)

GUAM (U.S.)

Islamabad

Rawalpindi

Lahore

New Delhi

Lucknow

Ganges R.

BANGLADESH

Dhaka

Calcutta

C H I N A

K U N L U N   M T S.

TIBET

Lhasa

Chang Jiang

(Yangtze R.)

Chongqing

Fuzhou

Guangzhou
(Canton)

Xiamen

Victoria

HONG KONG
(BR.)

Taipei

TAIWAN
(FORMOSA)

PESCADORES IS.

PACIFIC OCEAN

EQUATOR

MACAO
(PORT.)

PHILIPPINES

Manila

16

17

H I M A L A Y A S

BURMA

Vientiane

LAOS

Hanoi

Mekong R.

V I E T N A M

Manila Bay

SOUTH CHINA SEA

Bombay

Hyderabad

I N D I A

Rangoon

THAILAND

Bangkok

KAMPUCHEA

Phnom Penh

Ho Chi Minh City
(Saigon)

Bandar Seri Begawan

MOLUCCAS

IRIAN
JAYA

PAPUA
NEW GUINEA

10°S

Madras

BAY OF BENGAL

M A L A Y   P E N I N S U L A

BRUNEI

MALAYSIA

CELEBES

140°E

Calicut

ANDAMAN IS.
(INDIA)

NICOBAR IS.
(INDIA)

Kuala Lumpur

Singapore

Singapore

BORNEO

I N D O N E S I A

SRI LANKA

MALDIVES

Male

O C E A N

SUMATRA

Jakarta

JAVA

TIMOR

AUSTRALIA

120°E

100°E

80°E

807

Africa

South America

PACIFIC OCEAN

130°   120°   50°   110°   100°

Calgary   C   A   N

WASHINGTON
Seattle   Spokane
Olympia   Tacoma
Columbia
Portland
Salem

Regina

Columbia

Missouri   Great Falls
Helena
Butte   MONTANA

NORTH DAKOTA
Bismarck   Fa

OREGON
IDAHO

Yellowstone

Boise
Snake   R.
Pocatello

WYOMING
Casper

SOUTH DAKOTA
Pierre
Sioux

40°

Humboldt

Great
Salt
Lake   Ogden
Salt Lake
City

Cheyenne

NEBRASKA

Sacramento
Reno
Carson City
San Francisco
Oakland

NEVADA

UTAH

Platte

Denver

COLORADO
Pueblo

R.

Line

CALIFORNIA

Las Vegas

Colorado

Arkansas

KANSAS
Wichita

Los Angeles

Colorado   R.

ARIZONA

Phoenix

Albuquerque
Rio Grande
Santa Fe

NEW MEXICO

Amarillo

OKLA
Oklahoma City

San Diego

30°

Tucson

Pecos

El Paso

Fort Worth

T   E   X   A

120°

Colorado

Rio Grande

Austin

San Antonio

170°   180°   170°   160°   150°   140°

Barrow

70°

Cape Prince of Wales
Strait
SEWARD
PEN.
Nome

BERING
SEA

Yukon   R.
Fairbanks

Klondike

60°

160°

22°   30°

KAUAI

157°   30°

Corpus
Christi

NUNIVAK
ISLAND

Anchorage

NIIHAU

OAHU   Honolulu
Pearl Harbor

PRIBILOF
ISLANDS

KENAI
PEN.
Seward

MOLOKAI

Dutch Harbor

ALASKA
PEN.
Kodiak

GULF
OF
ALASKA

Juneau
Sitka

PACIFIC

LANAI
KAHOOLAWE

MAUI

155°

A   L   E   U   T   I   A   N   I   S   L   A   N   D   S

50°

Ketchikan
Prince Rupert

OCEAN

HAWAII
Hilo

20°

ALASKA

750 Miles

750 Kilometers

QUEEN
CHARLOTTE
ISLANDS

PACIFIC OCEAN

HAWAII

100 Miles

100 Kilometers

United States
Political

CANADA

Winnipeg

MINNESOTA
Duluth

L. Superior

Sault Ste. Marie

Quebec

St. Lawrence R.

MAINE
Fredericton
St. John

Augusta

Montreal

Ottawa

Burlington

Portland

VT.
Montpelier
N.H.
Concord
Manchester

WISCONSIN

MICHIGAN

L. Huron

Toronto

L. Ontario
Rochester
Syracuse
Albany

MASS.
Boston
Worcester
Providence

Minneapolis
St. Paul

Green Bay

Grand
Rapids

Flint

Hamilton

NEW YORK

Buffalo

Hartford
CONN. R.I.
New Haven

Madison

L. Michigan

Lansing

L. Erie

Erie

Scranton

New York

Sioux City

IOWA

Milwaukee

Detroit

Cleveland

PENNSYLVANIA

Newark
Trenton

NEW JERSEY

Chicago
Gary

Toledo

Akron

Pittsburgh

Harrisburg

Philadelphia
Wilmington

Mississippi R.

Des Moines

Peoria

Fort Wayne

OHIO

Dayton
Cincinnati

Columbus

WEST
VIRGINIA

Washington
D.C.

Baltimore
Dover

Annapolis

DELAWARE

maha

ILLINOIS

INDIANA

Indianapolis

Springfield

Ohio R.

Huntington

MARYLAND

Kansas City

Kansas City
Jefferson
City
St. Louis

Evansville

Frankfort

Charleston

Richmond

Louisville

VIRGINIA

Norfolk

peka

S

MISSOURI

KENTUCKY

Nashville

Knoxville

Raleigh

NORTH CAROLINA

Charlotte

Fort Smith

Memphis

Chattanooga

Columbia

ATLANTIC OCEAN

40°

Tulsa

OMA

ARKANSAS

TENNESSEE

SOUTH
CAROLINA

Little Rock

Red R.

Atlanta

Charleston

Dallas

Shreveport

Meridian

Birmingham

Columbus

GEORGIA

Savannah

Sabine R.

LOUISIANA

MISSISSIPPI

Jackson

ALABAMA

Montgomery

30°

Beaumont

Baton Rouge

Mobile

Jacksonville

Houston

New Orleans

Tallahassee

F

L

O

R

I

D

A

GULF OF MEXICO

Tampa

Miami

Key West

Straits of Florida

BAHAMAS

Havana

CUBA

80°

1000 Miles

1000 Kilometers

811

NORTH POLE

ARCTIC OCEAN

ELLESMERE I.

GREENLAND (DEN.)

JAN MAYEN (NOR.)

BANKS I.

VICTORIA I.

BAFFIN I.

ARCTIC CIRCLE

FAEROES (DEN.)

ICELAND

NORWAY

NORTH SEA

UNITED STATES

C A N A D A

NEWFOUNDLAND

UNITED KINGDOM

IRELAND

ALEUTIAN IS.

ST. PIERRE AND MIQUELON (FR.)

FRANCE

40° N

PORTUGAL

SPAIN

AZORES (PORT.)

UNITED STATES

MADEIRA IS. (PORT.)

MEDITER

BERMUDA (BR.)

ATLANTIC

CANARY IS. (SP.)

MOROCCO

TUNISIA

GUADALUPE (MEX.)

MEXICO

GULF OF MEXICO

BAHAMAS

OCEAN

TROPIC OF CANCER

WESTERN SAHARA (MOR.)

ALGERIA

20° N

REVILLAGIGEDO IS. (MEX.)

CUBA

DOMINICAN REPUBLIC

LEEWARD IS.

MAURITANIA

HAWAIIAN IS.

OAHU

HAWAII

JAMAICA HAITI

PUERTO RICO (U.S.)

CAPE VERDE IS.

SENEGAL

MALI

NIGER

UNITED STATES

JOHNSTON I. (U.S.)

CARIBBEAN SEA

WINDWARD IS.

GAMBIA

BURKINA FASO

VENEZUELA

GUINEA-BISSAU

GUINEA

KINGMAN REEF

PALMYRA

TERAINA

TABUAERAN

KIRITIMATI

PACIFIC OCEAN

CLIPPERTON I. (FR.)

COLOMBIA

SIERRA LEONE

LIBERIA

IVORY COAST

GHANA

NIGERIA

JARVIS I.

KIRIBATI

LINE IS.

MALDEN I.

STARBUCK I.

VOSTOK I.

CAROLINE IS.

GALÁPAGOS ISLANDS (ECUADOR)

ECUADOR

EQUATOR

KEY TO AFRICA:
1. TOGO
2. BENIN
3. SAO TOME AND PRINCIPE
4. EQUATORIAL GUINEA
5. CAMEROON
6. GABON

TOKELAU IS.

PENRHYN

MANIHIKI

FLINT I.

MARQUESAS IS.

PERU

BRAZIL

ASCENSION

AMERICAN SAMOA

COOK IS.

TUAMOTU ARCH.

SOCIETY IS.

TAHITI

ST. HELENA

NIUE

ROROTONGA

TUBUAI IS.

OENO I.

HENDERSON I.

BOLIVIA

PARAGUAY

TROPIC OF CAPRICORN

ST. HELENA GROUP (BR.)

20° S

FRENCH POLYNESIA

DUCIE I.

PITCAIRN I.

SALA-Y-GÓMEZ (CHILE)

EASTER I. (CHILE)

ARGENTINA

ATLANTIC OCEAN

URUGUAY

JUAN FERNÁNDEZ IS. (CHILE)

CHILE

TRISTAN DA CUNHA

GOUGH

40° S

FALKLAND IS.

SOUTH GEORGIA

BOUVET (NOR.)

FALKLAND ISLAND GROUP (BR.)

SOUTH SANDWICH IS.

60° S

ANTARCTIC CIRCLE

ANTAR

Antarctica is an international scientific

180° W   140° W   120° W   100° W   80° W   60° W   40° W   20° W

SOUTH POLE

60° N

80° N

CARIBBEAN LANDS

UNITED STATES

0 ———— 500 Miles
0 ———— 500 Kilometers

BAHAMAS

TURKS AND CAICOS IS. (BR.)

PUERTO RICO (U.S.)

U.S. VIRGIN IS.

BR. VIRGIN IS.

ST. BARTHELEMY (FR.)

CAYMAN IS. (BR.)

CUBA

DOMINICAN REPUBLIC

MEXICO

JAMAICA

HAITI

LEEWARD ISLANDS
1. ST.CHRISTOPHER AND NEVIS
2. ANGUILLA (BR.)
3. ANTIGUA AND BARBUDA
4. MONTSERRAT (BR.)

WINDWARD ISLANDS
5. DOMINICA
6. ST.LUCIA
7. ST. VINCENT AND THE GRENADINES

GUADELOUPE (FR.)

BELIZE

GUATEMALA

HONDURAS

MARTINIQUE (FR.)

EL SALVADOR

NICARAGUA

CORN IS. (NIC.)

ARUBA (NETH.)

NETH. ANTILLES (NETH.)

BARBADOS

GRENADA

COSTA RICA

PANAMA

TRINIDAD AND TOBAGO

COCOS (C.R.)

VENEZUELA

GUYANA

SURINAME

MALPELO (COL.)

COLOMBIA

FRENCH GUIANA (FR.)

Political Map of the World

Natural Scale 1: 100,000,000   Wagner's Near-Equal-Area Projection

---- International boundaries.

Line to show ownership groupings of islands;
ocean areas enclosed are mainly international waters.

□   States or dependencies so small their actual shapes cannot be shown.

——   Island Nations are underlined

```
0                                3000 Miles
0                    3000 Kilometers
```

Some Facts about Our States

	State	Date of admission	Capital	Area (sq. mi.)	Land area	Population (1988 est.)	Density[1]	Cities 100,000+	Population in SMSAs[2]
1	Delaware	1787	Dover	2,057	1,982	709,000	312	—	67%
2	Pennsylvania	1787	Harrisburg	45,333	44,966	11,936,000	264	4	85
3	New Jersey	1787	Trenton	7,836	7,521	7,672,000	996	4	100
4	Georgia	1788	Atlanta	58,876	58,073	6,222,000	97	4	62
5	Connecticut	1788	Hartford	5,009	4,862	3,211,000	647	5	93
6	Massachusetts	1788	Boston	8,257	7,826	5,855,000	739	3	91
7	Maryland	1788	Annapolis	10,577	9,891	4,535,000	434	1	93
8	South Carolina	1788	Columbia	31,055	30,255	3,425,000	106	—	60
9	New Hampshire	1788	Concord	9,304	9,027	1,057,000	106	—	55
10	Virginia	1788	Richmond	40,817	39,780	5,904,000	138	10	70
11	New York	1788	Albany	49,576	47,831	17,852,000	373	6	90
12	North Carolina	1789	Raleigh	52,586	48,798	6,413,000	123	5	54
13	Rhode Island	1790	Providence	1,214	1,049	986,000	908	1	93
14	Vermont	1791	Montpelier	9,609	9,267	548,000	56	—	22
15	Kentucky	1792	Frankfort	40,395	39,650	3,727,000	92	2	46
16	Tennessee	1796	Nashville	42,244	41,328	4,855,000	113	4	65
17	Ohio	1803	Columbus	41,222	40,975	10,784,000	263	7	79
18	Louisiana	1812	Baton Rouge	48,523	44,930	4,461,000	98	4	69
19	Indiana	1816	Indianapolis	36,291	36,097	5,531,000	152	5	68
20	Mississippi	1817	Jackson	47,716	47,296	2,625,000	54	1	28
21	Illinois	1818	Springfield	56,400	55,748	11,582,000	206	3	82
22	Alabama	1819	Montgomery	51,609	50,708	4,083,000	78	4	63
23	Maine	1820	Augusta	33,215	30,920	1,187,000	37	—	36
24	Missouri	1821	Jefferson City	69,686	68,995	5,103,000	72	4	66
25	Arkansas	1836	Little Rock	53,104	51,945	2,388,000	59	1	39
26	Michigan	1837	Lansing	58,216	56,817	9,200,000	160	8	81
27	Florida	1845	Tallahassee	58,560	54,090	12,023,000	192	8	90
28	Texas	1845	Austin	267,338	262,134	16,789,000	58	15	80
29	Iowa	1846	Des Moines	56,290	55,941	2,834,000	52	3	42
30	Wisconsin	1848	Madison	56,154	54,464	4,807,000	88	2	67
31	California	1850	Sacramento	158,693	156,361	27,663,000	158	26	95
32	Minnesota	1858	St. Paul	84,068	79,289	4,246,000	52	2	64
33	Oregon	1859	Salem	96,981	96,184	2,724,000	28	2	67
34	Kansas	1861	Topeka	82,264	81,787	2,476,000	29	3	49
35	West Virginia	1863	Charleston	24,181	24,070	1,897,000	81	—	37
36	Nevada	1864	Carson City	110,540	109,889	1,007,000	8	2	82
37	Nebraska	1867	Lincoln	77,227	76,483	1,594,000	21	2	45
38	Colorado	1876	Denver	104,247	103,766	3,296,000	29	5	80
39	North Dakota	1889	Bismarck	70,665	69,273	672,000	10	—	36
40	South Dakota	1889	Pierre	77,047	75,955	709,000	9	—	16
41	Montana	1889	Helena	147,138	145,587	809,000	6	—	24
42	Washington	1889	Olympia	68,192	66,570	4,538,000	64	3	80
43	Idaho	1890	Boise	83,577	82,677	998,900	12	1	18
44	Wyoming	1890	Cheyenne	97,914	97,203	490,000	5	—	15
45	Utah	1896	Salt Lake City	84,916	82,096	1,680,000	19	1	77
46	Oklahoma	1907	Oklahoma City	69,919	68,782	3,272,000	46	2	57
47	New Mexico	1912	Santa Fe	121,666	121,412	1,500,000	11	1	40
48	Arizona	1912	Phoenix	113,909	113,417	3,386,000	25	4	75
49	Alaska	1959	Juneau	589,757	569,600	525,000	1	1	43
50	Hawaii	1959	Honolulu	6,450	6,425	1,083,000	155	1	79
	Dist. of Columbia		Washington	67	61	622,000	10,016	1	100
	Puerto Rico		San Juan	3,435	3,421	3,261,000	943	5	
	Guam		Agana		209	120,000	531	—	
	American Samoa		Fagotogo		76	37,000	447	—	
	Virgin Islands		Charlotte Amalie		132	102,000	772	—	

[1]Density: persons per square mile of land area
[2]Percent of population living in Standard Metropolitan Statistical Areas (SMSAs)

Presidents and Vice-Presidents of the United States

President	Years in office	Party	Born	Died	State Born/Home	Vice-President
1 George Washington	1789–1797		1732	1799	Virginia	John Adams
2 John Adams	1797–1801	Federalist	1735	1826	Massachusetts	Thomas Jefferson
3 Thomas Jefferson	1801–1809	Republican	1743	1826	Virginia	Aaron Burr George Clinton
4 James Madison	1809–1817	Republican	1751	1836	Virginia	George Clinton Elbridge Gerry
5 James Monroe	1817–1825	Republican	1758	1831	Virginia	Daniel D. Tompkins
6 John Quincy Adams	1825–1829	Nat. Rep.	1767	1848	Massachusetts	John C. Calhoun
7 Andrew Jackson	1829–1837	Democratic	1767	1845	S.C./Tenn.	John C. Calhoun Martin Van Buren
8 Martin Van Buren	1837–1841	Democratic	1782	1862	New York	Richard M. Johnson
9 William Henry Harrison	Mar. 1841	Whig	1773	1841	Va./Ohio	John Tyler
10 John Tyler	1841–1845	Whig	1790	1862	Virginia	
11 James K. Polk	1845–1849	Democratic	1795	1849	N.C./Tenn.	George M. Dallas
12 Zachary Taylor	1849–1850	Whig	1784	1850	Va./La.	Millard Fillmore
13 Millard Fillmore	1850–1853	Whig	1800	1874	New York	
14 Franklin Pierce	1853–1857	Democratic	1804	1869	New Hampshire	William R. D. King
15 James Buchanan	1857–1861	Democratic	1791	1868	Pennsylvania	John C. Breckinridge
16 Abraham Lincoln	1861–1865	Republican	1809	1865	Ky./Ill.	Hannibal Hamlin Andrew Johnson
17 Andrew Johnson	1865–1869	Republican	1808	1875	N.C./Tenn.	
18 Ulysses S. Grant	1869–1877	Republican	1822	1885	Ohio/Ill.	Schuyler Colfax Henry Wilson
19 Rutherford B. Hayes	1877–1881	Republican	1822	1893	Ohio	William A. Wheeler
20 James A. Garfield	1881	Republican	1831	1881	Ohio	Chester A. Arthur
21 Chester A. Arthur	1881–1885	Republican	1830	1886	Vt./N.Y.	
22 Grover Cleveland	1885–1889	Democratic	1837	1908	N.J./N.Y.	Thomas A. Hendricks
23 Benjamin Harrison	1889–1893	Republican	1833	1901	Ohio/Ind.	Levi P. Morton
24 Grover Cleveland	1893–1897	Democratic	1837	1908	N.J./N.Y.	Adlai E. Stevenson
25 William McKinley	1897–1901	Republican	1843	1901	Ohio	Garret A. Hobart Theodore Roosevelt
26 Theodore Roosevelt	1901–1909	Republican	1858	1919	New York	Charles W. Fairbanks
27 William Howard Taft	1909–1913	Republican	1857	1930	Ohio	James S. Sherman
28 Woodrow Wilson	1913–1921	Democratic	1856	1924	Va./N.J.	Thomas R. Marshall
29 Warren G. Harding	1921–1923	Republican	1865	1923	Ohio	Calvin Coolidge
30 Calvin Coolidge	1923–1929	Republican	1872	1933	Vt./Mass.	Charles G. Dawes
31 Herbert C. Hoover	1929–1933	Republican	1874	1964	Iowa/Cal.	Charles Curtis
32 Franklin D. Roosevelt	1933–1945	Democratic	1882	1945	New York	John N. Garner Henry A. Wallace Harry S Truman
33 Harry S Truman	1945–1953	Democratic	1884	1972	Missouri	Alben W. Barkley
34 Dwight D. Eisenhower	1953–1961	Republican	1890	1969	Tex./N.Y., Pa.	Richard M. Nixon
35 John F. Kennedy	1961–1963	Democratic	1917	1963	Massachusetts	Lyndon B. Johnson
36 Lyndon B. Johnson	1963–1969	Democratic	1908	1973	Texas	Hubert H. Humphrey
37 Richard M. Nixon	1969–1974	Republican	1913		Ca./N.Y., Cal.	Spiro T. Agnew Gerald R. Ford
38 Gerald R. Ford	1974–1977	Republican	1913		Neb./Mich.	Nelson A. Rockefeller
39 Jimmy (James Earl) Carter	1977–1981	Democratic	1924		Georgia	Walter F. Mondale
40 Ronald Reagan	1981–1989	Republican	1911		Ill./Cal.	George Bush
41 George Herbert Walker Bush	1989–1993	Republican	1924		Mass./Tex.	J. Danforth Quayle

The Declaration of Independence

We Americans are luckier than most other people because the Founders of our new nation left us a short, clear, and simple list of reasons for the founding. The Declaration of Independence is our nation's birth certificate. It tells us in a few words what were the parent-ideas and hopes out of which the nation was born.

In the following pages we print the Declaration of Independence. We explain why it happened to say what it did, and what it has come to mean to Americans and to people everywhere in the world. The Declaration of Independence, like the Constitution, is a sacred document for Americans. This is because it is a *living* document. Of course it was written by living men in 1776 to suit the needs of American patriots in the Revolution. But it proved to have a life much longer than that of the men who adopted it. It is still very much alive. To understand why and how it lives will help us understand our country, and where it has been going in the centuries since 1776.

Why there had to be a Declaration of Independence, and how it fits into the story of the Revolution, is explained earlier in this book (pp. 6-10). In the following pages we provide in the center column the words of the Declaration precisely as Jefferson, helped by John Adams and Benjamin Franklin, wrote it. These very words were adopted by the Continental Congress in Independence Hall (which we can still visit) in Philadelphia on July 4, 1776. We have left their spelling, their punctuation, and their capitalization precisely as they wrote it. Even if this looks a little odd to us, it will help us remember that the Declaration was written two centuries ago. And this will not get in the way of our understanding.

In *Origins* we give some of the reasons why they wrote those words. In *Afterlife* we see what those words have come to mean in later years.

THE DECLARATION OF INDEPENDENCE

When in the Course of human events, it becomes necessary for one people to dissolve the political bands which have connected them with another, and to assume among the powers of the earth, the separate and equal station to which the Laws of Nature and of Nature's God entitle them, a decent respect to the opinions of mankind requires that they should declare the causes which impel them to the separation.

We hold these truths to be self-evident, that all men are created equal, that they are endowed by their Creator with certain unalienable Rights, that among these are Life, Liberty and the pursuit of Happiness. That to secure these rights, Governments are instituted among Men, deriving their just powers from the consent of the governed, That whenever any Form of Government becomes destructive of these ends it is the Right of the People to alter or to abolish it, and to institute new Government, laying its foundation on such principles and organizing its powers in such form, as to them shall seem most likely to effect their Safety and Happiness. Prudence, indeed, will dictate that Governments long established should not be changed for light and transient causes; and accordingly all experience has shewn, that mankind are more disposed to suffer, while evils are sufferable, than to right themselves by abolishing the forms to which they are accustomed. But when a long train of abuses and usurpations, pursuing invariably the same Object evinces a design to reduce them under absolute Despotism, it is their right, it is their duty, to throw off such Government, and to provide new Guards for their future security. Such has been the patient sufferance of these Colonies; and such is now the necessity which constrains them to alter their former Systems of Government. The history of the present King of Great Britain is a history of repeated injuries and usurpations, all having in direct object the establishment of an absolute Tyranny over these States. To prove this, let Facts be submitted to a candid world.

He has refused his Assent to Laws, the most wholesome and necessary for the public good.

He has forbidden his Governors to pass Laws of immediate and pressing importance, unless suspended in their operation till his Assent should be obtained; and when so suspended, he has utterly neglected to attend to them. He has refused to pass other Laws for the accommodation of large districts of people, unless those people would relinquish the right of Representation in the Legislature, a right inestimable to them and formidable to tyrants only.

He has called together legislative bodies at places unusual, uncomfortable, and distant from the depository of their public Records, for the sole purpose of fatiguing them into compliance with his measures.

He has dissolved Representative Houses repeatedly, for opposing with manly firmness his invasions on the rights of the people.

He has refused for a long time, after such dissolutions, to cause others to be elected; whereby the Legislative powers, incapable of Annihilation, have returned to the People at large for their exercise; the State remaining in the mean time exposed to all the dangers of invasion from without, and convulsions within.

He has endeavoured to prevent the population of these States; for that purpose obstructing the Laws for Naturalization of Foreigners; refusing to pass others to encourage their migrations hither, and raising the conditions of new Appropriations of Lands.

He has obstructed the Administration of Justice, by refusing his Assent to Laws for establishing Judiciary powers.

He has made Judges dependent on his Will alone, for the tenure of their offices, and the amount and payment of their salaries.

He has erected a multitude of New Offices, and sent hither swarms of Officers to harass our People, and eat out their substance.

He has kept among us, in times of peace, standing Armies without the Consent of our legislatures.

He has affected to render the Military independent of and superior to the Civil power.

He has combined with others to subject us to a jurisdiction foreign to our constitution, and unacknowledged by our laws; giving his Assent to their Acts of pretended Legislation:

For Quartering large bodies of armed troops among us:

For protecting them, by a mock Trial, from punishment for any Murders which they should commit on the Inhabitants of these States:

For cutting off our Trade with all parts of the world:

For imposing Taxes on us without our Consent:

For depriving us in many cases of the benefits of Trial by Jury:

For transporting us beyond Seas to be tried for pretended offences:

For abolishing the free System of English Laws in a neighbouring Province, establishing therein an Arbitrary government, and enlarging its Boundaries so as to render it at once an example and fit instrument for introducing the same absolute rule into these Colonies:

For taking away our Charters, abolishing our most valuable Laws, and altering fundamentally the Forms of our Governments:

For suspending our own Legislatures, and declaring themselves invested with power to legislate for us in all cases whatsoever.

He has abdicated Government here, by declaring us out of his Protection and waging War against us.

He has plundered our seas, ravaged our Coasts, burnt our towns, and destroyed the Lives of our people.

He is at this time transporting large Armies of foreign Mercenaries to compleat the works of death, desolation and tyranny, already begun with circumstances of Cruelty & perfidy scarcely paralleled in the most barbarous ages, and totally unworthy the Head of a civilized nation.

He has constrained our fellow Citizens taken Captive on the high Seas to bear Arms against their Country, to become the executioners of their friends and Brethren, or to fall themselves by their Hands.

He has excited domestic insurrections amongst us, and has endeavoured to bring on the inhabitants of our frontiers, the merciless Indian Savages, whose known rule of warfare, is an undistinguished destruction of all ages, sexes and conditions.

In every state of these Oppressions We have Petitioned for Redress in the most humble terms: Our repeated Petitions have been answered only by repeated injury. A Prince, whose character is thus marked by every act which may define a Tyrant, is unfit to be the ruler of a free people.

Nor have We been wanting in attentions to our Brittish brethren. We have warned them from time to time of attempts by their legislature to extend an unwarrantable jurisdiction over us. We have reminded them of the circumstances of our emigration and settlement here. We have appealed to their native justice and magnanimity, and we have conjured them by the ties of our common kindred to disavow these usurpations, which, would inevitably interrupt our connections and correspondence. They too have been deaf to the voice of Justice and of consanguinity. We must, therefore, acquiesce in the necessity, which denounces our Separation, and hold them, as we hold the rest of mankind, Enemies in War, in Peace Friends.

We, therefore, the Representatives of the united States of America, in General Congress, Assembled, appealing to the Supreme Judge of the world for the rectitude of our intentions, do, in the Name, and by Authority of the good People of these Colonies, solemnly publish and declare, That these United Colonies are, and of Right ought to be Free and Independent States; that they are Absolved from all Allegiance to the British Crown, and that all political connection between them and the State of Great Britain, is and ought to be totally dissolved; and that as Free and Independent States, they have full Power to levy War, conclude Peace, contract Alliances, establish Commerce, and to do all other Acts and Things which Independent States may of right do. And for the support of this Declaration, with a firm reliance on the protection of divine Providence, we mutually pledge to each other our Lives, our Fortunes and our sacred Honor.

Button Gwinnett	George Wythe	James Wilson	Wm: Whipple
Lyman Hall	Richard Henry Lee	Geo. Ross	Saml. Adams
Geo Walton	Th: Jefferson	Caesar Rodney	John Adams
Wm. Hooper	Benja. Harrison	Geo Read	Robt. Treat Paine
Joseph Hewes	John Hancock	Tho M: Kean	Elbridge Gerry
John Penn	Thos. Nelson jr.	Wm. Floyd	Step. Hopkins
Edward Rutledge	Francis Lightfoot Lee	Phil. Livingston	William Ellery
Thos. Heyward Junr.	Carter Braxton	Frans. Lewis	Roger Sherman
Thomas Lynch Junr.	Robt. Morris	Lewis Morris	Saml. Huntington
Arthur Middleton	Benjamin Rush	Richd. Stockton	Wm. Williams
Samuel Chase	Benja. Franklin	Jno Witherspoon	Oliver Wolcott
Wm. Paca	John Morton	Fras. Hopkinson	Matthew Thornton
Thos. Stone	Geo Clymer	John Hart	
Charles Carroll of	Jas. Smith	Abra Clark	
Carrollton	Geo. Taylor	Josiah Bartlett	

Note: This text of the Declaration of Independence is taken from the reprint in the Revised Statutes of the United States, corrected by comparison with the version printed in the journal of the Continental Congress. The original manuscript can be seen in the National Archives, Washington, D.C.

ORIGINS

The Preamble. The Declaration of Independence was directed not just to a few insiders—American colonists who wanted their independence—but to the whole world. It had to be plain and simple. The first part therefore had to state the "common sense" of the subject. The opening words of the Declaration, like the opening words of the Constitution, gave the basis for the whole argument. They expressed not only what most Americans believed, but also what would seem "self-evident" (needing no proof) to Britons of goodwill, and to people in France and other countries from whom the Americans wanted help.

Since Jefferson was not aiming to devise a new theory, it is not surprising that he wrote his draft in short order. On June 28, 1776, only about two weeks after he received the assignment, the energetic 33-year-old lawyer from Virginia managed to have his Declaration approved by the Committee and submitted to the Continental Congress. If he had needed a lot of research and reflection, it would have taken him much longer. He did not even need a library. He explained that he had purposely not referred to any books or pamphlets for special arguments. He wrote the Declaration in Philadelphia on a desk in the second-floor parlor of the house of a young German immigrant bricklayer where he was staying. He wanted to be sure that what he was saying simply summed up what educated people already knew from their schoolbooks.

The basis for government described here is precisely what Englishmen had accepted in their Glorious Revolution of 1688. All good Whigs in England still believed those principles. The Englishman John Locke had been the philosopher of that Glorious Revolution. His sacred three purposes of government were life, liberty, and property. Jefferson preferred "Life, Liberty, and the pursuit of Happiness."

The List of Grievances. Thomas Jefferson was a lawyer. He had studied law at William and Mary College. He was admitted to the Virginia bar in 1767 and was a successful practicing lawyer until the cause of Independence focused his talents on public issues. One of the main reasons why Jefferson was chosen to write the Declaration was that in 1774 he had written a brilliant *Summary View of the Rights of British America.* This eloquent little pamphlet brought him wide notice both as a learned lawyer and a lively stylist. There he had proven that the Parliament had no authority at all over the colonies. He did concede that the colonists, of their own free will, had submitted to the king as their connecting link with the home country.

And Jefferson was a careful lawyer. This explains why Jefferson's Declaration of Independence makes no mention at all of the British Parliament. On one occasion he mentions that "the present King of Great Britain" (George III) "has combined with *others*" for his nefarious purposes. Those "others" were, of course, the Parliament. But the lawyerly Jefferson would not do them the honor of naming them by name! From a lawyer's point of view the king was to blame, and had to take all the blame for allowing those "others" to oppress the colonies.

The list that Jefferson provides is detailed and technical. The colonists' rights, he says, were the traditional rights of all British subjects. This, of course, prevented the Declaration from having a radical sound. According to Jefferson's Declaration the colonists were now declaring their independence simply to preserve the rights that Britons had fought for and won over the past centuries.

We can already see here the need for compromise among the States, which would appear so plainly in the Constitution. The list of grievances that finally was approved by the Continental Congress was not precisely that which Jefferson included in his draft. Some sentimental members of the Continental Congress removed a few of Jefferson's personal remarks about George III. Out of tenderness to some delegates from the slave states, they also removed Jefferson's bitter attack on slavery and the slave-trade, for which he held the British king responsible.

AFTERLIFE

At the time, to the colonists, Jefferson's legalistic list of grievances seemed the heart of their case. These "facts submitted to a candid world" against the king of England justified the colonies' independence. The Preamble was only the "common sense" basis behind those grievances. In later years, after the United States had fought for and won independence, the facts of that day came to seem less interesting. To understand those facts required an understanding of history, of the sort we have tried to give in this book. Since they were in lawyers' language, they were easy to forget.

The Preamble, by contrast, stated the principles of free government. Jefferson's flowing language could not be forgotten. It is not surprising, then, that in the years since 1776 the Preamble has overshadowed all the rest of the document. Who can forget these words? "We hold these truths to be self-evident, that all men are created equal, that they are endowed by their Creator with certain unalienable Rights, that among these are Life, Liberty and the pursuit of Happiness. That to secure these rights, Governments are instituted among Men, deriving their just powers from the consent of the governed."

These words of the Preamble resound down the centuries. They have a wonderful ring, but Americans have not always agreed on what they meant.

Elizabeth Cady Stanton and her companions at the women's rights convention at Seneca Falls, New York, in 1848, issued their own "Declaration" modeled on Jefferson's work of 1776. They began "When, in the course of human events . . ." and went on to their own list of "self-evident" truths, and their grievances against man for oppressing woman.

The Civil War would have to be fought to secure agreement on what the Declaration meant when it said that "all men are created equal." When the southern states seceded they, too, declared that they were only following the principles of the Declaration of 1776.

Even today Americans disagree over precisely what a government should do to help Americans in the "pursuit of Happiness." But Jefferson's words in the Declaration of Independence still provide an American creed. We can all agree to this statement of principles. If the words had been more prosaic or more limited, they might not have lived. And we might have lacked the eloquent standard by which we can still judge ourselves.

The Declaration of Independence and the World. Jefferson's words have appealed to freedom-loving people everywhere. No other human document has been so inspiring to people with grievances against their government. The men and women who made the French Revolution of 1789 appealed to the Declaration. English reformers, and Irish rebels against English oppression, appealed to the Declaration. In the early 19th century, translated into Spanish, the Declaration inspired colonists in South America to become independent. It was translated into German and Italian to support liberal revolutions in the 1830s and 1840s. It was translated into scores of other languages, and everywhere has encouraged people fighting for freedom, helping them explain their cause to the world.

Jefferson himself knew that his Declaration was a voice for posterity and that it would have an Afterlife without end. He wrote his own epitaph. After a long life of countless achievements, he chose to have it written on his tombstone (along with his recognition as author of the Virginia statute for religious freedom and as father of the University of Virginia) that he was the author of the Declaration of Independence.

The Constitution of the United States

These pages give us the text of the Constitution, and they will help us understand why it was written this way, and how it has changed. For Americans, the Constitution is a sacred document. The Constitution itself prescribes that before taking office, each American President must "solemnly swear (or affirm) that I will . . . to the best of my Ability, preserve, protect and defend the Constitution of the United States." (Article II, section 1) While the Constitution is our sacred national document, it is not a fossil. It can be changed and has changed. Most of this book could be considered a history of how the Constitution has worked.

We have arranged the following pages on the Constitution to show that the Constitution was a *living* document. In the Convention in Philadelphia in the hot summer of 1787 the Framers had reasons for everything that they said. We can understand these reasons by our study of history. It was written by living people for their living needs. It would be changed slowly over the centuries to meet the needs of other living people, including ourselves.

In the beige sections (*The Text*) we print the Constitution as the Framers approved it on September 15 and signed it in Independence Hall in Philadelphia (a place we can still visit) on September 17, 1787. Their spelling, their punctuation, and their capitalizing of words may look a little odd to us. But we have left the document the way they wrote it, to remind us that it was written a long time ago. This, too, will remind us of the miracle of the survival of our Constitution as the frame of government of a great nation. None of the peculiarities will get in the way of our understanding.

In *Origins* we see some of the reasons that led men of the eighteenth century to write the words as they did. Here we have a glimpse of their arguments, disagreements, and compromises before they settled on the words we now read. All these are explained at greater length in the earlier pages of this book. The references to chapters and sections within chapters appear in brackets: [4:1] is Chapter 4, Section 1 and [int.] refers to the introductory chapter.

In *Afterlife* we see how the meaning of the document has changed to suit needs that the Framers never imagined. Some of their words were not clear, and the meanings of some words would change. These changes, too, are described in the earlier pages of this book.

The story of the Constitution itself is one of the most remarkable in all history. Like the life of a person, it is full of surprises—and disappointments. But the story as a whole must make Americans proud. We can still prosper under this Constitution written two centuries ago.

One of the best features of the document was that it was so short. It is shorter than the Constitution of any of the states. The Framers wanted to provide for the future, but they did not try to second-guess the future. They believed in change—otherwise they would not have dared to start a new nation and write a new constitution. They respected the wisdom of the future.

They left plenty of room for future Americans to make this Constitution serve their needs.

The Constitution survives because it is a living document. The Framers intended this Constitution to *live*. We help it live by understanding what they intended, why and how they wanted it to endure, why and how it has been changed, and how it can still be changed. And by seeing its wonderful simplicity and wisdom.

THE CONSTITUTION OF THE UNITED STATES

We the People of the United States, in Order to form a more perfect Union, establish Justice, insure domestic Tranquillity, provide for the common defence, promote the general Welfare, and secure the Blessings of Liberty to ourselves and our Posterity, do ordain and establish this Constitution for the United States of America.

ORIGINS

The Preamble. This is not merely an introduction, but one of the most important passages in the Constitution. It describes both the *basis* of government and the *purposes* of government. The Framers chose their words carefully.

A new basis. The weak Articles of Confederation of 1781 [int.] had been formed by "Delegates of the States." To make "a more perfect Union," the Constitution of the new nation was now ordained and established by "the People of the United States." To make a fresh start, the voters of the whole country (strictly limited at that time to certain white male property owners) delegated certain powers to the new national government, others to the states.

The purposes. The "in Order to" items were a list of the worries of Americans at the time. They wanted to "establish Justice" (which the British government had denied the colonies). They wanted to "insure domestic Tranquillity" (which Shays's Rebellion in Massachusetts, August 1786–February 1787 [int.], and other riots had threatened). They wanted better to "provide for the common defence" (the weak Continental Congress had almost lost the Revolution) [int.]. They wanted to "promote the general Welfare" (till then threatened by inflation and rivalries between the states). They wanted to "secure the Blessings of Liberty" not only to themselves but to their "Posterity" (that's us!), which required a firm and durable Constitution.

The Framers in the Federal Convention in Philadelphia in August–September 1787 worked over this language for the Preamble. The final form was given by Gouverneur Morris of Pennsylvania, who had signed the Articles of Confederation, had helped manage the troubled finances under the weak Articles, and had good reason to want a strong national government.

AFTERLIFE

The Preamble. While the Federalist Framers thought the meaning of this preamble was clear, it would not be so clear to all later generations. The Civil War would be fought partly over the precise meaning of the words. If the basis of government really was not "the People" of the whole United States but only the states—then what the states had made by coming together they could destroy by seceding. In 1819, Chief Justice John Marshall, drawing on the preamble, declared in *McCulloch* v. *Maryland* [int.], "The government of the Union . . . is emphatically and truly a government of the people. In form and in substance it emanated from them, its powers are granted by them, and are to be exercised directly on them, and for their benefit." But in the years before the Civil War, John C. Calhoun and other Southern secessionists did not agree.

The Civil War settled that issue.

The Constitution does not define *who* "the People" are. Like much else in the document the meaning of this phrase has changed. At first, "the People" were only white male property owners. Then all white males were included. Later black males were added by the 15th Amendment [2:3], then women by the 19th Amendment [10:1], and all citizens 18 years old or older by the 26th Amendment [21:3].

ARTICLE I

Section 1. All legislative Powers herein granted shall be vested in a Congress of the United States, which shall consist of a Senate and House of Representatives.

Section 2. The House of Representatives shall be composed of Members chosen every second Year by the People of the several States, and the Electors in each State shall have the Qualifications requisite for Electors of the most numerous Branch of the State Legislature.

Art. I
Sec. 2

No Person shall be a Representative who shall not have attained to the age of twenty five Years, and been seven Years a Citizen of the United States, and who shall not, when elected, be an Inhabitant of that State in which he shall be chosen.

ORIGINS

The Powers of Government and the Separation of Powers. The plan of the Constitution was wonderfully simple. The Framers believed that there were three main tasks of government: making the laws, enforcing (or "executing") the laws, and interpreting the laws. They described these in the first three Articles. Article I ("All legislative Powers") described the Congress. Article II ("The executive Power") described the President. Article III ("The judicial Power") described the Supreme Court and other courts.

The Revolution had been fought because Parliament had tried to tyrannize over the colonies. Now the Framers wanted to make all branches of government efficient, but prevent tyranny by any one of them. Therefore they kept each of these powers separate. Each would check the others, and the people would not have to fear any one.

The Articles of Confederation had provided nothing but a "firm league of friendship" among the sovereign states. There was no executive at all, and there was no national system of courts. Questions had to be decided by approval of at least nine

of "the united states in Congress assembled" where each state had one vote.

Legislative Powers. In Article I, the Framers took a bold step to remedy these weaknesses. The new Congress would represent not just the states, but "the People of the several States." And the Framers showed their hope to make a truly representative government by devoting more than half of the entire Constitution to this first Article describing the Congress.

Creating *two* houses of Congress was a crucial compromise between the large states (led by Virginia), who wanted members of Congress apportioned entirely by population, and the small states who wanted every state to have a single equal vote (as under the Articles of Confederation). There was already an example in England of a two-branched Parliament: a "lower" House of Commons, and an "upper" House of Lords. After much discussion and some bitterness, members of the Convention finally agreed to create a House of Representatives representing parts of the country according to their population, and a Senate where each state had an equal vote. Lawmaking powers were divided. The House of Representatives would have greater power over taxation and the ways of spending government money, for money bills had to begin there. The Senate would have greater control over foreign policy, for it had to approve treaties.

AFTERLIFE

Article I which set up the organization and structure of Congress has needed few changes over the years.

The freedom of each state to decide who can vote in federal elections has been limited by amendments to the Constitution. The Supreme Court has interpreted the 14th Amendment's "equal protection" clause as forbidding discriminatory practices by state election officials. The 15th and 19th amendments prohibited denying the franchise because of race, color, or sex. The 26th Amendment prohibited denying the franchise to persons 18 years old or older. The 24th Amendment outlawed the poll tax. It has needed further federal action to enforce the 15th Amendment [17:3, 20:1, and especially 21:1 on the Voting Rights Act of 1965].

Art. I
Sec. 2

Representatives and direct Taxes shall be apportioned among the several States which may be included within this Union, according to their respective Numbers, which shall be determined by adding to the whole Number of free Persons, including those bound to Service for a Term of Years, and excluding Indians not taxed, three fifths of all other Persons. The actual Enumeration shall be made within three Years after the first Meeting of the Congress of the United States, and within every subsequent Term of ten Years, in such Manner as they shall by Law direct. The Number of Representatives shall not exceed one for every thirty Thousand, but each State shall have at Least one Representative; and until such enumeration shall be made, the State of New Hampshire shall be entitled to chuse three, Massachusetts eight, Rhode-Island and Providence Plantations one, Connecticut five, New-York six, New Jersey four, Pennsylvania eight, Delaware one, Maryland six, Virginia ten, North Carolina five, South Carolina five, and Georgia three.

When vacancies happen in the Representation from any State, the Executive Authority thereof shall issue Writs of Election to fill such Vacancies.

The House of Representatives shall chuse their Speaker and other Officers; and ● shall have the sole Power of Impeachment.

ORIGINS

Another bold decision which we see here was to *list* the powers of the Congress (in section 8). These were called the "enumerated powers" of the federal government. The Articles of Confederation had provided no such list and this was one of the reasons for its weakness.

The large states (Virginia again in the lead) wanted Congress to have the power to veto laws passed by the states. But the smaller states were

fearful. Instead the delegates to the Convention finally agreed on a list of subjects (in section 10) on which the states were forbidden to pass their own laws. These included foreign policy, currency, and tariffs on imports or exports.

AFTERLIFE

A census of the population has been taken every ten years since 1790. The Congress decides how many members of Congress there will be. Each state is then informed how many representatives it may have on the basis of the census. In *Wesberry* v. *Sanders* (1964) the Supreme Court ruled that congressional districts within a state had to be roughly equal in population [21:1]. Since taxes were also to be apportioned among the states according to the census, the 16th Amendment (ratified in 1913) was required to allow an income tax to be imposed. In 1912 the maximum size of the House was set at 435. According to the census of 1980, after providing for states entitled to only one representative, the ratio is one member for about every 500,000 persons.

● The House "impeaches" and the Senate (sec. 3, pars. 6–7) tries the impeachment [int., 2:3, 21:3].

Art. I   **Section 3.** The Senate of the United States shall be composed of two Senators ■ from each State, chosen by the Legislature thereof, for six Years; and each Senator shall have one Vote.

Immediately after they shall be assembled in Consequence of the first Election, they shall be divided as equally as may be into three Classes. The Seats of the Senators of the first Class shall be vacated at the Expiration of the second Year, of the second Class at the Expiration of the fourth Year, and of the third Class at the Expiration of the sixth Year, so that one third may be chosen every second Year; and if vacancies happen by Resignation, or otherwise, during the Recess of the Legislature of any State, the Executive thereof may make temporary Appointments until the next Meeting of the Legislature, which shall then fill such Vacancies.

No Person shall be a Senator who shall not have attained to the Age of thirty Years, and been nine Years a Citizen of the United States, and who shall not, when elected, be an Inhabitant of that State for which he shall be chosen.

The Vice President of the United States shall be President of the Senate, but shall have no Vote, unless they be equally divided.

The Senate shall chuse their other Officers, and also a President pro tempore, in ▲ the Absence of the Vice President, or when he shall exercise the Office of President of the United States.

The Senate shall have the sole Power to try all Impeachments. When sitting for that Purpose, they shall be on Oath or Affirmation. When the President of the United States is tried the Chief Justice shall preside: And no Person shall be convicted without the Concurrence of two thirds of the Members present.

Judgment in Cases of Impeachment shall not extend further than to removal from Office, and disqualification to hold and enjoy any Office of honor, Trust or Profit under the United States: but the Party convicted shall nevertheless be liable and subject to Indictment, Trial, Judgment and Punishment, according to Law.

AFTERLIFE

■ The 17th Amendment (1913) provided for the election of senators directly by the people instead of by state legislatures [8:2].

▲ The 25th Amendment now provides for filling the Vice-Presidency when the office becomes vacant. Gerald Ford was the first person to be seleced by this procedure [21:3].

Art. I **Section 4.** The Times, Places and Manner of holding Elections for Senators and Representatives, shall be prescribed in each State by the Legislature thereof; but the Congress may at any time by Law make or alter such Regulations, except as to the Places of chusing Senators.

The Congress shall assemble at least once in every Year, and such Meeting shall ■ be on the first Monday in December, unless they shall by Law appoint a different Day.

AFTERLIFE

Under federal law all the states now hold elections for Congress on the first Tuesday after the first Monday in November in even-numbered years.
■ The meeting time of Congress was changed in the 20th Amendment, section 2 [12:1].

Art. I **Section 5.** Each House shall be the Judge of the Elections, Returns and Qualifications of its own Members, and a Majority of each shall constitute a Quorum to do Business; but a smaller Number may adjourn from day to day, and may be authorized to compel the Attendance of absent Members, in such Manner, and under such Penalties as each House may provide.

Each House may determine the Rules of its Proceedings, punish its Members for disorderly Behaviour, and, with the Concurrence of two thirds, expel a Member.

Each House shall keep a Journal of its Proceedings, and from time to time publish the same, excepting such Parts as may in their Judgment require Secrecy; and the Yeas and Nays of the Members of either House on any question shall, at the Desire of one fifth of those Present, be entered on the Journal.

Neither House, during the Session of Congress, shall, without the Consent of the other, adjourn for more than three days, nor to any other Place than that in which the two Houses shall be sitting.

AFTERLIFE

The right of each house to punish its own members has enabled them to discipline senators and representatives whose activities are judged to be improper. For example, under this clause Senator Joseph R. McCarthy was condemned in 1954, Representative Adam Clayton Powell was denied his seat in 1967 on the charge that he misused government funds, and Senator Herman Talmadge was "denounced" in 1979 for financial irregularities.

Art. I **Section 6.** The Senators and Representatives shall receive a Compensation for their Services, to be ascertained by Law, and paid out of the Treasury of the United States. They shall in all Cases, except Treason, Felony and Breach of the Peace, be privileged from Arrest during their attendance at the Session of their respective Houses, and in going to and returning from the same; and for any Speech or Debate in either House, they shall not be questioned in any other Place.

No Senator or Representative shall, during the Time for which he was elected, be appointed to any civil Office under the Authority of the United States, which shall have been created, or the Emoluments whereof shall have been encreased during such time; and no Person holding any Office under the United States, shall be a Member of either House during his Continuance in Office.

Section 7. All Bills for raising Revenue shall originate in the House of Representatives; but the Senate may propose or concur with amendments as on other Bills.

Every Bill which shall have passed the House of Representatives and the Senate, shall, before it become a Law, be presented to the President of the United States; If he approve he shall sign it, but if not he shall return it, with his Objections to that House in which it shall have originated, who shall enter the Objections at large on their Journal, and proceed to reconsider it. If after such Reconsideration two thirds of that House shall agree to pass the Bill, it shall be sent, together with the Objections, to the other House, by which it shall likewise be reconsidered, and if approved by two thirds of that House, it shall become a Law. But in all such Cases the Votes of both Houses shall be determined by yeas and Nays, and the Names of the Persons voting for and against the Bill shall be entered on the Journal of each House respectively. If any Bill shall not be returned by the President within ten Days (Sunday excepted) after it shall have been presented to him, the Same shall be a Law, in like Manner as if he had signed it, unless the Congress by their Adjournment prevent its Return, in which Case it shall not be a Law.

Every Order, Resolution, or Vote to which the Concurrence of the Senate and House of Representatives may be necessary (except on a question of Adjournment) shall be presented to the President of the United States; and before the Same shall take Effect, shall be approved by him, or being disapproved by him, shall be repassed by two thirds of the Senate and House of Representatives, according to the Rules and Limitations prescribed in the Case of a Bill.

AFTERLIFE

Although section 1 grants all legislative power to Congress, all bills must be submitted to the President. The President may then sign the bill and make it a law, or let it become a law without signing it. The President may also refuse to sign and return the bill with his reasons for doing so—that is, "veto" it. The bill can then become law only if each house passes it by a two-thirds majority. A bill sent to the President in the last ten days of a session of Congress does not become law if the President does not sign it. This is called a "pocket veto."

Andrew Jackson was the first president actively to use the veto power. He believed that the President had an equal right with the legislature and the courts to decide what was constitutional. He also thought that the President, as the only person elected by all the people, could veto measures passed by Congress if he disapproved of them even if they were clearly constitutional. Jackson vetoed more bills than all the Presidents who served before him put together. Among the other active Presidents, such as Lincoln, Theodore Roosevelt, and Wilson, none used the veto power more vigorously than Franklin D. Roosevelt. He vetoed more than 600 bills during his twelve years in office. Congress was able to override his veto only nine times.

Art. I **Section 8.** The Congress shall have Power To lay and collect Taxes, Duties, Imposts and Excises, to pay the Debts and provide for the common Defence and general Welfare of the United States; but all Duties, Imposts and Excises shall be uniform throughout the United States;

To borrow Money on the credit of the United States;

To regulate Commerce with foreign Nations, and among the several States, and with the Indian Tribes;

To establish an uniform Rule of Naturalization, and uniform Laws on the subject of Bankruptcies throughout the United States;

To coin Money, regulate the Value thereof, and of foreign Coin, and fix the Standard of Weights and Measures;

To provide for the Punishment of counterfeiting the Securities and current Coin of the United States;

To establish Post Offices and post Roads;

To promote the Progress of Science and useful Arts, by securing for limited Times to Authors and Inventors the exclusive Right to their respective Writings and Discoveries;

To constitute Tribunals inferior to the supreme Court;

To define and punish Piracies and Felonies committed on the high Seas, and Offences against the Law of Nations;

• To declare War, grant Letters of Marque and Reprisal, and make Rules concerning Captures on Land and Water;

ORIGINS

• On letters of marque, see [int.].

AFTERLIFE

One of the most disputed of the enumerated powers has been the right of Congress "to regulate Commerce." Exactly what the Framers meant both by "regulate" and by "Commerce" was unclear. In the case of *Gibbons* v. *Ogden* (1824) the Supreme Court laid down rules about a state establishing a monopoly [int.]. There Marshall also declared that Congress's power over commerce "may very well be restricted to that commerce which concerns more states than one"—that is, "interstate commerce." But Marshall also saw that commercial transactions taking place entirely within a state could influence commerce among the states. Since the late 1930s the Court has followed that line of reasoning to allow Congress a broad power to regulate commerce.

For example, the court has interpreted the "Commerce" clause in such a way that it not only allows the regulation of railroads, pipelines, and other clearly interstate activities, but also permits minimum wage regulation and prohibitions on child labor. In the case of *NLRB* v. *Jones and Laughlin Corp.* (1937), the Court declared that the Wagner Act [13:4], dealing with the rights of labor to organize and to bargain collectively, was constitutional. Justice Benjamin Cardozo stated that the power to regulate commerce was "as broad as the need that evokes it."

To raise and support Armies, but no Appropriation of Money to that Use shall be for a longer Term than two Years;

To provide and maintain a Navy;

To make Rules for the Government and Regulation of the land and naval Forces;

To provide for calling forth the Militia to execute the Laws of the Union, suppress Insurrections and repel Invasions;

To provide for organizing, arming, and disciplining, the Militia, and for governing such Part of them as may be employed in the Service of the United States, reserving to the States respectively, the Appointment of the Officers, and the Authority of training the Militia according to the discipline prescribed by Congress;

To exercise exclusive Legislation in all Cases whatsoever, over such District (not exceeding ten Miles square) as may, by Cession of Particular States, and the Acceptance of Congress, become the Seat of the Government of the United States, and to exercise like Authority over all Places purchased by the Consent of the Legislature of the State in which the Same shall be, for the Erection of Forts, Magazines, Arsenals, dock-Yards, and other needful Buildings;—And

To make all Laws which shall be necessary and proper for carrying into Execu- ■ tion the foregoing Powers, and all other Powers vested by this Constitution in the Government of the United States, or in any Department or Officer thereof.

AFTERLIFE

■ The meaning of this "necessary and proper" clause (or "elastic clause") was the dividing line between broad and strict constructionists. The first dispute occurred over Alexander Hamilton's proposal for a national bank [int.]. The Supreme Court under John Marshall in *McCulloch* v. *Maryland* (1819) agreed with the broad constructionists [int.]. Since the government was granted wide powers "on the due exercise of which the happiness and prosperity of the nation so vitally depends," Marshall ruled, it "must also be entrusted with ample means for their execution."

▲ **Section 9.** The Migration or Importation of such Persons as any of the States now existing shall think proper to admit, shall not be prohibited by the Congress prior to the Year one thousand eight hundred and eight, but a Tax or duty may be imposed on such Importation, not exceeding ten dollars for each Person.

ORIGINS

Absolute prohibitions on Congress.
▲ This clause was inserted to prevent Congress from outlawing the foreign slave trade before 1808.

AFTERLIFE

In 1808 Congress did outlaw the foreign slave trade.

Art. I Sec. 9	The Privilege of the Writ of Habeas Corpus shall not be suspended, unless when in Cases of Rebellion or Invasion the public Safety may require it. ▪ No Bill of Attainder or ex post facto Law shall be passed.

ORIGINS

On *habeas corpus*, see [1:1], pages 36–37.

▪ A *bill of attainder* is a legislative act pronouncing an individual guilty of a crime, usually treason, without a trial. It had been used by kings and queens to get rid of personal or political enemies.

An *ex post facto* law is a law passed after the fact, and was a way of punishing people whom the ruling powers disliked, even though they had not violated any existing law.

AFTERLIFE

During the Civil War, Abraham Lincoln suspended the writ of habeas corpus in certain areas [1:1]. When he suspended it in Maryland, Chief Justice Taney ruled in the *Merryman* case (1861) that only Congress had the right to suspend the writ of habeas corpus. Lincoln did not agree and continued to follow his own interpretation of the Constitution.

Art. I Sec. 9	No Capitation, or other direct, Tax shall be laid, unless in Proportion to the Census of Enumeration herein before directed to be taken.

AFTERLIFE

In *Pollock* v. *Farmers' Loan and Trust Co.* (1895), the Supreme Court ruled that a federal income tax was unconstitutional because it was a direct tax, but not laid in proportion to the census [6:5]. An income tax was made legal by the 16th Amendment (1913).

Art. I Sec. 9	No Tax or Duty shall be laid on Articles exported from any State. No Preference shall be given by any Regulation of Commerce or Revenue to the Ports of one State over those of another; nor shall Vessels bound to, or from, one State, be obliged to enter, clear or pay Duties in another. No Money shall be drawn from the Treasury, but in Consequence of Appropriations made by Law; and a regular Statement and Account of the Receipts and Expenditures of all public Money shall be published from time to time. No Title of Nobility shall be granted by the United States: And no Person holding any Office of Profit or Trust under them, shall, without the Consent of the Congress, accept of any present, Emolument, Office, or Title, of any kind whatever, from any King, Prince or foreign State.
Art. I	**Section 10.** No State shall enter into any Treaty, Alliance, or Confederation; grant Letters of Marque and Reprisal; coin Money; emit Bills of Credit; make any Thing but gold and silver Coin a Tender in Payment of Debts; pass any Bill of Attainder, ex post facto Law, or Law impairing the Obligation of Contracts, or grant any Title of Nobility.

<table>
<tr><td>Art. I
Sec. 10</td><td>No State shall, without the Consent of the Congress, lay any Imposts or Duties on Imports or Exports, except what may be absolutely necessary for executing it's inspection Laws: and the net Produce of all Duties and Imposts, laid by any State on Imports or Exports, shall be for the Use of the Treasury of the United States; and all such Laws shall be subject to the Revision and Controul of the Congress.</td></tr>
</table>

No State shall, without the Consent of Congress, lay any Duty of Tonnage, keep Troops, or Ships of War in time of Peace, enter into any Agreement or Compact with another State, or with a foreign Power, or engage in War, unless actually invaded, or in such imminent Danger as will not admit of delay.

ARTICLE II

- **Section 1.** The executive Power shall be vested in a President of the United States of America. He shall hold his Office during the term of four Years, and, together with the Vice President, chosen for the same Term, be elected, as follows

ORIGINS

- *"The executive Power."* The Presidency was one of the boldest inventions of the Framers. By creating a strong President, they showed their faith in representative government. They believed that a strong Congress and a strong judiciary would protect the people from any President's misuse of powers. During the Constitutional Convention there was much heated discussion of the problem of the executive. Some, like Roger Sherman of Connecticut, feared a strong President. They wanted him to be nothing but a kind of superpoliceman, who would see that the laws of Congress were enforced. But Gouverneur Morris wanted a President who would be "the guardian of the people, even of the lower classes, against Legislative tyranny," and many others agreed with him. His views finally prevailed.

During the Convention, the draft of this article was revised again and again. Some members, afraid that a single President might become a despot, argued for a three-man executive, one from each part of the country. Some wanted the President to be chosen by the Congress to be sure that he would enforce the will of Congress. The first draft they agreed on provided for a single executive, but had him chosen by the Congress. He was to be elected for a single term of seven years and could not be reelected.

Gradually in the Convention the movement for a strong, independent President made headway.

The ingenious device of an Electoral College allowed him to be elected, indirectly, by "the People." Then the Convention agreed that the President should be elected for four years with no limit on the number of his terms. More and more powers were given to him, including the power to make treaties (with the advice and consent of the Senate). He was given the power to veto acts of Congress. But his veto could be overridden by a two-thirds vote of both houses. And there was insurance against a despot, for the President could be removed from office "on Impeachment for, and Conviction of, Treason, Bribery, or other high Crimes and Misdemeanors."

The Framers were influenced not only by the fearful example of British tyranny over the colonies, but also luckily by the inspiring example of the heroic leader of the Revolution. "Many of the members cast their eyes toward General Washington as President," Pierce Butler of South Carolina who was at the Convention noted, "and shaped their ideas of the Powers to be given a President, by their opinions of his Virtue."

AFTERLIFE

While the President was given many powers in the Constitution, Article II does not say how the President is to use those powers. Whether the office is weak or strong depends on how the President interprets the Constitution and uses the powers it gives.

The powers of the office have grown, especially under such Presidents as Jackson, Lincoln, Theodore Roosevelt, Wilson, and Franklin D. Roosevelt. As Jefferson's purchase of Louisiana showed, even a President who considered himself a strict constructionist could act in such a way as to enlarge greatly the powers of the office [int.].

Art. II
Sec. 1

Each State shall appoint, in such Manner as the Legislature thereof may direct, a number of Electors, equal to the whole Number of Senators and Representatives to which the State may be entitled in the Congress: but no Senator or Representative, or Person holding an Office of Trust or Profit under the United States, shall be appointed an Elector.

The Electors shall meet in their respective States, and vote by Ballot for two Persons, of whom one at least shall not be an Inhabitant of the same State with themselves. And they shall make a List of all the Persons voted for, and of the Number of Votes for each; which List they shall sign and certify, and transmit sealed to the Seat of the Government of the United States, directed to the President of the Senate. The President of the Senate shall, in the Presence of the Senate and House of Representatives, open all the Certificates, and the Votes shall then be counted. The Person having the greatest Number of Votes shall be the President, if such Number be a Majority of the whole Number of Electors appointed; and if there be more than one who have such Majority, and have an equal Num- ▲ ber of Votes, then the House of Representatives shall immediately chuse by Ballot one of them for President; and if no Person have a Majority, then from the five highest on the List the said House shall in like Manner chuse the President. But in chusing the President, the Votes shall be taken by States, the Representation from each State having one Vote; a quorum for this Purpose shall consist of a Member or Members from two thirds of the States, and a Majority of all the States shall be necessary to a Choice. In every Case, after the Choice of the President, the Person having the greatest Number of Votes of the Electors shall be the Vice President. But if there should remain two or more who have equal Votes, the Senate shall chuse from them by Ballot the Vice President.

The Congress may determine the Time of chusing the Electors, and the Day on which they shall give their Votes; which Day shall be the same throughout the United States.

AFTERLIFE

▲ The election of 1800 in which Jefferson and Burr each received the same number of electoral votes brought about the replacement of paragraph 3 by the 12th Amendment in 1804 [int.]. In 1824 the election was thrown into the House, where John Quincy Adams was chosen over Andrew Jackson [int.]. Then in 1876, when Hayes defeated Tilden, the question of who was to count the electoral votes became a problem [2:4]. Again and again there have been movements for a constitutional amendment to abolish the Electoral College and provide that the President and Vice-President be chosen by a majority of votes cast by citizens throughout the nation. But these movements have been resisted by the smaller and less populous states and others. The "Electoral College" survives. The "Electors" meet in their respective state capitals and cast their ballots. The results are sent to Washington and counted in a session of the Congress.

Art. II
Sec. 1

No Person except a natural born Citizen, or a Citizen of the United States, at the time of the Adoption of this Constitution, shall be eligible to the Office of President; neither shall any person be eligible to that Office who shall not have attained to the Age of thirty five Years, and been fourteen Years a Resident within the United States.

In Case of the Removal of the President from Office, or of his Death, Resignation, or Inability to discharge the Powers and Duties of the said Office, the Same shall devolve on the Vice President, and the Congress may by Law provide for the Case of Removal, Death, Resignation or Inability, both of the President and Vice President, declaring what Officer shall then act as President, and such Officer shall act accordingly, until the Disability be removed, or a President shall be elected.

AFTERLIFE

In 1886 Congress enacted a law making the succession pass from the Vice-President to the members of the Cabinet in the order in which their offices were established. In 1947 this was changed. The purpose was to make it more likely that the President would be a person who had held some elective office. The succession now goes to the Speaker of the House, then to the President Pro Tempore of the Senate, and finally to the Cabinet officers. The 25th Amendment, however, makes it highly unlikely that succession will ever go beyond the Vice-President. Section 2 of that amendment provides that whenever a vacancy in the office of the Vice-President exists, the President shall nominate a Vice-President who shall take office with the approval of a majority of the members of Congress.

Art. II
Sec. 1

The President shall, at stated Times, receive for his Services, a Compensation, which shall neither be encreased nor diminished during the Period for which he shall have been elected, and he shall not receive within that Period any other Emolument from the United States, or any of them.

Before he enter on the Execution of his Office, he shall take the following Oath or Affirmation:—"I do solemnly swear (or affirm) that I will faithfully execute the Office of President of the United States, and will to the best of my Ability, preserve, protect and defend the Constitution of the United States."

Art. II

Section 2. The President shall be Commander in Chief of the Army and Navy of the United States, and of the Militia of the several States, when called into the actual Service of the United States; he may require the Opinion, in writing, of the principal Officer in each of the executive Departments, upon any Subject relating to the Duties of their respective Offices, and he shall have Power to grant Reprieves and Pardons for Offenses against the United States, except in Cases of Impeachment.

This provision insures that the military is clearly under civilian control. During the Civil War President Lincoln [1:1], who greatly enlarged the powers of the Presidency in other ways, played a major role in military affairs. In 1950 President Truman used his powers as Commander in Chief to commit troops to Korea and to remove General MacArthur from command [16:3]. Despite criticism from those who believed this provision did not give the President so much power, Eisenhower, Kennedy, Johnson, and Nixon used it to justify a variety of military moves [20:4].

Art. II
Sec. 2
He shall have Power, by and with the Advice and Consent of the Senate, to make Treaties, provided two thirds of the Senators present concur; and he shall nominate, and by and with the Advice and Consent of the Senate, shall appoint Ambassadors, other public Ministers and Consuls, Judges of the supreme Court, and all other Officers of the United States, whose Appointments are not herein otherwise provided for, and which shall be established by Law: but the Congress may by Law vest the Appointment of such inferior Officers, as they think proper, in the President alone, in the Courts of Law, or in the Heads of Departments.

The President shall have Power to fill up all Vacancies that may happen during the Recess of the Senate, by granting Commissions which shall expire at the End of their next Session.

Art. II
Section 3. He shall from time to time give to the Congress Information of the State of the Union, and recommend to their Consideration such Measures as he shall judge necessary and expedient; he may, on extraordinary Occasions, convene both Houses, or either of them, and in Case of Disagreement between them, with Respect to the Time of Adjournment, he may adjourn them to such Time as he shall think proper; he shall receive Ambassadors and other public Ministers; he shall take Care that the Laws be faithfully executed, and shall Commission all the Officers of the United States.

Art. II
Section 4. The President, Vice President and all Civil Officers of the United States, shall be removed from Office on Impeachment for, and Conviction of, Treason, Bribery, or other high Crimes and Misdemeanors.

On the impeachment and trial of Andrew Johnson, and the recommendation that Richard Nixon should be impeached, see [2:3], pages 66–67, and [21:3], pages 461–462.

For additional material on the Presidency, see also Amendments 20, 22, and 25.

ARTICLE III

Section 1. The judicial Power of the United States, shall be vested in one supreme Court, and in such inferior Courts as the Congress may from time to time ordain and establish. The Judges, both of the supreme and inferior Courts, shall hold their Offices during good Behaviour, and shall, at stated Times, receive for their Services, a Compensation, which shall not be diminished during their Continuance in Office.

ORIGINS

● *"The judicial Power."* The Articles of Confederation had provided no system of national courts. The Congress of the Confederation could only appoint special courts to settle disputes between states, and certain cases arising out of naval warfare during the Revolution. Under the Confederation a citizen was judged only by the courts of his state. But, of course, under the Confederation, there was no national system of laws to be interpreted.

Delegates to the Constitutional Convention agreed quickly and unanimously (on June 4, 1787) that a strong new nation, with a Congress empowered to pass many laws, required "that a national Judiciary be established." At first the New Jersey Plan, speaking for the small states, proposed only a "supreme Tribunal" with final powers over state courts and dealing only with federal matters. The compromise in Article III, proposed by James Madison of Virginia and James Wilson of Pennsylvania, created a Supreme Court for the nation, but left the question of lower courts to the future Congress. The belief that there had to be a national system of courts for a strong nation was confirmed when the first Congress met. By the Judiciary Act of 1789, they created a system of lower federal courts. Members of the Convention agreed (see Article VI) that there could not be a nation without some national system of courts, uniformly interpreting "the supreme Law of the Land" for every citizen.

The last three paragraphs of Article III aimed to protect citizens against the kind of despotic laws or interpretations of the law they had known before the Revolution. The Convention therefore guaranteed trial by jury in criminal cases.

In England over the centuries, tyrants had defined "treason" in any way that suited their purposes. The Framers gave "treason" a narrow and precise definition to protect innocent citizens against their unscrupulous enemies in power. This would encourage citizens to criticize their government without fear of being prosecuted as traitors. Citizens were protected too against "bills of attainder"—the name for laws that had sometimes been passed in England to convict people of crimes of which they had been acquitted or for which they had not been tried. Many supporters of the Constitution believed these safeguards were not enough. Their demands resulted in the "Bill of Rights," the first ten amendments.

The belief of the Framers that "a national Judiciary" was crucial to a new nation was soon to be justified. The Chief Justices of the Supreme Court, beginning with the first, John Jay, would prove effective champions of a national government of uniform laws.

AFTERLIFE

The Judiciary Act of 1789 [int.] provided for the establishment of "inferior courts." There are now district courts, circuit courts of appeals, and various other federal courts.

The Jeffersonian attempt to change the membership of the courts by impeachment [int.] was defeated as was the attempt by Franklin D. Roosevelt to change the Court by "packing" it with additional members [12:3].

The creation of national courts to enforce federal laws directly on citizens played an important part in establishing the power of the central government.

Art. III **Section 2.** The judicial Power shall extend to all Cases, in Law and Equity, arising under this Constitution, the Laws of the United States, and Treaties made, or which shall be made, under their Authority;—to all Cases affecting Ambassadors, other public Ministers and Consuls;—to all Cases of admiralty and maritime Jurisdiction;—to Controversies to which the United States shall be a Party;—to Controversies between two or more States;—between a State and Citizens of another State;—between Citizens of different States;—between Citizens of the same State claiming Lands under Grants of different States, and between a State, or the Citizens thereof, and foreign States, Citizens or Subjects.

In all Cases affecting Ambassadors, other public Ministers and Consuls, and those in which a State shall be Party, the supreme Court shall have original Jurisdiction. In all the other Cases before mentioned, the supreme Court shall have appellate Jurisdiction, both as to Law and Fact, with such Exceptions, and under such Regulations as the Congress shall make.

The Trial of all Crimes, except in Cases of Impeachment, shall be by Jury; and such Trial shall be held in the State where the said Crimes shall have been committed; but when not committed within any State, the Trial shall be at such Place or Places as the Congress may by Law have directed.

AFTERLIFE

The Supreme Court, in *Chisholm* v. *Georgia* (1793) ruled that a private citizen could bring a law suit against a state in a federal court. The 11th Amendment was adopted (1798) to make this impossible in the future.

The rights of individuals charged with crimes were further protected in the Bill of Rights (Amendments 4, 5, 6, 7, & 8) and later Supreme Court decisions [21:1].

Art. III **Section 3.** Treason against the United States, shall consist only in levying War against them, or in adhering to their Enemies, giving them Aid and Comfort. No Person shall be convicted of Treason unless on the Testimony of two Witnesses to the same overt Act, or on Confession in open Court.

The Congress shall have Power to declare the Punishment of Treason, but no Attainder of Treason shall work Corruption of Blood, or Forfeiture except during the Life of the Person attainted.

AFTERLIFE

For the precedent-setting trial of Aaron Burr on the charge of treason, see [int.].

ARTICLE IV

Section 1. Full Faith and Credit shall be given in each State to the public Acts, •
Records, and judicial Proceedings of every other State. And the Congress may by
general Laws prescribe the Manner in which such Acts, Records and Proceedings
shall be proved, and the Effect thereof.

Section 2. The Citizens of each State shall be entitled to all Privileges and Immunities of Citizens in the several States.

A Person charged in any State with Treason, Felony, or other Crime, who shall
flee from Justice, and be found in another State, shall on Demand of the executive
Authority of the State from which he fled, be delivered up, to be removed to the
State having Jurisdiction of the Crime.

No Person held to Service or Labour in one State, under the Laws thereof, es- ★
caping into another, shall, in Consequence of any Law or Regulation therein, be
discharged from such Service or Labour, but shall be delivered up on Claim of the
Party to whom such Service or Labour may be due.

Section 3. New States may be admitted by the Congress into this Union; but no ■
new State shall be formed or erected within the Jurisdiction of any other State;
nor any State be formed by the Junction of two or more States, or Parts of States,
without the Consent of the Legislatures of the States concerned as well as of the
Congress.

The Congress shall have Power to dispose of and make all needful Rules and
Regulations respecting the Territory or other Property belonging to the United ▲
States; and nothing in this Constitution shall be so construed as to Prejudice any
Claims of the United States, or of any particular State.

Section 4. The United States shall guarantee to every State in this Union a Re- ○
publican Form of Government, and shall protect each of them against Invasion;
and on Application of the Legislature, or of the Executive (when the Legislature
cannot be convened) against domestic Violence.

ORIGINS

Having described the three branches of the new
government—the Congress (legislative), the Presidency (executive), and the courts (judiciary)—and
the relations among these branches, the Framers
had still more to do. What about the relations between the states? What about criminals who fled
from one state to another? What about new
states? Could they be carved out of the existing
states? How could new states be admitted to the
Union? What was the central government required to do to preserve representative government
in the states? Did the national government have a
duty to prevent invasion into the states?

Article IV aimed to answer these questions. If

the nation was to expand, and yet avoid becoming
an empire with colonies, there had to be some way
to add new states. The Articles of Confederation
had made it difficult to add a new state, by requiring that nine of the original states had to agree.
Now the Framers wisely provided that new states
could be admitted to the Union by the vote of
Congress. Some delegates feared what might happen if new states were added endlessly toward the
west. Wouldn't the original Atlantic states be
overwhelmed? One delegate, Elbridge Gerry of
Massachusetts, actually proposed a clause providing
that the total number of representatives in the
House of Representatives from new states should
never be allowed to be greater than the number

from the original states. Wiser heads saw that this would produce a nation with second-class citizens. No such clause was adopted. Instead, the Framers decided to allow future Congresses to make the rules.

Delegates saw that Maine and Vermont and the western territories of Georgia, of North Carolina, and of Virginia were being made into states. They feared that some other states might be carved up in the future. These delegates were reassured by the provision that no state could be divided into two, nor joined to another, without the consent of its own legislature.

AFTERLIFE

• Without this clause, the United States would have been merely a league of states. This clause,

together with the "supremacy" clause in Article VI, helped weld the nation together, but it also proved to be a basis for many of the legal disputes over "states rights" before the Civil War.

★ This clause was the basis for the Fugitive Slave Laws [int.]. The provision became ineffective with the adoption of the 13th Amendment [1:5].

■ This section allowed the United States to grow and to become more than a continental nation [int.].

▲ It was this clause that allowed Congress to deal with the question of slavery in the territories [int.].

○ This section was used in the nineteenth century to deal with labor violence [6:1, 6:3].

ARTICLE V

The Congress, whenever two thirds of both Houses shall deem it necessary, shall propose Amendments to this Constitution, or, on the Application of the Legislatures of two thirds of the several States, shall call a Convention for proposing Amendments, which, in either Case, shall be valid to all Intents and Purposes, as Part of this Constitution, when ratified by the Legislatures of three fourths of the several States, or by Conventions in three fourths thereof, as the one or the other Mode of Ratification may be proposed by the Congress; Provided that no Amendment which may be made prior to the Year One thousand eight hundred and eight shall in any Manner affect the first and fourth Clauses in the Ninth Section of the first Article; and that no State, without its Consent, shall be deprived of its equal Suffrage in the Senate.

ORIGINS

Amendments. What would have happened if the Framers had not provided some way to amend the Constitution? Later generations might have been tempted to abandon the Constitution, and start all over again. Some delegates, like Charles Pinckney of South Carolina, thought their work was nearly perfect. They could imagine only that later generations would try to "undo" their good work. They opposed any scheme for amendments.

But most delegates saw that the Constitution was more likely to survive if it included some way of amendment to suit changing needs. Yet they

believed it should not be too easy to amend the Constitution. Otherwise, future generations would not respect the Constitution nor exert the effort needed to make it work. People then might be tempted to treat the Constitution like an ordinary law, easily changed by vote of Congress. Instead, the Framers hoped they were shaping a true "constitution"–the enduring foundation for preserving, making, and changing laws. They dared not leave it only to Congress to decide when an amendment was needed, or to block an amendment. So they provided that (even if two-thirds of Congress did not *propose* an amendment) two-thirds of the states could bring about the calling of a national convention to *propose* amendments. An amendment could then be *adopted* either by three-fourths of the state legislatures or by three-fourths of the state conventions called for that purpose.

To secure majority agreement to this amending clause, still other compromises were required. One (to reassure the slave states) provided that no amendment affecting the slave trade could be made before 1808. Another (to reassure the small states) provided that without its own consent no state could be deprived of its equal representation in the Senate.

AFTERLIFE

The Constitution has been amended 26 times, but so far there has never been a national convention to suggest amendments. And only in the case of the 21st Amendment has ratification been done by state conventions.

The Constitution has also been changed by interpretations made by the Supreme Court. The court has been called "a continuing constitutional convention." Its decisions on the commerce clause (above, page 563) have allowed the federal government far-reaching regulatory powers. Its decision in *Brown* v. *Board of Education* (1954) outlawed racial segregation in the classroom [17:3]. In other civil rights cases the Court has given the federal government increasing powers to enforce the equality of rights of all citizens. In *Gideon* v. *Wainwright* (1963) and other cases the Court has enlarged federal protection of the rights of the criminally accused—to have a lawyer, to be informed of their rights, and to be free from "cruel and unusual punishment."

ARTICLE VI

All Debts contracted and Engagements entered into, before the Adoption of this Constitution, shall be as valid against the United States under this Constitution, as under the Confederation.

This Constitution, and the Laws of the United States which shall be made in • Pursuance thereof; and all Treaties made, or which shall be made, under the Authority of the United States, shall be the supreme Law of the Land; and the Judges in every State shall be bound thereby, any Thing in the Constitution or Laws of any State to the Contrary notwithstanding.

The Senators and Representatives before mentioned, and the Members of the several State Legislatures, and all executive and judicial Officers, both of the United States and of the several States, shall be bound by Oath or affirmation, to support this Constitution; but no religious Test shall ever be required as a Qualification to any Office or public Trust under the United States.

ORIGINS

The Supremacy Clause. Under the Articles of Confederation, the decisions of the Congress of the Confederation were supposed to have the force of "law." But they really had no force at all. Since there was no federal system of courts, all decisions were left to the state courts. And when a rule of the Confederation Congress conflicted with a state law, the state courts ignored the Confederation's rule and simply enforced their own state law. Now this was changed. Under the Constitution, there would be a national court system. But suppose there was a conflict between a state law and a law passed by the new Congress. Which law should prevail? And who decided?

This was one of the most difficult problems facing the delegates to the Constitutional Convention. Some, including James Madison, wanted a scheme which would give the Congress power to veto conflicting state laws. Naturally the small states objected.

Luckily the proposed New Jersey Plan, speaking for the small states, contained a "supremacy clause" which saved the day. This clause declared that the Constitution, the acts of Congress, and treaties should be the supreme law of all the states. They would be state law just as much as if they had been adopted separately by the state legislatures. When this clause was proposed to the Convention, everybody agreed to it. Then (as we see in Article VI) the Constitution of the United States, the laws of the new federal Congress, and treaties made by the United States would be "the supreme law of the Land." In the future the Constitution and the laws of the new nation would be enforced, not only by a system of national courts (still to be created), but by the systems of state courts that had been at work since early colonial days. "And the Judges in every State shall be bound thereby, any Thing in the Constitution or Laws of any State to the Contrary notwithstanding."

The Virginia delegation proposed still another way (described here in Article VI) to enforce nationwide respect for the Constitution and laws of the new nation. Simply require all members of state legislatures and all executive and judicial officers of all the *states* (in addition to all officers of the United States) to take an oath or affirmation "to support this Constitution." Then all state officials would be solemnly reminded (under penalty of the criminal laws of perjury) that it was their duty to keep the laws of the new nation supreme! Incidentally the wise Framers took this occasion to make it plain that no official had to believe in God or in any particular religion to make his oath or affirmation binding. They forever banned any "religious Test" for "any Office or public Trust under the United States."

AFTERLIFE

On the repayment of the debt of the Confederation, see [int.].

● This clause became the basis for the American constitutional system. But the question of who was to decide the powers of the federal government was hotly debated (see [int.]). The Civil War was the final major battle over the question of the supremacy of the federal government.

ARTICLE VII

The Ratification of the Conventions of nine States, shall be sufficient for the Establishment of this Constitution between the States so ratifying the Same.

Done in Convention by the Unanimous Consent of the States present the Seventeenth Day of September in the Year of our Lord one thousand seven hundred and Eighty seven and of the Independence of the United States of America the Twelfth In witness whereof We have hereunto subscribed our Names,

Go. Washington—*Presidt and deputy from Virginia*

NEW HAMPSHIRE
John Langdon
Nicholas Gilman

MASSACHUSETTS
Nathaniel Gorham
Rufus King

CONNECTICUT
Wm. Saml. Johnson
Roger Sherman

SOUTH CAROLINA
J. Rutledge
Charles Cotesworth Pinckney
Charles Pinckney
Pierce Butler

GEORGIA
William Few
Abr Baldwin

VIRGINIA
John Blair—
James Madison Jr.

NORTH CAROLINA
Wm. Blount
Richd. Dobbs Spraight
Hu Williamson

PENNSYLVANIA
B Franklin
Thomas Mifflin
Robt Morris
Geo. Clymer
Thos. FitzSimons
Jared Ingersoll
James Wilson
Gouv Morris

NEW YORK
Alexander Hamilton

NEW JERSEY
Wil: Livingston
David Brearley.
Wm. Paterson.
Jona: Dayton

DELAWARE
Geo: Read
Gunning Bedford jun
John Dickinson
Richard Bassett
Jaco: Broom

MARYLAND
James McHenry
Dan of St Thos. Jenifer
Danl. Carroll

Note: This text of the Constitution of the United States is taken from the "literal print" of the document as reproduced in *The Constitution of the United States: Analysis and Interpretation* (Washington, D.C.: U.S. Government Printing Office, 1964). The original manuscript can be seen in the National Archives, Washington, D.C.

ORIGINS

Ratification. Down to the very last words of the Constitution, the delegates to the Convention showed their boldness and their willingness to learn from the unhappy recent experience of Articles of Confederation. The Constitutional Convention had been called merely to revise the Articles of Confederation. Under the Articles, no such revision could be made except by unanimous approval of all the state legislatures. Some legalistic delegates believed that the only proper procedure was to send the painfully drawn draft of the new Constitution to the Congress of the Confederation. They could then "recommend" that it be submitted to a convention in each of the states. But how long would be required for this cumbersome procedure?

At the very last minute, just as they were about to adjourn, the delegates took a bolder course. They would submit their work directly and at once to state conventions especially called for the purpose. Then as soon as any *nine* states had adopted the new Constitution it would go into force between them. A few laggards would not be allowed to sabotage the work. The remaining hold-out states would see themselves left in the cold. This final article, like the Preamble with which the Constitution began, showed that the new government owed its powers not to any older document, but directly to "the People of the United States."

AFTERLIFE

For the battle over ratifications, see [int.].

In Convention Monday, September 17th 1787.

Present The States of New Hampshire, Massachusetts, Connecticut, Mr. Hamilton from New York, New Jersey, Pennsylvania, Delaware, Maryland, Virginia, North Carolina, South Carolina and Georgia.

Resolved,

That the preceeding Constitution be laid before the United States in Congress assembled, and that it is the Opinion of this Convention, that it should afterwards be submitted to a Convention of Delegates, chosen in each State by the People thereof, under the Recommendation of its Legislature, for their Assent and Ratification; and that each Convention assenting to, and ratifying the Same, should give Notice thereof to the United States in Congress assembled. Resolved, That it is the Opinion of this Convention, that as soon as the Conventions of nine States shall have ratified this Constitution, the United States in Congress assembled should fix a Day on which Electors should be appointed by the States which shall have ratified the same, and a Day on which the Electors should assemble to vote for the President, and the Time and Place for commencing Proceedings under this Constitution. That after such Publication the Electors should be appointed, and the Senators and Representatives elected: That the Electors should meet on the Day fixed for the Election of the President, and should transmit their Votes certified, signed, sealed and directed, as the Constitution requires, to the Secretary of the United States in Congress assembled, that the Senators and Representatives should convene at the Time and Place assigned; that the Senators should appoint a President of the Senate, for the sole Purpose of receiving, opening and counting the Votes for President; and, that after he shall be chosen, the Congress, together with the President, should, without Delay, proceed to execute this Constitution.

By the Unanimous Order of the Convention

W. Jackson *Secretary.*

Go. Washington—*Presid.[t]*

AMENDMENT [I.]

Congress shall make no law respecting an establishment of religion, or prohibiting the free exercise thereof; or abridging the freedom of speech, or of the press; or the right of the people peaceably to assemble, and to petition the Government for a redress of grievances.

ORIGINS

The objections to the Constitution raised during the fight over ratification became the first ten amendments, or Bill of Rights [5:5, 6:2]. They limit the powers of the federal government and were born from English and colonial experience with despotic government. Submitted to the states in 1789, ratified in 1791.

The 1st Amendment was intended to insure freedom of religion, speech, press, assembly, and petition in the nation as a whole.

THE CONSTITUTION OF THE UNITED STATES   843

AFTERLIFE

The courts have always had difficulty deciding what limits can be placed on freedom of speech and the press. They have often used a formula first stated by the Supreme Court in *Schenk* v. *United States* (1919). In that case the Court concluded that when there was "a clear and present danger" that words will bring about "substantive evils," speech could be limited. But it is difficult to tell what is a "clear and present danger." And even this doctrine has not been uniformly applied, and speech and the press have sometimes been allowed to be limited for other reasons.

For the Court's application of the provision against the establishment of religion on the question of prayer and Bible reading in schools, see [21:1], page 449.

AMENDMENT [II.]

A well regulated Militia, being necessary to the security of a free State, the right of the people to keep and bear Arms, shall not be infringed.

AMENDMENT [III.]

No Soldier shall, in time of peace be quartered in any house, without the consent of the Owner, nor in time of war, but in a matter to be prescribed by law.

AMENDMENT [IV.]

The right of the people to be secure in their persons, houses, papers, and effects, against unreasonable searches and seizures, shall not be violated, and no Warrants shall issue, but upon probable cause, supported by Oath or affirmation, and particularly describing the place to be searched, and the persons or things to be seized.

ORIGINS

The right to keep and bear arms was insured by the 2nd Amendment.

After the experience with the British before the Revolution [int.], the 3rd Amendment restricted the government's right to quarter soldiers in private homes.

To prevent searches and arrests without reason by a tyrannical government the 4th Amendment was ratified.

AMENDMENT [V.]

No person shall be held to answer for a capital, or otherwise infamous crime, unless on a presentment or indictment of a Grand Jury, except in cases arising in the land or naval forces, or in the Militia, when in actual service in time of War or public danger; nor shall any person be subject for the same offence to be twice put in jeopardy of life or limb; nor shall be compelled in any criminal case to be a witness against himself, nor be deprived of life, liberty, or property, without due process of law; nor shall private property be taken for public use, without just compensation.

The 5th Amendment was intended to give broad protection to accused persons and to protect the owners of private property from having it taken by the government without the payment of a fair price.

AFTERLIFE

The 5th Amendment is a basic bulwark protecting the rights of individuals in criminal cases. Its pro-vision that no person "shall be compelled in any criminal case to be a witness against himself" has often been used by individuals who do not wish to testify in court or before congressional investigating committees. This is often referred to as "taking the Fifth Amendment." See also the 14th Amendment below.

AMENDMENT [VI.]

In all criminal prosecutions, the accused shall enjoy the right to a speedy and public trial, by an impartial jury of the State and district wherein the crime shall have been committed, which district shall have been previously ascertained by law, and to be informed of the nature and cause of the accusation; to be confronted with the witnesses against him; to have compulsory process for obtaining witnesses in his favor, and to have the Assistance of Counsel for his defence.

ORIGINS

The 6th Amendment attempted to insure that a defendant in a criminal case would receive a fair trial.

AMENDMENT [VII.]

In Suits at common law, where the value in controversy shall exceed twenty dollars, the right of trial by jury shall be preserved, and no fact tried by a jury shall be otherwise re-examined in any Court of the United States, than according to the rules of the common law.

AMENDMENT [VIII.]

Excessive bail shall not be required, nor excessive fines imposed, nor cruel and unusual punishments inflicted.

ORIGINS

The Constitution (Art III, sec. 2, par. 3) guarantees trial by jury in criminal cases. The 7th Amendment extends that guarantee to civil cases.

The 8th Amendment means that the courts should not ask for unreasonable amounts of bail (money paid to secure the release of an arrested person) or fines. The amendment also bars punishments that are cruel and unusual.

In 1972 in *Furman* v. *Georgia* the Supreme Court ruled that the death penalty was unconstitutional in Georgia because it was applied inconsistently— blacks were far more often executed than whites who had committed similar crimes. The Court did not, however, declare that the death penalty itself was necessarily a "cruel and unusual punishment."

AMENDMENT [IX.]

The enumeration in the Constitution, of certain rights, shall not be construed to deny or disparage others retained by the people.

AMENDMENT [X.]

The powers not delegated to the United States by the Constitution, nor prohibited by it to the States, are reserved to the States respectively, or to the people.

ORIGINS

In order to make it clear that the rights listed in the Constitution and its amendments were not the only rights of the people, the 9th Amendment was adopted.

The 10th Amendment made it clear that powers not given to the federal government in the Constitution remained with the states or with the people.

AMENDMENT [XI.]

The Judicial power of the United States shall not be construed to extend to any suit in law or equity, commenced or prosecuted against one of the United States by Citizens of another State, or by Citizens or Subjects of any Foreign State.

ORIGINS

In the case of *Chisholm* v. *Georgia* (1793) the Supreme Court ruled that a state did not have the right to protect itself from being sued by saying that it was a sovereign state and immune from suits by citizens of other states. To give states that right—known as sovereign immunity—this amendment was passed. Submitted to the states in 1794, ratified in 1798.

AMENDMENT [XII.]

The Electors shall meet in their respective states and vote by ballot for President and Vice-President, one of whom, at least, shall not be an inhabitant of the same state with themselves; they shall name in their ballots the person voted for as President, and in distinct ballots the person voted for as Vice-President, and they shall make distinct lists of all persons voted for as President, and of all persons voted for as Vice-President, and of the number of votes for each, which lists they

---

shall sign and certify, and transmit sealed to the seat of the government of the United States, directed to the President of the Senate;—The President of the Senate shall, in the presence of the Senate and House of Representatives, open all the certificates and the votes shall then be counted;—The person having the greatest number of votes for President, shall be the President, if such number be a majority of the whole number of Electors appointed; and if no person have such majority, then from the persons having the highest numbers not exceeding three on the list of those voted for as President, the House of Representatives shall choose immediately, by ballot, the President. But in choosing the President, the votes shall be taken by states, the representation from each state having one vote; a quorum for this purpose shall consist of a member or members from two-thirds of the states, and a majority of all the states shall be necessary to a choice. And if the House of Representatives shall not choose a President whenever the right of choice shall devolve upon them, before the fourth day of March next following, then the Vice-President shall act as President, as in the case of the death or other constitutional disability of the President—The person having the greatest number of votes as Vice-President, shall be the Vice-President, if such number be a majority of the whole number of Electors appointed, and if no person have a majority, then from the two highest numbers on the list, the Senate shall choose the Vice-President; a quorum for the purpose shall consist of two-thirds of the whole number of Senators, and a majority of the whole number shall be necessary to a choice. But no person constitutionally ineligible to the office of President shall be eligible to that of Vice-President of the United States.

ORIGINS

The 12th Amendment was brought about by the election of 1800, when the Democratic-Republicans' presidential candidate Jefferson and vice-presidential candidate Burr each received the same number of electoral votes. To avoid any chance of such an event occurring again, electors were now to vote for President on one ballot and for Vice-President on another [int.]. For elections in the House and disputed returns see [int.] and [2:4], pages 70-72. Submitted to the states in 1803, ratified in 1804.

AMENDMENT [XIII.]

Section 1. Neither slavery nor involuntary servitude, except as a punishment for crime whereof the party shall have been duly convicted, shall exist within the United States, or any place subject to their jurisdiction.

Section 2. Congress shall have power to enforce this article by appropriate legislation.

ORIGINS

The 13th, 14th, and 15th amendments were produced by the Civil War and its aftermath. See [2:2], pages 60 and 63, and [2:3], page 66.

The 13th Amendment abolished slavery, [1:3]. Submitted to the states in 1865, ratified in 1865.

AMENDMENT [XIV.]

Section 1. All persons born or naturalized in the United States and subject to the jurisdiction thereof, are citizens of the United States and of the State wherein they reside. No State shall make or enforce any law which shall abridge the privileges or immunities of citizens of the United States; or shall any State deprive any person of life, liberty, or property, without due process of law; nor deny to any person within its jurisdiction the equal protection of the laws.

ORIGINS

In the *Dred Scott* case (1857), Chief Justice Taney had stated that blacks were not citizens when the Constitution was adopted and were not covered by its provisions [int.]. By the 14th Amendment blacks were made citizens, and the privileges and immunities of citizens of the United States were extended to citizens of the states.

AFTERLIFE

The 14th Amendment is the most important amendment added to the Constitution since the Bill of Rights. The key part is Section 1 which contains the potent, but undefined phrases, "due process of law" and "equal protection of the laws."

Often in the 19th and early 20th centuries the Court used the amendment to protect corporations (which it defined as "persons") from state regulation, but in *Munn* v. *Illinois* (1877) and other later decisions the right of states and the federal government to regulate wage rates, hours, and other terms of employment was recognized [6:3].

Over time the amemdment has been increasingly interpreted to extend the protection of the Bill of Rights to citizens from actions by the states as well as against the federal government. Although in *Plessy* v. *Ferguson* (1896) [17:3] the Court upheld the "separate but equal" doctrine which legalized racial segregation, that was completely overturned in the series of decisions that culminated in *Brown* v. *Board of Education* (1954) [17:3]. In such cases as *Gideon* v. *Wainwright* (1963), *Escobedo* v. *Illinois* (1964), and *Miranda* v. *Arizona* (1966) [21:7] the Court greatly enlarged the rights of accused persons in state courts.

[XIV] **Section 2.** Representatives shall be apportioned among the several States according to their respective numbers, counting the whole number of persons in each State, excluding Indians not taxed. But when the right to vote at any election for the choice of electors for President and Vice President of the United States, Representatives in Congress, the Executive and Judicial officers of a State, or the members of the Legislature thereof, is denied to any of the male inhabitants of such State, being twenty-one years of age, and citizens of the United States, or in any way abridged, except for participation in rebellion, or other crime, the basis of representation therein shall be reduced in the proportion which the number of such male citizens shall bear to the whole number of male citizens twenty-one years of age in such State.

ORIGINS

The fear that southern states would keep blacks from voting prompted this provision. It provides that a state's representation in Congress may be cut if it denies the right to vote to any group of adult male citizens.

[XIV] **Section 3.** No person shall be a Senator or Representative in Congress, or elector of President and Vice President, or hold any office, civil or military, under the United States, or under any State, who, having previously taken an oath, as a member of Congress, or as an officer of the United States, or as a member of any State legislature, or as an executive or judicial officer of any State, to support the Constitution of the United States, shall have engaged in insurrection or rebellion against the same, or given aid or comfort to the enemies thereof. But Congress may by a vote of two-thirds of each House, remove such disability.

[XIV] ● **Section 4.** The validity of the public debt of the United States, authorized by law, including debts incurred for payment of pensions and bounties for services in suppressing insurrection or rebellion, shall not be questioned. But neither the United States nor any State shall assume or pay any debt or obligation incurred in aid of insurrection or rebellion against the United States, or any claim for the loss or emancipation of any slave; but all such debts, obligations and claims shall be held illegal and void.

[XIV] **Section 5.** The Congress shall have power to enforce, by appropriate legislation, the provisions of this article.

ORIGINS

This clause barred from federal office any former federal or state official who had served the Confederacy in the Civil War—unless Congress removed the ban by a two-thirds vote of each house.
● This section legalized the federal Civil War debt and voided all debts incurred by the Confederate states.

See p. 63 for further discussion of the origin of the 14th Amendment. Submitted to the states in 1866, ratified in 1868.

AMENDMENT [XV.]

Section 1. The right of citizens of the United States to vote shall not be denied or abridged by the United States or by any State on account of race, color, or previous condition of servitude.

Section 2. The Congress shall have power to enforce this article by appropriate legislation.

ORIGINS

The 15th Amendment attempted to insure that blacks would have the vote. Submitted to the states in 1869, ratified in 1870.

AFTERLIFE

The 15th Amendment did not, as it turned out, prevent blacks from being kept from the polls in the South. In the beginning, the Ku Klux Klan and other groups harassed and intimidated them [2:3]. Then a variety of legal tricks was used to deprive them of the vote [13:2]. It has needed strong federal activity to insure their right to vote (see [17:3, 19:4, 21:1] and especially [21:1] on the Voting Rights Act).

AMENDMENT [XVI.]

The Congress shall have power to lay and collect taxes on incomes, from whatever source derived, without apportionment among the several States, and without regard to any census or enumeration.

ORIGINS

In *Pollock* v. *Farmers' Loan and Trust Co.* (1895), the Supreme Court declared that an income tax was unconstitutional. As a result the 16th Amendment was passed [18:3]. Submitted to the states in 1909, ratified in 1913.

AMENDMENT [XVII.]

The Senate of the United States shall be composed of two Senators from each State, elected by the people thereof, for six years; and each Senator shall have one vote. The electors in each State shall have the qualifications requisite for electors of the most numerous branch of the State legislatures.

When vacancies happen in the representation of any State in the Senate, the executive authority of such State shall issue writs of election to fill such vacancies: *Provided,* That the legislature of any State may empower the executive thereof to make temporary appointments until the people fill the vacancies by election as the legislature may direct.

This amendment shall not be so construed as to affect the election or term of any Senator chosen before it becomes valid as part of the Constitution.

ORIGINS

The Framers of the Constitution distrusted "the people" in the mass and tried to restrict their role to electing only the representatives. The dominance of the electoral college by political parties soon gave the people control of presidential elections. But the Senate continued to be elected by the state legislatures, and since wealthy men were often able to use their cash to buy their elections, the Senate became a "rich man's club." This amendment gave the election of senators to the people [20:2]. Submitted to the states in 1912, ratified in 1913.

AMENDMENT [XVIII.]

Section 1. After one year from the ratification of this article the manufacture, sale, or transportation of intoxicating liquors within, the importation thereof into, or the exportation thereof from the United States and all territory subject to the jurisdiction thereof for beverage purposes is hereby prohibited.

[*XVIII*] **Sec. 2.** The Congress and the several States shall have concurrent power to enforce this article by appropriate legislation.

Sec. 3. This article shall be inoperative unless it shall have been ratified as an amendment to the Constitution by the legislatures of the several States, as provided in the Constitution, within seven years from the date of the submission hereof to the States by the Congress.

ORIGINS

In the moral fervor of World War I, national prohibition was enacted [10:1]. Submitted to the states in 1917, ratified in 1919.

AFTERLIFE

The "noble experiment" of Prohibition turned out to be a disaster. Millions of Americans became lawbreakers, and criminals took over the liquor trade [10:1].

AMENDMENT [XIX.]

The right of citizens of the United States to vote shall not be denied or abridged by the United States or by any State on account of sex.
Congress shall have power to enforce this article by appropriate legislation.

ORIGINS

After World War I, during which the work of women in the war effort had been important and conspicuous, women's suffrage was enacted [10:1]. Submitted to the states in 1919, ratified in 1920.

AFTERLIFE

The suffragists, who worked for the right to vote, had hoped that when women could go to the polls they would improve their chances to be treated equally. But women often failed to vote and did not vote as a bloc [13:3].

AMENDMENT [XX.]

Section 1. The terms of the President and Vice President shall end at noon on the 20th day of January, and the terms of Senators and Representatives at noon on the 3d day of January, of the years in which such terms would have ended if this article had not been ratified; and the terms of their successors shall then begin.

Sec. 2. The Congress shall assemble at least once in every year, and such meeting shall begin at noon on the 3d day of January, unless they shall by law appoint a different day.

The "Lame Duck" Amendment. A lame duck is an official who continues to serve to the end of his term even though he has not been reelected. Prior to this amendment a President leaving office was a "lame duck" for four months, since he left office on March 4. By pushing back the inauguration to January 20, the amendment shortened the time between when a President was elected (in early November) and when he took office. Submitted to the states in 1932, ratified in 1933.

[XX] **Sec. 3.** If, at the time fixed for the beginning of the term of the President, the President elect shall have died, the Vice President elect shall become President. If a President shall not have been chosen before the time fixed for the beginning of his term, or if the President elect shall have failed to qualify, then the Vice President elect shall act as President until a President shall have qualified; and the Congress may by law provide for the case wherein neither a President elect nor a Vice President elect shall have qualified, declaring who shall then act as President, or the manner in which one who is to act shall be selected, and such person shall act accordingly until a President or Vice President shall have qualified.

Sec. 4. The Congress may by law provide for the case of the death of any of the persons from whom the House of Representatives may choose a President whenever the right of choice shall have devolved upon them, and for the case of the death of any of the persons from whom the Senate may choose a Vice President whenever the right of choice shall have devolved upon them.

Sec. 5. Sections 1 and 2 shall take effect on the 15th day of October following the ratification of this article.

Sec. 6. This article shall be inoperative unless it shall have been ratified as an amendment to the Constitution by the legislatures of three-fourths of the several States within seven years from the date of its submission.

AMENDMENT [*XXI.*]

Section 1. The eighteenth article of amendment to the Constitution of the United States is hereby repealed.

Sec. 2. The transportation or importation into any State, Territory or possession of the United States for delivery or use therein of intoxicating liquors, in violation of the laws thereof, is hereby prohibited.

Sec. 3. This article shall be inoperative unless it shall have been ratified as an amendment to the Constitution by conventions in the several States, as provided in the Constitution, within seven years from the date of the submission hereof to the States by the Congress.

Disappointment over Prohibition, disgust at the activities of gangsters, and fear that disrespect for this one law would breed disrespect for all laws brought about the repeal of Prohibition in 1933 [24:1]. Submitted to the states in 1933, ratified in 1933.

AMENDMENT [XXII.]

[XXII]
Sec. 1

Section 1. No person shall be elected to the office of the President more than twice, and no person who has held the office of President, or acted as President, for more than two years of a term to which some other person was elected President shall be elected to the office of the President more than once. But this Article shall not apply to any person holding the office of President when this Article was proposed by the Congress, and shall not prevent any person who may be holding the office of President, or acting as President, during the term within which this Article becomes operative from holding the office of President or acting as President during the remainder of such term.

[XXII]

Sec. 2. This Article shall be inoperative unless it shall have been ratified as an amendment to the Constitution by the legislatures of three-fourths of the several States within seven years from the date of its submission to the States by the Congress.

ORIGINS

In 1947 for the first time in 14 years, the Republicans controlled both houses of Congress. Since President Washington there had been an unwritten tradition limiting a President to two terms. To strike at the Democrats and at Franklin D. Roosevelt, who had been elected four times, the Republicans proposed and supported this amendment making the tradition into law [16:2]. Submitted to the states in 1947, ratified in 1951.

AMENDMENT [XXIII.]

Section 1. The District constituting the seat of Government of the United States shall appoint in such manner as the Congress may direct:

A number of electors of President and Vice President equal to the whole number of Senators and Representatives in Congress to which the District would be entitled if it were a State, but in no event more than the least populous State; they shall be in addition to those appointed by the States, but they shall be considered, for the purposes of the election of President and Vice President, to be electors appointed by a State; and they shall meet in the District and perform such duties as provided by the twelfth article of amendment.

Sec. 2. The Congress shall have power to enforce this article by appropriate legislation.

ORIGINS

Since the District of Columbia was not a state, its residents had no vote in presidential elections. This amendment gave them the right to vote. Submitted to the states in 1960, ratified in 1961.

AFTERLIFE

Numerous proposals have been made for an amendment to give the District of Columbia representation in the House and in the Senate, but none has been adopted.

AMENDMENT [*XXIV.*]

Section 1. The right of citizens of the United States to vote in any primary or other election for President or Vice President, for electors for President or Vice President, or for Senator or Representative in Congress, shall not be denied or abridged by the United States or any State by reason of failure to pay any poll tax or other tax.

Section 2. The Congress shall have power to enforce this article by appropriate legislation.

ORIGINS

The "Anti-poll tax" Amendment. The poll tax was a tax everyone had to pay before he or she could vote [13:2, 19:4]. Some southern states used a poll tax as a way to prevent blacks from voting. Submitted to the states in 1962, ratified in 1964.

AFTERLIFE

As a result of this amendment and of the civil rights laws, black registration and voting increased rapidly in the 1960s [20:3]. Blacks elected mayors in many southern cities. Southern political candidates increasingly turned away from white supremacy and tried to win the votes of their black fellow citizens.

AMENDMENT [*XXV.*]

Section 1. In case of the removal of the President from office or of his death or resignation, the Vice-President shall become President.

Section 2. Whenever there is a vacancy in the office of the Vice-President, the President shall nominate a Vice-President who shall take office upon confirmation by a majority vote of both houses of Congress.

Section 3. Whenever the President transmits to the President pro tempore of the Senate and the Speaker of the House of Representatives his written declaration that he is unable to discharge the powers and duties of his office, and until he transmits to them a written declaration to the contrary, such powers and duties shall be discharged by the Vice-President as Acting President.

Section 4. Whenever the Vice-President and a majority of either the principal officers of the executive departments or of such other body as Congress may by law provide, transmit to the President pro tempore of the Senate and the Speaker of the House of Representatives their written declaration that the President is unable to discharge the powers and duties of his office, the Vice-President shall immediately assume the powers and duties of the office as Acting President.

Thereafter, when the President transmits to the President pro tempore of the Senate and the Speaker of the House of Representatives his written declaration that no inability exists, he shall resume the powers and duties of his office unless the Vice-President and a majority of either the principal officers of the executive department or of such other body as Congress may by law provide, transmit within four days to the President pro tempore of the Senate and the Speaker of the House of Representatives their written declaration that the President is unable to discharge the powers and duties of his office. Thereupon Congress shall decide the issue, assembling within forty-eight hours for that purpose if not in session. If the Congress, within twenty-one days after receipt of the latter written declaration, or, if Congress is not in session, within twenty-one days after Congress is required to assemble, determines by two-thirds vote of both houses that the President is unable to discharge the powers and duties of his office, the Vice-President shall continue to discharge the same as Acting President; otherwise, the President shall resume the powers and duties of his office.

ORIGINS

Americans remembered the problems caused by the incapacity of President Wilson and the deaths in office of eight Presidents and six Vice-Presidents.

The serious illnesses of President Eisenhower were the immediate reason for this amendment. It aimed to avoid a gap in the functioning of the Presidency if the elected President himself was not able to do his job. It also aimed to avoid in the future a situation (like that in the last months of President Wilson) when the President's wife or somebody else close to him might take over his decisions without legal authority. Submitted to the states in 1965, ratified in 1967.

AFTERLIFE

When Vice-President Agnew resigned in 1973, President Nixon nominated Gerald R. Ford to take his place [21:3]. After Ford became President, Nelson Rockefeller was made Vice-President by the procedure described in this amendment [23:1].

AMENDMENT [XXVI.]

Section 1. The right of citizens of the United States, who are 18 years of age or older, to vote shall not be denied or abridged by the United States or any State on account of age.

Section 2. The Congress shall have the power to enforce this article by appropriate legislation.

ORIGINS

During the war in Vietnam, many Americans began to feel that those who were old enough to be drafted and sent off to fight were old enough to vote. Submitted to the states in 1971, ratified in 1971.

AFTERLIFE

As with the 19th Amendment, which gave women the right to vote, the 26th Amendment had no far-reaching effects. Many citizens between 18 and 21 failed to go to the polls to vote.

Glossary

Abolitionist a person seeking the legal end of slavery in the United States (p. 240)

Abstract Expressionism style of painting dominant from the late 1940s to the early 1960s, in which no attempt was made to reflect objects realistically, and feeling was expressed through the use of color (p. 652)

administration one President's term in office; the officials who do the government's business during the term of a President (p.131)

admiralty courts law or courts dealing with cases involving shipping and navigation (p. 58)

advice and consent the power given the United States Senate by the Constitution to review and approve TREATIES and certain major appointments made by the President (p. 120)

affirmative action steps taken to increase the representation of women and minorities, especially in jobs and higher education, often by the use of timetables or QUOTAS (p. 724)

alien a citizen of a foreign country (p. 133)

Allies in World War I and World War II, the nations fighting against Germany and its associates, including the United States and Great Britain (p. 453)

ambassador a high-ranking diplomatic official representing his country in another country (p. 147)

amendment a change in or addition to a legal document, motion, bylaw, law, or constitution (p. 109)

amnesty a government pardon for a group of offenders (p. 308)

anarchy a complete absence of government; lawlessness, disorder, and confusion brought about by the absence of government (p. 104)

Anglo-Saxons the English people, or people of English descent, so called because the Angles, the Saxons, and the Jutes (Germanic tribes) settled in England in the fifth and sixth centuries A.D. (p. 379)

annex to attach new TERRITORY to an existing area, such as a city or a country (p. 249)

antebellum before a war; in American history, used to describe the period before the Civil War (p. 169)

antiballistic missile (ABM) a missile capable of destroying BALLISTIC MISSILES in flight (p. 705)

anti-Semitism prejudice against Jews (p. 529)

antitrust opposed to TRUSTS, MONOPOLIES, price-fixing, and other agreements that restrain trade (p. 357)

Appalachia the Appalachian mountain area, especially the region stretching from Pennsylvania to Alabama and Georgia (p. 69)

appeasement the policy of giving in to an aggressor nation in the hope that this will satisfy it and encourage it to stop being aggressive (p. 556)

arbitration the hearing and settling of a dispute by a third person who is not involved in the disagreement (p. 416)

aristocracy a privileged class of persons of high rank, such as the nobility; rule by such a class (p. 116)

armistice a temporary pause, agreed to by both sides, in a war or battle (p. 464)

arsenal a government building or buildings where arms and other war supplies are manufactured or stored; also, the war supplies themselves (p. 568)

ashcan school a group of American artists of the early twentieth century whose work realistically portrayed scenes from everyday city life (p. 337)

assembly line a moving workbench–a procedure in which automobiles or other items being manufactured move past workers and machines and are assembled piece by piece until completed (p. 495)

Atlantic Charter a joint declaration issued by President Franklin D. Roosevelt and British Prime Minister Winston Churchill on August 14, 1941, stating their common aims for the years after World War II: a peaceful world where all people would have the right of self-determination and adequate food and shelter (p. 564)

Atlantic Pact see NATO (p. 609)

automation the automatic performance by a machine of a manufacturing process or other task (p. 649)

Baby boom the rapid growth in the U.S. population between about 1945 and 1960 (p. 640)

balance of power a condition in which two countries or groups of countries are roughly equal in power, and neither can become dominant (p. 448)

balance of trade the relationship between the value of a nation's EXPORTS and the value of its IMPORTS in a given year. If imports are greater than exports, the balance is *negative*. If exports are greater than imports, the balance is *positive*. (p. 34)

balanced budget a BUDGET in which income and expenses are equal (p. 522)

ballistic missile   a rocket-powered object, often carrying a nuclear warhead, which is shot into the air and hits its ground target after a free fall (p. 668)

bank holiday   a day or several days when banks are closed and depositors cannot withdraw money; especially March 6 to March 10, 1933, when President Franklin D. Roosevelt temporarily closed all the nation's banks (p. 521)

belligerents   nations fighting a war, usually after a declaration of war (p. 555)

Bessemer converter   a furnace used for changing iron into steel (p. 351)

bilingual   able to speak two languages (p. 744)

bill of attainder   a legislative act pronouncing an individual guilty of a crime, usually TREASON, without a trial; specifically prohibited by Article I, sections 9 and 10 of the U.S. CONSTITUTION (p. 831)

Bill of Rights   the first ten AMENDMENTS to the U.S. CONSTITUTION (p. 111)

bipartisan   supported by two parties; in the United States, supported by both the DEMOCRATIC PARTY and the REPUBLICAN PARTY (p. 630)

Black Codes   laws passed, especially by the Southern states after the Civil War, to control the actions and limit the rights of blacks (p. 310)

Black Power   a movement among some blacks in the United States in the late 1960s to achieve social, political, and economic equality by rejecting integration and white assistance and attempting to unite all blacks in pursuit of these goals (p. 687)

blitzkrieg   a sudden invasion or "lightning war," first practiced by the Germans in World War II (p. 663)

bloody shirt   a method of campaigning used by Republicans after the Civil War, when they "waved the bloody shirt" to remind the voters that they had fought the war, freed the slaves, and saved the Union (p. 316)

Bolshevik   a member of the group within the Social Democratic party in Russia that favored seizing power by force (and ultimately did so) in the revolution of 1917; in the United States, an extreme left-wing radical (p. 448)

boycott   an organized refusal to buy or use a product, or to deal with a company or group of companies, as a protest or as a means of forcing them to take some action (p. 74)

broad construction   an interpretation of the U.S. CONSTITUTION that holds that government has the right to do everything necessary and proper to carry out any of the powers granted to it in the Constitution; compare STRICT CONSTRUCTION (p. 122)

budget   a detailed prediction of estimated income and expenses for a given period (p. 705)

bureaucracy   all the men and women, taken as a group, who run the agencies that do the everyday business of a government (p. 700)

Cabinet   the group of advisers to the President that is made up of the heads of the executive departments of the government (State, Defense, Treasury, etc.) as well as certain other important government officials (p. 521)

caravel   a fast, maneuverable three-masted sailing ship with a rounded hull, used by Spanish and Portuguese explorers in the late 1400s and early 1500s (p. 12)

carpetbaggers   Northerners who went South to acquire wealth or power during RECONSTRUCTION, after the Civil War. They were said to have arrived with no more belongings than they could carry in a carpetbag, an old-fashioned suitcase made of carpeting. The term is sometimes applied to any people who come from outside to interfere in local affairs. (p. 317)

casualties   in a war or battle, combatants who are killed, wounded, captured, missing in action, or in any way rendered unable to fight (p. 692)

caucus   a meeting of the members of a political party or a segment of that party, or of like-minded politicians, to try to reach decisions on matters of concern (p. 183)

census   an official counting of a population (p. 118)

charter   a legal document issued by a government to define the purposes and privileges of a CORPORATION (p. 37)

Chicano   an American of Mexican origin or descent (p. 732)

Christendom   collectively, those who believe in Jesus as the Christ (p. 16)

citizen   a person who by birth or NATIONALIZATION owes loyalty to, and receives the protection of, a nation's government; a resident of a locality, usually having the right to vote (p. 739)

civil liberties   certain rights guaranteed to the CITIZEN of a nation; in the United States, especially those rights protected by the BILL OF RIGHTS and the Fourteenth Amendment (p. 471)

civil rights   rights guaranteed to CITIZENS by the CONSTITUTION and laws of the nation, especially the rights of minorities to political, social, and economic equality (p. 680)

civil service   government jobs for which appointments and promotions are based on merit (often determined by an examination) rather than on political PATRONAGE (p. 395)

clemency   leniency or mercy shown towards an enemy, a criminal, or other offender (p. 746)

closed shop a work place where employees must be LABOR UNION members in order to be hired (compare UNION SHOP) (p. 605)

cloture a procedure for ending a debate or a FILIBUSTER in a legislature or meeting so the question at issue can be brought to a vote (p. 680)

cold war a hostility between nations that stops just short of open war; especially, the relationship of the United States and its free-world allies to the Soviet Union and its Communist allies and satellites in the decades after World War II (p. 598)

collective bargaining negotiations between a group of workers and their employer concerning wages, hours, and working conditions. The group of workers is usually represented in collective bargaining by a LABOR UNION. (p. 530)

colony a land area settled by a group of EMIGRANTS who continue to be subjects of their parent country; a people or TERRITORY that is ruled by another nation (p. 33)

commerce trade; the buying and selling of goods and services (p. 398)

commonwealth the name used instead of *state* by four of the United States (Kentucky, Massachusetts, Pennsylvania, and Virginia); the term used to designate the special status of Puerto Rico in the United States (p. 51)

company town a town built and controlled by a company, or a town that depends on a single company for most of its jobs (p. 390)

concentration camps camps where political opponents or other "enemies" of the state are confined, especially those established by Nazi Germany before and during World War II (p. 553)

confederacy a union, alliance, or league. During the Civil War, the Southern states called their union a confederacy. (p. 287)

Congress the legislative branch of the United States government, made up of the SENATE and the HOUSE OF REPRESENTATIVES (p. 76)

conquistadores Spanish word for "conquerors"; especially the Spanish adventurers who explored and conquered a large part of the western HEMISPHERE in the sixteenth century (p. 25)

Constitution the fundamental and supreme law of the United States (p. 95)

containment the United States policy after World War II of trying to keep the Soviet Union from expanding its area of influence and dominance (p. 600)

contraband goods that are illegal to import or export. During the Civil War, Northerners applied the term to slaves who fled the CONFEDERACY for the UNION. (p. 456)

convention a formal meeting of individuals, often delegates or representatives of others, to pursue common interests or goals; especially, a meeting of members of a political party to choose candidates for office and write a PLATFORM (p. 316)

convoy an organized group of merchant and/or passenger ships escorted and protected by naval vessels to ward off attack (p. 467)

corollary a principle that logically adds to or follows from another, as the Roosevelt Corollary was thought to follow from the Monroe Doctrine (p. 447)

corporation a group legally organized to act and to have its own rights separate from those of its members; a company in which the owners hold shares of STOCK and the firm has a separate legal identity from its owners; see JOINT STOCK COMPANY (p. 219)

coup d'état a sudden move to overthrow an existing government (p. 602)

currency coins and paper bills that serve as money (p. 298)

czar an emperor, king, or supreme ruler; the title of the ruler of Russia before the revolution of 1917 (p. 480)

Daguerreotype (duh-GARE-uh-type) an early form of photograph named after Louis Daguerre (1789-1851), its French inventor (p. 261)

de facto in fact or actuality (rather than by law) (p. 510)

default failure to pay a loan, mortgage, or other debt when it is due (p. 508)

deficit the amount by which money spent is greater than money received (p. 523)

deflation a widespread fall in prices (p. 394)

demilitarized zone an area where, by international agreement, no troops or armaments are allowed (p. 621)

democracy a form of government in which the people rule either directly or through freely elected representatives (p. 627)

Democratic party one of the two major political parties in the United States. It is a descendant of the Republican party established by Thomas Jefferson and James Madison in the early years of the republic. (p. 185)

demography the study of human populations and their characteristics (p. 639)

depression a long and severe decline in economic activity. The one that lasted from 1929 to about 1940 is known as the Great Depression. Compare RECESSION. (p. 103)

deregulation the reduction of government control over business and other activities (p. 771)

desegregation the elimination of SEGREGATION (p. 630)

détente a French word meaning relaxing or easing; in diplomacy, used especially to refer to an easing of tensions between nations (p. 705)

dictatorship a government in which one individual (the *dictator*) has absolute authority (p. 551)

diplomacy the art and practice of conducting relations between nations by peaceful means (p. 551)

disarmament the act of getting rid of military weapons (p. 487)

discrimination prejudice for or against someone based on race, religion, sex, or other classification (p. 722)

dividend a payment to a shareholder of a portion of the earnings of a CORPORATION (p. 500)

domino theory the idea that if one nation falls to the Communists, its neighbors will, too—just as a row of standing dominoes will fall if the first in line falls. President Eisenhower and others used this term in referring to the nations of Southeast Asia. (p. 691)

Dust Bowl the area of the United States that became so arid in the 1930s due to lack of rain that the topsoil became dust and in a strong wind blew away (p. 538)

Ecology the science that deals with the relationship of organisms and their environments (p. 684)

Electoral College jointly, all the electors chosen by the voters to cast the ballots of the states and the District of Columbia for President and Vice-President (p. 396)

emancipation the act of setting a person or people free (p. 295)

embargo a law or government order prohibiting trade with a foreign company or nation (p. 159)

embassy the building or buildings serving as the headquarters of the AMBASSADOR and other diplomatic personnel of a nation in a foreign country (p. 764)

emigrant a person who leaves one place—usually one country—to settle in another (p. 224)

empire a group of nations ruled by one supreme authority (p. 70)

encomienda a system of labor control in Spanish America, in which Spanish settlers exercised control over groups of American Indians and required those Indians to pay them a tribute in the form of crops or days of labor (p. 25)

entitlements payments from the government to which individuals are legally entitled because of age, unemployment, illness or incapacity, or status as veterans (p. 769)

e pluribus unum the motto of the United States. In Latin it means "one out of (or made from) many." (p. 139)

executive branch the part of the government charged with putting into effect the laws passed by the legislature; made up of the President, Vice-President, CABINET secretaries, and federal departments and agencies (p. 109)

ex post facto law a law passed "after the fact" that makes a previous action a crime although it was legal when it took place; specifically prohibited in Article I, Sections 9 and 10 of the U.S. CONSTITUTION (p. 831)

exports goods sent abroad, usually to be traded or sold (p. 70)

Federal relating to a union of states that recognize a single central government but retain certain powers for themselves (p. 108)

federalism the belief in or advocacy of a FEDERAL system of government; the federal form of government (p. 106)

Federalist party originally, the followers of Alexander Hamilton in the 1790s; believers in a strong central government (p. 124)

Federal Reserve System the nation's central bank; a system of 12 regional banks overseen by a central board in Washington, D.C. (p. 445)

filibuster a tactic that uses endless talk to prevent a vote on pending legislation; also, an illegal military operation by civilians of one country against another (p. 400)

financier a person who makes or oversees transactions involving large sums of money (p. 437)

foreclosure the act of taking possession of a mortgaged property (one against which money has been borrowed) when the debtor can no longer make the required payments (p. 402)

freedom riders people of different races who rode buses throughout the South in 1961 and attempted to force the integration of segregated facilities in public bus stations (p. 673)

free silver the making and issuing of silver coins in a fixed ratio to gold (p. 394)

frigate originally, a three-masted naval warship with 24 to 50 guns; today, a U.S. Navy vessel larger than a destroyer but smaller than a cruiser (p. 164)

frontier the border of a country; the edge of the unknown in a field of knowledge; in the United States, defined by the Bureau of the Census as the edge of settlement beyond which the land is occupied by two or fewer persons per square mile (p. 326)

Gag rule a rule in the HOUSE OF REPRESENTATIVES in 1836 that prevented the discussion of any antislavery petition (p. 249)

G.I. from "Government Issue"; applied to American soldiers in World War II and later wars (p. 603)

G.I. Bill of Rights also simply "G.I. Bill"; legislation, first passed in 1944, to help veterans readjust to civilian life, for example by supporting their college education (p. 603)

Gilded Age the title of a novel by Mark Twain and Charles Dudley Warner, the term is often applied to the gaudy, tawdry years from 1865 to 1900 (p. 393)

Glasnost a Russian word meaning a more open society (p. 782)

GNP see GROSS NATIONAL PRODUCT (p. 645)

gold standard a policy under which all paper money legally equals a certain amount of gold, and can be exchanged for that much gold on demand (p. 408)

GOP the REPUBLICAN PARTY, the "Grand Old Party" (p. 620)

grandfather clause laws passed in some Southern states giving the right to vote only to people who had that right on January 1, 1867, and to their descendants. This was a way to keep blacks from voting. (p. 542)

Grangers members of the Patrons of Husbandry, the farmers' league founded in 1867; so called because their lodges were called granges (p. 403)

greenbacks U.S. paper money, so called because of its color (p. 298)

gross national product (GNP) the total value of all the goods and services produced in a nation during a year (p. 645)

guerrilla warfare fighting by stealth and with small bands that make surprise raids against stronger forces (p. 774)

Habeas corpus, writ of a court order by which a judge may free a person who is being held in jail illegally or without just cause; protected by Article I, section 9 of the U.S. CONSTITUTION (p. 287)

hacienda Spanish for a large house or estate (p. 25)

hawks people who favor war or warlike policy; used especially during the Vietnam War (p. 694)

hemisphere half of the earth. The *northern* and *southern* hemispheres are separated by the equator; the *eastern* and *western* hemispheres are separated by a MERIDIAN with Europe, Asia, and Africa in one half and the Americas in the other. (p. 178)

Hessians German soldiers from the state of Hesse who were hired by the British to fight for them in the American Revolution; sometimes applied to anyone who fights for a foreign country for pay (p. 82)

holding company a company that owns (or "holds") and controls other companies (p. 357)

Hoovervilles the shantytowns built of cartons and wood scraps during the Great Depression of the 1930s; so called after President Herbert Hoover (p. 300)

House of Burgesses the lower house of the legislature in colonial Virginia and Maryland. Virginia's, established in 1619, was the first representative assembly among European settlers in the New World. In England, a *burgess* was a citizen of a borough (or town). (p. 35)

House of Representatives the lower house of the United States CONGRESS, whose members are elected for two-year terms; also, the lower house of most state legislatures (p. 107)

Immigrant a person who enters one country from another country with the intention of settling (p. 373)

immigration the movement of people from other countries into a country (p. 379)

impeach to bring a charge of wrongdoing by a government official before a proper legal body (p. 315)

imperialism the attempt to create an EMPIRE, either directly or through economic or political dominance (p. 424)

imports goods brought into a country from another country, usually to be traded or sold (p. 70)

impound to refuse to spend money that has been APPROPRIATED (set aside) for a specific purpose. In the Budget and Impoundment Act of 1974, Congress prohibited Presidents from impounding money it had voted to appropriate. (p. 748)

impressment the act of forcing a person to serve in the armed forces (p. 158)

inaugurate to induct into office formally (p. 142)

indentured servant a person who is required by an agreement to work for another person for a number of years, so called because of the perforation (indenture) that divides the two copies of the agreement (p. 35)

Industrial Revolution the revolution in manufacturing that began in about the middle of the eighteenth century with the introduction of power-driven machinery, and the social and cultural changes that followed (p. 218)

inflation a rapid, widespread rise in prices (p. 394)

initiative the procedure by which, in some states, a certain percentage of the voters can "initiate" or propose a law by PETITION and have it voted on by the people (p. 437)

injunction a court order preventing a certain action (p. 406)

interchangeable parts parts of a certain product that are mechanically produced to be the exact same size, shape, and weight as all similar parts. The use of interchangeable parts makes mass production techniques possible. (p. 222)

interlocking directorates boards of directors of several CORPORATIONS that have some of the same members, so that the businesses are to a degree under the same control; a device often used by FINANCIER J. P. Morgan (1837-1913) (p. 446)

international law the norms of behavior generally agreed to and followed by the nations of the world in their dealings with each other (p. 456)

internment confinement, especially in wartime (p. 571)

interstate between two or more states (p. 646)

Iron Curtain the line between Soviet-dominated Eastern Europe and the West, so called by Winston Churchill because the Soviets and their SATELLITE NATIONS prevented the free passage of people, information, and ideas across their borders (p. 600)

isolationism a policy of avoiding alliances and other types of involvement in the affairs of other nations (p. 555)

isthmus a narrow strip or neck of land running from one larger land area to another (p. 448)

Jim Crow laws laws in the Southern states in the nineteenth and twentieth centuries that forced the SEGREGATION of the races. The term came from the name of a song in a minstrel show. (p. 323)

jingoism aggressive nationalism (p. 421)

joint stock company a company whose owners hold shares of its STOCK (p. 30)

judicial branch the part of the government that includes courts of law and the administration of justice (p. 836)

junta (HOON-tuh) Spanish for a small group of individuals, often military officers, who rule a country (p. 776)

Keynesian (KANE-zee-uhn) following the economic theories of the English economist John Maynard Keynes (1883-1946) (p. 523)

Know-Nothing party the usual name for the American party, which was formed in 1849; so called because its members were sworn to secrecy, and when asked about the party's activities replied, "I don't know" or "I know nothing about it" (p. 264)

Ku Klux Klan (KKK) a secret society, first formed in the South after the Civil War, whose purpose was to insure white supremacy over blacks. In the 1920s a new Klan was formed, still favoring white supremacy, but opposed also to Jews, Catholics, BOLSHEVIKS, and many other groups they considered "un-American." More recently the Klan has appeared again all over the country to attempt to restore segregation and white supremacy. (p. 318)

Labor union workers organized as a group to seek higher wages, improved working conditions, and other benefits (p. 370)

lame duck an elected official whose term is about to end, and whose successor has been chosen but has not yet taken office; thus, someone who is no longer effective (p. 852)

land-grant colleges colleges that received land from the federal government under the Morrill Act of 1862 for the purpose of providing education in the agricultural and mechanical arts (p. 384)

latitude the angular distance calculated from the center of the earth north or south of the equator as measured in degrees. The North and South poles are each 90 degrees from the equator. All places that are the same distance from the equator in the same direction (north or south) are said to be located on the same PARALLEL, or line of latitude. (p. 4)

legal tender currency that can legally be used to pay a debt (p. 522)

legislative branch the part of the government that has the power to make laws; in the U.S. government, the CONGRESS, consisting of the SENATE and the HOUSE OF REPRESENTATIVES (p. 803)

Lend-Lease the World War II program under which the United States either lent or leased weapons, food, and services to our friends and the nations that would soon become our ALLIES, and especially to Great Britain and the Soviet Union (p. 563)

literacy tests a test of the ability to read and write once used by some Southern states to prevent blacks from voting (p. 543)

lithography a printing process for creating pictures. A stone (*lithos* means stone in Greek) or other flat surface is treated so that certain parts retain ink and repel water; next, the surface is covered with water and is inked. Then a piece of paper is pressed against it, picking up color only from the inked areas. The process can be repeated many times. (p. xvi)

lobby   to attempt to influence legislation; also, groups that attempt to do so. So called from the lobby outside a legislative chamber where people can meet their representatives. (p. 436)

lockout   during a labor dispute, the closing of a business (by locking the gates) to keep employees from entering (p. 604)

longitude   distance east or west of the prime MERIDIAN (the line of 0° longitude, which passes through Greenwich, England), as measured in degrees. The distance around the earth measures 360 degrees, because a degree is by definition 1/360 of the circumference of a circle. (p. 12)

Loyalists   colonists who remained loyal to England during the American Revolution; TORIES (p. 79)

lynch   to execute someone illegally by hanging, burning, or other means. So named after Colonel Charles Lynch of Virginia, whose informal "court" during the American Revolution was swift to punish LOYALISTS, often by whipping. (p. 481)

Machine   see POLITICAL MACHINE (p. 378)

mainstreaming   taking the handicapped out of special institutions and bringing them into the mainstream of American education (p. 742)

majority   more than half (p. 512)

Manifest Destiny   the idea, prevalent especially in the 1840s and 1850s, that it was America's obvious (manifest) and inevitable fate to occupy the entire continent (p. 250)

martial law   temporary rule by the military when civil government can no longer keep order (p. 33)

massive retaliation   the military policy of the United States announced by Secretary of State John Foster Dulles in January 1954, which threatened to respond to Soviet or Communist Chinese attacks on another country with an immediate all-out strike (p. 621)

Master Race   according to Nazi dictator Adolph Hitler (1889-1945), the so-called "pure" Germans who, because of their supposed racial superiority, had the right to conquer and rule other peoples (p. 551)

media   the outlets through which information reaches the public, such as television, radio, newspapers, magazines, and books. The word is the plural of *medium*. (p. 648)

mediation   the attempt of a neutral third party to settle a dispute (p. 455)

megalopolis   a number of cities so close together that they seem to create one giant city (p. 643)

mercantilism   the theory that money, especially gold and silver, is what makes a nation powerful. As applied to COLONIES, this meant that they existed only in order to enrich the mother country. (p. 56)

mercenaries   people who are paid to fight for a country other than their own (p. 82)

merchant marine   a nation's commercial ships (p. 157)

mestizo   Spanish for "mixed"; the term is applied to people who have both Spanish and Indian ancestors (p. 27)

metropolitan   relating to a large city or urban area (p. 643)

Middle Ages   the period in European history dating from approximately the fall of Roman civilization in the fifth century A.D. to the revival of learning during the RENAISSANCE in the fourteenth, fifteenth, and sixteenth centuries (p. 10)

middle passage   the sea voyage of black slaves from Africa to the western HEMISPHERE; so called because vessels in the trade made one trip (passage) to the coast of Africa, then the trip across the Atlantic to North or South America, and finally the passage back to their home ports (p. 229)

militarist   a person who advocates the predominance of the military (armed forces) and military ideas in a nation or region (p. 565)

military-industrial complex   the combination of interests of the armed forces and the industries that supply their needs. The term was used by President Dwight Eisenhower in his 1961 farewell address. (p. 637)

militia   all the able-bodied citizens capable of bearing arms (except ministers and members of a few other professions) who in colonial times and for many years thereafter met several times a year for drill and target practice in order to be able to serve as a defense force (p. 77)

monopoly   dominance in or control of a market for certain goods or services by a single company or combination of companies; see also TRUST (p. 175)

muckraking   investigating and exposing corruption and other illegal activities, especially as done by journalists during the Progressive era (p. 437)

Mugwump   a person who refuses to support his political party, especially the Republicans who worked to defeat James G. Blaine in 1884 (p. 398)

Nationalize   to take property, such as land or a business, from its private owners and place it under government control (p. 631)

NATO   the North Atlantic Treaty Organization, an alliance formed for mutual defense in 1949 under the North Atlantic Treaty, and now made up of 15 nations stretching from Canada to Turkey (p. 778)

natural aristocracy Jefferson's concept of a democratic ARISTOCRACY of the ablest, most industrious, and best educated, who would run the government (p. 719)

naturalization the granting of full citizenship to a foreigner (p. 133)

neutrality the policy of not taking sides in a dispute or a war (p. 455)

nonintercourse the suspension of trade with another country, especially as decreed by the Nonintercourse Act of 1809, which prohibited trade with Great Britain and France (p. 159)

nonpartisan not influenced by or supporting any political party or belief (p. 435)

nuclear freeze a halt in the manufacture and deployment (putting in place) of nuclear weapons (p. 780)

nuclear power energy produced from a controlled atomic reaction (p. 755)

nullification the declaration of an individual state that an act of the U.S. CONGRESS is null and void. Many Southern states claimed the right to do this in the years before the Civil War. (p. 133)

OPEC the Organization of Petroleum Exporting Countries; a group of oil-producing and exporting countries, first organized in 1960 to protect member nations' interests and control world oil prices (p. 749)

ordinance a government rule or law (p. 101)

organized labor collectively, all workers who are members of LABOR UNIONS (p. 370)

PAC see POLITICAL ACTION COMMITTEE (p. 753)

pacifist a person who is opposed to war, and refuses to fight under any circumstances (p. 458)

parallel an imaginary line of LATITUDE; so called because it runs parallel to the equator (p. 615)

pardon to forgive a punishable offense, and release the offender from further punishment (p. 746)

parity in agriculture, a level of crop prices designed to give farmers the same real income from their crops as they received between 1910 and 1914 (p. 524)

Parliament Great Britain's legislature (p. 55)

partisan devoted to a single political party and its beliefs (p. 435)

patronage the distribution of government jobs to political supporters; see also SPOILS SYSTEM (p. 155)

peculiar institution black slavery in the pre-Civil War South (p. 229)

per capita per person (p. 645)

Perestroika a Russian word meaning to restructure the economy, the party and the government (p. 782)

petition a written request to an individual or group in power (p. 80)

pioneers people who go into unoccupied or little-known regions, or people who explore new areas of knowledge (p. 374)

plantation an early settlement or COLONY; a large agricultural estate in the South, especially before the Civil War (p. 48)

platform a declaration of the principles, beliefs, and aims of a political party, usually adopted during its national CONVENTION. The individual sections of the platform are known as *planks*. (p. 609)

plurality in an election, the largest number of votes, but not a majority (p. 459)

Political Action Committee (PAC) an independent committee set up to receive funds and give them to a political candidate or candidates; legalized by the Federal Election Campaign-funding Reform Act of 1974 (p. 753)

political machine a political organization that works so smoothly and retains control so easily that it seems similar to a machine; found in many American cities in the late 1800s and early 1900s (p. 435)

poll tax a tax that must be paid before one can vote; once used in the South to discourage or prevent blacks from voting, and now prohibited in national elections by the Twenty-fourth Amendment to the U.S. CONSTITUTION (p. 453)

popular sovereignty the idea that the people in an area should decide for themselves the questions that concern them; especially, before the Civil War, that people in a TERRITORY should decide whether or not slavery should exist there (p. 258)

pork barrel federally financed improvement projects, such as dams, canals, and highways, that are designed to benefit a particular locality (p. 753)

preamble an introduction; especially, the opening statements of the Declaration of Independence and the U.S. CONSTITUTION (p. 80)

precedent something that happened or was done before and can now be used as an example to justify or explain similar occurrences or behavior (p. 134)

President the chief executive of a modern republic, especially of the United States (p. 109)

productivity in economics, a measure of the quantity of goods and services produced from a given amount of labor, equipment, land, and time (p. 497)

Prohibition the years from 1920 to 1933, when the Eighteenth Amendment to the U.S. CONSTITUTION was in effect, making it illegal to manufacture, sell, or transport alcoholic beverages in the United States (p. 491)

puppet government a government whose actions are completely controlled by another government, just as a puppet is manipulated by a person (p. 614)

Quarantine in foreign affairs, the isolation of a nation, carried out by refusing to communicate or trade with it and by preventing other nations from doing so (p. 565)

quota a predetermined maximum or minimum number of people who may or should be admitted to a group, institution, or nation (p. 613)

Racism the idea that a person's race determines his or her character or ability, and that one race is superior to others; prejudice against or preference for the members of one race (p. 723)

ratify to give formal approval (p. 109)

ration to limit the amount of something that each person may have. During World War II, such scarce items as sugar, butter, and gasoline were rationed in the United States. (p. 465)

real income the actual purchasing power of a person's income, rather than just the dollar amount (p. 470)

reapportionment the changing of the distribution of seats and the size of election districts for a legislature. Seats in the U.S. HOUSE OF REPRESENTATIVES must be reapportioned every ten years based on the results of the CENSUS. (p. 699)

recall a procedure established in some cities and states by which a percentage of the voters can remove an elected official from office at any time (p. 437)

recession a decline in economic activity, less severe and usually shorter than a DEPRESSION (p. 672)

Reconstruction the period (1867-1877) during which the former states of the CONFEDERACY were ruled by the federal government or by local Republican governments. Reconstruction lasted the full period only for Louisiana, Florida, and South Carolina. (p. 324)

Red a radical, anarchist, or Communist; so called because red was the color of the banner often used by revolutionaries, as in the Russian Revolution of 1917 (p. 483)

referendum a direct popular vote on a proposed new law or change in an existing law (p. 437)

refugee a person who flees from one country or region to seek refuge in another (p. 640)

regulation government control of the operations of business or other activities (p. 491)

Renaissance French for "rebirth"; the age, beginning about A.D. 1300 in Italy and later spreading throughout Europe, when there was a rebirth of art, literature, and learning; any period when there is a lively cultural life, as in the Harlem Renaissance of the 1920s (p. 10)

reparations payments required from a defeated nation for the damages and injuries it caused during a war (p. 473)

representative government a government in which the people are represented by delegates chosen in free elections (p. 107)

republic a form of government in which power is exercised by representatives elected by the people (p. 129)

Republican party Thomas Jefferson's party in the early days of the Republic; later, a new party launched in 1854 with the intent of opposing the spread of slavery into the TERRITORIES (p. 124)

reservations areas set aside (reserved) by the U.S. government for American Indian tribes (p. 332)

reverse discrimination the disadvantages suffered by others as a result of the special opportunities given to minorities in AFFIRMATIVE ACTION programs (p. 725)

revolution a sudden, violent change, especially the overthrow of a government (p. 67)

right-to-work laws laws in some states that forbid businesses to require workers to join a LABOR UNION as a condition of employment (p. 605)

SALT Strategic Arms Limitation Treaties: SALT I, signed in May 1972, and SALT II, signed in June 1979. Both aimed to slow down the nuclear arms race. SALT II was not ratified by the U.S. Senate. (p. 705)

salutary neglect the manner in which England governed the American colonies during much of the late 1600s and early 1700s; especially, the policy of weak enforcement of the laws regulating colonial trade (p. 58)

satellite nations nations that are subservient to another nation, especially the nations of Eastern and Central Europe that have been dominated by the Soviet Union since the years of World War II (p. 585)

scalawags an insulting name for white Southerners who were Republicans during RECONSTRUCTION (p. 317)

secession the act of withdrawing formally from a group; the attempt of eleven Southern states to withdraw from the UNION in 1860 and 1861 (p. 129)

sectionalism loyalty to and love of a region, such as the East, the Midwest, or the South (p. 129)

sedition an attempt to incite a rebellion against a national government (p. 133)

segregation separating people according to some standard–in American history, usually race–in schools, housing, industry, and public facilities (p. 323)

Senate the upper house of the U.S. CONGRESS, to which each state elects two members, called senators, for terms of six years each; also, the upper house in *bicameral* state legislatures (legislatures that have two houses) (p. 107)

seniority priority based on higher rank or longer term of service (p. 604)

separate but equal the standard by which the SUPREME COURT approved segregated facilities in *Plessy* v. *Ferguson* (1896). The Court overturned this decision in *Brown* v. *Board of Education* (1954), ruling that separate facilities were unequal. (p. 323)

separation of powers the doctrine that gives the powers of making, enforcing, and interpreting the laws to separate branches of government (LEGISLATIVE, EXECUTIVE, and JUDICIAL) (p. 109)

settlement house a private center providing social services for the poor in a needy neighborhood (p. 383)

sharecroppers farmers who do not own the land they work but pay rent to the owner in the form of a share of the crop they grow (p. 323)

shuttle diplomacy the conduct of international relations by traveling back and forth between two or more nations frequently; first applied to the activities of Henry Kissinger, who was Secretary of State in Richard Nixon's second term as President and Gerald Ford's term as President (p. 723)

sit-down strike a work stoppage in which employees refuse to leave the work place and occupy it in an attempt to force their employer to come to terms (p. 548)

sit-in a form of protest in which the participants occupy a building or a site in the hope of forcing their opponents to give in to their demands (p. 674)

SMSA Standard Metropolitan Statistical Area; a classification developed by the Office of Management and Budget for planning purposes, used to describe a central town and its outlying areas or a group of towns that make up a dense METROPOLITAN area (p. 643)

social security various programs of the federal government, some paid for by contributions from employers and employees, which provide economic assistance to the disabled, unemployed, and aged, as well as low-cost medical insurance for those over 65 (p. 530)

speakeasy an illegal bar during PROHIBITION (p. 494)

special interest groups groups of people who organize to take action on a particular issue (the environment, gun control, gun owners' rights, farm policy, etc.), hoping to influence public policy on that issue (p. 753)

specie money in the form of coins (p. 200)

speculator a person who gambles by buying or selling something, hoping to make a large profit (p. 99)

sphere of influence an area not within its own borders where the interests of one large nation are considered to be supreme (p. 426)

spoils system the procedure of rewarding political supporters with government jobs; partly abolished on the national level by the Pendleton Civil Service Act of 1883 (p. 190)

Stalwarts conservative Republicans who continued to favor the policies and procedures the party had followed during the Presidency of Ulysses S. Grant–and who especially opposed CIVIL SERVICE reform–in the years after Grant left office in 1877 (p. 395)

standard of living a rough measure of the material well-being of a person or group in a society (p. 645)

staple crop the main agricultural product grown in an area (p. 35)

states' rights the doctrine that seeks to limit the power of the federal government by interpreting the U.S. CONSTITUTION in a way that stresses the retained rights of the states and insists that the central government was granted only limited powers (p. 609)

status quo the way things are at a particular time (p. 169)

stock shares of ownership in a CORPORATION (p. 500)

stockholder the owner of STOCK (p. 500)

Strategic Defense Initiative (SDI) a defensive shield of advanced weapons, some operating in outer space, to make the United States safe from nuclear attack. Sometimes called "Star Wars." (p. 784)

strict construction an interpretation of the U.S. CONSTITUTION that holds that Congress and the President have no power to do anything unless the Constitution grants them that power in so many words; compare BROAD CONSTRUCTION (p. 122)

subpoena a legal order requiring someone or something to appear in court for questioning or inspection (p. 711)

subsidize when the government makes a monetary payment to assist an individual, organization, or cause (p. 683)

suburbs smaller towns surrounding large cities (p. 641)

suffrage the right to vote. The word comes from the Latin *suffragium,* which means "ballot" or "vote." (p. 436)

summit conference a meeting of the heads of state of two or more countries (p. 623)

superpower a nation far more powerful than most others; in the years since World War II, the United States and the Soviet Union (p. 760)

supply-side economics the theory that the government can best stimulate the economy by cutting taxes and encouraging investment in businesses, thus increasing the supply of goods (p. 767)

Supreme Court the highest federal court. Its powers are stated in Article III, of the U.S. CONSTITUTION. (p. 630)

Tactical atomic weapons smaller nuclear weapons, such as artillery shells, designed to be used on a conventional battlefield (p. 682)

tariff a charge placed by the government on certain imported goods (p. 508)

temperance when referring to alcohol, total abstinence from, or prohibition of, intoxicating beverages (p. 240)

tenant farmers farmers who rent the land they work (p. 540)

territory a political division of the United States before it becomes a state; a large area of land (p. 346)

terrorism the use of violence, intimidation, and coercion to achieve an end, to gain publicity for a cause, or to disrupt the normal functioning of society (p. 783)

Third World nations that profess not to be allied with either the Soviets and their SATELLITE NATIONS or the United States and its allies; especially the developing countries of Asia, Africa, and Latin America (p. 762)

Tories Americans who favored the British during the American Revolution; LOYALISTS (p. 77)

totalitarianism a form of rule in which the central government holds absolute control over the lives of its citizens (p. 613)

treason betrayal of one's country by making war on it or purposely aiding its enemies (p. 152)

treaty a formal agreement concluded between two or more countries (p. 14)

trust a MONOPOLY formed by combining the ownership of several formerly separate CORPORATIONS under a board of trustees (p. 357)

Ultimatum a final demand or set of demands, with the threat of serious consequences if the terms are not met (p. 174)

unalienable impossible to give up or surrender (p. 816)

unconditional surrender giving up without any terms or conditions decided upon beforehand (p. 541)

unconstitutional not allowed under the U.S. CONSTITUTION (p. 154)

underground railroad the informal network of escape routes and rest stops (stations) in the Northern states, and leading into Canada, by which slaves made their way to freedom (p. 260)

Union the separate states gathered together as the United States; the Northern states during the Civil War (p. 280)

union see LABOR UNION (p. 368)

union shop a business whose employees must join a LABOR UNION, but need not be members when they are hired; compare CLOSED SHOP (p. 605)

urban renewal the attempt to renew large areas of old cities, usually by tearing down old buildings and constructing new ones (p. 683)

utopia an imaginary place where everything is perfect; from two Greek words meaning "no place" (p. 391)

Veto under the U.S. CONSTITUTION, the power of the President to reject an act passed by Congress. (p. 599)

viceroy in the Spanish empire, the governor of a COLONY or a province (p. 26)

Viet Cong Vietnamese Communists in South Vietnam who fought against the South Vietnamese government forces and the United States forces in the Vietnam War (p. 671)

War criminals persons who commit acts during wartime that go beyond the bounds of accepted behavior, especially those tried for such acts after World War II (p. 607)

welfare various state and federal programs that aim to provide food, money, medical care, and other help to those in need (p. 316)

Whigs the name taken by the political party that opposed President Andrew Jackson, to imply a similarity to the English Whigs who had struggled against the king in the late 1700s (p. 198)

writ a written court order commanding an individual or organization to do (or stop doing) something (p. 287)

writ of habeas corpus see HABEAS CORPUS (p. 287)

Yellow press newspapers that, in order to attract readers, feature sensational, often distorted stories; especially the Hearst and Pulitzer papers of the late 1890s, which encouraged the United States to fight a war with Spain (p. 420)

Index

Middle East *and Arab countries by name*
Arapaho Indians, 329
Arawak Indians, 734
Archery, Georgia, 751
Architecture: Aztec, 6, 8; southwest American Indian, 8; Renaissance, 10; Jefferson and, 144; hotel, 189; in West, 227–229, 341–342; of department stores, 364–365; in growing cities, 375–377, 388–391
Ardennes, 583
Area Redevelopment Act, 672
Argentina, 451; and U.S. farmers, 408; Hoover and, 510; and World War II, 575; at war with Great Britain, 776
Aristocracy: in America in 1790s, 116–117; Jefferson on, 720
Arizona, 8, 25, 27, 252; becomes territory, 298, 346; mining in, 332; statehood for, 442; and Zimmermann note, 460; Mexican Americans in, 732
Arkansas: exploration of, 19; Reconstruction and, 317; 1930s migration from, 539; desegregation in, 629
Armada, Spanish, 28–29
Armaments: production in World War I, 466, 467, 469–470; 1920s arms race, 487; Nye investigation, 555; proposed conference on, 555–556; production in World War II, 569. *See also* Disarmament
Armed forces: cut after World War II, 603; reduced under Eisenhower, 621; Indians in, 739. *See also wars by name*
Armed Ship Bill, 460
Armies of the Night, The (Mailer), 654
Armistice: in World War I, 464, 471; in Korean War, 621
Arms limitation agreement, 760–761, 784, 792. *See also* Disarmament
Armstrong, Louis, 494
Armstrong, Neil, 701; *photo,* 702
Army, United States: Jefferson's reduction of, 144–145, 159; and Force Bill, 198; occupies South, 314–315; in West, 328–330; women in, 569; blacks in, 569, 570; McCarthy accuses, 626. *See also wars by name*
Army-McCarthy hearings, 626–627, *photo,* 626
Army Medical Corps, 426
Arnold, Benedict, 78, 87
Arnold, Hendrich, 248
Arroyo, Martina, 734
"Arsenal of democracy," 568
Art, American: colonial, 54–55; early painters, 180; Hudson River school, *painting,* 173; "ashcan school," 438, *il.,* 377; and the machine, 652–653. *See also artists by name*
Arthur, Chester A.: and Civil Service Reform, 395; and 1880 election, 395–396, *il.,* 396; as President, 396–397; dedicates Brooklyn Bridge, 387–388
Articles of Confederation, 96, 98–99, 106, 109
"Ashcan school" of painting, 438; *il.,* 377
Asia: Indian migration from, 6; search for route to, 2–5, 11–12, 14–16, 20–21, 29–30, 41; and Declaration of Independence, 81; and immigration laws, 483. *See also countries by name*
Assembly line, 495–497; Ford's, *il.,* 496
Astor, John Jacob, 243
Astoria, 243
Astrolabe, 12; *il.,* 4
Astronauts, 701
Aswan Dam, 631
Atlanta, Georgia: in Civil War, 301, 302–303, *il.,* 282; black mayor in, 643
Atlanta University, 312
Atlantic, battle of, 573
Atlantic cable, 216; song honoring, *il.,* 217

Atlantic Charter, 564
Atlantic Pact, 609. *See also* NATO
Atomic bombs: development of, 588–589; and World War II, 589–590; Soviets explode, 612; espionage cases, 612, 613; H-bomb tested, 621, 633; testing of, 670
Atomic energy: controlled release of, 589; international control, 599–600
Atomic Energy Act, 603–604, 624
Atomic Energy Commission (AEC), 604
Attorney General, 119
Attorney, United States, 119
Attucks, Crispus, 74
Audubon, John James, xvi
Austerlitz, Battle of, 156
Austin, Stephen F., 242
Austin, Texas, *lithograph,* 242
Australia: and U.S. farmers, 403; in World War II, 576, 577; defense pact with, 616; in SEATO, 622
Austria: and French Revolution, 125; defeated at Austerlitz, 156; and German immigration, 225; immigration from, 374; in World War I, 453; after World War I, 508; annexed by Germany, 556; Soviet Union and, 623
Automation, 649, 650
Automobiles: affect American life, 640, 645–646; automation and, 649; model changes, 650; in 1920s, 494, 503; Oliver Evans and, 212; pollution from, 684; safety, 684–685; and air pollution, 755–756; and foreign competition in 1980s, 769
Azores, 2, 3
Aztec Indians, 6, 8, 16, 27–28

B-17 bomber, 561, 579; *photo,* 580
"Baby boom" of 1950s, 640, 688; *photo,* 640–641
Backlash, white, 687; affirmative action and, 724–725
Bad Axe, Battle of, 195
Badger, Joseph, xvi
Baer, George F., quoted, 431
Baffin Island, 13
Baghdad Pact (1955), 622
Bagot, Charles, 174
Bahama Islands, 5
Baker, Howard, 741
Baker, Ray Stannard, 438
Balboa, Vasco Núñez de, 14
Balkans, and World War I, 453, 455
Ballinger, Richard A., 440–441
Balloon-frame construction, 227, 228
Balloons, in warfare, 560
Ballots, written, 187–188
Baltimore, Lord, 52
Baltimore, Maryland, 114, 116, 166, 189, 213, 216, 250, 393
Baltimore (ship), 417
Baltimore and Ohio Railroad, 369, 393
Bank of the United States: first, 122, 145, 172; second, 172, 175, 198–200, *cartoon,* 199; Tyler and, 249
Bankhead, John, 541
Bankhead-Jones Farm Tenant Act of 1937, 541–542
Banks and banking: Bank of the United States, 122, 145, 172, 175, 198–200, 249; Jackson and, 198–200; during and after Civil War, 298, reforms under Wilson, 444–446; and 1929 crash, 504; reforms under F. D. Roosevelt, 521–522
Banneker, Benjamin, 141

Bannock War of 1878, 332
Bantu, and slavery, 229
Baptists, 266
Barbary States: *map,* 145; piracy by, 145–146, 153, 155
Barbed wire, 345
Barkley, Alben W., 609
Barnett, D., 673
Barron, Captain, 157
Barton, Clara, 285; *photo,* 286
Baruch, Bernard M., 469–470, 599–600
Bastogne, Belgium, 583
Batista, Fulgencio, 636
Bavaria, 551
Bay of Pigs, 665
"Bear Flag," 252
Beauregard, P. G. T., 274
Becknell, William, 243
Beecher, Henry Ward, 262
Begin, Menachem, 762–763; *photo,* 762
Beijing (Peking), China, 426, 704–705
Beirut, Lebanon, 762, 775
Belgian War Relief, 469
Belgium: immigration, 223, 225; and Ostend Manifesto, 262; in World War I, 455, 458; in World War II, 560, 582; as postwar ally, 607
Belgrade, 454, 582
Belize, Mayas in, 6
Belknap, W. W., 319
Bell, John, 271, 272
Belleau Wood, France, 464
Bellow, Saul, 654
Belorussian, 599
Belpre, Ohio, 103
Benelux nations, 607
Benin, and slave trade, 229
Benson, Ezra Taft, 624
Bent, Charles, 243
Benton, Senator Thomas Hart, 200
Benton, Thomas Hart (painter), xvi; *paintings,* 478–479, 541
Benton Harbor, Michigan, 643
Bering Strait, 6
Berkeley, California, 689
Berle, Adolph A., Jr., 521
Berlin, Germany, 417; in World War II, 582, 584–586; after World War II, 607–608, 631, 635–636; blockade, 608, *photo,* 607; Kennedy and, 665, 666; wall and Brandenburg Gate, *photo,* 666
Berlin wall, 665
Bermuda, 31
Bernstein, Carl, 708
Bessarabia, 557
Bessemer, Henry, 390
Bessemer converter, 390; *painting,* 350–351
Bethlehem Steel Corporation, *painting,* 350–351
Bethune, Mary McLeod, 544–545, 547
Beveridge, Albert J., quoted, 418
Bible reading, in public schools, 699
Biddle, Nicholas, 198; quoted, 198; *cartoon,* 199
Bierstadt, Albert, xvi; *paintings,* 434
Bilingual education, 723, 724
Bill of Rights, 111. *See also amendments by number*
Bill of Rights, English, 95
Billeting Act of 1765, 72
"Billion-dollar" Congress, 401–402
Bipartisanship, on civil rights bills in Congress, 631
Birch, William, *engravings,* 105, 132
Birmingham, Alabama, 609, 674
Birney, James G., 240, 250
Birthrate, 639, 640
Bison, *see* Buffalo

Bissell, George H., 358–359
Bitter Cry of the Children, The (Spargo), 438
Black, Hugo, 628
Black Americans: in colonies, 35, 45–46, 47; in Revolution, 89; in slavery, 47, 95–96, 176, 228–231; and reform movements, 239–241; at Battle of New Orleans, 171; nullification and, 196; Dred Scott case, 257; in Civil War, 281, 298, *il.,* 297; in Reconstruction era, 308, 310–315, 316–318; *poster* honors, 317; abandoned after Reconstruction, 322–324; as cowboys, 339; and late 19th-century reform, 383, 385–386; and Lodge civil rights bill, 400; Populists and, 408; in World War I, 470, *il.,* 463; after World War I, 481, 483, 484, 492, 494; New Deal and, 542–545; organized labor and, 549; in World War II, 569–570, 572; Truman and, 605–606; in 1948 election, 609; equality struggle in 1950s, 627–630; migration after World War II, 641, 643–644; Kennedy and, 673–674; and Civil Rights Act of 1964, 680; in Cabinet, 683, 705; revolt in 1960s, 685–688; and equality issue, 721, 723–726. *See also* Abolition movement; Slavery
"Black Codes," 310–312
Black Hawk, Chief, 195, 271
Black Hills, South Dakota, 329, 332
Black Manhattan (Du Bois), 545
Black Muslims, 687
Black Power, 687–688, 689
"Black Renaissance" movement, 545
Black River Falls, Wisconsin, *photo,* 384
Black Thursday, 502–503
Blacklists, 611
Blacks: Balboa and, 14; revolt in Haiti, 147–148; brought from Africa, 230. *See also* Black Americans
Blackwell, Elizabeth, 239
Blackwell, Emily, 239
Blaine, James G., 320, 395, 397–399, 417; *cartoon,* 394
Bland, Richard, 394
Bland-Allison Act of 1878, 394
"Bleeding Kansas," 265; *lithograph,* 265
Blitzkrieg, 559–560
Block, Herbert (Herblock), xv
Block Island, Rhode Island, 21
Blockades: in War of 1812, 164; during Civil War, 283, *il.,* 284; of Berlin, 608; of Cuba, 669
Blood bank, 570
Board of Trade, colonial, 57, 58
Bodmer, Karl, xiv
Bogardus, James, 364, 389–390
Bois des Sioux City, *il.,* 226
Boland, Edward P., 774
Bolsheviks, 480, 481–483
Bombing: shelters in London, *photo,* 562; of Pearl Harbor, *photo,* 565; by B-17s, *photo,* 580; of Nagasaki, *photo,* 591. *See also* Air power; Atomic bombs
Bonds, government: and debt assumption in 1790, 120–122; in Civil War, 298; and gold drain, 406–407; sale in World War I, 469, *il.,* 458; World War II bonds, 572
Bonus Army, 507, 538
Bonus Bill, Calhoun's, 172
Bonus bill, for World War I veterans, 488
Books: McCarthy attacks, 626; output of, 654; power of 261–262, 331–332, 683–685. *See also* authors by name
Boone, Daniel, 103, 116
Booth, Edwin, 309
Booth, John Wilkes, 309
Borah, William E., 474; supports neutrality law, 558

Border states, in Civil War, 285, 287
Bork, Robert, 788
Bosch, Juan, 692
Bosnia, 454
Boss rule, 378, 436–437
Boston, Massachusetts: settlement of, 37; in American Revolution, 71, 73–74, 75; in 1789, 114; and railroads, 213; Irish in, 223; fire of 1872, 319, *il.,* 320–321; urbanization, 351
Boston (ship), 418
Boston Globe, 504
Boston Manufacturing Company, 219–221
Boston Massacre, 73–74; *il.,* 74
Boston Tea Party, 75
Bosworth, battle at, 28
Bourke-White, Margaret, xv
Bowie, James, 248
Boxer Rebellion, 426–427
Boycotts: colonial, 71, 73, 74, 75, *il.,* 71; of buses in Montgomery, 630; of grapes, 733; of Egypt, 749
Braceros, 732
Braddock, Edward, 60
Bradford, William, 36
Bradstreet, John, 60
Brady, Mathew, xv, 284; *photographs,* 259, 304, 307
Bradley, Omar, 615
"Brag" boats, 213
Brain Trust, 520–521
Brandeis, Louis D., 446
Brazil, 14, 229, 451, 575; and slavery, 230; in World War II, 575
Brazos River, 247
Breckinridge, John C., 271, 272
Breckinridge, Minnesota, *poster,* 226
Breed's Hill, 77
Brent, Margaret, 52
Brezhnev, Leonid, 705, 778
Briand, Aristide, 508
Bridges, building of, 386–388; *il.,* 354, 388
Bridgewater, Massachusetts, *il.,* 218
Brill, Wisconsin, *il.,* 344
"Brinkmanship," 621
Britain, Battle of, 561–562; bomb shelter, *photo,* 562
British East India Company, 75
British Guiana, 419–420, 563
British Orders in Council, in Napoleonic wars, 162, 164
British West Indies, 31, 70, 310
Brittany, 582
"Broad constructionists," 122
Brooke, Edward, 643
Brooklyn Bridge, 387–388; opening of, *il.,* 388
Brooks, Preston S., 265–266, 308
Brotherhood of Sleeping Car Porters, 570
Brown, John, *photo,* 264
Brown, William Wells, *il.,* 317
Brown v. *Board of Education of Topeka, Kansas* (1954), 628
"Brown Power" movement, 732
Brown University, 54
Brussels, Belgium, 582
Bryan, Charles W., 491
Bryan, William Jennings: 424; in 1896 election, 407–408; in 1900 election, 424–425; in 1908 election, 438; and 1912 election, 442; compared with Wilson, 444; and banking reforms, 445; as Secretary of State, 449, 456, 458; and 1924 election, 491; *photo,* 407
Bryn Mawr College, 385
Buchanan, James, 266–267, 268, 272
Budapest, Hungary, 582
Buddhists, in Vietnam, 671

Budget, Bureau of the, 487
Budget and Accounting Act, 487
Buell, D. C., 291
Buena Vista, Battle of, 252
Buffalo, 8, 19, 327–328, 330–331, 337; *painting,* 331
Buffalo, New York, 226, 429; and the Erie Canal, 210–211; Grover Cleveland as mayor, 397
"Buffalo Bill," 331
Buford (ship), 482–483
Bulgaria: in World War I, 455; in World War II, 582, 584; postwar control of, 584, 585; as Soviet satellite, 600
Bulge, Battle of the, 583
Bull market, 792
Bull Moose party, 442–443
Bull Run, first Battle of, 283, 288; second Battle of, 294
Bulls (papal decrees), 14, 20
Bunche, Ralph, 599
Bunker Hill, Battle of, 77, 87, 89, *il.,* 78
Burger, Warren, 705
Burgesses, House of, 35, 141
Burma, in World War II, 569, 575
Burma Road, 564, 569
Burnet, David G., 247
Burnside, Ambrose, 296
Burr, Aaron, 134, 152, 154
Bus transportation: Montgomery boycott, 630; for school integration, 723–724, *photo,* 724; for handicapped, 741–742
Bush, George, 780, 792; *photo,* 794
Bushmen, 229
Business and industry: Hamilton's report, 122, 124; and Tariff of 1816, 171–172; growth before 1860, 208–222; 237–238; after Civil War, 320, 351–370, 386–392; reform efforts, 398, 401, 403, 430–432, 434–435, 437–438; Wilson and reform, 444–447; in World War I, 465–466, 469–470; in 1920s, 491–492, 494, 495–497, 500–508; and New Deal, 521–522, 524, 525–526, 529–531, 534–535; in World War II, 568–569; postwar conversion, 604; Eisenhower and, 624; prosperity after World War II, 624, 645–650; Kennedy and, 671–673; Nixon and, 705–706; census and, 640; affirmative action by, 724–725; women's rights and, 726–731

Cabinet: creation of, 121; in presidential succession, 605
Cabinetwork, colonial, 55
Cabot, John, 20
Cahokia, Illinois, 87
Caine Mutiny, The (Wouk), 654
Caisson disease, 387
Cajamarca, Peru, 17
Calamity Jane, 332
Calder, Alexander, sculpture, *il.,* 596–597
Calhoun, Floride, 193
Calhoun, John C., 162, 257, 258, 268; Bonus Bill, 110; tariff and, 172; as Vice-President, 191–195; and nullification controversy, 193–195, 196–197; slavery and, 229; Texas and, 249–250
California, 233, 245, 255, 262, 298; Indians in, 8; settlement of, 25, 27, 242, 326; missions in, 27, *il.,* 27; Americans in, 244–246; annexation of, 250–251; Mexican-American War and, 252; statehood, 252–257; and slavery, 252–257; Crittenden Compromise, 272; immigrants in, 351;

Convoys, in World War I, 467
Cooke, Jay, 319
Coolidge, Calvin: Boston police strike and, 481; elected Vice-President, 486; as President, 488, 490, 491–492; foreign affairs under, 508–509; in 1924 election, 490–491; air force and, 561; quoted, 479, 501; *photos,* 490, 500
Coolidge, Grace, 490
Coolidge, John, 490
Cooper, James Fenimore, quoted, 187
Cooper, Thomas, 133
Cooperatives, farmers', 402
Copernicus, Nicolaus, 11
Copley, John Singleton, xvi; *paintings,* 46
Copying machines, 648–649
Coral Sea, Battle of, 576–577
Corbin Margaret, 88
Corn, Indian (maize); 6, 8, 33; planted by Pilgrims, 37; Embargo Act and, 159; western economy and, 219
Cornell, Alonzo B., 395
Cornwallis, Charles, 84, 87, 99; surrender of, 88; troops landing, *il.,* 86
Coronado, Francisco de, 19
Corporations: Industrial Revolution and, 219; development of, 358. *See also* Business and industry
Corporations, Bureau of, 432
"Corrupt Bargain," 184–185
Corruption: in Reconstruction era, 317; under Grant, 319–320; by Tweed Ring, 320–321; muckrakers and, 437–438; under Harding, 488–489; Prohibition and, 485; in labor unions, 603
Cortez, Hernando, 16–17, 19–20
Cosmopolitan (magazine), 437
Costa Rica, 774
Cotton: aristocracy and, 117; Embargo Act and, 159; gin invented, 117, 176; and depression of 1819, 192; northern textile mills, 218, 219; slavery and, 229; role in Civil War, 281; sharecropping and, 323–324; and Great Depression, 504, 525
Cotton gin, 117, 176
"Cotton Pickers," *painting,* 324
Coventry, England, bombing of, 562
Cow towns, 340; *map,* 340
Cowboys, 327, 338–339
Coughlin, Charles E., 529, 532
Council of Economic Advisers, 604, 672
Council of the Indies, 16, 25
Council of National Defense, 469
Council on Environmental Quality, 754
Counter-culture, 689
Courts, federal: establishment of, 119; proposed reform of, 534; busing and, 723–724; and Indian claims, 739. *See also* Supreme Court
Cox, Archibald, 709, 710–711, 788
Cox, James M., 474
Coxey, Jacob, 406; *il.,* 406
Cramer, Charles F., 488
Crawford, William H., 183
Crazy Horse, Chief, 329
Creation Science, 778
Credibility gap, L. B. Johnson's, 692
Crédit Mobilier scandal, 319, 396
Creek Indians, 125, 163
Creel, George, 470
Crime: Georgia colony and, 43; Prohibition and, 485; as recent political issue, 698, 699. *See also* Corruption
Crisis, The (Paine), 84
Crisis, The (black journal), 543, 570
Crittenden, John C., 272
Croatan Indians, 31
Croatan Island, 32

Crockett, Davy, 248
Cromwell, Oliver, 55–56
Cross-staff, 12
Crusade for Justice, 732
Cuba: Columbus and, 5; slavery expansion and, 262; *Trent* affair and, 290; war for independence, 420–421; post-independence, 425–426; treaties with, 426, 554; Roosevelt Corollary and, 450; in World War II, 575; Castro takes over, 636; Bay of Pigs, 665; missile crisis, 668–669, *photo,* 669; refugees from, 735–736; and Nicaragua, 748, 749
Cuban Americans, 735–736
Cullen, Countee, 545
Cullom, Shelby M., 398, 400
Culp's Hill, 300
Cumberland (ship), 292
Cumberland, Maryland, 208
Cumberland River, 290
Currency, *see* Money and currency problems
Currier and Ives, xvi; *lithographs,* 274, 321, 388
Currier, Nathaniel, *see* Currier and Ives
Curtis, Charles E., 510
Curtis, George W., 394, 398
Cushing, Caleb, 414
Custer, George A., *photo,* 285
Cutler, Manassah, 102
Cuzco, Peru, 6, 17
Czechoslovakia: created, 473; Munich Pact and, 556; postwar control of, 584–585; Communists take over, 602
Czolgosz, Leon, 429

D
-Day, 580–582; *photo,* 581
Da Gama, *see* Vasco da Gama
Dakota Territory, 346
Daladier, Edouard, 556
Dallas, Texas, 780; Kennedy death in, 675
Dame schools, 54
Danish West Indies, 416
Danvers, Massachusetts, 103
Darien, Panama, 14
Darrow, Clarence, 788
Dartmouth College, founded, 54
Dartmouth College Case (1819), 174
Darwin, Charles, 788
Daugherty, Harry, 486, 488–489
Daughters of Liberty, *il.,* 71
Davenport, Iowa, settlement of, 226
David, 39
Da Vinci, Leonardo, 10
Davis, David, 321
Davis, Jefferson, 257, 285, 288, 294, 295, 303
Davis, John W., 491, 528
Dawes, Charles G., 490
Dawes, William, 77
Dawes Act of 1887, 332
Deadwood, South Dakota, 332, 335
Deane, Silas, 79
Dearborn, Fort, (Chicago), 164
Death penalty, 699
Deaver, Michael, 792
Debates, political: Webster-Hayne, 193–194; Lincoln-Douglas, 268–269; Kennedy-Nixon, 661–662, *il.,* 661; Ford-Carter, 750; Carter-Reagan, 764; Reagan-Mondale, 780
Debs, Eugene V., 442–443, 471
Debt moratorium, 508
Debts, governmental: payment of, after Revolution, 118, 120–122; under Jefferson, 155; national bank and, 172; of Confederacy, 313, 317; under F. D. Roosevelt, 527
Decatur, Stephen, 145–146, 164

Declaration of Independence, 80–81, 154; and slavery, 239; equality and, 719; text, 816–821; *il.,* 81
Declaration of Rights and Grievances, 76, 131
Declaratory Act, 71
Deerfield Massacre, 59
Defense, Council of, 469
Defense, Department of, 606
Defense pacts, 623; in Suez War, 631–632
Deficits, federal budget: under New Deal, 523, 534, 536; Kennedy and, 672; under L. B. Johnson, 685; Nixon and, 705, 706; Ford and, 748; Reagan and, 767, 768, 769
Deflation: of 1870s, 394; of 1930s, 522
De Gaulle, Charles, 670
De Grasse, Admiral, 88
Delano, California, 712
Delaware: as colony, 41, 52, 58; ratifies Constitution, 110; slavery in, 287, 295, 296; and 1864 election, 302
Delaware Indians, 68, 127
Delaware River, 84
De Lôme, Dupuy, 420–421
Delta, rocket, 783
Delta Wedding (Welty), 654
Demobilization, in 1945–1946, 603
Democratic party: rise of, 185; seeks harmony in 1852 election, 260–261; splits in 1860 "solid South," 324, 396; rising appeal in cities, 493; F. D. Roosevelt and, 518–520; blacks flock to, 533; attracts women in 1930s, 545–546; 1948 splits in, 609–610. *See also* Elections
Democratic Republicans, 185, 198, 264
Demography, 639–640. *See also* Population
Demonstrations, *see* Protest demonstrations
Dempsey, Jack, 494
Denmark: early exploration, 12; Jay's Treaty and, 127; neutral in World War I, 455, 456; in World War II, 560, 564
Denver, Colorado, and Indians, 298; mining near, 332–335; establishment of, 326
Denver and Rio Grande Railroad, advertisement, *il.,* 433
Department stores, 363–364
Dependent Pension Act, 401
Depression: of 1784, 103–104; of 1819, 176, 192; of 1839, 201; of 1870s, 319–320; of 1892, 405–408; of 1930s, 502–508, 517–549
Deregulation, 771
Desegregation: in 1950s, 627–630; and Civil Rights Act of 1964, 680; of schools, 686, 723–726
Deserters, military, pardon for, 747
De Smet, Father Pierre, 341
Des Moines, Iowa, 226
De Soto, Hernando, 19
Destroyers, deal with Britain for, 563
Détente, 705
Detroit, Michigan, 61, 68, 166; and the Erie Canal, 211; settlement of, 226; black mayor in, 643; rioting in, 570, 688, *photo,* 688
De Vaca, Cabeza, 19
Developing nations, 736; and Point Four, 603
Dewey, George, 421, 422; *painting,* 419
Dewey, John, 651
Dewey, Thomas E.: in 1940 election, 562–563; in 1944 election, 583; in 1948 election, 609–610
Dewson, Mary (Molly), 545, 546, 547; *photo,* 546
De Zavala, Lorenzo, 247–248
Dias, Bartholomeu, 4
Diaz, Justino, 734
Dictionary, written by Webster, 181
Dickinson, Charles, 191
Dickinson, John, 54, 96
Dienbienphu, 621, 622